# Psychology

Third Edition

# Psychology

## Third Edition

---

## HENRY GLEITMAN
UNIVERSITY OF PENNSYLVANIA

---

W · W · NORTON & COMPANY · NEW YORK · LONDON

Printed in the United States of America
All Rights Reserved
Third Edition

**Library of Congress Cataloging-in-Publication Data**

Gleitman, Henry.
    Psychology/Henry Gleitman.—3rd ed.
    p.    cm.

    Includes index.
    1. Psychology.    I. Title.
BF121.G58    1991
150—dc20                      90-41937
ISBN 0-393-95955-4

The text of this book is composed in Times Roman, with the display type set in
Times Roman Bold.
Composition by New England Typographic Service, Inc.
Manufacturing by R. R. Donnelley & Sons Company.
Book design by Antonina Krass.
Illustrations by Delores Bego.

Cover illustration: *David,* by Michelangelo (Photograph by A. Moldvay/Art
Resource, New York)

Acknowledgments and copyrights appear on pages A93–A99, which constitute a
continuation of the copyright page.

W. W. Norton & Company, Inc., 500 Fifth Avenue, New York, N.Y. 10110
W. W. Norton & Company, Ltd., 10 Coptic Street, London WC1A 1PU

2 3 4 5 6 7 8 9 0

To three who taught me:

Edward Chace Tolman, to cherish intellectual passion
Hans Wallach, to recognize intellectual power
Lila Ruth Gleitman, to admire intellectual elegance

# The Contents in Brief

1. Introduction

# Contents

---

## PART I   Action

---

## PART II    Cognition

CHAPTER 9

## Language  333

BY LILA R. GLEITMAN AND HENRY GLEITMAN

# Preface

This is the third edition of my book *Psychology.* One reason for this revision is the obvious fact that like any other discipline, psychology advances and develops. Until a few decades ago, many psychologists tended to be somewhat defensive about the status of the field and were probably a bit too loud in proclaiming that "Psychology is a science!" Today there is no need for such defensive proclamations, for by now that assertion has become a simple statement of fact. In the decades that have passed psychology has assuredly become a "real" and vigorously progressing science.

As a field advances, so must the books that try to describe it. These advances, together with suggestions by students and colleagues who have used the text, prompted a number of changes that I describe below.

## THE OVERALL AIM: COHESION IN A DIVERSE FIELD

Before describing these changes, let me briefly review what has not changed: my original aims. In writing *Psychology,* I sought to present the field in all its diversity while yet conveying the sense in which it is a coherent intellectual enterprise. In pursuit of this goal, I did the following:

1. To present the different sub-areas of psychology, I organized the book around five main questions: How do humans (and where relevant, animals) act, how do they know, how do they interact, how do they develop, and how do they differ from each other?

2. To provide some intellectual cohesion, I considered each topic against the backdrop of one or two major ideas that could serve as an organizing and unifying framework. Thus the chapter on the biological bases of behavior opens with

Descartes's conception of the organism as a machine, and the next chapter treats various aspects of motivated behavior as manifestations of negative feedback. To relate the material across chapters, I used several overarching themes. For example, the various chapters that deal with cognition (Sensory Processes, Perception, Memory, Thinking, and Language) all involve variations on the two controversies of nature versus nurture and psychological atomism versus organization.

3. In many cases, the attempt at integration required taking a step backward to look at psychology's intellectual history, for a number of the field's endeavors are hard to explain unless one points to the paths that led up to them. Why did Thorndike study cats in puzzle boxes? Why did his conclusions have such an important effect on American psychology? Why were they challenged by Köhler and Tolman? It still pays to take a serious look at the work of such pioneers before turning to the present. Much as a river's water is clearer when it is taken from its source, so issues that have become more and more complex as detail has piled upon detail become more plain and evident when traced back to their origin.

## GENERAL ORGANIZATION

The most obvious difference between this and the previous editions is the expansion of the coverage of the topics of social psychology and personality, which are now treated in two chapters each. Further changes represent updatings (in some cases, major updatings) of the subject matter that are best described within an outline of the overall structure of the book. After an introductory chapter, the book is divided into five parts that reflect the perspectives from which most psychological phenomena can be regarded: Action, Cognition, Social Behavior, Development, and Individual Differences. In brief outline, they cover the following topics:

### Part I: Action

This part focuses on overt behavior and its physiological basis. It begins by considering the biological underpinnings of human and animal action, leading to a discussion of the nervous system and its operation (Chapter 2) and some phenomena of motivation (Chapter 3). It then asks how organisms can modify their behavior to adapt to new circumstances, a topic which leads to a discussion of classical and instrumental conditioning and modern behavior theory (Chapter 4).

In Chapter 2 *(Biological Bases of Behavior)* there is an increased emphasis on neurotransmitter processes at the synapse and on modern work on recovery of nervous function. Chapter 3 *(Motivation)* now includes sections on feeding disorders, drug addiction, and a discussion of the biological basis of reward. Chapter 4 *(Learning)* stresses recent developments in animal learning, including work on contingency and modern cognitive approaches to classical and instrumental conditioning.

## Part II: Cognition

This part deals with knowledge and how it is gained and used. It begins by asking how the senses provide us with information about the world outside (Chapter 5), and how this information is organized and interpreted to lead to the perception of objects and events (Chapter 6). Further questions concern the way this knowledge is stored in memory and retrieved when needed (Chapter 7), the way it is organized through thinking (Chapter 8), and the way knowledge is communicated to others through the medium of language (Chapter 9).

Many of the changes in this part reflect a greater concern with recent information-processing approaches. In Chapter 5 *(Sensory Processes)* the organization has been simplified by incorporating an appendix on some aspects of signal detection within the chapter. In Chapter 6 *(Perception),* the organization has been changed to give more prominence to some modern approaches to pattern recognition. Chapter 7 *(Memory)* highlights the changes in outlook from the stage theories of the sixties to the modern emphasis on encoding and retrieval and such current concerns as the role of schemas in memory and the difference between explicit and implicit memory. Chapter 8 *(Thinking)* includes new material on artificial intelligence, on reasoning, and on the role of framing in decision making. Chapter 9 *(Language and Language Development),* written by Lila Gleitman and myself, merged what were formerly two chapters into one that deals with language structure and processing as well as with language acquisition.

## Part III: Social Behavior

This part concerns our interactions with others. It begins with a discussion of built-in social tendencies in humans and animals, a topic to which ethology and evolutionary theory have made major contributions (Chapter 10). It proceeds by taking up the first influential attempt to understand how childhood affects human socialization by considering Freud and psychoanalytic concepts (Chapter 11), thus paving the way for the discussion of modern approaches to social development taken up later in the section on development. It then turns to modern social psychology, considering how people try to understand the social situation in which they find themselves, how they interpret their own internal states and emotions, and how they interact with others (Chapters 12 and 13).

There have been several changes in this section. Chapter 10 *(The Biological Bases of Social Behavior)* includes an expanded section on primate social behavior, as well as an expanded discussion of the relevance of sociobiological theories to human concerns. Like its counterpart in the previous edition, Chapter 11 *(The Individual and Society: The Contributions of Sigmund Freud)* discusses the contributions of psychoanalytic and related views to our conceptions of socialization. Two chapters are now devoted to issues in modern social psychology. Chapter 12 *(Social Cognition and Emotion)* focuses on the way individuals interpret social events, and includes discussions of attitudes and attitude change, attribution, impressions of others, and the interpretation of one's own internal states. Chapter 13 *(Social Interaction)* deals with the way individuals deal with others, and includes discussions of social exchange, attraction and love, conformity, obedience, and crowd behavior.

## Part IV: Development

This section contains two chapters on development. Chapter 14 *(Physical and Cognitive Development)* now merges what were formerly two chapters into one with a greater focus on recent, post-Piagetian approaches to mental growth, and includes a section on cultural differences in cognitive development. Chapter 15 *(Social Development)* updates its counterpart in the previous edition with expanded discussions of such topics as moral development, empathy, sex and gender. As previously noted, the subject matter of a former chapter on language development is now incorporated into one single chapter on language (Chapter 9).

## Part IV: Individual Differences

This part begins with a chapter on mental testing in general and intelligence testing in particular (Chapter 16), and then continues with two new chapters on personality assessment and theory (Chapters 17 and 18). It continues by looking at several varieties of psychopathology and asking how they arise (Chapter 19), and concludes by examining various methods of treatment and therapy (Chapter 20).

Chapter 17 *(Intelligence)* is updated in various ways, including more recent attempts to understand intelligence in information-processing terms. Two new chapters take up personality differences. Chapter 18 *(Personality I)* considers methods of personality assessment and discusses trait theory as one of four theoretical approaches to personality, with particular attention to the trait-situation controversy and to recent attempts to look for biological and genetic bases of personality differences. Chapter 19 *(Personality II)* takes up three other theoretical approaches to personality—the psychodynamic, behavioral, and humanistic. Both Chapter 19 *(Psychopathology)* and Chapter 20 *(Treatment of Psychopathology)* have been updated to include modern developments, such as the two-syndrome hypothesis of schizophrenia, new work on panic disorder, and new approaches to the evaluation of treatment outcome.

## THE READER AND THE BOOK

It is sometimes said that students in the introductory course want to learn about things that are relevant to themselves and to their own lives. But why should this be a problem? When you come right down to it, there is something odd about the idea that psychology is *not* relevant to anyone's particular life history—specialist and nonspecialist alike. Psychology deals with the nature of human experience and behavior, about the hows and whys of what we do, think, and feel. Everyone has perceived, learned, remembered and forgotten, has been angry and afraid and been in love, has given in to group pressure and been independent. In short, everyone has experienced most of the phenomena that psychology tries to explain. This being so, psychology cannot fail to be relevant.

It surely is relevant, but its relevance has to be pointed out. I've tried to do so by a liberal use of examples from ordinary experience and a frequent resort to metaphors of one kind or another, in the hope that in so doing I would show the direct relation of many psychological phenomena to the reader's own life.

In these attempts, the most important guide has been my own experience as a classroom teacher. There is little doubt that one of the best ways of learning something is to teach it, for in trying to explain to others, you first have to clarify it to yourself. This holds for the subject matter of every course I have ever taught, but most especially for the introductory course. Students in an advanced course will come at you with tough and searching questions; they want to know about the evidence that bears on a theory of, say, color vision or language acquisition, and about how that evidence was obtained. But students in an introductory course ask the toughest questions of all. They ask why anyone would ever want to know about color vision (or language acquisition or whatever) in the first place. And they also ask what any one topic has to do with any other. They ask such questions because they—unlike the advanced students—have not as yet accepted the premises of the field. They wonder whether the emperor is really wearing clothes. As a result, they made me ask myself afresh what the field of psychology is all about—what the emperor's clothes are really like when you look at them more closely.

This book as well as its predecessor grew out of my attempts to answer such questions over the years in which I taught the introductory course, to answer them not only to satisfy the students but also to satisfy myself.

## SUPPLEMENTARY MATERIALS

To help serve the needs of students, instructors, and teaching assistants, several supplementary materials are available with this text.

1. *For the student:*

There is a complete *Study Guide* for students, prepared by two of my colleagues and collaborators, John Jonides of the University of Michigan and Paul Rozin of the University of Pennsylvania. This *Study Guide,* a revised version of the guide the same authors wrote for the first and second editions of *Psychology,* should prove very useful to students who want some help and guidance in mastering the material in the text. Moreover, for every chapter, it provides experiments and observational studies that students can carry out on their own to get some first-hand experience with psychology's subject matter.

2. *For the instructor:*

There is an *Instructor's Manual,* prepared by Christine Massey of Swarthmore College, Hilary Schmidt of New Jersey Medical School and the Monell Institute, Alan Silberberg of American University, and myself, which offers specific suggestions for every textbook chapter, including discussion topics, demonstrations, and a bibliography. The manual also includes an annotated film and media guide prepared by James B. Maas of Cornell University.

John Jonides of the University of Michigan and Paul Cornwell of Pennsylvania State University, with the help of Tibor Palfai of Syracuse University, have prepared a *Test Item File,* which includes questions for all chapters and the statistical appendix. A proportion of these questions have been statistically analyzed at Syracuse and Pennsylvania State Universities; the resulting data are included in the printed *Test Item File.* Of course, this *Test Item File* is available on diskette in MS-DOS, Apple II, and Macintosh formats.

I have prepared a set of *Classroom Demonstrations* with the collaboration of Paul Rozin and Lila Gleitman, both of the University of Pennsylvania. Included are materials necessary to perform about thirty in-class experiments covering a range of phenomena, from the speed of the nervous impulse, through the Stroop effect, to a demonstration of sex stereotypes. Slides, transparencies, student worksheets, data summaries, and detailed instructions for the instructor are included. These demonstrations are adapted from those that I and my collaborators have used in our own teaching.

## ACKNOWLEDGMENTS

There remains the pleasant task of thanking the many friends and colleagues who helped so greatly in the various phases of writing this book and its predecessors. Some read parts of the manuscript and gave valuable advice and criticism. Others talked to me at length about various issues in the field which I then saw more clearly. I am very grateful to them all. These many helpers, and the main areas in which they advised me, are as follows:

### Biological Foundations

Elizabeth Adkins-Regan, *Cornell University;* Norman T. Adler, *University of Pennsylvania;* Robert C. Bolles, *University of Washington;* Brooks Carder; Dorothy Cheney, *University of Pennsylvania;* John D. Corbit, *Brown University;* Alan N. Epstein, *University of Pennsylvania;* Steven Fluharty, *University of Pennsylvania;* Charles R. Gallistel, *University of California, Los Angeles;* Harvey J. Grill, *University of Pennsylvania;* Jerre Levy, *University of Chicago;* Martha McClintock, *University of Chicago;* Peter M. Milner, *McGill University;* Douglas G. Mook, *University of Virginia;* Allen Parducci, *University of California, Los Angeles;* Judith Rodin, *Yale University;* Paul Rozin, *University of Pennsylvania;* Jonathan I. Schull, *Haverford College;* Robert Seyfarth, *University of Pennsylvania;* W. John Smith, *University of Pennsylvania;* Paul G. Shinkman, *University of North Carolina;* Peter Shizgall, *Concordia University;* Edward M. Stricker, *University of Pittsburgh.*

### Learning

Ruth Colwill, *Brown University;* Frank Costin, *University of Illinois;* Richard B. Day, *McMaster University;* Paula Durlach, *McMaster University;* Richard C. Gonzales, *Bryn Mawr College;* Robert Henderson, *University of Illinois;* Werner Honig, *Dalhousie University;* Francis W. Irwin, *late of University of Pennsylva-*

*nia;* Nicholas Mackintosh, *Cambridge University;* Robert Rescorla, *University of Pennsylvania;* Barry Schwartz, *Swarthmore College;* Richard L. Solomon, *University of Pennsylvania;* John Staddon, *Duke University.*

## Sensation and Perception

Linda Bartoshuk, *Yale University;* Julian E. Hochberg, *Columbia University;* Leo M. Hurvich, *University of Pennsylvania;* Dorothea Jameson, *University of Pennsylvania;* R. Duncan Luce, *University of California, Irvine;* Neil A. MacMillan, *Brooklyn College;* James L. McClelland, *Carnegie-Mellon;* Jacob Nachmias, *University of Pennsylvania;* Edward Pugh, *University of Pennsylvania;* Irwin Rock, *University of California, Berkeley;* Burton S. Rosner, *Oxford University;* Robert Steinman, *University of Maryland;* Denise Varner, *University of Washington;* Brian Wandell, *Stanford University;* James L. Zacks, *Michigan State University.*

## Cognition

Lynn A. Cooper, *Columbia University;* Robert G. Crowder, *Yale University;* Lila R. Gleitman, *University of Pennsylvania;* Francis C. Keil, *Cornell University;* Deborah Kemler, *Swarthmore College;* Stephen M. Kosslyn, *Harvard University;* John Jonides, *University of Michigan;* Michael McCloskey, *Johns Hopkins University;* Douglas Medin, *University of Illinois;* Morris Moscovitch, *University of Toronto;* Ulric Neisser, *Emory University;* Daniel N. Osherson, *Massachusetts Institute of Technology;* David Premack, *University of Pennsylvania;* Daniel Reisberg, *Reed College;* Miriam W. Schustack, *University of California, San Diego;* Myrna Schwartz, *University of Pennsylvania;* Michael Turvey, *University of Connecticut;* Rose T. Zacks, *Michigan State University.*

## Language

Sharon L. Armstrong, *Drake University;* Anne Fowler, *Bryn Mawr College;* John Gilbert, *University of British Columbia;* Roberta Golinkoff, *University of Delaware;* Barbara Landau, *Columbia University;* Anne Lederer, *University of Pennsylvania;* Elissa Newport, *University of Rochester;* Ruth Ostrin, *Medical Research Council, Cambridge, England;* Ted Suppala, *University of Rochester;* Kenneth Wexler, *Massachusetts Institute of Technology.*

## Social Psychology

Solomon E. Asch, *University of Pennsylvania;* Joel Cooper, *Princeton University;* Phoebe C. Ellsworth, *University of Michigan;* Frederick J. Evans, *Carrier Foundation, Bellemead, N.J.;* Alan Fridlund, *University of California, Santa Barbara;* Larry Gross, *University of Pennsylvania;* Michael Lessac; Clark R. McCauley, Jr., *Bryn Mawr College;* Stanley Milgram, *late of City College of New York;* Martin T. Orne, *University of Pennsylvania;* Albert Pepitone, *University of Pennsylvania;*

Dennis Regan, *Cornell University;* Lee Ross, *Stanford University;* John Sabini, *University of Pennsylvania;* Philip R. Shaver, *University of Denver;* R. Lance Shotland, *Pennsylvania State University.*

## Development

Thomas Ayres, *Clarkson College of Technology;* Renée Baillargeon, *University of Illinois;* Anne L. Brown, *University of Illinois;* Justin Aronfreed, *University of Pennsylvania;* Edwin Boswell, *Ardmore, Pennsylvania;* Adele Diamond, *University of Pennsylvania;* Carol S. Dweck, *Columbia University;* Margery B. Franklin, *Sarah Lawrence College;* Rochel Gelman, *University of California, Los Angeles;* Frederick Gibbons, *Iowa State University;* Ellen Gleitman, *Devon, Pennsylvania;* Susan Scanlon Jones, *Indiana University;* Philip J. Kellman, *Swarthmore College;* Ellen Markman, *Stanford University;* Elizabeth Spelke, *Cornell University;* Douglas Wallen, *Mankato State University;* Sheldon White, *Harvard University.*

## Intelligence

Jonathan Baron, *University of Pennsylvania;* James F. Crow, *University of Wisconsin;* Daniel B. Keating, *University of Minnesota;* Robert Sternberg, *Yale University.*

## Personality

Hal Bertilson, *Saint Joseph's University;* Jack Block, *Massachusetts Institute of Technology;* Nathan Brody, *Wesleyan University;* Peter Gay, *Yale University;* Lewis R. Goldberg, *University of Oregon, Eugene;* Ruben Gur, *University of Pennsylvania;* Judith Harackiewicz, *Columbia University;* John Kihlstrom, *University of Arizona;* Lester B. Luborsky, *University of Pennsylvania;* Carl Malmquist, *University of Minnesota;* Jerry S. Wiggins, *University of British Columbia.*

## Psychopathology

Lyn Y. Abramson, *University of Wisconsin;* Lauren Alloy, *Temple University;* Kayla F. Bernheim, *Livingston County Counseling Services;* John B. Brady, *University of Pennsylvania;* Gerald C. Davison, *University of Southern California;* Leonard M. Horowitz, *Stanford University;* Steven Mathysse, *McLean Hospital;* Sue Mineka, *Northwestern University;* Ann James Premack, *University of Pennsylvania;* Rena Repetta, *New York University;* Martin E.P. Seligman, *University of Pennsylvania;* Larry Stein, *University of California, Irvine;* Hans H. Strupp, *Vanderbilt University;* Paul L. Wachtel, *College of the City University of New York;* Ingrid I. Waldron, *University of Pennsylvania;* Richard Warner, *University of Southern California;* David R. Williams, *University of Pennsylvania;* Julius Wishner, *University of Pennsylvania.*

## Intellectual History

Mark B. Adams, *University of Pennsylvania;* David DeVries, *New York University;* Claire E. Gleitman, *New York University;* Alan C. Kors, *University of Pennsylvania;* Elisabeth Rozin, *Upper Darby, Pennsylvania;* Harris B. Savin, *Philadelphia, Pennsylvania.*

To state in detail how each of these persons helped me is impossible. But I do want to express special thanks to a few whose comments helped me to see whole topics in a new light for this edition. I owe special thanks to Ruth Colwill, Paula Durlach, Werner Honig, and Robert Rescorla, whose wise counsel and comments helped me understand how recent developments in the field of animal learning have given new life to many issues of its past; to Dorothy Cheney and Robert Seyfarth, who gave me valuable insights into empirical and theoretical issues in modern ethology; to Michael McCloskey and Douglas Medin, who provided unfailingly good advice in the areas of perception and cognition; to Robert Crowder, whose incisive comments on several drafts of the chapter on memory were invaluable; to Daniel Reisberg, who gave me important insights into new developments in the fields of memory and thinking and whose help went far beyond the bounds of collegial duty; to Jonathan Baron, Phoebe Ellsworth, and Rick McCauley, whose discussions of thinking, social processes, and intelligence helped me consider many aspects of these areas from a new perspective; to Adele Diamond, Susan Scanlon Jones, and Philip Kellman, who helped me to see the developmental forest as well as its trees; to Nathan Brody, whose many discussions and insightful comments on two chapters on personality I found invaluable; and to Lauren Alloy, whose comments and advice on facts and theories in the field of psychopathology were indispensable.

Yet another kind of thanks goes to Neil Macmillan who wrote "Statistics: The Collection, Organization, and Interpretation of Data," an appendix for *Psychology,* with a fine sense of balance between the demands of the subject matter and the demands of expositional clarity.

Four persons contributed in a special way: Lyn Abramson, John Jonides, Paul Rozin, and John Sabini. All four are distinguished scientists as well as dedicated teachers with considerable experience in the introductory course. They served as an editorial advisory group who counseled me on all aspects of this edition, sharing their knowledge of the subject matter as well as their experience in communicating it to beginning students. Lyn Abramson was particularly helpful in discussions of individual differences and psychopathology. John Jonides provided sharp criticisms and new perspectives, especially in the area of cognition. As always, Paul Rozin helped me see many facets of the field in a new way, especially its biological aspects. John Sabini shared his wide-ranging scholarly perspective, which was of particular help in the areas related to social processes.

In thanking all these persons I take particular pleasure from the fact that about half of them were once undergraduate and/or graduate students of mine. I find something reassuring in the reflection that those I once taught are now teaching me, though it's almost certain that I learned much more from them now than they ever learned from me.

To one person I owe a special debt: my wife, friend, and collaborator, Lila R. Gleitman. She read virtually all chapters of this manuscript and did what she always does to the things I do and think and write about—she makes them better. Much better. I can't thank her enough.

Several persons helped on this edition in still other ways. Kathy Hirsh-Pasek took photographs of her children to add to those illustrating previous developmental chapters. Further thanks go to my publisher, W. W. Norton, specifically to Roy Tedoff who managed the production of the book; to Antonina Krass who designed it; to Dolores Bego who executed the drawings and illustrations; to Amy Cherry who supervised the photo and art research, and to Jane Carter, Claire Gleitman, and Libby Miles who participated in that endeavor; to Ruth Mandel who lent us her sharp artistic eye; to Hank Smith who provided helpful and generous editorial advice and encouragement; and to Cathy Wick who served as a valuable adviser as well as editor of various ancillaries. I owe special thanks to Roberta Flechner for her untiring and admirable efforts in arranging the layouts, which somehow managed to fit the many pieces of the puzzle into a seamless whole.

My final thanks go to two other persons at Norton. One is its president, Donald Lamm. I met him over twenty-five years ago when he first gave me the idea to write this book. We have both aged (somewhat) in the interim, but he is still the same sharp-eyed critic that he was twenty-five years ago—his ideas are as brilliant (and often as outrageous) as ever, his puns as bad as ever, and my esteem and affection for him are as great as ever.

The other person at Norton I want to thank is my editor, Sandy Lifland. She is a person of exquisite taste and enormous personal tact and sensitivity, of extraordinary judgment and competence, and of an amazing ability to keep track of a multitude of details while never losing sight of the overall whole. It was a real pleasure to work with her.

H.G.

Merion, Pennsylvania
October 1990

# Psychology

Third Edition

# CHAPTER 1

# Introduction

What is psychology? It is a field of inquiry that is sometimes defined as the science of mind, sometimes as the science of behavior. It concerns itself with how and why organisms do what they do. Why wolves howl at the moon and sons rebel against their fathers; why birds sing and moths fly into the flame; why we remember how to ride a bicycle twenty years after the last try; why humans speak and make love and war. All of these are behaviors, and psychology is the science that studies them all.

## THE SCOPE OF PSYCHOLOGY

The phenomena that psychology takes as its province cover an enormous range. Some border on biology, others touch on social sciences such as anthropology and sociology. Some concern behavior in animals, many others pertain to behavior in humans. Some are about conscious experience, others focus on what people do regardless of what they may think or feel inside. Some involve humans or animals in isolation, others concern what they do when they are in groups. A few examples will give an initial sense of the scope of the subject matter.

### Electrically Triggered Images

Consider the relation between biological mechanisms and psychological phenomena. Some investigators have developed a technique of electrically stimulating the brains of human patients who were about to undergo brain surgery. Such operations are generally conducted under local rather than general anesthesia. As a result, the patients are conscious and their reports may guide the neurosurgeon in the course of the operation.

These and other procedures have shown that different parts of the brain have different psychological functions. For example, when stimulated in certain portions of the brain, patients have visual experiences—they see streaks of color or flickering lights. When stimulated in other regions they hear clicks or buzzes. Stimulation in still other areas produces an involuntary movement of some part of the body (Penfield and Roberts, 1959; Penfield, 1975).

Related findings come from studies that look at the rate at which blood flows through different parts of the brain. When any part of the body is especially active, more blood will flow to it—to deliver oxygen and nutrients, and carry away waste products—and the brain is no exception. The question is whether the blood flow pattern depends on what the patient does. The answer is yes. When the patient reads silently, certain regions of the brain receive more blood (and are thus presumably more active) than do others. A different blood flow pattern is found when the person reads aloud, yet another when he watches a moving light, and so on (Lassen, Ingvar, and Skinhoj, 1978).

## Ambiguous Sights and Sounds

Many psychological phenomena are much further removed from issues that might be settled by biological or medical investigations. To study these, one proceeds at the psychological level alone. An example is the perception of ambiguous visual patterns. Consider Figure 1.1, which is a photograph of a vase created for Queen Elizabeth on the occasion of her Silver Jubilee. It is usually seen as a vase, but it can also be seen as the profiles of the queen and her consort, Prince Philip.

The way ambiguous figures are perceived often depends on what we have seen just before. Take Figure 1.2, which can be seen as either a rat or an amiable gentleman with glasses. If we are first shown an unambiguous figure of a rat, the ambiguous picture will be seen as a rat. If we are first exposed to an unambiguous face, the ambiguous figure will be perceived as a face.

What holds for visual patterns also holds for language. Many utterances are ambiguous. If presented out of context, they can be understood in several different ways. An example is the following sentence:

*The mayor ordered the police to stop drinking.*

This sentence may be a command to enforce sobriety among the population at large. It may also be a call to end drunkenness among the police force. Just how it

**1.1 Reversible figure** *Photograph of a vase celebrating the twenty-fifth year of the reign of Queen Elizabeth in 1977. Depending on how the picture is perceptually organized, we see either the vase or the profile of Queen Elizabeth and Prince Philip. (Courtesy of Kaiser Porcelain Ltd.)*

**1.2 Perceptual bias** *(A) An ambiguous form that can be seen either as (B) a rat or (C) a man with glasses. (After Bugelski and Alampay, 1961)*

A　　　　　　　　B　　　　　　　　C

**1.3  The visual cliff**  (A) An infant is placed on the center board that is laid over a heavy sheet of glass and his mother calls to him. If he is on the "deep" side, he will not crawl across the apparent cliff. (Courtesy of Richard D. Walk) (B) A similar reaction in a kitten. (Courtesy of William Vandivert)

is understood depends on the context. A prior discussion of panhandlers and skid row probably would lead to the first interpretation; a comment about alcoholism among city employees is likely to lead to the second.

## The Perceptual World of Infants

Phenomena of the sort we've just discussed document the enormous effect of prior experience on what we see and do. But this does not mean that all psychological accomplishments are acquired by past experience. Some seem to be part of the innate equipment that all of us bring into the world when we are born. An example is the infant's reaction to heights.

Crawling infants seem to be remarkably successful in noticing the precipices of everyday life. A demonstration is provided by the so-called *visual cliff*. This consists of a large glass table, which is divided in half by a wooden center board. On one side of the board, a checkerboard pattern is attached directly to the underside of the glass; on the other side, the same pattern is placed on the floor three feet below. To adults, this arrangement looks like a sudden drop-off in the center of the table. Six-month-old infants seem to see it in much the same way. When the infant is placed on the center board and called by his mother, his response depends on where she is when she beckons. When she is on the shallow side, he quickly crawls to her. But when she calls from the apparent precipice, discretion wins out over valor and the infant stays where he is (Figure 1.3).

This result suggests that, to some extent at least, the perception of depth is not learned through experience, but is built into our system at the very start.

## Displays

Thus far, all our examples have dealt with individuals in isolation. But much of the subject matter of psychology is inherently social. This holds for animals no less than humans. For virtually all animals interact with others of their species, whether as mates, parents, offspring, or competitors.

In animals, many social interactions depend on largely innate forms of communication. An example is courtship in birds. Many species of birds have evolved elaborate rituals whereby one sex—usually the male—woos the other. Just what this wooing consists of depends on the species. Some males court by making themselves conspicuous: The peacock spreads his magnificent tail

3

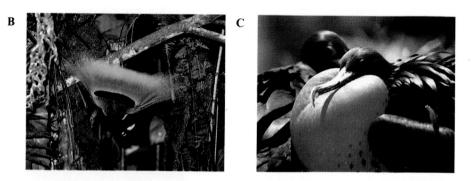

**1.4 Courting birds** *Birds have evolved many diverse patterns of courtship behavior that are essentially built-in and characteristic of a particular species. (A) The peacock displays his tail feathers. (Photograph by Keith Gunnar/Bruce Coleman) (B) The blue bird of paradise shows off his plumage while hanging upside down from a branch. (Photograph by B. Castes/Bruce Coleman) (C) The frigate bird puffs up his red throat pouch. (Photograph by William E. Ferguson)*

feathers, the blue bird of paradise displays his plumage while hanging upside down from a branch, and the red frigate bird inflates his red throat pouch. Other males take a more romantic approach: The bower bird builds a special cabin that he decorates with colored fruit and flowers. The males of other species offer gifts. In all cases, the fundamental message is the same: "I am a male, healthy, and willing peacock (or bird of paradise, or frigate bird, or whatever), and hope that your intentions are similar to mine" (Figure 1.4).

Such social communications are based on built-in signals called **displays,** which are specific to a particular species. They are ways by which one individual informs another of his current intentions. Some are mating displays, as in the case of courtship displays. Others are threats ("Back off or else!"; see Figure 1.5A). Still others are attempts at appeasement ("Don't hurt me. I am harmless!"). Some built-in displays form the foundation of emotional expression in humans. An example is the smile, a response found in all babies, even those born blind who couldn't have learned it by imitation. It is often considered a signal by which humans tell each other: "Be good to me. I wish you well." (See Figure 1.5B.)

**1.5 Displays** *(A) Threat display of the male mandrill, a large West African baboon. (Photograph by George H. Harrison/Grant Heilman) (B) The human smile. (Photograph by Suzanne Szasz)*

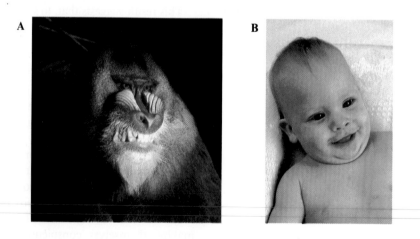

*1.6 **Panic** Richard Bosman, 1982.
(Collection of Robert H. Helmick;
courtesy Brooke Alexander, New York)*

## Complex Social Behavior in Humans

Human social interactions are generally much more subtle and flexible than those of animals. Male peacocks have just one way of going courting: They spread their tail feathers and hope for the best. Human males and females are much more complex, in courtship and many other social interactions. They try one approach, and if it fails, they will try another and yet another. If these fail, too, the partners will do their best to save the other's face. For much of human social life is based on the individual's rational appraisal of how another person will respond to his own actions: "If I do this . . . he will think this . . . then I will have to do this . . . ," and so on. Such subtleties are beyond the peacock. If his usual courtship ritual fails, he has no alternate strategy. He won't try to build bowers or offer flowers; all he can do is to display his tail feathers again and again.

While human social behavior has a strong element of rationality, there are some apparent exceptions in which we seem to act with little thought or reason. This is especially likely when we are in large groups. Under some circumstances, people in crowds behave differently than they do when alone. An example is panic (see Figure 1.6). When someone shouts "Fire" in a tightly packed auditorium, the resulting stampede may claim many more victims than the fire itself would have. At the turn of the century, a Chicago theater fire claimed over six hundred victims, many of whom were smothered or trampled to death by the frantic mass behind them. In the words of a survivor, "The heel prints on the dead faces mutely testified to the cruel fact that human animals stricken by terror are as mad and ruthless as stampeding cattle" (Brown, 1965). The task for psychology is to try to understand why the crowd acted differently from the way each of its members would have acted alone.

## A SCIENCE OF MANY FACES

These illustrations document the enormous range of psychology, whose territory borders on the biological sciences at one end and touches on the social sciences at

**Dreams** *Salvador Dali depicts a dream-like world in which various bizarre and disjointed images are interpreted by the dreamer to have symbolic meaning.* (The Great Paranoic, *by Salvador Dali, 1936; courtesy Museum Boymans-van Beuningen, Rotterdam)*

the other. This broad range makes psychology a field of multiple perspectives, a science of many faces.

To make this point concrete, we will focus upon one psychological phenomenon and show how it can be approached from several different vantage points. This phenomenon is *dreams.* Dreaming is a topic interesting in its own right, but it is also an especially good illustration of how psychology approaches any single phenomenon—not just from one point of view but from several.

Let us start out by describing dreaming as we all experience it. A dream is a kind of nocturnal drama to which the only price of admission is falling asleep. It is usually a series of scenes, sometimes fairly commonplace, sometimes bizarre and disjointed, in which the dreamer often figures as a participant. While this dream play unfolds, it is generally experienced as real. It seems so real in fact, that on waking one sometimes wonders whether the dream events might have happened after all. As a Chinese sage wrote over two thousand years ago, "Once upon a time, I, Chuang-tzu, dreamed I was a butterfly, fluttering hither and thither. . . . Suddenly I was awakened. . . . Now I do not know whether I was a man dreaming I was a butterfly, or whether I am a butterfly now dreaming I am a man" (MacKenzie, 1965).

How can such delicate, transient events ever become a suitable topic for scientific inquiry?

### Dreams as Mental Experiences

One way of looking at dreams is as conscious, mental experiences. According to an old account that goes back to the Greek philosopher Aristotle, the dream happenings are mental re-evocations of sights and sounds that occurred during the dreamer's waking life. Aristotle believed that the succession of these dream images from the past is experienced as real while it occurs because during sleep there is no competition from the clamor of waking reality and because the intellect is "dulled" during sleep (Aristotle, ca. 330 B.C.).

Later investigators tried to relate what people dream about to what happens to them both before and during sleep. One question concerns the effect of recent waking experiences. Aristotle was apparently correct in his belief that such recent events often re-emerge in dreams. This is especially so when the recent waking experience was highly emotional. For example, soldiers who have just gone through intense battle stress may relive their combat terrors in nightmare dreams (Pai, 1946).

Some writers have suggested that the dream images from the past are supplemented by external events that impinge upon the sleeper in the present. A widely cited example is the alarm clock, which is often said to turn into a peal of church bells or a fire engine in the dream. To test this hypothesis, several investigators have studied the effects of applying various forms of external stimulation during sleep. Numerous sleepers have been shaken, tickled, splashed with water, and shouted at—all to discover whether they would later report a dream that referred to these experiences. Sometimes they did. An example is a dream reported on awakening after an experimenter shouted "Help" into the sleeper's ears: "I was driving along the highway at home. Heard yelling and we stopped. A car was turned sideways in the road. I went down and saw the car was turned over on the side of the road. . . . There was a woman badly cut. We took her to the hospital" (Hall, 1966, p. 6). It is hard to resist the conclusion that, at some level, the dreamer heard and understood the shout "Help" even while asleep and then incorporated it within his dream narrative.

## Dreams as Behavior

Dreams as conscious, mental experiences are essentially private; they go on "inside" the individual. As such, dreams can be regarded as a form of behavior that is looked at from within, as if the actor were observing his own actions. Yet psychologists study most aspects of behavior from "outside," for much of what we do is directly apparent and overt and can therefore easily be seen by others. Humans and animals act. They run and fly and scurry about; they eat and fight and mate; they often perform new acts to attain their ends.

### OVERT BEHAVIOR

Can we study dreaming from the outside by taking this action-oriented view? On the face of it, the prospects don't seem too bright, for during sleep the body is by and large immobile. Even so, there is a way. For there is one thing the sleeper does while dreaming that is overt and can be observed from the outside: He moves his eyes.

This fact emerged after it became clear that there are two kinds of sleep: quiet sleep and active sleep. During quiet sleep, both breathing and heart rate are slow and regular, and the eyes are motionless. But during active sleep the pattern is different. Breathing and heart rate accelerate, and—most characteristic of all—the

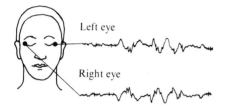

**1.7   Quiet and active sleep** *Record of eye movements picked up by electrodes at the side of each eye. The record shows the eye-movement pattern during active sleep, the period when sleepers dream. Both eyes move rapidly and in synchrony. (After Dement, 1974)*

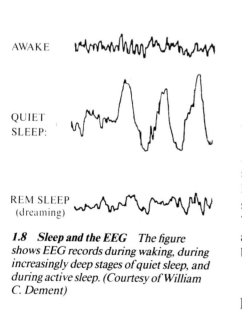

**1.8   Sleep and the EEG** *The figure shows EEG records during waking, during increasingly deep stages of quiet sleep, and during active sleep. (Courtesy of William C. Dement)*

eyes move back and forth behind closed eyelids in quick irregular darts. Periods of quiet and of active sleep (often called REM sleep because of the Rapid Eye Movements) alternate throughout the night, with a total of perhaps ninety minutes devoted to REM (Figure 1.7).

The crucial fact about REM sleep is that this is the period during which dreams occur. When subjects—the persons whose behavior is being studied—are aroused during REM sleep, about 85 percent of the awakenings lead to reports of a vivid dream. In contrast, subjects awakened from non-REM sleep recall dreams much less often (Dement, 1974).

There is little doubt that the rapid eye movements go along with dreaming. But some investigators take a further step. They suggest that these movements provide a clue to what the sleeper is dreaming of. In their view, the eye movements indicate that the sleeper is "looking at" whatever he sees in his dream world. Some evidence for this intriguing (though quite controversial) hypothesis comes from studies which show that the direction of the eye movements observed during a given REM period is appropriate to what the subject recalls having seen while dreaming. For example, when the predominant direction of eye movements was up and down, one subject dreamed that he had thrown basketballs, looking up at the net and shooting, then looking down to pick another ball off the floor. In contrast, another REM period, in which the eye movements were mostly from side to side, produced a dream in which the subject watched two people throwing tomatoes at each other (Dement and Kleitman, 1957).

### BIOLOGICAL UNDERPINNINGS OF BEHAVIOR

Evidence based on eye movements is one clue to the nature of dreaming. Another clue concerns its biological basis. Most psychologists take it for granted that whatever we do or think has some physical basis in the activity of our brains. Some promising first steps in this direction pertain to dreams. These came after the development of a number of methods for monitoring what people do when they are fast asleep. An important tool is the electroencephalogram, or EEG, which measures the overall activity of the sleeper's brain. The EEG traces the quick fluctuations of electrical activity over time, and its graphic record is sometimes called brain waves. Happily for sleep investigators, it soon proved possible to attach the multitude of required electrodes to the subjects without disturbing their sleep (Figure 1.8).

The results showed that the EEG patterns of sleep and waking differ markedly. As the subject falls into deeper and deeper stages of sleep, the brain waves become slow, large, and rather regular, indicating a lower level of brain activity. But this holds only for periods of quiet sleep. As this is interrupted by active (that is REM) sleep, the EEG becomes quite similar to that found when the subject is awake. This makes good sense, for it suggests that during REM sleep the brain is reasonably aroused and active—as well it should be since this is the time when we are busily engaged in dreaming.

## Dreams as Cognition

Like many other psychological phenomena, dreams reflect what we know, what we have experienced, remembered, or thought about—activities that psychologists call **cognition.** To be sure, the dream happenings didn't really take place. We didn't really fly through the air or have tea with Queen Elizabeth. But the components of the dream were surely drawn from the dreamer's own knowledge, which contains information about flying and the queen of England. How was this knowledge retrieved and woven into the dream story? How was the dream recalled on later awakening? And why is it that most of us remember so few of our dreams?

Some psychologists have tried to attack these and related questions by asking about the factors that make for better dream recall. They have come up with some evidence that people who remember more of their dreams are more likely to have better and sharper visual mental images in their waking life; perhaps their dreams are more memorable because they are experienced in a more vivid pictorial form (Cory et al., 1975). Another factor is the extent to which the dream experience is interfered with by what happens immediately after the sleeper awakes. In one study, subjects were asked to call the weather bureau immediately after waking up; after this, they had to write down a detailed description of any dreams they had that night. The results showed that weather reports and dreams don't mix. The subjects who made the call generally remembered that they had had a dream, but most of them could not remember what it was that they had dreamed about (Cohen and Wolfe, 1973).

## Dreams and Social Behavior

Human life is rarely solitary but is spent among a world of others—strangers and friends, partners and rivals, potential and actual mates. What holds for waking existence, holds for dreams as well. Most of them involve interaction with others. Some feature themes of aggression, such as competition, attack, and submission. Others concern friendship and sometimes sex. But whatever the plot, the cast usually includes some others. More than 95 percent of our dreams are peopled with others, and most revolve around our relations with them (Hall and Van de Castle, 1966).

### DREAMS AND THE CULTURE

Dreams concern major themes in the person's own life, but they take place within a larger framework, the dreamer's own culture. In our own society, a common dream is of appearing naked among strangers and being embarrassed. But such a dream would be unlikely among Australian aborigines who wear no clothing. Nor are many urban Americans likely to have nightmares in which they are chased by cows, which happens to be a common dream in western Ghana (Barnouw, 1963).

Culture affects not only what the dream is about but also how the dreamer thinks about it when she recalls it later on. In some societies, including our own, dreams are generally dismissed as nonsensical fancies, irrelevant to real life. Many preliterate cultures have a different view (Figure 1.9). Some regard dreams as supernatural visions and behave accordingly. Others take dreams very seriously even though they think of them as naturally occurring events. The Senoi, a tribe in Malaya, act as if they had all taken several courses in psychoanalysis. They believe that dreams indicate something about their inner lives and can pro-

**1.9   Iroquois cornhusk mask for dream ceremony**   *The Iroquois Indians regarded dreams as an important means for revealing hidden desires and held formal dream-remembering ceremonies during which special masks were worn. (Courtesy the Smithsonian Institution)*

vide clues for heading off problems before they become serious. Every morning Senoi children tell their father what they dreamed about the night before. The father then helps the children interpret their dreams. These may reveal some incipient conflict with others, as in a dream of being attacked by a friend. If so, the father may advise the child on how to correct matters, for example, by giving the friend a present (Stewart, 1951).

### DREAMS AND INTERNAL CONFLICT

The social aspect of dreaming lies at the heart of a famous (and controversial) theory of dreams proposed by Sigmund Freud. According to Freud, dreams are the product of an elaborate clash between two contending forces—the unconscious primitive urges of our biological heritage and the civilizing constraints imposed by society. In dreams we sometimes see one, sometimes the other side of the battle. Various forbidden impulses—mostly sex and aggression—emerge, but they are soon opposed by the thou-shalt-nots of our early upbringing. The result is a compromise. The forbidden material breaks through but only in a stealthy, censored masquerade. This disguise explains why dreams are so often odd and senseless. Their senselessness is only on the surface, a cunning mask that lets us indulge in the unacceptable wish without realizing that it is unacceptable (Freud, 1900).

According to Freud, some distortions involve various transformations of the unacceptable themes. One is symbolism. For example, he believed that sexual urges often emerge in symbolic guises. Thus, in his view, dreams of riding horses or walking up a staircase often mask erotic wishes. Here the symbols presumably bear some resemblance to that which they symbolize. The rhythmic movements of rising and falling in the saddle are similar to those of sexual intercourse, while ascending a staircase may be reminiscent of the way in which sexual passion mounts to a peak (Figure 1.10).

*1.10  Symbolism in dreams*  A film about Freud's early career includes a dream sequence in which he enters a deep tunnel that eventually leads him to a cavern where his mother sits, smiling, on a Cleopatra-like throne. The dream is a compact symbolic expression of how Freud saw himself: an explorer of subterranean unconscious motives who uncovered the hidden childhood lusts of all men and women. (From John Huston's 1963 film, Freud, with Montgomery Clift. Courtesy The Museum of Modern Art/Film Stills Archive)

Freud argued that these and many other symbolic transformations are the dreamer's way of smuggling the forbidden wish past the inner censor's eye. He believed that such defenses refer back to early childhood when the parents set up the various prohibitions that still haunt the adult in the present. Seen in this light, dreams reflect important social processes that pertain to the past, to the way in which the major social commandments were instilled in each of us by society's first agents, our parents.

## Dreams and Human Development

Thus far we have discussed dreams as they are experienced by adults. But of course dreams occur in childhood as well as in adulthood. Psychologists who are concerned with the course of human mental development have considered the different ways in which children and adults think about their dreams.

Developmental psychologists want to know how children acquire the basic intellectual operations that are part of adult human thought—how they learn to count, to understand that events have causes, and so on. For example, they ask how children learn that there is a difference between two realms of phenomena, those that we call subjective (thoughts, beliefs, and of course, dreams) and those that we call objective (the world of tangible things "out there"). To ask how this distinction is made is another way of asking how we attain our adult notion of objective reality, how we come to know that the tree in the garden—unlike a dream—will still be there after we blink our eyes.

This distinction is by no means clear in early childhood. Thus young children initially have great trouble in distinguishing dreams from waking life. A three-year-old awakes and tells her parents how much she loved the elephants at the circus yesterday. The parents correct her; she had not been at the circus yesterday. But the child indignantly sticks to her story and appeals to her brother for corroboration, for "he was there too." When her brother shakes his head in denial, she begins to cry, angrily insisting that she told the truth. Eventually she learns that there is a whole group of experiences that older people call "just dreams," no matter how real they seem to her (Levy, J., 1979).

The fact that the child finally recognizes the circus elephants—and the nightmare robbers and witches—as dreams does not mean that she has acquired an adult conception of what dreams are. Young children tend to think of them as physical objects. When asked whether dreams can be tall, a four-year-old replied, "*Yeah.* How tall? *Big, big, big* (spreads arms). Where are dreams? *In your bedroom.* In the daytime? *No, they're outside. . . .* What are they like? *They're made of rock.* Could they be heavy? *Yeah; and they can't break either*" (Keil, 1979, pp. 109–10).

It's quite a while before children think of dreams the way adults do. By six or seven, they believe that dreams are sent through the air, perhaps by the wind or by pigeons. Eventually they recognize that, as one eleven-year-old put it, "You dream *with the head* and the dream is *in the head*" (Piaget, 1972).

This realization that dreams are subjective events is no small achievement. As we will see later, the recognition that some experiences are subjective, inner happenings is not limited to dreams, but extends to many other conceptual attainments about the basic nature of the physical and psychological universe.

*That very night in Max's room a forest grew*

*and grew—*

**The distinction between dreams and waking reality is not always clear in childhood** *(From Sendak, 1963)*

*Wilhelm Wundt (1832–1920)*  *(Courtesy Historical Pictures Service, Chicago)*

*William James (1842–1910)*  *(Courtesy The Warder Collection)*

## Dreams and Individual Differences

There is a further aspect of dreams: They are a reflection of the fact that people are different. People vary in what they characteristically do and think and feel. And some of these differences between people are reflected in their dreams. Some simply pertain to the differing circumstances in the dreamers' lives. This point was made some two thousand years ago by the Roman poet Lucretius who noted that at night lawyers plead their cases, generals fight their battles, and sailors wage their war with the winds (Woods, 1947).

More interesting are differences that reveal something about the personalities of the dreamers. An example is a comparison of the dreams of normal people and of patients with a diagnosis of schizophrenia, a condition generally regarded as the most serious psychiatric disorder in our time. The difference between the two groups was enormous. The schizophrenics reported dreams that were highly bizarre and often morbid. The dreamer is eaten alive by an alligator; there are nuclear wars and world cataclysms. Themes of bodily mutilation were fairly common, as in a dream in which a woman killed her husband and then stuffed parts of his body into a camel's head. In contrast, the normals' dreams were comparatively mild and ordinary. This result fits in with what we know about schizophrenia. Schizophrenics often jump from one idea to the other without maintaining a firm line of thought. As a result, their behavior often appears bizarre. And they often report great personal turmoil and distress. It seems that their extremely bizarre and morbid dreams are simply an exaggeration of a condition already present in their waking life (Carrington, 1972).

## Perspectives on Psychology

We have seen that dreams can be looked at as conscious, mental experiences, as overt behaviors, as aspects of cognition, as indications of social patterns, as reflections of human development, and as expressions of the dreamer's individuality. What holds for dreams holds for most other psychological phenomena: They can all be viewed from several perspectives. Each perspective is valid but none is complete without the others, for psychology is a field of many faces and to see it fully, we must look at them all.

Given the many-faceted character of psychology, it is not surprising that those who have contributed to it came from many quarters. Some had the proper title of psychologist with appropriate university appointments in that discipline, including two of its founding fathers, Wilhelm Wundt of Germany and William James of the United States. But psychology was not built by psychologists alone. Far from it. Among its architects are philosophers, beginning with Plato and Aristotle and continuing to our own time. Physicists and physiologists played important roles and still do. Physicians contributed greatly, as did specialists in many other disciplines, including anthropology, and more recently, linguistics and computer science. Psychology, the field of many faces, is by its very nature a field of many origins.

In presenting the subject matter of psychology as it is today, we must try to do justice to this many-sidedness. In an attempt to achieve that, this book has been organized around five topics that emphasize somewhat different perspectives on the field as a whole. These five mirror the different ways in which we have just looked at dreams: ***action, cognition, social behavior, development,*** and ***individual differences.***

## THE TASK OF PSYCHOLOGY

Psychology is sometimes popularly regarded as a field that concentrates on the secret inner lives of individual persons—why Mary hates her mother and why George is so shy with girls. But questions of this sort are really not psychology's main concern. To be sure, there is an applied branch of psychology that deals with various adjustment problems, but it is only a special part of the field. The primary questions psychology asks are of a more general sort. Its purpose is not to describe the distinctive characteristics of a particular individual. Its main goal is to get at the facts that are general for all of humankind.

The reason is simple. Psychology is a science and, like all other sciences, it looks for *general principles*—underlying uniformities that different events have in common. A single event as such means little; what counts is what any one event—or object or person—shares with others. Ultimately of course, psychology—again, like all other sciences—hopes to find a route back to understand the individual event. It tries to discover, say, some general principles of adolescent conflict or parent-child relations to explain why George is so shy and why Mary is so bitter about her mother. Once such explanations are found, they may lead to practical applications: to help counsel and guide, and perhaps to effect desirable changes. But, at least initially, the science's main concern is with the discovery of the general principles.

Is there any field of endeavor whose primary interest is in individual persons, with the unique George and Mary who are like no other persons who ever lived or ever will live? One such field is literature. The great novelists and playwrights have given us portraits of living, breathing individuals who exist in a particular time and place. There is nothing abstract and general about the agonies of a Hamlet or the murderous ambition of a Macbeth. These are concrete, particular individuals, with special loves and fears that are peculiarly theirs. But from these particulars, Shakespeare gives us a glimpse of what is common to all humanity, what Hamlet and Macbeth share with all of us. Both science and art have something to say about human nature, but they go about it from different directions. Science tries to discover general principles and then to apply them to the individual case. Art focuses on the particular instance and then uses this to illuminate what is universal in us all.

Science and art are complementary. To gain insight into our own nature we need both. Consider Hamlet's description:

> What a piece of work is a man, how noble in reason, how infinite in faculties; in form and moving how express and admirable, in action like an angel, in apprehension like a god: the beauty of the world, the paragon of animals! (*Hamlet,* Act II, scene ii).

To understand and appreciate this "piece of work" is a task too huge for any one field of human endeavor, whether art, philosophy, or science. What we will try to do here is to sketch psychology's own attempts toward this end, to show what we have come to know and how we have come to know it. And perhaps even more important, how much we have not learned as yet.

# PART I

# Action

*The study of mind has many aspects. We may ask what human beings know, we may ask what they want, and we may ask what they do. Much of psychology is an attempt to answer the last question: What is it that humans do and why do they do it? In this section we will deal with the approach to mind that grows out of an interest in what all animals do, an approach that emphasizes behavior as the basic subject matter of psychology. We will focus on the particular version of this approach that is based on the notion that mind can be understood as a reflex machine. We shall see how the reflex notion has led to impressive achievements in our understanding of the structure and function of the nervous system, and how this notion has been modified to encompass the phenomena of motivation and of learning in animals and humans.*

# CHAPTER 2

# Biological Bases of Behavior

The ancients, no less than we, wondered why men and beasts behave as they do. What is it that leads to animal movement, impels the crab to crawl, the tiger to spring? Prescientific man could only answer *animistically:* There is some inner spirit in the creature that impels it to move, each creature in its own fashion. Today we know that any question about bodily movement must inevitably call for some reference to the nervous system; for to us it is quite clear that the nervous system is the apparatus which most directly determines and organizes an organism's reactions to the world in which it lives.

Modern advances in the study of this system have given us insights into its functioning that would have amazed the scientists who lived a century ago, let alone the ancients. Some of the new techniques allow us to observe the operations of small components of individual nerve cells (see Figure 2.1). Others permit us to eavesdrop on the workings of living human brains without seriously disturbing their owners (see Figure 2.2A and B). Our advances have been considerable. But to understand them more fully, we will take a look at some of the historical origins of our current conceptions.

We will soon ask many detailed questions about the structure and function of the nervous system—the apparatus that underlies human and animal action. But before we do so, we must ask a more general question: Broadly speaking, what must such a system accomplish?

**2.1 Observing the nervous system through a microscope** *A nerve cell in the spinal cord. (Photograph by Michael Abbey/Photo Researchers)*

## THE ORGANISM AS MACHINE

In modern times this question was first raised seriously by the French philosopher René Descartes (1596–1650), and his answer provides the broad outline

**2.2 Observing the living brain with PET scans** *(A) Horizontal plane of brain used in taking the PET (Positron Emission Tomography) scan. (B) Four PET scans taken while the subject rests, listens to someone talk, listens to music, or both. These scans indicate the degree of metabolic activity in different parts of the brain, viewed in horizontal cross-section as shown in the diagram with the front of the head on top. Red indicates the most intense activity and blue the least. Listening to speech activates the left side of the brain, listening to music activates the right side, and listening to both activates both sides. (PET scans taken by Dr. John Mazziotta, UCLA School of Medicine, et al./Science Photo Library/Photo Researchers)*

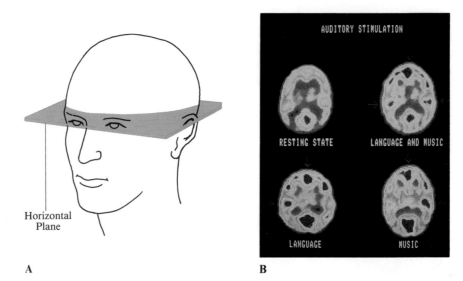

Horizontal Plane

A B

within which we think about such matters even now. Descartes lived in a period that saw the beginning of the science of mechanics. Kepler and Galileo were beginning to develop ideas about the movements of the heavenly bodies which some thirty years later led to Newton's *Principia.* Radically new views of man and his universe were being put forth. There were laws of nature that determined the fall of stones and the motions of planets: rigid, precise, and immutable. The universe was run by a system of pushes and pulls originally set in motion by God, the Great Watchmaker. At a more lowly level, these natural laws were mirrored in the workings of ingenious mechanical contrivances that were all the rage in the wealthy homes of Europe: clocks with cuckoos that would call the hour, water-driven gargoyles with nodding heads, statues in the king's garden that would bow to the visitor who stepped on a hidden spring. The action of a lever, the release of a spring—these could explain the operation of such devices. Could human thought and action be explained in similar mechanical terms?

## Descartes and the Reflex Concept

To Descartes all action, whether human or animal, was essentially a response to some event in the outside world. His human machine would work as follows. Something from the outside excites one of the senses. This transmits the excitation upward to the brain, which then relays the excitation downward to a muscle. The excitation from the senses thus eventually leads to a contraction of a muscle and thereby to a reaction to the external event which started the whole sequence. In effect, the energy from the outside is *reflected* back by the nervous system to the animal's muscles—the term **reflex** finds its origin in this conception (Figure 2.3).

Conceived thus, human doings could be regarded as the doings of a machine. But there was a problem. The same external event produces one reaction today and another tomorrow. The sight of food leads to reaching movements, but only when we are hungry. In short, the excitation from one of the senses will excite a nerve leading to one muscle on one occasion, but on another occasion it will ex-

**René Descartes** *(Courtesy National Library of Medicine)*

**2.3 Reflex action as envisaged by Descartes** *In this sketch by Descartes, the heat from the fire, A, starts a chain of processes that begins at the affected spot of the skin, B, and continues up the nerve tube until a pore of a cavity, F, is opened. Descartes believed that this opening allowed the animal spirits in the cavity to enter the nerve tube and eventually travel to the muscles which pull the foot from the fire. While the figure shows that Descartes anticipated the basic idea of reflex action, it also indicates that he did not realize the anatomical distinction between sensory and motor nerves. (From Descartes, 1662)*

cite a different nerve that may move an entirely different muscle. This means that Descartes's mechanism must have a central switching system, supervised by some operator who sits in the middle to decide what incoming pipe to connect with which pipe leading to the outside.

To describe these behavioral options mechanically was very difficult. Descartes was deeply religious and he was extremely concerned over the theological implications of his argument should he bring it to its ultimate conclusion. In addition he was prudent—Galileo had difficulties with the Inquisition because his scientific beliefs threatened the doctrines of the Church. So Descartes proposed that human mental processes were only semiautomatic. To handle the switching function he provided a soul (operating through a particular structure in the brain), which would affect the choice of possible nervous pathways.

Descartes shrank from taking the last step in his own argument, the reduction of human beings to the status of machines. Animals might be machines, but humans were more than mere robots. Later thinkers went further. They felt that the laws of the physical universe could ultimately explain all action, whether human or animal, so that a scientific account required no further "ghost in the machine"—that is, no reference to the soul. They ruthlessly extended Descartes's logic to human beings, arguing that humans differ from animals only in being more finely constructed mechanisms.

## The Basic Nervous Functions: Reception, Integration, Reaction

Psychologists today agree with Descartes that much of behavior can be understood as reactions to outside events: The environment poses a question and the organism answers it. This approach, like Descartes's, must lead to a tripartite classification of nervous functions: *reception* through the senses, *reaction* from the muscles and glands, and a *conduction* and *integration* system that mediates between these two functions.

As here conceived, the chain of events that leads to action typically begins outside of the organism. A particular physical energy impinges upon some part of the organism sensitive to it. This event we call a *stimulus* (a term that derives from the name of a wooden implement with a nail at one end used by Roman farmers some two thousand years ago to goad their sluggish oxen). The stimulus excites *receptors*, specialized structures capable of translating some physical energy into a nervous impulse. Once a receptor is stimulated, the excitation is conducted farther into the nervous system. Bundles of nerve fibers that conduct excitation toward the brain or spinal cord are called *afferent nerves* (from the Latin, *affere*, "to bring to"). These fibers transmit their message still farther; in the simplest case, to other fibers that go directly to the *effectors*, the muscles and glands that are the organs of action. Nerve fibers that lead to the effectors are called *efferent nerves* (from the Latin, *effere*, "to bring forth").

The transmission path from receptors to effectors is usually more circuitous than this, however. The afferent fibers often bring their messages to intermediate nerve cells, or *interneurons*, in the brain or spinal cord. These interneurons may transmit the message to the efferent nerve cells or send it on to yet other interneurons. Typically, many thousands of such interneurons have been "consulted" before the command to action is finally issued and sent down the path of the efferent nerve fibers.

We now turn to a more detailed discussion of the nervous system. We will deal with progressively larger units of analysis, first discussing the smallest functional and structural units of nervous activity (the nerve impulse and the nerve cell), then the interaction among different nerve cells (the synapse), and finally, the functional plan of the major structures of the nervous system.

## NERVE CELL AND NERVE IMPULSE

Neuroscientists know that the basic unit of nervous function is the *nerve impulse,* the firing of an individual nerve cell, or *neuron.* Our discussion begins with a brief look at the anatomy of the neuron.

### The Neuron

The neuron is the simplest element of nervous action. It is a single cell, with three subdivisions: the *dendrites,* the *cell body,* and the *axon* (see Figure 2.4). The dendrites are usually branched, sometimes enormously so. The axon may extend for a very long distance, and its end may fork out into several end branches. Impulses from other cells are received by the dendrites; the axon transmits the impulse to yet other neurons or to effector organs such as muscles and glands. Thus, the dendrites are the receptive units of the neuron, while the axon endings may be regarded as its effector apparatus.

Many axons are surrounded by a *myelin sheath,* a tube mainly composed of fatty tissue that surrounds the axon and insulates it from other axons. The tube is not continuous but consists of a number of elongated segments, with small uncoated gaps, the so-called *nodes of Ranvier,* between each segment.

A few details about neurons will give a feeling for their size and number. The diameter of an individual neuron is very small; cell bodies vary from 5 to about 100 microns in diameter (1 micron = 1/1,000 millimeter). Dendrites are typically short; say, a few hundred microns. The axons of motor neurons can be very long; some extend from the head to the base of the spinal cord, others from the spinal cord to the fingers and toes. To get a sense of the relative physical proportions of the cell body to the axon in a motor neuron, visualize a basketball at-

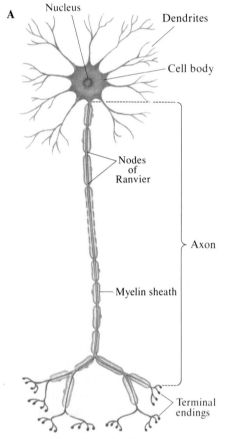

Nucleus

Dendrites

Cell body

Nodes of Ranvier

Axon

Myelin sheath

Terminal endings

*2.4 The neuron (A) A schematic diagram of the main parts of a "typical" neuron. Part of the cell is myelinated; that is, its axon is covered with a segmented, insulating sheath. (After Katz, 1952) (B) Highly magnified nerve cell in the human brain showing cell body and several dendrites. The long diagonal bands are branches from other nerve cells. (Nilsson, 1974)*

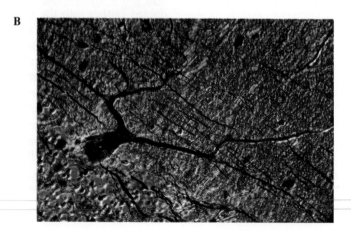

B

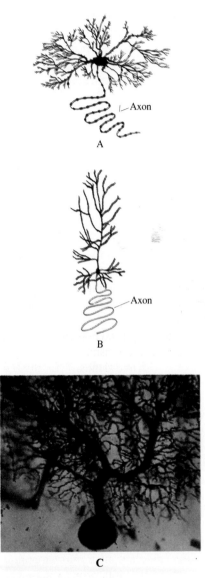

A

Axon

B

Axon

C

**2.5 Different kinds of neurons** *(A) A motor neuron of the human spinal cord. (B) A neuron in the human cerebral cortex, the part of the brain concerned with such higher mental functions as perception and planning. (After Kolb and Whishaw, 1980). (C) A specialized neuron in the cerebellum, a part of the brain which controls motor coordination. This kind of cell has been said to gather impulses from as many as 80,000 other neurons. The photomicrograph is from the cerebellum of a 12-month-old infant. It has been stained by a special chemical that shows the extent of the branching of the cell's dendrites. (© Guigoz/Dr. A. Privat/ Petit Format/Science Source/Photo Researchers)*

tached to a garden hose that stretches the whole fourteen-mile length of Manhattan Island. The total number of neurons in the human nervous system has been estimated to be as high as a 1,000 billion (Nauta and Feirtag, 1986). While this number may seem prodigious, it is somewhat sobering to realize that there is no way of getting more; a neuron, once lost, can't be replaced.*

The gap between the axon terminals of one neuron and the dendrites and cell body of another is called the synapse; this is the gap that has to be crossed for one neuron to stimulate the next. Such junctions often involve many more than two cells, especially in the brain, where a typical neuron may give and receive signals from 1,000 to 10,000 other neurons.

Different kinds of neurons are specialized for different tasks. We will mention only a few of the varieties. Some neurons are attached to specialized *receptor cells* that can respond to various external energies, such as pressure, chemical changes, light, and so on. These receptor cells can translate (more technically, *transduce*) such physical stimuli into electrical changes, which will then trigger a nervous impulse in other neurons. Receptor cells are like money changers, exchanging the various energies impinging from the other world into the only currency acceptable within the nervous system—the nervous impulse.

Neurons that convey impulses from receptors toward the rest of the nervous system are called *sensory neurons.* Sometimes the receptor is a specialized part of the sensory neuron; an example is the neurons that are responsible for sensing pressure on the skin. But in many cases, transduction and transmission are separate functions that are entrusted to different cells. In vision and hearing, there are receptor cells which transduce optic stimulation and air pressures into electrical changes in the cell. These changes in the receptors trigger impulses in sensory neurons that then transmit their information to other neurons in the nervous system.

Other neurons have axons that terminate in effector cells. An important example is the *motor neurons* that activate the *skeletal musculature,* the muscles that control the skeleton, such as those of the arms and legs. The cell bodies of the motor neurons are in the spinal cord or brain, and their long axons have terminal branches whose final tips contact individual muscle cells. When a motor neuron fires, a chemical event is produced at its axon tips which causes the muscle fibers to contract.

In complex organisms, the vast majority of nerve cells are *interneurons,* which have a functional position that is between sensory neurons and motor neurons. Interneurons come in many shapes and forms. They usually show considerable branching, which produces an enormous number of synaptic contacts (see Figure 2.5).

## The Electrical Activity of the Neuron

The biological function of a neuron is to receive and transmit impulses. How does it perform this function? The scientific understanding of the underlying electrical events required several advances in scientific instrumentation. One of these was the development of ever finer *microelectrodes,* some of which have tips

* Though some recent findings sound a more optimistic note, at least for male songbirds. Their brains shrink in the winter (when they don't sing) and expand in the spring (when they do). This annual increase in brain size is partially caused by the formation of new neurons during the spring which replace old neurons that die off in the fall (Nottebohm, 1987).

tapered to a diameter of 1 micron. Such electrodes can pick up currents from within a neuron without squashing the cell they are supposed to study. Equally important was the development of the *oscilloscope,* a device whose electrical response is amplified by vacuum tubes that send forth a stream of electrons that are swept across a fluorescent screen, leaving a glowing line in their wake. The pattern on the screen indicates what happened electrically during the entire (very brief) interval of the cell's activity. Yet another contribution was made by evolution, which provided the squid, an animal that contains several axons with giant diameters up to 1 millimeter—a great convenience for electrophysiological work on the nervous impulse.

### THE RESTING POTENTIAL

Figure 2.6 shows a microelectrode that is inserted on the inside of an axon while the other records from the surface of the fiber. In this manner one can record the *electrical potential* (the voltage) across the cell membrane. One fact emerges immediately. There is a difference in potential between the inside and the outside of the fiber when the cell is at "rest" (that is, not firing). The inside is electrically negative with respect to the outside. This *resting potential* is about −70 millivolts relative to the outside of the cell. This means that in its normal state the cell membrane is *polarized.* Its outside and inside are like the electrical poles of a miniature battery, with the outside positive and the inside negative.

### THE ACTION POTENTIAL

What happens when the neuron is aroused from rest? To find out, the surface of the fiber is stimulated by means of a third microelectrode which applies a brief electrical pulse. This pulse reduces the potential across the membrane for a brief instant. If the pulse is weak, nothing further will happen; there is no impulse. If the strength of the pulse is slowly increased, the resting potential drops still more, but there is still no impulse. This continues until the pulse is strong enough to decrease the potential to a critical point, the *threshold* (about 55 millivolts in mammals).

Now a new phenomenon occurs. The potential suddenly collapses; in fact, it overshoots the zero mark and for a brief moment the axon interior becomes positive relative to the outside. This brief flare lasts about 1 millisecond and quickly

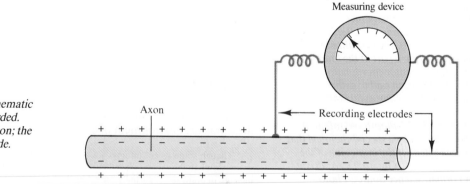

**2.6   Recording the impulse** *A schematic drawing of how the impulse is recorded. One electrode is inserted into the axon; the other records from the axon's outside. (After Carlson, 1986, p. 36)*

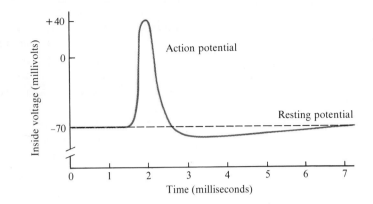

**2.7   The action potential**   *Action potential recorded from the squid giant axon. (After Hodgkin and Huxley, 1939)*

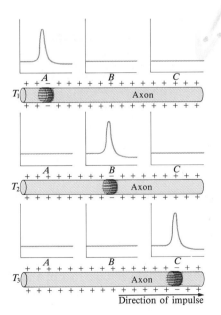

**2.8   The action potential as it travels along the axon**   *The axon is shown at three different moments in time—$T_1$, $T_2$, and $T_3$—after the application of a stimulus. The electrical potential is shown at three different points along the axon —A, B, and C. (After Carlson, 1986, p. 47)*

subsides. The potential then returns to the resting state. This entire sequence of electrical events is called the *action potential* (Figure 2.7).

The action potential is recorded from only one small region of the axon. What happens elsewhere in the fiber? Consider Figure 2.8. An *adequate stimulus*—that is, one that is above threshold—is applied to point *A* and the potential is measured at points *A, B,* and *C.* At first, an action potential is observed at *A;* at that time *B* and *C* are still at rest. A bit later, *A* returns to normal, while *B* shows the action potential. Still later, *B* returns to normal but an action potential is found at *C.* (Of course, these time intervals are exceedingly brief.) The change in potential is evidently infectious; each region sets off its neighbor much as a spark travels along a fuse.

*Explaining the action potential*   How do we explain these phenomena? Modern neurophysiology proposes a model based on physical and chemical interactions at the cell membrane. The neuron is enclosed in a very thin membrane which serves as a gatekeeper that governs the entrance and egress of various particles into the cell and out of it. The particles are *ions,* atoms or molecules that have gained or lost electrons, thus acquiring a negative or positive charge. An ion pumping mechanism leads to an excess of positively charged sodium ions ($Na^+$) on the outside of the cell, resulting in an electrical imbalance. This imbalance is maintained by the cell membrane, which contains special ion gates. During the cell's resting state, these gates are for the most part closed to sodium ions trying to enter from the outside.

When the neuron is stimulated, the polarization of the membrane (the difference between the electrical potential between the inside and the outside) is reduced. When this *depolarization* reaches the threshold value, the sodium gates of the membrane open, and sodium ions rush in, creating an excess of positively charged particles inside. Almost immediately the gates close again, and shortly after the resting potential returns to normal as potassium ions continue to leak out (for further details, see Figure 2.9).

Why does this excitation spread to neighboring regions? The reason is that the reversed polarization produces electric currents that flow toward neighboring regions of the membrane. This depolarizes them, which opens their sodium gates, and so on, from one region to another. The end result is the propagation of the impulse along the entire length of the axon.

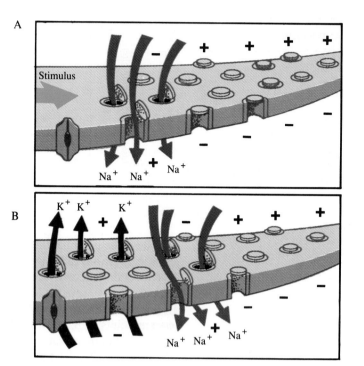

**2.9   Ion gates and the action potential**
*(A) When a stimulus is above threshold, special ion gates of the membrane open, and positively charged sodium ions ($Na^+$) surge inside. (B) Immediately thereafter, the gates that admitted $Na^+$ close, and the electrical balance is restored because some other positively charged ions—specifically potassium ions ($K^+$)—are now forced out. The whole process is repeated at an adjacent point in the axon. (After Starr and Taggart, 1989)*

*All-or-none and graded potentials*   One point should be stressed. The electrical response of the axon—that is, the action potential—is unaffected by the intensity of the stimulus, once the stimulus is at threshold level or above. Increasing the stimulus value above this level will not increase the intensity of the action potential or affect its speed of conduction to other points in the fiber. This phenomenon is sometimes referred to as the **all-or-none law** of axon reaction. The all-or-none law clearly implies that the stimulus does not provide the energy for the nervous impulse. It serves as a trigger and no more. Given that the trigger is pulled hard enough, pulling yet harder has no effect. Like a gun, a neuron either fires or does not fire. It knows no in-between.*

*Stimulus intensity*   We have seen that the axon obeys the all-or-none law. It appears that stimulus intensity has no effect once threshold is passed. Does this law make sense? Much of our everyday experience seems to deny it. We can obviously tell the difference between the buzz of a mosquito and the roar of a jet plane, even though both sounds are above threshold. How can we square such facts with the all-or-none law?

   In many cases what happens is that the more intense stimulus excites a *greater number of neurons.* This is precisely what we should expect, for we know that different neurons vary enormously in their thresholds. Thus, a strong stimulus will

---

* The all-or-none law holds for the action potential—that is, for conduction along the axon. As we will see shortly, the situation is different at the dendrites and cell body, where potentials are graded, being built up or lowered in a continuous rather than an all-or-none fashion.

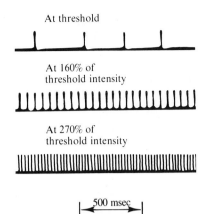

At threshold

At 160% of
threshold intensity

At 270% of
threshold intensity

|← 500 msec →|

**2.10 Stimulus intensity and firing frequency** *Responses of a crab axon to a continuous electric current at three levels of current intensity. The time scale is relatively slow. As a result, the action potentials show up as single vertical lines or "spikes." Note that while increasing the current intensity has no effect on the height of the spikes (the all-or-none law) it leads to a marked increase in the frequency of spikes per second. (After Eccles, 1973)*

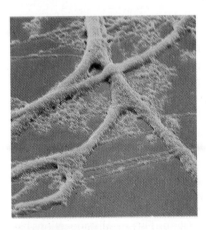

**Interaction among nerve cells** *An isolated nerve cell, magnified 20,000 times. The cell body is in contact with other cells through numerous extensions. The figure illustrates how nerve fibers cross each other to form an elaborate network. (Nilsson, 1974)*

stimulate more neurons than a weak stimulus. The weak stimulus will stimulate all neurons whose thresholds are below a given level; the strong stimulus will stimulate all of those, plus others whose threshold is higher.

While remaining strictly obedient to the all-or-none law, however, the individual neuron is nevertheless affected by stimulus intensity. This becomes apparent when we apply a continuous stimulus for somewhat longer intervals. Now we obtain not one impulse but a whole volley. We notice that the size of the action potentials remains the same whatever the stimulus intensity. What changes instead is the **impulse frequency.** The stronger the stimulus, the more *often* the axon will fire. This effect holds until we reach a maximum rate of firing, after which further increases in intensity have no effect (Figure 2.10). Different neurons have different maximum rates; the highest in man is of the order of 1,000 impulses per second.

## INTERACTION AMONG NERVE CELLS

In a way, the neurons of our nervous system are like 1,000 billion speakers, endlessly prattling and chattering to one another. But each of them has only one word with which to tell its story, the one and only word it can utter. It can choose only whether to speak its word or keep silent, and whether to speak it often or more rarely. Looked at in isolation, the individual speakers seem like imbeciles with a one-word vocabulary, babbling and being babbled at. But when taken as a whole, this gibbering becomes somehow harmonious. The trick is in the integration of the individual messages, the interplay of the separate components. The really interesting question for psychology, then, is not how a neuron manages to produce its word, but rather how it can talk to others and how it can listen.

### The Reflex

To study the interactions among different neurons, we begin with the simplest illustration of such interactions—the **reflex.** Descartes had pointed out that some of our actions are automatic—controlled by mechanical principles and not by the "will." Later progress in neuropsychology was made by studying animal motion that persists after the brain is gone. (What farmer had not seen a chicken running around the barnyard after its head was cut off?) Around 1750, the Scottish physician Whytt showed that such movements are controlled by the spinal cord. He found that a decapitated frog will jerk its leg away from a pinprick; but when deprived of *both* brain and spinal cord it no longer responded. Presumably, the frog's leg movement depended on the spinal cord.

The study of reflexes received some additional impetus during the French Revolution. Pierre Cabanis, friend and physician to some of its leaders, wondered whether consciousness survives beheading. He concluded that it does not and that the body's twitches after execution are mere reflex actions, automatisms without consciousness. This grim business was taken up again some forty years later by the German scientist Theodor Bischoff who performed a series of rather macabre experiments on the freshly separated head of an executed criminal. Even fairly intense stimuli produced no effects during the first minute after decapitation. Among the stimuli Bischoff employed, with perhaps greater devotion to science than human sensitivity, was the word "Pardon!" shouted into the ears of the severed head (Fearing, 1930).

Today we can list a host of reflexes, built-in response patterns executed automatically, without thought and without will. Vomiting, the rhythmic contraction of the intestines (peristalsis), erection of the penis, blushing, limb flexion in withdrawal from pain, sucking in newborns—the catalog is very large.

Can we classify these reflexes in any sensible fashion? There are several criteria. We can ask how many steps are part of the *reflex arc*—the reflex pathway that leads from stimulus to response. Some reflexes represent a chain of only two components, as in the case of an afferent neuron which contacts a motor neuron directly. More typically the chain is longer, and one or more interneurons are interposed between the afferent and efferent ends. We can also ask whether the reflex involves the brain (and if so, which part) or the spinal cord. When considering *spinal reflexes* we may want to distinguish further between those of *flexion* and those of *extension.* Flexion reflexes are typically associated with withdrawal, as when one pulls back one's arm from a burning fire. Extensor reflexes are often involved in postural reactions which uphold the body against gravity. Pressure on the soles of the feet stimulates the extensors, which thrust the leg upright.

## Inferring the Synapse

Until the turn of the century, most neurologists believed that the reflex pathway was across a long and essentially continuous strand of nervous tissue. The notion of the *synapse,* a gap between neurons across which they must communicate, is relatively modern. The critical studies which established the existence of the synapse and its role in nerve interaction were performed at the turn of the century by the English physiologist Sir Charles Sherrington (1857–1952). Sherrington's work was conducted at the level of behavior rather than that of electrophysiology. What he observed directly was reflex action in dogs, cats, and monkeys. How the synapse worked, he inferred.

Sherrington set out to study the *simple reflex,* that is, the reflex considered in splendid neurological isolation, unaffected by activities elsewhere in the nervous system. Of course he was well aware that such simplicity does not really exist, for even the lowliest spinal reflex is modified by higher centers in the spinal cord or the brain. An itch in your side will initiate a scratch reflex, but if you are the catchman in a trapeze act you will probably inhibit it. To remove the effect of higher centers, Sherrington used the *spinal animal,* usually a dog, whose spinal cord had been completely severed in the neck region. This cut all connections between the body (from the neck down) and the brain, so that spinal reflexes could be studied pure.

### EXCITATION

Sherrington's method was simple. He applied mild electric shocks to some point on the spinal animal's skin and observed whether this stimulus evoked a particular reflex response (Figure 2.11). His results indicated that there had to be conduction across at least two neurons—a sensory neuron from the skin receptor

*Sir Charles Sherrington* *(Courtesy National Library of Medicine)*

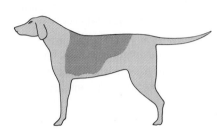

**2.11 Saddle-shaped area of spinal dog** *When a stimulus whose strength is above threshold is applied at any point in the "saddle," the animal will perform a scratching movement. (After Sherrington, 1906)*

and a motor neuron that activates muscle fibers. Sherrington asked whether conduction across neurons had the same characteristics as conduction within neurons. He discovered that it did not.

One line of evidence came from *temporal summation.* Sherrington showed that while one stimulus below threshold will not elicit the reflex, two or more of them (all equally subthreshold) may do so if presented in succession. The important point was that such temporal summation effects occurred even when the individual stimuli were spaced at intervals of up to half a second or thereabouts. But summation over such comparatively long time intervals does not occur within an individual axon fiber. The fact that temporal summation takes place anyway suggests that the summation process occurs somewhere else, presumably at the crossover point between neurons. The differences between conduction in reflex arcs and conduction in individual nerve fibers point to different mechanisms operating at the synaptic junction.

Sherrington supposed that there is some kind of excitatory process (presumably caused by the liberation of a then still undiscovered chemical substance from the ends of the axon) which accumulates at the synapse and builds up until it reaches a level high enough (the threshold level) to trigger the next neuron into action. This hypothesis clearly accounts for temporal summation. Every time cell *A* fires, a tiny amount of the excitatory substance is liberated into the synaptic gap between cell *A* and cell *B*. With enough repetitions of the stimulus, the total quantity of what Sherrington called the *central excitatory state* exceeds the threshold of cell *B* which then fires (Figure 2.12A).

Further evidence for Sherrington's general approach derives from the phenomenon of *spatial summation,* which highlights the fact that several neurons may funnel in upon one output. Consider two fairly adjacent points on a dog's flank, *A* and *B,* such that stimulating either of them alone will elicit a particular reflex if the stimulus is intense enough. Sherrington showed that subthreshold stimulation at *both* points will yield the reflex, even though this same weak stimulation would not suffice for either of these points in isolation. This indicates that two groups of nerve fibers converge upon one neural output—the *final common path.* At this juncture, the several converging neurons generate excitatory processes whose effects summate (Figure 2.12B).

**2.12 Arguments for synaptic transmission** *(A) Temporal summation. A subthreshold stimulus will not elicit the reflex but two or more stimuli will if presented successively at intervals of up to half a second. This indicates that the effects of the first stimulus were somehow stored and added to the effects of the second. (B) Spatial summation. Subthreshold stimuli applied to different points in the saddle area will not evoke a reflex if presented separately, but they will if presented simultaneously. This indicates that the excitatory effects from different regions are all funneled into the same common path.*

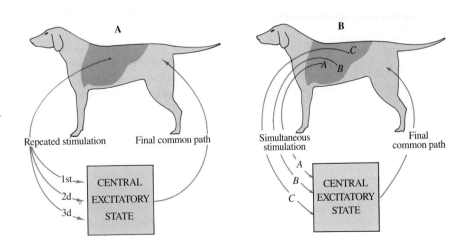

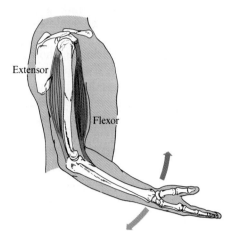

**2.13   An example of muscle antagonists**
*The figure shows how the members of an antagonistic muscle pair (biceps and triceps) oppose each other in flexing and extending the forearm.*

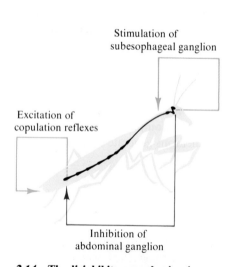

**2.14   The disinhibitory mechanism in the praying mantis**   *Excitation of the abdominal ganglion leads to copulatory movements in the male. But the sight of the moving female stimulates the subesophageal ganglion in the male's head. This in turn inhibits the abdominal ganglion so that copulation stops. Decapitation severs the subesophageal ganglion. The result is disinhibition and copulation resumes. Here, as in later diagrams, green indicates excitation and red inhibition. (Roeder, 1967)*

### INHIBITION

So far it would appear that neurons either vote "aye," thus adding to the central excitatory state at the synapse, or else abstain altogether. However, some neurons may signal "nay" and set up an inhibitory effect, actively opposing and preventing excitation.

One of the clearest demonstrations of such an effect is the phenomenon of ***reciprocal inhibition.*** Skeletal muscles typically come in antagonistic pairs—flexor and extensor (Figure 2.13). What happens to the flexor muscle when the extensor is excited and conversely? Patently, the antagonists must not both contract at the same time, like wrestlers straining against each other. For maximum mechanical efficiency, the force of the excited muscle should encounter no opposition whatever from its antagonist.

Using a spinal animal, Sherrington provided an experimental demonstration. He found that stimulation of a sensory site that caused the flexor to contract had a further effect. It also caused the extensor to relax so that it actually became limp —limper in fact than it was in the normal resting state. Sherrington concluded that this unusually low level of muscular contraction could only be explained by assuming that there was a counteracting process that nullifies the excitatory messages to the muscle fibers—*inhibition.*

These facts suggest that a neuron can receive both excitatory and inhibitory messages. The two processes summate algebraically; they pull in opposite directions and thus have opposite signs (with excitation positive, inhibition negative). Whether an efferent neuron fires (and thus activates a muscle fiber) depends upon many other neurons that form a synapse with it. Each of these cells gives a positive or negative signal or remains neutral and thereby determines whether the excitatory threshold of the efferent neuron is reached, and therefore, whether it fires or does not.

### DISINHIBITION

Impulses that have an inhibitory effect may derive from centers higher up than the spinal cord. The inhibitory effect of such brain centers is often discovered directly, by noting an *increase* in the strength of a reflex after the influence of this higher center is removed. Such an effect is called ***disinhibition.*** A classic example is spinal reflexes in frogs, which are more vigorous when all brain structures have been removed.

A rather ghoulish instance of disinhibition is provided by the love life of the praying mantis (see Figure 2.14). The female mantis is a rapacious killer. She seizes and devours any small creature unfortunate enough to move across her field of vision. Since the male mantis is smaller than the female, he too may qualify as food. This cannibalism is quite puzzling. How can the mantis survive as a species given a behavior tendency that counteracts successful fertilization?

According to one hypothesis, the female's predatory pattern is triggered almost exclusively by moving visual stimuli. The courting male's behavior is delicately attuned to this fact. As soon as he sees her he becomes absolutely immobile. Whenever she looks away for a moment he stalks her ever so slowly, but immediately freezes as soon as her eyes wheel back toward him—an inhibitory effect upon overall reflex activity. When close enough to her, he suddenly leaps upon her back and begins to copulate. Once squarely upon the female's back he is reasonably safe (her normal killer reflexes are elicited only by moving visual stimuli and he is mostly out of sight). But the dangers he must surmount to reach this place of safety are enormous. He must not miss her when he jumps; he must not slip while upon her. Should he fall, he will surely be grasped and eaten. Fairly often he does lose his balance, but even then all love's labour is not lost—for his genes, if not for him. The female commences to eat her fallen mate from the head on down. In almost all instances, the abdomen of the male now starts vigorous copulatory movements that are often successfully completed. Clearly, the male performs his evolutionary duty whatever his own private fate. But what is the mechanism?

It appears that the intact male's copulatory reflexes are inhibited by the sub-esophageal ganglion, located in his head. When this nerve cluster is removed, the animal will engage in endless copulatory movements even when no female is present. The same thing happens if the female chances to seize her mate and eat him. She first chews off his head and with it the subesophageal ganglion, thus dis-inhibiting the male's copulatory pattern which now resumes in full force—proof positive that love can survive beyond the grave (Roeder, 1935).*

## The Synaptic Mechanism

Sherrington could only guess at the specific physical mechanism that governs transmission at the synapse, but he did sketch some general guidelines. There had to be excitatory and inhibitory processes, accumulating over time, pooling effects from various neural inputs and adding algebraically. But what was their nature?

### SYNAPTIC TRANSMISSION

Sherrington and some of his contemporaries guessed that neurons communicate with their neighbors by means of some chemical substance that is released when the impulse reaches the end of the axon. The proof came in 1920 when Otto Loewi performed a crucial experiment. He dissected two frogs, removed their hearts, and placed each of the two hearts in separate, fluid-filled jars in which they kept on beating. One of the hearts still had the so-called vagus nerve attached to it; this nerve inhibits the heart muscle and slows down the heartbeat. Loewi electrically stimulated the vagus nerve for half an hour or so. All this time the other heart stayed in its own jar, and beat at its own, more rapid pace. After a while, Loewi took the fluid from the jar that held the first heart (whose beat had been slowed down by the vagus nerve) and poured it into the jar in which the second heart was kept. Almost immediately that second heart slowed down as well. The implication was clear. The stimulation of the vagus nerve liberated (at a region we now know acts just like a synapse) some substance whose effect on the heart muscle is to inhibit its function (see Figure 2.15). Loewi called that sub-

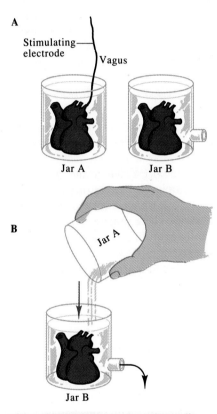

**2.15 Schematic illustration of Loewi's discovery of the action of neurotransmitters** *The hearts in two jars, A and B, are beating. (A) The vagus nerve that is still attached to the heart in jar A is stimulated, thus inhibiting its muscle and slowing down its heartbeat. (B) After an interval, the fluid in jar B is replaced by the fluid from jar A. The heart in jar B will now slow down almost immediately. (After Groves and Rebec, 1988)*

* A recent study suggests that this cannibalistic pattern may only occur under artificial conditions of captivity and when the female is virtually starved. Under more natural circumstances, males seem to manage to mate quite successfully without losing their heads in the process. But even if induced artificially, the phenomenon is an interesting if macabre illustration of the effect of disinhibition (Liske and Davis, 1984).

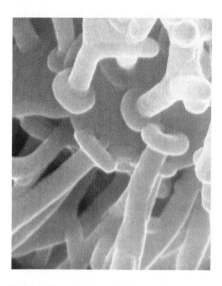

**2.16 The synapse** *Electron micrograph of synaptic knobs, the tiny swellings of the axon terminals that contain the vesicles. (Here magnified 11,250 times.) (Lewis et al., 1969)*

stance "vagus stuff." We now call it **acetylcholine** (usually abbreviated ACh), the first of a hundred or more substances now identified as **neurotransmitters** (Loewi, 1960; Eccles, 1982).

Loewi's experiment had only shown that the transmission of the neural message involves a chemical substance. We now know quite a bit more about the way in which this transmission occurs in actual neurons. Let's begin by distinguishing between the **presynaptic neuron** and the **postsynaptic neuron.** The presynaptic neuron sends the neural message; the postsynaptic neuron is the one the message is directed to. The process begins in tiny knobs of the axon terminals of the presynaptic neuron (see Figure 2.16). Within these swellings are numerous tiny sacs, or **vesicles,** which contain chemical substances called neurotransmitters. When the presynaptic neuron fires, the vesicles in its axon knobs release their transmitter load into the synaptic gap that separates the two cells. The transmitter molecules diffuse across this gap and come to rest upon the dendrite or cell body of the postsynaptic cell (see Figure 2.17A and B).

Once across the synaptic gap, how do transmitters perform their transmitting function? They do so by activating specialized receptor molecules in the postsynaptic membrane. When one of these receptors is activated, it opens or closes certain ion gates in the membrane. For example, some neurotransmitters open the gates to sodium ions. As these sodium ions enter the postsynaptic cell, that cell's resting potential is *decreased* (see Figure 2.17C and D). (We'll consider inhibitory effects shortly.) As more and more transmitter molecules are hurled across the synaptic gap, they activate more and more receptors, which drops the resting potential of the postsynaptic cell further and further. These drops accumulate and spread along the membrane of the postsynaptic neuron. Eventually they reach the point where that neuron's cell body adjoins its axon. When the drop gets large enough, the threshold is reached, the action potential is triggered, and the impulse will now speed down the postsynaptic cell's axon.

The changes in potential in the dendrites and cell body that are produced by the neurotransmitters are quite different from the action potential in the axon. For unlike the action potential (which is all-or-none), they are *graded* and add up in time: Small changes will accumulate as more and more transmitter molecules affect the postsynaptic cell (thus accounting for temporal summation). They also add up in space. Most neurons receive inputs from a great many presynaptic cells —in the brain, often from a thousand or more. As a result, transmitter molecules will arrive at several different regions of the postsynaptic membrane, and their effects will summate (thus accounting for spatial summation).

A similar mechanism accounts for inhibition. At some synapses, the presynaptic cell liberates transmitter substances that produce an *increase* in the resting potential of the postsynaptic neuron. This is in contrast to excitatory transmitter substances, which *decrease* the cell's resting potential.* As a result, a larger drop in resting potential will now be necessary to set off the action potential in the postsynaptic cell. Since most neurons make synaptic connections with neurons that excite them as well as others that inhibit them, the response of a given postsynaptic cell depends on a final tally of the various excitatory and inhibitory ef-

---

* Whether a transmitter is excitatory or inhibitory depends on its relation to the postsynaptic membrane. The same transmitter can be excitatory at some synapses and inhibitory at others. Thus acetylcholine excites the muscle fibers of the skeleton while inhibiting those of the heart.

**2.17   Schematic view of synaptic transmission**  *(A) Neuron A transmits a message through synaptic contact with Neuron B. (B) The events in the axon knob (the mitochondria shown in the figure are structures that help to produce the energy the neuron requires for its functioning). (C) The vesicle is released, and neurotransmitter molecules stream toward the postsynaptic membrane. (D) Transmitter molecules settle on the receptor site, an ion channel opens, NA⁺ streams in, and K⁺ leaks out. (After Bloom, Lazerson, and Hofstadter, 1988)*

fects that act upon it. If the net value is excitatory, and if this value exceeds the threshold, the cell will fire.

What happens to the transmitter molecules after they have affected the post-synaptic neuron? It wouldn't do just to leave them where they are, for they might continue to exert their effect long after the presynaptic neuron had stopped firing. Or they might wander off and trigger impulses at other synapses that they were never meant to affect. There are two mechanisms that prevent such false messages from being sent. Some transmitters are inactivated shortly after they've been discharged by a special "cleanup" enzyme that breaks them up into their chemical components. Others are removed from the synaptic cleft by *reuptake*, a process whereby they are, so to speak, sucked back into the presynaptic neuron.

### NEUROTRANSMITTERS

On the face of it, one might think that the nervous system only needs two transmitters: one excitatory and the other inhibitory. But nature, as so often, turns out to be exceedingly generous, for in actual fact there are a great number of different transmitter substances. About a hundred or so have been isolated thus far, and many more are sure to be discovered within the next decade.

We will mention just a few of these neurotransmitters here. One is Loewi's "vagus stuff," or *acetylcholine* (usually abbreviated *ACh*), which is released at many synapses and at the junction between motor neurons and muscle fibers (a junction that is a kind of synapse) and makes the fibers contract. Others include *serotonin (5HT),* a transmitter that is involved in many of the mechanisms of sleep and emotional arousal, and *GABA* (or to give its full name, gamma-amino-butyric acid), the most widely distributed inhibitory transmitter of the central nervous system. Yet others are *norepinephrine (NE)* and *dopamine (DA)* to which we will refer back in later discussions of drug effects and certain mental disorders. For now, we only want to note that neurons differ in the transmitters they release as well as the transmitters that affect them. Thus neurons sensitive to dopamine will not respond to serotonin or to GABA, and vice versa. It is as if different neurons spoke different languages. Some speak "Dopaminese," others speak "Serotonese," and so on.

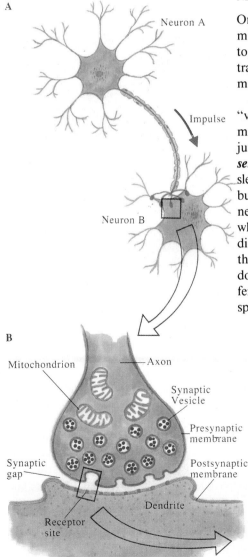

A

Neuron A

Impulse

Neuron B

B

Mitochondrion

Axon

Synaptic Vesicle

Presynaptic membrane

Postsynaptic membrane

Synaptic gap

Dendrite

Receptor site

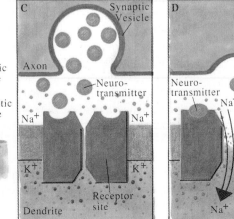

C

Synaptic Vesicle

Axon

Neuro-transmitter

Na⁺                    Na⁺

K⁺                    K⁺

Dendrite

Receptor site

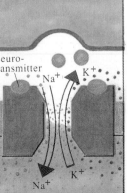

D

Neuro-transmitter

K⁺

Na⁺

Na⁺

K⁺

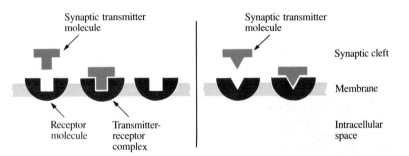

Synaptic transmitter molecule

Synaptic transmitter molecule

Synaptic cleft

Membrane

Receptor molecule

Transmitter-receptor complex

Intracellular space

**2.18 Lock-and-key model of synaptic transmission** *Transmitter molecules will only affect the postsynaptic membrane if their shape fits the shape of certain receptor molecules in that membrane much as a key has to fit into a lock. The diagram shows two kinds of transmitters and their appropriate receptors. (From Rosenzweig and Leiman, 1982)*

An attempt to understand these differences in chemical responsiveness is the so-called ***lock-and-key model*** of transmitter action. This theory proposes that transmitter molecules will only affect the postsynaptic membrane if their shape fits into certain synaptic receptor molecules much as a key must fit into a lock (see Figure 2.18). But the mere fact that a given molecule fits into the receptor is not enough to qualify it as a transmitter. The key must not just fit into the lock; it must also turn it. In the language of neurophysiology, the transmitter molecule must produce the changes in membrane potential that correspond to excitatory and inhibitory processes.

POISONS, DRUGS, AND NEUROTRANSMITTER ACTIVITY

The fact that communication between neurons depends on different neurotransmitter substances has wide implications for many aspects of psychological functioning. One is the effect of various drugs that enhance or impede the activity of transmitters at the synapse. Drugs that enhance this activity are technically called ***agonists,*** a term borrowed from Greek drama in which the agonist is the name for the hero. Drugs that impede a transmitter's action are ***antagonists,*** a term that refers to whoever opposes the hero (so to speak, the villain).

Many such drugs operate by increasing or decreasing the amount of available transmitter substance. Some agonists enhance a transmitter effect by blocking its reuptake, or by counteracting the cleanup enzyme, or by increasing the availability of some ***precursor*** (a substance required for the transmitter's chemical manufacture). Antagonists impede transmitter action through the same mechanisms operating in reverse: speeding up reuptake, augmenting cleanup enzymes, and decreasing available precursors. Still other drugs affect the synaptic receptors. Some are agonists that activate the receptors by mimicking the transmitter's action, much as a false passkey opens a lock. Others are antagonists that prevent the transmitter effect by binding themselves to the synaptic receptor and blocking off the transmitter, thus serving as a kind of putty in the synaptic lock.

*Acetylcholine and curare* An example of such a blocking action is provided by ***curare,*** a substance discovered by certain South American Indians who dipped their arrows in a plant extract that contained it, with deadly effect on animal prey and human enemies. Curare blocks the action of acetylcholine at the synaptic junctions between motor neurons and muscle fibers. The result is total paralysis and eventual death by suffocation since the victim is unable to breathe.

***Curare and paralysis*** *Certain South American Indians used curare-tipped arrows to immobilize and kill prey animals and human enemies. This Cofan man from Colombia is using a blowgun to hunt. (Photograph by B. Malkin/Anthro-Photo File)*

*Norepinephrine and amphetamine*   Curare exerts its effects by blocking a neurotransmitter. Other substances do the very opposite and enhance the activity of a transmitter at a synapse. An example is the effect of a group of drugs called the **amphetamines.** These drugs enhance the release of norepinephrine from the presynaptic neurons and also inhibit its reuptake. Norepinephrine is the transmitter for neurons that have to do with general bodily and psychological arousal. The greater the activity of such neurons, the more active and excited the individual is likely to be. It is therefore understandable that amphetamine acts as a powerful stimulant ("speed"). In moderate doses, it leads to restlessness, insomnia, and loss of appetite; larger doses and continued use may lead to frenetic hyperactivity and delusions. Certain other stimulants, in particular cocaine, have similar effects.

*Dopamine, schizophrenia, and Parkinson's disease*   The transmitter blockade produced by curare leads to catastrophic results. But other blockades may be beneficial. An example is the effect of various **antipsychotic drugs** such as **chlorpromazine** on the symptoms of schizophrenia, a serious mental disorder that afflicts about 1 percent of the population. In its more extreme forms, schizophrenia is characterized by delusions (believing what isn't so, such as conspiracies and persecution), hallucinations (perceiving what isn't there, such as hearing voices), or bizarre mannerisms and unusual postures that may be maintained for many hours. According to one hypothesis, schizophrenia is produced by an oversensitivity to the transmitter dopamine. Neurons that liberate dopamine have an arousing function in many parts of the brain. Adherents of the dopamine hypothesis believe that people who are overly responsive to this transmitter will be continually overaroused, which may ultimately lead to the symptoms of schizophrenia. One of the arguments for this theory comes from the fact that chlorpromazine, which blocks the effect of dopamine, has a pronounced effect in alleviating schizophrenic symptoms. While the dopamine hypothesis of schizophrenia is still a matter of dispute, many investigators do agree that disturbances in transmitter function play a role in the production of this and other mental disorders (see Chapter 19 for further discussion).

If the dopamine theory of schizophrenia is correct, the problem is an excess of (or an oversensitivity to) a certain transmitter, specifically dopamine. In other disorders, the problem is the very opposite. An important example is **Parkinson's disease,** which mostly afflicts persons in their later years. It is characterized by tremors, rigidity, and serious difficulties in initiating voluntary movements. Here too the cause is related to dopamine, but now as a case of too little rather than of too much, for in Parkinson's disease there is a gradual degeneration of dopamine-releasing neurons in a pathway of the brain that is crucial for movement. Some of the symptoms of Parkinson's disease are counteracted by the administration of L-DOPA, a substance that increases the dopamine supply of the brain, allowing the patient's surviving dopamine-releasing neurons to function more effectively. While this therapy alleviates many patients' symptoms, it does not constitute a real cure, for the progressive destruction of the dopamine-releasing neurons continues (Marsden, 1985).

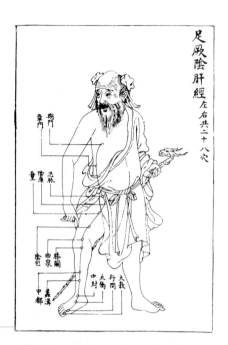

**2.19 Acupuncture** *Acupuncture is a complex system of treatment that grew up in ancient China and was based on the idea that disease is a disturbance in the balance of certain vital energies which were thought to circulate in certain channels. Their balance was to be restored by manipulating metal needles at special points along these channels. The figure is from a seventeenth-century Chinese treatise and illustrates the liver tract with twenty-eight special points. (From Blakemore, 1977, p. 42)*

### ENDORPHINS

Neurotransmitters have been implicated in yet another psychological process: the alleviation of pain (Bolles and Fanselow, 1982).

*The alleviation of pain*   There is little doubt that the perception of pain can be alleviated or even abolished by psychological means that serve as an **analgesic** (a pain reliever). There are many stories of athletes or soldiers at war who suffer injuries but don't feel the pain until the game or the battle is over. Related effects have been produced in the laboratory. Thus rats subjected to various forms of stress, such as being forced to swim in cold water, become less sensitive to pain (Bodnar, Kelly, Brutus, and Glusman, 1980). Similar results have been shown in humans. Paradoxically enough, mild electric shock to the back or limbs can serve as an analgesic. So can acupuncture, an ancient Chinese treatment in which needles are inserted in various parts of the body (see Figure 2.19; Mann, Bowsher, Mumford, Lipton, and Miles, 1973). In all these cases, the question is why.

The answer seems to be a matter of brain chemistry. It's long been known that the experience of pain can be dulled or entirely eliminated by various drugs, such as morphine and other opiates. These drugs are typically applied from the outside. But on occasion, the brain can be its own pharmacist. For when assailed by various kinds of stress (one of which is extremely painful stimulation), the brain can sometimes produce its own brand of opiates, which it then administers to itself. These are the so-called **endorphins**, (a contraction of *endogenous*—that is, internally produced—*morphines*), a group of neurotransmitters that are secreted by certain neurons within the brain. They do this by stimulating yet other neurons, which in their turn disrupt messages from the pain receptors sent up to the brain by a spinal cord tract (see Figure 2.20). Regular opiates such as morphine are chemically very similar to the endorphins and will therefore activate the same pain-inhibiting neurons (though, in fact, some of the brain's own endorphins are considerably more powerful than the artificially produced morphines dispensed by physicians; Snyder and Childers, 1979; Bloom, 1983).

What is the adaptive value of this roundabout system in which there is both pain and pain relief? The answer is that organisms need both. The pain is a crucial warning signal that tells an animal that it had better do something quickly to avert bodily harm. But once the warning is given, further pain may be incapacitating. A wounded deer must be able to ignore its wounds if it wants to escape the hunters.

*Placebos*   Many investigators believe that the endorphins play a similar role in the pain reduction produced by a **placebo,** a chemically inert substance that the patient believes will help him, such as the old family doctor's little sugar pill. There is good evidence that such placebos do sometimes alleviate pain and may have other beneficial effects (see Chapter 20 for a discussion of placebos in the context of psychotherapy).

To prove that the endorphins are involved in these and similar instances in which pain is reduced by "psychological" means, investigators turned to **naloxone.** This is a drug known to inhibit the effect of morphine and other opiates; it is generally given to addicts who have overdosed on heroin (which of course is yet another opiate). A number of studies have shown that naloxone also blocks the pain alleviation produced by acupuncture (Mayer, Price, Rafii, and Barber,

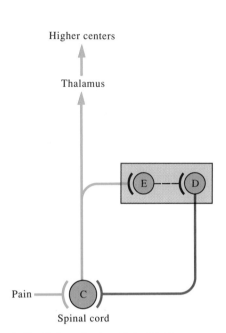

Higher centers

Thalamus

Pain

Spinal cord

**2.20 Pain and pain relief** *Highly schematic diagram of a proposed neural circuit to explain certain pain relief phenomena. As usual, green indicates excitation, red indicates inhibition. Pain stimuli excite neurons in the spinal cord (C) that carry pain information upwards to the thalamus. But they also excite endorphin-releasing neurons (E) in the midbrain which, through several intermediate steps, excite descending neurons (D) that inhibit the pain pathway in the spinal cord. This pain relief system can also be activated by the administration of morphine or by the electrical stimulation of the region of the midbrain that contains the E-neurons. (After Groves and Rebec, 1988, p. 265)*

1976). The same holds for placebos dispensed to patients who believe they are taking a pain killer. In one such study, patients were given a placebo after having a wisdom tooth extracted. This helped some of the patients, but had no effect when the patients were given naloxone in addition to the placebo (Levine, Gordon, and Fields, 1979). Some more recent studies have shown that while naloxone attenuates such placebo effects it does not abolish them completely. This indicates that there are some avenues to pain relief that do not involve the endorphin system (Watkins and Mayer, 1982; Grevert and Goldstein, 1985). An example is hypnosis, which is sometimes used as a means of surgical anesthesia. The mechanisms that produce this pain relief are still unknown, but they evidently do not involve endorphins since the analgesic effect of hypnosis is not abolished by naloxone (Mayer, 1979).

*Endorphins and exercise* Some authors believe that the exhilarating effect of repeated stressful exercise, such as jogging and marathon running, is also related to the endorphins. The runner continues to exert herself until she is exhausted and in pain. This builds up endorphins, which counteract the pain and produce a mood swing in the opposite direction. Eventually there may be something like an addiction—the jogger has to have her jogging fix to enjoy the endorphin-produced euphoria. Whether this interpretation is correct is still unknown, though there is evidence that stressful exercise does increase the secretion of endorphins (Carr et al., 1981).

## INTERACTION THROUGH THE BLOODSTREAM: THE ENDOCRINE SYSTEM

Thus far, we have considered the one primary instrument of communication within the body: the nervous system. But there is another organ system that serves a similar function: the **endocrine glands** (see Figure 2.21 and Table 2.1). Various endocrine glands (for example, the pancreas, adrenal glands, and pituitary) release their **hormone** secretions directly into the bloodstream and thus exert effects upon structures often far removed from their biochemical birthplace. As an example, take the **pituitary gland**. One of its components secretes a hormone that tells the kidney to decrease the amount of water excreted in the urine, a useful mechanism when the body is short of water (see Chapter 3).*

On the face of it, the integration that the endocrine glands give us seems to be very different from that which is provided by the nervous system. In the nervous system, messages are sent to particular addresses through highly specific channels. In contrast, the chemical messengers employed by the endocrine system travel indiscriminately to all parts of the body until they finally reach the one organ that is their destination. But at bottom, the two communication systems have a good deal in common, for ultimately they both use chemical substances to transmit information. In the nervous system, these are the neurotransmitters that excite or inhibit the postsynaptic cell; in the endocrine system, they are the hormones that affect specially sensitive cells in the target organ. To be sure, there is

---

* In addition to the endocrine glands, there are also **duct glands** (for example, salivary and tear glands), which have ducts that channel their secretions to the proper region of application.

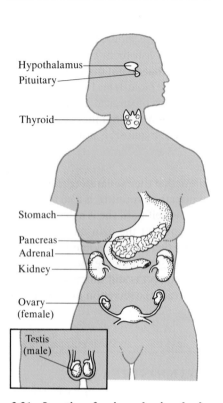

**2.21  Location of major endocrine glands and hypothalamus**

Table 2.1   THE MAIN ENDOCRINE GLANDS AND THEIR FUNCTIONS

| Gland | Functions of the released hormones |
|---|---|
| Anterior pituitary | Often called the body's master gland because it triggers hormone secretion in many of the other endocrine glands. |
| Posterior pituitary | Prevents loss of water through kidney. |
| Thyroid | Affects metabolic rate. |
| Islet cells in pancreas | Affects utilization of glucose. |
| Adrenal cortex | Various effects on metabolism; some effects on sexual behavior. |
| Adrenal medulla | Increases sugar output of liver; stimulates various internal organs in the same direction as the sympathetic branch of the ANS (e.g., accelerates heart rate). |
| Ovaries | One set of hormones (estrogen) produces female sex characteristics and is relevant to sexual behavior. Another hormone (progesterone) prepares uterus for implantation of embryo. |
| Testes | Produces male sex characteristics. Relevant to sexual arousal. |

an enormous difference in the distance these messengers have to travel. In the case of the neurotransmitters, it is the synaptic cleft, which is less than 1/10,000 mm wide; in the case of the endocrine system, it may be half the length of the entire body. But the fact that in both cases the medium of their message is chemical leads to a number of important similarities. Thus, several substances turn out to serve both as hormones and as neurotransmitters. For example, norepinephrine is the transmitter released by certain neurons that make blood vessels constrict; it is also one of the hormones secreted by the adrenal gland and has similar results.

## THE MAIN STRUCTURES OF THE NERVOUS SYSTEM

Our general approach has been to move from the simple to the increasingly complex. We first looked at the operation of the smallest functional unit of the nervous system, the neuron, and then considered the way in which two or more neurons may interact. We now turn to a third and still more complex level of analysis to discuss the function of large aggregates of neurons. What can we say about the function of those clumps of nervous tissue, each made up of millions of neurons, which comprise the gross structures of the brain and spinal cord?

## The Evolution of Central Control

The nervous system is analogous to a government, and its evolution can be understood as the gradual imposition of central control over local autonomy. A first step was the establishment of regional rule. Early in evolutionary history the cell bodies of many interneurons began to clump together to form *ganglia* (singular, *ganglion*). At first, these ganglia served primarily as relay stations that passed on sensory messages from the receptors to the muscles. But eventually they became much more than mere relay stations. The close proximity of the cells within these clumps of neural tissue allowed an ever-increasing number and complexity of synaptic interconnections. As a result, the ganglia became local control centers which integrated messages from different receptor cells and coordinated the activity of different muscle fibers. These regional centers were usually located close to the sites where important sensory information is gathered or where vital activity takes place.

As evolution progressed, the initial loose federation of ganglia gradually became increasingly centralized; some ganglia began to control others. The dominant ganglia were those that were located in the head. Their eventual preeminence grew out of the fact that the head contains the major receptors. To integrate the messages from the various receptors in the head, more and more neural machinery was required and the ganglionic centers which processed the incoming information became increasingly complex. They eventually started to coordinate the activity of ganglia elsewhere in the body until they finally emerged as the head ganglia in status as well as location—in short, they became the brain.

This tendency toward increasing centralization continued within the brain itself. The various structures of the brain tend to function hierarchically; there are higher centers which command lower centers, which in turn command still lower centers, and so on.

## The Peripheral and Central Nervous Systems

Taken as a whole, the human nervous system consists of a fine network of fibers that gradually merge into larger and larger branches which converge upon a central trunk line, like the tributaries of a stream. This system is composed of the central and peripheral nervous systems (see Figure 2.22). The *central nervous system* (usually abbreviated *CNS*) is made up of the brain and spinal cord. The *peripheral system,* as its name implies, comprises all nervous structures that are outside of the CNS.

Anatomists distinguish between two divisions of the peripheral nervous system —the somatic and the autonomic. The *somatic division* is primarily concerned with the control of the skeletal musculature and the transmission of information from the sense organs. It consists of various nerves that branch off from the CNS —efferent fibers to the muscles and afferent fibers from the skin, the joints, and the special senses. The *autonomic nervous system (ANS)* serves the many visceral structures that are concerned with the basic life processes, such as the heart, the blood vessels, the digestive systems, the genital organs, and so on.

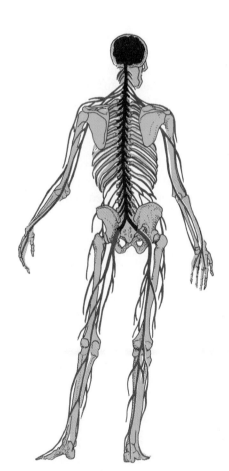

*2.22 Central and peripheral nervous system* The central nervous system (in red) and the peripheral nervous system (in orange). (After Bloom, Lazerson, and Hofstadter, 1988, p. 19)

The central nervous system can be described as a long tube that is very much thickened at its front end. The portion of the tube below the skull is the *spinal cord,* while the portion located in the skull is the *brain stem.* Two structures are attached to the brain stem. One is the pair of *cerebral hemispheres,* which are very large and envelop the central tube completely; the other is the *cerebellum* (literally, "little brain"), which is located lower down and is much smaller (see Figure 2.23).

Neuroanatomists find it convenient to consider the brain in terms of three major subdivisions: the *hindbrain, midbrain,* and *forebrain* (see Figures 2.23 and 2.24).

THE HINDBRAIN

The hindbrain includes the medulla and the cerebellum. The *medulla* is the part of the brain stem closest to the spinal cord; it controls some vital bodily functions such as heartbeat, circulation, and respiration. The *cerebellum* is a deeply convoluted structure that controls bodily balance and muscular coordination. It functions as a specialized computer whose 30 billion or more neurons integrate the enormous amount of information from the muscles, joints, and tendons of the body that are required both for ordinary walking and for the skilled, automatic movements of athletes and piano players.

THE MIDBRAIN

The midbrain contains several neural centers that act as lower level control centers for some motor reactions and that also have some limited auditory and visual functions (such as controlling eye movements). Of particular interest is a rather diffuse structure known as the *reticular formation,* which extends through the entire length of the brain stem from medulla to thalamus but is particularly prominent in the midbrain region. One of its functions is to serve as a general activator whose excitation arouses other parts of the brain, particularly the cerebral

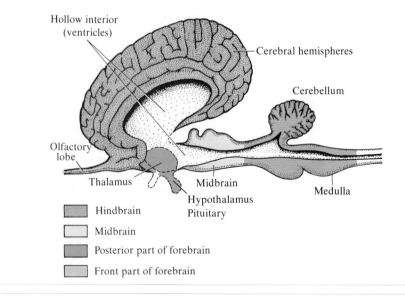

**2.23 The central nervous system** *This diagram is a highly schematic representation of the main parts of the brain. (After Lickley, 1919)*

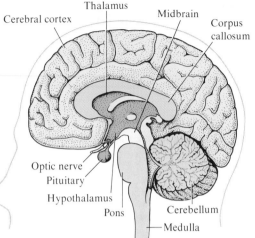

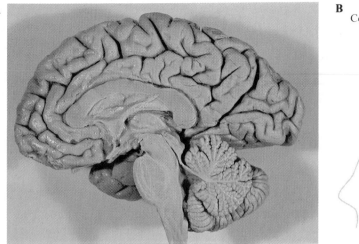

A — B

Cerebral cortex — Thalamus — Midbrain — Corpus callosum

Optic nerve — Pituitary — Hypothalamus — Pons — Cerebellum — Medulla

**2.24  The human brain**  *(A) A photograph of the brain cut lengthwise. (Photograph by Biophoto Associates, Photo Researchers) (B) A diagram of the brain, cut lengthwise. The colors are analogous to those used in Figure 2.23 to indicate hindbrain (red), midbrain (yellow), between-brain (dark green), and forebrain (light green). (After Keeton, 1980)*

hemispheres. Its deactivation seems related to sleep. We will return to these issues in a later section (see Chapter 3).

FOREBRAIN: THALAMUS AND HYPOTHALAMUS

Two of the forebrain structures represent the topmost region of the brain stem. They are the thalamus and the hypothalamus. The *thalamus* is a large system of various centers that serves as a kind of reception area to the cerebral hemispheres. Fibers from the eyes, the ears, the skin, and some motor centers, pass their information to the thalamus, which then forwards it upward to the cerebral cortex. The *hypothalamus* is intimately involved in the control of behavior patterns that stem from the basic biological urges (e.g., feeding, drinking, maintaining an appropriate temperature, sexual activity, and so forth; see Chapter 3).

FOREBRAIN: CEREBRAL HEMISPHERES

We finally turn to the structures that have traditionally been regarded as the functional summit of the behaving organism (or at least, of the thinking organism): the *cerebral hemispheres.* Anatomists usually distinguish several large parts within each hemisphere, called *lobes.* There are four such lobes, each named for the cranial bone nearest to it: the *frontal, parietal, occipital,* and *temporal.*

The outer layer of the cerebral hemispheres is called the *cerebral cortex,* and it is this region rather than the hemispheres as a whole that is thought to represent the pinnacle of neural integration. The cells in the cortex are densely packed and intricately interconnected; they are therefore capable of the most complex synaptic interconnections. While the cortex is only about 3 mm thick, it comprises a substantial proportion of the entire human brain. This is because the cerebral hemispheres are deeply folded and convoluted. Thus crumpled up, the cerebral surface that can be packed into the cranial cavity is very much increased (see Figure 2.25). The cortex is generally believed to be critical for the so-called "higher mental processes" (thinking, many aspects of memory, planned and voluntary

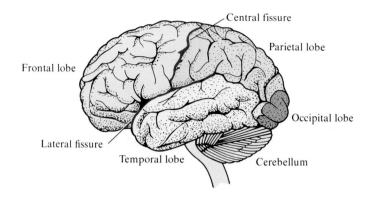

**2.25  The cerebral hemispheres, side view**

action) and is the most recent to emerge in the course of evolution. Fish have none at all, reptiles and birds have but a poor beginning, while in mammals there is considerable enlargement, especially in the primates.

FOREBRAIN: SUBCORTICAL STRUCTURES

A word or two should be added about several structures located in the subcortical regions of the cerebral hemispheres. One important group of structures are the **basal ganglia,** which are located near the base of the cortex and relay commands that coordinate large muscle movements. Some of the deficits in Parkinson's disease that we discussed before are caused by destruction of the dopamine circuits found in this area.

Another set of important structures is located near the center of the cerebral hemispheres, in a region that borders on the brain stem (see Figures 2.26 and 2.27) . These are often grouped together under the term **limbic system** (from *limbique,* "bordering"). Many limbic subsystems are part of what (in evolutionary

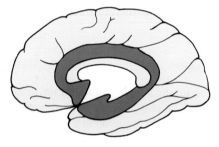

**2.26  The limbic system**  *A schematic diagram of the limbic system (in blue) shown in the side view. (After Russell, 1961)*

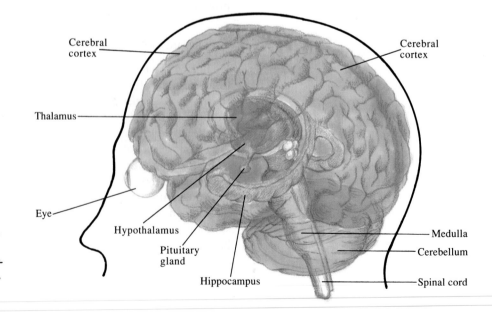

**2.27  Important structures of the limbic system**  *Thalamus, hypothalamus, and hippocampus as if seen through transparent hemisphere. (After Bloom, Lazerson, and Hofstadter, 1988)*

terms) is an older unit, sometimes called the "old cortex." The limbic system has close anatomical ties with the hypothalamus, and is involved in the control of emotional and motivational activities. We will later take a closer look at one particular limbic structure, the **hippocampus,** which plays an important role in various aspects of learning and memory (see Chapter 7).

## Hierarchical Function in the Nervous System

The various structures in the brain tend to function hierarchically; there are higher centers which command lower centers, which in turn command still lower centers, and so on. This hierarchical principle is the rule throughout the entire system (Gallistel, 1980).

To see how this hierarchical system operates, we will consider the behavior of cats whose brain has been cut (technically, "transected") at various anatomical levels of the system. Such transections sever the part of the nervous system below the cut from all control by the portion above. The question is what the part below the cut can do now that it is on its own.

Let's begin with a transection that leaves the animal with spinal cord and hindbrain and nothing else. The resulting "hindbrain animal" can still make the various limb and trunk movements that are required for standing, crouching, or walking. But it can't put them together. As a result, it is unable to stand or make walking movements unless supported by straps. Without support, it will collapse, unable to come up with more than disorganized reflex twitches if stimulated. Reduced to a hindbrain, the animal has become a mere biological marionette without a puppet master. As one author put it, the animal can move, but it cannot act (Gallistel, 1980).

Such acts are possible, however, if the transection is made just above the midbrain. Now the animal can stand without support, can walk, can shiver, chew, swallow, and hiss. The midbrain clearly performs some integrating function, for it somehow pulls the individual muscle movements together to form coordinated acts. But these acts don't fit into any larger behavioral scheme. The acts of a normal cat are organized into sequences that serve a larger goal. A hungry cat will walk to search for prey, will stalk the prey if one is found, and will then pounce, kill, and eat it. But a midbrain cat can't put its acts together. If starved, it won't look for food; if attacked, it won't flee. It acts, but it acts without point or purpose.

When the transection is made at a still higher level, so that the animal is left with most of its limbic system, lacking only the cortex, its separate acts are organized toward some purpose. It searches for food when hungry, looks for a warmer place when cold, escapes when harmed, and so on. In many ways it behaves much as a normal cat. But there is a difference—its performance is inept. When attacked by another cat, it will strike back, but quite ineffectively. Its blows will be poorly directed and easily avoided by its enemy. The limbic animal can coordinate its acts into a sequence that has an aim. But that sequence and the environment in which it is enacted must be very simple. If it is at all complex, the animal will fail. The limbic animal can act, and its acts have some purpose. But lacking a cortex, it is stupid (Bard and Rioch, 1937; Wetzel and Stuart, 1976; Gallistel, 1980).

# THE CEREBRAL CORTEX

We now turn to the cerebral cortex, the part of the nervous system that allows us to be intelligent. In cats, its presence may not be utterly necessary, although as we saw they are certainly in a bad way without it. But in our own species, its absence is catastrophic. For without a cortex there can be no planning, no complex sequence of motor movements, no perception of organized form, and no speech—in short, no semblance of anything that we call human.

## Projection Areas

Among the first discoveries in the study of cortical function was the existence of the so-called *projection areas.* These serve as receiving stations for sensory information or as dispatching centers for motor commands. ***Sensory projection areas*** are those regions of the cortex where the messages that come from the various senses (usually through some other relay stations) are first received. ***Motor projection areas*** are those from which directives that ultimately go to the muscles are issued. The term *projection* is here used in a geometrical sense: motor and sensory areas of the body are projected (mapped) onto particular regions of the cortex, resulting in a rough topographical correspondence between the location in the body and the location of the receiving or dispatching center in the cortex.

### MOTOR AREAS

The discovery of the cortical motor areas occurred when several physiologists opened the skull of a lightly anesthetized dog and then applied mild electric currents to various portions of its cerebral cortex. They discovered a region in the frontal lobe that controls movement. Stimulating a given point led to motion of the forelimb, stimulating another point led to motion of the trunk, and so forth. Exciting the left hemisphere led to movements on the right side of the body; exciting the right hemisphere caused movements on the left. This made good anatomical sense because most of the major efferent pathways from the brain cross over to the opposite side just as they leave the hindbrain.

Similar studies were conducted on human subjects by the Canadian neurosurgeon, Wilder Penfield. The stimulation was administered in the course of a brain operation. Such operations are usually administered under local rather than general anesthesia and patients are therefore able to report their experiences. Electrical stimulation applied to the open brain produces no pain. While pain receptors are located throughout the body and send their messages upward to the brain, the brain itself contains no such receptors.

The results of Penfield's studies showed that the cortical motor area in humans is in a region of the frontal lobe that is quite similar to that found in dogs. Stimulation there led to movement of some parts of the body, much to the surprise of patients who had no sense of "willing" the action, or of "performing it themselves." Systematic exploration showed that for each portion of the motor cortex, there was a corresponding part of the body that moved when its cortical counterpart was stimulated, with each hemisphere controlling the side of the body oppo-

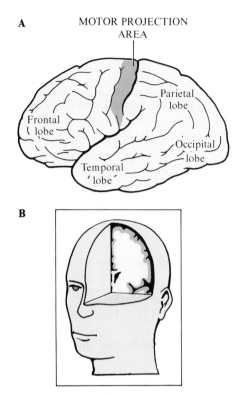

A
MOTOR PROJECTION AREA

Frontal lobe

Parietal lobe

Occipital lobe

Temporal lobe

B

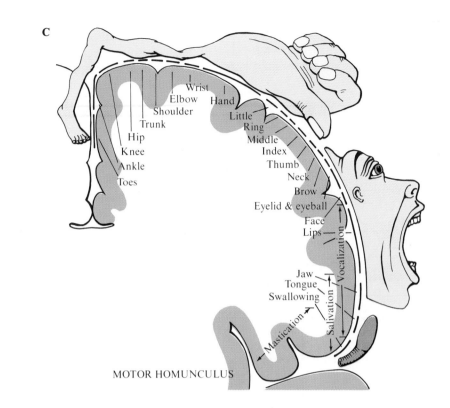

MOTOR HOMUNCULUS

Wrist
Elbow
Shoulder
Trunk
Hip
Knee
Ankle
Toes

Hand
Little
Ring
Middle
Index
Thumb
Neck
Brow
Eyelid & eyeball
Face
Lips

Jaw
Tongue
Swallowing

Mastication
Salivation
Vocalization

**2.28   The motor projection area of the human cortex**   *(A) The location of the motor projection area in a side view of the brain. (B) The head shows the plane of the cross-section of the figure. (C) The motor projection area of one hemisphere shown in a cross-section of the brain. The location and relative amount of cortical space allotted to each body region is graphically expressed as a motor homunculus. (After Penfield and Rasmussen, 1950)*

site to it. The results are sometimes expressed graphically by drawing a "motor homunculus," a schema of the body as it is represented in the motor projection area (Figure 2.28).

Inspection of the motor homunculus shows that equal areas of the body do not receive equal cortical space. Instead, parts of the body that are very mobile and capable of precisely tuned movement (for instance, the fingers, the tongue) are assigned greater cortical space compared to those employed for movements that are more gross and undifferentiated (for instance, the shoulder). What matters is evidently function, the extent and complexity of use (Penfield and Rasmussen, 1950).

Some related findings with various animals fit neatly into this picture. For example, consider the cortical representations of the forepaw in dogs and raccoons. Unlike the dog, the raccoon is a "manual" creature which explores the world with its forepaws; neatly enough, the forepaw cortical area in raccoons dwarfs its counterpart in dogs (Welker, Johnson, and Pubols, 1964).

SENSORY AREAS

Analogous stimulation methods have demonstrated the existence of cortical sensory areas. The ***somatosensory area*** is located in the parietal lobes. Patients stimulated at a particular point of this area report a tingling sensation somewhere on the opposite side of their bodies. (Less frequently, they will report experiences of cold, warmth, or of movement.) Again, we find a neat topographic projection. Each part of the body's surface is mapped onto a particular part of the cortical somatosensory area but again with an unequal assignment of cortical space. The parts of the body that are most sensitive to touch, such as the index finger and the

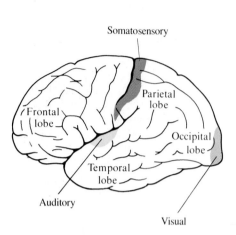

Somatosensory

Frontal lobe

Parietal lobe

Occipital lobe

Temporal lobe

Auditory

Visual

**2.29  Sensory projection areas of the human cortex**  *The location of the somatosensory, auditory, and visual projection areas in the brain. (After Cobb, 1941)*

tongue, enjoy a disproportionately larger cortical space allocation. And again we find a crossover effect. Each part of the body is mapped onto the hemisphere that is on the side that's opposite to it: the right thumb onto the left hemisphere, the left shoulder onto the right hemisphere, and so on.

Similar projection areas exist for vision and for hearing and are located in the occipital and temporal lobes respectively (Figure 2.29). Patients who are stimulated in the visual projection area report optical experiences, vivid enough, but with little form and meaning—flickering lights, formless colors, streaks. Stimulated in the auditory area, patients hear things, but again the sensation is rather meaningless and chaotic—clicks, buzzes, booms, hums. Some psychologists might argue that here we have "pure" visual and auditory input, the crude, raw materials of sensation, which are then shaped and interpreted as the excitation is transmitted to other areas of the brain.

## Association Areas

Less than one-quarter of the human cortex is devoted to the projection zones. The remaining regions are the ***association areas,*** which are implicated in such higher mental functions as planning, perceiving, remembering, thinking, and speech.* Most of the evidence comes from studies of human patients who have incurred damage (technically, ***lesions***) through tumors, hemorrhage, or blockage of cerebral blood vessels (popularly known as a stroke), or accident. Further evidence comes from a comparison of the anatomy of the cortex found in different mammals. In the rat, the bulk of the cortex is taken up by projection zones. In the cat, proportionally more cortical space is devoted to the association areas. The proportion is greater yet in monkeys, and it is greatest of all in man.

### METHODS FOR STUDYING LOCALIZATION

The traditional interpretation of the effect of lesions in association areas is that they impair the organization of messages that come from the sensory projection areas or that go to the motor projection areas. But just how do we know exactly where the lesions are? To be sure, their exact location will eventually be known through an autopsy, but both the physician (and no doubt the patient) would surely prefer to get an answer while the patient is still alive. Standard X-rays are of some help, but they only reveal very gross pathologies. Fortunately, several modern techniques have been developed that provide us with a much more precise picture of the anatomical structure of a living patient's brain.

One such technique is the so-called ***CAT scan*** (an abbreviation for ***Computerized Axial Tomography***). It employs a narrow beam of X-rays that is aimed through the patient's head and hits a detector on the opposite side. This beam slowly moves in a circular arc around the patient's head, and the detector moves along with it. Different brain tissues vary in density, and will therefore block the X-rays to different degrees. A computer eventually constructs a composite picture based on the X-ray views from all the different angles (see Figure 2.30).

---

* The term grew out of earlier belief that these are the regions where neural messages from the different senses meet and become associated.

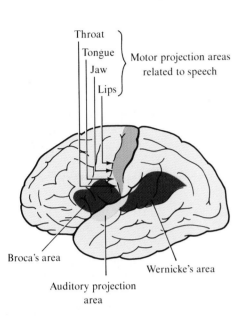

Throat
Tongue
Jaw
Lips

Motor projection areas
related to speech

Broca's area

Wernicke's area

Auditory projection
area

**2.36 Broca's and Wernicke's areas** *The diagram shows the two association areas most relevant to language. Destruction of Broca's area generally leads to expressive aphasia; destruction of Wernicke's area leads to receptive aphasia. Note the proximity to the relevant projection areas: Broca's area is closest to the regions that control the speech muscles, while Wernicke's area borders on the auditory projection zone.*

Unlike patients with expressive aphasia, those with receptive aphasia talk very freely and very fast, but while they utter many words, they say very little. The sentences they produce are reasonably grammatical, but they are largely composed of the little filler words that provide little information. A typical example is, "I was over the other one, and then after they had been in the department, I was in this one" (Geschwind, 1970, p. 904). In marked contrast with expressive aphasia, receptive aphasia shows no lack of function words. What's lacking are the so-called ***content words,*** the nouns and verbs that carry the bulk of the meaning.

Receptive aphasia is usually associated with left-hemisphere lesions (in right-handers) in various association areas of the temporal and parietal lobes. Many authorities believe that the crucial locus is ***Wernicke's area,*** a region that borders on the auditory projection zone and is named after a nineteenth-century neurologist who first described word deafness and other receptive aphasias (see Figure 2.36).

*Aphasia and sign language* In all cases of aphasia we've discussed thus far, there is a disruption of a spoken language such as English, or Hindi, or Swahili. But there is a small minority of persons who are deaf and who communicate through sign language. A number of investigators have shown that such sign languages, for example, American Sign Language, (*ASL*), are as complex as any of their vocal counterparts (see Chapter 9, pp. 374–75; Klima and Bellugi, 1979). What happens to deaf persons whose only language is ASL and who suffer a stroke in the left hemisphere? The general finding is that they suffer from a condition that is essentially equivalent to aphasia. They can move their hands and fingers, but they have serious difficulties in using them effectively to produce signs. Some lesions seem to impair the ability to produce particular signed words. Others impair the ability to put these signs together to form grammatical signed sentences. It appears that the left-hemisphere lesions that produce aphasia affect some mental function that is not specific to the ear-mouth channel. That function is human language, which evidently depends on some cerebral machinery that is pretty much the same whether the language is produced by tongue and mouth or by hands and fingers (Bellugi, Poizner, and Klima, 1983).

## One Brain or Two?

Anatomically, the two hemispheres appear to be quite similar, but there is abundant evidence that their functions are by no means identical. This asymmetry of function is called ***lateralization,*** and its manifestations include such diverse phenomena as language, spatial organization, and handedness—the superior dexterity of one hand over the other (Springer and Deutsch, 1981).

We have already seen that in right-handers aphasia is usually associated with lesions in the left hemisphere. Until fairly recently, neuroscientists interpreted this fact to mean that one hemisphere is *dominant* over the other. As a result, they called the (right-hander's) right hemisphere the "minor hemisphere," for they believed that it is essentially a lesser version of the left hemisphere, a hemisphere that lacks language functions, has less capacity for fine motor control, and so forth.

More recent evidence has rescued the right hemisphere from this poor relation status, for it now appears that it has some important functions of its own. Some of this evidence we've already encountered in our discussion of right-handers with lesions in the right hemisphere. As we've seen, these persons often suffer from various difficulties in the comprehension of various aspects of space and form; they concentrate on details but cannot grasp the overall pattern. Some have trouble recognizing faces; some suffer from the unilateral neglect syndrome; still others have great difficulties in dressing themselves; they put their arms in a pants leg or put a shirt on backwards (Bogen, 1969).

The results are more ambiguous for the 12 percent or so of the population that is left-handed (and also generally left-footed, and to a lesser extent, left-eyed and left-eared as well; Porac and Coren, 1981). Somewhat more than half of the left-handers have speech predominantly lateralized in the left hemisphere; in the rest, language is usually represented in both hemispheres. But overall, there seems to be less lateralization in left-handers than in right-handers, so that the functional capabilities of the left-handers' two hemispheres are more on a par. Thus, in left-handers, aphasia may often be produced by lesions to either hemisphere. But by the same token, left-handed aphasics have a greater chance for ultimate recovery, for the intact hemisphere is better able to take over the responsibilities formerly assigned to the hemisphere that suffered damage (Brain, 1965; Springer and Deutsch, 1981).

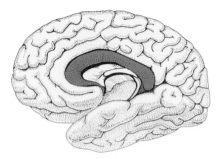

**2.37  The split brain**  *To control epilepsy, neurosurgeons sometimes sever the two hemispheres. This is accomplished by cutting the corpus callosum (in blue) and a few other connective tracts. The corpus callosum is shown here in a lateral cross-section.*

EVIDENCE FROM SPLIT BRAINS

*Dissociating the two hemispheres*  Some of the most persuasive evidence about the different functions of the two cerebral hemispheres comes from studies originated by Nobel laureate Roger Sperry using persons with **split brains** (Sperry, 1974, 1982). These are people whose **corpus callosum** has been surgically severed. The corpus callosum is a massive bundle of nerve fibers that interconnects the two hemispheres so that they can pool their information and function as a harmonious whole. This neurological bridge (and some other subsidiary ones) is sometimes cut in cases of severe epilepsy so that the seizure will not spread from one hemisphere to the other (Bogen, Fisher, and Vogel, 1965; Wilson, Reeves, Gazzaniga, and Culver, 1977). Once confined to a smaller cortical area, the seizures are less severe and less frequent. The operation clearly relieves suffering, but it has a side effect—the two hemispheres of the split brain become functionally isolated from each other and in some ways act as two separate brains (Gazzaniga, 1967; see Figure 2.37).

The effect of the split-brain operation is best demonstrated by setting a task that poses a question to one hemisphere and requires the answer from the other (see Figure 2.38). One method is to show a picture so that the neural message only reaches one hemisphere. This is done by flashing the picture for a fraction of a second to either the right or the left side of the patient's field of vision. The anatomical pathways of the visual system are such that if the picture is flashed to the

**2.38  A setup sometimes used in split-brain studies**  *The subject fixates a center dot and then sees a picture or a word on the right or left side of the dot. He may be asked to respond verbally, by reading the word or naming the picture. He may also be asked to respond without words, for example, by picking out a named object from among a group spread out on a table and hidden from view, so that it can only be identified by touch. (After Gazzaniga, 1967)*

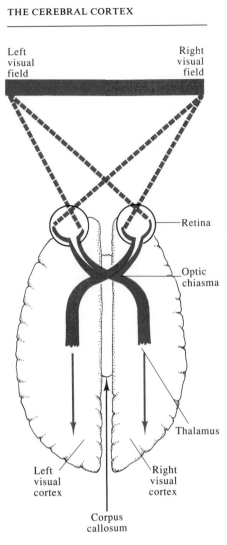

Left visual field

Right visual field

Retina

Optic chiasma

Thalamus

Left visual cortex

Right visual cortex

Corpus callosum

*2.39  The visual pathway*  *The visual pathway is so arranged that all points in the right visual field send their information to the left hemisphere; all those in the left field send theirs to the right hemisphere. Information from one hemisphere is transmitted to the other by way of the corpus callosum.*

right, it is projected to the left hemisphere; if presented to the left, it is projected to the right hemisphere (see Figure 2.39). The patient's job is merely to say what he sees. When the picture is on the right, he can easily do so, for the information is transmitted to the same hemisphere that can formulate a spoken answer—the left hemisphere (which as we've seen is the site of language knowledge and of speech). The situation is different when the picture is flashed on the left. Now the visual image is sent to the right hemisphere, but this hemisphere can neither provide a spoken reply, nor can it relay the information to the left hemisphere, which has the language capacity, because the bridge between the two has been cut (Gazzaniga, 1967).

This is not to say that the right hemisphere has no understanding of what it's been shown. One patient was unexpectedly shown a picture of a nude girl. When this picture was flashed to the left hemisphere, the patient laughed and correctly described what she had seen. When the same picture was presented to the right hemisphere, she said that she saw nothing, but immediately afterward she smiled slyly and began to chuckle. When asked what was so funny, she said, "I don't know . . . nothing . . . oh—that funny machine" (Gazzaniga, 1970, p. 106). The right hemisphere knew what it was laughing at. The left hemisphere heard the laughter but could only guess at the cause, for *it* didn't see what the right hemisphere had looked at.

An elegant demonstration of hemispheric differences uses stimuli that are composites of two pictures, in which the left half of one is joined to the right half of the other (Figure 2.40). These are briefly exposed, with their midline centered in the field of vision. Normal subjects see such pictures as they really are—bizarre monstrosities, such as the left half of a bee stuck onto the right half of an eye. In contrast, split-brain patients never seem to notice anything unusual. They either see a bee or they see an eye, but never both. Which of the two they choose depends upon which hemisphere is asked. Suppose the stimulus is the bee-eye combination, with the bee on the left (thus in the right hemisphere), the eye on the right (hence in the left hemisphere). In one condition, the subjects have to indicate what they just saw by pointing to one of several objects that are shown to them after the brief flash of the bee-eye combination. The choice objects include both a bee and an eye (drawn in complete form) and can be inspected at the subjects' leisure. In this task, language is irrelevant, for the subjects have to recognize only the similarity between two forms, regardless of the names. We have already seen that the right hemisphere is probably more critical for the perception of complex forms than the left. If so, the patients should point to the bee, for that is the only stimulus that the right hemisphere saw. This is just what happens.

In another condition, the task calls on language functions. Patients are again presented with a brief flash of the bee-eye combination. They are then shown pictures of several objects, such as a key and a pie, and they have to select the one whose name *rhymes* with the object they just saw. When tested in this manner, the patients will almost invariably choose the pie, an object whose name rhymes with the name of the only stimulus that was shown to the left hemisphere, the eye (Levy, Trevarthen, and Sperry, 1972; Levy, 1974).

*Is the right hemisphere utterly nonlinguistic?*  The split-brain studies give further proof that language is the province of the left hemisphere. But this doesn't mean that the right hemisphere has no language capacity at all. When a patient is asked to name a picture that is flashed to the left side (that is, to the right hemisphere),

**2.40 Composite figures used to test for hemispheric differences in split-brain patients** *(After Levy, Trevarthen, and Sperry, 1972)*

he sometimes makes a haphazard guess. But immediately afterwards, he often frowns or shakes his head. The right hemisphere evidently has some—limited—ability to understand what it hears. It sees the pictured object, and while it cannot produce the correct name—say, "ashtray"—it knows enough to understand that the name it just came up with—say, "coffeepot," couldn't possibly be right (Gazzaniga, 1967).

Further documentation of right-hemisphere language abilities comes from studies which show that split-brain patients can understand short written words flashed to the right hemisphere, and can tell whether a small string of letters, such as *house* and *pouse,* is or is not an English word (Zaidel, 1976, 1983; for some alternative interpretations, see Gazzaniga, 1983; Levy, 1983).

All the evidence for lateralization we've discussed thus far has come from patients with neurological deficits: some with lesions in one or another hemisphere, others with a severed corpus callosum. Can lateralization be demonstrated in normal populations? A considerable amount of recent research has shown that it can.

*Selective stimulation of the two hemispheres*  One approach uses the same experimental procedure that was so successfully employed with the split-brain patients. Various stimuli are briefly presented to either the right or the left visual field of normal subjects. Some of the stimuli are items that are presumably better dealt with by the left hemisphere: words or letters. Others are items that call on the special capacities of the right hemisphere: faces or other complex forms. The subject's task is to recognize the items and indicate his response as quickly and as accurately as he can.

In studies of this sort, the experimenters' primary interest is in the subject's **reaction time,** that is, in how long it takes him to respond. The logic of the experiment is simple. Suppose the stimulus is presented to the hemisphere that is most appropriate to it: words to the left, faces to the right. If so, this hemisphere can get to work immediately, decipher the stimulus, and come up with an answer. But suppose the stimulus is sent to the wrong cerebral address: words to the right and faces to the left. This calls for an extra step, for now the visual message must be forwarded to the other hemisphere by way of the corpus callosum. But this additional transmission step takes a certain amount of time. As a result, we would expect that subjects will be faster in recognizing words presented to the left hemisphere than to the right hemisphere. By the same token, we would expect them to respond more quickly to faces that are shown to the right hemisphere rather than to the left. By now, a fair number of experiments have shown that this is essentially what happens (e.g., Geffen, Bradshaw, and Wallace, 1971; Moscovitch, 1972, 1979).

*Monitoring the two hemispheres*  The reaction time studies just described show lateralization effects in normal subjects. But these effects have to be inferred from the subject's responses in a rather roundabout way. In recent years, neuroscientists have tried to observe the operation of the two hemispheres more directly and have devised a number of techniques to look in at the cortex from the outside.

One such tool is the PET scan we discussed earlier, which assesses the activity of different brain regions by measuring their metabolic action. A similar logic un-

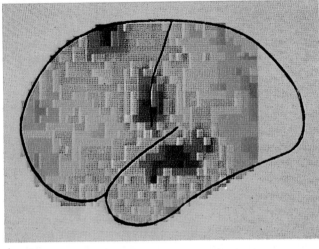

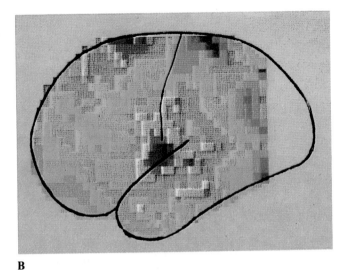

A                                                B

*2.41 Cerebral blood flow in right and left hemispheres during speech* Blood-flow maps obtained with the rCBF technique while subjects were speaking. In these maps, the brain surface was divided into squares, and a computer averaged the blood flow in each square. The rate of flow is indicated by the color, with green indicating average blood flow, shades of blue indicating flow rates below average, and shades of red flow rates above average. (A) Left hemisphere. Note that maximum blood flow occurred in the lower portion of the motor and somatosensory areas (the regions that control movement of the mouth, tongue, and larynx, or receive sensory input from them), the auditory projection area, and Broca's area. (B) Right hemisphere. There is considerably less activity in these regions. (Courtesy of Niels A. Lassen)

derlies the *rCBF (regional cerebral blood flow)* technique, which measures the blood flow in different cortical areas while the subject is engaged in various mental operations. Here the idea is that an increase in the activity of brain cells in a certain part of the cortex will call for an increase in the amount of blood supplied to that region. To determine the distribution of blood flow in the cortex, a mildly radioactive (but harmless) gas is injected into an artery (or is inhaled) and special radiation counters are placed at various points on the subject's skull. The subject is fully conscious and is asked to perform various tasks: to speak, read, follow a moving light, and so on. The distribution of counter readings at the various points on the skull will then give an index of the rate at which blood flows through a given region (Ingvar and Lassen, 1979).

The results of such studies provide a graphic proof that different cortical regions become activated during different tasks. In particular, they document the asymmetry of hemispheric functions. Figure 2.41 shows the rate of blood flow in the two hemispheres while subjects were speaking. In the left hemisphere, the blood flow was more extensive in just the areas where one would expect it to be: the lower portions of the motor and somatosensory cortex (which control and receive sensory information from the mouth, tongue, and larynx), the auditory projection zone, and Broca's area. In the right hemisphere, the activity was much less, especially in the mouth and auditory areas (Lassen, Ingvar, and Skinhoj, 1978).

TWO MODES OF MENTAL FUNCTIONING

The preceding discussion indicates that language and spatial organization are usually handled in two different areas of the brain. Some psychologists believe that this difference in localization goes along with a distinction between two fundamentally different modes of thought: one that involves words, the other spatial processes. This distinction is certainly in line with everyday observation. We often think in words—about scientific problems, about politics, about who likes whom; the list is endless. But we also mentally manipulate the world with little benefit of language—as when we visualize our living room with rearranged furniture or when we work a jigsaw puzzle. Many problems can be solved by either

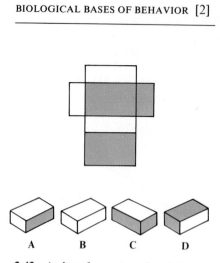

***2.42 An item from a test of spatial relations*** *The subject has to decide which of the figures, A, B, C, or D, can be made by folding the pattern above. (The correct answer is* D. *After Cronbach, 1970a)*

mode. We may find our way to a friend's home by referring to a mental map, or by memorizing a verbal sequence such as "first right turn after the third traffic light." But the two modes are somehow not intersubstitutable. How a corkscrew works is hard to describe in words; the pros and cons of a political two-party system are impossible to get across without them.

The difference between verbal and spatial modes of thought is explicitly recognized in the construction of many tests of intelligence. Different test items are provided to assess each mode separately. Verbal aptitude may be gauged by questions that involve vocabulary ("What does *formulate* mean?") or the abstraction of underlying similarities ("In what ways are waterpipes and streets alike?"). Spatial ability may be tested by items that require the subject to construct a design by arranging a set of colored blocks, or to visualize how a two-dimensional shape will appear when folded into a box (see Figure 2.42). In line with our previous discussion, performance on the various verbal tests is more impaired by lesions to the left hemisphere, while performance on spatial tests is more impaired by lesions to the right hemisphere (Levy, 1974).

Some theorists feel that there is a more fundamental difference in the functions of the two hemispheres that underlies the verbal-spatial distinction. In their view, the right hemisphere is specialized for the organization of space, whereas the left hemisphere concentrates upon organization in time. It is clear that spatial organization is critical for the perception of form, or the ability to visualize three-dimensional shapes given a two-dimensional pattern. But upon reflection, temporal organization is no less critical for language. The person who is insensitive to what comes first and what comes second cannot possibly speak or understand the speech of others. *Tap* is not the same word as *pat,* and the sentence "Wellington beat Bonaparte" is crucially different from "Bonaparte beat Wellington." To summarize this view, the right hemisphere is concerned with what goes where, the left with what comes when (Bogen, 1969; Tzeng and Wang, 1984).

While the space vs. time hypothesis is rather speculative, it is still more or less in line with the facts of hemispheric lateralization. The same is not always true of the many accounts written for the general lay audience. In the process of popularization, the facts have been progressively displaced by a rash of speculations that assert that the two hemispheres differ not just in their relative contributions to language function and spatial organization, but in many other underlying attributes as well. Thus it is sometimes claimed that the left hemisphere controls logical and sequential thought, that it analyzes, works with numbers, and deals in rationality. In contrast, the right hemisphere is said to be concerned with intuition, artistic creativity, and the comprehension of patterns that are grasped as a whole rather than being analyzed into their component parts. Some authors go as far as to relate the right-left hemispheric differences to the (alleged) difference between Western science and logic on the one hand and Eastern culture and mysticism on the other. By now, the popular myth has it that our own society overly encourages "left-brained" at the expense of "right-brained" functions and that we need special efforts to train the neglected right hemisphere (e.g., Ornstein, 1977). One author recommends "Ten Ways to Develop Your Right Brain," which include occasionally drowning out the presentation of information with a musical background and giving a thirty-second explanation of something and asking people to guess what you're getting at (Prince, 1978; cited in Springer and Deutsch, 1981). Whether such procedures actually help to strengthen intuitive thinking or complex pattern perception is exceedingly doubtful. But in any case, there is no reason to believe that the two hemispheres correspond to the distinctions (assuming such distinctions can really be made) between rational vs. intuitive thought, or analytic vs. artistic processes, or the difference between Western and Eastern philosophies of life. As Jerre Levy, a prominent investigator of hemispheric lateralization, puts it: ". . . The popular myths are misinterpretations and wishes, not the observations of scientists. . . . Normal people have not half a brain nor two brains but one gloriously differentiated brain, with each hemisphere contributing its specialized abilities. . . . We have a single brain that generates a single mental self" (Levy, 1985, p. 44).

## Recovery from Brain Injury

As we've seen, much of our knowledge of the brain comes from an analysis of the effects of various cerebral lesions. We now ask how people recover from cerebral injury and by what mechanisms they do so. It is self-evident that this topic is of great medical and general interest. But in addition, the facts about recovery have considerable scientific importance, for they throw yet further light on how the human brain works.

### REPAIR FROM WITHIN

Recovery from cerebral lesions varies enormously. Consider aphasia. In some cases, there is considerable recovery; for example, a stroke patient with aphasia may regain normal fluency and comprehension after a couple of months, though a certain difficulty in finding words (sometimes called **anomia**) usually remains. When shown a picture of a key, the patient may be unable to think of its name and say, "I know what it does . . . you use it to open a door" (Kolb and Whishaw, 1990). But in other cases, the recovery is considerably less, and the prospects for improvements are not too bright; if the individual has not recovered a year or so after the brain injury, the hopes for further gains are relatively small.

How can we explain these great variations in the degree to which patients recover from brain damage?

*Recovery of damaged but living neurons* A critical factor is whether some—or even all—of the neurons in the affected area were damaged rather than being destroyed outright. If so, many of the symptoms may be reversible. An example of such a reversible condition is the damage produced by the pressure brought on by the swelling following a head injury, an infection, or a tumor. If these conditions are removed, for example by draining some cerebral fluid to relieve cranial pressure, the damaged neurons may recover and the patient's symptoms will become less severe or even disappear entirely (Moscovitch and Rozin, 1989).

*Sprouting of collaterals* The outlook is much less favorable when neurons have been destroyed. For as we've seen, there is no replacement warranty for dead neurons; a neuron lost is lost forever. But even so, some possibilities of improvement remain. One possibility is the formation of new connections. The axons of some healthy neurons adjacent to the damaged cells will grow new branches, called **collateral sprouts,** which may eventually attach themselves to the synapses left vacant by the cells lost through injury (Veraa and Grafstein, 1981). Consider the effects of a certain lesion in the hypothalamus of a rat. In the first few days after the lesion, the animal just lies on its belly, unable to stand, let alone walk around, but after a few weeks there is recovery (Golani, Wolgin, and Teitelbaum, 1979). Some authors believe that some of the axons cut by this lesion gradually sprout new collateral branches that fill in for cells that were permanently destroyed. As a result, a smaller number of neurons can now do the work formerly done by many (Stricker and Zigmond, 1976).

Whether such sproutings will always be beneficial is by no means clear. Recovery will occur only if the newly grown branches attach themselves to the appropriate terminals. If the connections are made willy-nilly, the animal may end up worse off than it was before. This is analogous to what happens if a cable of telephone wires is cut. The trick is to reconnect the wires as they were, for anything else will produce telephonic chaos. As yet, we don't know exactly when sprouting will be helpful and when it won't, though there is evidence that both kinds of results can occur (Scheff and Cotman, 1977; Wall, 1980).

*Substitution of function* Another factor that can produce recovery is that the function of the damaged regions is taken over by other parts of the brain. This seems to occur in certain cases of recovery from aphasia; here the right hemisphere comes to perform some of the tasks originally handled by the left. Evidence comes from patients who show nearly complete recovery of language function subsequent to left-hemisphere lesions; in most of these cases, there is an increase in the blood flow to the right hemisphere (Knopman et al., 1984, cited in Rosenzweig and Leiman, 1989).

It appears then that the brain has a certain plasticity of function. Jobs performed by one region of the brain can be taken on by other parts when injury requires it. This plasticity is generally greater in the young. At least up to age eight, children who become aphasic regain speech function, regardless of how severe their impairment had been immediately after the brain injury (Woods and Teuber, 1978).

REPAIR FROM WITHOUT

Thus far, we've talked about cases in which the nervous system manages to repair itself, at least to some extent. Is there a way in which we can help that repair along?

We've seen that the brain cannot replace dead neurons. But there are some recent animal studies which suggest that someday neurologists may be able to provide some such replacement by transplanting neural tissue from outside. Thus far, this work is still in the early experimental stages, but initial results give some grounds for hope (Fine, 1986).

Several groups of investigators have created various kinds of lesions in the brains of rats and then transplanted tissues from the brains of rat fetuses into the affected areas (see Figure 2.43). The donors were fetuses rather than adults because fetal tissue is still relatively unformed and plastic. In one group of studies, the investigators partially destroyed a pathway of dopamine-releasing fibers in the midbrain. This pathway projects upwards to a region at the base of the cerebral hemispheres that is intimately involved in the control of voluntary movement. This is the same pathway whose gradual degeneration produces

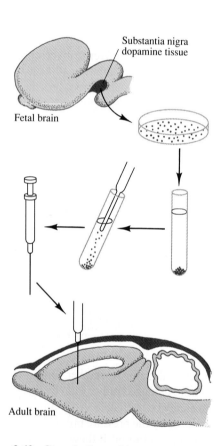

**2.43 Steps in the grafting procedure** *Fetal brain tissue is dissected from a fetal brain, is transferred to a dish with a saline solution, and is then treated to separate the fetal brain cells from connective tissue, blood vessels, and other tissue. It is then transferred to a syringe and injected into the appropriate region of an adult brain (After Björklund, Stenevi, Schmidt, Dunnett, and Gage, 1983)*

Substantia nigra dopamine tissue

Fetal brain

Adult brain

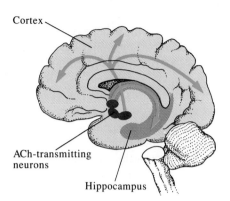

Cortex

ACh-transmitting
neurons

Hippocampus

*2.44 Acetylcholine pathways apparently involved in Alzheimer's disease* Acetylcholine-transmitting neurons located in regions at the base of the forebrain activate many regions of the cortex as well as the hippocampus. The degeneration of these neurons may be a major cause of Alzheimer's disease. (After Coyle, Price, and Delong, 1983)

Parkinson's disease in humans. The effect of the lesion on rats is essentially similar to that found in humans: a serious drop in the level of dopamine in the brains of the affected rats concurrent with massive motor disturbances (see p. 33). The implantation of tissues from the appropriate regions of the donors' brains led to an increase in the host brains' level of dopamine and considerable improvement in motor performance—a result that offers hope for a better therapy for Parkinson's disease than exists at present (Björklund, Stenevi, Schmidt, Dunnett, and Gage, 1983).

Another group of studies is of potential relevance to *Alzheimer's disease,* which afflicts 5 to 10 percent of all persons over age sixty-five (Gelman, 1989). This devastating disease is characterized by a progressive decline in intellectual functioning that begins with serious memory problems, continues with increasing disorientation, and culminates in total physical and mental helplessness. While Alzheimer's disease leads to degenerative changes throughout the brain, the worst destruction seems to befall a pathway of acetylcholine-releasing neurons that have their origin in a region at the base of the forebrain and extend to many cortical association areas as well as to the hippocampus (a structure that is important for memory). When enough of these cells are dead or dying, the cortical and hippocampal regions to which they project are no longer activated. As a result, there is loss of memory and cognitive functioning (see Figure 2.44; Coyle, Price, and DeLong, 1983, p. 1187).*

Can degenerative changes of this sort be reversed by brain transplants? They can in rats, at least to some extent. Some investigators worked on rats that had been subjected to lesions in acetylcholine-releasing pathways analogous to those destroyed in Alzheimer patients. Others used animals of a fairly advanced age (in rats, this is about two years of age). Both the lesioned and the aged rats showed substantial impairments on various tests of memory and spatial learning. Initially they couldn't learn certain simple mazes, or retain what they had learned from one occasion to the next. But after appropriate brain transplants, there was significant improvement (Björklund and Stenevi, 1984; Gage and Björklund, 1986).

Just how do these brain grafts lead to recovery? There are probably several answers. In part, the transplanted tissue may provide new cells for the host brain; in part, the graft may stimulate some of the host's intact neurons to release more transmitter substances; finally, the grafted tissue may encourage axon sprouting (Freed, de Medicacelli, and Wyatt, 1985).

What are the chances that these or similar techniques can be applied to human patients? As of yet, we can't say. There are obvious technological hurdles. But it's worth noting that if and when the transplantation techniques are ready for clinical application, there will be some serious ethical problems as well, because the most probable donors would be aborted human fetuses.

REHABILITATION

Recovery through processes of self-repair can only go so far, especially in adults, and transplantation therapy is as yet only a hope for the future. Can anything be done for the patient to help the recovery process along? The patient can sometimes be taught—very slowly and very patiently—to use impaired functions and

* Students interested in neuroanatomical details may want to know that the dopamine pathway involved in Parkinson's disease extends from the substantia nigra to the caudate nucleus, while the acetylcholine pathway involved in Alzheimer's disease originates in the nucleus basalis of Meynert.

**2.45 Rehabilitation** *Sometimes sheer persistence (and no doubt some good fortune in the site and extent of the lesion) leads to remarkable results. An example is the case of Patricia Neal, an Academy Award winning actress who had a stroke at the age of 39. The stroke paralyzed one leg, and left her unable to speak, read, and write. But an intensive rehabilitation program eventually enabled her to recover sufficiently so that four years later she could star in other films. (Neal, 1988; pictured in the TV movie The Homecoming; courtesy Globe Photos)*

to develop compensatory skills to make up for those lost or damaged. An example is making a patient sit on his good arm, thus forcing him to use the one that is semi-paralyzed. Days and weeks of practice will bring slow gains, but these gains often add up and help the patient develop self-sufficiency. How much this rehabilitation can accomplish depends on the injury and on the patient's capacity and will to continue the training process (see Figure 2.45). Sometimes sheer persistence (and no doubt some good fortune in the site and extent of the lesion) leads to remarkable results.

To sum up. While we know much more about the brain than we did only a decade or two ago, medical technology is as yet unable to do much to aid the recovery of the injured brain. But it looks as if we're on the threshold of a new era of progress in this crucial area. Considering that our population is aging at an ever-increasing rate, with a concomitant increase in the proportion of persons with degenerative brain disorders, that era can come none too soon.

## SOME PROBLEMS IN LOCALIZING BRAIN FUNCTION

The preceding discussion has outlined our current understanding of the localization of function in the human cortex and some prospects for its repair and rehabilitation. But there are some problems that complicate the analysis of any correlation between anatomical and psychological function.

### What Is the Psychological Function?

Much of our knowledge of human cerebral function comes from the study of lesions. But the fact that we know that the destruction of a given site leads to a particular deficit doesn't tell us how that site contributed to the function that was lost. An important first step toward an answer is to ask what that underlying function really is. Sometimes this is fairly clear, as in lesions of the sensory projection areas which cause defects in vision and hearing. But in some other cases, the explanation is much less obvious.

A good example is a famous case reported by the French neurologist Dejerine in 1892 (Geschwind, 1972). Dejerine's patient woke up one morning to discover that he could no longer read. He could speak and understand speech as before; in fact, he could write, though he could not read what he had written. His vision was unaffected with one exception—he could no longer see the right half of his visual field. Given the anatomical arrangement of the visual pathways, one neurological inference was inescapable: There was serious damage to the visual projection area of the left hemisphere. Should we conclude that this region is a "reading center"? Such an interpretation is wildly improbable. Man roamed earth for eons before the advent of writing and we could hardly expect the evolutionary process to provide neurological machinery for a purpose some million years ahead.

To explain the phenomenon we must first consider what reading is. Many authors believe that in most modern writing systems, the written word is a visual transcription of the spoken one (Gleitman, L., and Rozin, 1977). In their view, the child learns to read by associating certain visual forms with speech sounds and, through them, with meanings. Since the speech sounds and meanings are

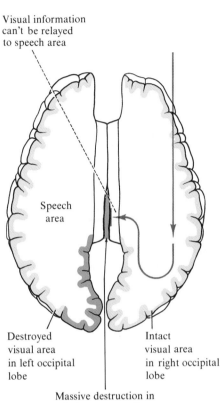

Visual information can't be relayed to speech area

Speech area

Destroyed visual area in left occipital lobe

Intact visual area in right occipital lobe

Massive destruction in posterior corpus callosum

**2.46  A disconnection effect**  *The figure shows lesions in the left occipital cortex and the posterior corpus callosum. Given these effects, vision depends entirely on the visual projection area in the right hemisphere. But this information can't be related to the speech area of the left hemisphere because the hemispheric bridge for visual messages is the posterior corpus callosum. As a result, the patient sees the word, but only as a meaningless set of forms. (After Geschwind, 1972)*

dealt with in the language areas of the left hemisphere, it is plausible to assume that these areas must participate in the act of reading. According to this view, the visual information has to be passed on to the language areas of the left hemisphere in order to be interpreted as language symbols—in order to be read. But suppose the pathway between the visual and the speech areas is no longer there? At postmortem examination, Dejerine found that his patient suffered such a disconnection. A large portion of his corpus callosum was destroyed, as was the visual projection area of the left hemisphere. This solved the riddle. The *right* visual cortex was unimpaired and so the patient could see. The language areas of the left hemisphere were intact, and so he could speak and comprehend. The motor system was unaffected, so he could write. But the destruction of the corpus callosum isolated the visual cortex of the right hemisphere from the language areas of the left. As a result, the patient saw printed text but could not read it (Figure 2.46). This effect is obviously quite similar to what is observed in split-brain patients.

This example highlights the fact that we must try to understand both terms of a psychoanatomical correlation. To understand the neural underpinnings of some aspect of behavior, whether language, memory, or whatever, we must understand something about that behavior itself, quite apart from its relation to cerebral anatomy. For psychology and neurophysiology go hand in hand. To claim that psychology will not progress until we know more about the brain is to assert only half the truth because the search for a neurophysiological underpinning necessarily requires some knowledge of what it is an underpinning of.

## Who's in Charge?

Another problem concerns hierarchical control. Who is in ultimate charge? We have previously seen that the nervous system is organized along the lines of a hierarchy, with higher centers controlling lower centers, which control yet lower ones. But where does the cortex fit in? Some nineteenth-century neurologists supposed that some regions of the cortex are at the very top of the hierarchy and hand down orders to all the rest. This notion fits in with our view that those functions that are most severely disturbed by cortical lesions—language, thinking, memory, and perception—are the "higher" mental processes, which presumably govern the "lower" ones. But many modern neuroscientists believe that this conclusion doesn't really follow. For the cortex does not control many of the lower functions. For example, rats—and for that matter, humans—continue to eat and seek food even though they may have suffered extensive cortical damage. Foods that they found highly palatable or distasteful before the lesion will still be palatable or distasteful afterwards (Grill and Berridge, 1985). This is not to say that the cortex does not play any role in food seeking (or drinking, or sexual behavior, or any other so-called "lower" functions). But there is no evidence that it governs them.

The best guess is that the nervous system is not organized according to a single hierarchy. It is not an absolute monarchy, with a cortical king who governs all else below (e.g., Arbib, 1972). Instead, it is composed of a number of hierarchies whose controls and functions overlap, with some in the cortex and some in subcortical structures. These hierarchies interact continuously, with one in charge on one occasion but not on another. So it probably makes no sense to say that any one of them is ruler. For the operation of the nervous system may well be analogous to that of a complex twentieth-century society such as ours. The United States in 1980 is not governed by *one* hierarchy, but by a number of interlocking ones. There are the three branches of the federal government, as well as the armed forces, the bureaucracies of the government agencies, the hierarchies of the large corporations, the labor unions, the media, and so on and so on. We are governed by a complex interaction of them all, and who will decide depends on many factors, including what it is that is to be decided.

Who's in charge? As yet, we know too little to be sure of any answer. But the best guess is: It depends.

## SUMMARY

1. Since Descartes, many scientists have tried to explain human and animal movement within the framework of the *reflex* concept: A stimulus excites a sense organ, which transmits excitation upward to the spinal cord or brain, which in turn relays the excitation downward to a muscle or gland and thus produces action. Descartes's general classification of nervous function is still with us as we distinguish between *reception, integration,* and *reaction.*

2. Later investigators showed that the smallest unit of the nervous system is the *neuron,* whose primary anatomical subdivisions are the *dendrites, cell body,* and *axon.*

3. The main function of a neuron is to produce a *nerve impulse.* This is an electrochemical disturbance that is propagated along the membrane of the axon. This occurs when the cell's normal *resting potential* is disrupted by a stimulus whose intensity exceeds the *threshold.* This stimulus produces a brief depolarization of the cell, which leads to an *action potential.* The action potential obeys the *all-or-none law:* Once threshold is reached, further increases of stimulus intensity have no effect on its magnitude. But the nervous system can nevertheless distinguish between different intensities of stimuli all of which are above threshold. One means is *frequency:* The more intense the stimulus, the more often the neuron fires.

4. To understand how neurons communicate, investigators have studied *reflex action,* which is necessarily based on the activity of several neurons. Results of studies with *spinal dogs* led Sherrington to infer the processes that underlie conduction across the *synapse,* the gap between the axon of one neuron and the dendrites and cell body of the next. Conduction within neurons was shown to obey different laws than conduction between neurons (that is, across the synapse). Evidence included the phenomena of *spatial* and *temporal summation.* Sherrington concluded that the excitation from several neurons funnels into a common reservoir to produce a *central excitatory state.*

5. Further studies argued for a *central inhibitory state.* Evidence came from *reciprocal inhibition* found in antagonistic muscles. Further work showed that a reflex can be activated either by increasing excitation or by decreasing inhibition. An example of the latter is the *disinhibition* produced by the destruction of higher centers which inhibit the reflex.

6. Sherrington's inferences of synaptic functions have been confirmed by modern electrical and chemical studies. Today we know that transmission across the synapse is accomplished by *neurotransmitters,* chemical substances that are liberated at the axon terminals of one neuron and exert excitatory or inhibitory effects on the dendrites and cell body of another. These transmitters cross the *synaptic gap* and affect *receptor molecules* located on the *postsynaptic membrane.* This creates *graded potentials* that summate and spread.

When they reach threshold value, they produce an action potential in the axon of the second neuron.

7. Important examples of neurotransmitters include *acetylcholine, norepinephrine* and *dopamine.* Of special interest is a group of neurotransmitters called *endorphins* whose activity serves to alleviate pain.

8. In addition to the nervous system, there is another group of organs whose function is to serve as an instrument of communication within the body. This is the *endocrine system,* whose glands secrete their *hormones* directly into the bloodstream, which will eventually carry them to various target organs.

9. A crude anatomical outline of the vertebrate nervous system starts out with the distinction between the *peripheral (somatic* and *autonomic)* and *central nervous systems.* The central nervous system consists of the *spinal cord* and the *brain.* Important parts of the brain are the *hindbrain* (including *medulla* and *cerebellum*), *midbrain* (including the *reticular formation*) and *forebrain* (including *thalamus, hypothalamus, cerebral hemispheres,* and *cerebral cortex*). Of special interest is a group of subcortical structures of the forebrain called the *limbic system.*

10. In general, the brain tends to function hierarchically, with higher centers commanding lower centers. Animals whose brain is cut so that they lack both midbrain and forebrain can still move but don't integrate their movements. Animals that lack the forebrain show integrated movements but without any goal.

11. The *cerebral cortex* is generally believed to underlie the most complex aspects of behavior. The *projection areas* of the cortex act as receiving stations for sensory information or as dispatching centers for motor commands. The remaining regions of the cortex are called *association areas.* Their function concerns such higher mental processes as planning, remembering, thinking, and speech.

12. A number of modern neurological tools, including the *CAT scan* and the *PET scan,* make it possible to diagnose and study lesions in the brains of living patients. Certain lesions of association areas lead to *apraxia,* a serious disturbance in the organization of voluntary action. Other lesions produce *agnosia,* a disorganization of perception and recognition. Still others cause *aphasia,* a profound disruption of language function, which may involve speech production, speech comprehension, or both.

13. In many ways, the two hemispheres are mirror images of each other. But to some extent, their function is not symmetrical. In most right-handers, the left hemisphere handles the bulk of the language functions, while the right hemisphere is more relevant to spatial comprehension. One source of evidence for this difference in hemispheric function, or *lateralization,* comes from the study of *split-brain patients* in whom the main connection between the two hemispheres, the *corpus callosum,* has been surgically cut. Further evidence is provided by the reaction times of normal persons when stimuli calling on verbal or spatial abilities are presented to either hemisphere. Direct observation of the operation of the two hemispheres can be obtained by measuring different rates of blood flow in the two hemispheres.

14. Recovery from cerebral lesions varies considerably from one patient to another. Some recovery is produced by *collateral sprouting,* whereby healthy neurons adjacent to the region of injury will grow new branches. In addition, some functions of the damaged regions are sometimes taken over by other, undamaged, parts of the brain. Recent work on the transplanting of neural tissue offers some hope that neurobiologists may ultimately provide some replacement for damaged tissue.

# CHAPTER 3

# Motivation

In this chapter, we will examine some of the simple motives that human beings share with other animals. These motives steer our behavior in certain directions rather than others; toward food, say, rather than toward shelter.

Our main concern will be with motives that are essentially unlearned and that pertain to the individual alone rather than to his interaction with others. Examples are hunger and thirst, the desire for safety, the need for rest. We will later take up two other kinds of motives. One concerns desires that are acquired through learning, such as the need to achieve, to attain prestige, or to amass possessions (see Chapters 12, 13, and 15). The other group is no less biologically based than hunger and thirst, but it involves motives that transcend the individual alone and focus on his relations with other persons, such as sex, filial love, and aggression (see Chapter 10).

## MOTIVATION AS DIRECTION

Most human and animal actions are directed. We don't simply walk, reach, shrink, or flee; we walk and reach *toward* some objects, shrink and flee *away* from others. The objects that are approached or withdrawn from may be in the organism's here and now, as when a kitten jumps toward a rolling ball. But often enough, the object exists in an as yet unrealized future. The hawk circles in the sky in search of prey, but there is none in sight as yet. In such a case, an inner motive (a purpose, a desire) leads to actions that bring the hawk closer to its food.

Directed action seems difficult to reconcile with Descartes's notion of humans and animals as reflex machines, however complex their internal wiring. This problem is most pronounced for actions that are directed toward some future

*Motivation as directed action*   *Cast adrift on a raft for weeks, the few survivors of a shipwreck direct all their efforts toward a nearby ship that might bring rescue. (*The Wreck of the Medusa *by Theodore Gericault, 1819; courtesy the Louvre)*

goal, for it is hard to see how an automaton can be imbued with purpose or desire. But difficulties arise even in the simplest case in which the direction is toward (or away from) an immediately present object. Consider the kitten reaching for the ball. What matters is not whether this flexor muscle is contracted or that extensor muscle relaxed, but rather whether the overall pattern of muscular activity gets the creature closer to the final end state—near the ball. The kitten may swipe at the ball with its right paw or its left, it may crouch more on one side or the other —all that matters is that, whatever the specific motor response, it will be toward the ball. Descartes's statues walked out and bowed when a visitor stepped on a hidden spring, but did they bow *to* the visitor? Suppose the visitor were to push the spring and then jump quickly to the left. The statue would surely lumber through its prescribed routine exactly as before, in stony disregard of the altered circumstance.

It is evident that a simple automaton is incapable of directed action. Can the machine be modified to overcome this lack? The answer is yes.

## Control Systems

Modern engineers have developed an immense technology based on machines that control their own activities and are in that sense directed. The basic principle upon which these devices are built is the notion of a *feedback system.* When a machine is in operation it performs some kind of action which may be mechanical, electrical, thermal, or whatever, but which in all cases engenders some changes in the external environment. If these changes in turn influence the further operation of the machine—if they feed back upon the machine—we have a control system based on feedback.

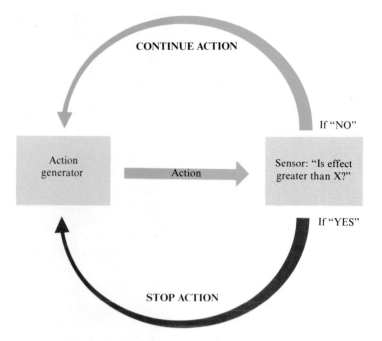

**CONTINUE ACTION**

If "NO"

Action generator

Action

Sensor: "Is effect greater than X?"

If "YES"

**STOP ACTION**

**3.1  Negative feedback**  *In negative feedback systems, the feedback stops or reverses the action that produces it. A sensing device indicates the level of a certain stimulus. If that level exceeds a certain setpoint, the action stops. The effect is self-regulation.*

In *positive feedback systems,* the feedback strengthens the very response that produced it. The result is an ever-increasing level of activity. A technological example is a rocket that homes in on airplanes. It is designed to increase its velocity the closer it gets to its target.

Of greater relevance to our present concern is *negative feedback* in which the feedback stops, or even reverses, the original response of the machine that produced the environmental change. Negative feedback underlies a large number of industrial devices called *servomechanisms* that can maintain themselves in a particular state. A simple example is the system that controls most home furnaces. A thermostat closes an electric contact for all temperatures below a given setting and opens it for all that are above it. The contact controls the furnace, which only operates when the contact is closed. In the winter, the result is a steady house temperature, for the furnace will burn fuel only if the temperature is below the critical level; once this is reached, the furnace shuts off, deactivated by its own negative feedback (Figure 3.1). In a sense, the thermostatically controlled furnace has a goal: It "aims" at a particular temperature.

Negative feedback systems exist at all levels of the nervous system and are responsible, at least in part, for directed action. In this chapter we will see how such systems underlie motivated actions of many kinds. Some concern the organism's regulation of various vital functions—temperature maintenance, food and water intake, and the like. Others involve the organism's reaction to threats from outside, whether fearful escape or raging attack.

## SELF-REGULATION

Can we apply the principles of negative feedback to the understanding of motivated action in which the direction is imposed from within? We will begin by considering those motives which grow directly out of the organism's regulation of its own internal state, such as its temperature, its water level, and its supply of food nutrients.

## Homeostasis

Some two hundred years after Descartes, another Frenchman, the physiologist Claude Bernard (1813–1878), emphasized the fact that the organism exists in an internal environment as well as an external one—the organism's own body fluids, its blood and its lymph. Bernard pointed out that this *internal environment* is kept remarkably constant despite considerable fluctuations of the environment outside. The striking constancy is shown by the salt and water balance of the body, its oxygen concentration, its pH (a measure of acidity), its concentration of various nutrient substances such as glucose, and its temperature (in warm-blooded animals). In healthy organisms, all of these oscillate within very narrow limits, and these limits define the organism's conditions for health and survival. Thus 60 to 90 milligrams per 100 cubic centimeters of blood is the acceptable range for the glucose concentration in the bloodstream of a healthy person. A drop below this level means coma and eventual death; a prolonged rise above it indicates disorders such as diabetes. The modern term for this stable internal equilibrium is **homeostasis** (literally, "equal state") and the mechanisms whereby it is achieved are sometimes said to reflect the "wisdom of the body" (Cannon, 1932).

## Temperature Regulation

A rather simple example of homeostatic balance is temperature regulation in birds and mammals. These animals are called warm-blooded because they have a large repertoire of homeostatic adjustments that keep their internal body temperatures at a fairly constant level, despite wide temperature variations in the surrounding environment.

### TEMPERATURE CONTROL FROM WITHIN

If the internal temperature of a warm-blooded animal is too high, various reflexive reactions produce heat loss. One is peripheral **vasodilatation,** a widening of the skin's capillaries. This sends warm blood to the body surface and results in heat loss by radiation. Other reactions that lead to cooling are sweating (in humans) and panting (in dogs), both of which produce heat loss by evaporation.

An opposed pattern is called into play when the internal temperature is too low. Now there is no sweating or panting, and instead of peripheral vasodilatation there is **vasoconstriction.** The capillary diameters narrow, so that the blood is squeezed away from the cold periphery and heat is conserved. Other reflexive reactions include **piloerection,** a ruffling of fur which creates a thick envelope of protective air. (The gooseflesh feeling is our feeble remnant of this reflex response, of little use to us now in our naked condition.)

These and other reflexive reactions are called into play when the temperature deviates too far from some internal temperature setpoint (Figure 3.2). But in some animals this setpoint can be changed. For example, a certain ground squirrel spends the winter in hibernation. As the outside temperature gets colder and

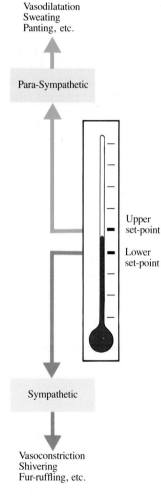

**3.2 Reflexive temperature regulation in mammals** *When the temperature deviates from an internal setpoint, various reflexive reactions will occur to restore the temperature to this setpoint.*

colder, his internal setpoint drops, so he finds a secluded burrow and falls into a torpor—a useful mechanism in times when food is very scarce. But while his new setpoint is low, it still functions. When the weather gets cold enough, he wakes up to keep from freezing to death (Heller, Cranshaw, and Hammel, 1978).

### TEMPERATURE CONTROL BY BEHAVIOR

The homeostatic mechanisms we have just described are essentially involuntary. They may be actions, but we don't feel that they are *our* actions; in fact, some of them concern only a fraction of the body's subsystems. For example, vasodilatation and vasoconstriction do not involve the skeletal musculature at all. But there is no question that when the need arises, these reflexive mechanisms are supplemented by voluntary actions that involve the organism as a whole. If a rat is placed in a cold cage, it will search for suitable materials and build a nest. That humans perform similar voluntary acts in the service of temperature regulation goes without saying: They wear coats when they are cold and wear as little as custom permits (or turn on an air conditioner if they have it) when they are hot. The important point is that these voluntary actions are still in the service of that same internal environment whose constancy is so crucial to survival. But there is one important difference: Now the organism actively changes its external environment so that its internal environment can stay the same.

### THE AUTONOMIC NERVOUS SYSTEM AND TEMPERATURE CONTROL

To understand how the nervous system marshals its forces to protect us against extreme heat and cold, we'll begin by looking at the involuntary side of temperature regulation. What controls the various reactions of the internal organs that accomplish this? The most direct control is exerted by the autonomic nervous system (ANS), which sends commands to the **glands** and to the **smooth muscles*** of the viscera (internal organs) and the blood vessels. The ANS has two divisions: the **sympathetic** and the **parasympathetic**. These two divisions often act as antagonists. Thus, the excitation of the sympathetic division leads to an acceleration of heart rate and inhibition of peristalsis (rhythmic contractions) of the intestines. Parasympathetic activation has effects that are the very opposite: cardiac deceleration and stimulation of peristalsis. This same antagonism is seen in temperature regulation. The sympathetic division acts to counteract cold; it triggers vasoconstriction, shivering, and fur-ruffling. In contrast, the parasympathetic helps to cool the body when it is overheated; it stimulates panting, sweating, and vasodilatation (see Figure 3.14, p. 82). We'll have more to say about the tug-of-war between the two autonomic divisions when we discuss fear and rage. For now, we merely note that the autonomic nervous system is an important agent in directing the control of the internal environment.

### SENSING THE INTERNAL ENVIRONMENT: THE HYPOTHALAMUS

The sympathetic and parasympathetic divisions control the various reflexive levers that help to maintain the internal environment. But what governs *them*? A crucial center is the hypothalamus (see Figure 3.3), which represents a certain

Hypothalamus

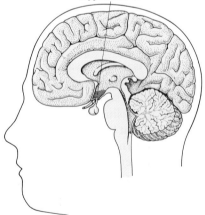

**3.3   The hypothalamus**   *Cross-section of the human brain with the hypothalamus indicated in blue. (After Keeton, 1980)*

---

* The individual fibers of these muscles look smooth when observed under a microscope, in contrast to the fibers of the skeletal muscles, which look striped.

triumph of anatomical miniaturization. Though weighing less than five grams it contains the controls for many of the biological motives.

Several regions within the hypothalamus control the two divisions of the autonomic nervous system whose excitation leads to the cooling and heating effects. The next question is how the hypothalamus decides which of the two divisions should act and by how much. Under normal conditions, temperature regulation is nearly perfect. This means that the organism somehow knows it own body temperature, can sense deviations from the normal level, and can then determine in which direction it should throw the autonomic two-way switch (for example, vasoconstriction versus vasodilatation) to restore the thermal balance. How does it do this?

The answer is that the hypothalamus contains its own thermometer: receptor cells that respond to the temperature of the body fluids in which the brain is bathed. These thermoreceptors are hooked up to the reflex controls so as to yield negative feedback—a hypothalamic thermostat. If this is so, one should be able to fool the hypothalamus by changing its temperature independently of the temperature of the skin and body; a hot hypothalamus should then cause sweating, regardless of the actual body temperature. This is just what happens. When a cat's anterior hypothalamus is heated by a warm wire, there is panting and vasodilatation despite the fact that the cat's body temperature may be well below normal (Magoun et al., 1938). The effect is analogous to what happens when hot air is directed at a home thermostat. The furnace will shut itself off, even though the house is actually freezing.

Vasoconstriction and vasodilatation are involuntary reflexes, more in the domain of physiology than that of behavior. Does the hypothalamic feedback device have similar effects upon actions that reach out into the external world (for instance, wearing a fur coat)? Indeed it does. As one example, consider a study that utilized the fact that rats in a cold chamber will press a bar for a brief burst of heat (Weiss and Laties, 1961; see Figure 3.4). The question was whether rats that had learned this skill in a cold environment would bar-press for heat if one cooled their brains rather than their bodies. The test was to run cold liquid through a very thin U-shaped tube implanted in the anterior hypothalamus (Satinoff, 1964). The rats turned on the heat lamp when their brains were cooled even though the outside temperature was reasonably neutral.

Tricking the hypothalamus can evidently affect integrated behavior patterns just as it does autonomic reactions like vasodilatation. The hypothalamus defines an internal need state for the rest of the nervous system, and this need state will then become an important criterion that determines the appropriateness of any given act.

It is worth noting that the region that controls involuntary temperature regulation (such as shivering and vasoconstriction) is not identical to the one that controls voluntary warming and cooling behaviors. When one of these was destroyed (an area just in front of the hypothalamus), the animals stopped pressing levers to turn heat lamps on or off, but there was no effect on involuntary reactions such as shivering and vasoconstriction. The result was reversed when another region was destroyed (this time an area at the side of the hypothalamus); now the autonomic reactions were abolished but the voluntary behaviors remained (Satinoff and Rutstein, 1970; Satinoff and Shan, 1971; Van Zoeren and Stricker, 1977). It appears there are separate circuits to handle two different ways of solving the same homeostatic problem; here, as in many other areas, evolution has provided multiple safeguards to protect the organism's vital functions (Satinoff, 1978).

*3.4 Performing a learned response to keep warm* A rat kept in a cold environment will learn to press a lever which turns on a heat lamp for a few seconds after each lever press. (Weiss and Laties, 1961)

***Osmotic dehydration*** *Although surrounded by water, sailors in a lifeboat are nevertheless dying of thirst, for drinking the seawater would only lead to further dehydration. (Scene from* Mutiny on the Bounty, *1935; courtesy Photofest)*

## THIRST

What holds for temperature holds for most other homeostatic regulations as well. An example is the body's water supply. The organism continually loses water—primarily through the kidneys, but also through the respiratory system, the sweat glands, the digestive tract, and occasionally, by hemorrhage.

How does the system act to offset these losses? One set of reactions is entirely internal. Thus, a loss of water volume leads to a secretion of the so-called ***antidiuretic hormone (ADH)*** by the pituitary gland. ADH instructs the kidneys to reabsorb more of the water that passes through them. As a result, less water is passed out of the body in the urine.

But as with temperature regulation, internal readjustments can only restore the bodily balance up to a point. ADH can protect the body against further water loss, but it cannot bring back what was lost already. Eventually, the corrective measures must involve some behavior by which the organism reaches out into the external world so as to readjust its internal environment. This behavior is drinking—in humans, an average of two to three quarts of water per day.

### Volume Receptors

How does the body know about its own condition? How does it know that what it needs is water? There are a number of receptors that provide this information. Some are located in the brain and monitor the total volume of blood and other body fluids outside of the cells. According to some investigators, the receptors perform this task by responding to a substance called ***angiotensin,*** which is produced by the kidneys when there is a decrease in the total amount of liquid that passes through them (Epstein, Fitzsimons, and Rolls, 1970). Other volume receptors are located inside of the heart and its surrounding veins, and they are excited by drops in blood pressure set off when there is a decrease in the total amount of body fluid. Their effect was shown by studies on dogs in which a small balloon was inserted into the large vein that leads to the heart. When this balloon was inflated, the dogs drank copiously. The balloon impeded the blood flow into the heart and caused a decrease in fluid pressure. This set off the pressure receptors which sent the brain the signals that led to drinking (Fitzsimons and Moore-Gillow, 1980; Rolls and Rolls, 1982).

## Osmoreceptors

Still another group of receptors keep track of the water *within* the body's cells. This depends on the concentration of certain minerals (especially sodium) that are dissolved in the fluid outside of the cell. Suppose the sodium content of the outside fluid is markedly increased (for example, by drinking salt water). While water can pass freely through the cell's membrane, many dissolved minerals cannot. The water will now flow in the direction that keeps the total concentration of dissolved materials equal on both sides of the membrane. As a result, any increase in the sodium content of the outside fluid dehydrates the cells as water is drawn out of them—a process called osmosis (see Figure 3.5). This of course is the reason why drinking salt water makes us *more* rather than less thirsty.

A number of studies have shown that there are receptor cells in the brain that are sensitive to these osmotic processes (and are therefore called ***osmoreceptors***). They respond to the concentration of their surrounding fluid solutions. Proof comes from studies in which tiny drops of salt water are injected into certain regions in or around the hypothalamus of a rat. The injection immediately leads to drinking. This is because the injection changes the concentration of the fluid that surrounds the receptor cell. It will now contain more dissolved materials (here, sodium) than the cell itself. As a result, water leaks out by osmosis, the receptor fires, and the animal begins to drink (Blass and Epstein, 1971; Rolls and Rolls, 1982).

It appears that there are at least three separate receptor systems that monitor the body's water levels; future research may find even more. Why so many? Here, as in the case of other disruptions of the organism's internal environment, we find that evolution has provided us with multiple defenses. There is a redundancy of mechanisms, so that if one fails another can take its place. We will find even greater redundancy when we turn to a more complex system of self-regulation: maintaining the body's nutrient levels by feeding.

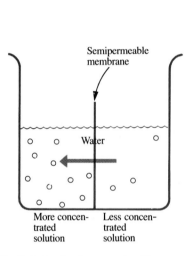

**3.5 Dehydration by osmosis** *If two solutions are separated by a membrane that allows the free flow of water but impedes the flow of substances that are dissolved in the water, water flows from the less concentrated region into the more concentrated one.*

## HUNGER

All animals have to eat and much of their lives revolve around food—searching for it, hunting it, ingesting it, and doing their best not to become food for others. There is no doubt that feeding is ultimately in the service of homeostasis, for no matter what food an animal eats or how he gets it, the ultimate biological consequence is always the same—to maintain appropriate nutrient supplies in the internal environment. But what are the actual mechanisms that determine whether humans and animals eat or stop eating? To put it another way, what is hunger and what is satiety?

## The Signals for Feeding

There are numerous signals that control food intake. Among the most important of these are stimuli that arise from within the animal's own body and somehow inform the brain of the current state of the nutrient supplies. That some such messages are sent is certain. Without them, neither humans nor animals would be able to control their food intake, and they generally do. If food is freely available, they usually tend to eat just about the right amount to keep a roughly constant weight as adults. What is regulated is calorie intake rather than the total volume of food that is eaten. This was demonstrated in a study in which the experimenter varied the calorie level of the diet he fed to rats by adulterating their food with nonnutritive cellulose. The more diluted the food, the more of it was eaten, in a quantity roughly adequate to keep the total calorie content constant (Adolph, 1947).

This self-regulation of food intake persists even when there is no guidance from taste and smell receptors. One experiment used rats whose food was always delivered directly into the stomach. The animals learned to press a bar that squirted a few drops of liquid food through a special tube which led into the stomach. The rats injected themselves with just about the right number of squirts to keep a level weight. When the food was diluted with an equal amount of water, they doubled their intake (Epstein and Teitelbaum, 1962).

### RECEPTORS IN THE BRAIN

How does the animal manage to adjust its food intake to its calorie needs? From the start, investigators focused on *glucose* (or blood sugar), which is the major source of energy for bodily tissues. They believed that somewhere in the body are receptors that detect changes in the way this metabolic fuel is utilized.

Many authors believe that some of the relevant receptors are in the brain itself, most likely the hypothalamus. These *glucoreceptors* are thought to sense the amount of glucose that is available for metabolic use (Mayer, 1955). Evidence comes from studies in which the hypothalamus was injected with a chemical that made its cells unable to respond to glucose. The result was ravenous eating. This treatment presumably silenced the glucoreceptors whose failure to fire was then interpreted as a fuel deficiency, which led to feeding (Miselis and Epstein, 1970).

### RECEPTORS IN THE STOMACH AND INTESTINES

Why does an animal stop eating? The receptors in the brain can't be the only reason. For they respond to fuel deficiency in the bloodstream, and this deficiency will not be corrected until after the meal has been at least partially digested. Yet, humans and animals will terminate a meal much before that. What tells them that it's time to stop?

Common sense suggests that feeding stops when the stomach is full. This is true enough, but it is only part of the story, for animals will stop eating even when their stomach is only partially full. This will only happen, however, if they have ingested a nutritious substance. If the stomach is filled with an equal volume of nonnutritive bulk, the animal will continue to eat. This suggests that the stomach walls contain receptors that are sensitive to the nutrients dissolved in the digestive juices. They signal the brain that nutrient supplies to the internal environment are on their way as food is about to enter the intestines. The result is satiety (Deutsch, Puerto, and Wang, 1978).

### SIGNALS FROM THE SMALL INTESTINE

Further satiety signals come from the **duodenum,** the first part of the small intestine. When food passes out of the stomach into the intestines, the duodenum begins to release a hormone from its mucous lining. There is good evidence that this hormone—**cholecystokinin,** or **CCK**—sends "stop eating" messages to the brain (Gibbs and Smith, 1984). When CCK is injected into the abdominal cavity of hungry rats and dogs, they stop feeding; when it is administered to people, it produces a sense that they've had enough (Stacher, Bauer, and Steinringer, 1979).

### SIGNALS FROM THE LIVER

Yet another source of information about the body's nutrient levels comes from the organ that acts as the manager of the body's food metabolism—the liver.

Immediately after a meal, glucose is plentiful. Since the body can't use it all, much of it is converted into other forms and put in storage. One such conversion goes on in the liver, where glucose is turned into **glycogen** (often called animal starch). Glycogen cannot be used up as a metabolic fuel. This is fine right after a meal, but eventually the stored energy has to be tapped. At that time, the chemical reaction goes the other way. Now the glycogen is turned into usable glucose.

Several recent studies suggest that the liver contains receptors that can sense in which direction the metabolic transaction goes, from glucose cash to glycogen deposits, or vice versa. If the balance tips toward glycogen manufacture, the receptors signal satiety and the animal stops eating. If the balance tips toward glucose production, the receptors signal hunger and the animal eats (Figure 3.6). The evidence that this happens in the liver comes from hungry dogs that were injected with glucose. If the injection was into the vein that goes directly to the liver, the dogs stopped eating. If the injection was anywhere else, there was no comparable effect (Russek, 1971; Friedman and Stricker, 1976).

Such evidence suggests that the internal stimuli for hunger and satiety arise at a rather earlier stage in the process of food extraction and storage than had been traditionally believed. If so, food-related homeostasis is not a last-ditch affair in which the system waits until the internal environment is already in precarious imbalance. Instead, the built-in hunger mechanism seems to be more prudent. It has an anticipatory character that corrects metabolic insufficiencies before they can possibly affect the internal environment that bathes the brain.

### SIGNALS FROM THE OUTSIDE

The self-regulation of food intake is remarkable, but it is not perfect. Humans and animals eat to maintain nutritive homeostasis; put another way, they eat because they are hungry. But they sometimes eat because they like the taste of a particular food. We eat dessert even though we may be full; our hunger is gone, but not our appetite.

Such facts show that eating is not solely determined by stimuli that come from within the body. For these are supplemented by various external signals. We

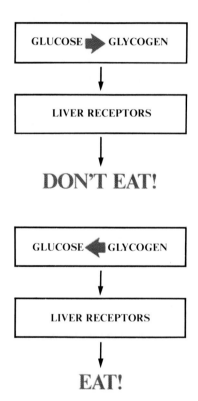

**3.6   The relation between the glucose-glycogen balance in the liver and eating**

**Peasant Wedding Feast**   *(Peter Brueghel the Elder, 1527; courtesy the Kunsthistorisches Museum)*

clearly do not eat for calories alone. Taste—and also smell and texture—is a powerful determinant of food intake for humans as well as animals. But palatability is not the only external signal for eating. Other signals are determined through learning. The expected mealtime is one example; the company of fellow eaters is another. A hen who has had her fill of grain will eagerly resume her meal if joined by other hens who are still hungry (Bayer, 1929).

External stimuli—say, the smell of a sizzling steak—can be a powerful inducement to start eating, but their effectiveness depends in part on the internal state of the organism. Sights, smells, and tastes can restore one's appetite, but if the meal was large enough, even the tastiest dessert will no longer be tempting. In line with this fact of everyday experience is a finding about food-sighting neurons in the hypothalamus of monkeys. In one group of studies, investigators implanted microelectrodes in the hypothalamus of waking monkeys and found some neurons in that area that fired when the animal was shown a peanut or a banana. But these cells only fired when the monkey was hungry. When the animal was first fed to satiety and *then* shown the same foods, the hypothalamic neurons did not respond. It would seem that at least in the hypothalamus, the eye is *not* bigger than the stomach (Mora, Rolls, and Burton, 1976; Rolls, 1978).

### Hypothalamic Control Centers

We have seen that there are many different signals for food intake. It was natural to suppose that these various messages are all integrated at one point in the nervous system where a final decision is made to eat or not to eat. The natural candidate for such a "feeding center" was the hypothalamus, which was already known to house controls for temperature regulation and water balance and which gave evidence of containing glucoreceptors. Psychophysiologists soon devised a theory of hypothalamic control of feeding that was analogous to the temperature system. It postulates two antagonistic centers, one corresponding to hunger, the other to satiety.

## DUAL-CENTER THEORY

According to dual-center theory, the hypothalamus contains an "on" and an "off" command post for eating. Two anatomical regions are implicated. One is located in the **lateral region** of the hypothalamus; it was said to function as a "hunger center" whose activation leads to food search and eating. The other is the **ventromedial region** which was thought to be a "satiety center" whose stimulation stops eating.

To buttress their claims about the functions of these regions, dual-center theorists pointed to the effects of lesions. Rats whose lateral hypothalamus has been destroyed suffer from **aphagia** (Greek, "no eating"). They refuse to eat and drink and will starve to death unless forcibly tube-fed for weeks (Teitelbaum and Stellar, 1954). Interestingly enough, eventually there is some recovery of function. After a few weeks the animals begin to eat again, especially if tempted by such delectables as liquid eggnog (Teitelbaum and Epstein, 1962).

The reverse occurs after lesions to the ventromedial region. Animals with such lesions suffer from **hyperphagia** (Greek, "excess eating"). They eat voraciously and keep on eating. If the lesion is large enough, they may become veritable mountains of rat obesity, finally reaching weights that are some three times as great as their preoperative levels. Tumors in this hypothalamic region (although very rare) have the same effects on humans (Miller, Bailey, and Stevenson, 1950; Teitelbaum, 1955, 1961).

While ventromedial lesions lead to rapid weight gain, this levels off in a month or two, after which the animal's weight remains stable at a new (and of course much greater) level. Once this new weight is reached, the animal eats enough to maintain it but no more (Hoebel and Teitelbaum, 1976). This suggests that the lesion produced an upward shift in the **setpoint** for weight regulation—the point that defines a kind of target value that determines food intake. As we will see, this interpretation may be relevant to explain some of the phenomena of human obesity (Nisbett, 1972; see Figure 3.7).

Details aside, dual-center theorists regard the two hypothalamic regions as mutually inhibitory centers, of which one serves as an on-switch for eating, the other as an off-switch. These switches are in turn activated by a number of internal and external signals. All of these signals act upon the feeding centers—some to trigger eating, others to inhibit it. Whether the organism eats will then depend on the summed value of them all: the level of various available nutrients in the bloodstream, satiety signals from the stomach, food palatability, learned factors, and so on (Stellar, 1954).

## DUAL CENTERS RECONSIDERED

The dual-center theory of feeding has held center stage for several decades. But it has been seriously questioned in recent years. The main grounds concern the effects of hypothalamic lesions. Some critics believe that some of the effects of these lesions are not directly on behavior, but rather on food metabolism (Stricker and Zigmond, 1976).

An example of this approach is a reanalysis of the effects of ventromedial lesions. According to the dual-center view, rats with such lesions overeat because of damage to some off-switch for feeding. But an alternative interpretation lays the blame on a disruption of fat metabolism.

A

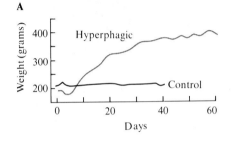

B

**3.7 Hyperphagia** (A) Curve showing the weight gain of hyperphagic rats after an operation creating a hypothalamic lesion. The weight eventually stabilizes at a new level. (After Teitelbaum, 1955) (B) Photograph of a rat several months after the operation. This rat weighed over 1,000 grams. (Courtesy Neal E. Miller, Rockefeller University)

Under normal conditions, animals store some of their unused nutrients in the form of fats. This tendency to save for later use can sometimes go too far, however. One effect of ventromedial lesions is that they produce an overreaction of certain branches of the parasympathetic system. This in turn increases the proportion of usable nutrients, especially glucose, that are turned into fat and cached away as adipose tissue. The trouble is that so much is stored that not enough is left over to serve as metabolic fuel. As a result, the animal stays hungry; it has to eat more to get the fuel that it needs. But since most of what it eats is turned into fat and stored away, the process continues and the animal has to keep on eating. It is in the position of a rich miser who has buried all of his possessions and has therefore no money to live on.

Evidence in favor of this general approach comes from studies which show that animals with ventromedial lesions get fatter than normals even when both groups are fed the identical amount. Whether such results are a decisive disproof of the dual-center theory is still a matter of debate (Friedman and Stricker, 1976).

## Food Selection

We've seen that the mechanisms that determine feeding are at least partially under the control of homeostasis. To that extent they resemble those that govern drinking and temperature regulation. But in many ways they are considerably more complex. One reason is that the control of food intake depends on two decisions. The animal (or its nervous system) must not only decide whether to eat, but also *what* to eat. How do animals and humans make this selection?

To some extent the selection is built into the nervous system. An example is the response to sweet and bitter tastes. When a human newborn's mouth is moistened with a sweet solution (say, sugar water), the infant's facial expression suggests pleasure; when the solution is bitter (say, quinine water), the newborn screws his face into a grimace and turns away (Steiner, 1974; see Figures 3.8A and B). This selectional bias makes good biological sense, for it leads to the best nutritional bet: In general, sweet substances have more nutritional value than others. In contrast, bitter tastes are found in many poisonous plants. Occasionally, the nutritional bet is lost: Saccharin is sweet and is generally preferred to less sweet substances, but it contains no calories whatsoever.

Can built-in preferences account for all of an animal's food choices? They might, if the animal lives on one (or only a very few) food items, such as the koala, whose diet consists almost entirely of eucalyptus leaves (Figure 3.9). But

**3.8  The response of newborn human babies to different tastes**  *Drops of different solutions were placed on the infants' mouths to record their reaction to (A) a sweet taste (sugar solution) and (B) a bitter taste (quinine solution). (From Steiner, 1977; photographs courtesy of Jacob Steiner)*

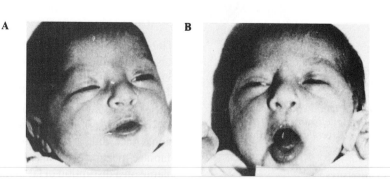

A          B

A

B

C

**3.9   Food selection**   *(A) Some animals such as zebras eat only plants. (Photograph by Laura Riley/Bruce Coleman) (B) Others such as lions eat only other animals. (Photograph by Joanne Zembal/ Black Star) (C) A few others subsist on a diet of just one food substance. In the case of the koala of Australia, this consists of eucalyptus leaves, which provide the animal with its water as well as nutrients. (Photograph by Helen Williams/Photo Researchers)*

the majority of animals are less specialized than the koala; their diet is made up of all sorts of foods. How do these animals know which substances in the world provide calories and which do not? Furthermore, how do they identify the various nutrients they require over and above calories: various vitamins, minerals, amino acids, and so on? For carnivores, the food selection problem is relatively easy. Since the animals they feed on have nutritional needs like their own, carnivores are assured of getting a balanced diet. Lions run no risk of vitamin deficiency unless they insist on eating vitamin-deficient zebras (Rozin, 1976c, 1982).

The food selection problem is more difficult for omnivores like ourselves who are culinary generalists and eat a wide variety of plant foods. The problem is that many plants lack some essential nutrients that animals need for survival. Worse yet, other plants contain poisons—an adaptive device that protects them from plant-eaters. To get the necessary nutrients, omnivores must somehow identify a large range of edible plants which, taken together, will satisfy all of their dietary needs, but they must also identify those that are toxic. How can this be done? Some animals have hit upon a rather simple solution. When it comes to food, they are *neophobic*—that is, afraid of anything that is new. When rats (who like humans are food generalists) are confronted with some substance they've never tasted before, they will initially shy away from it altogether. But eventually, they'll taste a very small amount, as it were, to "test" it. If it is a poison, they will get sick. But since they only ate a little, they will most probably recover. They will later associate the taste of that food with their sickness and will avoid this taste from then on.* On the other hand, if the food turns out to be safe, the animals will return in a day or two, take larger bites, and add this particular taste to their repertoire of acceptable food flavors (Rozin, 1976c).

Many human children exhibit a somewhat similar neophobia about foods once they are about two years old. From then on, they tend to be culinary conservatives who stick to foods they know and make sour faces if confronted with something new. But in humans this neophobia is less pronounced than it is in rats and is not too hard to override. One factor is built-in taste preferences, particularly for sweets. Babies may dislike new foods, but they are certainly willing to make exceptions for chocolate pudding. But even more important is the fact that unlike rats, people live in a culture, which allows them to benefit from the pooled experience of previous generations. Each rat has to learn anew whether a given

* Such acquired taste aversions have some important implications for our understanding of the learning process which will be discussed in a later section (see Chapter 4, pp. 136–38).

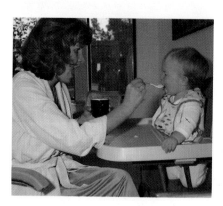

**The transmission of food preferences**
(Photograph by Suzanne Szasz)

food is safe, but a human child can rely on her mother. The child may fuss and scream about the spinach and cauliflower on her plate, but at least she doesn't have to worry that they might be poisonous. After a while, she will learn to eat the foods her culture prefers (Mother's apple pie), and to avoid those to which the culture has aversions or taboos (pork to Muslims and Jews).

Here, as so often, human culture plays a crucial role in channeling the satisfaction of biological needs. For leopards, food satisfies a caloric need; for humans, it serves many other functions as well. It can be a source of aesthetic satisfaction, is often used to make various symbolic statements, may underline social distinctions, and can help to cement social and family groups. After all, is there any American who believes that there are some special metabolic needs that arise in late November which require the specific nutrients provided by a turkey?

## Obesity

Both homeostatic and nonhomeostatic determinants of food intake are relevant to a problem partially created by the affluence of modern society which prior eras would have suffered only too gladly: obesity. Obesity is sometimes defined as a body weight that exceeds the average for a given height by 20 percent. Judged by this criterion, about one-third of all Americans are obese. Most of them would rather be slim, and their wistful desires offer a ready market for a vast number of diet foods and fads. In part, the reason is health (at least it is sometimes said to be). But more important are social standards of physical attractiveness. There are no corpulent matinee idols, no fat sex goddesses (Stunkard, 1975).

Most authorities agree that there are several reasons why people become fat. In some cases, the cause is a bodily condition. In others, it is a matter of eating too much.

### BODILY FACTORS IN OBESITY

Most of us take it for granted that body weight is a simple function of calorie intake and energy expenditure. To some extent this is undoubtedly true, but it is not the whole story. For there is good evidence that a number of constitutional factors can predispose one person to get fat, even if she eats no more (and exercises no less) than her next-door neighbor.

*Metabolic efficiency*   One reason may be a more proficient digestive apparatus; the person who manages to digest a larger proportion of the food she ingests will necessarily put on more weight than her digestively less efficient fellows. Another reason may be a different metabolic level; the less nutrient fuel is burnt up, the more is left for fatty storage. These constitutional differences may help to explain why some people gain weight much more readily than others (Sims, 1986).

Some recent studies suggest that such constitutional differences in metabolic efficiency depend partially on genetic makeup. One was a study on the effects of overeating on twelve pairs of identical male twins. Each of these men was overfed by about 1,000 excess calories per day above the amount required to maintain his initial weight. The activities of each subject were kept as constant as possible, and there was very little exercise. This regimen continued for a period of 100 days. Needless to say, all twenty-four men gained weight, but the amount they gained

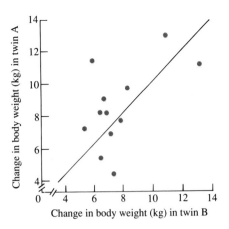

**3.10 Similarity of weight gains in identical twins** *Weight gains for twelve pairs of identical twins after 100 days of the same degree of overfeeding. Each point represents one twin pair, with the weight gain of twin A plotted on the vertical axis and the weight gain of twin B plotted on the horizontal axis. Weight gains are plotted in kilograms (1 kg = 2.2 lbs). The closer the points are to the diagonal line, the more similar the weight gains of the twins are to each other. (After Bouchard et al., 1990)*

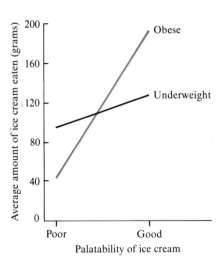

**3.11 Eating, palatability, and obesity** *In the experiment, obese and underweight subjects were given the opportunity to eat ice cream. If the ice cream tasted good, the obese subjects ate more than the underweight ones. The reverse was true if the ice cream did not taste good. (After Nisbett, 1968)*

varied substantially: from about ten to thirty pounds. A further difference concerned the parts of the body where the newly gained weight was deposited. For some subjects, it was the abdomen; for others, it was the thighs and buttocks. The important finding was that the amount each person gained was very similar to the weight gain of his twin (see Figure 3.10). Similarly for the location on the body where the weight was gained. If one twin gained in the abdomen, so did his twin; if another deposited the fat in his thighs and buttocks, his twin did too. These findings are a strong indication that people differ in the efficiency with which their bodily machinery handles excess calories, and that this metabolic pattern is probably inherited (Bouchard et al., 1990).

*Fat cells in the body* Another bodily factor concerns the fat cells in the body. In obese people, their number is some three times larger than in normal people (Hirsch and Knittle, 1970). To the obese person, these cells are an adipose albatross that cannot be removed. If a fat person diets, the fat cells will shrink in size, but their total number will remain unchanged. Some investigators suspect that the brain receives some signals that urge further eating until the shrunken fat cells are again refilled. If this is so, the once-fat can never truly escape their obese past. They may rigorously diet until they become as lean as a friend who was never fat, but their urge to eat will always be greater.

Some authors believe that the number of fat cells in the body is fixed sometime in early life, and is partly determined by genetic constitution and partly by feeding patterns in early childhood (Knittle and Hirsch, 1968). Others feel that additional fat cells can be added in adolescence and adulthood. If this is so, it is yet another argument against repeated bouts of diets followed by gradual regaining of the lost weight, for every weight gain generates additional fat cells that can never be lost (Sjöström, 1980).

BEHAVIORAL FACTORS

In some persons, obesity is evidently produced by a bodily condition. But for many others, the cause lies in behavior: They simply eat too much. The question is why. It is virtually certain that there is no one answer, for chronic overeating has not one cause but many.

*The externality hypothesis* Some years ago, a number of investigators subscribed to the ***externality hypothesis,*** which held that obese people are comparatively unresponsive to their own internal hunger state but are much more susceptible to signals from without (Schachter and Rodin, 1974). One line of evidence came from studies in which people were asked how hungry they are. In normal subjects, the response depended on the time since their last meal. But in obese people, there was no such correlation between the subjective experience of hunger and the deprivation interval. Further evidence came from experiments that seemed to show that obese subjects are rather finicky when it comes to food. If offered a fine grade of vanilla ice cream, they eat more than normal subjects. But if offered vanilla ice cream that has been adulterated with bitter-tasting quinine, they eat *less* of this mixture than do normals (Nisbett, 1968; see Figure 3.11).

According to some advocates of the externality hypothesis, this discrepancy in the sensitivity to external and internal cues for eating might be a contributing cause of obesity. Since he is presumably rather insensitive to his internal body state, the obese person will eat even though his body needs no further calories as long as there are enough external cues that prompt him on. And in food-rich twentieth-century America, such cues are certainly plentiful (Schachter, 1971).

*The restrained-eating hypothesis*    More recent studies have thrown doubt on the externality hypothesis. To begin with, the evidence for the greater sensitivity of obese persons to external cues turns out to be rather inconsistent. But to the extent that this oversensitivity does exist, its explanation may be quite different from what it was originally; it may be an *effect* of the obesity rather than its cause (Nisbett, 1972; Rodin, 1980, 1981).

In our society many people who are overweight consciously try to restrain their eating. After all, obesity is a social liability, so they make resolutions, go on diets, buy low-calorie foods, and do what they can to clamp a lid on their intense desire to eat. But the clamp is hard to maintain, for any external stimulus for eating will threaten the dieter's resolve. In effect, there is "disinhibition" of eating restraint (Herman and Polivy, 1980).

An interesting demonstration of the disinhibition of eating is provided by a study of "restrained" and "unrestrained" eaters. Persons judged as restrained said they were on a diet or expressed concerns about their weight. The subjects participated in what was described as an experiment on the perception of tastes. Initially, some subjects had to taste (and consume) one or two 8 oz. milk shakes, while control subjects tasted none. After this, the subjects were asked to judge the taste of ice cream. While performing this task, they were left alone with an unlimited supply of ice cream. How much would they eat? Unrestrained eaters ate a sensible, homeostatically appropriate amount: The more milk shakes they previously had consumed, the less ice cream they ate in the subsequent test. But the exact opposite was true of the restrained eaters. The more milk shakes they previously consumed the more ice cream they ate now. The prior exposure disinhibited their restraint and led to a motivational collapse—a phenomenon all too familiar to would-be dieters which some investigators have dubbed the "what the hell" diet-busting effect (Herman and Mack, 1975; see Figure 3.12).

*The setpoint hypothesis*    The restrained-eating hypothesis tries to explain some of the effects of obesity. But it has little to say about its cause. One possibility is that people differ in their setpoints for weight. These may reflect differences in constitution (for example, in the number of fat cells), which in turn may be partially determined by heredity (Foch and McClearn, 1980). Setpoints may also result from feeding experiences in childhood. Whatever their cause, these setpoints determine the weight an individual's system aims at as it regulates its internal economy. But if so, then many a person who is fat by the standards of official what-your-weight-should-be tables may weigh just the right amount considering his own particular setpoint. If he starves himself, he'll drop to a weight level below that level. But in the long run he probably won't stay there, for there'll always be a tendency to go back to the setpoint weight (Nisbett, 1972). Some authors point out that the tendency to maintain a given body weight affects energy expenditure as well as caloric intake. Thus when obese persons starve themselves, they don't lose anywhere as much weight as they should on the assumption (known to all dieters) that 3,500 calories equals one pound. The reason is that their body compensates for the calorie loss by a drastic reduction in metabolism (Keesey and Powley, 1986).

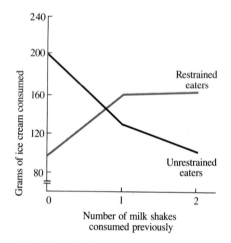

**3.12    The diet-busting effect in restrained eaters**    *In the experiment, restrained (blue) and unrestrained eaters (black) were asked to consume 0, 1, or 2 milk shakes in what they thought was an experiment on taste perception. They were later asked to judge the taste of ice cream and allowed to sample as much of it as they wished. The figure shows that restrained eaters ate considerably more ice cream if they had previously consumed one or more milk shakes previously. (After Herman and Mack, 1975)*

What can be done to help people who are overweight? Everyone knows that it's relatively easy to lose weight over the short run; the problem is to keep it off for good. Can it be done? Some authors are optimists and believe that obesity is a behavioral problem that can be remedied by retraining people to develop self-control and acquire appropriate habits of diet and exercise. Other authorities are more pessimistic, for they believe that weight depends largely on a person's set-point, which he can't escape from in the long run. Attempts at treatment include psychoanalysis, various forms of behavior therapy (techniques for modifying the individual's behavior by the systematic use of certain principles of learning; see Chapters 4 and 20), and self-help groups (for example, Weight Watchers International). There is considerable dispute over the extent to which any of these methods leads to long-term changes although there is some suggestion that the self-help groups do a fairly good job, especially for those who are only mildly overweight (Booth, 1980; Stuart and Mitchell, 1980; Stunkard, 1980; Wilson, 1980).

At this point it is difficult to decide whether the optimists have a better case than the pessimists. Thus far, the outcomes of the various procedures have not been studied systematically enough. For all we know, more effective treatment methods may be developed in the future. But suppose the pessimists turn out to be correct—suppose that there is a setpoint which decrees that weight is fate. If so, can we offer any hope to those who are overweight?

To begin with, one may question the widely held belief that being overweight is necessarily a disorder. It is often asserted that being overweight is a health hazard, and that over one-third of the U.S. population are too heavy (U.S. Public Health Service, 1966). But apart from cases of gross obesity, the relation between over-weight and life expectancy is still a matter of debate (Fitzgerald, 1981; see Figure 3.13). Some authors argue that for the great majority of individuals, obesity is a social and aesthetic problem, rather than a problem of physical health. (This is especially so for women, who are much more likely to regard themselves as over-weight than are men; Gray, 1977; Fallon and Rozin, 1985). Seen in this light, being slender is a social ideal, but we should not forget that it is an ideal of *our* society. Other cultures set different standards. The women painted by Rubens, Matisse, and Renoir were considered beautiful by their contemporaries; today they would be considered overweight. But does it really make sense to aspire to the body form of a fashion model if it is not one's own and perhaps can't be?

Many people who regard themselves as overweight try to become lithe and slender but often fail anyway. Perhaps the best advice to them is to accept themselves as they are.

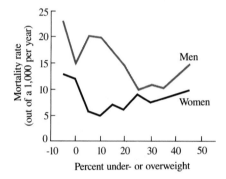

**3.13 Relation of obesity to mortality**
*The figure presents the mortality rate in a sample of 5,209 persons in Massachusetts for men and women from 45 to 74 years old between 1948 and 1964. The percent overweight is calculated by reference to mean weights for a given height. The figure shows that overweight does not increase the overall mortality risk, at least not for overweight percentages that are less than 50. (From Andres, 1980)*

### Anorexia and Bulimia

In some cases, the concern about being thin may be so extreme that it leads to certain eating disorders whose health hazards are much more serious than those produced by being somewhat overweight. One such condition is ***anorexia nervosa,*** which afflicts about 1 in 200 young women of the middle and upper classes in our society. Where the obese person is too fat and almost always eats too much, the anorexic is too thin (often dangerously so) and eats much too little. There are some cases of anorexia (literally "lack of appetite") that are caused by various or-

A

B                                    C

***Changing conceptions of the relation between body weight and attractiveness***
*An underlying cause of many eating disorders in Western women is their belief that being slender is beautiful. But is it? It depends. (A) The* Venus of Willendorf, *a prehistoric statuette, unearthed near Willendorf, Austria, that was sculpted some 30,000 years ago. Some archeologists believe that it depicts a fertility goddess; others, that it represents the female erotic ideal of the ice age. (Courtesy Naturhistorisches Museum, Wien) (B)* The Three Graces, *painted by the Flemish master Peter Paul Rubens in 1639. (Courtesy Museo del Prado) (C) Paulina Porizkova, a model in the 1980s. (Photograph by M. Carrard/Gamma-Liaison)*

ganic conditions; for example, in cancer patients undergoing chemotherapy which produces nausea and various food aversions. In contrast, anorexia nervosa is not produced by any known organic pathology but is at least in part brought on by psychological factors. Its defining feature is "the relentless pursuit of thinness through self-starvation, even unto death" (Bruch, 1973, p. 4).

Anorexics are intensely and continually preoccupied by the fear of becoming fat. They eat only low-calorie food, if they eat at all. In addition, they often engage in strenuous exercise, often for many hours each day. Of course, this regimen leads to extreme weight loss, sometimes reaching levels that are less than 50 percent of the statistical ideal. Further symptoms include the cessation of menstruation, hyperactivity, sleep disorders, and avoidance of sex. In perhaps 10 percent of the cases, the end result of this self-starvation is death. What leads to anorexia nervosa? Many investigators believe that it is produced by fears of being sexually unattractive, fears of sex, or rebellion against the parents. Others argue that the problem involves hormonal disturbances, as shown by the fact that anorexics have unusually low levels of reproductive and growth hormones. As yet, we don't know whether the hormonal imbalances are an effect rather than the cause of the psychological problems and the self-starvation diet. But it is very likely that the psychological factors—including the cultural obsession with slimness—are major contributors (Logue, 1986).

Another eating disorder is ***bulimia,*** which is characterized by repeated eating binges that are often followed by attempts to purge the calories just consumed by self-induced vomiting or laxatives. Unlike anorexics, bulimics are of roughly nor-

our day-to-day lives we rarely encounter emergencies that call for violent physical effort. But our biological nature has not changed just because our modern world contains no sabertooth tigers. We still have the same emergency system that served our primitive ancestors, and its bodily consequences may take serious tolls.

The disruptive effect of fear and anger upon digestion or upon sexual behavior is a matter of common knowledge. During periods of marked anxiety there are often complaints of constipation or other digestive ills. The same holds for impotence or frigidity. This is hardly surprising, since digestive functions and many aspects of sexual activity (for example, erection) are largely controlled by the parasympathetic system and are thus inhibited by intense sympathetic arousal. Moreover, the aftereffects of emotional arousal can sometimes be more permanent, causing profound and long-lasting bodily harm. Various disorders such as peptic ulcer, colitis, asthma, and hypertension can often be traced back to emotional patterns in the patient's life and are then considered psychophysiological disorders in which a psychological cause produces a bodily effect (see Chapter 19). Such psychophysiological effects are sometimes even more grievous and irrevocable, as in cases of hypertension and coronary disease that can lead to heart attacks and death (see Chapter 19).

## SLEEP AND WAKING

Thus far, our main concern has been with the *directive* function of motives. This direction can be primarily imposed from within, as in the case of the homeostatic motives such as thirst and hunger. It can also be initiated by stimulus conditions from the outside, as in fear and rage. Either way, the effects on behavior are readily described in terms of a negative feedback system. In the case of homeostatic motives, the organism acts so as to change the state of the internal environment; it eats or drinks until its water balance or nutrient levels are restored. In the case of rage and fear, it acts to change the conditions of the external environment that prompted the disturbance. The cat runs away to remove *itself* from a barking dog, or it hisses and scratches in a frantic attempt to remove the *dog.*

Motives have another function in addition to direction. They *arouse* the organism, which then becomes increasingly alert and vigorous. A given motive will thus act like both the tuner and the volume control of a radio. A thirsty animal seeks water rather than food or a sexual partner. And the thirstier it is, the more intensely it will pursue its goal. Psychologists have used various terms to describe this facet of motivation. Some call it **activation;** others prefer the term **drive.** They all agree that increased drive states generally lead to increased behavioral vigor. Thus, rats will run faster to water the longer they have been water-deprived.

We will now look at some of the biological mechanisms of activation as we consider its two extremes. One is a state of intense waking arousal, perhaps best typified by fear and rage. The other is sleep.

### Waking

In a sense, we may consider the sympathetic branch of the autonomic nervous system as an arousal system for the more primitive physiological processes of the

85

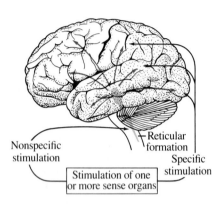

Nonspecific
stimulation

Reticular
formation

Specific
stimulation

Stimulation of one
or more sense organs

**3.19   The reticular activating system**
*The figure indicates the location and
function of the reticular structures in the
hind- and midbrain. When a sense organ is
stimulated, its message is relayed to a
particular region of the cortex, typically a
projection area. The sensory stimulation
also triggers the reticular system which
then arouses the cortex. As a result, the
areas of the brain that receive the specific
sensory message are sufficiently activated
so that they can interpret it.
(After French, 1957)*

body. Similar arousal systems operate to alert the brain. They activate the cortex so that it is fully responsive to incoming messages. In effect, they awaken the brain.

One of the most important of these is the ***reticular activating system*** or ***RAS***. This neurological system has its origin in the upper portion of the reticular formation, a network of interconnected cells that extends throughout the brain stem and has branches that ascend to much of the rest of the brain (Figure 3.19). Sleeping cats whose RAS is electrically stimulated will awaken; cats whose RAS is destroyed are somnolent for weeks (Lindsley, 1960). RAS activity not only leads to awakening but it also produces increasing levels of arousal once awake. Stimulation of the RAS in waking monkeys jolts them into an alert state of attention in which they look around expectantly.

What triggers the RAS? One factor is sensory stimulation. On the face of it, this is hardly surprising, for we all know that sleep comes more readily when it is quiet and dark. But the neurological chain of events that explains why intense stimuli lead to awakening is fairly complex. Oddly enough, the direct input from the sensory pathways to the cortex is not the primary cause of wakefulness. In one study, the investigators severed virtually all of the sensory tracts to the cortex in cats (Lindsley et al., 1950). When the cats were asleep the experimenters presented a loud tone and the cats woke up. But how could this be, if the path from ear to cortex was cut so that the cortex was isolated from any auditory input? The answer is that there is another, indirect pathway that leads through the RAS. All of the sensory pathways to the cortex send collateral side branches to the RAS. The information the RAS receives in this manner is very meager and unspecific; it amounts to no more than a statement that a sensory message is on its way up to the cortex without any further indication of what that message might be. But this is enough for the RAS which now functions as a general alarm. It arouses the cortex which can then interpret the specific signals sent over the direct sensory pathway. In effect, the RAS is like a four-year-old who has just been handed a telegram while his mother is asleep. The child cannot read but he awakens his mother who can.

Sensory stimulation is not the only source of RAS activation. Another comes from the cortex itself. There are descending fibers from the cortex that may excite the RAS which will then activate the cortex more fully. This circuit—cortex to RAS to cortex—probably plays an important role in many phenomena of sleep and waking. We sometimes have trouble in falling asleep because we "can't shut off our thoughts." Here cortical activity triggers the RAS which activates the cortex which again excites the RAS and so on. The importance of cortical activation of the RAS is also shown by the fact that some stimuli are more likely to wake us than others, regardless of their intensity—a baby's cry, the smell of fire, the sound of one's own name.

## Sleep

The primary focus of this chapter is on motivation, and thus on the direction and activation of behavior that motives bring about. In this context, sleep is of considerable interest because it seems to represent the very opposite of arousal. But it

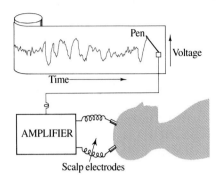

**3.20 Schematic diagram of EEG recording** *A number of scalp electrodes are placed on a subject's head. At any one time, there are small differences in the electrical potential (that is, the voltage) between any two of these electrodes. These differences are magnified by an amplifier and are then used to activate a recording pen. The greater the voltage difference, the larger the pen's deflection. Since the voltage fluctuates, the pen goes up and down, thus tracing a so-called brain wave on the moving paper. The number of such waves per second is the EEG frequency.*

has a more direct relevance as well. The desire for sleep is one of the most powerful of motives; if kept awake long enough, the urge to sleep will eventually take precedence over most other motives (which is one of the reasons why jailers sometimes use enforced sleeplessness to force confessions out of prisoners). What can we say about this state in which most of us spend a third of our lives?

### SLEEP AND BRAIN ACTIVITY

Sleep cannot be observed from within, since it is by definition a condition of which the sleeper is unaware. We must perforce study it from without. One way of doing this is by observing what the brain does while its owner is asleep.

Eavesdropping on the brain of waking or sleeping subjects is made possible by the fact that the language of the nervous system is electrical. When electrodes are placed at various points on the skull, they pick up the electrical changes that are produced by the summed activity of the millions of nerve cells in the cerebral cortex that is just underneath. In absolute terms these changes are very small; they are therefore fed to a highly sensitive amplifier whose output in turn activates a series of pens. These pens trace their position on a long roll of paper that moves at a constant speed (Figure 3.20). The resulting record is an ***electroencephalogram,*** or EEG, a picture of voltage changes over time occurring in the brain.

Figure 3.21 shows an EEG record. It begins with the subject in a relaxed state, with eyes closed, and "not thinking about anything in particular." The record shows ***alpha waves,*** a rather regular waxing and waning of electrical potential, at some eight to twelve cycles per second. This alpha rhythm is very characteristic of this state (awake but resting), and is found in most mammals. When the subject attends to some stimulus with open eyes, or when he is involved in active thought (for instance, mental arithmetic) with his eyes closed, the picture changes. Now the alpha rhythm is ***blocked;*** the voltage is lower, the frequency is much higher, and the pattern of ups and downs is nearly random.

### THE STAGES OF SLEEP

Several decades of work involving continuous, all-night recordings of EEGs and other measures have shown that there are several stages of sleep and that these vary in depth. Just prior to sleep, there tends to be an accentuated alpha rhythm. As the subject becomes drowsy, the alpha comes and goes; there are increasingly long stretches during which the pattern is random. The subject is now in a light, dozing sleep, from which she is easily awakened (Stage 1 in Figure 3.22). Over the course of the next hour she drifts into deeper and deeper stages, in which the EEGs are characterized by the complete absence of alpha and by waves of in-

**3.21 Alpha waves and alpha blocking** *(After Guyton, 1981)*

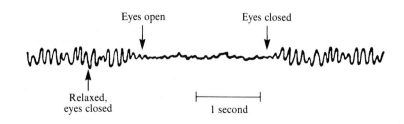

Eyes open    Eyes closed

Relaxed, eyes closed

1 second

(Stage 1)       (Stage 2)       (Stage 3)       (Stage 4)       Dreaming

**3.22   The stages of sleep**   *The figure shows EEG records taken from the frontal lobe of the brain, during waking, quiet sleep, and active sleep. (Courtesy of William C. Dement)*

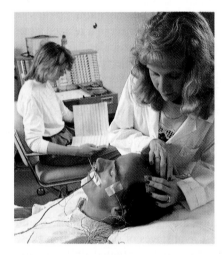

**Observing sleep**   *All-night recordings of EEGs of patients in sleep labs have revealed the several stages of sleep. (Photograph by Grant Leduc/Monkmeyer)*

creasingly higher voltage and much lower frequency (Stages 2 through 4 in Figure 3.22). In the last stages, the waves are very slow. They occur about once every second and are some five times greater in amplitude than those of the alpha rhythm. At this point the sleeper is virtually immobile and will take a few seconds to awaken, mumbling incoherently, even if shaken or shouted at. During the course of the night, the sleeper's descent repeats itself several times. She drops from dozing to deep, slow-wave sleep, reascends to Stage 1, drops back to slow-wave sleep, and so on for some four or five cycles.

The oscillations between different sleep stages are not merely changes in depth. When the sleeper reascends into Stage 1, he seems to enter a qualitatively different state entirely. This state is sometimes called ***active sleep*** to distinguish it from the ***quiet sleep*** found during the other stages. Active sleep is a paradoxical condition with contradictory aspects. In some ways it is as deep as sleep ever gets. The sleeper's general body musculature is more flaccid and he is less sensitive to external stimulation (Williams, Tepas, and Morlock, 1962). But judged by some other criteria, the level of arousal during active sleep is almost as high as during alert wakefulness. One sign is the EEG, which in humans is rather similar to that found in waking (Jouvet, 1967). Another is the appearance of dreams (of which more later), which are found in active rather than quiet sleep and during which we often feel as if we were active and thoroughly awake.

Of particular interest are the sleeper's eye movements which can be recorded by means of electrodes attached next to each eye. During quiet sleep, the eyes drift slowly and no longer move in tandem. But during active sleep a different pattern suddenly appears. The eyes move rapidly and in unison behind closed lids, as if the sleeper were looking at some object outside. These jerky, rapid eye movements (REMs) are one of the most striking features of active sleep, which is often called ***REM sleep.*** Young human adults enter this stage about four times each night (Figure 3.23).

THE FUNCTIONS OF SLEEP

What functions are served by sleep, whether in its active or quiet form? Surprisingly enough, the answer is still unknown.

*Sleep deprivation*   One way of trying to assess the benefits that sleep may bring is to observe what ills befall if it is prevented. This is the logic of sleep-deprivation experiments in which humans and animals are kept awake for days on end. The results suggest that there is indeed a need for sleep. If deprived of sleep, the organism seeks sleep just as it seeks food when it is starved. When sleep is finally allowed, the subjects sink down upon the nearest cot and try to make up for the sleep they have lost.

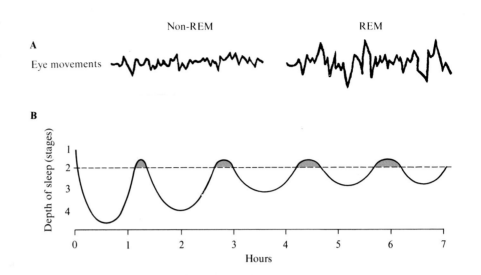

**3.23 REM and non-REM sleep** *(A) Eye movements during non-REM and REM sleep. The REM periods are associated with dreaming. (B) The alternation of non-REM and REM periods throughout the course of the night (REM periods are in color). Rapid eye movements and dreams begin as the person repeatedly emerges from deeper sleep to the level of Stage 1. (After Kleitman, 1960)*

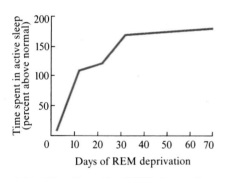

**3.24 The effect of lost REM sleep** *The figure shows an increase in the time cats spend in REM sleep after various periods of REM-sleep deprivation. The animals were deprived of REM sleep (but not non-REM sleep) for from 5 to 72 days by being awakened as soon as their EEG indicated the beginning of a REM period. On the first day when the animals were finally allowed to sleep undisturbed, there was an increase in the proportion of time spent in REM sleep rather than non-REM sleep. (Data from Cohen, 1972)*

The need of the sleep-deprived person is not just for sleep in general but also for the two major sleep states that comprise it. This is shown by studies on selective sleep deprivation in which the experimenter prevents one kind of sleep (for example, REM) but not the other. If he wants to deprive the subjects of REM sleep only, he simply wakes them up whenever the EEG and eye movements signal the beginning of a REM period. After the subjects wake up, they go back to sleep, are reawakened when they next enter the REM state, go back to sleep, are reawakened, and so on through the night. After a few nights of this, the subjects are allowed to sleep freely. They will now spend more time in REM than they normally do, as if to make up for the state of which they were deprived (Figure 3.24). The same holds for selective deprivation of the deep, slow-wave sleep of Stages 3 and 4. If lost one night, it is made up on another (Webb, 1972).

*Sleep as a restorative process* The sleep-deprivation experiments suggest that there is a need for sleep, but they do not tell us why. One possibility is that sleep is restorative, that it is a period during which some vital substance is resynthesized in the nervous system. In one form or another, this view was held at least as early as the Renaissance, as witness Shakespeare who regarded sleep as "a balm of hurt minds" that "knits up the ravel'd sleave of care." That sleep has some such function seems probable even though we have only a sketchy notion of what might be restored and how.

Some authors focus on the restorative functions of deep, slow-wave sleep (Stages 3 and 4). A number of studies suggest that slow-wave sleep is enhanced under conditions such as physical fatigue, where there is a greater need for bodily revival. There is some evidence that marathon runners sleep longer during the two nights after the race; their largest increase is in the times they spend during slow-wave sleep (Shapiro et al., 1981). This result fits in with the finding that a growth-promoting hormone is secreted primarily during slow-wave sleep (Takahashi, 1979).

Some authors believe that REM sleep also has a restorative function. They propose that while slow-wave sleep heals the exhaustion of the body, REM sleep mends the fatigue of the mind. As evidence, they point to studies that suggest that REM sleep goes up after a day of intense mental preoccupation or emotional stress. In one study, subjects wore prisms that turned the world upside down so that they had to adjust to a topsy-turvy environment. At night, there was a sharp increase in active sleep time. A similar effect seems to occur after a day of worry or depression. According to restoration theorists, learning (and perhaps various emotional reactions) requires the presence of certain transmitter substances in particular areas of the brain. The most likely candidates are the ***catecholamines.*** According to the theory, these substances are depleted when the organisms learn —or try to learn—new modes of adjustment. They are resynthesized during REM sleep. This claim is still mostly conjecture. Some supporting evidence comes from the effects of various drugs. Drugs which deplete catecholamine levels seem to enhance active sleep; those which augment the available catecholamine supply have the opposite effect (Hartmann, 1973).

*Sleep as an evolutionary relic*   Some investigators argue that while the desire for sleep is clearly an insistent motive, there is no reason to believe that it serves a vital bodily need. They agree that the sleepless person seeks sleep just as the starved one craves food. But they point out that while starvation eventually leads to death, there is no evidence that even prolonged sleep deprivation will have such dire effects; it will make people drowsy, a bit confused, and desperately anxious for sleep, but little more. One interpretation is that sleep is an evolutionary relic of former times, a built-in response system that once had an important adaptive function although it no longer does. A daily period of enforced near-immobility spent in some hiding place may have been quite useful to our animal ancestors; it would have helped them to conserve their energies and kept them out of the way of possible predators. Thus, according to some authors, human sleep may be nothing but a remnant of such an ancestral adaptive pattern. It is of little use to us now that we have electric light bulbs and need fear no predators except those of our own kind, but it is no less powerful even so (Webb, 1974).

To sum up, while we know a great deal about the phenomena of sleep and some of the mechanisms that bring it about, we are as yet unsure about its functions. The desire for sleep is a powerful motive, and some twenty-five years of an average lifetime are devoted to it. But it's still unclear what it is really good for. (For discussion, see Webb, 1979, 1982; Horne, 1988.)

## DREAMS

REM sleep was discovered fairly recently, but its discoverers almost immediately related it to a phenomenon surely known to humans since prehistoric times: dreaming.

*Dreaming and REM sleep*   When sleeping subjects are awakened during REM sleep, they generally report a dream: a series of episodes that seemed real at the time. Not so for quiet (that is, non-REM) sleep. When awakened from quiet sleep, subjects may say that they were thinking about something, but they rarely relate the kind of inner drama we call a dream (Cartwright, 1977). Further evidence links the duration of the dream events to the length of the REM period. Subjects who are awakened five minutes after the onset of REM tend to describe shorter dreams than subjects awakened fifteen minutes after the REM period begins. This result argues against the popular notion that dreams are virtually instantaneous, no matter how long they take to relate when later recalled. In actual

***Jacob's Dream*** *Dreams have often been regarded as a gateway between everyday reality and a more spiritual existence. An example is the biblical patriarch Jacob, who dreamed of angels descending and ascending a ladder between heaven and earth. (From the Lambeth Bible, England, 12th century; courtesy the Lambeth Palace Library)*

fact, the dream seems to take just about as long as the dream episode might have been in real life (Dement and Kleitman, 1957; Dement and Wolpert, 1958).

These findings suggest that the average adult dreams for about one and a half hours every night, the time spent in REM sleep. How can we square this statement with the fact that in everyday life many people seem to experience dreams only occasionally, and that some deny that they ever dream? The answer is that dreams are generally forgotten within minutes after they have occurred. In one study, subjects were awakened either during REM sleep or five minutes after a REM period had ended. In the first condition, detailed dream narratives were obtained on 85 percent of the narratives; in the second, there were none (Wolpert and Trosman, 1958).

Why dreams leave such fragile memories is something of a puzzle. One possibility is that the memory of the dream is ordinarily inaccessible because of a failure to relate the dream episode (when it occurs) to the many other memories of waking life (Koulack and Goodenough, 1976). This interpretation may explain some odd experiences in which we seem to remember something that we know did not occur. These may be recollections of a dream without the realization that it was a dream and not a real event.

*Do dreams have a function?* The ancients believed that dreams have a prophetic function. In our own time, several theorists have argued that their function is related to the sleeper's personal problems. The most influential account was that of Sigmund Freud, who maintained that during dreams a whole host of primitive and forbidden impulses—mostly concerning sex and aggression—start to break through the barriers we erect against them while awake. The result is a compromise. The prohibited materials emerge, but only in a heavily masked and censored form. Freud believed that this explains why our dreams are so often strange and senseless. According to Freud, they are only odd on the outside. If we look beneath the surface, we can recognize the disguised meaning, the hidden, unacceptable wishes that are cleverly masked and lie underneath (Freud, 1900).

During the last thirty years, more and more evidence has come up that has thrown considerable doubt on Freud's dream theory (for details, see Chapter 11). Today, many authors believe that dreams don't have the complex functions that Freud (let alone the ancients) maintained. In their view, the dream is simply a reflection of the brain's aroused state during active sleep. During this period, the cerebral cortex is active, and its activity is manifested in conscious experience—the dream. But this dream experience necessarily has a special form. The cortex may be active, but it is largely shut off from sensory input. Under the circumstances, its activity is not constrained by the demands of external reality. Memory images become more prominent than they are in waking life, for they do not have to compete with the insistent here and now provided by the senses. The recent experiences of the day are evoked most readily, and they will then arouse a host of previous memories and intermingle with them. The cortex is sufficiently active to connect and interpret these raw materials so that we experience a running, inner narrative. But this is often accomplished in a primitive, disjointed way; perhaps the cortex is not active enough to provide more than a crude organization (Hobson, 1988).

Since the cerebral activity of active sleep is unconstrained by sensory reality, the content of dreams is likely to reflect the individuality of the dreamer. The raw materials of the dream are peculiarly *hers: her* thoughts, *her* memories, *her* emo-

**91**

tions. Since objective sensory input is absent, these subjective sources are more prominent than they are in waking life. This is probably one of the reasons why dreams have so often been thought to have a deeper, personal meaning (see Chapter 11).

## WHAT DIFFERENT MOTIVES HAVE IN COMMON

The preceding sections have dealt with a number of motives that impel to action—hunger, thirst, fear, and so on. Some such as hunger are in the service of homeostasis and serve to maintain the internal environment. Others such as fear and rage are triggered by stimuli in the environment and are relevant to self-preservation. Still others, such as the craving for drugs, are acquired and ultimately deleterious but are no less compelling for all that. For a few others—the main example is sleep—the function is still unknown. These various motives are clearly very different, as are the goals toward which they steer the organism—food, water, escape from threat, a dose of heroin, a good night's sleep. But despite the differences between them, is there something that all these motives and these goals have in common?

### Level of Stimulation

A number of theorists have suggested that all—or at least most—motives can be described as a search for some ***optimum level of arousal*** or of general stimulation. One of the early controversies in the area was over the question of what this optimum level is.

#### DRIVE-REDUCTION THEORY

According to the drive-reduction theory proposed by Clark L. Hull some fifty years ago, the optimum level of arousal that organisms seek is essentially zero. Hull and his students were impressed by the fact that many motives seem directed at the reduction of some internal state of bodily tension which if continued would lead to injury or even death. Examples are food deprivation, water deprivation, pain, and so on. Hull believed that this is true for all motives. In his view, all built-in rewards produce some reduction of bodily tension (or, as he called it, of drive). This position amounts to the assertion that what we normally call pleasure is at bottom nothing else but the reduction of pain or discomfort. According to this view, what organisms strive for is the absolute minimum of all arousal and stimulation, a biopsychological version of the Eastern search for *Nirvana.*

In some ways, Hull's theory can be regarded as a homeostatic conception carried to its extreme form. As Hull saw it, anything an organism does is ultimately directed at getting rid of some noxious state—pain, nutrient deficit, or whatever. One immediate difficulty is posed by sex, a motive that is clearly not homeostatic in the sense in which hunger and thirst are. To explain sexual satisfaction in drive-reduction terms, Hull and his students argued that what is rewarding about sexual activity is the drop in tension that occurs during orgasm (Hull, 1943).

A

B

C

*Seeking stimulation* *People have invented many activities to experience the paradoxical joy of fear and danger. (A) Some of these activities induce excitement but are known to be safe in reality, such as riding on roller coasters. (B) Others are more dangerous but provide greater thrills, such as skydiving. (C) In yet other activities the fear and danger are experienced vicariously, as in watching horror movies. The figure shows a woman attacked by a shark in the 1975 film* Jaws. *(Photographs by Georg Gerster, Comstock; Guy Sauvage, Agence Vandystadt/Photo Researchers; movie still courtesy of the Kobal Collection)*

### AN OPTIMUM AROUSAL ABOVE ZERO

Hull's drive-reduction theory suggests that, in general, organisms seek minimum levels of stimulation, preferring peace and quiet to states of tension and arousal. But, in fact, this does not seem to be true. For there is little doubt that some experiences are actively sought after. One example is the taste of sweets or erotic stimulation. These are both felt to be positive pleasures rather than the mere removal of some irritant. One example concerns saccharin, a sweet substance that has no nutritive value and thus no effect on the bodily tension and deficit that underlies hunger. But rats and other animals will nevertheless drink a saccharine solution avidly (Sheffield and Roby, 1950).

Other findings concern sexual activity. In one study, male rats were run in a maze that had two end boxes. One was empty, while the other contained a sexually receptive female. When the male encountered the female, he usually mounted her. But an unsympathetic experimenter invariably separated the pair before ejaculation could occur. This meant that sexual tension was increased rather than decreased. But the males nevertheless chose the side of the maze that held the female. This shows that sexual stimulation is rewarding in its own right. Whether this point really required experimental substantiation is debatable, considering that so many humans engage in sexual foreplay and try to lengthen the time before orgasm (Sheffield, Wulff, and Backer, 1951).

Such evidence suggests that drive reduction is not the only goal. Similar conclusions emerge from work on curiosity and manipulation. Monkeys will go through considerable lengths to puzzle out how to open latches that are attached to a wooden board (see Figure 3.25). But when the latches are unlocked, nothing opens, because the latches never closed anything in the first place. Since unlatching gets the animal nothing, the response was presumably its own reward. In this regard, monkeys acted much like human beings, who in countless ways indicate that they often do things as ends in themselves, rather than as means to other ends.

**3.25 Curiosity and manipulation** *Young rhesus monkeys trying to open a latch. The monkeys received no special reward for their labors but learned to open the devices just "for the fun of it." (After Harlow, 1950; photograph courtesy of University of Wisconsin Primate Laboratory)*

According to Hull's theory, organisms always seek to diminish their level of arousal. But as we have seen, the evidence says otherwise. To be sure, we do try to reduce arousal if our arousal level is unduly high, as in intense hunger or fear or pain. But in many other cases we apparently try to increase it. This suggests that there is an above-zero optimum level of arousal. If we are above this optimum (for example, in pain), we try to reduce arousal. But if we are below it, we seek stimulation to ascend beyond it. This optimum undoubtedly varies from time to time and from person to person. According to some authors, some people are "sensation seekers" who generally look for stimulation, while others prefer a quieter existence (Zuckerman, 1979; see Chapter 18).

## Drugs and Addiction

The normal ways of coping with an arousal level that is too high or too low are by actively coping with the world outside. If we are overaroused, we move toward quiescence: we still our hunger, escape from pain, or go to sleep. If we are under-aroused, we seek stimulation. In some cases, this may reach rather high-pitched levels—by prolonged sex play, by watching an effective horror movie, by riding on a roller coaster. But there is another way to create a drastic change of arousal. We can use drugs that artificially give us a "high" or a "low."

### SOME DRUGS THAT CHANGE AROUSAL LEVEL

Our own interest concerns two major classes of drugs that have powerful psychological effects: those that act as behavioral **depressants** and those that act as **stimulants.**

Let's begin with the depressants. They include various sedatives (for example, barbiturates), alcohol, and the opiates (opium, heroin, and morphine).* Their general effect is to depress the activity of all the neurons in the central nervous system. On the face of it that may seem surprising since all of us have seen loud

---

* Strictly speaking, the opiates belong to a separate class. For unlike alcohol and other sedatives, they serve as narcotics (that is, pain relievers) and act on separate opiate receptors. In addition, one of their number—heroin—seems to be able to produce an unusually intense euphoric "rush," sometimes likened to intense sexual excitement, when taken intravenously.

and aggressive drunks who seem anything but lethargic or depressed. The paradox is resolved if we recognize that their hyperexcitability is a case of disinhibition. At the first stage of inebriation (or at low doses of alcohol ingestion), the depression hits inhibitory synapses in the brain before it affects the excitatory ones. The usual constraints are relaxed, and the individual may engage in activities that he normally might not. Sexual inhibitions will be loosened, as will inhibitions against aggression. There may also be some initial euphoria. But with further alcohol ingestion, the depressive effects will hit all of the cerebral centers. Now the excitement produced by disinhibition will give way to a general slowdown of activity. Attention and memory will blur, and bodily movement and speech will become increasingly uncoordinated, until finally the person will become completely incapacitated and lose consciousness.

The behavioral stimulants, which include amphetamine and cocaine, boost behavioral activity and can lead to an intense elevation of mood—a euphoric "rush" or "high" accompanied by feelings of enormous energy and increased self-esteem. This is especially so for cocaine, which some turn-of-the-century physicians (including Sigmund Freud) regarded as a miracle drug that produced boundless energy, exhilaration, and euphoria with no untoward side effects. This is unfortunately far from true, for the initial euphoria is bought at a considerable cost. Contrary to initial claims, amphetamines and cocaine often produce addictions that eventually become the user's primary focus in life. In addition, repeated use of cocaine (and amphetamines) can lead to extremely irrational states that resemble certain kinds of schizophrenia, in which there are delusions of persecution, irrational fears, and hallucinations (Siegel, 1984).

### TOLERANCE AND WITHDRAWAL

In many individuals, repeated drug use leads to *addiction.* One result is an increased *tolerance* for the drug, especially for the opiates, so that the addict requires ever-larger doses to obtain the same effect.

A second consequence of addiction goes hand in hand with increased tolerance. When the drug is withheld, there are *withdrawal symptoms.* In general, these are the precise opposite of the effects produced by the drug itself. Thus heroin users deprived of their drug feel hyperexcitable; they are extremely irritable, are restless and anxious, and suffer from insomnia. Similarly for the behavioral stimulants. The cocaine or amphetamine user's manic energy and elation give rise to severe emotional depression coupled with profound fatigue when the drug is withdrawn. The same antithesis holds for many physical symptoms. One characteristic of the opiates is that they lead to marked constipation. (They've been used for centuries to relieve diarrhea and dysentery.) But when the drug is withdrawn, the addict suffers violent diarrhea and related gastrointestinal symptoms (Julien, 1985; Volpicelli, 1989).

By its very nature, addiction tends to be self-perpetuating. To begin with, the addict wants to regain the intense pleasure of his drug-induced euphoria (which will become harder and harder because of his increased tolerance). Even more important, perhaps, is the fact that the addict (especially the opiate addict) wants to escape the pangs of drug withdrawal. To dull those pains, he has to take another dose of the drug. And so on.

Further factors that underlie addiction are various social and psychological problems—in the family, at the workplace, or whatever (Alexander and Hadaway, 1982). Such problems often existed before the drug use began. But they can only be worsened by the addiction, and another dose or another drink is a way of escaping them for a while (and making them even more serious in the long run).

## The Opponent-Process Theory of Motivation

What accounts for the phenomena of drug use and drug addiction? Some suggestions come from the *opponent-process theory*, which offers a broad outline of how many motives are acquired.* Opponent-process theory emphasizes the fundamental opposition of the various emotional feelings associated with pain and pleasure (such as fear and terror on the one hand, and joy and euphoria on the other). Its basic premise is that the nervous system has a general tendency to counteract any deviation from normalcy. If there is too much of a swing to one pole of the pain-pleasure dimension, say toward joy and ecstasy, an opponent process is called into play that tilts the balance toward the negative side. Conversely, if the initial swing is toward terror or revulsion, there will be an opponent process toward the positive side. The net effect is that there will be an attenuation of the emotional state one happens to be in, so that ecstasy becomes mild pleasure and terror loses some of its force. A further assumption of this theory is that repetitions of the initial emotional state will produce an increase in the power of the opponent process that is its antagonist (Solomon and Corbit, 1974; Solomon, 1980).

Opponent-process theory tries to account for some of the phenomena of drug addiction we have just discussed. Consider tolerance and withdrawal effects. According to the theory, the emotional reaction produced by a behavioral stimulant such as amphetamine produces an opponent process that pulls in the opposite direction. The more often the drug is taken, the stronger this opponent process becomes. The result is increased tolerance so that ever larger doses of the drug are required to produce an emotional high. The effect of the opponent process is revealed more starkly when the drug is withheld and there is no further pull toward the positive side of the emotional spectrum. Now all that remains is the opponent process whose strength has increased with every dose. This pulls the reaction in the opposite direction, resulting in the anguish of withdrawal (Solomon, 1980).

Some critics point to a problem with this interpretation. It essentially explains addiction as a way of escaping from the withdrawal symptoms. But in so doing it ignores how the addiction began in the first place. What made the addict start to take heroin in the first place, and take it frequently enough and at large enough doses to lead to tolerance and withdrawal? In addition, the critics deny that the withdrawal distress—while certainly unpleasant—is really as unbearable as it is sometimes said to be. According to this view, the drug must continue to produce some positive pleasure, rather than just the alleviation of withdrawal pain (Wise and Bozarth, 1987).

## The Biology of Reward

Thus far, we have discussed what the various motives that humans and animals strive to satisfy have in common psychologically. Another approach to this issue

---

* The term *opponent process* was originally used in the field of color vision where it designates neural processes that pull in opposite directions (see Chapter 5, pp. 193–94).

**3.26 Self-stimulation in rats** *The rat feels the stimulation of a pulse lasting less than a second. (Courtesy of Dr. M. E. Olds)*

has been through studies of the brain processes that come into play when an organism is rewarded. A number of investigators have asked whether there is a special region of the brain whose activation gives rise to what humans call "pleasure," a so-called "pleasure center" that is triggered whenever a motive is satisfied, regardless of which motive it is. They have tried to answer this question by studying the rewarding effects of electrical stimulation of various regions in the brain.

This general area of investigation was opened up in 1954 when James Olds and Peter Milner discovered that rats would learn to press a lever to give themselves a brief burst of electrical stimulation in certain regions of the limbic system (Olds and Milner, 1954; see Figure 3.26). Similar rewarding effects of self-stimulation have been demonstrated in a wide variety of animals, including cats, dogs, dolphins, monkeys, and human beings. To obtain it, rats will press a lever at rates up to 7,000 presses per hour for hours on end. When forced to opt between food and self-stimulation, hungry rats will typically opt for self-stimulation, even though it literally brings starvation (Spies, 1965).

### SPECIFIC AND GENERAL PLEASURE CENTERS

What explains the rewarding effect of self-stimulation? Two possibilities suggest themselves. One is that brain stimulation mimics certain *specific* natural rewards. Stimulation in one region might fool the brain into assuming there had been eating, stimulation in another that there had been copulation, and so on. Another possibility is that self-stimulation provides a more *general,* nonspecific kind of pleasure, something that all rewards share. Drinking, eating, and copulating are obviously different, but perhaps the different motivational messages they send to the brain ("have just drunk, eaten, copulated") ultimately feed into a common neurological system that responds to all of them in much the same way ("that sure felt good").

There is evidence that the stimulation of certain areas provides rather specific rewards. For example, animals will work to obtain electrical stimulation of the lateral zone of the hypothalamus (the "hunger center"). The extent to which they will work to get this reward depends on their hunger level. If they haven't eaten for a while, they will work much harder than they would otherwise. This suggests that the brain regards stimulation in this region as equivalent to food. Analogous effects are found for regions that are concerned with drinking or sexual behavior (Olds and Fobes, 1981).

The case for nonspecific reward effects is somewhat weaker. To begin with, there are a number of regions that lead to self-stimulation, but at a rate that is uninfluenced by food or water deprivation, sex hormones, and the like. Further evidence comes from studies of self-stimulation in human patients—schizophrenics or persons suffering from severe epilepsy. When asked to describe what the stimulation felt like, some patients showed specific reward effects. Most of these were sexual. The stimulation of one region made one patient feel that he had built up to a sexual orgasm. Other patients reported a more nonspecific, pleasurable feeling. They said they "felt good," "wonderful," and then they smiled, laughed, and continued to stimulate themselves by pressing the "happy button." Such results suggest that there might be a nonspecific reward system, a kind of general "pleasure center," that exists in addition to those specific to a particular motive (Heath, 1964; Rolls, 1975).

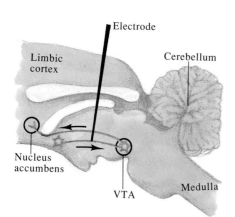

**3.27 Pathways implicated in the rewarding effect of brain stimulation** *The figure is a schematic cross-section of the lower part of a rat's brain, showing a descending pathway that stimulates dopamine-releasing neurons in the ventral tegmental area (VTA) that ascend to the nucleus accumbens. (After Rosenzweig and Leiman, 1989, p. 534)*

## THE DOPAMINE HYPOTHESIS OF REWARD AND DRUG EFFECTS

Can we say anything about the neurobiological underpinning of brain stimulation? Thus far, there are only some tentative steps toward an answer.

It is known that self-stimulation is most effective when it is applied to a bundle of nerve fibers called the ***medial forebrain bundle (MFB).*** According to some theorists, action potentials in some of these fibers will then trigger activity of a second (and as yet unknown) group of cells which extend from a certain region in the midbrain (the ***ventral tegmental area,*** or ***VTA***) to one in the base of the forebrain (the ***nucleus accumbens***) and release dopamine at their axon terminals (see Figure 3.27). That dopamine is involved is shown by the fact that when drugs that serve as dopamine antagonists are injected into the nucleus accumbens (that is, into the region of the second group's axon terminals), brain stimulation is much less effective. Conversely, if drugs that serve as dopamine agonists are injected into that same area, the opposite effect occurs: brain stimulation is very much more effective (Gallistel, Shizgal, and Yeomans, 1981; Stellar and Stellar, 1985; Wise and Rompre, 1989).

To explain these findings, some authors assume that the dopamine-triggered activation of fibers originating in the nucleus accumbens is interpreted by the brain as the neurological equivalent of "good . . . let's have it again"—which may well be just another version of the general pleasure center theory.

One virtue of this hypothesis is that it helps to explain some of the phenomena of drug addiction. Both cocaine and amphetamine are dopamine agonists that enhance the levels of dopamine at the synapse. Cocaine does so by blocking dopamine reuptake (so that the transmitter stays around for a longer period); amphetamine has the same effect and also enhances its release at the axon terminal. Once in the bloodstream, both drugs will eventually enter the nucleus accumbens and then trigger the "good . . . let's have it again" fibers. The opiates (and possibly alcohol) exert their effect by entering the VTA. There they stimulate the dendrites of these same dopamine-releasing cells (which happen to have opiate receptors) whose axons will then transmit the impulse to the nucleus accumbens. Whether the drug is a depressant such as heroin or a stimulant such as cocaine, the key to the addiction is that the drug provides something akin to pleasure, something that is "good . . . let's have it again." Withdrawal symptoms will help to strengthen the addiction, but they are not the only ingredient in creating or even in maintaining it (Wise, 1987; Wise and Bozarth, 1987; for discussion, see Gallistel, 1986).

### PRIMING AND OTHER PUZZLES

The "good . . . let's have it again" idea can't be the complete solution. For there are a number of other facts about brain stimulation that don't really fit (e.g., Gallistel, 1983). One problem is that the same rats who initially responded with such wild frenzy will ignore the lever altogether when put back in the experimental chamber after an interval of an hour or less. But they will resume their wild pressing if first given a few free brief electric pulses. It seems as if something in the brain has to be "primed" in order to reinstate the desire for the brain stimulation (see Figure 3.28). It appears that self-stimulation has several functions. It serves as a reward. But it also starts a positive feedback cycle in which every stimulation strengthens the tendency to get yet another stimulation, and so on. These two functions apparently have two different physiological underpinnings. While do-

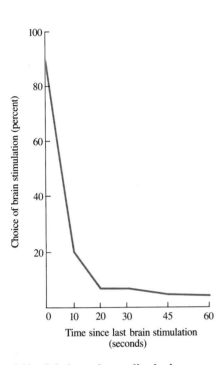

**3.28 Priming and rewarding brain stimulation** *Very thirsty rats were given a choice between two arms of a maze: one led to brain stimulation, the other to water. This choice was made either immediately after a burst of brain stimulation, or from 10 to 60 seconds after stimulation. The figure shows that the animals were much more likely to ignore their thirst and choose brain stimulation if they had been primed with such stimulation shortly before the choice. (Data from Deutsch, Adams, and Metzner, 1964)*

pamine antagonists disrupt the rewarding effect of brain stimulation, they do not abolish priming (Wasserman, Gomita, and Gallistel, 1982; for discussion, see Deutsch, 1960; Gallistel, 1973, 1983; Stellar and Stellar, 1985).

In this regard, the effect of self-stimulation may be similar to the effect of many natural rewards. When we start to eat, the first taste increases our desire for more food rather than decreasing it. In sexual behavior, this effect is even more striking. Each stimulation heightens the desire for further stimulation as sexual passion mounts to a higher and higher pitch. Of course, the positive feedback system is shut off eventually; feeding is finally stopped by satiety signals from the stomach and elsewhere, and sexual passion subsides with orgasm. The priming effect may well be just another instance of this general phenomenon. The difference is that the poor (or perhaps enviable) rat with a self-stimulating electrode in its head has no shut-off mechanism. There is no satiety signal and no orgasm, and so the rat keeps on self-stimulating and self-stimulating until the experimenter finally tears it away from the lever or it falls to the ground in sheer exhaustion.

As yet, we don't know how to put the various pieces of the brain stimulation puzzle together to create a coherent picture of its neurobiological underpinning. But there's reason to believe that when we do, we may understand much more than why rats (and dogs and dolphins) press levers that give certain portions of their brains small jolts of electric currents. We may understand the neurological basis of natural rewards and motives, what it is in the brain that makes humans and animals record certain events as events they want to re-experience (such as food when one is hungry, copulation when one is sexually aroused, and so on). And we may also understand something about the underlying biology of certain "unnatural" rewards like drugs to which some individuals may become addicted.

## The Nature of Motives

To sum up. During the past fifty years, there has been enormous progress in our understanding of the psychology and the physiological basis of the biological motives. But as yet, there is no agreement on one mechanism that explains their action. It may be that such a unitary mechanism doesn't really exist (although advocates of a general pleasure center would probably disagree). Like all scientists, psychologists are much happier when they get neat explanations, and one underlying mechanism would be so much neater than many different ones. But nature did not design organisms to make psychologists happy. And she may well have provided multiple mechanisms rather than just one.

A final point. This chapter was concerned with a number of built-in motives—the biological goals we must seek in order to survive. But whenever we looked at a motive in detail (as in the case of human food selection), we saw that the specific nature of these goals depends not only on our biology but also on what we have learned and have been taught. Just what we drink is not only a matter of our water balance: except for Count Dracula, none of us drink blood. By the same token, we have to maintain certain nutrient levels, but this doesn't mean that we'd be satisfied with a diet of grasshoppers. Similar concerns apply to what we fear and hate, or how we behave in sexual matters and when, where, and with whom. In all these cases, experience builds upon biology and gives form to the built-in basics with which we start. We learn—from the experience of our own lifetime, and through culture, from the lifetime of hundreds of prior generations.

Evolution gave us a set of built-in, biological goals, and a few built-in mechanisms for attaining them. Learning provides the way to modify these goals and to find ever more complex means to achieve them. We turn next to the mechanisms by which such learning occurs in humans and animals.

## SUMMARY

1. Most human and animal actions are motivated. *Motives* have a two-fold function: They *direct* behavior toward or away from some goal. They also serve to *activate* the organism, which becomes more aroused the greater the strength of the motive.

2. The biological basis of directed action is *negative feedback* in which the system "feeds back" upon itself to stop its own action. Built-in negative feedback is responsible for many reactions that maintain the stability of the organism's internal environment or *homeostasis*. Special cells in the hypothalamus sense various aspects of the body's internal state. An example is temperature. If this is above or below certain *setpoints,* a number of self-regulatory reflexes controlled by the sympathetic and parasympathetic divisions of the autonomic nervous system are triggered (for example, shivering). In addition, directed, voluntary acts (such as putting on a sweater) are brought into play.

3. Similar homeostatic mechanisms underlie a number of other biological motives. An example is *thirst.* The organism is informed about its water balance by *volume receptors* that monitor the total volume of its body fluids, and by *osmoreceptors* that respond to the concentration of certain minerals dissolved in these fluids. Water losses are partially offset by reflex mechanisms, including the secretion of the *antidiuretic hormone* (ADH), which instructs the kidneys to reabsorb more of the water that passes through them. In addition, the organism readjusts its own internal environment by directed action—drinking.

4. The biological motive that has been studied most extensively is *hunger.* Many of the signals for feeding and satiety come from the internal environment. Feeding signals include nutrient levels in the bloodstream (which probably affect *glucoreceptors* in the brain) and metabolic processes in the liver (especially the *glucose-glycogen* balance). Satiety signals include messages from receptors in the stomach and the small intestine (particularly a satiety hormone, *cholecystokinin,* or *CCK*). Other feeding and satiety signals are external, including the *palatability* of the food.

5. Many authors believe that the control of feeding is lodged in two antagonistic centers in the hypothalamus whose excitation gives rise to hunger and satiety respectively. As evidence, they point to the effect of lesions. Destruction of the supposed hunger center leads to *aphagia,* a complete refusal to eat. Destruction of the supposed satiety center produces *hyperphagia,* a vast increase in food intake.

6. Homeostatic factors determine *that* an animal feeds, but they have less of an effect on *what* it feeds on. Food selection is determined by a variety of factors, including built-in preferences and learning. Many animals are *neophobic*—afraid of anything that is new. They will only sample new foods in small amounts, developing a learned *taste aversion* if they turn out to be poisonous, and adding them to their diet if they prove to be safe.

7. A feeding-related disorder is *obesity.* Some cases are produced by various constitutional factors, including genetically based metabolic efficiency and an overabundance of fat cells. Others are the result of various behavioral factors. According to the *externality hypothesis,* overweight people are comparatively insensitive to internal hunger signals and oversensitive to external ones such as palatability. An alternative is the *setpoint hypothesis,* which asserts that overweight people have a higher internal setpoint for weight.

8. Other eating disorders are *anorexia nervosa* in which there is a pattern of relentless self-starvation, sometimes to the point of death, and *bulimia,* which is characterized by repeated binge-and-purge bouts.

9. In contrast to thirst and hunger, which are largely based on homeostatic factors from within, a number of motives are instigated from without. An example is the intense reaction to external threat. Its biological mechanisms include the operations of the *autonomic nervous system.* This consists of two antagonistic branches. One is the *parasympathetic nervous system,* which serves the vegetative functions of everyday life, such as digestion and reproduction. It slows down the heart rate and reduces blood pressure. The other is the *sympathetic nervous system,* which activates the body and mobilizes its resources. It increases the available metabolic fuels and accelerates their utilization by increasing the heart rate and respiration. Intense sympathetic activity can be regarded as an *emergency reaction,* which underlies the overt reactions of *fight* or *flight* and their usual emotional concomitants, rage or fear. The sympathetic emergency reaction is not always adaptive. It can produce temporary disruptions of digestive and sexual functions, and can also lead to more permanent psychophysiological disorders.

10. While the sympathetic system arouses the more primitive physiological processes of the body, a structure in the brain stem, the *reticular activating system,* or *RAS,* arouses the brain. The RAS awakens the cortex and is opposed by an antagonistic system which leads to sleep.

11. During sleep, brain activity changes as shown by the *electroencephalogram* or *EEG.* Each night, we oscillate between two kinds of sleep. One is *quiet sleep,* during which the cortex is relatively inactive. The other is *active sleep,* characterized by considerable cortical activity and *rapid eye movements* or *REMs,* a pattern of internal activity which is experienced as *dreams. Sleep-deprivation* studies show that when one or the other kind of sleep is prevented, it is to some extent made up later on. This suggests that there is a need for each of the two sleep states, but the biological functions served by either are as yet unknown. The best guess is that one or both forms of sleep serve a *restorative function* and also represent an evolutionary relic of *ancestral adaptive patterns.*

12. According to *drive-reduction theory,* all built-in motives act to reduce stimulation and arousal. Today most authors believe instead that organisms strive for an *optimum level of arousal.* If below this optimum, they try to increase arousal by various means.

13. One way of coping with an arousal level that is too high or too low is by the use of drugs. Some drugs act as *depressants,* including alcohol and the opiates. Others such as the *amphetamines* and *cocaine* act as *stimulants.* In many individuals, repeated drug use leads to *addiction,* accompanied by increased *tolerance* and *withdrawal effects* if the drug is withheld. The *opponent-process theory of motivation* tries to explain these and many other phenomena by arguing that all shifts of arousal level produce a counteracting process that acts to moderate the ups and downs. When the original instigator of the shift is removed, the opponent process is revealed more clearly, as in withdrawal effects.

14. Work on the rewarding effects of certain regions of the brain has led to speculations about possible *pleasure centers* in the brain. While there is evidence that stimulation of certain areas leads to specific reward effects, the evidence for nonspecific reward effects is somewhat weaker. According to the *dopamine hypothesis of reward,* the neural underpinning of such reward effects lies in the activation of fibers that originate in a brain structure called the *nucleus accumbens* and are triggered by dopamine. According to the hypothesis, their activation is the neurological equivalent of "Good . . . let's have it again!" A problem with any version of the reward effect hypothesis is the fact that self-stimulation requires some *priming.*

# CHAPTER 4

# Learning

Thus far, our discussion has centered on the built-in facets of human and animal behavior, the general neural equipment that provides the underpinning for everything we do, and the specific, innate feedback systems that underlie directed action. But much of what we do and are goes beyond what nature gave us. It is acquired through experience in our lifetime. People learn—to grasp a baby bottle, to eat with knife and fork, to read and write, to love or hate their neighbors, and eventually, to face death. In animals, the role of learning may be less dramatic, but it is enormously important even so.

What can psychology tell us about the processes whereby organisms learn? Many investigators have tried to reconcile the phenomena of learning with the reflex-machine conception that goes back to Descartes. The adherents of this approach, whose modern exponents are sometimes called **behavior theorists,** argued that the organism's *prewired* repertory of behaviors is supplemented by continual *rewirings* that are produced by experience. Some of these rewirings consist of new connections between stimuli. Thus, the sight of the mother's face may come to signify the taste of milk. Other rewirings involve new connections between acts and their consequences, as when a toddler learns that touching a hot radiator is followed by a painful burn. The behavior theorists set themselves the task of discovering how such rewirings come about.

The behavior theorists' interest in the learning process was admirably suited to the intellectual climate during the first part of this century, especially in the United States. For here was a society that was deeply committed to the individual's efforts to improve himself by pushing himself on to greater efforts and acquiring new skills—in numerous public schools and colleges, night classes for recent immigrants, dance classes for the shy, courses for those who wanted to "win friends and influence people," and martial-arts classes for those less interested in winning friends than in defeating enemies. There was—and in many ways, still is—an enormous faith in the near-limitless malleability of human beings, who were thought to be almost infinitely perfectible by proper changes in their environment, especially through education. Under the circumstances, it was hardly surprising that learning became (and still is) one of the paramount concerns of American psychology.

How should the learning process be studied? At least initially, most behavior theorists felt that there are some basic laws that come into play, regardless of what is learned or who does the learning—be it a dog learning to sit on command or a college student learning integral calculus. This early conception was very influential. It led to the view that at bottom even the most involved learned activities are made up of simpler ones, much as complex chemical compounds are made up of simpler atoms. Given this belief, it was only natural that the early investigators concentrated their efforts on trying to understand learning in simple situations and in (relatively) simpler creatures like dogs, rats, and pigeons. By so doing, they hoped to strip the learning process down to its bare essence so that its basic laws might be revealed.

As we will see, some of the beliefs of the early behavior theorists had to be modified in the light of later discoveries. They never succeeded in finding *one* set of laws that underlie *all* phenomena of learning in *all* organisms, including humans. But even so, their search led to the major discoveries that form the basis of much of what we know today. It is to these that we now turn.

## HABITUATION

The simplest of all forms of learning is *habituation.* This is a decline in the tendency to respond to stimuli that have become familiar due to repeated exposure. A sudden noise usually startles us—an adaptive reaction, for sudden and unfamiliar stimuli often spell danger. But suppose the same noise is repeated over and over again. The second time, the startle will be diminished, the third time it will hardly be evoked, and after that, it will be ignored altogether. Our startle response has become habituated. Much the same holds for many other everyday events. We have become so accustomed to the ticking of a clock in the living room that we are utterly unaware of it until it finally stops. By the same token, city dwellers become completely habituated to the noise of traffic but are kept awake by the crickets when they take a vacation in the country.

Habituation is found at virtually all levels of the animal kingdom. Mammals, birds, fish, insects, and snails perform various escape reactions when they first encounter a novel stimulus, but after several repetitions they come to ignore it. Thus marine snails initially withdraw their gills at the slightest touch, but they will stop responding after repeated stimulation. Similarly, male Siamese fighting fish adopt a striking fighting posture upon encountering another male of their own species (or when looking into a mirror), but after several such encounters they become less and less aggressive and eventually hold their peace (Figler, 1972; Peeke, 1984).

What is the adaptive significance of habituation? One of its major benefits is that it narrows down the range of stimuli that elicit escape reactions. After all, organisms have to eat and drink and mate to survive, and they can't do so if they spend all their time running away from imaginary enemies. Habituation allows

***Habituation in Siamese fighting fish***
*Male Siamese fighting fish adopt a fighting posture when they see another male, but after a while they habituate to his presence. (Photograph by Toni Angermeyer/Photo Researchers)*

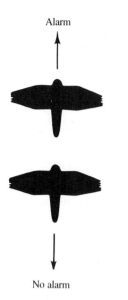

Alarm

No alarm

**4.1 Innate fear of hawks or habituation?**
*Young turkeys run for cover when a silhouette model is pulled in the direction of the model's short end which makes it look like a bird of prey, but not when it is pulled in the opposite direction which makes it look like a goose. (After Tinbergen, 1951)*

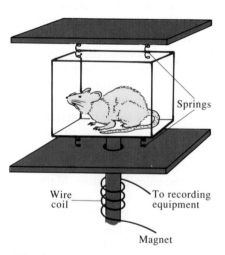

**4.2 An apparatus that measures the startle response in rats** *A small chamber is balanced on springs. The bottom of the chamber is attached to a magnet that is surrounded by a coil of wire. Sudden movements of the rat will lead to movements of the chamber that produce an electrical current in the wire. (After Hoffman and Fleshler, 1964)*

them to ignore the familiar and focus their emergency reactions on things that are new and may signal dangers (Wyers, Peeke, and Herz, 1973; Shalter, 1984).

An interesting example of the role of habituation in focusing escape reactions is the response of ground-living birds to the sight of birds flying above. Some early experiments studied the reaction of young turkeys to a cardboard silhouette of a bird pulled overhead on a string. The silhouette had a short end and a long end (see Figure 4.1). When pulled so that the long end pointed forward (which made it look like a goose with an outstretched neck), the young turkeys were nonchalant. But when it was pulled in the opposite direction, the birds became terrified and ran for cover. Now the short end pointed forward and the silhouette resembled a hawk. Some authors took this result as evidence that ground-living birds have a built-in fear reaction to birds of prey (Tinbergen, 1951). But further studies suggested that the effect was a result of novelty and habituation. In the turkeys' environment, long-necked geese and ducks flying overhead were fairly common, while hawks were hardly ever seen. As a result, the turkeys had become habituated to the one and not the other. The young birds began with a fear reaction to just about everything. Given time and habituation, familiarity bred neglect. As a result, their fear reaction could narrow down to the rather infrequent stimuli—the short-necked hawks overhead—that the animal indeed has good reason to fear (Schleidt, 1961).

Laboratory studies have shown that habituation comes in two varieties. One is a short-term effect that dissipates in a matter of minutes. A second is more long term; it lasts much longer and may persist for days or weeks. That these two are different makes intuitive sense. We gradually habituate to a certain noise; but after a year, the same sound might well frighten us again. These two facets of habituation were demonstrated in a study of rats that were exposed to a high-pitched, loud tone, presented for two seconds (Leaton, 1976). Initially, the stimulus produced a marked startle response; the rat literally jumped up in the air when it heard the tone (see Figure 4.2). To measure **short-term habituation,** the experimenters presented 300 of these tones within the space of five minutes. Presented in this manner, the startle quickly wore off. After 100 or so presentations, the animal ignored the now familiar tones. The experimenters first asked whether this nonchalance wore off over time. It evidently did, for when tested after a twenty-four-hour interval the rats jumped just as much as they did at the start of their last short-term training—a phenomenon called **spontaneous recovery.** To demonstrate **long-term habituation,** the investigators presented the same tone just once a day over an eleven-day period. They found that the startle response gradually declined over days. This shows that there is a long-term memory effect as well as a short-term effect. In some fashion, the animal compares what it now hears and sees with what else it has previously heard and seen, either in its immediate or its more remote past. To the extent that the current stimulus matches with what is in its memory, it is judged to be familiar and thus not "startling" (Wagner, 1979; Whitlow and Wagner, 1984). We will have occasion to revisit the distinction between short- and long-term memory storage in a later chapter (see Chapter 7).

## CLASSICAL CONDITIONING

In habituation, an organism learns to recognize an event as familiar, but he doesn't learn anything about the relation between that event and any other cir-

*Ivan Petrovich Pavlov* *(Courtesy Sovfoto)*

cumstances. Such learned relationships are called **associations.** There's little doubt that much of what we learn consists of various associations between events: between thunder and lightning, between the nipple and food, between the sound of a thumping motor and a large automobile repair bill. The importance of associations in human learning and thinking has been emphasized since the days of the Greek philosophers, but the experimental study of associations did not begin until the end of the nineteenth century. A major step in this direction was the work on conditioning performed by the great Russian scientist, Ivan P. Pavlov (1849–1936).

## Pavlov and the Conditioned Reflex

Ivan Petrovich Pavlov had already earned the Nobel Prize for his work on digestion before he embarked upon the study of conditioning which was to gain him even greater fame. His initial interest was in the built-in nervous control of the various digestive reflexes in dogs; most important to us, the secretion of saliva. He surgically diverted one of the ducts of the salivary gland, thus channeling part of the salivary flow through a special tube to the outside of the animal's body where it could be easily measured and analyzed. Pavlov demonstrated that salivation was produced by several innate reflexes, one of which prepares the food for digestion. This is triggered by food (especially dry food) placed in the mouth.

In the course of Pavlov's work a new fact emerged. The salivary reflex could be set off by stimuli which at first were totally neutral. Dogs that had been in the laboratory for a while would soon salivate to a whole host of stimuli that had no such effect on their uninitiated fellows. Not only the taste and touch of the meat in the mouth, but its mere sight, the sight of the dish in which it was placed, the sight of the person who usually brought it, even that person's footsteps—eventually all of these might produce salivation. Pavlov soon decided to study such effects in their own right, for he recognized that they provided a means of extending the reflex concept to embrace learned as well as innate reactions. The approach was simple enough. Instead of waiting for accidental events in each animal's history, the experimenter would provide those events himself. Thus he would repeatedly sound a buzzer and always follow it with food. Later he observed what happened when the buzzer was sounded and no food was given (Pavlov, 1927; Figure 4.3).

*4.3 Apparatus for salivary conditioning* The figure shows an early version of Pavlov's apparatus for classical conditioning of the salivary response. The dog was held in a harness, sounds or lights functioned as conditioned stimuli, while meat powder in a dish served as the unconditioned stimulus. The conditioned response was assessed with the aid of a tube connected to an opening in one of the animal's salivary glands. (After Yerkes and Morgulis, 1909)

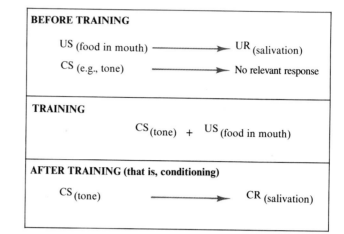

**BEFORE TRAINING**

US (food in mouth) ⟶ UR (salivation)

CS (e.g., tone) ⟶ No relevant response

**TRAINING**

CS (tone)   +   US (food in mouth)

**AFTER TRAINING (that is, conditioning)**

CS (tone) ⟶ CR (salivation)

*4.4   Relationships between CS, US, CR, and UR in classical conditioning*

The fundamental finding was simple: Repeated buzzer-food pairings led to salivation when the buzzer was presented alone (that is, unaccompanied by food) on occasional test trials. To explain this, Pavlov proposed a distinction between unconditioned and conditioned reflexes. ***Unconditioned reflexes*** he held to be essentially inborn and innate; these are unconditionally elicited by the appropriate stimulus regardless of the animal's history. An example is food in the mouth, which unconditionally elicits salivation. In contrast, ***conditioned reflexes*** were acquired, and thus they were conditional upon the animal's past experience, and according to Pavlov, based upon newly formed connections in the brain. (A stricter translation might have been "unconditional reflex" and "conditional reflex" respectively.)

According to Pavlov, every unconditioned reflex is based upon a (presumably built-in) connection between an ***unconditioned stimulus (US)*** and an ***unconditioned response (UR).*** In Pavlov's laboratory, these were food in the mouth (the US) and salivation (UR). The corresponding terms for the conditioned reflex are ***conditioned stimulus (CS)*** and ***conditioned response (CR).*** Here CS would be an initially neutral stimulus, that is, some stimulus (here, the buzzer) that does not elicit the CR without prior conditioning. The CR (here again, salivation) is the response elicited by the CS after some such pairings of CS and US. These various relationships are summarized in Figure 4.4 and constitute the basis of what is now known as ***classical conditioning.****

## The Major Phenomena of Classical Conditioning

Pavlov saw conditioning as a way of extending the reflex concept into the realm of learning. Later workers (especially in the United States) were not as convinced as he that the so-called conditioned reflex is in fact some kind of reflex, even one that is modified. As a result, they substituted the more neutral term "response" for "reflex," as in "unconditioned response." But until quite recently, most of

---

* The adjective *classical* is used, in part, as dutiful tribute to Pavlov's eminence and historical priority, and in part, to distinguish this form of conditioning from *instrumental conditioning* to which we will turn later.

them shared Pavlov's conviction that conditioning was essentially a change in what the animal does, and so, like he, they focused on the acquisition of the conditioned response. As we will see, later workers came to see conditioning in rather different ways than Pavlov did. But we will begin by describing his empirical discoveries with a minimum of editorial comment, for these findings laid the foundations for all subsequent theories of classical conditioning and indeed of much of learning generally.

### ACQUISITION OF CONDITIONED RESPONSES

Pavlov noted that the tendency of the CS to elicit the CR goes up the more often the CS and the US have been paired together. Clearly then, presenting the US together with (or more typically, subsequent to) the CS is a critical operation in classical conditioning. Such a pairing is said to *reinforce* the connection; trials on which the US occurs and on which it is omitted are called *reinforced* and *unreinforced trials* respectively.

*Measuring the strength of the CR*    There are a number of ways in which the strength of a CR can be measured. One is *response amplitude:* in Pavlov's experiments, this was the amount of saliva secreted when the CS was presented without the US. Another measure is *probability of response:* the proportion of trials on which the CR is made when the CS is presented alone. Yet another measure is *response latency:* the time from the onset of CS to the CR. In contrast to amplitude and probability of response, which increase as CR strength increases, response latency varies inversely with CR strength: The shorter the latency, the stronger the CR.

Figure 4.5 is an idealized *learning curve* in which strength of CR is plotted against successive reinforced trials. In this and other conditioning trials, the general trend is very clear and unsurprising: Response strength increases with the number of reinforced trials. What is less obvious is the shape of the curve, which is negatively accelerated (convex upwards) and rises to an asymptote (a final ceiling). As the figure shows, more is learned on any given trial than on the trial that succeeds it, until the curve levels off to its asymptote. We'll return to the shape of this curve in a later section (see p. 130).

*Second-order conditioning*    Once the CS-US relation is solidly established, the CS can serve to condition yet further stimuli. To give one example, Pavlov first conditioned a dog to salivate to the beat of a metronome, using meat powder as the US. After a number of such pairings, he presented the animal with a black square followed by the metronome beat, but without ever introducing the food. Eventually the sight of the black square alone was enough to produce salivation. This phenomenon is called *second-order conditioning.* The metronome, which served as the CS in first-order conditioning, now functioned as the US for a second-order conditioned response. In effect, the black square had become a signal for the metronome, which in turn signaled the appearance of food.

### EXTINCTION

The adaptive value of conditioning is self-evident. A zebra's chance of future survival is enhanced by conditioning. There's much to be gained by a conditioned

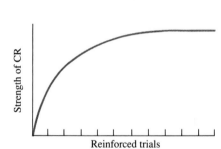

**4.5   An idealized learning curve**   *Strength of CR is plotted against number of reinforced trials. The curve presents the results of many such studies which by and large show that the curve is negatively accelerated. Strength of CR rises with increasing trials, but each trial adds less strength than the trial just before it.*

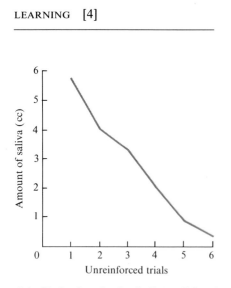

**4.6 Extinction of a classically conditioned response** *The figure shows the decrease in the amount of saliva secreted (the CR) with increasing number of extinction trials—that is, trials on which CS is presented without US. (After Pavlov, 1928)*

fear reaction to a place from which a lion has pounced some time before (assuming, of course, that the zebra managed to survive the CS-US pairing in the first place). On the other hand, it would be rather inefficient if a connection once established could never be undone. The lion may change its lair and its former prowling place may now be perfectly safe for grazing.

Pavlov showed that in fact a conditioned reaction can be undone. He demonstrated that the conditioned response will gradually disappear if the CS is repeatedly presented without being reinforced by the US; in his terms, the CS-US link undergoes *experimental extinction.* Figure 4.6 presents an extinction curve from a salivary extinction experiment. As usual, response strength is measured along the *y*-axis, while the *x*-axis indicates the number of extinction trials (that is, trials without reinforcement). As extinction trials proceed, the salivary flow dries up. In effect, the dog has learned that the CS is no longer a signal for food.

A conditioned response that has been extinguished can be resurrected. One means is through *reconditioning,* that is, by presenting further reinforced trials. Typically, reconditioning requires fewer reinforced trials to bring the CR to its former strength than were necessary during the initial conditioning session, even if extinction trials had been continued until the animal stopped responding altogether. The conditioned response was evidently not really abolished by extinction but instead was somehow masked.

The fact that the conditioned response is only masked rather than abolished by extinction is also shown by the phenomenon of *spontaneous recovery.* An extinguished CR will usually reappear after a rest interval during which the animal is left to its own devices. This effect is reminiscent of a similar phenomenon in habituation that bears the same name. In both cases, the sheer passage of time leads to the spontaneous recovery of a response; in the one case, the resurrected response had previously been habituated, in the other, it had been extinguished. The interpretation of these effects is still a matter of some debate. According to a recent analysis, the animal gradually loses interest in the CS as extinction proceeds and no longer looks or listens to it. After an interval away from the situation, it attends to the CS once again and therefore resumes responding. In principle, a similar analysis might account for the spontaneous recovery of habituation (Robbins, 1990).

GENERALIZATION

So far our discussion has been confined to situations in which the animal is tested with the *identical* stimulus that had served as the CS during training. But of course in the real world the stimuli are never really identical. The master's voice may signal food, but the exact intonation will surely vary from one occasion to another. Can the dog still use whatever it has learned before? If it can't, its conditioned response will be of little benefit. In fact, animals do respond to stimuli other than the original CS, so long as these are sufficiently similar.

This phenomenon is called *stimulus generalization.* A dog may be conditioned to respond to a tone of 1,000 hertz (cycles per second); nevertheless, the CR will be obtained not just with that tone, but also with tones of different frequencies, like 900 or 1,100 hertz. But the CR evoked by such new stimuli will show a *generalization decrement;* it will be weaker than the CR elicited by the original CS. The greater the difference between the new stimulus and the original CS, the larger this decrement will be. The resulting curve is called a *generalization gradient* (see Figure 4.7).

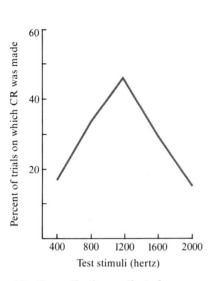

**4.7  Generalization gradient of a classically conditioned response**  *The figure shows the generalization of a conditioned blinking response in rabbits. The CS was a tone of 1,200 hertz and the US was electric shock. After the conditioned response to the original CS was well established, generalization was measured by presenting various test stimuli, ranging from 400 hertz to 2,000 hertz and noting the percent of the trials on which the animals gave the CR. The figure shows the results, averaged over several testing sessions. (After Moore, 1972)*

Stimulus generalization is not always beneficial. A kitten may be similar to a tiger; but a man who generalizes from one to the other is likely to be sorry. What he must do instead is discriminate.

The phenomenon of ***discrimination*** is readily demonstrated in the laboratory. A dog is first conditioned to salivate to a CS, for example, a black square (CS⁺). After the CR is well established, reinforced trials with the black square are randomly interspersed with nonreinforced trials with another stimulus, say, a gray square (CS⁻). This continues until the animal discriminates perfectly, always salivating to CS⁺, the reinforced stimulus, and never to CS⁻, the nonreinforced stimulus. Of course the dog does not reach this final point immediately. During the early trials it will be confused, or more precisely, it will generalize rather than discriminate. It will tend to salivate to CS⁻ (which, after all, is quite similar to CS⁺); by the same token, it will often fail to salivate when presented with CS⁺. Such errors gradually become fewer and fewer until perfect discrimination is finally achieved. Not surprisingly, the discrimination gets harder and harder the more similar the two stimuli are. As similarity increases, the tendency to respond to CS⁺ will increasingly generalize to CS⁻, while the tendency not to respond to CS⁻ will increasingly generalize to CS⁺. As a result, the dog will require many trials before it finally responds without errors.

One might think that the difficulty in forming discrimination is that the animal has trouble telling the two stimuli apart. But that is generally not the reason. The dog's problem is not that it can't form a sensory discrimination between CS⁺ and CS⁻. What is at fault is not its eyesight, for it can distinguish between the dark-gray and light-gray squares visually. Its difficulty is in discovering and remembering which stimulus is *right,* which goes with the US and which does not. Eventually the animal learns, but this doesn't mean that it has learned to see the stimuli differently. What it has learned is their significance; it now knows which stimulus is which.

## Extensions of Classical Conditioning

Thus far, our discussion has been largely restricted to the laboratory phenomena that Pavlov looked at: dogs salivating to buzzers, lights, and metronomes. Needless to say, conditioning would be of little interest if it only applied to those phenomena. But in actual fact, its scope is very much larger than that.

To begin with, classical conditioning has been found in a large variety of animal species other than dogs, including ants and anteaters, cats and cockroaches, pigeons and people. Any number of reaction patterns have been classically conditioned in animals. Thus, crabs have been conditioned to twitch their tail spines, fish to thrash about, and octopuses to change color. Responses conditioned in laboratory studies with humans include the galvanic skin response (where the US is typically a loud noise or electric shock) and the blink-reaction of the eyelid (where the US consists of a puff of air on the open eye; Kimble, 1961).

Nor is classical conditioning restricted to the laboratory, for there is little doubt that it plays a considerable role in our everyday life. Many of our internal feelings and urges are probably the result of classical conditioning. We tend to feel hungry at mealtimes and less so during the times between; this is so even if we fast a whole day. Another example is sexual arousal. This is often produced by a partner's special word or gesture whose erotic meaning is very private and is surely learned.

### CONDITIONED FEAR

Of special importance is the role of classical conditioning in the formation of various emotional reactions, especially those concerned with fear. A common consequence of a conditioned fear reaction is *response suppression.* The CS will evoke fear, which in turn will suppress whatever other activities the animal is currently engaged in. This is the basis of a widely used technique to study fear conditioning, the *conditioned emotional response (CER)* procedure. A hungry rat is first taught to press a lever for an occasional food reward. After a few training sessions, the rat will press at a steady rate. Now classical conditioning can start. While the animal is pressing, a CS is presented—a light or a tone that will stay on for, say, three minutes. At the end of that period, the CS terminates and there is a mild, brief electric shock (the US). Some twenty minutes later, the same CS-US sequence is repeated. After this, there is another twenty-minute interval during which neither the CS nor the US are presented, followed by yet another CS-US sequence, and so on (Estes and Skinner, 1941; Kamin, 1965). After twelve such trials, the response is completely suppressed (see Figure 4.8).

It is a plausible guess that many adult fears are based upon classical conditioning, acquired in much the same way that fear is acquired in the laboratory. These fears may be relatively mild or very intense (if intense enough, they are called *phobias*). They may be acquired in early childhood or during particular traumatic episodes in later life. An example is an Air Force pilot who bailed out of his plane but whose parachute failed to open until the last five seconds before he hit the ground. In such traumatic episodes, conditioning apparently occurs in a single trial. This seems reasonable enough, for it would certainly be unadaptive if the pilot had to bail out on ten separate occasions, each time barely escaping death, before he finally developed a conditioned fear reaction (Sarnoff, 1957).

### THE RELATION BETWEEN CR AND UR

The phenomenon of fear conditioning brings us to an important question that we have neglected up to now: What is the relation between the CR and the UR? In salivary conditioning, the CR and the UR seem to be rather similar, a fact that fits in very nicely with Pavlov's attempt to extend the reflex conception to encompass learned modifications of behavior. But on closer examination, the CR and the UR are rarely if ever identical. This is quite apparent in fear conditioning. When exposed to electric shock, the US, the animal makes little jumps and its heart beats faster; when it hears or sees the CS that signals the shock, it stops moving, tenses itself, and its heart beats more slowly. The difference between the CR and the UR is found even in salivary conditioning. To be sure, Pavlov's dogs salivated both when they heard or saw the CS and when they experienced the US. But when the dog responds to the US, its saliva is more copious and much richer in digestive enzyme than when it reacts to the CS.

All of this makes good biological sense. The CS is a signal for the US, but does not become a substitute for it. The response to the CS (the CR) is essentially a preparation for the US; while the response to the US (that is, the UR) performs the task for which the organism is now prepared (for discussion, see Zener, 1937; Holland, 1984; Hollis, 1984).

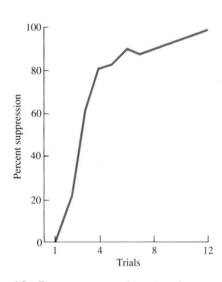

**4.8  Response suppression**  *A rat is trained to press a lever at a steady rate to gain food. The figure plots the extent to which this response is suppressed after successive presentations of a 3-minute light CS that is immediately followed by electric shock. After 12 such trials, suppression is at 100 percent, and the animal doesn't respond at all during the 3 minutes when the CS is presented. (Data from Kamin, 1969)*

CONDITIONING AND DRUG EFFECTS

In some situations, the CR is not just different from the UR, but is actually its very opposite. This effect is often encountered in studies on the conditioning of drug effects. Suppose a person gets many doses of insulin, which depletes blood sugar. It turns out that after a number of such insulin injections, the bodily reaction to various conditioned stimuli that accompany the drug is the exact opposite of the response to the drug itself: Given the CS, the blood-sugar level goes *up.* It is as if the body prepares itself for the chemical agent it is about to receive and does so by adopting a compensatory reaction that tilts the other way (Siegel, 1977).

This compensatory-reaction hypothesis has some important consequences for our understanding of drug addiction. Consider opiates such as morphine or heroin. These have various effects, such as relief from pain, euphoria, and relaxation. But after repeated administrations, stimuli that usually precede the injection of these drugs (for example, the sight of the hypodermic needle) produce effects that go in the opposite direction: depression, restlessness, and an increased sensitivity to pain. Some authors believe that these effects represent a compensatory reaction in which the response to the CS counteracts the reaction triggered by the US. As a result, the user develops drug tolerance. To make up for the conditioned compensatory reaction, he must inject himself with increasingly larger doses of the drug to obtain the same effect that was produced when he took it for the first time. But this will only work if he takes the drug under familiar circumstances, for if he takes it in a new environment, he runs the risk of a dangerous overdose. He has increased his drug dose to overcome the compensatory reaction of various conditioned stimuli. But in a new environment, there is a generalization decrement. Since many of the old conditioned stimuli are altered or missing, there is a weaker compensatory response. The result may be death by overdose—a lethal side effect of classical conditioning (Siegel, 1977, 1979).

That generalization effects of this sort may play this role in some cases of drug mortality is suggested by interviews with heroin overdose survivors. A number of these reported that on the occasion when they had injected themselves to near-fatal effect, their dose was no greater than usual. What differed were the circumstances under which they took the drug—the place, the company, and so on. Parallel results come from work with rats given heroin injections for a month, and then subjected to a larger dose in the same place or in a different environment. When the environment was altered, the larger dose was much more harmful (Siegel, Hinson, Krank, and McCully, 1982; Siegel, 1983).

The compensatory-reaction hypothesis is still a subject of considerable debate, however, for as yet it's unclear under what conditions a CR will be similar to the UR and under what others it will be the very opposite. In all likelihood both phenomena occur, and they depend on a number of different mechanisms, many of which are still unknown.* But whatever the ultimate upshot, it is clear that classical conditioning is much more than a laboratory curiosity limited to dogs, metronomes, and saliva. It is a phenomenon of enormous scope, a basic form of learning that pervades much of our life and is shared by flatworms and people alike (Eikelboom and Stewart, 1982; Hollis, 1982; Rescorla and Holland, 1982).

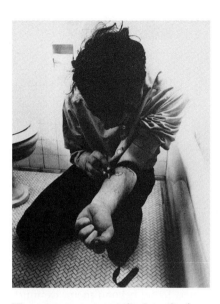

***The compensatory-reaction hypothesis and drug use*** *In an addict, the sight and feel of the hypodermic needle (or other drug-related stimuli) have become a CS for the counterreaction to the drug. If so, then a larger dose of the drug is needed to get the high. This may account for some overdose deaths, especially if the too-large dose was taken in an unfamiliar environment. (Courtesy of the Museum of the City of New York)*

---

* The compensatory-reaction hypothesis is similar to the opponent-process theory discussed in the previous chapter in assuming that various drug reactions are accompanied by processes that pull in the opposite direction. According to one hypothesis, such compensatory reactions are equivalent to conditioned opponent processes (Schull, 1979).

## INSTRUMENTAL CONDITIONING

Habituation and classical conditioning are two of the main forms of simple learning. Another is *instrumental conditioning* (which is also called *operant conditioning* or *instrumental learning*). An example of instrumental conditioning comes from the zoo. When a seal learns to turn a somersault to get a fish from the zoo attendant, it has learned an *instrumental response.* The response is instrumental in that it leads to a sought-after effect—in this case, the fish.

There are some important differences between instrumental and classical conditioning. The most important is the fact that in instrumental learning, reinforcement (that is, reward) depends upon the proper response. For the seal the rules of the game are simple: no somersault, no fish. This is not true for classical conditioning. There the US is presented regardless of what the animal does. Another difference concerns response selection. In instrumental learning, the response must be selected from a sometimes very large set of alternatives. The seal's job is to select the somersault from among the numerous other things a seal could possibly do. Not so in classical conditioning. There the response is forced, for the US unconditionally evokes it.

We could loosely summarize the difference between the two procedures by a rough description of what is learned in each. In classical conditioning the animal must learn about the relation between two stimuli, the CS and the US: Given CS, US will follow. In instrumental learning, the animal has to learn the relation between a response and a reward: Given this response, there will be reinforcement. But such statements are only crude descriptions. To get beyond them, we must discuss instrumental learning in more detail.

### Thorndike and the Law of Effect

The experimental study of instrumental learning began a decade or two before Pavlov. It was an indirect consequence of the debate over the doctrine of evolution. Darwin's theory was buttressed by impressive demonstrations of continuity in the bodily structures of many species, both living and extinct. But his opponents could argue that such evidence was not enough. To them the essential distinction between humans and beasts was elsewhere: in the human ability to think and reason, an ability that animals did not share. To answer this point it became critical to find proof of mental as well as of bodily continuity.

For evidence, the Darwinians turned to animal behavior. At first, the method was largely anecdotal. Several British naturalists (including Darwin himself) collected stories about the intellectual achievements of various animals as related by presumably reliable informants. Taken at face value, the results painted a flattering picture of animal intellect, as in accounts of cunning cats scattering bread crumbs on the lawn to entice the birds (Romanes, 1882). But even if such observations could be trusted (and they probably could not), they did not prove that the animals' performances were achieved in the way a human might achieve the same thing: by reason and understanding. To be sure of that, one would have to study the animals' learning processes from start to finish. To see a circus seal blow

**Edward L. Thorndike**  *(Courtesy The Granger Collection)*

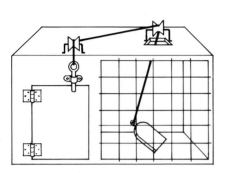

**4.9 Puzzle box** *This box is much like those used by Thorndike. The animal steps on a treadle which is attached to a rope, thereby releasing a latch that locks the door. (After Thorndike, 1911)*

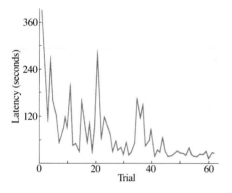

**4.10 Learning curve of one of Thorndike's cats** *To get out of the box, the cat had to move a wooden handle from a vertical to a horizontal position. The figure shows the gradual decline in the animal's response latency (the time it takes to get out of the box). Note that the learning curve is by no means smooth but has rather marked fluctuations. This is a common feature of the learning curves of individual subjects. Smooth learning curves are generally produced by averaging the results of many individual subjects. (After Thorndike, 1898)*

a melody on a set of toy trumpets is one thing; to conclude from this observation that it has musical understanding is quite another.

There was clearly a need for controlled experimental procedures whereby the entire course of learning could be carefully scrutinized. That method was provided in 1898 by Edward L. Thorndike (1874–1949) in a brilliant doctoral dissertation that became one of the classic documents of American psychology (Thorndike, 1898).

### CATS IN A PUZZLE BOX

Thorndike's method was to set up a problem for the animal. To gain reward the creature had to perform some particular action determined by the experimenter. Much of this work was done on hungry cats. The animal was placed in a so-called *puzzle box,* an enclosure from which it could escape only by performing some simple action that would unlatch the door, such as pulling a loop or wire or pressing a lever (Figure 4.9). Once outside, the animal was rewarded with a small portion of food and then placed back into the box for another trial. This procedure was repeated until the task was mastered.

On the first trial, the typical cat struggled valiantly; it clawed at the bars, it bit, it struck out in all directions, it meowed, and it howled. This continued for several minutes until the animal finally hit upon the correct response by pure accident. Subsequent trials brought gradual improvement. The mad scramble became shorter and the animal took less and less time to perform the correct response. By the time the training sessions were completed the cat's behavior was almost unrecognizable from what it had been at the start. Placed in the box, it immediately approached the wire loop, yanked it with businesslike dispatch, and quickly hurried through the open door to enjoy its well-deserved reward. The cat had certainly learned.

How had it learned? If one merely observed its final performance one might credit the cat with reason or understanding, but Thorndike argued that the problem was solved in a very different way. For proof he examined the learning curves. Plotting the time required on each trial (that is, the response *latency*) over the whole course of training, he usually found a curve that declined quite gradually (Figure 4.10). Had the animals "understood" the solution at some point during training, the curves should have shown a sudden drop with little change thereafter (for one would hardly expect further errors once understanding was reached).

### THE LAW OF EFFECT

Thorndike proposed that what the animal had learned was best described as an increase in the strength of the correct response. Initially, the cat has the tendency to perform a large set of responses, perhaps because of prior learning, perhaps because of built-in predispositions. As it happens, virtually all of these lead to failure. As trials proceed, the strength of the incorrect responses gradually weakens. In contrast, the correct response, which at first is weak, increasingly grows in strength. In Thorndike's terms, the correct response is gradually "stamped in" while futile ones are correspondingly stamped out. The improvements in the learning curves "represent the wearing smooth of a path in the brain, not the decisions of a rational consciousness" (Thorndike, 1911).

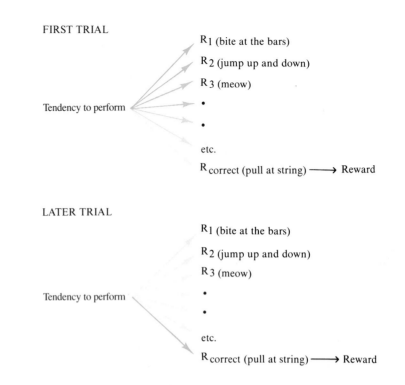

FIRST TRIAL

Tendency to perform

R₁ (bite at the bars)
R₂ (jump up and down)
R₃ (meow)
•
•
etc.
R correct (pull at string) ——→ Reward

LATER TRIAL

Tendency to perform

R₁ (bite at the bars)
R₂ (jump up and down)
R₃ (meow)
•
•
etc.
R correct (pull at string) ——→ Reward

**4.11   The law of effect**   *The figure is a schematic presentation of Thorndike's theory of instrumental learning. On the first trial, the tendency to perform various incorrect responses (biting the bars, jumping up and down) is very strong, while the tendency to perform the correct response (pulling the string) is weak or nonexistent. As trials proceed, the strength of these responses change. The incorrect responses become weaker and weaker, for none of these responses is immediately followed by reward. In contrast, there is a progressive strengthening of the correct response because this is followed more or less immediately by reward.*

According to Thorndike, some responses get strengthened and others weakened as learning proceeds. But what produces these different effects? Thorndike's answer was a bold formulation called the ***law of effect.*** The relevant features of his analysis are schematized in Figure 4.11, which indicates the tendency to perform the various responses, whether correct ($R_c$) or incorrect ($R_1, R_2, R_3$, etc.). The critical question is how the correct response gets strengthened until it finally overwhelms the incorrect ones that are at first so dominant. Thorndike's proposal, the law of effect, held that the consequences (that is, the effect) of a response determine whether the tendency to perform it is strengthened or weakened. If the response is followed by reward, it will be strengthened; if it is followed by the absence of reward (or worse yet, by punishment) it will be weakened. There was no need to postulate any further intellectual processes in the animal, no need to assume that the animal noticed a connection between act and consequence, no need to believe that it was trying to attain some goal. If the animal made a response and reward followed shortly, that response was more likely to be performed at a subsequent time.

This proposal neatly fits into the context of evolutionary thinking so dominant at the time. Thorndike emphasized the adaptive nature of the animal's activity which is gradually shaped to serve its biological ends. But the relationship to evolutionary theory is even closer for, as Thorndike pointed out, the law of effect is an analogue of the law of the survival of the fittest. In the life of the species, the individual whose genetic makeup fits it best for its environment will survive to transmit its characteristics to its offspring. In the life of the individual, learning provides another adaptive mechanism through the law of effect which decrees that only the fittest *responses* shall survive. As Thorndike put it, "It is a process of selection among reactions . . . by eliminating the unsuitable reaction directly by discomfort, and also by positively selecting the suitable one by pleasure. . . . It is of tremendous usefulness. . . . 'He who learns and runs away, *will live* to learn another day' " (Thorndike, 1899, p. 91).

### Skinner and Operant Behavior

Thorndike initiated the experimental study of instrumental behavior, but the psychologist who shaped the way in which most modern behavior theorists think about the subject is B. F. Skinner (1904–1990). Unlike Thorndike who believed that classical and instrumental conditioning are much alike, Skinner was one of the first theorists to insist on a sharp distinction between classical and instrumental conditioning. In classical conditioning, the animal's behavior is *elicited* by the CS; to that extent, the salivation is set off from the outside. But Skinner insisted that in instrumental conditioning the organism is much less at the mercy of the external situation. Its reactions are *emitted* from within, as if they were what we ordinarily call *voluntary.* Skinner called these instrumental responses **operants;** they operate on the environment to bring about some change that leads to reward. Like Thorndike, Skinner believed in the law of effect, insisting that the tendency to emit these operants is strengthened or weakened by its consequences (Skinner, 1938).

Behavior theorists have always searched for ever-simpler situations in the hope that the true laws of learning will show up there. Skinner's way of simplifying the study of operant behavior was to create a situation in which the same instrumental response could be performed repeatedly. The most common example is the experimental chamber (popularly called the Skinner box), in which a rat presses a lever or a pigeon pecks at a lighted key (Figure 4.12). In these situations, the animal remains in the presence of the lever or key for, say, an hour at a time, pressing and pecking at whatever rate it chooses. All of the animal's responses are automatically recorded; stimuli and reinforcements are presented automatically by automatic programming devices. The measure of response strength is **response rate,** that is, the number of responses per unit time.

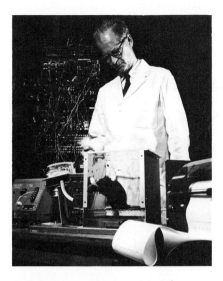

**B. F. Skinner** *(Photograph by Nina Leen, Life Magazine, © Time Inc.)*

*4.12 Animals in operant chambers* (A) A rat trained to press a lever for water reinforcement. (Photograph by Mike Salisbury) (B) A pigeon pecking at a lighted key for food reinforcement. Reinforcement consists of a few seconds' access to a grain feeder which is located just below the key. (Photograph by Susan M. Hogue)

A

B

**Shaping** *This dolphin has been trained by the method of successive approximations to jump through the hoop. (Photograph by Patrick Donehue/Photo Researchers)*

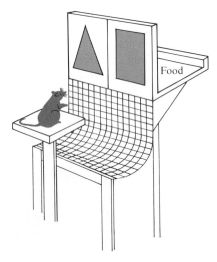

**4.13 Studying discriminative stimuli with the jumping stand** *The rat has to jump to one of two cards, say, a triangle or a square, behind which is a ledge that contains food. If the choice is correct, the card gives way and the animal gets to the food. If the choice is incorrect, the card stays in place, the rat bumps its nose and falls into the net below. (After Lashley, 1930)*

## The Major Phenomena of Instrumental Conditioning

Many of the phenomena of instrumental learning parallel those of classical conditioning. Consider *reinforcement.* In classical conditioning, the term refers to an operation (establishing a CS-US contingency) that strengthens the CR. In the context of instrumental learning, reinforcement refers to an analogous operation: having the response followed by a condition that the animal "prefers." This may be the presentation of something "good," such as grain to a hungry pigeon. The grain is an example of an *appetitive stimulus* (a stimulus for which the animal so to speak "has an appetite"). In Thorndike's terms, it is something that the animal does everything to attain and nothing to prevent. Reinforcement may also be the termination or prevention of something "bad," such as the cessation of an electric shock. Such a shock is an example of an *aversive stimulus,* one that the animal does everything to avoid and nothing to attain.

At a more technical level, we can also distinguish between *positive reinforcement* and *negative reinforcement.* Positive reinforcement refers to conditions in which the response produces an appetitive stimulus—a rat presses a lever to get food. Negative reinforcement refers to conditions in which the instrumental response eliminates or prevents an aversive stimulus—a rat jumping over a barrier to escape an electric shock.

As in classical conditioning, the probability of responding increases with an increasing number of reinforcements. And, again as in classical conditioning, the response suffers *extinction* when reinforcement is withdrawn.

### GENERALIZATION AND DISCRIMINATION

The instrumental response is not elicited by external stimuli but is, in Skinner's terms, emitted from within. But this doesn't mean that such stimuli have no effect. They do exert considerable control over behavior, for they serve as *discriminative stimuli.* Suppose a pigeon is trained to hop on a treadle to get some grain. When a green light is on, hopping on the treadle will pay off. But when a red light is on, the treadle-hopping response will be of no avail, for the pigeon gets no access to the food container. Under these circumstances, the green light becomes a positive discriminative stimulus and the red light a negative one (here indicated by $S^+$ and $S^-$ respectively). The pigeon will hop in the presence of the first and not when presented with the second. But this discrimination is made in an instrumental and not a classical conditioning context. The green light doesn't signal food the way a $CS^+$ might in Pavlov's laboratory. Instead, it signals a particular relationship between the instrumental response and the reinforcer, telling the pigeon as it were "If you hop now, you'll get food." Conversely for the red light, the $S^-$ tells the animal that there's no point in going through the treadle-hopping business right now.

A variety of techniques have been used to study the role of discriminated stimuli in affecting learned instrumental behaviors. Many of the results mirror those of generalization and discrimination in classical conditioning (see Figure 4.13).

An example is the study of stimulus generalization using operant techniques. Figure 4.14 shows a typical stimulus generalization gradient for color in pigeons. The animals were trained to peck at a key illuminated with yellow light, after

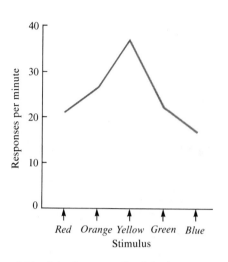

**4.14 Stimulus generalization of an instrumental response** *Pigeons were originally reinforced to peck at a yellow light. When later tested with lights of various colors, they showed a standard generalization gradient, pecking more vigorously at colors more similar to yellow (such as green and orange) than at colors farther removed (such as red and blue). Prior to being reinforced on the yellow key, their tendency to peck was minimal and roughly equal for all colors. (After Reynolds, 1968)*

which they were tested with lights of varying wavelengths. The resulting gradient is orderly. As the test light became less similar to the original S$^+$, the pigeons were less inclined to peck at it (Guttman and Kalish, 1956).

### SHAPING

How does an animal learn the particular instrumental response that will lead to reinforcement? The law of effect tells us that once that response has been made, then reinforcement will act to strengthen it. But what happens if that response isn't ever made in the first place? As it happens, pecking and lever pressing are fairly easy as such responses go; many animals hit upon them of their own accord. But we can make the response much more difficult. For example, we could set the rat's lever so high on the wall that it must stretch up on its hindlegs to depress it. Now the animal may never make the response on its own. But it can learn this response and even ones more outlandish if its behavior is suitably shaped. This is accomplished by the method of ***successive approximations.***

Take the problem of the elevated lever. The first step is to train the animal to approach the tray in which the food is delivered whenever the food-dispensing mechanism gives off its characteristic click. At random intervals, the click sounds and a food pellet drops into the tray; this continues until the rat shows that it is properly trained by running to pick up its pellet as soon as it hears the click. Shaping can now begin. We might first reinforce the animal for walking into the general area where the lever is located. As soon as it is there, it hears the click and devours the pellet. Very soon it will hover around the neighborhood of the lever. We next reinforce it for facing the lever, then for stretching its body upward, then for touching the lever with its paws, and so on until we finally complete its education by reinforcing it for pressing the lever down. The guiding principle throughout is immediacy of reinforcement. If we want to reinforce the rat for standing up on its hindlegs we must do it the instant after the response; even a one-second wait may be too long, for by then the rat may have fallen back on all fours and if we reinforce it then we will reinforce the wrong response.

By means of this technique, animals have been trained to perform exceedingly complex response chains. Pigeons have been trained to play Ping-Pong and dogs to plunk out four-note tunes on a toy piano. Such successes encouraged some enterprising psychologists to develop live advertising exhibits, featuring such stars as "Priscilla, the Fastidious Pig" to promote the sale of certain farm feeds (Breland and Breland, 1951). Priscilla turned on the radio, ate breakfast at a kitchen table, picked up dirty clothes and dropped them in a hamper, vacuumed the floor, and finally selected the sponsor's feed in preference to Brand X—a convincing tribute to the sponsor and to the power of reinforcement (Figure 4.15).

### CONDITIONED REINFORCEMENT

So far, our examples of reinforcement have included food or water or termination of electric shock, whose capacity to reinforce responses is presumably based upon built-in mechanisms of various kinds. But instrumental learning is not always reinforced by events of such immediate biological consequence. For example, piano teachers rarely reinforce their pupils with food or the cessation of electric shock; a nod or the comment "good" is all that is required. How does the Thorndikian approach explain why the word *good* is reinforcing?

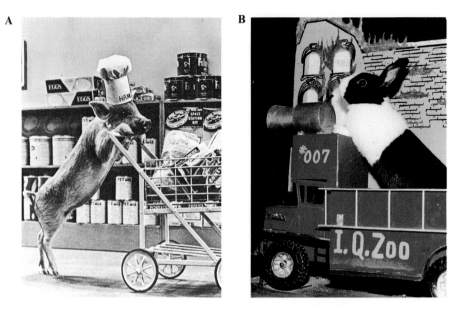

**4.15 Animals in show business** *(A) A pig trained by means of operant techniques to push a market cart. The animal was first reinforced for putting its front feet up on the handle, until it could raise up on the handle, and push the cart while walking on its hind feet. (B) A rabbit trained to get up in a firetruck, pull a lever a fixed number of times, and stay in the truck for a fixed interval so as to get reinforced. (Photographs courtesy of Animal Behavior Enterprises)*

**4.16 Conditioned reinforcement in chimpanzees** *Chimpanzee using token to obtain food after working to obtain tokens. (Courtesy Yerkes Regional Primate Research Center of Emory University)*

The answer is that a stimulus will acquire reinforcing properties if it is repeatedly paired with a primary reinforcer. It will then provide ***conditioned reinforcement*** if administered after a response has been made.

Numerous experiments give evidence that neutral stimuli can acquire reinforcing properties. For example, chimpanzees were first trained to insert poker chips into a vending machine to acquire grapes. Having learned this, they then learned to operate another device which delivered poker chips (Cowles, 1937; see Figure 4.16). Examples of this kind indicate that the critical factor in establishing a stimulus as a conditioned reinforcer is its association with primary reinforcement. It is then not surprising that the effect increases the more frequently the two have been paired. As we might also expect, a conditioned reinforcer will gradually lose its powers if it is repeatedly unaccompanied by some primary reinforcement. All of this argues that conditioned reinforcement is established by a process that is akin to, if not identical with, classical conditioning. The conditioned reinforcer serves as a CS that signals some motivationally significant US.

If conditioned reinforcers are so readily extinguished in the laboratory, why do they seem so much more permanent in human life? Nods do not lose their reinforcing value just because they haven't been paired with any primary reinforcer for a month or more. In part, the answer may be that the nod or the smile has enormous generality. It is associated not with one but with many different desirable outcomes. Even if extinguished in one context, it would still be maintained in countless others.

DELAY OF REINFORCEMENT

According to the law of effect, a response will be strengthened if it is followed by a reward. But the mere fact that a reward will follow is not enough. In general, the reward must follow rather quickly, for a reinforcer becomes less and less effective the longer its presentation is delayed after the response is made.

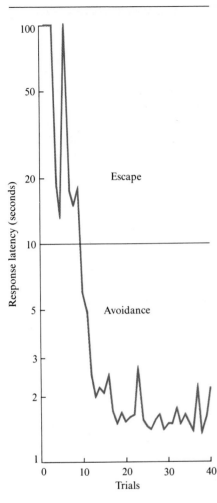

**4.23 The course of avoidance learning in a dog** *The figure shows response latencies of one animal in a shuttle box (where latency is the time from the onset of CS to the animal's response). A warning stimulus indicated that shock would begin 10 seconds after the onset of the signal. For the first nine trials the dog escaped. It jumped over the hurdle after the shock began. From the tenth trial on, the dog avoided: It jumped before its 10 seconds of grace were up. The jumping speed increased even after this point until the animal jumped with an average latency of about 1½ seconds. (Latency is plotted on a logarithmic scale. This compresses the time scale so as to put greater emphasis on differences between the shorter response latencies.) (After Solomon and Wynne, 1953)*

*Avoidance learning in human life* An enormous amount of ordinary human activity involves avoidance. We stop at red lights to avoid getting traffic tickets, pay bills to avoid interest charges, carry umbrellas to avoid getting wet, and devise excuses to avoid having lunch with a bore. We probably perform dozens of such learned avoidance responses each day, and most of them are perfectly useful and adaptive (Schwartz, 1989).

But some avoidance learning is essentially maladaptive and is often based on more potent aversive stimuli than a boring lunch. An extreme example is phobias. As already mentioned, some people have intense fears of various situations —heights, open spaces, dogs, elevators, and so on. As a result, they will develop elaborate patterns to avoid getting into these situations. In some cases, the phobia may be caused by traumatic experiences in the past as in the case of a woman who was trapped for several hours in a swaying elevator stuck between the fortieth and forty-first floor of an office building, and never used an elevator thereafter. Such an avoidance reaction is of little future use, for elevators ordinarily function perfectly well. But the trouble is that the avoidance response is self-perpetuating. It will not extinguish even if the aversive stimulus is no longer there. The reason is that the person (or animal) will not stay in the previously dangerous situation long enough to discover whether the danger is indeed still there. The woman who avoids elevators will never find out that they are now perfectly safe, for she won't ever use them again—a rather inconvenient behavior pattern if her own office happens to be above the forty-first floor.

Is there any way to extinguish avoidance responses? (The question is of considerable practical interest because it has implications for the therapy of phobias and related conditions.) In animals, the answer is "yes." The technique is to force them to "test reality" so that they can discover that the aversive stimulus is no longer there. In a number of studies, animals were first trained to jump back and forth in a shuttle box to avoid a mild shock. After they had learned the avoidance response, they were exposed to the stimulus that previously had signaled impending shock. They immediately tried to jump to the other side of the box, but they couldn't; their avoidance response was blocked by a floor-to-ceiling barrier that forced them to remain in the compartment. They necessarily remained and were visibly frightened. But, in fact, there was no shock. After a few such trials without shock, the avoidance reaction was extinguished. The idea is much like getting back on the horse that threw you—a good prescription for aspiring jockeys, assuming the horse won't throw them again (Baum, 1970; Mineka, 1979).

## COGNITIVE LEARNING

To the early behavior theorists, the essential thing about classical and instrumental conditioning was that both procedures modify action. This held for classical conditioning, which Pavlov saw as a rather primitive and mechanical extension of reflex action whereby the elicitation of certain responses (the UR's) is passed from one set of stimuli (the US's) to another (the CS's). It also held for instrumental conditioning, which Thorndike and Skinner regarded as the strengthening of certain responses by the mechanical effect of reinforcement.

From the earliest days of behavior theory, however, there was an alternative view that asserted that what really matters when animals (and humans) learn is

*Edward C. Tolman* *(Courtesy Psychology Department, University of California, Berkeley)*

that they acquire new *knowledge.* One of the most prominent exponents of this view was Edward C. Tolman (1886–1959), who argued that in both classical and instrumental conditioning an animal gains various bits of knowledge, or ***cognitions.*** These bits of knowledge are organized so that they can be utilized when needed. This is very different from asserting that the animal acquires a tendency to perform a certain response. As Tolman saw it, the response an animal acquires in the course of a learning experiment is only an index that a given cognition has been gained. It is an indispensable measuring stick, but it is not what is being measured. Rather the essence of what is learned is something within an animal, a private event that will only become public when the animal acts upon its newly acquired knowledge. Today such cognitions are often called ***representations,*** which correspond to (represent) certain events or relations between events in the animal's world (Dickinson, 1987).

Evidence that animals acquire cognitions came from a number of experiments designed to determine whether instrumental learning can occur without the performance of the relevant response. Many early behavior theorists had claimed that performance is an indispensable ingredient for instrumental learning, insisting that the animal "learns by doing" and in no other way. Several studies, however, suggest that this is not the case. For example, rats have been ferried from one end of a large room to another in transparent trolley cars. Later tests showed that they had learned something about the general features of the room even though they had not performed any relevant responses during their trolley-car ride (Gleitman, 1963). They had acquired what Tolman called a "cognitive map" that represents what is where and what leads to what (Tolman, 1948).

## A Cognitive View of Classical Conditioning

The cognitive approach has had considerable impact on current conceptions of animal learning, and may well be the dominant position in the field today. One of its effects was a reinterpretation of classical conditioning. Pavlov believed that the essential feature of classical conditioning is the newly achieved ability of one stimulus to elicit a response that was originally evoked by another. If it does, a well-conditioned animal should respond to the CS just as it does to the US. But as we have seen before, this is not the case. Even in Pavlov's original experiment, the UR and the CR were not really identical (the composition of the two salivary secretions differed), and in others, they could even be exact opposites (as in conditioning in which the US is heroin). We conclude that the animal acquires a representation about the relation between the two stimulus events. Instead of substituting for the US, the CS becomes a sign that the US will follow (Tolman, 1932; Rescorla, 1988).

### TEMPORAL RELATIONS BETWEEN THE CS AND THE US

It appears that what is learned in classical conditioning is an association between two events: the CS and the US. But how is this association acquired? In line with many philosophers who had thought about association, Pavlov believed that a necessary condition is temporal ***contiguity,*** that is, togetherness in time. As we will see, the answer is not quite as simple as that.

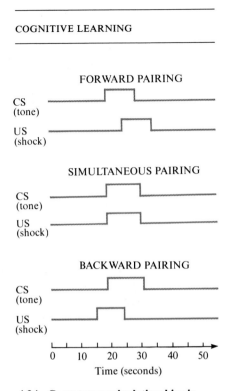

FORWARD PAIRING

CS (tone)

US (shock)

SIMULTANEOUS PAIRING

CS (tone)

US (shock)

BACKWARD PAIRING

CS (tone)

US (shock)

0    10    20    30    40    50

Time (seconds)

**4.24   Some temporal relationships in classical conditioning**

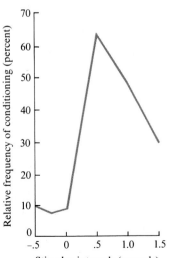

One way of finding out whether the CS-US association is based on contiguity in time is to vary the interval between the two stimuli as well as the order in which they are presented. A number of procedures do just that. In some, the CS precedes the US *(forward pairing)*, in others it follows the US *(backward pairing)*, and in yet others the two stimuli are presented at the same time *(simultaneous pairing)*. (See Figure 4.24.)

The general results of these procedures are as follows: Conditioning is best when the CS *precedes* the US by some optimum interval that is generally rather short (see Figure 4.25).* Presenting the CS and the US simultaneously is generally much less effective, and the backward procedure is even worse. On the other hand, the effectiveness of forward pairing declines rapidly when the CS-US interval increases beyond the optimum interval (Rescorla, 1988, p. 337).

How can we make sense of these facts? A reasonable suggestion is that the CS serves a signaling function: It prepares the organism for a US that is to come. Let us consider forward, simultaneous, and backward pairing in this light by likening the subject's situation to that of a driver setting out upon an unfamiliar road. Suppose our driver wants to go from Denver to Salt Lake City, and that some 150 miles out of Denver there is a dangerous hairpin turn over a ravine. How should the driver be warned of the impending curve? Presumably there will be a sign, "Hairpin Turn," which should obviously appear just a bit before the turn (analogous to forward pairing with a short CS-US interval). If the interval is too long it will be almost impossible to connect the sign with that which it signifies. We will lose some of our faith in the Highway Department if it sets up the sign, "Hairpin Turn," just outside the Denver city limits while the turn itself is three hours away (forward pairing with a long CS-US interval). Our faith will be really shaken if we see the sign prominently displayed just at the sharpest bend of the turn (simultaneous pairing). We finally begin to suspect a degree of malevolence if we discover the sign innocently placed on the road a hundred feet or so beyond the turn (backward pairing), though we should probably be grateful that we did not find it at the bottom of the ravine.

CONTINGENCY

It would seem that in classical conditioning an organism learns that one stimulus is a signal for another. The next task is to describe just what such a sign relationship between two events consists of.

---

* The precise value of that optimum interval depends on the particulars of the situation; it usually varies from about half a second to about ten seconds. In one form of classical conditioning, learned taste aversion, the optimum CS-US is very much longer, and may be of the order of an hour or more. This phenomenon poses obvious difficulties for a contiguity theory of conditioning—and much else besides—and will be discussed in a later section (see pp. 137–38).

**4.25   The CS-US interval in classical conditioning**   *The figure shows the results of a study on the effectiveness of various CS-US intervals in humans. The CR was a finger withdrawal response, the CS a tone, and the US an electric shock. The time between CS and US is plotted on the horizontal axis. Negative intervals mean that the US was presented before the CS (backward pairing), a zero interval means that the two stimuli were presented simultaneously, and a positive interval means that the CS began before the US (forward pairing). The vertical axis indicates the degree of conditioning. (After Spooner and Kellogg, 1947)*

Consider a dog in Pavlov's laboratory who is exposed to several presentations of a beating metronome followed by some food powder. The poor beast doesn't know that he is supposed to form a CS-US connection. All he knows is that every once in a while food appears. There are all sorts of stimuli in the laboratory situation. Of course he hears the metronome, but he also hears doors slamming, and a babble of (Russian) voices in the background, and he feels the strap of the conditioning harness. How does he discover that it is the metronome that is the signal for food rather than the scores of other stimuli that he was also exposed to? After all, no one told him that metronome beats are Professor Pavlov's favorite conditioned stimuli.

A useful way of trying to understand what happens is to think of the animal as an amateur scientist. Like all scientists, the dog wants to predict important events. (When his human counterparts succeed, they publish; when the dog succeeds, he salivates.) How can he predict when food will appear? He might decide to rely on mere contiguity, and salivate to any stimulus that occurs along with food presentation. But if so, he'd have to salivate whenever he was strapped in his harness or whenever he heard voices, for these stimuli were generally present when he was fed. But if the dog had any scientific talent at all, he would realize that the harness and the voices are very poor food predictors. To be sure, they occur when food is given, but they occur just as frequently when it is not. To continue in his scientific quest, the dog would look for an event that occurs when food appears and that does not occur when food is absent. The metronome beat is the one stimulus that fulfills *both* of these conditions, for it never beats in the intervals between trials when food is not presented. Science (or rather classical conditioning) has triumphed, and the dog is ready to announce his findings by salivating when the CS is presented and at no other times.

*Contingency versus contiguity*    The preceding account is a fanciful statement of an influential analysis of classical conditioning developed by Robert Rescorla (Rescorla, 1967). According to Rescorla, classical conditioning depends not only on CS-US pairings but also on pairings in which the absence of CS goes along with the *absence of US.* These two experiences—metronome/meat, and no metronome/no meat—allow the dog to discover that the occurrence of the US is **contingent** (that is, dependent) upon the occurrence of the CS. According to Rescorla, conditioning does not occur because the US is contiguous with the CS but rather because it is contingent upon the CS. By determining this contingency, the animal can forecast what is going to happen next. (Just how an animal manages to do this, is a point we'll take up later.)

Contingency need not be perfect. In nature it rarely is. A dark cloud generally precedes a storm, but it doesn't always. As a result, our weather predictions are never perfect. But we can nevertheless make some predictions about the weather that are better than chance, for it's more likely to rain when the sky is dark than when the sun is shining. The same holds in the conditioning laboratory in which we can arrange whatever relationship between CS and US we choose. We could decide that the metronome will be followed by food on say 80 percent of the trials, but that food will occur unheralded by the metronome on 20 percent of the trials. We have now created an imperfect contingency that will be harder to detect. But it is a contingency even so, for food is more likely after the CS than otherwise. To recognize such imperfect contingencies, the animal must keep track of four possible stimulus combinations that he will encounter. If the metronome is

**Table 4.1**  CONTINGENCY IN
CLASSICAL CONDITIONING

*Three tables illustrating three different CS/US contingency arrangements in a hypothetical experiment in which the CS is a tone and the US is meat powder. Each table presents a different tone/meat contingency based on twenty trials. The column labeled* p *shows the probabilities that meat will occur under a particular stimulus condition.*

*Meat contingent upon tone*

|         | Meat | No Meat | *p* |
|---------|------|---------|-----|
| Tone    | 8    | 2       | .80 |
| No Tone | 2    | 8       | .20 |

*Meat contingent upon absence of tone*

|         | Meat | No Meat | *p* |
|---------|------|---------|-----|
| Tone    | 3    | 7       | .30 |
| No Tone | 7    | 3       | .70 |

*Meat and tone independent*

|         | Meat | No Meat | *p* |
|---------|------|---------|-----|
| Tone    | 5    | 5       | .50 |
| No Tone | 5    | 5       | .50 |

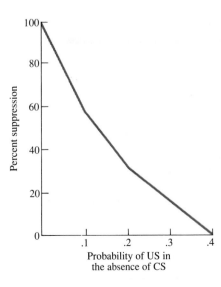

the CS, and meat is the US, these combinations are: metronome/meat, metronome/no meat, no metronome/meat, no metronome/no meat. To determine if getting meat is contingent upon the metronome, the animal must somehow compute two probabilities: the probability of getting meat when the metronome is sounded and the probability of getting meat when it is not. If the first probability is greater than the second, then getting meat is contingent on the metronome. If it is smaller than the second, getting meat is contingent upon the absence of the tone. Such a negative contingency is analogous to the relation between a sunny sky and rain—rain is more likely when the sun is *not* shining. An important final possibility is that the two probabilities are identical. If so, there is no contingency, and the two events are independent (see Table 4.1).

If this line of thinking is correct, it follows that temporal contiguity as such will not produce conditioning. For according to this view, conditioning will only occur if the probability of a US when the CS is present is greater than the probability of a US when the CS is absent. To prove his point, Rescorla exposed rats to various combinations of a tone CS and a shock US in a conditioned suppression experiment. In one set of conditions, the probability of receiving a shock when the tone was sounded was always the same (about .40). What varied was the probability that a shock would occur when no tone was sounded. The results were clear-cut. If the likelihood of a shock when the tone was on was the same as the likelihood of a shock when the tone was off, there was no conditioning. But if the likelihood of a shock was smaller when the tone was off than when it was on, conditioning did take place. The greater the difference in these probabilities, the stronger the level of conditioning the animal achieved (see Figure 4.26). The critical factor is evidently not contiguity, because the sheer number of CS-US pairings was identical for all groups. What mattered is whether the tone became an informative signal that told the animal that shock was more likely now than at other times (Rescorla, 1967, 1988).

*The absence of contingency*  What happens when there is no contingency whatsoever? On the face of it, there is nothing to learn. But in a situation in which there is fear and danger (for example, electric shock) the animal does learn something after all: It can never feel safe at any time.

Consider two situations. In one, there is a CS that signals that shock is likely to follow. When the CS appears, the animal will become more fearful. But there is a compensation. When there is no CS, the animal can relax, for now shock is less likely. The absence of the CS has become a ***safety signal.***

The situation is quite different when there is no stimulus that predicts when shock will occur. Now the animal is worse off than it is when there is a CS-US contingency, for it now has good reason to be afraid at all times. This unpleasant state of affairs is mirrored by a number of harmful physiological consequences. For example, rats who are exposed to unsignaled electric shock are much more likely to develop stomach ulcers than rats who receive just as many shocks, but with a signal that predicts their occurrence (Seligman, 1968; Weiss, 1970, 1977).

**4.26  Contingency in classical conditioning**  *The figure shows the results of fear conditioning as a function of contingency. The probability of the US in the presence of the CS was always .40, but the probability of the US in the absence of the CS varied from 0 to .40. Conditioning was measured by the degree of response suppression. (After Rescorla, 1966)*

The difference between signaled and unsignaled shock may be related to the distinction between *fear* and *anxiety,* made by clinical psychologists concerned with human emotional disorders. As they use the terms, fear refers to an emotional state that is directed at a specific object—of flying in airplanes, of snakes, or whatever. In contrast, anxiety is a chronic fear that has no particular object but is there at all times. A number of authors suggest that this unfocused anxiety state is in part produced by unpredictability. Patients whose dentists tell them "this may hurt" but at other times assure them "you won't feel anything now" will probably have fewer dental anxieties than those whose dentists never tell them anything (Seligman, 1975; Schwartz, 1989).

### THE ROLE OF SURPRISE

It appears that in classical conditioning animals learn that certain stimuli are signals for impending events. They do so by noting the contingency between these stimuli and the events they forecast (that is, the US's). But how does the animal manage to combine all of the information he gets in the conditioning procedure to determine which stimulus it is he should respond to? We have likened him to a scientist who tries to infer cause-and-effect relations. But of course this is just a metaphor. For it's very unlikely that the rats, dogs, and pigeons in classical conditioning laboratories keep a conscious mental record of their experiences, tallying trials on which the CS was followed by the US and trials on which the CS occurred and the US did not, and then computing probabilities and making appropriate deductions the way scientists do. Although in some ways they behave as if they do just that, the means whereby they achieve their results are almost certainly more automatic and mechanical than those employed by the human scientist.

The best guess is that classical conditioning in animals (and probably in humans too) is based on rather simple processes that operate on a trial-by-trial basis and somehow combine to produce a more complex result. The question is just what those simple mechanisms might be.

To answer this question, we must first ask some questions about the factors

*(Drawing by Chas. Addams; © 1981 The New Yorker Magazine, Inc.)*

that underlie the connection between a CS and a US. According to several theorists, the critical ingredient is the extent which the US is *surprising* (that is, unexpected). If the US is unexpected, the animal will form a connection between it and the CS that preceded it: the greater the surprise, the stronger that connection. If there is no surprise at all, there will be no connection at all (Kamin, 1968; Rescorla and Wagner, 1972).

*Blocking*  Evidence for the role of surprise comes from a series of studies performed by Leon Kamin, who discovered a phenomenon called the **blocking effect.** Kamin showed that when a stimulus is *redundant,* providing information that an organism already has, it will not become connected to the CS. If the animal already knows that the US is coming, it will not be surprised, and conditioning will not take place.

Kamin's basic experiment was run in three stages. In Stage 1, the rats heard a hissing noise that was followed by shock. As one might expect, this noise became a CS for conditioned fear. In Stage 2, the shock was preceded by *two* stimuli that were presented simultaneously: One was the same old hissing noise used in Stage 1, the other was a light. Stage 3 was a test in which the light was presented alone to see whether it would also produce a conditioned fear reaction. The results showed that it did not. When the light came on, there was no response suppression even though that stimulus had been a perfect predictor of shock. Somehow the old established stimulus (the noise) had blocked out the new stimulus (the light).

To prove that this blocking effect was indeed caused by the animals' previous experience with the tone, Kamin ran a control group. These controls never went through Stage 1, but began at Stage 2 (that is, light plus noise followed by shock) from the very outset, with no previous exposure to noise alone. When these control animals were later tested with the light alone, they exhibited a substantial conditioned fear response (Kamin, 1969; see Table 4.2 and Figure 4.27).

The blocking effect follows directly from the notion that the formation of a CS-US association depends on the extent to which the animal is surprised by the US. In Kamin's procedure, a well-established CS (the noise) is presented together with a new stimulus (the light); then *both* are followed by shock. In this situation, the new stimulus—the light—adds no further information. The animal already knows that it will be shocked. When the shock comes, the rat may be sad, it may be resigned—but it will not be surprised. As a result, it will not connect the light stimulus with the shock.

Here again the animals are a bit like human scientists who try to infer cause-and-effect relations. Consider the early scientists who asked themselves where maggots come from. Whenever they saw maggots, they saw rotten meat, and they never saw maggots anywhere else. As a result, they assumed that the maggots' appearance was contingent upon rotting meat (which they took as evidence for the theory that life is generated spontaneously). Once having discovered this contingency, they were blinded to other contingencies that were also present—such as

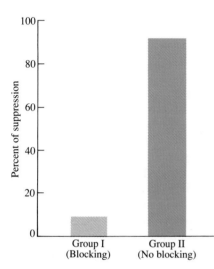

**4.27  The effect of blocking**  *Results for the test phase of Kamin's blocking experiment, in which the animals were presented with the light alone. Group I (in pink) showed virtually no response suppression (and hence no fear conditioning), indicating that the initial pairing of noise and shock in Stage 1 had blocked the recognition of the light-shock contingency during Stage 2. Group II (in blue), which had no such prior pairings, showed no blocking effect. (After Kamin, 1969)*

Table 4.2  BLOCKING

| Group | Stage 1 | Stage 2 | Test | Result |
|-------|---------|---------|------|--------|
| I | Noise → shock | (Noise + Light) → shock | Light alone | No conditioned fear |
| II | — | (Noise + Light) → shock | Light alone | Conditioned fear |

the fact that the meat had been lying around for a while (so flies could lay their eggs in it). Something similar holds for rats in classical conditioning. Once they've discovered a stimulus that signals the appearance of a US, they no longer connect other stimuli to the US, for they're no longer surprised when the US appears. The old stimuli block out the new, much as a scientist's old theory prejudices her to (blocks out) further facts.

*Blocking and contingency*    Can this blocking effect explain why animals respond to contingency rather than to contiguity? For the sake of simplicity, let's only compare the two extreme cases of zero contingency and perfect contingency. Let's start out with zero contingency, in which the US (say, a shock) is equally likely when the CS (say, a tone) is present and when it is absent. As we saw, in this noncontingency condition, the rat will *not* learn to connect the tone with the shock. To understand why this is so, we must first recognize that the experimental situation provides many other stimuli besides the tone CS; in particular, the various sights, sounds, and smells of the chamber in which the experiment is conducted. These other stimuli (let's call them box stimuli) are always present whenever the rat is in the box, both when a shock is given and when it isn't. As a result, the rat will come to expect a shock as soon as it is placed in the chamber. Now suppose the tone is sounded and a shock occurs. The rat won't connect the tone with the US because it expected the shock anyway. In effect, the box stimuli blocked out the tone. Note that the situation is quite different when the contingency is perfect. Now the shock will only occur when a tone is presented. Under these conditions, the tone is informative and provides the surprise that is necessary for conditioning.

The same general logic can explain the shape of the acquisition curve. As we saw, more is learned on the first trial than on the second, more on the second trial than on the third, and so on, until the curve reaches an asymptote. This fits in with the view that the strength of the linkage between the CS and the US depends on the degree to which the US is unexpected: The less the US is expected (that is, the greater the surprise), the stronger the link will be. Each trial presumably adds to the strength of that link. But the degree to which the US is unexpected will necessarily drop as the link between the two gets stronger and stronger. Eventually, there is no surprise left at all, and so further trials can add no further strength (Kamin, 1968, 1969; Rescorla, 1988; for more technical discussion, see Rescorla and Wagner, 1972; Mackintosh, 1983).

## A Cognitive View of Instrumental Conditioning

We have seen that what is learned in classical conditioning is a representation about the relation between two stimulus events, the CS and the US. There is reason to believe that a similar cognitive account applies to instrumental conditioning. As with classical conditioning, this interpretation goes back to Tolman. Thorndike and Skinner had argued that instrumental learning involves the strengthening of a particular response, such as pressing a bar in a Skinner box. In contrast, Tolman believed that the animal acquires an internal representation of the relation between the response and the reinforcer that followed it: It learns *that* the bar led to a food pellet. In effect, it acquires an association between an act and its outcome. This act-outcome representation might or might not be used on a

could escape by turning a treadwheel. A second group received the same shocks as the control rats but could do nothing about them. They suffered the same degree of physical stress, but unlike their counterparts in the control group, they learned that they had no control over their fate and so they became helpless. Later tests showed that animals who had been rendered helpless in this fashion produced fewer killer cells and were thus less able to stop tumor growth. This result fits in with other findings which show that learned helplessness in rats increases susceptibility to injected tumors (Visintainer, Volpicelli, and Seligman, 1982; Maier, Laudenslager, and Ryan, 1985).

Just why learned helplessness affects the immune system is still unknown. But whatever the mechanism, the fact that it does provides yet one further suggestion that learning about the contingencies (and in the case of learned helplessness, the lack of contingencies) between one's own actions and subsequent events in the world has profound effects on bodily functioning.

## Biological Constraints on Learning

In the early days of behavior theory, there was a widespread belief that animals are capable of connecting just about any CS to any US (in classical conditioning) or of associating virtually any response with any reinforcer (in instrumental conditioning). But during the last three decades, more and more evidence has accumulated that has undermined this position, which is sometimes called the ***equipotentiality principle.*** For it turned out that not all associations are equally easy to learn, and that what is easy and what is difficult depends in part on the animal that does the learning. By now, most investigators are convinced that there are certain built-in predispositions (often called ***biological constraints***) that determine what a given animal can learn and which sorts of learning it will find more difficult. These constraints are built into the animal's system and help to adjust it to the requirements of the environment in which it lives.

*Arbitrary learning by operant techniques* Animals can be trained to prefer all manner of arbitrary responses by operant techniques as in the case of this cat that plays the piano. But there are important biological constraints that make some responses more difficult to learn than others. The cat has trouble learning to press the piano keys for food because its natural tendency is to importune people (or as a kitten, its mother) to feed it. (Photograph courtesy of Animal Behavior Enterprises)

### CS-US RELATIONS IN CLASSICAL CONDITIONING

According to the equipotentiality principle, the associations between the CS and the US are essentially ***arbitrary.*** A dog in Pavlov's laboratory would presumably connect the unconditioned stimulus of the food powder with just about any conditioned stimulus the experimenter might present: a sounding metronome, a flashing light, or what have you. Similar arbitrary connections are commonplace in human life. The most obvious illustration is the relation between the sound of a word and its meaning. Except for a few onomatopoeic terms like *buzz, hiss,* and *cuckoo,* that relation is completely arbitrary. The same holds for many associations we pick up in the course of ordinary life, such as addresses, telephone numbers, and the like.

According to the equipotentiality principle, this arbitrariness is a basic feature of all learning. But this principle turns out to be wrong. For there is evidence that associations between two items are more readily formed if the items somehow belong together. An important example of the role of ***belongingness*** comes from classical conditioning, where a number of investigators have shown that certain CS's are more readily related to certain UC's than to others. In their view, the animal has a built-in predisposition, or ***preparedness,*** to form certain associations rather than others. The bulk of this evidence comes from *learned taste aversions* (Garcia and Koelling, 1966; Domjan, 1983).

*Belongingness and learned taste aversions*  It has long been known that rats are remarkably adept at avoiding foods they ate just before falling sick. This is the reason why it is very difficult to exterminate wild rats with poison: The rat takes a small bite of the poisoned food, becomes ill, generally recovers, and thereafter avoids the particular flavor. The animal has become bait shy. Similar effects are easily produced in the laboratory. The subjects (usually rats) are presented with a given flavor, such as water containing saccharin. After drinking some of this water, they are exposed to X-ray radiation—not enough to kill them, but enough to make them quite ill and nauseous. After they have recovered, they are given a choice between, say, plain water and a saccharine solution. They will now refuse to drink the saccharin even though they had much preferred this sweet-tasting drink prior to their illness.

Such learned taste aversions are usually believed to be based on classical conditioning in which the CS is a certain flavor (here, saccharin) and the US is being sick. The question is whether other stimuli such as lights or tones serve equally well as CS's for such taste aversions. A number of studies by John Garcia and his coworkers have shown that they do not, thus refuting the equipotentiality principle.

One of the earliest studies to make this point is an experiment by Garcia and Koelling in which thirsty rats were allowed to drink saccharine-flavored water. The water came from a drinking tube; whenever the rat licked the nozzle, a bright light flashed and a clicking noise sounded. Subsequently, some rats received a shock to their feet. Others were exposed to a dose of illness-producing X-rays. All of the animals developed a strong aversion. When again presented with water that was sweet and was accompanied by bright flashes and clicks, they hardly touched the drinking nozzle. All rats had presumably acquired a classically conditioned aversion. The US was either shock or illness. The CS was a stimulus

**A**

**B**

*Learned food aversions in birds*  In contrast to rats and humans, whose learned food aversions are usually based on taste and odor, most birds rely on visual cues. The figure shows the reaction of a bird who has just eaten a monarch butterfly, which contains distasteful and poisonous substances. The distinctive wing pattern of this butterfly provides the cue for an immediately acquired food aversion, for after one such mistake the bird will never again seize another monarch. (Courtesy of Lincoln P. Brower, University of Florida)

Table 4.4   BELONGINGNESS IN CLASSICAL CONDITIONING
In all groups: CS = saccharine taste + light + sound

| TRAINING US: | Shock | | X-ray illness | |
|---|---|---|---|---|
| TEST Water with: | Saccharine taste | Light + sound | Saccharine taste | Light + sound |
| RESULTS | No effect | Aversion | Aversion | No effect |

compound comprised of the flavor, the light, and the noise. But did the rats learn to avoid all of these stimulus features or only some?

To find out, the experimenters tested the rats in a new situation. They either gave them water that was saccharine-flavored but unaccompanied by either light or noise. Or they gave them plain, unflavored water that was accompanied by the light and sound cues that were present during training. The results showed that what the rats had learned to avoid depended upon the US. If they had been shocked (and felt pain), they refused water that was accompanied by light and noise but they had no objection to the sweet flavor. If they had been X-rayed (and became ill), the opposite was true—they avoided the saccharine flavor but were perfectly willing to drink when the water was preceded by light and noise (Table 4.4).

These results indicate that rats tend to link stimuli in certain fitting ways: In rats, taste goes with illness, sights and sounds with externally induced pain. These effects may well reflect a built-in belongingness relationship. This would make good biological sense. In the world of the rat, an omnivorous creature that selects its food mainly on the basis of its flavor, taste may well be the most reliable cue that warns of impending illness. If so, a natively given bias to associate sickness with preceding tastes is likely to have survival value. In effect, the rat cannot help but ask itself, "What did I eat?" whenever it has a stomachache (Garcia and Koelling, 1966).

If this is so, one might expect rather different results for animals who select their food on the basis of cues other than taste. An example are many species of birds that rely heavily on vision when choosing food. In one study, quail drank blue, sour water and were then poisoned. Some of the birds were later tested with blue, unflavored water; others were tested with water that was sour but colorless. The quail developed a drastic aversion to blue water. But they drank just about as much sour water as they had prior to being poisoned. Here, the learned food aversion was evidently based on color rather than on taste (Wilcoxin, Dragoin, and Kral, 1971). It appears that the built-in belongingness relation is species-specific. Certain birds have a natively given bias to link sickness with visual cues, while rats and other mammals link it to taste. This bias *prepares* them to learn certain relations rather than others (Seligman, 1970). In both cases, the preparedness fits in with the way the animal identifies food in its native habitat. (For an extension of the preparedness concept to phobias, see Chapter 19.)

*Learned taste aversions and the CS-US interval*   The equipotentiality principle is clearly false. This constitutes yet another argument against the role of contiguity in conditioning. In Garcia and Koelling's experiment, the noise and the

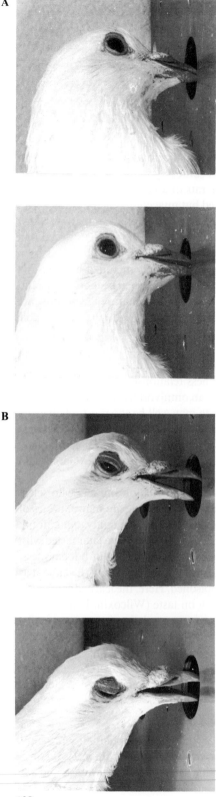

A

B

flashing light were no less contiguous to the illness-producing X-rays than was the flavor. But even so, only the flavor became an effective CS.

Yet another argument against the role of contiguity comes from studies of the CS-US interval in learned taste aversions. In most studies of classical conditioning, the most effective CS interval has been shown to be relatively short, of the order of a few seconds or less. But Garcia and other investigators showed that in learned taste aversions the optimum interval is about an hour and that learning will occur with intervals as long as twenty-four hours (Garcia, Ervin, and Koelling, 1966; Rozin and Kalat, 1971; Logue, 1979). Just why it is possible to associate illness with taste stimuli experienced an hour or more earlier is still a matter of debate (see Revusky, 1971, 1977; Rozin and Kalat, 1971). But whatever the mechanism that underlies it, the biological utility of this phenomenon is clear enough. After all, both the beneficial and harmful effects of ingested food are delayed by the fairly slow processes of absorption and digestion. Under the circumstances, a mechanism that allows an animal to connect its internal malaise with tastes experienced some time ago makes excellent adaptive sense.

ACT-OUTCOME RELATIONS IN INSTRUMENTAL CONDITIONING

The preceding discussion has shown that the CS-US relation in classical conditioning is not always arbitrary. A similar nonarbitrariness characterizes many instrumental learning situations (Shettleworth, 1972).

Consider a pigeon pecking away in a Skinner box. Here surely is the very prototype of arbitrary instrumental learning. But in fact, the relation between peck and what is pecked at is far from arbitrary. One line of evidence comes from the fact that it is exceedingly hard to train pigeons to peck so as to escape or avoid electric shock (Hineline and Rachlin, 1969). This doesn't mean that shock escape or shock avoidance are inadequate reinforcers for pigeons. Far from it. The birds readily learn to fly or hop or flap their wings in order to get away from shock. What they have trouble learning is to peck to bring about the same outcome. According to Robert Bolles, this is because many animals have built-in defense reactions to danger that are specific to their species. The pigeon is no exception. Its species-specific defense reaction is speedy locomotion, preferably airborne flight. Like all other animals, the bird can learn new avoidance responses, but only to the extent that these fit in with its natively given danger reaction. Hopping, flying, and wing-flapping qualify, for they are merely modifications of the basic defense pattern. But pecking does not, and it is therefore very hard to learn as an escape or an avoidance response (Bolles, 1970).

If pigeons have so much trouble learning to peck to escape or avoid, why are they so readily trained to peck for food? The reason is that pecking is what pigeons do naturally when they consume food. In effect, they are simply performing an anticipatory eating response. That something of this sort goes on is shown by how they peck when other reinforcers are used. In one study, thirsty pigeons had to peck at a key to obtain water. Their pecks were quite different from those seen with food reinforcement; they resembled the beak movements pigeons make while drinking (Figure 4.33). In another study, key-pecking brought access to a

*4.33 Key pecking for food and water* (A) The pictures show a pigeon's beak movements as it pecks a key to obtain water. The movements resemble those the bird makes when it drinks. (B) These pictures show quite different beak movements made when the bird is hungry and pecks a key for food. Now the movements resemble those the animal makes when it eats. (Photographs by Bruce Moore, from Jenkins and Moore, 1973)

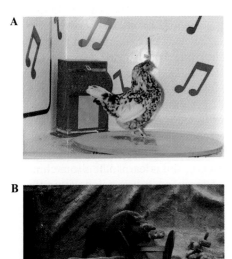

**Biological constraints on learning** *(A) The chicken pulls the loop on the jukebox to start the music, then "dances" on the platform by scratching the floor. The scratching is not reinforced but is a built-in tendency of the chicken when it seeks food. (B) The "gold-mining pig" tends to toss the nuggets around and root them even though this delays its reinforcement. Rooting is a natural tendency of the pig in food-seeking situations; in this case, it leads to "misbehavior" since it interferes with the desired operant response. (Photographs courtesy of Animal Behavior Enterprises)*

sexually receptive mate. Now the pigeons cooed as they pressed the key. All of this means that key-pecking is not an arbitrary instrumental response. In effect, the pigeon "eats" the key when working for food, "drinks" it when working for water, and "courts" it when working for sex. There clearly is an intimate relation between the response and its reinforcer (Schwartz, 1989).*

### THE "MISBEHAVIOR" OF ORGANISMS

Further evidence against the equipotentiality principle in instrumental conditioning comes from some observations by psychologists who trained animals to perform as live advertising exhibits (see pp. 117–18). By and large, their efforts were quite successful, but in some cases the animals "misbehaved." An example is a raccoon that was supposed to pick up several coins and then deposit them into a small piggy bank. The animal was first reinforced with food to pick up a coin. This was easy enough. After this, the raccoon was reinforced for dropping the coin into a container. This was more difficult, for the animal refused to let the coin go; it would rub it against the container, pull it back out, clutch it for a while, and release it only after considerable hesitation. The next step was even worse. Now the animal was required to pick *two* coins and then deposit them both. The raccoon refused. Instead of acting like a model savings bank customer, it rubbed the two coins together, dipped them into the container, pulled them out again, rubbed them together, and so on. It appeared that the raccoon reverted to a species-specific behavior pattern: Raccoons tend to rub food objects together, and dunk or "wash" them. Here, as in our previous examples, the relation between the instrumental response and its reinforcer is not arbitrary. The psychologists wanted the animal to learn an arbitrary response (deposit two coins) by reinforcing it with food. But the animal's own behavior drifted toward the response it was biologically predisposed to perform under these conditions (Breland and Breland, 1961).

### GENERALIST AND SPECIALIST

To sum up, it becomes clear that the way in which animals associate events is not arbitrary. Different species seem to come biologically prepared to acquire certain linkages rather than others. For instance, rats connect illness with taste but not with sights and sounds. Such built-in belongingnesses have the virtue of helping the animal to adapt to its particular ecological niche. But they have the drawback of making the animal into an intellectual specialist whose unusual gifts in noting certain relations are counterbalanced by its sluggishness in responding to others (Rozin and Kalat, 1971; Rozin, 1976a).

There is something ironic about all this. For the arbitrariness which both Pavlov and Skinner regarded as basic is something which people are more capable of than rats and pigeons. For people, a Skinner-box lever would indeed be an indif-

---

* A number of psychologists have interpreted such findings as evidence that key-pecking in a Skinner box is a classically rather than an instrumentally conditioned response. To some extent, this may be true. One line of evidence comes from a study in which naïve pigeons were left in a box whose key lit up periodically. The pigeons received food if they did *not* peck at the key during a six-second interval. But if they did peck, the key light went out and no food was presented. Here, food reward was contingent upon not pecking. But the pigeons pecked anyway. They simply couldn't help themselves (Williams and Williams, 1969). The CS-US contingency (here, lit key and food) evidently outweighed the response-outcome contingency (here, not pecking and food), which may be another way of saying that the response was in part a classically conditioned CR (Schwartz and Gamzu, 1977).

ferent means to an end, as readily pressed for food as for anything else. To this extent, the box might be suitable to study people rather than the animal subjects for which it was designed (Schwartz, 1974). This is not to say that the behavior theorists' devices can begin to do justice to the human intellect. After all, a Skinner box is hardly a place in which Plato or Shakespeare would show to full advantage. But while not remotely adequate to assess our intellectual maximum, it is an apparatus that seems to fit one fact of human learning: We are generalists who can relate just about anything to anything else. *We* can learn arbitrary relations.

Many psychologists believe that this is not the end of the story. Compared to animals, we are indeed generalists who can learn arbitrary relations. But we are also specialists, with built-in predispositions to learn certain relationships very quickly. One of these species-specific predispositions is for language. That language is learned is indubitable. Eskimo children come to speak Eskimo and Chinese children speak Chinese. But the question is how it is learned. It is something that virtually all human children acquire, without fuss or effort and within the first few years of life. By the time they are four or five, they all know how to speak their native tongues, uttering sentences of considerable complexity, most of which they could never have heard before. This is not because they are taught explicitly, for most children aren't. Instead, it probably reflects a built-in tendency to fit sounds, words, and larger units into a very general framework with which the organism comes already equipped. How this process works is as yet unknown (see Chapter 9). But it may be the counterpart of other specializations of the learning functions found elsewhere in the animal kingdom.

## COMPLEX COGNITION IN ANIMALS

The work on animal cognitions that we discussed earlier showed that animals may know something without manifesting this knowledge in their actions. But it did not focus directly on the intellectual capacities that this knowledge revealed. Evidence that bears on this point comes from a number of sources. One concerns spatial memory in animals; the other relates to insightful learning.

### Cognitive Maps

A number of contemporary investigators have extended Tolman's notion of a cognitive map that represents the spatial layout of the animal's world and indicates what is where and what leads to what (Tolman, 1948). By now we know that this spatial knowledge can be quite complex. One investigator studied rats in radial-arm mazes, which consist of a central platform from which a number of pathways extend like spokes in a wheel (Figure 4.34). Each arm of the maze contains one food pellet. A hungry rat is placed on the center platform and is allowed to move about at will. It generally explores a bit, and will then choose one of the arms, run to its end, find the food pellet, and eat it. The question is what will it do after it returns to the center? Its optimal strategy is *not* to revisit the arm on which it had just been—for this arm is now empty. What it should do is to visit each arm just once, thus getting the most food for the least effort. But to accomplish this, the rat must not only learn the spatial layout; it must also remember where on

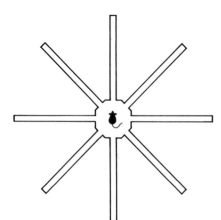

**4.34  A radial-arm maze**  *One pellet is placed at the end of each arm, and the rat is rewarded for choosing each arm once. (From Olton and Samuelson, 1976)*

that layout it has been and where it hasn't. The results show that the rats had these capacities. Given a radial maze of 8 arms, they chose an average of 7.9 different arms in 8 choices (Olton and Samuelson, 1976; Olton, 1978; Olton, 1979).

What rats can do, chimpanzees can do even better. Proof came from a chimpanzee version of an Easter-egg hunt. The experimenter took one animal at a time and carried it through a zig-zag course of a familiar, one-acre compound, while accompanied by an assistant who hid pieces of fruit in eighteen different locations. During this time, the chimpanzee merely watched through the bars of its carrying cage. A few minutes after the last piece of fruit had been hidden, the animal was released. It immediately dashed to one hiding place after another, unearthed the fruit hidden in each, and ate it. In general, the chimpanzee remembered most of the hiding places after only one trial of passive watching (Menzel, 1973; 1978).

Studies such as these suggest that the notion of a cognitive map may be more than a figure of speech. Perhaps something analogous to a map of the spatial environment is formed in the nervous system. Some authors have tried to find a physiological basis for such a mapping pattern in a certain region of the limbic system in the brain. This region contains neurons that seem to be sensitive to spatial information (O'Keefe and Nadel, 1978).

## Insightful Behavior

Thorndike had argued that problem solving in animals comes about by blind trial and error. But his conclusion was soon challenged by an early study of chimpanzees, undertaken by the German psychologist Wolfgang Köhler (1887–1968) only a decade or so after Thorndike's study of cats in a puzzle box.

Köhler believed that animals can behave intelligently. To be sure, Thorndike's cats had shown little signs of understanding, but perhaps cats are not the best subjects if one wants to determine the upper reaches of animal intellect. A closer relative of man, such as a chimpanzee, might prove a better choice. Even more important, Köhler believed that Thorndike had loaded the dice in favor of blind trial and error, for the problems he had posed his cats were often impossible to solve in any other way. Thus, even an intellectual supercat could never hit on the idea of yanking the wire that pulled the door latch except by pure chance; there was no other way, for all the strings and pulleys were hidden from the animal's view. To Köhler the real question was whether animals would behave intelligently if the conditions were optimum—when all of the ingredients of the solution were visibly present.

Köhler's procedure was simple. The chimpanzee was placed in an enclosed play area. Somewhere out of its reach was a desirable lure (usually some fruit, such as a banana). To obtain it, the ape had to employ some nearby object as a tool. In this the animals were remarkably successful. They learned to use sticks as rakes to haul in bananas placed on the ground just outside the cage, but beyond the reach of their arms. Sticks were equally useful to club down fruit which was hung too high overhead. Some chimpanzees used the sticks as a pole; they stood it upright under the banana, frantically climbed up its fifteen-foot length, and grasped their reward just as the stick toppled over (a considerable intellectual as well as gymnastic feat, demonstrating the virtues of a healthy mind in a healthy body). The chimpanzees also learned to use boxes as "climb-upon-ables," drag-

***Wolfgang Köhler*** *(Courtesy The Warder Collection)*

A        B        C        D

**4.35 Tool using in chimpanzees** *(A) Using a stick as a pole to jump up to a banana. (B) Using a stick as a club to beat down a banana. (C and D) Erecting three- and four-story structures to reach a banana. (From Köhler, 1925)*

**4.36 Tool making in chimpanzees** *Sultan making a double stick. (From Köhler, 1925)*

ging them under the banana and then stepping on top to claim their prizes. Eventually they even became builders, piling boxes on top of boxes and finally erecting structures that went up to four (rather shaky) stories, as Köhler spurred them on to ever-greater architectural accomplishments by progressively raising the height of the lure (Figure 4.35).

Occasionally the apes became toolmakers as well as tool-users. For example, when in need of a stick, they might break off a branch of a nearby tree. Even more impressive was the manufacture of a double stick. A particularly gifted chimpanzee called Sultan was faced with a banana far out of his reach. There were two bamboo sticks in his cage, but neither of them was long enough to rake in the lure. After many attempts to reach the banana with one stick or another, Sultan finally hit upon the solution. He pushed the thinner of the two sticks into the hollow inside of the thicker one and then drew the banana toward himself, his reach now enlarged by the length of two sticks (Figure 4.36).

Köhler denied that such achievements were the result of a mechanical strengthening and weakening of response tendencies. On the contrary, the animals behaved as if they had attained some ***insight*** into the relevant relationships, as if they *saw* what led to what.

Köhler offered several lines of evidence. To begin with, when the problem was once solved, the animals usually performed smoothly and continuously thereafter as if they "knew what they were doing," in marked contrast to Thorndike's cats who went on fumbling for many trials. In further opposition to Thorndike's findings was the fact that often the insightful solution came quite suddenly, sometimes after a pause during which the chimpanzee only moved its head and eyes as if to study the situation. Once the correct response was made, further errors were rare.

The most convincing evidence for the view that the chimpanzees learned by insight rather than by blind trial and error came from tests in which the situation was changed to determine what the animals would ***transfer*** from the original task. This is a method that serves to define what has been learned in any given situation. Teachers use just this approach to find out what their students have un-

**4.37 A device for studying discrimination learning in monkeys** *A monkey is presented with a stimulus tray that contains two (sometimes three or more) wells. In one of the wells is a desirable food reward, such as a raisin or a grape. The wells are covered with various objects, such as the sphere and cube shown in the figure. One of these objects is designated as the correct stimulus. The animal's task is to learn which of these objects is correct, push it aside, and pick up its reward from the well below. (After Harlow, 1949)*

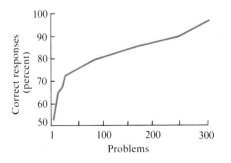

**4.38 Discrimination learning sets** *Monkeys were given 344 different discrimination problems, each for 6 trials. The curve shows the animals' average performance on the second trial. (After Harlow, 1949)*

derstood. Consider a young child who quickly answers "7" when confronted by the symbols "3 + 4 = ?" Has he really grasped the notion of addition? A simple test might be to present him with another problem, "4 + 3 =?" If he is now bewildered, he presumably has learned merely to give a specific answer to a specific question, but if his reply again is "7," he may be on the way to genuine arithmetic insight. Köhler used similar tests on his chimpanzees. For example, he took animals who had previously learned to use a box as a platform and presented the high lure again, but now with all boxes removed. The animals were quick to find other objects, such as a table or a small ladder, which they promptly dragged to the proper place. These were not the only substitutes. On one occasion, Sultan came over to Köhler, pulled him by the arm until he was under the banana, and then showed that in a pinch even the director of the Prussian anthropoid station would do as a climb-upon-able.

To Köhler, the main criterion for insight was wide and appropriate transfer. But is this kind of transfer really so hard to explain in behavior theory's terms? Can't one say that it is simply some form of stimulus generalization? A dog who has previously been conditioned to salivate to a tone of 1,000 hertz will also salivate when presented with 2,000 hertz. How is this different from the kind of transfer that we regard as a sign of understanding?

The answer is that in stimulus generalization transfer is only based on perceptual similarity. A variety of stimuli are seen (or heard or felt) as more or less alike and so they are responded to in a similar fashion. But in the case of the "3 + 4" example, the transfer is based on something else, on a common principle, on an abstract conceptual relationship. The important thing is not that "3 + 4" and "4 + 3" (not to speak of "2 + 5", "1 + 6" and so on) look alike. The important thing is that they are alike in meaning.

### ABSTRACT CONCEPTS IN ANIMALS

*Learning to learn in monkeys* A number of studies have shown that various primates can respond to certain abstract, conceptual aspects of a situation that transcend their perceptual characteristics. An example is **learning to learn** in monkeys. This phenomenon was studied extensively by Harry Harlow (1905–1981). Harlow trained rhesus monkeys on a long series of different discriminations. Each discrimination involved two stimulus objects that were never used again on any further problem. Thus, in the first discrimination, the monkey might have to choose between a small red square and a large blue circle; in the second, between a white line and a yellow dot; in the third, between a green pyramid and a black hemisphere. In one such study, the animals were trained on 344 separate discrimination problems (Figure 4.37). The results were dramatic. Learning the first few discriminations was difficult, but the animals became better and better the more new problems they encountered. After 300 of them, they solved each new problem in just one trial. In Harlow's terms, the monkeys had acquired a **learning set;** they had learned how to learn a certain kind of problem (Figure 4.38; Harlow, 1949).

What did the animals learn during this long series of different discrimination problems that finally enabled them to solve such tasks so efficiently? At first, each monkey was prone to certain kinds of errors that it made quite systematically—choosing the right side, or alternating sides from trial to trial, or always choosing the larger of the two objects. Such errors gradually dropped out, as if the

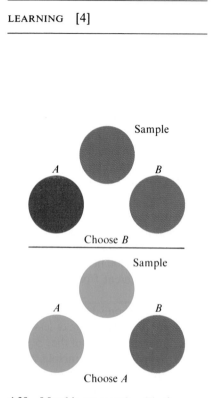

**4.39  Matching to sample**  *The figure shows the procedure of a typical matching-to-sample experiment. The top circle in each panel represents the sample. The subject's task is to choose the one circle among the two at the bottom which matches the sample in color. In the top panel of the figure, the correct choice is* B; *in the bottom panel, it is* A.

monkey realized that none of these factors was relevant to the solution. Once these error tendencies were eliminated, the animals could eventually adopt a new strategy, appropriate not just to one discrimination problem but to all of them. If you find food under some object, choose it again; if you don't, switch to the other. This "Win-stay, lose-shift" strategy obviously does not depend upon the specific stimuli employed in the task. It is based on a conceptual, not a perceptual, relationship (Harlow, 1959).

*Symbol manipulation in chimpanzees*    Further demonstrations of abstract concepts in animals have been obtained by David Premack who has tried to map the upper limits of the cognitive capacities in several chimpanzees, including his prize pupil, Sarah (Premack, 1976; Premack and Premack, 1983).

An example of such an abstract concept is the notion "same-different." Consider a situation in which an animal is shown three items. One serves as the sample; the other two are the alternatives. The animal's task is to choose the alternative that matches the sample. Suppose the alternatives are a triangle and a square. If so, the triangle is correct if the sample is a triangle; conversely, if the sample is a square. This procedure is called **matching to sample** (see Figure 4.39).

There is little doubt that animals other than primates can be taught to match if they are given enough trials to learn. Thus, pigeons can be taught to peck at a green rather than a yellow key if the sample is green, and to peck at the yellow key if the sample is yellow. But does that mean that they understand what sameness means? The question is whether they somehow understand that the relation between two yellow keys is the same as the relation between two equal tones or two identical triangles, that in all cases the two items are the same. To test whether the animal has this abstract concept of sameness, we have to determine whether there is any transfer from one matching-to-sample situation to another one in which the particular stimulus items are quite different. Take the pigeon that has learned to match green-green. Does this training facilitate learning to match red-red, or better yet, triangle-triangle? By and large, the answer seems to be no (Premack, 1978; but see also Zentall and Hogan, 1974). It can recognize that two reds are the same. But it does not recognize that this sameness is the identical relation that exists between two other equal stimulus items (see Figure 4.39).

The situation is quite different in chimpanzees. Having matched to sample on only three prior problems, Sarah and a few other animals readily handled new problems, performing perfectly on the very first trial. Even more impressive is the fact that Sarah learned to use two special tokens to indicate *same* and *different.* She was first shown two identical objects, such as two cups, and was then given a token whose intended meaning was *same.* Her task was to place this *same* token between the two cups. She was then presented with two different objects, such as a cup and a spoon, was given yet another token intended to mean *different,* and was required to place this *different* token between the cup and the spoon. After several such trials, she was tested with several pairs of items, some identical and some different, had to decide whether to place the *same* or the *different* token between them, and did so correctly (see Figure 4.40).

Such accomplishments show that chimpanzees can develop a way of thinking about the world that goes beyond the specific perceptual relations of the concrete moment. Like pigeons, they can of course respond to these concrete relationships, for example, the relationship between, say, red and red, circle and circle, A-flat and A-flat. But unlike pigeons, chimpanzees can also deal with some

**4.40  The same-different problem**  *(After A. Premack, 1976)*

**higher-order relationships,** the relations that hold between the various concrete relationships. They can therefore recognize that the relation between red and red is identical to that between circle and circle, and for that matter between hippopotamus and hippopotamus—that in all of these the relation is *sameness.*

### ACCESSING WHAT ONE KNOWS

The formation of abstract concepts is certainly one of the characteristics of what we normally call intelligence. But it is not the only one. Another criterion is whether the animal has some *access* to its own intellectual operations.

Consider a pigeon who finds its way home over large distances. That bird is a brilliant navigator. It refers to the stars, to the sun, to a number of landmarks, and somehow calculates the correct path with remarkable accuracy. But we don't therefore regard the bird as especially intelligent. The reason is that we are convinced that it doesn't really know what it is doing. Its brain constitutes a marvelous navigational computer. But the bird can't use that computer for any purpose other than that for which it was installed by evolution. It has no access to its own intellectual machinery.

In this regard, the pigeon is quite different from a human being. At least to some extent, we do have access to our own mental functioning. We think and remember and know that we think and remember. And we can use these and other intellectual capacities very broadly. This access to our own intellectual functions is by no means total; as we will see later on, it is especially limited in childhood (see Chapter 14). Our present point is only that this access is one of the defining features of intelligent behavior and is a characteristic of that intellectual generalist, man (Rozin, 1976a).

Some recent studies by Premack and his collaborators suggest that intellectual access is not confined to humans. They showed Sarah several videotaped scenes of a trainer struggling with different problems. In one scene, he tried to reach a banana suspended high above him. In another, he vainly stretched his arm toward a banana on the floor outside of a cage. After Sarah saw the tapes, she was shown different photographs of the trainer engaged in one of several actions. In one picture he was climbing on a box, in another he was shoving a stick under the wire mesh of the cage, and so on. Sarah's job was to pick the photograph that depicted the appropriate problem solution. Thus, if she was first shown a scene in

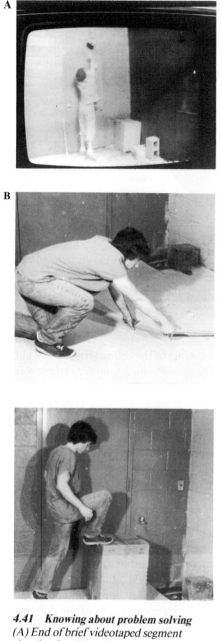

which the trainer struggled to reach an overhead banana, she had to choose the picture of a man stepping on a box. Sarah did quite well, succeeding in twenty-one out of twenty-four trials (Figure 4.41).

Sarah's success in this task suggests that the chimpanzee's problem-solving ability goes further even than Köhler had thought. To be sure, Sarah can solve a variety of spatial problems and can do so insightfully. But her ability may go beyond this. She not only solves problems, she also seems to know something *about* problem solving. She recognizes that the trainer has a problem, what this problem is, and how it should be solved. To this extent, she has some access to her own intellectual processes.

## TAKING STOCK

What is the upshot of the scientific study of animal learning that began with the studies of Pavlov and Thorndike some ninety years ago? It is clear that they and their intellectual descendants have discovered many vital phenomena of learning. Whether the principles they uncovered in their study of habituation, classical conditioning, and instrumental conditioning underlie all forms of learning is still a matter of debate. For certain complex intellectual achievements in animals and humans such as insightful understanding, abstract concepts, and—especially—human language may well be acquired in some different ways. But there is no question that the study of how CS-US and response-reinforcer relations are acquired and represented in animals will give important clues about the fundamental nature of some rock-bottom learning processes that are found in both humans and animals.

When we began our discussion, our initial focus was on *action,* on how classical and instrumental conditioning change what animals *do:* How Pavlov's dogs came to salivate at ticking metronomes they had never heard before; how Thorndike's cats came to perform all sorts of novel tricks. But as we saw, these changes of overt behavior are only one aspect of what has happened to these animals— they are the consequence of having learned rather than its essence. For unlike Pavlov and Thorndike, who focused on the overt behavior, modern investigators of animal learning have shown that at bottom classical and instrumental conditioning (and many other forms of learning too) depend on *cognition.* Rats—and dogs and pigeons—learn what events predict what other events and what actions produce what outcomes. These and other phenomena make it clear that psychological functions involve not just what animals and humans do, but also what they *know.*

Psychology must necessarily deal with both action and knowledge. In our discussion of animal learning we have straddled them both, for the field represents a kind of a bridge between these two major concerns. We will now cross the bridge completely, and move on to the study of cognition as a topic in its own right.

**4.41 Knowing about problem solving**
*(A) End of brief videotaped segment showing Sarah's trainer reaching for bananas that are too high for him. (B) Two pictured alternatives. One shows the trainer stepping on a box. The other shows him reaching along the ground with a stick. Sarah tended to choose the picture that showed the correct solution; in the present case, the trainer stepping on the top of the box. (From Premack and Woodruff, 1978)*

## SUMMARY

1. The simplest of all forms of learning is *habituation,* a decline in the tendency to respond to stimuli that have become familiar through repeated exposure.

## SUMMARY

2. In habituation the organism learns that it has encountered a stimulus before. In *classical conditioning,* first studied by I. P. Pavlov, it learns about the *association* between one stimulus and another. Prior to conditioning, an *unconditioned stimulus* or *US* (such as food) elicits an *unconditioned response* or *UR* (such as salivation). After repeated pairings of the US with a *conditioned stimulus* or *CS* (such as a buzzer), this CS alone will evoke a *conditioned response* or *CR* (here again, salivation) that is often similar to the UR.

3. The strength of conditioning is assessed by the readiness with which the CS elicits the CR. This strength increases with the number of *reinforced trials,* that is, pairings of the CS and the US. When a CS-US relation is well established, the CS can be paired with a second neutral stimulus to produce *second-order conditioning.*

4. Nonreinforced trials, during which the CS is presented without the US, lead to *extinction,* a decreased tendency of the CS to evoke the CR. According to some authors, the CR is masked rather than abolished by extinction, as shown by the phenomenon of *spontaneous recovery.*

5. The CR is elicited not only by the CS but also by stimuli that are similar to it. This effect, *stimulus generalization,* increases the greater the similarity between the CS and the new stimulus. To train the animal to respond to the CS but not to other stimuli, one stimulus (CS$^+$) is presented with the US, while another (CS$^-$) is presented without the US. The more similar the CS$^+$ is to the CS$^-$, the more difficult this *discrimination* will be.

6. Classical conditioning can involve many responses other than salivation; for example, conditioning of fear as assessed by the *conditioned emotional response (CER)* procedure. The CR is never identical, and often not even similar to the UR, which suggests that the CS serves as a signal for the US rather than as a substitute for it. In some cases, the CR is not just different from the UR but is its very opposite. A possible example is the development of drug tolerance.

7. In classical conditioning, the US is presented regardless of whether the animal performs the CR or not. In another form of simple learning, *instrumental conditioning* (or *operant conditioning*), something analogous to the US, reward or *reinforcement,* is only delivered upon performance of the appropriate instrumental response.

8. An early study of instrumental conditioning was conducted by E. L. Thorndike using cats that learned to perform an arbitrary response to escape from a *puzzle box.* As Thorndike saw it, what the animals learned involved no understanding but was rather based on a gradual strengthening of the correct response and a weakening of the incorrect one. To account for this, he proposed his *law of effect,* which states that the tendency to perform a response is strengthened if it is followed by a reward (reinforcement) and weakened if it is not.

9. During the past sixty years or so, the major figure in the study of instrumental conditioning has been B. F. Skinner, who was one of the first theorists to insist on a sharp distinction between classical conditioning in which the CR is *elicited* by the CS, and instrumental (which he calls *operant*) conditioning in which the instrumental response, or *operant,* is *emitted* from within. Operants are strengthened by *reinforcement,* but their acquisition may require some initial *shaping* by the method of *successive approximations.*

10. While some reinforcers are stimuli whose reinforcing power is unlearned, others are *conditioned reinforcers* that acquire their reinforcing power from prior pairings with stimuli that already have that capacity. One of the factors that determines the strength of instrumental conditioning is the *delay of reinforcement:* The shorter the interval between the response and the reinforcement, the stronger the response will be.

11. During *partial reinforcement,* the response is reinforced only some of the time. Responses that were originally learned under partial reinforcement are harder to extinguish than those learned when the response was always reinforced. The rule that determines the occasions under which reinforcement is given is a *schedule of reinforcement.* In *ratio sched-*

ules, reinforcement comes after a number of responses, which may be fixed or variable. In *interval schedules,* the animal is reinforced for the first response made after a given interval since the last reinforcement, which again can be fixed or variable.

12. Reinforcement can be provided by the presentation of *appetitive stimuli,* or by the termination or prevention of *aversive stimuli.* Aversive stimuli can weaken or strengthen instrumental responses, depending on the relation between the aversive stimulus and the response. In *punishment training,* the response is followed by an aversive stimulus; as a result, the animal learns *not* to perform it. In *escape learning,* the response stops an aversive stimulus that has already begun; in *avoidance training,* it averts it altogether. In both cases, the animal will then learn to make that response.

13. Pavlov, Thorndike, and Skinner believed that the essential aspect of both classical and instrumental conditioning is that they modify *action. Cognitive theorists* such as Köhler and Tolman and, more recently, Rescorla believe that what really matters when humans and animals learn is that they acquire new bits of knowledge or *cognitions.* According to many theorists, what is learned in classical conditioning is an association about two events, the CS and the US, such that the CS serves as a signal for the US. One line of evidence comes from studies of the effect of the CS-US interval. The general finding is that conditioning is more effective when the CS precedes the US by some optimum interval, which is typically rather short.

14. A number of investigators have asked how the animal learns that the CS is a signal for the US. The evidence shows that CS-US pairings alone will not suffice; there must also be trials on which the absence of CS goes along with the absence of US. This allows the animal to discover that the US is *contingent* (depends) upon the CS. The discovery of this contingency seems to depend on the extent to which the US is unexpected or "surprising," as shown by the phenomenon of *blocking.*

15. Unlike Thorndike and Skinner who argue that instrumental learning involves the strengthening of an instrumental response, cognitive theorists believe that it is based on an association between an act and its outcome. Evidence for this view comes from studies in which animals are trained to perform two responses that lead to two different outcomes, after which one of the outcomes is made less desirable. Subsequent tests indicate that the animals have learned which response led to what.

16. Contingency is crucial in instrumental conditioning just as it is classical conditioning. In instrumental conditioning, the relevant contingency is between a response and an outcome. When there is no such contingency, the organism learns that it has no *response control.* Threatening conditions in which there is no response control may engender *learned helplessness,* which often generalizes to other situations.

17. According to Pavlov, Skinner, and other early behavior theorists, the connections established by classical and instrumental conditioning are essentially *arbitrary.* This view is challenged by the fact that certain CS's are more readily associated with some US's than with others, as shown by studies of *learned taste aversions* in rats. These studies suggest that animals are biologically "prepared" to learn certain relations more readily than others. Similar preparedness effects occur in instrumental conditioning, for it turns out that some responses are more readily strengthened by some reinforcers than by others.

18. Cognitive theorists point out that animals are capable of rather complex cognitions. Evidence comes from work on spatial memory in rats and chimpanzees which shows that these animals can acquire rather elaborate *cognitive maps.* Further work concerns the ability to abstract *conceptual* relationships. Early evidence came from Köhler's studies of *insightful learning* in chimpanzees, who showed wide and appropriate transfer when later tested in novel situations. Later work showed that monkeys acquire *learning sets* and learn to learn when solving discrimination problems. Another example is provided by chimpanzees who can acquire certain *higher-order* concepts such as "same-different" and seem to have some *access* to their own cognitive operations.

alone; there must also be certain preexisting "categories" according to which this sensory material is ordered and organized. Examples are space, time, and causality—categories which, according to Kant, are *a priori,* built into the mind (or, as we would now say, into the nervous system). In Kant's view, there is no way in which we can see the world except in terms of these categories. It is as if we looked at the world through colored spectacles that we could never take off; if they were red, then redness would necessarily be part of everything we see. According to Kant, what experience does is to provide the sensory input that is then ordered according to the *a priori* categories. But the categories themselves, and the way in which they order the sensory information, are natively given.

## PSYCHOPHYSICS

The dispute between empiricists and nativists focused attention on the role of the senses and prodded later investigators into efforts to discover just how these senses function. The question they were concerned with can be stated very simply: What is the chain of events that begins with a stimulus and leads up to reports such as "a bitter taste," a "dull pressure," or a "brightish green"? The details of this sequence are obviously very different for the different senses. Vision differs from hearing, and both differ from taste—in the stimuli that normally excite them, in their receptors, in the qualities of their sensations. Even so, we can analyze the path from stimulus to sensory experience in quite similar ways, whatever the particular sense may be.

In all cases, one can crudely distinguish three steps in the sequence. First, there is the proximal stimulus. Second, there is the neural chain of events that this stimulus gives rise to. The stimulus is converted (technically, **transduced**) into an electrical signal, which is then translated into the only language that all neurons understand, the nerve impulse.* Once converted in this manner, the message is transmitted further and often is modified by other parts of the nervous system. Third, there is some sort of psychological response to the message, often in the form of a conscious, sensory experience (or sensation).

The sensory sequence can be looked at from several points of view. One concerns the **psychophysical** relations between some property of the (physical) stimulus and the (psychological) sensory experience it ultimately gives rise to, quite apart from the intervening neural steps. Another approach concerns the **psychophysiology.** Here the questions concern the neural consequences of a given stimulus input—how it affects the receptors and the neural structures higher up in the brain. For now, we will confine our discussion to psychophysical matters, leaving psychophysiological issues for later on.

The object of **psychophysics** is to relate the characteristics of physical stimuli to attributes of the sensory experience they produce. There are a variety of stimuli to which the human organism is sensitive. They include chemicals suspended in air or dissolved in water, temperature changes on the skin, pressure on the skin or within various parts of the body, pressure in the form of sound waves, and electromagnetic radiations within the visible spectrum. In each case, the sensory sys-

---

* This is typically a two-stage affair. The transduction process produces a graded potential in specialized receptor cells, which in their turn trigger a nerve impulse in other neurons.

tem will not respond unless the stimulus energy is above some critical level of intensity, the so-called ***absolute threshold.***

The range of stimuli to which a given sensory system reacts is actually quite limited. Human sight is restricted to the visible spectrum and human hearing to sound waves between 20 and 20,000 hertz (that is, cycles per second). But there are many organisms that respond to different ranges of stimulation and thus see and hear a world different from ours. Many insects see ultraviolet light, while dogs and cats hear sound waves of much higher frequency than we can. The bat has carried high-frequency hearing to a point of exquisite perfection. As it glides through the night it emits high-pitched screams of about 100,000 hertz which are used as a kind of sonar. They bounce off small objects in the air such as insects, echo back to the bat, and thus enable it to locate its prey.

## Measuring Sensory Intensity

Measuring the magnitude of a stimulus is in principle easy enough. We measure the physical stimulus energy—in pounds, in degrees centigrade, in footcandles, in decibels, or whatever. But matters become more difficult when we try to assess ***psychological intensity,*** the magnitude of a sensation rather than that of a stimulus.

Gustav Theodor Fechner (1801–1887), the founder of psychophysics, believed that sensations cannot be measured directly. In his view, sensations and the stimuli that produce them belong to two totally different realms—to use the terms many philosophers employ, that of the body and that of the mind. If this is so, how can one possibly describe them by reference to the same yardstick? Fechner argued that while sensations can't be compared to physical stimuli, they can at least be compared to each other. A subject can compare two of his own sensations and judge whether the two are the same or are different.

Consider the sensation of visual brightness produced by a patch of light projected on a certain part of the eye. We can ask, what is the minimal amount by which the original light intensity of the patch must be increased so that the subject experiences a sensation of brightness *just* greater than the one he had before? This amount is called the ***difference threshold.*** It produces a ***just-noticeable difference,*** or ***j.n.d.*** The j.n.d. is a psychological entity, for it describes a subject's ability to discriminate. But it is expressed in the units of the physical stimulus that produced it. (In our example, this would be millilamberts, a unit of illumination.) Fechner had found an indirect means to relate sensory magnitude to the physical intensity of the stimulus.

Before proceeding we should note that the absolute threshold may be considered as a special case of a difference threshold. Here the question is how much stimulus energy must be added to a zero stimulus before the subject can tell the difference between the old stimulus ("I see nothing") and the new ("Now I see it").

***Gustav Theodor Fechner*** *(Courtesy National Library of Medicine)*

### THE WEBER FRACTION

To Fechner, measuring j.n.d.'s was only the means to a larger goal—the formulation of a general law relating stimulus intensity to sensory magnitude. He believed that such a law could be built upon an empirical generalization first proposed by the German physiologist E. H. Weber (1795–1878) in 1834. Weber proposed that the size of the difference threshold is a constant ratio of the standard stimulus. Suppose that we can just tell the difference between 100 and 102 candles burning in an otherwise unilluminated room. If Weber is right, we would be able to just distinguish between 200 and 204 candles, 400 and 408, and so forth. Fechner was so impressed with this relationship that he referred to it as *Weber's law,* a label by which we still know it. Put algebraically, Weber's law is usually written as

$$\frac{\Delta I}{I} = C$$

where $\Delta I$ is the increment in stimulus intensity (that is, the j.n.d.) to a stimulus of intensity $I$ (that is, the standard stimulus) required to produce a just-noticeable increase, and where $C$ is a constant. The fraction $\Delta I/I$ is often referred to as the *Weber fraction.*

Fechner and his successors performed numerous studies to determine whether Weber's law holds for all of the sensory modalities. In a rough sort of way, the answer seems to be yes, at least for much of the normal range of stimulus intensity within each sense.* The nervous system is evidently geared to notice relative differences rather than absolute ones.

Weber's law allows us to compare the sensitivity of different sensory modalities. Suppose we want to know whether the eye is more sensitive than the ear. How can we tell? We certainly cannot compare j.n.d.'s for brightness and for loudness. To mention only one problem, the values will be in different units— millilamberts for the first, decibels for the second. The problem is circumvented by utilizing the Weber fractions for the two modalities. Being fractions, they are dimensionless and can therefore be used to compare the sensitivity of different senses. If $\Delta I/I$ is small, the discriminating power of the sense modality is great; proportionally little must be added to the standard for a difference to be observed. The opposite holds when $\Delta I/I$ is large. It turns out that we are keener in discriminating weight than smell; the Weber fraction for the first is 1/50, for the second it is only 1/14. Weber fractions for other sense modalities are presented in Table 5.1.

***E. H. Weber*** *(Courtesy National Library of Medicine)*

Table 5.1   REPRESENTATIVE VALUES FOR THE WEBER FRACTION FOR THE DIFFERENT SENSES

| *Sensory modality* | *Weber fraction* $(\Delta I/I)$ |
|---|---|
| Vision (brightness, white light) | .08 |
| Audition (loudness, noise) | .05 |
| Touch (vibration at fingertip) | .04 |
| Kinesthesis (lifted weights) | .02 |
| Taste (table salt) | .08 |
| Smell (butyl alcohol) | .07 |

SOURCE: Teghtsoonian 1971, and Cain, 1977.

* Weber's law tends to break down at the two extremes of the intensity range, especially at the lower end (for example, for visual stimuli only slightly above absolute threshold). At these intensities, the Weber fraction is larger than it is in the middle range.

Weber's law indicated that the more intense the stimulus, the more stimulus intensity has to be increased before the subject notices a change. By making a number of further assumptions, Fechner generalized Weber's finding to express a broader relationship between sensory and physical intensity. The result was *Fechner's law,* which states that the strength of a sensation grows as the logarithm of stimulus intensity,

$$S = k \log I$$

where $S$ stands for psychological (that is, subjective) magnitude, $I$ for stimulus intensity, and $k$ is a constant that depends on the value of the Weber fraction.

This law has been challenged on several grounds which are beyond the scope of this book. For our purposes, it is sufficient to note that a logarithmic law such as Fechner's makes good biological sense. The range of stimulus intensities to which we are sensitive is enormous. We can hear sounds as weak as the ticking of a watch twenty feet away and as loud as a pneumatic drill operating right next to us. Our nervous system has to have a mechanism to compress this huge range into some manageable scope, and this is precisely what a logarithmic transformation does for us.

## Detection and Decision

The goal of psychophysics is to chart the relationships between a subject's responses and various characteristics of the physical stimulus. But are these physical characteristics the only factors that determine what the subject does or says? What about her expectations or wishes? The early psychophysicists believed that such factors could be largely disregarded. But a more recent approach to psychophysical measurement insists that they cannot. This is *signal detection theory,* a very influential way of thinking about the way people make decisions.

To understand how beliefs and attitudes come into play in a psychophysical experiment, consider a study of absolute thresholds. On every trial, the harried subject is forced into a decision. Is a stimulus there or isn't it? The decision is often difficult, for at times the stimulus is so weak that the subjects may be quite uncertain of their judgment. Under the circumstances, their *response bias* will necessarily exert an effect. Such a response bias is a preference for one response over another (here "yes" or "no"), quite apart from the nature of the stimuli. Thus, some subjects will approach the task with a free-and-easy attitude, cheerfully offering "yes" judgments whenever they are in doubt. Others will take a more conservative line and will never respond with a "yes" unless they are quite certain. This will produce a difference in obtained thresholds that will necessarily be lower for the subjects who are more liberal with their "yes" responses. But this only reflects a difference in response bias, not in sensory sensitivity. Both groups of subjects can presumably hear or see or feel the stimuli equally well. They only differ in their willingness to report a stimulus when they are unsure.

## SIGNAL DETECTION

Such considerations make it clear that thresholds obtained with traditional techniques reflect two factors. One is sensitivity—how well the subject can hear or see the stimulus. The other is response bias—how readily the subject is willing to say "yes, I heard" when he is not certain. How can these two factors be separated?

The early psychophysicists tried to cope with this problem by using only subjects who were highly trained observers. In absolute threshold studies, such subjects were models of conservatism; they would never say "yes" unless they were completely certain. To maintain this attitude, the experimenters threw in an occasional "catch trial" on which there was no stimulus at all (Woodworth, 1938).

Signal detection theory has developed a more systematic way of dealing with response bias. To begin with, it has provided a somewhat different testing procedure, the so-called ***detection experiment,*** in which catch trials are part of the regular procedure rather than just an occasional check to keep the subjects on their toes (Green and Swets, 1966).

One version of this procedure is related to the measurement of the absolute threshold. Here the question is whether the subject can detect the presence of a stimulus. We take a fairly weak stimulus and present it on half the trials. On the other half of the trials (interspersed in random order), we present no stimulus at all. We will now look at two kinds of errors. One is a ***miss,*** not reporting a stimulus when one is present. The other is a ***false alarm,*** reporting a stimulus when in fact none is present. By the same token, there are two different kinds of correct responses: reporting a stimulus when it is actually there (a ***hit***) and not reporting one when none is present (a ***correct negative***) (see Table 5.2).

### THE PAYOFF MATRIX

The detection experiment can tell us what factors underlie response bias. One such factor is differential payoff. Suppose we (literally) pay a subject for every hit and correct negative but penalize him for every miss and false alarm according to a prescribed schedule of gains and losses called a ***payoff matrix.*** Thus the subject might gain 10 cents for every hit and 5 cents for every correct negative, while losing 10 cents for every miss and only 1 cent for every false alarm. Such a payoff matrix will lead to a bias toward "yes" judgments (Table 5.3). Suppose there are, say, fifty trials on which the subject has no sensory information on the basis of which she can decide whether the stimulus is present or not. If she consistently says "yes," she will on the average be correct on twenty-five trials (thus collecting $2.50) and wrong on the other twenty-five (thus losing $0.25) for a net gain of $2.25. In contrast, consistent "no" judgments will lead to a net loss ( + $1.25 for the correct negatives and − $2.50 for the false alarms).

If the stimulus is presented on half of the trials, the payoff bias can be calculated easily by comparing the sum of the values under the *Says "yes"* column with the sum under the *Says "no"* column. In this example, these sums are + 9¢ and − 5¢ respectively. Under the circumstances, the subject will do well to adopt a liberal criterion and give a "yes" judgment whenever she is in doubt.

Illustrations of the effect of payoff matrices abound in real life. There the differential payoff is usually reckoned in units larger than pennies. Consider a team of radiologists poring over an X-ray to look for a tiny spot that indicates the start of a malignant tumor. What are the penalties for error here? If the physicians de-

Table 5.2   THE FOUR POSSIBLE OUTCOMES OF THE DETECTION EXPERIMENT

|  | Responds "yes" | Responds "no" |
|---|---|---|
| Stimulus present | Hit | Miss |
| Stimulus absent | False alarm | Correct negative |

Table 5.3   PAYOFF MATRIX THAT WILL PRODUCE A "YES" BIAS

|  | Subject says "yes" | Subject says "no" |
|---|---|---|
| Stimulus present | + 10¢ | − 10¢ |
| Stimulus absent | − 1¢ | + 5¢ |

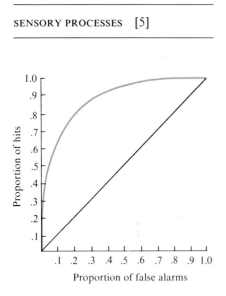

**5.3 The ROC curve** *The proportion of hits is plotted against the proportion of false alarms. The stimulus is kept constant but the response bias is systematically varied by asking subjects to adopt a more liberal attitude with their yeses. This bias becomes progressively larger as we move upward on the vertical axis (proportion of hits) and to the right on the horizontal axis (proportion of false alarms). Note that as the proportion of hits increases, so does the proportion of false alarms.*

cide there is no spot when there actually is one, their miss may cost the patient's life. If they decide that they see a spot when in fact there is none, their false alarm has other costs, such as the dangers of more elaborate clinical tests, let alone those of an operation. What the physicians ultimately decide will depend, both on what their eyes tell them as they inspect the X-ray and also on the relative costs of the two possible errors they may commit.

## SEPARATING SENSITIVITY AND RESPONSE BIAS

The preceding discussion showed that the subject's responses are jointly determined by his sensitivity to the stimulus and his response bias. If asked whether he hears a stimulus when presented with a thunderclap, he is almost certain to say "yes" even if his response bias is to say "no," for there is very little room for doubt given the intensity of the stimulus. But if the stimulus is relatively faint, he is very likely to say "no." Is there any way in which the effects of stimulus sensitivity and response bias can be disentangled? The detection procedure provides a means.

The first step is to vary response bias while keeping sensitivity constant. This can be done by changing the payoff matrix. Another way is to vary the proportion of trials on which no stimulus is presented—the fewer such trials, the greater the yes bias.

When response bias is varied in this fashion, the results are quite systematic. If we induce the subject to be more conservative, we find a reduction in the proportion of trials on which he is guilty of a false alarm. But at the same time, we also find a reduction in the proportion of hits. Similarly, upward shifts in the yes bias lead to an increase in the proportion of both hits and false alarms. These effects can be expressed graphically by plotting the two proportions against each other. The resulting function is known by the rather arcane designation of ***receiver-operating-characteristic curve,*** which is almost always abbreviated ***ROC curve*** (Figure 5.3).

The next step is to get an index of sensitivity that is uncontaminated by response bias. To do so, we obtain separate ROC curves for different levels of stimulus intensity (with each curve based on a separate detection experiment). The results are very striking. The stronger the stimulus, the more its ROC curve is bowed away from the main diagonal (Figure 5.4).

Why should this be so? To answer this question, consider a hypothetical detection experiment using a visual stimulus but a blind subject. Here the subject's sensitivity is obviously zero, so that his judgments must be based entirely upon response bias. For this blind subject, the stimulus does not exist, so that he is just as likely to obtain a hit as to strike a false alarm. In consequence, his ROC curve is necessarily the ***main diagonal.*** His yes bias can go up or down, but his proportion of hits and of false alarms will always be equal. Evidently, the main diagonal represents total insensitivity, an absolute inability to distinguish the presence of a

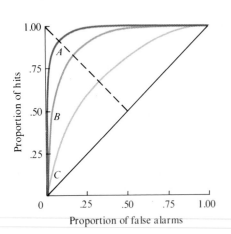

**5.4 ROC curves for stimuli of different intensities** *The figure shows ROC curves for three stimuli of increasing intensity (with A the strongest and C the weakest). Note that the stronger the stimulus, the more its ROC curve is displaced from the main diagonal. We can think of this diagonal as the ROC curve produced by a stimulus to which the subject is utterly insensitive. The displacement of the ROC curve from the main diagonal provides a pure index of sensitivity. It is measured along the second diagonal (broken line).*

stimulus from its absence. As sensitivity goes up, the ROC curve moves away from the diagonal. Thus, the displacement of the ROC curve from the main diagonal provides a pure measure of sensitivity for the stimulus on which the ROC curve is based; it is measured along the second diagonal (Figure 5.4).

### SIGNAL DETECTION AND THE DECISION PROCESS

There is one question that we have not really considered. Why does the subject have so much trouble distinguishing between the presence of a stimulus and its absence? Signal detection theory proposes an intriguing answer. It asserts that there really is no such thing as a zero stimulus.

The theory begins by assuming that psychophysical judgments are based on some underlying neural activity in the sensory system (whose exact nature is for now irrelevant) which can vary in magnitude. Let us call this hypothetical activity the *sensory process.* A sensory process can of course be produced by an actual, external stimulus (the *signal).* But signal detection theory proposes that a sensory process will occur even when in fact no stimulus is administered. The factors responsible for this are collectively described as *background noise.* Take an experiment in hearing and suppose that no sound is actually presented. This does not guarantee the absence of activity in the auditory system. Some sources of stimulation come from within the subject, such as the throbbing of the pulse. In addition, there is spontaneous activity in the nervous system, with many cells firing at random intervals without any external trigger. Under the circumstances, to say that there is no stimulus only means that the experimenter did not present one. From the subject's point of view, some stimulation is always there.

We can now state the subject's task in a detection experiment in another way. He must decide whether a given sensory process should be attributed to the signal superimposed on background noise or to the background noise alone; whether what he hears is a faint tone outside or his own heartbeat (or spontaneous neural firing or whatever) within. On the average, the signal (plus background noise) produces a process of greater magnitude than does the noise alone, an average value which rises with increasing signal strength. The subject's decision problem arises because the magnitude of the two sets of sensory processes fluctuates. Occasionally, one's heartbeat sounds louder than the experimenter's stimulus tone. But the more intense the stimulus, the less likely it is that such a confusion will occur.

To sum up, signal detection theorists offer a somewhat different conception of what a sensation is than did earlier psychophysicists. Fechner had no doubts that people have sensations and can report certain things about them. But according to signal detection theorists, subjects can't simply *report* that they have a sensation. The best they can do is to *decide* that they have a sensation—that their internal sensory experience is produced by a signal rather than by noise alone. And in this decision—as indeed, in many other decisions—they can be wrong.

### AN ANALYSIS OF THE DECISION PROCESS

For a more precise analysis of how signal detection theory envisages the decision process, consider Figure 5.5A. This is a *frequency distribution* of the intensity of the hypothetical sensory process when there is no stimulus, and thus only background noise. In this frequency distribution, the intensity of the sensory process

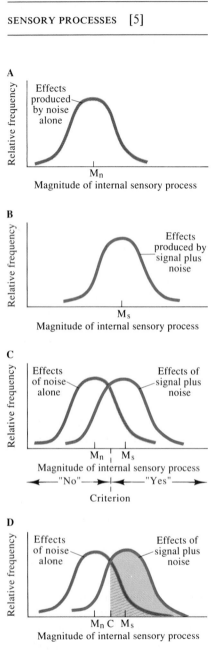

**A**

Relative frequency

Effects produced by noise alone

$M_n$

Magnitude of internal sensory process

**B**

Relative frequency

Effects produced by signal plus noise

$M_s$

Magnitude of internal sensory process

**C**

Relative frequency

Effects of noise alone

Effects of signal plus noise

$M_n$  $M_s$

Magnitude of internal sensory process

"No" ←→←→ "Yes"

Criterion

**D**

Relative frequency

Effects of noise alone

Effects of signal plus noise

$M_n$ C $M_s$

Magnitude of internal sensory process

**5.5  The decision process according to signal detection theory**  *(For explanation, see text.)*

is plotted on the horizontal axis and the frequency with which that intensity occurs on the vertical. The figure shows that the intensity is sometimes smaller and sometimes larger; most of the time it hovers around a mean, or average value that we will call $M_n$ (the mean of the noise-only distribution).

Now consider Figure 5.5B. This shows what happens when a stimulus is actually presented. Again, the intensity of the sensory process will fluctuate. But the values obtained now will in general be larger since we are dealing with trials on which there is *both* a signal and a background noise. As a result, the mean of this distribution, $M_s$, will be larger than $M_n$, the mean of the intensity values when there is noise alone.

How does the subject decide whether she heard (or saw, or felt) a stimulus or not? To see how signal detection theory deals with this problem, consider Figure 5.5C in which the noise-alone and the signal-plus-noise distribution are plotted on the same axis. As the figure shows, the two distributions overlap. This means that on some trials, the intensity of the sensory process when there is no stimulus (noise-alone) exceeds that which is generated when a stimulus is present (signal-plus-noise).

What can the subject do now? Her task, in effect, is to decide whether a given internal experience comes from the signal-plus-noise distribution or from the noise-only distribution. According to signal detection theory, the subject sets up a criterion and acts according to a decision rule. If the intensity of the sensory process is greater than this criterion, C, she decides that it came from the signal-plus-noise distribution and makes a "yes" judgment. If the value of the sensory process is less than C, she decides that it came from the noise-alone distribution and makes a "no" judgment.

Since the noise-alone and the signal-plus-noise distributions overlap, there is no way in which the subject can avoid errors. The nature of these errors will partially depend on the criterion. This is illustrated in Figure 5.5D. Because of the subject's decision rule, all the judgments to the left of the criterion, C, are "nos," while all the judgments to the right are "yeses." We can now read off the relative proportion of hits (saying "yes" when there was a stimulus) and false alarms (saying "yes" when there was no stimulus) from the figure. The proportion of "hits" is given by the portion of the area under the signal-plus-noise curve that falls to the right of C (and is here indicated in pink). The proportion of false alarms is indicated by the portion of the area under the noise-alone curve that falls to the right of the same criterion point (and is here indicated by stripes). Just where the criterion is placed depends on the subject's response bias. If she wants to minimize misses (saying "no" when a signal is actually presented), she has to shift her criterion to the left. This will decrease the number of misses, but it will also necessarily increase the number of false alarms.

EXTENSIONS TO OTHER FIELDS

The general approach of signal detection theory has applications to many areas of psychology outside of psychophysics. It is relevant whenever a person has to decide between two alternatives but can't be sure of the outcome. An example is the selection of college applicants. One error of admissions is a miss: An applicant is rejected who would have done well. Another error is a false alarm: An applicant is accepted who will be unable to graduate (for details, see Chapter 16). The important point is that in virtually all decision making some errors are inevitable and that these errors can be either misses or false alarms. There is always a trade-off between these two kinds of errors. If one wants to minimize the misses (rejected applicants who would have done perfectly well had they been accepted), one has to change the response bias toward "yes," which then inevitably increases the number of false alarms (accepted applicants who will flunk out). Conversely, if one wants to minimize the number of false alarms, one necessarily must increase the number of misses. Just which trade-off is chosen depends on the payoff matrix.

## SENSORY CODING

Thus far, our focus has been on the psychophysical relationships between the physical properties of the stimulus and the sensory experience it gives rise to. But sensory psychologists are not content with this alone. They also want to learn something about the intervening neural steps. One crucial issue that comes up in all such enterprises is the nature of the *sensory code* through which the nervous system represents various sensory experiences. A *code* is a set of rules whereby information is transformed from one set of symbols to another. An example is the Morse code used by telegraphers, in which letters are transformed into patterns of dots and dashes, so that dot-dash stands for *A,* dash-dot-dot-dot for *B,* and so on. What Samuel Morse did for telegraphy, the nervous system did for all the senses. Instead of dots and dashes, the nervous system *encodes* (that is, translates) the various properties of the stimulus into various characteristics of the nervous impulse. Many of the efforts of sensory psychophysiologists are directed at cracking these codes.

We'll shortly consider some of the discoveries that pertain to the codes within the different senses. But before doing so, we want to consider some general issues that apply to them all.

One question concerns *the code for psychological intensity,* such as changes in loudness and brightness. By and large, it appears that the relevant code is firing frequency: the more intense the stimulus, the greater the rate of neural firing (and the more intense the subjective experience; Borg, Diamant, Strom, and Zotterman, 1967). Another signal for sensory intensity is the sheer number of neurons that are triggered by the stimulus. The more intense the stimulus, the more neurons it will activate, which presumably will lead to an increase in the psychological magnitude.

Another question concerns the *code for sensory quality.* The different senses obviously produce sensations of different quality. For example, the sensations of pressure, A-flat, orange, or sour clearly belong to altogether different sensory domains (technically, to different *sense modalities*). To what factor shall we ascribe these differences in experienced quality? Is it the difference in the stimuli that produce these sensations? In 1826, the German physiologist Johannes Müller (1801–1858) argued that this answer was false. To be sure, visual sensations are usually produced by light waves, but occasionally other stimuli will serve as well. Strong pressure on the eyeballs leads us to see rings or stars (to the chagrin of boxers and the delight of cartoonists). Similarly, we can produce visual sensations by electric stimulation of various parts of the nervous system. Such facts led Müller to formulate his famous *doctrine of specific nerve energies.* According to this law, the differences in experienced quality are caused not by differences in the stimuli but by the different nervous structures which these stimuli excite,

**163**

most likely in centers higher up in the brain. Thus, were we able to rewire the nervous system so as to connect the optic nerve to the auditory cortex and the auditory nerve to the visual cortex we might be able to see thunder and hear lightning.

Some of Müller's successors extended his doctrine to cover qualitative differences within a given sense modality. For example, blue, green, and red are qualitatively different even though all three are colors. To the heirs of Müller, such a qualitative difference could only mean one thing: There had to be some decisive difference in the neural processes that underlie these different sensations, perhaps at the level of the receptors, perhaps higher up. This belief ultimately led to some fundamental discoveries about the physiological basis of various sensory experiences, such as color and pitch (Boring, 1942).

Müller's doctrine tells us that differences in sensory quality reflect a difference in some underlying neural process, but it leaves some room for debate about what the particular process is. In essence, there are two theoretical approaches. One is the ***specificity theory,*** which asserts that different sensory qualities are signaled by different neurons. These quality-specific neurons might be receptors, or they might be further up in the nervous system. In either case, they are somehow "labeled" with their quality, so that whenever they fire, the nervous system interprets their activation as "red" or "sour" or whatever their particular sensory quality might happen to be. The alternative position is the ***across-fiber pattern theory.*** This asserts that the code for quality comes from an overall pattern of activation across a whole set of fibers. In some sensory systems such as taste, the reactions of the sensory fibers are not too specific: Most of them respond to very many substances. What differs is the pattern of activation these substances produce, and this differential pattern may be the neural code that gives rise to the sensory quality. As we will see, the nervous system utilizes both specificity and pattern codes in different sensory systems (Goldstein, 1989; Rosenzweig and Leiman, 1989).

## AN OVERVIEW OF THE SENSES

The development of psychophysical methods, coupled with various physiological techniques, gave psychology a powerful set of tools with which to study the various senses. Our primary focus will be on just one sense, which we will consider in detail: vision. But we will first look briefly at several other sensory systems that provide us with information about various aspects of the world and about our own position within it.

### Kinesthesis and the Vestibular Senses

One group of senses informs the organism about its own movements and its orientation in space. Skeletal movement is sensed through ***kinesthesis,*** a collective term for information that comes from receptors in the muscles, tendons, and joints. Another group of receptors signals the rotation of the head. These are the receptors in the ***semicircular canals,*** which are located within the so-called ***vestibules*** of the inner ear (Figure 5.6). The three canals contain a viscous liquid that moves when the head rotates. This motion bends hair cells that are located at one end of each canal. When bent, these hair cells give rise to nervous impulses. The

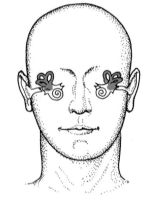

A

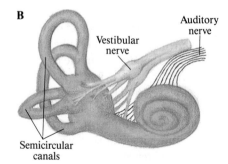

B

Vestibular
nerve

Auditory
nerve

Semicircular
canals

**5.6   The vestibular sense**   *(A) The location of the inner ears, which are embedded in bone on both sides of the skull. The vestibules are indicated in red. The rest of the inner ear is devoted to the sense of hearing. (After Krech and Crutchfield, 1958) (B) Close-up of the vestibular apparatus. (After Kalat, 1984, p. 139)*

sum total of the impulses from each of the canals provides information about the nature and extent of the head's rotation.

One vital function of the semicircular canal system is to provide a firm base for vision. As we walk through the world, our head moves continually. To compensate for this endless rocking, the eyes have to move accordingly. This adjustment is accomplished by a reflex system which automatically cancels each rotation of the head by an equal and opposite motion of the eyes. These eye movements are initiated by messages from the three semicircular canals which are relayed to the appropriate muscles of each eye. Thus, the visual system is effectively stable, operating as if it rested on a solid tripod.

## The Skin Senses

Stimulation of the skin informs the organism of what is directly adjacent to its own body. Not surprisingly, skin sensitivity is especially acute in those parts of the body that are most relevant to exploring the world that surrounds us directly: the hands and fingers, the lips and tongue. These sensitivities are reflected in the organization of the cortical projection area for bodily sensations. As we have seen, the allocation of cortical space is quite unequal, with a heavy emphasis on such sensitive regions as face, mouth, and fingers (see Chapter 2).

How many skin senses are there? Aristotle believed that all of the sensations from the skin could be subsumed under just one rubric, that of touch. But today most investigators believe that there are at least four different skin sensations: *pressure, warmth, cold,* and *pain.* How are these different sensory experiences coded by the nervous system? Here, as in the study of many other senses, the first line of inquiry was suggested by Müller's doctrine of specific nerve energies: If the sensory qualities are different, see whether there are different receptors that underlie them.

Are there different receptors that correspond to these different sensations? The answer is a qualified yes. There is good reason to believe that various sensations of pressure are produced by a number of different specialized receptors in the skin (see Figure 5.7). Some of these receptors are wrapped around hair follicles in the skin and sense movements of the hair. Others are capsules that are easily bent

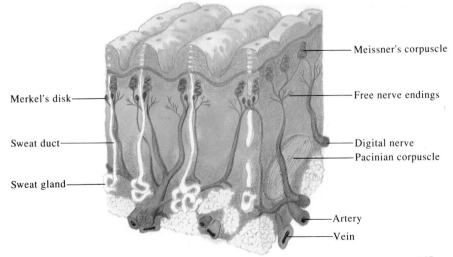

**5.7  A cross-section through the skin**  *The figure shows a number of structures that serve as receptors in hairless skin; for example, on the fingertips and palms. (After Carlson, 1986, p. 257)*

Merkel's disk

Sweat duct

Sweat gland

Meissner's corpuscle

Free nerve endings

Digital nerve
Pacinian corpuscle

Artery

Vein

by slight deformations of the skin. Some of these capsules respond to continued vibration; others react to sudden movement across the skin, still others sense steady indentation. It's clear that there is not one touch receptor but several.

Less is known about the underlying receptor systems for temperature and pain. Some of these experiences are probably signaled by free nerve endings in the skin that have no specialized end organs. These free nerve endings have been thought to provide information about cold and pain, but some of them may also be additional pressure receptors (Sherrick and Cholewiak, 1986).

Pain in particular has been the subject of much controversy. Some investigators believe that there are specialized pain receptors which are activated by tissue injury and produce an unpleasant sensation. Others hold that pain results from the overstimulation of any skin receptor. But whatever its receptor basis, there is little doubt that pain has a vital biological function. It warns the organism of potential harm. This point is vividly brought home by persons who have a congenital insensitivity to pain. On the face of it, the inability to experience this unpleasant sensation might seem to be a blessing, but nothing could be further from the truth. People who lack pain sensitivity often sustain extensive burns and bruises, especially in childhood; they never receive the first signals of danger so they don't withdraw the affected body parts. As a child, one such patient bit off the tip of her tongue while chewing food and sustained serious burns when kneeling on a hot radiator (Sternbach, 1963; Melzack, 1973; for a discussion of how the nervous system alleviates pain, see Chapter 2, p. 34).

## The Sense of Taste

The sense of taste has a simple function. It acts as a gatekeeper for the organism's digestive system by providing information about the substances that may or may not be ingested. Its task is to keep poisons out and usher foodstuffs in. In most land-dwelling mammals, this function is performed by specialized receptor organs, the **taste buds,** which are sensitive to chemicals dissolved in water. The average person possesses about 10,000 such taste buds, located mostly in the tongue but also in other regions of the mouth. Fibers from these receptors convey the message to the brain, first to the medulla and then further up to the thalamus and cortex.

### TASTE SENSATIONS

Most investigators believe that there are four basic taste qualities: *sour, sweet, salty,* and *bitter.* In their view, all other taste sensations are produced by a mixture of these primary qualities. Thus, grapefruit tastes sour and bitter, while lemonade tastes sweet and sour. What are the stimuli that produce these four basic qualities? As yet, we don't have a full answer. We do know that the salty taste is usually produced by inorganic molecules dissolved in water and the sour taste by acids. The story is more complicated for sweet and bitter sensations. Both are generally produced by complex organic molecules, but as yet there are no clear-cut rules that predict the resulting taste sensation. For example, "sweet" is produced by various sugars, but also by saccharin, a chemical compound that is structurally very different from sugar. Additional problems are posed by effects of concentration. Some substances, such as saccharin, that taste sweet in low concentrations taste bitter when their concentration is increased.

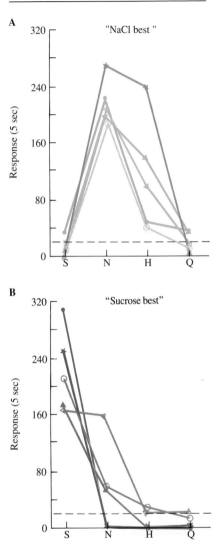

**5.8** *Response profiles of two kinds of taste fibers in the hamster* The figures show the number of responses to two kinds of fibers when stimulated by sucrose (S), sodium chloride (N), hydrochloric acid (H), and quinine (Q), which in humans give rise to the sensations of sweet, salty, sour, and bitter respectively. (A) Five fibers that respond best to sodium chloride, (B) five fibers that respond best to sucrose. (From Frank, 1973)

## CODING FOR TASTE QUALITY

What neural processes underlie the different taste qualities? According to specificity theory, these qualities are signaled by different fibers that carry the messages from the taste receptors to the brain. Electrical recording studies using rats and hamsters have shown that some of these fibers respond best when stimulated by sugar, others when stimulated by salt, still others by (very diluted) hydrochloric acid, and yet others by quinine, corresponding to the four primary taste sensations. According to specificity theorists, the taste quality conveyed by each taste fiber corresponds to the taste stimulus to which it responds most strongly. Thus, the fiber that responds best to sugar (the "sugar-best fiber") presumably signals sweet, the "quinine-best fiber" signals bitter, and so on. To the extent that any substance stimulates several taste fibers (and most substances do), the result will be a taste mixture. Evidence for this view comes from a comparison of two sugars: sucrose and fructose. Both rats and humans prefer sucrose to fructose, even though both sugars stimulate the sugar-best fibers (the ones that presumably signal "sweet"). The preference probably comes about because fructose also stimulates the salt-best fiber. As a result, its taste is a mixture of sweet and salty, which is less preferred. Whether these results are best explained by the specificity theory or by some version of the pattern theory is still a matter of debate (Bartoshuk, 1988; see Figure 5.8; adapted from Nowlis and Frank, 1981).

## TASTE AND SENSORY INTERACTION

The sense of taste provides an illustration of a pervasive principle that holds for most (perhaps all) of the other senses and that we will here call *sensory interaction.* It describes the fact that a sensory system's response to any given stimulus rarely depends on that stimulus alone. It is also affected by other stimuli that impinge, or have recently impinged, upon that system.

One kind of sensory interaction occurs over time. Suppose one taste stimulus is presented continuously for fifteen seconds or more. The result will be *adaptation,* a phenomenon that is found in virtually all sensory systems. If the tongue is continually stimulated with the identical taste stimulus, sensitivity to that taste will quickly decline. For example, after continuous exposure to a quinine solution, the quinine will taste less and less bitter and may finally appear to be completely tasteless. This adaptation process is reversible, however. If the mouth is rinsed out and left unstimulated for, say, a minute, the original taste sensitivity will be restored in full.

In another form of interaction, the adaptation to one taste quality may lead to the enhancement of another, an effect that is sometimes regarded as a form of contrast. For example, adaptation to sugar makes an acid taste even sourer than before (Kuznicki and McCutcheon, 1979). A related effect is the change in the taste of ordinary tap water after prior adaptation to various substances. Adaptation to a salty solution will make water taste sour or bitter; adaptation to one that's sweet will make it taste bitter (McBurney and Shick, 1971).

## The Sense of Smell

Thus far, our discussion has centered on the sensory systems that tell us about objects and events close to home: the movements and position of our own body, what we feel with our skin, and what we put in our mouth. But we clearly receive information from much farther off. We have three main receptive systems that enlarge our world by responding to stimuli at a distance: smell, hearing, and vision.

### THE OLFACTORY STIMULUS

Smell, or to use the more technical term, **olfaction,** provides information about chemicals suspended in air that excite receptors located in a small area at the top of our nasal cavity, the **olfactory epithelium** (see Figure 5.9). There is still considerable debate about the nature of the chemicals that act as effective olfactory stimuli ("odorants") and the way in which they set off the olfactory receptors. Several classification schemes exist for describing all odors by reference to a number of primary smell sensations, for example, *fragrant* (rose), *spicy* (cinnamon), and putrid (rotten eggs). But as yet, there is no agreement about the underlying principle that makes certain chemicals arouse one of these olfactory experiences rather than another. At present, the best guess is that olfactory quality is not coded by particular receptors—with, say, one group of receptors responding to stimuli we call fragrant and another receptor group responding to stimuli we describe as putrid. Instead, the relevant sensory code for quality is probably a *pattern* of excitation across different receptor groups.

### SMELL AS AN INTERNAL SENSE

Olfaction is a distance sense, but it is also a sense that can refer to things much closer by —in fact, to objects inside our own mouths (Rozin, 1982). We can smell the spaghetti on our plate, but we can also sense its flavor when we take a forkful in our mouth. That flavor—as indeed all flavors—depends largely on our sense of smell. For what we commonly call the "taste of food" is very rarely the sensation of taste alone; it is almost always a combination of taste, texture, tempera-

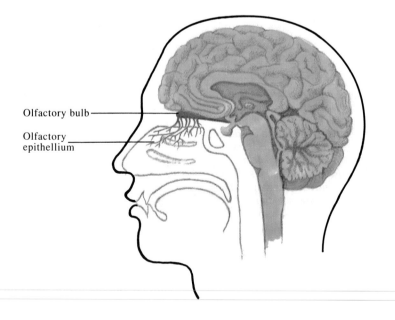

**5.9   The olfactory apparatus**   *Chemicals suspended in the air that flows through the nasal passages stimulate receptors in the olfactory epithelium which relay their information to a structure in the forebrain, the olfactory bulb. (After Amoore et al., 1964; Carlson, 1986)*

Olfactory bulb

Olfactory epithellium

ture, and—most important of all—smell. When our nose is completely stuffed up by a cold, food appears to be without any flavor. While we can still experience the basic taste sensations, the aroma is lost, and so the food seems "tasteless." If smell is gone, we can no longer distinguish between vinegar and a fine red wine, or between an apple and an onion. To be a gourmet (or a chef or a wine taster), you need a sensitive nose even more than you need a tongue.

### SMELL AS A DISTANCE SENSE

As a distance sense, smell plays a relatively minor part for humans. It is clearly less important to us than it is to many other species. In this regard we are similar to our primate cousins and to birds, in that these animals all left the odor-impregnated ground to move up into the trees, an environment in which other senses, especially vision, became more critical. In contrast, smell is of vital importance to many ground dwellers such as dogs. For them, it furnishes a guide to food and to receptive mates, and it may give warning against certain natural enemies. Modern psychophysical methods allow us to determine just how much more sensitive the dog's nose is compared to our own; it turns out that the ratio in sensitivities is about a thousand to one (Marshall and Moulton, 1981; Cain, 1988).

Compared to dogs and most other land-dwelling animals, we are evidently olfactory incompetents. But that doesn't mean that smell is of no relevance to human life. It does warn us of impending danger, as when we sniff escaping gas; it greatly adds to our enjoyment of food; and it provides the basis of the perfume and deodorant industries. According to some reports, it even helps to sell luggage and used cars; plastic briefcases saturated with artificial leather scents and second-hand cars permeated with a "new car" odor are said to have greater market value (Winter, 1976). In addition, smell evidently plays a role in identifying other persons. In one study, a psychologist asked men and women to wear T-shirts for twenty-four hours without taking a shower or using perfumes or deodorants. After the twenty-four hours were up, each (unwashed) T-shirt was sealed in a separate bag. Every subject was then asked to sniff the contents of three of these bags without looking inside. One contained his or her T-shirt, a second the T-shirt worn by another man, a third the T-shirt worn by another woman. About three-quarters of the subjects were able to identify their own T-shirt based only on its odor, and could also correctly identify which of the other T-shirts had been worn by a man or by a woman (Russell, 1976; McBurney, Levine, and Cavanaugh, 1977). This sensitivity to human odors starts in the nursery. Thus babies apparently respond to the odor of their own mother's breast and underarm odor in preference to the odors of a strange mother (Russell, 1976; Cernoch and Porter, 1985). Generally speaking, females perform better than males on these and other olfactory-related tasks (a difference that seems to be present from earliest infancy), and younger people do better than older ones (Balogh and Porter, 1986; Cain, 1988).

### PHEROMONES

In many species, olfaction has a function beyond those we have discussed thus far. It represents a primitive form of communication. Certain animals secrete special chemical substances called **pheromones** that trigger particular reactions in other members of their own kind. Some pheromones affect reproductive behavior. In many mammals, the female secretes a chemical (often in the urine) that signals that she is sexually receptive. In some species, the male sends chemical return messages to the female. For example, boars apparently secrete a pheromone that renders the sow immobile so that she stands rigid during mating (Michael and Keverne, 1968).

Other pheromones signal alarm. It appears that some animals can smell danger. To be more exact, they can smell a substance secreted by members of their own species who have been frightened. Thus rats who suffer an electric shock in an experimental chamber seem to exude a chemical that induces fear in other rats that are exposed to a whiff of the air from that same chamber (Valenta and Rigby, 1968).

Are there pheromones in humans? There may be some vestigial remains. One line of evidence concerns the development of *menstrual synchrony.* Women who live together, for example, in college dormitories, tend to develop menstrual cycles that roughly coincide with each other, even though their periods had been very different at the start of the school year (McClintock, 1971). Some recent studies suggest that this synchrony is primed by olfactory cues. Female subjects exposed to the body odor of a "donor" woman gradually shifted their menstrual cycles toward that of the donor, even though the subjects and the donors never saw each other (Russell, Switz, and Thompson, 1980).

Of potentially greater interest is the possibility of discovering an olfactory sex attractant that operates like a kind of pheromone. Thus far, there has been little to whet the financial appetites of perfume manufacturers or the erotic hopes of male or female Lonely Hearts. At best, there may be some faint remnants. One line of evidence comes from olfactory thresholds to certain musklike substances similar to that secreted by boars. Sexually mature women are vastly more sensitive to the smell of these compounds than are men or sexually immature girls. This sensitivity fluctuates with the woman's menstrual cycle and seems to reach a peak during ovulation. An intriguing speculation is that the receptive female's greater sensitivity to this odor points to the existence of a human male pheromone in our evolutionary past. Perhaps it is still present in a greatly attenuated form, but if so its effects are almost certainly too weak to be of any practical significance. Drenching himself in boar's musk and wearing Tom Cruise's unwashed T-shirt (or Mel Gibson's or Kevin Costner's) will not transform the universally rejected suitor into a matinee idol pursued by all women (or at least those near enough to smell him).

## Hearing

The sense of hearing, or *audition,* is a close relative of other receptive senses that react to mechanical pressure, such as the vestibular senses or touch. Like these, hearing is a response to pressure, but with a difference—it informs us of pressure changes in the world that may take place many meters away. In effect, then, hearing is feeling at a distance.

### SOUND

What is the stimulus for hearing? Outside in the world there is some physical movement which disturbs the air medium in which it occurs. This may be an ani-

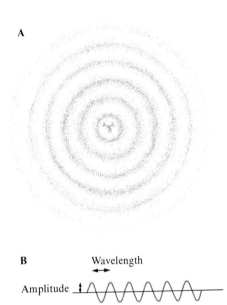

**5.10  The stimulus for hearing**  *(A) The figure depicts a momentarily frozen field of vibration in air. An insect vibrating its wings rapidly leads to waves of compression in the surrounding air. These waves travel in all directions like ripples in a pond into which a stone has been thrown. (B) The corresponding wave pattern is shown in simplified form. The amplitude of the wave is the height of each crest; the wavelength is the distance between successive crests. (From Gibson, 1966)*

mal scurrying through the underbrush or a rock dropping from a cliff or a set of vibrating vocal cords. The air particles directly adjacent to the movement are agitated, push particles that are ahead of them, and then return to their original position. Each individual air particle moves back and forth for just a tiny bit, but this is enough to set up a series of successive pressure variations in the air medium. These travel in a wave form analogous to the ripples set up by a stone thrown into a pond. When these **sound waves** hit our ears, they initiate a set of further mechanical pressure changes which ultimately trigger the auditory receptors. These initiate various further neural responses in the brain which ultimately lead to an experience of something that is heard rather than felt (which is yet another example of the operation of Müller's doctrine of specific nerve energies).

Sound waves can vary in both **amplitude** and **wavelength.** Amplitude refers to the height of a wave crest: the greater the intensity of the vibration, the higher this crest will be. Wavelength is simply the distance between successive crests. Sound waves are generally described by their **frequency,** which is the number of waves per second. Since the speed of sound is constant within any given medium, frequency is inversely proportional to wavelength (Figure 5.10).

Both amplitude and frequency are physical dimensions. Our brain translates these into the psychological dimensions of **loudness** and **pitch.** Roughly speaking, a sound will appear to be louder as its amplitude increases and will appear more high-pitched as its frequency goes up.

*Amplitude and loudness*  The range of amplitudes to which humans can respond is enormous. Investigators have found it convenient to use a scale which compresses this unwieldy range into a more convenient form. To this end, they developed a logarithmic scale that describes sound intensities in *decibels* (Table 5.4). Perceived loudness doubles every time the physical intensity (that is, the amplitude) goes up by 10 decibels. The physical stimulus intensity rises more steeply, increasing by a factor of 10 every 20 decibels (Stevens, 1955).

Table 5.4    INTENSITY LEVELS OF VARIOUS COMMON SOUNDS

| Sound | Intensity level (decibels) |
|---|---|
| Manned spacecraft launching (from 150 feet) | 180 |
| Loudest rock band on record | 160 |
| Pain threshold (approximate) | 140 |
| Loud thunder; average rock band | 120 |
| Shouting | 100 |
| Noisy automobile | 80 |
| Normal conversation | 60 |
| Quiet office | 40 |
| Whisper | 20 |
| Rustling of leaves | 10 |
| Threshold of hearing | 0 |

*Frequency and pitch*  The frequency of a sound wave is generally measured in **hertz** ($H_z$), or waves per second (so-called after the nineteenth-century German physicist Heinrich Hertz). The frequencies associated with some musical tones

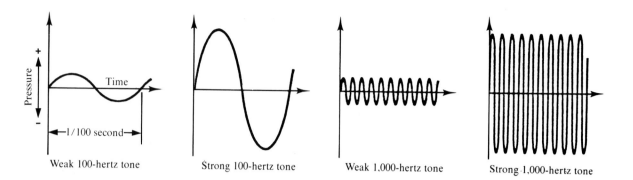

Weak 100-hertz tone     Strong 100-hertz tone     Weak 1,000-hertz tone     Strong 1,000-hertz tone

**5.11 Simple wave forms vary in frequency and amplitude** *Simple sound waves can be graphically expressed by plotting air-pressure change over time. The result is a so-called sine curve. These curves show the sine waves for a weak and a strong 100-hertz tone (relatively low in pitch) and a strong and a weak 1,000-hertz tone (comparatively high pitch). (After Thompson, 1973)*

are shown in Table 5.5. Young adults can hear tones as low as 20 hertz and as high as 20,000 hertz, with maximal sensitivity to a middle region in between. As people get older, their sensitivity to sound declines, especially at the higher frequencies.

*Simple and complex waves*   Thus far we have only dealt with simple wave forms. These are made up of waves that have only one frequency. Such waves are very rare in nature; they are produced by special electronic devices or by tuning forks. When such simple waves are expressed graphically, with pressure change plotted against time, they yield curves that correspond to the plot of the trigonometric sine function. Accordingly, such curves are called *sine waves* (Figure 5.11).

The sounds encountered in normal life are virtually never as simple as this. Instead, they are composed of many different waves, which differ in both frequency and amplitude. An example is this (relatively simple) *complex wave:*

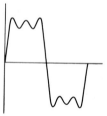

This complex wave can be physically produced by the acoustic mixture of three simple tones which correspond to three sine waves, as shown below:

The point of this example is that the auditory system can analyze complex waves into their component parts. We can hear the separate notes that make up a chord; the tones are mixed, but we can unmix them. This ability has its limits. If the sound is made up of a great number of unrelated waves, it is perceived as *noise,* which we can no longer analyze (Figure 5.12).

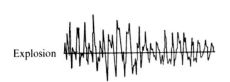

**5.12 An irregular sound wave—an explosion** *As in the previous figures, pressure change is plotted against time; but now there is no more regularity, so the wave form cannot readily be analyzed into its simpler components. (From Boring, Langfeld, and Weld, 1939)*

Table 5.5 SOUND FREQUENCIES OF SOME MUSICAL TONES

| Sound | Frequency (hertz) |
|---|---|
| Top note of grand piano | 4214 |
| Top note of piccolo | 3951 |
| Top range of soprano voice | 1152 |
| Top range of alto voice | 640 |
| Middle C | 256 |
| Bottom range of baritone voice | 96 |
| Bottom range of bass voice | 80 |
| Bottom note of contra bassoon | 29 |
| Bottom note of grand piano | 27 |
| Bottom note of organ* | 16 |

* Can be felt but not heard
SOURCE: After Geldard, 1972.

GATHERING THE PROXIMAL STIMULUS

Most of the ear is made up of various anatomical structures whose function is to gather the proximal stimulus—they conduct and amplify sound waves so that they can affect the auditory receptors (Figure 5.13). Sound waves collected by the outer ear are funneled toward a taut membrane which they cause to vibrate. This is the *eardrum* which transmits its vibrations across an air-filled cavity, the *middle ear,* to another membrane, the *oval window,* that separates the middle from the *inner ear.* This transmission is accomplished by way of a mechanical bridge built of three small bones that are collectively known as the *ossicles.* The vibrations of the eardrum move the first ossicle, which then moves the second, which in turn moves the third, which completes the chain by imparting the vibratory pattern to the oval window to which it is attached. The movements of the oval window set up waves in a fluid which fills the *cochlea,* a coiled tube in the inner ear which contains the auditory receptors.

Why did nature choose such a roundabout method of sound transmission? The major reason is that the cochlear medium is a fluid which like all liquids is harder to set into motion than air. To overcome this difficulty, the physical stimulus must be amplified. This amplification is provided by various features of the middle-ear organization. One involves the relative sizes of the eardrum and of

**5.13 The human ear** *Air enters through the outer ear and stimulates the eardrum which sets the ossicles in the middle ear in motion. These in turn transmit their vibration to the membrane of the oval window which causes movement of the fluid in the cochlea of the inner ear. Note that the semicircular canals are anatomically parts of the inner ear. (After Lindsay and Norman, 1977)*

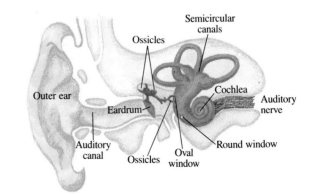

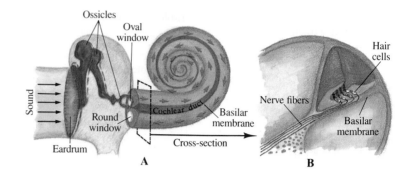

**5.14   Detailed structure of the middle ear and the cochlea**   (A) Movement of the fluid within the cochlea deforms the basilar membrane and stimulates the hair cells that serve as the auditory receptors. (After Lindsay and Norman, 1977) (B) Cross-section of the cochlea showing the basilar membrane and the hair cell receptors. (After Coren and Ward, 1989)

that portion of the oval window moved by the ossicles; the first is about twenty times larger than the second. The result is the transformation of a fairly weak force that acts on the entire eardrum into a much stronger pressure that is concentrated upon the (much smaller) oval window.

TRANSDUCTION IN THE COCHLEA

Throughout most of its length the cochlea is divided into an upper and lower section by several structures including the **basilar membrane.** The auditory receptors are so-called **hair cells** which are lodged between the basilar membrane and other membranes above it. Motion of the oval window produces pressure changes in the cochlear fluid which in turn lead to vibrations of the basilar membrane. As the basilar membrane vibrates, its deformations bend the hair cells and provide the immediate stimulus for their activity (Figure 5.14).

How does the activity of the auditory receptors lead to the sensory properties of auditory experience? Much of the work in the area has focused upon the perception of **pitch,** the sensory quality that depends upon the frequency of the stimulating sound wave.

*Basilar place and pitch*   According to the **place theory** of pitch, first proposed by Hermann von Helmholtz (1821–1894), different parts of the basilar membrane are responsive to different sound frequencies. In Helmholtz's view, the nervous system will then interpret the excitations from different basilar places as different pitches. The stimulation of receptors at one end of the membrane will lead to the experience of a high tone, while that of receptors at the other end leads to the sensation of a low tone.

Today we know that Helmholtz was correct at least in part. The classical studies were performed by Georg von Békésy (1899–1972) whose work on auditory function won him the Nobel Prize in 1961. Some of Békésy's experiments used cochleas taken from fresh human cadavers. Békésy removed part of the cochlear wall so that he could observe the basilar membrane through a microscope when the oval window was vibrated by an electrically powered piston. He found that such stimulation led to a wavelike motion of the basilar membrane (Figure 5.15). When he varied the frequency of the vibrating stimulus, the peak of the deformation produced by this wave pattern occurred in different regions of the membrane: high frequencies corresponded to regions close to the oval window, low ones to regions close to the cochlear tip (Békésy, 1957).

*Sound frequency and frequency of neural firing*   The place theory of pitch faces a major difficulty. As the frequency of the stimulus gets lower and lower, the defor-

*Georg von Békésy (1899–1972)*
*(Courtesy Nobel Stiftelsen)*

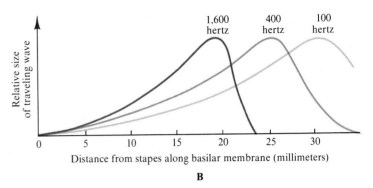

**A**

**B**

Relative size of traveling wave

1,600 hertz   400 hertz   100 hertz

Distance from stapes along basilar membrane (millimeters)

**5.15   The deformation of the basilar membrane by sound** *(A) In this diagram, the membrane is schematically presented as a simple, rectangular sheet. In actuality, of course, it is much thinner and coiled in a spiral shape. (B) The relation between sound frequency and the location of the peak of the basilar membrane's deformation. The peak of the deformation is located at varying distances from the stapes (the third ossicle, which sets the membrane in motion by pushing at the oval window). As the figure shows, the higher the frequency of the sound, the closer to the stapes this peak will be. (After Lindsay and Norman, 1977; Coren and Ward, 1989)*

***Hermann von Helmholtz (1821–1894)***
*(Courtesy National Library of Medicine)*

mation pattern it produces gets broader and broader. At very low frequencies (say, below 50 hertz), the wave set up by the tone deforms the entire membrane just about equally so that all receptors will be equally excited. But since we can discriminate low frequencies down to about 20 hertz, the nervous system must have some means for sensing pitch in addition to basilar location.

It is generally believed that this second means for sensing pitch is related to the firing frequency of the auditory nerve. For lower frequencies, the basilar membrane vibrates at the frequency of the stimulus tone and this vibration rate is then directly translated into the appropriate number of neural impulses per second, as evidenced by gross electrical recordings taken from the auditory nerve. The impulse frequency of the auditory output is further relayed to higher centers which somehow interpret it as pitch.

A further fact leads to some complications. A neuron cannot fire more often than about 1,000 times per second (see Chapter 2). While this would suggest that the impulse-frequency mechanism does not apply to tones higher than 1,000 hertz, its potential range has been extended to tones of still higher frequency by the *volley theory.* This proposes that impulse frequencies above 1,000 per second are generated by different squads of neurons, each of which is firing at a slightly different pace. For example, consider two neurons, both responding at a uniform rate of 1,000 impulses per second. If the second neuron starts to respond half a millisecond after the first, then the combined firing rate for both of them will be 2,000 impulses per second. In principle, this may allow even higher firing rates for the auditory nerve considered as a whole. Various lines of evidence suggest that some such mechanism may operate up to frequencies of about 4,000 hertz.

It appears then that pitch perception is based upon two separate mechanisms: higher frequencies are coded by the place of excitation on the basilar membrane, lower frequencies by the frequency of the neural impulses (which may involve the volley principle or some other means of sensing the timing pattern of neural firing). It is not clear where the one mechanism leaves off and the other takes over. Place of excitation is probably relatively unimportant at frequencies below 500–1,000 hertz and has no role below 50 hertz, while impulse frequency has little or no effect for tones above 5,000 hertz. In all probability, sound frequencies in between are handled by both mechanisms (Green, 1976; Goldstein, 1989).

## The Senses: Some Common Principles

In our discussion of the various senses, we have come across many ways in which they differ. We have also encountered a number of important phenomena that are not specific to any one sensory system but are found more generally.

**175**

First, in most sense modalities, the processing of external stimulus energies begins with various structures which gather and amplify these physical energies and thereby fashion a "better" proximal stimulus for the receptors to work on. An example is provided by the semicircular canals which contain a liquid that is set in motion by head rotation and then stimulates the hair cell receptors of the vestibular system.

Second, in all sense modalities, the next step involves the receptors which achieve the **transduction** of the physical stimulus energy into an electrical signal. In some sensory systems, particularly hearing and vision, the nature of this transduction process is reasonably well understood. In other systems, such as smell, it is still unknown.

Third, the processing of stimulus input does not stop at the receptor level. There are typically further neural centers at which **coding** occurs. The stimulus information is coded (so to speak, translated) into the various dimensions of sensation that we actually experience. Some of these dimensions involve intensity. In taste, we have more or less bitter; in hearing, we have more or less loud. Other dimensions involve differences in quality. In taste, we have the differences between bitter, sweet, sour, and salty; in hearing, we have differences in pitch.

Fourth, any part of a sensory system is in **interaction** with the rest of that system. This process of interaction pertains both to the immediate past and to present activity in neighboring parts of the system. We considered some examples of sensory interaction in the taste system, including the phenomena of adaptation (with continued exposure, quinine tastes less bitter) and taste contrast (sugar on one side of the tongue makes salt on the other side taste saltier).

## VISION

We now turn to a detailed discussion of vision, which in humans is the distance sense *par excellence.* The organization of this account will reflect characteristics which are common to most of the senses. Specifically, we will (1) describe the eye as a structure for gathering the visual stimulus, (2) examine the transduction of light energies by the visual receptors, (3) discuss some interaction processes found in vision, and (4) consider the coding processes that are involved in experiencing a particular sensory quality—in the case of vision, color.

### The Stimulus: Light

Most visual sensations have their point of origin in some external (distal) object. Occasionally, this object will be a light source which **emits** light in its own right; examples (in rather drastically descending order of emission energy) are the sun, an electric light bulb, and a glow worm. All other objects can only give off light if some light source illuminates them. They will then **reflect** some portion of the light cast upon them while absorbing the rest.

The stimulus energy we call light comes from the relatively small band of radiations to which our visual system is sensitive. These radiations travel in a wave form which is somewhat analogous to the pressure waves that are the stimulus for hearing. This radiation can vary in its **intensity,** the amount of radiant energy in

**5.24** **Contrast** *(A) "Arcturus" by Victor Vasarely. The luminous rays are not in the painting itself but are created by brightness contrast. Note that the painting consists of a series of frames, which surround other frames and become progressively darker as they go from center to periphery. (© by ADAGP, Paris, 1981, and by permission of the Hirshhorn Museum and Sculpture Garden, Smithsonian Institution) (B) The figure focuses on three of the frames in the painting. Consider squares 1, 3, and 4 in frame B. Squares 1 and 4 each have an entire side next to the brighter frame C above them. As a result, they look darker because of brightness contrast. But square 3 suffers little contrast, for it only touches on the brighter frame at its corner. It therefore looks brighter than the two squares 1 and 4 that are adjacent to it. For the same reason, squares 2 and 6 in frame A will seem to be darker than square 5. Since this happens for all the squares at the corners, the observer sees four radiating luminous diagonals. (Jameson, 1975)*

A

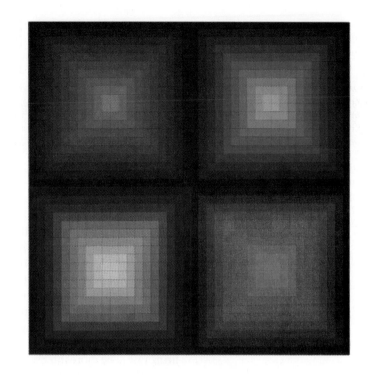

B

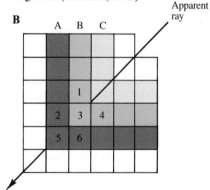

stimulus is outlined sharply. The contours of the retinal image are sharpened, for the visual system recreates, and even exaggerates, boundaries by the same mechanisms that generate Mach bands.

A PHYSIOLOGICAL ACCOUNT OF CONTRAST

What is the physiological mechanism that underlies brightness contrast? Today we know that the effect is based on the mutual inhibition of cells in the retina and higher up. The conclusive demonstration that this is so had to await the techniques of modern electrophysiology. But more than fifty years before this, such sensory psychologists as Ernst Mach and Ewald Hering (1834–1918) had postulated precisely such a process on the basis of what they observed in the sensory laboratory. In their view, the phenomena of contrast and Mach bands could be explained in no other way. In this regard, Mach and Hering resemble Sherrington

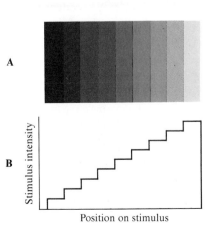

**5.25** **Mach bands** *(A) The series of gray strips is arranged in ascending brightness, from left to right. Physically, each strip is of uniform light intensity. This is graphically expressed in (B) which plots stimulus position against the physical light intensity, showing a simple series of ascending steps. But this is not what is seen, for the strips do not appear to be uniform. For each strip, the left edge (adjacent to its darker neighbor) looks brighter than the rest, while the right edge (adjacent to the lighter neighbor) looks darker. The explanation is contrast. The edges are closer to their darker or lighter neighbors, and will thus be more subject to contrast than the rest of the strip. The result is an accentuation of the contours that separate one strip from the next. (After Cornsweet, 1970; Coren, Porac, and Ward, 1978)*

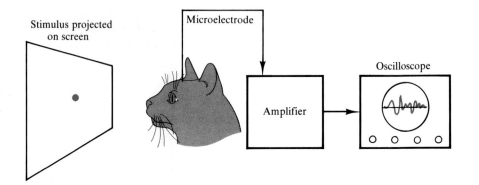

**5.26   Recording from the visual system of a cat**   *The experimental setup for recording neural responses from the visual system of a cat. An anesthetized cat has one eye propped open so that visual stimulation can be directed to particular regions of the retina. A microelectrode picks up neural impulses from a single cell in the optic system, amplifies them, and displays them on an oscilloscope. (After Schiffman, 1976)*

who inferred the synapse on the basis of behavioral data alone, many decades before there was any means for providing physiological proof.

The modern physiological account of contrast effects is based on single-cell recording methods. The first step is to place a microelectrode in a cat's optic nerve so that it picks up electrical activity from only one cell. The eye of an anesthetized animal is propped open and is stimulated by spots of light of varying intensities and at different locations (Figure 5.26). We find that there is a small region of the retina whose stimulation leads to an increase in the cell's normal firing rate. The more intense the light, the greater the cell's response. But this central region is surrounded by a region in which illumination has the opposite effect. Here, illumination depresses the cell's firing rate, and this depression increases with increases in the light intensity (Figure 5.27). The entire area of the retina in which stimulation by light affects the cell's firing rate—whether up or down—is called the *receptive field* of that cell.

*Lateral inhibition*   The results show that neighboring regions in the retina tend to inhibit each other. The reason is a process called *lateral inhibition* (in effect, it is inhibition exerted sideways). A simplified version of how this mechanism works is as follows: When any visual receptor is stimulated, it transmits its excitation upward to other cells that eventually relay it to the brain. But this excitation has a further effect. It also stimulates some neurons that extend sideways along the retina. These lateral cells make contact with neighboring cells whose activation they inhibit.

To see how lateral inhibition works, consider the retinal image produced by a gray patch surrounded by a lighter ring (Figure 5.28). For the sake of simplicity, we will only look at two neighboring receptor cells, *A* and *B*. *A* is stimulated by

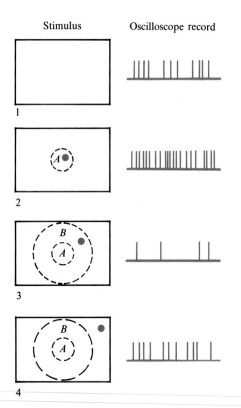

Stimulus    Oscilloscope record

**5.27   Receptive fields on the cat's visual system**   *Using the setup shown in Figure 5.26, stimuli are presented to various regions of the retina. The panels show the firing frequency of a particular ganglion cell. Panel 1 shows the base-level firing rate when no stimulus is presented anywhere. Panel 2 shows the effect when a stimulus is presented anywhere within an inner, central region, A, on the retina. When stimulated in A, the cell's firing rate goes up. Panel 3 shows what happens in response to a stimulus presented anywhere within the ring-shaped region, B, surrounding region A. Stimulation in B causes the cell's firing rate to go down. Panel 4, finally, shows what happens when a stimulus is presented outside of either A or B, the regions that together comprise the cell's receptive field. Now there is no significant change from the cell's normal base level. (From Kuffler, 1953)*

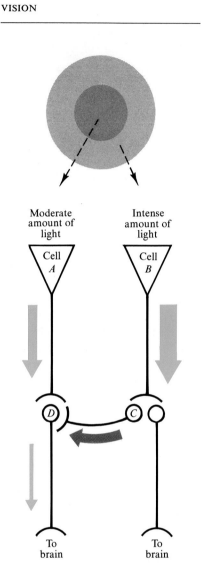

**5.28 Lateral inhibition and contrast**
*Two receptor cells, A and B, are stimulated by neighboring regions of a stimulus. A receives moderate stimulation; B receives an intense amount of light. A's excitation serves to stimulate the next neuron in the visual chain, cell D, which transmits the message further toward the brain. But this transmission is impeded by cell B, whose own intense excitation exerts an inhibitory effect on its neighbors. B excites a lateral cell, C, which exerts an inhibitory effect on cell D. As a result, cell D fires at a reduced rate. (Excitatory effects are shown by green arrows, inhibitory ones by red arrows.)*

the gray patch and receives a moderate amount of light. *B* is stimulated by the lighter ring and receives much more light. Our primary interest is in the excitation which cell *A*, the one stimulated by the gray patch, relays upward to the brain. The more cell *A* is stimulated, the more excitation it will relay further, and the brighter the patch will appear to be. The important point is that the excitation from cell *A* will not be passed on unimpeded. On the contrary. Some of this excitation will be cancelled by inhibition from neighboring cells. Consider the effect of cell *B*, whose stimulation comes from the lighter ring. That cell is intensely excited. One result of this excitation is that it excites a third cell *C* whose effect is inhibitory and exerted sideways (in short, a lateral inhibitor). The effect of this lateral cell *C* is to block the excitation that *A* sends upward.

Lateral inhibition is the basis of brightness contrast. Let's go back to the three cells in Figure 5.28. The more intensely cell *B* is stimulated, the more it will excite the lateral inhibitor, cell *C*. This explains why a gray patch on a black background looks brighter than the same gray patch surrounded by white. The black background does not stimulate cell *B*, so that the lateral inhibitor *C* will not be active. But a white background will stimulate cell *B*, which excites cell *C*, which in its turn diminishes the excitation cell *A* sends upward to the brain to inform it of the apparent brightness of the gray patch. The upshot of all this is contrast. The brain gets a visual message that is an exaggeration. What is dark seems darker, what is light seems lighter.

## Color

Despite their many differences, the sensory systems of hearing and of vision have some things in common. In both, the relevant stimulus energy is in wave form. And in both, wavelength is related to a qualitative psychological dimension—in one case pitch, in the other color. Much of the research in both domains has revolved around the question of how these sensory qualities are coded. We will here consider only one of these domains, that of color.

There is little doubt that color perception concerns sensory quality rather than intensity. The sensation red is different from green or blue in a way that cannot be described as a matter of more or less. Since Müller's formulation of the doctrine of specific nerve energies, sensory psychologists have assumed that such qualitative differences in sensation imply a difference in the neural processes that underlie these qualities. In their search for the color mechanism, they were guided largely by psychological facts, using them to infer neurological processes that could not be verified directly given the techniques of their time. As in the case of lateral inhibition, some of these inferences have ultimately been confirmed by physiological evidence, in some cases a century after they were first proposed.

### CLASSIFYING THE COLOR SENSATIONS

A person with normal color vision can distinguish over seven million different color shades. What are the processes that allow him to make these distinctions? One step in answering this question is to find a classification system that will allow us to describe any one of these millions of colors by reference to a few simple dimensions. In this task we concentrate on what we see and experience, on psychology rather than physics. What we want to classify is our color sensations

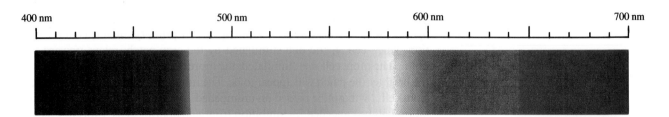

**5.29   The visible spectrum and the four unique hues**   *The visible spectrum consists of light waves from about 360 to 700 nanometers (1 nm = one millionth of a millimeter). White light contains all of these wavelengths. They are bent to different degrees when passed through a prism, yielding the spectrum with the hues shown in the figure. Three of the four unique hues correspond to part of the spectrum: unique blue at about 465 nm, unique green, at about 500 nm, and unique yellow, at about 570 nm. These values vary slightly from person to person. The fourth, unique red—that is, a red which has no apparent tinge of either yellow or blue—is called extraspectral because it is not represented by a single wavelength on the spectrum. It can only be produced by a mixture of wavelengths. (From Ohanian, 1984)*

rather than the physical stimuli that produce them. In doing so, we cannot help but discover something about the way our mind—that is, our nervous system—functions. Whatever order we may find in the classification of our sensations is at least partially imposed by the way in which our nervous system organizes the physical stimuli that impinge upon it.

*The dimensions of color*   Imagine seven million or so colored paper patches, one for each of the colors we can discriminate. We can classify them according to three perceived dimensions: hue, brightness, and saturation.

**Hue** is a term whose meaning is close to that of the word *color* as used in everyday life. It is a property of the so-called **chromatic colors** (for example, red and blue) but not of the **achromatic colors** (that is, black, white, and all of the totally neutral grays in between). Hue varies with wavelength (Figure 5.29). Thus, **unique blue** (a blue which is judged to have no trace of red or green in it), occurs on the spectrum at about 465 nanometers, **unique green** (which has no blue or yellow) at about 500 nanometers, and **unique yellow** (which has no green or red) at about 570 nanometers.

**Brightness** varies among both the chromatic and achromatic colors. Thus, ultramarine is darker than light blue and charcoal gray is darker than light gray (Figure 5.30). But the brightness dimension stands out most clearly if we consider achromatic colors alone. These differ in brightness only, while the chromatic colors may differ in hue (as we have seen) and in saturation (which we will discuss next). Note that white and black represent the top and bottom of the brightness

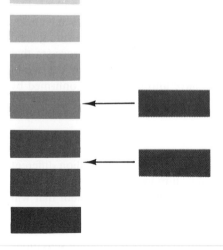

A                    B

**5.30   Brightness**   *Colors can be arranged according to their brightness. (A) This dimension is most readily recognized when we look at a series of grays, which are totally hueless and vary in brightness only. (B) Chromatic colors can also be classified according to their brightness. The arrows indicate the brightness of the blue and dark green shown here in relation to the series of grays.*

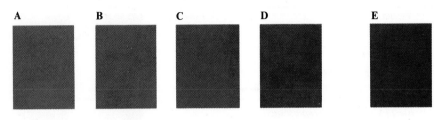

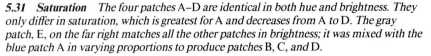

**5.31  Saturation**  *The four patches A–D are identical in both hue and brightness. They only differ in saturation, which is greatest for A and decreases from A to D. The gray patch, E, on the far right matches all the other patches in brightness; it was mixed with the blue patch A in varying proportions to produce patches B, C, and D.*

dimension. Thus, white is hueless and maximally bright; black is hueless and minimally bright.

*Saturation* is the "purity" of a color, the extent to which it is chromatic rather than achromatic. The more gray (or black or white) is mixed with a color, the less saturation it has. Consider the various blue patches in Figure 5.31. All have the same hue (blue). All have the same brightness as a particular, achromatic gray (which is also the same gray with which the blue was mixed to produce the less saturated blue patches, *A, B, C,* and *D*). The patches only differ in one respect: the proportion of blue as opposed to that of gray. The more gray there is, the less the saturation. When the color is entirely gray, saturation is zero. This holds for all colors.

*The color circle and the color solid*  Some hues appear to be very similar to others. Suppose we only consider the color patches that look most chromatic— that is, those whose saturation is maximal. If we arrange these on the basis of their perceptual similarity, the result is a circular series, the so-called ***color circle,*** such that red is followed by orange, orange by yellow, yellow-green, green, blue-green, blue and violet, until the circle finally returns to red (Figure 5.32).

The color circle embodies the perceptual similarities among the different hues. To complete our classificatory schema, we construct the so-called ***color solid*** which incorporates the color circle with the other two dimensions of perceived color, brightness, and saturation (Figure 5.33). Each of our original seven million

**5.32  The color circle**  *The relationship between maximally saturated hues can be expressed by arranging them in a circle according to their perceptual similarity. Note that in this version of the color circle, the spacing of the hues depends upon their perceptual properties rather than the wavelengths that give rise to them. In particular, the four unique hues are equally spaced, each 90 degrees from the next. (Hurvich, 1981)*

**5.33    The three dimensions of color**
*Brightness is represented by the central
axis, going from darkest (black) to
brightest (white). Hue is represented by
angular position relative to the color
circle. Saturation is the distance from the
central vertical axis. The farther the color is
from this axis, the more saturated it is.
The maximal saturation that is possible
varies from hue to hue; hence, the
different extensions from the central axis.
(Munsell Color, courtesy of Macbeth, a
division of Kollmorgen Corporation)*

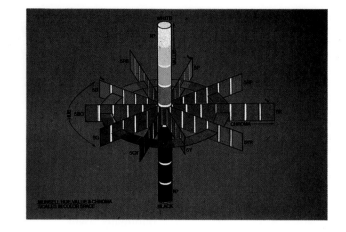

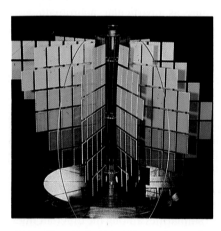

**5.34    The color solid**   *Every color can be
placed within a so-called color solid that is
based on the 3 dimensions of brightness,
hue, and saturation. The inside of the solid
is shown by taking slices that illustrate
variations in hue, brightness, and
saturation. (Munsell Color, courtesy of
Macbeth, a division of Kollmorgen
Corporation)*

color patches can be fitted into a unique position in this solid (Figure 5.34). Our classificatory task is thus accomplished.

COLOR MIXTURE

With rare exceptions, the objects in the world around us do not reflect a single wavelength; rather, they reflect different ones, all of which strike the same region of the retina simultaneously. Let us consider the results of some of these mixtures.

*Subtractive mixture*    Before proceeding, we must recognize that the kind of mixture sensory psychologists are interested in is very different from the sort artists employ when they stir pigments together on a palette. Mixing pigments on a palette (or smearing crayons together on a piece of paper) is **subtractive mixture.** In subtractive mixture, one set of wavelengths is subtracted from another set. The easiest demonstration is with colored filters, such as those used in stage lighting, which allow some wavelengths to pass through them while holding others back. Take two such filters, *A* and *B*. Suppose filter *A* allows passage to all light waves between 420 and 520 nanometers but no others. The broad range of light that comes through this filter will be seen as blue. In contrast, filter *B* passes light waves between 480 and 660 nanometers but excludes all others. The band of light waves that comes through this filter will be seen as yellow (Figure 5.35).

We now ask how we see light that has to pass through *both* filters. Filter *A* (the blue filter) blocks all light above 520 nanometers, while filter *B* (the yellow filter) blocks all light below 480 nanometers. As a result, the only light waves that can pass through this double barricade are those that can slip through the narrow gap between 480 and 520 nanometers, the only interval left unblocked by *both* filters. As it happens, light in this interval is seen as green. Thus, when the mixture is subtractive, mixing blue and yellow will yield green.

Thus far we have dealt with filters which let some wavelengths through while blocking others. The same account also applies to artists' pigments. Any pigment reflects only a certain band of wavelengths while absorbing the rest. Suppose we mix pigment *A* (say, blue) to pigment *B* (say, yellow). The result is a form of subtraction. What we will see is the wavelengths reflected by the blue pigment (420

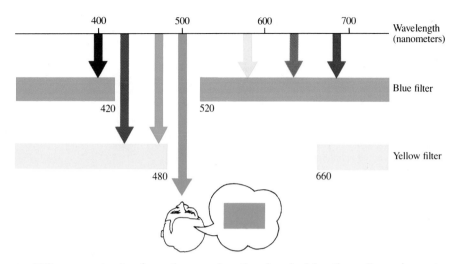

**5.35  Subtractive mixture**  *In subtractive mixture, the light passed by two filters (or reflected by two mixed pigments) is the band of wavelengths passed by the first minus that region which is subtracted by the second. In the present example, the first filter passes light between 420 and 520 nanometers (a broad-band blue filter), while the second passes light between 480 and 660 nanometers (a broad-band yellow filter). The only light that can pass through both is in the region between 480 and 520 nanometers, which appears green.*

to 520 nanometers) minus the wavelengths absorbed by the yellow pigment (everything below 480 nanometers). The effect is exactly the same as if we had superimposed a blue filter over a yellow one. All that is reflected is light between 480 and 520 nanometers, which is seen as green.

*Additive mixture*  In subtractive mixture, one set of wavelengths is removed from another set. In another kind of mixture, the procedure is the very opposite. This is ***additive mixture,*** which occurs when different bands of wavelengths stimulate the same retinal region simultaneously. Such additive mixtures can be produced in the laboratory by using filtered light from two different projectors which are focused on the same spot. As a result, the light from each filtered source will be reflected back to the same retinal area (Figure 5.36).

In real life, additive mixture has many uses. One is color television, in which the additive mixture is accomplished by three different sets of photosensitive substances. Another example is provided by the Pointillist painter Georges Seurat. He used dots of different colors that are too close together to be seen separately, especially when the picture is viewed from a distance (Figure 5.37).

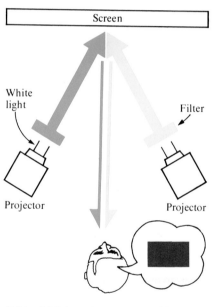

**5.36  Additive mixture**  *In additive mixture, the light passed by two filters (or reflected by two pigments) impinges upon the same region of the retina at the same time. The figure shows two projectors throwing blue and yellow filtered light upon the same portion of the screen from which it is reflected upon the same region of the retina. In contrast to what happens in subtractive mixture, the result of adding these two colors is gray.*

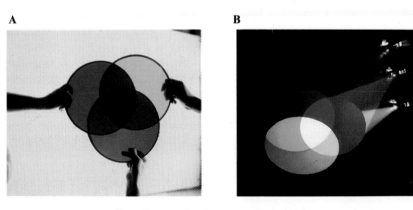

***Color mixture***  *The effect of (A) passing light through several filters (subtractive mixture), and (B) throwing different filtered lights upon the same spot (additive mixture). (Photographs by Fritz Goro/Life Magazine, © Time Warner, Inc.)*

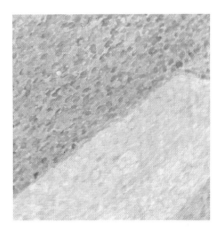

**5.37    Additive mixture in Pointillist art**    *The Channel of Gravelines (1890) by Georges Seurat. A detail of the painting (on the left) shows the separate color daubs which, when viewed from a distance, mix additively. The Pointillists employed this technique instead of mixing pigments to capture the bright appearance of colors outdoors. Pigment mixture is subtractive and darkens the resulting colors. (Courtesy Indianapolis Museum of Art, gift of Mrs. James W. Fesler in memory of Daniel W. and Elizabeth C. Marmon)*

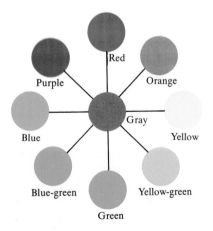

**5.38    Complementary hues**    *Any hue will yield gray if additively mixed (in the correct proportion) with a hue on the opposite side of the color circle. Such hue pairs are complementaries. Some complementary hues are shown here linked by a line across the circle's center. Of particular importance are the two complementary pairs that contain the four unique hues: red-green and blue-yellow.*

COMPLEMENTARY HUES

An important fact about additive color mixture is that every hue has a **complementary,** another hue which if mixed with the first in appropriate proportions will produce the color gray. An easy way to find complementaries is by reference to the color circle. Any hue on the circumference will yield gray if mixed (additively) with the hue on the opposite side of the color circle (see Figure 5.38). Of particular interest are the complementary pairs that involve the four **unique colors,** red, yellow, green, and blue. Blue and yellow are complementaries that produce gray upon additive mixture; the same holds for red and green. Hues that are not complementary produce mixtures that preserve the hue of their components. Thus, the mixture of red and yellow leads to orange (which still looks like a yellowish red) while that of blue and red yields a violet (which looks like a reddish blue).

At the risk of repetition, note that all of this holds only for additive mixture. When blue and yellow are additively mixed in the right proportions, the observer sees gray. This is in contrast to what happens when the mixture is subtractive, as in drawing a blue crayon over a yellow patch. Now the result is green. The same holds for red and green. Additive mixture of the two yields gray; subtractive mixture will produce a blackish brown.

COLOR ANTAGONISTS

The color-mixture effects we have just described suggest that color complementaries, such as blue and yellow on the one hand, and red and green on the other, are mutually opposed "antagonists" that cancel each other's hue. There are some further phenomena that lead to a similar conclusion.

190

**5.39 Color contrast** *The gray patches on the blue and yellow backgrounds are physically identical. But they don't look that way. To begin with, there is a difference in perceived brightness: the patch on the blue looks brighter than the one on the yellow, a result of brightness contrast. There is also a difference in perceived hue, for the patch on the blue looks somewhat yellowish, while that on the yellow looks bluish. This is color contrast, a demonstration that hues tend to induce their antagonists in neighboring areas.*

One effect is the chromatic counterpart of brightness contrast. In general, any region in the visual field tends to induce its complementary color in adjoining areas. The result is **simultaneous color contrast.** For example, a gray patch will tend to look bluish if surrounded by yellow, yellowish if surrounded by blue, and so on (Figure 5.39).

In simultaneous contrast, the complementary relation involves two adjoining regions in space. In a related phenomenon, the contrast is with an immediately preceding stimulus; it is a contrast in time rather than in space. Suppose we stare at a green patch for a while and then look at a white wall. We will see a reddish spot. This is a **negative afterimage** (Figure 5.40). Negative afterimages have the complementary hue and the opposite brightness of the original stimulus (which is why they are called negative). Thus, fixation on a brightly lit red bulb will make us see a dark greenish shape when we subsequently look at a white screen.

Afterimages are caused by events that occur in the retina and associated visual mechanisms. This is why, when the eye moves, the afterimage moves along with it. One reason for the effect is retinal adaptation. When we fixate a white disk on a black background, the pigments in the retinal region that corresponds to the disk will be stimulated more intensely than those in surrounding areas. During subsequent exposure to a homogeneous white surface, the more deeply stimulated regions will respond less vigorously and will thus report a lesser sensory intensity. The result is a dark gray negative afterimage. But peripheral adaptation is probably not the whole story. In addition, there may be a **rebound phenomenon.** While the inspection stimulus was still present, the excited regions may well have inhibited an antagonistic process. White held back black, blue inhibited yellow, and so on. When the stimulus is withdrawn, the inhibited processes rebound, like a coiled spring that is suddenly released.

**5.40 Negative afterimage** *Stare at the center of the figure for about a minute or two, and then look at a white piece of paper. Blink once or twice; the negative afterimage will appear within a few seconds showing the rose in its correct colors.*

### The Physiological Basis of Color Vision

What is the physiological basis of color vision? We will consider this issue by subdividing it into two questions: (1) How are wavelengths transduced into receptor activity? (2) How is the receptor output coded so that it yields the psychological attributes of color, such as the sensory experience of unique blue?

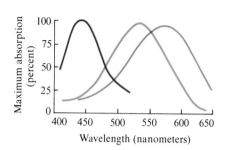

**5.41  Sensitivity curves of three different cones in the primate retina**  *The retinas of humans and monkeys contain three different kinds of cones, each with its own photopigments which differ in their sensitivity to different regions of the spectrum. One absorbs more of the shorter wavelengths (and is thus more sensitive to light in this spectral region), a second more of the middle wavelengths, a third more of the longer ones. The resulting sensitivity curves are shown here. (After MacNichol, 1964)*

*Ewald Hering*  (Courtesy National Library of Medicine)

## COLOR RECEPTORS

The raw material with which the visual system must begin is light of various intensities. Since we can discriminate among different wavelengths, there must be different receptors (that is, different types of cones) that are somehow differentially attuned to this physical dimension.

It turns out that normal human color vision depends on three different kinds of cone elements (which is why it is often called **trichromatic**). While each of these cone types responds to a broad range of wavelengths in the visible spectrum, their sensitivity curves differ in that one cone type is most sensitive to wavelengths in the short-wave region of the spectrum, the second to wavelengths in the middle range, and the third to the longer wavelengths (Bowmaker and Dartnall, 1980; MacNichol, 1986; see Figure 5.41).

The critical fact about all three cone elements is that their sensitivities overlap extensively so that most of the wavelengths of the visible spectrum stimulate each of the three receptor elements. This being so, how can we manage to discriminate different wavelengths? We can, because each receptor element will respond in differing degree depending upon the wavelength of the stimulus light. If the light is from the blue end of the spectrum, there will be maximum output from the cone element whose sensitivity is greatest in the short-wave region. If the light is from the orange end, it will elicit maximum activity from the cone element whose sensitivity is greatest in the long-wave region. As a result, each wavelength will produce a different ratio of the outputs of the three receptor types. Assuming that the nervous system can tell which receptor type is sending which message, wavelength discrimination follows.

## COLOR CODING: THE OPPONENT-PROCESS THEORY

The preceding analysis can explain how lights of different wavelengths are discriminated from each other, but can it account for why these lights *look* the way they do? One attempt to explain the psychological properties of color is the **trichromatic theory** (often called the **Young-Helmholtz theory** after Thomas Young and Hermann von Helmholtz who proposed it in the nineteenth century). According to the trichromatic theory, each of the three receptor types gives rise to the experience of one basic color. Stimulation of the short-wave receptor produces blue, stimulation of the medium-wave receptor produces green, and stimulation of the long-wave receptor produces red. According to the trichromatic theory, all other colors are essentially mixtures of the three colors that are said to be **primary**—red, green, and blue.

This interpretation of the way colors appear runs into a number of problems. Trichromatic theory asserts that all colors are produced by the mixture of the three primaries—red, green, and blue. But in fact, many colors don't look like mixtures of different proportions of red, green, and blue. Some do, such as purple, which looks like a mixture of red and blue. But many others do not. The most troublesome example is yellow, which *looks* like a primary but does not have primary status according to the trichromatic theory. An additional problem with trichromatic theory is that it cannot easily explain why the four unique hues form two complementary (and antagonistic) pairs: red-green and blue-yellow.

To explain phenomena of this kind we must assume some further neural mechanism that operates on the three receptor outputs and ultimately codes them into the sensory qualities we know as color. Such a further mechanism is proposed by the **opponent-process theory** formulated by Leo Hurvich and Dorothea Jameson which dates back to the nineteenth-century psychophysiologist, Ewald Hering. This theory asserts that there are six psychologically primary color qualities—red, green, blue, yellow, black, and white—each of which has a different neural process that corresponds to it. These six processes are not independent, but instead are organized into three opponent-process pairs: red-green, blue-yellow, and black-white. The two members of each pair are antagonists. Excitation of one member automatically inhibits the other (Hurvich and Jameson, 1957).

*The two hue systems* According to the opponent-process theory, the experience of hue depends upon two of three opponent-process pairs—red-green and blue-yellow. (As we will see, the black-white system is not relevant to perceived hue.) Each of these opponent-process pairs can be likened to a balance scale. If one arm (say, the blue process) goes down, the other arm (its opponent, yellow) necessarily comes up. The hue we actually see depends upon the position of the two balances (Figure 5.42). If the red-green balance is tipped toward red and the blue-yellow balance toward blue (excitation of red and blue with concomitant inhibition of green and yellow), the perceived hue will be violet. This follows, because the resulting hue will be a combination of red and blue, which is seen as violet. If either of the two scales is evenly balanced, it will make no contribution to the hue experience. This will occur when neither of the two antagonists is stimulated, and also when both are stimulated equally and cancel each other out. If both hue systems are in balance, there will be no hue at all and the resulting color will be seen as achromatic (that is, without hue).

*The black-white system* The brightness or darkness of a visual experience is determined by the activity of a third pair of antagonists, black and white. Every wavelength contributes to the excitation of the white system, in proportion to its intensity and the sensitivity of daylight vision to this point of the spectrum. The black process is produced by inhibition of the antagonistic white process. This is best exemplified by some phenomena of brightness contrast. A black paper placed against a dark gray background will look not black but a darker shade of gray. We can make it look pitch-black by presenting it against a brilliantly illuminated background. By doing so, we inhibit the white process within the enclosed region, which necessarily enhances the activity of its antagonist.

*The relation between color receptors and opponent processes* Can we reconcile the fact that there are three elements at the receptor level while there are four chromatic color opponents? Hurvich and Jameson have suggested a neural system that might produce the appropriate opponent-process reactions at some level beyond the receptor elements. The basic idea is that the three receptor elements have both excitatory and inhibitory connections with neurons higher up that correspond to opponent processes, and that one pole of each opponent process will be activated by excitation while its opposite pole will be activated by inhibition. (For details, see Figures 5.43A and B; adapted from Hurvich and Jameson, 1974).

THE PHYSIOLOGICAL BASIS OF OPPONENT PROCESSES

When the theory was first developed, the opponent processes were only an inference, based upon the perceptual phenomena of color vision. Today there is evi-

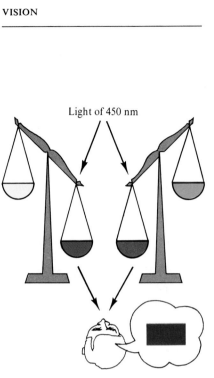

Light of 450 nm

Hue: Blue + Red = Violet

**5.42 The opponent-process hue systems** *The diagram shows how opponent-process theory interprets our response to light of a particular wavelength. In the example, the light is in the short-wave region of the visible spectrum, specifically, 450 nanometers. This will affect both the blue-yellow and the red-green systems. It will tip the blue-yellow balance toward blue, and the red-green balance toward red. The resulting hue will be a mixture of red and blue (that is, violet).*

A

Cone elements

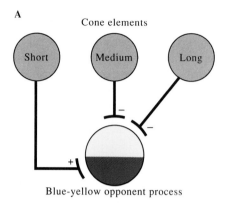

Blue-yellow opponent process

**5.43  From receptors to opponent-process pairs**  *A simplified presentation of a neural system in which all three receptor elements feed into two color opponent-process pairs. One pole of each opponent process is activated by excitation while its opposite pole is activated by inhibition. (A) The blue-yellow system.* This is excited by the short-wave receptors and inhibited by the medium- and the long-wave receptors. If excitation outweighs inhibition, the opponent-process signals blue; if inhibition outweighs excitation, it signals yellow; if excitation and inhibition are equal, there is no signal at all, and we see gray. *(B) The red-green system.* This is excited by both the short-wave and the long-wave receptor elements, and is inhibited by the medium-wave elements. If excitation outweighs inhibition, the system signals red; if inhibition outweighs excitation, it signals green; if excitation and inhibition are equal, there is no signal and we see gray. The assumption that this system is excited by both short- and long-wave receptors is made because the experience "red" occurs at the two extremes of the spectrum: short wavelengths produce the hues of violet or purple, which are perceived as having some red in them, while long wavelengths produce various oranges, which of course are also seen as having red in them. *(For discussion, see Hurvich and Jameson, 1974)*

B

Cone elements

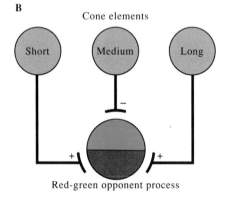

Red-green opponent process

dence that this inference was close to the neurophysiological mark. The proof comes from single-cell recordings (in the retina or higher up), which show that some neurons behave very much as an opponent-process theory would lead one to expect.

As an example, take a study of single-cell activity in the visual pathway of the rhesus monkey, whose color vision is known to be very similar to ours. Some of its visual cells behave as though they were part of a blue-yellow system. If the retina is stimulated by blue light, these cells fire more rapidly. The opposite holds true if the same area is exposed to yellow light—the firing rate is inhibited (Figure 5.44). This is exactly what should happen if the underlying color mechanism mirrors the perceptual phenomena. Blue should have one effect and yellow the opposite. Other cells have been discovered that show a similar antagonistic pattern when stimulated by red or by green light (de Valois, 1965).

COLOR BLINDNESS

A small proportion of the total population consists of people who do not respond to color as most others do. Of these the vast majority are men, since many such conditions are inherited and sex-linked. Some form of color defect is found in 8 percent of all males as compared to only .03 percent of females.

Color deficiencies come in various forms, some of which involve a missing visual pigment, others a defective opponent process, and many involve malfunction at both levels (Hurvich, 1981). Most common is a defect in which reds are confused with greens; least common is total color blindness in which no hues can be distinguished at all. Color defects are rarely noticed in everyday life, for color-blind persons ordinarily use color names quite appropriately. They call blood red and dollar bills green, presumably on the basis of other cues such as form and brightness. To determine whether a person has a color defect he or she must be tested under special conditions in which such extraneous cues are eliminated (Figure 5.45).

How do people with color defects see colors? We may know that a particular person cannot distinguish between red and green, but that does not tell us how these colors look to him. He cannot tell us, for he cannot know what sensory quality is lacking. The question would have remained unanswerable had it not

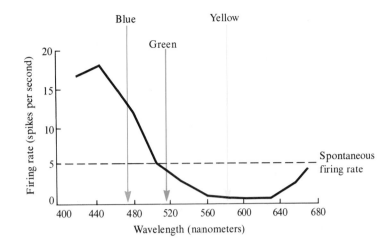

**5.44 Opponent-process cells in the visual system of a monkey** *The figure shows the average firing rate of "blue-yellow cells" to light of different wavelengths. These cells are excited by shorter wavelengths and inhibited by longer wavelengths, analogous to the cells in the human system that signal the sensation "blue." As the figure shows, shorter wavelengths lead to firing rates that are above the spontaneous rates obtained when there is no stimulus at all. Longer wavelengths have the opposite effect, depressing the cell's activity below the spontaneous firing rate. (Data from de Valois and de Valois, 1975)*

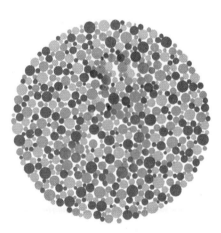

**5.45 Testing for color blindness** *A plate used to test for color blindness. To pick out the number in the plate, an observer has to be able to discriminate certain hues. Persons with normal color vision can do it and will see the number 3. Persons with red-green color blindness cannot do this.*

been for a subject who was red-green color blind in one eye and had normal color vision in the other. This subject (who happened to be one of the rare females with a color defect) was able to describe what she saw with the defective eye by using the color language of the normal one. With the color-blind eye she saw only grays, blues, and yellows. Red and green hues were altogether absent, as if one of the opponent-process pairs was missing (Graham and Hsia, 1954).

Let us take stock. We have looked at the way in which the different sensory systems respond to external stimuli, how they transduce the proximal stimulus and convert it into a neural impulse, how they code the incoming message into the various dimensions of our sensory experience, and how activity in any part of a sensory system interacts with the activity of other parts. All of this has led us to some understanding of how we come to see bright yellow-greens and hear high-pitched noises. But it has not yet addressed the question with which we started. How do we come to know about the objects and events outside—not just bright yellow-greens but grassy meadows, not just high-pitched noises but singing birds? That the sensory systems contribute the raw materials for such knowledge is clear enough. But how do we get from the sensory raw materials to a knowledge of the world outside? This question is traditionally dealt with under the heading of *perception,* the topic to which we turn next.

## SUMMARY

1. The study of sensory processes grew out of questions about the origin of human knowledge. John Locke and other *empiricists* argued that all knowledge comes through stimuli that excite the senses. We can distinguish two kinds of stimuli. One is the *distal stimulus,* an object or event in the world outside. The other is the *proximal stimulus,* the pattern of physical stimulus energies that impinges on a given sensory surface. The only way to get information about distal stimuli outside is through the proximal stimuli these give rise to. This leads to theoretical problems, for we perceive many qualities—depth, constant size and shape—that are not given in the proximal stimulus. Empiricists try to overcome such difficulties by asserting that much of perception is built up through learning by *association.* This view has been challenged by *nativists* such as Immanuel Kant who believe that the sensory input is organized according to a number of built-in categories.

**195**

2. The path to sensory experience or *sensation* begins with a proximal stimulus. This is *transduced* into a nervous impulse by specialized receptors, is usually further modified by other parts of the nervous system, and finally leads to a sensation. One branch of sensory psychology is psychophysics, which tries to relate the characteristics of the physical stimulus to both the quality and intensity of the sensory experience.

3. The founder of psychophysics, Gustav T. Fechner, studied sensory intensity by determining the ability of subjects to discriminate between stimulus intensities. Important measures of this ability are the *absolute threshold* and the *difference threshold.* The difference threshold is the change in the intensity of a given stimulus (the so-called *standard stimulus*) that is just large enough to be detected, producing a *just noticeable difference or j.n.d.* According to *Weber's law,* the j.n.d. is a constant fraction of the intensity of the standard stimulus. Fechner generalized Weber's law to express a wider relationship between sensory intensity and physical intensity. This is *Fechner's law,* which states that the strength of a sensation grows as the logarithm of stimulus intensity.

4. A way of disentangling sensory sensitivity and *response bias* is provided by *signal-detection theory.* In a typical *detection experiment,* the stimulus is presented on half of the trials, and absent on the other half. In this procedure, there can be two kinds of errors: *misses* (saying a stimulus is absent when it is present) and *false alarms* (saying it is present when it is absent). Their relative proportion is partially determined by a *payoff matrix.* When this payoff matrix is varied, the effects can be graphically expressed by an *ROC* curve. According to signal detection theory, distinguishing between the presence of a stimulus and its absence depends on a process in which the subject has to decide whether a *sensory process* is produced by the *signal* or some *background noise.* The probability that the subjects will make errors depends on the degree of overlap between the noise-alone and the signal-plus-noise frequency distributions. Whether these errors are more likely to be hits or misses depends on the criterion used in making a decision.

5. Investigations of the neural underpinning of sensation involve attempts to understand the *sensory codes* by which the nervous system represents sensory experiences. Of particular interest are qualitative differences that occur both between *sensory modalities* (e.g., A-flat versus red) and within them (e.g., red versus green). According to the *doctrine of specific nerve energies,* such qualitative differences are ultimately caused by differences in the nervous structures excited by the stimuli rather than by differences between the stimuli as such.

6. Underlying neural processes are described by two alternative views: *specificity theory,* which holds that the different sensory qualities are signaled by different neurons, and *across-fiber pattern theory,* which asserts that these differences are coded by the overall pattern of activation across a whole set of neurons. The best evidence indicates that the nervous system utilizes both specificity and pattern codes in different sensory systems.

7. Different sense modalities have different functions and mechanisms. One group of senses provides information about the body's own movements and location. Skeletal motion is sensed through *kinesthesis,* bodily orientation by the *vestibular organs* located in the *inner ears.*

8. The various *skin senses* inform the organism of what is directly adjacent to its own body. There are at least four different skin sensations: *pressure, warmth, cold,* and *pain.* Whether each of these four is produced by separate receptors is still a matter of debate.

9. The sense of *taste* acts as a gatekeeper to the digestive system. Its receptors are *taste buds* whose stimulation generates the four basic taste qualities of *sour, sweet, salty,* and *bitter.*

10. Smell or *olfaction* is both an internal sense that provides information about substances in the mouth and (with the sense of taste) gives rise to the experience of *flavor,* and

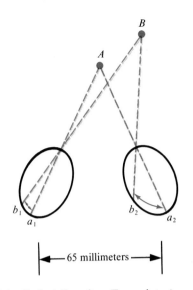

**6.1 Retinal disparity** *Two points, A and B, at different distances from the observer, present somewhat different retinal images. The distance between the images on one eye, $a_1b_1$, is different (disparate) from the distance between them on the other, $a_2b_2$. This disparity is a powerful cue for depth. (After Hochberg, 1978a)*

**6.2 Interposition** *When one figure interrupts the contour of another figure, it provides a monocular cue for depth. This is interposition. Because of interposition, the red rectangle in the figure is perceived to be in front of the blue one.*

## Binocular Cues

A very important cue to depth comes from the fact that we have two eyes. These look out on the world from two different positions. As a result, they obtain a somewhat different view of any solid object they converge on. This **binocular disparity** inevitably follows from the geometry of the physical situation. Obviously, the disparity becomes less pronounced the farther the object is from the observer. Beyond thirty feet the two eyes receive virtually the same image (Figure 6.1).

Binocular disparity alone can induce perceived depth. If we draw or photograph the two different views received by each eye while looking at a nearby object and then separately present each of these views to the appropriate eye, we can obtain a striking impression of depth. To achieve this stereo effect, the two eyes must converge as they would if they were actually looking at the solid object at the given distance.

## Monocular Cues

Binocular disparity is a very powerful (and probably innate) determinant of perceived depth. Yet, we can perceive depth even with one eye closed. Even more important, many people who have been blind in one eye from birth see the world in three dimensions. Clearly then, there are other cues for depth perception that come from the image obtained with one eye alone—the **monocular depth cues.**

Many of the monocular depth cues have been exploited for centuries by artists, and are therefore called **pictorial cues.** Examples include **linear perspective, relative size,** and **interposition.** In each case, the effect is an optical consequence of the projection of a three-dimensional world upon a flat surface. Objects that are farther away are also inevitably blocked from view by any other opaque object that obstructs their optical path to the eye (interposition; see Figure 6.2). Far-off objects necessarily produce a smaller retinal image than do nearby ones (linear perspective and relative size; Figures 6.3 and 6.4).

**6.3 Linear perspective as a cue for depth** *(Photograph by Roberta Intrater)*

A

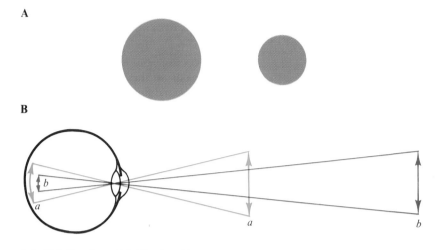

B

**6.4   Relative size**   *(A) All other things equal, the larger of two otherwise identical figures will seem to be closer than the smaller one. This is a consequence of the simple geometry of vision illustrated in (B). Two equally large objects, a and b, that are at different distances from the observer, will project retinal images of different size.*

A very powerful set of pictorial cues is provided by ***texture gradients,*** whose role was emphasized by James J. Gibson, a very influential theorist in the psychology of perception. Such gradients are ultimately produced by perspective. Consider what meets the eye when we look at cobblestones on a road or clumps of grass in a meadow. Gibson pointed out that the retinal projection of such objects must necessarily show a continuous change, a texture gradient, that depends upon the spatial layout of the relevant surfaces (Figure 6.5). Such texture gradients are powerful determinants of perceived depth. Discontinuities in texture gradients provide information about further spatial relationships between the various textured surfaces. Thus, the abrupt change of texture density in Figure 6.6 produces the impression of a sharp drop, a "visual cliff" (see also p. 204; Gibson, J., 1950, 1966).

A                                                      B

**6.5   Texture gradients as cues for depth**   *Uniformly textured surfaces produce texture gradients that provide information about depth: as the surface recedes, the texture density increases. (A) At a seashore, such gradients may be produced by rocks, or (B) a gannet colony. (Photographs by Hans Wallach and Robert Gillmor/Bruce Coleman)*

A                                                 B

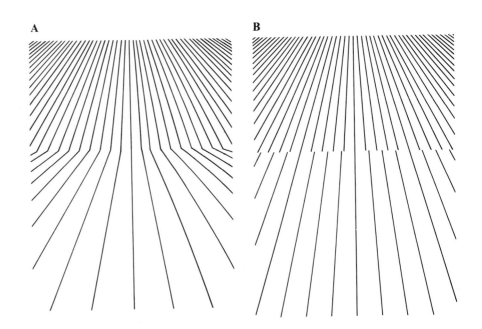

*6.6 The effect of changes in texture gradients* Such changes provide important information about spatial arrangements in the world. Examples are (A) an upward tilt at a corner; and (B) a sudden drop. (After Gibson, 1950)

## The Perception of Depth through Motion

Thus far we have encountered situations in which both the observer and the scene observed are stationary. But in real life we are constantly moving through the world we perceive. This motion provides a vital source of visual information about the spatial arrangement of the objects around us, a pattern of cues that once again follows from the optical geometry of the situation.

As we move our heads or bodies from right to left, the images projected by the objects outside will necessarily move across the retina. The apparent relative motion of these objects is an enormously effective depth cue, ***motion parallax.*** As we move through space, nearby objects seem to move very quickly and in a direction opposite to our own; as an example, consider the trees racing backward as one looks out of a speeding train. Objects farther away also seem to move in the opposite direction, but at a lesser velocity (Helmholtz, 1909; see Figure 6.7).

According to James Gibson, such movement-produced changes in the optic image are the major avenue through which we obtain perceptual information about depth relations in the world around us. Motion parallax is just one example of the perceptual role played by these changes. Another is the ***optic flow*** that occurs when we move towards or away from objects in the world. As we approach them, they get larger and larger; as we move away from them, they get smaller.

Objective motion

*6.7 Motion parallax* When an observer moves relative to a stationary environment, the objects in that environment will be displaced (and will therefore seem to move) relative to him. (The rate of relative displacement is indicated by the thickness of the pink arrows. The thicker these arrows, the more quickly the objects seem to move. The observer's movement is indicated by a blue arrow.) (After Coren and Ward, 1989)

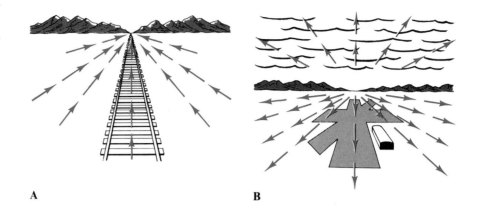

**6.8 Optic flow** (A) The optic flow field as it appears to a person looking out of the rear window of a railroad car. (From Bruce and Green, 1985) (B) The optic flow field as it appears to a pilot landing an airplane. (From Gibson, J., 1950, p. 121)

A                    B

Figure 6.8A shows the flow pattern for a person looking out of the back of a train; Figure 6.8B shows the flow pattern for a pilot landing an airplane (Gibson, J., 1950, 1979).

### Innate Factors in Depth Perception

In many organisms, important features of the perception of space are apparently built into the nervous machinery. An example is the localization of sounds in space. One investigator studied this phenomenon in a ten-minute-old baby. The newborn consistently turned his eyes in the direction of a clicking sound, thus demonstrating that some spatial coordination between eye and ear exists prior to learning (Michael Wertheimer, 1961).*

There is evidence that some aspects of visual depth perception are also innately given (or come in at such an early age that if they are learned, they must be learned very quickly). The facets of depth that apparently come in first are those that are based on perceived movement, such as motion parallax. Another example is the response to **looming,** a rapid magnification of a form in the visual field that generally signals an impending impact. To study this looming effect experimentally, several investigators have simulated the visual consequence of rapid approach by various means, for example by a rapidly expanding shadow cast on a screen. When exposed to these expanding patterns, crabs flatten out, frogs jump away, and infant monkeys leap to the rear of their cages. Human infants as young as two or three weeks of age blink their eyes as if they sense a coming collision, stiffen, and cry (Schiff, 1965; Ball and Tronick, 1971; Yonas, 1981).

Another demonstration of early (and possibly unlearned) visual depth perception is a classic study by Richard Walk and Eleanor Gibson. They noted that crawling infants are surprisingly (though by no means perfectly) successful in avoiding the precipices of their everyday lives (Walk and Gibson, 1961). The investigators studied infant behavior on the **visual cliff** (see Figure 6.9), which simulates the appearance of a steep edge but is safe enough to mollify the infants' mothers, if not the infants themselves. This device consists of a large glass table, about three feet above the floor, which is divided in half by a wooden centerboard. On one side of the board, a checkerboard pattern is attached directly to the

**6.9 An infant on the visual cliff** The infant is placed on the centerboard laid across a heavy sheet of glass and her mother calls to her. If the mother is on the "deep" side, the infant pats the glass, but despite this tactual information that all is safe, she refuses to crawl across the apparent cliff. (Photograph by Richard D. Walk)

---

* Appropriately enough for this nativist finding, the investigator was the son of Max Wertheimer, the founder of Gestalt psychology, a position with strongly nativist leanings, while the subject was his newborn grandchild.

Physical events

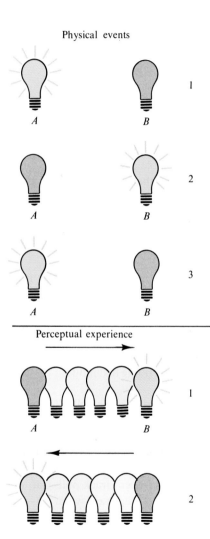

Perceptual experience

**6.10 Stroboscopic movement** *The sequence of optical events that produces stroboscopic movement. Light A flashes at time 1, followed by light B at time 2, then back to light A at time 3. If the time intervals are appropriately chosen, the perceptual experience will be of a light moving from left to right and back.*

underside of the glass; on the other side, the same pattern is placed on the floor. The apparent drop-off is perceived by adults, in part because of a sudden change in texture density, in part because of motion parallax and binocular disparity. But will six-month-old infants respond to any of these cues? The babies were placed on the centerboard, and their mothers called and beckoned to them. When the mother beckoned from the shallow side, the baby usually crawled quickly to her. But only a very few infants ventured forth when called from across the apparent precipice.

An empiricist might well argue that these findings are inconclusive because the babies had six months of previous experience. Unfortunately, there is no easy way of studying visual cliff behavior in younger infants. You can't very well ask where an infant will crawl to if he cannot get up on his knees. But motor coordination matures much earlier in many species, and various very young animals show appropriate cliff-avoidance as soon as they are old enough to move around at all. Kids and lambs were tested as soon as they were able to stand. They never stepped onto the steep side. Chicks tested less than twenty-four hours after hatching gave the same result (Walk and Gibson, E., 1961; Gibson, E., 1969; Walk, 1978).

## THE PERCEPTION OF MOVEMENT: WHAT IS IT DOING?

To see a large, unfriendly Doberman in front of you is one thing; to see him bare his teeth and rush directly at you is quite another. We want to know what an object is and where it is located, but we also want to know what it is doing. Put another way, we want to perceive events as well as objects. The basic ingredient of the perception of events is the perception of movement.

### Illusions of Movement

What leads to the perception of movement? One might guess that one sees things move because they produce an image that moves across the retina. But this answer is too simple. For in fact, we sometimes perceive movement even when none occurs on the retina.

#### STROBOSCOPIC MOVEMENT

Suppose we briefly turn on a light in one location of the visual field, then turn it off, and after an appropriate interval (somewhere between 30 and 200 milliseconds) turn on a second light in a different location. The result is **apparent movement** (sometimes called **stroboscopic movement** or the **phi phenomenon**). The light is seen to travel from one point to another, even though there was no stimulation—let alone movement—in the intervening region (Figure 6.10). This phenomenon is perceptually overwhelming; given the right intervals, it is indistinguishable from real movement. It is an effect that has numerous technological applications, ranging from animated neon signs to motion pictures (Wertheimer, 1912). These results suggest that one stimulus for motion is relative displacement over time. Something is here at one moment and there at the next. If the time intervals are right, the nervous system interprets this as evidence that this something has moved.

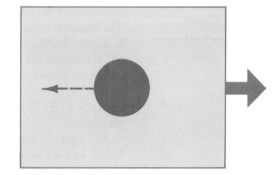

*6.11* **Induced movement**  *Subjects in an otherwise dark room see a luminous dot surrounded by a luminous frame. When the frame is moved to the right, subjects perceive the dot moving to the left, even though it is objectively stationary. (Duncker, 1929)*

INDUCED MOVEMENT

How does the perceptual system react when one of two objects is moving while the other is (physically) stationary? Consider a ball rolling on a billiard table. We see the ball as moving and the table at rest. But why not the other way around? To be sure, the ball is being displaced relative to the table edge, but so is the table edge displaced relative to the ball. One might guess that the reason is learning. Perhaps experience has taught us that balls generally move around while tables stay put. But the evidence indicates that what matters is a more general perceptual relationship between the two stimuli. The object that encloses the other tends to act as a frame which is seen as stationary. Thus, the table serves as a frame against which the ball is seen to move.

In this example, perception and physical reality coincide, for the frame provided by the table is truly stationary. What happens when the objective situation is reversed? In one study subjects were shown a luminous rectangular frame in an otherwise dark room. Inside the frame was a luminous dot. In actual fact, the rectangle moved to the right while the dot stayed in place. But the subjects saw something else. They perceived the dot as moving to the left, in the opposite direction of the frame's motion. The physical movement of the frame had induced the perceived movement of the enclosed figure (Figure 6.11).

The ***induced movement*** effect is familiar from everyday life as well. The moon apparently drifts through the clouds; the base of a bridge seems to float against the flow of the river current. In the second case, there may also be ***induced motion of the self.*** If the subject stands on the bridge that she perceives as moving, she perceives herself moving along with it. The same effect occurs when sitting in a train that's standing in a station. If a train on the adjacent track pulls out, we tend to feel ourselves moving though in fact we—and the train we're in—are stationary.

## Perceived Stability

Thus far, we have asked why things are seen to move. A related question is why they are generally seen as stable. The issue arises because our eyes are constantly moving, so that the retinal image shifts all the time. But if so, why do we perceive the world as stationary? One interpretation follows from the fact that eye movements don't produce relative displacements. When we move our eyes as we look at a chair, the retinal image of the chair is displaced, but so is the image of the

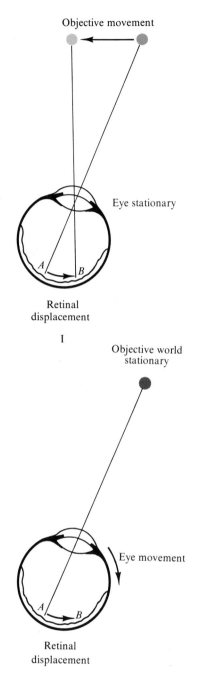

Objective movement

Eye stationary

Retinal
displacement

I

Objective world
stationary

Eye movement

Retinal
displacement

II

room which serves as its framework; as a result, there is no relative displacement. But this cannot be the whole story. As Helmholtz showed a century ago, movement will be seen if the eyes are moved by muscles other than their own. Close one eye and jiggle the outside corner of the other eye (gently!) with a finger. Now the world will move around, even though all relationships within the retinal image are kept intact. This shows that the perceptual system can respond to absolute displacement. But if it can do so when the eyes are pushed by a finger, why doesn't it when they are moved by the eye muscles that normally do the job?

Many students of visual perception believe that the nervous system achieves visual stability by compensating for retinal displacements that are produced by voluntary eye movements. Thus, when the brain signals the eye muscles to move, it computes the retinal displacement that such a movement would produce and then cancels out this amount in interpreting the visual input it receives. As a result, we will see a stationary point at rest, even though our eyes are moving. The brain evidently keeps track of what it told the eyes to do; say, to move 10 degrees to the right. It knows that the eye movement should produce a retinal displacement of 10 degrees in the opposite direction, and subtracts this from the visual signal (Figure 6.12).

## FORM PERCEPTION: WHAT IS IT?

We've asked how we see where an object is, and where it is going. But we have not dealt with the most important question of all: How do we perceive and recognize *what* an object is?

In vision, our primary means for recognizing an object is through the perception of its form. To be sure, we sometimes rely on color (a violet), and occasionally on size (a toy model of an automobile), but in the vast majority of cases, form is the major avenue for identifying what it is we see. The question is how. How do we recognize the myriad forms and patterns that are present in the world around us—triangles and ellipses, skyscrapers and automobiles, hands and faces?

In trying to answer this question, some investigators asked whether there are some primitive components into which all (or at least most) forms could be analyzed, and if so, what these components are.

### Elements of Form

The early empiricists believed that the elementary units out of which all forms are constructed are the simple visual sensations such as patches of color and brightness. In their view, these are gradually pieced together through learning. But

**6.12 Compensation for eye movements** *When the retinal image of some object is displaced, it may be because the object has moved, because the eye has moved, or both. In panel I, there is objective movement which produces a retinal displacement, as the dot's projection shifts from point A to point B on the retina. But panel II shows that the same retinal displacement can be produced by moving the eye (in the opposite direction from that of the dot in panel I) while the object remains stationary. From the retinal point of view, the displacements in panels I and II are identical. Fortunately, our brain allows us to see motion independent of eye movements by compensating for the displacements caused by changes in eye position. In panel II, the brain would decide that there was no movement because the motion of the eye is precisely equal (and opposite) to the displacement on the retina.*

**6.13 Cartoon pictures of normally arranged and scrambled faces** *Newborns spend about as much time looking at each; four-month-olds prefer to look at the normally arranged face. (From Fagan, J.F., 1976).*

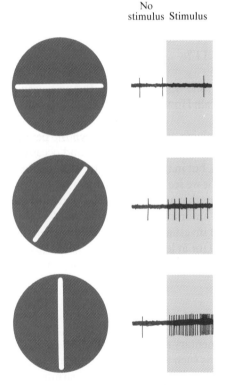

No
stimulus Stimulus

**6.14 Feature detectors in the visual system of the cat** *The response of a single cortical cell when stimulated by a slit of light in three different orientations. This cell, a simple unit, was evidently responsive to the vertical. A horizontal slit led to no response, a tilted slit led to a slight response, while a vertical slit led to a marked increase in firing. (After Hubel, 1963)*

modern investigators believe that the elementary building blocks of form are more complex than these early thinkers had supposed. In their view, such units of form as edges and angles are not pieced together through learning, but are instead extracted from the stimulus by processes that are part of our native equipment. Their beliefs are derived from the study of the innate mechanisms of form perception.

INNATE FACTORS IN FORM PERCEPTION

There is some evidence that at least some aspects of form perception are based on built-in processes. Some of the evidence comes from animals. A one-day-old chick will peck at small spheres in preference to small pyramids, even if kept in darkness from hatching to the time of the test. A prewired preference for round shapes together with the capacity to distinguish them is presumably useful to a creature whose primary foods are grain and seed (Fantz, 1957). Human form perception is less ready-made than the chick's; but even so, the visual world of a newborn infant is not a chaotic jumble of color and light. When a three-day-old infant is presented with a simple form, such as a triangle, its eyes do not move randomly. Photographs of the infant's cornea show that its eyes tend to orient toward those features of the pattern that help to define it, such as its edges and its vertices (Salapatek and Kessen, 1966; Salapatek, 1975).

Of special interest is the infant's early tendency to look at forms that resemble a human face, in preference to others (Fantz, 1961; Freedman, 1971; Fagan, 1976). This tendency is probably based on a preference for certain visual components that comprise a face, such as curved rather than straight contours (Fantz, 1970). Whatever its basis, such a built-in predisposition to look at facelike forms must have considerable survival value in an organism whose period of infar tile dependence is so long and so intense (Figure 6.13).

By about three months of age, there is evidence that the infant can recognize something about the mother's face in a photograph. When presented with color slides of their mother or of a strange woman, they preferred to look at the picture of their mother. This indicates that some aspects of the familiar facial pattern were recognized even in a novel, two-dimensional form (Barrera and Maurer, 1981). (For further discussion of infant perception, see Chapter 14.)

FEATURE DETECTORS

All in all, there seems to be good reason to believe that some aspects of form perception are innately given. But what are the mechanisms whereby the nervous system accomplishes this organization of the stimulus input? The last two or three decades have seen some steps toward an answer.

Electrophysiologists often record from single cells (see Chapter 2). By such techniques they have discovered how particular cells in a sensory system respond to simple stimuli such as light of a given wavelength (see Chapter 5). The same approach has been applied to stimuli that are much more complex and relational.

Two physiologists, Nobel prize winners David Hubel and Torsten Wiesel, studied the activity of single cortical cells in response to various visual stimuli. They found some cells that react to some of the elements of visual form—lines or edges or a particular orientation. One such cell might be excited by a thin sliver of light slanted at, say, 45 degrees, regardless of where on the retina the stimulus is presented (see Figure 6.14). This cell is called a ***feature detector;*** it analyzes the visual input to detect some fairly complex feature (such as orientation) and responds to this feature rather than to other aspects of the stimulus pattern. Hubel and Wiesel have discovered cells that detect even more complex features of visual form. An example is a cell that reacts to right angles (Hubel and Wiesel, 1959, 1979).

Later research has focused on cortical cells that signal other perceptual features. For example, some cells in the cortex are sensitive to binocular disparity (Hubel and Wiesel, 1970; Poggio and Fischer, 1978; Ferster, 1981). Other cells respond to directional movement; they fire if a line moves in one direction but won't fire if it moves in the direction that's opposite (e.g., Barlow and Hill, 1963; Vaultin and Berkeley, 1977).

### THE ADAPTATION OF FEATURE DETECTORS

Most psychophysiologists believe that the excitation of feature detectors leads to such perceptual experiences as angular orientation, binocular depth, movement, and the like. But they have no direct proof. To provide it, they would have to find detector cells in (unanesthetized) human subjects and ask them to describe what they perceive while the cell is firing. Such an experiment is obviously out of the question. Nevertheless, most investigators continue to believe that what they pick up with their electrodes is somehow implicated in what we perceive.

One means of studying feature detectors from the psychological perspective is based on the phenomenon of *adaptation.* We have previously encountered adaptation effects in the case of such relatively simple sensory qualities as hue. After prolonged fixation of a green patch, its apparent greenness will fade away and a neutral gray projected upon the same retinal region will look reddish (see Chapter 5). Effects of this sort laid the foundations for a theory of the opponent processes that underlie color. The same logic motivates the study of adaptation effects in more complex perceptual attributes (Anstis, 1975).

An example is the *aftereffect of visual movement.* If one looks at a waterfall for a while and then turns away to look at the riverbank, the bank and the trees upon it will be seen to float upward, a dramatic effect that is readily produced in the perceptual laboratory (Figure 6.15). We might expect just this result on the assumption that the direction of perceived movement is signaled by the activity of movement detectors that operate as opponent-process pairs. For example, one such pair might be composed of two kinds of movement detectors: one sensitive

*6.15 Aftereffect of movement* (A) The subject first looks at a band of downward moving lines for a minute or two. (B) He then looks at a stationary horizontal line. This line will now appear to be moving upwards. This effect is probably produced by the adaptation of a movement detector that signals downward motion.

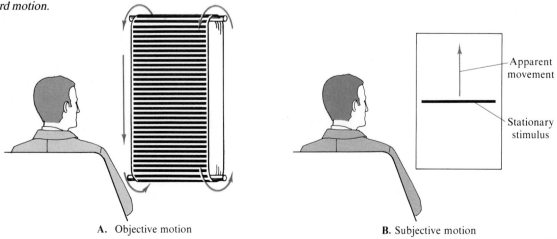

A. Objective motion

B. Subjective motion

Apparent movement

Stationary stimulus

to upward, the other to downward movement. If these two detectors interact like the members of the color opponent-process pairs, then the stimulation of either one will automatically lead to the inhibition of the other. If one has been stimulated for a long time (say, by exposure to a downward moving pattern), it will gradually adapt. As a result, the balance will swing toward the other member of the pair (that is, the upward movement detector). This changed balance is revealed when the moving target is withdrawn and the subject looks at a stationary pattern. This (objectively stationary) pattern is now seen to move upward. The effect is analogous to the red afterimage that follows prolonged fixation of a green patch. In both cases, there is adaptation of one member of an opponent-process pair.

Is there any way to determine whether a particular feature detector in humans is located in the retina or higher up in the brain? Needless to say, we can't resort to microelectrodes. But a number of investigators used another approach. They asked subjects to look at a stimulus that moved continuously in one direction, but to do so with one eye only; the other eye was covered. Would this lead to an aftereffect of movement when the subjects were then tested with the *other* eye? If so, the motion detectors that were adapted by the moving stimulus must be located at a point beyond the retina, some region in the brain where the information from both eyes is somehow combined. The results proved that this was indeed the case. Looking at a moving stimulus with one eye led to an appropriate adaptation effect when the test was conducted with the other eye (Mitchell, Reardon, and Muir, 1975).

## Perceptual Segregation

Suppose the observer looks at the still life in Figure 6.16A. To make sense of the picture, her perceptual system must somehow group the many visual elements of the scene appropriately. For one thing, it has to determine what is focal (for example, the fruit and the bowl) and what can at least temporarily be relegated to the background (for example, the green shutters, the table, and perhaps the pitcher). But there is still more to be done. Some objects will necessarily be partially occluded by others that stand or lie in front of them. Consider the portions A, B, C, D, and E of the figure shown in Figure 6.16B. To determine what any given object could possibly be, we must first perform an initial job of segregating the scene into subcomponents: decide whether portion B goes with A (half an apple combined with some grapes), or with C (half an apple with a piece of orange), or with D (half an apple with a banana), or finally with E (an apple).

This *visual segregation* process is sometimes called *perceptual parsing.* It performs the same function for vision that parsing performs for speech. When someone talks to us, our eardrums are exposed to a sound stream that is essentially unbroken. What hits the ears is a sequence of sounds such as:

*Thestudentsaidtheteacherisafool*

The listener parses the sound pattern by grouping some sounds together with others, forming units called words:

*The student said the teacher is a fool.*

*Max Wertheimer (1880–1943), one of the most influential figures in the psychology of perception. (Courtesy Omikron)*

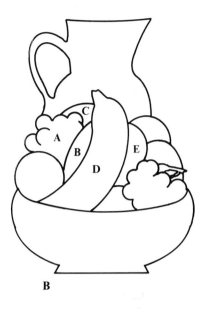

A                                                              B

**6.16   Perceptual segregation**   *(A) A still life. (Photograph by Jeffrey Grosscup) (B) An overlay designating five different segments of the scene shown in (A). To determine what an object is, the perceptual system must first decide what goes with what: does portion B go with A, with C, D, or E? Or with none of them?*

He may then parse further by grouping the words into larger units called phrases, as in:

> *The student, said the teacher, is a fool.*

In some cases, he may even discover that there are alternate ways of parsing, as in:

> *The student said, the teacher is a fool.*

The important point is that the parsing is not primarily in the stimulus. It is contributed by the listener, for the sound stream itself has no pauses between words and contains no commas. (This is why foreigners often sound as if they speak much faster than we do.) Until at least some basic parsing has been performed, the listener has no hope of comprehending what she has heard. To understand the meaning of the word *student,* she must first have segregated it from the surrounding sounds and heard it as a separate word.

What holds for words in speech, also holds for objects in the visual world. Visual segregation (or parsing) is the first step in organizing the world we see.

FIGURE-GROUND

Visual segregation begins with the separation of the object from its setting, so it is seen as a coherent whole that stands out against its background, as a tree stands out against the sky and the clouds. This segregation of **figure** and **ground** can be easily seen in two-dimensional pictures. In our still life, the apple is generally perceived as the figure, the tablecloth as the ground. But the same phenomenon also occurs with figures that have no particular meaning. Thus in Figure 6.17, the white splotch appears as the figure, which seems to be more cohesive and articulated than the green region, which is normally perceived as the ground. This darker ground is seen as relatively formless and as extending behind the figure.

**6.17   Figure and ground**   *The first step in seeing a form is to segregate it from its background. The part seen as figure appears to be more cohesive and sharply delineated. The part seen as ground is perceived to be more formless and to extend behind the figure.*

**6.18   Reversible figure-ground pattern**
*The classic example of a reversible figure-ground pattern. It can be seen as either a pair of silhouetted faces or a white vase.*

The differentiation between figure and ground is a perceptual achievement that is accomplished by the perceptual system. It is not in the stimulus as such. This point is made strikingly by ***reversible figures,*** in which either of two figure-ground organizations is possible. A classic demonstration is shown in Figure 6.18, which can be seen either as a white vase on a blue background or as two blue profile faces on a white background. This reversibility of figure-ground patterns has fascinated various artists, especially in recent times (see Figure 6.19).

According to one proposal, the figure-ground distinction corresponds to two different kinds of neural processing. One (in regions seen as figure) involves the analysis of fine detail, while another (in regions seen as ground) involves a cruder analysis appropriate to the perception of larger areas (Julesz, 1978). To test this hypothesis, subjects were presented with brief exposures to vertical and slightly tilted lines that were flashed on either of three locations of a line drawing of the vase-profile figure (see Figure 6.20). The subjects' task was to judge the orientation of the lines. In accordance with the detail-processing hypothesis, the subjects were much more accurate when the line was projected onto the area the subject happened to see as the figure than when it was projected onto the area they saw as the ground (Weisstein and Wong, 1986).

PERCEPTUAL GROUPING

Reversible figure-ground formations demonstrate that the same proximal pattern may give rise to different perceptual organizations. The same conclusion follows from the related phenomenon of perceptual ***grouping.*** Suppose we look at a collection of dots. We can perceive the pattern in various ways depending upon how we group the dots: as a set of rows, or columns, or diagonals, and so on. In each case, the figural organization is quite different even though the proximal stimulus pattern is always the same.

**6.19   Figure-ground reversal in the visual arts**   *The Trojan War as depicted by Salvador Dali. The scene of wild carnage conceals the image of the Trojan Horse, whose outline follows the gateway to the city. (Courtesy Esquire)*

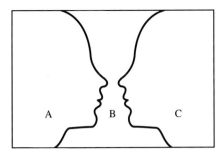

**6.20 Fine detail is more readily seen in the figure than the ground** *Subjects look at the vase-profiles figure as shown above, and have to determine whether lines that are briefly flashed at points A, B, or C are tilted or vertical. If the vase is seen as figure, they do much better when the stimuli are presented at B than at A or C. If the profiles are seen as figure, they do much better when the lines are presented at A or C rather than at B. (After Weisstein and Wong, 1986)*

What determines how a pattern will be organized? Some factors that determine visual grouping were first described by Max Wertheimer, the founder of *Gestalt psychology,* a school of psychology that believes that organization is basic to all mental activity, that much of it is unlearned, and that it reflects the way the brain functions. Wertheimer regarded these grouping factors as the laws of *perceptual organization* (Wertheimer, 1923). A few of these are discussed below.

*Proximity* The closer two figures are to each other *(proximity)* the more they will tend to be grouped together perceptually. Proximity may operate in time just as it does in space. The obvious example is auditory rhythm: four drum beats with a pause between the second and third will be heard as two pairs. Similarly, these six lines generally will be perceived as three pairs of lines:

*Similarity* Other things being equal, we tend to group figures according to their *similarity.* Thus, in the figure below, we group blue dots together with blue dots, and red dots together with red dots. As a result, we see rows rather than columns in the left panel, and columns rather than rows in the right panel.

What aspects of stimulus similarity lead to grouping? Color is clearly one. Another is orientation. When similarity of form (for example, *T*'s versus *L*'s) is pitted against orientation (upright *T*'s versus *T*'s tilted by 45 degrees), subjects generally group by orientation (Beck, 1966; see Figure 6.21). Certain simple visual features such as color, brightness, and orientation are evidently more important for segmentation than are visual properties like shape that depend on more complex relations between the stimuli such as the particular arrangement of their lines that defines the difference between a *T* and an *L* (Beck, 1982). This is just what we would expect if visual parsing is the first and thus more primitive step in visual organization.

**6.21 The effect of orientation and shape on perceptual grouping** *The demarkation between the upright T's and the tilted T's is more easily seen than that between the upright T's and the upright L's. (From Beck, 1966)*

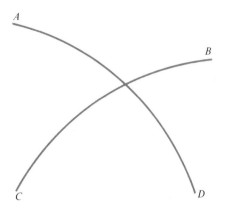

**6.22 Good continuation** *The line segments in the figure will generally be grouped so that the contours continue smoothly. As a result, segment A will be grouped with D and C with B, rather than A with B and C with D.*

*Good continuation* Our visual system seems to "prefer" contours that continue smoothly along their original course. This principle of grouping is called ***good continuation*** (Figure 6.22). Good continuation is a powerful organizational factor that will often prevail even when pitted against prior experience (Figure 6.23). This principle is used by the military for camouflage (Figure 6.24A). It also helps to camouflage animals against their natural enemies. For example, it helps to conceal various insects from predators who tend to see parts of the insect's body as continuations of the twigs on which it stands (Figure 6.24B).

*Closure* We often tend to complete figures that have gaps in them. Figure 6.25 is seen as a triangle despite the fact that the sides are incomplete.

A closurelike phenomenon yields ***subjective contours.*** These are contours that are seen, despite the fact that they don't physically exist (Figure 6.26). Some theorists interpret subjective contours as a special case of good continuation. In their view, the contour is seen to continue along its original path, and, if necessary, jumps a gap or two to achieve the continuation (Kanizsa, 1976).

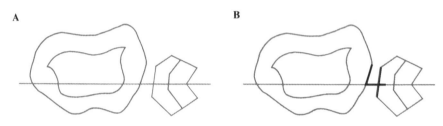

**6.23 Good continuation pitted against prior experience** *In (A), virtually all subjects see two complex patterns intersected by a horizontal line. Hardly anyone sees the hidden 4 contained in that figure—and shown in (B)—despite the fact that we have encountered 4's much more often than the two complex patterns which are probably completely new. (After Köhler, 1947)*

**6.24 Good continuation as the basis of camouflage** *(A) Here, camouflage is achieved by providing artificial contours that break up the outlines of the soldier's face and body. (Courtesy the United States Government) (B) Good continuation helps to conceal the insect from predators who tend to see parts of the insect's body as continuations of the twigs on which it stands. (Photograph by Farrell Grehan, Photo Researchers)*

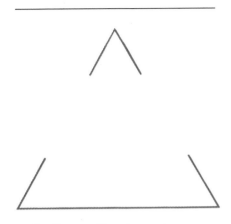

**6.25 Closure** *There is a tendency to complete—or close—figures that have a gap in them, as in the incomplete triangle shown here.*

Proximity, similarity, good continuation, and closure are among the factors that determine whether we see portions of the visual world as belonging together or apart. Is there a general rule that underlies these different grouping factors? Different theorists have come up with a number of proposals. We'll consider only one of these, the ***principle of maximum likelihood.*** This principle goes back to the nineteenth-century physiologist Hermann von Helmholtz, but it has many modern adherents (Helmholtz, 1910; Gregory, 1974; Hochberg, 1981; Rock, 1983). It asserts that we tend to interpret the proximal stimulus pattern as that external (that is, distal) stimulus object that most *probably* produced it (Pomerantz and Kubovy, 1986; Hochberg, 1988).

How would the maximum likelihood principle explain the grouping principles? Proximity is easy enough. Regions that are close together—and will therefore project images that are near each other on the retina—are generally portions of the same object. (Though there are exceptions, such as a worm on an apple.) The same holds for similarity. By and large, regions that are similar in color and texture also belong to the same object. (Though here too there are exceptions, such as a clown's costume or a patch quilt.)

This principle can also explain grouping by good continuation. Consider Figure 6.27A. Most observers tend to perceive this as two smooth intersecting lines rather than as two forms meeting at any angle (say, two fish kissing). Why should this be so? To answer this question, let's ask what Figure 6.27A might correspond to in the external world. One possibility is rather likely. It could easily be an image cast by two elongated objects, such as two branches of two trees that are at differ-

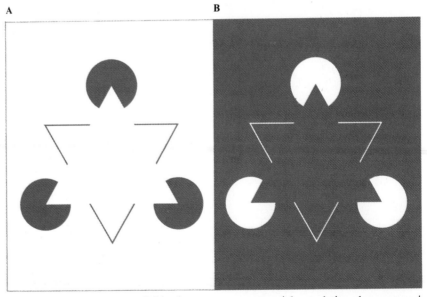

**6.26 Subjective contours** *Subjective contours are a special completion phenomenon in which contours are seen even where none exist. In (A), we see a white triangle whose vertices lie on top of the three blue circles. The three sides of this white triangle (which looks brighter than the white background) are clearly visible, even though they don't exist physically. In (B), we see the same effect with blue and white reversed. Here, there is a blue triangle (which looks bluer than the blue background) with subjective blue contours. (Kanizsa, 1976)*

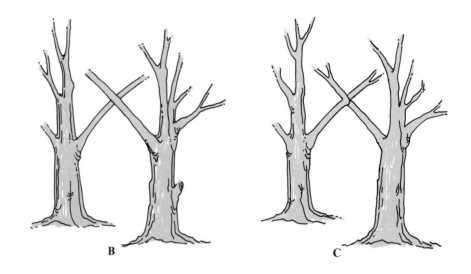

A

**6.27 Good continuation and the maximum likelihood principle** *(A) A figure that could be seen in two ways. (B) A likely alternative. (C) An unlikely alternative.*

ent distances from the observer (see Figure 6.27B). The two retinal images cast by, say, the two branches will intersect each other even when the vantage points from which the observer views them are varied considerably. There is another possibility that is much less likely. The figure may correspond to two angularly shaped objects, such as two elbow-shaped tree branches of the trees that happen to be viewed from just that orientation at which their two angles are seen to meet (Figure 6.27C). Note that this is exceedingly unlikely, for any slight change of vantage point will shift the angles, so that this pattern will no longer hold. (Perceiving two passionate fish is even more unlikely.) Under the circumstances, the perceptual system makes the bet that is most likely to correspond to external reality: it groups by good continuation.

VISUAL PARSING AND THE COMPUTATIONAL APPROACH

An important new perspective on visual parsing and many other aspects of form perception comes from the so-called ***computational approach,*** which combines principles of computer science with those of the psychology of visual perception (Schwab and Nusbaum, 1986). Its guiding theme is that many aspects of visual perception are the end result of a mathematical (hence, computational) analysis of what is given to the retina. Most theorists who subscribe to this conception believe that visual perception is based on several steps of ***information processing*** that transform (that is, "process") the retinal image into the cognitive end product: the perception of the objects and events in the world. This is generally thought to involve a series of successive stages, in which each stage further transforms the output of the previous stage.

An example of the computational approach is a set of proposals developed by David Marr and his associates about the early stages of visual processing (Marr, 1976, 1982; Frisby, 1980). According to Marr, the end product of visual parsing yields something like a simple sketch of the object that we're trying to recognize. This sketch is initially based on a number of simple features such as edges, their orientation, and certain aspects of depth, which are then appropriately grouped and segregated from their background (Marr, 1982). An example of how such a

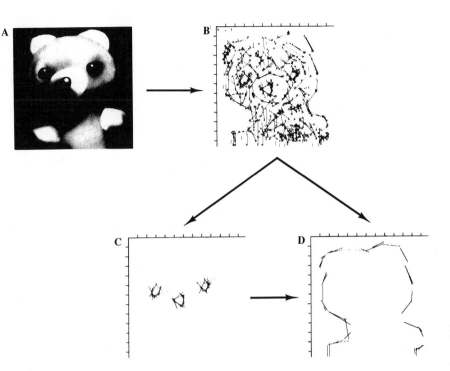

**6.28 From stimulus input to segmented sketch in Marr's account to pattern recognition** *(A) A photograph of a simple scene. (B) Feature description of that scene. (C) and (D) Two perceptual groupings derived from the feature description. (From Marr, 1976)*

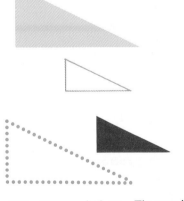

**6.29 Form equivalence** *The perceived forms remain the same regardless of the parts of which they are composed.*

sketch might be constructed by a suitable computer program is presented in Figure 6.28, which shows some of the processing steps, starting with a simple image of the object and moving on to a feature description, which is then parsed to yield an outline figure and some of the main subcomponents (Marr, 1976).

## Pattern Recognition

Thus far we have considered the first steps in perceiving an object—seeing it as a figure that stands out against its background and whose parts seem to belong together. The next step is to determine *what* that object is. To do this, the organism must match the form of this figure to the form of some other figure it has previously seen and recognize it appropriately. This process is called ***pattern recognition.*** One of the major problems of the psychology of perception is to determine how this is accomplished.

Humans and animals can recognize a form even when most of its component parts are altered. Consider two similar triangles. It doesn't matter whether they are small, rendered as solids or as line drawings, made up of dots or dashes. The perceived form remains the same (Figure 6.29). This phenomenon is sometimes called the ***transposition of form*** or ***pattern.*** A triangle is a triangle is a triangle, whatever the elements of which it is composed. Similar effects occur in the temporal patterning of sounds. A melody remains the same even when all of its notes are changed by transposing to another key, and the same rhythm will be heard whether played on a kettledrum or a glockenspiel.

Phenomena such as these were among the chief arguments of the Gestalt psychologists who insisted that forms are not perceived by somehow summing up all of the localized sensations that arise from individual retinal points of excitation. They argued instead that a form is perceptually experienced as a **Gestalt,** a whole that is different from the sum of its parts.* To recognize that a form is the same as one we have seen before, we must perceive certain relations among its component parts.

Most modern investigators of pattern recognition believe that the Gestalt psychologists had an important point. There is little doubt that a form is not just the sum of its parts: three angles alone do not make a triangle, no more than a mouth, a nose, and two eyes suffice to make a face. The trouble is that it is hard to specify just what relations among the parts create the pattern. We can do it separately for each figure: for a triangle, the three angles have to be properly aligned, for a face, the nose has to be between the eyes, and so forth. But thus far no one has succeeded in formulating a general description of the relations between the parts that will do justice to all patterns. As a result, while the importance of such relations is widely granted, most modern investigators haven't dealt with them at length.

There is another problem. The Gestalt psychologists' insistence on the importance of wholes is based on the phenomena of form transposition. There is indeed no doubt that a form will survive many transformations such as those of size, or color, or location on the retina. But this doesn't hold for *all* transformations. One important exception is orientation. If a form is rotated by, say, 90 degrees, it may not be recognized. Consider Figure 6.30. Most subjects find it hard to recognize, but they have no problem seeing what it is when it is presented in its normal position (see p. 221; from Rock, 1973).

Because of these and similar reasons, most investigators of pattern recognition have focused less on the wholes than on the parts of which those wholes are composed. They hoped by discovering the ways through which the proper parts could be identified, the pattern could be identified as well.

We now turn to a discussion of the mechanisms by which particular patterns are recognized, whether it is the letter *A,* or the face of our grandmother, or a picture of an apple. We will consider the steps in information processing by which the parts are transformed into patterns that we recognize as real objects and events in the world.

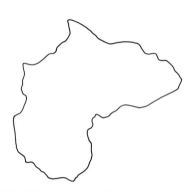

**6.30   Transposition of form has limits**
*This is a familiar form that corresponds to a well-known geographical outline. Can you recognize it? To see what it is, rotate the book clockwise by 90 degrees or turn to p. 221. (After Rock, 1973)*

### THE PANDEMONIUM MODEL

Some thirty years ago, an important approach to pattern recognition grew out of the efforts of computer scientists to develop machines that could "read" letters and numerals. Devices of this kind would have numerous practical applications, for example, sorting mail for the postal service or organizing bank records.

Many attempts to design such artificial recognition systems involved a chain of processing steps that began with the analysis of visual features. This approach was partially influenced by the neurophysiological work on feature detectors in the nervous system (see pp. 208–10). Under the circumstances, it seemed reasonable enough to endow systems of human (or machine) perception with a similar ability to extract elemental properties. A very influential system (or model) of this sort was one proposed by Oliver Selfridge (Selfridge, 1959). Suppose we have a machine that can scan the optical image of a letter. How can it decide that this letter is, say, a *T?* What the machine can do is start out by looking for the presence

* The term *Gestalt* is derived from a German word that means "form" or "entire figure."

or absence of certain visual features (for example, horizontal, vertical, or diagonal bars, curves to the right or left, and so on). It can then consult a list stored in its memory in which each capital letter is entered, together with the visual features that define it. By comparing the features in the stimulus with those of the letters on the list, it can begin to reach a decision. But there is a problem. A given feature (say, a vertical bar) is found not just in one letter, but in several (e.g., *P, R,* and *T*). If so, how can the machine decide which of these letters it is currently inspecting? Selfridge proposed that the choice is essentially by vote. If a feature in the stimulus matches up with a given letter on the memory list, it *activates* that letter to a certain degree. The more features match up, the stronger the activation. The final decision is then just a matter of comparing the levels of activation, with the choice falling on the letter whose level of activation is greater than that of any of the others.

Selfridge called his model *Pandemonium,* because he regarded perceptual analysis as analogous to the work of various demons who pass on the results of their analysis to demons higher up, with feature-demons shouting at (in our terms, activating) letter-demons, who in turn shout at a decision-demon, who finally decides in favor of whichever one shouts the loudest (Figure 6.31).

The simplest Pandemonium model only involves activation. But in later elaborations, there was also the inhibition of activation. Suppose one of the features of a letter stimulus is a horizontal bar. In a Pandemonium model supplemented with inhibition, that feature will not only activate all of the letters that contain this feature (such as *F* and *E*) but will also inhibit the activation of letters that do *not* contain that feature (such as *W* and *Q*). In the simplest version of Pandemonium, the demons merely try to shout as loudly as they can. In Pandemonium

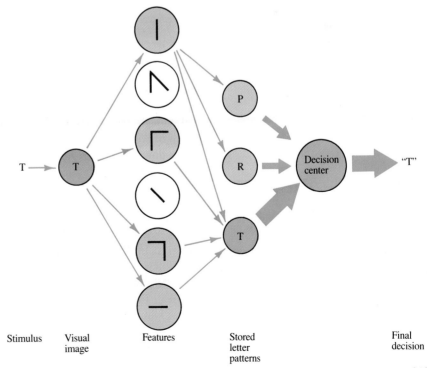

**6.31 The Pandemonium model** *The physical stimulus "T" gives rise to a visual image. This is then analyzed for the presence or absence of various component features, such as vertical or horizontal lines, various corners, and so on. Each feature stimulates the stored letter patterns that contain it. In this example, one of the feature units stimulates the pattern "P," one the pattern "R," and four the pattern "T." As a result, the "T" is more actively excited than the "P" and "R," which leads to the decision that the letter is "T." (After Goldstein, 1984)*

Stimulus  Visual image  Features  Stored letter patterns  Final decision

**A**

Geons

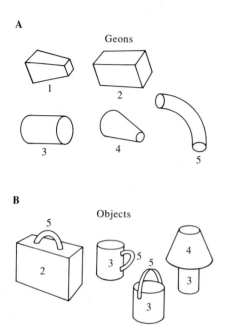

**B**

Objects

**6.32    Some proposed geometric primitives**    *(A) Some geons. (B) Some objects that can be created from these geons. (After Biederman, 1987)*

# THE CAT

**6.33    The effect of context on letter recognition**    *(After Selfridge, 1955)*

models in which there is inhibition, the demons do that but in addition they also clap their hands over the mouths of other demons whose letters don't fit the feature they have analyzed.

### A COMPONENT MODEL

Pandemonium's approach to pattern recognition may work for a relatively few simple forms like the set of letters and numerals (though it may encounter problems even there; e.g., Morton, 1969; Bruce and Green, 1985). But the features on which it is based seem too artificial to account for recognition of real objects in the world around us. In addition, they appear to be too small and atomistic to represent the basic units out of which the patterns of our perceptual experience are constructed.

Considerations of this sort led to several recent attempts that try to understand object recognition as a process that depends on our identification of perceptual components of objects that are somewhat broader than lines, curves, and angles. A model proposed by Irving Biederman lists some thirty such geometric primitives that he calls *geons* (a neologism for "geometric ions")—three-dimensional figures such as cylinders, cones, pyramids, and the like. (The recognition of the geons themselves is presumably handled by an earlier stage of pattern recognition.) According to Biederman, just about all the objects of the world can be—perceptually—analyzed into some number of such geons. When we encounter an object, we presumably perceive its component geons and their relationships, and then consult our visual memory to see whether there's an object that matches up. If we do, we recognize the object: "Ah, yes, Geon 4 on top of Geon 3—a desk lamp!" (Biederman, 1987; see Figure 6.32).

### TOP-DOWN PROCESSING

Thus far we have discussed pattern recognition as a ***bottom-up process***, which starts with component features (features or geons) and gradually builds up to larger units that are, so to speak, at the top. In Pandemonium, these would be letters, then words, then phrases; in Biederman's system, they would be geons, then objects in the world. But there are reasons to believe that bottom-up processing is not enough. Pattern recognition often involves ***top-down processes*** in which the chain of events begins with the activation of higher units, which then affect units lower down. Evidence comes from the fact that recognition is often affected by higher-level knowledge and expectations.

One demonstration of top-down processing in perception is provided by so-called ***context effects***. In some cases, context effects depend on stimuli that are simultaneously present with the affected stimulus. As an example, take the two words shown in Figure 6.33. The two middle "letters" of each word are physically identical, but they are usually seen as an *H* in *THE* and an *A* in *CAT*.

In other cases, the context is provided by experiences in the past (often the immediately preceding past). A good example is provided by ambiguous figures. Consider Figure 6.34A, which can be seen as either an old woman in profile or a young woman whose head is turned slightly away. In one study, subjects were first shown two fairly unambiguous versions of the figure (Figures 6.34B and C). When later presented with the ambiguous figure (Figure 6.34A), they perceived it in line with the ambiguous version they had been shown before (Leeper, 1935).

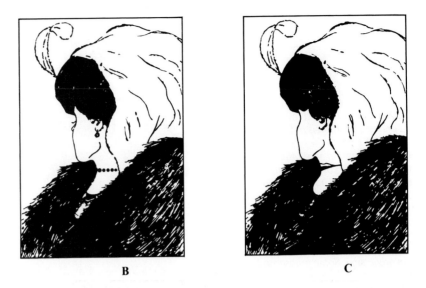

A                           B                           C

**6.34  An ambiguous figure**   *(A) This is ambiguous and is just as likely to be seen as a young woman or as an old woman. (B) and (C) are essentially unambiguous, and depict the young woman and old woman respectively. If the subjects are first shown one of the unambiguous figures, they are almost sure to see the ambiguous picture in that fashion later on. (After Boring, 1930; Leeper, 1935)*

Similar context effects can make us hear speech sounds where in fact there are none. Something of this sort occurs in everyday life, for when people talk they sometimes cough or clear their throat so that the speech stream is interrupted. But even so, we usually hear and understand them and never notice that there were physical gaps in their actual physical utterance. In a laboratory demonstration of this phenomenon subjects listened to tape-recorded sentences in which the speech sounds were tampered with, as in the sentence:

*The state governors met with their respective legislatures convening in the capital city.*

In this sentence the experimenter replaced the middle *s* in the word *legislatures* with a cough-like noise. Yet, virtually none of the subjects even noticed that any speech sound was missing. They somehow restored the deleted speech sound, and "heard" the *s* that was provided by the total context (Warren, 1970).

BIDIRECTIONAL ACTIVATION

Context effects demonstrate that there is some top-down processing. But this hardly means that bottom-up processing is unimportant. On the contrary. After all, if perceptual processing were only in the top-down direction, we would always see what we expect and think about—even if there were no stimulus whatever. To be sure, knowledge and expectations do help to interpret what we see and hear, but there has to be some sensory basis that confirms these interpretations. As a result, perceptual processing is generally in both directions: from the top down, but also from the bottom up.

*The familiar form on p. 218 when viewed in its normal position. It is the outline of Africa.*

**221**

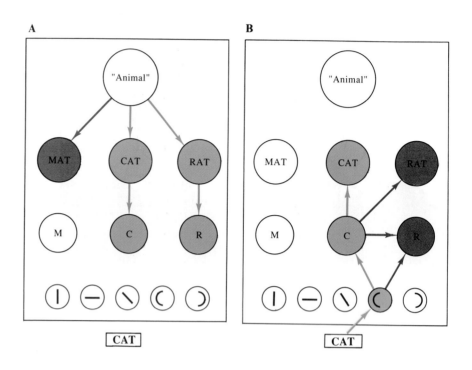

**6.35  Bidirectional activation**  (A) Top-down processing. *The first few milli-seconds of perceptual analysis of the stimulus word* CAT, *given the last two letters but no information about the first letter. Activation of the concept "Animal" activates the words* CAT *and* RAT *(among others), which then activate their first-position letters* C *and* R. *It also inhibits incompatible words such as* MAT *(again, among others). Activation is indicated in green; inhibition in red. (B) Bottom-up processing. Some milliseconds later, further perceptual analysis of the first letter of the stimulus word has activated the feature* curved-to-the-left, *which activates the letter* C, *adds to the ac-tivation of the word* CAT, *and also inhibits the letter* R *and the word* RAT. *The end result is that the word* CAT *is more intensely activated than all other words, and will reach recognition threshold. Activation is again in green, and inhibition in red. To keep things simple, many mutually inhibitory effects (e.g., between the words* CAT *and* RAT *) are not shown in the figure.*

This bidirectional aspect of perceptual processing has been incorporated into some recent models of pattern recognition systems that operate from the top down and the bottom up simultaneously. As an example, we'll take a problem in word recognition (see Figure 6.35). Suppose a perceiver is shown a three-letter word under very dim illumination. For the sake of simplicity, let's assume that in the first few milliseconds of the presentation, the system decides that the last two letters of the word are *AT*, but has as yet no information about the first letter. How does it choose between the many alternatives (e.g., *BAT, CAT, MAT, RAT, VAT*, and so on)? Let's suppose that the perceiver has just read a newspaper article on animals, which would presumably activate the words *BAT, CAT*, and *RAT*. These activations will in their turn lead to the inhibition of several other three-let-ter words that are inconsistent with the concept "Animal," such as *MAT* and *VAT*. They will also produce some top-down effects, activating the letters *B, C*, and *R*. A few more milliseconds pass, and some further perceptual analysis acti-vates the curved-to-the-left feature. Now processing becomes bottom up and goes in the other direction. There will now be some further activation of the letter *C*, together with the inhibition of the letters *B* and *R*. This in turn will strengthen the word *CAT* and weaken *RAT* and *BAT*, until the activation of the word *CAT* gets above the so-called recognition threshold (McClelland, Rumelhart, and Hinton, 1986). In effect we have an augmented Pandemonium model in which demons at every level of the hierarchy scream at each other upwards, downwards, and side-ways, until one word-demon finally wins the shouting match.

## PERCEPTUAL PROBLEM SOLVING

Bidirectional models of the kind just discussed fit in with the belief that much of perception is essentially a form of problem solving in which the observer tries to

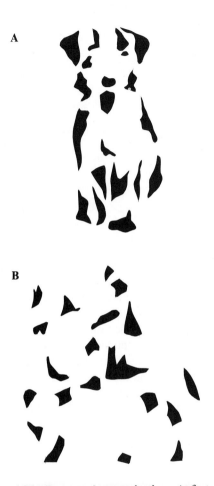

**6.36 Perceptual reorganization** *At first glance, (A) and (B) look like disorganized patches. But after looking at them for a while, they usually take on a new appearance as we see them as a dog (A), and a man on a horse (B), respectively. After they have been reorganized in this manner, it is difficult to see them as they appeared at first. (After Street, 1931)*

discover (consciously or, more commonly, without awareness) what it is that she sees. Such a process of problem solving come into play when we come to perceive and recognize new patterns.

## Creating New Patterns

Learning new perceptual patterns is a pervasive phenomenon of infancy and childhood. To be sure, infants come much better prepared to perceive the world than the early empiricists believed, for we now know that many aspects of the perception of depth, movement, and certain aspects of form are part of our native endowment. But it is inconceivable that built-in mechanisms can account for all the phenomena of form perception. There might be some preprogrammed systems that can detect complex shapes that are of special significance in the life of a given species. Perhaps humans have a primitive something-like-a-face detector that might help to establish the reaction to the mother at an early stage of infancy. But there has to be much more than that. Humans must discriminate among a multitude of patterns, and it is hardly possible that we carry specialized detector cells for them all—triangles, squares, apples, apple pies, champagne bottles, B-52s, cabbages, kings—the list is endless. At this stage we do not know where the natively given ends and where experience takes over. Edges, corners, or perhaps geons, may well be the ultimate innate units, but it is certainly clear that an enormous number of perceptual constellations are generated by the experience of the organism. Just how that process works is as yet unknown.

To some extent, the process of learning new patterns continues into adulthood. Thus, we sometimes manage to reorganize something that we see or hear so that it looks and sounds completely new. A foreign language may sound like gibberish before we learn to speak and understand it, but later on we can no longer remember the chaotic jumble we initially heard. Similar effects are found in visual perception. Consider Figure 6.36. At first, the patches look disorganized, but after a while they take on a new appearance as we discover that they represent a dog and a horse and rider respectively. Here, too, it is hard to recall what the patches looked like in their original, disorganized shape. According to several authors, such perceptual reorganizations amount to cognitive **constructions** created by the perceiver, perhaps created by an analogous process to that which operated in early childhood (Neisser, 1967; Hochberg, 1978a; Rock, 1983).

## Perceptual Hypotheses

The interplay of bottom-up and top-down processing fits in very nicely with the problem-solving approach to perception. Seen in this light, the perceptual system generally starts out with both a stimulus and a hypothesis. The perceptual hypothesis represents the top-down aspect of the process. It is tested as the system analyzes the stimulus (the bottom-up aspect) for some appropriate features. If these are found, the perceptual hypothesis gains plausibility and is either accepted or checked for further proof. If such features are not found, then a new hypothesis is considered, which is then tested by searching for yet other features, and so on.

Occasionally, we become consciously aware that some such process operates. This sometimes happens when we are presented with a visual display that initially

**6.37 Perceptual problem solving** *This is a picture of something. What? (Photograph by Ronald James)*

*"By George, you're right! I thought there was something familiar about it."*
*(Drawing by Chas. Addams; © 1957, 1985 The New Yorker Magazine, Inc.)*

makes no sense. An example is Figure 6.37. At first glance most observers don't know what to make of it. But as they continue to look at the figure, they develop hypotheses about what it might be (e.g., maybe this part is the leg of some animal, maybe the animal has a spotted hide). If they are lucky, they eventually hit on the correct hypothesis (a Dalmatian dog). When they finally see the dog, the top-down and bottom-up processes meet, and there is a perceptual insight, a visual "Aha!" Here the process of perceptual problem solving was quite conscious. But this is rare, for we usually see cars, trees, and people (and even Dalmatian dogs) without being aware that we are trying to solve any perceptual puzzles. But according to theorists who take the problem-solving approach to perception, much the same kind of thing occurs even then, though at much greater speed and outside of consciousness.

To sum up. Perceptual processing must include both bottom-up and top-down processes. Without bottom-up processing, there would be no effect of the external stimulus, and we would not perceive but only hallucinate. Without top-down processing, there would be no effect of knowledge and expectation, and we would never be able to guide and interpret what we see.

### The Logic of Perception

To the extent that perception involves a form of problem solving, it obeys a kind of logic. One of the laws of ordinary logic is that there can be no contradictions—a statement can't be both true and false at the same time. The perceptual system obeys a similar law. It operates to minimize perceptual contradictions and to make all parts mesh in a coherent whole. If the system detects a discrepancy, it does its best to rectify the situation (Rock, 1983).

attended ear shifts into a foreign language or if the tape is suddenly played backward (Cherry, 1953).

### THE FILTER THEORY OF ATTENTION

Results of this sort suggested that selective attention acts as a kind of filter. This filter is presumably interposed between the initial sensory registration and later stages of perceptual analysis. If the information is allowed through the attentional filter (that is, if it is fed into the attended ear), it can then be further analyzed—recognized, interpreted, and stored in memory. But if it does not pass through, it is simply lost. Early versions of this theory suggested that the filtering effect is all-or-none. Subjects in a dichotic listening experiment were thought to understand no part of the message that entered by way of the unattended ear (Broadbent, 1958).

This all-or-none theory turned out to be false, for there is good evidence that information which has some special significance is registered even if it is carried as part of the unattended message. The best example is the sight or sound of one's own name. No matter how intently we concentrate on the person next to us, we can't help but hear our own name in another conversation held on the other side of the room.

This everyday experience has been documented with the shadowing method. When subjects are forced to repeat a message that comes over one ear, word for word, they are almost completely oblivious to the irrelevant message that is fed into the other ear. But they do take notice when that irrelevant message contains the sound of their own name (Moray, 1959). This result suggests that the attentional filter does not block irrelevant messages completely. It only attenuates it, like a volume control that is turned down but not off. If the item is important enough (or perhaps familiar enough), then it may pass through the filter and be analyzed to some extent (Treisman, 1964).

Related evidence comes from a study in which subjects had to shadow sentences such as "They threw stones at the bank yesterday." Concurrently, the other ear was presented with either of two words: *river or money.* When questioned directly, the subjects couldn't recall which of the two words they had heard, if either. But some part of the meaning of these words must have come through nevertheless. The shadowed sentence contained the ambiguous word, *bank,* which can be understood as either a financial institution or as the side of a river. Which interpretation was chosen depended upon whether the unattended ear was presented with the word *money* or *river.* This shows that the subjects extracted some meaning from the unattended message even though they never knew they did (McKay, 1973).

## THE PERCEPTION OF REALITY

Of what use are all the mechanisms of perceptual organization we have considered throughout this chapter, whether innately given or based on learning? The answer is simple enough: They all help us to perceive reality. To be sure, the perceptual system may occasionally lead us astray, as in illusions of depth or movement, and sometimes it may actually leave us helpless, as in impossible figures.

But these are fairly rare occasions. By and large, the processes that lead to the perception of depth, movement, and form serve toward the attainment of a larger goal—the perception of the real world outside.

To see the real world is to see the properties of distal objects: their color, form, size, and location, their movement through space, their permanence or transience. But as we have noted before, organisms cannot gain experience about the distal stimulus directly; all information about the external world comes to us from the proximal stimulus patterns that distal objects project upon the senses. The trouble is that the same distal stimulus object can produce many different proximal stimulus patterns. Its retinal image will get larger or smaller depending upon its distance; its retinal shape will change depending upon its slant; the amount of light it projects on the retina will increase or decrease depending on the illumination that falls upon it.

Under the circumstances, it may seem surprising that we ever manage to see the real properties of a distal object. But see them we do. The best proof is provided by the *perceptual constancies:* a crow looks black even in sunlight; an elephant looks large even at a distance; and a postcard looks rectangular even though its retinal image is a trapezoid unless it is viewed directly head on. In all of these cases, we manage to transcend the vagaries of the proximal stimulus and react to certain constant attributes of the distal object such as its shape and its size.

## Empiricism and Nativism Revisited

How does the organism accomplish this feat? The attempts to answer this question are best understood as part of the continuing debate between the empiricist heirs of Locke on the one hand, and the nativist descendants of Kant on the other.

### THE EMPIRICISTS' ANSWER

Empiricists handle the problem by asserting that the sensation produced by a particular stimulus is modified and reinterpreted in the light of what we have learned through past experience. Consider perceived size. People five feet away look just about as tall as those at a fifty-foot distance. This is not merely because we *know* them to be average-sized rather than giants or midgets. The fact is that they really *look* equally tall provided there are cues that indicate their proper distance (Figure 6.43).

How can we explain this and similar phenomena? The most influential version of the empiricists' answer was formulated by Hermann von Helmhotz in the

**A**

**B**

*6.43   Perceived size and distance*   *(A) The actual image of the two men in the picture—which corresponds to the size of their retinal image—is in the ratio of 3 to 1. But this is not the way they are perceived. They look roughly equal in size, but at different distances, with one about three times farther off than the other. In (B) there are no cues that indicate that one man is farther away than the other. On the contrary. The figure was constructed by cutting the more distant man out of the picture, and pasting him next to the other man, with the apparent distance from the viewer equal for the two. Now they look very different in size. (After Boring, 1964; Photograph by Jeffrey Grosscup)*

late nineteenth century. According to Helmholtz, the perceiver has two sources of information. To begin with, there is the sensation derived from the size of the object on the retina. In addition, there are a number of depth cues that indicate how far away the object is. Prior learning has taught the perceiver a general rule: the farther away things are, the smaller will be the sensation derived from the retinal image. The perceiver can now infer the true size of the object, given its retinal size, its distance, and the learned rule that relates the two. As a result she adjusts her perception of size, shifting it downward if the object is seen as close by and upward if it is seen farther off. Helmholtz of course knew full well that we don't go through any *conscious* calculation of this sort when we look at objects and perceive their size. But he believed that some such process was going on anyway and he therefore called it ***unconscious inference*** (Helmholtz, 1909).

It's worth noting that the unconscious inference theory is really an early version of the top-down processing hypothesis in perception. Both positions insist that perception is only partially determined by the sensory stimulation, that perception is in part a kind of mental construction, based on various expectations and inferences of which the observer is often unaware. Thus contemporary theorists who argue that perception often involves a form of problem solving hold a view that is in many ways quite similar to that of Helmholtz (e.g., Hochberg, 1981, 1988; Rock, 1977, 1983, 1986).

### THE NATIVISTS' ANSWER

The nativists' reply is that the perception of size is directly given. They argue that the stimulus for the perceived size of an object is not the size of the retinal image as such. It is rather some relationship between that size and certain other attributes that pertain to depth.

A very influential modern version of this approach is that of James J. Gibson (1950, 1966, 1979). Gibson believed that such vital characteristics of an object as its size, its shape, and its distance from the observer are signaled by various ***higher-order patterns of stimulation*** to which the organism is innately sensitive.

As an example, let's return to size. To be sure, the size of the retinal image projected by an object must necessarily vary with its distance from the observer. But Gibson argued that this does not mean that there is no size information in the stimulus that hits the eye. One reason is that objects are usually seen against a background whose elements—leaves, pebbles, clumps of grass, or whatever—provide a texture. Since these elements are generally of about the same size, their size on the retina varies with distance and leads to texture gradients. As we've already seen, these texture gradients provide information about distance. But in addition, they also provide information about the relative size of objects in the world outside. For distance has the same effect on the retinal image of the object as it has on the retinal image of the adjacent texture elements of the object's background. In both cases, the retinal size decreases with increasing distance. As a result, there is a constant ratio between the retinal size cast by the object and the retinal size of its adjacent texture elements. According to Gibson, this ratio provides a higher-order stimulus relationship that remains *invariant* over changes of distance, and we pick up the information provided by this ratio directly, without any intermediate cognitive steps (such as unconscious inference). Gibson called this process ***direct perception.*** (See Figure 6.44.)

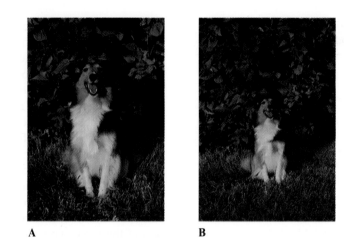

**A**                    **B**

**6.44  An invariant relationship that provides information about size**  (A) and (B) show a dog at different distances from the observer. The retinal size of the dog varies with distance, but the ratio between the retinal size of the dog and the retinal size of the texture elements made up of the bushes is constant. (Photographs by Jeffrey Grosscup)

The extent to which higher-order patterns of stimulation (such as the size ratio) provide information about various attributes of the world—of which size is only one—is still a matter of debate. Nor is it clear that perceivers are necessarily sensitive to all such higher-order patterns even if they do exist, or that the response to such patterns is part of our native endowment. These issues are by no means settled, as we will see when we turn to the empirical study of the various perceptual constancies.*

## Lightness Constancy

Virtually all objects reflect a certain proportion of the light that falls upon them. The exact proportion depends upon a physical property of the object itself, its *reflectance.* Some objects have a high reflectance (snow), others a low reflectance (coal). To say that an object is perceived as light or dark is really to say that we can tell something about its reflectance. Yet, we cannot possibly see the reflectance directly; all we get from the object is the amount of light it actually reflects on any given occasion, the *luminance.* But this luminance depends not only upon the object's reflectance but also upon the *illumination* that falls upon it. A white shirt in shadow may well reflect less light than does a gray shirt in brilliant sunlight. Under the circumstances, can we ever tell that the first is lighter than the second?

The fact is that we can, at least to some extent. A swan will not suddenly seem to turn gray when a cloud hides the sun; it appears just as white, but in shadow. This effect is called *lightness constancy.* The apparent lightness of an object remains fairly constant despite rather drastic changes in the illumination that falls upon it. This phenomenon is readily demonstrated in the laboratory. Subjects are shown two gray papers of equal reflectance. One paper, *A,* receives twice the illumination of another paper, *B,* which is in shadow (Figure 6.45). But even so, the

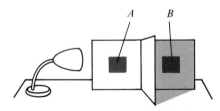

**6.45  Lightness constancy**  Subjects are shown two identical gray papers, A and B. A is illuminated while B is in shadow. As a result, A reflects much more light than B. Even so, the two are perceived to be about equal in lightness, a manifestation of lightness constancy. (After Rock, 1975)

* Some psychologists point out that one's stand on the unconscious inference versus direct perception debate is not necessarily tied up with one's position on the nature-nurture issue, even though the two have often been correlated in the past. At least in theory, there could be perceptual inferences that appeal to principles that are genetically preprogrammed. By the same token, a perceiver might learn to attend to a stimulus pattern that would provide direct information about some aspect of the real world, even if he had not done so initially (Pomerantz and Kubovy, 1986).

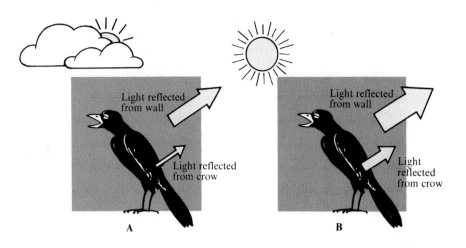

**6.46 Lightness constancy and brightness contrast** *In (A) the illumination on both bird and wall is moderate; in (B) it is much greater. The fact that illumination goes up increases the amount of light reflected by the bird, but it also increases the amount of light reflected by the wall that serves as its background. The two increases tend to cancel each other. Any increase in the light intensity of the background tends to inhibit the apparent lightness of the figure. This compensation effect acts in the direction of lightness constancy: The crow continues to look black even in brilliant sunshine.*

subjects judge the papers to be equally light, despite the fact that *A* reflects twice as much light as *B*.

How does lightness constancy come about? At least in part, it seems to be based on the same built-in processes that are responsible for brightness contrast (see Chapter 5). The basic idea is that illumination changes normally affect both the object in the foreground and the background against which it is seen. Consider a black crow that stands in front of a brown garden wall (see Figure 6.46). The sun is democratic, shining equally on the crow and on the garden wall. If it suddenly emerges from behind a cloud, the illumination on the crow (and hence its luminance) will go up. But the same holds for the wall. Its luminance will also increase and will then cause a decline in the apparent lightness of the crow. This is just another example of brightness contrast, which makes objects appear darker as the luminance of their background goes up. The result is an automatic compensation effect that works in the direction of lightness constancy (Wallach, 1948; Richards, 1977).

## Size and Shape Constancy

Lightness constancy is evidently due in the main to built-in mechanisms. Is the same true for the other perceptual constancies, such as those for size and shape? *Size constancy* is a term that describes the fact that the perceived size of an object is the same whether it is nearby or far away. A Cadillac at a distance of 100 feet will look larger than a Volkswagen 20 feet away. An analogous phenomenon is *shape constancy,* which refers to the fact that we perceive the shape of an object more or less independently of the angle from which it is viewed. A rectangular door frame will appear rectangular even though most of the angles from which it is regarded will produce a trapezoidal retinal image (see Figure 6.47).

How can we explain size and shape constancy? An essentially nativist approach such as Gibson's would try to account for the phenomena by looking for some higher-order stimulus pattern that remains invariant despite changes in distance or angle of orientation. As we saw earlier in the chapter, in the case of distance such a proposed invariant is provided by the relation between the target stimulus and the texture of the background. Suppose we approach a door in a

233

**6.47  Shape constancy**   *When we see a door frame at various slants from us, it appears rectangular despite the fact that its retinal image is often a trapezoid. (After Gibson, 1950)*

hallway. The door does not seem to change in size, even though its retinal image is expanding. But one thing remains unchanged: the ratio between the size of the images projected by the door and by the texture elements of the wallpaper in the hallway. Such size ratios may well contribute to the constancy phenomenon, but they are probably not the only factor. For size constancy is found even when there are no apparent texture elements in either the target stimulus or the background that might provide the basis for a size ratio. As long as there are any cues to depth at all—such as perspective, interposition, binocular disparity, motion parallax, and so on—size constancy remains. As the number of these cues is progressively diminished, size constancy declines (Holway and Boring, 1947; Harvey and Leibowitz, 1967; Chevrier and Delorme, 1983).

An invariant size ratio is evidently unable to explain all cases of size constancy. But if so, what can? According to Helmholtz, we somehow take account of the object's distance and compensate for it (by unconscious inference). Helmholtz believed that the size-distance relationship is acquired through long experience. He pointed out that young children sometimes mistake objects at a considerable distance for miniatures. When they look from a tower, they see the people below as tiny dolls—a phenomenon that is also seen in adults (Helmholtz, 1909; Day, Stuart, and Dickinson, 1980). Gibson would reply that at those distances the crucial texture elements are too far to be visible. This might explain why size constancy breaks down when the distance between observer and target gets large enough, but it cannot explain why that breakdown occurs at an earlier point in children than in adults (Zeigler and Leibowitz, 1957).

Perhaps Helmholtz was right in asserting that size constancy is learned. But if so, it must be learned fairly quickly, for size constancy seems to be present rather early in life (at least for moderate distances). Just how early is still a matter of some controversy, but it is certainly present by six months at the latest (Bower, 1966; McKenzie, Tootell, and Day, 1980; Day and McKenzie, 1981).

To test for size constancy in the first months of life, many investigators have resorted to the so-called ***habituation method*** (for details, see Chapter 14). The infant is presented with a visual stimulus until she gets habituated (that is, bored) and looks away. She is subsequently presented with a new stimulus. If she spends relatively little time looking at it, the presumption is that she regards it as quite similar to the old boring stimulus. But if she inspects the new stimulus with some interest and for a longer time, she presumably sees it as essentially different from the old one to which she had become habituated.

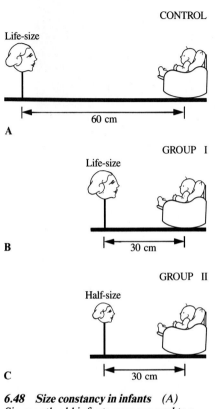

CONTROL

Life-size

60 cm

A

GROUP I

Life-size

30 cm

B

GROUP II

Half-size

30 cm

C

**6.48   Size constancy in infants**   *(A)
Six-month-old infants were exposed to a
model of a human head at a distance of 60
cm until they habituated. (B) One group
was then tested with the same head model
at a distance of 30 cm—same distal size
but altered retinal size. (C) A second group
was tested with the same head model
reduced to half its size but at the original
distance of 30 cm—same retinal size but
altered distal size. The infants in (C) spent
more time looking at the model than those
in (B), an indication of size constancy.*

A study that employed this method has shown size constancy in six-month-olds. The infants were first shown a model of a human life-sized head at a distance of 60 cm. After several trials with this figure, they habituated and looked elsewhere. The critical test involved two groups. Group I was shown the same head model at a distance of 30 cm—the distal size remained the same but the retinal size was changed. Group II was shown a head model identical in form but reduced by half and presented at a distance of 30 cm—here the distal size was changed while the retinal size remained the same (see Figure 6.48). The results showed that the infants in Group II spent much more time inspecting the stimulus than did those in Group I. It appears that a decrease in true size (with retinal image held constant) is a more effective change than a change in retinal size (with distal size held constant)—a strong indication that some measure of size constancy is present by the age of six months (McKenzie, Tootell, and Day, 1980). Such findings are certainly compatible with the view that at least some instances of size constancy are part of our native endowment, and are thus found at a very early age. But they are also compatible with the empiricist position, on the assumption that the relevant learning is acquired rather quickly.

What holds for size constancy, holds by and large for shape constancy as well. In both constancies, the observer requires some information in addition to the retinal image of the target stimulus: in size constancy, it is the distance to that target; in shape constancy, it is the slant from which it is viewed. When deprived of information about the slant of, say, a square tilted backward, he will respond to the shape of its retinal image—perceiving a trapezoid rather than a square. In further analogy to size constancy, shape constancy is found at a rather early age. By three months of age, infants seem to regard a tilted square as essentially equivalent to a square viewed straight on (Caron, Caron, and Carlson, 1979; Cook and Birch, 1984). By five to six months, infants seem to see the similarity between a face photographed in front view to one in semi-profile (Fagan, 1976). As in size constancy, the shape constancy effect may be based on learning, but if so, the learning must have occurred rather quickly.

## Inappropriate Compensation and Illusions

The preceding discussion shows that we compensate for distance when perceiving size. By and large, this perceptual strategy works. It leads to size constancy, one of the ways we have for seeing the world as it really is. But occasionally, this policy backfires and produces illusions.

A well-known example is the ***moon illusion.*** The moon looks considerably larger at the horizon than it does when up in the sky, even though its retinal image is equal in both cases. The main reason is that the horizon looks farther away than the overhead sky. But since the perceptual system compensates for perceived distance, the horizon moon is seen as larger. To test this hypothesis, subjects viewed artificial moons through special optical devices. They experienced the standard moon illusion. In line with the size-distance hypothesis, the illusion was greater the farther off the visible horizon appeared (Kaufman and Rock, 1962; see Figure 6.49).

A number of other illusions of size may be caused by a similar effect of perceived distance upon perceived size. The Müller-Lyer illusion (Figure 6.50) and

235

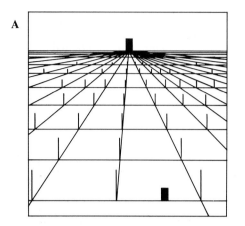

**6.49    The moon illusion** *(A) The black rectangle resting at the horizon seems to be larger than the one in the foreground, although both are objectively identical in size. The reason is apparent distance. Since the rectangle at the horizon seems farther off, it is perceived to be larger than the one that has the same retinal size but appears to be nearer. (After Rock and Kaufman, 1962) (B) When the moon is at the horizon, depth cues such as perspective and interposition indicate that the moon is far away. As a result, the moon seems larger. When the moon is overhead, the depth cues are less prominent, so the moon appears smaller.*

**6.50    The Müller-Lyer illusion** *(A) In the Müller-Lyer illusion, the center line in the left figure seems longer than its counterpart on the right, though the two lengths are identical. This illusion may be another effect of misleading perspective cues. This can be seen by noting that the Müller-Lyer figure is present whenever one looks at the corners of rooms or buildings. (B) shows the interior corner of a room, in which the lines of the ceiling and floor correspond to the outward-pointing fins of the figure whose center line looks longer than in C, presumably because it appears to be farther away. In contrast, (C) shows the outer edge of a building with receding perspective lines. Here, the perspective lines correspond to the arrow heads of the figure whose center line looks shorter, presumably because it appears to be closer by. (Coren and Girgus, 1978)*

the Ponzo illusion (Figure 6.51), both named after their discoverers, are two examples. In both cases, perspective cues indicate that one part of the figure is more distant than another. This leads to a faulty compensation in which the part that seems farther away is perceived to be larger than it really is (Gregory, 1963, 1966; Coren and Girgus, 1978).

This interpretation seems to fit at least some of the size illusions. Thus, the Ponzo illusion (Figure 6.51) is considerably stronger when it is displayed as part of a photograph rather than as a line drawing. This is presumably because depth cues are generally more powerful in a photograph than a schematic line drawing (Leibowitz, Brislin, Perlmutter, and Hennessy, 1969). Other studies show that the Ponzo illusion is stronger for older than younger children. This makes sense if one assumes that older children have more experience with depth cues, especially as they appear in pictures (Coren and Girgus, 1978).

Illusions are special cases in which reality is misperceived. In ordinary life, such mistakes are rare because our perceptual systems are geared to see the world as it really is—allowing us to bypass the continual fluctuations of the proximal stimulus so that we can grasp the enduring properties of the distal reality outside.

But while illusions are fairly rare, they are exceedingly useful to those who want to understand how perception works. By studying illusions, we can learn about the mechanisms upon which our normal perception of reality is based.

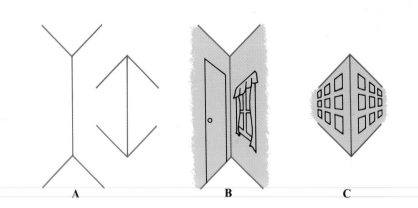

**6.51 The Ponzo illusion** *The two horizontal bars seem to be unequal, with the one on top apparently larger than the one below. In actuality, the two horizontal lines are perfectly identical. This illusion is produced by perspective cues which make the top bar appear to be farther away and thus larger, an effect similar to that which leads to the moon illusion.*

Some of these mechanisms are built in; illusory effects such as brightness contrast have shown the way to their discovery. Other mechanisms involve learning and past experience. The perspective illusions just discussed are a case in point. But so, of course, are many other perceptual phenomena (such as the recognition of form) which we have seen to be enormously affected by memory of the past and expectations of the future, for there is a wide region in which it is not quite clear where seeing ends and knowledge begins.

## THE REPRESENTATION OF REALITY IN ART

The mechanisms of perceptual organization evolved to serve in the struggle for survival that all organisms must wage. They allow us to see reality as it actually is, so that we can perceive what is out there in the world that we must seek or must avoid. But it is part of our humanity that we have managed to turn these perceptual mechanisms to a use that goes beyond the stark necessities of sheer survival: the representation of reality in art.

The psychology of visual art is yet another illustration of the overlap between seeing and knowing that we've repeatedly encountered in our previous discussions of perceptual phenomena. We will see that an acute awareness of this overlap is found in the artists who try to represent the perceptual world on paper or on canvas.

### Seeing and Knowing

Consider Figure 6.52, a tomb relief carved in Egypt some four thousand years ago. Why did the artist depict the figure as he did, with eyes and shoulders in front view and the rest of the body in profile? His fellow Egyptians were surely built as we are. But if so, why didn't he draw them "correctly"?

The answer seems to be that Egyptian artists drew, not what they could see at any one moment or from any one position, but rather what they knew was the most enduring and characteristic attribute of their model. They portrayed the various parts of the human body from the vantage point that shows each form in its most characteristic manner: the front view for the eyes and shoulders, the profile for the nose and feet. The fact that these orientations are incompatible was evidently of no concern; what mattered was that all of the components were represented as the artist knew them to be (Gombrich, 1961).

**6.52 Carved tomb relief of a government official, ca. 2350–2280 B.C.** *The conventions of Egyptian art required the main parts of the human body to be represented in its most characteristic view. Thus, heads are shown in profile, arms and legs from the side, but eyes are depicted in full-face view, as are the shoulders and the chest. (Courtesy The Egyptian Museum, Cairo)*

### The Renaissance: Scenes through a Window Frame

The illustrations of Egyptian art show the enormous role of the known in the visual representation of the seen. One may argue that this simply reflects the fact that these artists never set themselves the task of mirroring nature as it appears to the eye. Does the artist copy more precisely if his purpose is to do just that?

The most striking examples come from the Renaissance masters who conceived the notion that a picture should look just like a real scene that is viewed through a window from one particular orientation. The painting's frame is then

**6.53 Perspective in Renaissance art**
The Annunciation *by Crivelli (ca.
1430–1495). Note the loving attention to
perspective detail, such as roofs and arches
extending far back. (Courtesy the National
Gallery, London)*

the frame of this window into the artist's world. One major step toward achieving this end was the discovery of the geometrical laws of perspective. This was supplemented by the systematic use of other pictorial cues for depth such as interposition.

In effect, the Renaissance masters seemed to believe that to catch visual reality, one's picture should correspond to the image the model casts on the eye also. This motivated their search for means to portray depth on a flat canvas (Figure 6.53). The same conception also served as the starting point for such empiricists as Locke and Berkeley, whose concern was with the nature of perception. The empiricists asked how the painters' means of portraying depth—the pictorial cues—could lead to the experience of depth if the image on the eye is two-dimensional.

### The Impressionists: How a Scene Is Perceived

The Renaissance painters tried to represent a scene as it is projected on the eye. Other schools of painting set themselves a different task. Consider the French Impressionists of the late nineteenth century. They tried to recreate certain perceptual experiences that the scene evokes in the observer, the impression it makes rather than the scene itself. One of their concerns was to render color as we see it in broad daylight. Their method was to create a seeming patchwork of different daubs of bright colors (Figure 6.54). These are clearly separate when looked at directly. But when viewed from the proper distance they change appearance, especially in the periphery where acuity is weak. The individual patches now blur together and their colors mix. But when the eyes move again and bring that area of the picture back into the fovea, the mixtures come apart and the individual patches reappear. Some authors believe that this continual alternation between mixed colors and separate dots gives these paintings their special vitality (Jameson and Hurvich, 1975).

This patchwork technique has a further effect. It enlists the beholder as an active participant in the artistic enterprise. Her active involvement starts as soon as she tries to see the picture as a whole rather than as a meaningless jumble of colored patches. This happens when the separate patches blur: when they are viewed from the periphery or from a few steps back. Now the picture suddenly snaps into focus and a whole emerges. This is both similar to and different from what happens in ordinary life. There we move our eyes to bring some part of the world to a region of greater acuity, the fovea. In the museum, we sometimes move our eyes (or our entire body) to bring a picture to a region of lesser acuity, away from the fovea. In either case, active movement leads to the perception of a figural whole (Hochberg, 1978b, 1980).

*6.54* **Bend in the Epte River, near Giverny** *(1888) by Claude Monet* *Monet, one of the leaders of Impressionism, was engaged in a life-long attempt to catch the fleeting sensations of light in nature. If the painting is viewed from farther back or out of foveal vision, the form becomes clearer and less impressionistic. What is lost is the brilliant shimmer of light and color. The oscillation between these two modes of appearance contributes to the total esthetic effect. (Courtesy Philadelphia Museum of Art: The William L. Elkins Collection)*

### The Moderns: How a Scene Is Conceived

The Impressionists tried to engender some of the perceptual experiences a scene evokes in the observer. Later generations went further and tried to capture not just how the scene is *perceived* but how it is *conceived;* how it is known as well as seen. Modern art provides many examples, as in Pablo Picasso's still life showing superimposed fragments of a violin (Figure 6.55). Here perception and knowledge are cunningly merged in a sophisticated return to some of the ways of Egyptian artists (Gombrich, 1961).

Some modern artists are not satisfied to add conceptual elements to their visual representations. They want to create ambiguity by setting up visual puzzles that can't be solved. One way is to pit knowledge against visual perception, as in Picasso's faces that are seen in profile and front-face at the same time. Another is to build contradictions within the perceptual scene itself. An example is a painting by the turn-of-the century Italian Giorgio de Chirico (Figure 6.56). One reason for the disturbing quality of this picture is the fact that de Chirico used incompatible perspectives. The structure on the left converges to one horizon, that on the right to a horizon far below the other, while the wagon in the middle does not converge at all. The result is an insoluble visual problem, an eerie world which cannot be put in order.

De Chirico's streets do not look like real streets and Picasso's violins are a far cry from those one sees in a concert hall. In this regard, these modern painters ap-

*6.55* **Violin and Grapes** *by Pablo* **Picasso, 1912** *(Courtesy Museum of Modern Art, New York, Mrs. David M. Levy bequest)*

**6.56** Melancholy and Mystery of a Street *by Georgio de Chirico, 1914* *(Private Collection, U.S.A.)*

pear quite different from many of their predecessors whose representations were closer to the world as it appears to the perceiver. But we have to realize that no artists, whether Renaissance masters, Impressionists, or moderns, ever try to fool the observer into thinking that he is looking at a real scene. They neither can nor want to hide the fact that their painting is a painting. It may spring to life for a moment and look like a real person or a real sunset, or it may briefly conjure up a vivid memory of what a face or a violin looks like when viewed from several angles. But whether it emphasizes the seen or the known, it is also recognized as a flat piece of canvas daubed with paint.

According to some authors, this perceptual duality is an important part of the beholder's esthetic experience as he looks at a work of representational art. In a well-known poem by Robert Browning, a duke points to his "last duchess painted on the wall,/Looking as if she were alive." The key words are *as if.* One reason why visual art leads to an esthetic experience may be because it provides us with a halfway mark between seen reality and painted appearance, because it presents a visual *as if* (Hochberg, 1980).

In our discussion of visual art we have taken yet another step across the wide, shadowy region where perception and conception, seeing and knowing merge. In the next chapter we cross the boundary altogether and consider how we remember objects and events that no longer stimulate our senses.

## SUMMARY

1. The fundamental problem of *perception* is how we come to apprehend the objects and events in the world around us. In the field of visual perception, the major issues concern the way in which we see *depth, movement,* and *form.*

2. The visual world is seen in three dimensions even though only two of these are given in the image that falls upon the eye. This fact has led to an interest in *depth cues.* Among these are *binocular disparity* and various *monocular cues* such as *interposition* and *perspective.* Of special interest are *texture gradients,* which are powerful determinants of perceived depth. More important still is the motion of our own heads and bodies. This leads to *motion parallax* and various patterns in the *optic flow,* all of which provide vital information about the distance of objects from each other and from ourselves.

3. Many aspects of depth perception are apparently built into the nervous machinery. Evidence comes from the behavior of very young humans or animals, as in reactions to *looming* and to the *visual cliff.*

4. Retinal displacement alone cannot explain the perception of movement as shown by the phenomena of *apparent movement* and *induced movement,* and by the fact that the nervous system compensates for displacements produced by movements of the eye.

5. One issue in the psychology of form perception is whether there are primitive components into which forms can be analyzed, and if so, what these components are. Much of the work on this topic gained impetus from the discovery that some aspects of form seem to be built in as shown by the perceptual achievements of very young humans and animals. Attempts to find the physiological mechanisms that underlie these achievements have concentrated on *feature detectors,* both in the retina and in the brain. These are cells that respond to certain relational aspects of the stimulus, such as edges and corners, as shown by single-cell recordings. The adaptation of such feature detectors may explain certain changes of perceptual experience after prolonged exposure to a certain kind of stimulus, as in the *aftereffect of visual movement.*

6. Before the perceiver can recognize a form, he must first engage in a process of *visual segregation* and *parse* the visual scene. This involves the segregation of *figure* and *ground.* This is not inherent in the proximal stimulus but is imposed by the perceptual system, as shown by reversible figure-ground patterns. Further segregation produces *perceptual grouping,* which depends upon factors such as *proximity, similarity, good continuation,* and *closure.* Some authors believe that all of these parsing phenomena are manifestations of a *maximum likelihood principle*—the tendency to interpret a proximal stimulus pattern as that external stimulus object that most probably produced it.

7. A crucial fact in form perception is *transposition of form.* A perceived form may remain the same even if all of its constituent parts are altered. This phenomenon is the keystone of *Gestalt psychology,* a theory that emphasizes the importance of wholes created by the relationship between their parts.

8. An important approach to *pattern recognition* grew out of efforts of computer scientists to develop machines that could identify visual forms such as letters. Most such attempts start with the view that pattern recognition typically involves two kinds of processes. One is *bottom-up processing,* which starts with the stimulus and "works up" by subjecting it to a *feature analysis,* which begins with lower-level units (such as slanted lines) that then activate higher-level units (such as letters and words). The other is *top-down processing,* which is based on expectations and hypotheses and begins with the activation of higher-level units that then activate lower-level ones.

SUMMARY

9. Top-down and bottom-up processes typically operate jointly. Top-down processes provide *perceptual hypotheses* that are then tested by bottom-up processes. This kind of *perceptual logic* sometimes fails, as in the case of *impossible figures.*

10. Perception is selective, for all aspects of a stimulus are not given equal weight. This selection is partially achieved by physical orientation, as in the case of *eye movements.* It is also achieved by a central process, *selective attention.* Methods for studying attention include *selective looking,* as in *visual search,* and *selective listening,* as in *dichotic presentation,* in which one message is *shadowed.*

11. The ultimate function of perceptual organization is to help the organism perceive the outside world as it really is. An illustration is the *constancies* in which the perceiver responds to certain permanent characteristics of the distal object despite various contextual factors—illumination, distance, and orientation—which lead to enormous variations in the proximal stimulus. In *lightness constancy,* the perceiver responds to the object's *reflectance* and tends to ignore the level of illumination that falls upon it. In *size and shape constancy,* the perceiver responds to the actual size and shape of the object more or less regardless of its distance and orientation.

12. Attempts to resolve the discrepancy between what the proximal stimulus gives us and what we actually see go back to two main approaches, the *empiricist* and *nativist.* Empiricists explain this discrepancy by referring to *unconscious inference* based on a learned rule (in the case of size constancy, the rule that farther objects lead to smaller retinal sensations). Nativists emphasize *invariant higher-order stimulus relationships* that are directly given (in the case of size constancy, invariant size ratios in the retinal image).

13. The evidence indicates that lightness constancy is in large part based upon the same built-in processes that yield brightness contrast. The verdict is less clear-cut for size and shape constancy, but if those constancies are based on learning, that learning must occur quite early in life. Some of the compensations for distance that produce size constancy sometimes produce misperceptions, as in the case of the *moon illusion.*

14. The psychology of visual art is a further illustration of the overlap between perception and thinking. The artist represents both what he sees and what he knows. *Renaissance* painters represented scenes seen through a window frame; the *Impressionists* tried to re-create certain perceptual experiences the scene evokes in the beholder; while many modern artists try to represent the scene as it is conceived and thought about.

*A cartoonist's view of the problem of seeing versus knowing* (Drawing by Alain; © 1955, 1983 The New Yorker Magazine, Inc.)

# CHAPTER 7

# Memory

Our discussion of perception, and especially of visual perception, has emphasized the way in which psychological events are organized in space. Locke and Berkeley to the contrary, our perceptual world is not a jumbled mosaic of isolated sensory fragments, but an organized, coherent whole in which every piece relates to every other. We now turn to the subject of *memory* in which organization plays an equally prominent part. Where perception concerns the organization of space, memory—or at least many aspects of memory—concerns organization in time.

Memory is the way in which we record the past and later utilize it so that it can affect the present. It is hard to think of humans (or any animal that is able to learn) without this capacity. Without memory, there would be no then but only a now, no ability to employ skills, no recall of names or recognition of faces, no reference to past days or hours or even seconds. We would be condemned to live in a narrowly circumscribed present, but this present would not even seem to be our own, for there can be no sense of self without memory. Each individual wakes up every morning and never doubts that he is *he* or she is *she.* This feeling of personal identity is necessarily based upon a continuity of memories which links our yesterdays to our todays.

## STUDYING MEMORY

The preceding comments underline the overwhelming importance of memory to psychological functioning. To see how psychologists have tried to study this process, we have to make a few preliminary points.

To start with, we should note that any act of remembering implies success at three aspects in the memory process. Consider a person working on a crossword

**The Persistence of Memory** by Salvador Dali. Memory persists, sometimes in distorted form. (Courtesy of the Museum of Modern Art)

puzzle who is trying to think of an eight-letter word meaning "African anteater." If she comes up with the answer, we can be sure that she succeeded in all three aspects of remembering. The first is *acquisition.* To remember, one must first have learned; the puzzle solver must first have encountered and noted this particular item of zoological exotica. During this acquisition phase, the relevant experiences leave some record in the nervous system, the *memory trace.* Next comes *storage,* during which the memory traces are squirreled away and held in some more or less enduring form for later use (probably the next crossword puzzle). The final phase is *retrieval,* the point at which one "tries to remember," to dredge up this particular memory trace from among all the others we have stored. Many failures to remember are failures of retrieval and not of storage. Our crossword expert may be unable to come up with the correct answer at the time, but when she later sees the solution, she realizes that she'd known it all along: "Of course. It's *Aardvark!"*

The preceding discussion makes it clear that there can be no remembering without prior acquisition. But just what does this acquisition consist of? The subject presumably encountered the word *aardvark* on some previous occasion. But to understand just what she remembered and how, we have to know more than that some such encounter took place. We must also know how the item was *encoded.* Taken from computer science, the term *encoding* refers to the form (that is, the code) in which an item of information is stored. In most cases, there are a number of possible codings. The subject might have encoded the word as a sound pattern, or as a particular letter sequence, or in terms of its meaning, or as all of these. What she later remembers will generally reflect this encoding.

Encoding, storage, and retrieval are the three aspects of the memory process. Encoding and retrieval represent the start and the end of this process, and are the two aspects that can be studied more or less directly and that we will focus upon in this chapter. (For some discussion of storage, see pp. 278–79, 282–87.)

**Card games and memory** *Many card games make considerable demands on memory. Pictured here are children hard at work "playing" the game of "Memory." (Photograph by Kathy Hirsh-Pasek)*

There are two major methods psychologists employ to study these memory processes. The first is ***recall*** in which the subject is asked to *produce* an item or a set of items. Our anteater illustration is one example of a recall question. Others are "Where did you park your car?" or "What is the name of the boy who sat next to you in the third grade?" The experimental psychologist often tests for the recall of materials learned in the laboratory; this assures that any failures in recall aren't simply failures of original acquisition. The second method is ***recognition.*** A person is shown an item and has to indicate whether she has encountered it before, either in general ("Did you see this face before?") or in a particular context ("Is this one of the girls who played on your high school field hockey team?"). In the laboratory, the subject is usually asked to pick out the previously learned item from among several false alternatives. Examples are multiple-choice or true-false tests, which obviously put a greater premium on recognition than do essay or short-answer fill-in examinations whose emphasis is on recall.

## ENCODING

We'll begin our discussion by asking how memories are formed in the first place. The first step is encoding. We will begin our account by considering an important theory of memory, which we will here call the ***stage theory.*** As we'll see, this theory has been in some ways superseded by later discoveries, but its formulations still provide the framework for much of our current thinking about the topic.

### The Stage Theory of Memory

Memory has often been compared to a storehouse. This conception goes back to the Greek philosophers and to St. Augustine who described the "roomy chambers of memory, where are the treasures of countless images . . ." This spatial metaphor that likens memories to objects that are put into storage compartments, are held for a while, and are then searched for, is a recurrent theme in both ancient and modern thought.

An influential account developed some twenty years ago represents a modern variation on this same spatial metaphor but casts it within the framework of an information processing approach. Unlike Augustine who believed that there is one memorial warehouse, this theory asserts that there are several such storage systems, each with different properties (Broadbent, 1958; Waugh and Norman, 1965; Atkinson and Shiffrin, 1968).

The belief that there are several memory stores comes from the fact that memory may reach back for years but may also concern events that occurred just moments ago. We usually think of memory in terms of a past that is reckoned in hours, days, or years. But a moment's reflection tells us that memory comes into play as soon as the stimulus has disappeared from the scene. An example is a telephone number we look up and retain just long enough to complete the dialing; here the interval between acquisition and retrieval is a matter of mere seconds, but it is a memory all the same.

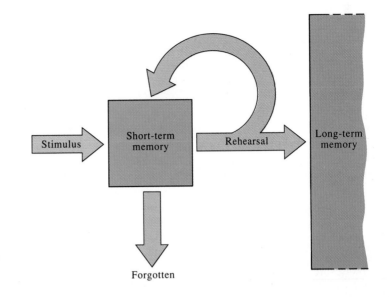

**7.1   The relation between the short-term and long-term memory system as envisaged by stage theory**   *The figure is a schematic representation of the relation between the two memory systems as stage theory conceived it. Information is encoded, and it enters the short-term store. To enter the long-term store, it must remain in short-term memory for a while. The means for maintaining it there is rehearsal. (Adapted from Waugh and Norman, 1965)*

These simple facts provide the starting points for the stage theory of memory. One of its assertions is that there are several memory systems. Of these, the most important are **short-term memory,** which holds information for fairly short intervals, and **long-term memory,** in which materials are stored for much longer periods, sometimes as long as a lifetime.* The second, and even more important assertion of the theory is that information enters these two systems in successive stages: to get to the long-term system, information must first pass through the short-term store (see Figure 7.1).

### SHORT-TERM MEMORY

There is reason to believe that memories for relatively recent and remote events differ in some important ways. Some pertain to the way in which these memories are consciously experienced. Others concern the storage capacity of the two postulated memory systems.

*Conscious experience and short-term memory*   According to many psychologists, an important difference between short-term and long-term memory concerns consciousness. Events that just occurred and are still in consciousness are thought to be in short-term memory, while those that are no longer in consciousness but can be brought back by recall or recognition are in long-term memory. When considered in this way, short-term and long-term memory are sometimes called **primary memory** and **secondary memory** respectively (James, W., 1890).

This distinction appears to fit the way in which we consciously experience our remembered past. Much of our past is experienced as gone and done with. The movie seen last night, the dinner enjoyed an hour ago, are in the past tense; they are remembered, not perceived. But this is not so for certain events that hap-

---

* The original theory asserted that there is an additional stage that precedes the others, which is a **sensory register** in which sensory material is held for a second or two (Sperling, 1960; Atkinson and Shiffrin, 1968), but some recent critiques have challenged this assumption (e.g., Haber, 1983).

pened just a few moments back. We hear a melody, and seem to perceive much or all of it in the present, even though the first chord has already ebbed away by the time the last note of the musical phrase reaches our ears. What is still in short-term (primary) memory is experienced as *now;* what has to be dredged up from long-term (secondary) memory is experienced as *then.*

*The capacity of short-term memory*   The **storage capacity** of short-term memory is markedly different from that of long-term memory. The capacity of long-term memory is enormous: The size of an average college student's reading vocabulary (about 80,000 words, according to one estimate) is documentation enough. In contrast, the capacity of short-term memory is exceedingly limited.

One way to determine the capacity of short-term memory is by measuring the **memory span,** the number of items an individual can recall after just one presentation. For normal adults, this span is remarkably consistent. If the items are randomly chosen letters or digits, the subject can recall about seven items, give or take about two. This quantity, 7 plus or minus 2, has been called the **magic number,** a widely quoted term originated by George Miller (Miller, 1956). According to Miller, this number represents the holding capacity of the short-term system, the number of items that will fit into its store at any one time. There is some debate about whether this number, 7 plus or minus 2, is really an accurate description of short-term capacity, but all investigators are agreed that this capacity is very small indeed.

### SHORT-TERM MEMORY AS A LOADING PLATFORM

What is the relation between short-term and long-term memory? The stage theory of memory asserts that the road into long-term memory necessarily passes through the short-term store. Seen in this light, short-term memory can be regarded as a loading platform into the huge long-term warehouse. A parcel that stays on the platform long enough may be picked up and placed in the warehouse. But the vast majority of the parcels never make it.

*Forgetting of recent memories*   Material in short-term memory is very short-lived. While reading the morning newspaper, we briefly note all kinds of extraneous matter; the coffee tastes bitter, a child is crying next door, there is a printer's error on the editorial page. But only a few moments hence these experiences are as if they had never been. One reason may be *decay:* The memory trace becomes eroded over time by some unknown physiological process, so its details become progressively less distinct. Another possibility is *displacement:* Items are somehow pushed out of memory by other items, perhaps those that enter later or those already there. The best evidence to date suggests that both factors play a role, that some packages on the platform rot away (decay) while others are shoved off by other packages (displacement). In either case, it is clear that they are not allowed to remain on the platform very long.

This rapid forgetting from short-term memory may be a blessing in disguise, for without it, our memory systems would be clogged with a clutter of useless information. Switchboard operators would be in poor shape if they were unable to forget a number immediately after they had dialed it. Given its limited capacity, the loading platform has to be cleared very quickly to make room for new packages as they arrive (Bjork, 1970).

**Overloading capacity**   *The limited cognitive capacity of the working memory system has its physical analogue in the demands sometimes made upon us in modern technological society as caricatured in this scene from Charlie Chaplin's 1936 film,* Modern Times. *(Courtesy the Kobal Collection)*

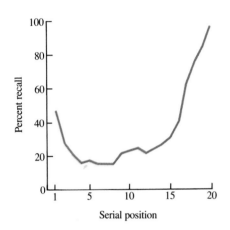

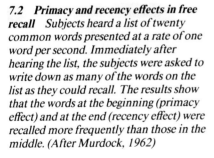

**7.2 Primacy and recency effects in free recall** *Subjects heard a list of twenty common words presented at a rate of one word per second. Immediately after hearing the list, the subjects were asked to write down as many of the words on the list as they could recall. The results show that the words at the beginning (primacy effect) and at the end (recency effect) were recalled more frequently than those in the middle. (After Murdock, 1962)*

*Transfer into long-term memory* According to stage theory, some items on the platform are eventually moved into the long-term store by an essentially mechanical transfer process. As we've seen, most packages disappear before this transfer can happen, but a few do remain on the platform for a while and thus become candidates for memorial tenure. Stage theorists believe that one reason why they will remain long enough to be transferred is *rehearsal.* By repeating an item over and over again, a subject will necessarily hold it in short-term memory, which increases the probability that this item will eventually be transferred into the long-term store.

These hypotheses about the relations between short- and long-term memory systems fit rather well with certain well-known facts obtained by the method of *free recall.* The subject hears a list of unrelated items, such as common English words, presented one at a time, and is asked to recall them in any order that she wants to. If the items are presented only once, and if their number exceeds the memory span, the subject cannot possibly produce them all. Under these circumstances, the likelihood that any one item will be recalled depends upon where in the list it was originally presented. Items that were presented at the beginning or the end of the list will be recalled much more often than those that were in the middle. The *primacy effect* describes the enhanced recall of items at the beginning; the *recency effect* designates the greater recall for those at the end (see Figure 7.2).

Stage theorists believe that the recency effect is produced because the items that were presented at the end of the list are retrieved from short-term memory. These items are generally reported first. They are still clear in the subject's memory because she heard them just a few seconds ago. As a result, she quickly recites them before they disappear from the short-term store. According to stage theory, the recency effect simply reflects this phenomenon: the fact that three or four items are still in the short-term store when the subject begins to recall, and that these items are the first she reports.*

According to stage theory, the items at the beginning of the list are presumably retrieved from long-term memory. One reason for this interpretation of the primacy effect is that the early items have had more opportunity for rehearsal and thus for transfer into the long-term store. For example, if the first three items are *camera, boat,* and *zebra,* the subject could give her full attention to rehearsing *camera* after hearing it. She would then have to divide her attention between rehearsing *camera* and *boat* after hearing the second item, divide it yet more to rehearse *camera, boat,* and *zebra* after hearing the third, and so on. The more attention a word gets, the more likely that word will make it to the long-term warehouse. Since the attention is greater for the words at the beginning than those that come later on, those first words have a memorial advantage over those that come later.

To sum up. The items at the beginning of the list benefit from the greater opportunity for rehearsal, which increases their chance to get into long-term memory (the primacy effect). The words at the end of the list benefit from the short time interval between their presentation and recall, which increases the chance that they will still be in short-term memory when the subject begins to report (the recency effect).

* Some authors use the recency effect to estimate the capacity of the short-term store. If assessed in this manner, its capacity is of the order of three items (Crowder, 1976).

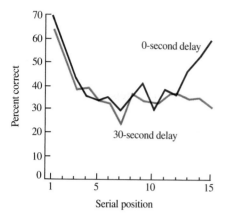

**7.3   The recency effect and short-term storage**   *Subjects heard several fifteen-word lists. In one condition (black), free recall was tested immediately after they heard the list. In the other condition (color), the recall test was given after a thirty-second delay during which rehearsal was prevented. The long delay left the primacy effect unaffected but abolished the recency effect, indicating that this effect is based on retrieval from short-term storage. (After Glanzer and Cunitz, 1966)*

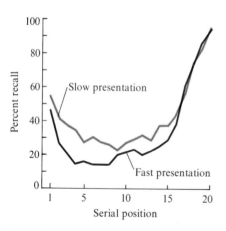

**7.4   The primacy effect and long-term storage**   *The figure compares free-recall performance when item presentation is relatively slow (two seconds per item) and fast (one second per item). Slow presentation enhances the primacy effect but leaves the recency effect unaltered. The additional second per item presumably allowed more time for rehearsal which leads to long-term storage. (After Murdock, 1962)*

Supporting evidence for these interpretations comes from various manipulations of the primacy and recency effects. One important factor is the interval between the last item on the list and the signal to recall. If this interval is increased to thirty seconds (during which the subject performs some mental tasks such as counting backwards so she can't rehearse), the primacy effect remains unchanged but the recency effect is completely abolished. This is just what one would expect if the last items are stored in short-term memory from which forgetting is very rapid (see Figure 7.3). Other procedures diminish the primacy effect. An example is the rate at which items are presented. If this rate is relatively fast the subject has less time for rehearsal. As a result, there is less transfer to long-term storage. We would therefore expect a reduced primacy effect but no particular change in the recency effect, and this is again what happens (see Figure 7.4).

NEUROPSYCHOLOGICAL EVIDENCE FOR THE STAGE THEORY

One of the most persuasive arguments for the separation between short- and long-term memory came from work on brain-damaged persons. Some of these patients suffer deficits that seemed to fit well with the idea that short-term memory and long-term memory represent two distinct memory systems. In some patients, the primary difficulty seems to be with forming new long-term memories; in others, the problem is with the short-term store.

*Impairments in long-term storage*   Certain lesions in the temporal cortex (specifically, in the **hippocampus** and other structures near the base of the brain) produce a memory disorder called **anterograde amnesia** (anterograde, "in a forward direction"). The patient often has little trouble in remembering whatever he had learned prior to the injury: his difficulty is learning anything new thereafter. Such lesions can occur in various ways. They are found in certain chronic alcoholic patients who suffer from **Korsakoff syndrome** (named after the Russian physician who first described it). They sometimes accompany senility. In a famous case, they were a tragic side effect of neurosurgery that was undertaken to minimize seizures in H.M., a patient with severe epilepsy (see Figure 7.5).

H.M.'s hippocampal lesion occurred when he was twenty-nine. Following the surgery he had a normal memory span. But he seemed to be incapable of adding any new information to his long-term storage. He often could not recognize anyone he had not met before the surgery, no matter how often they met afterward. He was unable to find his way to the new house his family moved into after his operation. When told that his uncle had died he was deeply moved, but then forgot all about it and repeatedly asked when his uncle would come to visit. On each occasion he was informed once more of his uncle's death, and every time his grief was as intense as before; to him, each time he was told was the first (Milner, 1966; Milner, Corkin, and Teuber, 1968; Marslen-Wilson and Teuber, 1975; Corkin, 1984).

While H.M.'s long-term storage system apparently became almost completely closed to any new memories, his memories prior to the operation remained largely intact, especially for events that happened more than a year or so before the surgery. He could still read and write and engage in lively conversation. In many ways, his intellectual functioning was unimpaired. This is not uncommon in patients suffering damage to the hippocampus and related systems. Korsakoff's original patient could still play a competent game of chess though he could not remember how any given position on the chess board came about.

**7.5  Regions of the brain where damage can cause memory loss**  *A cutaway section of the human brain showing regions of the hippocampus and associated structures whose destruction caused H.M.'s massive memory deficits. Patients with Korsakoff's syndrome tend to have lesions in regions that lie higher up, including the thalamus, while patients with Alzheimer's disease show damage in the base of the forebrain. (Adapted from Mishkin and Appenzeller, 1987)*

Area where damage leads to Alzheimer's disease

Area where damage leads to Korsakoff's syndrome

Surgery for epilepsy (as in H.M.) destroys these areas

*Impairments in short-term storage*  H.M.'s deficit suggested a normal short-term system, coupled with an inability to transfer materials from the short-term to the long-term store. There are some brain-damaged patients whose defects are the precise opposite. One such patient showed some mild aphasic symptoms, but no general intellectual impairment. His defects involved the short-term system. He had a memory span of about two, and on tests of free recall he had a much diminished recency effect. But his long-term memory was essentially normal as shown on various tests of memorization. Here seemed to be yet further confirmation of the distinction between short- and long-term memory (Shallice and Warrington, 1970; Basso, Spinnler, Vallar, and Zanobio, 1982).

OVERCOMING THE SHORT-TERM BOTTLENECK

Stage theory asserts that in order to enter long-term storage, items must first pass through short-term memory. But as we have seen, the short-term loading platform has a limited capacity. It can handle only a small number of packages at any one time. In view of this bottleneck, how do we manage to deposit so much material in the long-term store? Stage theory's answer is organization. The capacity limit of the loading platform is on the number of packages, which is exceedingly small (perhaps $7 \pm 2$). But what these packages contain is up to us. If we can pack the input more efficiently, we may squeeze more information into the same number of memorial units.

*Recoding into larger chunks*  As an example consider a subject who tries to recall a series of digits that he heard only once:

$$1\ 4\ 9\ 1\ 6\ 2\ 5\ 3\ 6\ 4\ 9\ 6\ 4\ 8\ 1$$

If he treats this as a series of fifteen unrelated digits, he will almost surely fail. But if he recognizes that the digits form a pattern, specifically

$$1\ 4\ 9\ 16\ 25\ 36\ 49\ 64\ 81$$

his task has become absurdly easy. He only has to remember the underlying relationship "the squares of the digits from 1 to 9," and the fifteen components of the series are easily recreated.

251

**The role of chunking in remembering a visual display** *Could anyone possibly remember all the figures in this bewildering array? He might, if he knew Netherlandish proverbs of the sixteenth century, for that is what the painting depicts. To mention only some, there is (going from left to right): a man who "butts his head against the wall," another who is "armed to the teeth" and "ties a bell to the cat," and two women of whom "one spins while the other winds" (malicious gossips). Going further left, we see a woman who "puts a blue cloak over her husband" (deceives him), a man who "fills the hole after his calf was drowned," and another who "throws roses [we say pearls] before swine." Recognizing these scenes as illustrations of familiar proverbs will organize the visual array and thus help to remember its many parts. (Detail of* Netherlandish Proverbs *by Pieter Brueghel, 1559; courtesy Gemäldegalerie, Staatliche Museen PreuBischer Kulturbesitz, Berlin)*

A similar example is the letter series

C I A F B I I B M T W A

This is again quite difficult if interpreted as a series of twelve unrelated letters. But if it is reorganized by three-letter groupings, specifically

CIA FBI IBM TWA

the recall task is again perfectly trivial.

In both of these examples, the subject has repackaged the material to be remembered. He has ***recoded*** the input into larger units that are often called ***chunks.*** Each chunk imposes about the same load on memory as did each of the smaller units that are contained within it. But when eventually unpacked, each of these chunks yields much more information.

Much of the job of recoding items into larger chunks (often called ***chunking***) has occurred in our early life. To an adult, a word is already a coherent whole, not merely a sequence of sounds. Still higher units of memorial organization are involved in the memory for sentences. The memory span for unrelated words is about six or seven items, but we may well recall a fairly long sentence after only a single exposure. This fact even holds for sentences that make little sense, such as *The enemy submarine dove into the coffee pot, took fright, and silently flew away.* This dubious bit of naval intelligence consists of fourteen words, but it clearly contains fewer than fourteen memorial packages: *the enemy submarine* is essentially one unit, *took fright* is another, and so on.

### SOME PROBLEMS OF THE STAGE THEORY

The stage theory of memory dominated much of the field's thinking for several decades. But as time went on, there was a reevaluation.

*Some further neuropsychological findings*   As we've seen, brain damage can produce two opposite patterns of memory defects. Some patients show normal short-term memories coupled with massive defects in long-term learning ability, while others can learn perfectly well but show grossly defective short-term memory performance. On the face of it, these two patterns of memory impairment seem to provide powerful evidence for the distinction between short-term and long-term memory which stage theory postulates. But on further reflection this is not so clear.

The problem is that some of the persons whose short-term performance is so very deficient can acquire new information and lead perfectly active and successful lives. One works as a personal secretary, another runs a shop and looks after a household. But how could they manage to do all this if the only road to long-term memory runs through the short-term system? It would seem that the short-term store can't have the enormous significance that stage theory assigns to it (Basso et al., 1982; Vallar and Baddeley, 1984).

*Maintenance rehearsal*   An even more important challenge to stage theory came from some findings on the effect of rehearsal. Stage theory asserts that when an item is rehearsed, it is more likely to enter long-term memory. According to stage theory, this transfer from a short-term loading platform to the long-term warehouse depends entirely on how long that item has been on the platform. The longer it sits there, the greater will be its probability of being transferred. According to this view, rehearsal helps because it keeps the item in the short-term store for a longer period, and keeps it from rotting away or being displaced before that transfer can happen. But there is evidence that entering long-term memory is by no means as automatic as this.

It turns out that one form of rehearsal does relatively little in the long run. This is called ***maintenance rehearsal,*** through which the subject mentally holds on to the material for a little while but does nothing more. We use this form of rehearsal when we try to retain a telephone number just long enough to complete the call. We repeat it to ourselves until we begin dialing and then promptly forget it. Experimental evidence on the effect of maintenance rehearsal comes from an ingenious study that varied the time in which items remained in short-term memory. The subjects listened to a number of lists of words, and they were asked to monitor each list for words beginning with a certain letter. The lists varied in length. At the end of each list, the subjects had to report the last word on the list that began with that letter. Suppose the letter was *G* and that the list was as follows:

> *Daughter,     Oil,     Rifle,     Garden,     Grain,     Table,*
> *Football,     Anchor,     Giraffe,     Pillow,     Thunder.*

In this situation, the subject has to hold one G-word in short-term memory until the next one appears. Thus *Garden* will be replaced by *Grain* which will make way for *Giraffe* and so on until the end of the list is reached, at which time the subject has to come up with the *last* G-word—in the present case, *Giraffe.* This arrangement guarantees that some of the G-words are held longer in short-term memory than others are; thus *Grain* will stay longer than *Garden.* The question was whether this increased stay in the short-term store increased the chance that *Garden* would be transferred to long-term memory. To find out, the experimenters gave a final—and quite unexpected—test after the end of the session when many such lists had been presented. They simply asked the subjects to report as many of the G-words they had heard as they could. The results showed that the time an item had been in short-term memory had no effect—*Garden* was recalled just as often as was *Grain* (Craik and Watkins, 1973). The results of this and further studies indicate that maintenance rehearsal confers little or no benefit in aiding recall (Rundus, 1977).

## A Changed Emphasis: Active Memory and Organization

The preceding discussion highlighted some of the problems of the stage theory of memory. These difficulties eventually led to a theoretical reorientation in the way psychologists today think of memory processes. One change concerns the conception of short-term memory. Another is an emphasis on the role of processing and organization.

### THE CONCEPT OF ACTIVE MEMORY

As we saw, stage theorists conceived of short- and long-term memory as memory depots in a traffic flow in which information was moved from a small short-term loading platform to the more spacious long-term store. Today, however, most theorists believe that long-term memories are formed by a more active process in which the subject's own ways of encoding and organizing the material play a major role. As a result, they regard short-term memory not so much as a temporary storage platform but rather as a mental workbench on which various items of experience are held while they are sorted, manipulated, and organized. According to this view, whether the materials will be retained in memory and eventually retrieved does not depend upon a simple transfer from one storage container to

***Active memory at work*** *Cardplayers have to call on active memory to decide which cards were played most recently and which should be played next. (*The Cardplayers, *by Paul Cezanne; courtesy The Metropolitan Museum of Art, Bequest of Stephen C. Clark, 1960)*

another. Instead, it depends on how this material is processed (that is, encoded). The more elaborate the processing, the greater the likelihood of later recall and recognition.

Considerations of this sort led many psychologists to abandon the concept of short-term memory as a mere storage depot (Crowder, 1982). It also led many of them to prefer the terms *active memory* or *working memory* (or William James's *primary memory)* to the older designation *short-term memory.* The newer terms focus on the way in which memories are *processed* rather than on the hypothetical *structures* in which these memories are held. Seen in this light, the key difference is between those portions of our memory system that are currently *activated* (and acted upon) on the one hand—that is active memory—and those that are currently *dormant* on the other—that is, long-term memory. This new conception can easily account for the findings that first led to the belief in a short-term memory store with a limited capacity. As modern investigators think about it, what's limited is not the storage area but rather the processing capacity. There is only so much cognitive processing (or mental effort) the system can engage in at any time, for active memory deals with whatever is currently thought about and dealt with. This may be something we want to remember, if only for a moment, like a telephone number before it is dialed. Or it may be some mental task such as multiplying two-digit numbers in our heads, where we have to keep track of the numbers, the partial products, and the point we're at in the problem.

If this is correct, the appropriate metaphor for the limited capacity of the working memory system is not really a loading platform that can *hold* only so many parcels. It is rather an overworked operative at the memory workbench who can only *pack* so many parcels—can only do so much chunking and organizing and linking materials to prior memories—at any one time. It's as if he (or she, or it) has only so many mental hands (Baddeley, 1976, 1986).

PROCESSING AND ORGANIZING: THE ROYAL ROAD INTO MEMORY

Our previous discussion has already pointed to the importance of how the subject encodes the incoming material for later recall. Certain ways of encoding (such as those produced by chunking) evidently promote better recall; others (such as those produced by maintenance rehearsal) are of much less help. What is it that the more helpful forms of encoding have in common?

*Depth of processing* An influential attempt to explain why some encodings help recall more than others argued that success in remembering depends on the *depth* at which the incoming information has been processed (Craik and Lockhart, 1972). The advocates of this *depth of processing* approach have performed many experiments that compare the effect of "shallow" and "deep" processing on later recall. For verbal materials, the term "shallow" is generally used for encoding of superficial characteristics such as sound, while "deep" refers to meaning. In one such study, subjects were briefly shown forty-eight words as part of an experiment that they were told was concerned with perception and speed of reaction. As each word was presented, the subject was asked one of three possible questions. One had to do with the word's physical appearance ("Is it printed in capital letters?"); another concerned the word's sound ("Does it rhyme with *train?*"); while a third concerned the word's meaning ("Would it fit into the sentence: *The girl placed the _____ on the table?*"). The first question would presumably lead to the shallowest encoding, the third to the deepest. After the subjects had gone through the entire list of forty-eight words, they were given an unexpected final task: They were asked to write down as many of the words they had seen as they could remember. The results were in line with the depth of processing hypothesis. Words that called for the shallowest processing (typeface) were recalled worst of all; words that required an intermediary level (sound) were recalled a bit better; and words that demanded the deepest level (meaning) were recalled best of all (Craik and Tulving, 1975).

Some of the original formulations of the depth of processing hypothesis have come under attack. For example, some critics charged that there is really no satisfactory definition of *depth* (Baddeley, 1978). But even so, one of the key assertions of this approach still stands: What is remembered depends crucially on how it was originally encoded.

*Organization*   The depth of processing hypothesis emphasized the importance of meaning. A related view stresses **organization.** We already encountered the importance of organization when we took up chunking. Further evidence comes from a number of further findings that elaborate on the nature of the chunking and organizational process.

Chunks like the first nine squares, well-known acronyms such as FBI, and English words are taken from the subject's prior experience; all she has to do is to recognize them. But in many cases, the would-be memorizer will not be lucky enough to have all the material neatly pre-chunked; she has to perform some of the chunking herself if she wants to remember successfully.

A recent experiment gives dramatic proof of the power of recoding in creating newer and larger chunks that expand our normal capacity for a particular memory task. The heroic subject was an undergraduate who devoted some 230 hours to the task of becoming a virtuoso at recalling strings of digits. In each session he heard random digits presented at a rate of one per second and then tried to recall the sequence. If his recall was correct, the sequence was increased by one digit; if it was incorrect, it was decreased by one digit. After more than twenty months of this, the subject's digit span had risen enormously: from an initial starting point of seven to a final level of almost eighty (Figure 7.6). What happened was that the subject had learned to recode the digit sequences into meaningful subparts, thus creating larger chunks. He was a long-distance runner who competed in major athletic events. This led him to express three- and four-digit groups as running times for various races (e.g., 3492 became "3 minutes 49 point 2 seconds, near world record time"), a device supplemented with ages (893 became "89 point 3, very old man") and dates (1944 was "near end of World War II"). These recoded strings of digits became chunked groups in memory. This was neatly shown by the subject's pause as he produced the digits in recall—virtually all of his pauses fell between the groups rather than within them (Ericsson, Chase, and Faloon, 1980).

Chunking is a way to relate incoming items to each other so that they can be more readily recalled. But these relationships will often go unrecognized unless we can relate the materials to what we already know. This organization may help us to understand what we hear or see with powerful effects on later recall. An example is an experiment in which two groups of subjects were presented with a tape-recorded passage and were asked to try to understand and remember it. The passage was as follows:

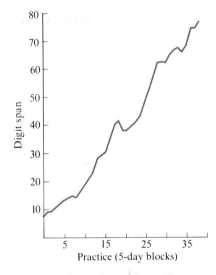

**7.6   Chunking makes perfect**   *The figure shows an enormous increase in memory span after twenty months of practice during which the subject learned to code digit sequences into meaningful subparts. (After Ericsson, Chase, and Faloon, 1980)*

The procedure is actually quite simple. First you arrange things into different groups depending on their makeup. Of course, one pile may be sufficient depending on how much there is to do. If you have to go somewhere else due to lack of facilities that is the next step, otherwise you are pretty well set. It is important not to overdo any particular endeavor. That is, it is better to do too few things at once than too many. In the short run this may not seem important, but complications from doing too many can easily arise. A mistake can be expensive as well. The manipulation of the appropriate mechanisms should be self-explanatory, and we need not dwell on it here. At first, the whole procedure will seem complicated. Soon, however, it will become just another facet of life. It is difficult to foresee any end to the necessity for this task in the immediate future, but then one never can tell (From Bransford and Johnson, 1972, p. 722).

Both groups of subjects heard the identical passage and were treated identically in all regards but one. One group heard the passage without any further information as to what it was about. The other group was told: "The paragraph you will hear will be about washing clothes." Not surprisingly, the two groups performed very differently on both tests of comprehension and of general recall (total number of ideas in the paragraph). Once they knew the sentences were about washing, the sentences in the paragraph could be related to what the subjects already knew. This meaningful encoding helped later recall (Bransford and Johnson, 1972).

MNEMONICS

The general principles of memorial organization we have just discussed also underlie a very practical endeavor whose roots go back to ancient times—the development of techniques for improving one's memory, often called ***mnemonics.***

*Mnemonics through verbal organization*    The ancients were well aware that it is much easier to remember verbal material if it is organized. They were particularly partial to the use of verse, a phonological organization of word sequences which maintains a fixed rhythm and rhyme. Without such aids, preliterate societies might never have transmitted their oral traditions intact from one generation to the next. Homeric bards could recite the entire *Iliad,* but could they have done so had it been in prose? Verse is still used as a mnemonic when it seems necessary to impose some sort of order upon an otherwise arbitrary set of items (e.g., "Thirty days hath September/April, June, and November").

*Mnemonics through visual imagery*    Some of the most effective mnemonics ever devised involve the deliberate use of mental imagery. One such technique is the ***method of loci,*** which requires the learner to visualize each of the items she wants to remember in a different spatial location (locus). In recall, each location is mentally inspected and the item that was placed there in imagination is thus retrieved. This method provides a scheme that allows orderly retrieval. It requires a deliberate effort to relate the items that must be memorized to distinctive features of the retrieval scheme, and to do so through visual imagery. The efficacy of this mnemonic system has been tested by several experimental studies. Subjects who recalled by the method of loci recalled up to seven times more than their counterparts who learned in rote manner. In one such study, college students had to learn lists of forty unrelated concrete nouns. Each list was presented once for about ten minutes, during which the subjects tried to visualize each of the forty objects in one of forty different locations around the college campus. Tested immediately, they recalled an average of thirty-eight of the forty items; tested one day later, they still managed to recall thirty-four (Ross and Lawrence, 1968).

*Why does imagery help?* Why are images such a powerful aid to memory? One of the reasons may be that they are yet another way of forming a new chunk in memory. By creating a mental image, the subject joins two unrelated items so that they form a new whole. When part of the chunk (the imagined locus) is presented, the entire chunk is retrieved, yielding the part required for recall.

Some evidence for this view comes from studies that show that mental images will only facilitate recall if they tend to unify the items to be associated into a coherent whole. Consider a subject who has to learn a list of noun-noun pairs such as *eagle-locomotive* and is instructed to use imagery as an aid to memory. She can construct mental pictures that bring the items into some kind of unitary relationship, for example, an eagle winging to his nest with a locomotive in his beak. But she may form an image whose constituents are merely adjacent and do not interact, such as an eagle at the side of a locomotive. Several recent experiments demonstrate that unifying mental images produce much better recall than non-unifying images (Wollen, Weber, and Lowry, 1972). A similar effect is found when the test items are real pictures. If shown a drawing of a doll standing on a chair waving a flag, subjects quickly reply "chair and flag" when asked to recall the objects that were pictured with the doll. Their recall score is substantially lower if they were shown a picture of the doll, chair, and flag, drawn as separate, unrelated objects (Figure 7.7).

*The usefulness of mnemonics in everyday life* Mnemonic systems provide effective means for imposing organization upon otherwise disparate materials, such as a foreign vocabulary list or nonsense materials developed in the psychological laboratory. But we are not often confronted by such arbitrary pairings. A student reading a history text does not have to impose an organization. His job is to discover the organization that is already inherent in the material. When he does so, the various treaties and battles will fall into an appropriate mental scheme, linked to each other and to relevant historical matters that have been learned before. But imagery mnemonics will not help to provide this scheme. A visual image that links, say, General Custer and Chief Sitting Bull, will be of little use in helping the student understand the conflict between the American Indians and the encroaching settlers.

**7.7 Interactive and noninteractive depictions** *Subjects shown related elements, such as a doll standing on a chair and waving a flag (A) are more likely to associate the words* doll, flag, *and* chair *than subjects who are shown the three objects next to each other but not interacting (B), (After Bower, 1970)*

A

B

In short, the best prescription for recall is to organize and understand the material at the time it is learned. If this material is devoid of inherent organization, some organization must be imposed upon it. In that case mnemonic devices, especially imagery, are a useful tool. If the material is already organized, the best approach is to discover that organization and to chunk the various items in terms of it.

## RETRIEVAL

We've considered some of the ways in which memories are acquired. We will now ask how they are retrieved from storage.

That memory storage is not the same as memory retrieval is obvious to anyone who has ever blocked on a familiar name. We may know (that is, have stored) a name, a fact, an event, or whatever, and still be unable to retrieve it on a particular occasion. In such cases, the memory trace is said to be *inaccessible.* Access to the trace may be restored by an appropriate **retrieval cue,** a stimulus that opens the path to the memory. This point has often been demonstrated experimentally. Subjects are presented with a list of words that belong to various categories and are then tested for free recall. They may neglect to recall any word from a particular rubric. If now prompted by the category name, they readily produce several of the appropriate items (Tulving and Pearlstone, 1966).

The phenomenon of retrieving a memory that at first seemed altogether lost is well-known. The very words in which we describe our memorial functions testify to the distinction between storage and retrieval: We are *re*minded, we *re*member, we *re*collect—even our vocabulary suggests that what is now brought up was not available before. The recollection of temporarily inaccessible memories by appropriate retrieval cues is usually a rather humdrum event. We can't recall where we parked on a shopping trip, are reminded that our first stop was in a drugstore, and suddenly remember squeezing the car into a narrow space just across the street. But occasionally the effect is much more dramatic. Some persons have reported being unable to recall some of the simplest geographical features of the hometown they left years before. They finally returned for a visit, barely reached the outskirts, and suddenly all of the memories flooded back, often with a sharp pang of emotions that had been felt years before. Physical places are only one source of retrieval cues that may bring back the past. A word, a mood, a smell, a visit from a school friend not met for decades—any of these may trigger memories we thought were utterly lost.

### The Relation between Original Encoding and Retrieval

What are the characteristics of an effective retrieval cue? It is obvious that not every reminder will in fact *re*mind us, will in fact retrieve what is stored. The best guess is that success is most likely if the context at the time of retrieval approximates that during original encoding. This is sometimes called the principle of **encoding specificity** (Tulving and Osler, 1968; Tulving and Thomson, 1973).

One obvious test is to vary the physical conditions during which the subject learns and is later asked to remember. A rather dramatic illustration is provided

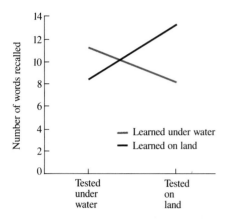

**7.8 The effect of changing the retrieval situation** *Scuba divers learned a list of 36 unrelated words above water (black) or 20 feet underwater (color) and were then tested above or underwater. The figure shows that retention was better when the retrieval situation was the same as that in which encoding took place. (Godden and Baddeley, 1975)*

**Retrieval cues in the movies** *A scene from Charlie Chaplin's 1931 film,* City Lights, *which shows the little tramp with a millionaire, played by Harry Myers, who befriends him one night while drunk, doesn't recognize him the next morning when he is sober, but greets him as an old friend when he gets drunk again the following night. While nowhere as extreme as this, such* **state-dependent memory effects** *have been observed in the laboratory. (Eich, 1980; courtesy Photofest)*

by a study of scuba divers who had to learn a list of unrelated words either on shore or underwater and who were later tested for recall in either the same or the alternate environment in which they had learned. The results showed a clear-cut context effect: what was learned in the water was best recalled in the water and similarly for what was learned on land (Godden and Baddeley, 1975; see Figure 7.8).

Similar effects can be obtained without going underwater. One experimenter presented subjects with a large list of words. A day later he brought them back for an unexpected recall test that took place in either the same room or a different one that varied in size, furnishings, and so on. Recall was considerably better for subjects who were tested in the same physical environment. But the investigator found a simple way of overcoming this context effect. A different group of subjects was brought to the new room, but just prior to the recall test these subjects were asked to think about the room in which they had learned the lists—what it looked like, what it made them feel like. By doing so, they mentally recreated the old environment for themselves. On the subsequent recall test, these subjects performed no worse than those for whom there was no change of rooms. It appears that what matters is not so much that the retrieval cues physically match the conditions of acquisition; what counts is how the subject thinks about these conditions at the time he tries to recall (Smith, S.M., 1979).

### Elaborative Rehearsal

The role of retrieval cues may help to explain why some ways of encoding are so much better than others for later recall. We've seen that organization helps, that chunking (which is a close relative of organization) helps, that deeper processing helps. But why? One might think that these superior ways of encoding allow us to *store* the material more efficiently. Perhaps they do. But they have an even more important effect—they make material easier to *find* when we later try to retrieve it. The key to good encoding is to provide means for later retrieval.

Evidence comes from a comparison of two forms of rehearsal. As we've previously seen, maintenance rehearsal, in which material is passively held in short-term memory, is of little help in recall. But there is another kind of rehearsal that has a powerful effect. That is ***elaborative rehearsal.*** This is a general term for the mental activities by means of which the subject organizes the items he wants to remember. He may organize them, recode them into fewer chunks, or relate them to each other and to other material in long-term memory—all of these are ways that help him store the material more efficiently. But this kind of rehearsal has another and even more important function: It increases the likelihood of later retrieval. If the subject is asked to recall, say, a list of words, then any one of these words that comes to mind will help him to retrieve more of the others. In addition, whatever else he saw and thought about at the time of rehearsal will also be connected to some of the items and may later serve as a retrieval cue. In the ancient world, all roads led to Rome and so the traveller could always find it. Much the same holds true for elaborative rehearsal. Every elaboration builds another path by which the material can later be reached; the more such paths exist, the easier retrieval will be (Craik and Tulving, 1975).

Evidence comes from a study in which the degree of elaboration was varied. Subjects were presented with sentences in which one word was missing. Some of these were rather simple, such as: "He cooked the _____." Others were more complex, such as: "The great bird swooped down and carried off the struggling _____." The subjects' task was to decide whether a given target word (for example, *chicken*) could appropriately fit the sentence frame. After sixty such trials, the subjects were (unexpectedly) asked to recall as many of the target words as they could. In line with the elaboration rehearsal hypothesis, the more complex sentence frames led to better recall. The richer encoding contexts presumably built more and better retrieval paths (Craik and Tulving, 1975).

## Memory Search

Many investigators believe that retrieval is generally preceded by an internal process called *memory search.* In most cases, this process occurs without our awareness and at great speed, as when answering the question: "Which president of the United States had the first name 'Abraham'?" But there are times when we do become aware that some such process is going on, as we consciously sift and sort among our memories until we finally recall just who it was that did what to whom on which occasion many years ago.

### SEARCH STRATEGIES

In a recent study of such conscious search processes, subjects were asked to try to recall the names of their high school classmates after intervals of from four to nineteen years. Their recall accuracy was checked by consulting their high school yearbooks. The subjects came up with a fair number of names in the first few minutes of this attempt. After this, they said that they couldn't remember any more. But the experimenters asked them to keep on trying anyway. And so they did, for ten sessions of one hour each. As they continued their efforts, they surprised themselves by dredging up more and more names, until they finally recalled about a third of the names of a class of 300 (Williams and Hollan, 1982).

While going about this task, the subjects were asked to think aloud. Their comments fit the analogy to a physical search. They seemed to hunt for the sought-for names as one might search for a tangible object, inspecting one likely memory location after another. Their efforts were rarely haphazard, but seemed often based on well-formulated search strategies. For example, they mentally looked through their various classes, clubs, and teams, or scanned internal pictures to locate yet another person whom they would then try to name:

> . . . It's like I want to think of, sort of prototypical situations and then sort of examine the people that were involved in those. And things like P.E. class, where there was . . . Ah . . . Gary Booth. Umm, and Karl Brist . . . Umm . . . I can think of things like dances. I guess then I usually think of . . . of girls . . . Like Cindy Shup, Judy Foss, and Sharon Ellis . . . I mean it's sort of like I have a picture of the high school dance. . . . (Williams and Hollan, 1982, p. 90)

### THE TIP-OF-THE-TONGUE PHENOMENON

Needless to say, search isn't always successful. Some forgotten names are never retrieved, no matter how hard we try. But occasionally, we experience a kind of

*External aids to memory*  *People often rely on external memory aids. Some remind us of events in our past, such as family albums and diaries. Others remind us of plans for future actions, such as calendars, memo pads, and shopping lists. (Photograph by Nina Leen/Life)*

**Instructions**

Here are the dictionary definitions of twelve uncommon words. Please look at each definition in turn. Try to think of the word. There are several possibilities:

1. You may be pretty sure that you know the word. Or you may be quite sure that you don't know it. In *either* case, just move on to the next definition on the list.
2. You may feel that you know the word, but can't recall it just now. In fact, it may be "on the tip of your tongue." If so, quickly do the following:

a. Guess the letter of the first word.

b. Try to think of one or two words that sound similar to the one you're trying to find.

Follow this procedure as you go through the whole list of definitions. Then turn to the next left-hand page for the list of the words that fit these definitions.

**Definitions**

1. A blood feud in which members of the family of a murdered person try to kill the murderer or members of his family
2. A protecting charm to ward off spirits
3. An old coin of Spain and South America
4. A dark, hard, glassy volcanic rock
5. A secretion from the sperm whale used in the manufacture of perfume
6. A building used for public worship by Moslems
7. An Egyptian ornament in the shape of a beetle
8. The staff of Hermes, symbol of a physician or of the medical corps
9. A sword with a short curved blade, used by the Turks and Arabs
10. A Russian sled drawn by three horses
11. A navigational instrument used in measuring altitudes
12. A narrow strip of land by which two larger bodies of land are connected

***7.9 The tip-of-the-tongue phenomenon*** *This figure may provide an opportunity to demonstrate how something can be close to being retrieved from memory but not quite. (Adapted from Foard, 1975)*

halfway point, when we seem to recall something but not quite. When this occurs, we feel as if the searched-for memory is on "the tip of the tongue," but we are unable to go beyond. There is no better description of what this experience feels like than that by William James:

> Suppose we try to recall a forgotten name. The state of our consciousness is peculiar. There is a gap therein; but no mere gap. It is a gap that is intensely active. A sort of wraith of the name is in it, beckoning us in a given direction, making us at moments tingle with the sense of our closeness, and then letting us sink back without the longed-for term. If wrong names are proposed to us, this singularly definite gap acts immediately so as to negate them. They do not fit into its mold. And the gap of one word does not feel like the gap of another, all empty of content as both might seem necessarily to be when described as gaps. (W. James, 1890, vol. 1, p. 251)

There is evidence that the tip-of-the-tongue experience described by James is a good reflection of how close to the mark we had actually come in our memory search, that we were really "getting warm," though unable to reach the exact spot. In one study college students were presented with the dictionary definitions of uncommon English words such as *apse, sampan,* and *cloaca.* The subjects were asked to supply the words that fit these definitions. The experimenters were concerned with those occasions on which subjects were unable to recall the target word but felt that they were on the verge of finding it (see Figure 7.9). Whenever this happened, they were asked to venture some guesses about what the target word sounded like. These guesses turned out to be closely related to the target. Given that the target word was said to be at the tip-of-the-tongue, its initial letter was guessed correctly over 50 percent of the time. Similar results were found when the subjects were asked to guess at the number of syllables. When asked to supply some other words which they thought sounded like the target, the subjects were usually in the correct phonological neighborhood. Presented with the definition "a small Chinese boat" for which the proper answer is *sampan,* subjects who said they almost remembered but not quite, supplied the following as sound-alikes: *Saipan, Saim, Cheyenne,* and *sarong* (Brown and McNeill, 1966; Koriat and Lieblich, 1974).

## Implicit Memory

Up to now, we've considered only methods of retrieval that are *explicit,* specifically recall and recognition. In both procedures, the subject is asked a question that refers to her prior experience. She may be tested for recall: "Tell me the name of one of your former high school teachers." Or she may be asked for recognition: "Was Mr. Halberdam one of your former high school teachers?" In either case, the question explicitly refers to the subject's remembered past. But retrieval need not be explicit. An example comes from the performance of well-practiced skills. The pianist is not consciously aware of when and where he learned to finger the keys as he strikes a chord, nor does the golfer consciously remember where and how he perfected his golf swing while swinging the club. We know of course that the achievements of these skilled performers are honed by constant practice and thus depend on memory. To play the chord or hit the ball, both pianist and golfer necessarily retrieve something from memory, but these retrievals are *implicit* rather than explicit, for there is typically no awareness of "remembering" at the time. In consequence, the memory that underlies such retrievals is sometimes called ***implicit memory*** (Graf and Schacter, 1985; Schacter, 1987).

Implicit memory has been the subject of many laboratory investigations (see Lewandowsky, Dunn, and Kirsner, 1989). In one such study the subjects were shown a number of words after which they were given two tests of memory. The first was a test of explicit memory, in which a standard recognition procedure was employed. The second was a test of implicit memory, in which the subjects' task was to identify words that were flashed on a screen for 35 milliseconds. Some of these words were the same as those that had been on the original list. The results of this second test showed ***repetition priming:*** Words that were on the original list were identified more readily than words that were not. The crucial finding was that this priming effect held even for words that the subjects failed to recognize on the previous test of explicit memory. In short, subjects may have implicit memory for items that they cannot consciously—that is, explicitly—remember (Jacoby and Witherspoon, 1982).

Similar implicit memory effects have been shown using a number of other priming procedures. An example is word completion, in which subjects are presented with a word fragment (such as C_O_O_I_E for CROCODILE) and have to complete it with the first appropriate word that comes to mind. Here priming is indicated by an increased tendency to use words that were shown on a previous list (Jacoby and Dallas, 1981; Tulving, Schacter, and Stark, 1982; Graf and Mandler, 1984).

One might suppose that implicit modes of retrieval are not really different from the more explicit kinds except for being more sensitive. But there are differences, for implicit memory tasks seem to tap some different aspects of memory than do traditional tests of recall and recognition. One example concerns depth of processing, which affects explicit and implicit memory differently. We've previously seen that subjects who encode words for meaning (deep processing) tend to remember these words better than subjects who encode them by sound or visual appearance (shallow processing), and that they benefit more from elaborative rehearsal than from mere maintenance rehearsal. But recall and recognition are tests of explicit memory. When the test is for implicit memory, these effects do not hold. Thus repetition priming is unaffected by whether the items were encoded deeply or shallowly, or whether the subjects employed maintenance or elaborative rehearsal. All that matters is that the items have previously been seen (Jacoby and Dallas, 1981; Graf, Mandler, and Haden, 1982).

Such results do indeed suggest that explicit and implicit retrieval tasks tap some different memory functions. Some authors believe that these differences are based on different memory systems, perhaps served by different areas of the brain. In large part, their view is based on the fact that brain-damaged patients with amnesia show massive deficits in explicit memory tasks but much less disruption on implicit ones (Squire and Cohen, 1984; see pp. 286–87).

## Retrieval from Active Memory

So far, all our discussions have dealt with retrieval from a passive (that is, long-term) store. The sought-for materials might be words from an experimenter's list, or names of former classmates, or uncommon items in the subject's own vocabulary—in every case, they were generally not in the would-be retriever's consciousness at the time she was asked to recall. They were typically in her passive, not her active memory. Here it makes some intuitive sense to talk of retrieval or of search. Can one talk about retrieval when the items are in active (or short-term) memory—when they are right on the memory workbench and thus, so to speak, in plain view? One might guess that in such cases there is no retrieval process at all, that there is no need for any kind of mental search at all. But in fact, the situation is not quite so simple. For it turns out that retrieval from active memory is not instantaneous but requires some mental search and comparison.

The evidence comes from a series of elegant experiments by Saul Sternberg. His subjects were first shown a short list of letters, the memory set, which might contain as few as one or as many as seven items. Suppose the memory set was $C$, $F$, and $M$. The subjects were then shown a single item (e.g., $W$) and had to indicate whether it was or was not a member of that memory set. What are the retrieval processes that allow the subject to accomplish this task? One thing is clear. To decide whether the target item was or was not presented a moment before, it must be compared with the items that are now in active memory. For each comparison, the memory system must decide whether the target stimulus is an adequate match for the trace. How are these comparisons conducted? One possibility is *parallel search* (Figure 7.10A). This proposes that the stimulus letter $W$ is simultaneously compared to each of the three items in the memory set. The second alternative is *serial search.* In serial search the comparisons occur successively. The stimulus $W$ is first compared to $C$, then to $F$, and finally to $M$ (Figure 7.10B).

To decide between these alternatives, Sternberg measured the reaction time from the moment the target stimulus appeared until the subject made his response (pressing either a "Yes" or a "No" key). To find out whether the search process is conducted serially or in parallel, he determined how reaction time is af-

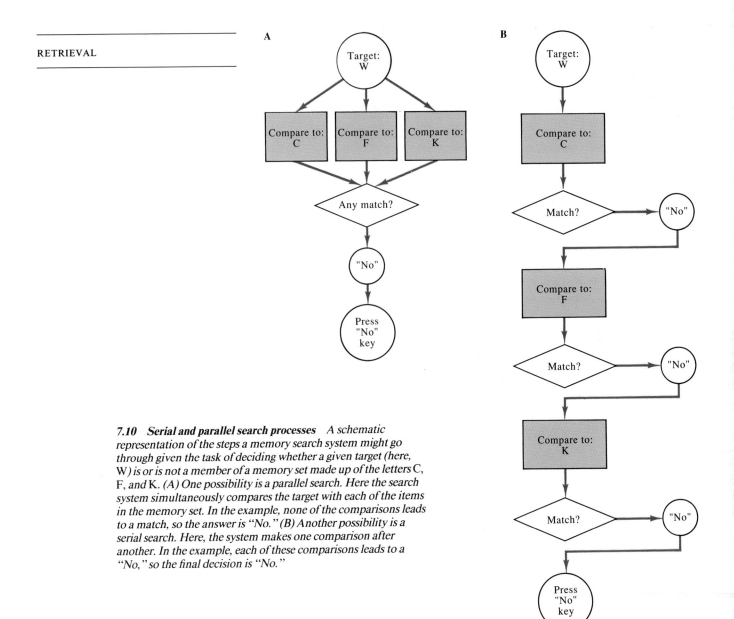

**7.10  Serial and parallel search processes**  *A schematic representation of the steps a memory search system might go through given the task of deciding whether a given target (here, W) is or is not a member of a memory set made up of the letters C, F, and K. (A) One possibility is a parallel search. Here the search system simultaneously compares the target with each of the items in the memory set. In the example, none of the comparisons leads to a match, so the answer is "No." (B) Another possibility is a serial search. Here, the system makes one comparison after another. In the example, each of these comparisons leads to a "No," so the final decision is "No."*

fected by the number of items in the memory set. Suppose the process is handled in parallel. If so, then the size of the memory set should have no effect, for the various comparisons between the target and the items in memory are assumed to proceed simultaneously (Figure 7.11A).

The results should be quite different if the search is serial, for now the comparisons are assumed to occur one after the other. On the assumption that each comparison takes the same amount of time, reaction time should be a linear function of the size of the memory set (Figure 7.11B).

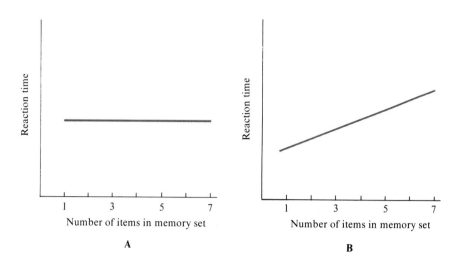

**7.11 Predicted results in Sternberg's experiment** *(A) If the search through short-term memory is parallel, the time to decide whether a given item is a member of the memory set should be the same regardless of the number of items. If so, the curve that relates reaction time and the size of the memory set would be a horizontal line. The height of this reaction-time function would depend on the time required for processes other than the comparison, such as the time required to recognize the target letter, the time to press the key, and so on. (B) If the search is serial, reaction time must increase with the size of the memory set, since each additional item in the set requires an additional comparison. The slope of the predicted line is the increase in reaction time added by any one comparison.*

The results actually obtained fit the hypothesis that the search process is serial: The relation between reaction time and size of memory set is best rendered by a straight line (Figure 7.12). As Sternberg sees it, the slope of this line corresponds to the time it takes to compare the target stimulus to one of the items in the memory set. This slope has generally been found to have a value of about 30 milliseconds. It appears that the search process is serial but is conducted at an exceedingly rapid rate (Sternberg, S., 1969).*

## CONCEPTUAL FRAMEWORKS AND REMEMBERING

Remembering depends upon encoding and retrieval. But both of these are affected by still another factor that we've discussed only in passing: what the learner already knows. For all remembering takes place against a backdrop of prior knowledge that necessarily colors whatever enters memory. Without prior knowledge, we could not understand the words we hear, their connection with each other, or their relation to events in the world.

Organization helps us to remember, but this organization is almost always based on connecting what we hear and see with what we already know. It's easier to recall the first nine squares than the sequence 149162536496481 (because we know about numbers and squares) and easier to recall some disconnected sentences that are preceded by the title "Doing the laundry" than if they're not (because we know about laundry routines). To give another example, consider a study in which subjects listened to a taped description of half an inning of a fictional baseball game. Some of the subjects were very knowledgeable about the game; others were not (though they had a rough idea of the rules of the game). When later asked to write down as much of the taped account as they could, the more expert subjects did far better than the subjects whose knowledge of the game was slight (Spilich, Vesonder, Chiesi, and Voss, 1979).

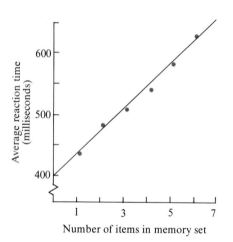

**7.12 Actual results of Sternberg's study** *The figure shows the actual results of one of Sternberg's experiments. The average reaction time over all trials at a given memory set size is shown by the circles. The results clearly support the prediction made by the serial search hypothesis. (After Sternberg, S., 1970)*

---

* A number of later critics have argued that Sternberg's results don't necessarily prove that the search process he studied is serial, but a discussion of this controversy is beyond the scope of this book (e.g., Townsend, 1971; Sternberg, S., 1975).

The utilization of prior knowledge in memory is analogous to the effect of top-down processing in perception. As in perception, such top-down effects can be enormously helpful. But again as in perception, our knowledge and expectations can lead us astray. For just as we can misperceive, so we can—and often do—misremember.

## Memory Distortions

The most influential experiments on memorial distortions were performed by the British psychologist Frederic Bartlett almost sixty years ago. Bartlett's subjects were asked to reproduce stories taken from the folklore of other cultures; thus, their content and structure were rather strange to Western ears. The reproductions showed many changes from the original. Some parts were subtracted, others were overelaborated, still others were additions that were completely new. In effect, the subjects had built a new story upon the memorial ruins of the original. This memorial reconstruction was generally more consonant with the cultural conceptions of the subjects than with the story they had actually heard. For example, certain supernatural plot elements were reinterpreted along more familiar lines.

In another variant of the same experiment, Bartlett used the method of *serial reproduction.* The original was presented to one subject, who reproduced it from memory for the benefit of a second, whose reproduction was shown to a third, and so on for a chain of up to ten subjects (Bartlett, 1932). With this technique (an experimental analogue of rumor transmission), each subject's memorial distortions became part of the stimulus for the next one down the line; the effect was to grossly amplify the reconstructive alteration (Figure 7.13).

### THE EFFECT OF SCHEMAS AND SCRIPTS

Numerous experiments document Bartlett's claim that memories for events or narratives are strongly affected by the framework of prior knowledge in terms of which they are understood. In one study, subjects were asked to read a descrip-

**7.13 Remembering studied by the method of serial reproduction** *Ten subjects were used in the experiment. Subject 1 saw the original figure and was asked to reproduce it after half an hour. His reproduction was shown to subject 2 whose reproduction was shown to subject 3, and so on through subject 10. The figure shows the original drawing and the 10 serial reproductions, illustrating a massive reconstruction process. (After Bartlett, 1932)*

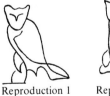

Original drawing    Reproduction 1    Reproduction 2    Reproduction 3    Reproduction 4

Reproduction 5    Reproduction 6    Reproduction 7    Reproduction 8    Reproduction 9    Reproduction 10

267

tion of a home while taking either of two different viewpoints: that of a prospective home buyer or that of a burglar. Later recall showed that the different perspectives affected what was remembered: in the case of the "home buyers," a leaky roof; in the case of the burglars, a valuable coin collection (Anderson and Pichert, 1978). In another study, subjects who were told about a person's visit to the dentist falsely recalled hearing some details that typically occur in a dentist's office (checking in with the receptionist, looking at a magazine in the waiting room, and so on) even though these were never explicitly mentioned (Bower, Black, and Turner, 1979).

In all these cases, the subjects' memory was affected by their knowledge of the world. They had some ideas of how home buyers, burglars, and dental patients are likely to behave, and they fit their particular recollections into the general outlines of this knowledge. Following Bartlett, many contemporary psychologists describe such conceptual frameworks as *schemas.* As used in this context, the term refers to a general cognitive structure into which data or events can be entered, typically with more attention to the broad brush strokes than to specific details. Many aspects of our experience are redundant: when prospective buyers look at a house they inspect the roof and basement; when patients visit the dentist, they generally check in with a receptionist, and so on. A schema is an effective summary of this redundancy, and can therefore help us interpret and supplement the details of our remembered experience (Schwartz and Reisberg, 1991). A special subcase of a schema is a *script,* which describes a characteristic scenario of behavior in a particular setting, such as a restaurant script (whose sequence includes being seated, looking at the menu, ordering the meal, eating the food, paying the bill, and leaving), or the visit-to-the-dentist script we've considered before (Schank and Abelson, 1977).

EYEWITNESS TESTIMONY

The schema-induced distortions we've discussed thus far were not particularly damaging. To be sure, the subject's memory for the particular details was faulty, but that hardly mattered since she recalled the gist. Under the circumstances, there was no harm done, since our ultimate object is to remember what a statement is all about, not its detailed phrasing. One might even argue that schematized remembering is beneficial since its efficiency lets us package, store, and retrieve more material than we could otherwise manage in an information-cluttered world.

The trouble is that this enhanced efficiency has a down side, for sometimes the details *are* of considerable importance. They are to the student who has to remember a specific chemical formula or the locations of the cranial nerves or the particulars of a novel. And they are to lawyers and judges who are concerned with the accuracy of eyewitness testimony. In all these cases, schematic distortion can have deleterious effects.

Witnesses are sometimes quite confident of various circumstances that fit their assumptions but don't fit the actual facts. An accident occurred months ago, and its details have dimmed over time; as he tries to retrieve this past event the witness may fill in the gaps by an inference of which he is quite unaware.

A series of studies by Elizabeth Loftus and her associates has highlighted this problem of schematized memory processes in eyewitness testimony. An important factor is the way in which recall is questioned. In one study, subjects viewed a

brief film segment of a car accident. Immediately afterward they were asked a number of questions that were in either of two forms:

> "Did you see the broken headlight?"

or

> "Did you see a broken headlight?"

The results showed that subjects who were questioned about *the* headlight were more likely to report having seen one than subjects who were asked about *a* headlight. This was so whether the film actually showed a broken headlight or did not. In effect, the use of the definite article, *the,* makes the query a leading question, one which implies that there really was a broken headlight and that the only issue is whether the subject has noticed it. No such presupposition is made when the indefinite article, *a,* is used (Loftus and Zanni, 1975).

Another study showed that suitable leading questions during a first interrogation may lead to a reinterpretation of a recently witnessed account. When later questioned again, the witness will recall this reinterpretation. Subjects were again shown film segments of a car accident. Shortly afterward some were asked leading questions such as, "Did you see the children getting on the school bus?" A week later, all subjects were asked the direct question, "Did you see a school bus in the film?" In actual fact, there was no school bus. But when compared to controls, subjects who were originally asked the leading question that presupposed the school bus were three to four times more likely to say that they had seen one (Loftus, 1975).

These results are of considerable relevance both to the legal process and to the psychology of memory. To legal scholars they reemphasize the crucial importance of how questions are worded, not only in the courtroom but also in prior interrogations. To students of memory, they underline the fact that remembering is in part a reconstructive process in which we sometimes recreate the past while we try to retrieve it.

WHAT PRODUCES SCHEMA-BASED DISTORTIONS?

That schematic processing leads to memory distortions seems clear enough. But what are the mechanisms that lead to these distortions?

*Reconstruction at retrieval*　One possibility is that the distortions are really reconstructions. According to this view, the subject *reconstructs* the past from her partial knowledge in the process of trying to remember it. Take the film clip of the auto accident. According to the reconstruction hypothesis, the subject has forgotten whether or not she saw a broken headlight. She fills the gap in her memory by making an inference: Since the experimenter asked her about *the* headlight there must have been one. The subject tries to remember what she actually saw, but she ends up reporting what she decides she *must* have seen. Here, as in perception, top-down processing may produce a form of mental problem solving. In perception, the subject acts as if she asks herself: "What can it possibly be?" In memory, the equivalent question is: "What could it possibly have been?" In the first case, the inference concerns the present; in the second, it concerns the past. And in both cases, the inference may very well have been unconscious (see Chapter 6).

It is probably not surprising that reconstructive errors of this kind are more frequent the more time elapses between the original encoding and the retrieval test. With increasing time, there is increasing forgetting, which in turn leads to greater reliance on inference to patch up the holes in memory (Anderson and Pichert, 1978; Spiro, 1980).

*Rewriting memories* Some authors believe that schemas can do more than just fill gaps; they may actually alter memories one already has. An example is a study in which subjects were shown slides of an automobile collision. Later on, the subjects were asked either of two questions: "How fast were the cars going when they hit each other?" or "How fast were the cars going when they smashed into each other?" A week later the subjects were asked whether they had seen any broken glass in any of the slides they had been shown. (In actual fact, there was none.) Subjects who had been asked about the cars that "*smashed* into each other" were much more likely to report having seen such glass than subjects who were asked about the cars that "*hit* each other." It appears that a question that was posed *after* the subjects had seen the slides affected how they remembered them (Loftus and Palmer, 1974).

In this and similar studies, earlier memories seem to be changed to adjust to some later interpretation, as if the past were rewritten and updated to fit into our view of the present. Such retrospective alterations of memory are called ***accommodative distortions.*** Whether such phenomena really prove that old memories are quite so easily erased and updated is still a matter of debate (Belli, 1989; Loftus and Hoffman, 1989; Tversky and Tuchin, 1989; Zaragoza and McCloskey, 1989).

## The Limits of Memory

There is ample evidence that memory is often fallible and subject to distortion. But the phenomena of retrieval also tell us that more is retained in memory than we can typically dig out and recall on any one occasion. This fact has led to a search for special techniques for recovering memories that have some particular importance; for example, trying to help witnesses remember what a suspect said or did.

### MEMORY, HYPNOSIS, AND THE COURTROOM

A case in point is hypnosis. A number of U.S. law enforcement agencies have used this as a device to prompt witness recall in criminal investigations. A witness is hypnotized, told that he is back at a certain time and place, and asked to tell what he sees. On the surface, the results—in either the real world or in laboratory studies—are quite impressive. A hypnotized witness identifies an assailant as he mentally returns to the scene of the crime; a hypnotized college student is brought back to the age of six and relives his sixth birthday party with appropriately childlike glee. There is little doubt that these hypnotized people are convinced that they are actually re-experiencing these events, that what they recall really happened. But upon investigation, it often turns out that the hypnotically prodded memories are actually false. In one courtroom case, a suspect turned out to have been abroad at the time the hypnotized witness recalled having seen him

**7.14   Remembering studied through drawings done while under hypnosis**
*(A) Drawings done at age six (blue). (B) Drawings done while subject was hypnotized and told that he was six years old (black). Note some interesting differences between the pictures, for example, the tepee, which is much more detailed in (B): the spelling of* balloon: *and a sense of overall design present in (B), and altogether lacking in (A). (From Orne, 1951)*

during an assault (Orne, 1979). Similar points apply to the description of childhood events elicited under hypnosis. Convincing details such as the name of a first-grade teacher turn out to be quite false when later checked against available records. Some of the subjects were asked to draw a picture while mentally back at the age of six. At first glance, their drawings looked remarkably childlike. But when compared to the subjects' own childhood drawings made at that very age, it is clear that they are much more sophisticated. They represent an adult's conception of what a childish drawing is, rather than being the real thing (Figure 7.14; Orne, 1951).

How can we explain these results? It would seem that hypnosis does not have the near-magical powers often attributed to it (Barber, 1969; Orne and Hammer, 1974; Hilgard, 1977). Hypnosis does not enable us to relive our past at will (nor, for that matter, does it permit feats of agility or strength of which we would otherwise be incapable). What it does do is to make people unusually anxious to believe in and cooperate with another person, the hypnotist, and to do what he asks of them (within the bounds of certain mutually understood limitations). If he asks them to remember, they will do their very best to oblige. They will doggedly stick to the task and rummage through their minds to find any possible retrieval cue. And so of course would we all, whether hypnotized or not, providing that we wanted to remember badly enough. But what if we don't succeed? If we are not hypnotized, we will eventually concede failure. But hypnotized persons will not. They try to please the hypnotist who has told them to recall and has assured them that they can. And so they do what the hypnotist asks. They produce memories—by creatively adding and reconstructing on the basis of what they already know. As we have seen, such reconstructions are a common feature in much so-called remembering. The difference in hypnosis is that the subject has little or no awareness that his reconstructions and confabulations are just that, rather than being true memories; being hypnotized, he is convinced that his fabrications are the real thing.

Some evidence comes from a study on the susceptibility to leading questions. The experimenter employed the familiar technique of showing subjects videotapes of an accident and later asking them to recall certain details, in some cases while hypnotized and in others while not. Some of the probes were leading questions, while others were more objective in phrasing. As we just saw, such leading questions lead to errors even without hypnosis. But they lead to even more errors in hypnotized subjects than in controls. When asked whether they had seen "*the* license plate . . . " (which in fact was not visible), some of the hypnotized subjects not only said yes but actually volunteered partial descriptions of the license plate number. Findings of this sort cast some serious doubts on the uncritical use of hypnosis in real-life judicial settings (Putnam, 1979).

THE TAPE RECORDER THEORY OF MEMORY

Over and above what these findings may tell us about hypnosis, they also have some implications for what is sometimes called the tape recorder (or, to update it, the videotape recorder) theory of memory. According to this view, the brain contains a virtually imperishable record of all we have ever heard or seen or felt. The only trick is to find a way to turn the recorder back to some desired portion of the tape. But the evidence indicates that this suggestion is exceedingly implausible. All techniques that claim to provide such memory "playbacks"—the major ex-

ample is hypnosis—have been found wanting. Under the circumstances, our best guess is that the tape recorder theory is false. To be sure, we retain much more than we can retrieve at any given moment. But this doesn't mean we retain every bit of sensory information we encounter. Some is never entered, some is lost if not rehearsed and organized, and some is altered to fit in with incoming material (Loftus and Loftus, 1980; Neisser, 1982b).

### The Limits of Distortion

In the last chapter we saw that perception is an active process. It depends on incoming stimuli, but it does not provide a mere copy, for the incoming sensory information is often reshaped and transformed. A similar point applies to memory. It depends on what is stored, but a given act of remembering provides us with more than a frozen slice of the past; it often fills in gaps and reconstructs as we unwittingly try to fit our past into our present (Neisser, 1967).

But these acts of cognitive construction and reconstruction have some limits, in memory as well as in perception. For while there are numerous ways in which a memory can be distorted, such distortions don't always occur. Far from it. After all, we do remember many details of experiences we've been exposed to, and many of those fit into no particular cognitive mold. And even in cases in which various schemas have led to distortions of recall, subsequent tests of recognition show that more is remembered than seems so at first (Alba and Hasher, 1983).

In sum. Our memory is neither wholly distorted nor wholly accurate. The tape recorder theory of memory is false. But so is the theory that everything we remember is changed and distorted by inference and reconstruction.

In these regards, memory is again much like perception. Both are affected by processes that work from the top down as well as by those that start from the bottom up. Perception without any bottom-up processing (that is, without any reference to stimuli) would amount to continual hallucination. Memory without bottom-up processing (that is, without any reference to memory traces) would amount to perpetual delusion, a mere will-o'-the-wisp in which the remembered past is continually constructed and reconstructed to fit the schemas of the moment. Both top-down and bottom-up processes operate in both cognitive domains.

The use of schemas—that is, top-down processing—clearly has a cost, for it can lead to distortions of memory. But it also confers great benefits. Our cognitive machinery is limited: There's only so much that we can encode, and store, and retrieve. As a result, we are forced to schematize and simplify so that we can impose order on the world we perceive and think about. But the very tools that help us to understand and remember occasionally backfire so that we misremember.

## VARIETIES OF LONG-TERM MEMORY

We've discussed long-term memory as if it were all of a piece, like a huge warehouse in which all our memories are stored, regardless of their form and content.

But during the past twenty years or so, a number of authors have tried to make some further distinctions that may provide some clue as to how this warehouse is arranged.

## Generic Memory

One important distinction is between episodic memory and what is often called generic memory. *Episodic memory* is the memory for particular events (episodes) of one's own life: what happened when and where, as when recalling that one ate fried chicken the other night. This contrasts with *generic memory,* which is memory for items of knowledge as such, independent of the particular occasion on which one had acquired them, such as the capital of France, the square root of 9, and the fact that Aaron Burr shot Alexander Hamilton in a duel. In effect, a person's generic memory is the sum total of his acquired knowledge—the meanings of words and symbols, facts about the world, what objects look like, and various general principles, schemas, and scripts.

Most of the studies on memory we have described thus far are primarily about episodic memory. Consider an experiment in which subjects have to memorize a list of nouns such as *submarine, typewriter, elephant,* and so on. When the experimenter tests for later recall, his interest is in what the subjects learned at the time of the experiment—that the list they were presented with included *elephant* and *typewriter* but not *gazelle* and *thermometer.* This is not to say that there were no generic memories that the subjects brought to bear on the tasks. After all, they knew and understood all the words on the list. But the experimenter was not interested in their generic memories. Had he been, he would have asked questions such as "What is an elephant?" (Tulving, 1972).

One of the most important components of generic memory is *semantic memory,* the memory that concerns the meanings of words and concepts. As some authors conceive it, our entire vocabulary is this store: every word, together with its pronunciation, all of its meanings, its relations to objects in the real world, the way it is put together with other words to make phrases and sentences. How do we ever find any one bit of information in this near-infinity of verbal knowledge? One thing is certain. When we search for an item—say, a synonym for *quiet*—we don't go through all of the items in the semantic store by a serial search. If we did, the hunt might last for days or weeks. The fact that we can come up with *silent* in a second or less shows that we make use of a much more efficient retrieval system. To use a library analogy, the person who takes out a book doesn't have to rummage through all of the volumes on each shelf in order to find the one he wants. He can obtain his book much faster because there is an organized system according to which the books are arranged in the stacks.

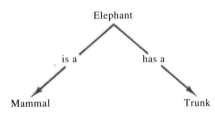

**7.15 Network structure in semantic memory models** *The figure shows a small section of a semantic memory model, with nodes ("elephant" "mammal" "trunk") connected through associative links. Some networks employ "labeled associations" that indicate the particular relations between the nodes (such as "is a" "has" and so on).*

### A HIERARCHICAL NETWORK

Semantic memory is surely organized, but just what does its organization consist of? Collins and Quillian were among the first to propose a *network model* in which the words and concepts stored in semantic memory are linked through a complex system of relationships (somewhat analogous to the networks we've encountered in the preceding chapter when discussing pattern recognition). In such networks, the words or concepts are indicated by *nodes,* while the associations between them are indicated by lines or arrows (see Figure 7.15).

273

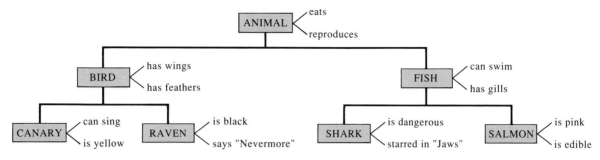

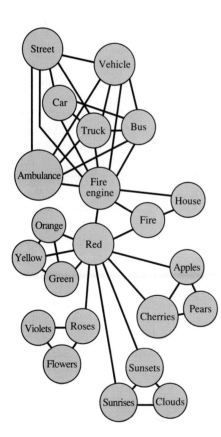

**7.16   A hierarchical theory of semantic memory**   *To decide whether the sentence "Ravens have feathers" is true, given the organization of the entries here pictured, one has to "look up" the information at the second level, under* bird.

**7.17   The spreading activation model**
*The figure shows a—very small—portion of the semantic network postulated by the spreading activation model. The shorter the path, the stronger the semantic relation. (After Collins and Loftus, 1975, p. 412)*

The original model proposed by Collins and Quillian was hierarchical. In such a semantic hierarchy a particular word (say, *canary*) would be stored under the higher-order category that subsumes it (here, *bird*), which in turn would be stored under a yet higher category (here, *animal*), and so on. Certain properties (or *features*) that describe each of these terms would then be stored under the node that's most appropriate. Under *canary,* one would presumably store such features as: "is yellow," "can sing." Under *bird,* one might store features such as: "has wings," "has feathers." Similarly for yet higher categories such as *animal,* or *living thing* (see Figure 7.16; Collins and Quillian, 1969).

Collins and Quillian's hierarchical model was very neat but as so often, nature is much less neat than theorists would like her to be. To mention only one problem, membership in many semantic categories does not seem to be all-or-none. Thus when subjects are asked to rate various birds according to the degree to which they are "typical birds," robins are rated to be most typical, *chickens* less so, and *penguins* birds by courtesy only (Rosch, 1973a, 1973b). These differences in typicality seem to affect the way in which semantic memory is accessed. For example, subjects are faster in agreeing that "X is a bird," if X is a typical bird like a canary rather than a marginal case like a penguin or an ostrich (Rips, Shoben, and Smith, 1973; Rips, Smith, and Shoben, 1978). Such effects suggest that the relation between items of information in the semantic memory is not as neat and tidy as the hierarchical position had supposed (e.g., Conrad, 1972; for further discussion, see Chapter 9).

A NETWORK MODEL BASED ON SEMANTIC DISTANCE

The difficulties of the hierarchical model led to the formulation of several alternatives. One was the ***spreading activation model*** developed by Collins and Loftus, in which semantic relationships were built directly into the network. In this network, shorter arrows between two nodes indicated a closer semantic relationship—based on hierarchical position (as in *canary–sing*) or on similarity in meaning (*apple–orange*) or on well-learned associations (*Pepsi-Cola*). Collins and Loftus proposed that nodes can be activated—again analogous to a similar process in pattern recognition—and that this activation spreads to other nodes. This effect will be greater (and occur more quickly) for nodes that are nearby than for others that are farther off, for the activation tends to dissipate as it spreads (Collins and Loftus, 1975; see Figure 7.17).

How can this spreading activation hypothesis be tested? One line of evidence came from a study in which broad semantic categories were activated. Subjects were asked to think of a word that begins with a certain letter and belongs to some

semantic category. Suppose she is asked for a word that is a *G-fruit*. The experimenter measures the reaction time from the presentation of the category term *fruit* and the response (say, *grapes*). Shortly thereafter the subject gets tested once more. On some occasions, the same category is again called for, though with a different initial letter, as in *S-Fruit*. Now, the time to retrieve a suitable word (say, *strawberries*) is quite a bit shorter than it was the first time. What seems to have happened is that a semantic category is activated and remains that way for a while, like a section in a library that is lit up by a previous user who leaves the lights on when she departs. This part of the library will now become easier to find (Loftus, 1973).

Further evidence comes from several experiments on **semantic priming.** In a classic study, the subjects were presented with two strings of letters, with one string printed above the other (Meyer and Schvaneveldt, 1971). Three examples are:

| NURSE | NURSE | NARDE |
|-------|-------|-------|
| BUTTER | DOCTOR | DOCTOR |

The subjects' job was to press a "yes" button if *both* letter sequences were real words (that is, for NURSE-BUTTER and NURSE-DOCTOR), and a "no" button if one or both of the two were not (that is, for NARDE-DOCTOR). Our only interest is in the two pairs that required a "yes" response. (In such tasks, the "no" items are only there to make sure that the subject does what he is supposed to.) The results showed that the reaction time was shorter when the two words were related in meaning (as in NURSE-DOCTOR) than when they were unrelated (as in BREAD-DOCTOR). It appears that the sight of the word NURSE *primed* the system to respond to related words such as DOCTOR but had no such facilitating effect on unrelated words such as BUTTER. This is in line with the Collins and Loftus model: The node corresponding to NURSE was activated, and this activation spread to nearby nodes (e.g., DOCTOR) on the network. Simply put, it means that words are stored and filed according to their semantic relatedness (Blank and Foss, 1978; McKoon and Ratcliff, 1979).

## Visual Memory

Important as words and the abstract concepts that underlie them may be, they are not all that we remember. We also seem to have memory systems that preserve some of the characteristic attributes of our senses. The idea is not just that we know that, say, people's waists are between their head and their toes. Of course we do, but that isn't all. We also seem to be able to somehow retrieve this betweenness from a mental image that has some of the characteristics of the original visual experience. As some authors (beginning with Shakespeare) have put it, we see it in "our mind's eye." While similar claims have been made for other senses —hearing with the mind's ear (composers), feeling with the mind's fingers (blind persons)—our primary concern will be with visual memory.

### RATING ONE'S OWN IMAGES

The first attempt to study visual imagery goes back a hundred years ago when Sir Francis Galton (1822–1911), the founder of the field of individual differences,

asked people to describe their own images and to rate them for vividness (Galton, 1883). The results showed that individuals differed widely. Some people said they could call up past scenes at will and see them with the utmost clarity. Others (including some well-known painters) denied ever having had images at all. But these differences in how people described their own experiences have surprisingly little to do with how they actually performed on various tasks that seemed to call for visual memory. One study showed that there was no correlation between self-rated image vividness and performance on an objective test that measured memory for spatial designs (Di Vesta, Ingersoll, and Sunshine, 1971). Nor is there any relationship between the way subjects rate their own images and the degree to which they benefit from imagery mnemonics (Baddeley, 1976).

### EIDETIC IMAGERY

Since self-judgments of imagery seemed to be of little use, psychologists turned to more sophisticated procedures. In addition to asking what the image appeared to be like, they asked what it enabled the subject to do. For example, is the image a mental picture from which we can read off information as if it were an actual visual scene outside? By and large, the answer is no. But there are some exceptions. The most striking is *eidetic imagery,* which is characterized by relatively long-lasting and detailed images of visual scenes that can sometimes be scanned and "looked at" as if they had real existence outside. In one study, a group of schoolchildren was shown a picture for thirty seconds. After it was taken away, the subjects were asked whether they could still see anything and, if so, to describe what they saw (Leask, Haber, and Haber, 1969). Evidence for eidetic imagery is contained in the following protocol of a ten-year-old boy, who was looking at a blank easel from which a picture from *Alice in Wonderland* had just been removed (Figure 7.18).

*7.18   Test picture for study of eidetic imagery   This picture from* Alice in Wonderland *was shown for half a minute to elementary schoolchildren, a few of whom seemed to have an eidetic image of it. (Illustration by Marjorie Torrey)*

EXPERIMENTER: Do you see something there?
SUBJECT: I see the tree, gray tree with three limbs. I see the cat with stripes around its tail.
EXPERIMENTER: Can you count those stripes?
SUBJECT: Yes (pause). There's about 16.
EXPERIMENTER: You're counting what? Black, white or both?
SUBJECT: Both.
EXPERIMENTER: Tell me what else you see.
SUBJECT: And I can see the flowers on the bottom. There's about three stems but you can see two pairs of flowers. One on the right has green leaves, red flower on bottom with yellow on top. And I can see the girl with a green dress. She's got blond hair and a red hair band and there are some leaves in the upper left-hand corner where the tree is (Haber, 1969, p. 38).

Eidetic imagery is relatively rare. Only 5 percent of tested schoolchildren seem to have it, and the proportion is almost surely smaller in adults. According to one author, this difference between children and adults may only indicate that children tend to rely more on imagery in their thinking, perhaps because their verbal and conceptual memory systems are not as yet sufficiently developed (Kosslyn, 1980, 1984). In any case, there is no reason to believe that this form of imagery is an especially useful form of mental activity. Contrary to popular belief, memory

experts don't generally have eidetic imagery (or photographic memory as it is sometimes popularly referred to); their skill is in organizing material in memory, rather than in storing it in picture form.

### OTHER FORMS OF VISUAL MEMORY

With the possible exception of eidetic imagery—which as we've seen is a rare and rather elusive phenomenon—visual memory is not a simple reembodiment of stored visual sensation. Our perceptions are not like photographs, and so our visual memories can't be either. But they may nevertheless contain certain pictorial attributes that are also found in visual perception. A number of studies suggest that this is indeed the case.

*Mental rotation*   One line of evidence comes from studies on **mental rotation.** The subjects were shown a digit or a number, either in their normal version or in mirror-reversed form (that is, *R* or Я). But in addition, the figures were tilted so that the subject might encounter a normal *R* rotated by, say, 180 degrees. Or she might be presented with a mirror-reversed *R*, rotated by, say, 60 degrees (see Figure 7.19). The subject's task was to press one button if the stimulus was normal, another if it was mirror-reversed.

The reaction time proved to be a regular function of how far the characters were tilted away from the upright position. As the orientation of the letters changed from the upright (that is, 0 degree rotation) through 60 degrees to 180 degrees, reaction times increased. The same was true for the mirror-reversed letters. The authors interpret their results as evidence for a separate visual memory system. In their view, the subjects mentally rotated an image of the stimulus they were presented with until it was upright. Once they had brought it to this position, it could be compared to the visual memory of the normal and mirror-reversed characters. The fact that reaction time was a function of angle shows that this mental rotation takes time; in the present case, it took about 30 milliseconds for every 10 degrees (Cooper and Shepard, 1973; Shepard and Cooper, 1982).

*Image scanning*   Another line of evidence comes from studies on **image scanning.** In one such study, the subjects were first shown the map of a fictitious island containing various objects: a hut, a well, a tree, a meadow, and so on (see Figure 7.20). After memorizing this map by copying it repeatedly, the subjects performed a reaction time task. The experimenter named two objects on the map (say, the hut and the meadow). The subjects' task was to conjure up a mental image of the entire island and then to imagine a little black speck zipping from the first location to the second. The results showed that their reaction time was directly proportional to the distance between the two points. This result would be no surprise had the subjects scanned a physical map with their *real* eye. That the same holds true when they scan an image with their *mind's* eye is rather remarkable (Kosslyn, Ball, and Reiser, 1978).

*Images are not pictures*   The preceding discussion makes it clear that visual images share some of the properties of pictures. But this does not mean that they *are* pictures. Some evidence for this view comes from a study by Chambers and Reisberg who presented their subjects with a figure (that they had never seen be-

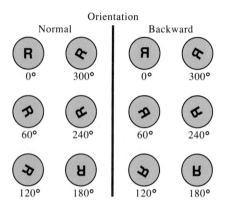

Orientation

Normal | Backward

**7.19   Mental rotation**   *Normal and backward versions of one of the characters used in the mental rotation study, showing the orientations in which it appeared as a test stimulus. (Adapted from Cooper and Shepard, 1973)*

**7.20   Image scanning**   *Subjects were asked to look mentally at a map of a fictional island and then to imagine a speck zipping from one location to another. (After Kosslyn, Ball, and Reiser, 1978)*

**7.21 Images are not pictures** *The rabbit-duck figure, first used in 1900 by Joseph Jastrow. (After Attneave, 1971)*

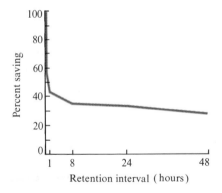

**7.22 Forgetting curve** *The figure shows retention after various intervals since learning. Retention is here measured in percentage saving, that is, the percent decrease in the number of trials required to relearn the list after an interval of no practice. If the percentage saving is 100 percent, retention is perfect—no trials to relearn are necessary. If the percentage saving is 0 percent, there is no retention at all, for it takes just as many trials to relearn the list as it took to learn it initially. (After Ebbinghaus, 1885)*

fore) that is normally reversible: If it is seen as oriented toward the left, it looks like the head of a duck; if oriented to the right, it looks like the head of a rabbit (Figure 7.21). The subjects' first task was to form a mental image of this figure. At a later time, when the picture was no longer physically present, they were asked to call up this image and describe what it looked like. All subjects "saw" either a duck or a rabbit with their mind's eye, and some said they saw it very vividly. They were then asked whether their image might look like something else. Not one of the subjects came up with a reversal, even after many hints and considerable coaxing. The results were very different when the subjects subsequently *drew* the figure and looked at their own drawing. Now everyone came up with the perceptual alternative. To Chambers and Reisberg these results indicated that a visual image is not a picture. It is instead a mental product that is based on a picture, but that is already encoded to some extent—perhaps as a duck, perhaps as a rabbit. To the extent that it is so encoded, it has lost its pictorial innocence. It is no longer ambiguous because it has already been interpreted. (See Chambers and Reisberg, 1985; for further discussion, see Finke, Pinker, and Farah, 1989; Reisberg and Chambers, 1990.)

## FORGETTING

In popular usage, the word *forgetting* is employed as a blanket term whenever memory fails. But as we have seen, memorial failures have many causes. Some arise from faulty storage procedures, while others are produced by conditions at the moment of recall. We now turn to the relation of such failures to the **retention interval** that intervenes between original learning and the time of the test.

At least on the face of it, forgetting increases with retention interval. Yesterday's lesson is fresher today than it will be tomorrow. This fact was well known to Hermann Ebbinghaus (1850–1909), who began the experimental study of human learning by constructing lists of **nonsense syllables**—two consonants with a vowel in between that do not form a word, such as *zup* and *rif*—and then serving as his own subject as he memorized their serial order. He was the first to plot a **forgetting curve** by testing himself at various intervals after learning (using different lists for each interval), and then asking how much effort he had to expend to relearn the list to the level previously achieved. He found that there was a *saving:* Relearning the list took fewer trials than did the original learning. As one might expect, the saving declined as the retention interval increased. The decline was sharpest immediately after learning and became more gradual thereafter (Ebbinghaus, 1885; see Figure 7.22).

### Theories of Forgetting

What accounts for the fact that the retention of long-term memories seems to decline the longer the time since learning? There are several theories designed to explain this and related phenomena.

#### DECAY

The most venerable theory of forgetting holds that memory traces gradually *decay* as time passes, like mountains that are eroded by wind and water. The ero-

sion of memories is presumably caused by normal metabolic processes whose impact wears down the memory trace until it fades and finally disintegrates.

While this theory has considerable intuitive appeal, there is so far little direct evidence in its favor. One study tried to provide an indirect test by varying body temperature. Like most chemical reactions, metabolic processes increase with increasing temperature. If these reactions are responsible for memorial decay, then forgetting should be a function of the body temperature during the retention interval. This prediction has been tested with cold-blooded animals such as the goldfish whose body takes on the temperature of its surroundings. By and large, the results have been in line with the hypothesis: the higher the temperature of the tank in which the fish is kept during the retention interval, the more forgetting takes place (Gleitman and Rozin, as reported in Gleitman, 1971).

But some other findings complicate this picture. There is good evidence that forgetting is determined not simply by the duration of the retention interval, but by what happens during this time. Experiments on human subjects have shown that recall is substantially worse after an interval spent awake than after an equal period while asleep (Jenkins and Dallenbach, 1924). Later studies suggest that the favorable effect of sleep on retention only holds for quiet, slow-wave sleep (Ekstrand, 1972; Ekstrand, Barrett, West, and Maier, 1977).

Such results pose difficulties for a theory that assigns all of the blame for forgetting to decay, for they show that time itself does not cause all of the loss. To explain such findings within a theory of decay, one would have to assert that the relevant processes that erode the memory trace are slowed down (or counteracted) during one or all of the sleep states.

### INTERFERENCE

A rather different theory of forgetting is *interference.* According to this view, a forgotten memory is neither lost nor damaged, but is only misplaced among a number of other memories that interfere with the recovery of the one that was sought. Seen in this light, our inability to remember the name of a high school friend is analogous to what happens when a clerk cannot find a letter he received a year ago. The letter is still somewhere in his files, but it has been hopelessly buried in a mass of other letters that he filed both before and since.

Memorial interference is easily demonstrated in the laboratory. A major example is *retroactive inhibition* in which new learning hampers recall of the old. In a typical study, a control group learns some rote material such as a list of nonsense syllables (List *A*) and is tested after a specified interval. The experimental group learns the same list as the control group and is tested after the same retention interval. But in addition it must also learn a second list (List *B*) that is interpolated during the retention interval (Table 7.1). The usual result is a marked inferiority in the performance of the experimental group; the interpolated list interferes with (inhibits) the recall of List *A*.

Table 7.1   RETROACTIVE INHIBITION EXPERIMENT

|  | Initial period | Retention interval | Test period |
|---|---|---|---|
| Control group | Learns list *A* | —————— | Recalls list *A* |
| Experimental group | Learns list *A* | Learns list *B* | Recalls list *A* |

279

Table 7.2 PROACTIVE INHIBITION EXPERIMENT

| | Initial period | | Retention interval | Test period |
|---|---|---|---|---|
| Control group | _____ | Learns list *B* | _____ | Recalls list *B* |
| Experimental group | Learns list *A* | Learns list *B* | _____ | Recalls list *B* |

A similar effect is ***proactive inhibition*** in which interference works in a forward (proactive) direction. The usual procedure is to have an experimental group learn List *A* followed by List *B,* and then test for recall of List *B* after a suitable retention interval. The critical comparison is with a control group which learns only List *B* (Table 7.2). In general, the experimental group does worse on the recall test.

### CHANGE OF RETRIEVAL CUES

Decay theory holds that the memory trace gradually fades away with time, while interference asserts that the trace gets lost among other traces acquired both before and after. There is a further alternative which argues that memorial success or failure is primarily determined by the retrieval cues presented at the time of recall.

*Changes in retrieval cues with increasing retention interval* We have already seen that a change in retrieval cues disrupts remembering. But can this effect explain why forgetting increases with an increasing retention interval? To maintain the hypothesis that the critical factor is cue alteration, one must assume that such an alteration becomes ever more likely with the passage of time. There are some cases for which this may well be true. Certain memories may have been acquired in a particular locale; over the years the neighborhood changes as some houses are torn down and new ones are built, thus altering the physical cue situation and thereby decreasing the chance of retrieval.

The retrieval cue hypothesis is a very plausible account of some aspects of forgetting. But it probably cannot explain them all. Forgetting increases as a function of the time since learning even when the retrieval conditions appear essentially unchanged. Some evidence comes from studies with animal subjects where all facets of the situation are under the experimenter's control. In one study, rats were trained to run an alley for food reward. Some of them were tested one day after original learning; others, after sixty-eight days. All of the physical conditions of the experiment—the location and illumination of the alley, the home cages, the animal's own weight—were kept identical throughout the entire period. Even so, there was a massive effect of the retention interval. The animals tested some two months after training were much more hesitant in the alley than they were before, as if they had forgotten what they were supposed to do (Gleitman, 1971).

*Childhood amnesia* Some authors appeal to the retrieval cue hypothesis to explain the phenomenon of ***childhood amnesia***—the fact that most of us can't recall events of our very early childhood. When college students are asked to report any events they can remember that occurred in early life, the average age of their

***The child's world is in many ways utterly different from the adult's*** *According to some authors, childhood amnesia is partially produced by the enormous change in the retrieval cues available to the adult. (Photo courtesy of Suzanne Szasz)*

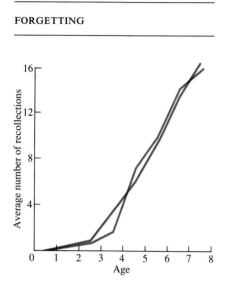

**7.23 Number of childhood memories**
*College students were asked to recall childhood experiences. The figure plots the average number of events recalled as a function of the age at which they occurred for men (blue) and for women (red). Women recall a bit more at the earliest ages, which may reflect the fact that the maturation of girls is generally ahead of that of boys. (Data from Waldfogel, 1948)*

earliest recollection is about three and a half years (Waldfogel, 1948; Sheingold and Tenney, 1982; see Figure 7.23). One possible cause is a massive change of retrieval cues. The world of the young child is utterly different from the world she will occupy some ten or fifteen years later. It is a world in which tables are hopelessly out of reach, chairs can be climbed upon only with great effort, and adults are giants in size and gods in ability. Whatever memories the child may store at this time are necessarily formed and encoded within this context; thus the appropriate retrieval context is necessarily absent from the adult's environment (Schachtel, 1947; Neisser, 1967).

An alternative hypothesis appeals to encoding differences rather than to changes in retrieval cues. According to some authors, infants and very young children store memories—especially explicit memories—less efficiently than older children and adults. This may be because some relevant neural structures are not yet sufficiently mature (Nadel and Zola-Morgan, 1984). It may also be because these very young children have not yet developed the necessary schemas within which experiences can be explicitly organized, encoded, and rehearsed (White and Pillemer, 1979).

In summary, we must conclude that each of the theories of forgetting proposed thus far can account for some of the aspects of the phenomenon but not all. Interference and change of retrieval cues play a major role, but neither of them can readily explain why forgetting increases with the passage of time. While the evidence for decay is by no means solid, it nevertheless seems reasonable to suppose that some such process does occur and is partially responsible for the effect of retention interval.

*Childhood memories  While there is childhood amnesia for the events of the first two or three years, some early memories do remain, often in a jumbled and kaleidoscopic fashion. Thus the paintings of the Russian emigre artist Marc Chagall (1887–1985) show composite images of his early life in a Russian village, including a cow being milked, his mother, a child's naive picture of a Russian village, and so on. (I and the Village, 1911, oil on canvas, 6'3⅝" × 59⅝". Collection, The Museum of Modern Art, New York, Mrs. Simon Guggenheim Fund)*

## When Forgetting Seems Not to Occur

The fact that there is forgetting doesn't mean that it always occurs. For memory doesn't always fail, even after very long time intervals.

### LONG-LASTING SEMANTIC MEMORIES

Some evidence was provided by Harry Bahrick who studied the long-term retention of materials in semantic memory. Bahrick was interested in what people remember from what they learned in school. To this end, he gave a Spanish reading comprehension test to nearly 800 persons who had studied Spanish either in high school or in college for three or four years. They were tested at intervals that ranged from one week to fifty years since their last Spanish course. The results showed that quite a bit is forgotten in the first two or three years after learning. But after this, the test performance levels off until much later in life, where aging effects probably account for the bulk of the later memory loss (see Figure 7.24). Educators will probably be gratified by the fact that even after fifty years the test performance reflects how well the language was learned originally. On average, students who had earned an A performed better than those who had received a C, even after half a century had passed (Bahrick, 1984).

The important finding is that some fraction of what had been learned originally remained intact without any further forgetting. In Bahrick's terms, these memories—vocabulary items, idioms, bits of grammar—moved into what he called a *permastore.* The semantic memory of an adult contains much information that is essentially permanent. We don't forget the meaning of ordinary words, or the rules of arithmetic, or many individual bits of information. In part, this may be because such materials are extremely well-learned in the first place. But in part, it may be because such items—and hopefully much of what we learn in school—have an inherent structure that protects them from forgetting, a structure that Ebbinghaus's nonsense syllable series certainly lacked (Neisser, 1989).

### FLASHBULB MEMORIES

Bahrick's findings concerned semantic memory. Are there some episodic memories that are also essentially immune to forgetting? According to Roger Brown and James Kulik, certain unexpected and emotionally important events produce *flashbulb memories,* which are extremely vivid and essentially permanent. They believe that such memories are like a photograph that preserves the scene when a flashbulb is fired. Some of the events that trigger the flash may be private and personal, such as an early morning telephone call that tells of a parent's death. Others may involve news of powerful national import such as the assassination of President Kennedy or the space shuttle disaster. Brown and Kulik found that most people recall where they were at the time they learned of President Kennedy's assassination and also what they did, who told them, and so on. On the face of it, these detailed memories are surprising. That a president's assassination is an important and memorable event is obvious, but why should so many Americans recall the humdrum circumstances in which they personally found themselves at the time, such as "the weather was cloudy and gray," or "I was carrying a

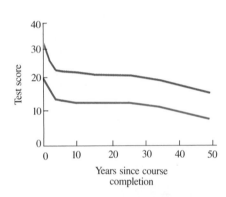

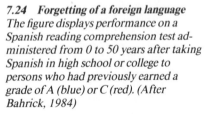

**7.24   Forgetting of a foreign language**
*The figure displays performance on a Spanish reading comprehension test administered from 0 to 50 years after taking Spanish in high school or college to persons who had previously earned a grade of A (blue) or C (red). (After Bahrick, 1984)*

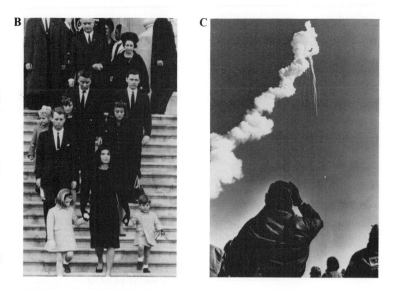

*Events that have produced flashbulb memories* *(A) The attack on Pearl Harbor, (B) after the Kennedy assassination, (C) the space shuttle disaster. (Courtesy the Bettmann Archive)*

carton of Viceroy cigarettes which I dropped?" According to Brown and Kulik, the reason is that such surprising and emotionally powerful events set off a mental flashbulb that preserves the entire scene along with perfectly mundane and unremarkable details (Brown and Kulik, 1977; see also Pillemer, 1984; McCloskey, Wible, and Cohen, 1988).

The flashbulb hypothesis has been the subject of considerable debate. The main issue is whether such memories are really created by a special mechanism that fixes the circumstances of the moment with a special "flashbulb" clarity. The best guess is that such a special mechanism does not exist. To begin with, there is some debate about the accuracy of these memories; they may be vivid, but that does not mean that they are fully correct (e.g., Neisser, 1982a, 1986; Thompson and Cowan, 1986; McCloskey, Wible, and Cohen, 1988). In addition, much of what was remembered may have been rehearsed in subsequent conversations with others. But if so, what was entered in memory did not depend on a hypothetical flashbulb set off in the head. All in all, there is good reason to doubt the existence of a special flashbulb mechanism.

A question remains. Even if some aspects of the so-called flashbulb memories are inaccurate, a surprising amount of detail is still preserved. Why would one recall such trivia as the state of the weather or a dropped carton of cigarettes? According to Ulric Neisser, the reason is that vivid and emotionally arousing public events may serve to connect the time course of the world at large with our own private lifeline. Most of us see little relation between our own personal history and the history of the world at large. We define our past and present by crucial points in our own biography: say, graduating from college, getting married, catching and recovering from pneumonia. The fact that the bout of pneumonia coincided with a change in the French cabinet or a Yankee no-hitter is of little consequence. But every once in a while a gripping public event occurs that forms a link between our own personal timeline and the world's. By remembering where we were when Kennedy was shot or when the space shuttle exploded, we somehow fit our own narratives into those of millions of others. To quote Neisser: ". . . such memories are . . . the places where we line up our own lives with the course of history itself and say 'I was there' " (Neisser, 1982a).

## DISORDERED MEMORIES

Thus far, our discussion has largely centered on people with normal memories. But during the last thirty years, some of the most intriguing questions about human memory have been raised by studies of people with drastic defects in memory functions that are caused by various kinds of damage to the brain (Rozin, 1976b; Cermak, 1979; Squire, 1987; Mayes, 1988).

### Anterograde Amnesia

We have previously mentioned H.M., who suffered from *anterograde amnesia* produced by lesions in the hippocampus and nearby regions of the limbic system. In the case of H.M. and others like him the primary deficit is a massive impairment in the ability to store any new information. But their memory for what happened before the injury is often quite good, especially for events that happened a year or two previously (Marslen-Wilson and Teuber, 1975; see Figure 7.25). Since they remember the distant past and experience the immediate present, they are often aware that there is a large gap in between. Some of H.M.'s comments give some idea of what such an amnesic state is like:

> Right now, I'm wondering. Have I done or said anything amiss? You see, at this moment everything looks clear to me, but what happened just before? That's what worries me. It's like waking from a dream; I just don't remember. [And on another occasion] . . . Every day is alone in itself, whatever enjoyment I've had, and whatever sorrow I've had. (Milner, 1966; Milner, Corkin, and Teuber, 1968)

### Retrograde Amnesia

Various brain injuries may lead to *retrograde amnesia* (retrograde, "in a backward direction") in which the patient suffers a loss of memories for some period *prior* to the accident or the stroke. That period may be relatively brief, perhaps a matter of days or weeks. But in some cases, the retrograde amnesia covers a much longer span, and may be reckoned in years. Some retrograde effects often go along with anterograde amnesia. Thus H.M. has difficulty remembering events that happened one to three years before his operation, but he has perfectly normal memory for those that occurred before then (Mayes, 1988).

What accounts for the loss of memories for events preceding the cerebral injury? According to some authors, one of the causes is *trace consolidation.* This is a hypothetical process by which newly acquired memory traces undergo a gradual change through which they become established (consolidated) ever more firmly. This consolidation effect may be on storage—young traces need time to become more resistant to forgetting, for until then they are as vulnerable as a cement mixture before it has hardened. The effect may also be on retrieval—like a newly acquired library book that will be difficult to find until the librarian takes the time to fill out its card for the catalogue and to file it properly (Weingartner and Parker, 1984).

| 1940s | 1950s | 1960s | 1970s | 1980s |

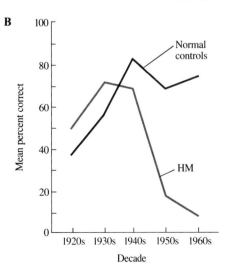

**7.25 Remote and recent memory in amnesics** *(A) Sample items adapted from the "famous faces" test in which patients are asked to identify faces of individuals who reached fame in a particular decade (Albert, Butters, and Levin, 1979; Butters and Albert, 1982). One would expect that patients with anterograde amnesia would perform normally in identifying persons that were well-known prior to the onset of their disorder and more poorly with persons that became widely known after this. The figure shows three faces for each of the decades from 1940 to 1990. Their names are listed on page 287. (B) Results on the famous faces test for H.M. (color) and normal controls (black) for the years from 1920 to 1960. Note that the performance of H.M. was essentially equivalent to that of normals in identifying persons reaching prominence between 1920 and 1930. Like the normals, he did poorly for faces that predate 1930 when he was still a preschool child. But he performed much more poorly than the two controls on faces from the period after his operation (which was performed during the early 1950s). (Adapted from Marslen-Wilson and Teuber, 1975)*

285

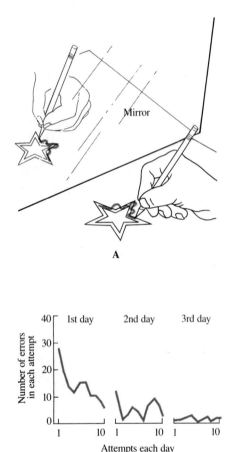

**7.26 An example of what amnesics can learn** *(A) In mirror drawing subjects have to trace a line between two outlines of a figure while looking at their hand in a mirror. (Kolb and Whishaw, 1990) (B) Initially, this is very difficult, but after some practice subjects get very proficient at it. The same is true for amnesics. The figure shows H.M.'s improvements on this task over a period of three days. (Milner, Corkin, and Teuber, 1968)*

Whether retrograde amnesia effects can be explained in this manner is still a matter of debate. One trouble is the fact that retrograde amnesia often extends back for several years prior to the injury. If so, consolidation could not explain the deficit unless one assumes—and some authors do, while others don't—that it is an exceedingly drawn-out process that may continue for very long time periods (Squire and Cohen, 1979, 1982; Squire, 1987).

## Explicit and Implicit Memory Revisited

For quite a while, it was thought that H.M. and other patients with the amnesic syndrome could not acquire any long-term memories at all. But with further study, it turned out that this wasn't true. They can be classically conditioned, they can learn to trace the correct path through a maze, and they can acquire certain skills like mirror-tracing, and reading mirror-imaged print. With practice, their performance gets better and better. But each time they are brought back into the experimental situation, they continue to insist that they have never seen the conditioning apparatus or the maze before, and that they don't remember anything at all (Corkin, 1965; Weiskrantz and Warrington, 1979; Cohen and Squire, 1980).

How can we make sense of these findings? Anterograde amnesics are evidently quite competent at retaining skills such as mirror-tracing (they do just about as well as normals, despite their insistence that they don't remember anything about it; see Figure 7.26). On the other hand, they are utterly incompetent at many ordinary long-term memory tasks; for example, they don't recognize an experimenter they have met on twenty different occasions. The one kind of memory is spared; the other is not. What is the essential difference?

Some authors believe that the essential distinction is between what computer scientists call *procedural* and *declarative knowledge.* Procedural knowledge is "knowing how": how to ride a bicycle, or how to read mirror writing—areas in which the amnesic's memory is relatively unaffected. According to this view, such skills are essentially programs (that is, procedures) for executing certain motor or mental operations. In contrast, declarative knowledge is "knowing that": that there are three outs in an inning, that raisins are made of grapes, that I had chicken for dinner last Thursday. To know something procedurally does not guarantee that one also knows it declaratively. Professional baseball players "know" the procedures for swinging a bat, but not all of them can explain just what it is that they know. Conversely, most physicists probably know (and can describe) the underlying mechanics of a baseball swing, but few will be able to perform competently when given a bat and asked to hit a ball. Neuroscientists who argue that this distinction explains what amnesics can remember and what they can't also believe that procedural and declarative memories depend on different neural systems (Cohen and Squire, 1980; Squire, 1986).

A somewhat different explanation centers on the distinction between explicit and implicit memory (see p. 263). The memories may be there, but they may be implicit, so that the patient doesn't know that he has them. As a result, he cannot answer questions like "Do you remember?" or "Do you recognize?" when they pertain to events that occurred after he sustained the cerebral damage. Some evidence that the amnesics' deficit concerns explicit but not implicit memory comes from priming procedures. When amnesic patients are shown a number of words and are later asked to recall or recognize them, they fail completely. But the re-

*(Cartoon by Abner Dean)*

sults are quite different when they are presented with fragments of the words and asked to complete them by forming the first words that come to mind. Now there is evidence that something was remembered. The patient who was previously shown ELEPHANT and BOOKCASE will properly complete the fragments _L_P_A_T and B_O_C_S_, even though he will not recognize either word if explicitly asked whether he'd just seen it before (Warrington and Weiskrantz, 1978; Diamond and Rozin, 1984). Interestingly enough, this implicit memory effect will work only if the patient does not connect it with any intentional attempt to retrieve the word from memory. If he is explicitly asked to recall the previously presented words by using the fragments as cues, he will fail again (Graf, Mandler, and Squire, 1984).

Whether the explicit-implicit distinction is better or worse than the procedural-declarative one at capturing the essence of what the amnesic can and cannot learn is as yet unclear. It would seem that the two categories overlap, though they are probably not identical (Schacter, 1987). Perhaps there is no *one* distinction that does justice to the findings since amnesia is almost surely not a unitary disorder; not every impaired memory is necessarily impaired in the same way (Squire and Cohen, 1984). In any case, there are many further questions. What is it about the development of declarative knowledge or of explicit, conscious access that makes them so vulnerable to brain damage? Why is procedural knowledge spared? As we begin to find some answers, it is likely that they will shed light not only on the amnesic disorders but on memory functions in general (Crowder, 1985).

## TAKING STOCK

In looking back over this chapter, we are again struck by the intimate relation between the fields of perception, memory, and thinking. It is so often unclear where one topic ends and another begins. To give just one example, consider memory search. As we saw, trying to recall the names of one's high school classmates apparently involves many of the same thought processes that are called upon when we try to figure out how to solve a geometry problem. To the extent that this is so, it is clear that much of memory involves thinking. And as we saw previously, the same is also true of perception. For there, too, the perceiver becomes a thinker as he tries to solve perceptual problems and make sense out of ambiguous or impossible figures. In the next chapter, we will consider the topic of thinking in its own right.

***Names of famous faces:*** 1940s *Douglas MacArthur, Betty Grable, Joe DiMaggio.* 1950s *Mamie Eisenhower, Joe McCarthy, Adlai Stevenson.* 1960s *Nikita Khrushchev, Coretta Scott King, Golda Meir.* 1970s *Anwar Sadat, Betty Ford, Patty Hearst.* 1980s *Robert Bork, Geraldine Ferraro, Bjorn Borg.*

## SUMMARY

1. Any act of remembering implies success in each of three phases: *acquisition,* during which a *memory trace* is formed and *encoded; storage* over some time interval; and *retrieval,* which may be tested by *recognition* or *recall.*

2. According to the *stage theory* of memory, an earlier and very influential approach to memory, there are two main memory systems. One is *short-term memory* (*STM,* also called *primary memory* or *active memory*), in which information is held for fairly short

intervals. The other is *long-term memory* (*LTM,* also called *secondary memory*), in which information is stored for much longer periods. According to stage theory, to get to the long-term memory system, material must first pass through the short-term store.

3. An important difference between STM and LTM is in their *capacity.* That of LTM is enormous; that of STM is very limited as shown by studies of *memory span.* Since stage theory assumes that the only gateway to LTM is through STM, there is an obvious bottle-neck. This is overcome by *recoding* the incoming material into larger *chunks.*

4. The recall of an item heard just before may be from STM or LTM. Studies of *free recall* with lists of unrelated items have provided a way of determining from where such items are retrieved. According to stage theory, the *primacy effect* obtained by use of this procedure is associated with retrieval from long-term storage, while the *recency effect* reflects retrieval from short-term memory.

5. Some further evidence that seemed to support stage theory's claims for the relations between STM and LTM came from cases of *anterograde amnesia.* Some of these patients have normal short-term capacity but have little or no long-term recall or recognition for events subsequent to the time they suffered the damage to their brain.

6. The key assumption of stage theory—that STM is a gateway to LTM—has been challenged by several findings. One is the fact that in certain cases of brain damage there is a marked deficit in the capacity of STM but little or no defect in LTM functioning. The other is the finding that *maintenance rehearsal,* is which material is simply held in STM, confers little or no long-term benefits.

7. These challenges led to a theoretical reorientation in the way memory is conceived today. One change concerns STM, which is now regarded as the currently activated portion of LTM and is usually called *active memory* or *working memory.* The other change is in an emphasis on how the subject encodes and processes incoming material. This includes demonstrations that memory is better after *deep processing* than after *shallow processing,* is helped by *chunking* and *organization,* and is further aided by relating the material with what is already known. These general principles of memorial organization underlie *mnemonics,* techniques for helping memory, which include various forms of verbal organization and the use of *visual imagery.*

8. Remembering depends in part upon the presence of appropriate *retrieval cues.* According to the principle of *encoding specificity,* remembering is most likely if the context at the time of retrieval is identical to that present at the time of original encoding. One reason why certain forms of encoding (for example, organization and understanding) are better than others is that they help in later retrieval. This also explains the effect of *elaborative rehearsal,* which, unlike *maintenance rehearsal,* helps in remembering because it provides appropriate retrieval paths.

9. Retrieval from long-term memory is often preceded by a process of *memory search.* In some cases, the search reaches a halfway point, where we seem to recall something but not quite, and we experience the *tip-of-the-tongue phenomenon.*

10. Retrieval from active memory has been studied by *reaction time* procedures. The results suggest that this retrieval is based on a *serial* rather than a *parallel search* process. Evidence comes from the relation between reaction time and the number of items in the *memory set,* which shows that each additional item adds a constant time increment.

11. In some cases, the memory that underlies retrieval is *implicit* rather than *explicit,* for there is no awareness of remembering at the time that this memory is utilized. Examples come from the exercise of learned skills, and from *repetition priming.*

12. In many cases, remembering depends on prior knowledge, which affects encoding and later retrieval by relating the incoming material to various conceptual frameworks

called *schemas* and *scripts.* The utilization of such frameworks can sometimes lead to *memory distortions* as originally shown by Bartlett. Modern studies of eyewitness testimony have elaborated this point by demonstrating that what is remembered can be seriously affected by building various *presuppositions* into the request for recall. Related work has shown that hypnotized subjects will reconstruct memories to please a hypnotist. Although genuinely convinced that what they recall really happened, the hypnotized subject often turns out to be incorrect and to be easily affected by leading questions.

13. There is some question about the mechanisms that underlie schema-based memory distortions. Some authors believe that they are mainly *reconstructions* in which gaps in memory are filled by conscious or unconscious inference. Others believe that schemas produce *accommodative distortions,* which don't just fill gaps but represent genuine alterations in one's memory.

14. A distinction is often made between two varieties of LTM, *episodic* and *generic* memory. An important component of generic memory is *semantic memory,* whose organization has been described by various *network models* and which has been studied by various techniques for assessing memory search, including *memory activation.* According to an early hypothesis, this network is *hierarchical.* More recent proposals feature networks based on *semantic distance* and receive support from studies of *semantic priming.*

15. Some LTM systems seem to be essentially visual. An extreme and rather rare example is *eidetic memory.* More common are other forms of visual memory that are not a simple reembodiment of the original visual impression but preserve some of the pictorial properties of the original. Evidence comes from work on *mental rotation* and *image scanning.*

16. Other things equal, forgetting increases the longer the time since learning. This point was first demonstrated by Ebbinghaus who plotted the forgetting of associations between *nonsense syllables.* The causes of forgetting are still a matter of debate. One theory holds that traces gradually *decay* over time, though this view is complicated by the fact that forgetting is greater if the subject is awake rather than asleep during the retention interval. Another view argues that the fundamental cause of forgetting is *interference* produced by other, inappropriate memories. This approach leans heavily on two forms of interference produced in the laboratory, *retroactive* and *proactive inhibition.* Yet another theory asserts that forgetting is primarily caused by *retrieval cue changes* at the time of recall. This position is sometimes used to explain the phenomenon of *childhood amnesia.*

17. Under some circumstances, forgetting doesn't seem to occur. There is evidence that some semantic memories last for a very long time, as in the case of a language learned in school, some remnants of which seem to remain in *permastore.* Other evidence for long-lasting memories are *flashbulb memories,* as in remembering where one was at the time one heard that President Kennedy was assassinated.

18. Certain injuries to the brain, particularly to the *hippocampus* and surrounding regions, can produce disorders of memory. In *anterograde amnesia,* the patient's ability to fix material in long-term memory is damaged. In *retrograde amnesia,* the loss is for memories just prior to the injury, and is sometimes attributed to a disruption of *trace consolidation.* An important current issue is why patients with severe anterograde amnesia can acquire certain long-term memories (learning a maze, benefiting from seeing a word by later repetition priming) but not others (remembering that they have seen the maze or the word before). According to one hypothesis, the crucial distinction is between *procedural* and *declarative knowledge;* according to another, it is between *implicit* and *explicit memory* (that is, between remembering and knowing that one remembers).

# CHAPTER 8

# Thinking

In ordinary language, the word *think* has a wide range of meanings. It may be a synonym for *remembering* (as in "I can't think of her name"), or for *attention* (as in the exhortation "Think!"), or for *belief* (as in "I think sea serpents exist"). It may also refer to a state of vague and undirected reverie as in "I'm thinking of nothing in particular." These many uses suggest that the word has become a blanket term which can cover virtually any psychological process that goes on within the individual and is essentially unobservable from without.

But thinking also has a narrower meaning which is graphically rendered in Rodin's famous statue of "The Thinker." Here, the meaning of thinking is best conveyed by such words as *to reason* or *ponder* or *reflect.* Psychologists who study thinking are mainly interested in this sense of the term. To distinguish it from the others, they refer to ***directed thinking,*** a set of internal activities that are aimed at the solution of a problem, whether it be the discovery of a geometric proof, of the next move in a chess game, or of the reason why the car doesn't start. In all of these activities, the various steps in the internal sequence are directed and dominated by the ultimate goal, the solution of the problem.

## THE COMPONENTS OF THOUGHT

An old endeavor in the study of thinking is the search for the elements that make up thought. Some psychologists have proposed that the ultimate constituents of thought are images; others have felt that they are abstract mental structures such as concepts. We will look at both suggestions in turn.

*Thinking* *(Aristotle Contemplating the Bust of Homer, 1653, by Rembrandt; courtesy The Metropolitan Museum of Art, purchased with special funds and gifts of friends of the Museum, 1961)*

## Mental Imagery

One of the oldest proposals is that thought consists of mental images as seen by the mind's eye (or heard by the mind's ear; see Chapter 7). According to Berkeley and other British empiricists, all thought is ultimately comprised of such images, which enter and exit from the stage of consciousness as the laws of association bid them. But later studies have shown that it is very unlikely that thought is the simple kaleidoscope of mental pictures (or sounds and touches) that this view claims it to be. Imagery plays an important role in thinking, but by no means an exclusive one, for much thought goes on without images. Around the turn of the century, several psychologists asked subjects to describe everything that "went through their minds" as they tried to solve various intellectual problems. The solution frequently came without a trace of imagery (and also without words). The subjects reported that when their thought was both wordless and imageless they often had a sense of certain underlying relationships, such as the experience of "this doesn't go with that" or a "feeling of *if* or *but*" (Humphrey, 1951). Mental images are evidently one of the elements of thought. But they are not the only ones.

## Abstract Elements

Mental images are in some ways picture-like. There are some constituents of thinking, however, that are not picture-like at all. Unlike images, they are essentially abstract and symbolic. A good example (though by no means the only one) is words.

291

A

B

*Some representations are picture-like; others are abstract* *(A) A photograph of Ambroise Vollard, a French art dealer at the turn of the century. (B) A cubist portrait of Monsieur Vollard by Pablo Picasso. Note that while Picasso's rendering is by no means literal, there is still enough of a pictorial similarity to the model that the portrait is still recognizable. While this painting is a picture-like representation, the model's name— Ambroise Vollard—is not. It stands for him, but it is not like him, for both names and words are abstract representations rather than picture-like ones. (Picasso's* Portrait of Ambroise Vollard, *1909. Moscow, Pushkin Museum; courtesy Scala/Art Resource*)

Consider a picture of a mouse and compare it to the word *mouse.* The picture is in some ways quite different from the real animal. It *represents* a mouse rather than actually being one. But even so, the picture has many similarities to the creature that it represents, for it looks quite a bit like a real mouse. In contrast, take the word *mouse.* This word stands for the same long-tailed, big-eared, and bewhiskered creature that the picture represents. But unlike the picture, the word has no similarity to the mouse whatever. The relation between the sound "mouse" (or the written, five-letter word *mouse*) and the little long-tailed animal that it represents is entirely arbitrary and symbolic.

Many psychologists believe that the kind of thinking that utilizes mental imagery differs from the kind that underlies words and sentences much as pictures differ from words. In their view, the language-related form of thinking is more symbolic and abstract than the picture-like form that uses imagery. The attempt to describe the components of this more abstract level of thinking is relatively recent, at least for psychologists. But some of the key items of such a description are already in the vocabulary of related disciplines such as logic and linguistics. Examples are the terms *concept* and *proposition.*

## CONCEPTS

The term ***concept*** is generally used to describe a class or category that subsumes a number (sometimes an infinite number) of individual instances. An example is *dwelling,* which includes *hut, house, tent, apartment,* and *igloo.* Other concepts designate qualities or dimensions. Examples are *length* and *age.* Still others are relational, such as *taller than.* Relational concepts don't apply to any one item in isolation. One can't be *taller than* except in relation to something else to which one's height is being compared. (For more detail, see Chapters 7 and 9).

## PROPOSITIONS

Concepts describe classes of events or objects or relations between them. They are what we generally think about. In so doing, we tend to combine them in various ways. The British empiricists emphasized one such mental combination: the simple associative train of thought in which one idea leads to another. A more important way of relating concepts is by asserting something about them, for example, "dogs generally bite postmen." Such statements are called ***propositions.*** They make some assertion that relates a ***subject*** (the item about which an assertion is made; e.g., *dogs*) and a ***predicate*** (what is asserted about the subject; e.g., *generally bite postmen*) in a way that can be true or false.

That much of our thought is propositional requires little proof. The propositions we entertain may be true or false, profound or silly—what matters is that they are propositions, that they link mental elements in certain ways. In what form do such propositions exist psychologically? One possible hypothesis is that they are elaborate images. But as the philosopher Jerry Fodor has shown, this cannot be. Consider the proposition that is expressed by the sentence: "Napoleon is dead." Can this be expressed by way of a mental image? A vivid imager might conjure up an image of the emperor in an open coffin, with weeping veterans of his wars passing by to pay their last respects. But is this image equivalent to the proposition? By no means. This image implies many propositions other than the one at hand: "Napoleon was buried with his sword," "Napoleon was rather fat when he died," "Napoleon's veterans loved him," and so on. The trouble with pictures (whether real or imagined) is that one can say so many things about them. The proposition is a way of singling out the aspects of the world that one wants to make some assertion about (Fodor, 1975).

It appears that propositions cannot be based on images. But they are not equivalent to the sentences in which they are expressed either, as shown by the fact that the same proposition can be expressed in several forms. People who speak both English and German know that "The dog bites the cat" and "Der Hund beisst die Katze" mean precisely the same thing. The same holds within the same language. Consider "The dog bites the cat" and "The cat is bitten by the dog." Again, the same proposition is asserted. Something is being said (and presumably thought) about the hapless cat that does not depend upon the particular form in which this proposition is cast.

To sum up, it seems that there are two different thinking modes. One involves thinking in mental images which, like pictures, resemble whatever it is they represent. A second mode of thinking is more abstract and symbolic, and it involves mental structures such as concepts and propositions. (Some of these matters were touched on in the discussion of semantic memory in Chapter 7; others will be dealt with when we take up language, in Chapter 9.)

## PROBLEM SOLVING

Thus far our concern has been with the elements of which thought is composed. We now turn from the question of *what* to the question of *how.* How does thinking operate as we try to solve the myriad of problems encountered in life, whether trying to fix a broken lawn mower, smoothing over an awkward social situation, or solving an anagram?

Regarded in this context, thinking is an activity. It is something an organism does. Locke, Berkeley, and their many descendants believed that this stream of activity is produced by a chain of associated ideas, each triggered by the one before. The fundamental difficulty of this position is that thinking, like every other activity of the organism, is organized.

The individual items in any activity an organism is engaged in generally do not stand in isolation but take their meaning from the overall structure in which they are embedded. This holds for thought as well as action. A famous paper by Karl Lashley illustrates this point with examples from the psychology of language (Lashley, 1951). Uttering a sentence is not just a matter of stringing one word after another, for the selection of a word often depends not only on the immediately preceding word but upon others spoken both earlier and later. In English, we say "The dog runs" rather than "the dog run," for verb and subject must agree with each other. This agreement rule governs our speech even when the subject comes many words after the verb, as in "Down the street runs the excited, barking, hungry, flea-bitten *dog.*" The fact that we produce the verb with a third-person singular *s* indicates that there is a broad mental scheme that precedes the actual utterance and determines its various parts. In effect, there was a mental plan that provided the outline according to which the specific words were produced (Miller, Galanter, and Pribram, 1960; Dell, 1986; Levelt, 1989).

What holds for speech holds for many other activities, including problem solving. The problem solver goes through a sequence of internal steps. These steps are organized in a special way: They are directed toward a goal—the solution of the problem. Consider a taxi driver who is trying to decide on the best route from the city to the airport. According to a simple chain-association hypothesis, the initial stimulus ("Get me to the airport in time for a 9:15 flight") triggers various internal responses (such as "superhighway," "crosstown express," etc.) until the correct solution is finally evoked (Figure 8.1). But this interpretation cannot readily explain why the would-be solutions that come to mind, whether right or wrong, are usually relevant to the problem at hand. Nor can it explain how such potential solutions are accepted or rejected. If they were merely aroused by associative connections, the problem solver would be adrift in a sea of irrelevancies: "crosstown express" might evoke "uptown local" or "crossword puzzle." Instead, each mental step is determined not just by the step before but by the original problem. This sets the overall direction which dominates all of the later steps and determines how each of them is to be evaluated. The taxi driver considers the superhighway and rejects it as he recalls some road construction along the way, thinks of the crosstown express and dismisses it because of rush-hour traffic, and so on. The original problem acts like a schematic frame, waiting to be filled in by a "fitting" solution. Given this frame, the irrelevant word association "crossword puzzle" never enters his mind.

## Hierarchical Organization and Chunking

We have encountered the notion of hierarchical organization while discussing the role of chunking in memory (see Chapter 7). A similar principle governs directed thinking. To the taxi driver, the idea "take the crosstown express" is a sort of master plan that implies various subsidiary actions: entering from the appropriate one-way street, maneuvering out of the truck lane, following the signs to the airport exit, and so on. To the experienced driver all of these substeps require no fur-

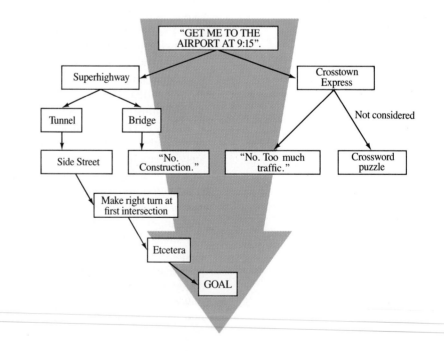

**8.1   Problem solving as directed by the goal**   *The taxi driver's goal determines the thought processes throughout. Some would-be solutions are considered and rejected as inappropriate. Others (e.g., crossword puzzles), although associatively related, aren't even called to mind.*

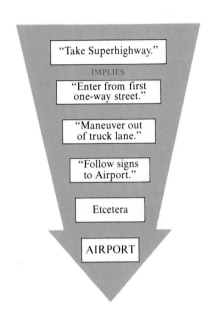

**8.2 Hierarchical organization of a plan**
*Plans have subcomponents which have subcomponents below them, as here illustrated by the taxi driver's task.*

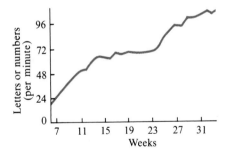

**8.3 An apprentice telegrapher's learning curve** *The curve plots the number of letters or digits the operator can receive per minute against weeks of practice. Note the plateau in the learning curve. The curve stays level from weeks 15 to 25 and then starts to rise again. According to Bryan and Harter, the new rise indicates the use of larger chunks. (After Bryan and Harter, 1899)*

ther thought, for they are a consequence of hierarchical organization which resembles that of a disciplined army. The colonel who orders his regiment to attack does not have to specify the detailed commands his second lieutenants issue to their platoons. Given the order from above, the subcommands follow (Figure 8.2).

The ability to subsume many details under a larger chunk is one of the crucial features of directed activity, including the internal activity we call thinking. As we shall see, much of the difference between master and apprentice is in the degree to which subcomponents of the activity have been chunked hierarchically. To the master, the substeps have become automatic.

### DEVELOPING SKILLS

The role of chunking in directed activity is particularly clear when we study how people become proficient at various skills such as typing, driving a car, or playing golf. In all such activities, becoming skillful depends upon a qualitative change in how the task is performed.

The first experimental study in this area was done about ninety years ago by Bryan and Harter. These psychologists were trying to discover how telegraph operators master their trade. Their subjects were Western Union apprentices whose progress at sending and receiving Morse code messages was charted over a period of about forty weeks. Figure 8.3 plots one student's improvement at receiving, measured in letters per minute. What is interesting about this learning curve is its shape. Following an initial rise, the curve flattens into a *plateau,* after which it may rise again until it reaches another plateau, and so on. According to Bryan and Harter, such plateaus are an indication that the learner gradually transforms his task. At first he merely tracks individual letters, getting progressively faster in doing so as practice proceeds. But with time, the effective units he deals with become larger and larger: first syllables and words, then several words at a time, then simple phrases. The plateau represents the best the learner can do given a unit of a lower level (say, letters); once this lower level is completely mastered, a higher level of organization—a larger chunk—is possible and the learning curve shoots up once more (Bryan and Harter, 1897).

Similar effects are observed in the acquisition of many other skills, such as typing, or driving a car, or playing golf. In all such activities, becoming skillful involves a qualitative change in how the task is performed (Keele, 1982). To the novice, typing proceeds letter by letter; to the expert, the proper units are much larger, including familiar letter groupings, words, and occasionally phrases. Similarly, the beginning driver laboriously struggles to harmonize clutch, gas pedal, steering wheel, and brake, to the considerable terror of innocent bystanders. After a while, those movements come quite routinely and are subsumed under much higher (though perhaps equally dangerous) chunks of behavior, such as overtaking another car. An even simpler example is dressing. To the small child every article of clothing represents a major intellectual challenge; she beams with pride when she finally gets the knack of tying her shoelaces. To an adult the unit is "getting dressed" and its various components are almost completely submerged within the larger chunk. We decide to dress and before we know it we are almost fully clothed. Somehow our shoes get laced but we never notice, unless the laces break.

| **A** | **B** |
|-------|-------|
| ZYP | RED |
| QLEKF | BLACK |
| SUWRG | YELLOW |
| XCIDB | BLUE |
| WOPR | RED |
| ZYP | GREEN |
| QLEKF | YELLOW |
| XCIDB | BLACK |
| SUWRG | BLUE |
| WOPR | BLACK |
| SUWRG | RED |
| ZYP | YELLOW |
| XCIDB | GREEN |
| QLEKF | BLUE |
| WOPR | GREEN |
| QLEKF | BLUE |
| WOPR | RED |
| ZYP | YELLOW |
| XCIDB | BLACK |
| SWRG | GREEN |

**8.4   The Stroop effect**   *The two lists, (A) and (B), are printed in four colors—red, green, blue, and yellow. To observe the Stroop effect, name the colors (aloud) in which each of the nonsense syllables in list (A) is printed as fast as you can, continuing downward. Then do the same for list (B), calling out the colors in which each of the words of the list is printed, again going from top to bottom. This will very probably be easier for list (A) than for list (B), a demonstration of the Stroop effect.*

## AUTOMATIZATION

The automatization of subcomponents in skilled activities, however, has a side effect. Once the plan is set into motion, its execution may be difficult to stop. An example is reading. When we see a billboard on a highway, we can't help but read what it says, whether we want to or not. The forms on the sign proclaim that they are letters and words; this is enough to trigger our automatized reading routines (La Berge, 1975). A striking demonstration of this phenomenon is the so-called *Stroop effect* (Stroop, 1935). Subjects are asked to name the colors in which groups of letters are printed and to do so as quickly as they can (Figure 8.4). In one case, the letter groups are unrelated consonants or vowels. In this condition, the subjects have little trouble. After a little practice, they become very proficient at rattling off the colors, "red, green . . ."

The subjects' task becomes vastly more difficult in a condition in which the letters are grouped into words, specifically color names. Diabolically enough, these are not the names of the colors in which the words are printed. Now the subjects respond much more slowly. They are asked to say "green, red, yellow. . ." But they can't help themselves from reading the words "yellow, black . . ." for reading is an automatized skill. As a result, there is violent response conflict. This conflict persists even after lengthy practice. One way subjects finally manage to overcome it is by learning to unfocus their eyes. By this maneuver, they can still see the colors but can no longer recognize the words (Jensen, 1965).

## THE CHUNKING PROCESS

At present we know very little about the mechanisms that underlie the chunking process. Associationists propose that the explanation involves *chaining.* In their view, many skilled acts are highly overpracticed stimulus-response chains in which the first movement provides the kinesthetic stimulus for the second, which produces the stimulus for the third, and so on. This interpretation is almost certainly false. As Karl Lashley pointed out, a trained pianist may reach a rate of sixteen successive finger strokes a second when playing an arpeggio. This speed is too high to allow time for a sensory message to reach the brain and for a motor command to come back to the fingers (Lashley, 1951). We can only conclude that there is a learned neural program that allows the successive finger movements to occur without alternative sensory monitoring, but the nature of the mechanism that underlies this process is still a matter of debate (e.g., Shiffrin and Schneider, 1977; Newell and Rosenbloom, 1981; Logan, 1988).

We may not understand precisely how this complex chunking is acquired, but there is little doubt of its importance. It is hard to imagine any organized, skilled behavior in which this process does not play a role. In Bryan and Harter's words, "The ability to take league steps in receiving telegraphic messages, in reading, in addition, in mathematical reasoning and in many other fields, plainly depends upon the acquisition of league-stepping habits . . . The learner must come to do with one stroke of attention what now requires a half a dozen, and presently, in one still more inclusive stroke, what now requires thirty-six." The expert can, if necessary, attend to the lower-level units of his skill, but for the most part these have become automatic. This submergence of lower-level units in the higher chunk frees him to solve new problems. "Automatism is not genius, but it is the hands and feet of genius" (Bryan and Harter, 1899, p. 375).

NAGMARA

BOLMPER

SLEVO

STIGNIH

TOLUSONI

**8.5  Anagrams** *Rearrange the letters on each line to form a word. (For the solution, see p. 299.)*

**8.6  Concrete object problem** *Assemble all six matches to form four equilateral triangles, each side of which is equal to the length of one match. (For solution, see Figure 8.19, p. 304.)*

**8.7  Nine-dot problem** *Nine dots are arranged in a square. Connect them by drawing four continuous straight lines without lifting your pencil from the paper. (For solution, see Figure 8.14, p. 301.)*

## SEARCHING FOR SOLUTIONS

Psychologists have devised many experimental situations to study human problem solving. Subjects have been asked to decipher anagrams (Figure 8.5), to manipulate various concrete objects so as to produce a desired result (Figure 8.6), or to find the solution to various geometrical problems (Figure 8.7). Considering this variety of tasks, it is hardly surprising that there are differences in the way in which they are attacked; a subject who tries to join nine dots with one continuous line will call upon a somewhat different set of mental skills than one who has to rearrange the letters *STIGNIH* into an English word. The question is whether there is a common thread that runs through all attempts at problem solving, no matter what the particular problem may be. Many psychologists believe that hierarchical organization is such a common feature.

The role of organization in problem solving was highlighted in a classic study by the Gestalt psychologist Karl Duncker, who asked his subjects to "think out loud" while they tried to find the solution (Duncker, 1945). One of Duncker's problems was cast in medical terms:

> Suppose a patient has an inoperable stomach tumor. There are certain rays which can destroy this tumor if their intensity is large enough. At this intensity, however, the rays will also destroy the healthy tissue which surrounds the tumor (e.g., the stomach walls, the abdominal muscles, and so on). How can one destroy the tumor without damaging the healthy tissue through which the rays must travel on their way?

Duncker's subjects typically arrived at the solution in several steps. They first reformulated the problem so as to produce a general plan of attack. This in turn led to more specific would-be solutions. For example, they might look for a tissue-free path to the stomach and so propose to send the rays through the esophagus. (A good idea which unfortunately will not work—rays travel in straight lines and the esophagus is curved.) After exploring several other general approaches and their specific consequences, some subjects finally hit upon the appropriate general plan. They proposed to reduce the intensity of rays on their way through healthy tissue and then turn up this intensity when the rays reach the tumor. This broad restatement of what is needed eventually led to the correct specific means, which was to send several bundles of *weak* rays from various points outside so that they meet at the tumor where their effects will summate (Figure 8.8, p. 298).

## MASTERS AND BEGINNERS

Some people solve certain problems better than others do. One reason is experience; the trained mechanic is more likely to hit on the why and wherefore of automotive failure than is his young apprentice. But what exactly does experience contribute? A major factor is chunking, which plays a similar role in problem solving to that played in the execution of various skills. Experts approach a problem in different ways than beginners. They think in larger units whose components are already contained within them and thus require no further thought.

An interesting demonstration of how chunking makes the master comes from a study of chess players conducted by the Dutch psychologist Adrian de Groot whose findings have been corroborated and extended by several American inves-

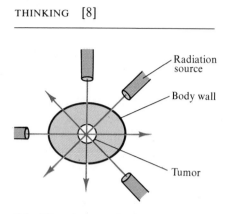

**8.8   The solution to the ray-tumor problem**  *Several weak rays are sent from various points outside so that they will meet at the tumor site. There the radiation of the rays will be intense, for all the effects will summate at this point. But since they are individually weak, the rays will not damage the healthy tissue that surrounds the tumor. (After Duncker, 1945)*

**8.9   Memory for chess positions in masters and average players**
*(A) An actual chess position which was presented for five seconds after which the positions of the pieces had to be reconstructed. Typical performances by masters and average players are shown in (B) and (C) respectively, with errors indicated in red. (After Hearst, 1972)*

tigators (de Groot, 1965; Chase and Simon, 1973a, 1973b). The chess world ranks its members according to a ruthlessly objective hierarchy of merit based on a simple record of who beats whom. Grandmasters are at the top, followed by masters, experts, down to Class *D* players at the lower rungs of the chess ladder. De Groot, himself a chess master, posed various chess problems to members of each merit category (including two former world champions) and asked them to select the best move. All of the masters chose continuations that would have won the game, while few of the other players did. But why? De Groot and many later theorists believed that the reason was in the way the players organized the problem. The chess master structures the chess position in terms of broad strategic concepts (e.g., a king-side attack with pawns) from which many of the appropriate moves follow naturally. In effect, the master has a "chess vocabulary" of more and larger chunks. If so, one would expect him to grasp a chess position in a shorter time. This is indeed the case. Players of different ranks were shown chess positions for five seconds each and were then asked to reproduce them a few minutes later. Grandmasters and masters did so with hardly an error; lesser players (including mere experts) performed much more poorly (see Figure 8.9). This is not because the chess masters have better visual memory. When presented with bizarre positions that would hardly ever arise in the course of a well-played game, they recall them no better than novices do. Their superiority is in the conceptual organization of chess, not in the memory for visual patterns as such.

Some later studies have shown that the superiority of the chess masters is not entirely produced by better chunking. They are also better in evaluating chess positions and look further ahead in their mental calculations (Charness, 1981; Holding and Reynolds, 1982; Holding, 1985). But chunking clearly plays a role in this mental skill, just as it does in telegraphy, typing, and various athletic pursuits (e.g., Allard, Graham, and Paarsalu, 1980).

At least in part, the essence of expertise is twofold. To begin with, experts know more than novices. And in addition, they have developed an organization of the relevant subcomponents, which allows them to solve their problems in terms of fewer but vastly larger steps. Whether the skill is reading or typing or playing a musical instrument, its mastery depends on the acquisition of newer and better chunkings.

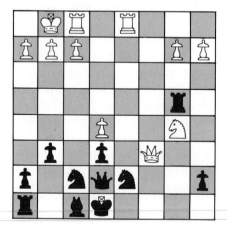

A. Actual position

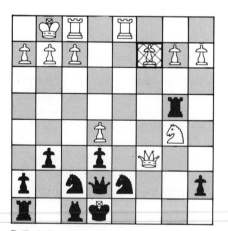

B. Typical master player's performance

C. Typical average player's performance

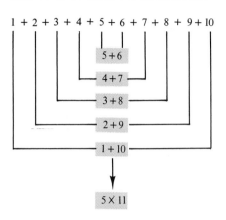

$$1 + 2 + 3 + 4 + 5 + 6 + 7 + 8 + 9 + 10$$

5 + 6

4 + 7

3 + 8

2 + 9

1 + 10

↓

5 × 11

**8.10  Reorganizing a series of sums**
*Young Gauss's solution amounts to the insight that in a series of numbers 1 + 2 . . . + 10, the numbers increase by one going from left to right and decrease by one going from right to left. As a result, the sum of the extreme pairs (1 + 10) must equal the sum of the next-to-extreme pair (2 + 9) and so on. Given this insight, it can be generalized to a series of any length. Thus 1 + 2 . . . + 1,000 = 500 (1 + 1,000). (After Wertheimer, 1945)*

ANAGRAM

PROBLEM

SOLVE

INSIGHT

SOLUTION

*Solution to Figure 8.5 (p. 297)*

It is possible that processes similar to chunking underlie the cognitive growth that occurs in childhood. As infants grow into toddlers, and toddlers into children, they gradually acquire many concepts that adults take for granted, so that they eventually comprehend space, time, and causality in much the way their parents do. It may be that the way in which they achieve this has much in common with the route that beginners take in becoming masters in a particular skill. We will return to this issue in a later discussion of cognitive development (see Chapter 14).

Acquiring the appropriate chunkings is in part a matter of experience. But in part, it is also a matter of talent, for some people can see chunks where the rest of us cannot. When the mathematician Karl Friedrich Gauss was a young boy in grammar school, his teacher asked the class to add all the numbers from 1 to 10. Young Gauss got the answer almost immediately. Unlike his classmates, he did not chug through all of the tedious steps of the summation. He recognized that the series 1 + 2 + 3 . . . + 10 can be rewritten as a sum of 5 pairs each of which equals 11. (His reorganization of the series is rendered graphically in Figure 8.10.) Given this insight, he quickly came up with the correct answer, 55, no doubt to the considerable amazement of the teacher.

This process of reorganizing bits and pieces so that they form a unified whole is also found in artistic creation. Mozart describes it in one of his letters:

> Those ideas that please me I retain in memory, and am accustomed, as I have been told, to hum them to myself. If I continue in this way, it soon occurs to me how I may turn this or that morsel to good account, so as to make a good dish of it, that is to say agreeably to the rules of counterpoint, to the peculiarities of the various instruments, etc. All this fires my soul, and provided that I am not disturbed my subject enlarges itself and becomes methodized and refined, and the whole, though it be long, stands almost complete and finished in my mind, so that I can survey it, like a fine picture or a beautiful statue—at a glance. Nor do I hear in my imagination the parts successively, but I hear them, as it were, all at once. What a delight this is, I cannot tell. . . . What has been thus produced, I do not easily forget, and this is perhaps the best gift I have my divine maker to thank for. (Quoted in Humphrey, 1951, p. 53)

## Obstacles to Problem Solving

So far, we have primarily dealt with situations in which problem solvers succeed. How can we explain their all too many failures? In many cases, the solution is simply out of reach. The problem solver lacks some necessary informational prerequisites or relevant chunkings—as when a ten-year-old is unable to solve a problem in integral calculus. But failure often occurs even when all the necessary ingredients for solution are known perfectly well, for the would-be problem solver may get stuck in a wrong approach and may not be able to get unstuck. When finally told the answer, his reaction often shows that he was blind rather than ignorant: "How stupid of me. I should have seen it all along." He was victimized by a powerful ***mental set*** that was inappropriate for the problem at hand.

### FIXATION

A well-known study shows how mental set can make people rigid. They became ***fixated*** on one approach to the task, which made it hard for them to think of it in

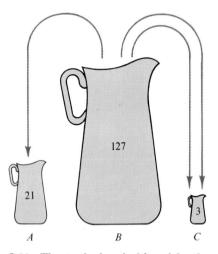

**8.11 The standard method for solving the three-container problem** *(After Luchins, 1942)*

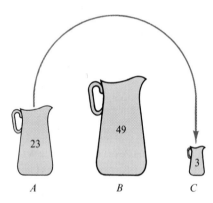

**8.12 A simpler method for solving certain three-container problems** *(After Luchins, 1942)*

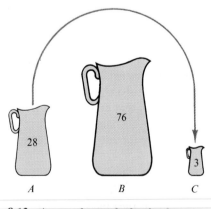

**8.13 A case where only the simple method works** *(After Luchins, 1942)*

any other way. The subjects were presented with a series of problems. They were told that they had three jars of known volume. Their job was to use these to obtain (mentally) an exact quantity of water from a well. In one problem, for example, the subjects had three containers—*A, B,* and *C*—which held 21, 127, and 3 quarts respectively. Their task was to use these three jars to obtain 100 quarts. After a while, they hit upon the correct method. This was to fill jar *B* (127 quarts) completely, and then pour out enough water to fill jar *A* (21 quarts). After this, they would pour out more water from jar *B* to fill jar *C* (3 quarts), empty jar *C* and fill it again from jar *B.* The remaining water in jar *B* was the desired quantity, 100 quarts (Figure 8.11).

On the next few problems, the numerical values differed (Table 8.1). But in all cases, the solution could be obtained by the same sequence of arithmetical steps, that is, $B - A - 2C$. Thus, $163 - 14 - 2 \times 25 = 99$; $43 - 18 - 2 \times 10 = 5$, and so on.

After five such problems, the subjects were given two critical tests. The first was a problem that required them to obtain 20 quarts, given jars whose volumes were 23, 49, and 3 quarts. Now most of the subjects showed a mechanization effect produced by mental set. They dutifully performed the laborious arithmetical labors they had used before, computing $49 - 23 - 2 \times 3 = 20$. They did so, even though there was a simpler method that takes only one step (Figure 8.12).

Subsequent to this was a second critical problem. The subjects were now asked to obtain 25 quarts, given jars of 28, 76, and 3 quarts. Note that here the only method that will work is the direct one; that is, $28 - 3 = 25$ (Figure 8.13). But the mental set was so powerful that many subjects failed to solve the problem altogether. They tried the old procedure, which is inappropriate ($76 - 28 - 2 \times 3$ does not equal 25), and so could not hit on an adequate alternative. The set had made them so rigid that they became mentally blind (Luchins, 1942).

Similar effects have been demonstrated in other problem situations. In many of these there is no need to induce the misleading set by instructions or prior practice, for it is usually engendered by the perceptual arrangement of the problem situations. Examples of such perceptually induced sets are the nine-dot problem (Figure 8.14) and the horse-and-rider problem (Figure 8.15).

SET AND MOTIVATION

In fairy tales, the hero is sometimes required to solve a riddle or suffer death but, being a fairy-tale hero, he invariably succeeds. In real life, he would have a harder time, for problem solution, unfairly enough, becomes more difficult when the need for it is especially great. This is because of the relation between set and moti-

Table 8.1   THE THREE-CONTAINER PROBLEM

| Desired quantity of water (quarts) | Volume of empty jar (quarts) | | |
| --- | --- | --- | --- |
| | A | B | C |
| 99 | 14 | 163 | 25 |
| 5 | 18 | 43 | 10 |
| 21 | 9 | 42 | 6 |
| 31 | 20 | 59 | 4 |

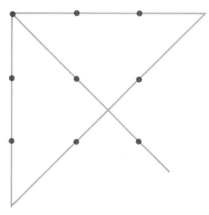

**8.14   The solution of the nine-dot problem**   *The problem (Figure 8.7) is solved by going outside of the square frame into which the dots are perceptually grouped. The lines have to be extended beyond the dots as shown. Most subjects fail to hit on this solution because of a perceptual set imposed by the square arrangement.*

A

B

**8.15   Horse-and-rider problem**   *The task is to place (B) on (A) in such a way that the riders are properly astride the horse. (After Scheerer, Goldstein, and Boring, 1941; for solution, see Figure 8.20, p. 304.)*

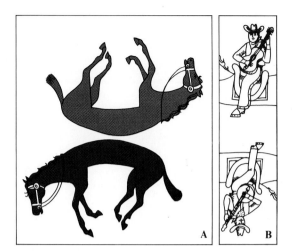

A         B

vation. The greater the motivation toward solution, the stronger are the sets with which the problem is approached. If these sets happen to be appropriate, well and good. But if they are inappropriate, increased motivation will be a hindrance, for sets will then be that much harder to break. Since difficult problems—almost by definition—are problems that tend to engender the wrong set, their solution will be impeded as motivation becomes intense.

Evidence for these assertions comes from several experiments which show that flexibility goes down when motivation becomes intense enough. In one such study, the subjects were posed a practical problem. The problem was to mount two candles on a wall, given only the candles, a box of matches, and some thumbtacks (Figure 8.16). The solution is to empty one of the boxes, tack it to the wall, and then place the candles upon it. The difficulty of this particular problem is caused by *functional fixedness.* This is a set to think of objects in terms of their normal function: a box is to put things in and not on top of. The tendency to maintain this set (that is, functional fixedness) was increased by motivation. Subjects who expected no particular reward solved the problem more quickly than subjects who were told that they might win a $20 reward (Glucksberg, 1962).

## Overcoming Obstacles to Solution

The preceding discussion highlighted some of the conceptual and motivational obstacles that lie in the face of problem solution. Apart from acquiring some further knowledge and some relevant cognitive chunks (and keeping calm about the $20 reward that accompanies success), is there anything one can do to surmount them? Thus far, no one has found a problem solver's panacea that can apply to any and all of his difficulties. But some psychologists have offered a few suggestions.

**8.16   Functional fixedness**   *(A) The problem is to mount two candles on the wall, given the objects shown. (B) To solve the problem, one has to think of a new function for the box. (After Glucksberg, 1962; photographs by Jeffrey Grosscup)*

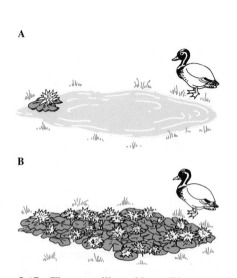

A

B

**8.17 The water-lily problem** *Water lilies double in area every 24 hours. On the first day of summer, there is one water lily as in (A). On the 60th day, the lake is all covered, as in (B). On what day is the lake half-covered?*

WORKING BACKWARDS

One useful method of solving problems is to work backwards. As an example consider the following problem:

Water lilies double in area every twenty-four hours. On the first day of summer, there is one water lily on a lake. It takes sixty days for the lake to become covered with water lilies. On what day is the lake half covered?

Here the problem solver will run into trouble if she tries to work it out by brute force: On Day 1, there is one lily; on Day 2, there are two; on Day 3, there are four, and so on. The trick is to shift gears and look at the problem backwards. If the lake is fully covered on Day 60, it must be half-covered on the day before since lilies double in area every day, which means that the answer is Day 59 (after Sternberg and Davidson, 1983; see Figure 8.17).

Another example that can be solved using the same general approach is the following:

Fifteen pennies are placed in front of two players. When it is his turn, a player must remove some pennies from the pile—no less than one, but no more than five. The players alternate turns. The object of the game is to take the last penny off the table. Is there a method of play that guarantees victory to the player who has the first turn?

To solve the problem, one must again work backwards. You begin by asking how many pennies you should seek to have in the pile on your last turn so as to guarantee that you will be the winner. The answer is anywhere from one to five pennies. If that's the situation, you can pick up whatever pennies are left on the table and thus be the winner. Once we understand this, you can take the next step and ask how many pennies you should leave in the pile for your opponent on the move just before. The answer is six pennies, for if so, he will be forced to leave you from one to five pennies regardless of what he does on his move. It follows that if you can leave your opponent with twelve pennies on his previous move, you've won. For no matter how many pennies he takes, you can guarantee that he'll have exactly six pennies on the next turn (e.g., if he takes one, you take five; if he takes two, you take four, and so on). This tells you how you can assure yourself of victory if you are the first player: Take three pennies from the pile and leave your hapless opponent with twelve (from Wickelgren, 1974).

In these two examples, the working backwards method is guaranteed to work. But it doesn't work with all problems, and even when it does it is not necessarily the best procedure. When the solution requires a great deal of specialized information, as in problems in physics, novices (students in a college physics course) are more likely to work backwards than experts (their instructors). The expert recognizes the point of the problem and can therefore mount a direct attack; the novice can only feel her way, and so starts backwards from the goal (Larkin, McDermott, Simon, and Simon, 1980).

FINDING AN APPROPRIATE ANALOGY

Some problems seem to have a similar structure. Such similarities are often seen in the problems of everyday life. The school counsellor who advises teenagers is likely to find that the problem she hears about today reminds her of one she has heard about a few months back, and her experience with the first generally helps her in understanding the second. What holds for the real world also holds for the laboratory. Sometimes new problems are solved by analogy with similar ones encountered earlier.

In one study subjects were first exposed to an analogue of the ray-tumor problem. They read a story about a general who had to attack a fortress but faced a dilemma: The fortress was protected against attack because all the roads that led to it were mined. While the mines were set to be detonated by a large body of men passing over them at one time, small groups of men would not set them off. Given this situation, the general divided his army into small groups and dispatched each of them to a different road. When he gave the signal, they each marched to the fortress, where they converged and attacked successfully. After reading this story, the subjects were given the ray-tumor problem (Gick and Holyoak, 1980, 1983).

The structural similarity between the ray-tumor problem and the general's dilemma is clear enough: In both cases, a force must be initially dispersed and later brought to convergence. But does exposure to the one problem help subjects to solve the other one? It does, if they see the analogy. If they are given a hint that the military story may help them, about 80 percent of them solve the ray-tumor problem compared with only 10 percent of the control subjects. But if the subjects merely hear the general's story without being informed of its relevance, the beneficial effect is much weaker (about 20 percent). Mere exposure to an analogy is evidently not enough if the analogy is not recognized as such. But it may come to mind if it is somehow made more memorable. After hearing an additional story analogue (the second featured an oil-well fire extinguished by the use of multiple converging hoses), the number of subjects who solved the ray-tumor problem rose to about 45 percent (Gick and Holyoak, 1983).

It's clear that analogies can help in finding a solution. But the analogy must be the right one. This point is illustrated by another study in which experts and novices were asked to classify physics problems according to their similarity. Novices sorted the problems according to their surface similarity, for example, by whether they involved inclined planes or pulleys. In contrast, experts classified the problems according to the underlying physical principles that applied to them, such as the law of conservation of energy (Chi, Feltovich, and Glaser, 1981). The trick is to find the right analogy and to see its relevance.

### CHANGING THE REPRESENTATION

In many cases, a problem seems difficult because it is not correctly interpreted. To solve it, it has to be looked at in a new way; technically speaking, it requires a change in the way it is *represented.* Below are two examples:

> Suppose Joe and Frank have the same amount of money. How much must Joe give Frank so that Frank has $10 more than Joe?

Here the crucial recognition is that Frank's gain is necessarily Joe's loss. Every dollar Joe gives to Frank must be represented as a net change of *two* dollars: one gained by Frank and one lost to Joe. Since we need a net change of $10, the answer is $5. (For another problem in which the solution depends on a change of representation, see Figure 8.18).

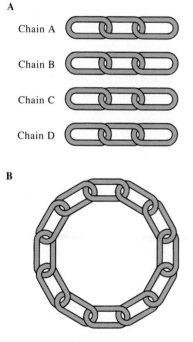

A

Chain A

Chain B

Chain C

Chain D

B

**8.18 The cheap-necklace problem** *(A) You are given four separate pieces of chain that are each three links in length as shown below. It costs 2 cents to open a link and 3 cents to close a link. All links are closed at the beginning of the problem. Your goal is to connect all 12 links of chain into a single circle as shown in (B). The total cost must be no more than 15 cents. (From Wickelgren, 1974. The solution is described on p. 306).*

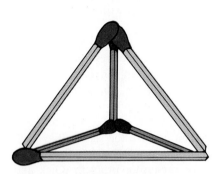

**8.19 Solution of the matchstick problem** *To arrange six matches (see Figure 8.6) into four equilateral triangles, the matches have to be assembled into a three-dimensional pyramid. Most subjects implicitly assume the matches must lie flat. (After Scheerer, 1963)*

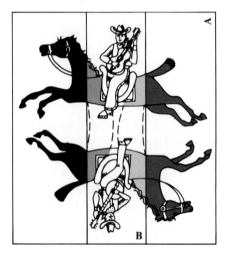

**8.20 Solution of the horse-and-rider problem** *To solve the horse-and-rider puzzle (see Figure 8.15) requires a change of perceptual set. (A) must be rotated 90 degrees so that the two old nags are in the vertical position. One can now see that the head of each (vertical) can join (horizontally) with the hindquarters of the other. The final step is to slide (B) over the middle of (A) and the problem is solved. (After Scheerer, Goldstein, and Boring, 1941)*

## Restructuring

We've already seen that the solution of a difficult problem often involves a dramatic shift in the way in which the problem is viewed. This shift may be very sudden and is then experienced as a flash of insight, a sense of "aha" that occurs when the misleading set is finally broken. Restructuring is especially clear in problems that impose a false conceptual set. To solve the nine-dot problem, the subject has to move out of the square frame imposed by the dots (see Figure 8.14). In a similar vein, the match problem requires working in three dimensions rather than two (Figure 8.19), while the horse-and-rider problem can only be solved by a 90-degree rotation of the drawing which recombines the fore- and hindquarters of the misshapen horses to form two new animals entirely (Figure 8.20).

Gestalt psychologists have proposed that this kind of perceptual restructuring lies at the heart of most problem solving in both animals and humans (see Chapter 4). So far, little is known about the mechanisms that underlie the restructuring effect, but there is reason to believe that it is a central phenomenon in the psychology of thinking. (For a contrary view, see Weisberg and Alba, 1981.)

### CREATIVE THINKING

The creative thinker is one who generates a problem solution that is both new and appropriate. At the top of the pyramid are such giants as Archimedes, Descartes, and Newton, whose creations define whole chapters of intellectual history. On another level are the anonymous copywriters who develop new advertising slogans for spray deodorants. But whether great or humble, these real-life achievements are quite similar to those of the problem solver in the psychological laboratory. They represent a conceptual reorganization of what was there before.

According to the creators' own accounts, the critical insights typically occur at unexpected times and places. There is usually a period of intense preparation during which the thinker is totally immersed in the problem and approaches it from all possible angles. But illumination tends not to come then. Quite the contrary. After the initial onslaught fails, there is usually a period of retreat during which the problem is temporarily shelved. Rest or some other activity intervenes, and then suddenly the solution arrives, not at the writer's desk or the composer's piano, but elsewhere entirely—while walking in the woods (Helmholtz), or riding in a carriage (Beethoven, Darwin), or stepping onto a bus (the great mathematician Poincaré), or, in the most celebrated case of all, while sitting in a bathtub (Archimedes; see Figure 8.21).

Such effects have sometimes been attributed to a process of ***incubation*** (Wallas, 1926). According to this view, a thinker does not ignore the unsolved problem altogether when she turns away from it in baffled frustration; she continues to work on it, but does so "unconsciously." This hypothesis adds little to our understanding, for it merely substitutes one mystery for another. Unless we know the why and wherefore of unconscious thought (whatever that may be), we know no more than we did before.

Many psychologists suspect that such so-called incubation effects are produced by a change in mental set (e.g., Wickelgren, 1974; Anderson, 1990). To find the

**8.21   Archimedes in his bathtub**   *A sixteenth-century engraving celebrating a great example of creative restructuring. The Greek scientist Archimedes (287–212 B.C.) tried to determine whether the king's crown was made of solid gold or had been adulterated with silver. Archimedes knew the weight of gold and silver per unit volume but did not know how to measure the volume of a complicated object such as a crown. One day, in his bath, he noticed how the water level rose as he immersed his body. Here was the solution: the crown's volume is determined by the water it displaces. Carried away by his sudden insight, he jumped out of his bath and ran naked through the streets of Syracuse, shouting "Eureka! I have found it!" (Engraving by Walter H. Ryff, courtesy The Granger Collection)*

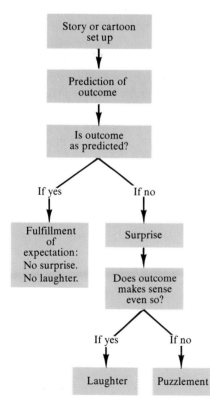

**8.22   A cognitive analysis of the appreciation of humor**   *The joke or cartoon sets up an expectation. The experience of humor will arise (1) if this expectation is not fulfilled and (2) if the outcome nevertheless makes sense. (After Suls, 1972)*

solution, the problem solver must shake off one or more false approaches. These become increasingly restricting the longer she stays at the task, all the more so since her motivation is very intense. Leaving the problem for awhile may very well break the mental set. As time elapses, the false set may be forgotten, and the drastic change of retrieval cues (to the woods or to the bathtub) will prevent its reinstatement. Once the false set is dropped, there is a chance that the true solution may emerge. Of course, it is only a chance that may come to fruition if one is totally familiar with all the ins and outs of the problem and (especially) if one has the talents of a Beethoven or an Archimedes. Just taking a bath is unfortunately not enough.

### RESTRUCTURING AND HUMOR

At least on the face of it, there is a certain similarity between insightful problem solution and humor. A joke does not strike us as funny unless we "get the point." Conversely, insights sometimes have a comic aspect, especially when one recognizes how absurdly simple the solution really is.

Several writers suggest that the essential similarity lies in the fact that both insight and humor involve a dramatic shift from one cognitive organization to another (e.g., Suls, 1972, 1983; see Figure 8.22). The joke teller creates one expectation during the early stage of the narrative, and then betrays it when he comes to the punch line. There is surprise followed by the realization that the unexpected ending makes some sense after all (Gleitman, 1990).

305

***Solution to the cheap-necklace problem***
*The obvious (but incorrect) approach to the problem (Figure 8.18, p. 303) is to try to link the four chains together: A to B to C to D and then back to A. The trouble is that this procedure will cost too much. To solve the problem, one has to shift the representation and see that one of the chains (say, A) can provide the connecting links to connect the other three chains. The first step is to destroy a chain by opening all three links in A (at a total cost of 6 cents). The first link is used to connect B and C (creating a 7-link chain), the second to join this new chain with D (making an 11-link chain), and finally the third to join the ends of this 11-link chain together, at a total cost of 9 cents. One of the reasons why this problem is quite difficult is that its solution requires a detour: In order to make a larger chain (that is, the final necklace) one has to destroy one of the smaller ones. (From Wickelgren, 1974)*

As an example, consider the story about three men, a doctor, a lawyer, and an engineer, all of whom are to be executed on a guillotine. As they step up to the scaffold, each is given a choice of lying face up or face down. The doctor is the first and decides that one should confront one's fate directly, so he opts to lie face up. The blade drops, but then stops with a loud squeak just one foot above the doctor's body. There is much amazement, and then the prisoner is released. Next is the lawyer. He is sure that legal precedent would lead to his own release if the blade were to stop for him as it had for the doctor, so he too lies face up. Again the blade stops short, and again the prisoner is released. It's now the engineer's turn. He decides his best bet is to go with whatever worked before. As he lies face up, he too can see the blade overhead. But then, just before the blade descends, he turns to the executioner and says, "Say, wait—I think I see what your problem is up there."

The story is set up to lead to the expectation of another ending, perhaps a third failure. The actual ending is unexpected and incongruous, but it makes sense even so—the engineer can't resist solving an engineering problem, even if it kills him. But incongruity as such is not enough, for without a viable cognitive alternative into which the ending fits, there will be no humor. If the engineer had asked the executioner to lend him a handkerchief, there would have been no joke at all, only puzzlement.

In other cases, the cognitive structure of the joke is more subtle. Consider the story about a mountain climber who slipped over a precipice and barely hung on to a long rope with a thousand-foot drop gaping underneath. There was no one with him, and he knew he couldn't hold on much longer. In his fear and despair, he looked up to the heavens and shouted: "Is there anyone up there who can help me?" There was a long pause and then a deep voice was heard from above: "You will be saved if you show your faith by letting go of the rope." The mountain climber looked down at the deep abyss beneath him, and then looked up again and cried: "Is there anyone *else* up there who can help me?"

Here, the joke sets up a puzzle—what will the mountain climber do now? His response is unexpected. He both has faith and he doesn't. Not content with hearing from one deity, he wants to hear from yet another, trying to get a better bargain. A similar relation between humor and puzzles is apparent in many cartoons. For example, when a viewer first sees the famous skiing cartoon of Charles Addams, he tries to figure out what is going on. The solution is incongruous, but it fits, and is therefore funny (see Figure 8.23).

**8.23 Humor in a cartoon** *(Drawing by Chas. Addams; © 1940, 1968 The New Yorker Magazine, Inc.)*

Surprise and reinterpretation are probably not the only cognitive factors required for humor to occur. Another ingredient is the comparison of the two cognitive structures that are juxtaposed. The critical element can be seen in *both* contexts. This simultaneous membership of an item in two radically different cognitive contexts seems to be a crucial aspect of humor. Thus, one of Oscar Wilde's dowagers, on interviewing a potential son-in-law, asks:

> LADY BRACKNELL: . . . Now to minor matters. Are your parents living?
> JACK: I have lost both my parents.
> LADY BRACKNELL: To lose one parent, Mr. Worthing, may be regarded as a misfortune; to lose both looks like carelessness.
>
> (Wilde, *The Importance of Being Earnest,* Act 1)

The humor derives from the sudden jolt caused by the second meaning of "lost," which is then contrasted with the first.

While cognitive restructuring is an important and perhaps a necessary condition for the production of humor, it is clearly not a sufficient one. A whole variety of emotional and motivational factors are also involved. Thus humor can serve as a relatively harmless outlet for aggressive or sexual wishes that can't be indulged directly, as in sarcastic wit and "dirty jokes." A further condition is that the new and unexpected meaning (the point of the joke) has to be emotionally acceptable to the listener. Jokes about Hitler's extermination camps are not funny to anyone. This point holds even for the so-called "sick joke." We can (barely) accept, "Yes, yes, Mrs. Lincoln, but how did you like the play?" because 1865 is over a hundred years in the past. An equivalent line about Mrs. John F. Kennedy is unpardonable.

## ARTIFICIAL INTELLIGENCE: PROBLEM SOLVING BY COMPUTER

The preceding discussion has emphasized the role played by hierarchical organization in thinking. But how does this organization come about? How does the problem solver hit upon the right plan of attack and how does she recognize that it is right when she thinks of it? These questions are as yet unanswered, but there have been some promising leads.

One interesting avenue of research comes from attempts to program computers so as to simulate certain aspects of human thinking. The impetus for this work stems from the belief, held by many psychologists, that humans and computers are similar in one important regard—they are both *information-processing systems.* We have already seen several examples of the information-processing approach in our discussions of perception and memory. When we talk of items that are temporarily activated in working memory, are recoded into fewer and more compact chunks, and are later retrieved by various hierarchical search procedures, we are describing a system in which information is systematically converted from one form into another. There is a formal similarity between this sequence of inferred events in human memory and the actual steps of a computer program that handles the storage, recoding, and retrieval of various materials (such as library titles, tax returns, and so on). In an analogous way, what we

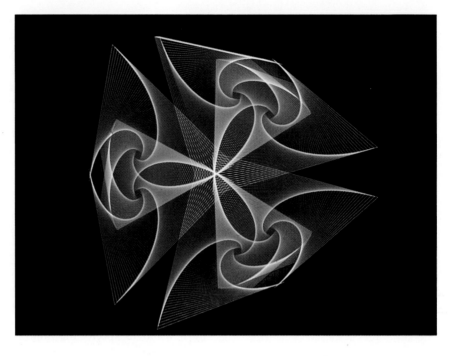

***Computer-generated visual design***   *By now, computers are used to assist in many human endeavors. The figure shows a computer design generated from a graphic program that incorporates various geometrical algorithms. ("Tri-Vail" © 1968 Melvin L. Prueitt)*

call "thinking" may be the systematic manipulation of the hierarchically arranged conceptual chunks stored in our brain.

To be sure, the underlying physical machinery is very different. Computers use hardware made of magnetic cores and transistors, while biological systems are built of neurons. But this difference does not prohibit a similarity in their operations. Two different computers may be built with either electronic tubes or transistors, but they may be fed the same programs even so—and they will both compute the same functions. Similarly—for at least some purposes—it may not matter that digital computers are built of steel and ceramic chips while an organism's mental machinery is built of neurons. To students of ***artificial intelligence,*** the important point is that both computers and human beings are information-processing systems (Turing, 1950). They therefore regard it as likely that the study of one will help in the understanding of the other.

A further advantage of the computer simulation of thought comes from the fact that machines are painfully literal. The program must be spelled out in absolutely precise detail, for the computer will balk if presented with vague or overgeneralized instructions. This limitation is a blessing in disguise. It forces the scientist to formulate his notions in completely rigorous and explicit terms.

### Algorithms and Heuristics

Several investigators have deliberately forced their "thinking" programs to be as humanlike as possible. The most prominent among these are Allen Newell and Nobel laureate Herbert Simon, who have programmed computers to play chess, to discover and prove theorems in symbolic logic, and to decipher cryptograms. They began by studying how human subjects deal with these problems, discovered their typical strategies by use of the think-aloud technique we discussed earlier and then incorporated these problem-solving plans into the instructions fed to their computer. Interestingly enough, the computer does fairly well if it attacks these problems as human subjects say they do (Newell and Simon, 1972).

Newell and Simon found it useful to distinguish between two major kinds of solution strategies. One is an *algorithm,* a procedure in which all of the operations required to achieve the solution are specified step by step. Examples are the various manipulations of arithmetic. An algorithm guarantees that a solution will be found in time, but this time may be very long in coming. Consider a person working on a crossword puzzle who is trying to find a synonym for "sharp-tongued" that will fit into _c_ _bi_. An algorithm exists: Insert all possible alphabetic combinations into the four empty spaces and check each result against an unabridged dictionary. While this procedure is certain to produce "acerbic," it should appeal to few puzzle solvers, for it will require the inspection of nearly 460,000 possibilities.

In actual practice, crossword puzzles are solved by procedures which, though not as sure, are much less slow. These are *heuristics,* which are various tricks and rules of thumb that have often worked in the past and may do so again, such as guessing at a suffix given the word's grammatical class (*ic* is a good bet for an adjective), forming hypotheses on the basis of likely letter sequences in the language (if *c* is the second letter, the first must be an *s* or a vowel), and so on. The various procedures for overcoming obstacles to problem solving which we have discussed before, such as working backwards, finding analogies, and changing the way the problem is represented, are algorithms of a similar sort—they are by no means guaranteed to work, but they often do. The great majority of problems people face are solved by such heuristic procedures rather than by algorithms, for human life is short and human processing capacity is limited. Physicians reach their diagnoses by first considering a few hypotheses that seem most plausible and then testing those. If instead they looked at every possibility, the patient would be dead before being diagnosed.

If the problem is complex enough, even high-speed computers must resort to heuristics (Boden, 1977). Consider the analysis of a chess position some ten moves ahead. The total number of possibilities (based on moves, replies, replies to replies, and so on) has been estimated at an astronomical billion billion billion. Under the circumstances, an algorithm is out of the question. (If the inspection of each possibility takes one-millionth of a second, the inspection of all of them would be completed after 1,000 billion years.) On the other hand, heuristics work remarkably well. Modern chess programs require the computer to search for moves that satisfy certain subgoals such as material superiority (e.g., give a pawn for a queen but not vice versa) and various strategic objectives such as occupation of the center squares (which limits the opponent's mobility). Notice that this approach resembles that of the human player. His ultimate goal is to checkmate his opponent, but he is not likely to achieve it unless he proceeds hierarchically; instead of evaluating each move in terms of the final goal, he considers it in the light of the subgoals that lead up to it. Chess programs that employ heuristics of this sort have become very powerful (Holding, 1985). They combine what is essentially brute force (the ability to search at extremely high speeds) with the ability to evaluate positions. Under the circumstances, it is not surprising that they are

**8.24 Chess computers as expert systems** *Grandmaster Arthur Bisguier inspecting a variety of chess microcomputers commercially available in 1982. By now, the best of these machines can hold their own against a player rated as a master but are unlikely to defeat players of Bisguier's stature. These chess computers can be regarded as expert systems because their knowledge is entirely limited to chess. (Photograph by Bruce Helm, U.S. Chess Federation)*

closing in on the game's human champions. One such program, Deep Thought, has already defeated several grandmasters (Byrne, 1989; see Figure 8.24).

Programs based on heuristics have scored some successes in other fields. An example is a program that can prove theorems in symbolic logic (Newell, Shaw, and Simon, 1958). Its general scheme is to work backward from the desired end. The program tries to find a means to the final goal, then a means to achieve that means (which now becomes a subgoal), and so on. To accomplish this, it considers whatever state it "desires" (the goal or subgoal), and then tries to minimize the difference between this and the present state by various operations (e.g., algebraic transformations). Newell and Simon give a simplified example of how a similar strategy might be used by people faced with the ordinary problems of everyday life:

> I want to take my son to nursery school. What's the difference between what I have and what I want? One of distance. What changes distance? My automobile. My automobile won't work. What is needed to make it work? A new battery. What has new batteries? An auto repair shop. I want the repair shop to put in a new battery; but the shop doesn't know I need one. What is the difficulty? One of communication. What allows communication? A telephone . . . and so on (Newell and Simon, 1972, p. 416).

### EXPERT SYSTEMS

A promising new trend in the field of artificial intelligence is the development of ***expert systems.*** These are problem solving programs with a very narrow scope. They deal only with problems in a highly limited domain, such as some subfield of organic chemistry, law, or medicine. Because they are so specialized, their memory can be stocked with a considerable amount of know-how in their own area.

An example is MYCIN, a computer program designed to assist physicians in the treatment of infectious diseases. MYCIN is not just a stored table that lists drugs to combat this or the other microorganism. It can diagnose, suggest therapies, estimate their effectiveness, and will even explain how it arrived at its decisions if asked. The physician "informs" the computer of the patient's symptoms and of the results of various blood tests and bacterial cultures. The computer will then consult its memory for lists of potentially useful drugs and will then choose among them by following various decision rules (which consider the patient's age, other medications, side effects, and so on) and make a recommendation, indicating the statistical probability of success. If "asked," it will indicate how it arrived at its decision. If appropriately "instructed," it will add to or modify its rules; for example, it may note that a particular antibiotic ought not to be administered to a patient with a certain allergy (Shortliffe, Axline, Buchanan, Merigan, and Cohen, 1973; Duda and Shortliffe, 1983; Buchanan and Shortliffe, 1985). Below is a condensed excerpt from a MYCIN consultation on the diagnosis and therapy of a patient (here called Jane Brown). (MYCIN's comments are in capitals and the consulting physician's are in lower case.)

ARE THERE ANY POSITIVE CULTURES OBTAINED FROM JANE BROWN?
No
    [More questions]
HAS JANE BROWN RECENTLY HAD SYMPTOMS OF PERSISTENT HEAD-ACHE, OR OTHER ABNORMAL NEUROLOGIC SYMPTOMS (DIZZINESS, OR LETHARGY, ETC.)?
Yes
    [More questions]
HAS JANE BROWN RECENTLY HAD OBJECTIVE EVIDENCE OF ABNOR-MAL NEUROLOGIC SIGNS (COMA, SEIZURES, ETC.)?
Yes
    [More questions]
THE . . . CULTURES WILL BE CONSIDERED TO BE ASSOCIATED WITH *MENINGITIS*
    [Now questions about treatment]
DOES JANE BROWN HAVE A CLINICALLY SIGNIFICANT ALLERGIC REAC-TION TO ANY ANTIMICROBIAL AGENT?
No
IS JANE BROWN PREGNANT OR BREAST FEEDING?
No
DO YOU HAVE REASON TO SUSPECT IMPAIRED RENAL FUNCTION?
No
JANE BROWN'S WEIGHT IN KILOGRAMS?
51.3
MY PREFERRED THERAPY RECOMMENDATION IS AS FOLLOWS. GIVE THE FOLLOWING IN COMBINATION:
  1. ETHAMBUTOL
    [Details on dosage]
    COMMENTS: PERIODIC VISION SCREENING TESTS ARE RECOM-MENDED FOR OPTIC NEURITIS.
  2. INH
    [Details on dosage]
  3. RIFAMPIN
    COMMENTS: ADMINISTER DOSE ON EMPTY STOMACH

(Adapted from Duda and Shortliffe, 1983)

A number of studies have assessed the effectiveness of the MYCIN program by comparing its recommendations with those of over a dozen infectious disease specialists. The results indicate that the program performs at or near the level of expert physicians, at least in narrowly defined problem areas. Since MYCIN can be continually updated and improved, it is possible that it, or some similar program, may be used in medical practice before long. Whether the patients will take to MYCIN's bedside manner is another question. (And some physicians apparently have certain reservations; see Teach and Shortliffe, 1985.)

Is MYCIN intelligent? In a sense, it obviously isn't. Its very strengths are its weaknesses. It "knows" only about infectious diseases. If it is asked about a broken bone or a psychiatric condition, it will be utterly lost. It is a highly specialized expert that may eventually become a valuable though rather limited assistant. But it is not a model of the human intellect, for it simulates only a few human mental operations. Like other expert systems that are now being developed, MYCIN is meant to be an aid to human intelligence, not a substitute. All the same, its operations may be a microcosm of how the human mind solves some very limited problems and so, in the end, it may provide a genuine contribution to our understanding of the psychology of human thought.

## Some Limitations of Artificial Intelligence

Computer simulation has added a new and exciting dimension to the study of cognitive processes. But so far at least, it still has some serious limitations as an approach to human thinking. We have just noted that expert systems such as MYCIN are both too rigid and too narrow-minded to be considered "truly intelligent." But current artificial thinking machines have additional problems that are even more serious.

### WELL-DEFINED AND ILL-DEFINED PROBLEMS

The problems that existing computer programs can handle are **well-defined.** There is a clear-cut way to decide whether a proposed solution is indeed the right one. Examples are algebraic proofs (Are the terms identical on both sides of the equation?), chess problems (Is the opposing king checkmated?), and anagrams (Is the rearranged letter sequence a word that appears in the dictionary?).

In contrast, many of the problems people face in real life are **ill-defined.** Consider an architect who is asked to design a modern college dormitory. Exactly what is a correct solution? Some proposals can obviously be rejected out of hand —for example, if there are no provisions for bathrooms—but there is no definite criterion for what is acceptable. Similarly for many other problem activities, such as completing a sonnet or organizing a lecture or planning a vacation. In all of these cases, the critical first step is to define the problem so that it can be answered and so that the answer can be evaluated. The architect begins by asking questions about the number of students who are to be housed, the facilities that must be included, the surrounding terrain, the available budget—all in an attempt to transform an ill-defined problem into a well-defined one. The progress of human knowledge is often a matter not of problem solution but of problem definition and redefinition. The alchemist looked for a way to change lead into gold; the modern physicist tries to discover the atomic structure of matter.

"This one writes some fine lyrics, and the other one has done some beautiful music, but they just don't seem to hit it off as collaborators." (©1978 by Sidney Harris—American Scientist Magazine)

famous nineteenth-century mathematician, entitled his treatise on the laws of logic "An Investigation into the Laws of Thought," with little doubt that the laws that governed the one would also govern the other (Henle, 1962). Today, this belief is no longer held as widely. For by now, there is ample evidence that people are very prone to errors of reasoning. As a result, some psychologists have argued that the laws of logic have more to say about how people *should* think than about how they really *do* think, for in their view humans are not quite as rational as one would like to believe.

## Deductive Reasoning

In *deductive reasoning,* the reasoner tries to determine whether certain conclusions can or cannot be drawn—that is, deduced—from a set of initial assertions. The decision as to whether the deduction is valid or not depends entirely on the initial assertions coupled with some basic logical operations such as affirmation, negation, and so on.

### ANALYZING SYLLOGISMS

A classical example of deductive reasoning is the analysis of *syllogisms,* an enterprise that goes back to Aristotle. Each syllogism contains two premises and a conclusion. The question is whether the conclusion logically follows from the premises (see Figure 8.27). A few examples of such syllogisms (some valid, others invalid) are:

**8.27 Syllogistic argument** *Insisting upon the execution of the Cheshire Cat, the King of Hearts argued that anything that has a head can be beheaded, including the Cheshire Cat, which at this stage of the story consists of nothing but a head. (Lewis Carroll,* Alice in Wonderland, *p. 55)*

> All A are B.
> All B are C.
> Therefore: All A are C. (valid)

> All A are B.
> Some B are C.
> Therefore: Some A are C. (invalid)

Or, stated in more concrete terms:

> All American Eagles are patriots.
> All patriots are redblooded.
> Therefore: All American Eagles are redblooded. (valid)

To give another example:

> All heavenly angels are accomplished harp players.
> Some accomplished harp players are members of the American musicians' union.
> Therefore: Some heavenly angels are members of the American musicians' union. (invalid)*

Until the nineteenth century, most philosophers were convinced that the ability to evaluate syllogisms of this kind was an essential aspect of human rational-

---

* Note that the validity of the syllogisms only depends on whether the conclusion follows *logically* from the premises. The empirical plausibility of the conclusion (e.g., that the angels of heaven are unionized) has nothing to do with the matter.

ity. Under the circumstances, it was a bit disheartening when experimental psychologists demonstrated that subjects make a considerable number of errors on syllogism tasks.

One cause of errors is the subjects' tendency to perform inappropriate logical transformations. They hear the statement "All A are B" and somehow interpret it as if it were symmetrical. As a result, they convert it to: "All A are B and all B are A." Such invalid conversions will then of course lead to invalid judgments (Revlin and Leirer, 1980). An example is "All owls are birds," which of course does not permit the conclusion "All birds are owls."

### THE TROUBLESOME CONDITIONAL

There are certain logical constructions that most people—logicians excepted—have trouble evaluating. These are the so-called ***conditional statements,*** which are if-then constructions such as:

If A, then B,

or, to put it in more concrete form:

If it is Sunday, John goes to the ballgame.

What conclusions can be drawn from statements of this kind? One follows from what we'll here call the ***positive rule of if-then inference.*** According to the positive rule, if the first part of the statement (that is, A) is true, then the second part (that is, B) must also be true. In other words, given that:

If it is Sunday, John goes to the ballgame.
It is Sunday.

It follows that:

John goes to the ballgame.

The "If A, then B" statement allows us to draw another conclusion, which follows from what we'll call the ***negative rule of if-then inference.**** If we know that B is false, it follows that A must also be false. Thus, given that:

If it is Sunday, John goes to the ballgame.
John does not go to the ballgame.

It follows that:

It is not Sunday.

This second conclusion is not so readily apparent as the first, perhaps because it requires some additional steps of inferential reasoning in which the initial statements are transformed into their opposites: "I know that if it is Sunday, John goes

---

* In logic, the positive and negative rules of if-then inference are called *modus ponens* and *modus tollens* respectively.

to the ballgame. I also know that John is *not* going to the ballgame. This means that it cannot be Sunday."

A number of experimental findings demonstrate that the application of the negative rule is considerably more difficult than that of its positive counterpart. If presented with if-then statements and asked to evaluate what conclusions can be drawn from them, virtually all subjects apply the positive rule, but many of them fail to follow with the negative rule (Taplin and Staudenmayer, 1973).

The failure to apply the negative rule of if-then inference is highlighted by a very influential study by Wason. He presented subjects with four cards laid out on a table, as shown below:

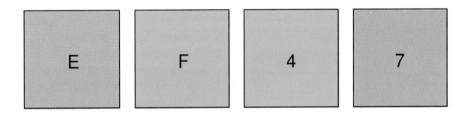

The subjects were informed that each of the cards has a letter on one side and a number on the other. Their job was to test the following hypothesis: "If a card has a vowel on one side, it has an even number on the other side." They were told that to do so, they had to flip over some card or cards, but they could only flip over that card (or those cards) required to test the hypothesis—no more and no less (Wason, 1966).

Wason found that most of his subjects followed the positive rule by turning over the E.* But very few solved the problem completely by following the negative rule and also turning over the 7. (If the card with the 7 turns out to have a vowel on the other side, the hypothesis is disconfirmed.)

How can one explain this result? The best guess is that people don't generally use formal logic in solving problems. What they do instead is to refer to various experiences that they have previously found useful in reasoning tasks. Evidence comes from a number of studies in which the Wason selection task was presented in a more concrete form. In one study, the subjects were University of Florida students who had to put themselves in the position of a police officer trying to make sure that people conform to a drinking-age rule: "If a person is drinking beer, then the person must be over nineteen years of age." They were told that the officer is given four cards that give information about four people sitting at a table: On one side of each card is the person's age, on the other side is the beverage he or she is drinking. As in Wason's original selection task, the subject's job was to turn over the appropriate cards to decide whether or not each person was violating the rule. The four cards were labeled:

---

* Many subjects flipped both the E and the 4. Note that flipping the 4 doesn't help solve the problem, for even if there is no vowel on the other side the rule isn't falsified. It only says that if there is a vowel, then there'll be an even number. It does not say that *only* if there is a vowel, there'll be an even number. In these and subsequent illustrations of the selection problem, the two cards that should be flipped over are colored blue, while cards that are irrelevant are colored green.

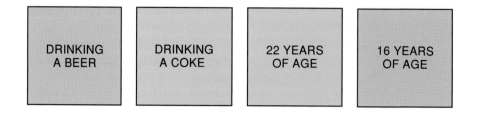

Formally speaking, the task was identical to that used by Wason, but the results were quite different. In Wason's task only 4 percent of the subjects solved the problem fully; in the more concrete version posed by the drinking-age problem, 73 percent of the subjects did so (Griggs and Cox, 1982).

What accounts for this difference? In part, it may be a matter of specific personal experience: At the time of the experiment the legal age for drinking alcoholic beverages was nineteen years in the state of Florida. But in part, the benefit of casting the Wason task in this concrete form may come from the use of certain broad, pragmatic reasoning schemas the subjects have previously utilized. To prove this point, some investigators cast the Wason task in a yet different form. They asked subjects to imagine themselves in the role of an immigration officer trying to make sure that passengers entering a country had been inoculated against cholera. To do so, the officer had to look at a form one side of which indicated whether the passenger was entering the country or was in transit; the other whether he or she had been innoculated against cholera. The task was again handled with cards that had to be turned over:

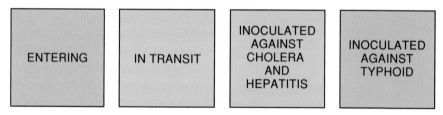

The results were similar to those obtained in the drinking-age study: most of the subjects followed both the positive and negative rules by turning over the two appropriate cards ("Entering," and "Inoculated against typhoid"). Here, most subjects lacked the relevant personal experience, never having coped with immigration laws. But then, how did they manage to reason properly? According to the authors, they succeeded because the task could be understood within a more general framework, the ***permission schema:*** "If a person fulfills condition A, then he or she is permitted to do B." While they had no experience with the particular rules that govern immigration, they recognized that those are just special cases of the more general permission rule, and they knew how to reason about that (Cheng and Holyoak, 1985; Cheng, Holyoak, Nisbett, and Oliver, 1986).

## Inductive Reasoning

In deductive reasoning, we typically go from the general to the particular. We apply some general rule or rules ("All men are mortal") and ask how it applies to a particular case ("John Smith is mortal"). In ***inductive reasoning,*** this process is

"There it comes again."

*(Illustration by Henry Gleitman)*

reversed. Here we go from the particular to the general. We consider a number of different instances and try to determine—that is, *induce*—what general rule covers them all.

Induction is at the very heart of the scientific enterprise, for the object of science is to determine what different events have in common. To do so, scientists formulate various **hypotheses**—tentative assumptions about what constitutes the general rule from which the individual observations can be derived. Hypotheses are developed by laymen as well as scientists. All of us try to see some general pattern in the world around us, as in trying to explain the behavior of a moody daughter or a troublesome automobile. The hypotheses we come up with may not be particularly profound ("She's a teenager" or "It's a lemon"), but profound or not they are attempts to comprehend an individual case by subsuming it under a more general statement.

What do people do to determine whether their hypotheses are correct? A number of investigators have concluded that there is a powerful ***confirmation bias.*** By and large, people seek evidence that will confirm their hypotheses, but they only rarely set out to see whether their hypotheses are false.

An illustration is provided by a study in which subjects were presented with the three numbers "2–4–6" and were told that they were an example of a series that conforms to a general rule which the subjects were asked to discover. To do this, they had to generate a three-number series of their own. Every time they produced such a series, the experimenter would tell them whether it did or not fit the rule. The subjects always indicated why they chose a particular series, and after a number of trials they announced their hypothesis. This continued until the subject succeeded or finally gave up.

The rule the experimenter had in mind was exceedingly simple: "Any three numbers in increasing order of magnitude." It was so simple in fact that the subjects took quite a while before they discovered what it was. But the real issue was how they went about their task. All of them soon developed one or another hypothesis. But whenever they did, they almost always generated a series that fit this

**The confirmation bias in science** *Galileo vainly trying to persuade a group of university professors to look through his telescope. (From a National Theatre production of* Galileo *by Bertolt Brecht; photograph by Zoe Dominic)*

hypothesis—to confirm it. They very rarely generated a series that was not consistent with their current hypothesis, and would *dis*confirm it.

For example, one subject began with the notion that the rule was: "You start with any number and then add 2 each time." She came up with four successive series: "8–10–12," "14–16–18," "20–22–24," and "1–3–5" and was told each time that they conformed to the experimenter's rule. She then announced her hypothesis, was informed that it was false, and developed a new hypothesis: "The middle number is the average of the other two." To test this hypothesis she first offered "2–6–10" and then "1–50–99." After learning that each of these conformed to the correct rule, she announced her new hypothesis, and was again told that it was false. She continued to formulate new hypotheses, for example, "the difference between the first and second number is equal to the difference between the second and third." She again tested the hypothesis by looking for confirmations, generating the series "3–10–17" and "0–3–6," was again told that each of them conformed to the rule, and again discovered that this hypothesis too was incorrect. Eventually, she did hit on the correct hypothesis. But what is interesting is that she hardly ever tested any of her hypotheses by generating a sequence that was *in*consistent with them. For example, she never tried a sequence such as "2–4–5," a quick way to show that the "add 2" hypothesis was wrong (Wason, 1960, 1968; Wason and Johnson-Laird, 1972).

The confirmation bias shown in the 2–4–6 experiment is a very pervasive phenomenon. It is not restricted to the psychologist's laboratory, for it is also found in the real-world behavior of scientists and engineers. They too tend to seek confirmations of their hypotheses and are disinclined to seek evidence that contradicts them. When Galileo provided visible proof that Jupiter has moons that rotate around it, some of his critics were so incensed at this challenge to their geocentric views of the universe that they refused even to *look* through his telescope (Mitroff, 1974; Mahoney, 1976).

There is little doubt that the confirmation bias can be a genuine obstacle to understanding, for in many ways, disconfirmations are more helpful in the search for truth than are confirmations. *One* disconfirmation shows that a hypothesis is false, but countless confirmations cannot really prove that it is true.

What accounts for the confirmation bias? A plausible guess is that humans have a powerful tendency to seek order in the universe. We try to understand what we see and hear, and impose some organization upon it. The organization may not be valid, but it is better than none at all, for without some such organization we would be overwhelmed by an overload of information. But this benefit also has a corresponding cost, for our confirmation bias often condemns us to remain locked within our false beliefs and prejudices (Howard, 1983). Our tendency to come up with plausible hypotheses often serves us well. But we would be better off if we would be more ready to consider their falsity and would heed Oliver Cromwell's advice to a group of clergymen: "I beseech you, in the bowels of Christ, think it possible you may be mistaken."

## Decision Making

Deductive reasoning is about certainties: If certain premises are true, then certain conclusions will follow. There are no exceptions. If it is true that John Smith is a man and that all men are mortal, then it inevitably follows that John Smith is mortal. The situation is very different in inductive reasoning, in which we try to find (that is, induce) a general rule when given a number of individual instances. Once this rule is induced, we will then try to apply it to new instances. But in contrast to deductions, inductions can never be certain but only probable. This even holds for Mr. Smith's mortality. For in actual fact, the proposition "All men are mortal" is only an induction. To be sure, this induction is based on all of human history in which every single man that ever lived was ultimately observed to die. That John Smith will be an exception is therefore exceedingly unlikely—in fact, astronomically improbable. But death (or for that matter, taxes) is not an *absolute* certainty in the sense in which deductively arrived truths always are.

In ordinary life, we are usually concerned with probabilities that are much less clear-cut, and evaluating these probabilities is often crucial. Baseball batters have to estimate the likelihood that a pitcher will throw a fast ball; brokers must judge the probability that a certain stock will rise; patients who contemplate elective surgery must do their best to weigh the relevant medical risks. How do people form the relevant probability estimates? And how do they utilize them to decide whether to swing at the pitch, buy the stock, or undergo surgery? These questions are the province of an area of psychology (and other social sciences) called *decision making.** 

### COGNITIVE SHORTCUTS FOR ESTIMATING PROBABILITIES

Technically, the probability that a particular event will happen is defined by a ratio: the frequency of that event (for example, the number of times a coin falls "heads") divided by the total number of observations (the number of times the coin is tossed). But in actual practice we often don't know these frequencies. And even if we do, we often find it difficult to use them properly. According to Amos Tversky and Daniel Kahneman, we instead make use of various heuristics, which as we've seen are rules of thumb, cognitive shortcuts that often serve us well enough. But as Tversky and Kahneman point out, they sometimes lead to serious errors when they are used to estimate likelihoods (Tversky and Kahneman, 1973, 1974).

*The representativeness heuristic* One such rule of thumb is called the ***representativeness heuristic.*** When people have to make a judgment about the probability that a particular object or event belongs to a certain category, they often do this by comparing the similarity of the particular instance to a prototype of the category (that is, a representative case of that category). As a result, they may seriously misjudge the actual probabilities. A representativeness heuristic often comes into play when we have to make judgments about people. In one study, Kahneman and Tversky presented subjects with the following thumbnail sketch of an individual:

> Jack is a 45-year old man. He is married and has four children. He is generally conservative, careful, and ambitious. He shows no interest in political and social issues and spends most of his time on his many hobbies which include carpentry, sailing, and mathematical puzzles.

* For a discussion of the relation between these probability estimates and the costs associated with different kinds of errors, see Chapters 5 and 16.

One group of subjects was told that this description was drawn at random from a group of seventy engineers and thirty lawyers, and were asked to indicate their judgment of the probability that the person described by the sketch was an engineer. A second group of subjects was given the identical task with only one difference: They were told that the description was drawn at random from a group of seventy lawyers and thirty engineers.

The results showed that both groups estimated that the odds that Jack was an engineer were more than 90 percent. They evidently concluded that the thumbnail sketch described a person with hobbies and interests that were more stereotypical of an engineer than of a lawyer. To that extent Jack seemed more representative of an engineer than of a lawyer. That the subjects took this information into account in making their judgment is not too surprising. What is surprising is that the group that was told that engineers accounted for only 30 percent of all the cases did not take this fact into account at all. It appears that the subjects completely ignored the ***base rate,*** the proportion of the category—here, engineers—that were in the original sample. The concrete description and its similarity to the stereotype overwhelmed all other factors in the estimate (Kahneman and Tversky, 1972, 1973).

One possibility is that such failures to take base rates into account may reflect a general tendency to give more weight to the vivid, prototypical, and concrete case, and less to the pale statistics. But there is another factor that may well contribute to the effect. This has to do with the listener's presumptions about the nature of conversation (whether oral or written).

In talking to others, we generally assume that whatever they say is somehow relevant to the conversation (Grice, 1975). The reader would surely be puzzled if the next sentence in this paragraph were "Eating lollipops before dinner will ruin your appetite," for while this sentence is probably true it is surely not relevant to what is going on *now.* What holds for lollipops also holds for what we're told about Jack. In Tversky and Kahneman's experiment, the subjects are provided with all sorts of information about this man whose profession they are supposed to guess—that he has certain hobbies, that he is careful and precise about his work, and so on. Given the presumption of relevancy, it is of little surprise that the subjects take these items of information into account. They seem to regard these concrete details as more important than the base rates they are also told about (e.g., thirty engineers and seventy lawyers); perhaps they assume that the more specific and concrete the information, the more relevant it is.

*The availability heuristic*    Another rule of thumb used in inductive reasoning is the ***availability heuristic.*** This is a cognitive shortcut for estimating the frequency of certain events by considering how many such events come readily to mind (are currently available to memory). One study involved guesses of how often certain letters appear in different positions in English words. As an example, take the letter *R.* Considering all the words in the language, does it occur more frequently in the first position or in the third position of all the words in the language? Over two-thirds of the subjects said that it is more common in the first than the third position. In actuality the reverse is true. The reason for the errors is availability. The subjects made their judgments by trying to think of words in which *R* is the first letter (e.g., *r*ed, *r*ose, *r*ound) and of words in which it is the third (e.g., er*r*ing, bo*r*ing, ca*r*t, st*r*ong). They then compared the number they managed to generate in each category. But this method leads to a wrong estimate because our memorial dictionary (as well as Webster's) is organized according to the first rather than to the third letter in each word. As a result, words that start with an *R* are much more easily retrieved (that is, more available) than those whose third letter is an *R*. As a result, their frequency is seriously overestimated (Tversky and Kahneman, 1973).

The availability heuristic can have serious practical consequences. What are the chances that the stock market will go up tomorrow or that a certain psychiatric patient will commit suicide? The stockbrokers and psychiatrists who have to decide on a particular course of action must base their choice on their estimate of these probabilities. But this estimate is likely to be affected by the availability heuristic. The stockbroker who remembers a few vivid days on which the market went up may overestimate the chances of an upswing; the psychiatrist who remembers one particular patient who unexpectedly slashed his wrists may underestimate the likelihood of eventual recovery of his other patients.

Another example is the assessment of a politician's chances in an election. The people who surround him generally tend to overestimate how well he will do. In part, this may be caused by wishful thinking, but in part, it may be another manifestation of the availability heuristic. Evidence comes from interviews of the reporters who covered the election campaign of Senator George McGovern, the unsuccessful Democratic candidate for President in 1972. These reporters had spent much of the campaign with McGovern and hardly any with his opponent, the incumbent President Richard Nixon. Senator McGovern lost by a landslide, yet on the night of the election these highly experienced reporters believed that the election would be much closer. The reporters were affected by the enthusiastic crowds of McGovern supporters they had been exposed to. Of course, they knew these were a biased sample, but they couldn't help but be affected anyway. The wildly cheering crowds were much more vivid than the pale statistics of the polls they read (Figure 8.28). This led to an increased availability to memory, which then colored the reporters' estimates of McGovern's national support (Nisbett and Ross, 1980).

**8.28 The availability heuristic as a cause of political misjudgment** *The photo shows Senator George McGovern surrounded by enthusiastic crowds of supporters during his unsuccessful presidential campaign in 1972. Reporters who covered his campaign mistakenly believed that the election outcome would be much closer than it was. (Photograph by Owen Franken/Stock, Boston)*

BIASES IN JUDGING OUTCOMES: FRAMING

The representativeness and availability heuristics can produce biases in estimates of the probability that some event will occur. Certain other heuristics affect our judgment of the desirability of those events.

One such heuristic is the way the choice is *framed.* Consider the following example, in which one group of subjects was presented with this problem:

> Imagine that the U.S. is preparing for the outbreak of an unusual Asian disease, which is expected to kill 600 people. Two alternative programs to combat the disease have been proposed. Assume that the exact scientific estimate of the consequences of the two programs are as follows:
>
> If Program A is adopted, 200 of these people will be saved.
>
> If Program B is adopted, there is 1/3 probability that 600 people will be saved, and 2/3 probability that no people will be saved.
>
> Which of the two programs would you favor?

Given this problem 72 percent of the subjects opted for Program A. They preferred the guarantee of 200 lives saved to a one-third chance of saving them all.

The results were quite different for a second group of subjects who were given the same problem but with a different formulation of the two programs, again applied to 600 people. For this group of subjects, the alternatives were:

If Program A is adopted, 400 people will die.

If Program B is adopted, there is 1/3 probability that nobody will die, and 2/3 probability that 600 people will die.

Given this formulation, 78 percent of the subjects chose Program B. To them the certain death of 400 people was less acceptable than a two-thirds probability that all 600 persons would die (Tversky and Kahneman, 1981).

The crucial point here is that the two problems are formally identical. The only difference between them is the way in which the alternative outcomes are framed. In the first case, they are characterized as gains, as "lives saved" (e.g., 200 out of 600). In the second case, they are characterized losses, as "lives lost" (e.g., 400 out of 600). But these different descriptions obviously have a massive effect. In the first case (gains), they lead to the decision to take a certain gain and avoid any risk. In the second, they lead to the decision to take a risk in order to avoid a certain loss.

What explains this effect? To answer this question we must first ask why people are afraid to take risks when trying to obtain gains but more willing to take them when trying to avoid losses.

*The diminishing returns principle*  According to some theorists, this difference in risk taking stems from a ***principle of diminishing returns*** in the judgment of subjective magnitude. We've encountered that principle previously in the study of sensory processes (see Chapter 5). As we saw then, the difference in the subjective brightness produced by 10 candles and 20 candles is larger than the difference between 100 and 110 candles. What matters is the difference in the ratios between them, not the difference in their absolute magnitudes. A similar principle describes other psychological magnitudes, including the value we place on various pains and pleasures. The obvious example is the value we place on money. The subjective value of money increases as the amount of money increases. But the evidence (collected by both psychologists and economists) indicates that the subjective value of every additional dollar decreases the more dollars the person has already. Put in other words, the psychological difference between zero dollars and $100 is greater than that between $100 and $200, which is greater than that between $200 and $300, and so on—again, what counts is something like a ratio rather than a difference in absolute magnitudes (Kahneman and Tversky, 1984; Baron, 1988; Dawes, 1988; see Figure 8.29).

Given this psychological law of diminishing returns, we can explain why people are unwilling to take risks when dealing with gains. Suppose they are offered a choice between getting a sure gain of $100 and a coin toss that will net them $200 if the coin comes up "heads" but give them nothing if it comes up "tails." Most people will pocket the $100 bill and walk away from the gamble. Given the diminishing returns curve of subjective value they are behaving quite rationally. The additional $100 they gain if they win isn't worth as much to them (psychologically) as the first $100 they must give up if they lose. But if so, they are getting poor odds, and hence they are quite right to refuse the bet.

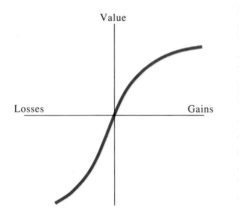

Value

Losses                          Gains

**8.29  A curve of subjective value**  *Note that absolute gains and losses follow a curve of diminishing returns. The same absolute gain becomes subjectively smaller as gains increase. The same holds for losses. (Adapted from Kahneman and Tversky, 1984)*

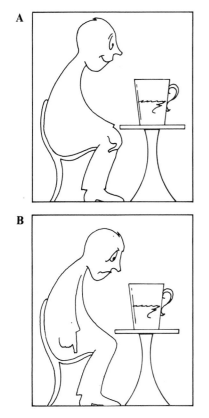

**Is the glass half full or half empty?** A hoary version of the framing effect is the contrast between the optimist who regards the glass as half full (a gain) and the pessimist who sees the same glass as half empty (a loss).

The same logic can explain why people are willing to take risks when dealing with losses. Here too the reason is the curve of diminishing returns. To be sure, the negative value (let's call it the distress) produced by a $200 loss is undoubtedly greater than that produced by a loss of $100. But the distress produced by every lost dollar declines the more money has already been lost. As a result, the first $100 loss hurts more than the second, and so on. Given this diminishing returns curve, the relation between losses and risk taking makes sense. Consider a person who has already lost $100 and is now given a choice between accepting the loss or taking a 50:50 gamble of losing nothing if he wins or losing an additional $100 if he loses. Since the $100 loss is more distressful than the loss of an additional $100, he may well feel that he is getting good odds (at least psychologically speaking). That people do indeed behave in line with these predictions—accepting risk to cancel losses that they would not have taken for (objectively) equivalent gains is well established in the psychological laboratory. It is also a well-known fact to casino operators who know that losers will try even harder to "get even."

Thus far, all our examples involved monetary gains and losses. But the same logic can be applied to other gains and other losses. The framing study used an example that involved lives saved, which is surely a gain. Here, the prediction would be that people prefer a sure gain to a gamble. And this is just what they do. Given a choice between 100 lives saved, and a 50:50 chance of saving none versus saving 200, subjects generally refuse the gamble. In the framing study, the second version of the problem was about death, clearly a loss. Here we would predict the exact opposite. Given a choice between, say, 100 certain deaths, and a 50:50 chance gamble of no deaths at all versus 200, subjects should take the risk, and this is just what they do. (In the framing study, the numbers were somewhat different, but the logic was the same.)

*Changing losses to gains by framing* The diminishing returns curve explains why trying to obtain gains leads to different risk-taking behavior than trying to avoid losses. But it does not tell us why a slight change in wording shifts the subject's cognitive perspective, emphasizing gains in the one case and losses in the other. The best guess is that it is analogous to the many context effects we have described in previous chapters: An ambiguous letter-like form looks like an *H* in the word *THE* and an *A* in the word *CAT*; a list of unrelated sentences takes on meaning once it's clear what it is they're describing (the laundry), and so on (see Chapters 6 and 7). Similar processes may explain framing effects. Kahneman and Tversky liken such effects to a shift in the physical perspective from which a scene is viewed: The scene remains the same, but it looks different depending on the vantage point. By the same token, a different way of describing a choice can determine whether one focuses on gains or on losses.

The framing process seems to occur in a number of real-world situations. The most obvious examples concern the marketplace. In these days of paying in plastic, a number of retailers (for example, gas stations) have two prices for the same service or merchandise: one for cash, the other for credit. Retailers generally prefer to describe this price difference as a "cash discount" rather than as a "credit card surcharge." Needless to say, the dollar amount is identical; what differs is which of the two prices is treated as the "normal" reference point. By using the word "discount," the reference standard is the credit card price; as a result, the discount is seen as a gain. Conversely, the term "surcharge" frames the cash price as the reference point; if so, the surcharge is seen as a loss. Since people are more willing to give up gains than to suffer losses, they don't mind paying by credit card and feel that they're getting a bargain if they pay in cash.

## Are People Really Irrational?

The preceding discussion has considered a large body of evidence that throws a rather poor light on human rationality. People make many errors in deductive reasoning; they often misunderstand or misconvert the premises and so come up with an incorrect conclusion. They make errors in inductive reasoning; they are primarily concerned with demonstrating that their hypotheses are correct and don't try to discover whether they are wrong. They are also very prone to error when they have to make decisions in the face of uncertainty; they use a number of heuristics that may lead to mistakes in estimating the probability of events. Intellectually, we evidently have much to feel modest about. But if so, how could humanity possibly have achieved what it has in mathematics, philosophy, music, and science?

To begin with, despite our many errors, it seems likely that some aspects of rational thinking are part and parcel of our mental apparatus, in much the sense in which the fundamental operations of arithmetic (addition, subtraction, multiplication, and division) are built into a pocket calculator. But the calculator will not yield correct results if its owner punches in the wrong numbers or inadvertently presses the key for addition instead of the one for subtraction. In the same way, the capacity for logical thinking may very well be part of our makeup, even though we don't always make use of it, or use it incorrectly. But the fact that this capacity is there allows for the possibility of its use if certain other factors are present. But what are these other factors?

One depends on human history. There is little doubt that most of our great intellectual achievements are at bottom collective. They depend on countless prior generations, each of which bequeathed some bits of new knowledge and some new ways of gaining yet further knowledge to the generation that followed it. Because of them, we possess an immense arsenal of intellectual tools, including various techniques of formal thinking. Our mental machinery has some limited capacity for deductive and inductive reasoning, but this capacity is not finely honed until experience makes it so—the individual's own and that of his ancestors before him.

Of course, this is not all. For even if we have the necessary intellectual tools, we may not use them. We may know statistics and still fall prey to the representativeness and availability heuristics; we may be trained in science and still be subject to the confirmation bias. But here, too, we are helped by the fact that much of human thought is a collective enterprise. An individual scientist may very well be biased toward confirmation and may not be inclined to look for evidence that disproves her hypothesis. But there are other scientists who will not have the same compunction. Many of them will not entertain the same hypothesis, and so they will be only too glad to do what's necessary to disprove *hers*. The collective upshot is likely to be a victory for rationality.

This is not to say that reason will always win out in the end. It surely does not. Many of the errors of thought we've discussed are still with us after millennia of

*"But we just don't have the technology to carry it out." (©1976 by Sidney Harris— American Scientist Magazine)*

human history, and they are found whether we're alone or in groups. But this doesn't prove that we are not rational beings. At worst our rationality is bounded —by habit, circumstance, and by the fact that our processing capacity is limited (Simon, 1956).

Some of the leading investigators in this area have drawn an analogy between errors of thought and perceptual illusions (Tversky and Kahneman, 1983). If the analogy holds, there is yet further hope for human rationality. Both kinds of errors are distortions: in the one, we misjudge truth or probability; in the other, we misperceive the world of concrete reality. But the fact that there are perceptual illusions does not mean that by and large we don't see reality as it actually is. Perceptual illusions are an exception and not the rule, for by and large our perceptual machinery generally does a fine job of informing us about the world. It may be that errors of thought have a similar status—that they are special distortions of patterns of thought that ordinarily work and serve us perfectly well.

If we take the analogy between errors of thought and perceptual illusions seriously, there is a further consequence. Some of the perceptual illusions have helped us understand the processes whereby we see without error. The classical case is brightness contrast, which is crucial in the understanding of many perceptual and psychophysiological phenomena (see Chapter 5). It remains to be seen whether the study of errors of thought will have an analogous effect in helping psychologists understand the processes of ordinary thinking in which we do tolerably well. After all, in ordinary life, we don't manage all that badly. We usually find our way from place to place, devise sensible courses of action, and have beliefs about daily-life phenomena that are generally formed on fairly good evidence. Perhaps the *special* cases in which we go wrong may help us understand the *general* machinery of thinking by means of which we often go right.

A final point. There's an interesting irony in the fact that psychologists who study human thinking and computer scientists who try to build intelligent machines find their subjects inadequate in precisely opposite ways. Psychologists who study the various biases in decision making point out that their human subjects are not as rational as one might wish. They sometimes bemoan the fact that people aren't more like computers and would like to teach them to become more so. For computers don't ignore base rates, or judge probability by what's currently available; nor are they subject to framing effects. Computer scientists bemoan the opposite fact. They tear their hair out when their programs yield such algorithmically correct, but stupidly irrelevant answers as "Yes, SIR!!!" or "None," and so they wish that their computers were more like people and want to teach them to become more so.

Human thinking involves a heady mixture of exactness and inexactness, of algorithmic and heuristic procedures that computers have not as yet achieved and perhaps never will. There may be a permanent difference in *kind*—not just a present difference in *size*—between human and computer thinking. For while computers are getting ever more powerful—with enormous memorial stores, incredible processing speeds, and huge interlocking networks of commands—it's by no means clear that they are coming closer to reproducing the kaleidoscopic reach, the flexibility and the creativity of human thought. In the current infancy of artificial intelligence, it is of course too early to be secure about any such pessimistic assessment. But meanwhile, don't ask a computer for its best guess if you want to figure out who killed Laura Palmer of "Twin Peaks" fame.

## A BACKWARD LOOK AT PERCEPTION, MEMORY, AND THINKING

In looking back over the three domains of cognition—perception, memory, and thinking—we can only repeat a theme we have struck before. There are no clear boundaries that demark these three domains. In describing perception, we often cross over the border into memory. For the way we perceive familiar objects—let alone such ambiguous figures as the young woman–old woman picture—is based in part on how we perceived them in the past. But perception also shades into thinking. We look at the moon at the horizon, decide that it must be larger than it first appears because it looks farther off, and promptly perceive it in line with this (presumably unconscious) inference. Nor is it clear where memory leaves off and thinking begins. Much of remembering seems like problem solving. We try to re-call to whom we lent a certain book, conclude that it has to be Joe, for we know no one else who is interested in the book's topic, and then suddenly have a vivid recollection of the particular occasion on which he borrowed it (and the way he swore that he'd return it right away). But if remembering is sometimes much like thinking, thinking can hardly proceed without reference to the storehouse of memory. Whatever we think about—which route to take on a vacation trip, how to fill out a tax form—requires retrieval of items from various memory systems.

All of this shows that there are no exact boundaries between perception, memory, and thinking. These areas are not sharply separated intellectual domains, with neat lines of demarcation between them. They are simply designations for somewhat different aspects of the general process of cognition. We will now turn to the one aspect of cognition that we have thus far discussed only in passing—language. It, too, is intertwined with the other domains of cognition, but unlike perception, memory, and thinking, which are found in many animals, language is unique to human beings.

## SUMMARY

1. A classical issue in the study of thinking concerns the *elements* that make up thought. According to one view, all thought is necessarily composed of *mental images.* While there is good evidence that some thinking has the picture-like quality of imagery, most psychologists doubt that all thinking is of this kind. They feel that there is another, more abstract and symbolic mode of thinking that involves mental structures such as *concepts* and *propositions.*

2. Considered as an activity, thinking is *directed.* In problem solving, all steps are considered as they fit into the overall structure set up by the task. This structure is typically *hierarchical,* with goals, subordinate subgoals, and so on. This hierarchical structure is not unique to problem solving but may be a general characteristic of any directed activity.

3. Increasing competence at any directed activity goes together with an increase in the degree to which the subcomponents of this activity have become chunked and *automatized.* In learning to send and receive Morse code, as in the attainment of many skills,

learning curves exhibit *plateaus,* followed by a later rise, suggesting the acquisition of progressively larger units. Similar chunking seems to occur in many forms of mental activity, including problem solving, and differentiates masters and beginners in many endeavors such as mental calculation, musical composition, and playing chess.

4. Problem solving is not always successful. One reason may be a strong, interfering *mental set,* which makes the subject *rigid,* and which is especially hard to overcome under conditions of intense motivation.

5. Investigators of thinking have come up with a few suggestions to overcome obstacles to problem solving. One is *working backwards* from the goal, another is trying to *find an analogy,* yet another is *changing the mental representation* of the problem. Sometimes the solution involves a radical *restructuring* by means of which a misleading set is overcome. Such restructurings may be an important feature of much of *creative thinking.* Accounts by prominent writers, composers, and scientists suggest that restructuring often occurs after a period of *incubation.* Restructuring may also play a role in *humor,* which often occurs when an unexpected cognitive organization turns out to make sense after all.

6. An influential approach to problem solving comes from work on *artificial intelligence,* which tries to simulate certain aspects of human thinking. A number of solution strategies have been incorporated into several computer programs, including *algorithms* and *heuristics.* Some further extensions feature the use of *expert systems.* Among the limitations of current artificial intelligence programs as an approach to human thinking includes their difficulty in dealing with *ill-defined problems* and a certain *single-minded directedness.* Even more important is their lack of *common sense,* a knowledge about many aspects of the world together with an understanding of what is *relevant* to the problem at hand.

7. While the solution of *spatial problems* often depends on mental imagery, it is sometimes based on a more abstract, conceptual form of thinking. Evidence comes from studies which indicate that geographical knowledge is often organized in a conceptual rather than picture-like form. Further evidence shows that spatial thinking need not be visual, as indicated by studies on *cognitive maps* in persons born blind.

8. Studies of *deductive reasoning* show that people are prone to various errors in thinking. Errors of reasoning in dealing with *syllogisms* are caused by a number of factors, including the tendency to perform inappropriate logical transformations.

9. A special problem in deductive reasoning is posed by *conditional statements* such as "if A, then B." While people have relatively little trouble with using the *positive rule of if-then inference* (if A is true, then B must be true), they have difficulty with the *negative rule* (if B is false, then A must be false). The difficulty in applying the negative rule has been demonstrated by the failure of subjects to solve a *selection task* devised by Wason. This task is extremely difficult unless it is phrased in a concrete form that suggests familiar heuristics, such as a *permission schema.*

10. In deductive reasoning, the thinker tries to deduce a particular consequence from a general rule or rules. In *inductive reasoning,* the direction is reversed, for here the thinker tries to induce a general rule from particular instances. An initial, tentatively held induction is a *hypothesis.* A number of studies have pointed to a powerful *confirmation bias* that makes subjects seek evidence that will confirm their hypothesis rather than look for evidence that would show their hypothesis to be false.

11. *Decision making* involves the estimation of probabilities and the utilization of these estimates in deciding on a course of action. To make such estimates, people often make use of certain *heuristics.* These are cognitive rules of thumb that often serve us well enough but

that may also lead to serious errors. One such rule of thumb is the *representativeness heuristic:* estimating the probability that an object belongs to a category by comparing the object to a prototype of the category while ignoring other factors such as *base rates.* Another rule of thumb is the *availability heuristic:* estimating the frequency of an event by how readily an example of such an event comes to mind.

12. Some heuristics affect the judgment of the desirability of certain events. A major example is the way outcomes are *framed,* which affects whether they are interpreted as gains or as losses. The effects of framing depend partially on a *diminishing returns principle,* which states that the subjective value of money (or other gains, such as lives saved) decreases as the amount of money gained increases. The same principle holds for losses. As a result, people prefer a sure gain to a gamble to gain still more, but they will take risks to avoid a loss rather than settle for a certain smaller loss.

# CHAPTER 9

# Language

## By Lila R. Gleitman and Henry Gleitman

When we consider the social forms and physical artifacts of human societies, we are struck by the diversity of cultures in different times and places. Some humans walk on foot, others travel on camels, and still others ride rockets to the moon. But in all communities and all times, humans are alike in having language. This essential connection, between *having language* and *being human,* is one reason why those interested in the nature of human minds have always been particularly intrigued with language.

To philosophers such as Descartes, language was that function which most clearly distinguished between beasts and humans, and was "the sole sign and only certain mark of thought hidden and wrapped up in the body." Descartes held that humans were utterly distinct from the other animals because all humans have language, while no other animals have anything of the sort. But this claim comes up against an immediate objection: There are about 4,000 languages now in use on earth (Comrie, 1987). Obviously, these are different from one another, for the users of one cannot understand the users of another. In what sense, then, can we speak of "language in general" rather than of French or English or Hindi? The answer is that human languages are at bottom much more alike than they seem at first glance to be. For example, all languages convey thought by the same *means:* They all use words and sentences to organize ideas. In contrast, animal communications often have something like words (for instance, a cat can purr happily and hiss angrily), but they never have complicated sentences (such as *I'm going to stop purring and start hissing unless you give me that catnip immediately).*

Another similarity is in the *ideas* human languages can express. When the United Nations ambassador from France makes a speech, numerous translators immediately whisper its equivalent in English, Russian, Arabic, and so on, to the listening ambassadors from other countries. The fact that the French speech can

**The biblical account of the origin of different languages**  *According to the Bible, all men once spoke a common language. But they built a tall structure, the Tower of Babel, and tried to reach the heavens. To punish them for their pride and folly, God made them unable to understand each other, each group speaking a different language. (*Tower of Babel *by Pieter Brueghel, the Elder, c. 1568; courtesy the Kunthistoriches Museum, Vienna)*

readily be translated suggests that, by and large, the same things that can be said in French can be said in English and Russian as well. This is true despite the fact that the Russian and English listeners may disagree with what the French diplomat is saying. But the translation will allow them to *know* that they disagree, so that they are in a position to stomp out of the room in a rage, or make a counter-speech—which will also be translatable. In our discussion of language, we will use English as our main example. But it is important to keep in mind that what we say about English generally goes for the other human languages as well.

## MAJOR PROPERTIES OF HUMAN LANGUAGE

There are five major properties of all human languages that psychology must describe: language is *creative* (or *novel*), it is highly *structured* (or *patterned*), it is *meaningful,* it is *referential* (that is, it refers to and describes things and events in the real world), and it is *interpersonal* or *communicative* (involving the thoughts of more than one person at a time).

### Language Is Creative

At first glance, language might seem to be merely a complicated habit, a set of acts by ear and mouth that have been learned by memorization and practice. According to this view, the explanation of talking is simple: Each of the memorized speech acts is simply performed whenever the appropriate circumstances arise. Our mothers said *That's a rabbit* when they saw a rabbit. Having observed this, we now say *That's a rabbit* when we see a rabbit. But this position of language as habit is hard to maintain, for speakers can and will utter and understand a great many sentences that they have never uttered or heard before. To see this point, it is only necessary to realize that, in addition to *That's a rabbit,* each of us can also say and understand:

> *That's a rabbit over there.*
> *A rabbit is what I see over there.*
> *Obviously, that's a rabbit.*
> *How clearly I recall that the word for that animal is* rabbit.
> *Well bless my soul, if that isn't a rabbit!*

And so on, with hundreds of other examples. A little child who has memorized all these sentences must be industrious indeed. But the situation is really incredibly more complicated than this, for we can talk about objects and creatures other than rabbits, including aardvarks and Afghans, apples and armies, and proceeding all the way to zebras and Zyzzogetons.

Furthermore, the sheer number of English sentences rules out habit as the explanation for language use. A good estimate of the number of reasonably short (20 words or fewer) English sentences is $10^{30}$. Considering the fact that there are only $3 \times 10^9$ seconds in a century, a learner memorizing a new sentence every second would have learned only a minute fraction of them in the course of a lifetime. But the fact is that we can all say and understand most of them (Postal, 1968).

In sum, we effortlessly create and interpret new sentences on the spot. Only a very few such as *How are you?, What's new?,* and *Have a nice day* are said and heard with any frequency. All the rest are at least partly new—new to the person who says them and new to his listeners as well. To express all the thoughts, we combine a limited—though large—number of words into sentences. Thus language is a system that allows us to reach a limitless end from limited means: Our stock of memorized, meaningful words is finite, but we nevertheless have the capacity to speak of an infinite number of new things and events. We can do so because our language system allows us to combine the old words in novel ways.

## Language Is Structured

While language use is creative in the sense that we can and do invent new sentences all the time, it is also restricted: There are unlimited numbers of strings of English words that—accidents aside—we would never utter. For example, we do not say *Is rabbit a that* or *A rabbit that's* even though these are fairly comprehensible ways to say *That's a rabbit.* Speakers construct their utterances in accord with certain abstract principles of language structure. These ***structural principles*** underlie the way in which we combine words to make up new sentences, and they are honored by every normal individual—without special thought, and without any formal training in school. These principles are generally not known consciously, but are *implicit.* Even so, they govern our use of language and allow us to compose and understand boundless new sentences.

Language is not unique in being unlimited and structured, for a number of other behavior patterns have a similar potential for systematic and novel use. Consider arithmetic. Surely we don't know the sum of, say, 5,384 and 9,253 off-

**The power of an "H"** *A scene from the stage version of* My Fair Lady, *in which the cockney flower girl, Eliza (Julie Andrews) is taught by Henry Higgins (Rex Harrison) how to pronounce an "H" the way the British upper classes do. She thus becomes a lady. This shows that following prescriptive rules can sometimes confer important social advantages (Labov, 1970: photograph by Leonard McCombe/LIFE MAGAZINE, © Time Warner, Inc.)*

hand. But we can readily calculate it, for we know a set of laws—the rules or principles of arithmetic. Similarly, we can drive cars to destinations where we have never traveled before, solve chess problems we have never previously encountered, and blush at embarrassments we have never experienced before. Thus many behavioral systems have the unbounded character that we have just shown for language.

We should point out that the structural principles of language (sometimes called *descriptive rules*) have to be distinguished from certain *prescriptive rules* handed down from various authorities about how they think we *ought* to speak or write. Prescriptive rules are the so-called "rules of grammar" that many of us learned painfully at school in the fourth grade (and thankfully forgot in the fifth), such as "Never say ain't" or "A sentence cannot end with a preposition." These recipes for speech and writing often do not conform to the actual facts about natural talking and understanding. For example, most of us have no qualms about ending sentences with a preposition (as in the sentence, *Who did you give the packages to?*) or even two prepositions (as in *What in the world are you up to?*). In some cases it sounds rather odd not to do so, as Winston Churchill pointed out when spoofing this "rule" by insisting that *This is the kind of language up with which I will not put!*

The *structural principles* we will be concerned with in this chapter are those that every normal speaker honors without effort or formal instruction—for example, the principle by which we invariably say *the rabbit* rather than *rabbit the*. It is these regularities that are fundamental to understanding language as a universal human skill. In fact, most human cultures outside of America and Western Europe do not have prescriptions for "proper" speech at all.

## Language Is Meaningful

Each word in a language expresses a meaningful idea (or concept) about some thing (e.g., *camera* or *rabbit*), action (*run* or *rotate*), abstraction (*justice* or *fun*), quality (*red* or *altruistic*), and so on. The purpose of language is to express all these meanings to others, so we have no choice but to learn a conventional word for each.

But people talk in whole sentences rather than just one word at a time. This is because the grammatical patterns that we discussed in the previous section also contribute to meaningfulness. For example, the words *dogs, cats, bite* express very different meaningful thoughts depending on how they are put together: *Dogs bite cats,* or *Cats bite dogs.*

## Language Is Referential

Language users know more than how to put words together into meaningful and grammatical sentences. They also know which words refer to which things, scenes, and events in the world. If a child said *"That's a shoe"* (a sentence whose grammar is impeccable and whose meaning is transparent) but did so while pointing to a rhinoceros, we would not think she had learned English very effectively. This is the problem of *reference:* how to use language to describe the world of real things and events—saying *shoe* to make reference to a shoe, but saying *rhinoceros* to refer to a rhinoceros.

***Adam gives names to the animals*** *The belief that knowledge of word meanings sets humans above animals goes back to antiquity. An example is the biblical tale illustrated in this painting by William Blake which shows Adam assigning names to the animals. According to some ancient legends, this act established Adam's intellectual superiority over all creation, including even the angels. In one such tale, the angels were unable to call the animals by name, but Adam could: " 'Oh Lord of the world! The proper name for this animal is ox, for this one horse, for this one lion, for this one camel!' And so he called all in turn, suiting the name to the peculiarity of the animal" (Ginzberg, 1909, vol. 1, p. 62). Notice that Adam thinks that words sound like what they mean. (William Blake's* Adam Naming the Beasts; *Stirling Maxwell Collection, Pollok House, Glasgow Museums & Art Galleries)*

The problem of reference is quite a complex one just because speech is not an automatic response of the nervous system. Even though the word *lemon* refers to lemons, one does not have to cry out *"Lemon!"* every time one sees a lemon. The source of language events has to do with the contents of the mind, what one is thinking about. Of course, if one sees a lemon, the probability that one is thinking about lemons is increased; but it is by no means a certainty. Seeing a lemon does not evoke the cry *Lemon!* in anything like the sense that seeing a lemon evokes salivation from a hungry viewer, or in the sense that seeing a lemon in bright light evokes a bluish afterimage. Salivation and visual afterimages are direct psychophysiological reactions (responses) to identifiable events (stimuli). But sentences about lemons are not automatic reactions to seeing lemons. Sentences are expressions of our state of mind, and this can vary with relatively little regard to what is going on "out there in the real world."

## Language Is Interpersonal

Many aspects of human language are within the individual and are thus the property of each single human mind. But language is a process that goes beyond the individual, for it is a social activity in which the thoughts of one mind are conveyed to another. To accomplish these social ends, each speaker must know not only the sounds, words, and sentences of his language, but also certain **principles of conversation.** These principles govern the way in which language is used appropriately under varying circumstances.

Suppose, for example, that one sees a lion in the parlor and wants to tell a companion about this. It is not enough that both parties speak English. One has to estimate the listener's mental state, capacities, motivations, and relations to oneself in order to speak appropriately. If the companion is a sharpshooter with a revolver, one might say:

*Quick, shoot! There is a lion in the parlor.*

But if the companion is an artist, one might say:

*Quick, draw! Lion of a gorgeous shade of ochre in the parlor.*

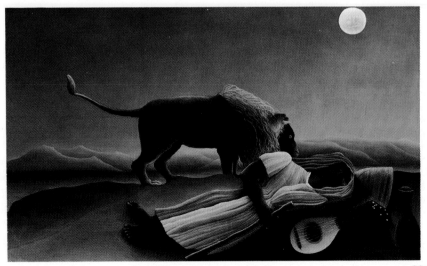

**The stimulus-free property of language use**   *How many sentences can you think of to describe this painting? (Henri Rousseau's* The Sleeping Gypsy, *1897, oil on canvas, 5′1″ × 6′7″. Collection, The Museum of Modern Art, New York. Gift of Mrs. Simon Guggenheim)*

To a biologist, one might say:

*Quick, look! Member of the genus* Felis leo *in the parlor.*

And to an enemy,

*Lovely morning, isn't it? See you later.*

Clearly, what one says about a situation is not just a description of that situation, but depends upon one's knowledge, beliefs, and wishes about the listener. To communicate successfully, then, one must build a mental picture of "the other" to whom speech is addressed (Austin, 1962; Clark and Clark, 1977; Clark, H., 1978; Prince, E., 1981; Schiffrin, 1988).

The same problem arises for the listener, of course. To determine the sense of what one has heard, one must make an estimate of the speaker and the circumstances of her utterances. Suppose, for example, someone said "Can you pass me the salt?" To know how to respond appropriately, one must ask oneself (implicitly, of course) "Does this speaker think my arms are broken?" (in which case the answer should be "Yes, I can" or "No, I can't," depending on whether one's arms *are* in fact broken). But if one is hale and hearty, the ordinary supposition would be that this was just a polite way of requesting one to pass the salt. And now the answer should be, "Sure. Here you are," accompanied by the action of passing the salt (Searle, 1969; Clark, H., 1979; Sperber and Wilson, 1986).

In sum, the actual speech acts that pass between people are merely hints about the thoughts that are being conveyed. Talking would take just about forever if one literally had to say all, only, and exactly what one meant. Rather, the communicating pair takes the utterance and its context as the basis for making a series of complicated inferences about the meaning and intent of the conversation. A listener who fails to make these inferences is taken as an incompetent at best and a bore at worst. A person who blandly answers "Yes!" when you say "Could you tell me the time?" has failed to obey the principles of conversation that make communication possible (Grice, 1968).

## THE STRUCTURE OF LANGUAGE

All human languages are organized as a hierarchy of structures. At the bottom of the hierarchy, each language consists of little snippets of sound; and at the other end, of sentences and conversations. We begin by describing the basic building blocks: the 40 or so phonemes, the 80,000 or so morphemes, and the hundreds of thousands of words.

### Phonemes

To speak, we move the various parts of the vocal apparatus from one position to another in a rapid sequence while expelling a column of air up from the lungs and out through the mouth (see Figure 9.1). Each of these movements shapes the column of air from the lungs differently, and thus produces a distinctive speech sound (MacNeilage, 1972). Many of these differences among speech sounds are ignored by the listener. Consider the word *bus,* which can be pronounced with

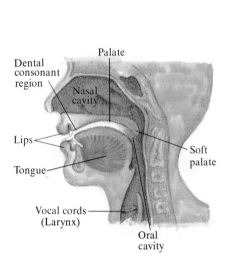

**9.1   The human vocal tract**  *Speech is produced by the air flow from the lungs which passes through the larynx (popularly called the voice box) containing the vocal cords and from there through the oral and nasal cavities which together make up the vocal tract. Different vowels are created by movements of the lips and tongue which change the size and shape of the vocal cavity. Consonants are produced by various articulatory movements which temporarily obstruct the air flow through the vocal tract. For some consonants the air flow is stopped completely. Examples are* p, *where the stoppage is produced by bringing both lips together; and* t *where it is produced by bringing the tip of the tongue to the back of the upper teeth. Some other consonants are created by blocking the air flow only partially, for example* th *(as in* thick*), produced by bringing the tip of the tongue close to the upper teeth but without actually touching. (After Lieberman,* 1975*)*

Labels in figure: Dental consonant region, Palate, Nasal cavity, Lips, Tongue, Vocal cords (Larynx), Soft palate, Oral cavity

**9.2 The hierarchy of linguistic structures** *Every sentence is composed of phrases, which are composed of morphemes (simple units of meaning such as strange and the plural -s), which in turn are composed of phonemes (the units of speech sound, such as p and ə). The phonemes are described by symbols from the phonetic alphabet because English spelling is not always true to the sounds of words.*

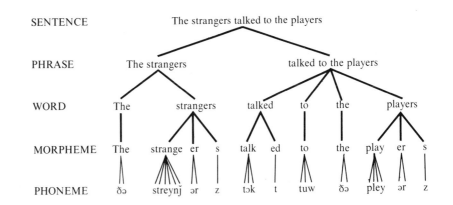

more or less of a hiss in the *s*. This difference is irrelevant to the listener, who interprets what was heard to mean 'a large vehicle' in either case. But some sound distinctions do matter, for they signal differences in meaning. Thus neither *butt* nor *fuss* will be taken to mean 'a large vehicle.' This suggests that the distinctions among *s, f,* and *t* sounds are relevant to speech perception, while the difference in hiss magnitude is not. The distinctions that are perceived to matter are called **phonemes.** They are the perceptual units of which speech is composed (Liberman, 1970; see Figure 9.2, which illustrates the entire hierarchy of linguistic structures).

UNDERSTANDING UNFAMILIAR SPEECH

Because of the construction of the human speech apparatus, children can learn to pronounce a couple of hundred different speech sounds clearly and reliably. But each language restricts itself to using only some of them. English uses about forty.* Other languages select differently from among the possible phonemes. For instance, German uses certain gutteral sounds that are never heard in English, and French uses some vowels that are different from the English ones. Once children have learned the sounds used in their native tongue, they usually become quite rigid in their phonemic ways: It becomes difficult for them to utter or perceive any others. This is one reason why foreign speech often sounds like a vague and undifferentiated muddle, rather than like a sequence of separable sounds.

Another difficulty in understanding unfamiliar speech—even in one's own language—has to do with the sheer rate at which the speech sounds are produced in sequence; adults can understand speech at the rate of 250 words per minute (Foulke and Sticht, 1969), which converts to about 16 phonemes per second. There are rarely gaps or silences that mark off one speech unit from the next in everyday speech. This holds not only for the successive phonemes, but for the words and phrases as well. All these units usually run into each other, so that it is difficult to tell where one ends and the other starts. Thus when one person speaks of a *gray tabby,* her listener may hear *a great abbey.*

---

* The English alphabet provides only twenty-six symbols (letters) to write these forty phonemes, so it often uses the same symbol for more than one. Thus, the letter *O* stands for two different sounds in *hot* and *cold,* an "ah" sound and an "oh" sound. This fact contributes to the difficulty of learning how to read English.

COMBINING PHONEMES

As speakers of a language, we have learned the phonemes that constitute its sound elements. But we have learned something further as well—the way these phonemes can be combined into words. Some of these choices are a matter of historical accident. For instance, English happens to have a word *pledge,* composed phonemically of the sounds p-l-e-j. But it does not happen to have a word *medge,* composed of m-e-j. But some of the facts about how phonemes combine in words are systematic rather than accidental choices.

To see this point, consider the task of an advertising executive who tries to find a name for a new breakfast food. She will have to find some sequence of phonemes that has not already been used to mean something else. Will any new arrangement of phonemes do? The answer is no. To begin with, some, such as *gogrps* or *fpibs,* would be hard to pronounce. But even among phoneme sequences that can be pronounced, some seem somehow un-Englishlike. Consider the following possibilities: *Pritos, Glitos,* and *Tlitos.* They can all be pronounced, but one seems wrong: *Tlitos.* English speakers sense intuitively that English words never start with *tl,* even though this sequence is perfectly acceptable in the middle of a word (as in *motley* or *battling*). So the new breakfast food will be marketed as tasty, crunchy *Pritos* or *Glitos.* Either of these two names will do, but *Tlitos* is out of the question. The restriction against *tl*-beginnings is not a restriction on what human tongues and ears can do. For instance, one Northwest Indian language is named *Tlingit,* obviously by people who are perfectly willing to have words begin with *tl.* This shows that the restriction is a structural principle of English specifically. Few of us are conscious of this principle, but we have learned it and similar principles exceedingly well, for we honor them in our actual language use (Chomsky and Halle, 1968).

***Noam Chomsky***

## Morphemes and Words

At the next level of the linguistic hierarchy (see Figure 9.2), fixed sequences of phonemes are joined into morphemes. The ***morphemes*** are the smallest language units that carry bits of meaning. Like phonemes, the morphemes of a language can be combined only in certain ways. Some words consist of a single morpheme, such as *and, run,* or *strange.* But many morphemes cannot stand alone and must be joined with others to make up a complex word. Examples are *er* (meaning 'one who') and *s* (meaning 'more than one'). When these are joined with the morpheme *strange* (meaning 'alien' or 'odd') into the complex word *strangers (strange + er + s),* the meaning becomes correspondingly complex ('ones who are odd or alien'). Each of these morphemes has a fixed position within the word. Thus *er* has to follow *strange* and precede *s*; other orders (such as *erstranges* or *strangeser*) are not allowed (Aranoff, 1976).

The morphemes such as *strange* that carry the main burden of meaning are called ***content morphemes.*** The morphemes that add details to the meaning but also serve various grammatical purposes (such as the suffix *er* or the connecting word *and*) are called ***function morphemes.***

The average speaker of English has acquired about 80,000 morphemes by adulthood (Miller and Gildea, 1987), knows the meaning of each, and how they are positioned within words. If we counted vocabulary by words rather than morphemes, normal people would be credited with several hundred thousand of these, for then *strange, stranger, strangers,* etc., would each count as a separate item.

## Phrases and Sentences

The system of words in a language is very rich and allows us to express an enormous variety of meanings with great precision. Nevertheless, we cannot memorize a new word for each of the hundreds of millions of thoughts that we want to express. Therefore, we combine our limited—though large—stock of words into whole sentences. We may remark either *The lion kicked the gnu* or *The gnu kicked the lion.* Both these sequences of words are meaningful, but there is a difference in the meaning that is of some importance—at least to the lion and the gnu. The term **syntax** (from the Greek, *arranging together*) is the name for the system that arranges (or groups) words together into meaningful phrases and sentences. This topic has been extensively investigated by the American linguist, Noam Chomsky (Chomsky, 1957, 1975, 1980, 1987; for overviews of syntactic theory, see Newmeyer, 1983; Sells, 1985; Radford, 1988).

Just as a morpheme is an organized grouping of phonemes, and a word is an organized grouping of morphemes, so a **phrase** is an organized grouping of words. The phrases are the building blocks of which sentences are composed. Consider the sentence

> *The French bottle smells.*

This sentence is **ambiguous:** It can be understood in two ways depending on how the words are grouped into phrases; either

> *(The French bottle) (smells).*

or  *(The French) (bottle) (smells).*

Thus by the choice of phrasing (that is, word grouping), the word *bottle* comes out a noun in the first interpretation, so that sentence is telling us something about French bottles. But *bottle* comes out a verb in the next interpretation, in which case the sentence is telling us about what the French put into bottles—namely, smells (that is, perfumes). For another example, see Figure 9.3.

The phrase is thus the unit that organizes words into meaningful groupings within the sentence. Just as for phoneme sequences and morpheme sequences, some phrase sequences (like those we just considered) are acceptable, while others are outlawed; for example, *(The French) (smells) (bottle).*

**9.3  How phrase structure can affect meaning**  *On being asked what a Mock Turtle is, the Queen tells Alice "It's the thing Mock Turtle Soup is made from." Needless to say, this is a misanalysis of the phrase* mock turtle soup *as (mock turtle) (soup). It ought to be organized as* (mock) (turtle soup)—*a soup that is not really made out of turtles (and is in fact usually made out of veal). (Lewis Carroll,* Alice in Wonderland, *1865/1969, p. 73)*

## THE LINGUISTIC HIERARCHY AND MEANING

We have seen that language consists of a small number of sound units (the forty or so phonemes) organized into fixed sequences (the 80,000 or so morphemes and hundreds of thousands of words), which in turn are organized into the boundless number of sentences. In sum, as we ascend the linguistic ladder there are more and more units at every level. How can the human mind deal with this ever-expanding number of items? There is only one possible answer: We don't learn the billions of sentences in the first place. Instead, we acquire generalizations that allow us to construct any sentence. It is the fact that organization of units exists at each level of the hierarchy that makes language use possible in the first place. Without systematic knowledge of such patterns, we would not be able to learn, speak, or understand a language—there would just be too much to handle.

But why do humans go to the trouble of acquiring language? The answer, of course, is just that it allows us to convey boundless thoughts from one human mind to another human mind. Of primary interest, then, are the higher-level units and patterns of language: the meaningful words, phrases, and sentences. In the following sections, therefore, we will take up the questions of word and sentence meaning in detail.

## The Meaning of Words

The question, "What do words mean?" is one of the knottiest in the whole realm of language (see Putnam, 1975; Fodor, 1983; 1988). The subfield that deals with this question, **semantics,** has thus far been able to give only a few, rather tentative answers. As so often, the first step is to eliminate some of the answers that appear to be false.

### MEANING AS REFERENCE

One of the oldest approaches to the topic equates word and phrase meaning with **reference.** According to this position, the meaning of a word or phrase is whatever it refers to in the world. Thus this view asserts that words and certain phrases are essentially names. Proper names such as *Steffi Graf, Australia,* and the *Eiffel Tower* are labels for a particular person, place, and object. The reference theory of meaning claims that expressions such as *tennis player, continent,* and *building* function in a similar manner. According to this view, the only difference between such expressions and true proper names is that the former are more general: *tennis player* refers to various male and female players and to champions as well as duffers: *Steffi Graf* refers to one player and no one else.

The reference theory of meaning runs into several difficulties. One is that some words or phrases are perfectly meaningful even though it is hard to know exactly what they refer to. Some of these are abstract expressions such as *justice, infinity,* and *historical inevitability.* One cannot point to a real "infinity" somewhere out there in the world. Others are imaginary, such as *unicorn* and *the crown prince of South Dakota,* which presumably have no real-world referents at all. Yet these expressions do not seem to be "meaningless" or "semantically empty."

A famous example of the distinction between meaning and reference was pointed out by the German philosopher, Gottlob Frege (1892): The expression *the morning star* has one meaning (namely, 'the last star visible in the eastern sky as dawn breaks'), and the expression *the evening star* has quite a different meaning (namely, 'the first star visible in the western sky as the sun sets'). Yet both of these expressions refer to one and the same object in the sky (namely, the planet Venus). Thus two expressions can have different meanings and yet refer to the same thing. It follows that there is a distinction between the meaning of a word or

*Is this the entry for bird in your mental dictionary?*   *bird n. [ME, fr. OE bridd]. Any of a class (Aves) of warm-blooded vertebrates distinguished by having the body more or less completely covered with feathers and the forelimbs modified as wings.*

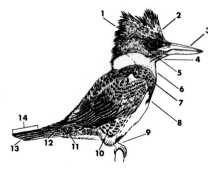

*bird 2 (kingfisher):* 1 *crest,* 2 *crown,* 3 *bill,* 4 *throat,* 5 *auricular region,* 6 *breast,* 7 *scapulars,* 8 *abdomen,* 9 *tarsus,* 10 *upper wing coverts,* 11 *primaries,* 12 *secondaries,* 13 *rectrix,* 14 *tail (Webster's 9th Collegiate Dictionary)*

phrase and the things that this word or phrase refers to in the world. The meaning of a word is the idea or concept that it expresses. The referents of the word are all those things in the real (or imaginary) world that fall under that concept.

### THE DEFINITIONAL THEORY OF MEANING

We have just concluded that the meaning of a word is a concept (or *category*). Some words describe concepts that refer to only one thing or creature in the real or imaginary world, such as *Madonna* or *Pinocchio,* while other words such as *dog* or *unicorn* are more general, describing categories that have many referents. But is the meaning of a word always just a simple concept, irreducible to simpler elements? Most theories of word meaning assert that only a relative handful of the words in a language describe elementary "simple" concepts. The rest are labels for bundles of concepts. Thus the words *feathers, flies, animal, wings* might describe simple concepts, but all of these ideas are bundled together in the (relatively) complex word *bird.* One approach of this kind is the *definitional theory of meaning.* It holds that meanings are analyzable into a set of sub-components, organized in our minds much as they are in standard dictionaries. This approach starts out with the fact that there are various meaning relationships among different words and phrases. Some words are similar in meaning *(wicked-evil),* others are opposites *(wicked-good),* still others seem virtually unrelated *(wicked-ultramarine).* According to the definitional proposal, these relationships can be explained by assuming that words are *bundles of semantic features* (Katz and Fodor, 1963; Katz, 1972). As an example, take the word *bachelor.* This word clearly has something in common with *uncle, brother, gander,* and *stallion.* As speakers of English, we know that all of these words carry the notion *male.* This point is forcefully made by considering various sentences that most English speakers will regard as odd (or, to use the technical term, *anomalous*). Thus, the sentence *My _____ is pregnant* sounds very peculiar if the missing word is any of the members of the bachelor-related group listed below:

|      |          |              |
|------|----------|--------------|
|      | uncle    |              |
|      | brother  |              |
| My   | gander   | is pregnant. |
|      | stallion |              |
|      | bachelor |              |

Demonstrations of this sort suggest that words like *stallion* and *bachelor* are not simple in meaning, but rather are composed of a number of meaning atoms —the semantic features. Further demonstrations with anomalous sentences show that *bachelor* contains additional features such as 'unmarried' and 'adult.' This explains why the following sentences are also odd in meaning:

> *My sister is married to a bachelor.*
> *I met a two-year-old bachelor yesterday.*

The ultimate aim of this kind of analysis is to describe the meanings of words as packages that bundle together a limited set of primitive semantic attributes or *features.* For *bachelor,* these might be 'never married,' 'human,' 'adult,' and 'male'; for *stallion,* they would include 'adult,' 'male,' and 'horse.' Words like *stallion* and *bachelor* will be perceived to be related because when an individual

***Can a white rose be red?*** *The Queen had ordered the gardeners to plant a red rose bush but they planted a white one by mistake. They're now trying to repair their error by painting the white roses red. On the definitional theory of meaning, this seems reasonable enough. For the expressions* red rose bush *and* white rose bush *differ by only a single feature—red versus white. But if so, why are they so terrified that the Queen will discover what they did? (From Lewis Carroll,* Alice in Wonderland, *1865/1969, p. 62)*

343

looks up the features for each of these words in her mental dictionary (or **lexicon**), she will find that the meaning atom 'male' is listed for both of them. Taken together, the semantic features constitute a definition of a word. According to this theory, we carry such definitions in our heads as the meanings of words.

### THE PROTOTYPE THEORY OF MEANING

The definitional theory faces a problem, for some members of a meaning category appear to exemplify that category better than others do. Thus a German shepherd seems to be a more doglike *dog* than a Pekinese, and an armchair seems to be a better example of the concept of *furniture* than a reading lamp. This seems to be at odds with the analysis we have described thus far, whose aim was to specify the necessary and sufficient attributes that *define* a concept. When a dictionary says that a bachelor is "an adult human male who has never been married," it claims to have said it all. Whatever fits under the umbrella of this definitional feature list is a bachelor. Whatever does not, is not. But if so, how can one bachelor be more bachelorlike (or one dog more doglike) than another?

The question is whether the semantic categories described by words are really as all-or-none as the definitional theory would have it. Several investigators have made a strong case for an alternative view, called the ***theory of prototypes*** (Rosch, 1973b; Rosch and Mervis, 1975; Smith and Medin, 1981).

The facts that the prototype theory tries to account for can be easily illustrated. Close your eyes and try to imagine a bird. It is pretty safe to guess that you just imagined something like a robin or sparrow, not a buzzard, ostrich, or goose. There is something quintessentially *birdy* about a robin, while a goose does not seem such a good example of a bird. The definitional theory would have considerable trouble explaining why this is so. According to this theory, some feature or features associated with the concept *bird* (such as 'has feathers,' 'lays eggs,' 'flies,' 'chirps') are both necessary and sufficient to pick out all birds and only birds. But if geese and robins are both said to be birds because they share these necessary and sufficient features, what makes the robin more birdy than the goose?

According to the prototype theory, the answer is that the meaning of many words is described as a whole set of features, no one of which is individually either necessary or sufficient. The concept is then held together by what some philosophers call a ***family resemblance structure*** (Wittgenstein, 1953). Consider the way in which members of a family resemble each other. Joe may look like his father to the extent that he has his eyes. His sister Sue may look like her father to the extent that she has his nose. But Joe and Sue may have no feature in common (he has his grandfather's nose and she has Aunt Fanny's eyes), and so the two of them do not look alike at all. But even so, the two are physically related through a family resemblance, for each has some resemblance to their father (see Figure 9.4).

In sum, a family resemblance structure is like a collection of attributes. Probably no single member of the family will have them all. Nor will any two members of a family have the same ones (except for identical twins). But all will have at least some. Some individuals will have many of the family features. They are often called the "real Johnsons" or "prototypical Smiths." They are the best exemplars of the family resemblance structure because they have, say, the most Johnson-attributes and the least Jones-attributes. Other family members are marginal. They have only the nose or the little freckle behind the left ear.

**9.4   The Smith brothers and their family resemblance**   *The Smith brothers are related through family resemblance, though no two brothers share all features. The one who has the greatest number of the family attributes is the most prototypical. In the example, it is Brother 9, who has all the family features: brown hair, large ears, large nose, moustache, and eyeglasses. (Courtesy Sharon Armstrong)*

A

B

C

**Prototypes** *Members of the bird category. (A) A prototypical bird—the robin, (B) An untypical bird—the ostrich, (C) An exceedingly untypical bird—the penguin. (Photographs by Joseph Van Wormer, Bruce Coleman, and M. P. Kahl, all courtesy of Bruce Coleman)*

Many investigators believe that what holds for the Smiths and the Johnsons may hold for many word concepts, such as *bird,* as well. For in fact, there is little doubt that, except for professional biologists, most people don't really know the features that all birds have in common (and which could thus serve as a definition for *bird*). Thus, contrary to our first guess, not all birds fly (ostriches don't fly). And not everything that lays eggs is a bird (giant tortoises lay eggs). Not all birds chirp (crows do not chirp, they caw), and some chirpers (crickets) are not birds. What are we left with from our list of defining features? Nothing but a pile of feathers! But feathers alone do not make something a bird. Hats have feathers too. And, after all, if one plucked all the feathers out of a robin, it would be a mutilated robin, but it would still be a bird for all that. (You think this unfair? What would *you* call it? A hippopotamus?)

According to prototype theorists, birdiness is largely a matter of the total number of bird features a given creature exhibits. No one of these features is necessary and none is sufficient, but animals that have few (such as penguins and ostriches) will be judged to be poor members of the bird family, while those that have many (such as robins) will seem to be exemplary members. According to the theory, these judgments are based on a comparison with an internal ***prototype*** of the concept. Such prototypes represent mental averages of all the various examples of the concept the person has encountered. In the case of birds, people in our culture have presumably seen far more robins than penguins. As a result, something that resembles a robin will be stored in their memory system and will then be associated with the word *bird.* When the person later sees a new object, he will judge it to be a bird to the extent that it resembles the prototype in some way. A sparrow resembles it in many ways and so is judged to be "a good bird"; a penguin resembles it just a little and hence is "a marginal bird"; a rowboat resembles it not at all and hence is judged to be no bird.

Evidence for the prototype view comes from the fact that when people are asked to come up with typical examples of some category, they generally produce instances that are close to the presumed prototype (e.g., *robin* rather than *ostrich*). A related result concerns the time required to verify category membership. Subjects respond more quickly to the sentence *A robin is a bird* than to *An ostrich is a bird* (Rosch, Mervis, Gray, Johnson, and Boyes-Braem, 1976; for a related discussion, see Chapter 7).

### COMBINING DEFINITIONAL AND PROTOTYPE DESCRIPTIONS

It appears that both the definitional and the prototype approaches to word meaning have something to offer. The prototype view helps us to understand why robins are better birds than ostriches. But the definitional theory explains why an ostrich is nevertheless recognized as a bird. Perhaps we can combine both views of meaning rather than choosing between them.

Consider the word *grandmother.* This word designates people who are 'mothers of a parent.' Thus *grandmother* clearly has a set of necessary and sufficient attributes that neatly define it. The definitional theory seems just right for words like this. But now reconsider. Everyone knows that a grandmother is a person who bakes cookies, is old and gray, and has a kindly twinkle in her eye. When we say that someone is *grandmotherly,* we are referring to such prototypical attributes of grandmothers, not to geneology. But some grandmothers lack these typical properties. Zsa Zsa Gabor is a mother of a parent, but she is hardly gray or

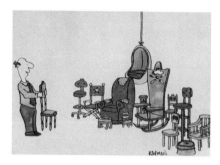

*"Attention, everyone! I'd like to introduce the newest member of our family."*
*(Drawing by Kaufman; © 1977 The New Yorker Magazine, Inc.)*

twinkly. And we all know some kindly lady who is gray and twinkly but never had a child; she may be grandmotherly, but she is not a grandmother (Lakoff and Johnson, 1980; Landau, 1982).

The most plausible assumption is that people have two partly independent mental representations for the meaning of a word. They know about prototypical attributes that are good symptoms of being a grandmother, such as being old and gray. They probably store a list (or perhaps a picture) of such attributes (or prototypical features) as a handy way of picking out likely grandmother candidates. But they also store defining grandmother features (e.g., 'mother of a parent'). These definitional features determine grandmother limits, and tell one how to use the prototype appropriately (Miller and Johnson-Laird, 1976; Smith and Medin, 1981; Armstrong, Gleitman, and Gleitman, 1983).

## Organizing Words into Meaningful Sentences

While individual words describe things, events, and so forth, the word groups that constitute phrases describe the endless varieties of complex categories for which the 80,000 words would be insufficient. Thus, once in a lifetime, we might want to speak of *three of the spotted ostriches on Joe Smith's farm.* We could not possibly memorize enough word items for all such complex categories that we could construct and might want to talk about, so we combine the words together in patterned ways to express our more complex concepts.

Sentence meanings are even more complex. They have to do with the various relations *among* the concepts that we want to express. Basic sentences introduce some concept that they are about (this is called the **subject of the sentence)** and then **propose** or **predicate** something of that concept (called the **predicate of the sentence**). Thus when we say *The boy hit the ball,* we introduce *the boy* as the subject or topic, and then we propose or predicate of the boy that he *hit the ball.* This is why sentence meanings are often called **propositions:** *The boy hit the ball* proposes (of the boy) that he hit the ball.

**A grammar lesson at the Mad Hatter's Tea Party**    The meanings of words change in different linguistic constructions, so grammatical patterns are of great importance for communication.
March Hare:    "You should say what you mean."
Alice:    "I do—at least I mean what I say—that's the same thing, you know."
Hatter:    "Not the same thing a bit! Why, you might just as well say that 'I see what I eat' is the same thing as 'I eat what I see'!"
March Hare:    "You might just as well say that 'I like what I get' is the same thing as 'I get what I like.'"

*(From Lewis Carroll,* Alice in Wonderland, *1865/1969, p. 44)*

**A**
SURFACE: Smoking volcanoes
can be dangerous

**B**
SURFACE: Smoking volcanoes
can be dangerous

UNDERLYING PROPOSITIONS:
Volcanoes smoke This can be dangerous

UNDERLYING PROPOSITIONS:
Someone smokes volcanoes This can be dangerous

**9.10 Ambiguity of underlying structure**

in our earlier example of *great abbeys* and *grey tabbies.* Finally, there is word-meaning ambiguity. This occurs whenever words have more than one meaning. Thus *Someone stepped on his trunk* will give rise to different mental pictures depending on whether *his trunk* refers to a traveller with a suitcase, a tree surgeon, or a kneeling elephant (see The Tale of the Mouse, p. 352).

## COMPREHENSION

How do listeners understand the sentences they encounter? All they hear are sequences of words that occur one after another. But these sequences are only the surface forms of the sentences. To understand what the sentences mean, the listeners must somehow recover their underlying structure. How can they do this?

**9.11 An analogy between linguistic and perceptual ambiguity** *Linguistic ambiguities are in some ways quite similar to perceptual ambiguities of the kind we encountered in Chapter 6. For in both cases, a stimulus can be interpreted in either of two different ways. (A) Ambiguity in visual perception. The same figure can be seen as either two profiles or a vase. (B) Ambiguity in sentence perception. The same sentence can refer to volcanoes that smoke or to volcanoes that are smoked.*

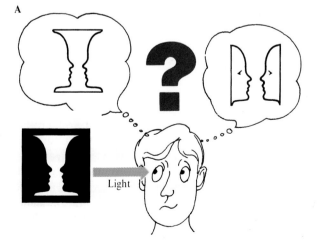

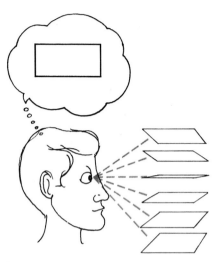

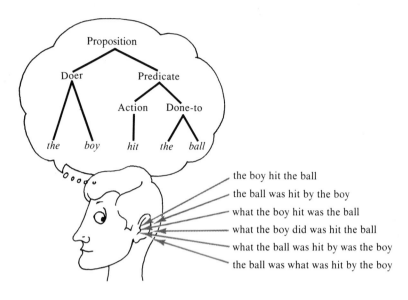

**A**                                    **B**

**9.12  An analogy between linguistic
paraphrase and perceptual constancy**
*Linguistic paraphrase is in some ways sim-
ilar to perceptual constancies of the kind
we discussed in Chapter 6. For in both
cases, we interpret superficially different
patterns of stimulation as roughly
equivalent. (A)* Shape constancy. *When
we look at a tabletop, the image that
actually falls on our eye is a trapezoid
whose exact shape depends on our
orientation to the table. But shape constancy allows us to perceive the unchanging
rectangular shape that gives rise to these
images. (B)* Paraphrase. *The ear literally
hears a variety of surface sentences, but the
linguistic system interprets them all as
containing the same proposition.*

After all, few listeners are lucky enough to encounter utterances such as *Focus on
the done-to: John saw Mary.* Instead, they hear *Mary was seen by John.* How do
they reconstruct the underlying logic from the surface forms?

In some ways, the problem of the listener is similar to that of the visual perceiver who has to determine the real shape of an object given its retinal image.
This retinal shape changes with the object's orientation to the observer. But the
observer can nevertheless perceive the object's actual shape, for he has a number
of cues, such as perspective, that tell him about the orientation from which the
object was viewed. Given these cues, the observer can now reconstruct the actual
shape of the object perceptually (see Figure 9.12, and Chapter 6 for discussion).

Something analogous happens with language. Here, the underlying structures
give rise to various surface forms. But these forms still bear telltale traces of the
underlying structures to which they are related. These telltale traces are generally
the appearance of certain function words, such as *by* or *who.* An example is the
presence of a pattern such as *is verb-en by* (as in *is taken by, is given by,* and so
on). This particular pattern is a good hint that we are dealing with a passive surface structure and that the focus therefore is on the done-to. Similarly, as we shall
see, other function words, such as *who* and *or,* are a good clue that there is more
than one proposition in the sentence being heard (Kimball, 1973).

### The Sentence Analyzing Machinery

Just how are these clues utilized to reconstruct the underlying structure from the
surface form? According to several psycholinguists, the ***Sentence Analyzing
Machinery*** (let us call him—or her—SAM) operates in terms of several general
strategies, two of which are discussed below. Depending on how easy or hard
the sentence is to analyze by use of these strategies, the sentence will be correspondingly easy or hard for subjects to understand. (For general descriptions
of sentence comprehension, see Frazier and Fodor, J. D., 1978; Cairns, 1984;
Tanenhaus, 1988.)

## THE SIMPLEST FORM: DOER, ACT, DONE-TO

Several demonstrations have shown that SAM starts out with a strong bias about what kind of sentence he is about to hear: It is one in which the propositional roles appear in the order doer, act, done-to (or, using grammatical terminology, subject, verb, object).

The strategy of tentatively casting the first noun phrase in the role of the doer is quite useful, for in ordinary speech the active form of sentences (e.g., *John hits Fred*) is much more frequent than the passive *(Fred is hit by John)*. But infrequent or not, passive sentences do occur. Here, SAM's doer-first strategy necessarily fails, for in passive sentences the done-to comes before the doer. Now SAM has to correct himself. He recognizes his error when he gets far enough along to arrive at the words *is* and *by,* which occur in passive sentences. Having found these clues, he will revise his first guess and reassign the first noun phrase as done-to (and the second noun phrase as doer). But this revision takes some effort.

Evidence comes from studies of reaction time. The first-noun-did-it strategy necessarily implies that it will take a bit longer to understand a passive sentence than its corresponding active form. One investigator had subjects listen to sentences such as *The dog is chasing the cat* and *The cat is chased by the dog.* Immediately afterward, the subjects were shown one of two pictures— a dog chasing a cat or a cat chasing a dog. Their job was to decide whether the sentence did or did not describe the picture. The subjects reached the decision faster when the sentence was in the active rather than the passive form (Slobin, 1966; see Figure 9.13).

If SAM truly prefers to hear simple propositions in which the phrases occur in the order doer, act, done-to, he should also experience some difficulty with sentences in which one proposition occurs smack in the middle of another one, e.g., *The boy who ate a hamburger hit the ball.* Here, the proposition *The boy hit the ball* is interrupted by another proposition *(who ate a hamburger).* What is the effect of this interruption? Imagine SAM pursuing his doer, act, done-to strategy. For our new sentence, SAM does hear a noun phrase first *(the boy),* to which he happily assigns the role of doer. At this point, SAM is hoping to hear a verb, to which he can assign the role of action. But the next word in the complex sentence is *who,* surely not a verb. SAM must now do a kind of mental double take, analyzing the interrupting proposition *(who ate a hamburger)* before returning to finish the main sentence *(The boy . . . hit the ball).*

Of course we can all decipher such interrupted sentences, which are frequent in everyday speech, but careful measurement of reaction time shows that they require more effort than sentences like *The boy ate a hamburger and the boy hit the ball,* which presents the propositions one at a time, each in the order doer, act, done-to (Bever, 1970; Wanner and Maratsos, 1978).

## FUNCTION WORDS THAT SIGNAL PROPOSITION BOUNDARIES

In the example sentence just mentioned *(The boy who ate a hamburger hit the ball),* the boundary between the two propositions is signaled by the word *who.* Thus just as in the case mentioned earlier (the cueing of passive by the words *is* and *by*), it is the role of function words to reveal the structure of the sentence to the listener.

But in some cases, English allows us to omit such a function word in quick speech. For instance, we can say either *The princess kissed the frog whom the king*

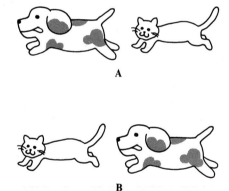

**9.13 Deciding who is doer and who is done-to** *Subjects were presented with sentences such as* The cat chases the dog *and* The dog is chased by the cat. *They were then shown either (A) or (B) and had to decide whether the sentence described the picture. Reaction times were faster for active than for passive sentences. (Slobin, 1966)*

*knighted* or we can leave out the *whom,* saying *The princess kissed the frog the king knighted.* Evidently SAM gets a bit confused as to how to separate out the propositions when this clue from the function word is missing, and so takes longer to understand such sentences (and occasionally misinterprets them altogether; Bever, 1970).

PUSHING SAM BEYOND HIS CAPABILITIES: A LINGUISTIC ILLUSION

We mention now a case where comprehension fails. Just as for the case of visual perception (see Chapter 6), some of the best evidence for understanding how the nervous system accomplishes its tasks in the usual case comes from looking at the rare cases where this machinery fails. Thus we saw that impossible figures defeat the observer, who sees a drawing of what appears to be an object but at the same time is perplexed because its parts don't seem to fit together in a natural way. Similar situations occur in sentence understanding, where the machinery that works most of the time will go haywire for the occasional unusual sentence. Here is one such case:

> *The horse raced past the barn fell.*

If you are like most English readers, your first impression will be that this is a totally ungrammatical sentence, one that has an "extra" verb *(fell)* that just doesn't fit. Yet there is good reason to believe that this sentence is both grammatical and meaningful (see Figure 9.14). Almost all listeners acknowledge it to be so once they have compared it to a related sentence. The trick is to notice that it is just a short form of

> *The horse who was raced past the barn fell.**

Why is *The horse raced past the barn fell* so hard to understand? The reason is that this sentence doesn't respond too readily to SAM's favorite analyzing strategies. For one thing, it doesn't consist of two separate cases of doer and action, one after the other, as in *The horse was raced past the barn, and the horse fell.* Instead, it inserts the second proposition *(The horse was raced past the barn)* in the middle of the first proposition *(The horse fell),* and this insertion comes after its doer (the *horse*) but *before* its action *(fell).* As if that weren't enough, the sentence makes things even more difficult by omitting the function words *who* and *was:* It says *raced past the barn* rather than *who was raced past the barn.* This is perfectly permissible—that is, grammatical—but as we have seen, such omissions make sentences much harder to understand. Finally, to add insult to injury, the proposition is in the passive *(the horse was raced past the barn)* rather than the active form in which doer is first and action is second (as in *Someone raced the horse past the barn).*

Every one of these features adds further complexity to the act of deciphering the sentence into the who-did-what-to-whom form. Rolled all together into one sentence, they overwhelm the processing capacity of the listener or reader. No wonder SAM doesn't comprehend.

---

* If the sentence still seems hard to understand, try comparing it to the further sentences: *The horse taken past the barn fell* and *The horse who was taken past the barn fell.* These sentences are easier to understand because the form of the word *take (taken,* a so-called *passive participle)* could never be the main verb of the sentence. In contrast, *race* happens to have the same form for both past tense *(raced)* and passive participle (again, *raced*), much to the confusion of all!

The horse (who was) raced past the barn
(by the jockey)

———— fell.

**9.14 Interpreting the sentence The horse raced past the barn fell.**

Consider how SAM proceeds. Since he expects to hear a doer followed by an act, he goes down a garden path as he starts to listen, and then he interprets "The—horse—raced—past—the—barn" as one of his favorite cases in which *the horse* is doer, *raced* is the act, and *past the barn* is the place where the action takes place. But now, to his chagrin, SAM hears "fell." SAM cannot recover from his first guess and gives up. He is betrayed by the very machinery of normal comprehension that serves him so well in 99 percent of the cases, foiled by the one unusual sentence that doesn't fit. Here, as so often, we learn something quite precise about the mental gymnastics of ordinary and successful understanding by looking at a case where SAM registers "TILT!" and does *not* understand.

### The Interaction of Syntax and Semantics

Our discussion of comprehension has focused on how we use syntactic information as a clue to sentence meaning. But several authors have pointed out that this process may be heavily affected by semantic factors, ranging all the way from the meanings of the words uttered to the sense of the conversation as a whole (Marslen-Wilson, 1975; Kintsch and vanDijk, 1977; Crain and Fodor, J.D., 1985; Crain and Steedman, 1985; McClelland and Kawamoto, 1986; Stowe, 1987; Carlson and Tanenhaus, 1988). It is all these additional factors that keep conversation from being drowned in confusion by the pervasive ambiguity of word, phrase, and sentence structure.

To take a simple example, there is some evidence that the meaning of a passive sentence is recovered as quickly as the meaning of an active sentence if the words used give strong semantic cues to the overall propositional thought. Thus *The flowers were watered by the girl* can hardly be misunderstood to mean *The flowers watered the girl,* so the passive sentence in this case is rapidly understood through attention to its semantics (Slobin, 1966; see Figure 9.15).

In summary, the process of comprehension is marvelously complex, taking into consideration factors of multiple kinds. It is all the more amazing that we understand almost every sentence we hear in a snap. The difference in effort for the so-called easy ones and the so-called hard ones is usually just a few tenths of a second. Thus the facts of comprehension are one important instance of the intricacy of language knowledge that is somehow embodied in the brains of all normal adults.

**9.15 Semantic cues to propositional thought** *The passive sentence* The flowers are watered by the girl *takes no longer to understand than the active sentence* The girl waters the flowers, *since its meaning will surely be understood as pictured in (A) rather than in (B).*

A          B

*Lewis Carroll's poignant tale of how an animal's mind would be different if it had language*   Alice came to a forest where nothing had a name. She met a fawn that walked trustingly by her side: "So they walked together through the wood, Alice with her arms clasped lovingly around the soft neck of the Fawn, till they came out into another open field [where things had names]. And here the Fawn gave a sudden bound into the air, and shook itself free of Alice's arm. 'I'm a Fawn!' it cried out in a voice of delight. 'And dear me! You're a human child!' A sudden look of alarm came into his beautiful brown eyes, and in another moment it had darted away at full speed." (Carroll, Through the Looking Glass, *1871/1946, p. 227).*

## THE GROWTH OF LANGUAGE IN THE CHILD

Now that we have surveyed the boundless forms and contents of language, and some of the computational complexities of comprehension, it seems impossible that any save the most brilliant person could possibly learn it. Yet we know that language is as natural and inevitable a part of human nature as chirping is to birds, roaring is to lions, and barking is to dogs. Whatever their talent, their motivation, or their station in life, normal children learn their native tongue to a high level of proficiency during the preschool years. This holds for children reared in poverty on the streets of New York and in the deserts of North Africa as much as it does for British upper-class children reared by nannies and sent to posh nursery schools.

### The Problem of Language Learning

Language seems to pose awesome problems for the mere babes who must learn it. It is not even obvious which sounds are relevant and which can be ignored. The infant listening to adults is exposed to an enormous jumble of sounds. Some of these sounds constitute speech, but others are coughs, hums, whistles, and even animal imitations ("and the big cow said 'Moooooooooo' "). How does the learner ever sort through this jumble of noise to discover which of the sounds she hears are speech sounds and which are not?

Let's suppose the infant has somehow managed to solve this task, and knows which sounds are relevant to language. How does she relate these sounds to meanings? Here matters become even more complicated. One problem is that the same speech events seem to refer to different things at different times. Thus the caregiver may say "dog" when the child sees a Great Dane, but also when the child sees the very different looking Boston terrier or even a fluffy stuffed toy. How does the learner discover the category (namely, dog) that is to cover such widely different things? (Carey, 1985). Symmetrically, sometimes the child will hear different speech signals when she observes a single thing, for parents may refer to the pet in the house as "Spot," "the dog," "that animal," or even "that housewrecker." And oftentimes, when the child is attending closely to the dog, the adult may say something quite irrelevant, such as "Time for your nap, honey." Under the circumstances, how does the child ever discover that the word *dog* refers to dogs, while *nap* refers to sleeping? (Carey, 1982; Pinker, 1984; Gleitman, L., 1990).

It is clear that the young language learner is confronted with a confusing welter of sounds and information about the world. But she somehow makes sense out of all this jumble even so. If she is a learner of English, she extracts the general fact that the sound "see" means 'gaze with the eyes'; if she is a learner of Spanish, she extracts the different fact that the same sound "see" (as in "Si!") means 'yes.' The question is how.

### Is Language Learning the Acquisition of a Skill?

Language learning is more than mere imitation. It is true that young children say "dog" and not "perro" or "chien" if they are exposed to English, so in this sense they are imitating the language community around them. But the real trick in word learning and use is creative: The word *dog* must apply to new dogs that the learners see. What served as a label for the pet bulldog must apply to the neighborhood poodle as well.

What goes for words goes for sentences too. Young children utter sentences they have never heard before. For instance, a mother may say to her child "I love you, Jane." But in response Jane may say "I hate you, Mommy" or "I'm going to crayon a face on this wall." These sentences are clear, though unwelcome, creative language acts of Jane's. They could not possibly have been learned by imitation.

Another popular hypothesis about language learning is that it is based on explicit *correction* or *reinforcement* by parents. According to this view, grammatical mistakes are immediately pointed out to the young learner, who subsequently avoids them. But in fact, this hypothesis is false (Morgan and Travis, 1989). In actual practice, mistakes in grammar and pronunciation generally go unremarked, as in the following exchange:

2-year-old: Mamma isn't boy, he a girl.
Mother:     That's right.

The situation is quite different if the child makes an error of fact. In that case, the mother often does provide a correction:

> 2-year old:  And Walt Disney comes on Tuesday.
> Mother:      No, he does not.

(Brown and Hanlon, 1970)

These findings are perfectly reasonable. Parents are out to create socialized and rational beings, not little grammarians, and so they correct errors of conduct and fact, not errors of grammar.

## LANGUAGE DEVELOPMENT

As we have just seen, imitation, correction, and reinforcement can't bear too much of the burden in explaining language learning. Children don't come to the task of acquiring their native tongue as little robots who can only notice and copy whatever they hear, whenever they hear it. How then are we to explain the growth of speech and comprehension? We will begin by tracing the child's progress during the first few years of life.

### The Social Origins of Speech Production

Infants begin to vocalize from the first moments of life. They cry, coo, and babble. They make sounds such as "ga" and "bagoo" that sound very much like words—except that these babbles have no conventional meaning. This is shown by the fact that deaf infants, who cannot hear others' vocalizations, babble in the same way (Lenneberg, 1967). But in the hearing infant, vocalization soon takes on a social quality, for three-month-olds will vocalize more when an adult vocalizes to them (Collis, 1975; Bloom, K., 1988).

Though true speech is absent in the first year of life, prelinguistic children have their own ways of making contact with the minds, emotions, and social behaviors of others. Quite early in life, babies begin to exchange looks, caresses, and touches with caregivers. Several investigators have suggested that these gestures are precursors and organizers of the language development to follow. The idea is that the gesture-and-babble interaction helps children to become linguistically socialized; to realize, for instance, that each participant in a conversation "takes a turn," and responds to the other (Bruner, 1974/1975; Sinclair, 1970, 1973).

Thus language knowledge is essentially social and interpersonal from the beginning. Though the capacity to learn it is built into the individual brain of the child, specific knowledge of a particular language requires social interactions between more than one person at a time. To speak to another, one has to have an idea—no matter how primitive—that the other lives in the same, mutually perceived, world (Bates, 1976; Bates and McWhinney, 1982).

*Social origins of speech*   *(Photograph by Erika Stone)*

### Discovering the Forms of Language

Infants' first attempts to speak are rather unimpressive. But careful analysis shows that they know more about language than they seem to at first glance. For

**A**

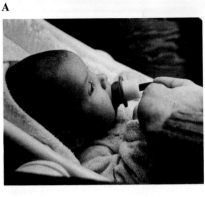

**B**

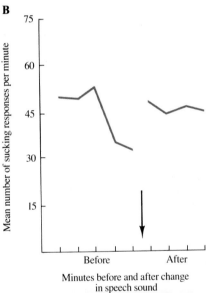

Minutes before and after change
in speech sound

**9.16  Sucking rate and speech perception
in the infant**  *(A) An infant sucks to hear
"ba" or "ga." (Photograph courtesy of
Philip Morse, Boston University) (B)
The graph shows the sucking rate of
four-month-olds to "ba" or "ga." The
infants soon become habituated, and the
sucking rate drops. When a new stimulus is
substituted ("ga" for "ba" and "ba" for
"ga"), the infant dishabituates and sucks
quickly once again. Similar results have
been obtained for one-month-olds. The
point of the shift is indicated by the arrow.
(From Eimas, Siqueland, Jusczyk, and
Vigorito, 1971)*

at a very early age, they make some perceptual distinctions about the sounds they
hear that are crucial to later language learning.

### THE RUDIMENTS OF PHONEME DISCRIMINATION

We have previously seen that all languages are built out of a few basic sound distinctions: the phonemes. But these linguistic sound atoms vary somewhat from
language to language. Thus in English, there is a crucial difference between "l"
and "r" (as in *lob* vs. *rob*). Though physically these sounds are quite similar, each
of them falls within a different phoneme in English, whose speakers have no trouble producing and perceiving the distinction. In contrast, this distinction has no
linguistic significance in Japanese, where "l" and "r" sounds fall within the same
phoneme. In consequence, Japanese speakers can neither produce nor perceive a
distinction between them. How does the infant learn which sound distinctions
are the phonemes of his language?

The answer is that initially infants respond to just about all sound distinctions
made in any language. They discover the phonemes of their native tongue by
*learning to ignore* the distinctions that don't matter. Their first step in understanding, say, Japanese, is to learn not to become speakers of all the other 4,000
languages on earth (Jusczyk, 1985).

Evidence comes from studies which show that two-month-old babies can distinguish between such sounds as "ba" and "pa," "la" and "ra," and so forth. The
experimenters used a version of the habituation method (see Chapter 14; pp.
557–58). The babies were given a pacifier, and whenever they sucked on it the
syllable "ba" was broadcast over a loudspeaker. The infants quickly learned that
their sucking led to the sound, and they began sucking faster and faster to hear it
some more. After awhile, the babies habituated to the "ba" sound and their sucking rate diminished. At this point, the experimenters changed the broadcast
sound from "ba" to "pa." The babies now started to suck again at a rapid rate.
They had become dishabituated. This result indicates that they could discriminate between the two sounds (see Figure 9.16; Eimas, Siqueland, Jusczyk, and Vigorito, 1971).

Infants in the first year of life are sensitive to just about every contrast that
occurs in *any* human language, but their sensitivity to foreign contrasts diminishes significantly by twelve months of age (Werker and Tees, 1984). This is consistent with the idea that infants must be prepared by nature to learn any
language on earth. After all, they arrive without a passport that tells them which
language they are going to hear. But the diminished sensitivities of twelve-month-
olds suggest that babies recalibrate their perceptions just as true speech and understanding begin, thus concentrating selectively on the distinctions that matter
in their own linguistic community.

### THE RUDIMENTS OF THE SENTENCE UNIT: "MOTHERESE"

We have seen that a crucial characteristic of language is that it includes syntax—
general principles for combining the finite stock of words into infinitely many
sentences. To discover the principles of syntax, infants first must recognize what
a sentence is—where one ends and the next one begins.

One cue that helps infants is a special way of speaking that is almost universally
employed by adults when they talk to babies. This special speech style has come
to be called, somewhat whimsically, **Motherese** (Newport, Gleitman, and Gleit-

***Learning language requires a receptive human mind.*** *Ginger gets plenty of linguistic stimulation but is prepared by nature only to be Man's Best Friend. (The FAR SIDE cartoon by Gary Larson is reprinted by permission of Chronicle Features, San Francisco, California)*

man, 1977). Of course, "Motherese" is something of a misnomer, for this style of speaking is adopted by fathers as well as mothers and by strangers as well as relatives when they are talking to an infant (Fernald, Taeschner, Dunn, Papousek, De Boysson-Bardies, and Fukui, 1989). It is characterized by a special tone of voice, with high pitch, slow rate, and exaggerated intonations (Fernald and Kuhl, 1987). (Just hold a baby and talk to her; you will discover that you naturally use Motherese and will feel quite awkward if you try to sound the way you do when you talk to your Psych I professor.)

There is good evidence that infants prefer Motherese to adult-to-adult speech, even though they as yet understand neither. One investigator conditioned four-month-old babies to turn their heads to the left or right so they could listen to speech sounds that came out of two loudspeakers. When the baby turned his head toward the loudspeaker on the right, he heard Motherese (produced not by his own, but by another child's mother). When he turned to the left, he heard adult-to-adult talk. The infants soon began to turn their heads to the right, indicating a preference for Motherese despite the unfamiliarity of the speaker's voice (Fernald and Simon, 1984).

This remarkable coadjustment between adult and child—the caregiver finding it irresistible to speak in a special way to infants, and the infants finding that style of speech bewitching to listen to—is a first hint of how our species is biologically adapted for the task of learning language. Indeed, such early observers as Charles Darwin (1877) had already noticed these protolinguistic interactions between mothers and their infants, and he called Motherese "the sweet music of the species."

The tones of Motherese and the responsive cooing of the infant are among the behavioral patterns related to the affective bonding between caregiver and child (Fernald, 1984). But Motherese has more specific uses in language learning as well. Motherese has acoustic properties that make it useful for learning to recognize the phrases and sentence units in speech. Both in adult speech and in Motherese there are certain sound cues that mark off the boundaries between phrases and sentences. These include changes of pitch: The pitch tends to start high at the beginnings of sentences and to go down at their ends. Another characteristic is the presence of pauses (brief periods of silence) that often occur at the boundaries between phrases and between sentences. But these cues (and their co-occurrence) are much more reliable and clear in the exaggerated style of Motherese than in speech among adults. As a result, the Motherese style may help the infant to recognize sentence units and their phrase components (Morgan and Newport, 1981; Gleitman, L., and Wanner, 1982; Morgan, 1986; Gleitman, Gleitman, Landau, and Wanner, 1988).

Evidence comes from a recent experiment in which the investigators asked whether seven-month-olds prefer to hear speech in which these two cues (pitch fall and silent interval) occur together to speech in which they do not. To find out, they inserted extra-long pauses (one second in length) in recorded Motherese. The pause was inserted either at the end of sentences in that speech (where a fall in pitch naturally occurred) or some arbitrary distance earlier (three words from the end of the sentence, a place where the pitch usually did *not* fall). A loudspeaker on the child's left broadcast the speech in which the pauses co-occurred with the fall in pitch; a loudspeaker on the right broadcast the speech in which the pause was placed elsewhere. The infants showed a marked preference for the speech that came from the left in which the fall in pitch and the pause coincided (as shown by the fact that they turned their heads toward this rather than toward the other loudspeaker). This could hardly be because the infants preferred pauses at the end of sentences—for they presumably didn't know as yet what sentences are. What they preferred was speech in which a pause went along with a fall in pitch. A pause in the middle of sentences, where the pitch was still high, evidently sounded less natural (Hirsh-Pasek, Kemler-Nelson, Jusczyk, Cassidy, Druss, and Kennedy, 1987).

This preference for the coincidence of falling pitch and pause will be useful for the babies in later language learning. For they eventually must learn what is a sentence and what is not, and this coincidence will provide an important clue. It may well be that infants are specially tuned by nature to notice just those aspects of the sound stream that will be important to language learning—and that their caregivers are specially tuned by nature to make these properties available by exaggerating them in Motherese.

## The One-Word Speaker

Children begin to understand a few words that their caregivers are saying as early as five to eight months of age. For example, some six-month-olds will regularly glance up at the ceiling light in response to hearing their mother say "light." Actual talking begins sometime between about ten and twenty months of age. Almost invariably, children's first utterances are one word long. Some first words refer to simple interactions with adults, such as *hi* and *peekaboo*. Others are names, such as *Mama* and *Fido*. Most of the rest are simple nouns, such as *duck* and *spoon,* adjectives such as *hot* and *big,* and action verbs such as *give* and *push.* And lest one think that child rearing is all pleasure, one of the first words is almost always a resounding *No.* The early vocabulary tends to concern things that can be moved around and manipulated or that move by themselves in the child's environment. For example, children are less likely to talk about ceilings than about rolling balls. And this early vocabulary refers more often to attributes and actions children can perceive in the outside world, such as shape or movement, than to internal states and feelings, such as pain or ideas (Nelson, 1973; Huttenlocher, Smiley, and Charney, 1983).

Missing altogether are the function words and suffixes, such as *the, and,* and *-ed.* These are among the most frequent items the child hears, but they are never uttered by beginners even so. There are several reasons for the lateness of these function items. One has to do with how hard they are to perceive. As we just saw, infants are especially interested in such properties of the sound wave as high pitch. But the function words are usually not stressed and occur with low pitch in the caregiver's speech. A second reason is that the function morphemes are grammatical items. Since the young children say only one word at a time, they presumably have little need to utter morphemes whose central role is to organize groups of words into sentence form (Gerken, Landau, and Remez, 1990).

### WORD MEANING AT THE ONE-WORD STAGE

It is hard to find out precisely what young children mean by the words they say. To be sure, we hear the tots say "rabbit" and "ball" but what exactly do these words mean to their young users? One reason for our relative ignorance about

*(Photograph by Erika Stone, 1989)*

**9.17 Symmetrical problems for child learners and investigators of child language** *(A) The child's helpful mother points out a rabbit, saying "rabbit." The child sees a rabbit—but also sees an animal, an ear, and the ground beneath the rabbit. Which one does the mother mean by the word* rabbit*? (B) The mother's (and the investigator's) problem in understanding young children's speech is much the same. The child may say "rabbit" when she observes a rabbit, but for all the mother knows the child may have made an error in learning, and thus may mean something different by this word.*

these earliest word meanings is that the same scene or event can often be described in many ways, depending on the particular words chosen. The very same creature can be described as *Peter, the rabbit, the animal, the creature with a tail,* and so forth. Therefore, even if a young child says "rabbit" on seeing a rabbit, he may mean 'tail' or 'animal' or 'white' or even 'runs by' for all we know.

The same problem that makes it hard for investigators to find out exactly what the children mean ought to make it hard for the children themselves to discover these meanings. Even if the helpful mother points out a rabbit to her child, saying "rabbit," the child still has a big job to do. He has to make up his mind whether the word *rabbit* means a particular animal (in which case *rabbit* is a name, such as 'Peter Rabbit'), anything that falls within the animal kingdom (in which case *rabbit* means 'animal'), anything within a particular species (so *rabbit* means 'rabbit'), or even some property, part, or action of a rabbit (in which case *rabbit* means 'white' or 'tail' or 'hops'; see Figure 9.17).

Because such problems for the learner are real, beginners often **undergeneralize** the meaning of a word: They may know that the word *house* refers to small toy buildings but not that it also refers to large real buildings. And they may **overgeneralize** the meanings of other words. They may think that the word *Daddy* refers to any man, not just their own father. These overgeneralizations and undergeneralizations are common for the first seventy-five or so words the child utters, but very rare thereafter (Rescorla, 1980). At later stages of learning, the child is almost always exactly on the mark in using words to refer to the right things in the world. We shall return in later discussion to how the child manages to be right overwhelmingly often despite the real problem of rabbits, rabbit parts, and the like. But for now it is important to realize that even the young overgeneralizer is surprisingly correct in what he has learned. Though he just about always observes the ground whenever he observes a rabbit (and hears the word *rabbit*)—because rabbits can't fly and thus are always found near the ground—still, he virtually never mistakenly learns that *rabbit* means 'ground' (or that *ground* means 'rabbit'). His only error is to make the category a bit too broad or narrow at first.

Developmental psychologists have different theories about the child's earliest word meanings. Some investigators take a ***functional*** approach. They believe that children use words to classify things together that act alike in their world—a ball is that which one throws and bounces in the playground (Nelson, 1973). Others argue for a ***featural*** approach. These investigators believe that children use words to designate things that look alike in at least some regards, things that share certain perceptual features. Thus *ball* may be overgeneralized to anything that is round, including faces, balls, and the moon (Clark, 1973). Still others believe that early word meanings are based on ***prototypes.*** In their view, children call things "ball" to the extent that they resemble a particular ball which serves as the model (prototype) for the entire concept (Anglin, 1975; deVilliers, 1980; Keil and Batterman, 1984). Of course these primitive meanings will change and develop as the children acquire more and more information (Chi, Glazer, and Rees, 1982) and reorganize the categories of their physical and mental world (Carey, 1985).

### PROPOSITIONAL MEANING AT THE ONE-WORD STAGE

There is another question about children's first words: Are these little foreshortened sentence attempts? That is, do children have a proposition and attitude in mind when they say "Doggie!" as a dog runs by? To listening adults, it does seem as though children have in mind a comment, request, question, or command. Thus adults are inclined to interpret "Eat" as 'The duck is eating' when the child says it as he watches a duck eat, but as 'Eat this cookie!' if it is said as the child forces a cookie into a stuffed duck's beak. Many investigators of child language believe young children have propositional ideas in mind even when they are speaking only one word at a time (Shipley, Smith, and Gleitman, L., 1969; Sachs and Truswell, 1978).

One basis for this belief is that one-word speakers fill out their speech with accompanying gestures (Greenfield and Smith, 1976). A child may say "rabbit" and also reach toward a rabbit at the same time, so the meaning 'Give me that rabbit' or 'I want that rabbit' comes across to the watching, listening, adult. Moreover, one-word speakers differentiate their requests, comments, and demands by intonation: Their pitch goes up when they seem to be requesting information and down when they seem to be making a demand (Gallagan, 1987).

The strongest evidence comes from recent experiments in which children as young as sixteen months of age (who themselves speak only one word at a time) look at brief movies that depict different happenings. The subjects sit on their mothers' laps and can see two video screens, one to their left and one to their right (Figure 9.18). Each screen shows cartoon characters known to the babies, en-

**9.18 Set-up for the selective looking experiment** *The child sits on the mother's lap and listens to a taped sentence while two video screens show two cartoon characters performing different actions. A hidden observer notes which screen the child is looking at. The mother wears a visor that covers her eyes, to make sure that she does not see which screen shows which action and thereby give inadvertent clues to the child. (Courtesy Roberta Golinkoff)*

Computer

Hidden speaker

Hidden tape deck

Hidden tape deck

Hidden observer

Child on mother's lap

**9.19  Stimuli for the selective looking experiment**  *One screen shows Big Bird tickling Cookie Monster, the other shows Cookie Monster tickling Big Bird.*

gaged in various actions (Figure 9.19). On the screen to the left, Big Bird is tickling Cookie Monster, and on the screen to the right, Cookie Monster is tickling Big Bird. Half the children hear a voice saying "Oh look! Big Bird is tickling Cookie Monster." The other children hear the reverse sentence ("Oh look! Cookie Monster is tickling Big Bird."). Hidden observers now record which screen the children turn their attention to. The finding is that the toddlers look primarily at the screen that matches the sentence they have heard. To understand what matches and what does not match, their only clue is the syntax of the sentence they have heard. Thus the experiment proves that even babies who can speak only in single words understand the logic of simple sentences in terms of the drama of who-did-what-to-whom (Hirsh-Pasek, Golinkoff, Fletcher, De-Gaspe-Beaubien, and Cauley, 1985).

## The Two-Word (Telegraphic) Speaker

Many drastic changes take place beginning at about the second birthday. The child's vocabulary begins to spurt, rising to many hundreds of words. Soon, she begins to put words together into primitive sentences, and then we are aware most poignantly that another human mind is among us.

### SYNTAX AND PROPOSITIONAL MEANING IN TWO-WORD SPEECH

Though we can clearly recognize propositional ideas in these first "sentences," these hardly sound like adult speech. Generally, each rudimentary sentence is only two words long, and each of its components is a content word. The function morphemes are still largely missing, and so these sentences sound like the short ones we often use in telegrams and newspaper headlines: "Throw ball!," "Daddy shoe," "No eat!" (Brown, R., and Bellugi, 1964).

These sentences show some organization, however, despite their simplicity. From the earliest moments of "telegraphic speech," the words seem to be serially ordered according to the propositional roles. The child who says "Throw ball" usually does not say "Ball throw" to mean the same thing (Braine, 1963; Bloom, L., 1970; deVilliers and deVilliers, 1973). Thus young English speakers will put the doer of the action first and will say "Mommy throw!" if they want the mother to throw the ball; and they will put the done-to last and say "Throw ball!" in approximately the same circumstances. So mothers of two-year-old learners of English would probably be right in feeling a bit miffed if their child said "Throw Mommy!"

Thus we see that two-year-olds' correct use of word order to express different sentence meanings is consistent with the comprehension that they showed even earlier (in understanding who did what to whom in the Cookie Monster and Big Bird videos). In fact, these short sentences are ordinarily so clear in meaning that one may wonder why children bother to learn anything more. But see Figure 9.20 for a demonstration of how ambiguous two-word speech sometimes is.

### EXPLAINING TWO-WORD SPEECH

Why are children's early sentences so short? We have discussed one reason: The function words have low pitch and thus are less salient in the sound wave as children perceive it. Accordingly, it is hard to learn them (Gleitman, L., and Wanner, 1982). Another factor is the sheer problem of memory and information handling that makes construction of a complex sentence plan difficult, so the child reduces what she says to "the bare essentials" required to make communication go through (Bloom, L., 1970; Bloom, P., 1990).

But a third factor has been suggested recently. Several authors believe that learners are neurologically "programmed" to expect human language to have a certain specific syntactic organization. Variation away from this "universal linguistic structure" is only on a very few details (or *parameters*) in the real languages of the world. All the same, there is a little variation. One example has to do with expressing the subject noun phrase. In adult English, one must say "I am going to the store." One does not say "Am going to the store." But most of the languages of the world do not require the subject of the sentence to be uttered when its meaning is clear from the conversation. Thus in Spanish, one usually

**9.20  The ambiguities of two-word speech**  *The two-word utterances of young children, while systematic and meaningful, are quite ambiguous. The three panels from the children's story* Higgledy Piggledy Pop, *by Maurice Sendak, show why one young child might want to learn more about adult syntax. (A) An adventurous dog takes a job as nurse to Baby. He must get Baby to eat, or he will be fed to the lion down in the basement. Here Baby refuses the food, saying "No eat!" (I will not eat). (B) Here, the dog eats up the food Baby has refused. Baby finds this objectionable, and so cries out "No eat!" (Don't eat my porridge!). (C) Baby has angrily pushed the button so the dog-nurse will fall down to the waiting lion; but Baby has accidentally fallen also. To avoid being eaten by the lion, Baby cries out "No eat!" (Don't eat me up!). (From Maurice Sendak, 1979)*

A

B

C

**9.21    The parameter setting theory of language learning**    *(A) Children hearing English and children hearing Spanish both come from nature's factory with the switch set to allow subject omission (SO). (B) The English speaker eventually resets his switch to disallow this (No SO); the Spanish speaker does not.*

says "Hablo Español" (literally, "Speak Spanish") rather than the fuller "Yo hablo Español" ("I speak Spanish").*

Some investigators believe that children are preprogrammed to expect that the language they are learning will allow this dropping of the subject because this is the fact about *most* human languages. According to this view, the option of omitting the subject is a kind of "initial setting" in the child's head for the mental machinery that is devoted to language learning. The learners come from nature's factory, so to speak, set to think that the language they are learning will be organized in such-and-such a way. For the case we are discussing, the first hypothesis of young English speakers, just like young Spanish speakers, is that one can omit the subject; so these learners say "Throw ball" instead of "I throw ball" (see Figure 9.21A). Learning that the subject is required in English is therefore a relatively late acquisition, for it violates the factory setting, which the child must "switch" after sufficient exposure to English. In contrast, Spanish-speaking children can just stick to their initial hypothesis and leave out obvious subjects for the rest of their lives (Figure 9.21B, Hyams, 1986).

## Later Stages of Language Learning: Syntax

By two-and-a-half years or so, children progress beyond the two-word stage. Their utterances now become longer (Figure 9.22). They can say little sentences that contain all three terms of a basic proposition, and function words have begun to appear. Their utterances are still short and simple, but—at least initially —they are quite correct as far as they go. Soon, however, a new phenomenon appears. Children start to make various kinds of errors in their word formation and in their syntax. An example concerns the *-ed* suffix which represents 'pastness.'

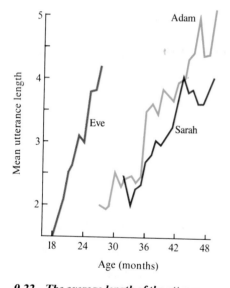

**9.22    The average length of the utterances produced by three children**    *The mean utterance length in three children between 1½ and 4 years of age. The utterance length is measured in morphemes, where* dolls *counts as two morphemes (doll + s). Note the variations among the children, who were all within a normal range. (After Brown, Cazden, and Bellugi-Klima, 1969)*

---

* The languages allowing the subject to be dropped are, not surprisingly, usually the ones that have an **agreement morpheme** attached to the verb itself (e.g., the *-o* in *hablo,* which signals first-person, and thus identifies the missing doer as "I"). More generally, the approach to language acquisition (called **learnability theory**) that we are now discussing is a direct outgrowth of formal linguistic studies. Such approaches are based on an examination of the grammars of the languages of the world. Once these grammars are described, these investigators ask (again, generally by formal analysis): What must the child's mind be like, such that he or she could learn any of these language systems? (Chomsky, 1965; Wexler and Culicover, 1980; Baker and McCarthy, 1981; Borer and Wexler, 1987; Roeper and Williams, 1987; Pinker, 1984; Lust, 1987).

At the age of two and three, children use correct regular forms of the past tense (as in *walked* or *talked*), as well as correct irregular ones (such as *ran, came,* and *ate*). But at the age of four and five, these same children often say "runned," "comed," and "eated" (Ervin, 1964; Cazden, 1968; Brown, R., 1973; Kuczaj, 1977). And they resist change even when they hear their parents use the correct form, as in the following exchange:

Child:  My teacher holded the baby rabbits and we patted them.
Mother:  Did you say your teacher held the baby rabbits?
Child:  Yes.
Mother  What did you say she did?
Child:  She holded the baby rabbits and we patted them.
Mother:  Did you say she held them tightly?
Child:  No, she holded them loosely.

(Bellugi, 1971)

What has happened to this child who in earlier years said "held" but who now doggedly keeps saying "holded"? The answer seems to be that the child is now seeking general patterns that hold over the whole vocabulary or set of sentence structures. If some words choose to be exceptions to these patterns, so much the worse for these words. Thus the child now overgeneralizes the use of certain structures though, as we saw earlier, she no longer overgeneralizes the meanings of words. (For an alternative view, see Rumelhart and McClelland, 1986; for discussion, see Pinker and Prince, A., 1988).

Another example is the use of nouns as verbs. The child has heard "John bats the ball," where *bat* means 'hit with a bat,' so he invents "Don't Woodstock me!" to mean 'Don't hit me with a Woodstock toy' (Clark, E., 1982). A more complicated case is the invention of so-called **causative verbs** (Bowerman, 1982; Pinker, 1989). Children evidently notice that there are many ways to express causation in English. Given a sentence like "The door opened," one can express the causal agent in this affair by saying "John made the door open," "John got the door to open," or "John opened the door." So since children know sentences like "I giggle," they make an analogy from *open* and say "Daddy giggled me" to mean 'Daddy made me giggle.'

## Further Stages of Language Learning: Word Meaning

We have already discussed some of the difficulties children *should* confront when they try to discover which word stands for which meaning. But in reality, they experience very little difficulty. Five-year-olds have a vocabulary of 10,000 to 15,000 words, whereas at fifteen months they had a vocabulary of only about twenty-five words. This means they must be acquiring about ten words a day—every day, every week, every month. It is likely that none of us adults could do as well.

### CAREGIVER AIDS TO WORD LEARNING

Part of the explanation for this remarkably rapid learning may come from the quite regular ways in which mothers talk to their children, for syntax often contains useful hints about what a word could mean. Let's return to the problem of learning which word means 'ear' and which means 'rabbit' (see Figure 9.17, p.

*(Photograph by Roberta Intrater, 1980)*

366). It turns out that when mothers refer to the whole rabbit, they use simple sentences ("This is a rabbit") and often point to the rabbit at the same time. But when they want to refer to the ear, they first refer to the whole rabbit, and then use such words as *his* in referring to the part: "This is a rabbit; these are his ears" (Shipley, Kuhn, and Madden, 1983).

### PERCEPTUAL AND CONCEPTUAL BIASES IN CHILD LEARNERS

We see that caregivers' speech style helps language learners to decide which words are about the whole objects and which words are about their parts. It turns out that children have some biases, or "best guesses," of their own that also contribute to their solution of the word learning problem.

Much of the child's word learning is explained by how she is disposed to carve up *(categorize)* the world that she observes. Some ways of conceptualizing experience are natural to humans while others are less natural (Rosch, 1973a; Keil, 1979; Fodor, 1983). Thus the child can learn more easily if she assumes that each word represents some "natural" organization of experience.

One indication of this is the fact that young children acquire the "basic-level" words (e.g., *dog*) before the superordinates *(animal)* or subordinates *(Chihuahua)* (Rosch, 1978). One might think this is just because the basic-level words are used most frequently to children. But this does not seem to be the explanation. In some homes, the words *Spot* or *Rex* (specific names) are used much more often than *dog* (a basic-level term), for obvious reasons. And it is true that in this case the young learner will soon utter "Spot" and not "dog." But she has first learned it as a basic-level term all the same. This is shown by the fact that she will then utter "Spot" to refer to the neighbor's dog as well as her own. She overgeneralizes *Spot* just enough to convert it from a specific name to the basic level of categorization—evidently, the most natural level for carving up experience (Mervis and Crisafi, 1978; Shipley and Kuhn, 1983).

Further evidence comes from experimental attempts to teach new words to children. The method is to point to a new object and label it with a new (nonsense) word, and then to determine *what else* other than the first sample object the child will apply this new label to. Thus if an experimenter points toward an object and says "That's biff," children will almost always guess that "biff" names the whole object rather than, say, some of its parts, or the material of which it is made, its color, and so forth (Markman and Hutchinson, 1984). This is despite the logical problem that when one points toward an object one simply can't help pointing toward its color (e.g., green) and substance (e.g., plastic or pewter) at the same time. Even more interesting, if one then shows this child other objects that are *shaped just like the original sample object* but differ from it in size or color, the child will take these as more biffs. But the same child will reject, as "not biffs," objects that have *even slightly different shapes.* Evidently, colors and textures are not as salient in the child's perceptual organization as shapes, so the slightest change in the latter will convince the learner that the new item is something wholly different from the one previously called "a biff" (Landau, Smith, and Jones, 1988).

### THE INTERPLAY OF STRUCTURE AND MEANING IN WORD LEARNING

We have seen that children organize word meanings according to conceptual categories: the ways in which they understand the world. But children also seem to have pretty strong ideas about language itself: how a language can express these categories. One example concerns synonyms. Though many words are similar in meaning, it is hard to find exact and perfect synonyms in the simple vocabulary of any language. Young children apparently take this as a matter of principle: Any one concept can have only one word that refers to it (Clark, E., 1987; for an alternative view, see Gathercole, 1987).

Evidence again comes from experiments on new word learning. This time, the investigators showed some preschoolers a *familiar* kind of object, one that the children already had a word for (say, a cup made of pewter) and said "That's biff." Other children were shown an *unfamiliar* object (say, a pair of tongs made of pewter) and also told "That's biff." Afterwards, the children were shown a collection of new objects and asked to select "more biffs." The children who had been introduced to tongs picked out all other tongs they saw, including those of different colors and substances (e.g., plastic ones as well as pewter ones). This again shows that children think that all objects with the same shape should have the same linguistic title. But the children who had been introduced to the cup behaved differently. They selected all pewter objects (that is, pewter tongs, cups, spoons, and so forth). These latter children apparently reasoned that they already knew a name for cups (namely, *cup*) and therefore *biff* could not mean 'cup.' So despite their initial bias that new words stand for whole objects, they had to find "something else" that the word meant. They did not believe that the new word was simply a synonym for the word they knew (Markman and Wachtel, 1988).

### WORD CLASSES AND WORD MEANINGS

Children are disposed to organize the world into overarching categories—things, events, properties, and so forth. But what is more, they appear to believe that language will classify words according to related categories—nouns, verbs, and adjectives—in a way that is consistent with the conceptual categories (Braine, 1976; Pinker, 1984).

This phenomenon was demonstrated in an experiment with three- and four-year-olds in which the experimenter showed children a picture in which a pair of hands seemed to be performing a kneading sort of motion, with a mass of red confetti-like material that was overflowing a low, striped, container (Figure 9.23). The children were introduced to the picture in sentences that used nonsense words, but either as verbs ("In this picture can you see *sibbing?*"), common nouns *("Can you see a sib?")*, or mass nouns *("Can you see any sib?").** The children who had been asked to show *sibbing* made kneading motions with their hands, those asked to show *a sib* pointed to the container, and those asked about *any sib* pointed to the confetti (Brown, R., 1957; see also Katz, Baker, and MacNamara, 1974; Carey, 1982).

Thus children use their growing knowledge of word classes and their semantic correlates to discover what a new word refers to, even though the scene itself can be interpreted in many ways (Pinker, 1984; Gleitman, L., et al., 1988). Symmetrically, as we have seen with such examples as *Don't Woodstock me!,* and *Daddy*

**9.23 Word classes and word meanings**
*When asked "In this picture can you see any sibbing?" (verb), children pointed to the hands; when asked "Can you see a sib?" (common noun), they pointed to the blue bowl; and when asked "Can you see any sib?" (mass noun), they pointed to the pink confetti. (Adapted from Brown, R., 1957)*

---

\* A **common** or **count noun** is one that (1) requires a specifier such as *the* or *two* (compare *The dog walks down the street* with the ungrammatical *Dog walks down the street*), and (b) generally refers to the kinds of entities that can be counted (e.g., *One dog, two dogs*). A **mass noun** (1) occurs without a specifier (compare *Water flows through the pipes* with the ungrammatical *A water flows through the pipes*), and (2) generally refers to stuff that can't be counted, e.g., *water, confetti,* or *sand.*

*giggled me!,* they can use their knowledge of language structure to decide how to use these new words in novel sentence structures that their parents surely never taught them.

In sum, children proceed in their learning in two directions at once. They will use the forms of new words as clues to their meanings (e.g., "Since this new word was just used as a noun, it probably describes a thing"). But they will also use their knowledge of words to predict their forms ("Since this Woodstock toy is now an instrument for hitting me on the head, I can use it as a verb"). Using both kinds of evidence, the children efficiently "bootstrap" their way into knowledge of the tens of thousands of words and the ways these can be used in sentences (Grimshaw, 1981; Pinker, 1989; Gleitman, L., 1990).

## LANGUAGE LEARNING IN CHANGED ENVIRONMENTS

Thus far, our focus has been on language development as it proceeds normally. Under these conditions, language seems to emerge in much the same way in virtually all children. They progress from babbling to one-word speech, advance to the two-word telegraphic stage, and eventually graduate to complex sentence forms and meanings. The fact that this progression is so uniform and universal has led many psycholinguists to the view that children are biologically pre-programmed to acquire language. Further evidence for this view stems from studies of language development under certain unusual conditions, when children grow up in environments that are radically different from those in which language development usually proceeds. Which aspects of the early environment are essential for language learning? One line of evidence comes from reports of children who grew up in the wild or under conditions of virtual social isolation.

### Wild Children

There are some remarkable examples of children who wandered (or were abandoned) in the forest, and who survived, reared by bears or wolves. Some of these cases have been discussed by the psycholinguist Roger Brown (1958). In 1920, some Indian villagers discovered a wolf mother in her den together with four cubs. Two were baby wolves, but the other two were human children, subsequently named Kamala and Amala. No one knows how they got there and why the wolf adopted them. Brown tells us what these children were like:

> Kamala was about eight years old and Amala was only one and one-half. They were thoroughly wolfish in appearance and behavior: Hard callus had developed on their knees and palms from going on all fours. Their teeth were sharp edged. They moved their nostrils sniffing food. Eating and drinking were accomplished by lowering their mouths to the plate. They ate raw meat . . . At night they prowled and sometimes howled. They shunned other children but followed the dog and cat. They slept rolled up together on the floor . . . Amala died within a year but Kamala lived to be eighteen . . . In time, Kamala learned to walk erect, to wear clothing, and even to speak a few words. (Brown, 1958, p. 100)

**9.24 A modern wild boy** *Ramu, a young boy discovered in India in 1976, appears to have been reared by wolves. He was deformed, apparently from lying in cramped positions, as in a den. He could not walk, and drank by lapping with his tongue. His favorite food was raw meat, which he seemed to be able to smell at a distance. After he was found, he lived at the home for destitute children run by Mother Theresa in Lucknow, Uttar Pradesh. He learned to bathe and dress himself, but never learned to speak. He continued to prefer raw meat, and would often sneak out to prey upon fowl in the neighbor's chicken coop. Ramu died at the age of about 10 in February, 1985. (New York Times, Feb. 24, 1985; photographs courtesy Wide World Photos)*

The outcome was much the same for the thirty or so other wild children about whom we have reports. When found, they were all shockingly animal-like. None of them could be rehabilitated so as to use language at all normally, though some, including Kamala, learned to speak a few words (Figure 9.24).

## Isolated Children

Kamala and Amala were removed from all human society. Some other children have been raised by humans, but under conditions that were almost unimaginably inhumane, for their parents were either vicious or deranged. Sometimes, such parents will deprive a baby of all human contact. "Isabelle" was hidden away, apparently from early infancy, and given only the minimal attention necessary to sustain her life. Apparently no one spoke to her (in fact, her mother was deaf and did not speak). Isabelle was six years old when discovered. Of course she had no language, and her cognitive development was below that of a normal two-year-old. But within a year, this girl learned to speak. Her tested intelligence was normal, and she took her place in an ordinary school (Davis, K., 1947; Brown, R., 1958). Thus Isabelle at seven years, with one year of language practice, spoke about as well as her peers in the second grade, all of whom had had seven years of practice.

Rehabilitation from isolation is not always so successful. A child, "Genie," discovered in California about twenty years ago, was fourteen years old when found. Since about twenty months, apparently, she had lived tied to a chair, was frequently beaten, and never spoken to—but sometimes barked at, for her father said she was no more than a dog. Afterwards, she was taught by psychologists and linguists (Fromkin, Krashen, Curtiss, Rigler, and Rigler, 1974). But Genie did not become a normal language user. She says many words, and puts them together into meaningful propositions as young children do, such as "No more take wax" and "Another house have dog." Thus she has learned certain basics of language. Indeed, her semantic sophistication—what she means by what she says—

is far beyond young children. Yet, even after many years of instruction, Genie did not learn the function words that appear in mature English sentences, nor did she combine propositions together in elaborate sentences (Curtiss, 1977).

Why did Genie not progress to full language learning while Isabelle did? The best guess is that the crucial factor is the age at which language learning began. Genie was discovered after she had reached puberty while Isabelle was only six. As we shall see later, there is some reason to believe there is a ***critical period*** for language learning. If the person has passed this period, language learning proceeds with greater difficulty.

## Language without Sound

The work on wild and isolated children argues that a necessary condition for learning language is some contact with other humans. If one's early life is spent entirely among animals, the effects are irreversible. If it is spent among people who do not talk to one, language may still be acquired later on if the crucial learning period has not been passed as yet. Our next question concerns the more specific factors of the learner's human environment. What aspects of this environment are essential for language to emerge?

It has sometimes been suggested that an important ingredient is exposure to language sounds. According to this view, language is intrinsically related to the way we organize what we hear. If so, language cannot develop in the absence of sound.

This hypothesis is false. For there is one group of humans that is cut off from auditory-vocal language—the deaf, who cannot hear it. Yet this doesn't mean that they have no language. Most deaf people eventually learn to read and write the language of the surrounding community of hearing persons. But they also have a manual-visual, or ***gestural system.*** One such system is ***American Sign Language*** (or ***ASL***).

Are gestural systems genuine languages? One indication that they are is that these systems are not derived by translation from the spoken languages around them, but are independently created within and by communities of deaf individuals (Klima, Bellugi, et al., 1979). Further evidence comes from comparing ASL to the structure and development of spoken languages. ASL has hand shapes and positions of which each word is composed, much like the tongue and lip shapes that allow us to fashion the phonemes of spoken language (Stokoe, 1960). It has morphemes and grammatical principles for combining words into sentences that are similar to those of spoken language (Supalla, 1986; see Figure 9.25).

Finally, babies born to deaf users of ASL (whether or not the babies themselves are deaf) pick up the system from these caregivers through informal interaction rather than by explicit instruction, just as we learn our spoken language (Newport and Ashbrook, 1977).* And they go through the same steps on the way to adult knowledge as do hearing children learning English. It is hard to avoid the conclusion that ASL and other gestural systems are true languages (Klima, Bellugi et al., 1979; Supalla and Newport, 1978; Newport, 1984).

***Deaf youngsters signing***  *(Courtesy of New York School for the Deaf)*

---

* In fact, the expert sign-language translators seen on television are usually hearing children of deaf parents. They grow up in a bilingual environment, with ASL learned from their parents and English learned by contact with hearing children and adults, so they achieve perfect knowledge of both and thus are the best translators.

Thus language does not depend on the auditory-vocal channel. When the usual modes of communication are denied to humans of normal mentality, they come up with an alternative that reproduces the same contents and structures as other language systems. It appears that language is an irrepressible human trait: Deny it to the mouth and it will dart out through the fingers.

## Language without a Model

The evidence we have reviewed shows that language emerges despite many environmental deprivations. Still, each case seemed to have one requirement—some adults who knew a language and could impart it to the young. But this must leave us puzzled about how language originated in the first place. Is it a cultural artifact (like the internal combustion machine or the game of chess) rather than a basic property of human minds, an invention that happened to take place in prehistoric times? Our bias has been the opposite, for we have argued that humans are biologically predisposed to communicate by language. But our case would have been much better if Kamala and Amala had invented a language of their own, down there in the wolf's den. Why didn't they? There are many ways to write off or ignore this case—maybe they were too busy learning to be good wolves, and maybe a human language is of no special use for learning to devour raw chickens. Is there a better test than those provided by the tragic cases of brutal mistreatment and neglect so far considered?

It certainly would be interesting if we could find a case of mentally normal children living in a socially loving environment but not exposed to language use by the adults around them. Feldman, Goldin-Meadow, and L. Gleitman (1978) found six children who were in such a situation. These children were deaf, and so they were unable to learn spoken language. Their parents were hearing; they did not know ASL and decided not to allow the children to learn a gestural language. This is because they shared the belief (held by some groups of educators) that deaf children can achieve adequate knowledge of spoken language by special training in lip reading and vocalization. The investigators looked at these children before they had acquired any knowledge of English, for a number of prior studies had shown that under these circumstances deaf children will spontaneously gesture in meaningful ways to others (Tervoort, 1961; Fant, 1972). The question was which aspects of communication these youngsters would come up with as they developed.

The results showed that the children invented a sizeable number of pantomimic gestures that the investigators could comprehend. For example, they would

*9.25 Some common signs in ASL* (A) *The sign for* tree. *One difference between ASL and spoken language is that many of the signed words physically resemble their meanings. This is so for* tree, *in which the upright forearm stands for the trunk and the outstretched fingers for the branches. But in many cases, such a resemblance is not present. Consider (B) which is the modern sign for* help, *whose relation to its meaning seems as arbitrary as that between most spoken words and their meanings. Even so, such a relation was once present, as shown in (C), a nineteenth-century sign for* help. *At that time, the sign was not arbitrary; it consisted of a gesture by the right hand to support the left elbow, as if helping an elderly person cross a street. (B) grew out of (C) by a progressive series of simplifications in which signs tend to move to the body's midline and use shorter, fewer, and more stylized movements. All that remains of (C) is an upward motion of the right palm. (Frishberg, 1975; photographs of and by Ted Supalla)*

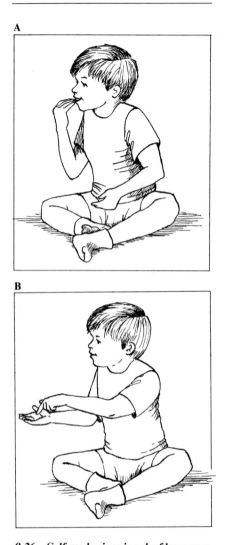

A

B

*9.26   Self-made signs in a deaf boy never exposed to sign language*   *A two-sign sequence. (A) The first sign means "eat" or "food." Immediately before, the boy had pointed to a grape. (B) The second sign means "give." The total sequence means "give me the food." (Goldin-Meadow, 1982; drawing courtesy Noel Yovovich)*

flutter their fingers in a downward motion to express *snow,* twist their fingers to express a twist-top *bottle,* and flap their arms to represent *bird* (see Figure 9.26).

The development of this "language" showed many parallels to ordinary language learning: The children gestured one sign at a time in the period (about eighteen months of age) when hearing learners speak one word at a time. At two and three years of age they went on to two- and three-word sentences and so on. And in these basic sentences, the individual gestures were serially ordered by semantic role. This is strong evidence for a rudimentary syntactic organization, just like that of children who hear German or French—or see ASL—produced by adults.

On the other hand, we should not lose sight of severe limitations of these homemade systems. First, they are limited to the elementary basics of language as we know it, with function words and elaborately organized sentences absent (Goldin-Meadow, 1982). And there is a yet more serious limitation that goes back to the social and interpersonal nature of ordinary language use: The parents of these children used gestures to them very rarely, and their sporadic gesturing was in terms of isolated "words" and pointings to things in view, with no syntactic organization (Goldin-Meadow and Mylander, 1983). The result was that social interaction in this medium was quite restricted, for it takes more than one individual—inventive as he or she may be—to make a living language. We can be thankful, then, that these children once they reached the age of four or five began to receive instruction in reading English, and were eventually introduced to a full sign language (ASL) by meeting other deaf individuals.*

In sum, these studies provide us with a fairly pure case of a group of children who were isolated from language stimulation, but not from love and affection. The findings show that the capacity to organize thought using the word and syntax principles of language is a deep-seated property of the human mind, at least in its basics if not in its elaborations. In this sense, we have no need to ask further about the origins of human language. Our best guess is that as human nature origseinated in evolutionary history, language inevitably made its appearance too. Yet the same studies show us the necessarily interpersonal and interactive nature of human communication, which must become stymied and dysfunctional in the end if there is no "other" with whom it can be used.

### Children Deprived of Access to Some of the Meanings

Children usually learn the meanings of words in situations in which they can determine the referents of those words. Thus it is certainly easier to learn the meaning of the word *horse* if that word is said in the presence of a horse. Only the rarer, and late-acquired, words like *zebu* usually have to be looked up in the dictionary (and even for these, we are helped if the dictionary provides a picture). To the extent that referents of the words and sentences help the learner, we should expect that blind learners have significant difficulties in learning a language. For often

---

* The degree of success with lip-reading and vocalization of English, as well as reading acquisition, by deaf children is variable, with the level attained closely related to the degree of deafness. Even the slightest hearing capability helps enormously. But there is growing evidence that the most natural alternative for profoundly deaf children is to learn and use ASL, for in this manual-visual medium they have no language handicap at all, as we showed in a previous section.

A

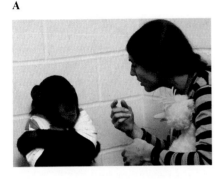

B

*Chimpanzees signing*    *A young chimpanzee making the sign for (A) "hug" and (B) "apple." (Terrace, 1979; photograph courtesy Herbert Terrace)*

Recent claims for another species, the pygmy chimpanzee, are even stronger, given a communication system that combines a visual geometric symbol set and the response to spoken English words. It is claimed that these animals quite often come up with novel combinations of words and that their language knowledge in general is broader than that of common chimpanzees (Savage-Rumbaugh, McDonald, Sevcik, Hopkins, and Rupert, 1986; Savage-Rumbaugh, 1987). Our final assessment of primate linguistic intelligence will depend to some degree on further documentation of such effects.

Current evidence allows us to conclude only that chimpanzees can learn words and show some propositional thought. There is little satisfactory evidence that they can create (or understand) syntactic structures that are the human vehicles for expressing propositional thought. Thus—at least so far, though the debate continues—they cannot be said to be "linguistic animals." (For discussion of some of these issues, see Seidenberg and Pettito, 1979; Van Cantfort and Rimpau, 1982.)

IS IT LANGUAGE?

To sum up, recent years have seen a tremendous growth of scientific interest in the question of whether chimpanzees (and dolphins, gorillas, and other advanced animals) can acquire language. Of course, the idea of talking to animals is not a new one, appearing in the mythology of many cultures (not to speak of Dr. Doolittle). This idea for some reason has always held a fascination for many people who dream of interspecies communication (as witness the popularity of some recent movies in which chimpanzees not only talk and think, but also display impressive courage and an outstanding moral sense). The investigations we have discussed, however, go beyond such mythic motivations and are deeply grounded in the question of comparative (evolutionary) psychology. For it would be strange if we could see absolutely no link to the spectacular use of language by humans in the behavior of our closest neighbors on the evolutionary ladder.

What current evidence supports is that there are some precursors and prerequisites (such as primitive propositional thought) to our language capacities that are observable in trained chimpanzees. However, these very findings have led to great controversy. Some scientists have concluded from them that there is little qualitative difference in this regard between us and these primates—only a difference in degree. Others conclude that the chimpanzees' accomplishments are too sporadic and limited to be of much interest for understanding the minds of either chimpanzees or humans. Many other scientists find no merit at all in calling these chimpanzee behaviors "language" in any useful sense. Their view is that

dividual words (i.e., that *water-bird* means 'a bird of the water' and not 'water for a bird'). This is not too plausible because this particular form/meaning interpretation is not inevitable, but rather is a fact about current-day English grammar, where we put the modifying word *(water)* before the main word *(bird)* to create such compounds. English was not always this way. Today we would say, for example, *penny-pincher* to mean 'one who pinches pennies' (that is, a miser). But in an earlier stage of English, the requirement was to put the main word first, and so people said *pinch-penny* for that same meaning. Are we to believe that the chimpanzee understands the current status of English morphology and syntax, and so follows the new rule rather than the historically earlier one? Many critics would say it is easier—barring much, much stronger evidence—to say that the chimpanzee had just seen both water and a bird and so uttered these two signs one after the other without regard to (1) their particular serial order, or (2) the semantic significance of that serial order.

these trained behaviors are no more convincing than the tricks of dancing circus poodles, whose accomplishments are never taken to prove that dogs, like humans, are two-legged animals.

Whether the chimpanzees' accomplishments should be called *language,* then, seems to depend on one's definition of that term. We can choose to say that trained chimpanzees use language. But in doing so, we have changed the technical meaning of the term so as to exclude from consideration the learning, speech, and comprehension machinery shown by every nonpathological human. Worse, we have even changed the common-sense meaning of the term *language.* For one thing is certain: If any of our children learned or used language the way Washoe or Sarah does, we would be terror-stricken and rush them to the nearest neurologist.

## LANGUAGE AND ITS LEARNING

In our survey of the nature of language, we emphasized that human communication systems are at rock bottom the same all over the world. To be sure, the words themselves sound different so the speakers of different languages cannot understand each other. Still, every language turned out to consist of a hierarchy of structures that represent a complex interweaving of meaning and form. The effect is that, if we share a language, we can communicate about all the endless social, emotional, and intellectual matters that concern us as humans.

Language is marvelously ornate and intricate—so much so that we must be boggled by the idea that human babies can learn any such thing. And yet they do, as we have seen. In all the nurturant (and even most of the horribly abusive) circumstances in which human babies find themselves, language makes its appearance and flourishes. Our nearest primate cousins even given the utmost in social and linguistic support do not approach the competence and sophistication of the most ordinary three-year-old human child. What makes this learning possible?

We have argued throughout that language is the product of the young human brain, such that virtually any exposure conditions will suffice to guide acquisition of any language in the world. In retrospect, this is scarcely surprising. It would be just as foolish for evolution to have created human bodies without human "programs" to run these bodies than to have created giraffe bodies without giraffe programs or white-crowned sparrow bodies without white-crowned sparrow programs.

But we must close by reemphasizing that specific languages must be learned by human babies, even though the capacity to accomplish this is given in large part by nature. This is because the manifestations of the human language capacity are certainly variable, particularly in the sounds of the individual words. To reiterate a point with which we began: Greek children learn Greek, not Urdu or Swahili. For this reason, we have had to view the language acquisition task as a complex interaction between the child's innate capacities and the social, cognitive, and specifically linguistic supports provided in the environment. Perhaps, in light of the efficiency and sure-handedness with which (as we saw) human babies accomplish this feat, you might feel disposed to buttonhole the next baby you meet in the street to compliment her for being born a human being.

# SUMMARY

1. Language has five major properties. It is *creative* or novel: All normal humans can say and understand sentences they have never heard before. It is *structured:* Only certain arrangements of linguistic elements (phonemes, words, and so forth) are allowed. It is *meaningful:* Each word or combination of words expresses a meaningful idea (or concept). It is *referential:* It relates to things, scenes, and events in the extralinguistic world. It is *interpersonal:* It enables us to communicate with more than one person at a time.

2. Languages are organized as a hierarchy of structures. The lowest-level units are *phonemes,* the sound elements of language. Each language uses somewhere between twelve and sixty phonemes and has specific arrangements of the phonemes it uses. Each language also has *morphemes,* which are the smallest language units that carry bits of meaning. There are *content morphemes,* which carry the bulk of meaning, and *function morphemes,* which carry the structure of the sentence. *Phrases* are groupings of morphemes that carry more complex meanings than single morphemes and words. Phrases are combined into *sentences* according to the principles of syntax. There are infinitely many phrases and sentences in a language.

3. Word and phrase meaning is not identical to word and phrase reference, for some expressions can refer to the same thing and yet have different meanings. The *definitional theory of meaning* holds that each word describes a bundle of more elementary semantic features. Each word is "defined" as some small set of features that are individually necessary and jointly sufficient to pick out that word from all other words in the language. The *prototype theory of meaning* responds to the fact that it is hard to find necessary and sufficient definitions for all words. The most widely held theory of word meaning today combines the definitional and prototype theories. The definitional part picks out properties that a concept must have. The prototype part concerns the most "typical" properties, the ones that most members of the concept share in common.

4. Human thought is in terms of whole *propositions,* consisting of a subject or topic, and a *predicate* (that which is said about the subject or topic). The linguistic expression of a proposition is a simple sentence, consisting of a *noun phrase* (representing the subject or topic) and a *verb phrase* (representing the predicate). Sentence structures are represented by hierarchical tree diagrams, which show the relations among the phrases and words that make up the full sentences.

5. Sentences have both a *surface structure,* which describes their structural parts (the phrases and words) and the order in which these are uttered in speech, and an *underlying structure,* which describes their meaning. The underlying structure consists of the sentence as interpreted into a proposition containing *doer, act,* and *done-to,* and various *attitudes* to this proposition, such as negative, doer focus, and question.

6. Sentence relations can be described according to various properties of surface and underlying structure. Two sentences that are the same in surface structure but different in underlying structure are *ambiguous.* Two sentences that are the same in underlying structure but different in surface structure are *paraphrases.*

7. Listeners hear only surface structure but, to comprehend, must recover the underlying structure. The psychological machinery in people's heads that accomplishes comprehension is called the *Sentence Analyzing Machinery,* or *SAM.*

8. Language learning is more than skill acquisition, for the learning cannot be fully described as a habit acquired through imitation and reinforcement since children come to know more than they ever could have heard.

9. Infants are responsive to linguistic simulation almost from birth. For instance, they have been shown to be responsive to differences among just about all the phonemes used in the various languages of the world. Learning a specific language's phoneme structure involves learning not to notice those distinctions not made in one's native language. Infants are especially responsive to a form of speech known as *Motherese*—talk used by parents—which is characterized by large variations in pitch and by pauses at phrase boundaries.

10. Most infants begin talking in *one-word sentences* at about one year of age and rapidly acquire a large vocabulary. They seem to have propositional ideas in mind, and some appreciation of syntactic structure, even at this early stage.

11. At about two years of age, children begin using rudimentary *two-word* or *telegraphic sentences* that contain content words but typically omit function morphemes and words. These first sentences are short because of the difficulty of planning complex speech events and perhaps because of their initial "preprogramming" concerning the design characteristics of human languages. Still, these short sentences have a good deal of structure.

12. Language learning takes place successfully in many radically different environments. It fails only if children are removed from all human company or violently isolated and abused. Even if one is deaf, one learns a language. In this case, the language will be a signed (visual-manual) language rather than a spoken (auditory-vocal) one.

13. Children isolated from opportunities to learn the language around them invent some of it for themselves. An example is deaf children not exposed to signed languages who invent pantomimic gestures for words and propositions.

14. In contrast to the cases of changed environmental conditions, which children of normal mentality generally overcome, are cases of changed conditions of mentality. When the brain is unusual or deficient, radical changes in language learning are seen.

15. An important case of a "changed brain" that learns a language is the second-language learner who is chronologically older than the usual first-language learner. The less mature brain and the mature brain appear to have different capacities. The finding is that the younger the second-language learner, the more likely he or she is to acquire the new language adequately.

16. Deaf children not exposed to signed languages present the opportunity to see whether age of exposure affects the learning of a *first* language. The age at which deaf children are first exposed to a signed language predicts their skill with this language, even if they are tested twenty or thirty years after they begin using one.

17. Because experimental evidence makes it clear that language learning is based on special properties of the young human brain, we should not expect to find that human language can be fully or even adequately learned by other higher animals such as chimpanzees and dolphins. Nevertheless, chimpanzees have been shown to have rather good word-learning capacities, though nowhere as good as those of a two-and-a-half-year-old human. They also seem to be able to think propositionally to some degree; that is, to think in terms of who-did-what-to-whom. There is little or no credible evidence, however, that chimpanzees can acquire even the rudiments of syntactic principles.

18. Summarizing all the evidence, language learning results from the interaction between a young human brain and various social, cognitive, and specifically linguistic supports provided in the environment. Language is perhaps the central cognitive property whose possession makes us "truly human." If aliens came from another planet but spoke like us, we would probably try to get to know them and understand them—rather than trying to herd them or milk them—even if they looked like cows.

# PART III

# Social Behavior

In the preceding chapters, we have asked what organisms do, what they want, and what they know. But thus far we have raised these questions in a somewhat limited context, for we have considered the organism as an isolated individual, abstracted from the social world in which it lives. For some psychological questions this approach may be perfectly valid. Robinson Crusoe's visual system was surely no different on his lonely island than back home in London. But many other aspects of behavior are impossible to describe by considering a single organism alone, without reference to its fellows. Consider a male parrot feeding a female in a courtship ritual, a monkey mother clasping her infant closer at a stranger's approach, two stags locking antlers during the rutting season, or the front runner of a band of wild hunting dogs cutting off a fleeing zebra's escape—all of these activities are social by definition. Courtship, sex, parental care, competition, and cooperation are not merely actions. They are interactions in which each participant's behavior is affected by the behavior of the others.

Social interactions are vital in the lives of most animals: after all, successful reproduction (that is, sex and parental care) is what survival is all about. In humans, the role of social factors is even more powerful than in animals, for our world is fashioned not only by our contemporaries but by generations preceding whose vast cultural heritage structures the very fabric of our lives. Most of our motives are social for they concern other people—the desire to be loved, to be accepted, to be esteemed, perhaps to excel, and in some cases, unhappily, to inflict pain and hurt. The all-importance of social factors extends even to motives that, on the face of it, seem to involve only the isolated organism, motives such as hunger, thirst, and temperature maintenance. These motives as such may pertain primarily to the individual, but the ways in which they are satisfied are enormously affected by the social context in which we live. We eat food that is raised by a complex agricultural technology based on millennia of human discovery, and we eat it, delicately, with knife and fork, according to the etiquette of a long-dead king. Even the isolated Robinson Crusoe was no exception. In Defoe's tale, Crusoe's survival depended upon a few items of valuable debris he managed to salvage from his sunken ship. Thus his existence was not truly solitary: he was still bound to a world of others—by a few nails, a hammer, and a plank or two. Robinson Crusoe was on an island, but even he was not an island entire to himself.

In the following chapters we will discuss these social factors in some detail, as they bear on our actions, motives, thoughts, and knowledge.

# CHAPTER 10

# The Biological Basis of Social Behavior

A classic question posed by philosophers is, "What is the basic social nature of man?" Are greed, competition, and hate (or, for that matter, charity, cooperation, and love) unalterable components of the human makeup, or can they be instilled or nullified by proper training? To answer these questions, we will have to consider not just humankind but some of its animal cousins as well.

## THE SOCIAL NATURE OF HUMANS AND ANIMALS

Are human beings so built that social interaction is an intrinsic part of their makeup? Or are they essentially solitary creatures who turn to others only because they need them for their own selfish purposes? The English social philosopher Thomas Hobbes (1588–1679) argued for the second of these alternatives. In his view, man is a self-centered brute who, left to his own devices, will seek his own gain regardless of the cost to others. Except for the civilizing constraints imposed by society, men would inevitably be in an eternal "war of all against all." According to Hobbes, this frightening "state of nature" is approximated during times of anarchy and civil war. These were conditions Hobbes knew all too well, for he lived during a time of violent upheavals in England when Stuart royalists battled Cromwell's Puritans, when commoners beheaded their king in a public square, and when pillage, burning, and looting were commonplace. In such a state of nature, man's life is a sorry lot. There are "no Arts; no Letters; no Society; and which is worst of all, continuall fear, and danger of violent death; And the life

**Thomas Hobbes** *(Painting by John Michael Wright; courtesy The Granger Collection)*

391

of man solitary, poore, nasty, brutish, and short" (Hobbes, 1651, p. 186). Hobbes argued that under the circumstances, men had no choice but to protect themselves against their own ugly natures. They did so by entering into a "social contract" to form a collective commonwealth, the State.

Hobbes's psychological starting points are simple enough: Man is by nature asocial and destructively rapacious. Society is a means to chain the brute within. Only when curbed by social fetters does man go beyond his animal nature, does he become truly human. Given this position, the various social motives that bind us to others (such as love and loyalty) presumably are imposed through culture and convention. They are learned, for they could not possibly be part of our intrinsic makeup.

## Natural Selection and Survival

During the nineteenth century, Hobbes's doctrine of inherent human aggression and depravity was garbed in the mantle of science. The Industrial Revolution seemed to give ample proof that life is indeed a Hobbesian battle of each against all, whether in the marketplace, in the sweatshops, or in the far-off colonies. Ruthless competition among men was regarded as just one facet of a more general struggle for existence that is waged among all living things. This harsh view of nature had gained great impetus at the start of the nineteenth century when Thomas Malthus announced his famous law of population growth. According to Malthus, human and animal populations grow by geometrical progression (for example, 1, 2, 4, 8, 16, . . .) while the food supply grows arithmetically (for example, 1, 2, 3, 4, 5, . . .). As a result, there is inevitable scarcity and a continual battle for survival.

When Charles Darwin (1809–1882) read Malthus's essay, he finally found the explanatory principle he had been seeking to account for the evolution of living things. He, as others before him, believed that all present-day plants, animals, and even humans, were descended from prior forms. The evidence came from various sources, such as fossil records that showed the gradual transformation from long-extinct species to those now living. But what had produced these changes? Within each species there are individual variations; some horses are faster, others are slower. Many of these variations are part of the animal's hereditary makeup and thus are bequeathed to its descendants. But will an individual animal have descendants? That depends on how it fares in the struggle for existence. As a matter of fact, most organisms don't live long enough to reproduce. Only a few seedlings grow up to be trees; only a few tadpoles achieve froghood. But certain characteristics may make survival a bit more likely. The faster horse is more likely to escape predatory cats than its slower fellow, and it is thus more likely to leave offspring who inherit his swiftness. This process of ***natural selection*** does not guarantee survival and reproduction; it only increases their likelihood. In consequence, evolutionary change is very gradual and proceeds over eons (Darwin, 1872a).

***Charles Darwin***   *(Painting by J. Collier; courtesy of The National Portrait Gallery, London)*

### PERSONAL AND GENETIC SURVIVAL

Natural selection leads to the "survival of the fittest." But just what does it mean to be fit? Thus far, our examples of better "fitness" involved attributes that make

*Genetic survival*  The peacock's long tail feathers are a cumbersome burden that may decrease his chances of escaping predators and thus his own personal survival. But this is more than offset by his increased chances in attracting a sexual partner, thereby assuring survival of his genes. (Photograph by G. K. Brown, Ardea London Ltd.)

*A woven nest*  Many animals have genetically determined behavior patterns characteristic of their species. An example is nest weaving in the thick-billed African weaverbird. (Photo courtesy of Brian M. Rogers/Biofotos)

*personal survival* more likely: the faster horse, the more ferocious cat, and so on. But personal survival as such is not what the evolutionary game is about. The trick is to have reproductive success—to have offspring who will pass your genes along. A horse that manages to live two or three times longer than any of its fellows but that for some reason or another stays celibate has not survived in an evolutionary sense. Personal survival (at least until sexual maturity) is a prerequisite for *genetic survival,* but it alone is not enough.

Seen in this light, it's clear that "fitness" is determined by all characteristics that enhance reproductive success, whether or not such characteristics contribute to the individual's own personal survival. Consider the magnificent tail feathers of the peacock. His long, cumbersome tail may somewhat *decrease* his chance to escape predators, but it hugely contributes to his evolutionary fitness. The peacock has to compete with his fellow males for access to the peahen; the larger and more magnificent his tail, the more likely will she respond to his sexual overtures. From an evolutionary point of view, the potential gain was evidently greater than the possible loss; as a result, long tail feathers were selected for. Much the same holds for many other characteristics that are of advantage in sexual competition. This is especially so among males (for reasons we'll discuss later on, see p. 408). Some of these characteristics are rather general, such as strength and aggressiveness. Others, such as the brightly colored plumage of many male birds and the large antlers of the stag, are more specialized. But whatever the particulars of a given attribute, its contribution to the animal's fitness is the extent to which it leads to reproductive success.

### INHERITED PREDISPOSITIONS TO BEHAVIOR

The inherited characteristics that increase the chance for biological survival (that is, reproduction) may concern bodily structures such as the horse's hooves or the stag's antlers. But Darwin and his successors pointed out that natural selection may also involve behavior. Squirrels bury nuts and beavers construct dams; these behavior patterns are characteristic of the species and depend on the animals' **genes,** the basic units of heredity. Whether these genes are selected for or not depends upon the **adaptive value** (that is, the biological survival value) of the behavior they give rise to. A squirrel who has a genetic predisposition to bury nuts in autumn is presumably more likely to survive the winter than one who doesn't. As a result, it is more likely to have offspring who will inherit the nut-burying gene (or genes). The end product is an increase in the number of nut-burying squirrels.

Granted that behavior can be shaped by evolution, what kind of behavior is most likely to evolve? And, most important to us, what kind of built-in predispositions are most likely to characterize humankind? Many nineteenth-century thinkers answered in Hobbesian terms. They reasoned that man is an animal and that in the bitter struggle for existence all animals are shameless egoists by sheer necessity. At bottom, they are all solitary and selfish, and man is no exception. To the extent that humans act sociably and on occasion even unselfishly—mating, rearing children, living and working with others—they have learned to do so in order to satisfy some self-centered motive such as lust or hunger.

On the face of it, this Hobbesian view seems to fit evolutionary doctrine. But on closer examination, Darwinian theory does not imply anything of the sort. It holds that there is "survival of the fittest," but "fittest" only means most likely to survive and to have offspring; it says nothing about being solitary or selfish. Dar-

**Konrad Lorenz**   *(Photograph by Nina Leen)*

**Niko Tinbergen**   *(Photograph by Nina Leen)*

win himself supposed that certain predispositions toward cooperation might well be adaptive and would thus be selected for. We now know that something of this sort is true, for animals as well as human beings. As we shall see, there is considerable evidence that, Hobbes to the contrary, humans and animals are by nature social rather than asocial and that much of their social behavior grows out of natively given predispositions rather than running counter to them.

## Built-in Social Behaviors

Most systematic studies of built-in social behavior have been conducted within the domain of ***ethology,*** a branch of biology that studies animal behavior under natural conditions. Led by the Europeans Konrad Lorenz and Niko Tinbergen, both Nobel Prize winners, ethologists have analyzed many behavior patterns that are characteristic of a particular species and seem to be primarily built-in or instinctive. Many of these instinctive, ***species-specific*** behavior patterns are social; they dictate the way in which creatures interact with others of their own kind. Some involve a positive bond between certain members of the same species—courtship, copulation, care of the young. Others concern reactions of antagonism and strife—the struggle for social dominance, competition for a mate, and dispute over territory.

### FIXED-ACTION PATTERNS

The early ethologists believed that many species-specific social reactions are based on genetically pre-programmed ***fixed-action patterns,*** which in turn are elicited by genetically pre-programmed ***releasing stimuli.*** An example of such a fixed-action pattern is the begging response of newly hatched herring gulls. They beg for food by pecking at the tips of their parents' beaks. The parent will then regurgitate some food from its crop and feed it to the young. What is the critical stimulus that "releases" the chick's begging pecks? To find out, Tinbergen offered newly hatched gull chicks various cardboard models of gull heads and observed which ones they pecked at the most. The most successful model was one that was long and thin and had a red patch at its tip (see Figure 10.1). These are the very characteristics of an adult herring gull's beak, but the newly hatched chick has never encountered a parent's beak previously. Tinbergen concluded that evolution had done a good job in pre-programming the chick to respond to certain stimulus features so as to recognize the parent's beak at first sight (Tinbergen, 1951).

More recent studies suggest that the relation between releasing stimuli and species-specific fixed-action patterns is not quite as rigidly fixed and prewired as Tinbergen's account suggests. For it appears that the baby gulls' begging response is partially shaped by experience. Right after hatching, the chicks peck at any red spot that moves horizontally across their field of vision, whether it is attached to a gull's head or not. But after two days in the nest with their parents, they peck only when confronted with a proper herring gull's beak. This suggests that the genes provide a crude first outline, as Tinbergen's work suggested. But then the chick's own experience must refine and build upon this outline (Hailman, 1967).

Many releasing stimuli are produced by an animal's own behavior. An important example of such response-produced stimulus releasers are ***displays.*** Displays produce an appropriate reaction in another animal of the same species and are

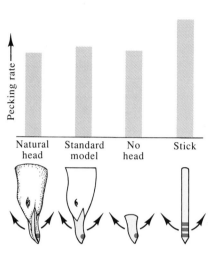

**10.1 Stimulus releasers for pecking**
*The figure indicates the pecking rate of a herring gull chick when presented with various models. As the figure indicates, a flat cardboard model is a bit more effective than a real head and a disembodied bill works almost as well. Best of all was a stick with spots on it moving back and forth horizontally. (Adapted from Keeton and Gould, 1986, p. 558)*

**10.2 Defending the nest** *A small Australian bird, the willie wagtail, attacks a bird of prey, the kookaburra, who has come too close to its nest. (Photograph by Jen and Des Bartlett/Bruce Coleman)*

thus the basis of a primitive, innate communication system. The gull chick's begging peck is an elementary signal whose meaning is genetically given to both chick and parent: "Feed me! Feed me now!" (Tinbergen, 1951).

THE SOCIOBIOLOGICAL APPROACH

The analysis of chick pecking we have just discussed concentrated on the causes of behavior that are in the organism's own past (often the immediately preceding past): the particular stimuli that elicit the behavior, the physiological mechanisms that underlie it, and the developmental factors (such as learning) that help to shape it further. But there is another level of causation that precedes the particular organism's own past by countless generations: the animal's own evolutionary history, which created the built-in bias toward that behavior through natural selection. In the last twenty years, a new branch of biology called *sociobiology* has arisen that focuses on these long-past causes with particular reference to the evolutionary basis of various *social* behaviors (Wilson, 1975). Most behavioral scientists agree that sociobiology has provided valuable insights about social behavior in animals. What is much more controversial is the sociobiologists' contention that similar analyses can be applied to human social patterns, a topic to which we turn in a later section (see pp. 409–10, 421–22).

## BIOLOGICAL SOURCES OF AGGRESSION

We will begin our discussion of built-in social patterns by considering the biological basis of aggression. In humans, some of the causes of aggression are events in the immediate present, such as threats and frustrations that provoke anger and hostility. Other causes stem from the individual's own past and prior learning. Our present concern is with sources that lie in our inherent makeup, the biological roots of aggression that derive from our evolutionary past. To uncover these, we have to study animals as well as humans, for the biological sources of human aggression are often obscured by cultural factors and tradition.

### Conflict between Species: Predation and Defense

Most psychobiologists restrict use of the term **aggression** to conflict between members of the same species. When an owl kills a mouse, it has slaughtered for food rather than murdered in hatred. As Lorenz points out, the predator about to pounce upon his prey does not look angry; the dog who is on the verge of catching a rabbit never growls nor does it have its ears laid back (Lorenz, 1966). Neurological evidence leads to a similar conclusion. Rat-stalking (predatory attack) and arched-back hissing (aggression or self-defense) are elicited by the stimulation of two different areas of a cat's hypothalamus (Wasman and Flynn, 1962). Predatory attack is an outgrowth of the hunger motive and not of aggression; the hypothalamic site whose stimulation gives rise to rat-stalking also elicits eating (Hutchinson and Renfrew, 1966).

Somewhat closer to true aggression is the counterattack lodged by a prey animal against a predatory enemy (see Figure 10.2). Flocks of birds sometimes **mob** an intruding cat or hawk. A colony of lovebird parrots will fly upon a would-be attacker in a body, flapping their wings furiously and uttering loud, shrill squeaks. In the face of this commotion, the predator often withdraws to look for a less troublesome meal (Dilger, 1962). Defense reactions may also occur when a hunted animal is finally cut off from retreat. Even normally reticent creatures may then become desperate fighters, as in the case of the proverbial cornered rat.

Aside from these defense behaviors, aggression is the exception rather than the rule among members of different species. In an aquarium filled with tropical fish, like attacks like but leaves unlike alone. Vicious fights between unrelated species such as tigers and pythons have been photographed for wildlife films, but they are rare; the animals involved are either half-starved or they are goaded into the un-natural contest by having their escape route blocked (Lorenz, 1966).

## Conflict between Like and Like

There is probably no group among the animal kingdom that has foresworn aggression altogether; fighting has been observed in virtually all species. Fish chase and nip each other; lizards lunge and push; birds attack with wing, beak, and claw; sheep and cows butt heads; deer lock antlers; rats adopt a boxing stance and eye each other warily, until one finally pounces upon the other and begins a furious wrestling match with much kicking and leaping and occasionally serious bites (see Figure 10.3).

Among vertebrates, the male is generally the more aggressive sex. In some mammals, this difference in combativeness is apparent even in childhood play. Young male rhesus monkeys, for instance, engage in more vigorous rough-and-tumble tusslings than do their sisters (Harlow, 1962). A related result concerns the effect of **testosterone,** a male sex hormone. High testosterone levels in the bloodstream accompany increased aggressiveness in males; the reverse holds for decreased levels. This generalization seems to hold over a wide range of species including fish, lizards, turtles, birds, rats and mice, monkeys, and human males (Davis, 1964).

### SECURING RESOURCES

What do animals fight about? Their struggles are about scarce **resources**—something valuable in their world that is in short supply. Such a resource may be a food source or a water hole; very often it is a mate. To secure a modicum of such resources many animals stake out a claim to a particular region which they will then defend as their exclusive preserve, their private **territory.**

An example is provided by male songbirds. In the spring, they endlessly patrol their little empires and furiously repel all male intruders who violate their borders. Contrary to the poet's fancy, the male bird who bursts into full-throated song is not giving vent to inexpressible joy, pouring out his "full heart in profuse strains of unpremeditated art." His message is more prosaic. It is a warning to male trespassers and an invitation to unattached females: "Have territory, will share."

A biological benefit of territoriality is that it secures an adequate supply of resources for the next generation. The songbird who chases his rivals away will probably leave more offspring than the one who doesn't, for his progeny will have

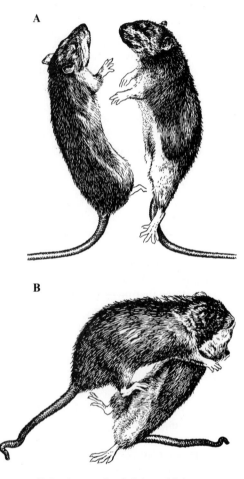

**10.3 Aggressive fighting** *Male rats generally fight in fairly stereotyped ways, including (A) a "boxing position" that often escalates into (B) a leaping, biting attack. (From Barnett, 1963)*

**Aggressive encounter between male bighorn rams**  *(Courtesy Stouffer Productions, Animals Animals)*

**Bull seal threatening an intruder** *(Photograph by Robert W. Hernández/ Photo Researchers)*

a better start in life. Once his claim is staked out he can entice the female, offering his territory as a kind of dowry.

A side effect of territoriality is that it often serves to keep aggression within bounds. Good fences make good neighbors, at least in the sense that they keep the antagonists out of each others' hair (or fins or feathers).

One mechanism whereby territoriality limits combat is rather simple. Once a territory is established, its owner has a kind of home-court advantage in further disputes (Krebs, 1982). On his home ground he is courageous; if he ventures beyond it, he becomes timid and is readily repulsed. As a result, there are few actual conflicts other than occasional border skirmishes. This behavior pattern is utilized by circus trainers who make sure that they are the first to enter the training ring and that the animals come in later. As a result, the ring becomes the trainer's territory and even the great cats are more readily cowed (Hediger, 1968).

LIMITING AGGRESSION

A certain amount of aggression may be biologically adaptive. This is especially so for males who compete for access to females. For example, a more aggressive songbird will conquer a larger and more desirable territory, which will help him attract a mate. In addition, his territory confers further advantages such as more seeds or more worms, which further help his progeny who will get more and better food in their early days as nestlings. As a result, we would expect some selection for aggressiveness. But this holds only up to a point, for while aggression may confer some benefits, it also has its costs. Combat is dangerous and can lead to death or serious injury. In addition, it distracts the animal from other vital pursuits. The male who is continually fighting with his sexual rivals will have little time (let alone energy) left to mate with the female after his competitors have fled. Under the circumstances, natural selection strikes a compromise; there is aggression, but a number of factors keep it firmly in hand.

One way of avoiding catastrophic damage to life and limb is to assess the strength of the enemy. If he seems much stronger (or more agile, or better armed) than oneself, the best bet is to proclaim a cease-fire and concede defeat, or better yet, never to start the battle altogether. Many male animals behave just that way. An example is provided by red deer stags who compete with each other for fe-

**10.4   Ritualized fighting**   *Two South African wildebeest males in a harmless ritualized dual along an invisible but clearly defined mutual border between their territories. (Photograph by Lennard Lee Rue III/Bruce Coleman)*

**10.5   Threat displays**   *(A) Some species threaten by making themselves appear larger and more impressive, as when lizards expand their throat skin fold. (Photograph by Joseph T. Collins/Photo Researchers) (B) Other species threaten by shouting at the top of their lungs, like the howler monkeys, who scream at each other for hours on end. (Photograph by Wolfgang Bayer/Bruce Coleman)*

males. In the autumn, stags who hold a harem are challenged by other stags. In the first stage of this contest, the harem owner and the challenger roar at each other, sometimes for days on end. If the harem owner can keep on roaring longer and louder, the intruder will generally back off—a reasonable decision, since a stronger roar is most likely produced by a stronger stag (Krebs and Davies, 1987). Similar strategies for avoiding the costs of a bloody defeat are found in many species of sheep and deer whose males engage in a ritualized form of combat as if under an internal compulsion not to inflict serious wounds (see Figure 10.4).

The limitation on violence appears in other ways as well. Many conflicts are settled by blustering diplomacy before they erupt into actual war. For example, male chimpanzees try to intimidate each other by staring, raising an arm, or uttering fearsome shouts. This approach is found throughout the entire animal kingdom: Whenever possible, try to get your way by threat or bluff rather than by actual fighting. This holds even for creatures as large as elephants and as fierce as tigers. Both these and other creatures make use of **threat displays,** a much less costly method for achieving one's aim than actual combat (see Figure 10.5).

In some cases, serious fighting will occur even so, for animals no less than human generals may miscalculate their chances of victory. But some ways of limiting the cost of defeat still remain. In wolves, the loser may "admit defeat" by

A

B

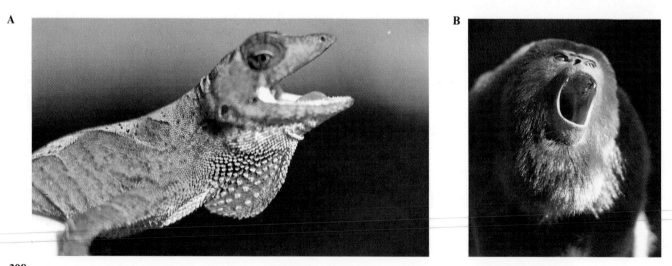

adopting a special submissive gesture, such as begging like a puppy or rolling on his back. This an *appeasement display* that is functionally equivalent to our white flag of surrender. Unlike some human warriors, the victorious wolf is without rancor. He generally accepts the loser's submission, and all fighting stops (Lorenz, 1966). The adaptive value of such submissive signals is clear enough. They allow today's loser to withdraw from the field of battle so that he can come back in a year or two when he is older, wiser, and when he may very well win a rematch. The evolutionary rule is simple enough: Don't fight unless the probable gains (in reproductive success) outweigh the costs. If you lose and run away (or make an appeasement display), you may live to fight (and copulate) another day.

DOMINANCE AND SUBMISSION

Animals that live in groups often develop a social order based on *dominance hierarchies.* Such hierarchies can be quite complex among troops of primates. For example, in baboons, the dominant male has usually achieved his status through victory in several aggressive encounters. After this, his status is settled for a while, and lower-ranking baboons generally step aside to let the "alpha male" pass, and nervously scatter if he merely stares at them.

In the early days of ethology, many investigators saw such hierarchies as a way of lessening aggression. In their view, once a hierarchy was formed, it was fairly stable. As a result, everyone "knew his place," thus minimizing combat and friction for the good of all (e.g., Lorenz, 1966). This view has been seriously challenged. To begin with, it is difficult to believe that baboons or rhesus monkeys have somehow entered into a Hobbesian social contract, as if they knew what was good for the group as a whole (or that they cared). Nor do such hierarchies abolish all internal friction. Much of an alpha male's life is spent in efforts to maintain his place at the top—harassing his subordinates, approaching them until they back away, staring at them until they look down, and if necessary, attacking them with teeth and nails. In these endeavors, the alpha male often depends on alliances with other males (often his own brothers) who will join him to fight off his rivals and who in turn are supported by him in their future aggressive encounters (Walters and Seyfarth, 1986; see Figure 10.6A).

Why should the animals spend so much time to achieve and maintain dominance? The answer is that rank has considerable privileges. The alpha male has first choice of sleeping site, enjoys easier access to food, and has priority in mating (see Figure 10.6B). Such perquisites undoubtedly make life more pleasant for

*10.6   Dominance hierarchies*   (A) The two baboons at the right jointly threaten the larger baboon on the left who could defeat either of them alone but won't risk fighting them both. (Courtesy L. T. Nash, Arizona State University) (B) A dominant male baboon with a harem of females and young. (Courtesy of Bruce Coleman)

A

B

the alpha male than for his less-fortunate fellows. But even more important may be the long-run evolutionary value of rank, for in terms of genetic survival, the higher-ranking animal is more "fit." Since he has easier access to females, he will presumably leave more offspring (Smith, 1981; Silk, 1986).

Thus far, our primary focus has been on dominance relations among primate males. This followed the initial emphasis of investigators in this area who focused on male-male aggression. To be sure, the males' aggressive encounters are quite obvious, as they fight and strut and bellow. Many authors took this as evidence that the social order among most primates (and by implication, our own) was ultimately based on the political struggles among males. But recent research shows that this conclusion is far off the mark. For in many primate societies, females compete no less than males and develop hierarchies that are often more stable than those of males. Moreover, female rank has important long-term consequences, for mothers tend to bequeath their social rank to their offspring, especially to their daughters (Hrdy and Williams, 1983; Walters and Seyfarth, 1986).

### TERRITORIALITY IN HUMANS

Is any of the preceding discussion of animals relevant to human behavior? At least on the surface there are parallels that have led some writers to suppose that concepts such as territoriality, dominance hierarchy, and the like, apply to humans as well as to animals. There are certainly some aspects of human behavior that resemble territoriality. Even within the home, different members of a family have their private preserves—their own rooms or corners, their places at the dinner table, and so on. Other territorial claims are more temporary, such as a seat in a railroad car, whose possession we mark with a coat, a book, or a briefcase if we have to leave for a while.

A related phenomenon is ***personal space,*** the physical region all around us whose intrusion we guard against. On many New York subways, passengers sit on long benches. Except during rush hour, they will carefully choose their seats so as to leave the greatest possible distance between themselves and their nearest neighbor (Figure 10.7).

In one study, personal space was deliberately violated. Experimenters went to a library and casually sat next to a person studying there, even though a more distant chair was available. After some fidgeting, the victim tried to move away. If

*10.7 Personal space (A) Relatively even spacing in ring-billed gulls (Photograph by Allan D. Cruikshank © 1978/ Photo Researchers) (B) Some ethologists believe that the maintenance of personal space in humans is a related phenomenon. Vacationers at a beach on the Baltic Sea in Germany keep a precise distance between each couple or family unit. (Photograph by J. Messerschmidt/Bruce Coleman)*

A

B

this was impossible, books and rulers were neatly arranged so as to create a physical boundary (Felipe and Sommer, 1966). A desire to maintain some minimum personal space is probably nearly universal, but the physical dimensions seem to depend upon the particular culture. In North America, acquaintances stand about two or three feet apart during a conversation; if one moves closer, the other feels crowded or pushed into an unwanted intimacy. For Latin Americans, the acceptable distance is said to be much less. Under the circumstances, misunderstanding is almost inevitable. The North American regards the Latin American as overly intrusive; the Latin American in turn feels that the North American is unfriendly and cold (Hall, 1959).

How seriously should we take such parallels between humans and animals? There is no doubt that many people—though not all—care deeply about private ownership, whether of things, of real estate, or more subtle private preserves. The question is whether this concern stems from the same evolutionary roots as does the territoriality of the songbird, whether humans really respond to a built-in "territorial imperative" that, according to some writers, is part of our genetic ancestry and cannot be disobeyed (Ardrey, 1966).

The best guess is that while the overt behaviors may sometimes be similar, the underlying mechanisms are not. Territoriality in robins is universal and innately based; but in humans it is enormously affected by learning. For example, there are some societies in which private ownership is relatively unimportant, which certainly suggests that cultural factors play a vital role.

## THE BIOLOGICAL BASIS OF LOVE: THE MALE-FEMALE BOND

The preceding discussion has made it clear that there is some biological foundation for strife and conflict. The tendencies toward destruction are kept in bounds by a set of counteracting tendencies such as territoriality and ritualized fighting. As we shall see, they are also controlled and modified by learning, especially during childhood in humans, and their expression is greatly affected by situational factors (see Chapters 12 and 15).

But over and above these various inhibiting checks on aggression, there is a positive force that is just as basic and deeply rooted in the biological makeup of animals and humans. The poets call it love. Scientists use the more prosaic term *bonding*, the tendency to affiliate with others of one's own kind.

The forces of social attraction are most obvious between mate and mate, and between child and parent. But positive bonds occur even outside of mating and child care. Examples are the social relationships cemented by *grooming* in monkeys and apes who sit in pairs while the groomer meticulously picks lice and other vermin out of the groomee's fur (Figure 10.8). The animals evidently like to groom and be groomed over and above considerations of personal hygiene; it is their way of forming a social bond, and it works. Grooming occurs most commonly among kin (brothers and sisters, cousins, and so on), although it may also occur among unrelated animals. But whether they be kin or unrelated, animals who groom most often are also the most closely bonded by other measures of primate togetherness: They sit together, forage for food together, and stick together in alliances against common antagonists (Walters and Seyfarth, 1986).

*10.8   Grooming in baboons   (Photograph by Mitch Reardon/Photo Researchers)*

It has sometimes been suggested that a comparable human practice is small talk, in which we exchange no real information but simply talk for the sake of "relating" to the other person. Other people are part of our universe, and we need them and want their company. Much the same is probably true for our primate cousins. They groom each other, whether or not they have vermin. We talk to each other, whether or not we really have something to say.

## Sexual Behavior

In some very primitive organisms, reproduction is asexual; thus amoebas multiply by a process of simple cell division. This form of procreation seems to work well enough, for amoebas are still among us. It appears that contrary to one's first impression, sex is *not* necessary (at least, not for reproduction). But if so, why do the vast majority of animal species reproduce sexually? Perhaps sexual reproduction is more enjoyable than the asexual varieties, but its biological advantage lies elsewhere. It comes from the fact that it assures a greater degree of genetic variability.

An amoeba that splits into two has created two replicas of its former self. Here natural selection has no differences to choose between, for the second amoeba can be neither better nor worse in its adaptation to the environment than the first since the two are genetically identical.

Things are quite different in sexual reproduction. Here specialized cells, *sperm* and *ovum,* must join to form a fertilized egg, or *zygote,* which will then become a new individual. This procedure amounts to a kind of genetic roulette. To begin with, each parent donates only half of the genetic material: Within some limits, it is then mere chance that determines which genes are contained in any one sperm or ovum. Chance enters again to determine which sperm will join with which ovum. As a result, there will be inevitable differences among the offspring. Now natural selection can come into play, perhaps favoring the offspring with the sharper teeth, or the one with the more sexually attractive display, which will then enhance the survival of the gene that produced these attributes.

## Sexual Choice

For sexual reproduction to occur, sperm and ovum have to meet in the appointed manner, at the proper time, and in the proper place. Many structures and behavior patterns have evolved to accomplish these ends. Our first concern is with those that underlie sexual choice and determine who mates with whom.

### ADVERTISING ONE'S SEX

The first job of a would-be sexual partner is to proclaim his or her sex. Many animals have anatomical structures whose function is precisely that; for example, the magnificent tail feathers of the male peacock or the comb and wattle of the rooster (see Figure 10.9). These structures are often crucial for appropriate mating behavior. In one species of woodpecker, the male has a moustache of black feathers while the female does not. An unkind ethologist trapped a female and attached a moustache. When she later flew back to her nest, her mate attacked her

*10.9 Advertising one's sex* The comb and wattle of this barred rock rooster proclaim that he is a male. (Photograph by Garry D. McMichael, 1987/Photo Researchers)

mercilessly, presumably under the impression that he was warding off an intruding male (Etkin, 1964).

In humans, structural displays of sex differences are less pronounced, but they are present nonetheless. A possible example is the enlarged female breast whose adipose tissue does not really increase the infant's milk supply. According to some ethologists, it evolved as we became erect and lost our reliance upon smell, a sense which provides the primary information about sex and sexual readiness in many mammals. Under the circumstances, there had to be other ways of displaying one's sex. The prominent breasts of the female may be one such announcement among hairless, "naked apes" (Morris, 1967).

COURTSHIP RITUALS

*Advertising one's intentions* In many animals, sexual display involves various species-specific behavior patterns, called **courtship rituals.** These are essentially ways of advertising one's amorous intentions. Some of these rituals are mainly a means to exhibit the structural sex differences, as in the male peacock spreading his tail feathers. Others are much more elaborate. Thus penguins bow deeply to each other while rocking from side to side, and certain grebes complete an elaborate aquatic ballet by exchanging gifts of seaweed (Figure 10.10).

In some species, courtship rituals may also involve alternating bouts of approach and withdrawal, of coy retreat and seductive flirtation. What accounts for these apparent oscillations between yes and no? There is an underlying conflict between attraction and fear; neither animal can really be sure that the other is not hostile. Each must therefore inform the other that its intentions are not aggressive. This is especially true of the male, who in many species performs various appeasement rituals that allay the female's fears.

*Indicating one's species* Courtship rituals have a further function. They not only increase the likelihood that boy meets girl, but they virtually guarantee that the two will be of the same species. This is because these rituals are so highly species-specific, as in the case of the gift-exchanging grebes. In effect they are a code, whereby each member of the pair informs the other that he belongs, say, to the duck species *anas platyrhynochos,* rather than to *bucephala clangula* or *tachyeres patachonicus,* or some other duck species that no self-respecting *anas platyrhynochos* would want to mate with. The effect of such species-specific courtship codes

**10.10 Courtship rituals** *(A) The male bower bird tries to entice the female into an elaborate bower decorated with berries, shells, or whatever else may be available, such as colored clothespins. (B) Grebes engage in a complex aquatic ballet. (C) The male tern courts by feeding the female. (Photographs from left to right by Philip Green; Bob and Clara Calhoun/Bruce Coleman; Jeff Foott/Bruce Coleman)*

A

B

C

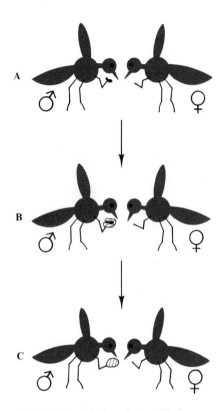

**10.11  The evolution of courtship in dancing flies**  *(A) In some species, the male catches a prey animal and gives it to the female to eat during copulation; this keeps her busy so she is less likely to eat him. (B) In other species, the male first wraps the prey in a balloon of secreted silk. This keeps the female even busier since she has to unwrap the prey. (C) Finally, in the dancing fly, the male gives the female a ball of silk without anything in it. (After Klopfer, 1974)*

is that they make it more likely that the mating will produce fertile offspring. For contrary to popular view, different species can interbreed if they are related closely enough. But the offspring of such "unnatural" unions is often infertile; an example is the mule, a result of crossing a horse with a donkey. Species-specific courtship rituals have evolved to avoid such reproductive failures.

*The evolutionary origin of courtship rituals*  We've discussed the general function of courtship rituals, but what can we say about the evolutionary history of a particular ritual or display? Displays leave no fossils so there is no direct method for reconstructing their biological past. One possible approach is to compare displays in related species. By noting their similarities and differences, the ethologist tries to reconstruct the evolutionary steps in their history, much as a comparative anatomist charts the family tree of fins, wings, and forelegs.

An example of how this comparative method works when applied to species-specific behaviors is an analysis of an odd courtship ritual in a predatory insect, the dancing fly (Kessel, 1955). At mating time, the male dancing fly secretes a little ball of silk which he brings to the female. She plays with this silk ball while the male mounts her and copulates. How did this ritual arise? The courtship patterns in a number of related species give a clue. Most flies of related species manage with a minimum of precopulatory fuss; the trouble is that the female may decide to eat the male rather than mate with him. However, if she is already eating a small prey animal, the male is safe. Some species have evolved a behavior pattern that capitalizes on this fact. The male catches a small insect and brings it to the female for her to eat while he mates with her. In still other species, the male first wraps the prey in a large silk balloon. This increases his margin of safety, for the female is kept busy unwrapping her present. The dancing fly's ritual is probably the last step in this evolutionary sequence. The male dancing fly wastes no time or energy in catching a prey animal, but simply brings an empty ball of silk, all wrapping and no present. Copulation can now proceed unimpeded since the female is safely occupied—perhaps the first creature in evolutionary history to realize that it is the thought and not the gift that matters (Figure 10.11).

WHO MAKES THE CHOICE

The preceding discussions have centered on the various factors that bring male and female together. But, interestingly enough, the two don't have an equal voice in the ultimate decision. In most species, the female finally decides whether or not to mate. The biological reason is simple—the female shoulders the major cost of reproduction. If she is a bird, she supplies not only the ovum but also the food supply for the developing embryo. If she is a mammal, she carries the embryo within her body and later provides it with milk. In either case, her biological burden is vastly greater than the male's. If a doe's offspring fails to survive, she has lost a whole breeding season. In comparison, the stag's loss is minimal—a few minutes of his time and some easily replaced sperm cells. Under the circumstances, natural selection would favor the female who is particularly choosy about picking the best possible male; that is, the male whose genetic contribution will best ensure their offsprings' survival. From the male's point of view, the female seems coy or "plays hard to get." But in fact this is not just playacting for, to the female, reproduction is a serious business with heavy biological costs (Trivers, 1972).

There are a few interesting exceptions. One example is the sea horse, whose young are carried in a brood pouch by the male. In this animal, the male exhibits greater sexual caution and discrimination than the female. A similar effect is found in the phalarope, an arctic seabird whose eggs are hatched and whose chicks are fed by the male (Figure 10.12). Here a greater part of the biological burden falls on the male, and we should expect a corresponding increase in his sexual choosiness. This is just what happens. Among the phalaropes, the female does the wooing. She is brightly plumaged, and aggressively pursues the dull-colored, coyly careful male (Williams, 1966).

## Reproduction and Timing

Once male and female have met, the next step is to arrange for the union of their respective sperm and ovum. Terrestrial animals have evolved a variety of sexual mechanics to accomplish this end. In general, the male introduces his sperm cells into the genital tract of the female, where the ovum is fertilized. The problem is synchronization. The sperm has to encounter a ready ovum, and the fertilized egg can develop only if it is provided with the appropriate conditions. Under these circumstances, timing is of the essence. In birds and mammals, the timing mechanism depends on a complex feedback system between brain centers and hormones.

### ANIMAL SEXUALITY AND HORMONES

*Hormonal cycles*   Except for the primates, mammals mate only when the female is in heat, or *estrus.* For example, the female rat goes through a fifteen-hour estrus period every four days. At all other times, she will resolutely reject any male's advances. If he nuzzles her or tries to mount, she will kick and bite. But during estrus, the female responds quite differently to the male's approach. She first retreats in small hops, then stops to look back, and wiggles her ears provocatively (McClintock and Adler, 1978). Eventually, she stands still, her back arched, her tail held to the side, in all respects a willing sexual partner.

What accounts for the difference between the female's behavior during estrus and at other times? The crucial fact is a simple matter of reproductive biology. The time of estrus is precisely the time when the female's ova are ripe for fertilization. Evolution has obviously provided a behavioral arrangement that is exactly tuned to reproductive success.

The mechanism is an interlocking system of hormonal and neurological controls that involves the pituitary gland, the hypothalamus, and the ovaries. In effect, there are three phases: (1) During the first, follicles in the ovary mature under the influence of pituitary secretions. The follicles produce the female sex hormone *estrogen.* As the concentration of estrogen in the bloodstream rises, the hypothalamus responds by directing the pituitary to change its secretions. In consequence, follicle growth is accelerated until the follicle ruptures and releases the mature ovum. (2) This triggers the second phase during which the animal is in estrus. Estrogen production climbs to a steep maximum and stimulates certain structures in the hypothalamus which make the animal sexually receptive. (3) The third phase is dominated by the action of another female sex hormone, *progesterone,* which is produced by the ruptured follicle. Its secretion leads to a thick-

**10.12   Plumage pattern in the male and female phalarope**   *The phalarope male hatches and feeds the chicks. Since he carries a larger share of the biological cost of reproduction, he is more coy and choosy than the female. As the drawing indicates schematically, the female phalarope (bottom) is larger and more colorfully plumaged than the male (top). (Hohn, 1969)*

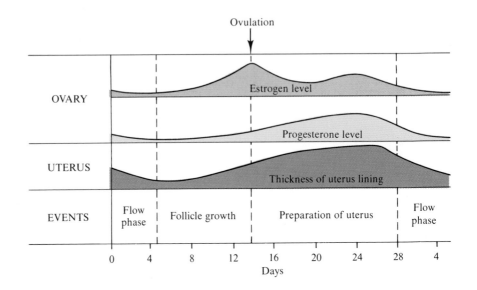

**10.13   The main stages of the human menstrual cycle**   *The figure shows estrogen and progesterone levels and thickness of the uterus lining during the human menstrual cycle. The cycle begins with the growth of a follicle, continues through ovulation and a maximum estrogen level, is followed by a phase during which the uterus becomes prepared to receive the embryo, and ends with a flow phase during which the thickened uterus lining is sloughed off. (After Keeton, 1980)*

ening of the uterus lining, a first step in preparing the uterus to receive the embryo. If the ovum is fertilized, there are further steps in building an appropriate womb. If it is not, the thickened uterus walls are reabsorbed and another cycle begins. In humans and some primates, too much extra tissue is laid on to be easily reabsorbed; the thickened uterus lining is therefore sloughed off as ***menstrual flow*** (Figure 10.13).

*Hormonal changes and behavior*   Some hormonal changes affect behavior dramatically. When male rats are castrated, they soon lose all sexual interest and capacity, as do female rats without ovaries. But sexual behavior is quickly restored by appropriate injections of male or female hormones, specifically testosterone and estrogen.

Many investigators believe that behavioral effects of hormones are caused by neurons in the hypothalamus that contain receptors with which certain hormone molecules from the bloodstream combine. When this occurs, it leads to neural changes in the hypothalamus that trigger sexual appetite and behavior. This hypothesis has been tested by injecting minute quantities of various hormones into several regions of the hypothalamus. The total amounts were negligible and could hardly affect the overall hormone concentration in the blood. Will the hypothalamic sexual control system be fooled by the local administration of the hormone, as is its thermostatic counterpart when it is locally cooled or heated (see Chapter 3)? It evidently is. A spayed female cat will go into estrus when estrogen is implanted in her hypothalamus (Harris and Michael, 1964). Analogous effects have been obtained with ***androgens*** (that is, male hormones) administered to castrated male rats (Davidson, 1969; McEwen et al., 1982; Feder, 1984).

Hormones affect behavior, but the relation can also work the other way around. What an animal does and what it sees and feels will often have drastic effects on its hormonal secretions. An example is the effect of copulation on progesterone secretion in female rats. Some progesterone is secreted during the normal cycle, but not enough to permit the implantation of the fertilized egg in the uterus. Yet more progesterone is released as a reflex response to sexual stimulation. In rats, the male evidently has two reproductive functions. He supplies the sperm, but he also supplies the necessary stimulation which triggers the extra progesterone secretion without which there can be no pregnancy. This is shown by the fact that when the male rat ejaculates too quickly, no pregnancy results. There has been too little stimulation to set off the female's hormonal reflex (Adler, 1969).

HUMAN SEXUALITY AND HORMONES

The major difference between animal and human sexuality concerns the flexibility of sexual behavior. When does it occur, how, and with whom? Compared to animals, we are much less automatic in our sexual activities, much more varied, much more affected by prior experience. Human sexuality is remarkably plastic and can be variously shaped by experience, especially early experience, and by cultural patterns (see Chapters 11 and 15).

The difference between animal and human sexual behavior is especially marked when we consider the effects of hormones. In rats and cats, sexual behavior is highly dependent upon hormone levels; castrated males and spayed females stop copulating a few months after the removal of their gonads (Figure 10.14). In humans, on the other hand, sexual activity may persist for years, even decades, after castration or ovariectomy, provided that the operation was performed after puberty (Bermant and Davidson, 1974).

The liberation from hormonal control is especially clear in human females. To be sure, women are subject to a physiological cycle, but this has relatively little impact on sexual behavior, at least when compared to the profound effects seen in animals. The female rat or cat is chained to an estrus cycle that commands her to be receptive during one period and prevents her from being so at all other times. There are no such fetters on the human female, who is capable of sexual behavior at any time during her cycle, and also capable of refusing.

Although we are evidently not the vassals of our hormones that most animals are, this is not to say that hormonal factors have no effect. Androgen injections into men with abnormally low hormone levels will generally increase their sex drive (Davidson, 1986). An important demonstration of this concerns the effects of androgen administration on male homosexuals. The androgen-injected homosexual becomes more sexually active; but, contrary to a common misconception, his renewed sexual vigor is toward homosexual partners just as before (Kinsey, Pomeroy, and Martin, 1948).

Another demonstration of hormonal effects comes from studies of the menstrual cycle. While women can respond sexually at virtually all points of their cycle, there are still some variations within that period. Sexual desire and activity tend to be highest during the middle of the cycle, when ovulation occurs (Hamburg, Moos, and Yalom, 1968; Bancroft, 1986). These effects are not very pronounced; they probably represent a small remnant of the old animal estrus cycle, buried under layers of evolutionary change.

## Evolution and Mating Systems

In many species, the male and female part company after copulation and may very well never meet again. But in others, the partners remain together for a breeding season or even longer. In many cases, their arrangement involves *poly-*

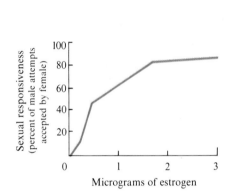

**10.14   Estrogen and sexual behavior**
*The effect of estrogen injections on the sexual responsiveness of female rats was measured by the number of male attempts at mounting that were accepted by the female. The females' ovaries had been removed, so they could not produce estrogen themselves. The hormone was injected daily in the doses shown above. Sexual behavior was measured eight days after hormone treatment began. (After Bermant and Davidson, 1974)*

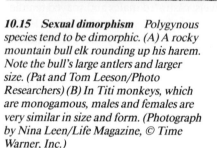

**10.15 Sexual dimorphism** *Polygynous species tend to be dimorphic. (A) A rocky mountain bull elk rounding up his harem. Note the bull's large antlers and larger size. (Pat and Tom Leeson/Photo Researchers) (B) In Titi monkeys, which are monogamous, males and females are very similar in size and form. (Photograph by Nina Leen/Life Magazine, © Time Warner, Inc.)*

**Birds as monagamous** *Birds tend to mate and stay together during a mating season as both parents are needed for successful incubation of their young. Here a black-bowed albatross male courts a female on the nest that will serve as home for their offspring. (Photograph by Robert W. Hernandez/The National Audubon Society Collection/Photo Researchers)*

*gyny,* and the resulting family consists of one male, several females, and their various offspring. In a very few others, the mating system is *polyandry,* which works the other way around, with one female and several males. And in still others, the mating pattern is *monogamy,* with a reproductive partnership based on a special, more or less permanent tie between one male and one female.

MATING SYSTEMS IN ANIMALS

What accounts for the different mating systems found in different parts of the animal kingdom? A clue comes from the different patterns found in mammals and birds. Some 90 percent of all birds are monogamous: They mate and stay together throughout a breeding season. In contrast, more than 90 percent of all mammals are polygynous, with one male monopolizing a number of females. Why should this be so?

Sociobiologists seek the answer through some kind of evolutionary economics: the patterns that evolved are such as to maximize each individual's reproductive success. Consider the reproductive problem faced by birds. In many species, successful incubation requires both parents: one who sits upon the eggs, another who forages for food to nourish the bird that's sitting. After hatching, finding food for a nestful of hungry chicks may still require the full-time efforts of both birds. Under the circumstances, monogamy makes reproductive sense for both sexes: the father has to help the mother after she lays her eggs, or else no chicks will survive into adulthood.

The situation is quite different for most mammals. Here there is no incubation problem; since the fetus grows within the mother's womb, she is still able to forage for her own food during the offspring's gestation. In addition, the mother has the exclusive job of feeding the offspring after birth, for only females can secrete the milk on which the infants live. Now the reproductive calculus leads to a different conclusion. The male does not have to invest time and effort in taking care of his offspring; instead, his best bet for maximizing his own reproductive success lies in mating with as many females as he possibly can. To accomplish this, he has to become attractive to females (by developing the most impressive antlers, or

whatever), and he has to win in the competition with many other males, all of whom have the identical goal. The end result is polygyny, with one successful male monopolizing a number of females.

There's an interesting anatomical correlate of mating arrangements in the animal kingdom. Almost invariably, polygyny is accompanied by **sexual dimorphism,** a pronounced anatomical difference in the size or bodily structures of the two sexes. The more polygynous the species, the more dimorphic it tends to be, with the males larger and often more ornamented than the females, as shown by the peacock's tail, the stag's antlers, and the male elephant seal's disproportionate size (Figure 10.15A). In contrast, monogamous species such as the gibbon show no such dimorphism (Figure 10.15B).

### MATING PATTERNS IN HUMANS

A number of authors have tried to extend this general line of reasoning to account for the evolution of human sexual and mating behavior. They start out with the observation that humans are somewhat dimorphic: On average, the human male is about 10 percent larger than the female. Since such dimorphism is correlated with polygyny in animals, one might expect some similar tendency in humans.

*The sociobiological perspective*   To bolster their case, sociobiologists refer to a number of findings that in their view point in this direction. One is the anthropological evidence. A review of 185 cultures showed that the majority formally allowed polygyny. Only 16 percent of the cultures had monogamous marriage arrangements that permitted only one spouse to each partner (Ford and Beach, 1951). Related findings come from a number of studies of our own culture. These strongly suggest that, on average, men have a greater desire for a variety of sexual partners than do women (Symons, 1979).

Sociobiologists argue that these differences are ultimately rooted in our biological nature. In their view, men want greater sexual variety because for them it is reproductively adaptive: the more women they mate with, the more children they father. In contrast, women are much more cautious in evaluating potential sexual partners and more interested in a stable, familial relationship—a good reproductive strategy since, as we've seen, the biological parental investment of a female is almost always greater than a male's. Such built-in patterns are presumably no longer relevant in a modern world in which birth control techniques have managed to uncouple sex from reproduction. But according to the sociobiologists, these remnants of our biological past are still with us just the same. They were once reproductively adaptive, and they continue to influence our behavior even though their adaptive role is diminished or altogether gone.

*The cultural perspective*   The sociobiological view has been severely challenged. One line of attack concerns the role of culture. Many critics argue that differences in sexual attitudes are a product of society rather than of biological predispositions and reflect a cultural rather than a built-in double standard. In their opinion, polygyny is a natural outgrowth of cultural conditions in which men are dominant and women are perceived as property. As to the differences in men's and women's desire for sexual variety, they regard it as a product of early social

**Polygynous tendencies in humans**   *The archetype of the philandering male is Don Juan, or to use his Italian name, Don Giovanni. In Mozart's opera, Don Giovanni boasts of having seduced 1,975 women of every age and rank, but is eventually punished for his polygynous sins and dragged down to hell. (From a 1989 production of* Don Giovanni, *with Erie Mills and John Cheek, © 1989 Martha Swope)*

training: boys are taught that many sexual conquests are a proof of "manliness," while girls are taught to value home and family and to seek a single partner.

By way of retort, some writers point to the different sexual practices of male and female homosexuals (Symons, 1979). It turns out that male homosexuals are vastly more interested in sexual variety than are female homosexuals. Their sexual relations tend to be briefer, more casual, and to involve many more partners than those of female homosexuals. Thus one study of 151 lesbians and 581 gay men in West Germany found that only 1 percent of the women reported having sexual relations with more than ten partners, while 61 percent of the men said they had (Schäfer, 1977). Such findings have been interpreted as evidence for a biological rather than a cultural interpretation on the assumption that persons who have rejected heterosexuality are unlikely to have succumbed to a culturally induced double standard. Seen in this light, gay men behave like heterosexual men and lesbians like heterosexual women because of their biological nature. Whatever their other differences, in the last analysis, they are men and women and their sexual attitudes and desires cannot help but be shaped by this rock-bottom biological fact. But this interpretation does not necessarily follow. For it's perfectly possible that the culture has taught gay men (no less than their heterosexual brothers) that being manly is to have a lot of sexual experiences, and has taught lesbians (no less than their heterosexual sisters) that a woman should be faithful to just one partner (Gagnon and Simon, 1973).*

Critics of the sociobiological approach have no quarrel with the sociobiologists' efforts to understand animal behavior in an evolutionary perspective. Their critique is aimed at the attempt to extend these concepts to the human level. After all, terms such as *monogamy* have quite a different meaning when applied to, say, geese and humans. In geese, the term describes the fact that two parents stay together for one breeding season to hatch and raise their young; in humans, the term describes an arrangement that only makes sense in the context of a network of social and legal patterns. Evolution may have shaped many of our impulses and desires, but we simply don't know how these in turn have shaped the culture in which humans live and mate and bring up their children. Since this is so, it is rank speculation to assert that the reproductive economics that underlie an elephant seal's attempts to set up a harem are at bottom the same as those that account for the philandering found in some human males (Kitcher, 1985).

## THE BIOLOGICAL BASIS OF LOVE: THE PARENT-CHILD BOND

There is another bond of love whose biological foundations are no less basic than those of the male-female tie—the relation between mother and child (and in many animals, the relation between father and child as well). In birds and mammals some kind of parental attachment is almost ubiquitous. In contrast to most fish and reptiles that lay eggs by the hundreds and then abandon them, birds and mammals invest in quality rather than quantity. They have fewer offspring, but they then see to it that most of their brood survives into maturity. They feed them, clean them, shelter them, and protect them during some initial period of

---

* Some of these patterns have no doubt been changed in recent years in the wake of the AIDS epidemic.

dependency. While under this parental umbrella, the young animal can grow and become prepared for the world into which it must soon enter and can acquire some of the skills that will help it survive in that world. This period of initial dependency is longest in animals that live by their wits, such as monkeys and apes, and is longest of all in humans.

## The Infant's Attachment to the Mother

In most birds and mammals, the young become strongly attached to their mother. Ducklings follow the mother duck, lambs the mother ewe, and infant monkeys cling tightly to the mother monkey's belly. In each case, separation leads to considerable stress: the young animals give piteous distress calls, and quack, bleat, and keen continuously until the mother returns. The biological function of this attachment is a simple matter of personal survival. This holds for humans as well as animals. For there is little doubt that in our early evolutionary history a motherless infant would probably have died an early death—of exposure, starvation, or predation. There are very few orphanages in nature.

The mechanisms that lead to this attachment will be discussed in a later section (see Chapter 15). For now, we will only say that while some theorists believe that the main factor is the child's discovery that the mother's presence leads to the alleviation of hunger, thirst, and pain, there is strong evidence that the attachment is more basic than that. For the distress shown by the young—whether birds, monkeys, or humans—when they are separated from their mother occurs even when they are perfectly well-fed and housed. It appears that the infant's attachment to its mother is based on more than the satisfaction of the major bodily needs. The infant evidently comes predisposed to seek social stimulation, which is rewarding in and of itself.

**Orangutan mother and child**   (Photograph by Roy P. Fontaine/The National Audubon Society Collection/Photo Researchers)

## The Mother's Attachment to the Infant

For the infant, the function of the mother-child bond is simple personal survival. For the mother, the biological function is again a matter of survival, but for her, the survival is genetic rather than personal, for unless her young survive into adulthood, the parents' genes will perish. But what are the mechanisms that produce the parents' attachment? Robins and gibbons behave like proper parents: they care for their young and protect them. But they surely don't do this because they realize that their failure to act in this way would lead to genetic extinction. The real reason must lie elsewhere. One possibility is that there are some built-in predispositions toward parental behavior. If such predispositions do exist, they would then be favored by natural selection.

There is good evidence that the young of many animal species have a set of built-in responses that elicit caretaking from the parents. To give only one example, many baby birds open their mouths as wide as they can as soon as the parent arrives at the nest. This "gaping" response is their means of begging for food (see Figure 10.16). Some species of birds have special anatomical signs that help to elicit a proper parental reaction. An example is the Cedar Waxwing, whose bright red mouth lining evidently provides a further signal to the parent: I'm young, hungry, and a Cedar Waxwing!

**10.16   Gaping in young birds**   *(A) The gaping response of the young yellow warbler serves as a built-in signal that elicits the parents' feeding behavior. (Photograph by John Shaw/Bruce Coleman) (B) Cuckoos are parasites who lay their eggs in other birds' nests. The figure shows a young cuckoo being fed by its foster parent, a reed warbler. The young cuckoo, at about twenty-four hours old, instinctively ejects any eggs or young of its host from the nest, so that it alone is the sole occupant. Its large orange-red gaping mouth provides a powerful stimulus in eliciting feeding. The unwitting warbler will continue to feed the cuckoo even when it has grown to several times the "parent's" size. (Courtesy of Ian Wyllie, Monks Wood Experiment Station)*

Child care in humans is obviously more complex and flexible than it is in Cedar Waxwings, but it too has biological foundations. The mother-child relation grows out of a number of built-in reaction patterns, of child to mother and mother to child. The human infant begins life with a few relevant reflex patterns, including some that help him find the mother's nipple and suck at it once it is found. He also has an essentially innate signal system through which he tells the mother that he is in distress: he cries. Analogous ***distress calls*** are found in many animals, for when the young chirp, bleat, mew, or cry, the mother immediately runs to their aid and comforts them.

According to ethologists, evolution has further equipped the infant with a set of stimulus features that function as innate releasers of parental, and especially maternal, feelings. The cues that define "babyness" include a large, protruding forehead, large eyes, an upturned nose, chubby cheeks, and so on. Endowed with these distinctive properties, the baby looks "cute" and "cuddly," something to be picked up, fussed over, and taken care of. The case is similar for the young of various animals who share aspects of the same "baby schema." Various commercial enterprises are devoted to the deliberate manufacture of cuteness. Dolls and Walt Disney creatures are designed to be babied by children, while certain lap dogs are especially bred to be babied by adults (Figure 10.17).

Nature has provided the infant with yet another trick to disarm even the stoniest of parental hearts: the smile. In some fashion, smiling may begin within the first month: it is often considered a built-in signal by which humans tell each other. "I wish you well. Be good to me." There is reason to believe that it is innate. Infants who are born blind smile under conditions that also produce smiling in sighted children, as when they hear their mother's voice. They obviously could not have learned this response by imitation.

## COMMUNICATING MOTIVES

The preceding discussion has given ample testimony that many animal species exist within a social framework in much the same way that humans do. What one creature does often has a crucial effect on the behavior of another of its own kind. As we have seen, the major means of exerting such social influences is the signaling display.

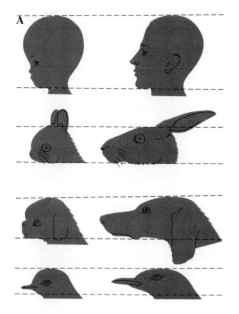

**10.17   The stimulus features of "babyness"**  *"Cute" characteristics of the "baby schema" are common to humans and a number of animals. (A) These include a rounded head shape, protruding forehead, and large eyes below the middle of the head (after Lorenz, 1943). These properties, as well as a rounded body shape and large head-to-body ratio, produce cuteness in a lap dog (B). (Photograph by Michael S. Renner/Bruce Coleman)*

## Expressive Movements: Animal Display

Displays represent a simple mode of communication whereby animals inform each other of what they are most likely to do in the immediate future. The crab waves its claws and the wolf bares its fangs; these threat messages may save both sender and receiver from bodily harm if the message is heeded.

How do ethologists determine what message is conveyed by a given display? Since the sender is an animal, they cannot ask it directly. They can try, however, to infer the message by noting the correlation between a given display and the animal's behavior just before and after its occurrence. For example, if a certain posture is generally followed by attack, then it is usually called a threat display; if it is usually followed by mating, it is probably a courtship signal, and so on.

Some ethologists interpret such correlations between displays and subsequent behavior by assuming that in effect displays communicate the animal's present

*The evolutionary origin of the human smile   According to some authors, the human smile grew out of the "fear grin." This is an appeasement display found in monkeys and other primates which usually signifies submission but may also indicate reassurance, when directed by a dominant animal to a subordinate (van Hooff, 1972). (A) The fear grin in a young chimpanzee. (George Holton, 1986/Photo Researchers) (B) A smile in a three-month-old infant. (© 1988 James Sugar/Black Star)*

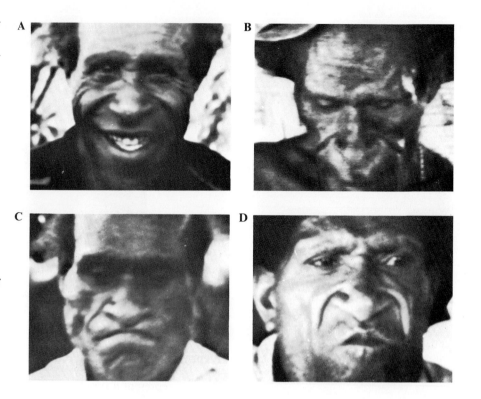

**10.18    Attempts to portray emotion by New Guinea tribesmen**    Acting out emotions appropriate to various situations: (A) "Your friend has come and you are happy" (B) "Your child has died" (C) "You are angry and about to fight" (D) "You see a dead pig that has been lying there for a long time." (© Paul Ekman, 1971)

motive state—its readiness to fight or to mate, its need for food or parental attention, and so forth. For this reason, displays are sometimes said to "express" the animal's inner state and are therefore described as ***expressive movements.***

## The Expression of Emotions in Humans

In humans, built-in social displays are relegated to a lesser place. After all, we have the much richer communication system provided by human language. But even so, we do possess a set of displays that tell others something about our feelings and needs—our various emotional expressions.

### THE UNIVERSALITY OF EMOTIONAL EXPRESSIONS

Humans have a sizable repertory of emotional expressions, most of them conveyed by the face. We smile, laugh, weep, frown, snarl, and grit our teeth. Are any of these expressive patterns our human equivalent of displays? If so, they should be universal to all humans and innately determined (Ekman, 1973; Ekman and Oster, 1979; Fridlund, Ekman, and Oster, 1983).

In one study, American actors posed in photographs to convey such emotions as fear, anger, and happiness. These pictures were then shown to members of different cultures, both literate (Swedes, Japanese, Kenyans) and preliterate (members of an isolated New Guinea tribe barely advanced beyond Stone-Age culture). When asked to identify the portrayed emotion, all groups came up with quite similar judgments. The results were much the same when the procedure was reversed. The New Guinea tribesmen were asked to portray the emotions appro-

priate to various simple situations such as happiness at the return of a friend, grief at the death of a child, and anger at the start of a fight. Photographs of their performances were then shown to American college students who readily picked out the emotions the tribesmen had tried to convey (Figure 10.18).

These results indicate that there may be some emotional expressions that are common to all humans. This conclusion fits observations of children born blind. These children cry, smile, and laugh under essentially the same conditions that elicit these reactions in sighted children. In fact, much the same is true even of children born both blind and deaf. It would be hard to argue that these children had *learned* the emotional expressions considering that their sensory avenues of both sight and sound had been blocked off from birth (see Figure 10.19).

At least in part, such built-in expressions may serve a similar function as do animal displays. They act as social signals by which we communicate our inner states to others, a way of saying what we are likely to do next.

THE ROLE OF CULTURE

These findings do not imply that smiling and other emotional expressions are unaffected by cultural conventions. According to some accounts, Melanese chieftains frown fiercely when greeting each other at a festive occasion, and Samurai mothers are said to have smiled upon hearing that their sons had fallen in battle (Klineberg, 1940). But such facts do not disprove the claim that facial expressions are built-in social signals; they only show that such signals can be artificially masked and modified. How and when such artifice comes into play, however, depends on the culture.

Some evidence for this view comes from studies in which American and Japanese subjects were presented with a harrowing documentary film of a primitive puberty rite. As they watched the film, their facial expressions were recorded with a hidden camera. The results showed that when alone, the facial reactions of the Japanese and American subjects were virtually identical (see Figure 10.20). But the results were quite different when the subject watched the film in the company of a white-coated experimenter. Now the Japanese looked more polite and smiled more than the Americans (Ekman, 1977; for further discussion, see Fridlund, 1990).

**10.19  The smile in blind children**  *(A) Smile in a child born blind. (Courtesy The Lighthouse, N.Y.C.) (B) Smiling in a child born both blind and deaf. (Courtesy I. Eibl-Eibesfeldt)*

**10.20  Spontaneous facial expressions** *(A) A Japanese and (B) an American student watched a film that depicted a rather gruesome scene. The figure shows their expressions when they were alone. Under these conditions, their facial expressions were virtually identical. But when they watched in the presence of another person, the Japanese masked his expression of unpleasant emotions more than the American did. (From Ekman and Friesen, 1975)*

## The Difference between Display and Language

How are display repertories different from the communication achieved by human language? There is an obvious similarity. In both cases, the behavior of one organism affects that of its fellows. But the differences between these two communication systems far outweigh the similarities.

### CREATING NEW MESSAGES

One obvious difference is in the complexity and flexibility of the two communicative systems. Consider the relative size of the two "vocabularies." Most mammals have some twenty to forty distinguishable display signals. This contrasts with an estimated vocabulary size of at least 50,000 words for the average human adult. The contrast is even sharper when we compare the way in which these vocabulary items are combined. Human language is based on a ***productive*** principle. Given the rules for putting words together (syntax), the speaker can construct any number of new messages that he has never heard before (see Chapter 9). Not so for animal displays. The display system is rigid. Each stickleback, robin, and rhesus monkey sends only messages that were sent by previous sticklebacks, robins, and rhesus monkeys. There is no room for originality in the language of display.

One reason is that in animal display systems there is no provision for rearrangements of parts so as to make a new whole. Consider the messages of the jackdaw. This bird has two distinct calls that beckon others to fly with it—a high-pitched call that sounds like *kia,* uttered when the jackdaw migrates southward in the autumn, and a lower-pitched call that sounds like *kiaw* uttered when the bird returns home in the spring. Yet another jackdaw call is *zick-zick-zick* which occurs during courtship. There is also an angry, *rattle*like sound, emitted when the jackdaw is about to attack an enemy (Lorenz, 1952). These various calls are useful in helping the jackdaw communicate with its fellows, but they should not be considered as the analogues of words in a language. If they were, the jackdaw should be able to shuffle the individual calls to create new and ever more complex messages. They might produce a sentence in Jackdawese: *"Kia, rattle-rattle; Kiaw, zick-zick-zick."* Freely translated, this sentence might read, "Let us fly south to fight the enemy and then fly home to make love." No jackdaw—or indeed, any animal but man—has ever achieved such a linguistic feat.

### THE CONTENT OF THE MESSAGES

Thus far, we've looked at the difference between the ways displays and true language systems express their messages. But there also tends to be a difference in what the messages convey. For the most part, displays are a way of telling a fellow creature what one is about to do.* In effect, they are statements about the sender's

*(Photograph by Benny Ortiz)*

* This statement must be qualified, for a number of primates have recently been found to have displays that signal different kinds of predators. Thus vervet monkeys have different alarm calls depending upon the nature of the predator they have sighted: one for an eagle, another for a leopard, and yet another for a python snake (Seyfarth, 1980; Cheney and Wrangham, 1986).

interpersonal motives at a given time and place. If this is indeed what most displays are about, we can understand why the relative poverty of the system is no barrier to communication. There is no need for a large vocabulary or a productive combinatorial system because there is a limit on the number of things an animal wants to do to (or with) another of its own kind: flee, attack, feed or be fed by, groom or be groomed by, copulate, and a few others.

In contrast, human language must precisely describe the world outside and is thus virtually unlimited in its topics. For this, a productive system is absolutely crucial. The variety of possible events and relationships in the world is infinite, and only a system that is capable of an infinite number of utterances can do justice to this variety.

Some evidence for a fundamental difference in the content of the messages of display and of human language comes from our own experience. We obviously don't use our display systems to tell others about the external world. We don't smile, blush, or embrace so as to inform each other about the Pythagorean theorem or the leak in the upstairs toilet. But conversely, we sometimes feel "at a loss for words" to express emotion and motive (the proper content of display messages). Such matters are often difficult to put into words, or at least words seem inadequate when we finally manage to do so. "I love you" is hard to say and, even if said, is somehow not enough. "I'm very sorry" is pallid as an expression of grief or consolation. In these situations, the more primitive display system is more appropriate because the signal to be sent concerns interpersonal feelings. The beloved is touched, the bereaved is cradled, and these "simple" gestures seem somehow right. Nothing more is gained by speech, because what matters has already been displayed.

## SELF-SACRIFICE AND ALTRUISM

The preceding pages have provided ample evidence that animals are necessarily social: they fight and compete with each other, mate, reproduce, and communicate. Still further work by ethologists suggests that under certain conditions they may even behave as if they were "unselfish altruists."

It's of course well known that many animals go to considerable lengths to defend their offspring. Various birds have evolved characteristic ways of feigning injury such as dropping one wing and paddling around in circles to draw a predator away from their nests (see Figure 10.21). On the face of it, such acts appear heroically unselfish, for the parents court the danger that the predator will seize them. But here again we come up with the difference between personal and genetic survival. For what seems unselfish from the vantage of the individual looks different from a biological point of view (Wilson, 1975). The mother bird who does not divert a potential attacker may very well live longer because she has played it safe. But from an evolutionary perspective what counts is not her own survival but the survival of her genes. And these are more likely to perish if she flies off to safety; while she hides in the bushes, the marauding cat will eat her chicks. As a result, she will have fewer offspring to whom she can pass on her genes, including the very gene or genes that underlie her maternal indifference. Those of her offspring that do survive will in turn have fewer offspring, and so on, until her genetic attributes will disappear.

**10.21 A misleading display** In feigning injury, the killdeer, a small American bird, runs and flies erratically from predators that approach its nest, often flopping about as if it has a broken wing. (Photograph by Wayne Lankinen/Bruce Coleman)

**10.22  Alarm call**  *Ground squirrels give alarm calls when they sense a nearby predator. Such alarm calls are more likely to be given by females rather than males. The females usually have close relatives living nearby. As a result, their alarm call is more likely to benefit genetically related rather than unrelated individuals, which suggests that it is based on kin selection. (Photograph by Georg D. Lepp/Bio-Tec Images)*

## Altruism in Animals

Seen in this light, parental self-sacrifice can be understood in evolutionary terms. Can a similar analysis be applied to unselfish acts that benefit individuals who are not one's own children? Such apparently altruistic acts are found in various animal species.* A case in point is the warning signal given off by many species at the approach of a predator (see Figure 10.22). When a robin sees a hawk overhead, it gives an alarm call, a special cry that alerts all members of the flock and impels them to seek cover. This alarm call is based on a built-in, inherited tendency and is essentially unlearned. All robins emit this cry when in danger, and they do so even if raised in complete isolation from their fellows. There is no doubt that this alarm benefits all robins who hear it. They crouch low and hide, so their chances of escape are enhanced. But what does it gain the bird who sounds the alarm? Doesn't it place him in greater danger by increasing the likelihood that the hawk will detect *him?* Why does the robin play the hero instead of quietly stealing away and leaving his fellows to their fate? There are several possible factors, each of which may play a role.

### ENLIGHTENED SELF-INTEREST

One possibility is that this act of avian heroism is not as unselfish as it seems, for it may well increase the warner's own chance of personal survival in the long run. If a particular robin spies a hawk and remains quiet, there is a greater chance that some bird in the flock will be captured, most likely another bird. But what about tomorrow? A hawk who has seized a prey in a particular location will probably return to the very same place in search of another meal. And this meal may be the very same robin who originally minded his own business and stayed uninvolved (Trivers, 1971).

### KIN SELECTION

There is another alternative. Let us assume that our heroic robin is unlucky, is seized by the hawk, and dies a martyr's death. While this act may have caused the robin to perish as an individual, it may well have served to preserve some of that bird's genes. This may be true even if none of the birds in the flock are the hero's own offspring. They may be relatives who carry some of his genes, brothers and sisters who share half of the same genes, or nieces and nephews who share one-fourth. If so, the alarm call may have saved several relatives who carry the alarm-calling gene and who will pass it on to future generations of robins. From an evolutionary point of view, the alarm call had survival value—if not for the alarm caller or its direct offspring, then for the alarm-calling gene (Hamilton, 1964; Maynard-Smith, 1965).

According to this view, altruistic behavior will evolve if it promotes the survival of the individual's kin. This ***kin-selection*** hypothesis predicts that unselfish behavior should be more common among relatives than unrelated individuals.

---

* In modern biological usage, the term *altruism* is reserved for cases in which the good deed benefits neither the doers nor their own offspring.

There is some evidence that this is indeed the case. Certain deer snort loudly when alarmed, which alerts other deer that are nearby. Groups of does tend to be related; bucks, who disperse when they get old enough, are less likely to be related. The kin-selection hypothesis would then predict that does should be more likely to give the alarm snort than bucks. This is indeed what happens. Similar results have been obtained for various other species (Hirth and McCullough, 1977; Sherman, 1977).

### RECIPROCAL ALTRUISM

There is yet another possible mechanism that leads to biologically unselfish acts. Some animals—and we may well be among them—may have a built-in Golden Rule: Do unto others, as you would want them to do to you (or to your genes). If an individual helps another, and that other later reciprocates, the ultimate upshot is a benefit to both. For example, male baboons sometimes help each other in aggressive encounters, and the one who received help on one occasion is more likely to come to the other's assistance later on (Packer, 1977).

A built-in predisposition toward reciprocity may well be one of the biological foundations of altruism in some animals (and perhaps ourselves as well). If the original unselfish act doesn't exact too great a cost—in energy expended or in danger incurred—then its eventual reciprocation will yield a net benefit to both parties. A tendency toward reciprocal altruism of this kind, however, presupposes relatively stable groups in which individuals recognize one another. It also presupposes some safeguards against "cheating," accepting help without reciprocating. One such safeguard might be a link between a disposition toward altruism and a disposition to punish cheaters (Trivers, 1971).

## Altruism in Humans

There is little doubt that humans are capable of considerable self-sacrifice. Soldiers volunteer for suicide missions, and religious martyrs burn at the stake. In addition to these awesome deeds of heroism are the more common acts of altruism—sharing food and money, offering help, and the like. Can such human acts of altruism be understood in the biological terms that apply to the alarm calls of birds and monkeys?

### THE SOCIOBIOLOGISTS' VIEW

According to Edward Wilson, the founder of sociobiology, the answer is yes, at least to some extent. While Wilson emphasizes the enormous variations among human social systems, he notes that there are certain common themes, which he regards as grounded in our genetic heritage. Of these, the most important is kinship. Wilson and other sociobiologists suggest that, by and large, we will be most altruistic to our closest relatives. According to Wilson, the person who risks death in battle or through martyrdom probably helps to ensure the survival of the group of which he is a member—and thus of his own genes, since this group probably includes his own kin. As with the robin, the individual hero may die, but his genes will survive (Wilson, 1975; 1978).

*Braving death for an ideal*    *During the Civil War, a vastly outnumbered group of black Union soldiers attacked an impregnable fortress held by the Confederate forces, suffering enormous casualties. They were willing to die for the abolition of slavery and to show that blacks are just as capable of sacrificing themselves for an ideal as whites are. From the 1989 film Glory, directed by Edward Zwick. (Photo courtesy of Photofest)*

Sociobiologists believe that this position is supported by the fact that kinship is of considerable importance in just about all human societies, as attested to by the elaborate terms used to describe the precise nature of kinship relations: brother, sister, uncle, cousin, second-cousin-once-removed, and so on. At least in our culture, the likelihood that one person will make a sacrifice for another increases the closer the two are genetically related to each other. In one study, a fairly large sample of American women was asked who had helped them on occasions when they required assistance (of money, emotional support, and so on). The results showed that they were three times more likely to have been helped by their parents, siblings, or children (who share half their genes) than by half-siblings, aunts, uncles, nieces, nephews, and grandchildren or grandparents (who share only a quarter of their genes). This is not to say that genetically unrelated friends (let alone husbands) did not provide help, for indeed they did. But according to the authors, help among friends was probably based on *reciprocal* altruism. If a subject's friend gave her money (or time or emotional support), there was a mutual expectation that the assistance would be reciprocated at some later time. Among kin, such expectation of later repayment was less common (Essock-Vitale and McGuire, 1985).

Other sociobiologists have expanded this kinship-selection argument even further. As they see it, kinship selection underlies a human tendency toward *tribalism*—putting the welfare of one's own group ahead of others. This argument has further consequences. The individual's own resources are usually limited, but we have seen that even so he will often share them with his kin. But for the same reasons he is more likely to engage in conflict *outside* his immediate kin, and by extension, outside of his tribe.

Me against my brother; me and my brother against our cousins; me, my brother, and my cousins against our friends; me, my brothers, cousins, and friends against our enemies in the village; all of these and the whole village against the next village . . . (Old Arab proverb)

the root of this or the other symptom. Many of these events dated back to a particularly traumatic period during which she nursed her dying father. An example was a nervous cough which she traced to an occasion at her father's bedside. She heard the sound of dance music coming from a neighbor's house, felt the wish to be there, and was immediately struck by guilt and self-reproach. She covered up her feelings with a nervous cough, and thereafter coughed uncontrollably whenever she heard rhythmic music. The symptom disappeared when the forgotten episode was remembered (Freud and Breuer, 1895).

## Resistance and Repression

Eventually Freud abandoned hypnosis altogether, in part because not all patients were readily hypnotized. He found that crucial memories could be recovered even in the normal, waking state through the method of *free association.* The patients are told to say anything that enters their mind, no matter how trivial and unrelated it might seem, or how embarrassing, disagreeable, or indiscreet. Since all ideas are presumably related by an associative network, the emotionally charged "forgotten" memories should be evoked sooner or later. At first, this procedure seemed to work and yielded results similar to those obtained through hypnotic probes. But a new difficulty arose, for it became clear that the patients did not really comply with Freud's request. There was a *resistance* of which the patient was often unaware:

> The patient attempts to escape . . . by every possible means. First he says nothing comes into his head, then that so much comes into his head that he can't grasp any of it. Then we observe that . . . he is giving in to his critical objections, first to this, then to that; he betrays it by the long pauses which occur in his talk. At last he admits that he really cannot say something, he is ashamed to. . . . Or else, he has thought of something but it concerns someone else and not himself. . . . Or else, what he has just thought of is really too unimportant, too stupid and too absurd. . . . So it goes on, with untold variations, to which one continually replies that telling everything really means telling everything (Freud, 1917a, p. 289).

Freud noticed that the intensity of resistance was often an important clue to what was really important. When a patient seemed to struggle especially hard to change a topic, to break off a train of thought, she was probably close to the recovery of an emotionally charged memory. Eventually it would come, often to the patient's great surprise. But if this was so, and if the recovery of these memories helped the patient to get better (as both Freud and his patients believed), why then did the patients resist the retrieval of these memories and thus obstruct their own cure? Freud concluded that the observed phenomenon of resistance was the overt manifestation of some powerful force that opposed the recovery of the critical memories into consciousness. Certain experiences in the patient's life—certain acts, impulses, thoughts, or memories—were pushed out of consciousness, were *repressed,* and the same repressive forces that led to their original expulsion were mobilized to oppose their reentry into consciousness during the psychiatric session.

What are the ideas whose recollection is so vehemently resisted, which have to be repressed and kept out of mental sight? According to Freud, they are always connected with some wish or impulse that the person is unable to face without

***Anna O.*** *In the annals of psychoanalysis, Anna O. figures only as a famous case history. But in real life, Anna—or to use her true name, Bertha Pappenheim—was much more than that. After she recovered from her various disorders, she became a distinguished pioneer in the field of social work, as well as a militant and effective champion of women's rights in Eastern Europe.*

suffering intense anxiety. Repression is a defense; the unacceptable wish and various thoughts associated with it are pushed out of consciousness to ward off intolerable pain. The repressed wishes are invariably linked to the basic biological urges, especially the sexual ones, whose full expression is forbidden by society.

Freud also concluded that the critical repressions date back to early life, when the instinctual urges of the child first clash with the restraints imposed by society as embodied in his parents. As evidence he cited his clinical observations. In patient after patient, the eventual recovery of a repressed memory merely led to further resistance, which ultimately gave way to reveal a repressed memory earlier on, and so on back to the early years of childhood.

Freud believed that the repressed material is not really eradicated but remains in the *unconscious.* This is a metaphorical expression which only means that the repressed ideas still exert a powerful effect. Again and again, they push up from below, like a jack-in-the-box, fueled by the biological urges that gave rise to them in the first place, or triggered by associations in the here and now. As these repressed ideas well up again, they also bring back anxiety and are therefore pushed down once more. The result is a never-ending unconscious conflict. This conflict often leads to a compromise in which the rejected wishes are expressed, but in a censored form. According to Freud, many symptoms of psychopathology represent conflict solutions of this kind. An example is a patient who repeatedly pulls off her blouse with one hand and pulls it back on with the other. Freud would probably argue that this is a dramatized sexual fantasy in which the patient plays two roles—a lover who is trying to undress her and that part of herself that tries to resist.

The task Freud set for himself was the analysis (as he called it, the ***psychoanalysis***) of these conflicts, the discovery of their origins, of their effects in the present, of their removal or alleviation. But he soon came to believe that the same mechanisms which produce the symptoms of psychopathology also operate in normal persons, that his discoveries were not just a contribution to psychiatry, but were a foundation for a general theory of human personality.

## UNCONSCIOUS CONFLICT

Our sketch of Freud's theory of the nature and development of human personality will concentrate on those aspects that seem to represent the highlights of a complex theoretical formulation that was continually revised and modified during the course of Freud's long career. In this description, we will separate two aspects of Freudian theory. We will begin with the conception of the mechanisms of unconscious conflict. We will then deal with Freud's theory of the origins of these conflicts in the individual's life history, and of their relation to the development of sexual identity and morality.

### The Antagonists of Inner Conflict

Freud's theories concern the forces whose antagonism produces unconscious conflict and the effects produced when they clash. But who fights whom in unconscious conflict?

***Inner conflicts as envisaged by Plato*** *The Greek philosopher Plato anticipated Freud's tripartite division of the mind by over two thousand years. In one of his* Dialogues, *he likened the soul to a chariot with two horses that often pull in opposed directions. The chariot's driver is Reason, the two horses are Spirit (our nobler emotions ) and Appetite. This Renaissance medallion depicts Plato's image of the internal conflict.*

When conflict is external, the antagonists are easily identified: David and Goliath, St. George and the Dragon, and so on. But what are the warring forces when the conflict is inside of the individual? In essence, they are different behavior tendencies, such as Anna O's sexually tinged desire to be at a dance and her conflicting reactions of guilt at leaving a dying father. One of the tasks Freud set himself was to classify the tendencies that participate in such conflicts, to see which of them are usually arrayed together and fight on the same side. The eventual result was a threefold classification of conflicting tendencies within the individual, which he regarded as three more or less distinct subsystems of the human personality: the *id,* the *ego,* and the *superego.* In some of Freud's writings, there is a tendency to treat these three systems as if they were three separate persons that inhabit the mind. But this is only a metaphor that must not be taken literally; *id, ego,* and *superego* are just names for three sets of very different reaction patterns. They are not persons in their own right (Freud, 1923).

### THE ID

The *id* is the most primitive portion of the personality, from which the other two are derived. It contains all of the basic biological urges: to eat, drink, eliminate, be comfortably warm and, most of all, to gain sexual pleasure.* The id's sole law is the *pleasure principle*—satisfaction now and not later, regardless of circumstances and whatever the cost.

The id's blind strivings for pleasure know no distinction between self and world, between fantasy and reality, between wishing and having. Its insistent urges spill out into reflex motor action, like emptying the bladder when it is full. If that doesn't work, the clamoring for pleasure leads to primitive thoughts of gratification, fantasies of wish fulfillment that cannot be distinguished from reality.

### THE EGO

At birth, the infant is all id. But the id's shrill clamors are soon met by the harsh facts of external reality. Some gratifications come only after a delay. The breast or the bottle are not always present; the infant has to cry to get them.

The confrontations between hot desire and cold reality lead to a whole set of new reactions that are meant to reconcile the two. Sometimes the reconciliation is by appropriate action (saying "please"), sometimes by self-imposed delay (going to the bathroom), sometimes by suppression of a forbidden impulse (not touching one's genitals). These various reactions become organized into a new subsystem of the personality—the *ego.* The ego is derived from the id and is essentially still in its service. But unlike the id, the ego obeys the *reality principle.* It tries to satisfy the id (that is, to gain pleasure), but it does so pragmatically, in accordance with the real world and its real demands. As time proceeds, the opposition between need and reality leads to the emergence of more and more skills, all directed to the same end, as well as a whole system of thought and memories that grows up concurrently. Eventually, this entire system becomes capable of looking

---

* These urges are sometimes called instincts, but that is a misnomer caused by an unfortunate translation of Freud's original term.

at itself and now deserves the name Freud gave it, ego or self. Until this point, there was no "I" but only a mass of undifferentiated strivings (appropriately named after the Latin impersonal pronoun *id,* literally "it").

### THE SUPEREGO

The id is not the ego's only master. As the child grows older, a new reaction pattern develops from within the ego that acts as a kind of judge that decides whether the ego has been "good" or "bad." This new mental agency is the ***superego*** which represents the internalized rules and admonitions of the parents, and through them, of society. Initially, the ego only had to worry about external reality. It might inhibit some id-inspired action, but only to avert some future trouble: You don't steal cookies because you might be caught. But a little later, the forbidden act is suppressed even when there can never be any real punishment. This change occurs because the child starts to act and think as if he himself were the parent who administers praise and reproof. A three-year-old is often seen to slap his own hand as he is about to play with mud or commit some other heinous deed; he sometimes mutters some self-righteous pronouncement like "Dirty. Bad." This is the beginning of the superego, the ego's second master, which praises and punishes just as the parents did. If the ego lives up to the superego's dictates, the reward is pride. But if one of the superego's rules is broken, the superego metes out punishment just as the parents scolded or spanked or withdrew their love. There is then self-reproach and a feeling of guilt.

The formation of the superego puts the ego in a difficult position, for its two masters often issue conflicting commands. The promptings of the id are all too often in forbidden directions; if the ego gives in, the superego will punish it. What's worse is that both masters are essentially infantile. We have seen that the id's demands are blind and unreasoning, but the superego's strictures are also rooted in childish irrationality. The superego was formed when the child's cognitive abilities were still quite primitive. At that time, it could only internalize what it understood then—blind do's and don'ts. As a result, the superego is essentially irrational; Freud regarded it as largely unconscious. It issues absolute imperatives that are not accessible to reason. If the ego obeys, it must throttle various urges of the id, even if those are merely expressed in a thought or a memory. To accomplish this feat, the ego must resort to repression.

In summary, Freud's threefold division of the personality is just a way of saying that our thoughts and actions are determined by the interplay of three major factors: our biological drives, the various ways we have learned to satisfy these drives and master the external world, and the commands and prohibitions of society. Freud's contribution is his insistence that the conflicts among these three forces are inside the individual, that they are derived from childhood experiences, and that they are waged without the individual's conscious awareness.

## The Nature of Unconscious Conflict

We now turn to Freud's formulation (here drastically simplified) of the rules by which these inner wars are waged. In rough outline, the conflict begins when id-derived urges and various associated memories are pushed underground, are repressed. But the forbidden urges refuse to stay down. They find substitute outlets whose further consequence is a host of additional defenses that are erected to re-

**The Furies and the superego**   *According to Greek mythology, the pangs of guilt, which Freud attributed to the superego, are caused by outside forces—the Furies, who pursue and torment evildoers. (From a scene in Peter Hall's 1981 production of Aeschylus's Oresteia at the London National Theatre; photograph by Nobby Clark)*

inforce the original repression, hold off the id-derived flood, and allow the ego to maintain its self-regard (Freud, S., 1917a, 1926; Freud, A., 1946).

REPRESSION AND ANXIETY

What underlies repression? Freud came to believe that the crucial factor is intense *anxiety,* an emotional state akin to fear (see Chapter 3). According to Freud, various forbidden acts become associated with anxiety as the child is scolded or disciplined for performing them. The parents may resort to physical punishment or they may merely register their disapproval with a frown or reprimand; in either case, the child is threatened with the loss of their love and becomes anxious. The next time he is about to, say, finger his penis or pinch his baby brother, he will feel a twinge of anxiety, an internal signal that his parents may leave him, and that he will be abandoned and alone.

Since anxiety is intensely unpleasant, the child will do everything he can in order to remove it or to ward it off. If the cause is an external stimulus, the child's reaction is clear. He runs away and thus removes himself from the fear-inducing object. But how can he cope with a danger that comes from within? As before, he will flee from whatever evokes fear or anxiety. But now the flight is from something inside himself. To get rid of anxiety, the child must suppress that which triggers it—the forbidden act.

Freud's concept of repression applies to the thought no less than the deed. We can understand that a four-year-old boy who is punished for kicking his baby brother will refrain from such warlike acts in the future. But why does the boy stop *thinking* about them and why does he fail to remember the crucial incident, as Freud maintains? One answer is that thinking about an act is rather similar to performing it. This is especially so given the young child's limited cognitive abilities. He has not as yet fully mastered the distinction between thought and action. Nor does he know that his father can't really "read his mind," that his thoughts are private and thus immune from parental prosecution. The inhibition therefore applies not just to overt action, but to related thoughts, memories, and wishes.

SUPPLEMENTARY MECHANISMS OF DEFENSE

Repression can be regarded as the primary, initial *mechanism of defense* that protects the individual against anxiety. But repression is often incomplete. Often enough the thoughts and urges that were pushed underground refuse to stay buried and surge up again. But as they do, so does the anxiety to which they are associated. As a result, various further mechanisms of defense are brought into play to reinforce the original dam against the forbidden impulses.

*Displacement*  One such supplementary defense mechanism is *displacement.* When a geyser is dammed up, its waters usually penetrate other cracks and fissures and eventually gush up elsewhere. According to Freud, the same holds for repressed urges, which tend to find new and often disguised outlets. An example is *displaced aggression,* which develops when fear of retaliation blocks the normal direction of discharge. The child who is reprimanded by her parent turns on her playmate or vents her anger on the innocent household cat. According to many social psychologists, the same mechanism underlies the persecution of minority groups. They become convenient scapegoats for aggressive impulses fueled by social and economic unrest.

433

**Rationalization** *The expression "sour grapes" comes from a fable by Aesop, which tells of a fox who desperately desired some grapes that hung overhead. When the fox discovered that the grapes were so high that he could not reach them, he said that he never really wanted them, for they were much too sour. (From* Baby's Own Aesop *by Walter Crane, engraved and colored by Edmund Evans; reproduced from the print collection of the New York Public Library, Astor, Lenox, and Tilden Foundations)*

*Reaction formation*    In displacement, the forbidden impulse is rechanneled into a safer course. Certain other mechanisms of defense are attempts to supplement the original repression by blocking off the impulse altogether. An example is **reaction formation** in which the repressed wish is warded off by its diametrical opposite. The young girl who jealously hated her sister and was punished for hostile acts may turn her feelings into the very opposite; she now showers her sister with an exaggerated love and tenderness, a desperate bulwark against aggressive wishes that she cannot accept. But the repressed hostility can still be detected underneath the loving exterior; her love is overly solicitous and stifling and the sister probably feels smothered by it.

*Rationalization*    In reaction formation, there is an attempt (albeit not too successful) to keep the forbidden wishes at bay. Some other mechanisms represent a different line of defense; the repressed thoughts break through but they are reinterpreted and are not recognized for what they are. One example of this is **rationalization** in which the person interprets some of his own feelings or actions in more acceptable terms. The cruel father beats his child mercilessly but is sure that he does so "for the child's own good." Countless atrocities have been committed under the same guise of altruism; heretics have been tortured to save their immortal souls and cities have been razed to protect the world against barbarism. Rationalization is also employed at a more everyday level, as a defense not only against repressed wishes but against any thought that would make the individual feel unworthy and anxious. An example is the sour-grapes phenomenon. The jilted lover tells his friends that he never really cared for his lost love; eventually he believes it himself.

*Projection*    Another example of a defense mechanism in which cognitive reorganization plays a major role is **projection.** Here the forbidden urges well up and are recognized as such. But the person does not realize that these wishes are his own; instead, he attributes them to others. "I desire you" becomes "You desire me," "I hate you" becomes "You hate me"—desperate defenses against repressed sexual or hostile wishes that can no longer be banished from consciousness (Freud, 1911).

*Isolation*    In yet another defense mechanism, the dangerous memories are allowed back into consciousness; what's held back is their relation to the patient's motives and emotions. The memories themselves are retained, but they are *isolated* (so to speak, compartmentalized) from the feelings that go along with them. This mechanism is sometimes seen in people who have suffered severe distress, such as concentration camp survivors or rape victims. Some of these persons are able to relate their experiences in precise detail but are unable to recall the emotions that accompanied them.

## Origins of Unconscious Conflict

Freud believed that the unconscious conflicts he uncovered always referred to certain critical events in the individual's early life. His observations of his patients convinced him that these crucial events are remarkably similar from person to person. He concluded that all human beings go through a largely similar se-

***Hidden meanings*** *This painting* Hide and Seek *by the Russian emigré artist Pavel Tchelitchew shows the different aspects of childhood development as hiding in the branches of a gnarled tree. (*Hide and Seek, *1941–42, oil on canvas, 6′ 6½″ x 7′ ¾″, collection, the Museum of Modern Art; reproduced by permission)*

quence of significant emotional events in their early lives, that some of the most important of these involve sexual urges, and that it is this childhood past that shapes their present (Freud, 1905).

STAGES OF PSYCHOSEXUAL DEVELOPMENT

Freud's theory of psychosexual development emphasizes different stages, each of which is built upon the achievements of those before. (In this regard it resembles Jean Piaget's theory of cognitive growth, which we will take up in Chapter 14.) In Freud's view, the child starts life as a bundle of pleasure-seeking tendencies. Pleasure is obtained by the stimulation of certain zones of the body that are particularly sensitive to touch: the mouth, the anus, and the genitals. Freud called these regions ***erogenous zones,*** for he believed that the various pleasures associated with each of them have a common element which is sexual.* As the child develops, the relative importance of the zones shifts. Initially, most of the pleasure seeking is through the mouth (the ***oral stage***). With the advent of toilet concerns, the emphasis shifts to the anus (the ***anal stage***). Still later, there is an increased interest in the pleasure that can be obtained from stimulating the genitals (the ***phallic stage***). The culmination of ***psychosexual development*** is attained in adult sexuality when pleasure involves not just one's own gratification but also the social and bodily satisfaction brought to another person (the ***genital stage***).

How does the child move from one stage to the next? In part, it is a matter of physical maturation. For example, bowel control is simply impossible at birth, for the infant lacks the necessary neuromuscular readiness. But there is another element. As the child's bodily maturation proceeds, there is an inevitable change in what the parents allow, prohibit, or demand. Initially, the child nurses, then he

*One of his arguments for regarding oral and anal stimulation in infancy as ultimately sexual was the fact that such stimulation sometimes precedes (or replaces) sexual intercourse in adulthood.

is weaned. Initially, he is diapered, then he is toilet trained. Each change automatically produces some frustration and conflict as former ways of gaining pleasure are denied. (For some of Freud's hypotheses about the long-term effects of such conflicts during the oral and anal stages of adult personality, see Chapter 18, pp. 716–17.)

### THE OEDIPUS COMPLEX

We now turn to that aspect of the theory of psychosexual development that Freud himself regarded as the most important—the family triangle of love and jealousy and fear that is at the root of internalized morality and out of which grows the child's identification with the parent of the same sex. This is the **Oedipus complex,** named after the mythical king of Thebes who unknowingly committed the two most awful crimes—killing his father and marrying his mother. According to Freud, an analogous family drama is reenacted in the childhood of all men and women. Since he came to believe that the sequence of steps is somewhat different in the two sexes, we will take them up separately. We will start with his theory of how genital sexuality emerges in males (Freud, 1905).

*First act: Love and hate*   At about three or four years of age, the **phallic stage** begins. The young boy becomes increasingly interested in his penis, which becomes a source of both pride and pleasure. He masturbates and this brings satisfaction, but it is not enough. His erotic urges seek an external object. The inevitable choice is his mother (or some mother substitute). After all, he has already become attached to her through the various gratifications she provided during the oral stage. It seems only logical to direct his phallic urges to this source of all other pleasure. In some cases, this tendency is intensified by the mother herself who takes a special interest in her "little man." (An analogous pattern is seen in fathers who very often are especially fond of their daughters.) The little boy wants to be near his mother, wants to touch and caress her. In addition, he perhaps has some vaguely erotic fantasies about her when he touches his penis. He has found his first sexual partner.

**Oedipus Rex**   *From a 1955 production directed by Tyrone Guthrie with Douglas Campbell in the title role, at Stratford, Ontario. (Courtesy Billy Rose Theatre Collection, The New York Public Library at Lincoln Center, Astor, Lenox and Tilden Collections)*

unusually slow or if it is accompanied by increased heart rate or a marked galvanic skin response, that word is presumably emotion-arousing for her. Using this method, one experimenter selected a set of neutral and emotional words for each subject (Jacobs, 1955). When these were later used as the responses in a paired-associate task, the subject had more trouble in producing the emotional than the neutral items. One way of explaining the result is to assume that as the emotionally loaded word was about to be retrieved from memory, it triggered anxiety which blocked further efforts at retrieval.

Seen in this light, repression may turn out to be a special case of retrieval failure. We have previously seen that recall is enormously dependent upon the presence of an appropriate retrieval cue. We forget the street names of the city we grew up in, but most of them come back when we revisit the city after many years. The same may hold for memories that Freud said are repressed. Perhaps they are not really held back by some imperious censor; perhaps they are rather misfiled under a hard-to-reach rubric and cannot be retrieved for this reason. One might want to add some further assumptions about the role of anxiety in maintaining this state of affairs. Perhaps anxiety blocks refiling; perhaps it impedes the use of appropriate retrieval cues (Erdelyi and Goldberg, 1979).

## Problems of Freud's Dream Theory

The preceding discussion suggests that unconscious conflict and defense are probably genuine phenomena. To this extent, Freud's general position has been upheld. But the verdict has been less favorable on some of his more specific assertions. An example is his theory of dreams.

*The Nightmare* This painting by Henry Fuseli (painted in 1783 and said to have decorated Freud's office) highlights what seems to be one of the difficulties of Freud's dream theory. If all dreams are wish fulfillments, what accounts for nightmares? According to Freud, they are often dreams in which the latent dream is not sufficiently disguised. The forbidden wish is partially recognized, anxiety breaks through, and the sleeper suffers a nightmare. (Courtesy The Detroit Institute of Arts)

## Testing Freud's Theories of Repression and Defense

The fact that we are unaware of many of our own mental processes was by no means unknown to psychologists before Freud arrived on the scene. They knew that we often retrieve material from memory without conscious awareness, and that many mental operations drop out of consciousness as we automatize them by constant practice, such as the way in which we tie our shoelaces (see Ellenberger, 1970). Yet it was Freud's influence that made the term "unconscious" a part of everyday language. In addition, the term "unconscious" meant more to Freud than mental processes of which the individual is unaware. To him, it mostly referred to mental processes—acts, wishes, thoughts, perceptions—that are *kept out* of consciousness by an elaborate system of internal censorship: the mechanisms of defense headed by repression. This notion of repressive forces is the cornerstone of psychoanalytic thought. What is the evidence for unconscious processes in this more narrow, Freudian sense? Our primary concern will be with cases that involve memory and are thus akin to what Freud called repression.

### CLINICAL EVIDENCE FOR REPRESSION

One study tried to provide some objective evidence for a repressionlike effect during psychoanalytic sessions. During such sessions (as of course, in ordinary life) patients sometimes have a momentary lapse of memory. They say, "I just had a thought, but it slipped my mind." Eventually they think of what they had wanted to say, often within the same session. Are these memory lapses related to the patient's emotional preoccupations? Freud would certainly have guessed that they are, that they occur when the patient is thinking (or is about to think) of something that is especially charged with emotion.

In a test of this hypothesis, several hundred tape-recorded psychoanalytic sessions were examined for instances of such momentary forgetting. When did such lapses occur? The investigator examined the topics the patient talked about just before and just after the memory lapse. He then compared these topics with those dealt with during control intervals (taken from other sessions in which there were no lapses). The results indicate that the lapses did not occur at random; they were much more likely during periods when the patient dealt with a crucial emotional theme (Luborsky, 1973; Luborsky, Sackheim, and Christoph, 1979).

### LABORATORY STUDIES OF ANXIETY AND RECALL

There have been many efforts to produce repression and related effects in the laboratory (see Eriksen and Pierce, 1968). But this task is far from easy. According to psychoanalytic theory, motivated forgetting is a defense against anxiety. One would therefore expect that materials that are associated with anxiety will be recalled less readily than neutral items. But how can the experimenter be sure that the critical material is really anxiety-provoking for the subject?

To cope with this problem, several investigators pre-selected their items to fit each subject's own pattern of anxieties. One way of doing this is by an initial word-association test. The subject is given a list of words; she has to reply to each with the first word that comes to mind. If her reaction to any one stimulus word is

have become part of our culture and Freudian lore (often vulgarized) has become a staple of our popular literature, our stage, and our screen.

## A REEXAMINATION OF FREUDIAN THEORY

Thus far, we have presented Freud's views with a minimum of critical comment. (Our discussions of Freud's theory of female psychosexual development and the psychoanalytic approach to myths and literature were exceptions.) We now shift our perspective to consider some of his assertions in the light of present-day thought and evidence.

By what criteria can one determine whether Freud's assertions are in fact correct? Freud's own criterion was the evidence from the couch. He considered the patient's free associations, his resistances, his slips of the tongue, his dreams, and then tried to weave them into a coherent pattern that somehow made sense of all the parts. But can one really draw conclusions from this kind of clinical evidence alone? Clinical practitioners cannot be totally objective no matter how hard they try. As they listen to a patient, they are more likely to hear and remember those themes that fit in with their own views than those that do not. (This point is especially pertinent to Freud who never took notes during psychoanalytic sessions.) Would a clinician with different biases have remembered the same themes?

The issue goes deeper than objective reportage. Even if the analyst could be an utterly objective observer, he could not possibly avoid affecting that which he observes. His own theoretical preconceptions would be inevitably noticed by his patients, whose dreams and free associations would very likely be colored by them. The trouble is that there is no way of disentangling the effect of the analyst (and of his theories) upon the patient's mental productions (which we want to use as evidence for or against these theories).

Yet another problem is conceptual. Scientific theories lead to certain predictions; if these fail, the theory is refuted. But are Freud's assertions theories in this sense? What specific predictions do they lead to? Consider the hypothetical case of a boy raised by a harsh, rejecting mother and a weak, alcoholic father. What will the boy be like as an adult? Will he seek dominating women who will degrade him as his mother did? Will he try to find a warm, comforting wife upon whom he can become dependent and thus make up for the mothering he never had as a child? There is no way of predicting on psychoanalytic grounds. Each outcome makes perfectly good sense—*after* it has occurred.

Another problem with many psychoanalytic arguments is that the analyst's theory often determines whether a patient's statement should or should not be accepted at face value. Suppose a woman insists that she hates her mother. The analyst will probably believe her. But if she swears that she loves her mother, the analyst may conclude that she, like Shakespeare's lady, "doth protest too much." He may then interpret her protestations of love as meaning the exact opposite, as reflecting a reaction formation against her "real" feelings of hate. The trouble with this kind of two-way reasoning is that it becomes difficult to find any sort of disproof. (For a discussion of this and related issues see Grünbaum, 1984.)

Such considerations suggest that if we want to test Freud's assertions, we must look for more objective evidence and must be more rigorous in the way in which we interpret it. We will begin by considering some work that bears on Freud's theories of repression and unconscious defense.

**Hamlet confronting his mother in her bedroom**   *A scene from Lawrence Olivier's 1948 film* Hamlet. *Olivier's conception of the role of Hamlet was seriously affected by Ernest Jones's psychoanalytic interpretation of the play. His casting of a young attractive actress, Eileen Herlie, for the part of Hamlet's mother helped to underscore the Oedipus theme. (Courtesy Universal Pictures)*

myths. The artistic production reflects the artist's own inner conflicts and has impact upon others because it strikes the same unconscious chords in them. Perhaps the most famous example of psychoanalytic literary interpretations is Freud's analysis of *Hamlet,* later elaborated by his student Ernest Jones (Jones, 1954). The central puzzle of the play is Hamlet's indecisiveness. He waits until the end of the fifth act before he finally avenges his father's death upon his hated uncle, a delay that causes his own death as well as the death of virtually everyone else in the play, innocent as well as guilty. To Freud and Jones, the clue to Hamlet's inaction is the Oedipus complex. Hamlet is paralyzed because he must kill a man who did precisely what he himself unconsciously wanted to do, kill his father and marry his mother. According to Freud and Jones, the play grips the audience because it stirs the same latent conflicts in them.

Shakespearean scholars are by no means agreed on the virtues of this interpretation, though some find it interesting. But the issue goes further than that. Suppose we accept the interpretation that Freud and Jones offer. Is this *the* key to Hamlet, which is then shorn of all its mysteries, like a completed crossword puzzle that is discarded once it is solved? The truth is that there is no one key, there is no one meaning of *Hamlet,* for a work of art is necessarily ambiguous. As with myths and legends, this or the other interpretation may help to illuminate them, but it does not explain them away. *Hamlet* may be about Oedipal conflicts, but many hack novels have the same theme. What makes the one a great literary treasure while the others are forgotten almost immediately?

These points argue against the overenthusiastic application of psychoanalytic interpretation to literary works. But for good or ill (probably for both), Freud's impact on literature and literary criticism has been enormous. Most literary critics today have at least a passing acquaintance with Freud's basic works, and many major authors have been consciously affected by him. By now, his insights

Stated in the most general terms, Freud's theory asserts that dreams tend to reflect the current emotional preoccupations of the dreamer, including those of which he is unaware, often portrayed in a condensed and symbolic form. This is probably quite true. Thus, patients who await major surgery reveal their fears in what they dream about during the two or three nights before the operation. Their fears are rarely expressed directly; few, if any, of their dreams are about scalpels or operating rooms. The reference is indirect, in condensed and symbolized form, as in dreams about falling from tall ladders or standing on a high, swaying bridge, or about a decrepit machine that needs repair (Breger, Hunter, and Lane, 1971).

Such evidence indicates that dreams do express whatever motives are currently most important. But Freud's theory went much further than this. As we saw, he believed that the manifest dream is a censored and disguised version of the latent dream that lies underneath and represents a wish fulfillment. This conception of dreams has been much criticized. To begin with, there is considerable doubt that all (or even many) dreams are attempts at wish fulfillments, whether disguised or open. In one study, subjects were made extremely thirsty before they went to sleep. Since thirst is hardly a forbidden urge, there is no reason to suppose an internal censorship. However, none of the subjects reported dreams of drinking. Since they were so thirsty, why didn't they gratify themselves in their dreams (Dement and Wolpert, 1958)?

Another problem is the fact that the same urge is sometimes freely expressed in dreams, but heavily disguised on other occasions. Tonight, the sleeper dreams of unabashed sexual intercourse; tomorrow night, she dreams of riding a team of wild horses. For sake of argument, let us agree that riding is a symbol for intercourse. But why should the censor disguise tomorrow what is so freely allowed tonight?

One investigator, C. S. Hall, has come up with a plausible suggestion (Hall, 1953). According to Hall, the dream symbol does not *disguise* an underlying idea; on the contrary, it *expresses* it. In Hall's view, the dream is a rather concrete mental shorthand that embodies a feeling or emotion. Riding a horse, plowing a field, planting a seed—all of these may be concrete renditions of the idea of sexual intercourse. But they are not meant to hide this idea. Their function is much the same as the cartoonist's picture of Uncle Sam or John Bull. These are representations of the United States and of England, but they are certainly not meant as disguises for them. During sleep, more specifically during REM sleep (see Chapter 3), we are incapable of the extreme complexity and abstractness of waking mental life. We are thus reduced to a more concrete and archaic form of thinking. The wishes and fears of our waking life are still present at night, and we dream about them. But the way in which these are now expressed tends to be more primitive, a concrete pictorialization that combines fragments of various waking concerns and serves as a kind of symbolic cartoon.

## Biology or Culture?

While many psychologists agree with Freud's thesis that there is unconscious conflict, they are more skeptical of his particular assertions of what these conflicts are. One of their major quarrels is with Freud's insistence that the pattern of these conflicts is biologically based and will therefore be found in essentially the same form in all men and all women.

## THE EMPHASIS ON SOCIAL FACTORS

Since Freud believed that the key to emotional development is in biology, he assumed that its progression followed a universal course. In his view, all humans pass through oral, anal, and phallic stages and suffer the conflicts appropriate to each stage. This conception has been challenged by various clinical practitioners, many of whom used Freud's own psychoanalytic methods. These critics felt that Freud had overemphasized biological factors at the expense of social ones. This point was first raised by one of Freud's own students, Alfred Adler (1870–1937). It was later taken up by several like-minded authors who are often grouped together under the loose label *neo-Freudians,* including Erich Fromm (1900–1980), Karen Horney (1885–1952), and H. S. Sullivan (1892–1949).

According to the neo-Freudians, human development cannot be properly understood by focusing on the particular anatomical regions—mouth, anus, genitals—through which the child tries to gratify his instinctual desires. In their view, the important question is how humans relate, or try to relate, to others—whether by dominating, or submitting, or becoming dependent, or whatever. Their description of our inner conflicts is therefore in social terms. For example, if they see a mother who toilet trains her child very severely, they are likely to interpret her behavior as part of an overall pattern whereby she tries to push the child to early achievement; the specific frustrations of the anal stage as such are of lesser concern to them. Similarly for the sexual sphere. According to Freud, the neurotic conflict centers on the repression of erotic impulses. According to the neo-Freudian critics, the real difficulty is in the area of interpersonal relationships. Neurosis often leads to sexual symptoms, not because sex is a powerful biological motive that is pushed underground, but rather because it is one of the most sensitive barometers of interpersonal attitudes. The man who can only relate to other people by competing with them may well be unable to find sexual pleasure in his marriage bed; but the sexual malfunction is an *effect* of his neurotic social pattern rather than its *cause.*

The same emphasis on social factors highlights the neo-Freudian explanation for how these conflicts arise in the first place. In contrast to Freud, it denies that these conflicts are biologically pre-ordained; they rather depend upon the specific cultural conditions in which the child is reared. According to the neo-Freudians, the conflicts that Freud observed may have characterized *his* patients, but this does not mean that these same patterns will be found in persons who live at other times and in other places.

## THE REJECTION OF CULTURAL ABSOLUTISM

One set of relevant findings came from another discipline, *cultural anthropology,* which concerns itself with the practices and beliefs of different peoples throughout the world. There are evidently considerable variations in these patterns, with accompanying variations in the kind of person who is typical in each setting. Personality characteristics that are typical in our culture are by no means universal, a result that was beautifully tuned to the antibiological bias of the neo-Freudians.

A well-known example concerns cultural variations in the roles that different societies assign to the two sexes. An influential study by the American anthropologist Margaret Mead, "Sex and Temperament," compared the personality traits of men and women in three New Guinea tribes that lived within a hundred-mile

*Margaret Mead* (Courtesy The American Museum of Natural History)

radius. Among the Arapesh, both men and women were mild, cooperative, and, so to speak, "maternal" in their attitudes to each other and especially to children. Among the neighboring Mundugomor, both sexes were ferociously aggressive and quarrelsome. In yet another tribe, the Tchambuli, the usual sex roles were reversed. The women were the hale and hardy breadwinners who fished and went to market unadorned. While the women managed the worldly affairs, the men gossiped and pranced about, adjusted elaborate hairdos, carved and painted, and practiced intricate dance steps (Mead, 1935, 1937). The neo-Freudians took such findings as a strong argument against the cultural absolutism which regards the patterns of modern Western society as the built-in givens of human nature.

Several anthropologists have criticized Mead's account as an oversimplification. They point out that there are probably some universal sex roles after all; for example, warfare is generally conducted by the men, even among the Tchambuli. They argue that some of the differences between male and female aggressiveness may very well be due to biological factors, for aggression is in part under hormonal control; as androgen levels rise, both human and animal males become more aggressive (see Chapter 10). What culture does is to determine how this aggression is to be channeled and against whom, whether it is to be valued, and how much of it is allowed. (For recent discussions of Mead's work, see Freeman, 1983, 1986; Brady, 1983; Patience and Smith, 1986.)

## Critiques of Freud's Theories of Development

It's rather ironic that Freud, whose views of childhood development had such a powerful influence on Western thought, never himself studied children. His theories of early development were mostly based on his adult patients' recollections, dreams, and free associations. Under the circumstances, it was essential to gather evidence on actual childhood behavior.

Today the study of human development is a flourishing enterprise. We will describe it in some detail in Chapters 14 and 15. For now our concern is with evidence that bears directly on Freud's theories of child development. While some of Freud's broader concepts are still of considerable influence, the verdict has not been too favorable on his more specific hypotheses. (For an overview, see Zigler and Child, 1972.)

The most influential of Freud's assertions about early childhood concerns sexuality and the Oedipus complex. Our major source of information in this area comes from studies of other cultures. On the whole, the evidence was welcome grist to the neo-Freudian mill: The Oedipus conflict is not universal but depends upon cultural variations in the family constellation.

This point was first raised some fifty years ago by the English anthropologist Bronislaw Malinowski on the basis of his observations of the Trobriand Islanders of the Western Pacific (Malinowski, 1927). The family pattern of the Trobriand Islanders is quite different from our own. Among the Trobrianders, the biological father is not the head of the household. He spends time with his children and plays with them, but he exerts no authority. This role is reserved for the mother's brother who acts as a disciplinarian. The Trobriand Islanders thus separate the roles that in Freud's Vienna were played by one and the same person.

According to Freud, this different family pattern should make no difference. There should still be an Oedipus complex in which the father is the hated villain

*Freud at age sixteen with his mother, Amalie Nathanson Freud* *Freud was his mother's first-born and her favorite, a fact that may have affected his theory of the human family drama. As he put it, "A man who has been the indisputable favorite of his mother keeps for life the feeling of a conqueror, that confidence of success that often induces real success." (E. Jones, 1954, p. 5; photograph courtesy Mary Evans/Freud copyrights)*

*Freud looking at a bust of himself sculpted for his seventy-fifth birthday* by O. Nemon *(Courtesy Wide World Photos)*

for, after all, it is he who is the little boy's sexual rival. But this did not turn out to be the case. Malinowski saw no signs of friction between sons and fathers, though he did observe a fair amount of hostility directed at the maternal uncle. The same held for dreams and folk tales. The Trobriand Islanders believe that there are prophetic dreams of death; these generally involve the death of the maternal uncle. Similarly there are no myths about evil fathers or stepfathers; again, the villain is typically the mother's brother. If we accept Freud's notion that dreams (and myths) involve unconscious wishes and preoccupations, we are forced to conclude that the Trobriand boy hates his uncle, not his father. In sum, the child has fears and fantasies about the authoritarian figure in his life, the man who bosses him around. This is the father in Freud's Austria, but the uncle on the Trobriand Islands. His fears are not about his mother's lover as such, for the Trobriand boy does not hate the father who plays this role.

## FREUD'S CONTRIBUTIONS IN RETROSPECT

We have seen that many of Freud's beliefs have not been confirmed. There are good grounds to doubt Freud's essentially Hobbesian view of human nature. There is little evidence for his general theory of psychosexual development, even less for his male-centered conception of feminine psychology, and there is a good reason to believe that he overemphasized biological givens at the expense of cultural factors. We have also seen that Freud can be criticized not just for what he asserted but for the way in which he tried to prove his claims. By now, there is general agreement that the psychoanalytic couch is not a source of objective fact, and that many of Freud's theoretical proposals are rather vague and metaphorical, so that it is not clear how one can decide whether they are right or wrong.

All in all, this is a formidable set of criticisms. But even so, many psychologists would maintain that, wrong as he probably was in any number of particulars, Sig-

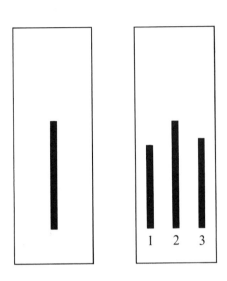

**12.1 The stimulus cards in Asch's social pressure experiment** *The cards are drawn to scale. In the actual experiment, they were generally placed on the ledge of a blackboard, separated by forty inches. (Asch, 1956)*

**12.2 The subject in a social pressure experiment** *(A) The true subject (center) listens to the instructions. (B) On hearing the unanimous verdict of the others, he leans forward to look at the cards more carefully. (C) After twelve such trials, he explains that "he has to call them as he sees them." (Photographs by William Vandivert)*

An amusing example of the social nature of many of our beliefs is provided by an experiment in which several social psychologists asked a number of their students to stop in the middle of a crowded thoroughfare in New York City and to look up at the sixth floor window of an office building on the other side of the street. When only one such person looked up, it had virtually no effect on the passersby. But when the number of the upward lookers became fifteen, almost half of the passersby stopped and looked up too. What happened is perfectly obvious. The people who saw the others look up surely believed that there was something to see. (After all, who would be paranoid enough to assume that the upward lookers were social psychologists conducting an experiment?) For at bottom we are all convinced that we all share the same physical reality. Within limits (not everyone has perfect eyesight; some people are color blind), what you can see, I can see too. Given our natural—perhaps morbid—curiosity, what would be more natural than to stop and look up too to discover just what it was that *they* saw (Milgram, Bickman, and Berkowitz, 1969).

But the shared aspects of human knowledge go deeper than this, for our very notion of physical reality is at least in part a matter of mutual agreement. This point was made very dramatically in a classic study performed by Solomon Asch (Asch, 1956).

In Asch's experiment, nine or ten subjects are brought together in a laboratory room and shown pairs of cards placed a few feet in front of them. On one card is a black line, say, 8 inches long. On the other card are three lines of varying lengths, say 6 1/4, 8, and 6 3/4 inches (Figure 12.1). The subjects are asked to make a simple perceptual judgment. They have to indicate which of the three lines on the one card is equal in length to the one line on the other card. Then the experimenter tells the subjects that this procedure is only a minor prelude to another study and casually asks them, in the interest of saving time, to indicate their judgments aloud by calling them out in turn (the three comparison lines are designated by the numbers 1, 2, and 3 printed underneath them). This procedure continues for a dozen or so pairs of cards.

Considering the sizable differences among the stimuli, the task is absurdly simple except for one thing: There is only one "real" subject. All of the others are the experimenter's secret confederates. They have arranged their seating order so that most of them will call out their judgments before the real subject's turn comes around. After the first few trials, they unanimously render false judgments on most of the ones thereafter. For example, the confederates might declare that a 6 1/4-inch line equals an 8-inch line, and so on, for a dozen more trials. What does the real subject do now? (See Figure 12.2.)

Asch found that the chances were less than one in four that the real subject would be fully independent and would stick to his guns on all trials on which the

A

B

C

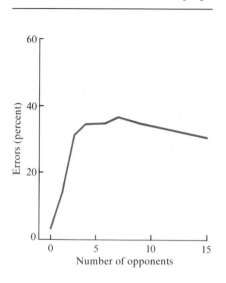

12.3 *The effect of social pressure* The extent to which the subject yielded against the size of the group pitted against him is demonstrated by this figure. In this situation, the effect of group size seems to reach a maximum at three, though other studies (such as Gerard, Wilhelmy, and Conolley, 1968) have found that conformity continues to rise beyond this point as the number of opponents increases. (After Asch, 1955)

*The interpersonal nature of reality* A scene from the 1939 film Gaslight, with Charles Boyer and Ingrid Bergman, in which a scheming husband terrifies his young wife into doubting her own sanity. (Courtesy the Kobal Collection)

group disagreed with him (Figure 12.3). Most subjects yielded to the group on at least some occasions, in fine disregard of the evidence of their senses—a result with rather uncomfortable implications for the democratic process. When interviewed after the experiment, most of the yielding subjects made it clear that the group didn't really affect how they *saw* the lines. No matter what everyone else said, the 8-inch line still looked bigger than the 6 1/4-inch line. But the subjects wondered whether they were right, became worried about their vision and sanity, and were exceedingly embarrassed at expressing their deviance in public (Asch, 1952, 1956; Asch and Gleitman, 1953).

For our present purposes, our primary concern is not so much with what the subjects *did,* but rather with how they *felt.* In this regard, most of them were alike. Some yielded and some were independent (see Chapter 13), but assuming they did not suspect a trick (and few of them did), they were generally very much disturbed. Why all the furor? The answer is that Asch's procedure had violated a basic premise of the subjects' existence: However people may differ, they all share the same physical reality. Under the circumstances, it is small wonder that Asch's subjects were deeply alarmed by a discrepancy they had never previously encountered. (Needless to say, the whole experiment was carefully explained to them immediately afterwards.)

What accounts for the assumption of a socially shared reality? We can only speculate. One possibility is that the notion that others perceive more or less the same world that we do is a built-in facet of the human animal. Another is that this notion is part and parcel of a more general consistency that provides the criterion for what we mean when we say that an object is "real." For example, when something is real, the senses provide *consistent* information about it. Macbeth sees a dagger but cannot touch it and therefore regards it as "a dagger of the mind, a false creation proceeding from the heat-oppressed brain." Another criterion is consistency across time. Real objects provide what one philosopher called a "permanent possibility of a sensation." You may look away from a tree, but it is still there when your gaze returns to it a moment later (J. S. Mill, 1865). At least in principle, the general notion of a fixed reality that is "out there" and independent of our momentary point of view is a rock-bottom concept that we all accept. If it is challenged, we become deeply disturbed. It may be that the definition of reality —perhaps from the outset, perhaps through learning—includes not only agreement among different perceptions and memories within one person but also agreement with those of others. As a result, the belief that others see, feel, and hear pretty much as we do becomes a cognitive axiom of our everyday experience. When this axiom is violated, as it is in Asch's experiment, a vital prop is knocked out from under us, a prop so basic we never even realized that it was there.

## Social Comparison

The Asch study shows what happens when the clear evidence of one's senses is contradicted by the verdict of a unanimous group. But suppose that our own perception does not provide a clear-cut answer. This would happen, for example, if the lines differed by only a small amount. If left to our own devices, we would try to obtain some further sensory evidence. We might look at the lines once more

***Social comparison*** *The two museum visitors don't seem quite sure what to make of Marisol's sculpture* The Family *and compare reactions. (Photograph by Burt Glinn/© 1964 Magnum Photos)*

but from a different angle, or try to measure them with a ruler. But if we can't do that, then it's only reasonable to listen to what others have to say. Their judgment can then be used in lieu of further information provided by our own eyes or hands. If the others should now disagree with us, we might well change our own answer on their say-so. Several studies have shown that this is precisely what occurs in an Asch-type experiment in which the discrimination is fairly difficult. There is more yielding and very little emotional disturbance (Crutchfield, 1955; for further discussion of conformity effects, see Chapter 13, pp. 511–14).

This general line of reasoning may explain why people seek the opinion of others whenever they are confronted by a situation that they do not fully understand. To evaluate the situation, they need more information. If they cannot get it first hand, they will try to compare their own reactions to those of others (Festinger, 1954; Suls and Miller, 1977). The need for such ***social comparison*** is especially pronounced when the evaluations pertain to social issues, such as the qualifications of a political candidate or the pros and cons of fluoridating the water supply.

## Cognitive Processes and Belief

The preceding discussion has shown that people try to make sense of the world they encounter. But how? In effect, they do this by looking for some consistency among their own experiences and memories, and then turning to other people for comparison and confirmation. If all checks out, then well and good. But what if there is some incongruity? The Asch study showed what happens when there is a serious incongruity between one's own experiences (and the beliefs based upon them) and those reported by others. But suppose the incongruity is among the person's own experiences, beliefs, or actions? Many social psychologists believe that this will trigger some tendency to restore cognitive consistency—to reinterpret the situation so as to minimize whatever inconsistency may be there.

What kinds of mechanisms might explain this general tendency to reinterpret aspects of our experience so that they fit together sensibly? A very influential approach was developed by Leon Festinger who proposed that any perceived inconsistency among various aspects of knowledge, feelings, and behavior sets up an unpleasant internal state that he called *cognitive dissonance,* which people try to reduce whenever possible (Festinger, 1957).

One of the earliest examples is provided by a study of a sect that was awaiting the end of the world. The founder of the sect announced that she had received a message from the "Guardians" of outer space. On a certain day, there would be an enormous flood. Only the true believers were to be saved and would be picked up at midnight of the appointed day in flying saucers. (Technology has advanced considerably since the days of Noah's Ark.) On doomsday, the members of the sect huddled together, awaiting the predicted cataclysm. The arrival time of the flying saucers came and went; tension mounted. Finally, the leader of the sect received another message: To reward the faith of the faithful, the world was saved. Joy broke out, and the believers became more faithful than ever (Festinger, Riecken, and Schachter, 1956).

Given the failure of a clear-cut prophecy, one might have expected the very opposite. A disconfirmation of a predicted event should presumably lead one to abandon the beliefs that produced the prediction. But cognitive dissonance theory says otherwise. By abandoning the belief that there are Guardians, the person who had once held this belief would have to accept a painful dissonance between her present skepticism and her past beliefs and actions. Her prior faith would now appear extremely foolish. Some members of the sect had gone to such lengths as giving up their jobs or spending their savings; such acts would lose all meaning in retrospect without the belief in the Guardians. Under the circumstances, the dissonance was intolerable. It was reduced by a belief in the new message which bolstered the original belief. Since other members of the sect stood fast along with them, their conviction was strengthened all the more. They could now think of themselves not as fools, but as loyal, steadfast members of a courageous little band whose faith had saved the earth.

*(Drawing by Rea; © 1955, 1983, The New Yorker Magazine, Inc.)*

**Attitudes** *Attitudes are a combination of beliefs, feelings, and evaluations, coupled with some predisposition to act accordingly. (Left: photograph by Sylvia Johnson/Woodfin Camp, 1989. Right: photograph by Susan McElhinney, 1980/Woodfin Camp)*

## ATTITUDES

Social beliefs are accompanied by strong feelings. Take the conviction that abortion is murder—a far cry from the many beliefs we hold that are completely unencumbered by emotion, such as our nonchalant assurance that the sum of the angles of a triangle is 180 degrees. Emotionally tinged social views of the former kind are generally called attitudes. Since various people often have different attitudes, they tend to interpret many social situations differently; the same crowd may look like a group of peaceful demonstrators to one observer and like a rioting mob to another.

As modern social psychologists use the term, an **attitude** is a rather stable mental position held toward some idea, or object, or person. Examples are attitudes toward nuclear power, the legalization of marijuana, school integration, or packaged breakfast foods. Every attitude is a combination of beliefs, feelings, and evaluations, and some predisposition to act accordingly. Thus, people who differ in their attitudes toward nuclear power will probably have different beliefs on the subject (e.g., "nuclear power plants are—or are not—unsafe"), will evaluate it differently (from extreme *pro* to extreme *con*), and these differences will make them more likely to take some actions rather than others (e.g., to support or protest the construction of a new nuclear plant).

### Attitudes and Behavior

Attitudes can be measured in a number of ways. The most widely used methods involve some form of self-report. For example, the subject might be given an **attitude questionnaire** with items that relate to the matter at hand. Thus, in a questionnaire on nuclear power and related issues, subjects might be given a statement such as: "Accidental explosions in nuclear plants pose some danger; but this risk is relatively small compared to the economic and social benefits of cheap and abundant energy." They would then be asked to select a number between, say, + 10 and − 10 to indicate the extent of their agreement or disagreement. The sum of a person's responses to a number of statements that all tap the same concerns may then provide a quantitative expression of that person's attitude.

Do attitudes as measured by self-report predict what people actually do? The question has led to controversy, for some earlier reports suggested that the relationship is much weaker than one might have thought. During the thirties when there was considerable prejudice against Orientals, Richard LaPiere traveled through the country with a Chinese couple and stopped at over fifty hotels and motels and at nearly two hundred restaurants. All but one hotel gave them accommodations, and no restaurant refused them service. Later on the very same establishments received a letter that asked whether they would house or serve Chinese persons. Ninety-two percent of the replies were "No" (LaPiere, 1934). It appeared that there was a major inconsistency between people's attitudes as verbally expressed and their actual behavior.

The results of this and some related studies led some social psychologists to doubt whether the attitude concept is particularly useful. If attitudes don't predict behavior, what is the point of studying them in the first place? (Wicker, 1969). But upon further analysis, this pessimism proved to be unwarranted. For later studies showed that under many circumstances attitudes do indeed predict behavior. Thus voter preferences during the four presidential campaigns of 1952 to 1964 as expressed in preelection interviews were a pretty good predictor of later behavior in the voting booth: 85 percent of the persons interviewed voted in line with their previously expressed preference. For the most part, those who shifted had initial preferences that were rather weak (Kelley and Mirer, 1974).

It appears that attitudes often do predict behavior. But if so, how can we explain the fact that they don't always do so? One possible factor concerns situational pressures that may override other considerations. This holds for personality characteristics (being sociable or withdrawn, bold or fearful, and so on). Just about everybody stops at a red light, regardless of whether they are bold or anxious; and just about everybody is hushed at a funeral, regardless of whether they are sociable or shy (see Chapter 18 for further discussion). What holds for personality characteristics also holds for attitudes. LaPiere's Chinese couple consisted of two young students who were attractive and well-groomed and who were accompanied by a white professor. Here, the situational pressures probably made refusal difficult and embarrassing. Under the circumstances, they may well have combined to override the ethnic prejudice.

Even more important is how specifically the attitude is defined. The more general one's definition, the less likely is it to predict a particular bit of behavior. One study analyzed the relation between general attitudes to environmentalism and a particular act: volunteering for various activities of the Sierra Club. They found no relation. But when they tested the attitudes toward the Sierra Club as such, they found a substantial correlation between attitude and action; those who had stated strongly positive views toward the club were much more likely to volunteer (Weigel, Vernon, and Tognacci, 1974). In a similar vein are the results of a study on women's attitudes to birth control. Positive attitudes toward birth control *in general* showed only a negligible correlation with the use of oral contraceptives during a two-year period. But attitudes toward using birth control pills *in particular* correlated quite well with their actual use during this period (Davidson and Jaccard, 1979).

A

B

**You don't have to be Jewish**

**to love Levy's**
real Jewish Rye

*Attempts at persuasive communication*
*Two advertising messages that try to change consumer attitudes toward various products. (A) links a perfume to exotic glamour; (B) asserts that a certain bread will appeal to any ethnic group whatever. (Courtesy Guerlain; Best Foods Baking Group)*

## Attitude Change

While attitudes have a certain resilience, their stability is threatened at every turn; especially in modern mass society where our attitudes and beliefs are under continual assault. Hundreds of commercials urge us to buy one product rather than another, political candidates clamor for our vote, and any number of organizations exhort us to fight for (or against) arms control, or legalized abortion, or environmental protection, and so on and so on. When we add these mass-produced appeals to the numerous private attempts at persuasion undertaken by our friends and relatives (let alone our would-be lovers), it is hardly surprising that attitudes sometimes do change. Social psychologists have spent a great deal of effort in trying to understand how such attitude changes come about.

### PERSUASIVE COMMUNICATIONS

A number of investigators have studied the effectiveness of so-called ***persuasive communications.*** These are messages that openly try to persuade us: to stop smoking, to outlaw abortion, to favor capital punishment, or—on a more humble level—to choose one brand of toothpaste rather than another. Among the factors that determine whether a given message has its desired effect are the person who sends the message and the message itself (Cialdini, Petty, and Cacioppo, 1981; McGuire, 1985).

*The message source* One factor that determines whether someone will change your mind on a given issue is who that someone is. To begin with, there is the element of ***credibility.*** Not surprisingly, communications have more of an effect if they are attributed to someone who is an acknowledged expert than to someone who is not. Thus a recommendation that antihistamines should be sold over the counter was more effective when ascribed to the *New England Journal of Medicine* than to a popular mass circulation magazine; a positive review of an obscure modern poem was more likely to lead to upward reevaluations of that poem if the review was attributed to T.S. Eliot rather than to another student (Hovland and Weiss, 1952; Aronson, Turner, and Carlsmith, 1963).

Expertise is important, but so is ***trustworthiness.*** For the would-be persuader will have a much harder time if we believe that she has something to gain from persuading us. A number of studies have shown that communicators are more effective when they argue for a position that seems to be against their own self-interest. In one study, students were shown statements that argued either for or against the strengthening of law enforcement agencies and that were attributed either to a prosecuting attorney or to a criminal. Statements in favor of stronger law enforcement had more effect when they were thought to be made by the criminal than by the prosecutor; the reverse was true for statements in favor of weaker law enforcement (Walster, Aronson, and Abrahams, 1966). When a used car salesman tells you *not* to buy a car from his lot, you are likely to believe him. (Unless you believe that the other lot to which he refers you belongs to his brother-in-law.)

***Another attempt to persuade*** *An American advertisement from around 1900. (Frontispiece from* The Wonderful World of American Advertising, 1865–1900 *by Leonard de Vries and Ilonka van Amstel, Chicago: Follett, 1972)*

*The message*　However important the messenger, the message she delivers is surely more important yet. What are the factors that determine whether that message will change attitudes?

One would assume that one important element is the kind of argument on which the persuader rests her case. These arguments are sometimes strong and compelling, as in pleas to stop smoking because it leads to lung cancer. They are sometimes weak and unconvincing, as in appeals to buy a certain cereal because a particular baseball star says it is his favorite breakfast food. On the face of it, one might assume that strong arguments would be more effective than weak ones. But according to some authors, this isn't necessarily so (Petty and Cacioppo, 1985).

This somewhat paradoxical prediction is the core of the so-called ***elaboration-likelihood model*** of persuasion. According to this model, there are two routes to persuasion. One is the ***central route to persuasion,*** in which we follow the message with some care and mentally elaborate its arguments with yet further arguments and counterarguments of our own. We would take this route if the issue is one that matters to us, and if we're not diverted by other matters. Here content and information are what matter, and strong arguments will indeed be more effective in changing our minds than will weak arguments. But the situation is quite different if the message comes by way of the ***peripheral route to persuasion.*** We'll be induced to take this route if we don't care much about the issue, or if the message isn't clearly heard because of background noise, or if we are otherwise distracted. If so, then content and arguments matter little. What counts instead is how or by whom or in what surroundings the message is presented.

Some evidence in line with this model comes from a study on the effects of distraction on persuasion in which the investigators tried to change students' attitudes in favor of a rather steep proposed college tuition increase. Some of the students were given a weak argument: the extra money would be used to plant better shrubs on the campus. Others heard a stronger argument: the money would be used to hire more and better professors and to improve library facilities. Half of the students heard one of these two messages without distraction; the other half heard it while simultaneously monitoring a computer screen to determine whether certain letters did or did not appear. As predicted by the elaboration-likelihood model, when there was no distraction the stronger argument led to more persuasion than the weaker one. When the subject was distracted, however, the superiority of the better argument was abolished (Petty, Wells, and Brock, 1976).

The so-called central route to persuasion involves reasoned thought. But just what is the peripheral route? According to some authors, it often represents a kind of mental shortcut. After all, there are only so many things we can pay attention to, and so we use some rules of thumb, or ***heuristics,*** to help us decide whether to accept or reject the message (Eagly and Chaiken, 1984; Chaiken, 1987). Such heuristics may include the speaker's apparent expertise ("experts know what they're talking about"), or likability ("nice people can be trusted"), or the sheer number or length of the arguments that are presented, regardless of how good they are ("the more arguments they give, the more likely that they are right"). Such heuristics in reacting to persuasive communications are reminiscent of heuristics in decision making; both are mental shortcuts we resort to because our cognitive capacity is limited (see Chapter 8, p. 309, for a further discussion of heuristics).

COGNITIVE DISSONANCE AND ATTITUDE CHANGE

We've already seen that attitudes can affect behavior. But the relation can also go the other way. For in some situations, what an individual does will lead to a change in his attitudes. According to some social psychologists, this effect is produced by a tendency to reduce cognitive dissonance analogous to that which we've considered in the context of a change in beliefs.

*Post-decision dissonance*  Suppose there is some inconsistency between a person's attitudes and her behavior. Suppose further that the behavior is something she has already done. How can she reconcile the inconsistency now? She can't change her behavior, for that's past and done with. All she can do is to readjust her present attitude.

Dissonance theorists point to a number of phenomena that demonstrate attitude changes that preserve some harmony between past acts and present attitudes. Some involve reevaluations that occur after some irrevocable decision has been made. Suppose a person has to choose between two alternatives: to attend one college rather than another, or to buy one make of automobile rather than another. If both options are attractive, the final decision will necessarily lead to dissonance—for whichever alternative is chosen means giving up the other. According to the theory, there will now be a tendency to reduce dissonance by reevaluating the two alternatives: the one that was finally chosen will seem more attractive and the one that was rejected will seem less attractive than it did before. A number of studies have given results in line with this prediction (e.g., Brehm, 1956). In one such study, the investigators asked bettors at a race track to estimate their horse's chances. Some bettors were asked to make this estimate just before they reached the betting window; others were asked to make the estimate immediately after they made their bets. The results were in line with dissonance theory: Bettors were much more certain that their horse would win after they had placed their bet than just before (Knox and Inkster, 1968).

*Justification of effort*  Some related findings concern retrospective explanations of prior efforts. People often make considerable sacrifices to attain a goal—backbreaking exertion to scale a mountain, years and years of study to become a cardiologist. Was it worth it? According to dissonance theory, the goal will be esteemed more highly the harder it was to reach. If it were not, there would be cognitive dissonance. Support comes from common observation of the effects of harsh initiation rites, such as fraternity hazing. After the ordeal is passed, the initiates seem to value their newly found membership all the more. Similar effects have been obtained in the laboratory. Subjects admitted to a discussion group after going through a fairly harsh screening test put a higher value on their new membership (Aronson and Mills, 1959; Gerard and Mathewson, 1966).

*Forced compliance*  A related result is the effect of ***forced compliance.**** The basic idea is simple. Suppose someone agrees to give a speech in support of a view that

***Justification of effort***  *Newly accepted members of a group tend to value their group membership all the more if their initiation was especially harsh, as in the case of Marines who have gone through boot camp. (Photograph by James Nachtwey/ Magnum)*

---

* The term *forced compliance* was coined to describe the phenomenon when it was first demonstrated experimentally (Festinger and Carlsmith, 1959). It is a bit of a misnomer since the subject is not really "forced" to lie about his attitudes but is rather persuaded or coaxed. Modern social psychologists prefer the more accurate—if more clumsy—designation *counter-attitudinal advocacy.*

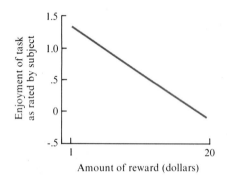

**12.4　The effect of forced compliance on attitude**　*After being paid either $1 or $20 to tell someone that a boring task they had just performed was very interesting, subjects were asked to rate their own true attitude. As the figure shows, subjects who were only paid $1 gave a much higher rating than those paid $20. (After Festinger and Carlsmith, 1959)*

is contrary to his own position, as in the case of a bartender arguing for prohibition. Will his public act change his private views? The answer seems to depend upon why he agreed to make the speech in the first place. If he was bribed by an enormous sum, there will be little effect. As he looks back upon his public denunciation of alcohol, he knows why he did what he did; $500 in cold cash is justification enough. But suppose he gave the speech with lesser urging and received only a trifling sum. If we later ask what he thinks about prohibition, we will find that he has begun to believe in his own speech. According to Festinger, the reason is the need to reduce cognitive dissonance. If the bartender asks himself why he took a public stand so contrary to his own attitudes, he can find no adequate justification; the few dollars he received are not enough. To reduce the dissonance, the compliant bartender does the only thing he can: He decides that what he said wasn't really all that different from what he believes.

A number of studies have demonstrated such forced compliance effects in the laboratory. In a classic experiment, subjects were asked to perform several extremely boring tasks, such as packing spools into a tray and then unpacking and turning one screw after another for a quarter turn. When they were finished, they were induced to tell another subject (who was about to engage in the same activities) that the tasks were really very interesting. They were paid either $1 or $20 for lying in this way. When later asked how enjoyable they had found the tasks, the well-paid subjects said that they were boring, while the poorly paid subjects said that they were fairly interesting. This result is rather remarkable. One might have guessed that the well-paid liar would have been more persuaded by his own arguments than the poorly paid one. But contrary to this initial intuition—and in line with dissonance theory—the exact opposite was the case (Festinger and Carlsmith, 1959; see Figure 12.4). A number of other studies have performed variants on the original experiment with essentially the same results (e.g., Rosenfeld, Giacalone, and Tedeschi, 1984).

DISSONANCE RECONSIDERED

The reevaluation of prior decisions and the effect of forced compliance seem to be ways of reducing dissonance. But just what is the dissonance that is here reduced? In the early days of dissonance theory, dissonance was regarded as essentially equivalent to logical inconsistency, like the inconsistency between the belief that the earth moves around the sun and the belief that it is at the center of the solar system. There is little doubt that cognitions are often adjusted to become consistent in just this sense. A person who hears the mumbled sentence *The woman shaved himself* is likely to hear it as *The man shaved himself* or *The woman shaved herself,* so that noun and pronoun are in agreement. The question is whether all cases of dissonance reduction boil down to an analogous tendency to keep cognitions logically consistent. In the early days of dissonance theory, this is precisely what its adherents believed. But more recent evidence suggests that dissonance reduction is not always a cognitive matter. A number of studies indicate that we often try to reduce the dissonance between our acts and beliefs for more emotional reasons. One such factor is an effort to maintain a favorable picture of ourselves (Aronson, 1969; Steele and Liu, 1983; Cooper and Fazio, 1984).

Consider the retrospective reevaluation of whether some achievement was worth its cost. People who have made a great sacrifice to attain some goal will value it more than those who achieved the goal with little effort. The original in-

argue that he had an off day but that he will be sure to win a rematch, while his opponents will insist that it only proves their own favorite is the better of the two (Winkler and Taylor, 1979).

*Cognitive accounts*   What accounts for the self-serving bias? There are a number of competing views. On the face of it, this bias seems to be a good argument for the role of motivation in the perception of social causality. But some authors have argued that cognitive factors may play a role even here. They point out, for example, that people usually expect to succeed rather than to fail, and there is evidence that expected outcomes are more likely to be attributed to internal rather than external causes (Miller and Ross, 1975; Nisbett and Ross, 1980). But since the self-serving bias is still present when expectations of success and failure are equalized and becomes more pronounced when the subject is made to believe that the task indicates something important to their self-esteem, motivation is surely a factor as well.

*Motivational accounts*   But just what is the motive that accounts for the bias? Perhaps the most obvious hypothesis is that the bias is just another case of impression management. The experimenter asks a subject why she thinks she succeeded or why she failed. The subject doesn't want to lose face in public, and therefore explains her performance to put herself in the best possible light, regardless of what she herself may think. In effect, she is trying to delude the experimenter rather than herself. While such maneuvers probably play a role, however, they cannot account for the entire effect. For self-serving biases occur even when subjects experience failure but don't think the experimenter knew about it. Under these conditions, they have no reason to protect their public image, for that is never threatened. But they show a self-serving bias even so. They presumably try to protect the picture they hold of themselves, now deluding *themselves* instead of—or in addition to—others (Greenberg, Pyszczynski, and Solomon, 1982; Schlenker, Hallam, and McCown, 1983).

## PERCEIVING ONESELF

We have discussed some of the ways in which we see various qualities in others. What about the way in which we see such qualities in ourselves? We all have a conception of our own selves, what we are really like and why we do what we do: "I am a certain kind of person with such and such capacities, beliefs, and attitudes." But how do such self-concepts arise?

### The Self-Concept and Others

One crucial element is some reference to other people. For there is little doubt that there can be no full-fledged "I" without a "you" or "they," for a crucial component of the self-concept is social. According to many authors, the child begins to see herself through the eyes of the important figures in her world and thus acquires the idea that she is a person—albeit at first a very little person—just as they

*(Photograph by Suzanne Szasz)*

477

are (Mead, 1934). As the social interactions become more complex, more and more details are added to the self picture. In effect, the child sees herself through the mirror of the opinions and expectations of those of others—mother, father, siblings, friends—who matter to her. Her later behavior cannot help but be shaped by this early "looking-glass self" (Cooley, 1902). Examples of such effects include the roles in which society casts children from the moment of birth: black, white, male, female, and so on. (For different theoretical approaches to the development of the self-concept, see Chapters 10, 14, and 15.)

## Self-Perception and Attribution

According to the looking-glass theory we learn who we are by finding out through others. But isn't there a more direct method? Can't we discover who we are and what we feel simply by observing ourselves?

According to some authors, the answer is no. In their view, our conceptions of self are attained through an attribution process no different in kind from that which allows us to form conceptions of other people. The advocates of this **self-perception theory** maintain that, contrary to common-sense belief, we do not know our own selves directly (Bem, 1972). In their view, self-knowledge can only be achieved indirectly, through the same attempts to find consistencies, discount irrelevancies, and interpret observations that help us to understand other people.

One line of evidence concerns the relation between attitude and behavior. Common sense argues that attitudes cause behavior, that our own actions stem from our feelings and our beliefs. To some extent, this is undoubtedly true. The pro-segregationist is unlikely to join a civil rights demonstration. But under some circumstances, the cause-and-effect relation is reversed. For as already noted in our discussion of cognitive dissonance, sometimes our feelings or beliefs are the *result* of our actions.

A simple example is our liking for people. Naturally enough, we are more prone to do favors for the people we like than for those we do not. But occasionally there is a reverse effect. This is the basis of Benjamin Franklin's cynical advice on how to win someone's good graces: Get that person to do you a small favor, such as lending you a book, and he will end up beholden to *you*.

Whether Franklin's advice was ever followed by any of his revolutionary colleagues is unknown, but his suggestion was tested in a study in which subjects were made to act either kindly or harshly to someone else. The subjects had to supervise two "learners" in a learning task. They were told to compliment one of the learners whenever he made a right response. In contrast, they had to criticize the other learner harshly for any error. After the session was over, the subjects were asked to rate the learners' personalities. Benjamin Franklin would have been pleased to know that the subjects had a more favorable judgment of the learner they had praised than the one to whom they had issued reproofs (Schopler and Compere, 1971). The subjects were presumably unable to attribute their own acts entirely to the instructions imposed by the experimenter. Under the circumstances, they had to find some additional reasons within themselves: "I couldn't have been that unpleasant unless I disliked him."

A similar effect involves the "foot-in-the-door" technique, originally perfected by traveling salesmen. In one study, suburban homeowners were asked to comply with an innocuous request, to put a 3-inch square sign in their window advocat-

***The foot-in-the-door effect and the environment*** *The foot-in-the-door effect can start at an early age. The photo shows young children induced to do their bit for conservation. Whether the cans they collect now make much of a difference matters less than that these acts are likely to lead to greater efforts in the future as the children come to think of themselves as environmentalists. (Photographs by S. C. Delaney/EPA)*

ing auto safety. Two weeks later, another experimenter came to visit those home-owners who agreed to display the small sign. This time they were asked to grant a much greater request, to permit the installation of an enormous billboard on their front lawns, proclaiming "Drive Carefully" in huge letters while obstructing most of the house. The results showed that agreement depended upon prior agreement. Once having complied with the first, small request, the subjects were much more likely to give in to the greater one (Freedman and Fraser, 1966).

One interpretation of this and similar findings is a change in self-perception (Snyder and Cunningham, 1975). Having agreed to put up the small sign, the subjects now thought of themselves as active citizens involved in a public issue. Since no one forced them to put up the sign, they attributed their action to their own convictions. Given that they now thought of themselves as active, convinced, and involved, they were ready to play the part on a larger scale. Fortunately for their less-involved neighbors, the billboard was in fact never installed—after all, the request was only part of an experiment. But in real life we may not be let off so easily. The foot-in-the-door approach is a common device for persuading the initially uncommitted; it can be used to sell encyclopedias or political convictions. Extremist political movements generally do not demand violent actions from newcomers. They begin with small requests like signing a petition or giving a distinctive salute. But these may lead to a changed self-perception that ultimately may ready the person for more drastic acts.*

This line of argument may have some bearing on our understanding of how social systems function. The social world casts people in different roles that prescribe particular sets of behaviors; representatives of labor and management will obviously take different positions at the bargaining table. But the roles determine attitudes as well as behavior. If one has to act like a union representative, one starts to feel like one. The same holds for the corporation executive. This point has been verified in a study of factory workers both before and after they had become a union steward or had been promoted to foreman (Lieberman, 1956).

In short, our attitudes are affected by what we do and are expected to do. To some extent at least, the role makes the man or the woman. If one is appointed a judge, one begins to feel judicious.

## EMOTION: PERCEIVING ONE'S OWN INNER STATES

We have seen that there is evidence that we come to know some of our own attitudes by a process of self-attribution. Some social psychologists have proposed that a similar process may affect the subjective experience of emotion. We say that we feel love, joy, grief, or anger. But are we always sure exactly what emotion we experience? In one of Gilbert and Sullivan's operettas, a character notes that the uninitiated may mistake love for indigestion. While this is probably an over-statement, something of the sort may be valid for all of us. We often have to inter-

*The misattribution of one's own inner state* According to one of the characters in Gilbert and Sullivan's operetta Patience, *"There is a transcendentality of delirium—an acute accentuation of the supremest ecstasy—which the earthy might easily mistake for indigestion."* (From a production by the New York Gilbert and Sullivan players; photograph by Lee Snider, 1987)

---

* These phenomena are very reminiscent of the effects of forced compliance and justification of past effort we discussed previously in the context of dissonance reduction. Under the circumstances, it may not be surprising that some authors have suggested that such effects are best explained by self-perception theory rather than by a tendency to reduce cognitive dissonance. The resulting controversy between adherents of the dissonance position and of the self-perception approach is beyond the scope of this book (Bem, 1967, 1972).

pret our internal states, have to decide whether the knot in our stomach is fear (say, of an impending examination), or is impatient anticipation (say, of a lovers' meeting). According to some psychologists, some such interpretive processes are involved whenever we experience an emotion (Schachter and Singer, 1962; Mandler, 1975, 1984). To put their views in perspective, we will begin with a discussion of some earlier theories of emotion.

### The James-Lange Theory

The topic of emotion has perplexed generations of investigators. Psychologists and biologists have had reasonable success in uncovering some of the objective, bodily manifestations of emotional states; examples are the emotional concomitants of fear and rage (see Chapter 3) and emotional expressions such as the smile (see Chapter 10). But what can we say about the way our emotions are experienced subjectively, how they feel "inside"?

Many nineteenth-century psychologists tried to catalogue various emotional experiences, much as they had classified the different sensations provided by the senses (such as red, sour, A-flat). But their efforts were not too successful. There were simply too many emotional experiences that people reported, and the classifications that were proposed did not seem to do justice to the richness of these subjective feelings. In addition, there were disagreements about the precise meaning of emotional terms. How does sadness differ from dolor or weariness or dejection? Different people reported different shades of meaning and there seemed to be little hope of agreement as long as the description was confined to the subjective experience alone (which of course is private by definition).

A different approach to the problem was proposed by William James. To James, the crucial facet of emotion was that it is an aspect of what a person *does.* In fear, we run; in grief, we weep. The common-sense interpretation is that the behavior is caused by the emotion. James stood common sense on its head and maintained that the causal relation is reversed; we are afraid *because* we run:

> Common-sense says, we lose our fortune, are sorry and weep; we meet a bear, are frightened and run; we are insulted by a rival, are angry and strike. The hypothesis here . . . is that we feel sorry because we cry, angry because we strike, afraid because we tremble . . . Without the bodily states following on the perception, the latter would be purely cognitive in form, pale, colorless, destitute of emotional warmth. We might then see the bear, and judge it best to run, receive the insult and deem it right to strike, but we should not actually *feel* afraid or angry. (James, 1890, v. II, p. 449)

These phrases are the core of what is now known as the ***James-Lange theory of emotions.*** (Carl Lange was a contemporary of James and offered a similar account.) In effect, the theory asserts that the subjective experience of emotion is neither more nor less than the awareness of our own bodily changes in the presence of certain arousing stimuli. These bodily changes might be produced by skeletal movements (running) or visceral reactions (pounding heartbeat), though later adherents of James's theory emphasized the visceral responses and the activity of the autonomic nervous system that underlies them (Figure 12.6).

The James-Lange theory has been the focus of considerable controversy. One of the major criticisms was raised by Walter Cannon, the pioneer in the study of

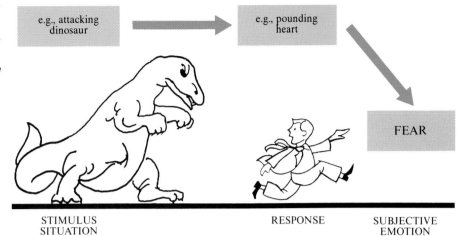

**12.6   The sequence of events as conceived by the James-Lange theory of emotions** *According to the James-Lange theory, the subjectively experienced emotion is simply our awareness of our own response to the anger- or fear-arousing situation. We see a dangerous object (an attacking dinosaur will do as well as any other), this triggers a bodily response (running, pounding heart), and the awareness of this response is the emotion (here, fear).*

e.g., attacking dinosaur

e.g., pounding heart

FEAR

STIMULUS SITUATION    RESPONSE    SUBJECTIVE EMOTION

autonomic functioning (see Chapter 3). Cannon pointed out that sympathetic reactions to arousing stimuli are pretty much the same, while our emotional experiences vary widely. Take the relation between rage and fear. Cannon pointed out that these two emotions are accompanied by just about the same autonomic discharge. But if so, the James-Lange theory must have a flaw since we are certainly able to distinguish between these two emotional experiences (Cannon, 1927).

A different objection concerns the effect of autonomic arousal. In several early studies, this was accomplished by injecting subjects with adrenaline. This triggered sympathetic activation with all its consequences—palpitations, tremor, and sweaty palms. According to the James-Lange theory, these are among the internally produced stimuli that give rise to the intense emotions of fear and rage. But in fact the subjects did not experience these emotions. Some simply reported the physical symptoms. Others said they felt "as if" they were angry or afraid, a kind of "cold emotion" that they knew was not the real thing (Landis and Hunt, 1932). These findings seemed to constitute a further argument against the James-Lange theory. The visceral reactions are evidently not a sufficient condition for the emotional experience.

## The Cognitive Arousal Theory of Emotion

In contrast to the James-Lange theory, which emphasizes the role of bodily feedback, an alternative account focuses on cognitive factors. After all, emotional experiences are usually initiated by certain external events—a letter with tragic news, a loved one's return. Events such as these bring grief or joy, but before they can possibly affect us emotionally they must be appraised and understood. Suppose we see a man who throws a spherical object toward us. Our emotional reaction will surely be different if we think the object is a ball than if we believe that it is a hand grenade. The emotion depends on some cognitive interpretation of the situation that in turn depends on what we see, what we know, and what we expect (Arnold, 1970).

Can a cognitive approach to emotion be combined with the James-Lange emphasis on bodily feedback? Proponents of Stanley Schachter's ***cognitive arousal***

**12.7 The sequence of events as conceived by Schachter and Singer's cognitive evaluation theory of emotions** *According to Schachter and Singer, subjectively experienced emotion is the result of an evaluation process in which the subject interprets his own bodily reactions in the light of the total situation. Any number of external stimuli (ranging from attacking dinosaurs to competition in a race) may lead to the same general bodily reaction pattern—running and increased heart rate. The subjective emotion depends upon what the subject attributes these bodily responses to. If he attributes them to a danger signal (the dinosaur) he will feel fear. If he attributes them to the race, he will feel excitement.*

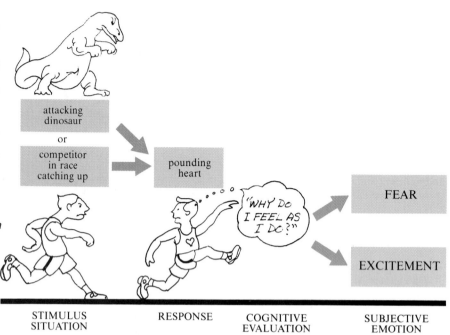

attacking dinosaur

or

competitor in race catching up

pounding heart

"WHY DO I FEEL AS I DO?"

FEAR

EXCITEMENT

STIMULUS SITUATION    RESPONSE    COGNITIVE EVALUATION    SUBJECTIVE EMOTION

*theory* believe that it can. As they see it, various stimuli may trigger a general state of autonomic arousal, but this arousal will provide only the raw materials for an emotional experience—a state of undifferentiated excitement and nothing more. This excitement is shaped into a specific emotional experience by cognitive appraisal and interpretation. In effect, this amounts to an attribution process. A person's heart beats rapidly and her hands are trembling—is it fear, rage, joyful anticipation, or a touch of the flu? If the individual has just been insulted, she will interpret her internal reactions as anger and will feel and act accordingly. If she is confronted by William James's bear, she will attribute her visceral excitement to the bear and experience fear. If she is at home in bed, she will probably assume that she is sick. In short, according to cognitive arousal theory, emotional experience is produced, not by autonomic arousal as such, but rather by the interpretation of this arousal in the light of the total situation as the subject sees it (Schachter and Singer, 1962; Schachter, 1964; Mandler, 1984; see Figure 12.7).

THE MISATTRIBUTION OF AROUSAL

To test this general conception, Schachter and Singer performed a now classic experiment in which subjects were autonomically aroused but did not know what caused the arousal. Toward this end, the subjects were injected with a drug that they believed to be a vitamin supplement but that was really adrenaline (epinephrine). Some subjects were informed of the drug's real effects, such as increase in heart rate, flushing, tremor, and so on. Other subjects were misinformed. They were told that the drug might have some side effects, such as numbness or itching, but they were not informed of its actual bodily consequences. After the drug had been administered, the subjects sat in the waiting room while waiting for what they thought was a test of vision. In actual fact, the main experiment was conducted in this waiting room with a confederate posing as another subject while the experimenter watched through a one-way screen. One condition was set up to produce anger. The confederate was sullen and irritable and eventually stalked out of the room. Another condition provided a context for euphoria. The confederate was ebullient and frivolous. He threw paper planes out of the window, played with a hula hoop, and tried to engage the subject in an improvised basketball game with paper balls. Following their stay in the waiting room, the subjects were asked to rate their emotional feelings (Schachter and Singer, 1962).

The critical question was whether the prior information about the drug's effects had influenced the subjects' reactions. Schachter and Singer reasoned that those subjects who had been correctly informed about the physiological consequences of the injection would show less of an emotional response than those who had been misinformed. The informed subjects could attribute their tremors and palpitations to the drug rather than to the external situation. In contrast, the misinformed subjects had to assume that their internal reactions were caused by something outside—the elation of the euphoric confederate or the sullenness of the angry one. Given this external attribution, their emotional state would be in line with the environmental context—euphoric or angry as the case might be. The results were more or less as predicted. The misinformed subjects in the euphoria condition described themselves as more joyful than their correctly informed counterparts and were somewhat more likely to join in the confederate's mad antics. Analogous results were obtained in the anger condition.

### EXTENSIONS OF THE MISATTRIBUTION OF AROUSAL EFFECT

*False feedback*    Related effects were found by a number of studies that played several variations on the misattribution theme. In one such study, male subjects were provided with *false feedback* about their own internal sensations in matters of romance. They were allowed to listen to an amplification of their own heartbeats while looking at slides of nude females. These amplified heartbeats were in fact rigged by the experimenter; they were sometimes faster and sometimes slower than the subjects' own. The subject's task was both pleasant and simple. He had to rate the attractiveness of each nude. The results showed that the subjects based their judgments not just on what they saw but also on what they heard —or thought they heard. If their heartbeat was rapid, they were more likely to judge the nude as especially attractive. She had to be, for she made their hearts race. It appears that in erotic situations, we listen to our hearts in a more than figurative sense (Valins, 1966).

*Excitation transfer*    Other studies looked at emotional spillover. Autonomic arousal usually takes a while to subside; as a result, some bodily aftereffects of fear or anger or even physical exercise remain for quite a bit longer than we might expect. Such aftereffects may lead to *excitation transfer effects* (Zillman, 1983). In one study, some subjects first engaged in a bout of strenuous physical activity on an exercise bicycle. A few minutes after they finished pedaling, they were angered by a confederate in an adjacent room who administered a number of (mild) electric shocks as a way of signaling disagreement on various attitudes they discussed over an intercom. When subsequently given a chance to retaliate, they were more aggressive (that is, administered more severe shocks) than control sub-

***Excitation transfer***    *There is some evidence that the arousal immediately following intense exercise can lead to a misattribution of one's own reaction to emotion-producing stimuli. Whether competitive athletes to whom strenuous exercise is a matter of course are subject to this effect is an open question. (Photograph by Michael Nichols/Magnum)*

jects who were tested after their heart rate and blood pressure had returned to base levels. (Needless to say, no shocks were really delivered.) A similar effect was found for sexual excitement in response to erotic films; here too, arousal was enhanced by preceding physical exercise (Zillman, Katcher, and Milavsky, 1972; Cantor, Zillman, and Bryant, 1975). The explanation readily follows from Schachter's theoretical position. Some residual bodily aftereffects of the previous physical exercise are still present even though the subject doesn't know it. He is still aroused, but doesn't know why. As a result, he misattributes his arousal to the situation in which he currently finds himself and in so doing amplifies his own emotional feelings. If provoked, he becomes even angrier; if sexually aroused, he becomes more excited still (Valins, 1966).

## Beyond Cognitive Arousal Theory

Cognitive arousal theory has come in for some criticisms. A number of authors have pointed to various problems with the original Schachter and Singer study; some of the effects were rather small or inconclusive, and several later investigators did not succeed in replicating the full range of results predicted by cognitive arousal theory (Reisenzein, 1983). But the main point at issue goes beyond the details raised by that experiment. It concerns cognitive arousal theory's contention that visceral arousal can lead to any and all emotional experiences, depending upon the person's interpretation of the situation. Some later studies suggest that emotional experience is not quite as flexible as this. Thus injections of epinephrine may be more likely to lead to negative emotional experiences (such as fear and anger) than to positive ones (such as euphoria) regardless of the context in which they occur (Marshall and Zimbardo, 1979; Maslach, 1979; for a rebuttal, see Schachter and Singer, 1979).

The issue is by no means settled, but a plausible position is one that stands midway between the James-Lange and Schachter theories. As we saw, the Schachter-Singer approach starts out with the assumption that all human emotions have the same bodily underpinning. But this assumption can be questioned. Some investigators claim that there are differences in the autonomic patterns that accompany such emotions as anger, sadness, and fear (e.g., Ax, 1953; Funkenstein, 1956; Schwartz, Weinberger, and Singer, 1981). Other investigators make similar claims but base them mainly on differences in facial expressions. According to these authors, these different bodily and facial patterns characterize a number of different *fundamental emotions* (Ekman, 1971, 1984; Izard, 1977). If so, the autonomic raw materials may not allow themselves to be shaped into virtually any emotional experience as Schacter and Singer had supposed.

### FUNDAMENTAL EMOTIONS AND FACIAL EXPRESSION

The hypothesis that there are a few fundamental emotions that are revealed by distinctive patterns of facial expression goes back to Charles Darwin (Darwin, 1872b). Just how many of these elemental emotions are there? One account lists six: happiness, surprise, anger, sadness, disgust, and fear (Ekman, 1985; see Figure 12.8). Others offer different lists, numbering from eight to ten (e.g., Izard, 1971; Plutchik, 1980). But specific numbers aside, all theorists who subscribe to this general conception accept Darwin's original belief that these fundamental

**12.8 Six fundamental emotions** *The photos depict the facial expressions that some investigators regard as characteristic of six fundamental human emotions: (A) happiness, (B) surprise, (C) sadness, (D) anger, (E) disgust, and (F) fear. (From Matsumoto and Ekman, 1989; photographs courtesy of David Matsumoto)*

A

B

C

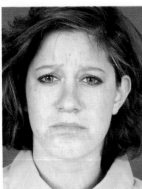

D

E

F

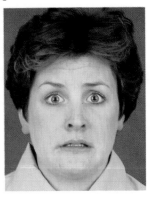

emotions represent several broad behavior patterns that serve vital adaptive functions. Thus, anger is thought to accompany impulses to destroy barriers, expressed by lowered brows, widened eyes, and open mouth with exposed teeth—signals to one's fellows that they better get out of one's way. Similarly for the expression of disgust (or in its milder form, contempt), which goes with riddance reactions such as vomiting, and so on, and is signaled by an expression in which the nose is wrinkled as if to shut out a smell and the lips are pursed and thrust forward as if to spit something out (Plutchik, 1970, 1984; Izard, 1977).

In a previous chapter, we've seen that the same expressive signals are used and recognized in many cultures, that they emerge at a very early age, that they are displayed in blind and deaf children who could not have learned them by observation, and that they must therefore be regarded as part of our built-in human heritage (see Chapter 10, pp. 414–17). But as we've also seen, this doesn't mean that they can't be overlaid by all sorts of learned *display rules*—about when such signals may or may not be shown overtly. (For discussion, see Fridlund, 1990.)

JAMES-LANGE REVISITED: THE FACIAL FEEDBACK HYPOTHESIS

Suppose we grant that there are six to ten fundamental emotions tied up with expressive patterns. Why is it that these emotions—anger, fear, disgust, and so on—feel subjectively different? Some authors suggest that the reason is sensory feedback from the facial muscles. A smile necessarily produces a different pattern of muscular contractions than a frown; sensory messages from the facial muscles to the brain could then serve as signals for the subjective feelings of joy or anger. This is the *facial feedback hypothesis,* which is a special variant of the James-Lange theory. It suggests—at least in principle—that you become angry because you scowl (Izard, 1977).

Some apparent support for the facial feedback hypothesis came from experiments in which expressions were *posed.* An example is a study in which different parts of the subject's face were manipulated until they led to certain expressions; for example, pushing the brows down to generate a frown. The experimenter tried to prevent the subject from becoming aware that her muscular contortions corresponded to a frown or a smile by attaching electrodes to her face on the pretext that this would monitor the electrical activity of different muscles. The subjects were asked to maintain these grimaces for a short time while exposed to various stimuli such as cartoons. Their emotional reactions seemed to be in line

**The face and emotion**    *A grieving Cyprus woman. Whether such emotions can be induced by adopting the appropriate facial expression is a matter of debate. (Photo by Constantine Manos/Magnum)*

with their facial contortions; if their muscular pattern was that of a smile, they rated cartoons as funnier than if it was that of a frown (Laird, 1974).

Later authors asked whether the subjects in the facial manipulation experiment had really been oblivious to the fact that their face assumed the expressions we call "smile" or "frown." A subsequent study in which this problem was corrected indicated that the muscular pattern as such has little effect (though the issue is still controversial, see Tourangeau and Ellsworth, 1979; Izard, 1981; Tomkins, 1981; Ellsworth and Tourangeau, 1981; Winton, 1986). If so, the problem may be that there is a difference between spontaneous facial expressions (which may well enhance the emotional experience) and posed ones (which probably do not). (For futher discussion, see Zuckerman, Klorman, Larrance, and Spiegel, 1981.)

All in all, the facial feedback hypothesis seems to have fared not much better than its earlier autonomic counterpart. As we've seen, injecting epinephrine as such does not lead to emotion; nor does a facial expression as such. But autonomic arousal may indeed affect emotion if it occurs in an appropriate situational context. It boosts emotional experience if there is a threatening (or anger-provoking, or sexually exciting) object. Much the same holds for facial expression. If this occurs in a natural, emotion-arousing context, it probably contributes to and intensifies the overall emotional feeling tone. According to one theorist, this is not so much because the subject receives sensory feedback from the facial muscles. It is rather because of facial *"feed-forward"*: an awareness of a motor command that tells the muscles the facial expression (of a smile or a snarl) the subject is about to initiate (Leventhal, 1984).*

FUNDAMENTAL EMOTIONS AND COGNITION

Whatever the ultimate verdict on the facial feedback hypothesis, there are a number of further problems about the way in which emotional experience arises. One concerns the fact that the number of fundamental emotions is rather small. The largest number that has been suggested is ten. But we surely can distinguish between many more emotional experiences than this—for example, between sadness, resignation, regret, grief, and despair, and between happiness, jubilation, rapture, and serene delight. But how can we do this if we possess at most ten different fundamental emotions?

The best guess is that further distinctions have to be made by just the kind of interpretive process that Schachter and Singer had described. A situation arouses the bodily states (and expressive reactions) corresponding to one of the fundamental emotions. This in turn produces an emotional experience—say of fear, or anger, or joy, or sadness. But its exact nature is then further shaped by the situation as the individual interprets it to be. And since the number of situations that the individual can face is countless, the number of emotional experiences that he can feel is countless as well—each with its own complexity and subtle shadings.

* A related view asserts that facial expressions are communicative gestures rather than expressions of internal emotional states. If so, they should occur more frequently when other people are around—either in actuality or at least in one's imagination—than when they are not, and this seems to be the case (Fridlund, 1990).

## Complex Emotions

Thus far we have considered emotions that we may have shared with our primate predecessors and perhaps some even more primitive creatures earlier in our ancestral line. Many of these may well have had some version of what we call rage, fear, disgust, and joy (or at least lust); they fought competitors (rage), escaped from predators (fear), spat out noxious substances (disgust), and joined with mates (joy). But there are some emotions that seem peculiarly human, for they require a level of symbolic processing that is probably restricted to our own species. Examples are such emotional experiences as pity, anger, guilt, and regret, all of which depend on a complex attributional analysis of why we or someone else failed or succeeded in some endeavor, an analysis that even the cleverest chimpanzee is probably incapable of.

### PITY, ANGER, AND GUILT

Consider the emotions of anger, pity, and guilt. Each of them is aroused by some misfortune: the loss of a job, failing an examination, and so on. According to Bernard Weiner, which particular emotion is felt depends on our perception of how this misfortune came about. If we believe that the outcome was essentially controllable, we feel anger; if we regard it as uncontrollable, we feel pity. If we hear that Joe failed an important exam because he went to a party the night before, we feel a bit angry (all the more so, if we really like him and wanted him to do well). But if he failed the exam because he had been ill all semester, we're more likely to feel sorry for him. In the first case, we feel that the failure was Joe's own fault; in the second, he failed but couldn't help it (Weiner, B., 1982).

In these examples, the emotion is provoked by another person, for it is he who performed (or did not perform) the act that led to the unfortunate outcome. But a

*Anger as a social emotion*  A four-year-old in self-righteous anger at a playmate who is using one of her toys and won't relinquish it. (Photograph by Suzanne Szasz)

rather similar analysis applies when the emotional target is one's own self. Here too what matters is whether one could or could not control the outcome. If it was controllable, we feel guilt (which in a sense is anger directed at the self). If it was not controllable, we feel self-pity.

Support for these assertions comes from studies in which subjects were asked to report their emotional reactions to various scenarios. In one study, the subjects read stories about an individual who approached another person and asked for financial aid. If the story indicated that the reason was ill health (uncontrollable), the subjects' response was pity and concern. If it was because the person in need didn't like to work (controllable), the reaction was anger (Meyer and Mulherin, 1980). Similar results were obtained when subjects were asked to describe some incidents in their own lives that made them feel anger or guilt. Below are descriptions of an anger-provoking and a guilt-producing incident respectively:

> My roommate brought her dog into our no-pet apartment without asking me first. When I got home, she wasn't there, but the barking dog was . . . [and] the dog had relieved itself in the middle of the entry. . . .

> A friend and I studied together and I interfered with her studies by talking, wasting time, etc. On the midterm, I . . . got a strong B, while she got a D. I felt guilty about this. (Weiner, 1982, pp. 199–200)

In both incidents, the key is that the unfortunate outcome was controllable. The thoughtless act that aroused the anger was obviously the dog owner's fault. While the dog's bladder was not hers to control, its unsupervised stay in the apartment certainly was. Similarly for the guilt incident. The writer didn't have to interfere with her friend's studies, and so she felt guilty (Weiner, 1982).

Still further complexities are introduced by the fact that certain emotions—such as anger and guilt—involve an appreciation of a moral order. Consider anger. Imagine that you are waiting on a line, say, to buy a pair of World Series tickets. By the time you reach the ticket office you find out that there are no more tickets left; the man just in front of you bought the very last pair. Do you get angry at that man? You may get angry at your bad luck and curse the fates, but you won't get angry at *him.* You somehow recognize that his position on the waiting line gave him the *right* to the tickets. The situation would have been very different if he had pushed himself ahead of you in the line. Now you would become fiercely angry, because you would perceive his act as a moral *transgression* (Averill, 1978; Sabini and Silver, 1982).

To be sure, anger may well be based on a fundamental emotion that is related to within-species aggression. Dogs snarl and bare their fangs in rage. But in humans, anger is evidently more than this. We've seen that it involves the appreciation of another person's intentions and capacities. But beyond that, it also involves some sense of moral rights and transgressions. At that point, it is not rage, but *out*rage. Given all that, it clearly transcends its simple biological roots.

### REGRET

Yet another emotion that transcends simple arousal or the few fundamental emotions is *regret,* a reaction produced by comparing the outcomes of whatever one did with what one might have done. It is the emotion of the *might have been.*

*Anger at moral transgression* Waiting on line to avoid righteous anger. (Drawing by Chas. Addams; © 1960, 1988, The New Yorker Magazine, Inc.)

We've all had the experience of almost achieving some desired goal but just missing out. Somehow such near-misses are much more painful than attempts that don't come close at all. The man who gets a lottery ticket that differs from the winning number by just one digit feels much worse than the one whose number is way off the mark. The same holds for the football player who *almost* catches the winning touchdown pass or the businessman who *almost* makes the big sale. This general phenomenon has been documented in a number of studies in which subjects were presented with various scenarios and had to indicate their reaction. One example concerns a missed plane:

> Mr. Crane and Mr. Tees were scheduled to leave the airport on different flights, at the same time. They travelled from town in the same limousine, were caught in a traffic jam, and arrived at the airport 30 minutes after the scheduled departure time of their flights.
>
> Mr. Crane is told that his plane left on time. Mr. Tees is told that his flight was delayed, and left five minutes ago.
>
> Who is more upset?
>
> (From Kahneman and Tversky, 1982, p. 203)

It is no surprise that the nearly unanimous answer was Mr. Tees who suffered the near-miss. But why should this be so, considering that the objective situation of the two men was completely identical since they both missed their planes? Kahneman and Tversky believe the near-miss is more upsetting because it is much easier to imagine how one might have arrived earlier by five minutes rather than by half an hour. If the limousine had only made one traffic light, if the baggage had only been unloaded a bit more quickly, if only . . .

Kahneman and Tversky call this tendency to refer to such imaginary replays (or simulations) of what was and what might have been the ***simulation heuristic;*** it is yet another of the various mental shortcuts (e.g., the availability heuristic, see Chapter 8) that we use in making decisions and evaluating outcomes.

A number of further findings represent variations on the same general theme. In one study, subjects read about two persons who died of exposure after surviving a plane crash to a remote area. In one condition, they learned that the victim made it to within one-quarter mile of safety; in the other, that he came within seventy-five miles. They were then asked to determine a fair amount of compensation for the victims' families. The subjects recommended a considerably higher sum for the family of the victim who came so close than for the family of the one who perished further away. They evidently felt that the fate of the first victim who came so close was worse (so to speak, more "unfair") than that of the second. In their imaginary reconstructions, they found it easier to construct a mental simulation for undoing the first victim's fate than for undoing that of the second—if he'd only known how close he was, if he'd just been able to take a few more steps.

A similar account may explain why misfortunes that are caused by some exceptional departure from routine seem especially regrettable. That someone died on the *Titanic* is terrible enough, but it appears more terrible yet if he only got his ticket because of a last-minute cancellation by a passenger who suddenly fell sick. It's apparently easier to create a mental script for undoing an unusual circumstance than to imagine how more usual event patterns can be altered (Kahneman and Miller, 1986).

***Regret*** *The sadness of "It might have been." (Drawing by Chas. Addams; © 1956, 1984, The New Yorker Magazine, Inc.)*

The experience of regret highlights the difficulty of referring all of our subjective emotional feelings to a few fundamental emotions. Regret is not just sadness, or a mixture of sadness with another fundamental emotion. Dogs may conceivably experience some inner state akin to what we call sadness; they seem to grieve for a lost master and look profoundly depressed after learned helplessness training. But it's hard to imagine that they could possibly feel regret. To credit them with that emotion is to suppose that they can mentally rummage through unrealized possibilities. But unlike dogs, humans are able to compare what *is* with what *might have been.* As a result, they can experience the special sadness of regret.

## Emotion and the Theater

There is a certain emotional experience that is in some ways quite unlike those we encounter in everyday life—the emotion we feel when watching a play or a movie. Is it a real emotion? Sometimes it seems to be. Some plays or movies can obviously move us to tears. As children, we weep at Lassie's illness; as adults, at Juliet's death. In retrospect, we may insist that while watching the play or the movie, we were "really in it" and had come to accept the characters' joys and sorrows as though they were real. But did we truly? Consider a great performance of *Oedipus Rex,* climaxed by that awesome scene in which Oedipus blinds himself. We may say that while watching the play we believed that what happened on stage was reality. In fact, we did no such thing. If we had, we would have experienced horror instead of tragic awe; we would have rushed for help, perhaps shouting, "Is there an ophthalmologist in the house?" In fact, we never believe that the stage Oedipus is real; at best, we are willing to suspend our *dis*belief, as the poet Coleridge put it so aptly. But in the fringes of our consciousness there is always the feeling that we are sitting in a comfortable theater armchair. We may suspend disbelief, but this does not mean that we believe.

The emotion we experience in the theater cannot be identical to the one we feel in the real world. But then, what is it? Let us assume that when we witness certain events that befall others in real life—a tearful reunion, a fistfight, a death scene—we experience real emotions. When analogous events occur on stage or on the screen, they trigger a similar arousal. But the cognitive context is quite different, for we still know that we are sitting in a darkened theater hall. The experience is analogous to the "cold fear" produced by injecting adrenaline, an "as if" emotion that occurs in subjects who cannot attribute their arousal to any external cause.

The special esthetic flavor of the theatrical experience probably depends upon just this "as if." But this quality requires a delicate balance between disbelief and belief, between too little arousal and too much. On the one hand, there must be some sense of "being in it," or the experience will be cold and dispassionate, like that of the bored usher who has seen the same show over and over again. On the other hand, too much arousal will also defeat the esthetic goal, for the "as if" feeling will then be lost altogether. A theatrically naïve audience may believe that what happens on stage is the real thing, as in children's theater where the four- and five-year-olds shout fearful warnings at Snow White when the evil old witch approaches. Their seven-year-old cousins are less naïve, and thus more capable of enjoying the genuine dramatic experience. They feel aroused and excited, but

**Emotion and the actor**  *A scene from Shakespeare's* King Lear *in which the old king, half-crazed with impotent fury, screams at the world during a raging storm. Lear was surely in a state of vehement frenzy. But was the actor who portrayed him? (Peter Ustinov and Robin Phillips in a 1979 Stratford, Ontario, Festival production; photograph by Robert C. Ragsdale)*

## SUMMARY

ing that of situational factors. This attribution bias is reversed when we ourselves are the actor rather than the observer. Reasons for the *actor-observer difference* include the fact that we know ourselves better than anyone else and that actors and observers have different perspectives. An additional reason is the *self-serving bias,* which tends to make people deny responsibility for their failures while taking credit for their successes.

10. According to *self-perception theory,* similar attribution processes determine how we perceive ourselves. In line with this theory is evidence that people realign their self-perception to fit their behavior.

11. An influential application of self-perception theory is Schachter and Singer's *cognitive arousal theory,* which is a revision of the *James-Lange theory of emotions.* Cognitive arousal theory argues that the emotion we feel is an interpretation of our own autonomic arousal in light of the situation to which we attribute it. Misattribution effects of autonomic arousal focus on *false feedback* and *excitation transfer.*

12. Many investigators doubt that one arousal process underlies all emotions. They suggest that there are some six to ten *fundamental emotions* that correspond to different *facial expressions.* According to the *facial feedback hypothesis,* the subjective experience of emotions is partially based on the sensory information provided by the facial muscles when we smile, scowl, or wrinkle our nose.

13. Certain complex emotions seem to be uniquely human because they require an unusual level of symbolic processing. Some depend on the judgments that a bad outcome was controllable (anger) or that it was not (pity). Others depend on the construction of cognitive scenarios that involve "what might have been" (regret). Still others depend on an "as if" experience, such as the emotion we feel while watching a performance in the theater.

# CHAPTER 13

# Social Interaction

In the previous chapter, we discussed the ways in which we try to understand the social world around us. Our primary emphasis was on social cognition: our attitudes and how they are changed, our impressions of people, our interpretation of why they do what they do, and finally, the way that we ourselves interpret our own actions and experiences. In this chapter, our focus will be on action, or more precisely, *inter*action, as we ask how people deal with each other, influence each other, and act in groups.

We will consider three major kinds of interaction. Some are *one-on-one,* as when two friends have dinner or a customer tries to bargain with a used-car salesman. Others are *many-on-one,* as when a group of teenagers pressures one in their midst to wear the same clothes as all the others. Still another kind of interaction is *many-on-many,* as in riots or panics when many persons affect many others and are affected by them in turn.

## RELATING TO OTHERS: ONE-ON-ONE INTERACTIONS

How do people interact on a one-on-one basis? To a large extent, the answer depends on the relationship the actors have with each other. We deal one way with comparative strangers, another with people we know and like, and yet another with those we know but don't like. But according to many social scientists, there are some common threads that run through most of our relationships, no matter how tenuous or strong they may be. We'll begin by looking at the ways in which we interact with comparative strangers.

**Social exchange** *The photo shows fruit vendors in Beijing. The process of social exchange is most obvious when it is economic. (Photograph by Hiroji Kubota/Magnum Photos)*

## Social Exchange

A number of theorists believe that one common principle that underlies the way people deal with others is *social exchange.* According to this view, each partner in a relationship gives something to the other and expects to receive something in return. Just what is exchanged depends on the relationship. If it is economic, as between buyers and sellers or employees and employers, the exchange will involve goods or labor for money. If it is between friends, lovers, or family members, the exchange will involve valued intangibles such as esteem, loyalty, and affection. According to social exchange theory, all (or at least, most) human relationships have this underlying give-and-take quality. If one partner gives and receives nothing in return, the relationship will disintegrate sooner or later (Kelley and Thibaut, 1978).

## Reciprocity

The social exchange perspective is essentially economic, and thus quite appropriate to the realm of material transactions. In the marketplace, money provides a common standard by which the value of commodities can be assessed. As a result, the value of what is given and received can be compared. This is much harder (and perhaps impossible) to accomplish when the exchange involves such "commodities" as praise or loyalty, let alone love. Whether the social exchange approach applies to all social interactions is therefore a matter of debate, but that it applies to *some* is indubitable. One important example is the operation of the *reciprocity principle.* This is a basic rule that affects many aspects of social behavior. We feel that we somehow must repay whatever we have been given: a favor for a favor, a gift for a gift, a smile for a smile. As one author points out, this sense of social indebtedness is so deeply ingrained that it has been built into the vocabulary of several languages: thus, "much obliged" is a virtual synonym for "thank you" (Cialdini, 1984).

The reciprocity rule is extremely powerful and pervasive. When Cicero asserted that "There is no duty more indispensable than that of returning a kindness," he was not just talking about the Romans of his time, but also about us and about virtually all cultures and societies past and present. In the Trobriand Islands, inland islanders give vegetables to the fishermen on the shore, who will later repay the gift with fish, which then becomes a further gift, which in turn calls for a vegetable repayment, and so on: a reciprocity system in which "neither partner can refuse, neither may stint, neither may delay" (Malinowski, 1926). Such exchanges often yield mutual gain, as in the case of the farmers and the fishermen who obtain nutritional benefits. But over and above such material advantages, the gift exchange has a further social function. It creates a web of mutual obligations that knits the members of a society together. In fact, there are a number of societies in which gift giving creates a ritualized cycle of obligations that are never completely cancelled; any one gift represents a repayment for a previous gift with a little bit extra—an extra just large enough to require still another gift in return, and so on (Gouldner, 1960).

***The gifts of the Magi***  *The social exchange position can be stretched too far, for sometimes we give without expectation of return. (Courtesy S. Apollinare Nuovo, Ravenna)*

According to Robert Cialdini, the reciprocity principle can become a powerful tool of persuasion (Cialdini, 1984). Cialdini points out that incurring a favor necessarily leads to a sense of indebtedness. We feel that we must repay a donor, even if we never wanted his gift in the first place. As a result, we are sometimes manipulated into compliance, saying "yes," or buying some merchandise or making donations—all despite the fact that we never really wanted to. As an example, Cialdini describes the techniques of the Hare Krishna Society in soliciting donations. Members of this sect approach airport travellers and press a flower into their hands. The traveller typically wants to return the unwanted gift, but the Krishna member will not take the flower back, insisting sweetly that "It is our gift to you." The member's next step is to request a donation to the society. Many travellers feel that under the circumstances they have no choice. Since they took the gift (no matter how unwillingly), they feel that they have to reciprocate. Their only defense—and many travellers resort to it—is to beware of Krishnas bearing gifts!

Still another kind of behavior often affected by the reciprocity rule is bargaining. The seller states his price. The potential buyer says "No." Now the seller makes a concession by offering the item (the house, the car, or whatever) at a lower price. This very concession exerts a pressure on the buyer to increase *her* offer; since he offered a concession, she feels that she ought to give a little on her side too.

The reciprocal concession effect has been the subject of several laboratory investigations. In one study, an experimenter approached persons walking on a university campus and first made a very large request. He asked them to work as unpaid volunteer counselors in a juvenile detention center for two hours a week over a two-year period. Not a single subject agreed. The experimenter then made a much smaller request: that they accompany a group of boys or girls from the juvenile detention center on a single two-hour trip to the zoo. When this smaller request came on the heels of the large request that had been refused, 50 percent of the subjects consented. In contrast, only 17 percent of the subjects acceded to the smaller request when this was not preceded by the prior, larger demand. In the first case, there was an apparent concession; in the second, there was not. The sheer fact that the experimenter seemed to make a concession was enough to make the subjects feel that they should now make a concession of their own (Cialdini, Vincent, Lewis, Catalan, Wheeler, and Darby, 1975). This method for achieving compliance has been dubbed the *door-in-the-face technique* by way of contrast to the *foot-in-the-door technique,* in which compliance with a small request makes the subject more likely to comply with the larger one (see Chapter 12, pp. 478–79). Both techniques take their names from the tricks of door-to-door salespeople (Cialdini, 1984).

## Altruism

Social exchange theory suggests (and the reciprocity principle derived from it insists) that no one ever gets anything for nothing. There is no such thing as a free lunch. But this harsh judgment on human nature seems to be contradicted by the fact that people sometimes act unselfishly. Or do they?

There is ample evidence that people often fail to help others who are in distress. The widespread indifference of pedestrians to the beggars and the homeless all around them is by now a daily fact of American city life. The classic example of public apathy to a stranger's plight is the case of Kitty Genovese who was attacked and murdered on an early morning in 1964 on a street corner in Queens, New York. The assault lasted over half an hour, during which time she screamed and struggled while her assailant stabbed her repeatedly until she finally died. It later developed that thirty-eight of her neighbors had watched the episode from their windows. But none of them had come to her aid. No one even called the police (Rosenthal, 1964). Why was there this appalling inactivity?

### THE BYSTANDER EFFECT

One factor may be a lack of altruistic motivation. Perhaps people in a big city simply don't care about the fate of strangers, no matter how terrible it may be. But according to Bibb Latané and John Darley, the failure to help is often produced by the way the people understand the situation. It's not that they don't care, but that they don't understand what should be done. Here as in many other contexts, social action (and interaction) is heavily affected by social cognition (see Chapter 12).

*Ambiguity* Consider the passerby who sees a man lying unconscious on a city street. How can he tell whether the man is ill or is drunk? The situation is ambiguous. A similar confusion troubled some of the witnesses to the Genovese slaying. They later reported that they weren't quite sure what was going on. Perhaps it was a joke, a drunken bout, a lover's quarrel. If it was any of these, intervention might have proved very embarrassing.

*Pluralistic ignorance* The situation is further complicated by the fact that the various witnesses to the Genovese tragedy realized that many others were seeing just what they did. For as they watched the drama on the street unfold, they saw the lights go on in many of the windows of the building. As a result there was ***pluralistic ignorance.*** Each of the witnesses looked to the others to decide whether there really was an emergency. Each was ignorant of the fact that the others were just as unsure as they. The sheer fact that the various witnesses could see each other through the windows reassured them that nothing urgent was going on.

*Diffusion of responsibility*    The fact that each observer knew that others observed the same event made it difficult to realize that the event was an emergency. But this fact had yet another consequence. It made intervention less probable even for those witnesses who did recognize (or at least suspect) that the situation *was* an emergency. For these persons were now faced with a ***diffusion of responsibility.*** No one thought that it was *his* responsibility to act. After all, while many of the observers might have felt some impulse to help, they also had self-centered motives that held them back. Some didn't want to get involved, others were afraid of the assailant, still others were apprehensive about dealing with the police. The conflict between the desire to help and to mind one's own business was finally resolved in favor of inaction through the knowledge that others witnessed the same event. Everyone assumed that since so many others saw just

**13.1    The bystander effect**

what they did, surely one of them would do something about it or had already done it (such as calling the police). As a result, no one did anything (see Figure 13.1).

This general line of reasoning has been tested in a number of experiments. In one, subjects were asked to participate in what they thought was a group discussion about college life with either one, three, or five other persons. The subjects were placed in individual cubicles and took turns in talking to each other over an intercom system. In actuality, there was only one subject; all the other discussants were tape recordings. The discussion began as one of the (tape-recorded) confederates described some of his own personal problems, which included a tendency toward epileptic seizures in times of stress. When he began to speak again during the second round of talking, he feigned a seizure and gasped for help. The question was whether the subject would leave his own cubicle to assist the stricken victim (usually, by asking the experimenter's help). The results demonstrated the so-called ***bystander effect:*** the larger the size of the group that the subject is in (or thought he was in), the *less likely* he is to come to the victim's assistance (Darley and Latané, 1968; see Figure 13.2).

The bystander effect has been obtained in numerous other situations. In some, a fellow subject seems to have an asthma attack; in another, the experimenter appears to faint in an adjacent room; in still others, the laboratory fills with smoke. But whatever the emergency, the result is always the same: the larger the group the subject is in (or thinks he is in), the smaller the chance that he will take any action—in dramatic accord with the diffusion of responsibility hypothesis (Latané and Nida, 1981; Latané, Nida, and Wilson, 1981).

Some further studies have shown that the effect of other bystanders depends in part on what the subjects think about their competence in the situation. In one experiment, the subject was convinced that the only other person who knew about the emergency was in another building, too far to help. Now there was no bystander effect. The subject responded as she would have if she had been alone. Under these circumstances, there was no one to whom she could pass the buck (Bickman, 1971). Conversely, the subject will tend to do nothing if she believes that another bystander is better qualified to handle the problem. Thus, subjects in a variation of the epileptic-seizure experiment were less likely to intervene if they thought that one of the other members of the discussion group was a medical student (Schwartz and Clausen, 1970).

### THE COSTS OF HELPING

The work on the bystander effect indicates that people often don't recognize that a need for help exists and that even when they do, they may not act because they think that others will. But suppose the situation is not ambiguous and that responsibility for helping is not diffused? Will they then help a stranger in distress?

One factor that determines whether they will or won't is the physical or psychological cost to the prospective helper. The greater that cost, the smaller the chance that he will in fact help. In some cases, the cost is physical danger. In others, it is simply time and effort. In one study, students had to go from one campus building to another to give a talk. They were told to hurry, since they were already late. As they rushed to their appointments, these students passed by a shabbily dressed man who lay in a doorway groaning. Only 10 percent stopped to help the victim. Ironically enough, the students were members of a theological seminary, and the topic of their talk was the parable of the "Good Samaritan"

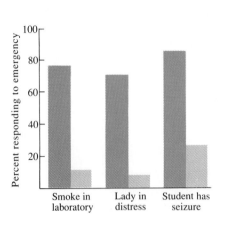

**13.2  Group inhibition of bystander intervention in emergencies**  *When people are alone (in blue) they are more likely to respond in an emergency than when they are—or think they are—with others (in pink), in part because of diffusion of felt responsibility. (A) Percent of subjects who respond to smoke coming through a vent in the laboratory. (B) Percent of (male) subjects who came to the help of a female confederate who apparently had suffered a fall. (C) Percent of subjects who respond to a fellow subject who seems to have suffered a seizure. (Data from Darley, 1968; Latané and Rodin, 1969)*

**The Good Samaritan** *(Painting by Luca Giordano, 1634–1705, the Musée des Beaux Arts, Rouen; Lauros-Giraudon/Art Resource)*

who came to the aid of a man lying injured on a roadside. It appears that if the cost—here in time—is high enough, even theological students may not behave altruistically (Darley and Batson, 1973).

Another cost is physical aversion and disgust. In one study, an investigator feigned illness and collapsed in a subway car. Bystanders were *less* likely to come to the victim's aid if blood trickled from his mouth. In part, this reaction may have been prompted by physical disgust. But in part, it may have been a matter of the potentially greater cost in time and effort. If there is internal bleeding, the victim must be taken to a hospital; if the bleeding was caused by an assailant, that assailant might come back and attack the helper too; the potential helper might make things worse (and would perhaps be blamed) by moving the victim, and so on (Piliavin and Piliavin, 1972).

What is costly to one potential helper may not be equally so to another. Take physical danger. It is probably not surprising that bystanders who intervene in cases of assault are generally much taller, stronger, and better trained than bystanders who do not intervene, and are almost invariably men (Huston, Ruggiero, Conner, and Geis, 1981).

THE SELFISH BENEFITS OF UNSELFISHNESS

Providing help can yield benefits as well as costs. Some of the benefits are various signs of social approval, as in the case of a wealthy donor who is sure to make a lavish contribution as long as everyone watches. Other benefits have to do with avoiding embarrassment. Many city dwellers give two or three quarters to a beggar not because they want to help him but because it's easier to give than to say no. Occasionally the benefits of giving involve romance. In one study, the investigators posed as motorists in distress, trying to flag passing cars to provide help with a flat tire. The passing cars were much more likely to stop for a female than for a male, and the cars that stopped were generally driven by young men alone. The best guess is that the young men's altruism was not entirely unalloyed by sexual interest (West, Whitney, and Schnedler, 1975).

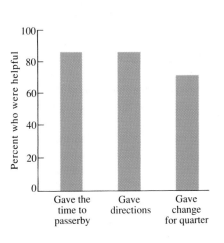

13.3 *Small acts of helping in a large city* *Various minor and prosaic acts of helping strangers are by no means uncommon even in a big city. (Data from Gerard, Wilhelmy, and Conolley, 1968)*

**Altruism** *Helping victims of a highway collapse during the San Francisco earthquake of 1989. (UPI/Bettmann Newsphotos)*

IS THERE ANY GENUINE ALTRUISM?

The preceding discussion paints a somewhat unflattering portrait of human nature. It seems that we often fail to help strangers in need of assistance and that when we do, our help is often rather grudging and calculating. But that picture is too one-sided. For while people can be callous and indifferent, they are also capable of true generosity and altruism (see Figure 13.3). Some people sometimes share food, give blood, contribute to charities, and administer artificial respiration to accident victims. Yet more impressive are the unselfish deeds of living, genetically unrelated donors who gave one of their kidneys to a stranger who would otherwise have died (Sadler et al., 1971). And still others are commemorated by Jerusalem's Avenue of the Righteous, dedicated to the European Christians who sheltered Jews during the Nazi Holocaust, risking (and often giving) their own lives to save those to whom they gave refuge (London, 1970).

Such acts of altruism probably stem from several motives. One is *vicarious distress;* by and large people become distressed when they perceive the distress of others. Vicarious distress may motivate us to help the sufferer—if we can relieve *her* pain, our own (vicarious) pain will be relieved in turn. But if this is our only motive, there's no guarantee that we will help the victim since we can relieve our vicarious distress quite easily by averting our eyes and turning away from the victim. A more reliable motive for helping is *empathic concern,* in which the main desire is to relieve the *other person's* suffering. There is some evidence that some people tend to be more empathically concerned than others. Such persons will offer more help to someone in need, are more likely to contribute to charity, and will help someone even if no one knows that they did so (Chlopan, McCain, Carbonell, and Hagen, 1985; Fultz, Batson, Fortenbach, McCarthy, and Varney, 1986).

What is the origin of altruistic motives? Some of them may have biological roots. For example, there is evidence that vicarious distress starts in the nursery: three-day-old infants begin to wail when they hear another baby's cries (for details, see p. 597). This pattern of concern toward others may grow out of some of the built-in tendencies toward altruism we discussed in Chapter 10 (see pp. 419–21). But human generosity sometimes goes further than reciprocal altruism and kin selection. While people tend to be more giving to their close relatives than to others, some of them make gifts to strangers—ranging from food, to one of their kidneys, or even to their own lives. And their gifts have no strings of reciprocity attached to them.

Such acts of altruism suggest that human behavior is not always selfish. This probably undermines the claim that *all* social interactions can be understood as a form of exchange. To be sure, acts of altruism in which the giver gets no benefits at all—no gratitude, no public acclaim—are fairly rare.* The true miracle is that they exist at all. One aspect of our humanity is that we can go beyond the calls of social exchange and reciprocity.

---

* It is sometimes argued that even the most self-sacrificing hero is at bottom no less selfish than anyone else. For even if no one else ever knows of his unselfish efforts, he himself does, thus gaining an increased sense of self-esteem and the satisfaction of knowing that the person he has helped is now better off. Thus at bottom the apparent altruist is selfish after all. This argument twists the ordinary meaning of the word "selfish." At some level, every individual—including the noblest of martyrs—seeks certain rewards. Whether someone should be considered selfish or unselfish depends on *which* rewards he seeks to gain. A man who seeks the reward of seeing *someone else* feel better is by definition acting unselfishly (Sabini, 1992, in press).

## Attraction

Thus far, we've primarily looked at social interactions with virtual strangers. What happens when the interactions are with people to whom we are closer and about whom we have stronger feelings? We'll begin by asking about the factors that attract us to others.

Could we ever hope to discover what it is that determines who will become friends or even lovers? On the face of it, it seems hard to believe that we will. For we've all been exposed to the romantic notions of our culture. We've all read and seen countless novels and movies that show millionaires befriending tramps, princes marrying showgirls, and Beauty enamored of the Beast—each teaching the lesson that friendship and most especially love are not ruled by reason. But as we will see, while romantic love has some irrational and complex aspects, the factors that determine much of the attraction that humans have for each other are surprisingly simple.

### PROXIMITY

One of the most important determinants of attraction and liking is sheer *physical proximity.* By now, dozens of studies have documented the fact that if you want to predict who makes friends with whom, the first thing to ask is who is nearby. Students who live next to each other in a dormitory or sit next to each other in classes develop stronger relations than those who live only a bit farther away. Similarly, members of a bomber crew become much more friendly to fellow crewmen who work right next to them than to others only a few feet away (Berscheid and Walster, 1978; Berscheid, 1985).

What holds for friendship also holds for mate selection. The statistics are rather impressive. For example, there is evidence that more than half of the couples who took out marriage licenses in Columbus, Ohio, during the summer of 1949 were persons who lived within sixteen blocks of each other when they went out on their first date (Clarke, 1952). Much the same holds for the probability that an engagement will ultimately lead to marriage; the farther apart the two live, the greater the chance that the engagement will be broken off (Berscheid and Walster, 1978).

Why should proximity be so important? One answer is that you can't like someone you've never met, and the chances of meeting that someone are much greater if he is nearby. But why should getting to know him make you like him?

One reason may be *familiarity.* There is a good deal of evidence that people tend to like what's more familiar. This seems to hold for just about any stimulus, whether it's a word in a foreign language, or a melody, or the name of a commercial product, or the photograph of a stranger's face—the more often it is seen or heard, the better it will be liked (Zajonc, 1968; Brickman and D'Amato, 1975; Moreland and Zajonc, 1982). The same familiarity process probably plays an important role in determining what we feel about other people. The hero of a well-known musical comedy explains his affection for the heroine by singing "I've grown accustomed to her face." In a more prosaic vein, the laboratory provides evidence that photographs of strangers' faces are judged to be more likable the more often they have been seen (Jorgensen and Cervone, 1978). Another study

*"Do you really love me, Anthony, or is it just because I live on the thirty-eighth floor?" (Drawing by Claude; © 1959, 1987, The New Yorker Magazine, Inc.)*

**13.4 Familiarity and liking** *The figure shows two versions of a rather well-known lady. Which do you like better—the one on the right or the one on the left? (Courtesy Documentation Photographique de la Réunion des Musées Nationaux)* *(Please turn to p. 504.)*

applied this general idea to the comparison of faces and their mirror images. Which will be better liked? If familiarity is the critical variable, then our friends should prefer a photograph of our face to one of its mirror image, since they've seen the first much more often than the second. But we ourselves should prefer the mirror image, which for us is by far the more familiar. The results were as predicted by the familiarity hypothesis (Mita, Dermer, and Knight, 1977; see Figure 13.4).

SIMILARITY

Do people like others who are similar to themselves, or do they prefer those who are very different? To put it differently, which bit of folk wisdom is more nearly correct: "Birds of a feather flock together" or—perhaps in analogy with magnets—"Opposites attract." It appears that birds have more to teach us in this matter than magnets do, for the evidence suggests that, in general, people tend to like others who are similar to themselves. For example, elementary school students prefer other children who perform about as well as they do in academics, sports, and music (Tesser, Campbell, and Smith, 1984), and "best friends" in high school resemble each other in age, race, year in school, and high school grades (Kandel, 1978).

Whether similarity of personality characteristics such as sociability and extraversion plays a similar role in determining attraction is still unclear. There is some evidence that similarity on these and related personality traits is greater in happy than in unhappy marriages (Dymond, 1954; Cattell and Nessleroade, 1967), but the issue is not yet settled (e.g., Levinger, 1983).

Personality characteristics may or may not affect marital choice and stability, but such relatively more objective attributes as race, ethnic origin, social and educational level, family background, income, and religion certainly do. This also holds for such behavioral patterns as the degree of gregariousness and drinking and smoking habits. A widely cited study has shown that engaged couples in the United States are similar along all of these dimensions (Burgess and Wallin, 1943). The authors interpreted these findings as evidence for *homogamy*—a powerful tendency of like to marry like. A recent study has shown that homogamy plays a role in determining a couple's stability; couples who had stayed together after two-and-one-half years were more similar than those who had broken apart (Hill, Rubin, and Peplau, 1976).

***Homogamy*** American Gothic by *Grant Wood, 1930 ( Photograph © 1989 The Art Institute of Chicago, all rights reserved)*

Is homogamy really produced by the effect of similarity on mutual liking? Or is it just a byproduct of proximity, of the fact that "few of us have an opportunity to meet, interact with, become attracted to, and marry, a person markedly dissimilar from ourselves"? (Berscheid and Walster, 1978, p. 87). The answer to this chicken-and-egg problem is as yet unknown. But whether similarity is a cause of the attraction, or is a side effect of some other factors that led to it initially, the end product is the same: like pairs with like, and no heiress ever marries the butler except in the movies. We're not really surprised to discover that when a princess kisses a frog he turns into a prince. What would really be surprising is to see the frog turn into a *peasant* whom the princess then marries all the same.

PHYSICAL ATTRACTIVENESS

There is little doubt that for a given time and culture there is considerable agreement as to how physically attractive a particular man or woman is. Nor is there any doubt that this factor is overwhelmingly important in determining a person's appeal—or at least, his or her initial appeal—to members of the opposite sex. The vast sums of money spent on cosmetics, fashions, diets, and various forms of plastic surgery are one kind of testimony; our everyday experience is another. Under the circumstances, one may wonder whether there is any need to document the point experimentally, but in any case, such documentation does exist. In one study, freshmen were randomly paired at a dance and later asked how much they liked their partner and whether they wanted to go out with him or her at some future time. The main factor that determined each person's desirability as a future date was his or her physical attractiveness (Walster, Aronson, Abrahams, and Rottman, 1966). Similar results were found in a study of the clients of a commercial video-dating service who selected partners after consulting files that included a photograph, background information, and detailed information about interests, hobbies, and personal ideals. When it came to the actual choice, the primary determinant was the photograph: both male and female clients selected on the basis of physical attractiveness (Green, Buchanan, and Heuer, 1984).

*Matching for attractiveness* Physical attractiveness is clearly a very desirable quality. But if we all set our sights on only those who occupy the very top of this dimension, the world would soon be depopulated—there are simply not enough movie queens and matinee idols to go around. One would therefore assume that people behave in a more sensible fashion. They may well covet the most attractive of all possible mates, but they also have a fairly reasonable perception of their own social desirability (which is determined in part by their own physical attractiveness). In consequence, they will seek partners of roughly comparable social assets; while trying to get a partner who is most desirable, they also try to avoid rejection. This ***matching hypothesis*** predicts a strong correlation between the physical attractiveness of the two partners (Berscheid, Dion, Walster, and Walster, 1971). This hypothesis is well supported by everyday observations ("They make such a fine couple!") and has been repeatedly documented in various empirical observations (Berscheid and Walster, 1974; White, 1980). In one study, dating couples were observed in bars, theater lobbies, and various social events, and they were rated for physical attractiveness. There was a remarkable similarity in the rated attractiveness of the two partners (Silverman, 1971).

*Revisiting Figure 13.4 The familiarity-leads-to-liking hypothesis would predict a preference for the right panel—a retouched photograph of the Mona Lisa (see p. 503). The panel on the left is a mirror image of that photograph, which is presumably the less familiar of the two.*

*What underlies physical attractiveness?* Our discussion has assumed that physical attractiveness is a given and that people pretty much agree on who is and who is not attractive. But why should this be? Why should one set of particular features, one set of bodily proportions, represent the apex of attractiveness for so many people in our time and culture? As yet we don't know.

So far we are only beginning to discover just what it is that constitutes physical attractiveness in our own culture. According to one study, American college men judge women as more attractive if their face has certain features that are perceived as "cute" and tend to be found in children, such as (relatively) large and widely separated eyes, a small nose, and a small chin. If this result holds up in other cultures (for which there is no evidence thus far), a sociobiologist might suggest that this is because perceived youthfulness is a sign of fertility. The trouble is that there are a number of other features judged to be attractive that are associated with maturity rather than immaturity; for example, wide cheekbones and narrow cheeks (Cunningham, 1986).

In any case, there is little reason to suppose that the standards of attractiveness —of face or body—are essentially the same across different times and places. To be sure, some similarities do exist. Signs of ill health and deformity (which might suggest a poor genetic bet) are considered unattractive in all cultures. The same holds for signs of advancing age (which generally signal lower fertility, especially in females). In addition, all cultures want males to look male and females to look female, although the specific cues that weigh in this judgment (and that are considered attractive) vary widely. Beyond this, however, the differences probably outweigh the similarities.

Consider the kind of female body build preferred by males. Are plump women more attractive than slim ones? You will probably agree with enthusiasm if you happen to be a Chukchi of Northeast Siberia or a Thonga of Mozambique. But your views will be very different if you are a Dobuan from New Guinea to whom corpulence is disgusting. While men in many cultures are especially attracted to women with wide hips and a broad pelvis (presumably an advantage for childbearing), men in one or two of the cultures on which data exist strongly dislike women with these bodily characteristics (Ford and Beach, 1951).

*Attractiveness* *People ornament themselves in virtually every culture but choose different ways for doing so (A) Balinese dancer (Photograph by George K. Fuller), (B) Ahka girl from a village in Thailand (Photograph by George K. Fuller), (C) Masai girl in Kenya (John Moss/ Photo Researchers)*

B

C

A

*Tattooed Maori man and woman* *Some cultures employ tattooing as both ornamentation and a sign of enhanced prestige. Among the Maori of New Zealand, both men and women of sufficient social standing were heavily tattooed, with the chief's tattoos most lavish of all. (Top: from The New York Public Library, Astor, Lenox, and Tilden Foundations. Bottom: © Morri Manning/ Black Star, 1978)*

What holds for body build holds even more for facial features. Different cultures seem to have different conceptions of facial beauty. What's more, some of them have permanent means of facial adornment that at least some members of our own culture would probably find rather repellent. Some peoples have developed complex systems for sculpting decorative patterns of scar tissue; others have created elaborate schemes of tattooing the face and body of both men and women. Some of these practices seem quite odd from our own perspective. An example is a custom of the Ainu (indigenous inhabitants of Japan who are now largely assimilated) who used to tattoo elaborate moustaches on their young girls' faces, without which they would not be considered attractive and could not possibly hope to attract a husband.

It's clear that there are considerable variations in what constitutes attractiveness. One culture's sex goddess may very well be another's lonely heart. What conclusions can we draw from all this? Our best guess is that the phenomenon of heterosexual attraction as such, the fact that men are attracted to women and women to men, is largely based on built-in factors. Some of the bodily characteristics that differentiate the sexes, such as the female's breasts, may have evolved to serve precisely such a function (see Chapter 10). But the phenomenon of differential attraction, the fact that some men and women are more attractive than others, cannot be explained without some appeal to learning. The Ainu male must surely learn that tattooed moustaches are a sign of physical beauty—while to us, and probably most other peoples, they assuredly are not.

## Love

Attraction tends to bring people closer together. If they are close enough, their relation may be that of "love." According to some authorities, psychologists might have been "wise to have abdicated responsibility for analysis of this term and left it to poets" (Reber, 1985). But wise or not, in recent years psychologists have tried to say some things about this strange state of mind that has puzzled both sages and poets throughout the ages.

Psychologists have tried to distinguish between different kinds of love. Some of the resulting classification systems are rather complex. One such scheme tries to analyze love relationships according to the presence or absence of three main components: *intimacy, passion,* and *commitment,* thus yielding eight different patterns (see Table 13.1; Sternberg, R., 1986, 1988).

Whether we're as yet at the stage at which one can really make such fine distinctions as such systems propose is debatable. But most psychologists would agree that there are at least two crude categories. One is ***romantic***—or ***passionate—love,*** the kind of love that one "falls into," that one is "in." The other is ***companionate love,*** a less violent state that emphasizes companionship and mutual trust and care.

### ROMANTIC LOVE

Romantic love has been described as essentially passionate: "a wildly emotional state [in which] tender and sexual feelings, elation and pain, anxiety and relief, altruism and jealousy coexist in a confusion of feelings" (Berscheid and Walster, 1978). The extent to which the lovers feel that they are in the grip of an emotion they can't control is indicated by the very language in which they describe their love: They "fall in love," "are swept off their feet," and "can't stop themselves" (Solomon, 1981).

These tumultuous emotions are sharply focused on the beloved, who is almost always seen through a rosy glow. The lover constantly thinks about the beloved and continually wants to be in his or her company, sometimes to the point of near obsession. Given this giddy mixture of erotic, irrational, obsessed passions and idealized fantasy, it's understandable why Shakespeare felt that lovers have much in common with both madmen and poets. They are a bit mad because their emotions are so turbulent and their thoughts and actions so obsessive; they are a bit poetic because they don't see their beloved as he or she really is but as an idealized fabrication of their own desires and imaginings.

*Romantic love and theories of emotions* A number of investigators have argued that if romantic love is an emotion, then theories such as Schachter's cognitive arousal theory (see Chapter 12, pp. 481–84) should apply to it just as they do to fear, anger, and euphoria. According to Schachter, an emotion has two components. One is a state of physiological arousal. The other is the appropriate cognitive context in the light of which that arousal is interpreted. According to some authors, much the same holds for romantic love (Walster and Berscheid, 1974; Walster and Walster, 1978).

Let's begin with the context. This includes our various ideas of what love and falling in love are all about. Our notions of romantic love—that there is *the* right person and none else will do, that it can occur at "first sight," that one is often "helpless in the throes of love," that the beloved is a paragon of all possible virtues, and so on and so on, are at least in part cultural inventions. They were fashioned by a historical heritage that goes back to Greek and Roman times (with tales of lovers hit by Cupid's arrows), were revived during the Middle Ages (with knights in armor slaying monsters to win a lady's favor), and were finally mass-produced by the Hollywood entertainment machine (with a final fade-out in

**Romantic love** *The blindness of romantic love is epitomized by Titania, Queen of the Fairies, in Shakespeare's* Midsummer Night's Dream. *Titania is magically made to fall in love with a man who has been turned into an ass. (From a 1984 production at Stratford, Ontario, with Patricia Connolly and Brian Bedford; photograph by David Cooper)*

Table 13.1   A TAXONOMY OF KINDS OF LOVE BASED ON THE TRIANGULAR THEORY*

| Kind of love | Intimacy | Passion | Commitment |
|---|---|---|---|
| No love | − | − | − |
| Liking | + | − | − |
| Infatuation | − | + | − |
| Empty love | − | − | + |
| Romantic love | + | + | − |
| Companionate love | + | − | + |
| Fatuous love | − | + | + |
| Consummate love | + | + | + |

* As the terms are used here, *infatuation, romantic love* and *consummate love* represent an increasing degree of bondedness as passion is first combined with intimacy (romantic love) and then with commitment as well (consummate love). Sternberg describes *fatuous love* in which there is passion and commitment but no intimacy as the "kind of love we sometimes associate with Hollywood, or with whirlwind courtships in which a couple meets on Day X, gets engaged two weeks later, and marries the next month."
SOURCE: Sternberg, 1986, p. 124.

which boy and girl embrace to live happily ever after).* This complex set of ideas about what love is, together with an appropriate potential love object—attractive, of the right age, more or less available, and so on—constitute the context that may lead us to interpret physiological arousal as love.

What leads to the relevant bodily arousal? One obvious source is erotic excitement, although other forms of stimulation may have the same effect. We've previously seen that physiological arousal produced by sheer physical exertion can enhance sexual feelings (see Chapter 12, p. 483). In a similar vein, fear, pain, and anxiety may heighten general arousal and thus lend fuel to romantic passion. In a widely cited experiment, investigators compared the reactions of young men who crossed either of two bridges. One was a long, narrow, wobbly suspension bridge, precariously suspended over a shallow rapids 230 feet below. The other was a solid, well-built bridge, sitting only 10 feet above a small river. As each man crossed the bridge, he was approached by an attractive young woman who asked him to fill out a questionnaire for her to help her with a class project. Some of the men did indeed call the young woman later (ostensibly to discuss the experiment, but really to ask her for a date). But the likelihood of their doing so depended on the bridge on which they met. If it was the rickety suspension bridge—which presumably would elicit some fear and excitement—the chances were almost one in three that the men would call. If it was the safe and solid bridge, the chances were only one in twenty (Dutton and Aron, 1974; but see also Kenrick and Cialdini, 1977; Kenrick, Cialdini, and Linder, 1979).

*The rocky course of romantic love*    This general approach may help us understand why romantic love seems to thrive on obstacles. Shakespeare tells us that the "course of true love never did run smoothly" but if it had, the resulting love might have been lacking in ardor. The fervor of a wartime romance or of an extramarital affair is probably fed in part by danger and frustration, and many a lover's passion becomes all the more intense for being unrequited. In all these cases, there is increased arousal, whether through fear, frustration, or anxiety. This arousal continues to be interpreted as love, a cognitive appraisal that fits in perfectly with our ideas about romantic love, for these include suffering as well as rapture. An interesting demonstration of this phenomenon is the so-called **Romeo-and-Juliet effect** (named after Shakespeare's doomed couple whose parents violently opposed their love). This describes the fact that parental opposition tends to *intensify* the couple's romantic passion rather than to diminish it. In one study, couples were asked whether their parents interfered with their relationship. The greater this interference, the more deeply the couples fell in love (Driscoll, Davis, and Lipitz, 1972). The moral is that if parents want to break up a romance, their best bet is to ignore it. If the feuding Montagues and Capulets had simply looked the other way, Romeo and Juliet might well have become bored with each other by the end of the second act.

*Romantic love as an adventure*    A related characteristic of romantic love is that it has some of the qualities of an adventure (Simmel, 1911; Sabini, 1992, in press). Initially the word "romance" described a certain kind of tale written in

***Rocky course of romantic love***    *Parental opposition tends to intensify Romeo and Juliet's passion. Pictured here is the balcony scene from Prokofiev's ballet,* Romeo and Juliet. *(From a 1990 performance by American Ballet Theater; photograph by Martha Swope)*

---

* While various Hindu myths and Chinese love songs make it clear that romantic love is found in other times and places than our own, it's unlikely that any other cultural epoch has taken it quite as seriously as ours does; thus love as a precondition for marriage is a relatively new and Western concept (e.g., De Rougemont, 1940; Hunt, 1959; Grant, 1976).

***Romance and the knightly quest for
adventure*** *A painting based on a
16th-century Italian epic celebrating the
heroic deed of Roger, a valorous knight
doing battle with a sea monster to rescue
the virtuous Angelica. (*Roger and
Angelique, *by Jean-Auguste-Dominique
Ingres, 1819; © Photo Réunion des
Musées Nationaux)*

***Companionate love*** *When passion and
obsession ebb, the companionship and affection of companionate love, as shown
here, may follow. (© Paul Fusco/
Magnum)*

medieval French (a language derived from Latin, or "Roman") about the won-
drous feats of knights in armor who fought dragons and monsters and undertook
quests to win some lady's love. In time, the word's meaning centered on the
knight-meets-lady aspect of these stories and became more or less synonymous
with "love affair." Some of its original sense still inheres in the way the term "romantic" is used today, for it suggests some of the quality of fanciful adventure
that the medieval romances described.

This adventurous aspect of romance is probably one of its great attractions,
even in our own, prosaic age. It's in the nature of an adventure that one doesn't
quite know how it will turn out. Adventures imply a certain amount of novelty
and a bit (sometimes quite a bit) of danger. Climbing a steep mountain cliff is an
adventure, as is skydiving. And so is beginning a romance. It's probably no accident that when someone says "I had an adventure," we often assume that what's
meant is a love affair. This adventurous aspect of the romance may be yet another way to provide physiological arousal and to perpetuate the emotion of romantic love.

### COMPANIONATE LOVE

It's widely agreed that romantic love tends to be a short-lived bloom. That wild
and tumultuous state, with its intense emotional ups and downs, with its obsessions, fantasies, and idealizations, rarely if ever lasts forever. Eventually there are
no further obstacles, no further surprises, no further room for fantasy and ideal-
ization. The adventure is over, and romantic love ebbs. Sometimes it turns into
indifference (if not active dislike). Sometimes it is transformed into a related but
gentler emotion—***companionate love.*** This is sometimes defined as the "affection

**509**

we feel for those with whom our lives are deeply intertwined. This is not to say that the earlier passion doesn't occasionally flare up again. But it no longer has the obsessive quality that it once had, where the lover is unable to think of anything but the beloved (Berscheid and Walster, 1978).

## SOCIAL INFLUENCE: MANY-ON-ONE INTERACTIONS

Up to now, our discussion has focused upon one-on-one interactions: some between comparative strangers, others between friends and lovers. In such interactions, other people often affect what we do, as in the case of a salesman trying to sell a car to a potential customer, or a would-be lover who tries to persuade his beloved to reciprocate his affections. But there are instances in which the interaction is more complex and in which the social effects come from many persons simultaneously.

Such situations are usually discussed under the general heading of *social influence.* In these cases, the interaction is of the form of many-on-one: the influence of many others converges upon one individual. In some cases, the influence of others may make us tailor our behavior to *conform* to theirs. In others, it will make us obey them and *comply* with their orders. And in still other instances, the others exert their influence upon us in an even simpler way—by their *mere presence* as an audience.

### Social Facilitation: Social Influence by Mere Presence

It has long been known that the presence of other people has an effect on us. An example is laughter. Every comedian knows that laughter is contagious; each guffaw triggers another and then yet another, a fact that led to the use of canned TV laughter on the theory that if the home audience hears the (dubbed) laughs of others, they will laugh along (Wilson, 1985). Similar effects have been demonstrated by many investigators who compared people on various tasks that they performed either alone or in the presence of others. The initial results suggested that the social effect is always beneficial. When together with others who are engaged in the same task, people race bicycles faster, learn simple mazes more quickly, and perform more multiplication problems in the same period of time. Such effects have been grouped under the general title *social facilitation* (Allport, 1920).

Other studies, however, have indicated that the presence of others can sometimes be a hindrance instead of a help. While college students are faster at solving simple mazes when working together with others, they are considerably slower when the mazes are more complex (Hunt and Hillery, 1973; Zajonc, 1965, 1980). An audience can evidently inhibit as well as facilitate. How can such divergent results be reconciled?

According to Robert Zajonc, the explanation is that the presence of others leads to a state of increased drive or arousal. Such an increase would resolve the apparent contradiction if we assume that such increased arousal strengthens the tendency to perform highly *dominant* responses—the ones that seem to come "automatically." If so, then we should expect that the presence of others will improve performance when the dominant response is also the correct one—as in performing simple motor skills, or learning simple mazes. But when the task gets

*Social facilitation* Audiences generally enhance the performance of an accomplished professional. But the effect on novices is not always beneficial. (Photograph by Gale Zucker/Stock, Boston)

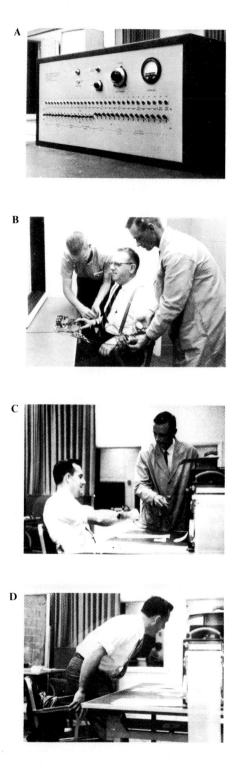

It appears that obedience to inhuman orders is in part a function of the total situation in which a person finds himself. Under some social systems—Hitler's Germany, Stalin's Russia—the conditions for compliance or tacit acceptance are so powerful that an outsider might well pause to wonder whether "there but for the grace of God go I."

*The Milgram study* The importance of situational factors in producing obedience is highlighted by the results of one of the best-known experiments of modern social psychology, a study conducted by Stanley Milgram (1963). Milgram's subjects were drawn from a broad spectrum of socioeconomic and educational levels; they were recruited by a local newspaper ad offering $4.50 per hour to persons willing to participate in a study of memory. Milgram's subjects arrived at the laboratory where a white-coated experimenter told them that the study in which they were to take part concerned the effect of punishment on human learning.

The subjects were run in pairs and drew lots to determine who would be the "teacher" and who the "learner." The task of the learner was to master a list of paired associates. The task of the teacher was to present the stimuli, record the learner's answers, and—most important—to administer punishment whenever the learner responded incorrectly. The learner was conducted to a cubicle where the experimenter strapped him in a chair, to "prevent excess movement," and attached the shock electrodes to his wrist—all in full view of the teacher. After the learner was securely strapped in place, the teacher was brought back to the main experimental room and seated in front of an imposing-looking shock generator. The generator had 30 lever switches with labeled shock intensities, ranging from 15 volts to 450 volts in 15-volt increments. Below each of the levers there were also verbal descriptions ranging from "Slight Shock" to "Danger: Severe Shock." The labels below the last two levers were even more ominous; they were devoid of any verbal designation and were simply marked "XXX" (Figure 13.5).

The teacher presented the items that had to be memorized. He was instructed to move on to the next item on the list whenever the learner responded correctly but to administer a shock whenever an error was made. He was told to increase the level of punishment with each succeeding error, beginning with 15 volts and going up by one step for each error thereafter until 450 volts was reached. To get an idea what the learner experienced, the teacher first submitted to a sample shock of 45 volts, the third of the 30-step punishment series, which gave an unpleasant jolt. During the experiment, all communications between teacher and learner were conducted over an intercom, since the learner was out of sight, strapped to a chair in the experimental cubicle.

Needless to say, the shock generator never delivered any shocks (except for the initial sample) and the lot drawing was rigged so that the learner was always a confederate, played by a mild-mannered, middle-aged actor. The point of the experiment was simply to determine how far the subjects would go in obeying the experimenter's instructions. Since the learner made a fair number of errors, the shock level of the prescribed punishment kept on rising. By the time 120 volts was reached, the victim shouted that the shocks were becoming too painful. At

*13.5   The obedience experiment*   (A) The "shock generator" used in the experiment. (B) The learner is strapped into his chair and electrodes are attached to his wrist. (C) The teacher receives a sample shock. (D) The teacher breaks off the experiment. (Copyright 1965 by Stanley Milgram. From the film Obedience, distributed by the New York University Film Library)

150 volts he demanded that he be let out of the experiment. At 180 volts, he cried out that he could no longer stand the pain. At 300 volts, he screamed that he would give no further answers and insisted that he be freed. On the next few shocks there were agonized screams. After 330 volts, there was silence.

The learner's responses were of course predetermined. But the real subjects—the teachers—did not know that, so they had to decide what to do. When the victim cried out in pain or refused to go on, the subjects usually turned to the experimenter for instructions. In response, the experimenter told the subjects that the experiment had to go on, indicated that he took full responsibility, and pointed out that "the shocks may be painful but there is no permanent tissue damage."

How far do subjects go in obeying the experimenter? When the study was described to several groups of judges, including a group of forty psychiatrists, all predicted considerable defiance. In their view, only a pathological fringe of at most 2 percent of the subjects would go to the maximum shock intensity. But these predictions were far off the mark. In fact, about 65 percent of Milgram's subjects continued to obey the experimenter to the bitter end. This proportion was unaffected even when the learner mentioned that he suffered from a mild heart condition. This isn't to say that the obedient subjects had no moral qualms. Quite the contrary. Many of them were seriously upset. They bit their lips, twisted their hands, sweated profusely—and obeyed even so.

Is there a parallel between obedience in these artificial laboratory situations and obedience in the all-too-real nightmares of Nazi Germany or Cambodia? In some ways, there is no comparison, given the enormous disparities in scope and degree. But Milgram believes that some of the underlying psychological processes may be the same in both cases.

*Being another person's agent*   In Milgram's view, one of the crucial factors is a personal history in which there is a continual stress on obedience to legitimate authority, first within the family, then in the school, and still later within the institutional settings of the adult world. The good child does what he is told; the good employee may raise a question but will accept the boss's final decision; the good soldier is not even allowed to question why. As a result, all of us are well practiced in adopting the attitude of an agent who performs an action that is initiated by someone else. The responsibility belongs to that someone else, and not to us.

One way of reducing the sense of personal responsibility is to increase the psychological distance between one's own actions and their end result. This phenomenon was studied in Milgram's laboratory. In one variation, two teachers were used. One was a confederate who was responsible for administering the shocks; the other was the real subject who was asked to perform such subsidiary tasks as reading the stimuli over a microphone and recording the learner's responses. In this new role, the subject was still essential to the smooth functioning of the experimental procedure. If he stopped, the victim would receive no further shocks. But even so, the subject might be expected to feel further removed from the ultimate consequence of the procedure, like a minor cog in a bureaucratic machine. After all, *he* didn't do the actual shocking! Under these conditions, over 90 percent of the subjects went all the way (Milgram, 1963, 1965; see also Kilham and Mann, 1974).

If obedience is increased by decreasing the subject's sense of personal responsibility, does the opposite hold as well? To answer this question, Milgram *decreased*

**13.6 Obedient subject pressing the learner's hand upon the shock electrode** *(Copyright 1965 by Stanley Milgram. From the film* Obedience, *distributed by the New York University Film Library)*

the psychological distance between what the subject did and its effect upon the victim. Rather than being out of sight in an experimental cubicle, the victim was now seated directly adjacent to the subject who was told to administer the shock in a brutally direct manner. He had to press the victim's hand upon a shock electrode, holding it down by force if necessary. (His own hand was encased in an insulating glove to protect it from the shock; see Figure 13.6). Now compliance dropped considerably, in analogy to the fact that it is easier to drop bombs on an unseen enemy than to plunge a knife into his body when he looks you in the eye. But even so, 30 percent of the subjects still reacted with perfect obedience. (For further discussion of this and related issues, see Miller, 1986.)

*Cognitive reinterpretations*   To cope with the moral dilemma posed by compliance with immoral orders, the obedient person develops an elaborate set of cognitive devices to reinterpret the situation and his own part in it. One of the most common approaches is to put on psychic blinders and try to shut out the awareness that the victim is a living, suffering fellow being. According to one of Milgram's subjects, "You really begin to forget that there's a guy out there, even though you can hear him. For a long time I just concentrated on pressing the switches and reading the words" (Milgram, 1974, p. 38). This ***dehumanization*** of the victim is a counterpart to the obedient person's self-picture as an agent of another's will, someone "who has a job to do" and who does it whether he likes it or not. The obedient person sees himself as an instrument; by the same token, he sees the victim as an object. In his eyes, both have become dehumanized (Bernard, Ottenberg, and Redl, 1965).

The dehumanization of the opponent is a common theme in war and mass atrocity. Victims are rarely described as people, but only as bodies, objects, numbers. The process of dehumanization is propped up by euphemisms and bureaucratic jargon. The Nazis used terms such as "final solution" (the mass murder of six million persons) and "special treatment" (death by gassing); the nuclear age contributed "fallout problem" and "preemptive attack"; the Vietnam War gave us "free-fire zone" and "body count"—all dry, official phrases that are admirably suited to keep all thoughts of blood and human suffering at a reasonably safe distance.

By dehumanizing the victim, moral qualms are pushed into the background. But for all but the most brutalized, these qualms can't be banished forever. To justify continued obedience, such queasy feelings may be suppressed by reference to some higher, overriding moral ideology. In Milgram's study, the subjects convinced themselves that science had to be served regardless of the victim's cries; in Nazi Germany, the goal was to cleanse humanity by ridding it of Gypsy and Jewish "vermin." In a related kind of self-justification, the fault is projected on the victims; they are considered to be subhuman, dirty, evil, and only have themselves to blame. In part, this cognitive reorientation may stem from a primitive belief that by and large the world is "just"; if someone is punished, there is probably a good reason. This general conception has been tested in several laboratory experiments. The results suggest that persons who suffer some misfortune are judged to have deserved it (Lerner, 1971). An extreme example of the same phenomenon was reported when the British forced a group of German civilians to march through a nearby Nazi death camp in the days just after the war. One of the civilians was overheard to remark, "What terrible criminals these prisoners must have been to get such punishment" (Cohn, in Dicks, 1972, p. 262).

The cognitive reorientation by which a person no longer feels responsible for his own acts is not achieved in an instant. Usually, inculcation is by gradual steps. The initial act of obedience is relatively mild and does not seriously clash with the person's own moral outlook. Escalation is gradual so that each step seems only slightly different from the one before. This of course was the pattern in Milgram's study. A similar program of progressive escalation was evidently used in the indoctrination of death-camp guards. The same is true for the military training of soldiers everywhere. Draftees go through "basic training," in part to learn various military skills, but much more important, to acquire the habit of instant obedience. Raw recruits are rarely asked to point their guns at another person and shoot. It's not only that they don't know how; most of them probably wouldn't do it.

### Social Impact Theory

The preceding discussion has dealt with several different forms of social influence, including social facilitation and inhibition, conformity, and obedience. According to Bibb Latané's *social impact theory* all of these forms of social influence can be understood by thinking of the individual as exposed to a field of social forces that converge upon him much as a number of light bulbs cast light upon a target surface. How much light will be cast depends on their number, the strength of each bulb, and how close the bulbs are to the target. According to Latané, the impact of social forces converging on one individual works in a similar manner. The total impact will depend on the number of persons who affect the target individual, how strong (in age, status, or power) each of these persons is, and how close they are to him in space or time (see Figure 13.7, freely adapted from Latané, 1981).

**13.7   Multiplication of social impact**
*(Freely adapted from Latané, 1981)*

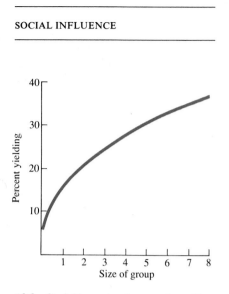

**13.8 Social impact and group size** *The figure shows yielding in a situation analogous to Asch's social pressure experiment with unanimous majorities of differing size. (After Gerard, Wilhelmy, and Conolley, 1968)*

Evidence for the role of strength comes from work on stage fright: performers are more anxious when anticipating playing before audiences of higher than of lower status (Latané and Harkins, 1976). There is also evidence for the role of immediacy: performing for a live audience produces more stage fright than performing for one that watches a video monitor in another room (Borden, 1980). Evidence for the effect of number is even more convincing, for in virtually all many-on-one situations, the influence the "many" exert on the "one" goes as their number increases.\* The larger the unanimous majority, the greater the conformity; the larger the audience, the greater the stage fright; the larger the crowd looking up at the sky, the more others will look up too. These effects are illustrated in Figure 13.8. As the figure shows, each additional individual increases the social impact, though with diminishing returns. Adding one person to a group of two will produce a much greater increase in social impact than adding one to a group of eight.

Thus far, we've only considered cases where the social influence exerted by several different sources converges upon one single target individual. In such cases, the impact goes up with their number (though, to be sure, with diminishing returns). What happens when that influence is spread out over more than one target? According to Latané, this will diffuse the impact, which will now be divided over all the targets. The more targets there are, the less social impact will hit any one of them (see Figure 13.9; adapted from Latané, 1981). Evidence comes from a study of stage fright in participants at a college talent show. The acts at the show had from one to ten performers. The stage fright of these performers de-

\* On the face of it, obedience might seem to be an exception since the command is usually issued by just one person and is enormously effective even so. But as we've already mentioned, this one person personifies many others—in Milgram's case, it was Science; in the military, it is the State—so the exception may be more apparent than real.

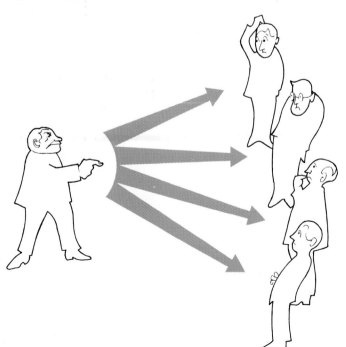

**13.9 Diffusion of social impact** *(Freely adapted from Latané, 1981)*

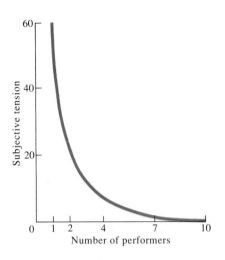

**13.10 Diffusion of social impact and performance anxiety** *Ratings of nervousness obtained prior to a college talent show from persons who performed alone or with 2, 4, 7, or 10 others. (After Jackson and Latané, 1981)*

pended on the number of co-performers in the act: the greater their number, the less the stage fright of any one member of the act (Jackson and Latané, 1981; see Figure 13.10).

A similar dispersion of social impact is relevant to the bystander effect we have discussed in another context (see p. 499). The likelihood that any one person will provide help in an emergency decreases as the number of bystanders increases. Here diffusion of social impact is partially produced by the diffusion of responsibility, for the obligation to help is spread out over all the onlookers, and each can ask, "Why me? Why not the others?"

A final example of diffusion of social impact comes from a phenomenon called **social loafing.** This describes the fact that when individuals work as a group on a common task, all doing the same thing, they often generate less effort than they would if they worked alone. An example is pulling at a rope. In one study, one man working alone pulled with an average force of 139 pounds, while groups of eight pulling together only averaged 546 pounds, which is less than four times the solo rate. In another study, students were asked to clap and cheer as loudly as they could; sometimes alone, sometimes in groups of two, four, or six. Here too the results showed social loafing: each person cheered and clapped less vigorously the greater the number of others he was with (Latané, Williams, and Harkins, 1979). There is an old adage "Many hands make light the work." The trouble is that they don't make it as light as they should.

What accounts for social loafing? The best guess is that each individual worker passes the buck and lets the others do more of the pulling or cheering. After all, there is no way for anyone to know just how hard each person works. If so, they can't be blamed if the group does badly (nor praised if it does well). Evidence that this is so comes from a study in which individuals were made to believe that their own contribution to the group effort was readily identifiable. When this was done in a study of group cheering, social loafing was almost completely abolished (Williams, Harkins, and Latané, 1981).

**Social loafing** *In a tug-of-war, everyone seems to pull as hard as he can, but the total force exerted by the group tends to be less than the solo rate times the number of its members. (Photograph by Jodi Cobb, 1985/Woodfin Camp)*

## CROWD BEHAVIOR: MANY-ON-MANY INTERACTIONS

In this chapter we've considered two broad classes of social interaction. The first involved *one-on-one* interactions between two persons who might be relative strangers or friends and lovers. In a second group, the interactions were of *many-on-one*—cases of social influence in which the impact of a number of others converged on an individual producing social facilitation or inhibition, conformity, or obedience. We now turn to a third class of social interactions in which the relation is *many-on-many.* These are group interactions in which a number of persons interact with a number of others simultaneously. An important example is ***crowd behavior.**

There is little doubt that under some circumstances people in crowds behave differently from the way they do when alone. In riots or lynch mobs, they express aggression at a level of bestial violence that would be inconceivable if they acted in isolation. In other situations, crowds may become frantically fearful, as in panics that may sweep a tightly packed auditorium when someone shouts "Fire." Yet another example is provided by occasional reports of crowds that gather to watch some disturbed person on a high ledge of a tall building, and then taunt the would-be suicide and urge him to jump.

What does the crowd do to the individual to make him act so differently from his everyday self? In analogy to the attempt to explain blind obedience, we can distinguish between two contrasting views. One holds that the crowd transforms the individual completely so that he loses his individuality and becomes deindividuated and essentially irrational. Another position holds that crowd behavior is not quite as irrational as it appears at first, but that it can be explained—at least in part—as a function of the individual's cognitive appraisal of the total situation.

### Deindividuation and Crowd Behavior

An early exponent of the deindividuation approach was Gustav Le Bon (1841–1931), a French writer of conservative leanings whose disdain for the masses was reflected in his theory of crowd behavior. According to Le Bon, persons in a crowd become wild, stupid, and irrational, giving vent to primitive impulses that are normally suppressed. Their emotion spreads by a sort of contagion, and rises to an ever-higher pitch as more and more crowd members become affected. In consequence, fear becomes terror, hostility turns into murderous rage, and the crowd member becomes a savage barbarian—"a grain of sand among other grains of sand, which the wind stirs up at will" (Le Bon, 1895).

A number of social psychologists have tried to translate some of these ideas into modern terms. To them, the key to crowd behavior is ***deindividuation,*** a state in which an individual in a group loses the awareness of himself as a separate individual. This state is more likely to occur when there is a high level of arousal

* The many-on-one and many-on-many distinction is not hard and fast. At bottom, most many-on-many interactions are probably composed of a large number of many-on-one interactions, as each member in a panicky crowd or a rioting mob is influenced by the collective force of the mass of others.

A

B

*Deindividuation* (A) Some deindividuation effects are harmless. (B) Others represent a menace to a humane, democratic society. (Top: © 1983 by Michael Sheil/Black Star. Bottom: © Detroit Free Press, 1988, Pauline Lubens/Black Star)

and anonymity. Deindividuation tends to disinhibit impulsive actions that are normally under restraint. Just what the impulses are that are disinhibited by deindividuation depends on the group and the situation. In a carnival, the (masked) revelers may join in wild orgies; in a lynch mob, the group members will kill and torture (Festinger, Pepitone, and Newcomb, 1952; Zimbardo, 1969; Diener, 1979).

To study deindividuation experimentally, one investigation focused on the effect of anonymity in children who were trick-or-treating on Halloween. Some came alone; others came in groups. Some were asked for their names by the adults in the homes they visited; others were not. All children were then given an opportunity to steal pennies or candy when the adult left the room on some pretext. The children were much more likely to steal if they came in groups and were anonymous. Thus an increase in wrongdoing may have occurred because anonymity made the child less aware of himself as a separate individual—that is, made him deindividuated—with a resulting disinhibition of petty thievery. But there may have been a simpler and perfectly rational reason: being anonymous, the child was less afraid of being caught (Diener, Fraser, Beaman, and Kelem, 1976).

Further evidence on the role of anonymity comes from a cross-cultural study of the prescribed code for warriors before they go to battle. Some of the cultures were judged to be more ferocious in warfare than others—their warriors killed all enemies on the spot, fought to the death in all battles, or took prisoners so that they could torture them later. Other cultures were judged to be (comparatively) less ferocious. This difference in the way each culture waged war was correlated with the warriors' appearance as they went into battle. Warriors of the more ferocious cultures were more likely to paint their face or body, or to wear a special tribal mask. War paint and masks may well be a means to make a warrior feel less of an individual and more of a member of his group—to become deindividuated and thus capable of violent acts that characterize his culture's warfare (Watson, 1973). A somewhat similar function may be performed by the modern military uniform, which tends to make its wearer feel anonymous; if he pulls the trigger, he does so as a faceless agent of his government and not of his own volition (Redl, 1973).

Another illustration comes from a study of crowds that taunt would-be suicides. One investigator examined a number of cases in which crowds were present when a person threatened to jump off a building, bridge, or tower. In some of these cases, members of the crowd baited the victim—shouting "Jump," screaming obscenities, and in one case, throwing stones and debris at the rescue squad. In other cases, there was no baiting. Baiting was more common when the crowd was quite large and when the potential suicide occurred at or toward night time and thus under the cover of darkness—conditions that would enhance anonymity and deindividuation (Mann, 1981).

## Cognitive Factors and the Panicky Crowd

Is crowd behavior really as irrational as the deindividuation approach suggests? To be sure, phenomena such as panics indicate that people in groups sometimes act in ways that have disastrous consequences which none of them foresaw or desired. This shows that crowd behavior can be profoundly maladaptive, but does it

***Panic*** *In June of 1985, a riot broke out at a soccer match in Brussels resulting in the collapse of a stadium wall that killed 38 persons and injured more than 200 others. The photo gives a glimpse of the resulting panic. (Photograph by Eamonn McCabe, The Observer)*

prove that the individual members of the crowd acted irrationally? Several social psychologists have argued that it does not (Brown, 1965). They point out that in certain situations, such as fires in crowded auditoriums, the optimum solution for all participants (that is, escape for all) can only come about if they all trust one another to behave cooperatively (that is, not to run for the exits). If this trust is lacking, each individual will do the next best thing given her motives and her expectations of what others will do. She will run to the exit because she is sure that everyone else will do the same, hoping that if she runs quickly enough she will get there before them. The trouble is that all others make the same assumption that she does, and so they all arrive more or less together, jam the exit, and perish.

According to this cognitive interpretation, intense fear as such will not produce crowd panic, contrary to Le Bon's assertion. What matters are people's beliefs about escape routes. If they think that the routes for escape (the theater exits) are open and readily accessible, they will not stampede. Nor will panic develop if all escape routes are thought to be completely blocked, as in a mine collapse or a submarine explosion. Such disasters may lead to terror or apathetic collapse; but there will be none of the chaos that characterizes a panicky crowd. For panic to occur, the exits from danger must be seen to be limited or closing. In that case, each individual may well think that he can escape only if he rushes ahead of the others. If everyone thinks this way, panic may ensue (Smelser, 1963).

### THE PRISONER'S DILEMMA

Roger Brown believes that some facets of escape panic can be understood in terms of a problem taken from the mathematical theory of games (Brown, 1965). It is generally known as the ***prisoner's dilemma*** (Luce and Raiffa, 1957). Consider the hypothetical problem of two men arrested on suspicion of bank robbery. The district attorney needs a confession to guarantee conviction. He hits on a diabolical plan. He talks to each prisoner separately and offers each a simple choice—confess or stay silent. But he tells each man that the consequences will depend, not just on what he does, but also on his partner's choice. If both confess, he will recommend an intermediate sentence of, say, eight years in prison for each. If neither confesses, he will be unable to prosecute them for robbery but he will charge them with a lesser crime such as illegal possession of a gun and both will get one year in jail. But suppose one confesses and the other does not? In this case the two men will be dealt with very differently. The one who confesses will be treated with extra leniency for turning state's evidence; he will receive a suspended sentence and won't go to jail at all. But the one who remains silent will feel the full force of the law. The D.A. will recommend the maximum penalty of twenty years.

As the situation is set up, there are four possible combinations of what the prisoners may do. Both may remain silent; Prisoner A may confess while B does not; B may confess while A does not; both may confess. Each of the four sets of decisions has a different consequence or **payoff** for each of the two prisoners. The four sets of decisions and the payoffs associated with each yield a so-called **payoff matrix** as shown in Table 13.2.

Table 13.2   PAYOFF MATRIX FOR THE PRISONER'S DILEMMA

|  |  | *Prisoner* B: | |
|---|---|---|---|
|  |  | Stays silent | Confesses |
| *Prisoner* A: | Stays silent | 1 year for *A*<br>1 year for *B* | 20 years for *A*<br>No jail for *B* |
|  | Confesses | No jail for *A*<br>20 years for *B* | 8 years for *A*<br>8 years for *B* |

Given this payoff matrix, what can the prisoners do? If both remain silent, the consequence is reasonably good for each of them. But how can either be sure that his partner won't double-cross him? If A remains silent while B tells all, B is even better off than he would be if both kept quiet; he stays out of jail entirely, while poor, silent A gets twenty years. Can A take the chance that B will not confess? Conversely, can B take this chance on A? The best bet is that they will *both* confess. The D.A. will get his conviction, and both men will get eight years.

In a sense, the prisoners' behavior is maladaptive, for the outcome is far from optimal for each. But this doesn't mean that either of the two men behaved irrationally. On the contrary. Paradoxically enough, each picked the most rational course of action considering that he couldn't be sure how his partner would decide. Each individual acted as rationally as possible; the ironic upshot was an unsatisfactory outcome for each. In the best of all possible worlds they would have been able to trust each other, would have remained silent, and been in jail for a much shorter period.

evidently in the midst of a municipal election. Modern archeologists have found some of the election slogans on the excavated walls: "Vote for Vatius, all the whoremasters vote for him" and "Vote for Vatius, all the wife-beaters vote for him." While the techniques of the anti-Vatius faction may be a bit crude for our modern taste, they certainly prove that the psychology of the smear campaign has a venerable history (Raven and Rubin, 1976).

Phenomena of this sort suggest that there are some invariant properties of human social behavior which can provide the foundation for a genuine science of social psychology.

## SUMMARY

1. Social interactions can be classified as those that are *one-on-one*, those that are *many-on-one*, and those that are *many-on-many*. According to some theorists, all one-on-one interactions depend on *social exchange* as shown by the operation of the *reciprocity rule.*

2. In investigating *altruism*, social psychologists have found that people often fail to help others in an emergency. One reason is the *bystander effect*. The more people that are present, the less likely that any one of them will provide help, in part because of *pluralistic ignorance*, in part because of *diffusion of responsibility*. When altruism does occur, it is often triggered by *vicarious distress*. But this alone won't lead to altruistic behavior unless it is accompanied by *empathic concern*.

3. Social psychologists have studied some of the factors that attract people to each other. They include *physical proximity, familiarity, similarity*, and *physical attractiveness*. There is evidence in favor of the *matching hypothesis*, which predicts a strong correlation between the physical attractiveness of the two partners. *Love* is an especially close relation between two partners. Some authors distinguish between *romantic love*, in which the emotions are intensely focused, and *companionate love*, which is less turbulent and more long-lasting.

4. A number of many-on-one situations involve *social influence*. In some cases, all that matters is the mere presence of others, which produces *social facilitation and inhibition*.

5. Another case of social influence is *conformity*. One reason for conformity is *informational*: we may believe that the group has knowledge we don't possess. Another reason is *motivational*: we go along because we want to be liked. A dissenting minority often leads to a massive reduction in the force toward conformity and may produce genuine changes in what people think and feel.

6. Still another form of social influence is *obedience*. Blind obedience has sometimes been ascribed to factors within the person, as in studies on the *authoritarian personality*. But situational factors may be even more important, as shown by Milgram's obedience studies. His findings suggest that obedience depends on the psychological distance between one's own actions and their end result. When this distance is increased—by decreasing one's sense of responsibility, by *depersonalization*, and by means of various *cognitive reinterpretations*—obedience increases too.

7. According to *social impact theory*, various phenomena of social influence can be understood by thinking of the individual as the target in a field of social forces. In certain situations—such as audience effects and conformity—the social forces converge upon one individual. In others, the impact is diffused over several other targets, as in the bystander effect and *social loafing*.

531

8. In *many-on-many interactions,* a number of persons interact with a number of others simultaneously. An example is *crowd behavior,* as in panics or riots. According to one account, the behavior of such crowds is essentially irrational. According to another interpretation, it is not as irrational as it appears at first. The *prisoner's dilemma* shows that under certain conditions there can be collective irrationality even though all of the participants behave rationally as individuals.

9. Other forms of apparently irrational crowd behavior are violent *group hostility* and *apathy.* In violent crowds, there is *deindividuation,* a weakened sense of personal identity. But part of the explanation may lie in the way the individual members of the group interpret the situation. An important factor is *diffusion of responsibility,* which applies to both sins of commission (as in rioting mobs) and sins of omission (as in bystander apathy).

# PART IV

# Development

*How do psychologists try to explain the phenomena they describe? Thus far, we've primarily dealt with two main approaches. One is concerned with* mechanism—*it tries to understand how something works. A second approach focuses on* function —*it tries to explain what something is good for. But there is yet another approach to explanation in psychology which focuses on* development. *This approach deals with questions of history—it asks how a given state of affairs came into being.*

*In the next two chapters, our concern will be with this developmental perspective on psychological phenomena. We will ask how various psychological processes arise in the organism's history—how we come to see and remember, reason and think, feel and act as we now do; how it is that we are no longer children, but for better or worse have become adults in mind as well as body.*

# CHAPTER 14

# Physical and Cognitive Development

***Children as miniature adults*** *Children dressed as did the adults of their time and class as shown in this 1786 Dutch painting. (*Helena van der Schalke, *by G. ter Borch, Courtesy Rijksmuseum, Amsterdam)*

At the beginning of the nineteenth century, many thinkers became increasingly interested in all forms of progressive change. They lived at a time of dramatic upheavals—the French Revolution, which ushered in a period of continued political unrest, and the Industrial Revolution, which transformed the social and economic structure of Europe and North America. These massive changes suggested that human history is more than a mere chronicle of battles and successive dynasties, but that it also reveals an underlying pattern of social development toward greater "progress" (Bury, 1932). Given this intellectual background, many scientists became interested in development wherever they saw it: in the history of the planet as it changed from a molten rock and formed continents and oceans; in the history of life as it evolved from simple early forms to myriad species of fossils and plants. One aspect of this intellectual movement was an increasing concern with the life history of individual organisms, starting from their embryonic beginnings and continuing as they develop toward maturity.

All animals develop, and so do we. The duckling becomes a duck, the kitten a cat, the human baby an adult. For in this regard all humans are alike. It doesn't matter whether they are Gandhi or Hitler, Joan of Arc or Isaac Newton—they all started life as infants. Is there any common pattern in the progression that marks the developmental history of each human life? If so, what is it? The attempt to answer these questions is the province of developmental psychology.

## WHAT IS DEVELOPMENT?

There seem to be some characteristics that apply to many aspects of human development, at least in a very general way, whether it is **physical development**, the maturation of various bodily structures; **motor development**, the progressive attainment of various motor skills; **cognitive development**, the growth of the child's intellectual functioning; or **social development**, changes in the way the child deals with others. According to many developmental psychologists, one such characteristic is **differentiation** as revealed in the physical development of the embryo and childhood behavior.

### Development as Differentiation

The concept of differentiation grows out of some early discoveries in embryology, which charts the history of the individual organism as it develops from a single egg and assumes the complex shape and function of its adult form. The German biologist Karl Ernst von Baer (1792–1876) pointed out that embryological development involves a progressive change from the more general to the more particular, from the simpler to the more complex—in short, **differentiation.** In embryonic development, anatomical differentiation is directly apparent. Initially there is one cell, then several cell layers, then the crude beginnings of the major organ systems, until the different organs and their component parts gradually take shape. Von Baer argued that this is the reason why embryos of very different species are so similar at early stages of development and utterly dissimilar at later stages (see Figure 14.1). Initially, the embryo only manifests the very general body plan characteristic of a broad class of animals. Thus a very young chick embryo looks much like the embryo of any other vertebrate animal at a similar stage of its development. The embryonic structures that will eventually become wings are quite similar to those structures of a very young human embryo that will eventually become human arms. As embryonic development proceeds, special features begin to emerge and the chick embryo begins to look like a bird, then like some kind of fowl, and still later like a chicken (Gould, 1977).

Von Baer's differentiation principle was initially regarded as a description of anatomical development and nothing else. But a number of psychologists suggested that a similar differentiation principle also applies to the development of behavior. Consider the development of grasping movements in human infants. When reaching for a small block, they initially curl their entire hand around the block; still later, they oppose the thumb to all four fingers. By the time they are

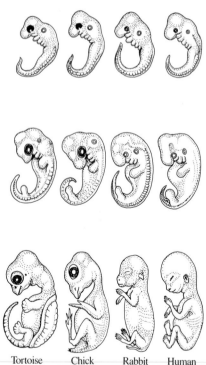

Tortoise    Chick    Rabbit    Human

**14.1   Differentiation during embryonic development**   *The figure shows three stages in the embryonic development of four different vertebrates—tortoise, chick, rabbit, and human. At the first stage, all of the embryos are very similar to each other. As development proceeds, they diverge more and more. By the third stage, each embryo has taken on some of the distinctive characteristics of its own species. (From Keeton, 1980. Redrawn from Romanes, 1901)*

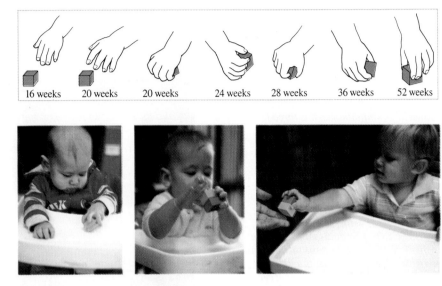

**14.2 The development of manual skills**
*The diagram shows the progressive differentiation in the infant's use of the hand when holding an object. At 16 weeks of age, he reaches for the object but can't hold on to it. At 20 weeks, he grasps it using the hand as a whole, with no differentiated use of the fingers. Between 24 and 36 weeks, the fingers and thumb become differentiated in use, but the four fingers operate more or less as a whole. By 52 weeks of age, hand, thumb, and fingers are successfully differentiated to produce precise and effective pincer movements. (Adapted from Liebert, Polous, and Strauss, 1974) Photos illustrate the same point at 23, 28, and 58 weeks. (Photographs by Kathy Hirsh-Pasek)*

16 weeks   20 weeks   20 weeks   24 weeks   28 weeks   36 weeks   52 weeks

*23 weeks*        *28 weeks*        *58 weeks*

one year old, they can victoriously coordinate hand, thumb, and one or two fingers to pick up the block with an elegant pincer movement (although such ultimate triumphs of manual differentiation as picking up a tea cup while holding the little finger extended will probably have to wait until they are old enough to read a book on etiquette) (Halverson, 1931; see Figure 14.2).

## Development as Growth

One of the most obvious characteristics of all development is growth. Organisms "grow up" as they change from a fertilized egg to a fetus, and after birth, they continue to grow in many different dimensions ranging from sheer physical size to mental complexity.

### GROWTH BEFORE BIRTH

Each human existence begins at conception when a sperm and egg cell unite to form the fertilized egg. This egg divides and redivides repeatedly and produces a cellular mass that attaches itself to the wall of the uterus. Two weeks after conception, the mass of cells (now called an *embryo*) begins to differentiate into separate cell layers. From now until birth, growth and development proceed at a rapid pace (see Figure 14.3). At one month after conception, the embryo is a fifth of an inch long and looks like a little worm. At two months after conception the mass of cells is about one inch in length and is now called a *fetus.* Just one month later, the fetus has grown to about three inches in length and has begun to look like a miniature baby with some functioning organ systems and a number of early reflexes, including sucking movements when the lips are touched. In another four months (that is, seven months after conception), the fetus has grown to sixteen

537

**14.3   Early stages of human prenatal development**   *(A) Six-week-old embryo, shown in its amniotic sac. It is three-fifths of an inch long, and its eyes, ears, and limbs are beginning to take shape but are still at a comparatively early stage of differentiation. For example, the hands have not yet differentiated into separate fingers. (B) Seven-week-old embryo, now nearly an inch long. Differentiation is further along as witness the presence of fingers. (C) Three-month-old fetus, three inches long. By now the fetus's features are recognizably human. Fingers and toes are fully formed, and there are external ears and eyelids. (D) Four-month-old fetus pushing against amniotic sac. The fetus is more than six inches long, with all organs formed. (From Nilsson, 1974)*

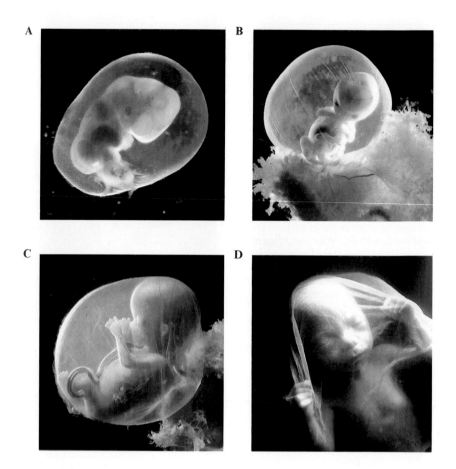

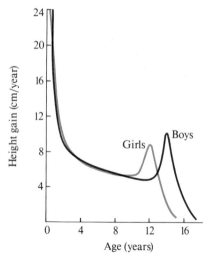

**14.4   Physical growth**   *Heights of British boys (black) and girls (color) from birth until 19 years of age. Physical growth continues for almost 20 years after birth with a special spurt at adolescence. (From Tanner, 1970)*

inches, has a fully developed reflex pattern, can cry, breathe, swallow, and has a good chance of survival if it should be delivered prematurely at this time.

These stages of our prenatal life attest to the massive changes in sheer size and structural complexity that take place over this period. In addition to these gross gains, however, there are also many subtler ones that have far-reaching effects. Some of the most important of these concern the developing nervous system. In the later stages of prenatal growth, the neurons begin to mature, and their axons and dendrites form increasingly complex branches and interconnections with other nerve cells (Schacher, 1981).

GROWTH AFTER BIRTH

Physical growth continues for almost two decades after birth, with a special spurt at adolescence (see Figure 14.4). The growth of the child's body is accompanied by the no less striking growth of her mind—in the way she perceives, thinks, speaks and understands, and reacts to others. The details of these accomplishments will be discussed in later sections. For now we only note that some of these feats are probably based on the continuation of events that began before birth. Of particular importance is the growth of neural interconnections beginning in fetal life and continuing long into infancy, as illustrated in Figure 14.5, which shows

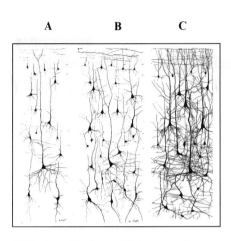

**14.5 Growth of neural interconnections**
*Sections of the human cortex in (A) a newborn, (B) a three-month-old, and (C) a fifteen-month-old. (Conel, 1939, 1947, 1955)*

**Capacity for learning** *Learning from culture is not accomplished overnight. A ten-month-old baby is trying to master the intricacies of eating with a spoon. (Photograph courtesy of Kathy Hirsh-Pasek)*

sections of the human cortex in a newborn, a three-month-old, and a fifteen-month-old child (Conel, 1939, 1947, 1955). According to a recent analysis, there is a tenfold increase in the average number of synapses per cortical neuron in the first year of life (Huttenlocher, 1979). This increasing neural complexity may well be one of the reasons for the increase in mental capacities as development proceeds.

### THE SLOW RATE OF HUMAN GROWTH AND ITS EFFECTS

Nine months after conception, the fetus is presumably ready to enter the outer world. But is it really ready? Left to its own devices, it obviously is not. It is singularly helpless and inept, more so by far than the young of most other mammals. To be sure, a newborn calf has to suckle and follow its mother, but it can walk at birth, and it can pretty well manage on its own after a fairly short period. But in humans (and to a lesser extent, in monkeys and apes), a considerable degree of development continues far beyond birth. For example, in most mammals the newborn's brain is just about fully formed. Not so in primates, and most especially not so in Man. The human newborn has achieved only 23 percent of her adult cranial capacity at birth, and is still only at 75 percent of this final value when she is about two and a half years old (Catel, 1953, cited in Gould, 1977).

What holds for brain growth also holds for other aspects of physical development. At birth, the bones of the skull are not yet joined together and certain wrist bones are still made of cartilage. All in all, the human newborn is further removed from adulthood than is the newborn of most other species. In a way, we are all born premature.

A number of authors believe that this retarded rate of development is what most distinctively makes us human, for the inevitable result is a long, protracted period of dependency. In some ways, this is quite inconvenient—for child and parent alike. But in many others, there are great benefits. For such a long period of dependency is tailor-made for a creature whose major specialization is its capacity for learning, and whose basic invention is *culture*—the ways of coping with the world which each generation hands on to the next. As there is so much to learn, the young have much to gain by being forced to stay a while with those who teach them.

### THE NEWBORN'S EQUIPMENT

What does a newborn bring into the world to serve as a foundation for further psychological development? Here, we will only ask about her motor and sensory capacities.

*The infant's response capacities* Initially infants have little control of their motor apparatus. Newborns can do very little—they thrash around in an uncoordinated manner and can't even hold up their heads. By four months of age they'll be able to sit up with support and reach for visible objects (which they often miss). But what do they do in the meantime?

Part of the answer is that newborns start life with a neurological survival kit that will see them through their first period of helplessness: a set of early reflexes.

Some reflexes of early infancy have to do with clinging to the person who supports her. An example is the ***grasp reflex***—when an object touches the infant's

539

**A vital reflex in the newborn**   *The sucking reflex is initiated when an appropriate object is inserted three or four centimeters into the mouth. (Photograph by Kenneth Garrett 1984/Woodfin Camp)*

palm, she closes her fist tightly around it. If the object is lifted up, the infant hangs on and is lifted up along with it, supporting her whole weight for a minute or more. This and some related reflexes are sometimes regarded as a primitive heritage from our primate ancestors, whose infants cling to their mothers' furry bodies.

Other infantile responses pertain to feeding. An example is the ***rooting reflex.*** When the cheek is lightly touched, the baby's head turns toward the source of stimulation, her mouth opens, and her head continues to turn until the stimulus (usually a finger or nipple) is in her mouth. When this point is reached, sucking begins.

Many infantile reflexes disappear after a few months. In some cases, the reflex is eventually replaced by a more directed response. Thus infants stop reflexive grasping when they are about three or four months old, but this doesn't mean that they will never again grasp objects in their hands. Of course they will. But when they do (at about five months of age), they'll do so because they want to— their grasp has become voluntary rather than reflexive. Such voluntary actions could not be performed (however clumsily) before various parts of the cerebral cortex had matured sufficiently to make them possible. But until this point, the infantile reflexes had to serve as a temporary substitute.

*The infant's sensory capacities*   While newborns' motor capacities are initially very limited, their sensory channels function rather nicely from the very start. Evidence comes from changes in their rates of breathing, of sucking, and of similar indices in response to stimulation. Newborns can hear; they can discriminate between tones of different pitch and loudness. They also prefer their mother's voice to that of a strange female (DeCasper and Fifer, 1980; Aslin, 1987). Newborns can see; while quite short-sighted and unable to focus on objects farther off than about four feet, they can readily discriminate brightness and color, and they can follow a moving stimulus with their eyes (Bornstein, 1985; Aslin, 1987). In addition, they are sensitive to touch, smell, and taste (Crook, 1987).

All in all, infants seem to come rather well equipped to *sense* the world they enter. But do they come pre-equipped to *interpret* what it is they see, hear, or touch? This is a disputed issue to which we will return in a later section. For now we merely note that the young infant is quite competent to receive sensory inputs. Whether he has some built-in knowledge of what these inputs might signify (as nativists would argue) or has to acquire this knowledge by relating various sensory inputs to each other (as empiricists would have it) is another matter.

## Development as Orderly Progression

In prenatal growth some events necessarily come before others. The embryo consists of primitive tissue layers before it develops organs; the skeleton is made of cartilage before it becomes bone. Developmental psychologists point out that similar patterns of orderly progression characterize development after birth.

A good example is motor development. There is a regular sequence of achievements that begins with the ability to hold the head erect, followed by the ability to roll over, then to creep, crawl, sit up, stand up, take a step or two, and finally to walk, first shakily and then with increasing confidence. The average ages of these accomplishments are shown in Figure 14.6. As the figure shows, there is a good deal of variability in the age at which a given baby masters each skill. But a few

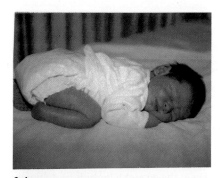

2 days

2 months

6 months

8 months

FETAL POSITION
0 month

CHIN UP
1 month

CHEST UP
2 months

REACH AND MISS
3 months

SIT WITH SUPPORT
4 months

SIT ON LAP
GRASP OBJECT
5 months

SIT ON HIGH CHAIR
GRASP DANGLING OBJECT
6 months

SIT ALONE
7 months

STAND WITH HELP
8 months

CREEP
10 months

WALK WHEN LED
11 months

PULL TO STAND
BY FURNITURE
12 months

CLIMB STAIR STEPS
13 months

STAND ALONE
14 months

WALK ALONE
15 months

**14.6   The development of locomotion**   *(A) The average age at which babies master locomotor skills, from holding their chins up to walking alone. These ages vary considerably. (From Shirley, 1961) (B) A pictorial record of these milestones in the life of one child. (Photographs courtesy of Kathy Hirsh-Pasek)*

months more or less make little difference for later development. What matters is that each step in the sequence comes before the next. No baby can walk before he can crawl.

Somewhat similar progressions are found in aspects of intellectual development. An example is the acquisition of language (see Chapter 9). Here too there is an orderly sequence. Initially the baby coos, then he babbles, then he utters the first word or two, then he develops a small, first vocabulary but is limited to one-word sentences, then he increases his vocabulary and utters two-word sentences, after which both vocabulary and sentence complexity increase until they finally

10 months          10 months          14 months

Table 14.1   CHARACTERISTIC LINGUISTIC ACHIEVEMENTS IN THE FIRST 30 MONTHS

| Age | Linguistic achievement |
|---|---|
| 3 months | cooing |
| 4 months | babbling |
| 10 months | first word |
| 18 months | about 20 words; one-word utterances |
| 24 months | about 250 words; two-word utterances |
| 30 months | about 500 words; three-plus utterances |

SOURCE: From Lenneberg, 1967, pp. 128–30.

reach adult levels. Table 14.1 gives a rough idea of the ages at which these achievements occur. As with motor development, there is a good deal of variability among different infants. Some may begin to talk by ten months, others as late as twenty, but age of initial language onset is no predictor of later linguistic competence. The important point is that linguistic development follows the same general progression for all children. Here, as in so many other areas, development generally proceeds by an orderly sequence of steps, and this holds for the growth of our minds as well as our bodies.

## THE PHYSICAL BASIS OF DEVELOPMENT

What produces the many changes that constitute development? One of the bases for these changes is the genetic blueprint that dictates much of the course of the organism's development from the moment of conception—it determines whether it will grow up to be a man or a mouse, an earthworm or a bald-headed eagle. Another basis is the organism's environment—both before and after it is born.

### The Mechanism of Genetic Transmission

An organism's genetic makeup is encoded in the *genes*, the units of hereditary transmission. These genes are a set of instructions that determine growth and steer the organism's development from fertilized cell to mature animal or plant. They are stored within the *chromosomes* in the cell's nucleus, with each chromosome holding a thousand or more of such genetic commands. In organisms that reproduce sexually, the chromosomes come in corresponding pairs; one member of each pair is contributed by the mother, the other by the father (see Figure 14.7).

SEX DETERMINATION

The genetic commands that determine whether a given animal will be male or female are inscribed in a pair of so-called sex chromosomes. In males, the two members are different: One is called an *X chromosome*; the other is somewhat

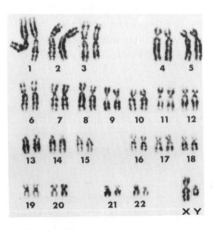

**14.7   The human chromosome pairs**   *The figure shows the 23 pairs of chromosomes in a human male. The twenty-third pair determines the individual's sex. In males, one member of each pair is an X-chromosome, the other a Y-chromosome. In females, both are X-chromosomes. (Photograph courtesy of M. M. Grumbach)*

*Genetic effects on behavior* *(Drawing by Shanahan; ©1989 The New Yorker Magazine, Inc.)*

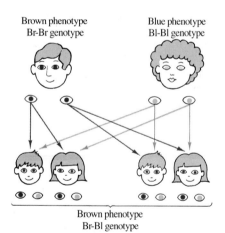

Brown phenotype
Br-Br genotype

Blue phenotype
Bl-Bl genotype

Brown phenotype
Br-Bl genotype

*14.8   Phenotype and genotype in the transmission of eye color   Eye color of the children of a brown-eyed and a blue-eyed parent if the brown-eyed parent's genotype is brown-brown. All of the children's eyes (phenotypes) will be brown, although their genotypes will be brown-blue. In the figure, genotypes are indicated by a pair of schematic eye-color genes under each face.*

smaller and is called a *Y chromosome*. In females, both members of the pair are X chromosomes. Which sex the child will be depends entirely on the father. For while every egg cell contains one X chromosome, sperm cells contain either an X chromosome or a Y chromosome. Depending upon which of the two kinds joins up with the egg cell, the resulting fertilized egg (or *zygote*) may contain an XX pair (a female) or an XY pair (a male).

### DOMINANT AND RECESSIVE GENES

Any given gene is located at a particular place on a given chromosome. Since chromosomes come in pairs, both members of each pair have corresponding loci at which there are genes that carry instructions about the same characteristic (for example, eye color). These two related genes—one contributed by each parent—may or may not be identical. Consider eye color. If both of the genes for eye color are identical (blue-blue or brown-brown), the result is simple: The eye color will follow suit. But suppose they are different. Now the overt expression of the genetic blueprint depends upon still other relationships between the two members of the gene pair. In humans, the brown-eyed gene is *dominant;* it will exert its effect regardless of whether the other member of the gene pair calls for brown or blue eyes. In contrast, the blue-eyed gene is *recessive.* This recessive blue-eyed gene will lead to blue eyes only if there is an identical (that is, blue-eyed) gene on the corresponding locus of the paired chromosome.

There are many other human traits that are (largely) based on a single gene pair, such as dark hair, dimples, and thick lips (dominant); and baldness, red hair, and straight nose (recessive). Some are more deleterious, and many of those are recessive. Examples range from mild conditions such as susceptibility to poison ivy and red-green color blindness, to hemophilia (in which the blood does not clot so that a person may bleed to death from a minor injury). Since these and most other damaging genetic characteristics are recessive, their expression is relatively rare. There will be no overt effect unless both parents transmit the recessive gene. This fact may partially account for the widespread cultural prohibition against incest. The offspring of close relatives run a much greater risk of serious genetic defects (let alone susceptibility to poison ivy).

The phenomenon of gene dominance illustrates a crucial distinction in the study of heredity. On the one hand, there is the overt appearance of an organism —its visible structure and behavior. This is the *phenotype,* the characteristic we actually observe in a given individual. But this phenotype is by no means equivalent to the organism's genetic blueprint, its *genotype.* As we have seen, two people who have brown eyes may well have different genotypes for eye color; one may be brown-brown, the other brown-blue (see Figure 14.8). Nonetheless, the phenotypes are the same, for if a blue-eyed gene is present it will be masked by its brown-eyed counterpart.

## Environments at Different Points in Development

Thus far, our focus has been on the genetic basis for the organism's development. What about the environment? It's obvious that a genetic blueprint without a proper environment will remain an unrealized potentiality. A given genetic potential cannot express itself without an appropriate environment—Isaac Newton could not possibly have rewritten the laws of the physical universe if he had been kept in a black, soundproof box from birth to adulthood. This underlines the fact (did anyone ever doubt it?) that development involves *both* heredity and environment. But the relation between the two is more subtle than that, for what is meant by *environment* continually changes as development proceeds.

### THE ENVIRONMENT BEFORE BIRTH

*Early embryonic development*   The embryo has various tissues that will ultimately become its inner organs, muscles, skin, and nervous system. How does any given cell in the embryo know how to fulfill its proper destiny—to become part of a mouth, or of a spinal cord, or whatever? After all, every cell of the organism has the same genes, so that they all presumably get the same genetic instructions. But if so, how do they manage to develop differently?

Part of the answer is that the fate of any given cell is partially determined by the cells that are adjacent to it and form its physical environment. Evidence comes from studies of salamander embryos. At an early stage of their development, they have an outer layer of tissue whose cells can turn into skin or teeth. They will become teeth if they make contact with certain other cells in the mouth region that belong to an inner layer of the embryo. Proof comes from studies in which parts of the flank of a salamander embryo were cut out and then transplanted into the embryo's mouth region. Had those cells stayed where there were, they would have eventually developed into the skin of the flank region. Having been brought into a different cell environment, however, they became teeth (Spemann, 1967).

*The development of sexual structures*   In an early stage of embryonic development, the environment consists of other cells. Somewhat later, development is affected by another kind of environment that we have discussed previously in another context—the internal environment that consists of the organism's own body fluids, especially its bloodstream (see Chapter 3). In mammalian embryos this is intimately linked up with the mother's blood supply. Various hormones that circulate within the embryo's blood or that of its mother will have a vital effect on the future course of development. An example is the development of sexual structures and behavior.

What determines whether an individual is biologically male or female? One might guess that the answer is just a matter of genetics—you are male if you are chromosomally XY, and female if you are XX. But the actual story is more complicated than that.

At around six weeks of age, the human embryo has primordial gonads and some external grooves and swellings that as yet give no indication of the baby's sex. A week or so later, the chromosomes initiate the differentiation of ovaries and testes, but the external genital apparatus still gives no clue as to whether its owner is male or female (see Figure 14.9). Now it is up to the hormones. In a genetic male, the XY chromosome pair leads to the formation of testes. Once formed, these produce **androgen,** the male sex hormone. The presence of this hormone in the bloodstream leads to the differentiation of the external genitals, and now the fetus is on the way to becoming a little boy.

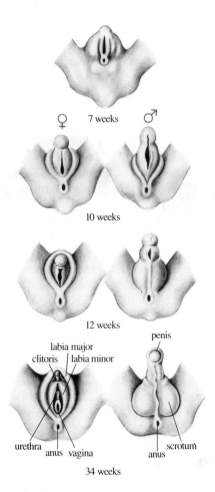

♀   7 weeks   ♂

10 weeks

12 weeks

penis

labia major
clitoris / labia minor

urethra
anus   vagina

scrotum
anus

34 weeks

**14.9   The development of external genitals in the human fetus**   At 7 weeks, the genitalia of human male and female fetuses are virtually indistinguishable. Some differentiation is seen at 10 weeks, and becomes increasingly more pronounced in the weeks thereafter. At 34 weeks, the distinctive characteristics of the different genitalia are fully apparent. (From Keeton, 1980)

*The creation of Eve  According to the Bible, Eve was created subsequent to Adam. But biologically, the order is reversed. (Panel from the Sistine Chapel ceiling, by Michelangelo, 1508–1512. Courtesy of Scala Art Resource)*

The pattern is different for females. The XX chromosome pair will lead to the formation of ovaries, but the formation of the female's external genitals does not depend on hormones except indirectly. As long as no androgen circulates in the bloodstream, the fetus will develop the appropriate female organs. In mammals, the basic developmental plan evidently calls for the building of a female, and it will run its course in that direction if left undisturbed. It would seem that biologically—if not biblically—speaking, Adam is created after Eve (Money and Ehrhardt, 1972; Money, 1980).

We'll later discuss certain hormonal malfunctions that produce certain developmental abnormalities (see Chapter 15). For now our primary point is to reiterate that development depends on an interaction between genetic makeup and environmental conditions. The chromosome pairs define an individual's genetic sex. But the way in which that sex is actually shaped depends upon the organism's internal environment—the presence or absence of male hormones in its bloodstream.

### THE ENVIRONMENT AFTER BIRTH

After birth, the crucial environmental events that affect development are those in the surrounding physical and social world. But here, too, what is important in one period of the individual's life has a lesser effect in another. The point is obvious in the case of social development. Who could doubt that the relevant social environment of a six-month-old baby is totally different from that of a teenager, even if both should be exposed to the identical sights and sounds?

The same point applies to the cognitive realm. We will later discuss theories of how children come to understand the world around them. But no one can doubt that this world is different at three months and at three years if for no other reason than that the babbles heard in early infancy are not heard as language until two years later. Under the circumstances, it is clear that what we call "environment" is not the same at different ages. Imagine a three-month-old who hears an older sibling's loud (and no doubt well-intentioned) shout "Surprise!" as the parents put some new toy in the baby's crib.* In all likelihood, the baby would cry in fear, for all *he* heard was a loud noise. At three years of age, the same shout would probably produce joyous squeals of anticipation, for now the sound has meaning and that meaning is vastly more important than its auditory intensity.

SENSITIVE PERIODS

The preceding discussion underlines a fact that everyone has always known—that what is important at one stage in life may not be so at some later point. But various developmental theorists have expanded this idea to make a much stronger claim. They argue that there are certain *critical periods* in development during which certain important events will have an impact that they would not have (or would have to a much lesser extent) at earlier or later times.

The hypothesis of critical periods was derived from embryological development. Take the differentiation of organ tissue. We've previously seen that at a very early stage, parts of an embryo's outer tissue may become skin or teeth, depending upon the cells they are adjacent to. If transplanted at this time, they will take the shape appropriate to their new surroundings. But at a later point in time, this plasticity is gone. Skin and teeth have become unalterably differentiated; if the teeth are transplanted from mouth to flank and vice versa, then a skin flap will form in the mouth and the flank will sport teeth—proof positive that a critical period has been passed (Spemann, 1967).

Many developmental psychologists believe that similar critical periods exist after birth or hatching. An example is the attachment of the young of many species to their mother, an attachment that is generally much more readily formed at an early age (see Chapter 15). In humans, the main example is the acquisition of language, which as we've seen is also easier at younger ages (see Chapter 9). But the periods during which these developmental attainments are possible are not as rigidly fixed and all-or-none as the critical periods when the organism is an embryo. As a result, they are now called *sensitive periods* rather than critical periods.

## Environment and Maturation

As noted earlier, development is orderly and progressive. Infants sit up before they can walk, and babble before they can talk. What accounts for this well-nigh inevitable schedule of early developmental achievements?

A number of developmental psychologists believe that many of these achievements (especially of motor and sensory development) are produced by *maturation*—an inevitable unfolding of behavior patterns that is genetically programmed into the species and is independent of specific environmental conditions. They believe that this sequence of behavioral milestones is analogous to the ordered progression that characterizes physical growth. The particular rate of this behavioral schedule may vary somewhat from one baby to the next, but the steps in that schedule are essentially the same for all—crawling precedes

---

* Though some younger siblings argue that *nothing* an older sibling ever does could possibly be well intentioned. (Personal communication from the author's younger brother, G. Gleitman, 1985.)

walking, and uncoordinated reaching precedes precise grasping. Maturation theorists believe that these achievements result primarily from the growth and development of the infant's brain and musculature and that they have little to do with experience.

### MATURATION AND PRACTICE

The orderliness of early development argues that it is heavily based on maturational processes. How are such processes affected by practice?

A number of investigators focused on motor development by comparing infant-rearing practices in different cultures. In some societies—for example, the Hopi and Navaho Indians—the infant is swaddled and bound to a cradle or carrying board, with his activity severely inhibited for much of the first year of life (see Figure 14.10). Despite some initial reports to the contrary (Dennis, 1940), the bulk of the evidence suggests that such early restrictions do have a retarding effect on later motor milestones (e.g., among the Mayan Indians; Brazelton, 1972), while systematic practice in various motor activities leads to some acceleration (e.g., in certain Kenyan communities; Super, 1976).

Do these studies prove that the maturation concept should be discarded? Not really. For the effects of immobilization or special practice are relatively slight—the onset of walking may occur a bit earlier or later, but the child's ultimate performance is pretty much the same in either case. The important developmental achievement is to walk at all, and this is very probably based on maturation.

In line with this conclusion are studies using twins, one of whom was trained in such basic motor activities as walking or climbing stairs. The results showed that while practice may help, it doesn't have long-run effects. If a twin practiced before he was "ready," he did indeed surpass his untrained twin. But the gains were short-lived. For once the other twin was given similar practice after reaching the appropriate maturational point, he quickly caught up with his specially educated twin and attained the same level of locomotor proficiency (Gesell and Thompson, 1929; McGraw, 1935).

All in all, it looks as if certain activities that are basic to the species—sitting, walking, climbing—occur as a function of maturation. They can be modified somewhat by experience, but they will emerge—more or less on schedule—regardless of specific practice.

### SPECIFIC VS. NON-SPECIFIC EXPERIENCE

Various achievements of early development such as walking seem to depend on maturation. But that does not mean that the organism's environment has no effect. What is relatively unimportant is *specific* experience—such as training in how to walk. But there is a good deal of evidence that certain *general* kinds of experience exert important effects on a number of sensory and motor patterns. For example, animals reared in total darkness in early life will not develop certain structures of the visual system that allow them to see properly when they are later exposed to light (Gottlieb, 1976b).

A very influential series of studies showed that just as sensory deprivation can retard maturation, environmental enrichment can help it along. In these experiments, rat pups were placed in either an "impoverished" or an "enriched" environment right after they were weaned. The animals in the "impoverished"

***14.10 Learning, maturation, and walking***
*A Shoshone infant strapped into a cradle. (Shosone Indian Reservation, Wyoming; Photograph by Victor Englebert/Photo Researchers)*

**14.11   Effects of environmental enrichment**   *After eighty days in the enriched environment of this rat playground, the animals had 23 percent more neural interconnections than control animals. (Photo courtesy of Dr. Mark Rosenzweig)*

environment were individually housed in a standard laboratory cage with continual access to a water bottle and to food. In contrast, the animals in the "enriched" environment were housed in groups of about twelve in a large cage that was a veritable rats' playground: It contained a variety of objects that served as "toys" that the rats could climb upon, walk across, and run in and out of, and that were changed daily to provide additional opportunities for informal learning (Rosenzweig and Bennett, 1972; Renner and Rosenzweig, 1987; see Figure 14.11). After eighty days of exposure to these different environments, the brains of the animals were examined. The results showed that the brains of the environmentally enriched rats were heavier than those of the environmentally impoverished rats. It's not that the number of neurons in the brains of the two groups was any different. What differed instead was the number of neural branchings and interconnections. In one study, the enriched animals were estimated to have about 9,400 synapses per neuron, while the impoverished animals only had about 7,600 (Turner and Greenough, 1985). The increase in the number and complexity of synaptic junctions associated with exposure to a varying environment may well be the biological basis on which later behavioral development depends (Schapiro and Vukovich, 1976).

The organism's genetic instructions dictate the maturation of many of its early achievements. But these dictates cannot be obeyed without a proper environment in which maturation can take place.

## PIAGET'S THEORY OF COGNITIVE DEVELOPMENT

Thus far, our discussion of development has focused on physical growth and changes in motor behavior. But the child grows in mind as well as body—in what she knows, how she comes to know it, how she thinks about it, and in the fact that she can tell it to others (sometimes interminably so). This intellectual growth that accompanies the progress from infancy to adulthood is generally called *cognitive development.*

We will organize our discussion of the child's mental growth around the work of the Swiss psychologist Jean Piaget (1896–1980). Piaget's conceptions have been enormously influential. He was the first to develop methods for studying the ways in which infants and children see and understand the world, the first to suggest that these ways are profoundly different from those of adults, and the first to offer a systematic theoretical account of the process of mental growth from infancy to adulthood. As we will see, Piaget's formulations have aroused considerable controversy; many of his empirical claims have been disputed, and most of his theoretical proposals have come under serious attack. But even so, we cannot begin the study of cognitive development without first considering Piaget's views. For these views shaped the way in which all subsequent investigators thought about the subject matter.

Piaget believed that mental growth involves major qualitative changes. This hypothesis is relatively recent. According to the eighteenth-century empiricists, the child's mental machinery is fundamentally the same as the adult's, the only difference being that the child has fewer associations. Nativists also minimized the distinction between the child's mind and the adult's, for they viewed the basic categories of time, space, number, and causality as given *a priori,* being part of the native equipment that all humans have at birth. Thus both empiricists and nativists regarded the child as much like an adult; the first saw him as an adult-in-training, the second as an adult-in-miniature. In contrast, Piaget and many other developmental psychologists usually look for qualitative differences and try to chart the orderly progression of human intellect as the child grows into an adult.

Piaget's original training was as a biologist, which may be one of the reasons why his conception of intellectual development bears many resemblances to the way an embryologist thinks of the development of anatomical structures. The human fetus doesn't just get larger between, say, two and seven months; its whole structure changes drastically. Piaget argued that mental development is characterized by similar qualitative changes. He proposed that there are four main stages of intellectual growth, whose overall thrust is toward an increasing emancipation from the here-and-now of the immediate, concrete present to a conception of the world in increasingly symbolic and abstract terms. These stages are the period of *sensory-motor intelligence* (from birth to about two years), the *preoperational period* (two to seven years), the period of *concrete operations* (seven to eleven years), and the period of *formal operations* (eleven years and on). The age ranges are very approximate and successive stages are often thought to overlap and blend into each other.

*Jean Piaget* (Photograph by Yves DeBraine, Black Star)

## Sensory-Motor Intelligence

According to Piaget, at first there is nothing but a succession of transient, unconnected sensory impressions and motor reactions. For mental life during the first few months contains neither past nor future, no distinction between stable objects and fleeting events, and no differentiation between the *me* and the *not me.* The critical achievement of the first two years is the development of these distinctions.

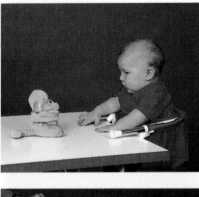

**14.12 Object permanence** *(A) A six-month-old looks intently at a toy. (B) But when the toy is hidden from view, the infant does not search for it. According to Piaget, this is because the infant does not as yet have the concept of object permanence. (Photograph by Doug Goodman 1986/Monkmeyer)*

OBJECT PERMANENCE

Consider an infant holding a rattle. To an adult, the rattle is an object, a *thing,* of whose existence he has no doubt, whether he looks at it or briefly looks away. The adult is sure of its existence, for he is certain that he will see it once more when he looks at it again. But does the rattle exist as a thing in the same sense to the infant? Does the infant have the notion of ***object permanence***?

According to Piaget, there is little object permanence in the first few months of life. The infant may look at a new toy with evident delight, but if it disappears from view, he shows little concern (see Figure 14.12). It seems as if what's out of sight is also out of mind and does not really exist for the infant. Piaget described one such incident when his daughter was seven months old:

> . . . Jacqueline tries to catch a celluloid duck on top of her quilt. She almost catches it, shakes herself, and the duck slides down beside her. It falls very close to her hand but behind a fold in the sheet. Jacqueline's eyes have followed the movement, she has even followed it with her outstretched hand, but as soon as the duck has disappeared —nothing more (Piaget, 1951, pp. 36–37).

Needless to say, infants eventually come to live in a world whose objects do not capriciously appear and disappear with the movement of their eyes. At about eight months of age, they start to search for toys that have been hidden or that have fallen out of their cribs. But for quite a while, their search pattern has some peculiar limitations.

Consider a nine-month-old who sees an experimenter hide a toy monkey in one place, say, under a cover to her right. She will happily push the cover off and snatch the monkey. The experimenter now repeats the process a few times, always hiding the monkey in the same place, under the same cover to the child's right; she'll keep on pulling the cover off and retrieve the monkey. Now the experimenter introduces a change in the procedure. Very slowly and conspicuously and in full view of the child, he now hides the toy in a different place, say, under a cover to the child's left. The child watches his every movement with grave attention—and then does exactly what she did before. She searches under the cover on the right where she *previously* found the monkey, even though she saw the experimenter hide the toy in another place just a moment before. This phenomenon is often called the ***A-not-B effect***, where *A* designates the place where the object was first hidden, and *B* the place where it was hidden last.

This *A-not-B* effect has been repeatedly demonstrated by both Piaget and many other investigators (Harris, 1987). According to Piaget, it demonstrates that the child does not yet have a clear understanding that objects exist in their own right. Piaget believed that the young infant's notion of the object includes her own action in retrieving it, as if her reaching toward place *A* where she found it previously were as much a part of the monkey as is the monkey's tail (Piaget, 1952; Flavell, 1985).

According to Piaget, the notion that objects exist on their own, and continue to exist even if they are not seen, heard, felt, or reached for, is a major accomplishment of the sensory-motor period. This notion emerges as the infant gradually interrelates his various sensory experiences and motor reactions. Eventually he coordinates the sensory spaces provided by the different modalities—of vision, hearing, touch, and bodily movement—into one real space in which all of the world's objects—himself included—exist.

### SENSORY-MOTOR SCHEMAS

The newborn starts life with a rather limited repertoire of built-in reactions, such as gross bodily movements in response to distress, sucking and swallowing reflexes, and after a few days, certain orienting responses such as head and eye movements. These recurrent action patterns are the first mental elements—or *schemas*—through which the infant organizes the world that impinges upon her. At first, these various schemas operate in isolation. A one-month-old infant can grasp a rattle and can also suck it or look at it. But she will perform these actions only if the stimulus object is directly applied to the relevant sensory surface. She will suck the rattle if it touches her mouth and will grasp it if it's pressed into her palm. But she is as yet unable to grasp whatever she's sucking or to look at whatever she's grasping. The coordination of all these patterns takes time and is not complete until she's about five months of age. How is this integration achieved?

According to Piaget, the answer lies in the joint action of the two processes that in his view are responsible for all facets of cognitive development: *assimilation* and *accommodation*. At any given point, the child has to be able to interpret the environment in terms of the mental schemas he has at the time; the environment is *assimilated* to the schema. But the schemas necessarily change as the child continues to interact with the world around her; they *accommodate* to the environment. In the case of the sucking response, the initial schema only applies to the nipple. But with time, the infant starts to suck other objects such as her rattle. Piaget would say that by doing this she has assimilated the rattle into her sucking schema. The rattle is now understood and dealt with as a "suckable." But the process does not stop there. After all, rattles are not the same as nipples; while both are suckable, they are not suckable in quite the same way. This necessarily leads to new discriminations. As a result, the sucking schema adjusts (that is, accommodates) to the new object to which it is applied. This process continues, with further assimilations followed by yet further accommodations, until finally looking, reaching, grasping, and sucking have all merged into one unified exploratory schema (Piaget, 1952).

*Assimilation and accommodation* The three-month-old has assimilated the rattle into her sucking schema and has accommodated the schema so that it now includes the rattle as a suckable object. (Photograph by Steve Skloot/Photo Researchers)

### BEGINNINGS OF REPRESENTATIONAL THOUGHT

The last phase of the sensory-motor period (about eighteen to twenty-four months) marks a momentous change in intellectual development. Children begin to conceive of objects and events that are not immediately present by representing (that is re-presenting) some prior experience with these to themselves. Such *representations* may be internalized actions, images, or words. But in all cases, they function as symbols that stand for whatever they may signify but are not equivalent to it.

One demonstration of this change is the achievement of full object permanence. At eighteen months or so, children actively search for absent toys and are surprised (and sometimes outraged) if they don't find them under the sofa cover where they saw the experimenter hide them; it is reasonable to infer that they have some internal representation of the sought-for-object. Even more persuasive are examples of ***deferred imitation*** in which children imitate actions that occurred some time past, such as a playmate's temper tantrum observed a day ago. A related phenomenon is make-believe play, which is often based on deferred imitation.

## The Preoperational Period

Given the tools of representational thought, the two-year-old has taken a gigantic step. A year ago, he could interact with the environment only through direct sensory or motor contact; now he can carry the whole world in his head. But while his mental world now contains stable objects and events that can be represented internally, it is still a far cry from the world of adults. The two-year-old has overcome the initial chaos of separate sensations and motor impressions, but only to exchange it for a chaos of ideas (that is, representations) that he is as yet unable to relate in any coherent way. The achievement of the next five years is the emergence of a reasonably well-ordered world of ideas. According to Piaget, this requires higher-order schemas that he calls ***operations,*** which allow the internal manipulation of ideas according to a stable set of rules. In his view, genuine operations do not appear until about seven or so, hence the term ***preoperational*** for the period from two to seven years.

### FAILURE OF CONSERVATION

*Conservation of quantity and number* A revealing example of preoperational thought is the young child's failure to ***conserve quantity.*** One of Piaget's experimental procedures uses two identical glasses, *A* and *B*, which stand side by side and are filled with the same amount of some colored liquid such as orangeade. A child is asked whether there is more orangeade in the one glass or in the other, and the experimenter obligingly adds a drop here and pours a drop there until his subject is completely satisfied that there is "the same to drink in this glass as in that." Four-year-olds can easily make this judgment.

The next step involves a new glass, *C*, which is much taller but also narrower than *A* and *B* (see Figure 14.13). While the child is watching, the experimenter pours the entire contents of glass *A* into glass *C*. He now points to *B* and *C*, and

*14.13 Conservation of liquid quantity Patrick, aged 4 years, 3 months, is asked by the experimenter, "Do we both have the same amount of juice to drink?" Patrick says yes. (B) The experimenter pours the juice from one of the beakers into a new, wider beaker. When now asked, "Which glass has more juice?," he points to the thinner one. (Photographs by Chris Massey)*

A

B

asks, "Is there more orangeade in this glass or in that?" For an adult, the question is almost too simple to merit an answer. The amounts are obviously identical, since *A* was completely emptied into *C*, and *A* and *B* were set to equality at the outset. But four- or five-year-olds don't see this. They insist that there is more orangeade in *C*. When asked for their reason, they explain that the liquid comes to a much higher level in *C*. They seem to think that the orangeade has somehow increased in quantity as it was transferred from one glass to another. They are too impressed by the visible changes in appearance that accompany each transfer (the changing liquid levels) and do not yet realize that there is an underlying reality (the quantity of liquid) that remains constant throughout.

By the time children are about seven years old, they respond much like adults. They hardly look at the two glasses, for their judgment needs little empirical support. "It's the same. It seems as if there's less because it's wider, but it's the same." The experimenter may continue with further glasses of different sizes and shapes, but the judgment remains what it was: "It's still the same because it always comes from the same glass." To justify their answer, the children point to the fact that one can always pour the liquid back into the original glass (that is, *A*), and thus obtain the same levels. They have obviously understood that the various transformations in the liquid's appearance are *reversible*. For every transformation that changes the way the liquid looks, there is another that restores its original appearance. Given this insight, children at this age recognize that there is an underlying attribute of reality, the quantity of liquid that remains constant (is *conserved*), throughout the various perceptual changes. (For comparable results with malleable solids like clay or plasticene, see Figure 14.14.)

A related phenomenon is **conservation of number.** The child is first shown a row of six evenly spaced bottles, each of which has a glass standing next to it. The child agrees that there are as many bottles as there are glasses. The experimenter now rearranges the six glasses by setting them out into a much longer row while leaving the six bottles as they were. Here the turning point comes a bit earlier, at about five or six. Up to that age, children generally assert that there are more glasses (or disks, or checkers, or whatever) because "they're more spread out" (see Figure 14.15). From about six on, there is conservation; the child has no doubt that there are just as many bottles in the tightly spaced row as there are glasses in the spread-out line. In all these conservation tasks, the older child's explanation emphasizes reversibility—liquid can be poured back in the taller glass, and the long line of glasses can be reassembled into a compact row.

**14.14 Conservation of mass quantity**
*In parallel to the failure to conserve liquid quantity is the preschooler's failure to conserve mass. Tyler, aged 4 years, 5 months, is shown two balls of Play-doh which she adjusts until she is satisfied that there is the same amount of Play-doh in both. The experimenter takes one of the balls and rolls it into a long, thin "hot dog." When now asked which has more Play-doh in it, she points to the hot dog. (Photograph by Chris Massey)*

**14.15 Conservation of number** *(A) The experimenter points to two rows of checkers, one hers, the other Tyler's. She asks, "Do I have as many checkers as you?," and Tyler nods. (B) One row of checkers is spread out and the experimenter says, "Now, do we still have the same?" Tyler says no and points to the spread-out row, which she says has more. (Photographs by Chris Massey)*

A

B

*Attending to several factors simultaneously* Why are preschool children unable to appreciate that the amount of a substance remains unaffected by changes of shape or that the number of objects in a given set does not vary with changes in the spatial arrangement? According to Piaget, part of the problem is the child's inability to attend to all of the relevant dimensions simultaneously. Consider conservation of liquid quantity. To conserve, the children must first comprehend that there are two relevant factors: the height of the liquid column and the width. They must then appreciate that an *increase* in the column's height is accompanied by a *decrease* in its width. Initially, they center their attention only on the height and do not realize that the change in height is compensated for by a corresponding change in width. Later on, say at five, they may well attend to width on one occasion and to height on another (with corresponding changes in judgment). But to attend to both dimensions concurrently and to relate them properly requires a higher-order schema that reorganizes initially discrete perceptual experiences into one conceptual unit.

In Piaget's view, this reorganization occurs when the child focuses on the transformations from one experience into another, rather than on the individual transformations by themselves. The child sees that these transformations are effected by various reversible overt actions, such as pouring the contents of one glass into another. The overt action eventually becomes internalized as a reversible operation so that the child can mentally pour the liquid back and forth. The result is conservation of quantity (Piaget, 1952).

In summary, the preoperational child is the prisoner of his own immediate perceptual experience and tends to take appearance for reality. When a seven-year-old watches a magician, she can easily distinguish between her perception and her knowledge. She *perceives* that the rabbits come out of the hat, but she *knows* that they couldn't possibly do so. Her four-year-old brother has no such sophistication. He is delighted to see rabbits anytime and anywhere, and if they want to come out of a hat, why shouldn't they?

EGOCENTRISM

The inability of preoperational children to consider two physical dimensions simultaneously has a counterpart in their approach to the social world. They cannot understand another person's point of view, for they are as yet unable to recognize that different points of view exist. This characteristic of preoperational thought is often called **egocentrism.** As Piaget uses the term, it does not imply selfishness. It is not that children seek to benefit at the expense of others; it is rather that they haven't fully grasped that there are other selves.

An interesting demonstration of egocentrism involves a literal interpretation of "point of view." If two adults stand at opposite corners of a building, each knows that the other sees a different wall. But according to Piaget, preoperational children don't understand this. In one study, children were shown a three-dimensional model of a mountain scene. While the children viewed the scene from one position, a small doll was placed at various other locations around the model. The child's job was to decide what the doll saw from *its* vantage point (see Figure 14.16). To answer, the child had to choose one of several drawings that depicted different views of the mountain scene. Up to four years of age, the children didn't even understand the question. From four to seven years old, their response was fairly consistent—they chose the drawing that showed what they saw, regardless of where the doll was placed (Piaget and Inhelder, 1956).

**14.16 The three-mountain test of egocentrism** *The child is asked to indicate what the doll sees. The results suggest that the child thinks the doll sees the scene just as she does, including the little house which is of course obstructed from the doll's vantage point. (After Piaget and Inhelder, 1967)*

## Concrete and Formal Operations

Seven-year-olds have acquired mental operations that allow them to abstract some of the essential attributes of reality such as number and substance. But according to Piaget, these operations are primarily applicable to the relations between concrete events (hence the term *concrete operations*). They do not really suffice when these relations must be considered entirely in the abstract. Eight- or nine-year-olds can perform various simple manipulations on specific numbers they are presented with, but they generally fail to understand that certain results will hold for any number whatsoever. They may realize that 4 is an even number and 4 + 1 is odd, and similarly for 6 and 6 + 1, 8 and 8 + 1, and so on, but they are by no means sure that the addition of 1 to any even number must always produce a number that is odd. According to Piaget, the comprehension of such highly abstract and formal relationships requires *formal operations,* operations of a higher order which emerge at about eleven or twelve years of age. Given formal operations, the child's thought can embrace the possible as well as the real. He can now entertain hypothetical possibilities, can deal with what *might be* no less than what *is.*

An illustration of the role of formal operations comes from a study in which children had to discover what makes a pendulum go fast or go slow. They were shown how to construct a pendulum by hanging some object from a string. They were also shown how to vary the length of the string, the weight of the suspended object, and the initial force that set the pendulum in motion. Children between seven and eleven typically varied several factors at a time. They might compare a heavy weight suspended from a long string with a light weight suspended from a short string, and would then conclude that a pendulum swings faster the shorter its length and the lighter its weight. Needless to say, their reasoning was faulty, for the way to determine whether a given factor (e.g., weight) has an effect is to hold all others (e.g., length) constant. Children below about eleven cannot do this, for they can operate only on the concretely given. They are unable to consider potential cause-and-effect relationships, which must first be deliberately excluded and then tested for later on. In contrast, older children can plan and execute an appropriate series of tests. Their mental operations proceed on a more formal plane so that they can grasp the notion of "other things being equal" (Inhelder and Piaget, 1958).

The period of formal operations is the last important milestone in the child's intellectual progression that Piaget and his co-workers have charted in some detail. Their account of the developmental steps that led up to this point has been enormously influential. But this doesn't mean that it has gone unchallenged. We will now consider some of the efforts to look at Piaget's description of human cognitive development with a more critical eye.

## PERCEPTION AND MOTOR ACTION IN INFANCY

One important challenge to Piaget's work concerns his views of what is given at the very start of life. A number of modern developmental psychologists contend that Piaget—who in this regard was much like the early British empiricists—had seriously underestimated the infant's native endowment. These critics deny that the infant's mind is the mere jumble of unrelated sensory impressions and motor reactions that Piaget had declared it to be, for they believe that some of the major categories by which adults organize the world—such as the concepts of space, time, objects, and causality—have primitive precursors in early life. They have buttressed their position by systematic studies of perception and action in very young infants.

### Links between Eye and Ear

Some recent findings concern the way in which the infant links sights, sounds, and touches. Normally, such sensory impressions provide information that refers to the same object or event outside. A cup breaks, and we see it shatter and also hear the crash. As adults, we don't ordinarily experience these visual and auditory messages separately; they both seem to refer to the same event—the breaking cup. But according to Piaget (and the British empiricists before him), the infant is initially quite unaware that these auditory and visual experiences are in some way related. For Piaget believed that, at first, the various senses are utterly separate doorways to the real world and that they become interconnected only after a period of learning and mental growth.

A number of investigators suggest that at least some intersensory relations may be present at the very outset (Spelke, 1987). Evidence comes from the fact that very young infants are remarkably sensitive to various correspondences between sights and sound. When shown films of a speaker's face in which the voice is sometimes synchronized and sometimes not, infants as young as three months will spend more time looking at the voice-synchronized face (Dodd, 1979). This phenomenon is not limited to speech. In one series of studies, four-month-olds were shown two films side by side. One featured a game of peek-a-boo, the other showed a hand that repeatedly struck various percussion instruments with a baton. Simultaneously, the infants heard either the peek-a-boo or the percussion soundtrack. The results were clear-cut—the infants spent almost twice as much time looking at the film that was appropriate to the soundtrack than at the film in which the sound did not match the sight (Spelke, 1976, 1981; see Figure 14.17 for some related results).

Analogous links between touch and vision have been reported in twenty-nine-day-old infants (Meltzoff and Borton, 1979). And some intersensory correspondence seems to exist even in newborns; when presented with a click to either the right or the left, they move their eyes to the appropriate side (Wertheimer, 1961; Harris, 1983). Such results suggest that there are some built-in connections between the information provided by the two sensory channels of sight and hearing.

### The Perception of Objects

The preceding discussion suggests that there are early and perhaps built-in correspondences between the different sensory channels and between sensory input and motor reaction. Other evidence bears on an even more fundamental Piage-

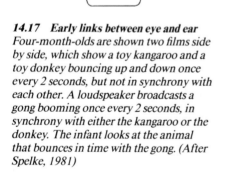

**14.17   Early links between eye and ear** *Four-month-olds are shown two films side by side, which show a toy kangaroo and a toy donkey bouncing up and down once every 2 seconds, but not in synchrony with each other. A loudspeaker broadcasts a gong booming once every 2 seconds, in synchrony with either the kangaroo or the donkey. The infant looks at the animal that bounces in time with the gong. (After Spelke, 1981)*

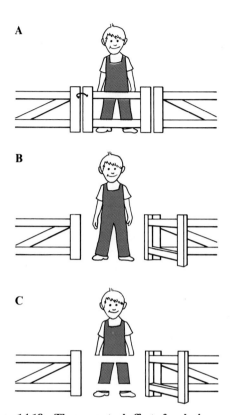

**14.18 The perceptual effect of occlusion**
*(A) A child occluded by a gate is perceived as a whole person behind a gate, so that he will look like (B) when the gate is opened, rather than being perceived as (C) a child with gaps in his body.*

tian (and empiricist) claim: the view that infants begin life with no conception that the world outside consists of real objects that exist independently of whether they are touched or seen.

### PERCEIVING OCCLUDED OBJECTS

One series of studies hinged on the perceptual effect of ***occlusion.*** Consider Figure 14.18A, which shows an object that partially obscures (occludes) the view of an object behind it. When adults encounter this sight, they will surely perceive it as a boy behind a gate. They are completely certain that when the gate is opened so that the partial occlusion is removed, they will see a whole boy (Figure 14.18B) and would be utterly astounded if the opened gate revealed a boy with gaps in him (Figure 14.18C). This ability to perceive partly hidden objects as they really are is continually called upon in our everyday life, for most of the things we see are partly concealed by others in front of them. But even so, we perceive a world of complete objects rather than disjointed fragments (see Chapter 6).

What accounts for the adult's ability to perceive partly hidden objects? To some extent, it is surely a matter of learning. We know that people have no gaps in them, and that even if they do, they can't stand unsupported in mid-air. But does this mean that Piaget is correct and that the infant starts life with no idea at all that there are external objects outside? Some authors believe it does not. In their view, the infant comes pre-equipped with some primitive concept of a physical world that contains unitary objects whose parts are connected and stay connected regardless of whether the object is partially hidden. Their evidence comes from experiments which show that under some conditions four-month-old infants seem to perceive occluded objects in much the same manner that adults do. Most of these experiments employed the ***habituation procedure*** (Figure 14.19).

**14.19 The habituation procedure** *(A) A four-month-old's face, looking at a small slowly rotating pyramid in front of her (the pyramid can be seen in the mirror that is behind the infant and above her head). (B) Habituation: The infant becomes increasingly bored and looks away. (C) Dishabituation: The infant sees a new object (the rotating cube shown in the mirror) and looks again. This dishabituation effect provides evidence that the infant perceives a difference between the first and the second stimulus (that is, the pyramid and the cube). (Photographs courtesy of Phillip Kellman)*

A

B

C

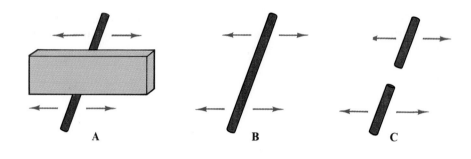

A          B          C

**14.20 The perceptual effect of occlusion in early infancy** *Four-month-olds were shown a rod that moved back and forth behind an occluding block as shown in (A). After they became habituated to this display and stopped looking at it, they were shown two new displays, neither of which was occluded. (B) was an unbroken rod that moved back and forth. (C) was made of two aligned rod pieces that moved back and forth together. The infants spent much more time looking at (C) than at (B). (After Kellman and Spelke, 1983)*

In one such study, the infants were shown a rod that moved back and forth behind a solid block that occluded the rod's central portion (Figure 14.20A). This display was kept in view until the infants became bored (that is, habituated), and stopped looking at it. The question was whether the infant perceived a complete, unitary rod, despite the fact that this rod was partially hidden. To find out, the experimenters presented the infants with two new and unoccluded displays. One was an unbroken rod that moved back and forth (Figure 14.20B). The other consisted of two aligned rod pieces, that moved back and forth in unison (Figure 14.20C). If the infants saw the original display as a complete rod that moved behind the block, they would presumably regard the broken rod as a novel stimulus. If so, they would keep on looking at it for a longer time than at the (now unobstructed) complete rod. This is just what happened. The fact that the top and bottom of the rod in the original display were seen to move together behind the block apparently led to the perception that they were connected. This suggests that some notion of a real physical object exists even at four months of age (Kellman and Spelke, 1983; Kellman, Spelke, and Short, 1986).

KNOWING ABOUT OBJECTS

The preceding discussion suggests that very young infants have some conception that objects exist even though they are not fully seen. They evidently see objects rather than disjointed fragments. Do they also understand certain rock-bottom principles of the physical world, such as the fact that two objects can't occupy the same space at the same time?

To answer that question, four-and-a-half-month-olds were shown a miniature stage in the middle of which was a medium-sized yellow box. In front of the box was a screen that was hinged on a rod attached to the stage floor. Initially, that screen was laid flat so that the box behind it was clearly visible, but the screen was then rotated upwards like a drawbridge, hiding the box from view (Figure 14.21A). There were two conditions. In one condition, the screen rotated backwards until it reached the no longer visible box, stopped, and then rotated for-

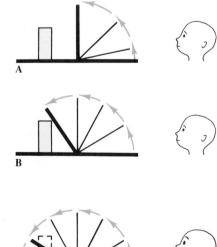

A

B

C

**14.21 Knowing about objects** *A four-and-a-half-month-old infant is looking at a stage on which he sees an upright, brightly colored box. In front of the box is a screen that initially lies flat and then (A) starts to rotate upward. In the first condition (B), the screen stops rotating as soon as it hits the box. In the second condition (C), when the screen is at a point high enough to hide the box, the box is surreptitiously removed and the screen continues to rotate backwards. The infant seems to find this quite surprising as shown by the fact that he continues to look at the stage much longer than he did in the first condition. Infants seem able to distinguish possible from impossible events. (After Baillargeon, 1987a)*

wards and returned to its initial position at which point the box became visible again (Figure 14.21B). In the other condition, the screen rotated backwards until it reached the occluded box and then kept on going as though the box was no longer there. Once it finished the full 180 degree arc, it reversed direction, and swiveled all the way backwards, at which point the box was revealed again (the box being surreptitiously removed and replaced as required; see Figure 14.21C; Baillargeon, Spelke, and Wasserman, 1985; Baillargeon, 1987a).

To an adult, these two conditions present the observer with two radically different events. The first of these makes perfect physical sense: Since two objects can't occupy the same space at the same time, the screen necessarily stops when it encounters the solid box. But the second event is physically impossible: If one assumes the box is still where it was originally seen to be, the screen couldn't possibly pass through it.

This is all very well for adults, but do infants see the world the same way? The answer seems to be yes. They spent much less time looking at the stage in the first condition than they did in the second. In the first condition, the screen did what it "was supposed to": it came to a halt when it came-up against the—presumably still present—solid box. But in the second condition, the screen behaved rather oddly, for it apparently passed through a solid object. The four-month-olds evidently found the second condition more surprising—or puzzling—than the first. This suggests that, Piaget notwithstanding, these young infants had some notion of object permanence, for they evidently believed that the yellow box they had seen before continued to exist even though it was now occluded. It also suggests that young infants have some notions of the principles that govern objects in space; they evidently know that two objects (here, the screen and the yellow box) can't occupy the same place at the same time.

Some further experiments showed that infants also know that objects generally keep their shape or size even when temporarily occluded. Five-month-old infants were shown two toy rabbits that moved on a track behind a screen whose middle section had been removed so that it had a window. As the rabbits traveled along the track, they disappeared at one end of the screen and reappeared at the other, but *without* appearing at the window. This made good sense for one of the rabbits, for that one was shorter than the lower edge of the window; under the circumstances, one wouldn't have expected to see its head through the window (Figure 14.22A). But it made much less sense for the other rabbit, which was taller than the window's lower edge, so that *its* head *had* to be visible through the window, unless it somehow shrank as it moved behind the screen and then promptly expanded again when it reappeared on the other side (Figure 14.22B). Here too the infants seemed to react much as an adult might. They looked much longer at the tall rabbit, as if they expected it to appear in the screen window and were surprised that it did not (Baillargeon and Graber, 1987). In so doing, they gave yet another indication that they believe that objects maintain their identity and their physical characteristics even when temporarily hidden (Baillargeon, 1987b).

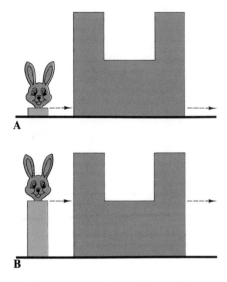

**14.22 Reasoning about objects** *Infants of about five months of age saw (A) a short rabbit move behind a screen and then emerge on the other side. The screen had a window but its lower edge was too high for the rabbit to be visible as it moved across. In (B), the infants saw a tall rabbit that again moved behind the screen and emerged on the other side, but was not seen through the window even though it was clearly tall enough to be visible. This "impossible" event was made possible by having the rabbit stopping behind the tall part of the screen on the left, and a bit later, having a second, identical, rabbit reappearing from behind the tall part of the screen on the right. (After Baillargeon and Graber, 1987)*

OBJECT PERMANENCE AND THE SEARCH PROCESS

Results of this kind do not really prove that some foundation for object perception is built in. After all, the subjects in these studies had already lived for four months, and some learning may well have occurred during this period. But the

**14.23   A dissociation between what the infant knows and what the infant does**   *(A) A seven-month-old looks at a toy that has just been placed in B, one of the two wells. (B) He continues to look at well B after both wells are covered. (C) When finally allowed to reach for the toy, he uncovers well A in which he found the toy on a previous trial rather than well B in which he saw the toy being placed. In this particular sequence he actually still looks at B while uncovering A, suggesting a dissociation between what the infant knows and what he does. (Courtesy Adele Diamond)*

results make such a built-in basis far more plausible than had been previously supposed (Spelke, 1983).

All in all, there is reason to believe that Piaget and the empiricists to the contrary, infants come remarkably pre-equipped to see the world as it really is. But if so, how can we explain the findings that led Piaget to argue for the lack of object permanence in infancy, such as infants' persistent failure in retrieving objects that are out of sight? Most modern investigators feel that there is no real inconsistency. They hold that while infants may believe that objects exist, they are exceedingly inept in *searching* for them. Much of the work that led to this conclusion comes from studies on the *A-not-B* effect (discussed earlier in this chapter), the infant's tendency to search at a place where he found a hidden toy previously rather than at a place where he has just seen it hidden.

What accounts for the *A-not-B* effect? One factor may be the infants' inability to inhibit whatever response is currently dominant. Since they've repeatedly reached toward *A* before, that reaching pattern is presumably momentarily potent; if not held in check, it will override all competing response alternatives. In line with this hypothesis is the fact that in a few cases infants *look* at *A* even though they *reach* for *B*, as if they knew where the object was but couldn't tell their arms what they had learned with their eyes (see Figure 14.23). Some investigators believe that the ability to override dominant action tendency depends on the maturation of a certain region in the frontal lobe (specifically, the prefrontal cortex, a region just in front of the motor projection area). Evidence comes from work on monkeys with lesions in this area; they show the deficits in the same tasks (Diamond, 1988, 1989; Diamond and Goldman-Rakic, 1989).

Thus there is good reason to believe that Piaget was wrong about the infant's failure to have a notion of object permanence. The best guess is that the very young infant has an idea that there are objects out in the world that have a separate existence apart from himself. What he does not have as yet is much of an idea of how to deal with those objects—for example, how to find them when they are hidden from view.

## THE PRESCHOOLER AND THE STAGE CONCEPT

The preceding discussion showed why many critics feel that Piaget has underestimated the infant's native cognitive endowments. If these critics are right, the starting point of mental growth is higher than that which Piaget assumed it to be. But what about the process of development from then on? As Piaget described it, cognitive development goes through several distinct **stages** that are in some ways analogous to the stages found in embryological development. This stage notion of development has been the subject of considerable debate. No one doubts that there is mental growth, that the child changes in the way she thinks as she gets older. But is this growth best described as a progression through successive stages?

### The Meaning of Mental Stage

What do we mean by *stage?* There is one sense of the term that is essentially empty. Suppose someone announces that "Johnny is going through the thumb-sucking stage." This is just a cumbersome way of saying that Johnny is currently sucking his thumb, for it asserts nothing further. The same is true for a whole host of similar statements, such as "Jane is in the no-saying stage," or "Joey is in the covering-the-wall-with-crayons stage," which respectively inform us that Jane generally says "no" and that Joey crayons the wall, regrettable facts we already knew and to which nothing more is added by calling them stages.

When Piaget used the term *stage* he tried to say considerably more than this. In effect, he took the embryological analogy seriously. In this context, a developmental stage has two characteristics. One is that development at a given stage is more or less *consistent*. That is, the characteristics of a given embryological stage hold pretty much across the board—the development of the gastrointestinal tract is more or less on a par with the development of the circulatory system, and so on. A second characteristic is that embryological stages tend to be *discrete* rather than continuous. There is a qualitative difference between a tadpole and a frog; to be sure, the change from one to the other takes a while, but by the time the creature is a frog, its tadpole days are emphatically over. As Piaget is generally interpreted, his claim was that the same two characteristics—consistency and discreteness—apply to cognitive development. A number of critics have questioned whether they really do. For the most part, these critics have focused on the preschooler's abilities.

## The Question of Consistency

How consistently do children behave in various intellectual tasks at any given time in their development? According to a strict interpretation of Piaget's stage theory, children who succeed in tests of conservation should also perform well on other indices of the same stage (that is, the stage of concrete operations), such as taking another person's social or visual point of view. But in fact, the correspondence between these different indices is fairly low; a child may be able to conserve mass or number and fail on tests of point of view. Unlike an embryo, the child does not seem to obey one single developmental clock that synchronizes all aspects of his mental growth. While this result does not constitute a decisive disproof of the Piagetian view, it is not exactly what a simple stage theory might lead one to expect (Gelman and Baillargeon, 1983).*

## The Question of Discreteness

How discrete are developmental stages? As Piaget's account is often understood, many cognitive capacities that mark one period of development are totally absent at prior periods. Consider conservation of quantity or number. According to a simple discrete-stage hypothesis, these should be totally absent at an early age, say, five years old and younger. They are then thought to emerge, virtually full blown, when the curtain finally opens on the next act of the developmental

---

* The issue of what is meant (or what should be meant) by a developmental stage has led to a considerable amount of rather technical discussion that is beyond the scope of this book. (For some examples, see Brainerd, 1978; Case, 1985; Flavell, 1985). One problem is caused by the fact that Piaget's theory seems to have some escape clauses because he admits that there are some "slippages" in the process of development. To give only one example, Piaget attributes the fact that children may show conservation on one task but not on another to such factors as differences in task difficulty which mask the actual developmental stage the child is in (Piaget, 1954).

drama, the period of concrete operations. A number of modern investigators disagree, for they deny that cognitive development is essentially all-or-none. As these critics see it, various cognitive achievements such as conservation have primitive precursors that appear several years earlier than the Piagetian calendar would predict (Gelman, 1978; Gelman and Baillargeon, 1983).

### EGOCENTRISM REVISITED

One area of reevaluation concerns the concept of egocentrism. According to Piaget, young preschool children are unable to appreciate the difference between another's point of view and their own. But recent studies show that a modicum of this ability is found in children between two and four.

One study used a picture-showing task. Children from one to three years of age were asked to show a photograph to their mother who was seated opposite them. At two and a half and three years of age, all children turned the picture so that it faced the mother. But this implies that they had some conception of the difference between one person's angle of regard and another's. If they had been totally egocentric, they should have shown their mothers the back of the picture while continuing to look at it from the front (Lempers, Flavell, and Flavell, 1977; see also Figure 14.24).

### A SECOND LOOK AT CONSERVATION

Another phenomenon whose reexamination suggests that preschoolers are less inept than Piaget supposed is conservation, especially conservation of number. We have previously described the standard Piagetian finding: When preschoolers are asked to compare two rows that contain the same number of, say, toy soldiers, they often say that the longer row contains more soldiers, in an apparent confusion of length and number. But recent studies show that children as young as three have surprising precursors of number conservation if the test conditions are suitably arranged.

In one procedure, the children were shown two toy plates, each with a row of toy mice attached with velcro. One plate might have two mice, while the other had three. One plate was designated the "winner," the other the "loser." Each plate was then covered by a can and shuffled around while the children were instructed to keep track of the winner—a small-fry version of the venerable shell

**14.24 A simplified test of egocentrism**
*Poor performance on Piaget's test of egocentrism may have resulted from the fact that the spatial layout of his three-mountain task is unduly complicated. In a later study, three- and four-year-olds were shown various three-dimensional displays such as (A) and (B), as well as a three-mountain scene (C). Grover, a doll, was shown to drive a toy car around each layout. When he stopped the car, the child was asked to turn an identical display on another table until "you are looking at it the same way Grover is." The children did quite well with all displays except (C), the three-mountain scene. This one probably caused trouble because the children couldn't distinguish the mountains as readily as they could distinguish the toy objects in (A) and (B). (Borke, 1975; photograph courtesy of H. Borke)*

A

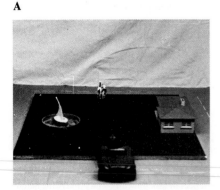

B

C

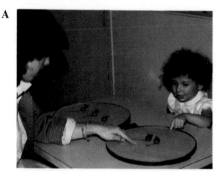

**14.25 Gelman's mouse-plate test**
*(A) The experimenter points to the plate that has two mice and says it is the "winner" while three-year-old Carly watches. (B) After the experimenter covers the plates and rearranges the plates by a sleight-of-hand trick, (C) Carly points to the correct "winner" and then looks at the experimenter with surprise and says, "Hey—they're spreaded out!" (Photographs courtesy of Hilary Schmidt)*

game. After each trial, the plates were uncovered, and the children received a prize if they could correctly identify the winner and the loser. After several such trials, the real test was conducted. The experimenter surreptitiously substituted a new plate for the original winner. In one case, the new plate contained the same number of mice as the original, but the row was made longer or shorter. In the other case, the row length stayed unchanged, but a mouse was added or subtracted. The results showed that spatial arrangement made little difference. But changes in number had dramatic consequences even at three and four years of age. The children were surprised, asked where the missing mouse was, and searched for it (Gelman, 1972; see Figure 14.25).

Such findings suggest that the number concepts of later periods are built upon foundations established much earlier. One such foundation is counting. Some initial rudiments of this skill appear as early as two and a half. At this age, children may not yet know the conventional number terms. But nevertheless they may have grasped some aspect of what the counting process is all about. For example, some children employ an idiosyncratic number series. Thus one two-year-old consistently used "one, two, six," and another used "one, thirteen, nineteen." But what is important is that they used these series consistently. They realized that each of these number tags has to be applied to each object in the set on a one-to one basis, that the tags must always be used in the same order, and that the last number applied is the number of items in the set. And this realization is the foundation on which counting rests (Gelman and Gallistel, 1978).

Phenomena of this kind argue against the notion that cognitive development proceeds by sudden, dramatic leaps. The achievements of the concrete-operational period do not come out of the blue. If we look carefully enough, we see that they have preludes in much earlier childhood years. It may well be true that there are stages of intellectual growth that have to be passed in an ordered sequence. But there are no neat demarcations between stages and no sharp transitions. The stages of cognitive development are not as all-or-none as the changes from tadpole to frog (let alone from frog to prince).

## Sequence or Stages?

What can we conclude about Piaget's stages of mental development? The evidence as a whole suggests that the child's mental growth does not proceed as neatly as a simple stage theory might lead one to expect (Flavell, 1985).

Does this mean that Piaget's cognitive milestones have no psychological reality? Not really. The cognitive sequence may not be as neat as one might have wished, but there is little doubt that some such sequence exists. Consider the difference between seven-year-olds and preschoolers. Despite all the precursors of concrete operations at four or even earlier, there is no question that seven- and eight-year-olds have something preschoolers lack—the ability to apply their insights to a much wider range of problems (Fodor, 1972). Three-year-olds can tell the difference between two and three mice regardless of how they are spaced on the table. But they haven't fully grasped the underlying idea—that number and spatial arrangements are in principle independent and that this is so for all numbers and all spatial arrangements. As a result, they fail—and will continue to fail until they are six or seven years old—the standard Piagetian test for conservation of number in which they have to recognize that two rows of, say, nine buttons contain the same number of buttons, regardless of how the rows are expanded or compressed. This task baffles the preschool child, who finds the number in each row too large to count and gets confused. Seven-year-olds have no such problems. They can count higher, but that's not the issue. They know that there is no need to count, that the number of buttons in each row has to be identical, regardless of the way they are arranged. As a result, they can conserve number in general.

What holds for conservation of number holds for many other intellectual achievements that are generally associated with the first school years. Most of them have precursors, often at much earlier ages than Piaget led us to suppose. But these preschool abilities usually represent isolated pockets of knowledge that can't be applied very widely. The seven- or eight-year-old's understanding of physical, numerical, and social reality is considerably more general, so much so that it seems qualitatively different from what went on before. By simplifying the task in various ways, experimenters can induce preschoolers to perform more creditably. But the interesting fact remains that by the time the child is seven or eight years old, no such simplification is necessary. A seven- or eight-year-old conserves with barely a glance at the containers in which the liquid is sloshed around. He *knows* that the liquid quantity is unaffected no matter how the containers are shaped.

## THE CAUSES OF COGNITIVE GROWTH

Thus far, we have looked at cognitive growth and seen that there is some question of how it might be best described (e.g., stage or sequence). We now turn to attempts at explanation. Trying to explain cognitive development has turned out to be even more difficult than trying to describe it (Siegler, 1989). As so often in the field of cognition, the attempts to come up with an adequate explanation have fluctuated between the two poles of the nature-nurture controversy.

### The Nativist Approach: Maturation

Some investigators are inclined toward a nativist interpretation. There is of course no doubt that native endowment must play some role in cognitive development. The human infant begins life with a potential that is quite different from that of his near and distant cousins in the rest of the animal kingdom, and no amount of training and nurturing can ever erase these differences in the equipment with which the varying species begin. Worms won't fly, platypuses won't form higher-order chunkings, and polar bears won't conserve liquid quantity, no matter what environments they are reared in. Our native equipment is thus a necessary precondition for all development. But can this endowment explain the orderly progression of cognitive development?

Some theorists believe that it can. They believe that development is largely driven by some form of physical ***maturation,*** a pre-programmed growth process based on changes in underlying neural structures that are relatively independent of environmental conditions. Maturation is obviously an important factor in

A

B

C

**14.26 Development as maturation?**
*(A) A butterfly emerging from its crysalis and (B) walking are largely matters of maturation. (C) Is the cognitive growth that underlies a seven-and-a-half-year-old's success in a Piagetian conservation task to be understood in similar terms? (Photographs by Pat Lynch/Photo Researchers; Ray Ellis/Photo Researchers; Chris Massey)*

motor development—for example, flying in sparrows and walking in humans. These are behavior patterns that are characteristic of all adult members of the species. They emerge as the organism matures, but their development is relatively unaffected by environmental changes (except those extreme enough to cripple or kill).

Could cognitive development be a matter of maturation (in part or whole), in the sense in which walking is (Figure 14.26)? There is good evidence for a maturational contribution during the first two years of life. There is a tenfold increase in the number of synaptic connections in the cortex between birth and twelve months of age, and a still further increase until about age two. Yet further changes last into the school years (Siegler, 1989).

A number of authors have argued that maturational changes of this kind underlie many aspects of human cognitive development. In their view, there is something inexorable about cognitive development, especially up to age seven or eight (Wohlwill, 1973). This view is buttressed by the fact that, at least in broad outline, mental growth seems rather similar in children of different cultures and nationalities. While children of different cultures master intellectual tasks such as conservation at somewhat different ages, they usually pass these landmarks in the same order. Thus Arab, Indian, Somali, and British children show the same progression from nonconservation of quantity to conservation (Hyde, 1959). This is reminiscent of physical maturation. Different butterflies may emerge from their chrysalis at slightly different times, but none is a butterfly first and a chrysalis second. The timing of the transitions may well be affected by environmental conditions: in humans, by culture; in butterflies, by temperature. But according to the maturational hypothesis, the order of the stages is predetermined by the genetic code.

## The Empiricist Approach: Specific Learning

The simplest alternative to a maturation-centered approach is one that emphasizes learning by exposure to the environment. The most extreme version of this view is that of the empiricists who followed in the footsteps of John Locke (see Chapter 5). To them, the human mind starts out as a blank wax tablet, a *tabula rasa,* upon which experience gradually leaves its mark. But can such a radical empiricist position explain the systematic sequence of cognitive development that Piaget and other investigators have chronicled?

Piaget argued that simple learning theories of the kind espoused by the early empiricists—and by their modern heirs such as Pavlov and Skinner—will not do. According to such theories, learning is the acquisition of relatively specific skills —such as figure skating—that in principle could be mastered at any age. But this is precisely what Piaget denied. According to Piaget, four-year-olds cannot possibly be taught how to use a measuring cup correctly, no matter how attractive the reinforcements or how many the number of trials. He argued that four-year-olds lack the prerequisite concepts of number and quantity (which they cannot attain before the concrete-operational level), so that any attempt to teach them is as fruitless as trying to build the third story of a house without a second story underneath it. This view has obvious relevance to educational policy. If Piaget is right, then there is little point in efforts to teach children this or that aspect of the curriculum before they are "ready" for it.

In an attempt to test this claim, several investigators have tried to determine whether children can be trained to reach certain cognitive landmarks such as conservation ahead of schedule. The results are a bit ambiguous. Formerly, most investigators concluded that specific training has little impact. In some cases, conservation was speeded up by special coaching, but later checks revealed that the children had not really understood the underlying principles and quickly reverted to their previous, nonconserving ways (e.g., Smedslund, 1961). But some later studies showed more substantial effects. In some cases, these were brought about by mere observation; for example, six-year-old nonconservers who watched conservers perform showed subsequent conservation of mass or number (Botvin and Murray, 1975; Murray, 1978). But the best guess is that the children already had most of the necessary conceptual ingredients at the time they were "trained." If so, then training (or watching another child) did not really teach conservation; it only helped to uncover what was already there (Gold, 1978; Gelman and Baillargeon, 1983).

Related findings come from a study conducted in a Mexican village whose inhabitants made pottery and whose children helped and participated in this activity from early on. When tested for conservation of mass, these children turned out to be more advanced than their North American counterparts (or those studied by Piaget in Switzerland). Having spent much of their lives working at a potter's wheel, they were more likely to know that the amount of clay is the same whether it is rolled into a ball or stretched into a long, thin sausage (Price-Williams, Gordon, and Ramirez, 1969). But these effects of pottery making were relatively specific. They led to an advance on tests of conservation of mass but to little else. (For further discussion, see Greenfield, 1976; Price-Williams, 1981; Rogoff, Gauvain, and Ellis, 1984.)

All in all, there is little doubt that environment must play *some* role in cognitive development. To acquire liquid conservation, one presumably has to live in a world in which liquids exist. If a frozen planet like Jupiter had inhabitants whose cognitive potential was like our own, their young would never know that when water is poured from a wide jar into a tall, thin beaker the amount of water stays unchanged. But this is not to say that the environment shapes human (or Jovian) children in the simple, passive way proposed by an extreme empiricist position.

### Piaget's Approach: Assimilation and Accommodation

Piaget's own view was that neither maturation nor specific learning could by themselves account for cognitive development. As he saw it, the child's mental progress is propelled by the twin engines of developmental change that we mentioned earlier, assimilation and accommodation. At any one stage, the environment the child faces is interpreted in terms of the mental schemas she has at that point in time—the environment is assimilated to the schemas. But these schemas cannot help but change as the child continues to interact with the world around her—the schemas accommodate to the environment. Without active involvement with the environment, there will be no such accommodation and hence no mental growth.

Piaget's conception of these two opposite processes, assimilation and accommodation, may be a useful way of emphasizing the fact that organism and environment interact in producing mental growth. But is it an explanation? Many psychologists argue that it is not, for Piaget offered no mechanism whereby schemas are changed through accommodation. Lacking such a mechanism, we do not really understand why children go from one stage of thought into another.

## The Information-Processing Approach: Chunking and Strategies

A recent suggestion for explaining cognitive development is in terms of information processing. According to this approach, all cognitive activities are ways of handling—that is, **processing**—information. Whenever a person perceives, remembers, or thinks, he has to acquire, retrieve, or transform information (see Chapters 6, 7, and 8). If adults think differently (and with greater success) than children, this is presumably due to the fact that they process information differently.

In recent years, information-processing concepts have been applied to many aspects of cognitive development, including perception, language, thinking, and memory (Siegler, 1983). We will focus on just one of these areas, the development of memory.

### THE CHILD AS A LIMITED MENTAL PROCESSOR

There is little doubt that on many conventional tests of recall, younger children do worse than older ones. Take memory span—the number of items a subject can reproduce after just one presentation. This number is roughly equal to the child's age until she is about five: one item at eighteen months, three at three-and-a-half years, and four at four-and-a-half years, compared to a digit span of seven or eight in adulthood (see Figure 14.27).

What has happened during development that makes us so much better at remembering than young children are? Several theorists (sometimes called neo-Piagetians) believe that the reason is maturation. Initially, the child's mind is like a small computer, with limited storage and processing capacity. But as her brain grows, so does her memory capacity. This in turn allows her to develop a whole set of cognitive skills that she could never have acquired previously (Pascale-Leone, 1978; Case, 1978, 1985). But there is reason to believe that maturational processes are only part of the story.

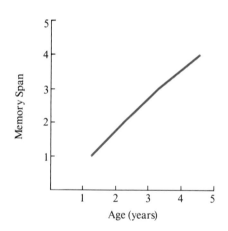

**14.27 Memory span in young children** *(After Case, 1978)*

### THE CHILD AS NOVICE

There is evidence that the young child's poor performance at memory tasks is caused, at least in part, by the fact that she knows so little and has rather limited strategies for remembering the little that she does know (Flavell and Wellman, 1977; Brown, Bransford, Ferrara, and Campione, 1983; Chi, 1978, 1985).

In a previous section, we saw that in the course of acquiring skills as in becoming a typist or a telegraph operator, the performance of the learner changes qualitatively. He has presumably formed various higher-order *chunks,* so that he no longer responds to individual letters but to letter groupings and words (see Chapter 8). It may be that much of cognitive development can be understood as a similar process that all human beings go through as they go from infancy to adulthood.

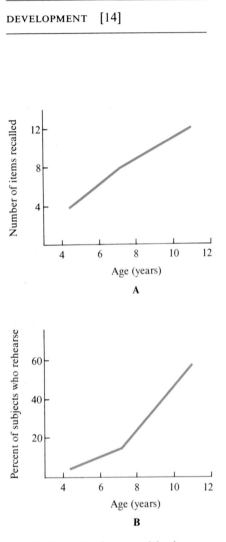

**14.28   Strategies for memorizing in children**   *(A) Nursery-school children, first-graders, and fifth-graders were shown a number of pictures and were asked to try to remember. The figure shows recall as a function of age. (B) While the subjects watched the stimuli, the experimenters observed them for signs of rehearsal— naming the pictures, moving the lips while watching, and so on. The figure shows the proportion of all children who rehearsed. In the older children, there was quite a bit of rehearsal, but there was very little for the first-graders and virtually none for the nursery-school children. Absence of rehearsal has also been found for retarded subjects. (Data from Appel et al., 1972)*

This view assumes that the difference between child and adult is in large part a matter of expertise—the adult has had the time to develop many conceptual chunkings that the child still lacks. But suppose we found some task on which the child is the expert and the adult the novice? One investigator studied memory for chess positions in adults and ten-year-olds. Experts generally do much better than novices because they can draw on more and larger chunks (see Chapter 8, pp. 297–98). But the study had a novel twist because here the children were the experts (they were recruited from local chess clubs), while the adults were the novices. Now that the tables were turned, what mattered was specific mastery rather than overall level of cognitive development. The children recalled many more chess positions than did the adults (Chi, 1978).

According to some authors, such findings suggest that intellectual growth is largely produced by the acquisition of more and more knowledge. In their view, some of this knowledge is in the form of cognitive capital goods—tools for acquiring new knowledge. These are strategies for learning and thinking that become increasingly efficient and more widely applicable as the child gets older. As a result, he can become an expert in many areas.

### THE CHILD AS A POOR STRATEGIST

*Strategies for remembering*   When an adult is presented with a series of items and told to repeat them a moment later, she does her best to "keep them in mind." She rehearses, perhaps by repeating the items mentally, perhaps by organizing them in various ways. But the very young child doesn't do this, for he hasn't yet learned how. Some first precursors of rehearsal are found at age three. In one study, three-year-olds watched while an experimenter placed a toy dog under one of two containers. The experimenter told the children that he'd leave the room for a little while, but that they should tell him where the dog was hidden as soon as he came back. During the interval, some children kept on looking at the hiding place and nodding "yes"; others steadfastly maintained their eye on the wrong container while shaking their head "no"; yet others kept their hand tightly grasping the correct container. They had found a way of building a bridge between past and present by performing an overt action—keeping the toy dog in their mind by marking its location with their body. Piaget, who believed that all mental activity is ultimately an outgrowth of overt action, might well have been pleased at this outcome (Wellman, Ritter, and Flavell, 1975).

Keeping one's hand on the to-be-remembered object may be a forerunner of rehearsal, but it's still a far cry from the real thing. Genuine rehearsal does not occur spontaneously until around age five or six. One experiment used subjects of five, seven, and ten years of age. The stimuli were pictures of seven common objects (e.g., a pipe, a flag, an owl, etc.), and the experimenter slowly pointed at three of them in turn. The children's job was to point at the three pictures in the same order after a fifteen-second interval. During this interval their eyes were covered (by a specially designed space helmet) so they couldn't bridge the interval by looking at the pictures, or by surreptitiously pointing at them. Not surprisingly, the older children did better on the recall test than the younger ones (Figure 14.28). Was this because they had greater memory capacity? The main cause lay elsewhere. One of the experimenters was a trained lip reader who observed that almost all of the ten-year-olds were silently mouthing the words—that is, rehearsing—compared to only 10 percent of the five-year-olds. The older children re-

**15.1 The need for contact comfort** *A frightened rhesus monkey baby clings to its terry-cloth mother for comfort. (Photograph by Martin Rogers/Stock, Boston)*

**15.2 Contact comfort in humans** *(Photograph by Suzanne Szasz)*

was made of soft terry cloth. The wire figure was equipped with a nipple that yielded milk, but no similar provision was made for the terry-cloth model. Even so, the monkey infants spent much more time on the terry-cloth "mother" than on the wire figure. The terry-cloth figure could be clung to and could provide what Harlow called "contact comfort" (Figure 15.1). This was especially clear when the infants were frightened. When placed in an unfamiliar room or faced with a mechanical toy that approached with clanking noises, they invariably rushed to the terry-cloth mother and clung to her tightly. The infants never sought similar solace from the wire mothers, who were their source of food and nothing more (Harlow, 1958).

These results are in complete opposition to the cupboard theory. The monkey infant evidently loves its mother (whether real or terry cloth), not because she feeds it, but because she feels so "comforting." Some of the characteristics of the figure toward whom the monkey can direct its attachment are evidently pre-programmed. In monkeys, these presumably include the way the figure feels to the touch. Whether touch is equally important to human infants is as yet unclear, but very likely it plays some role. Frightened young humans run to their mothers and hug them closely just as rhesus infants do (Figure 15.2). Children also like stuffed, cuddly toys such as teddy bears, whom they hold tightly when they feel apprehensive. Perhaps Linus's security blanket is a kind of terry-cloth mother. It may or may not be; but contrary to the cupboard theory, it is emphatically not a substitute tablecloth.

BOWLBY'S THEORY OF ATTACHMENT

What is the alternative to the cupboard theory? According to John Bowlby, attachment results because infants are born with a number of interrelated built-in tendencies that make them seek direct contact with an adult (usually the mother).

One facet of attachment seeking is positive. The infant evidently enjoys being with his mother and interacting with her. From birth on, he is well-equipped for social interaction. He quickly comes to recognize and prefer his mother's voice and even her smell (MacFarlane, 1975; DeCasper and Fifer, 1980). If he is contented, he is generally calm, gurgles, and (starting at about six weeks) will produce a full-blown social smile. The mother—and other important adults—will happily reciprocate; when the baby smiles, they smile back. As the infant gets older and acquires some locomotor control, he will do whatever he can to be in the adult's company—reaching toward the mother and father to be picked up, crawling toward them, and so on (Campos, Barrett, Lamb, Goldsmith, and Sternberg, 1983).

Bowlby believes that attachment seeking has a second, more negative cause. This is a built-in fear of the unknown and unfamiliar, which is yet another reason why the young of most mammals and birds become attached and stay close to some object that has become familiar to them. But while this is an important factor it is not the only one. For there seems to be an innate bias to become attached to things that have certain stimulus properties rather than others—as in the case of infant monkeys, who prefer soft, furry terry cloth to hard wire. In the real world, the most likely object of attachment will be the mother. She has been around throughout the infant's short life and has therefore become familiar. And she obviously has the appropriate stimulus properties for the young of her species: if she is a duck, she quacks; if she is a rhesus monkey, she is furry.

Why do infants have the built-in fear of the unfamiliar? According to Bowlby, this fear has a simple survival value. Infants who lack it would stray away from their mother and would be more likely to get lost and perish. In particular, they might well fall victim to predators, for beasts of prey tend to attack weak animals that are separated from their fellows.

Needless to say, infants don't know enough about the world to fear specific predators. But Bowlby argues that the built-in fear is initially quite unspecific. He conjectures that the fear aroused by the mother's absence is analogous to what psychiatrists call *free-floating anxiety.* This is a state in which the patient is desperately afraid but doesn't know what he is afraid of; he therefore becomes all the more afraid. Given this anxiety, even mild external threats become enormous to the child; the increased need for reassurance may lead to wild clinging and "childish" dependency, as in the dark or during a thunderstorm. This may occur even when the threat comes from the parents themselves. A child who is severely punished by his parents often becomes even more clinging and dependent than before. The parents caused the fear, but they are the ones who are approached for reassurance. This is analogous to the dog who licks the hand that whipped him. The whipping led to fear and pain, but whom can the dog approach for solace but his master?

IMPRINTING

According to Bowlby, the fear of the unfamiliar produces an attachment to a familiar object. In the real world of animals, this object is generally the mother. But it needn't be. Harlow's studies have already shown us that the focus of filial devotion is not rigidly predetermined by the genes, as witness the love borne for the terry-cloth mother.

A similar point is made by *imprinting* in birds, which has been studied extensively by the European ethologist Konrad Lorenz. Imprinting is a kind of learning that occurs very early in life and provides the basis for the chick's attachment to its mother. When a newly hatched duckling is first exposed to a moving stimulus, it will approach and follow this stimulus as soon as it is able to walk (at about twelve hours after hatching). If the duckling follows the object for about ten minutes, an attachment is formed; the bird is imprinted. In nature, the moving stimulus is the duckling's mother and all is well. But in the laboratory, it need not be. The duckling may be exposed to a moving duck on wheels, or to a rectangle sliding back and forth behind a glass window, or even to Konrad Lorenz's booted legs. In each case, the result is the same. The duckling becomes imprinted on the wooden duck or on the rectangle or on Lorenz; it follows one of these objects as if it were its mother, uttering piteous distress calls whenever it is not nearby. The real mother may quack enticingly so as to woo her lost offspring back, but to no avail; the imprinted duckling continues to follow the wooden duck or the moving rectangle or Lorenz (Hess, 1959, 1973).

Imprinting occurs most readily during a sensitive period that in ducklings lasts for around two days, with a maximum sensitivity at some fifteen hours after hatching (Hess, 1959). Subsequent to this period, imprinting is difficult to achieve (see Figure 15.3). According to Lorenz, this phenomenon reflects a decline in the plasticity of some part of the young bird's brain—a decline that is somehow tied to a physiological clock (Gottlieb, 1961). Another possible explanation is that ducklings are difficult to imprint after the sensitive period is past

**Free-floating anxiety**    *(Photograph by Suzanne Szasz)*

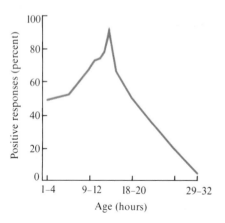

**15.3    Imprinting and the critical period**    *The curve shows the relation between imprinting and the age at which a duckling was exposed to a male moving model. The imprinting score represents the percentage of trials on which the duckling followed the model on a later test. (After Hess, 1958)*

*Imprinting in ducklings*  *Imprinted ducklings following Konrad Lorenz. (Courtesy Nina Leen)*

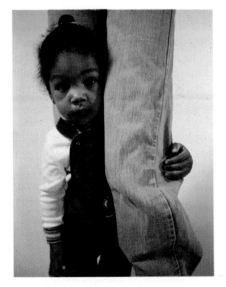

*(Photograph by J. Blyenberg/Leo de Wys)*

because by then they have become thoroughly afraid of all new objects. When exposed to the wooden duck (or Lorenz's boots or a moving rectangle), the bird flees instead of following. Having lived for several days, it has learned something about what is familiar, and it can therefore appreciate—and fear—what is strange. Some evidence for this position comes from the fact that older ducklings can be imprinted on new objects if they are forced to remain in their presence for a while. One group of investigators exposed five-day-old ducklings to a moving rectangle. The ducklings tried to flee and huddled in a corner. After a while, their fear diminished. At this point, they began to follow the rectangle and gave distress calls when it was withdrawn. They had become imprinted even though they were long past the sensitive period (Hoffman, 1978; for still another account, see Bateson, 1984).

## Separation and Loss

The attachment to the mother has a corollary: A separation from her evokes distress. During the first few months of life, the infant will accept a substitute, perhaps because there is as yet no clear-cut conception of the mother that differentiates her from all other persons. But from somewhere between six and eight months of age, the infant comes to know who his mother is; he now cries and fusses when he sees her leave. The age at which children begin to register this protest against separation is pretty much the same across such diverse cultures as African Bushmen in Botswana, U.S. city dwellers, Indians in a Guatemalan village, and members of an Israeli kibbutz (Kagan, 1976).

### LONG SEPARATION AND PERMANENT LOSS

To the child, seeing the mother leave is bad enough, but it's even worse if she doesn't return shortly. Lengthy separations can have serious effects. Infants of

579

**15.4   Grief in apes and humans**  *Two orphans, a young chimpanzee after losing his mother and an orphaned nineteenth-century boy. (Left: photograph by Jane von Lawick-Goodall. Right: courtesy Barnardo Photo Library)*

seven months or older who are placed in a hospital for a short stay fret and protest and seem negative and frightened. After returning home, they remain anxious for a while, as if terrified of another separation. They continually cling to their mother, scream when left alone by her, are unusually afraid of strangers, and may even become suspicious of such familiar persons as fathers and siblings (Schaffer and Callender, 1959).

Similar effects are often seen in older children. One study dealt with two- and three-year-olds who were placed in a residential nursery for some weeks. During the first few days, they cried frequently and desperately clung to some favorite toy they had brought along. After a while their crying abated, but not their distress. They became apathetic and hostile and lost previously acquired bowel control (Heinicke and Westheimer, 1966).

As children get still older, they become increasingly secure in the knowledge that the mother will be there when needed; they can therefore accept increasingly long separations. According to some psychologists, this emotional knowledge provides a basic trust that then serves as the foundation for further attachments and allows the child to become independent, to become an adult (Erikson, 1963).

However firm our trust, eventually all of us must face the grim reality of irrevocable separation (Figure 15.4). According to some authors, the grief experienced by adults at a loved one's death is in many ways akin to the separation anxiety of a child away from her mother. The first symptoms of grief are often crying, as in the mother-separated infants. Following this—again similar to the separated infants—the symptoms are those of hopeless despair: numb apathy, withdrawal, and profound depression (Bowlby, 1973). Similar effects are sometimes seen in ape and monkey mothers whose infants have died. They refuse to abandon the dead body, and carry it with them until it is only skin and skeleton.

ASSESSING ATTACHMENT

The reaction to separation provides a means for assessing the kind of attachment a particular infant has to his mother. A widely used procedure is the so-called "Strange Situation" devised by Mary Ainsworth and her colleagues for children of about one year of age (Figure 15.5). The child is first brought into an unfamiliar room that contains many toys, and he is given an opportunity to explore and play while the mother is present. After a while, a stranger enters, talks to the mother and then approaches the child. The next step is a brief separation—the mother goes out of the room, and leaves the child alone with the stranger. A reunion follows—the mother comes back and the stranger leaves (Ainsworth and Bell, 1970; Ainsworth, Blehar, Waters, and Wall, 1978).

The behavior of one-year-olds falls into several broad categories. One group (over two-thirds of the children in one of Ainsworth's studies) is described as "securely attached." As long as the mother is present, these children explore, play with the toys, and even make wary overtures to the stranger. They show some distress when the mother leaves, but greet her return with great enthusiasm. The remaining children show various behavior patterns that Ainsworth and her colleagues regard as signs of "insecure attachment." Some are described as "resistant." They don't explore even in the mother's presence, become intensely upset and very panicky when she leaves, and act emotionally ambivalent during the reunion, running to her to be picked up and then angrily struggling to get down. Others are described as "avoidant." They are distant and aloof from the very outset, show little distress when the mother leaves, and ignore her when she returns.

Ainsworth and other adherents of attachment theory believe that these behavior patterns reflect fairly stable characteristics, at least for the first few years of life. Thus children who were rated as securely attached in the Strange Situation at fifteen months of age were judged to be more outgoing, popular, and well-adjusted in nursery school at age three and a half (Waters, Wippman, and Sroufe, 1979).

Attachment theorists regard these findings as evidence that the Strange Situation provides a good index of the parent-child relationship and that this relationship is a major determinant of later social and emotional adjustment. But this cause-and-effect interpretation has not gone unchallenged. Some authors point out that correlations between behavior at fifteen months (in the Strange Situation) and at three and a half (in nursery school) don't prove that early attachment relations exert an effect on the child's later adjustment. One possibility is that the correlation was based on the fact that the child's social environment stayed pretty much the same. A mother who was gentle and loving when her child was fifteen months of age, probably remained gentle and loving during the next two years. Similarly for the mother who was short-tempered and rejecting. Under the circumstances, we can't be sure that the child's behavior in nursery school can be traced to the mother-child interaction two years earlier, for it could just as well be caused by the mother's current attitude (Lamb, Thompson, Gardner, Charnov, and Estes, 1985). Another possibility is that the entire effect is caused by the child's own (in part, built-in) temperament. Some children are more irritable—or more gentle and sociable—than others, and this difference is likely to remain for a while at least. If so, the correlation was caused by something within the child rather than something in the attachment relation in early childhood (Kagan, 1984).

### ASSESSING THE ROLE OF THE FATHER

Ainsworth's general approach has provided a means for studying various other aspects of early social development. An example is the infant's relation to the father. Thus far, we've concentrated entirely on the child's attachment to the

**15.5 A diagrammatic sketch of the "Strange Situation"** M indicates the mother, and S the stranger. (Adapted from Ainsworth, Blehar, Waters, and Wall, 1978, p. 34)

A

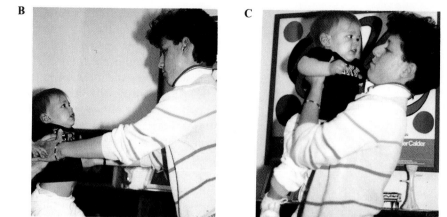

B

C

**15.6 Stranger anxiety** *An eleven-month-old taken from his father's lap by a stranger (Photograph by Stephanie Arch, courtesy Kathy Hirsh-Pasek)*

mother. Is the father left out in the cold? To find out, one investigator used the Strange Situation with fathers as well as mothers and found signs of distress when the father left and some clinging and touching when he returned (see Figure 15.6). It appears that the emotional life of the child is not exclusively wrapped up in the mother. But the mother seems to be more important, at least at an early age. There was more distress at the mother's departure than at the father's and more enthusiasm at her return (Kotelchuk, 1976).

It appears that young children become attached to fathers as well as to mothers, but further evidence indicates that the attachments to the two parents have some different characteristics. A number of studies have shown that fathers are more likely to play with their infants (and young children) than mothers are. In addition, their play is more physical and vigorous; they may lift or bounce their babies or toss them in the air. In contrast, mothers generally play more quietly with their infants, and stress verbal rather than physical interactions. As a result, while the mother may be the parent the child is more likely to run to for care and comfort, the father is often the preferred playmate. This difference in the response to the two parents begins in early infancy, when there are more smiles for the mother and more giggles for the father. By the time the children are toddlers, two out of three pick the father as the one they want to play with. Mother is security and comfort; father is fun (Lamb, 1977; Clarke-Stewart, 1978; Parke, 1981).

What accounts for the differences in the way the two parents respond to their young child? One can make a case for both nature and nurture. In part, the distinction is surely based on social and economic circumstances. By and large, fathers are less involved in the actual caregiving process (though there is some evidence that this is changing; see Pleck, 1985; Ricks, 1985). As a result, their interactions with their children are quite different from those of the mother:

*(Photograph by Rick Rusing/Leo de Wys)*

In our family, when Ron comes home from work, the kids squeal with delight. He gets down on the floor with them and roughhouses; he tosses the baby in the air; he gives them horsey rides on his back. Then he says, "Okay, kids, that's it," and he hands the baby back to me. When *I* come home from work, the kids say, "Feed me, feed me." (Clarke-Stewart, Perlmutter, and Friedman, 1988, p. 195)

But cultural factors alone may not be the sole explanation. Some evidence comes from a comparison of fathers who were their infant's secondary caregivers (the usual role in our culture) and fathers who were the primary caregivers. The behavior of these two groups of fathers was quite similar. Both groups engaged in much more physical play with the infants than the mothers did (Field, 1978). This might suggest that some aspects of the father-mother difference are based on different biological predispositions. After all, rough-and-tumble play is much more common in male than in female primates, whether monkeys, apes, or humans (see Chapter 10). But one can well counter that the male-female behavioral difference is so deeply ingrained by learned societal patterns that it is very hard to dislodge. Nature and nurture are exceedingly hard to disentangle.

## How Crucial Is Early Experience?

Theoretical details aside, Sigmund Freud made two major claims about human social development. One was that the initial human social relationship is ultimately based on the gratification of basic creature needs. The other held that what happens in early childhood determines all future development (see Chapter 11). As we saw, there is good reason to believe that Freud's first claim is false, for it appears that humans—no less than ducks, lambs, and monkeys—are built to be social beings from the very outset. What can we say about his second claim? Here, there is still a great deal of controversy.

We will begin by describing some of the evidence that seems to be in line with Freud's belief in the all-important role of early experience.

### THE ABSENCE OF ATTACHMENT

What happens when the initial attachment of the child to the mother is not allowed to form? The effects are apparently drastic.

*Motherless monkeys* We previously considered Harlow's studies on rhesus monkeys raised with substitute mothers made of terry cloth. Some later studies asked what happens when monkey infants are reared without any contact at all. The infants were isolated for periods that ranged from three months to one year. During this time, they lived in an empty steel chamber and saw no living creature, not even a human hand.

After their period of solitary confinement, the animals' reactions were observed in various test situations. A three-month isolation had comparatively little effect. But longer periods led to dramatic disturbances. The animals huddled in a corner of the cage, clasped themselves, and rocked back and forth. When they were brought together with normally reared age-mates, the results were pathetic. There was none of the active chasing and playful romping that is characteristic of monkeys at that age. Whenever the normals took an aggressive lunge at them, the monkeys reared in isolation were unable to fight back. They withdrew, huddled, rocked—and bit *themselves* (Figure 15.7).

This social inadequacy persisted into adolescence and adulthood. One manifestation was a remarkable incompetence in sexual and parental matters. For-

A

B

**15.7 Motherless monkeys** *(A) A monkey reared in isolation, huddling in terror in a corner of its cage. (B) An isolated monkey biting itself at the approach of a stranger. (Courtesy Harry Harlow, University of Wisconsin Primate Laboratory)*

**15.8 Motherless monkeys as mothers** *Female monkeys raised in isolation may become mothers by artificial impregnation. They usually ignore their infants. Sometimes, as shown here, they abuse them. (Courtesy Harry Harlow, University of Wisconsin Primate Laboratory)*

merly isolated males were utterly inept in the business of reproduction: As Harlow put it, "Isolates may grasp other monkeys of either sex by the head and throat aimlessly, a semi-erotic exercise without amorous achievements." Formerly isolated females resisted the sexual overtures of normal males. Some were eventually impregnated, in many cases by artificial means. When these motherless monkeys became monkey mothers themselves, they seemed to have no trace of love for their offspring. In a few cases, there was horrible abuse. The mothers crushed the infant's head to the floor, chewed off its toes or fingers, or bit it to death (Figure 15.8). Early social deprivation had evidently played havoc with the animals' subsequent social and emotional development (Suomi and Harlow, 1971; Harlow and Harlow, 1972; Harlow and Novak, 1973).

*Humans reared in institutions* Can we generalize from infant monkeys to human children? There is reason to suspect that there are some important similarities. After all, the monkey is related to *Homo sapiens,* however distantly; and like humans, monkeys go through a long period of development before they attain adulthood. In any case, it appears that human infants reared under conditions of comparative social isolation (although needless to say, not as drastic as that imposed on the monkeys) suffer somewhat analogous deficits.

The evidence comes from studies of infants reared in institutions. In many cases, they received perfectly adequate nutrition and bodily care; the problem was that there was very little social stimulation. In one institution the infants were kept in separate cubicles for the first eight months or so as a precaution against infectious disease. Their brief contacts with adults were restricted to the times when they were fed or diapered. Feeding took place in the crib with a propped-up bottle. There was little social give and take, little talk, little play, and little chance that the busy attendant would respond to any one baby's cry (Goldfarb, 1955; Provence and Lipton, 1962).

When these infants were compared to others who were raised normally, there were no differences for the first three or four months. Thereafter, the two groups

*Imitating an absent model* *The child may dress up to feel like an adult out of a desire for competence and mastery of the universe. (Photograph by Erika Stone)*

FEEDING AND TOILET TRAINING

To answer questions of this sort, one must first decide which particular aspects of the parents' behavior one wants to focus on. Until thirty years ago, developmental psychologists interested in these general issues were heavily influenced by psychoanalytic theories. As a result, they concerned themselves with aspects of child rearing that Freud and his followers had made so much of. They asked about the effects of different practices associated with feeding, weaning, and toilet training. Does breast feeding produce happier (or unhappier) infants? What about early weaning or early toilet training? As it turned out, the answer is that these (and many other) child-rearing particulars have little or no effect (Orlansky, 1949; Zigler and Child, 1969; Zigler, Lamb, and Child, 1982).

CHILD-REARING STYLES

In recent years, developmental psychologists have taken a different approach. Instead of concentrating on specific child-rearing practices, they have turned their attention to the general home atmosphere in which the child is raised (Baumrind, 1967, 1971; Maccoby and Martin, 1983).

*Different kinds of parents* In a number of studies, parents were asked to describe the way they dealt with their children and were also observed with them in various situations. Several patterns of child rearing emerged. One is the so-called *autocratic* pattern in which the parents control the child strictly, and often quite sternly. The rules they set down are essentially edicts whose infraction leads to severe (and frequently physical) punishment. Nor do they attempt to explain these rules to the child, who has to accept them as a simple manifestation of parental power: "It's because I say so, that's why."

At the opposite extreme is the *permissive* pattern in which children encounter few don'ts and even fewer do's. The parents try not to assert their authority, impose few restrictions and controls, tend not to have set time schedules (for, say, bedtime or watching TV), and rarely use punishment. They also make few demands on the children—such as putting toys away, or doing schoolwork, or helping with chores.

Autocratic parents brandish parental power; permissive parents abdicate it. But there is a third pattern that is in some ways in between. It is called *authoritative-reciprocal* because the parents exercise their power but also accept the reciprocal obligation to respond to the child's point of view and his reasonable demands. Unlike the permissive parents, they govern; but unlike the autocratic ones, they try to govern with the consent of the governed.

Parents whose pattern is authoritative-reciprocal set rules of conduct for their children and enforce them when they have to. They are fairly demanding, assign duties, expect their children to behave maturely and "act their age," and spend a good deal of time in teaching their children how to perform appropriately. But they also encourage the child's independence, and allow a good deal of verbal give-and-take.

*Different kinds of children* Are there any differences between children that are raised in these three different styles? One investigator observed preschoolers in various settings. She found that children raised autocratically were more withdrawn, lacked independence, and were more angry and defiant (especially the

*"They never pushed me. If I wanted to retrieve, shake hands, or roll over, it was entirely up to me." (Drawing by Frascino; ©1971 The New Yorker Magazine, Inc.)*

boys). Interestingly enough, children at the opposite end of the spectrum had similar characteristics. Thus children whose parents were permissive were not particularly independent and (if boys) they were more prone to anger. In addition, they seemed very immature and lacked social responsibility. In contrast, the children raised in the authoritative-reciprocal mode were more independent, competent, and socially responsible. Here, as so often, there seems to be a happy medium.

There is evidence that the parental pattern experienced when the child was three or four is related to the way the child behaves in later years. When observed at the age of eight or nine, children whose parents had been judged to be either autocratic or permissive five years earlier seemed to be relatively low in intellectual self-reliance and originality. Once again, the children raised in the authoritative-reciprocal style fared best. They were more self-reliant when faced by intellectual challenges, strove for achievement, and were socially more self-confident and at ease (Baumrind, 1977).

## The Child's Effect on the Parents

Thus far, we have discussed socialization as something that is done *to* the child. But in recent years, developmental psychologists have become increasingly insistent that socialization is a two-way street. For the child is more than a lump of psychological clay that is shaped by various social agencies. In actual fact, he actively participates in his own rearing. His own behavior affects that of the parent, whose behavior then in turn affects him. To the extent that this is true, the parents don't just socialize the child. They are also socialized by him (Bell, 1968; Bell and Harper, 1977).

One of the main reasons why socialization works in both directions is that infants differ from the very day they are born. For example, there are differences in **temperament** that probably have a built-in, genetic basis (see Chapter 17). One infant may be relatively placid and passive; another may be more active and assertive. These differences persist over at least the first two years of life and may last much beyond. The mother will respond quite differently to these two infants. If we later study the correlation between what the mother did and how the child behaves, we will find a correlation. But in this case, the order of cause and effect is the reverse of the one that is actually expected. A difference in the child led to a difference in the way his parents dealt with him (Thomas, Chess, and Birch, 1970; Osofsky and Danzger, 1974; Olweus, 1980). This is another way of saying that children help to make their own environments. To the extent that they are genetically different in either temperament or ability, their parents, siblings, and eventually their peers, cannot help but treat them differently (Scarr and McCartney, 1983).

Such reversed cause-and-effect relations can never be ignored as possible (although probably only partial) explanations of correlations between the way a child was reared and his personality. As an example consider the effect of physical punishment. As already mentioned, there is some evidence which suggests that parents who resort to physical punishment have children who tend to be more aggressive than average (Feshbach, 1970; Parke and Slaby, 1983). If this relationship is genuine, how should we interpret it? One possibility is that the parents provide a model for their child who learns to do to others what his parents have done unto him. But there is an alternative. Some children may be more aggressive to begin with, and they are the ones who are more likely to be spanked. The relation may be even more complex. The more aggressive child will probably be punished more severely; this will lead to more aggression in the child, which will then provoke yet further parental countermeasures.

The best guess is that all these cause-and-effect relationships exist side by side. The parents' behavior affects the child, but the child's behavior also affects the parents—a continual, interactive pattern in which the characteristics of all parties in the family act as both cause and effect.

## THE DEVELOPMENT OF MORALITY

Initially, the child's social world is largely confined to the family. His first lessons in social behavior are taught in the limited family context: pick up your toys, don't push your baby brother, and so on—circumscribed commands and prohibitions that apply to a very narrow social setting. But his social sphere soon grows to include young peers: at home, in day-care centers, in preschool settings, still later in the schools. These peers become increasingly important and their approval is then sought as eagerly (if not more eagerly) than that of his parents. Eventually the child's social universe expands still further as he acquires rules of social thought and action that are vastly broader than the simple commands and prohibitions of his toddler years. For these rules pertain not just to the persons he meets face-to-face but to countless others he has never met and probably never will meet. Among the most important of these rules are those of moral conduct.

### Not Doing Wrong

All societies have prohibitions that its members must learn to obey despite various temptations to the contrary. It's easy enough to set up external sanctions that enforce the prohibitions from the outside. Children rarely steal from the cookie jar when their parents are present. The trick is to make them resist temptation when they are not being watched. The person who does not steal or cheat because he thinks that he will be caught is not moral; he's merely prudent. One aim of socialization is to instill moral values that are *internalized,* so that the individual will shun transgressions because he feels that they are wrong and not because he is afraid of being punished.

INTERNALIZATION AND THE SUPEREGO

What leads to the internalization of right and wrong? According to Freud, the primary agent of internalization is the *superego,* a component of the personality that controls various forbidden impulses by administering self-punishment in the form of guilt and anxiety (see Chapter 11). The child kicks his little brother, and the parents punish him. As a result, the forbidden act (or, for that matter, the mere thought of that act) becomes associated with anxiety. As a result, the child will feel a pang of anxiety the next time he starts to attack his younger brother. To stop this painful feeling, he must stop that which triggered it: the thought, let alone the execution, of the forbidden behavior. The superego is the sum total of all such internalized inhibitions, a remnant of our childhood that remains with us

*Internalization* A four-year-old reproaches her doll: "Bad girl! Didn't I tell you to keep out of the dirt?" In imitating how her mother scolds her, the child is taking the first steps toward internalizing the mother's prohibitions. (Photograph by Suzanne Szasz)

for the rest of our lives and makes sure that we commit no wrong. The external authorities that once punished our transgressions have long stopped watching the cookie jar. But they no longer have to because they now inhabit our minds, where we can no longer hide from them.

### INTERNALIZATION AND MINIMAL SUFFICIENCY

This general view of the inhibition of forbidden acts makes certain predictions about the relation between child rearing and moral behavior. If the superego is a remnant of punishment administered during childhood, one might expect that the internalization of prohibition is most pronounced in children whose parents relied on sheer power in raising them—whether this power was exercised by the use of physical punishment, or deprivation of privileges, or threats of withdrawal of love and of abandonment. But this prediction turns out to be false. For a number of studies suggest that prohibitions are *less* internalized in children whose parents primarily relied on power in its various forms than in children whose parents took pains to explain just why a misdeed was wrong and why the child ought to behave differently. The children of power-asserting (autocratic) parents were more likely to cheat for a prize when they thought no one was looking, and they were less likely to feel guilt about their misdeeds or to confess them when confronted (Hoffman, 1970).

One proposal tries to deduce these and other phenomena of socialization from the so-called principle of **minimal sufficiency.** This states that a child will internalize a certain way of acting if there is just enough pressure to get him to behave in this new way, but not enough so that he feels he was forced to do so. This principle seems to fit a number of experimental findings. An example is a study in which children were prohibited from playing with a particularly attractive toy. For some children, the prohibition was backed with a mild threat (e.g., "I will be a little bit annoyed with you"); for others, the threat was severe (e.g., "I will be very upset and very angry with you"). When later tested in a rather different situation in which they thought they were unobserved, the mildly threatened children resisted temptation more than the severely threatened ones. The punishment led to internalization, but it did so only if it was *not* the most memorable part of the child's experience.

The same principle may help account for some of the effects of child rearing we've discussed in a prior section. We saw that the children of authoritative-reciprocal parents are more likely to internalize their parents' standards than the children of autocratic or permissive parents. This is in accord with the minimal sufficiency hypothesis. Autocratic parents supply too much force to induce their children to behave in the appropriate way, so their children become outwardly compliant but will not change their inner attitudes. Permissive parents apply no force at all, so their children never change their behavior in the first place—they won't even comply outwardly, let alone internalize. But authoritative-reciprocal parents somehow manage to strike the proper balance. They apply a force just strong enough to get their children to change their behavior, but mild enough so that the children come to believe that they performed the moral act of their own free will (Lepper, 1983).*

***Minimal sufficiency*** *If the older sister's scolding is of minimal sufficiency, it may lead to internalization. (Photograph by Roberta Intrater)*

---

* This is reminiscent of the effects of forced compliance on attitudes. As we saw in Chapter 12, subjects who are pressured into performing some action that runs counter to their own attitudes, will tend to change this attitude if the pressure (the threat or the bribe) is relatively small, but will not change the attitude if the pressure is large (Festinger and Carlsmith, 1959; Aronson and Carlsmith, 1963).

## Doing Good

Thus far, our discussion of moral action has dealt with the inhibition of forbidden acts. But moral action pertains to do's no less than to don'ts, to doing good as well as not committing evil. In a previous chapter we've considered the fact that humans are capable of positive moral actions that call for some personal sacrifice and altruism (see Chapter 13). We now ask how this capacity develops in the child.

Thus far, we are still far from an answer. A number of studies show that even very young children try to help and comfort others, and occasionally share with them (Rheingold, Hay, and West, 1976; Radke-Yarrow, Zahn-Waxler, and Chapman, 1983). The question is why.

According to a Hobbesian view of human nature, such apparently unselfish acts are much more egoistic than they appear to be on the surface. Perhaps the child only gives to others in order to reap some ultimate benefit for himself, such as avoiding censure and obtaining social approval. There is some evidence that this hypothesis is false, for in fact children who are more popular and self-confident to begin with are more likely to help others than are children who are less popular. This suggests that altruism is more likely when one's own needs for social approval are already satisfied. But if so, its main motivation is probably not the desire to gain yet further social approval (Hoffman, 1975a).

### EMPATHY

Such findings argue against the Hobbesian position that humans are by nature self-centered. A further argument comes from studies of *empathy* in very young infants. Empathy is a direct emotional response to another person's emotions; we see a patient writhe in pain in a hospital bed and we ourselves experience vicarious distress (Aronfreed, 1968; see also Chapter 13). Some precursors to such empathic reactions are found in the first two days of life. On hearing a newborn's cry, one-day-old infants cry too and their hearts beat faster (Simner, 1971; Sagi and Hoffman, 1976).

What accounts for such empathic reactions at this tender age? According to one hypothesis, the reason is classical conditioning. In this view, the response of crying becomes conditioned to the sound of crying. Initially, crying was evoked by some pain or discomfort. But soon the sound of the infant's own crying became a conditioned stimulus for further crying. Since another baby's cry resembles the infant's own, it will elicit his own cry as a conditioned response (in addition to various other distress reactions, such as increased heart rate). An alternative hypothesis is that some empathic reactions are innately given, a position that is by no means implausible given the facts on built-in alarm and distress reactions in many animals (see Chapter 10). As yet it is too early to choose between these two views. But whichever turns out to be correct, it is clear that some forerunner of what may later become a feeling for others is found at the very start of life.

The newborn's response to another baby's cry is just the first step in the development of empathic feelings for others. Initially, there is probably no clear separation between "self" and "other," and the infant may not really know that he is reacting to *another* child's distress. Genuine empathy, in which one feels for an-

**From empathy to altruism** *Empathy is a likely precursor of altruism. The child who feels the pain of others is more likely to be altruistic. (*St. Thomas of Villanueva as a Child Distributing His Clothes among the Beggar Boys *by Bartolome Murillo, 1670; © Cincinnati Art Museum)*

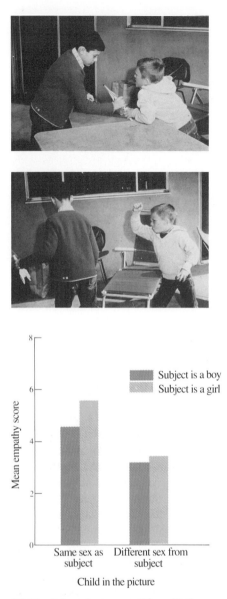

**15.12  It is easier to empathize with those who are similar**  *(A) Six- and seven-year-olds were presented with sequences of pictures such as this. After looking at each sequence, the child was asked "How do you feel?" Empathy was scored as a feeling that corresponded to that of the child in the picture (here, anger). (Courtesy of Norma Feshbach) (B) The children's empathy scores (the maximum score was 8). As the figure shows, the boys (in blue) felt greater empathy when the child in the picture was a boy than when it was a girl; the girls (in pink) felt more empathy when it was a girl than when it was a boy. (Adapted from Feshbach and Roe, 1968)*

other while yet perfectly aware that this other is not oneself, probably doesn't come much before the end of the first year. At about two years of age, children can put it in words: "Her eyes are crying—her sad" or "Janie crying, want mommy" (Bretherton, McNew, and Beeghly-Smith, 1981; see Figure 15.12).

FROM EMPATHIC DISTRESS TO UNSELFISH ACTION

The mere fact that one feels empathy doesn't mean that one will do anything about it. For to help one's fellows, one has to do more than just feel for them. One also has to act on this feeling. And one has to know how.

Consider a two-year-old girl who sees an adult in pain—say, an uncle who has cut his finger with a knife. In all likelihood, she will feel empathy and become distressed herself. But what will she do? A number of anecdotes suggest that she will give her uncle whatever *she* finds most comforting herself—for example, her favorite doll. While appreciating her kindly sentiments, the uncle would probably have preferred a band-aid or a stiff drink. But the child is as yet too young to take his perspective and doesn't realize that his needs are not the same as hers (Hoffman, 1977a, 1979, 1984).*

As we develop, we become increasingly able to tell what other people are likely to feel in a given situation and how to help if help is needed. But even that is not enough to ensure that we will act unselfishly. For helping is only one means of getting rid of the empathic distress that is caused by the sight of another person's pain. There is an easier but more callous method: one can simply look away. This often occurs in the big city, with its many homeless and victims of violence, where empathy may seem a luxury one can no longer afford. It may also occur in war or other situations where people "harden their hearts" to become immune to the sufferings of others (see Chapter 13).

Such arguments indicate that while empathy is a likely precursor of altruism, it does not guarantee it. In fact, there may be some circumstances in which empathy will interfere with appropriate helpful action. An interesting finding concerns a group of nurses who worked in a ward for severely ill persons. Those nurses who seemed to experience the greatest degree of empathy for their patients were the least effective. The reason was simple. They couldn't bear their patients' pain, and so they tried to have as little contact with them as possible (Stotland, Mathews, Sherman, Hansson, and Richardson, 1978).

## Moral Reasoning

Thus far, our focus has been on the development of moral behavior. What about the development of moral thought? What happens to the child's conception of right and wrong as he grows up? Much of the research on this topic has been strongly influenced by Piaget's cognitive developmental approach.

* Some authors make a distinction between **empathic distress,** in which the primary focus is on the unpleasant feelings the victim's plight arouses in *us,* and **sympathetic distress,** in which there is a desire to help the other person—not merely to relieve one's own empathic distress but to relieve *his* distress. According to this view, empathic distress is a more primitive forerunner of sympathetic distress, which does not occur until the child is about two (Hoffman, 1984).

## PIAGET AND THE CHILD'S CONCEPTION OF MORALITY

As we saw in our discussion of cognitive development, Piaget believed that children before age five or six are relatively egocentric, being unable to see the world from any perspective other than their own (see Chapter 14). According to Piaget, this same egocentric pattern is revealed when the child has to make a moral judgment. Our adult conceptions of crime and punishment place great emphasis upon the perpetrator's intention and carefully distinguish between accident and design. But this distinction requires an ability to take account of another person's motives. Young children cannot readily do this, anymore than they can take account of width in a liquid conservation task while attending to height. In consequence, they tend to consider only the extent of the injury produced by the deed, regardless of the motive. In one of Piaget's studies, children had to judge which of two boys was the naughtier. John accidentally tripped, fell against a cupboard, and smashed fifteen cups. In contrast, Henry only broke one cup, which he knocked to the floor while climbing the cupboard to steal some forbidden jam. Younger children generally judged John to be the greater villain who should be punished more severely; after all, he had broken fifteen cups! Older children were much more likely to consider intent (Piaget, 1932).*

## KOHLBERG'S STAGES OF MORAL REASONING

Piaget's account of moral development is the basis of a more elaborate stage theory devised by Lawrence Kohlberg, who has tried to extend it to adolescence and adulthood. Kohlberg's basic method is to confront subjects with a number of stories that pose a moral dilemma. An example is a story about a man whose wife will die unless treated with a very expensive drug that costs $2,000. The husband scraped together all the money he could, but it was not enough. He promised to pay the balance later, but the pharmacist still refused to give him the drug. In desperation, the husband broke into the pharmacy and stole the drug. The subjects were asked whether the husband's act was right or wrong and why (Kohlberg, 1969).

Kohlberg analyzed the subjects' answers and concluded that moral reasoning proceeds through a series of successive stages. Roughly speaking, there is a progression from a primitive morality guided by personal fear of punishment or desire for gain ("If you let your wife die, you'll get in trouble"), through stages in which right or wrong are defined by convention, by what people will say ("Your family will think you're an inhuman husband if you don't"), to the highest stage in which there are internalized moral principles that have become one's own ("If you didn't steal the drug, you wouldn't be blamed and you would have lived up to the outside rule of the law, but you wouldn't have lived up to your own standards of conscience"). As one might expect, there is a rough correlation between Kohlberg's levels and age. But even in adulthood only a small proportion of the subjects give answers that correspond to Kohlberg's highest level. In a recent study that made use of a revised set of Kohlberg's criteria, no subject below the age of

* Whether the situation is as clear-cut as Piaget believed is debatable. After all, we saw that even very young children have some primitive empathic notion of another person's joy or distress, which indicates that the child's egocentrism is by no means complete. In fact, there is evidence that if the judgment task is made somewhat easier, then intentions are considered even by six-year-olds (e.g., Feldman, Klosson, Parsons, Rholes, and Ruble, 1976).

Table 15.1  KOHLBERG'S STAGES OF MORAL REASONING

| Stage of moral reasoning | Moral behavior is that which: |
|---|---|
| **Preconventional morality** | |
| Level 1 | Avoids punishment |
| Level 2 | Gains reward |
| **Conventional morality** | |
| Level 3 | Gains approval and avoids disapproval of others |
| Level 4 | Is defined by rigid codes of "law and order" |
| **Postconventional morality** | |
| Level 5 | Is defined by a "social contract" generally agreed upon for the public good |
| Level 6 | Is based on abstract ethical principles that determine one's own moral code |

SOURCE: Adapted from Kohlberg, 1969.

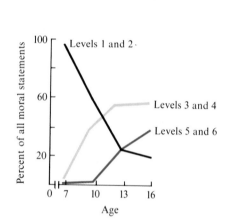

**15.13  Level of moral reasoning as a function of age**  With increasing age, the level of moral reasoning changes. In this figure, the percent of all moral judgments made by children at various ages falls into one of three general categories defined by Kohlberg. At seven, virtually all moral judgments are in terms of avoiding punishment or gaining reward (Kohlberg's levels 1 and 2). At ten, about half the judgments are based on criteria of social approval and disapproval or of a—rigid— code of laws (Kohlberg's levels 3 and 4). From thirteen on, some of the children refer to more abstract rules—a generally agreed-upon social contract or a set of abstract ethical principles (Kohlberg's levels 5 and 6). (After Kohlberg, 1963)

twenty was judged to have reached Stage 5, and Stage 6 was not found at all (Colby, Kohlberg, Gibbs, and Lieberman, 1983; Colby and Kohlberg, 1986). Considering that Kohlberg considers this final stage to be the level that characterized such moral giants as Mahatma Gandhi and Dr. Martin Luther King, the failure of his subjects (and no doubt, most of us) to attain it, is probably not too surprising (Figure 15.13; Table 15.1).

### MORAL REASONING IN MEN AND WOMEN

Are there sex differences in moral orientation? An influential discussion by Carol Gilligan suggests that there may be. In her view, men tend to see morality as a matter of *justice,* ultimately based on abstract, rational principles by which all individuals can be treated fairly. As one eleven-year-old boy put it in describing the moral dilemmas posed by Kohlberg: "It's sort of like a math problem with humans." Women in contrast see morality in more concrete, social terms. To them, the focus is on *caring*—on compassion, on human relationships, on special responsibilities to those with whom one is intimately connected. Given these different emphases, one might expect women to score lower than men when moral reasoning is assessed by Kohlberg's yardstick. For as Gilligan sees it, Kohlberg's system has a built-in sex bias in which the moral outlook usually adopted by men is judged to be more advanced than that which is more characteristic of women. Kohlberg calls the highest steps on his moral staircase "postconventional morality," which is defined by just those abstract, rational principles that tend to fit in with the way in which men see the moral order. The moral outlook of women, on the other hand, with their emphasis on helping others, would be judged to be on one of Kohlberg's lower steps. Under the circumstances, it would not be surprising to find that women obtain lower scores on Kohlberg's tests than men (Gilligan, 1982).

Psychologists interested in moral reasoning were quick to ask whether men really achieve "higher" levels of moral reasoning as defined by Kohlberg. It turns out that they don't. According to several authors, a systematic check of the work performed on the topic reveals no reliable sex differences in moral reasoning on

Kohlberg's test; of 108 studies, only 8 showed a superiority of males over females (4 or 5 went in the opposite direction) (Brabeck, 1983; Walker, 1984; but see Baumrind, 1986). But if so, what remains of Gilligan's critique?

Gilligan states that she herself never said that women *can't* reason at Kohlberg's "highest" level; the point is that they usually *choose* not to do so. As she sees it, the female perspective emphasizes human relationships, attachments, and personal responsibilities rather than the abstract conceptions of rights and justice emphasized by the male perspective (Gilligan, 1986). That such a difference in emphases exists is suggested by various empirical findings, including the fact that girls seem to place a greater value on going out of one's way to help other people and show more emotional empathy than do boys (Hoffman, 1977b). Just why women emphasize the perspective of care rather than of abstract justice is still unsettled. The best guess is that it is a result of different patterns of socialization that stress different values for boys and girls (Hoffman, 1984).

Is either perspective preferable to the other? Virtually everyone agrees that the answer is no, and that an appropriate conception of morality must include both justice and compassion. As Kohlberg points out, both of these orientations are built into the New Testament's Golden Rule. That rule is formulated in two ways. One insists on justice: "Do unto others as you would have them do unto you." The other urges care and compassion: "Love thy neighbor as thyself" (Kohlberg and Candee, 1984).

### MORAL REASONING AND MORAL CONDUCT

Are stages of moral reasoning related to ethical conduct? To some extent they may be. Thus a number of studies found that delinquents were at a lower stage of moral reasoning than nondelinquents of the same age and IQ. Other studies suggest that individuals at higher, principled levels of moral reasoning are less likely to cheat in an ambiguous situation in which they are unobserved and are more likely to maintain their position against the pressure of other people's views. But taken as a whole, the results suggest that the relation between moral reasoning and moral conduct is far from perfect (Blasi, 1980; Rest, 1983; Gibbs, Clark, Joseph, Green, Goodrick, and Makowski, 1986). To some extent, this result is reminiscent of the relatively low correlations between social attitudes and behavior we encountered in a previous chapter (see Chapter 12). Kohlberg's stages (just like attitudes) don't specifically pertain to conduct. They indicate whether an individual *describes* certain moral principles, but they don't tell us much about the individual's actual behavior, which may or may not be ruled by the moral principles he described (for discussion, see Rest, 1984; Blasi, 1984; Kohlberg, Levine, and Hewer, 1984).

But there is a further problem. For Kohlberg's stages don't just indicate what an individual's moral principles are. They also concern that person's *ability to describe* these principles and reason on the basis of them. Kohlberg has indeed shown that this ability increases with age and mental development. But this is not particularly surprising. After all, the same holds for the ability to describe and reason about various other rules of mental life—for example, those that pertain to space, to number, and to language. Seen in this light, what is really surprising is that Kohlberg's stages correlate with behavior as *well* as they do. One reason why they don't correlate any better may be that they have less to do with the develop-

***Moral reasoning in men and women*** *The belief that men and women focus on different aspects of morality has ancient roots. A classical example is Sophocles's tragedy* Antigone *which revolves around the irreconcilable conflict between Antigone, who insists on burying a slain brother, and her uncle Creon, the king, who issues a decree forbidding anyone from doing so on pain of death. To Antigone, the ultimate moral obligation is to the family; to Creon, it is to the state and its laws. (From a 1982 production at the New York Shakespeare Festival, with F. Murray Abraham and Lisa Banes; photograph by Martha Swope)*

ment of morality than with the development of something we might call "meta-morality" (in analogy with the metacognitive processes we've described in a previous section): the ability to reflect on moral rules, regardless of whether one lives by them (see Chapters 8 and 14).

## THE DEVELOPMENT OF SEX AND GENDER

Thus far, our emphasis has been on social development considered as growth and expansion. But social development is more than that. Like physical and cognitive development, it involves growth, but this growth is not just a matter of increasing size. It is also accompanied by increasing differentiation. For as the child gets older, she becomes increasingly aware of the fact that people differ from each other and from herself. In so doing, she also gains a clearer conception of her own self and of her own personality—what she is really like, in her own eyes and in those of others.

Seen in this light, social development goes hand in hand with the development of a sense of personal identity. One of the most important examples of this is sexual identity—of being male or female and all that goes with it.

Biologically, sexual identity seems simple enough. It may refer to XX vs. XY chromosome pairs or to the external genitals. But what does it mean psychologically? It refers to three issues. One is *gender identity*—our inner sense of whether we are male or female. A second is *gender role*—a whole host of external behavior patterns that a given culture deems appropriate for each sex. A third is *sexual orientation*—the choice of a sexual partner, which is by and large—though of course not always—directed toward the opposite sex. Gender identity, gender role, and sexual orientation are among the most important determinants of a person's social existence.* How do they come about?

***Social learning of gender roles***
*(Photograph by Suzanne Arms/ Jeroboam)*

### Gender Roles

Gender roles pervade all facets of social life. The induction into one or the other of these roles begins with the very first question that is asked when a human being enters the world: "Is it a boy or a girl?" As soon as the answer is supplied, the process of gender typing begins, and the infant is started along one of two quite different social paths. Some of the patterns of gender typing have probably changed in the wake of the women's movement of the sixties and seventies, but many differences in child rearing persist.

---

* It has become customary to distinguish between *sex* and *gender*. The term *sex* is generally reserved for aspects of the male-female difference that pertain to reproductive functions (for example, ovaries versus testes, vagina versus penis) or that are likely to be linked to genetic factors (for example, differences in average height and muscular strength). It is also used to designate erotic feelings, inclinations, or practices (for example, heterosexual, homosexual). The term *gender* refers to social or psychological aspects of being seen as a man or woman or regarding oneself to be so. It is one thing to be a male, it is another to be a man. The same holds for being a female and being a woman (Stoller, 1968). A special note about the term *sex difference*. As here employed, this term will be used to designate male-female differences when no presupposition is made about either a biological or a cultural origin.

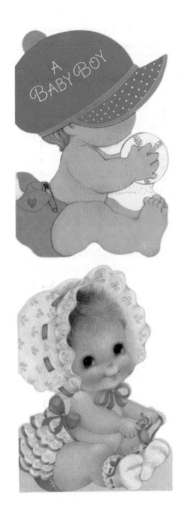

**Gender-role stereotypes**  *Once parents and others recognize an infant's sex, they will treat him or her differently. Notice the difference in the cards sent to parents congratulating them on the birth of a son or daughter. (© Hallmark Cards, Inc., used with permission)*

The stereotype is simple enough: The infant is dressed in either pink or blue; the child plays with either dolls or trucks; the adult woman's place is in the home, while the man's is in the marketplace—or the buffalo hunting grounds, or whatever. Society not only has different expectations about what the two sexes should *do*; it also has different conceptions of what they should *be*. In our own culture, the male has been expected to be more aggressive and tough, more restrained emotionally, and more interested in things than in people. The contrasting expectations for females are greater submissiveness, greater emotional expressiveness, and an interest in people rather than in things.

There is no doubt that these gender-role stereotypes have a considerable effect on the way we perceive people, even newborns and very young infants. In one study, mothers of young infants were asked to participate as subjects in an experiment on "how children play." The mothers were introduced to a six-month-old baby, little "Joey" or "Janie," and they were asked to play with him or her for a few minutes. In fact, the six-month-old was a "baby actor" who dressed up as a boy or girl regardless of its actual sex. The results showed that the subjects' behavior depended on whether they thought they were playing with "Joey" or "Janie." To "Joey" they offered toys such as a hammer or a rattle, while "Janie" was invariably presented with a doll. In addition, the subjects physically handled "Joey" and "Janie" differently. In dealing with "Joey," they often tended to bounce "him" about, thus stimulating the whole body. In contrast, their response to "Janie" was gentler and less vigorous (Smith and Lloyd, 1978).

The children soon behave as the adults expect them to. Starting at about age one and a half, they begin to show gender-typed differences. By three years of age, they prefer different toys and play with peers of their own sex (Huston, 1983). As they grow older, they become increasingly aware of male and female stereotypes. In one study, both male and female children had to decide whether certain characteristics were more likely in a man or a woman. Over 90 percent of a group of U.S. eleven-year-olds thought that the adjectives *weak, emotional, appreciative, gentle, soft-hearted, affected, talkative, fickle,* and *mild* probably described a woman, and that the adjectives *strong, aggressive, disorderly, cruel, coarse, adventurous, independent, ambitious,* and *dominant* probably described a man. Boys and girls had just about the same gender-role stereotypes (Best, Williams, Cloud, Davis, Robertson, Edwards, Giles, and Fowles, 1977).

There is little doubt that many of these gender-role stereotypes are reinforced by parents and peers. When young children play with toys that are judged to be inappropriate—as when a boy plays with a dollhouse—their parents are likely to express disapproval. This is especially so for fathers, who vehemently object to any such behaviors in their sons. By and large, girls are allowed more latitude in such matters. A girl can be a tomboy and get away with it; a boy who is a sissy is laughed at (Langlois and Downs, 1980).

## Constitutional Factors and Sex Differences

What accounts for the difference in current gender roles? We will consider both constitutional and social factors in an attempt to understand how biology and society conspire to make boys into men and girls into women.

Which of the differences between the sexes are based on constitutional differences? Apart from the obvious anatomical and physiological differences that pertain to reproduction, there are of course differences in average size, strength, and physical endurance. But what about *psychological* differences? There is no doubt that such differences do exist and that some of them fit cultural stereotypes. The question is whether any of these differences—in aggression, independence, emotional expressiveness, social sensitivity, and so on—are biologically given, whether they accompany the sexual anatomy the way menstruation goes along with a female XX chromosome pair.

Before proceeding, note two preliminary cautions. The first is that any psychological difference between the sexes is one of averages. The *average* three-year-old girl seems to be more dependent than her male counterpart; she is more likely to ask for help, to cling, and to seek affection (Emmerich, 1966). But this doesn't mean that the two groups don't overlap. For there are certainly many three-year-old girls who are *less* dependent than many three-year-old boys. After all, the same holds true even for many physical differences. There is no doubt that men are, on the average, taller than women. But it is equally clear that a considerable number of women are taller than many men.

A second caution concerns interpretation. Suppose we obtain a difference. What accounts for it? It might be a difference in biological predispositions. But it may also reflect the society in which the children are raised. In our society—as indeed, in many others—boys are encouraged to be independent, to be "little men," beginning at a very early age, and the obtained difference in dependency may simply reflect this cultural fact. Here, as in so many other areas, nature and nurture are difficult to disentangle.

AGGRESSION

If there is one sex difference that might well be constitutional in origin, at least in part, it is aggression. Males tend to be more active and assertive than females. This difference is apparent from the very outset; male infants are more irritable and physically active than female infants. At two or three, boys are much more likely to engage in rough-and-tumble play and mock fighting than are girls (a difference also seen in apes and monkeys; see Figure 15.14). By four or five, they are more ready to exchange verbal insults and to repel aggression by counterattack. The difference continues into adulthood. While acts of physical violence are relatively rare among both sexes, they are very much more common among men than women; thus among adolescents, arrests for violent crimes occur five times more often among males than females (Johnson, 1979). A similar pattern of results holds in different social classes and in such widely different cultural settings as Ethiopia, India, Kenya, Mexico, Okinawa, and Switzerland (Whiting and Whiting, 1975; Maccoby and Jacklin, 1974, 1980; Parke and Slaby, 1983).

It is probably not surprising that this sex difference is more pronounced for physical aggression than for other forms of aggression. When aggression is measured by rating the degree of verbal hostility, or by asking how intense a shock a subject is willing to administer to another person, the difference is not as striking (Hyde, 1981). But even so, it is still quite marked.

The fact that this sex difference in aggression—especially in its physical manifestations—is found so early in life, is observed in so many different cultures, and is also seen in our primate relatives, suggests a constitutional origin—all the more

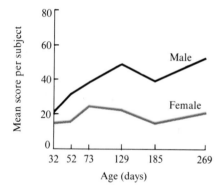

**15.14   The development of rough-and-tumble play in male and female rhesus monkeys**   *Roughhouse play in two male and two female rhesus monkeys during the first year of life. The scores are based on both frequency and vigor of this activity, in which monkeys wrestle, roll, or sham bite—all presumably in play, since no one ever gets hurt. Roughhouse play is considerably more pronounced in males than in females, a difference that increases during the first year of life. (After Harlow, 1962)*

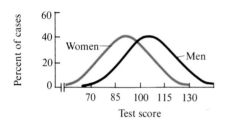

**15.15   Sex differences in spatial ability**
*Results on a spatial-mathematical test which included questions such as "How many times between three and four o'clock do the hands of a clock make a straight line?" The curve plots the percentage of subjects who receive a particular score (with men in black and women in color). As the curve shows, the men perform better than the women, though the two curves overlap considerably. (Data from Very, 1967, with test scores adjusted by a method called normalization)*

so given the fact that aggressiveness is enhanced by the administration of male sex hormones (see Chapter 10).

### PATTERN OF INTELLECTUAL APTITUDES

There is another psychological difference that is often said to be based on biological givens—a different pattern of intellectual abilities. On the average, men do better on tests of spatial and mathematical ability than do women (Figure 15.15; Maccoby and Jacklin, 1974, 1980; Halpern, 1986). Until fairly recently, it was generally believed that the reverse held for verbal abilities. But according to some recent studies, the superiority of women over men on verbal tasks may be much smaller than had previously been assumed (Hyde and Linn, 1988).

What accounts for the sex difference in cognitive aptitudes, especially in spatial-mathematical abilities? In part, it may simply reflect a difference in the way boys and girls are brought up. But various lines of evidence suggest that social factors are only part of the story. An example is a study of SAT scores in 40,000 male and female adolescents. The investigators found the usual sex difference on spatial and mathematical tasks even when they limited their comparison to boys and girls who had taken the same high school math courses and had expressed the same degree of interest in mathematics (Benbow and Stanley, 1983; Benbow, 1988).

A number of authors feel that such sex differences in mathematical aptitude are ultimately produced by a difference in certain spatial abilities. An example is the ability to visualize objects in space, which is often assessed by asking subjects to rotate a three-dimensional object in their imagination to decide whether it is a rotated version of another figure or whether it is its mirror image. Since a number of branches of mathematics rely on such abilities—for example, geometry, topology, trigonometry, and much of calculus—it does not seem too far-fetched to assume that the sex difference in this ability underlies those in quantitative aptitude and achievement (Burnett, Lane, and Dratt, 1979; Hunt, 1985a; Halpern, 1986).

A number of investigators have searched for a constitutional basis for the male-female difference in spatial abilities. Some believe that the key to the puzzle is in different maturation rates. There is some evidence that children who mature later tend to do better on spatial tests than children who mature earlier. An intriguing hypothesis is that this effect is related to the different functions of the two cerebral hemispheres. As we've previously seen, the right hemisphere is specialized for spatial tasks, the left for language (see Chapter 2). By making the assumption that the right hemisphere matures more slowly than the left, and that neurological maturation comes to an effective end at the time of puberty, we can account for most of the evidence. The usual male-female difference in cognitive orientation would then follow from the fact that girls generally reach puberty before boys. If so, their right (spatial) hemisphere is stopped at an earlier point of neurological organization (Waber, 1977, 1979).

## Social Factors and Sex Differences

While some psychological sex differences may have biological roots, even more important is the way in which boys and girls are socialized. We will begin our discussion by taking a second look at the two characteristics for which there is some

605

evidence of a biologically based sex difference: aggression and the discrepancy between spatial and verbal aptitudes. We'll see that even here there is some reasonable evidence that social effects augment and interact with whatever constitutional difference may have been there to start with.

### ARE CONSTITUTIONALLY GIVEN DIFFERENCES REALLY CONSTITUTIONAL?

There may well be a greater initial predisposition toward aggression in boys than in girls, but cultural pressures serve to magnify whatever sex differences exist at the outset. Parents will generally allow (and even foster) a degree of aggressiveness in a boy that they would not countenance in a girl. Thus fathers often encourage their sons to fight back when another boy attacks them (Sears, Maccoby, and Levin, 1957). The result of such differential training is that the initial built-in bias toward a sex difference in behavior is considerably exaggerated.

Similar considerations may apply to the discrepancy between spatial and verbal aptitudes. In our society, girls are expected to do better in English than in math. This belief is shared by teachers, parents, and pupils, who all help to make it come true. As a result, even the girl who does have the appropriate genetic potential may do worse on spatial and mathematical tests than her ability warrants.

### SEX REASSIGNMENT IN CHILDHOOD

The most dramatic examples of the effect of social factors in the determination of gender identity and gender role come from studies of children who at birth were declared to be of one sex but who were later reassigned to the other. This sometimes occurs if the newborn is a ***hermaphrodite,*** with reproductive organs that are anatomically ambiguous so that they are not exclusively male or female. In such cases, parents and physicians sometimes decide to reverse the initial sex assignment. Corrective surgery is undertaken, the sex is officially reassigned, and the child is raised accordingly. The results suggest that if the reassignment occurs early enough—according to some investigators, up to eighteen months, according to others, up to three or four years—the child adjusts to a remarkable degree. It becomes a he or a she, in part because this is how other people now regard it (Money and Ehrhardt, 1972).

*The effects of reassignment*   The reports of parents leave no doubt that the child is seen very differently before and after the reassignment. One case involved a child that was genetically male. It had a male's XY chromosome pair and testes. But the external genitals were otherwise more similar to a female's than to a male's. At birth the child was pronounced a boy, but the decision was reversed seventeen months later, at which time there was corrective surgery. According to the parents, there was an immediate change in the way the child was now treated. Even her three-year-old brother reacted differently and showed a "marked tendency to treat her much more gently. Whereas before he was just as likely to stick his foot out to trip her as he went by, he now wants to hold her hand to make sure she doesn't fall" (Money and Ehrhardt, 1972, p. 124).

Even more startling is the case of two normally born male identical twins, one of whom suffered a surgical accident at the age of seven months—his penis was amputated flush with the abdominal wall. After lengthy medical consultation, the parents decided upon sex reassignment. In cases of this sort, there is consider-

***Social factors and sex differences***   *Social effects augment constitutional differences. (Photograph by Roberta Intrater)*

*A four-year-old and her doll    Is she trying to live up to her gender identity or simply acting like a parent? (Photograph by Erika Stone)*

dog if it wanted to, or if its whiskers were cut off. This suggests that the lack of gender constancy is just another reflection of the preschooler's failure to comprehend the underlying constancies of the universe. After all, children at this stage of cognitive development do not conserve liquid quantity, mass, or number (see Chapter 14).

According to Kohlberg, the child's identification with the parent of the same sex *follows* the acquisition of gender identity. Once they recognize that they are boys or girls, they will try to live up to their sense of gender identity, to act in a manner that befits their own self-concept. They will now look for appropriate models—and the most readily available ones are their mothers and fathers—that can show them how to get better and better at being a male or a female.

## Sexual Orientation

The majority of men and women are ***heterosexual.*** They seek a partner of the opposite sex. But for a significant minority, the sexual orientation is otherwise; their erotic and romantic feelings are directed primarily or exclusively toward members of their own sex; they are ***homosexual.*** What are the factors that determine which sexual orientation is adopted?

### THE INCIDENCE OF HOMOSEXUALITY

According to a survey made in the 1940s that is still regarded as the most reliable study of sexual patterns among American males, 4 percent of American males are exclusively homosexual during their lifetime (Kinsey, Pomeroy, and Martin, 1948). The comparable incidence of exclusive homosexuality among women seems to be lower—about 2 percent (Kinsey, Pomeroy, Martin, and Gebhard, 1953). It is clear that a substantial number of men and women are erotically oriented toward a partner of their own sex despite the fact that our society sharply stigmatizes such behavior. This cultural taboo is by no means universal. According to one cross-cultural survey, two-thirds of the societies studied regarded homosexuality as normal and acceptable, at least for some persons or for some age groups (Ford and Beach, 1951). In certain historical periods the practice was glorified and extolled, as in classical Greece where Pericles, the great Athenian statesman, was regarded as rather odd because he was *not* attracted to beautiful boys.

Homosexuality illustrates the fact that sexual orientation, gender identity, and gender role are in principle independent. Most male homosexuals think of themselves as men and are so regarded by others; the analogous point holds for female homosexuals (Marmor, 1975).

### THE NATURE OF HOMOSEXUALITY

Is homosexuality an illness that requires a cure if any can be found? Or is it simply a different form of sexual expression that happens to be disapproved of in this culture at this time?

According to one—now largely discredited—psychiatric view, homosexuality is pathological, based on incapacitating fears of the opposite sex and "incompatible with life" (Bieber et al., 1962; Bieber, 1965). The primary evidence for this position came from a widely cited study of 106 male homosexuals under psychiatric

**611**

treatment who were described as unusually disturbed and unhappy. But this study suffers from several flaws. One concerns the sample of homosexuals upon which the conclusions were based. This sample is biased since it included only persons who sought psychiatric help. Such people are almost certain to be more disturbed than the population at large and are not representative of the many homosexuals who never enter a psychiatrist's office.

In an effort to meet these objections, several investigators have compared nonpatient homosexuals to nonpatient heterosexuals of equal age, educational level, and intelligence. The results of such studies show that the differences between homosexuals and heterosexuals are much less than had been supposed. Some investigators found no difference whatever (Hooker, 1957; Thompson, McCandless, and Strickland, 1971). Others found that homosexuals (especially male homosexuals) were somewhat more likely to lack confidence, to suffer from low self-esteem, and to clown at their own expense (Saghir and Robins, 1973). But such differences are probably best explained by the fact that homosexuals in our society are members of a minority group that is often the target of scorn and discrimination. Self-hatred and protective clowning are common characteristics in any persecuted minority (Hooker, 1965).

In any case, the real issue is not whether homosexuals as a group are as happy or well-adjusted as heterosexuals are as a group. Given the stigma attached to their orientation, it would be surprising if they were. The question is whether homosexuality as such necessarily implies personal disturbance and neurosis. The answer seems to be no. Under the circumstances, there is no reason to maintain that homosexuality is a psychological disorder. In 1974, this view became part of the official position of the American Psychiatric Association, which voted that "homosexuality by itself does not necessarily constitute a psychiatric disorder" (Marmor, 1975, p. 1510).

To be sure, some homosexuals may want to change their sexual orientation, and if they do, a therapist might try to help them. But this undertaking is by no means easy, especially for persons who have been exclusively homosexual. Freud himself was doubtful that it could be done. Later psychoanalysts were more optimistic, but they rarely reported lasting changes in more than about one-third of the cases treated.

The safest conclusion seems to be that sexual orientation—both heterosexual and homosexual—is a fairly stable condition. It can be changed in some cases but not easily. Nor do most homosexuals *wish* for such a change. Homosexuality is not a disease nor a personality disturbance. But neither is it a simple matter of personal choice that can be done or undone more or less at will.

WHAT CAUSES HOMOSEXUALITY?

What leads to homosexuality? So far, there is no clear answer. It may well be that this question simply represents the other side of the question, "what leads to heterosexuality?" This second question is rarely asked because most people take the heterosexual preference for granted. Yet if we did know how to explain the origin of heterosexuality, we would probably be much closer to an understanding of how homosexuality comes about as well.

*Experience in childhood*    Some of the attempts at an explanation focus on the role of childhood experience. The most famous example is Freud's theory of male

THE NATURE OF THE TRANSITION

Compared to other animals, humans attain sexual maturity rather late in their development. This is just another facet of an important difference between ourselves and our animal cousins—a lengthened period of immaturity and dependence that provides more time for each generation to learn from the one before. When is this period over?

Biology has set a lower limit at roughly age fifteen for girls and seventeen for boys when physical growth is more or less complete. But the point that marks the beginning of adulthood is decreed by social conditions as well as biology. As an example, a study of colonial New England families shows that the age at which sons become autonomous from their parents changed over the course of four generations. The sons of the first settlers stayed on their parents' farm until their late twenties before they married and became economically independent. As farm land became scarcer and other opportunities opened in the surrounding villages and towns, the sons left home much earlier, learned a trade, married, and became autonomous at a younger age (Greven, 1970). But with the onset of mass education in the mid-nineteenth century, this pattern was reversed again. Instead of leaving to become an apprentice or take a job, more and more youths continued to live with their families and remained in school through their late teens. This allowed them to acquire the skills required for membership in a complex, technological society, but it postponed their social and economic independence and their full entry into the adult world (Elder, 1980).

Culture evidently has an important say in the when and how of the transition period. It also sets up special occasions that mark the end of that period or highlight certain points along the way. A number of human societies have ***initiation rites*** that signify induction into adulthood (Figure 15.18). In some preliterate cultures, these are violent, prolonged, and painful, especially in certain puberty rites

A

B

*15.18 Initiation rites  These rites signify induction into adulthood, as in (A) a bar mitzvah, or (B) a South African ceremony in which young men of about 19 are initiated into full manhood by having to live in isolation for 2 months after a ritual circumcision. During this period, they are smeared with white clay to indicate that they are in a state of transition and in contact with ancestral spirits. (*Left: photograph by Blair Seitz, 1986/Photo Researchers.* Right: *photograph by Omas D. W. Friedmann/Photo Researchers)*

for boys that involve ceremonial beatings and circumcision. According to some anthropologists, such initiation rites are especially severe in cultures that try to emphasize the dramatic distinction between the roles of children and adults, as well as between those of men and women. In our own society, the transition to full adulthood is much more gradual, with milestones that refer not just to biological changes but also to various educational and vocational attainments. It is therefore not too surprising that we have not one initiation rite but many (none of which would ever be regarded as especially severe): confirmations and bar (or bas) mitzvahs, "sweet sixteen" parties, high school and college graduations, and so on. Each of them represents just one more step on a protracted road to adulthood (Burton and Whiting, 1961; Muuss, 1970).

Cultural factors also determine the time at which other benchmarks of development are reached. An example is the age at which virginity is lost, which has steadily decreased in our own society during the past few decades, reflecting a change in sexual mores for both men and women. This change is undoubtedly caused by many factors, not the least of which is the existence of increasingly effective methods of birth control which allow the separation of the emotional and recreational functions of sexuality from its reproductive ones.

IS ADOLESCENCE ALWAYS TURBULENT?

There is a traditional view of adolescence which holds that it is inevitably a period of great emotional stress. This notion goes back to the romantic movement of the early nineteenth century, when major writers such as Goethe wrote influential works that featured youths in desperate conflict with a cynical, adult world that drove them to despair, suicide, or violent rebellion. This position was later endorsed by a number of psychological theorists, including Sigmund Freud and many of his followers. To Freud, adolescence was necessarily a period of conflict, since this is the time when the sex urges repressed during the closing phase of the Oedipal conflict can no longer be denied and clash violently with the unconscious prohibitions previously set up. Further conflicts center on struggles with the older generation, especially the same-sex parent, that were repressed in childhood but now come to the fore (see Chapter 11).

This traditional view of adolescence has been seriously challenged by several modern writers who argue that the turbulence of the period is by no means inevitable. Whether there is marked emotional disturbance depends on the way the culture handles the transition. Some evidence for this view comes from studies of preliterate cultures in which the shift from childhood to adulthood is very gradual. Among the Arapesh of New Guinea, the young increasingly participate in adult activities as they get older. The child begins by tilling her parents' garden and eventually tills her own. Given the relatively simple social and economic structure of Arapesh life, the change is not very drastic. Correspondingly, there seems to be no psychological crisis among the Arapesh during adolescence (Mead, 1939).

However enviable, the gentle adolescent transition of the Arapesh is difficult to achieve in our modern industrial society. It's hard to see how a five-year-old can help his father at his job if that job happens to be computer programming. Accordingly, one might expect a fair level of disturbance during adolescence in our own society. And indeed, such emotional disturbance is a theme often sounded by the mass media and much modern literature (for example, J. D. Salinger's

*Catcher in the Rye).* But in fact, a number of studies suggest that such turbulence is by no means universal among modern American adolescents. Several investigators find that for many adolescents "development . . . is slow, gradual, and unremarkable" (Josselson, 1980, p. 189). What probably matters is the particular social and psychological setting, which surely differs from individual to individual in a complex society such as ours.

### TRYING TO FIND A PERSONAL IDENTITY

It appears that adolescence is not necessarily a time of troubles. But even so, it does pose a number of serious problems as the adolescent has to prepare to become an autonomous individual in his or her own right. A number of writers have tried to understand some characteristic adolescent behavior patterns in light of this ultimate goal.

*Establishing a separate world*   Unlike fledglings, adolescents in our society remain in the nest for quite a while after they can fly (or perhaps more precisely, get their driver's license). This probably makes it all the more essential for them to establish some elements of a separation between themselves and the world of their parents. As one means to this end, many adolescents adopt all kinds of external trappings of what's "now" and what's "in," such as distinctive tastes in dance steps, clothing, and idiom (Figure 15.19). These often change with bewildering rapidity as yesterday's adolescent fads diffuse into the broader social world and become today's adult fashions (as witness men's hair styles). When this happens, new adolescent fads spring up to maintain the differentiation (Douvan and Adelson, 1958).

*The identity crisis of adolescence*   According to Erikson, the separation from the adult's sphere is only one manifestation of what adolescents are really trying to achieve. Their major goal throughout this period is to discover who and what they really are as they go through what he calls an ***identity crisis.*** In our complex culture, there are many social roles, and adolescence is a time to try them on to see which one fits best—which vocation, which ideology, which group membership. The adolescent's primary question is, "Who am I?" and to answer it, he strikes a succession of postures, in part for the benefit of others, who then serve as a mirror in which he can see himself. Each role, each human relationship, each

*15.19   Adolescent fads   New adolescent fads spring up to maintain the differentiation between the adolescents' own world and that of the adults around them. They then disappear rather quickly to be replaced by yet newer fads. The photos show some such fads prominent at various times. (A) seventies—streaking, (B) eighties—punk hair styles. (Left: photograph by Ted Crowell/Black Star. Right: photograph by Jerry Howard/Positive Images)*

A

B

(Top: *Photograph by Roberta Intrater;* Bottom: *photograph by Michael Nichols/Magnum)*

world view is first temporarily adopted on an all-or-none basis with no room for compromise. Each is at first a costume. When the adolescent finds that some costume fits, it becomes the clothes of his adult identity. Most adolescents eventually succeed, but the process of identity seeking has its difficulties:

> . . . The danger of this stage is role confusion . . . . To keep themselves together they temporarily overidentify, to the point of apparent loss of identity, with the heroes of cliques and crowds. This initiates the stage of "falling in love," which is by no means entirely, or even primarily, a sexual matter . . . . To a considerable extent adolescent love is an attempt to arrive at a definition of one's identity by projecting a diffuse ego image on another and by seeing it thus reflected and gradually clarified. This is why so much of young love is conversation . . ." (Erikson, 1963, p. 262)

## Adulthood

Erikson describes a number of further stages of personality development. In young adulthood, the healthy individual has to achieve the capacity for closeness and intimacy through love, or else suffer a sense of isolation that will permit only shallow human relationships. In early middle age, she has to develop a sense of personal creativity that extends beyond her own self. This includes a concern for others, for her work, for the community of which she is a part. And toward the end of life, there is a final crisis during which each person has to come to terms with his or her own life and accept it for what it was, with a sense of integrity rather than of despair. Erikson eloquently sums up this final reckoning: "It is the acceptance of one's own and only life cycle as something that had to be and that, by necessity, permitted of no substitutes . . . healthy children will not fear life if their elders have integrity enough not to fear death" (Erikson, 1963, pp. 268–69).

### RECENT ATTEMPTS TO FIND COMMON STAGES

Erikson's developmental scheme is a literary and moving account of the human odyssey through life, but in what sense is it a true description? Are the crises he listed *the* crises through which all of us must pass, and are their characteristics what he described them to be? A number of modern investigators have studied adults at various stages of their life to find out what, if any, patterns are common to a given time of life. By and large, most of them have described a number of developmental periods that resemble some of Erikson's "ages of man" (Gould, 1978; Levinson, 1978). Others have tried to find similarities between youthful patterns and adult fulfillment when the same person is interviewed some thirty years later (Vaillant, 1977; see Chapter 18).

A stage of adult development that has received considerable attention from both Erikson and later authors is the so-called "mid-life transition" (which sometimes amounts to a mid-life crisis), in which the individual reappraises what she has done with her life thus far and may reevaluate her marriage and her career. It is a period when the individual begins to see physical changes that show that the summer of life is over and its autumn has begun, a recognition that may occur earlier in women than in men (in part, because of the psychological impact of menopause). There is a shift in the way one thinks about time, from "How long have I lived?" to "How much time do I have left?" Some investigators point out

*(Photograph by Eve Arnold, Magnum)*

that the middle-aged person is in the middle in more than one sense as she observes her children grow up and her own parents age and die:

> It is as if there are two mirrors before me, each held at a partial angle. I see part of myself in my mother who is growing old, and part of her in me. In the other mirror I see part of myself in my daughter . . . . (Neugarten and Datan, quoted in Colarusso and Nemiroff, 1981, p. 124)

### HOW UNIVERSAL ARE THE STAGES OF ADULT DEVELOPMENT?

There is enough consistency in the results obtained by various investigators of adult development to suggest that the stages and transitions they describe apply fairly widely to people in our time and place. But are they universal? When we considered various stage theories of child development, we asked whether these stages occur in all cultures. The same question can be asked about adult development. Is there a mid-life transition among the Arapesh? Does a Kwakiutl man of fifty go through an agonizing reappraisal of what he's done with his life to date? If the answer is no, then we have to ask ourselves what the various stages described by Erikson and other students of the adult life-span really are.

Thus far, there is little concrete evidence one way or the other, so we can only guess. Certain adult milestones are clearly biological. In all cultures, humans reach puberty, mate, have children, begin to age, go through female menopause

621

*The ages of man*  Jacob Blessing the Sons of Joseph *by Rembrandt, 1656 (Copyright by Staatliche, Kunstsammlungen Kassel. Photograph by M. Busing)*

or male climacteric, age still further, and finally die. But the kind of crises that confront persons at different points of the life cycle surely depend on the society in which they live.

An example of the effect of social conditions on adult crises is the transition into old age. Over a century ago in the U.S., different generations often lived close together as part of an extended family system. There was much less segregation by age than there is now; children, parents, and grandparents frequently lived under the same roof or close to each other in the same neighborhood. In times of economic hardship, older people contributed to the family's resources even when they were too old to work—by caring for the children of working mothers, helping with the housekeeping, and so on. Older people—especially women—had yet another function: they were often sought out for advice on matters of child rearing and homekeeping. But today, the elderly have no such recognized family role. They usually live apart, are effectively segregated from the rest of society, are excluded from the work force, and have lost their role as esteemed advisers. Given these changes, it follows that the transition into old age today is quite different from what it was 150 years ago. People still age as they did then—although the proportion of persons who live into their seventies has increased radically—but they view aging differently (Hareven, 1978).

Facts of this sort suggest that various aspects of the stages proposed by students of adult development may be quite specific to our society and can therefore not be said to be universal. But if so, can we say anything about the life cycle that goes beyond the narrow specifics of our own time and social condition? Perhaps the best suggestion comes from a lecture by Erikson in which he tried to define adulthood:

> . . . In youth you find out what you *care to do* and who you *care to be* . . . . In young adulthood you learn whom you *care to be with.* . . . In adulthood, however, you learn what and whom you can *take care of.* . . (Erikson, 1974, p. 124)

Seen in this light, the later phases of the life cycle can perhaps be regarded as the culmination of the progressive expansion of the social world that characterizes the entire course of social development from early infancy on. In a way, it is a final expansion in which our concern turns from ourselves to others and from our own present to their future (and in some cases, the future of all mankind).

This may or may not be a good description of what genuine adulthood *is*. But it seems like an admirable prescription for what it *ought* to be.

## SUMMARY

1. The infant's *socialization* begins with the first human bond he forms—his *attachment* to his mother (or other caregiver). Studies of infant humans and monkeys indicate that this attachment is not caused by the fact that the mother feeds them, but rather because she feels so "comforting." A separation from the mother generally leads to *separation anxiety.*

2. Developmental psychologists have tried to assess the quality of the child's attachment to the mother by observing the behavior of infants and young children in the "Strange Situation." There is some evidence that the quality of attachment at about fifteen months of age predicts behavior two years later, but there is some controversy as to whether this reflects a long-term effect of the early mother-child relationship or is based on other factors, such as persisting patterns in the mother-child relationship or some continuity of childhood temperament.

3. Some theorists have proposed that the attachment to the mother can only be formed during a *sensitive period* in early life, In part, this position derives from work on *imprinting* in birds. According to this view, if such an early attachment is not formed, later social development may be seriously impaired, as indicated by studies of motherless monkeys and children reared in institutions. But later work on monkey isolates and adopted children suggests that this impairment is not necessarily irrevocable.

4. The process of *socialization* continues with child rearing by the parents. Some important differences in the way children are reared depend on the dominant values of the culture of which the parents are a part. Modern attempts to explain the mechanisms that underlie socialization include *social learning theory* which emphasizes *modeling,* and *cognitive developmental theory* which emphasizes the role of understanding as opposed to imitation.

5. The evidence indicates that different modes of weaning or toilet training have little or no long-term effects. What seems to matter instead is the general home atmosphere, as shown by the effects of *autocratic, permissive,* and *authoritative-reciprocal* patterns of child rearing. On the other hand, how the parents treat the child is partially determined by the child's own characteristics, as suggested by studies on infant *temperament.*

6. One aspect of moral conduct concerns the *internalization* of prohibitions. According to some theorists, punishment is more likely to lead to such internalization if the threatened punishment fits the principle of *minimal sufficiency.* Another aspect of moral conduct involves altruistic acts. Studies of *empathy* suggest that some precursors of altruism may be present in early infancy.

7. The study of *moral reasoning* has been strongly affected by Piaget's cognitive developmental approach. An influential example is Kohlberg's analysis of progressive stages in moral reasoning. According to a later critique by Carol Gilligan, there are some important sex differences in moral orientation, with men emphasizing justice and women stressing human relationships and compassion.

8. Socialization plays a role in determining various senses of being male or female, including *gender identity, gender role,* and *sexual orientation.*

9. Certain psychological differences between the sexes may be based on biological differences. One is *aggression,* which tends to be more pronounced in men. Another is a tendency for males to perform better on spatial tests of mental ability than women do. Such biologically based differences—if any—are undoubtedly magnified by socially imposed gender roles. The importance of such roles is illustrated by the effects of *sex reassignment* in childhood.

10. Each of the three main theories of socialization—psychoanalysis, social learning theory, and cognitive developmental theory—tries to explain how social factors shape our sense of being male or female. Psychoanalysis asserts that the basic mechanism is *identification.* Social learning theory proposes that it is *imitation* of the parent of the same sex. Cognitive developmental theorists believe that identification comes after the child acquires gender identity, which presupposes an understanding of *gender constancy.* Some of these theoretical differences grow out of differences of emphasis. Psychoanalysis focuses on sexual orientation, social learning theory concentrates on gender role, and cognitive developmental theory is most interested in gender identity.

11. In the past, some psychiatrists regarded homosexuality as a psychological disorder, but this view is now largely discredited. Its causes are still unclear. Constitutional factors probably play a role, but some aspects of early childhood learning may also be relevant. Whatever its causes, this sexual orientation (no less than heterosexuality) is a fairly stable condition that can be changed only with difficulty, if at all.

12. Development continues after childhood is past. Some theorists, notably Erik Erikson, have tried to map later stages of development. One such stage is *adolescence,* which marks the transition into adulthood.

# PART V

# Individual Differences

*People are different. They vary in bodily characteristics such as height, weight, strength, and hair color. They also vary along many psychological dimensions. They may be proud or humble, adventurous or timid, gregarious or withdrawn, intelligent or dull—the list of psychological distinctions is very large. Thus far such individual differences have not been our main concern. Our emphasis has been on attempts to find general psychological laws that apply to all persons, whether in physiological function, perception, memory, learning, or social behavior. To be sure, we have occasionally dealt with individual differences, as in the discussions of handedness, color blindness, and variations in imagery. But our focus was not on these differences as such; it was rather on what they could tell us about people in general—on how color blindness could help to explain the underlying mechanisms of color vision or how variations in child rearing might help us understand some aspects of socialization. In effect, our concern was with the nature of humankind, not with particular men and women.*

*We now change our emphasis and will consider individual differences as a topic in its own right. We will first deal with the measurement of psychological attributes, specifically intelligence and personality traits. We will then turn to the discussion of psychopathology and attempts to treat it, a field in which the fact that people are in some ways different—sometimes all too different—is starkly clear.*

# CHAPTER 16

# Intelligence: Its Nature and Measurement

In twentieth-century industrialized society, especially in the United States, the description of individual differences is a flourishing enterprise that has produced a multitude of psychological tests to assess various personal characteristics, especially those that pertain to intellectual aptitude. This effort is a relatively recent phenomenon, for until the turn of the century most psychologists preferred to study the "generalized human mind" without worrying about the fact that different minds are not identical.

As we will see, the interest in individual differences grew in part from an effort to apply evolutionary ideas to humanity itself. But even more important was the social climate of the times, which provided a fertile soil for such concerns. The study of individual differences makes little sense in a society in which each person's adult role is fully determined by the social circumstances of his or her birth. In a caste society there is no need for vocational counselors or personnel managers. In such a society farmers beget farmers, soldiers beget soldiers, and princes beget princes; there is no point in administering mental tests to assist in educational selection or job placement. The interest in human differences arises only if such differences matter, if there is a social system that will accommodate them.

In a complex, industrialized society like our own, with its many different socioeconomic niches and some mobility across them, we have the precondition for a systematic assessment of human characteristics. Such a society will try to find a means, however imperfect, for selecting the proper person to occupy the proper niche.

Mental tests were meant to supply this means. They were devised as an instrument to help in educational and occupational selection, for use in various forms

*Francis Galton (1822–1911), a pioneer in the study of individual differences. (Courtesy National Library of Medicine)*

of personal guidance and diagnosis. As such, they are often regarded as one of the major contributions of psychology to the world of practical affairs. However, for this very reason, the discussion of test results and applications necessarily touches upon social and political issues that go beyond the usual confines of scientific discourse. Under the circumstances, it is hardly surprising that some of the questions raised by testing, especially intelligence testing, are often debated in an emotionally charged atmosphere. Should a student be denied admission to a college because of his or her scholastic aptitude test score? Are such tests fair to disadvantaged ethnic or racial groups? Are scores on such tests determined by heredity, by environment, by both? This chapter will not be able to provide definitive answers to all of these questions. Some involve judgments about social and political matters; others hinge on as yet unresolved issues of fact. Our primary purpose is to provide a background against which such questions have to be evaluated.

## MENTAL TESTS

Mental tests come in different varieties. Some are tests of **achievement;** they measure what an individual can do *now,* his present knowledge and competence in a given area—how well he understands computer language or how well he can draw. Other tests are tests of **aptitude;** they predict what an individual will be able to do *later,* given the proper training and the right motivation. An example is a test of mechanical aptitude, which tries to determine the likelihood that an individual will do well as an engineer after an appropriate training period. **Intelligence tests** are sometimes considered as tests of a very general cognitive aptitude, including the ability to benefit from schooling. Still another kind of test is a **test of personality,** which tries to assess an individual's characteristic behavior dispositions—whether she is generally outgoing or withdrawn, placid or moody, and so on.

We will begin our discussion by considering the nature of mental tests in general, regardless of what in particular they try to measure. We must begin by realizing that mental tests are in many ways different from tests used in medicine and the physical sciences. To be sure, there is a similarity on the face of it. A high score on a psychological test, such as a mechanical aptitude test, suggests a better than average ability for work in engineering; a certain reaction on chemical tests used by obstetricians indicates pregnancy. But there are some important differences as well. For one thing, the relation between the test result and what it signifies is much more tenuous in psychology than in the physical or biological sciences. To begin with, there is a difference in predictive accuracy. A high mechanical aptitude test score makes it more likely that the individual will succeed in engineering, while a certain chemical reaction on the obstetrician's test makes pregnancy a virtual certainty. More important yet is the fact that for most medical tests we have a much better understanding of why the test result signifies what it does. When a physician diagnoses the heart's condition from an electrocardiogram, the inference is fairly direct, for the test provides a graphic record of the heartbeat. Mental testers are usually in a less fortunate situation, for they can point to few theoretical links between their tests and what these tests try to measure. To understand the reasoning that underlies the construction and use of mental tests, we will have to take a detour and look at the general problem of variability and of its measurement.

## The Study of Variation

The study of how individuals vary from each other grew up in close association with the development of statistical methods. Until the nineteenth century, the term *statistics* meant little more than the systematic collection of various state records (*state*-istics) such as birth and death rates or the physical measurements of army recruits. In poring over such figures, the Belgian scientist Adolphe Quetelet (1796–1874) saw that many of them fell into a pattern. From this, he determined the ***frequency distribution*** of various sets of observations, that is, the frequency with which individual cases are distributed over different intervals along some measure. For example, he plotted the frequency distribution of the chest expansion of Scottish soldiers, noting the number of cases that fell into various intervals, from 33 to 33.9 inches, 34 to 34.9 inches, and so on (Table 16.1).

Table 16.1  QUETELET'S DISTRIBUTIONS OF CHEST MEASURES OF SCOTTISH SOLDIERS

| Measures of the chest in inches | Number of men per 10,000 |
| --- | --- |
| 33 | 4 |
| 34 | 31 |
| 35 | 141 |
| 36 | 322 |
| 37 | 732 |
| 38 | 1,305 |
| 39 | 1,867 |
| 40 | 1,882 |
| 41 | 1,628 |
| 42 | 1,148 |
| 43 | 645 |
| 44 | 160 |
| 45 | 87 |
| 46 | 38 |
| 47 | 7 |
| 48 | 2 |

### VARIABILITY

Two facts are immediately apparent. The scores tend to cluster around a central value. One of the most common measures of this central tendency is the ***mean,*** or average, which is obtained by summing all of the values and dividing by the total number of cases. But the clustering tendency is by no means perfect, for there is variability around the average. All Scottish soldiers are not alike, whether in their chest sizes or anything else. An important measure of variability in a distribution is the ***variance (V).*** This is computed by taking the difference between each score and the mean, squaring this difference, and then taking the average of these squared differences. For many purposes, a more useful measure of variability is the ***standard deviation (SD)*** which is simply the square root of the variance.*

Quetelet's main contribution was the realization that, when put on a graph, the frequency distributions of various human physical attributes have a characteristic bell-shaped form. This symmetrical curve approximates the so-called ***normal curve*** which had already been studied by mathematicians in connection with games of chance. The normal curve describes the probability of obtaining certain combinations of chance events. Suppose, for example, that someone has the patience to throw six coins for over a hundred trials. How often will the coins fall to yield six heads, or five, four, three, two, one, or none? The expected distribution is shown in Figure 16.1, which also indicates what happened when a dedicated statistician actually performed the experiment. As more and more coins are thrown on any one trial, the expected distribution will approach the normal curve (Figure 16.2).

According to Quetelet, the variability found in many human characteristics can be explained in similar terms. He believed that nature aims at an ideal value —whether of height, weight, or chest size—but that it generally misses the mark, sometimes falling short and sometimes overshooting. The actual value of an at-

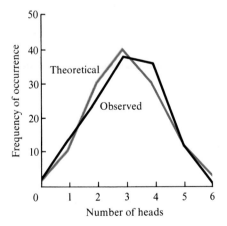

**16.1  Theoretical and observed distribution of number of heads in 128 throws of heads in 128 throws of six coins**  (*After Anastasi, 1958*)

* For a fuller description of these and other statistical matters which will be referred to in this chapter, see the Appendix, "Statistics: The Collection, Organization, and Interpretation of Data."

**16.2   The normal curve**   *(A) The probability of the number of heads that will occur in a given number of coin tosses. (B) When the number of coins tossed approaches infinity, the resulting distribution is the normal curve. The fact that this curve describes the distribution of many physical and mental attributes suggests that these attributes are affected by a multitude of independent factors, some pulling one way and some another.*

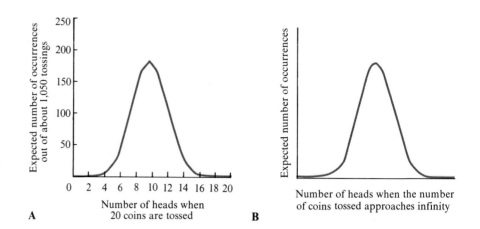

A

Number of heads when
20 coins are tossed

B

Number of heads when the number
of coins tossed approaches infinity

tribute such as height depends upon a host of factors, some of which lead to an increase, others to a decrease. But each of these factors is independent and their operation is determined by chance. Thus nature is in effect throwing a multitude of coins to determine any one person's height. Each head adds, say, a millimeter to the average, and each tail subtracts one. The result is a frequency distribution of heights that approximates a normal curve.

### VARIABILITY AND DARWIN

After Darwin published his *Origin of Species,* variability within a species was suddenly considered in a new perspective. Darwin showed that it provides the raw material on which natural selection can work. Suppose that the average finch on a particular island has a fairly long and narrow beak. There is some variability; a few finches have beaks that are shorter and wider. These few would be able to crack certain hard seeds that the other finches could not open. If these hard seeds suddenly become the primary foodstuffs in the habitat, the short-beaked finches might find themselves at a reproductive advantage. They would outlive and thus outbreed their long-beaked comrades and eventually a new species might be born (or more precisely, hatched). Seen in this light, variability is far from being an error of nature that missed the ideal mark as Quetelet had thought. On the contrary, it is the very stuff of which evolution is made (Figure 16.3).

### CORRELATION

Could this line of reasoning be applied to variations in human characteristics? It might, if these characteristics could be shown to be hereditary, at least in part. This assumption seemed reasonable enough for physical attributes of the kind that Quetelet had tabulated, but is it appropriate for mental characteristics such as intellectual ability? A half-cousin of Darwin's, Francis Galton (1822–1911) spent much of his life trying to prove that it is. Most of the subsequent work in the area rests on the statistical methods he and his followers developed to test his assertions.

An important part of Galton's program called for the assessment of the similarity among relatives. The trouble is that such relationships are not perfect. Children tend to be like their parents, but only to some extent. The problem was to

**16.3   Darwin's finches**   *In 1835 Charles Darwin visited the Galapagos Islands in the Pacific Ocean and observed a number of different species of finches. They eventually provided an important stimulus to his theory of natural selection, as he supposed that "one species had been taken and modified for different ends." The figure shows two of these finches. One has a rather narrow beak and is a woodpecker-like bird that lives in trees and feeds on insects. The other is a large-beaked seed-eater. (After Lack, 1953)*

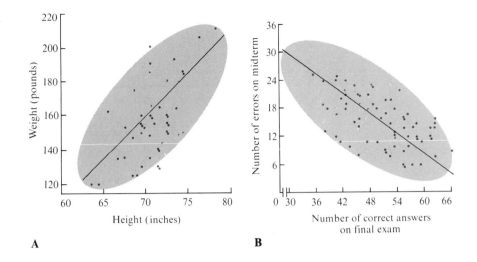

**16.4   Correlation**   *(A) A scatter diagram of the heights and weights of 50 male undergraduates. Note that the points fall within an ellipse which indicates the variation around the line of best fit. The correlation for these data was +.70. (Technically, there are two lines of best fit. One predicts weight from height; the other predicts height from weight. The line shown on the diagram is an average of these two.) (B) A scatter diagram of the test performances of 70 students in an introductory psychology course. The diagram plots number of errors in a midterm against number of correct answers on the final. The correlation was −.53. If errors (or correct answers) had been plotted on both exams, the correlation would of course have been positive.*

A                                              B

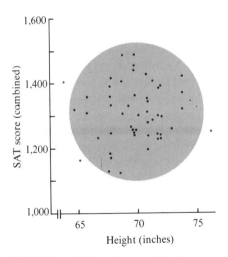

**16.5   A correlation of zero**   *A scatter diagram of the scholastic aptitude scores and the heights of 50 undergraduate males. Not surprisingly, there was no relation as shown by the fact that the points fall within a circle. The correlation was +.05, which for all essential purposes is equivalent to zero.*

find some measure of this relationship. Put more generally, the question was how one could determine whether a variation along one characteristic could be accounted for by a variation along another. The two characteristics might be the height of a father and that of his son. They might also be characteristics within the same individual such as a person's height and the same person's weight.

Take as an example an individual's weight. How is this related to his height? The first step is to construct a ***scatter diagram*** in which one axis represents weight and the other height. Each person will be represented by one point corresponding to his position along the weight and height axes (see Figure 16.4A). Inspection of the scatter diagram reveals that the two variables are related, for they covary: that is, as height goes up, so does weight. But this covariation, or ***correlation,*** is far from perfect. We can draw a ***line of best fit*** through the points in the scatter diagram, which allows us to make the best prediction of a person's weight given his height. But this prediction is relatively crude, for there is considerable variability around the line of best fit.

Galton and his students developed a mathematical expression that summarizes both the direction and the strength of the relationship between the two measures. This is the ***correlation coefficient*** which varies between + 1.00 and − 1.00 and is symbolized by the letter *r*. The plus or minus sign of the correlation coefficient indicates the direction of the relationship. In the case of height and weight this direction is positive: as height increases so does weight (16.4A). With other measures, the direction is negative: as the score on one measure increases, the score on the other declines (Figure 16.4B).

The strength of the correlation is expressed by its absolute value (that is, its value regardless of sign). A correlation of *r* = .00 indicates no relation whatsoever. An example might be the relation between a student's height and his scholastic aptitude score. If we plot the scatter diagram, the points will be arranged in a circle. There is no way of predicting a student's scholastic aptitude from his height, so there is no single line of best fit (Figure 16.5).

As the absolute value of *r* increases, the dots on the scatter diagram form an ellipse around the line of best fit. As the correlation goes up, the ellipse gets thinner and thinner. The thinner the ellipse, the less error there is as we try to predict the value of one variable (say, weight) when given the value of the other (say, height).

When the absolute value of *r* reaches 1.00 (whether + 1.00 or − 1.00), the ellipse finally becomes a straight line. There is no more variation at all around the line of best fit; the correlation is perfect and prediction is error-free. However, such perfect correlations are virtually never encountered in actual practice; even in the physical sciences there is bound to be some error of measurement.

While correlations are a useful index of the degree to which two variables are related, they have a limitation. The fact that two variables are correlated says nothing about the underlying causal relationship between them. Sometimes, there is none at all. Examples are correlations that are produced by some third factor. The number of umbrellas one sees on a given day is surely correlated with the number of people who wear raincoats. A Martian observing the human scene might conclude that umbrella-carrying causes raincoat-wearing or vice versa; our own earthly wisdom tells us that both are caused by rain.

## Evaluating Mental Tests

While the correlation techniques developed by Galton and his students were initially meant to investigate the extent to which relatives resemble each other, they were soon extended to other problems. One important application was to mental testing for which they provided the underlying statistical methodology.

A mental test is meant to be an objective yardstick to assess some psychological trait or capacity on which people differ (for example, artistic and mechanical aptitude; see Figures 16.6 and 16.7). But how can one tell that a given test actually accomplishes this objective?

### RELIABILITY

One important criterion of the adequacy of a test is its ***reliability,*** the consistency with which it measures what it measures. Consider a spring balance. If the spring is in good condition, the scale will give virtually identical readings when the same object is repeatedly weighed. But if the spring is gradually losing its elasticity, repeated weighings will give different values. If it does this, we throw away the scale. It has proved to be unreliable.

The same logic underlies test reliability. One way of assessing this is by administering the same test twice to the same group of subjects. The correlation between test and retest scores will then be an index of the test's reliability.

One trouble with the ***test-retest method*** is that the performance on the retest may be affected by what the subject learned the first time around. For example, some people may look up the answers to questions they missed. To avoid this problem, testers sometimes develop ***alternative forms*** of a test; if the two alternate forms are exactly equivalent, reliability can be assessed by using one form on one occasion and another on a second. Since any two halves of a single test can be considered "alternate forms," reliability is often measured by the ***split-half technique*** (correlating subjects' scores on, say, all of the odd items with their scores on all of the even items). If both halves correlate highly, we consider the test reliable; if they don't, we regard it as unreliable.

Most standard psychological tests now in use have ***reliability coefficients*** (that is, test-retest or split-half correlations) in the .90s or in the high .80s. Tests with lower reliability are of little practical use in making decisions about individuals.

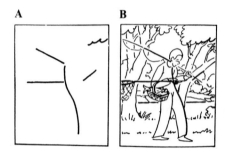

**16.6  A test of art aptitude**  *The person tested is presented with (A). Using the lines in this card as a start, he has to make a completed drawing. (B) A completed sample. The test score is based on ratings by an experienced art teacher. These scores correlated quite well (.66) with grades in a special art course for high-school seniors. (Cronbach, 1970b. Test item from the Horn Art Aptitude Inventory, 1953; courtesy Stoelting Co., Chicago)*

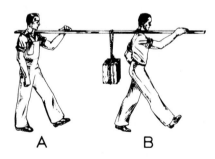

**16.7  A test of mechanical comprehension**  *One of the items asks, "Which man carries more weight?" (Sample item from the Bennett Test of Mechanical Comprehension; courtesy The Psychological Corporation)*

High reliability alone does not guarantee that a test is a good measuring rod. Even more critical is a test's *validity,* which is most simply defined as the extent to which it measures what it is supposed to measure.

Again consider the spring scale. If the spring is made of good steel, the scale may be highly reliable. But suppose someone decides to use this scale to measure *length.* This bizarre step will produce an instrument of high reliability but virtually no validity. It measures some attribute very precisely and consistently but that attribute is not length. As a test of length, the scale is invalid.

In the case of the scale, we can readily define the physical attribute that it is meant to measure and this lets us assess validity. But how can we define the psychological attribute which a mental test tries to assess?

*Predictive validity*   One approach is to consider the test as a *predictor* of future performance. If a test claims to measure scholastic aptitude, a score on that test should predict later school or college performance. The same holds for tests of vocational aptitude, which ought to predict how persons later succeed on the job. One index of a test's validity is the success with which it makes such predictions. This is usually measured by the correlation between the test score and some appropriate *criterion.* For scholastic aptitude, a common criterion is the grade-point average the student later attains. For vocational aptitude, it is some measure of later job proficiency. For example, aptitude tests for salespersons might be validated against their sales records.

Validity coefficients (that is, the correlations between test scores and criteria) for scholastic aptitude are generally in the neighborhood of .50 or .60, which means that the prediction is far from perfect. This is hardly surprising. For one thing, the tests probably don't provide a perfect index of one's "capacity" (ignoring for the time being just what this capacity might be). But even if they did, we would not expect validity coefficients of 1.00, for we all know that school grades depend on many factors in addition to ability (for example, motivation).

An important fact about validity coefficients is that their magnitude depends upon the *range of ability* within the group in which they are determined. As this range is narrowed, the correlation between test score and criterion declines. This relationship holds for all correlation coefficients. Consider the correlation between height and weight. If we choose to narrow the range by excluding jockeys and basketball players, the height-weight correlation will be reduced. If we narrow the range more drastically by, say, looking only at persons between 5'7'' and 5'8'', the correlation will become virtually insignificant.

The same phenomenon occurs in the field of testing. Scholastic aptitude tests do a reasonably good job in predicting high school and college grades. However, they tend to be less useful in predicting how a student will perform in graduate or professional school. The reason is that the postgraduates are already preselected. They have survived many years of schooling and are thus screened for academic ability, at least to some extent. As a result, the range of scholastic aptitude within this group is necessarily less than that found within the population at large. Since the differences in scholastic aptitude within this preselected group are relatively small, they are of less value in predicting future academic performance (Figure 16.8). But this does not mean that the test has no bearing on the prediction of fu-

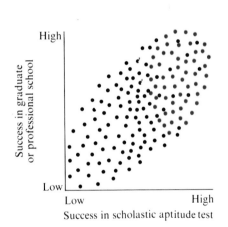

*16.8   The effect of preselection upon correlation*   *Hypothetical data which show the relation between some scholastic aptitude test taken in high school and success in graduate or professional school. When we look at the records of those who actually entered postgraduate schools (color), we find little if any relation to aptitude scores in high school. If there had been no preselection—that is, if every high school student eventually ended up in graduate or professional school—the resulting scatter diagram would include all dots (both black and color) and would indicate a sizable correlation. (After Cronbach, 1970a)*

ture performance. It may not be able to predict success in graduate or professional school for those who are already admitted. But it can be used for the larger, as yet, unselected population. For example, it may help a vocational guidance counselor in advising a high school student who is considering, say, a career in medicine (Cronbach, 1984).

*Construct validity*    Predictive validity is not the only way of assessing whether a test measures what it claims to measure. Another approach is to establish that the test has **construct validity** (Cronbach and Meehl, 1955). This is the extent to which the performance on the test fits into a theoretical scheme—or construct—about the attribute the test tries to measure. For example, suppose someone tries to develop a test to assess behavioral tendencies toward depression (see Chapter 19). The validity of such a test would not be established by correlating it with any *one* factor, such as feelings of helplessness. Instead, the investigator would try to relate the test to a whole network of hypotheses about depression. To the extent that the results do indeed fit into this larger pattern, they confer construct validity on the test. In terms of the medical analogy we used before, present-day chemical tests of pregnancy have both construct and predictive validity. They have construct validity because modern medical science knows enough about the hormonal changes during pregnancy to understand why the chemical reacts as it does. They also have predictive validity, for they correlate almost perfectly with the highly visible manifestations of pregnancy which appear a short time later.

STANDARDIZATION

To evaluate a test, we need one further item of information in addition to its reliability and validity. We have to know something about the group on which the test was **standardized.** A person's test score by itself provides little information. It can, however, be interpreted by comparing it with the scores obtained by other people. These other scores provide the **norms** against which an individual's test scores are evaluated. To obtain these norms, the test is first administered to a large sample of the population on which the test is to be used. This initial group is the **standardization sample.**

A crucial requirement in using tests is the comparability between the subjects who are tested and the standardization sample that yields the norms. If these two are drawn from different populations, the test scores may not be interpretable. Consider a scholastic aptitude test standardized on ten-year-olds in 1920. Its norms will surely not apply today to ten-year-olds whose schooling undoubtedly differs in many ways. There will be no way of evaluating a particular test score, for the comparison is with ten-year-olds today rather than seventy years ago.

A similar issue crops up when tests are administered to persons whose cultural backgrounds are different from that of the standardization sample. This problem is by no means hypothetical; examples are the cultural differences between ethnic and racial groups and between rural and urban dwellers. Some test items clearly discriminate in favor of one group or another. When urban schoolchildren were asked questions like "What is the largest river in the United States?" or "How can banks afford to pay interest on the money you deposit?" they did considerably better than rural schoolchildren of the same age. The difference was reversed for questions like "Name a vegetable that grows above ground" or "Why does seasoned wood burn more easily than green wood?" (Shimberg, 1929).

## Using Tests for Selection

Suppose we have a test of good reliability and reasonable validity. How is it used? One important application in our society is as a selection device. A well-known example is an aptitude test for pilot training developed by the Army Air Force during World War II. A large number of separate subtests were constructed for this purpose, including tests of motor coordination, reaction time, perceptual skills, and general intellectual ability. These subtests were administered to over 185,000 men who went through pilot training. The initial question was how each of these subtests correlated with the criterion—success or failure in training. The scores of each subtest were then weighted to produce a composite score that gave the best estimate of the criterion. The use of this composite pilot aptitude test score led to an appreciable improvement in trainee selection. Without the test, the failure rate was 24 percent. By using the test, the failure rate was cut to 10 percent. This was accomplished by setting a ***cutoff score*** on the test below which no applicant was accepted (Flanagan, 1947).

Given a reasonable validity coefficient, the use of tests evidently helps to reduce the number of selection errors. The overall number of such errors declines as the validity coefficient of the test increases. But some errors will always be present, for validity coefficients are never at 1.00; in fact, most vocational aptitude testers count themselves lucky if they manage to obtain validity correlations of .40 or .50.

The important point is that selection errors are of two kinds. On the one hand, there are "false accepts," persons who are accepted but who will fail. On the other hand, there are "false rejects," people who are rejected but who would have performed adequately. What determines which of the two kinds of errors will predominate? The answer depends upon the choice of the cutoff score. Suppose we decide to use a very stringent cutoff point. The result will be a marked reduction in the number of false accepts; but there is a price, an increased frequency of false rejects. We can reduce the number of false rejects by picking a lower cutoff score; but again there is a trade-off, a concomitant increase in the number of false accepts (Figure 16.9).

**16.9   Selection errors and cutoff scores**
*Applicants to pilot training are selected on the basis of an aptitude test. The line of best fit indicates the prediction of trainee performance from aptitude test score; the ellipse shows the variation around this line. The choice of a cutoff aptitude score, below which no applicant is accepted, determines the nature of selection errors. (A) A high cutoff score will increase the proportion of false rejects relative to false accepts. (B) A low cutoff score has the reverse effect.*

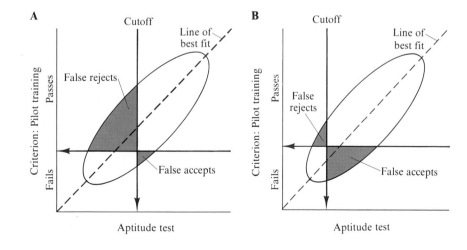

What cutoff score is the appropriate one? The answer hinges on the costs and benefits the selector assigns to each of the four possible outcomes: false accepts, false rejects, correct accepts (accepted applicants who succeed), and correct rejects (rejected applicants who would not have succeeded). These costs and benefits yield a *payoff matrix* similar to some we have already encountered (see Chapters 5 and 12).

Just what these costs and benefits are depends upon a number of social, economic, and institutional values. Let us consider only the selection errors. Which is the more harmful? It obviously depends. In selecting combat pilots, there is a premium on avoiding false accepts. Pilot training is extremely costly. A trainee who doesn't make the grade represents a serious loss: in instruction time, in tying up expensive equipment, and—in case of really extreme failure—in life and limb. From the point of view of the Air Force, a false reject is much less serious. A rejected applicant who would in fact have succeeded as a pilot is still perfectly useful as a member of the ground crew. Under the circumstances, a high cutoff score makes good sense. In other selection situations, however, the payoff matrix may be very different. Suppose that there is a serious shortage in a particular occupation, say, engineering. If the number of applicants to engineering schools is relatively low, the schools would be well advised to set a lower cutoff point on an engineering aptitude test. Given the increased need for engineers and the reduced pool of applicants, there are good reasons to minimize false rejects. Graduating a few additional engineers may now be worth the price of a larger number of student dropouts.

The payoff matrix that underlies a selection procedure obviously varies with the situation. It also varies according to one's perspective. The best example is the contrast between the institution that does the selecting and the applicant. A college with a large number of applicants might well decide to reduce the number of false accepts. But many applicants will see things very differently, especially if they have applied only to this one school. From their point of view, the worst error is to be falsely rejected (Table 16.2). This is not to say that the payoff matrices of selector and potential selectee are always different. Occasionally they are in harmony. In picking combat pilots, the Air Force wants to minimize the number of false accepts. But so do the applicants. When poor job performance may mean a fiery death, a high cutoff score is in the best interest of both parties.*

To conclude, the use of tests in selection involves several factors. To begin with, there is the question of how well the test predicts performance, whether in school or on the job. To answer this question we need to know the test's reliability and validity. But since prediction is necessarily imperfect, we have the further question of where to set the cutoff point. And this decision cannot be settled on the basis of the test alone. It is inextricably tied up with all kinds of value judgments that determine the payoff matrix for the possible outcomes.

---

* There is a formal similarity between the selection problem just discussed and the decision subjects have to make in a detection experiment. In a detection study, a subject can make two kinds of errors: "false alarms" (reporting a stimulus when in fact there is none) and "misses" (failing to report a stimulus when in fact there is one). False alarms are analogous to false accepts, while misses are analogous to false rejects. In both the selection problem and the detection experiment, the choice between yea and nay is partially determined by a cutoff value, which in turn depends on a payoff matrix (see Chapter 5).

Table 16.2  TWO PAYOFF MATRICES FOR ACCEPTING COLLEGE APPLICANTS (IN ARBITRARY UNITS)

*A. From the perspective of the college*

|  | Passes | Fails |
|---|---|---|
| Accept | *Correct accept (+ 5):*<br><br>Delighted | *False accept (− 5):*<br><br>Waste of resources |
| Reject | *False reject (− 1):*<br><br>Not too serious, for there are more applicants than openings | *Correct reject (+ 1):*<br><br>Satisfaction in having decided correctly |

*B. From the perspective of the applicant*

|  | Passes | Fails |
|---|---|---|
| Accept | *Correct accept (+ 5):*<br><br>Delighted | *False accept: (− 1)*<br><br>A wasted year but not completely since something was gained any way |
| Reject | *False reject (− 10):*<br><br>A calamity | *Correct reject (+ 1):*<br><br>OK, if really so |

## INTELLIGENCE TESTING

What is ***intelligence?*** In a crude sense, of course, we all have some notion of what the term refers to. The dictionary is full of adjectives that distinguish levels of intellectual functioning such as *bright* and *dull, quick-witted* and *slow.* Intelligence tests try to get at some attribute (or attributes) that roughly corresponds to such distinctions. But the test constructors did not begin with a precise conception of what it was they wanted to test. There was no consensus as to a definition of intelligence, and those definitions that were offered were usually so broad and all-inclusive as to be of little use. Intelligence was said to be a capacity, but what is it a capacity for? Is it for learning, for transfer, for abstract thinking, or judgment, comprehension, reason, or perhaps all of these? There was no agreement. Edward Thorndike suggested a first approximation according to which intelligence was to be defined "as the quality of mind . . . in respect to which Aristotle, Plato, Thucydides, and the like, differed most from Athenian idiots of their day." While this seemed sensible enough, it hardly went beyond the intuitive notions people had long before psychologists appeared on the scene (Thorndike, 1924).

## Measuring Intelligence

Given the difficulty in defining intelligence, devising tests for this hard-to-define attribute was an undertaking of a rather different sort from constructing a specialized aptitude test for prospective pilots. The pilot aptitude test has a rather clear-cut validity criterion. But what is the best validity criterion for intelligence tests? Since the nature of intelligence is unclear, we can't be sure of what the appropriate validity criterion might be.

But our theoretical ignorance notwithstanding, we do have intelligence tests, and many of them. They were developed to fulfill certain practical needs. We may not understand exactly what it is that they assess, but the test consumers—schools, armies, industries—want them even so. The fact is that for many practical purposes these tests work quite well.

### TESTING INTELLIGENCE IN CHILDREN

The pioneering step was taken by a French psychologist, Alfred Binet (1857–1911). As so often in the field of individual differences, the impetus came from the world of practical affairs. By the turn of the century, compulsory elementary education was the rule among the industrialized nations. Large numbers of schoolchildren had to be dealt with and some of them seemed mentally retarded. If they were indeed retarded, it appeared best to send them to special schools. But mere backwardness was not deemed sufficient to justify this action; perhaps a child's prior education had been poor, or perhaps the child suffered from some illness. In 1904, the French minister of public instruction appointed a special committee, including Binet, and asked it to look into this matter. The committee concluded that there was a need for an objective diagnostic instrument to assess each child's intellectual state. Much of what we now know about the measurement of intelligence comes from Binet's efforts to satisfy this need.

*Alfred Binet*   *(Courtesy National Library of Medicine)*

*Intelligence as a general cognitive capacity*   Binet and his collaborator, Théophile Simon, started with the premise that intelligence is a rather general attribute that manifests itself in many spheres of cognitive functioning. This view led them to construct a test that ranged over many areas. It included tasks that varied in both content and difficulty—copying a drawing, repeating a string of digits, recognizing coins and making change, explaining absurdities. The child's performance on all these subtests yielded a composite score. Later studies showed that this composite measure correlated with the child's school grades and with the teacher's evaluations of the child's intelligence.

Binet and other intelligence testers have sometimes been criticized on the ground that some—perhaps all—of their test items depend upon prior knowledge. One obviously cannot define a word without having seen or heard it, nor can one make change for a franc without exposure to arithmetic and French currency. But Binet did not regard this as a drawback. He felt that there is no such thing as pure, disembodied intelligence which develops independently of environmental input. In constructing his tests he tried to use only items whose content was in principle familiar to all of the children that he tested. He believed that once this condition is met, the test score makes sense. Each child has had some contact with a common culture; one assesses the children's underlying capacity by noting what they have picked up from this environment and how they can put it together in different ways.

*The intelligence quotient, IQ*  Binet made another assumption about intelligence. He believed that it develops with age until maturity is reached. Here too his ideas fit our intuitive notions. We know that an average group of six-year-olds is no intellectual match for an average group of eight-year-olds. It's not just that they know less; they're not as smart. This conception provided the basis for the test's scoring system.

Binet and Simon first gave the Form L-M test to a standardization sample composed of children of varying ages whose test performance provided the norms. Binet and Simon noted which items were passed by the average six-year-old, and so on. (Items that were passed by younger but not by older children were excluded.)

The resulting classification of the test items generated a ladder of tasks in which each rung corresponds to a number of subtests that were successfully passed by the average child of a given age. Testing a child's intelligence was thus tantamount to a determination of how high the child could ascend this ladder before the tasks finally became too difficult. The rung she attained indicated her **mental age** (usually abbreviated MA). If she successfully coped with all items passed by the average eight-year-old and failed all those passed by the average nine-year-old, her MA was said to be eight years. Appropriate scoring adjustments were made when the performance pattern did not work out quite as neatly; for example, if a child passed all items at the seven-year-old level, 75 percent of those at the eight-year-old level, 25 percent of those at the nine-year-old level, and

*A boy taking the Stanford-Binet (Form L-M)*  (Photograph by Mimi Forsyth/ Monkmeyer)

Table 16.3  REPRESENTATIVE TASKS FROM THE STANFORD-BINET (FORM L-M)

| Age | Task |
|---|---|
| 2½ | Points to toy object that "goes on your feet"<br>Names *chair, flag*<br>Can repeat two digits |
| 4 | "In daytime it is light, after night it is . . . ."<br>"Why do we have houses?" |
| 6 | "What is the difference between a bird and a dog?"<br>"An inch is short, a mile is . . . ."<br>"Give me _____ blocks" (up to ten) |
| 9 | "Tell me a number that rhymes with *tree*."<br>"If I buy 4 cents worth of candy and give the store keeper 10 cents, how much money will I get back?"<br>Repeats four digits in reversed order |
| 12 | Defines *skill, muzzle*<br>"The streams are dry _____ there has been little rain."<br>" 'In an old graveyard in Spain, they have discovered a small skull which they believe to be that of Christopher Columbus when he was about ten years old.' . . . What is foolish about that?"<br>Repeats 5 digits in reversed order |

SOURCE: Modified from Terman and Merrill, 1973.

***Block design test***  *This twelve-year-old girl is arranging blocks so that they will match the pictured arrangement on the card. This block design test is one of the twelve parts of a children's version of Wechsler's intelligence test, the WISC-R (Wechsler's Intelligence Scale for Children-Revised), which provides scores that indicate overall IQ, verbal IQ, and performance IQ. (Photograph by Nancy Hays/Monkmeyer)*

none beyond. Table 16.3 presents representative test items from the Stanford-Binet (Form L-M), an American adaptation of the Binet-Simon test. This test was replaced by the Stanford-Binet Intelligence Scale: Fourth Edition, in 1986.

The MA assesses an absolute level of cognitive capacity. To determine whether a child is "bright" or "dull" one has to compare her MA with her chronological age (CA). To the extent that her MA exceeds her CA, we regard the child as "bright" or advanced; the opposite is true if the MA is below the CA. But a particular lag or advance clearly has different import depending upon the child's age. A six-year-old with an MA of three is obviously more retarded than a ten-year-old with an MA of seven. To cope with this difficulty, a German psychologist, William Stern (1871–1938), proposed the use of a ratio measure, the ***intelligence quotient*** or ***IQ***. This is computed by dividing the MA by the CA. The resulting quotient is multiplied by 100 to get rid of decimal points. Thus,

$$IQ = \frac{MA}{CA} \times 100$$

By definition, an IQ of 100 indicates average intelligence; it means that the child's MA is equivalent to his CA and thus to the average score attained by his age-mates in the standardization sample. By the same token, an IQ greater than 100 indicates that the child is above average; an IQ of less than 100 that he is below average.

Stern's quotient measure has various drawbacks. The major problem is that the top rung of Binet's mental age ladder was sixteen (in some later revisions of the Stanford-Binet the ceiling was higher). In some ways this makes good sense, for intelligence does not grow forever, any more than height does. But since CAs keep on rising beyond the MA ceiling, the IQ (defined as a quotient) cannot help but decline. Consider the IQ of an adult. If her CA is 48 and her MA is 16, the use

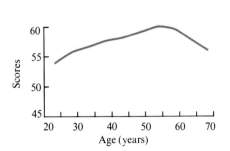

Scores

45 50 55 60

20 30 40 50 60 70
Age (years)

**16.17 Mental test scores as related to age when studied by a variation of the longitudinal method** *The scores, which cover a fifty-year age range, were obtained over a seven-year period from several adult populations, the youngest of which was twenty at the beginning of the study and the oldest in their sixties. (After Schaie and Strother, 1968)*

*Fluid and crystallized intelligence* It appears that the precipitous decline of intelligence with age reported by earlier investigators was an artifact that was avoided by the longitudinal comparisons. But does this mean that there is no decline until age sixty or even later? Further work has shown that it depends on just what abilities are being tested. Many facets of verbal abilities show little decline until age seventy. The results of tests of vocabulary are even more encouraging to those of later years; there is no drop in vocabulary even at age eighty-five (Blum, Jarvik, and Clark, 1970). In contrast, nonverbal abilities that are tapped by such tests as the Progressive Matrices decline earlier, usually around age forty (Green, 1969). The most pronounced drops are found for tests that depend on quick recall, especially when there is no memory organization that can help retrieval. An example from everyday life is memory for names, whose gradual worsening is bemoaned by many persons as they get older. An example from the laboratory is the word fluency test, in which the subject has two minutes to write down as many words as he can think of that start with a particular letter. Such mental calisthenics are best left to the young; declines in word fluency are very steep and are seen as early as thirty (Schaie and Strother, 1968).

Some authors believe that the different age curves obtained for different subtests of intelligence scales reflect an important distinction between two underlying intellectual abilities (Cattell, 1963). One is **fluid intelligence**, which is the ability to deal with essentially new problems. The other is **crystallized intelligence**, which is the repertoire of information, cognitive skills, and strategies acquired by the application of fluid intelligence to various fields.

Examples of tasks that emphasize fluid intelligence are scrambled sentences and number series. Consider the set of words shown below:

*Tree pick an climbed man our apple the to*

When a person is asked to rearrange these words so as to make a meaningful sentence, she can't just rely on what she has previously learned but has to reason it out. The same holds for number series, such as the one below in which the task is to find the number that is next in the series:

*3   8   12   15   17*

In contrast, tasks that primarily rely on crystallized intelligence are exemplified by tests of vocabulary (e.g., what is *amenuensis*?) or of calculation (e.g., $6 \times 7 - 4 \times 5 = ?$).

According to the theory, fluid intelligence declines with age, beginning in middle adulthood or earlier. But crystallized intelligence does not drop off. On the contrary, it will continue to grow until old age if the person is in an intellectually stimulating environment. From the point of view of actual functioning in middle age and beyond, the drop in the one ability may be more than compensated for by the increase in the other.* The older person has "appropriated the collective intelligence of the culture for his own use" (Horn and Cattell, 1967). By so doing, he has not only amassed a store of knowledge larger than the one he had when he was younger, but he has also developed better ways of organizing this knowledge, of approaching problems, and of filing new information away for later use.

---

* Some of these issues are still a matter of debate (see Horn and Donaldson, 1976; Baltes and Schaie, 1976).

These cognitive achievements are similar to those we discussed in Chapter 8 in which we considered the distinction between "masters" and "apprentices." The masters have chunked and organized the material at a different level than the apprentices. On balance, then, the slight loss in fluid intelligence can be tolerated if made up for by an increase in crystallized intelligence.

## THE INFORMATION-PROCESSING APPROACH TO INTELLIGENCE

What has the psychometric approach taught us about intelligence? We know that the instruments devised by Binet and his successors can diagnose the extreme form of intellectual deficit we call mental retardation; they can also predict school success, at least as defined in a middle-class, twentieth-century industrial world. We have considered the hypothesis that these instruments measure an underlying set of abilities, of which some are more and some less general. Finally, these tests show marked changes in performance over age—an initial sharp improvement followed by a moderate decline on some subtests in later years.

Many of these results are of considerable practical importance. Since tests are used in diagnosis, guidance, and selection, they often have an important impact on individual lives. But has any of this helped us to understand the processes that underlie more or less intelligent behavior? Does it explain why individuals fail (or succeed) on a particular problem? The psychometric approach provides tools whereby we can compare how people perform relative to each other; their relative standing gives us a measure of a presumed attribute we call intelligence. But it provides little insight into the mechanisms that lead to problem solution or to failure. It tells us that some people are better and others worse at the various mental tasks that intelligence tests pose, but it doesn't tell us why.

A number of psychologists believe that the answer will come from an analysis of the relevant cognitive operations that intelligence tests call for. The basic idea is to link differences in test performance to differences in the way individuals process information as they perceive, attend, learn, remember, and think. This general approach to the analysis of individual differences in mental abilities is reminiscent of similar attempts in the study of various aspects of cognition and cognitive development (see Chapters 7, 8, and 14).

### Simple Cognitive Correlates

Some investigators have concentrated on relatively simple cognitive operations and have tried to correlate differences in the way these are carried out with differences in intelligence-test performance. In the main, they have concentrated on processes that involve memory.

An example is looking up well-known items in long-term memory. When we hear the word *mouse* and recognize it, we presumably make contact with some memory file that includes all sorts of information about small, bewhiskered, long-tailed rodents that go by that name. The same memory file is presumably accessed when we see the word *mouse* in print and also when we see a picture of a mouse. Many cognitive psychologists believe that this process of accessing well-established memories is a fundamental step in many mental tasks. To speak and understand, we must look up words in a mental dictionary; to read, we must look up the letters. According to some investigators, differences in the speed with which people perform this memory look-up operation may be one of the factors that underlie differences in intelligence-test performance (Hunt, Lunneborg, and Lewis, 1975; Hunt, 1976, 1985). Each individual look-up will only take a few milliseconds. But those milliseconds will soon add up in tasks that involve thousands of such look-up operations, for example, reading or arithmetic.

To test this general hypothesis, a number of investigators have used the ***lexical identification task***, which is designed to measure the speed with which words are accessed in long-term memory. A subject is presented with strings of letters, such as *bread* and *blead*, and is asked to decide whether the string is a word or is not as quickly and accurately as he can. His speed of lexical access is measured by the time it takes him to make this decision.* The results of several studies show that memory look-up times assessed by this and similar methods are shorter in persons who do well on conventional tests of verbal intelligence than in those who do less well. The difference is especially marked when the comparison is between normal subjects and groups at the lower extremes of the population, such as brain-damaged persons (Hunt, 1978). But to a lesser extent, such differences also have been obtained within normal populations; for example, between college students with high and low scores on tests of verbal intelligence or on tests of reading comprehension (Hunt, Lunneborg, and Lewis, 1975; Jackson and McClelland, 1975, 1979).

## Complex Cognitive Components

Simple cognitive operations such as memory look-up may be correlated with intelligence-test performance, but a number of investigators doubt that studying these operations will go very far in helping us to understand what intelligence really is. Intelligence may depend on the smooth operation of certain simple, rock-bottom cognitive processes, but it is not equivalent to them. Consider the performance of a ballet dancer. She can't dance if she can't walk and run and jump, but dancing is more than walking, running, and jumping. It involves the intricate organization of various higher-level motor actions such as pirouettes, combinations of ballet steps, and so on. These cannot be performed without the lower-level operations (that is, walking, running, and jumping), but this doesn't mean that the two levels are identical. Much the same may be true for intelligence. To reason about a problem in arithmetic, one has to recognize the numbers (e.g., 1 means "one") and one may have to retrieve the multiplication table (e.g., $2 \times 3 = 6$). But recognizing numbers and retrieving from the multiplication table are not the same as reasoning with arithmetic.

Such considerations led to attempts to study some of the higher-level rather than the lower-level cognitive processes that underlie intelligence. In attempts to discover what some of these higher-level processes are, several investigators turned to items in standard intelligence tests. Their object was to find the ***cogni-***

---

* Strictly speaking, it is the time he takes to make this yes-no decision minus the time it takes him to react to the strings when no decision is asked for.

*tive components* such tasks call for, most of which would presumably be higher-level processes (Sternberg, 1977).

One such undertaking was Robert Sternberg's analysis of ***analogical reasoning.*** Analogy problems are a staple of many intelligence tests, and they are often regarded as a particularly good measure of Spearman's *g*-factor. Below are several examples:

> *Hand* is to *foot* as *finger* is to (*arm, leg, thumb, toe*).
> *Pistol* is to *bow* as *bullet* is to (*gun, sword, arrow, blade*).

Or, to give a somewhat more difficult item:

> *Washington* is to *one* as *Lincoln* is to (*five, ten, twenty*).

Sternberg's interpretation of how such problems are solved has the step-by-step quality of a computer program (in this it resembles other information-processing approaches to thinking and problem solving; see Chapter 8). He believes that the problem is solved in separate stages (which he calls components). The first step is the identification of some potentially relevant attributes of each term (e.g., both Washington and Lincoln were presidents; Washington was the first and Lincoln the sixteenth president). After this, the subject tries to infer some possible relations between the first and second terms of the analogy (e.g., Washington was the first president, and his portrait is on the one-dollar bill), and then she tries to map possible relations between the first and third terms (both Washington and Lincoln were presidents and both appear as portraits on U.S. currency). The last step is to decide which of the alternatives offered is the appropriate term to complete the analogy. To accomplish this, the subject takes the various relations he inferred for the *Washington–one* pair and tries to apply them to create an appropriate match for *Lincoln.* One such relation is *president–the first.* This doesn't fit, for Lincoln was the sixteenth president, not the fifth, tenth, or twentieth. But there is another relation that is appropriate—*portrait of Washington–one-dollar bill.* This works, for Lincoln's portrait is on the five-dollar bill and "five" is one of the options. At this point, everything matches up, the subject makes his choice, and the analogy is solved (Sternberg, 1977; see Figure 16.18).

Will an analysis of complex cognitive task components help us to understand what intelligence really is? To answer this question, we have to know whether the components isolated by Sternberg and other investigators have some reasonable level of generality. Do the same components underlie performance on different intellectual tasks? Do they correlate reasonably well with traditional measures of intelligence? A considerable amount of research is and has been directed at these issues (for overviews, see Sternberg, 1982, 1985).

Some promising results come from a study in which subjects were presented with various tests of reasoning (Sternberg and Gardner, 1983). Some were analogies such as:

> *Mouth* is to *taste* as *eye* is to (*help, see*).
> *Tree* is to *forest* as *soldier* is to (*army, general*).

(for which the correct answers are *see* and *army* respectively.)

Others were classification tasks in which the subject had to indicate with which of two pairs of words the word at the left fits best, for example:

> *Italy:*    (a) *Germany, France* (b) *Vietnam, Korea*
>
> *oven:*    (a) *refrigerator, air conditioner* (b) *furnace, stove*

**16.18** *Washington is to One as Lincoln is to Five.*

(In which the correct choices are *Germany, France* and *furnace, stove* respectively.)

In all cases, the subjects had to respond as quickly and accurately as they could. There was a remarkable correspondence between decision times on these and similar tasks and the subjects' scores on several standard psychometric tests of abstract reasoning. The average correlation was −.65, a very encouraging result for the complex cognitive components theory. (As before, the correlation was negative because shorter decision times correspond to higher reasoning scores.)

## Strategies and Intellectual Functioning

Concepts derived from information processing have provided still another approach to the study of individual differences in intellectual functioning. This approach asks whether subjects use various flexible mental **strategies** for solving problems, for learning, and for remembering. We have previously discussed such cognitive strategies in the context of cognitive development (see Chapter 14). As we saw, a normal adult can master memory tasks that are generally beyond the reach of a normal six-year-old. One reason is that the adult uses a well-developed repertoire for solving problems, for learning, and for remembering. Suppose she is asked to memorize unrelated materials, such as the words

*tulip plumber tiger sweater lily tailor daisy*
*raincoat monkey butcher zebra jacket.*

She will surely do her best to rehearse this list of items and try to impose some kind of order upon it. For example, she might try rhythmic grouping, say, by repeating the items in threes, as in "*tulip plumber tiger . . . sweater lily tailor . . . daisy raincoat monkey . . .*" and so on. Or she might try to file the words in a mental catalogue according to their semantic categories, first the flowers, then the occupations, then the animals, as in "*tulip, lily, daisy . . . plumber, tailor, butcher . . .*" and so on. Any of these organizational devices will help her do much better in later tests of recall.

### STRATEGIES AND MENTAL RETARDATION

The utilization of such cognitive strategies may account for some of the intellectual differences between adults. Much of the evidence comes from studies in the use of strategies for remembering (see Chapter 7). Such strategies, if they exist at all, are much more primitive in retarded subjects who attack memory tasks with little or no resort to organization. Mentally retarded persons are less likely to rehearse, to group items in a list, or to show recall clustering by semantic categories (Brown, 1974; Campione and Brown, 1977; Campione, Brown, and Ferrara, 1982). Similar results have been found in young children (Flavell and Wellman, 1977).

### TRYING TO TEACH THE MISSING STRATEGIES

Is there any way of teaching retardates some of the strategies for problem solving and remembering that they so grossly lack? This question has important applications: if the answer is yes, then some aspects of retardation may be remediable. The results of some investigations have given a glimmer of hope. They have showed that mildly retarded subjects can be trained to rehearse; for example, by being required to repeat the items cumulatively and aloud (Brown, Campione, Bray, and Wilcox, 1973). This induced rehearsal leads to recall performance virtually identical to that of adults.

These results would be extremely encouraging except for one discordant note. According to many investigators, the newly acquired strategies are often abandoned shortly after they are taught. Furthermore, they tend not to be generalized to tasks other than the one in which they were acquired (Campione and Brown, 1977). An example is training in the use of semantic categories, which shows little transfer to new lists with different verbal materials (Bilsky, Evans, and Gilbert, 1972).

Does this mean that trying to teach retarded persons cognitive strategies is essentially fruitless? A number of investigators have shown that the answer is no. For the newly taught strategies *will* transfer if the retarded person is also explicitly taught that they can and should be used in other situations. Suppose he is trained to use a particular mode of rehearsal; for example, grouping the items in a list by threes, and repeating them out loud. He will then have to be carefully reminded to use this technique on each trial. He'll also have to be trained to use the same technique with different lists and somewhat different methods of presentation. If this is done carefully enough, the strategy will be learned and will show a reasonable degree of a transfer (Campione, Brown, and Ferrara, 1982). Similar techniques have been employed to help schoolchildren who are not retarded but are poor at learning from texts (Brown, Campione, and Day, 1981).

### STRATEGIES FOR USING STRATEGIES

Why is it that retarded persons and young children are so narrow in their use of the strategies they are taught so that they won't generalize them without slow and explicit instruction? If retardates learn to remember a set of names by rehearsing them aloud, why don't they apply the same principle to a shopping list? According to several writers, what is lacking is a "master plan" for dealing with memory tasks in general, a strategy for using strategies (Flavell, 1970). Normal adults adopt this higher-order strategy as a matter of course whenever they try to learn. They know that remembering telephone numbers, or traffic directions, or the names of the twelve cranial nerves, are at bottom similar memory tasks. They also know that trying to learn them means using some aids to learning—the lower-order strategies of rehearsal, rhythmic and semantic grouping, or whatever. Both young children and retardates lack this general insight. They don't recognize what all memory tasks have in common and what they all require for their mastery. Young children will get it in time; retardates may never attain it.

As we look back, it is clear that we are still far from an understanding of the processes that underlie differences in intellectual performance. To put it another way, we have taken only a few tentative steps toward the construct validation of intelligence tests. Psychologists concerned with the study of cognitive processes have provided us with some promising leads, including the notion of cognitive components and the role of various strategies that young children and mentally retarded persons lack. But these are only guideposts for the future. Thus far, we have no general theory of intelligence. We may be able to measure intelligence, but as of yet we don't know what it really is.

## NATURE, NURTURE, AND IQ

While it is far from clear just what intelligence tests really measure, this state of affairs has not deterred psychologists—nor indeed, the general public—from making intelligence-test performance one of the major foci of the nature-nurture controversy, debating it with a stormy passion rarely found in any other area of the discipline (see Block and Dworkin, 1976; Eysenck vs. Kamin, 1981; Fancher, 1987).

### Some Political Issues

The vehemence of the debate over intelligence-test performance is understandable considering that mental testing is a field in which the concerns of the scientist impinge drastically upon those of the practical world. In our society, those who are well off tend to do better on intelligence tests than those who are disadvantaged. The same holds for their children. What accounts for this difference? There is some tendency for social groups to be biased in favor of different answers to this question. This bias was especially marked some seventy years ago when the prevailing social climate was much more conservative. Then—and to a lesser extent even now—advantaged groups were more likely to believe that intelligence is largely inherited. This assertion was certainly comforting to those who benefited from the status quo since it suggested they got what they "deserved."

In contrast, spokesmen for the disadvantaged took a different view. To begin with, they often disparaged the tests themselves, arguing that the tests are not fair to their own subculture. In addition, they argued that intellectual aptitudes are much more determined by nurture than nature. In their view, differences in intelligence, especially those between different ethnic and racial groups, are determined predominantly by environmental factors such as early home background and schooling. Seen in this light, the children of the poor obtain lower test scores, not because they inherit deficient genes, but rather because they inherit poverty.

These contrasting views lead to different prescriptions for social policy. An example of the impact of a hereditarian bias is the rationale behind the United States immigration policy between the two World Wars. The Immigration Act of 1924 set definite quotas to minimize the influx of what were thought to be biologically "weaker stocks," specifically those from Southern and Eastern Europe. To prove the genetic intellectual inferiority of these immigrants, a congressional committee pointed to their army intelligence-test scores, which were indeed substantially below those attained by Americans of Northern European ancestry.

In actual fact, the differences were primarily related to the length of time that the immigrants had been in the United States prior to the test; their average test scores rose with every year and became indistinguishable from native-born Americans after twenty years of residence in the United States. This result undermines the hypothesis of a hereditary difference in intelligence between, say, Northern and Eastern Europeans. But the congressional proponents of differential immigration quotas did not analyze the results so closely. They had their own reasons for restricting immigration, such as fears of competition from cheap labor. The theory that the excluded groups were innately inferior provided a convenient justification for their policies (Kamin, 1974).

*"Immigration Restriction. Prop Wanted."*

**Anti-immigration sentiment in the United States**  *A cartoon that appeared in the January 23, 1903, issue of the* Philadelphia Inquirer *calling for more restrictive immigration laws. (Courtesy of the New York Public Library)*

**659**

A more contemporary example of the relation between psychological theory and social policy is the argument over the value of compensatory education programs for preschool children from disadvantaged backgrounds. Such programs have been said to be failures because they often don't lead to improvement in later scholastic performance. Assuming this is true (and it may well not be), the question is why. A highly controversial paper by Arthur Jensen suggested that the difference in the intellectual performance of the advantaged and the disadvantaged groups is partially caused by a genetic difference between the groups. Given this hereditarian position, Jensen argued that environmental alterations can at best mitigate the group difference; they cannot abolish it (Jensen, 1969).

Jensen's thesis has been vehemently debated on many counts, some of which we will discuss below. For now, we will only note that the failure of any given program (assuming it was really a failure) does not prove the hereditarians' claim. Perhaps the preschool experience that was provided was not of the right sort; perhaps it was inadequate to counteract the overwhelming effects of ghetto life (Hunt, 1961). In any case, there is by now a growing consensus that Jensen and others have underestimated the effectiveness of preschool education on school performance in later years (Zigler and Berman, 1983). Such preschool experiences may or may not raise the childrens' intelligence-test scores.* But further analyses have shown that, regardless of their effect on IQ scores, many such programs have had positive effects on the childrens' school performance in later years. Thus low-income children who have participated in such programs seem to perform more acceptably in later grades (from fourth to twelfth grades) than children who had no such experience; they were less likely to be held back in grade, less likely to drop out of school, and so on (Lazar and Darlington, 1982).

## Genetic Factors

Thus far, our emphasis has been on the social and political aspects of the nature-nurture issue in intelligence, the considerations that bias people to take one or another side of the issue. But while it is interesting to know what people prefer to believe about the world, our primary concern is with what the world is really like. What is the evidence about the contributions of heredity and environment in producing differences *within* groups (for instance, among American whites) and *between* groups (for instance, between American whites and blacks)?

### GENETIC TRANSMISSION

Before turning to the relationship between intelligence-test performance and genetic endowment, let us review a few points about the transmission of genetic characteristics, some of which were discussed in a previous chapter (see Chapter 14, pp. 542–43).

---

* Some preschool experiences apparently do seem to raise intelligence-test scores, both here and in underdeveloped regions elsewhere in the world, especially if they are accompanied by health measures, nutritional supplements, and various efforts to help the mother through job training, remedial education, and the like (e.g., McKay, Sinisterra, McKay, Gomez, and Lloreda, 1978; Garber and Heber, 1982). Other programs were less successful, especially when evaluated some years after the preschool experience (see Coleman et al., 1966; Bronfenbrenner, 1975).

*Phenotype and genotype* A key distinction in any discussion of hereditary transmission is that between *phenotype* and *genotype*. The phenotype corresponds to the overt appearance of the organism—its visible structure and behavior. But this phenotype is by no means equivalent to the organism's genotype, which describes the set of the relevant genes. Each genetic instruction is carried out by two corresponding genes, one from each parent. If one member of a gene pair is *dominant* while the other is *recessive*, the first will mask the effect of the other, thus producing a difference between phenotypic expression and the underlying genotype. Another way in which a genotype may be kept from overt expression is by the interaction between genotype and environment. This interaction is especially important during the early stages in the organism's development since a particular genetic command can only be executed if certain physical characteristics (oxygen concentration, hormone levels, temperature) both within and outside of the developing body are within a certain range.

As an example, consider the dark markings on the paws, tail, and eartips of a Siamese cat. These markings are not present at birth, but they appear gradually as the kitten matures. The genealogical records kept by cat breeders leave no doubt that these markings in the mature animal are determined by heredity. But this does not mean that they emerge independently of the environment. The dark markings will only appear if the kitten's extremities are kept at their normal temperature, which happens to be lower than that of the rest of the animal's body. If the extremities are deliberately warmed during early kittenhood by such devices as leggings and tail- and earmuffs, they will not turn darker—in apparent defiance of the creature's genotype (Ilyin and Ilyin, 1930).

This example underlines the fact that genes do not operate in a vacuum. They are instructions to a developing organism, instructions that will be followed only within a given range of environmental conditions. It therefore makes no sense to talk of heredity alone or environment alone, for there is no trait that does not depend upon both. There can be no organism without a genotype, and this genotype cannot ever express itself independently of the environment.

*The inheritance of behavior* There is ample evidence that many behavioral characteristics are affected by hereditary makeup. Basset hounds are relatively lethargic, German shepherds are relatively excitable, and the offspring of their cross-matings have temperaments in between (James, 1941). Some behavioral tendencies seem to be determined by a single gene. An example is the response to intense, high-pitched noises in mice. Some mice are relatively unaffected by such stimuli while others react with violent epileptic seizures. Breeding experiments have shown that this proneness to seizures is carried by a single recessive gene (Collins and Fuller, 1968).

An illustration of a human psychological characteristic that is determined by a single gene is a severe form of mental retardation, *phenylketonuria* or *PKU*. In the United States, about one baby in every fifteen thousand is born with this defect. PKU is caused by a deficiency in an enzyme that allows the body to transform *phenylalanine,* an amino acid (a building block of proteins), into another amino acid. When this enzyme is missing, phenylalanine is converted into a toxic agent that accumulates in the infant's bloodstream and damages his developing nervous system. Analyses of the incidence of PKU among the siblings of afflicted children and among others in their family trees indicate that this disorder is produced by a single recessive gene.

**661**

Although PKU is of genetic origin, it can be treated by appropriate environmental intervention. The trick is a special diet that contains very little phenylalanine. If this diet is introduced at an early enough age, retardation can be minimized, or even eliminated.

This result demonstrates the fallacy of the popular believe that what is inborn is necessarily unchangeable. The genes lay down certain biochemical instructions that determine the development of a particular organ system. If we understand the genetic command clearly enough, we may eventually find ways to circumvent it. In the case of PKU, we are already on the way to doing so (McClearn and DeFries, 1973).

*Polygenic inheritance*   Most of the preceding discussion concerned hereditary traits that are for the most part produced by the action of one gene pair. Such characteristics are usually all-or-none, such as being brown-eyed or blue-eyed. But what about attributes that vary continuously, such as height or intelligence, which partially depend on genetic factors? The answer is ***polygenic inheritance***, in which the trait is controlled not by one but by many gene pairs. Take height. Some gene pairs pull toward increased stature, others toward lesser stature; the individual's ultimate genetic potential for height (for now, ignoring environmental effects) is then determined by the combined action of all the height-controlling gene pairs. To the extent that intelligence (or any other psychological attribute that varies continuously) is partially determined by hereditary factors, the same logic applies to it.

GENETICS AND IQ

How can we find out whether differences in human intelligence (at least as measured by intelligence-test performance) have a genetic basis? To do so, we have to infer the underlying genotypes from the observable phenotypic behavior. One strategy is to examine the similarities between relatives, an approach that dates back to Francis Galton. Galton found that eminence (which he measured by reputation) runs in families; eminent men were more likely to have eminent relatives than the average person (Galton, 1869). Similar results have been repeatedly obtained with intelligence-test scores. For example, the correlation between the IQs of children and parents, or between the IQs of siblings, runs in the neighborhood of .45 (Bouchard and McGue, 1981). From Galton's perspective, such findings document the inheritance of mental ability. But the environmentalist has a ready reply. Consider eminence. The relatives of an eminent person obviously share his or her social, educational, and financial advantages. As a result, there is a similarity of environmental background, as well as an overlapping set of genes. The same argument applies to the interpretation of the correlations between the IQs of close relatives.

A similar problem arises in another connection. IQs tend to be fairly stable; the ten-year-old with an IQ of 130 will probably get a roughly similar score at age fifteen. Supporters of the genetic theory of intelligence have often argued that this constancy of the IQ shows that intelligence tests measure an inborn capacity, "native intelligence," which is an essentially unalterable characteristic of an individual and is genetically based. This argument has been used as a justification of such educational practices as early assignment to one or another school track. But IQ constancy is no proof that intelligence is fixed or inborn. To the extent that this constancy occurs, it only demonstrates that a child tends to maintain his relative standing among his age-mates over time. This may be because of a genetically given attribute that remains unchanged with age. But it may also be because the child's environmental advantages stay pretty much the same as time goes on. If a child is born in a slum, the odds are pretty good that she will still be there at twelve; the same holds if she is born in a palace. Once again, the evidence is inconclusive.

During the last fifty years, psychologists have developed a variety of research designs that were meant to disentangle hereditary and environmental factors. We will consider two main attempts to accomplish this end: (1) the study of twins, and (2) the study of adopted children.

*Twin studies* **Identical twins** originate from a single fertilized egg that splits into two exact replicas which then develop into two genetically identical individuals (see Figure 16.19). In contrast, **fraternal twins** arise from two different fertilized eggs. Each of two eggs in the female reproductive tract is fertilized by a different sperm cell. Under the circumstances, the genetic similarity between fraternal twins is no greater than that between ordinary siblings. Since this is so, a comparison between identical twins and fraternal twins of the same sex is of considerable interest, if one is willing to assume that the twins' environments are no more similar if they are identical than if they are fraternal. Given this premise, it follows that if identical twins turn out to be more similar on some trait than fraternals, one can conclude that this trait is in part genetically determined.

One review summarizes the results of several dozens of studies. The overall result shows that the correlation between the IQs of identical twins is substantially larger than that between the IQs of fraternal twins. Based on roughly 10,000 twin

**16.19  Identical twins**  *Photographs of a pair of identical twins taken at 18 months, 5, 15, and 50 years. (Photographs courtesy of Franklin A. Bryan)*

Table 16.8   CORRELATIONS BETWEEN THE IQS OF FAMILY MEMBERS

| | |
|---|---|
| Identical twins reared together | .86 |
| Fraternal twins reared together | .60 |
| Siblings reared together | .47 |
| Child and natural parent by whom child is reared | .42 |
| Child and biological mother separated from the child by adoption | .31 |
| Child and unrelated adoptive mother | .17 |

SOURCE: Data on twins, siblings, and children reared with natural parents from Bouchard and McGue, 1981; data on adopted children from Horn, Loehlin, and Willerman, 1979.

pairs in all, the average correlations are .86 for identicals and .60 for fraternals (Bouchard and McGue, 1981). Some further findings on familial similarity in IQ scores are presented in Table 16.8.

On the face of it, this pattern of results seems like clear-cut evidence for a genetic component in the determination of IQ. But a number of criticisms have been leveled at these and related studies. One argument bears on the assumption that the similarity in the environments of identical and fraternal twins is essentially equal. But is it really? Since identical twins look alike, there may be a tendency to treat them the same way. Ultimately, parents and teachers may develop the same expectations for them. In contrast, fraternal twins are no more or less similar in appearance than ordinary siblings and may thus evoke a more differentiated reaction from others. If this is so, the comparison of the IQ correlations between identical and fraternal twins is not as neat a test of the nature-nurture issue as it seemed at first (Anastasi, 1971; Kamin, 1974).

In a study designed to meet this criticism, over three hundred twins were classified as identical or fraternal according to two criteria. One was by a comparison of twelve blood-type characteristics. This is a reliable and objective method for assessing genotype identity. To be judged identical, both members of a twin pair must correspond on all of the twelve indices. Another criterion involved the subjects' own belief in whether they are identical or fraternal. This belief is presumably based on how similar the twins think they are and how similarly they feel that they are treated. In a sizable number of twins this subjective judgment did not correspond to the biological facts as revealed by the blood tests. Which of the two ways of classifying a twin is a better predictor of the similarity in intelligence-test scores? The results suggest that the primary determinant is the true genotype. When the classification was by blood tests, there was the usual effect; identical twins scored more similarly than did fraternals. But when the classification was based on the twins' own judgments, this effect was markedly reduced. This result suggests that the greater intellectual similarity of identical as compared to fraternal twins is not an artifact of different environments. The best guess is that the effect occurs because intelligence-test performance is in part genetically determined (Scarr and Carter-Saltzman, 1979).

*Adopted children*   Another line of evidence comes from studies of adopted children. One study was based on three hundred children who were adopted immediately after birth (Horn, 1983; Horn, Loehlin, and Willerman, 1979, 1982). When these children were later tested, the correlation between their IQs and those of their *biological* mothers (whom they had never seen) was greater than the corresponding correlation between their IQs and those of their *adoptive* mothers (.28 versus .15). Other investigators have shown that this pattern persists into adolescence. When the adopted child is tested at age fourteen, the correlation between

to grow on his farm next year, adding that it's difficult to make both ends meet . . . and "I vomited yesterday" and "What day is it today?" . . . And if you let him go on, he will never stop. . . . (Edmonds, *The Characters of Theophrastus*, 1929, pp. 48–49)

Even more influential than such literary efforts were those of the playwrights. The very origin of the word *personality* suggests a possible relationship between the dramatic rendering of character and the psychologists' attempts to describe and understand it. The word comes from *persona,* the mask that Greek actors wore to indicate the character that they played.

In their comic drama, the Greeks and the Romans tended to think of people as *types,* a tradition that has continued in various forms to the present day. Their comedy created a large cast of stock characters: the handsome hero, the pretty young maiden, the restless wife, her jealous husband, the angry old man, the sly servant, the panderer, the kind-hearted prostitute, the boastful soldier, the pedant, and so on. Many of these types were resurrected in later times and other countries. An example is the comic theater of Renaissance Italy, the *commedia dell' arte,* which boasted a large stable of such stock characters, each invariably played by the same actor, and always with a mask that indicated who he was. While modern movie and television actors usually don't wear masks (the Lone Ranger is one exception), they often represent stock characters even so. The hero and villain of the Western and the busybody and conniving schemer of the television soap opera are only a few of such instantly recognizable types.

Over the ages, there have been many discussions of the appropriate conception of dramatic and literary character. One concerned the use of type characters in drama and literature. Some critics argued that such characterizations are necessarily flat and two-dimensional and could not possibly do justice to an individual; in reality, even the most passionate lover is not just passionate, for he surely has other attributes as well. They therefore felt that drama and literature should avoid all such stock characters and instead only present fully rounded, complex characters, such as Hamlet, who are essentially like no one else. Such rounded characters are as difficult to describe perfectly as a person in real life, and are therefore capable of surprising us (Forster, 1927). But other critics disagreed and felt that while simplified types could not possibly do full justice to any individual, they accomplished another and equally important aim: they showed what all people of a certain kind have in common rather than that which distinguishes them as individuals (Johnson, 1765).

Other arguments concerned the relative importance of internal versus external forces in determining what a character does. Some critics insisted that all dramatic action ultimately springs from within and grows out of the character's own essential nature, while others disagreed and pointed to the role of the external situation, as in the case of realistic modern dramas, such as *Death of a Salesman,* whose heroes do what they do because their social or economic situation forces them to. Yet another issue concerns the character's self-knowledge. Do her actions spring from goals of which she is aware, or is she reacting to unconscious forces that she herself does not recognize? (Bentley, 1983).

Some of these arguments between different schools of drama and literature are mirrored in current debates between different psychological theories of personality. As we will see, the drama of types is a distant cousin of modern **trait theory,** which holds that personality is best understood by the description and analysis of underlying personality traits (see this chapter, pp. 688–92). The insistence that

A

B

***Characters in 16th and 17th century Italy's Commedia dell' arte*** *(A) Pantalone, the rich, stingy, old merchant, who is invariably deceived by his servants, his children, and his young wife. (B) Pulcinella, a sly and boisterous comic. (Courtesy Casa Goldoni, Venezia; photographs by Paul Smit, Imago)*

675

characters be rounded and to some extent unpredictable would be congenial to a *humanistic approach* to personality, which maintains that what is most important about people is how they achieve their own selfhood and actualize their human potentialities (see Chapter 18, pp. 732–39). The insistence that a character's action is prompted by external circumstances is related to some formulations of the *behavioral approach* (sometimes called the behavioral-cognitive approach), which defines personality differences by the way in which different people act and think about their actions, and insists that these acts and thoughts are produced by the situation that the individuals face now or have faced on previous occasions (see Chapter 18, pp. 722–32). And the belief that characters may act because of unconscious impulses is of course a dominant view of *psychodynamic theory,* which argues that the crucial aspects of personality stem from deeply buried, unconscious conflicts and desires (see Chapter 18, pp. 713–22).

We will refer back to some of the issues raised by the representation of dramatic character in both this and the following chapter, because they will provide us with a useful metaphorical framework within which to approach our present topic.

Before turning to a detailed discussion of these four orientations, we should make a preliminary distinction. Some of these orientations focus on personal*ity* (so to speak, in the singular). They look for the laws that explain how the various aspects of our psychological functioning—the way we think and feel and desire and act—are put together to form the patterning we call personality. Such approaches tend to focus on the factors that govern personality formation *in general;* as a result, they are much more likely to focus on what Jim and John have in common than on what they do not. Other approaches are really perspectives on personal*ities* (so to speak, on personality in the plural). Their emphasis is on how various personalities *differ,* on what makes Jim different from John and why.

Needless to say, all orientations to personality are concerned with both human sameness and human difference, with personality considered in both the singular and the plural. But as we will see, their emphases differ. Our own focus, both in this and in the following chapter, will be on those aspects of these theoretical orientations that describe and try to explain the differences between persons.

Before turning to these theories of personality, we must first consider some of the methods by which differences in personality have been assessed.

## METHODS OF ASSESSMENT

There is an implicit assumption that underlies Theophrastus's sketches and any drama that uses character types, and that assumption is shared by most subsequent authors who have concerned themselves with personality: The personality patterns ascribed to their characters were assumed to be essentially consistent from time to time, and from situation to situation. The hero was generally heroic, the villain villainous, and the garrulous man kept on talking regardless of who listened (or rather, tried not to listen). Some of the traits by which modern students of personality describe people are more subtle than those that define the stock characters of the classical or Renaissance stage, but for many investigators the key postulate of this *trait theory* still exists. They assume that these traits characterize a person's behavior in a variety of situations. This is just another way of saying that a knowledge of an individual's personality traits will permit us to pre-

***Masks in modern theater***  *Masks are sometimes employed in modern drama in an allusion to their early use in classical times. (From a 1986 production of Harrison Birtwhistle's opera* The Mask of Orpheus *at the English National Opera; © Catherine Ashmore, London)*

**Character types in the Nō drama of Japan** *In the traditional Nō drama of Japan, character is indicated by a mask. The mask shown in the figure is that of a mystical old man with godlike powers. Before donning the mask, the actor who performs this part must go through various rituals of purification, because after he puts it on, the actor "becomes" the god. (Photograph by George Dineen/ Photo Researchers)*

dict what he is likely to do, even in situations in which we have never observed him (Allport, 1937).

Personality tests were devised in an attempt to supply the information that makes such prediction possible. In a way, they are analogous to an actor's audition; the director asks him to try out for a part by reading a page or two from a scene. Such an audition is a test that tries to determine (by no means perfectly) whether the actor *can play* a certain part. In contrast, a personality test is a test that tries to determine (again, far from perfectly) whether a person *is* that part.

## Structured Personality Tests

As in the case of intelligence measurement, the impetus for the development of personality tests came from the world of practical affairs. But the parallel is even closer than that, for both kinds of tests began as instruments to determine certain undesirable conditions. Binet's test was originally designed to identify mentally retarded children. The first personality test had a parallel diagnostic aim. It was meant to identify emotionally disturbed United States Army recruits during World War I. This test was an "adjustment inventory" consisting of a list of questions that dealt with various symptoms or problem areas (for instance, "Do you daydream frequently?" and "Do you wet your bed?"). If the subject reported many such symptoms, he was singled out for further psychiatric examination (Cronbach, 1970a).

The parallel between tests of intelligence and those of personality ends when we turn to the question of how these tests are validated. Binet and his successors had various criteria of validity: teachers' evaluations, academic performance, and, perhaps most important, chronological age. It turns out that validity criteria are much harder to come by in the field of personality measurement.

### THE MMPI: CRITERION GROUPS FROM THE CLINIC

To provide an objective validity criterion, some later investigators turned to the diagnostic categories developed in clinical practice. Their object was to construct a test that could assess a person's similarity to this or the other psychiatric criterion group—hysterics, depressed patients, schizophrenics, and so on. The best-known test of this sort is the **Minnesota Multiphasic Personality Inventory,** or **MMPI,** which first appeared in 1940 and is still one of the most widely used personality tests on the current scene, both in clinical practice and research (Lanyon and Goldstein, 1982). It was called multiphasic because it was developed to assess a number of psychiatric patterns simultaneously.

*Constructing the MMPI*   The authors of the MMPI began by compiling a large set of test items taken from previously published inventories, from psychiatric examination forms, and from their own clinical hunches. These items were then administered to several patient groups with different diagnoses as well as to a group of normal subjects. The next step was to eliminate all items that did not discriminate between the patients and the normal controls and to retain those items that did. The end result was the MMPI in substantially its present form—an inventory of 550 items, the responses to which can be analyzed by reference to ten major scales. The score on each of these scales indicates how the subject's answers compare with those of the relevant criterion group (Table 17.1).

Table 17.1   SOME MMPI SCALES WITH REPRESENTATIVE EXAMPLE ITEMS*

| Scale | Criterion group | Example items |
|---|---|---|
| Depression | Patients with intense unhappiness and feelings of hopelessness | "I often feel that life is not worth the trouble." |
| Paranoia | Patients with unusual degree of suspiciousness, together with feelings of persecution and delusions of grandeur | "Several people are following me everywhere." |
| Schizophrenia | Patients with a diagnosis of schizophrenia, characterized by bizarre or highly unusual thoughts or behavior, by withdrawal, and in many cases by delusions and hallucinations | "I seem to hear things that other people cannot hear." |
| Psychopathic deviance | Patients with marked difficulties in social adjustment, with histories of delinquency and other asocial behaviors | "I often was in trouble in school, although I do not understand for what reasons." |

* In the example items here shown, the response appropriate to the scale is "True." For many other items, the reverse is true. Thus, answering "False" to the item "I liked school" would contribute to the person's score on the psychopathic deviance scale.

*Using the MMPI*   In actual practice, interpreting an MMPI record is a complicated business. Clinicians don't merely look at the absolute scores obtained on any one scale. Instead, they consider the various scale values in relation to each other. This is most easily done by inspecting **score profiles** which present the scores on every scale in graphic form (Figure 17.1). An example is the interpretation of scores on the so-called depression scale. This consists of items which dif-

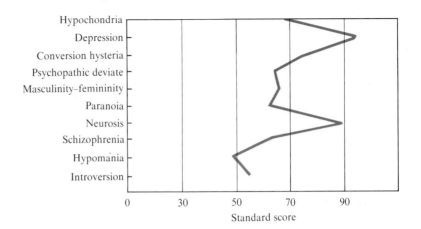

**17.1 MMPI profile** *The profile is of an adult male seeking help in a community health center. The scales are those described in Table 17.1. The scores are based on the performance of the standardization group. Scores above 70 will occur in about 2.5 percent of the cases; scores above 80 in about .1 percent. The profile strongly suggests considerable depression and neurotic anxiety. (After Lanyon and Goldstein, 1971)*

ferentiated a group of patients diagnosed to be in a depressive state from normal persons. But a high score on this scale alone tells little more than that the patient is very unhappy. If we want to know more about the nature of this disturbance, we have to look at the profile as a whole (Meehl, 1956).

*Validity scales* One trouble with self-administered personality inventories is that the subjects can easily misrepresent themselves. To cope with this and related problems, the originators of the MMPI added a set of further items that make up several so-called validity scales. One is a simple lying scale. It contains items like "I gossip a little at times" and "Once in a while I laugh at a dirty joke." The assumption is that a person who denies a large number of such statements is either a saint (and few of those take personality tests) or is lying. Another validity scale consists of a number of bizarre statements like "There are persons who are trying to steal my thoughts and ideas" and "My soul sometimes leaves my body." To be sure, some of these statements are accepted by severely disturbed psychiatric patients, but even they endorse only a small proportion of them. As a result, we can be reasonably sure that a person who checks an unusually large number of such items is either careless, or has misunderstood the instructions, or is trying to fake psychiatric illness. If the score on these and similar validity scales is too high, the test record is discarded as invalid.

### THE CPI: CRITERION GROUPS FROM NORMAL LIFE

While the MMPI can be employed to test normal subjects, it has some limitations when used in this way. The main problem is that the criterion groups that defined the scales were composed of psychiatric patients. This prompted the development of several new inventories constructed according to the same logic that led to the MMPI, but with normal rather than with pathological criterion groups. One of the best known of these is the *California Psychological Inventory,* or *CPI.* The CPI is especially aimed at high school and college students. It tests for various personality traits such as dominance, sociability, responsibility, sense of well-being, and so on.

As an example of how scales for these and other traits were derived, consider *dominance.* High school and college students were asked to name the most and the least dominant persons within their social circles. The persons who comprised these two extremes were then used as the criterion groups that defined the dominance-submission dimension. From here on, the procedure paralleled that which led to the construction of the MMPI. A large set of items (many of them taken from the MMPI) was administered to both groups, and those items that differentiated between the groups were kept to make up the dominance scale. Other traits were defined in a similar manner and several validity scales were added to assess the subjects' test-taking attitudes (Gough, 1975).

### THE VALIDITY OF PERSONALITY INVENTORIES

The originators of the MMPI, the CPI, and other personality inventories based on criterion groups, took considerable pains to provide their instruments with a solid, empirical foundation. To evaluate the success of their efforts, we must look at the validity of these tests.

*Predictive validity*   The usual way to assess validity is to determine the degree to which a test can predict some real-world events. There is evidence that personality tests do indeed have some predictive power. For instance, among college women during the fifties and sixties, the sociability scale of the CPI correlated with how often the subject went out on dates and whether she joined a sorority. Other scales correlate with how subjects are rated by their peers (Hase and Goldberg, 1967).

The trouble is that while personality inventories can predict, their efficiency in doing so is quite low. The correlations between test scores and validity criteria are generally in the neighborhood of +.30. This contrasts poorly with the validation coefficients of intelligence tests (usually assessed by correlating IQ and academic performance), which are about +.50. The contrast is even sharper if we compare the usefulness of these personality tests with the predictive efficiency of common-sense measures such as relevant past behavior in related situations. The result is simple. The best predictor of future performance (for example, psychiatric breakdown, delinquency) is past performance. A dramatic and widely cited example is provided by a study which showed that the thickness of a mental patient's file folder correlates +.61 with the probability of his rehospitalization following his release (Lasky et al., 1959).

*Construct validation*   The low predictive validity coefficients of personality inventories may not be grounds for as much chagrin as one might assume at first. For what most personality tests try to get at is some *hypothesized* psychological entities, such as traits, that are presumed to underlie overt behavior. In effect, the trait—whether sociability, or psychopathic deviance, or whatever—is a theoretical concept devised by the psychologist in an effort to make sense, not just of one set of observations, but of many. To validate such a construct, one has to devise and test hypotheses about the relation between the underlying trait and various behavioral effects. This is **construct validation,** an approach we have discussed previously, in the context of intelligence testing (see Chapter 16).

Construct validation is often built upon a set of diverse relationships between the test scores and rather different behavioral manifestations. An example is provided by the psychopathic deviance scale (Pd) of the MMPI, a scale originally based upon those items that differentiated a group of delinquents from other groups (see Table 17.1). Not too surprisingly, normal (that is, nondelinquent)

Assessing the validity of Rorschach interpretation is a difficult task. We will consider this issue together with similar ones raised by the other major projective technique in current use, the **Thematic Apperception Test,** or **TAT** developed by Henry Murray and his associates (Morgan and Murray, 1935).

### THE THEMATIC APPERCEPTION TEST (TAT)

To Rorschach, content was a secondary concern. To the originators of the TAT, it was the primary focus, for their emphasis was on a person's major motives and preoccupations, defenses, conflicts, and ways of interpreting the world.

*Administration* The TAT test materials are a number of pictures of various scenes (Figure 17.4). The subject is asked to tell a story about each picture, to describe what is happening, what led up to the scene, and what the outcome will be.

*Interpretation* In clinical practice, TAT interpretation is usually a rather free-wheeling affair. Each story suggests a hypothesis which is then checked and elaborated (or discarded) by looking at later stories. The desired end product is a picture of the person's major motives and conflicts, pieced together by interpreting the TAT stories in the light of all previously available information, of which the case history is probably the most important.

An illustration of this impressionistic and global approach to TAT interpretation is provided by the case of Morris, a twenty-six-year-old securities salesman, one of whose conflicts centered upon his sex life. He was puzzled why sex was relatively unimportant to him, and he had at least as many homosexual as heterosexual experiences. Condensations of two of his TAT stories are presented below:

**17.4 A picture of the type used in the TAT**

> *Picture of a naked man . . . in the act of climbing a rope up or down:* The man is a eunuch in Ethiopia . . . and there this man Ahab, as he was called by the Arabs, lived for 20 years as servant in the sheik's harem. Surprisingly, instead of developing the usual lackadaisical castrated attitude that comes to eunuchs . . . this Ahab was constantly tormented by the presence of all the women and his complete inability to do anything about it . . . he decided he must escape . . . threw a rope out of the window . . . and let himself down. . . . Fate was against him. He got to the bottom: four of the servants of the Arab chief were there, ready to grab him. . . . He died in the most unique way the chief could think up . . . in a room with a couple of colonies of red ants.

> *Picture of a young man standing with downcast head buried in his arm. Behind him is the figure of a woman lying in bed:* "Jesus, what a shape! Positively indecent! . . ." His first thought was that the man was "going to the bathroom to make sure he doesn't catch anything!" He then said that the scene was in Hawaii, where a man and a girl were "sitting and drinking on a terrace." After "six drinks, they stagger upstairs and land on the bed"; a couple of minutes later, the man goes to the bathroom to throw up. (Janis, Mahl, Kagan, and Holt, 1969, pp. 700–701)

In both these stories heterosexual love comes to an unhappy end. The same holds true for two other stories in this person's TAT record that contained heterosexual themes. There is also the fact that each of these four stories was set in such distant places as Ethiopia and Hawaii. To the TAT interpreter this meant that Morris was unable to imagine any heterosexual involvement in the here and now. In contrast, homosexual themes occurred in contemporaneous settings close to home. A related fact concerns another TAT picture which shows a male embrac-

**685**

**17.5 Projective techniques for use with children** *Special projective techniques have been developed for use with children. An example is the Children's Apperception Test, CAT, that consists of ten pictures in which all characters are animals. (Courtesy Leopold Bellak)*

**17.6 The Blacky pictures** *A projective technique in which the subject tells a story about 12 cartoons featuring a little dog Blacky who is shown in a number of settings corresponding to different stages of the psychoanalytic theory of development. Pictured here is the cartoon depicting Oedipal conflicts. (From Blum, 1949; courtesy Psychodynamic Instruments, Ann Arbor, Michigan)*

ing a female. But in Morris's story, the sexes are misperceived. The male is seen as a mother, the female as the mother's weak and pudgy son who has to lean on her. This confusion of sexual identity goes together with the theme of castration that is quite explicit in one of the two stories summarized here. According to the TAT interpreter, this theme is linked to Morris's life history. His father deserted the family when Morris was only eight, a fact which may have contributed to Morris's unsure sense of being a heterosexual male (Janis et al., 1969).

Interpretations of this sort are very beguiling. They suggest facets of an individual's personality which might never have been revealed otherwise. But are these facets actually there? To what extent can we trust the projective tester's interpretations? Are these interpretations equally astute when the tester does not have the benefit of hindsight, when she does not know the salient facts of the subject's life history?

*Offshoots of the TAT* A number of further projective techniques are essentially offshoots of the TAT. Some were specially devised for use with younger children, such as the **Children's Apperception Test,** which consists of a number of cartoon pictures of animals or humans in various family situations (see Figure 17.5, from Bellak, 1986). Others were said to mirror classical Freudian issues, such as the Blacky test, which depicts a little dog, Blacky, in a number of settings that were meant to evoke the unconscious conflicts of the oral, anal, and Oedipal stages (Blum, 1950; see Figure 17.6). Still other TAT derivatives focus on just one particular motive, for example the need for achievement or for power (e.g., McClelland, Atkinson, Clark, and Lowell, 1953; McClelland, 1975), in contrast to the original TAT, which tries to assess the entire gamut of an individual's needs and conflicts.

VALIDITY OF PROJECTIVE TECHNIQUES

By now, there must be nearly ten thousand published articles that are explicitly devoted to the Rorschach and the TAT. Considering all this effort, the upshot has been disappointing. According to some experts, these techniques have some limited validity; according to others, they have little or none (Holt, 1978; Kleinmuntz, 1982).

*Validity and the Rorschach* Individual Rorschach indices—especially those that don't refer to content—show little or no relation to external validity criteria. In one study of psychiatric patients, over thirty different measures from the Rorschach records (for instance, the number of responses using the whole inkblot) were studied to see whether there was any relation to later diagnosis. There was none. Similar results apply to nonpsychiatric populations. For example, a preponderance of human movement responses is said to indicate creativity, but a group of eminent artists were no different from ordinary persons in this regard (Zubin, Eron, and Shumer, 1965).

Studies of this kind have sometimes been criticized as too "atomistic," for they compare individual indices one by one in various criterion groups. Wouldn't it be better to use the test as a whole, and to allow the judge to read the entire record verbatim (or even to administer the test) and then predict the criterion on the basis of this overall, "global" knowledge? One study that meets these conditions used twelve eminent Rorschach experts who tried to assess various aspects of the personalities of various patients on the basis of their complete Rorschach records. The external criterion was the pooled judgment of a number of psychiatrists who read each patient's case history, obtained in six or so interviews of several hours each. The mean correlation between the Rorschach experts' predictions and the psychiatrists' judgments was +.21. Global assessment on the basis of the verbatim record evidently has some modest validity (Little and Shneidman, 1959).

Some recent efforts by John Exner suggest that the clinical usefulness of the test may be increased by using a more rigorous system for administration, scoring, and interpretation (Exner, 1974, 1978; Exner and Clark, 1978). The system he developed to accomplish this has evidently led to a considerable improvement in the test's reliability, as shown by a large increase in its test-retest stability. Whether it will also increase the test's diagnostic power (that is, its validity) is as yet unclear.

*Validity and the TAT*    The TAT has fared no better than the Rorschach in those validity studies that assessed its ability to predict psychiatric diagnosis. In one case study, the TAT was administered to over a hundred male veterans, some in mental hospitals and others in college. There was no difference between normals and patients, let alone between different psychiatric groups (Eron, 1950).

While such results indicate that the TAT may have drawbacks as a diagnostic tool for psychiatric classification, the test does seem to have some validity for more limited purposes. A number of studies have shown that the TAT may be a fair indicator of the presence of certain motives, though probably not of all. One group of investigators worked with subjects who had not eaten for various periods of time. When presented with TAT-like pictures, some of which suggested food or eating, hungry subjects came up with more stories whose plots concerned hunger or food-seeking than a control group of sated subjects (Atkinson and McClelland, 1948). Related findings have been obtained with various other motives, including aggression, sexual arousal, the need for achievement, and so on. The success of these efforts represents a kind of construct validation of the TAT as an assessment device for at least some motives.

*Projective techniques and incremental validity*    Given the verdict of these various validation studies, many projective experts have become convinced that their devices are not really tests at all, but instead are really adjuncts to a clinical interview (Zubin, Eron, and Shumer, 1965). Rorschach and TAT scores make little sense to a practitioner who has not administered the tests personally or at least read the verbatim records. They are also hard to interpret without a knowledge of the subject's background and life history, but proponents of these techniques argue that when they are used as part of the total clinical evaluation, they help to provide a richer understanding of the person.

We have seen that when the Rorschach or TAT are used in this manner, they do indeed have some modest predictive validity for diagnosis. But according to some critics, predictive validity is not enough; the real issue is whether these tests have **incremental validity** (Meehl, 1959). The question is how much additional (that is, incremental) information these techniques provide over and above that which is contained in case histories and similar data that have to be gathered anyway. To give and score a Rorschach and/or a TAT is very time-consuming; since this is so, these tests ought to provide a reasonable increment in information. But the available evidence suggests otherwise. Several studies have shown that when clinical psychologists were asked to make inferences about a subject's personal characteristics, they were just as accurate with only the case history to go on as they were when provided with additional data in the form of the Rorschach or TAT records (Kostlan, 1954; Winch and More, 1956).

## TRAIT THEORY

Personality tests have a very practical purpose: they are meant as an aid in diagnosis and counseling. But psychologists who study the topic of personality have aims that go beyond such applications, no matter how socially useful those might be. They want to understand the kinds of differences that personality tests uncover, to find a useful framework within which to describe such differences, and to discover how they come about. In their efforts to answer these questions, they appeal to several so-called "personality theories."

Most of the theories of personality that have been developed thus far aren't really theories in the conventional sense. They are not specific enough to make the clear-cut predictions that would help us choose between them. What they are instead are different orientations from which the subject of personality is approached. We will begin with the *trait* approach, which tries to describe individuals by a set of characterizing attributes.

Trait theory is first of all an attempt to be descriptive. It tries to find some way to characterize people by reference to some underlying basic traits. But just which traits are basic? The comic stages of classical and Renaissance days—and modern trait theory—imply not merely that a particular person has a characteristic personality, but that this personality can be categorized along with those of others who are in some ways equivalent. But what are the categories along which people should be grouped together? The early playwrights (and many film makers) picked a few attributes that were easy to characterize and caricature—the tight-lipped silence of the Western hero who speaks only with his guns, the virtuous chastity of the eternal heroine, the cowardice of the braggart soldier (who in Shakespeare's hands transcends his type and becomes Falstaff). But are these

A                                       B

*Stock characters in the Hollywood Western* (A) *The hero (played by William S. Hart) and a woman in distress in* Wild Bill Hickok, *and (B) the hero (played by Roy Rogers) and the villain (played by George Hayes) in* Young Buffalo Bill. *(Courtesy Movie Stills Archives)*

the personality traits that are really primary for the description of human personality?

The trait theorists' search for an answer is a bit like an attempt to find a few general principles that underlie the multitude of masks on, say, an Italian Renaissance stage. At first glance, these masks are very different, as different as the many persons we encounter in real life. Is there a way to classify these masks according to a few basic dimensions? Put another way, can we classify human personality by reference to a few fundamental traits?

## The Search for the Right Taxonomy

In a way, much the same question is faced during the early stages of any science. At this point, a major task is the development of a useful *taxonomy,* or classification system. Consider the early biologists. They recognized that the various creatures differ in a multitude of ways—their size and color, the absence or the presence of a skeleton, the number and kind of appendages, and so on. The biologists had to decide which of these distinctions provided the most useful classification categories. Exactly the same issue faces the psychologist who studies personality differences. The dictionary lists 18,000 trait names (Allport and Odbert, 1936). But without some kind of taxonomy, how can we decide which of these are basic traits and important for classifying all people?

### CLASSIFICATION THROUGH LANGUAGE

One step towards a taxonomy of personality traits grew out of an examination of the language used to describe personality attributes (Allport and Odbert, 1936). Advocates of this procedure argue that the adjectives used to describe people embody the accumulated observations of many previous generations. A systematic sifting of trait words would then give clues about individual differences whose description has been important enough to withstand the test of time (Goldberg, 1982).

This line of reasoning led to the development of a widely used personality inventory by Raymond Cattell (1957). Cattell's starting point was a set of 4,500 terms taken from the 18,000 trait words in an unabridged dictionary. This list was drastically reduced by throwing out difficult or uncommon words and eliminating synonyms. Finally 171 trait names were left. A group of judges was then asked to rate subjects by using these terms. Their ratings were subsequently factor analyzed by using methods similar to those employed in the study of intelligence-test performance—that is, by finding out which items correlated highly with one another while correlating little or not all with others. The resulting item clusters were then inspected to see what they had in common, yielding what Cattell thought were some sixteen primary dimensions of personality. Each of these dimensions was defined by a pair of adjectives that describe the opposite poles of the dimension, such as outgoing versus reserved, suspicious versus trusting, tense versus relaxed, happy-go-lucky versus sober, and so on (Cattell, 1966).

Later work by other investigators managed to reduce the number of primary dimensions to a smaller set. A widely quoted study by Warren Norman featured five major dimensions of personality: extroversion (sometimes called extraversion), emotional stability, agreeableness, conscientiousness, and cultural sensitiv-

***The seven dwarfs as character types*** *Doc, Sleepy, Grumpy, Dopey, Sneezy, Happy and Bashful. (From Walt Disney's* Snow White; *courtesy the Kobal Collection)*

Table 17.3 THE NORMAN FIVE-FACTOR TAXONOMY OF PERSONALITY TRAITS

| Factor names | Scale dimensions |
|---|---|
| Extroversion | Talkative/Silent<br>Frank, open/Secretive<br>Adventurous/Cautious<br>Sociable/Reclusive |
| Agreeableness | Good-natured/Irritable<br>Not jealous/Jealous<br>Mild, gentle/Headstrong<br>Cooperative/Negativistic |
| Conscientiousness | Fussy, tidy/Careless<br>Responsible/Undependable<br>Scrupulous/Unscrupulous<br>Persevering/Quitting, fickle |
| Emotional stability | Poised/Nervous, tense<br>Calm/Anxious<br>Composed/Excitable<br>Not hypochondriacal/Hypochondriacal |
| Culture | Artistically sensitive/Artistically insensitive<br>Intellectual/Unreflective, narrow<br>Polished, refined/Crude, boorish<br>Imaginative/Simple, direct |

SOURCE: Adapted from Norman, 1963.

ity. Norman's model is hierarchical in the sense that several lower-level traits (for example tidy/careless, persevering/fickle) can be regarded as manifestations of a higher-order factor (here, conscientiousness; see Table 17.3, from Norman, 1963).

NEUROTICISM AND EXTROVERSION/INTROVERSION

While many later studies have come up with five-factor descriptions of personality that are quite similar to Norman's (see Goldberg, 1981; Brody, 1988), others have suggested that the underlying dimensions may be fewer. The most influential alternative is that proposed by Hans Eysenck, who tried to encompass personality differences in a space defined by just two dimensions: neuroticism/emotional stability and extroversion/introversion (which correspond to two of Norman's dimensions).

*Neuroticism* is equivalent to emotional instability and maladjustment. It is assessed by affirmative answers to questions like "Do you ever feel 'just miserable' for no good reason at all?" And "Do you often feel disgruntled?" *Extroversion-introversion* are terms that refer to the main direction of a person's energies, toward the outer world of material objects and other people or toward the inner world of one's own thoughts and feelings. The extrovert is sociable, impulsive, and enjoys new experiences, while the introvert tends to be more solitary, cautious, and slow to change. Extroversion is indicated by affirmative answers to questions such as "Do you like to have many social engagements?" and "Would you rate yourself as a happy-go-lucky individual?"

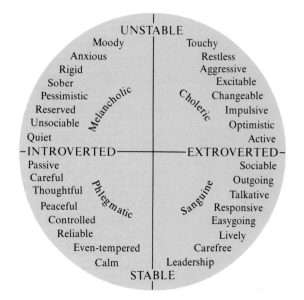

**17.7  Eysenck's two-dimensional classification of personality**   *Two dimensions of personality—neuroticism (emotional instability) and extroversion-introversion—define a space into which various trait terms may be fitted. Eysenck points out that the four quadrants of this space seem to fit Hippocrates's temperaments. Introverted and stable—phlegmatic; introverted and unstable—melancholic; extroverted and stable—sanguine; extroverted and unstable—choleric. (Eysenck and Rachman, 1965)*

As Eysenck sees it, neuroticism and extroversion-introversion are independent dimensions. To be sure, both introverts and many neurotics have something in common: they are both unsociable and withdrawn. But, in Eysenck's view, their lack of sociability has different roots. The healthy introverts are not afraid of social activities: they simply do not like them. In contrast, neurotically shy persons keep to themselves because of fear: they want to be with others but are afraid of joining them.*

It's worth noting that Eysenck's two-dimensional classification defines a conceptual space into which many trait terms can be fitted (see Figure 17.7). To the extent that it or similar classification systems succeed in doing so, they are analogous to the classification schemes that have proved so successful in the field of sensory psychology; for example, the color solid, which accommodates all possible colors on the basis of just three dimensions—brightness, hue, and saturation (see Chapter 5, pp. 187–88).

Eysenck points to an interesting relation between his own two-dimensional space and the venerable four-fold classification of temperaments proposed by the ancient Greek physician Hippocrates (ca. 400 B.C.). Hippocrates believed that there are four human temperaments that correspond to four different personality types: **sanguine** (cheerful and active), **melancholic** (gloomy), **choleric** (angry and violent), and **phlegmatic** (calm and passive). He believed that these temperaments reflected an excess of one of four bodily humors; thus sanguine persons were thought to have relatively more blood, melancholy persons to have an excess of black bile, phlegmatic persons to have an excess of phlegm, and choleric

---

* A more recent version of Eysenck's system adds a third dimension independent of the other two, called **psychoticism**—a characteristic related to aggressive, antisocial, cold, impulsive, and self-centered attributes. This new dimension evidently encompasses two more of Norman's five dimensions: *agreeableness/disagreeableness* and *conscientiousness/irresponsibility*. The fifth, which Norman calls **cultural sensitivity,** is presumably related to cognitive and educational traits, including intelligence (Eysenck and Eysenck, 1975, 1983; for critique, see Claridge, 1983).

persons an excess of yellow bile (see Figure 17.8). Today the humor theory is a mere historical curiosity, but Hippocrates's four-fold classification is in some ways still with us. For the four quadrants of Eysenck's two-dimensional space seem to fit Hippocrates's four temperamental types. The category introverted and stable corresponds to phlegmatic, introverted and unstable to melancholic, extroverted and stable to sanguine, and extroverted and unstable to choleric (Eysenck and Rachman, 1965).

IS FACTOR ANALYSIS THE PROPER ROAD TO A TAXONOMY?

A number of psychologists have taken issue with factor analytical approaches such as Eysenck's. They point out that there is no guarantee that the factors extracted by such methods are the "real" dimensions of personality, since the end product of the analysis has to depend on what is fed into it. The factors describe the coherence among a certain set of items; if some items were added and others subtracted, the pattern of coherence (and thus the factors) might well be different. While this critique has definite merit, there is no denying the fact that the two main dimensions of Eysenck's classification—extroversion and emotional instability—seem to come up again and again even if different tests are used. In fact, there is some evidence that these dimensions may apply not just to our own culture but to others, since much the same factor pattern was obtained when translated versions of personality scales were administered in such diverse societies as Bangladesh, Brazil, Hong Kong, and Japan. This is not to say that people in these different cultures do not differ on various personality traits, for they certainly do. For example, extroversion scores are very much higher in the United States than in Japan. What is the same is the way the responses to the items hang together; as a result, the same dimensions of personality emerge (Eysenck and Eysenck, 1983).

We are surely far from having established a genuine taxonomy of personality differences. But if and when we do, it is likely that Eysenck's two main dimensions will find some place within it.

## TRAITS VERSUS SITUATIONS

Different trait theorists may argue about the kind and number of trait dimensions with which to describe personality. Yet on one thing they all agree: There are personality traits that are stable and enduring properties of the individual. But during the last two decades, this basic credo has come under serious attack. One reason was the predictive validity of personality tests. For while tests such as the MMPI and the CPI predict behavior, they don't predict it all that accurately.

*17.8 An early taxonomy of personality* *A medieval illustration of one of the earliest attempts to classify human personality, Hippocrates's four temperaments: sanguine (cheerful and active), melancholic (gloomy), choleric (angry and violent), and phlegmatic (calm and passive). According to Hippocrates, these temperaments reflected an excess of one of four bodily humors; thus sanguine persons were thought to have relatively more blood. Today the humor theory is a mere historical curiosity, but some aspects of Hippocrates's classification are still with us. (Courtesy the Bettmann Archive)*

*Traits versus situations   Do the fighters punch each other because they want to win the prize money (situation) or because they are angry men (trait)? The blows probably hurt just as much either way. (George Bellows,* Stag at Sharkey's, *1909, courtesy The Cleveland Museum of Art, Hinman B. Hurlbut Collection)*

Critics of the trait approach suggest that the tests don't do as well as one might wish because that which they are trying to measure—a set of stable personality traits—isn't really there. To put it another way, perhaps there is no real consistency in the way people behave at different times and in different situations.

## The Difficulties of Trait Theory

The concept of stable personality traits was seriously challenged by Walter Mischel, whose survey of the research literature led him to conclude that people behave much less consistently than a trait theory would predict (Mischel, 1968). A classic study concerns honesty in children (Hartshorne and May, 1928). Grade-school children were given the opportunity to lie, cheat, or steal in a wide variety of settings: in athletic events, in the classroom, at home, alone, or with peers. The important finding was that the child who was dishonest in one situation (cheating on a test) was not necessarily dishonest in another setting (an athletic contest). There was some consistency, but it was rather unimpressive; a later reanalysis of the results came up with an average intercorrelation of +.30 (Burton, 1963). The correlations were greater the greater the similarity between the two situations in which honesty was assessed. Honesty in one classroom situation was more consistent with honesty in another classroom situation than with honesty assessed at home.

Mischel argued that a similar lack of cross-situational consistency is found for many other behavior patterns. Examples are aggression, dependency, rigidity, and reactions to authority. The intercorrelations among different measures of what seems to be the same trait are often low and sometimes nonexistent. In Mischel's view, the fact that personality tests have relatively low validities is just another demonstration of the same phenomenon. A personality test taps behavior in one situation while the validity criterion of that test assesses behavior in another context. Since cross-situational consistency tends to be low, so are validity coefficients.

693

*Consistency across situations?* *(A) In some situations, most people behave the same way. (B) In others, most people behave differently. A major task of personality psychology is to discover whether they behave consistently across different situations. (Photographs by Bob Krist/Black Star; and Jan Halaska/Photo Researchers)*

### SITUATIONISM

The failure to find behavioral consistency has been taken as an argument against the importance of personality characteristics in determining what a person will do. But if these are not relevant, what is? One answer is ***situationism,*** the notion that human behavior is largely determined by the characteristics of the situation rather than by those of the person. That this is so for some situations is indubitable. Given a red light, most drivers stop; given a green light, most go—regardless of whether they are friendly or unfriendly, stingy or generous, dominant or submissive, and so on. Situations of this sort produce predictable reactions in virtually all of us. But according to situationism, the same principle applies to much or nearly all of human behavior. Consider the enormous effect of social roles which often define what an actor must do with little regard to who the actor is (see Chapter 12). To predict how someone will act in a courtroom, there is little point in asking whether he is sociable or extravagant with money or whether he gets along with his father. What we really want to know is the role that he or she will play—judge, prosecutor, defense attorney, or defendant. Seen in this light, what we do depends not on who we are, but on the situation in which we find ourselves.

This is not to say that situationists deny the existence of individual differences. They certainly agree that various demographic and socioeconomic factors are powerful determinants of human behavior. Examples are age and sex, marital status, ethnic background, occupation, and income. Nor do they dispute the important effect of differences in ability, especially cognitive ability. As they see it, all of these factors determine the kinds of situations a person is likely to encounter or to have encountered (and thus learn from). But in their view, it is these situations, rather than personality traits, that determine what people actually do.

### CONSISTENCY AS AN ILLUSION

If this view is right, the underlying consistency of the personalities of our friends and acquaintances (and perhaps our own) is more or less illusory. But if so, how can one explain the fact that most people have been subject to this particular illusion since the days of Greek drama and no doubt much before?

*Consistency as an illusion* *At a class reunion people may think that their old classmates haven't changed at all. They really have changed, but they act as they once did because they have returned to the old situation. Here we see Kathleen Turner in the 1986 film* Peggy Sue Got Married, *as she once again puts on the crown and holds the flowers as "homecoming queen" at her 25th class reunion. (Courtesy the Kobal Collection)*

According to critics of trait theory, one explanation is that people's personalities seem to be stable because we tend to see them in the same social setting. But the critics make an even more important point. In their view, personality traits are mental constructions devised by the observer who watches another person's actions and tries to make sense out of them. They believe that people are often faced with an overload of information, which they then try to reduce and simplify (e.g., Shweder, 1975; Ross, 1977; Nisbett and Ross, 1980). As a result, they are prone to various kinds of errors of inference that produce the belief that there are consistent personality traits.* Critics of trait theory argue that such errors show that personality descriptions are more in the eyes of the beholder than in the person she beholds (Cantor and Mischel, 1977, 1979).

## In Defense of Traits

The emphasis on situations provided a useful corrective to those who sought to explain everything people do as a manifestation of their own inner nature. But if pushed to the extreme, this position becomes just as questionable as the one it had tried to correct. For in this form it can be interpreted as asserting that personality does not exist at all. Whether any psychologist has actually gone to this extreme is doubtful; certainly Mischel never did (Mischel, 1973, 1979). But the very possibility that someone might climb all the way out on this particular theoretical limb was enough to produce a spirited counterreaction against Mischel's attack on the trait concept.

### CONSISTENCY OVER TIME

The reaction to the situationist position took several forms. Many authors felt that there is considerable personal consistency over time (Block, 1971, 1977). Proof comes from a number of longitudinal studies that show a fair degree of behavioral consistency over sizable stretches of the life span. Thus in one study, dependability in males as judged in high school correlated quite well with ratings of the same attribute made by different judges some ten or more years later ($r = +.55$; Block, 1971). In another study, male adults between seventeen and eighty-five years of age were given the same personality inventory at six- and twelve-year intervals. The correlations between their scores on the first and second administration of the inventory (on traits such as dominance, sociability, and emotional stability) ranged from $+.59$ to $+.87$ (Costa, McCrae, and Arenberg, 1980).

### CONSISTENCY ACROSS SITUATIONS

Consistency over time there might be, but what about consistency across situations, which was the major focus of Mischel's critique? According to Seymour Epstein, this cross-situational consistency is much higher than Mischel had supposed. In Epstein's view, studies that seem to show low cross-situational consistency usually employ only a small sample of behaviors. As a result, the

---

* We've previously considered some of these errors in our discussion of attribution processes and person perception; for example, the fundamental attribution error, illusory correlations, and oversimplified schemas and stereotypes (see Chapter 12).

assessment of the relevant trait is necessarily unreliable. But if so, the correlation between two (unreliable) measures of this trait cannot help but be low or nonexistent. To determine whether people behave consistently from one situation to another, the behavior in each situation (e.g., cheating in class and cheating on the athletic field) must be measured not just once, but on a number of different occasions.

To buttress his position, Epstein observed subjects' moods, behavior, and various physiological indices on about thirty days. He found that correlations from one day to any other day were very low. He then compared correlations based on the average score on any two days, then on any three days, and so on. As the number of observations increased, the correlations rose from about .30 to .80 (Epstein, 1979, 1980).

Epstein interprets these findings as evidence for cross-situational consistency. But Mischel and his collaborators reply that they are essentially demonstrations of consistency in time and not across situations, though this is still a matter of considerable debate (Mischel and Peake, 1983; Epstein, 1983).

### THE CRITERION OF CONSISTENCY

Another issue concerns the criterion of cross-situational consistency. Whether such consistency is found may well depend on what behaviors the experimenter defined as different or equivalent for the purposes of assessing a given trait.

A number of authors argue that behavioral inconsistency is often more apparent than real, for two reactions that are at first glance quite dissimilar may turn out to be a manifestation of the same underlying trait when examined more closely (e.g., Moskowitz, 1982; Buss and Craik, 1983; Rorer and Widiger, 1983). In the words of a recent review, "trait theory is more impressive—and more interesting—when it displays not literal consistency from one situation to another but predictability or coherence in what appear to be different behaviors" (Loevinger and Knoll, 1983, p. 209).

Some good examples come from the study of development. Consider aggression. In males, aggression is fairly consistent between childhood and adolescence, but it takes different overt forms at different ages. Young boys pummel each other with their fists; young men rarely do more than shout in anger (Kagan and Moss, 1962). Another example concerns the distinction between the attributes *happy/outgoing* and *somber/reserved.* When different judges were asked to assess this trait in persons first studied at age six and then again at age fifteen, their ratings were quite similar, yielding correlations of about +.60. This consistency disappeared, however, when the judges were asked to rate overt behavior only. But as the author saw it, this result made sense. The five-year-old who is reserved and somber shows this by a low level of physical vitality. At ten, the same underlying attribute manifests itself as cautiousness and emotional vulnerability. Still later, during adolescence, this basic pattern goes together with a sense of inferiority (Bronson, 1966).

A similar point was made in a study of infants' attachment to their mother at twelve and eighteen months of age. By and large, the infants' patterns of behavior ("securely attached" or "avoidant") were similar when tested at these two ages (see Chapter 15). But this doesn't mean that the particular details of what each infant did both times were identical. On one occasion, an infant may have toddled

*Aggression in boys and men* The same trait is often (though not always) expressed differently at different ages. *(*Left: *Photograph by Wayne Miller/Magnum.* Right: *Photograph by Paul Kennedy/Leo de Wys)*

over to his mother; on another, he may have remained where he was but smiled, turned toward her, and showed her a toy. On the surface, these two reactions are different enough. But the investigators decided to group them together as instances of the same broad class of "secure attachment." Given this broader definition of attachment, they found considerable consistency from one age to the next. Had they decided to use a narrower criterion, there would have been little or no consistency (Waters, 1978; Sroufe, 1979).

Here, as in so many other aspects of behavior, a superficial difference disguises a deeper sameness. At a surface level, the two sentences *John eats the apple* and *The apple is eaten by John* are obviously different. But at a deeper level, they are in many ways alike and mean much the same thing (Chapter 9).

## The Interaction between Person and Situation

A number of psychologists feel that the debate between situationists and trait theorists has focused on the wrong distinction. As originally formulated, the question was whether an individual's actions are better predicted by the situation or by his or her own personal characteristics. But there is a third alternative: the critical factor may be the ***interaction*** between person and situation (e.g., Magnusson and Endler, 1977).

### THE PERSON-BY-SITUATION INTERACTION

The term *interaction* is used here in a technical sense. To understand what it means in this context, consider a hypothetical experiment in which we study the reactions of several pairs of individuals to two different situations. The response will be anxiety as indicated by the galvanic skin response (GSR); the two situations are waiting to take a test and being threatened with electric shock. Let's call the subjects Jane and Carol, Mary and Claire, and let us assume that the GSR scale runs from 0 (no anxiety) to 12 (maximal anxiety). Two extreme outcomes are displayed in Tables 17.4 and 17.5.

697

Table 17.4 AN EFFECT OF SITUATION

|  |  | Situation | | Average for each person |
|---|---|---|---|---|
|  |  | Test | Shock | |
| Person | Jane | 3 | 9 | 6 |
|  | Carol | 3 | 9 | 6 |
| Average for situation | | 3 | 9 | |

Table 17.5 AN EFFECT OF INDIVIDUAL DIFFERENCES

|  |  | Situation | | Average for each person |
|---|---|---|---|---|
|  |  | Test | Shock | |
| Person | Mary | 3 | 3 | 3 |
|  | Claire | 9 | 9 | 9 |
| Average for situation | | 6 | 6 | |

The results shown in Tables 17.4 and 17.5 are diametrically opposed. Table 17.4 depicts a powerful effect of the situation. For these two subjects, Jane and Carol, shock is evidently much more frightening than the test. But there is no effect of individual differences since Jane and Carol behave identically. In Table 17.5 we see the reverse. Here, there is a massive effect of individual differences; Claire is evidently much more fearful than is Mary. But in this second example, the situations are essentially equivalent in the fear they provoke.

These two illustrations fit the extreme positions that ascribe all behavior either to the situation or to personality differences. Needless to say, there are much more plausible intermediate outcomes in which both factors play a role. But our concern is with another alternative, which has quite different theoretical implications. Consider the pattern of results shown by yet another pair of subjects as indicated in Table 17.6.

Table 17.6 AN INTERACTION EFFECT

|  |  | Situation | | Average for each person |
|---|---|---|---|---|
|  |  | Test | Shock | |
| Person | Anne | 3 | 9 | 6 |
|  | Donna | 9 | 3 | 6 |
| Average for situation | | 6 | 6 | 6 |

What is important about the results of Table 17.6 is that they do not exhibit effects of the situations as such nor of the individual differences as such. When we look at average GSRs, Anne and Donna prove equally fearful. The same holds for the difference between the situations; *on the average,* the test and the threatened shock produce equal GSRs. But there is a new twist that is obscured by the averages. The two situations produce radically different effects in the two persons. Anne is evidently much more afraid of the shock than of the test, while the opposite holds for Donna. In statistical language, a relationship of this kind, in which the effect of one variable (fear-evoking situation) depends upon another variable (individual differences) is called an *interaction.*

The test-shock experiment here described is a highly simplified version of a large number of studies that have actually been carried out. An example is a study in which subjects were asked to describe their usual reaction to various threats

***Person-by-situation interaction*** *Like some other fantasy heroes, Superman is utterly fearless when faced by physical danger, but is shy and timid—at least as his alter Ego, Clark Kent—when around women. (*Top: *Courtesy the Kobal Collection.* Bottom: *Courtesy Photofest)*

(Endler and Hunt, 1969). Some of these perils involved loss of self-esteem (failing an examination), others physical danger (being on a high ledge on a mountaintop), still others a threat whose nature was still unclear (getting a police summons). The results showed that both individual differences and situations affected behavior to some extent. Some people seemed more generally fearful than others, and some situations ("being approached by cars racing abreast") evoked more fear than others ("sitting in a restaurant").

What is more interesting is that the bulk of these effects were produced by the person-by-situation interaction. Put in other words, people tend to be frightened (or angered or reassured) by different things. A simple situationism is evidently untenable; the man who is terrified of heights may well be a passionate scuba diver. But this finding also undercuts the usefulness of general traits such as "anxiety." To predict behavior better, such traits should be qualified; for example, "anxiousness in an interpersonal setting," "anxiousness when facing physical danger," "anxiousness in the face of the unknown." By this utilization of the person-by-situation interaction, the notion of stable personality differences can be maintained. But there is a price, for the process of qualification may be endless. Consider "anxiousness when facing physical dangers." Should this be further qualified so that we separately consider "anxiousness when facing inanimate nature," "anxiousness when facing threatening strangers," and "anxiousness in the presence of animals," with the last of these subdivided into "anxiousness with cats," "anxiousness with dogs," "anxiousness with horses"? The end result of such subdivisions can only be an enormous subdivision of ever more finely drawn traits (Cronbach, 1975; Nisbett, 1977).

RECIPROCAL INTERACTION

We've seen that different situations may affect different persons differently. But the interaction between person and situation may go deeper than this. For in many cases, the relation between situation and person is *reciprocal.* For people often play a major role in choosing the situations they confront—the places they live in, the work they do, the friends they associate with. And those choices are partially determined by their personality traits: The extrovert will generally find a lively party while the introvert will seek a quiet corner where she can curl up with a book. The situation may (and often does) determine a person's behavior, but the person's traits often determine what that situation is (Snyder, 1981; Endler, 1982).

People have a hand in choosing their situations, but that's not all; in many cases, they actually create them. In an experimental demonstration of this phenomenon, subjects were asked to participate in a study of how people become acquainted with each other. To that end, they were asked to converse on the telephone with a member of the opposite sex. Some of the men were led to believe that the woman they were to speak to was physically attractive; others, that she was physically unattractive. The woman knew nothing about this. Her part of the conversation was recorded separately from the men's and was later presented to outside judges who were completely ignorant of the circumstances of the experiment. The results showed that the woman who was perceived (unbeknown to them) as physically attractive was judged to have talked in a more friendly, attractive, and sociable manner than the woman whose conversational partners regarded her as less attractive.

The reason is simple. The men's actual behavior (that is, the way they talked on the telephone) was in line with their expectations before they ever picked up the phone. As rated by judges (who only heard the men's part of the conversation), the conversational manner of the men who believed that the woman on the other end of the telephone was attractive was more sociable, interesting, outgoing, and humorous than that of the men who believed that she was unattractive. The men's initial expectations led to different behaviors from the very outset, and these differences provoked different responses from the woman. These in their turn confirmed the men's initial expectations—a good example of a self-fulfilling prophecy (Snyder, Tanke, and Berscheid, 1977).

Reciprocal effects of this sort are pervasive throughout the domain of human interaction. They are a commonplace in the psychiatric clinic where many unhappy individuals don't recognize that the situations that trouble them so greatly are partially of their own creation. Further examples come from developmental psychology, where many investigators have pointed to the fact that children of different temperaments elicit different reactions from their parents (e.g., Scarr and McCartney, 1983; see Chapter 15 for a fuller discussion).

## Consistency as a Trait

By now there is general agreement that, when properly defined, traits do exist. We've seen that a major criterion for determining whether such traits are present is cross-situational consistency in behavior. But recently, psychologists have come to realize that consistency itself—the degree to which people do much the same thing in different situations—varies from person to person! To the extent that this is true, cross-situational consistency may be regarded as a trait in its own right.

### SOME PEOPLE ARE MORE CONSISTENT THAN OTHERS

Most of us are affected by both our personal characteristics and by the demands of the situation. But the extent to which one or the other of these predominates

*The extremes of the self-monitoring scale* (A) Woody Allen as the high self-monitor, Zelig, the man who can fit in with anybody, anywhere, anytime. (B) Woody Allen as the hero of most of his other movies who remains Woody Allen, the ultimate low self-monitor, who stays true to himself regardless of the situation. (Pictured with Calvin Coolidge and Herbert Hoover in Zelig, 1983, courtesy the Kobal Collection; with Diane Keaton in Annie Hall, 1977, courtesy Photofest)

A

B

Table 17.7 SOME REPRESENTATIVE ITEMS FROM THE SELF-MONITORING SCALE

1. I can look anyone in the eye and tell a lie with a straight face (if for a right end). (True)*

2. In different situations and with different people, I often act like very different persons. (True)

3. I have trouble changing my behavior to suit different people and different situations. (False)

4. I can only argue for ideas which I already believe. (False)

* In the items shown, the key after each question is in the direction of self-monitoring. Thus high self-monitors would presumably answer "True" to questions 1 and 2, and "False" to questions 3 and 4.
SOURCE: Snyder, 1987.

varies from person to person. It goes without saying that there are some social situations that affect most people equally and allow little play for personal variations. At a funeral, everyone is quiet and restrained. But at a picnic, differences in sociability and energy level will be readily apparent (Price and Bouffard, 1974; Monson, Hesley, and Chernick, 1982). What about situations that are more ambiguous? Here some people will tend to behave much more consistently than others.

*Self-monitoring* One of the factors that determines the extent to which people adjust their behavior to fit the social situation is the degree to which they try to control the impression they make on others, so that they can be "the right person in the right place at the right time." The tendency to do this is assessed by the ***self-monitoring scale,*** developed by Mark Snyder (for some representative items, see Table 17.7). High self-monitors care a great deal about the appearance of the self they project in a given social situation. By constantly adjusting to the situation, they are necessarily inconsistent; they'll act like cultured highbrows when with art lovers, and boisterous sports fans when with a group of college athletes. In effect, they always seem to ask themselves: "How can I be the person this situation calls for?" In contrast, low self-monitors are much less interested in how they appear to others. They want to be themselves whatever the social climate in which they find themselves. As a result, their behavior is much more consistent from situation to situation (Snyder, 1987).*

On the face of it, the high self-monitor seems to cut a rather less admirable figure than his low self-monitoring counterpart. But as Snyder points out, whether such value judgments apply depends on the way in which the self-monitoring pattern fits into the rest of the individual's life. The high self-monitor is probably rather pleasant to be with, and his diplomatic skill and adaptability may well be

* One might guess that high self-monitoring is just another aspect of extroversion since the social skills of high self-monitors would seem to be closely related to the extroverted style of life. There is indeed a correlation between the self-monitoring scale and tests of extroversion, but it is very slight. It appears that the two traits are at bottom quite different. High self-monitors can readily be the life of the party, but they will only be so when it seems appropriate. They know when the situation calls for greater decorum, say, at an upper-class tea party or in an art gallery, and then they will be properly reserved. The extrovert is much more likely to be gregarious and outgoing even in such situations (Snyder, 1987).

an asset in dealing with the many roles created by a complex society such as ours. The virtues of the low self-monitor are even more apparent; there's much to be said for the man of integrity who is the same today as he'll be tomorrow and to himself is true. But at the extremes, neither approach is particularly appealing. An extremely high self-monitor may very well be a shallow, unprincipled poseur. And an extremely low self-monitor may manage to turn the virtues of his pattern into vices as consistent adherence to principle becomes blind and stubborn rigidity. To march to the music of a different drummer is not necessarily admirable. It depends on what the music is (Snyder, 1987).

*Consistency and mental disorder*   When insensitivity to the situation becomes extreme enough, we are in the realm of mental disorder. Mentally disturbed persons are generally less (usually much less) responsive to the demands of a situation than are normals. As a result, they show more behavioral consistency across situations. Normal people smile about births and cry about deaths; psychiatrically depressed patients may cry about both. The same applies to other forms of mental illness. The patients' responses are governed more by factors within themselves—depressions, violent elations, delusions—than by the situation that confronts them. As a result, their behavior is often viewed by others as inappropriate to the occasion (which is one of the reasons why they are in the psychiatric ward). But in consequence, they also manifest more cross-situational consistency than do the rest of us (for some relevant findings, see Moos, 1969).

### PEOPLE DIFFER IN WHAT THEY ARE CONSISTENT ABOUT

Trait theorists generally assume that all people can be classified in line with the same trait dimensions. Some people are sociable and others are withdrawn, some are emotionally stable and others are not; whatever their differences, however, they can all be described by the same categories. But this assumption may not be true, because some trait dimensions may be irrelevant (or at least less relevant) for some people than for others.

This general idea found some support in an influential study by Bem and Allen (1974). They agreed that traits imply cross-situational consistency in behavior, but they argued that people may very well differ in the trait categories that are applicable to *them.* If so, they ought to be cross-situationally consistent in one trait domain area and inconsistent in another. To determine whether this is so,

**People differ in what they're consistent about**   *The two members of the* Odd Couple *are utterly consistent about being respectively fussy and neat on the one hand (Felix), and messy and sloppy on the other (Oscar). But that doesn't mean that their behavior is necessarily consistent in other respects. (Tony Randall and Jack Klugman in the TV version of the* Odd Couple; *courtesy Paramount Pictures © 1989)*

they asked subjects to assess themselves on several trait dimensions, such as friendliness and conscientiousness, by rating their overall level ("In general, how friendly and outgoing are you?") and their own consistency ("How much do you vary from situation to situation in how friendly and outgoing you are?"). In addition, the experimenters obtained a number of behavioral measures (e.g., observing the subjects in a group discussion to assess friendliness) as well as ratings by parents and peers.

The results suggest that people do indeed differ in what they are consistent about. If the subjects described themselves as consistently friendly (or unfriendly), the various indices of their behavior and others' ratings correlated rather highly (+.57). But if they described themselves as rather inconsistent, these indices correlated much more poorly (+.24). A similar pattern was found for conscientiousness. According to Bem and Allen, these results indicate that different people may have to be characterized by different trait categories. Their findings, however, are still a matter of some controversy (e.g., Chaplin and Goldberg, 1984).

## Person Constancy

In the light of all this, what can we say about the assumption that there is an underlying unity in how any one individual acts and thinks and feels, a basic consistency that we call personality? The evidence indicates that this assumption —which goes back to the ancient dramatists and before—still stands.

We all have an intuitive belief in something like "person constancy," a phenomenon analogous to "object constancy" in perception (see Chapter 6). A chair is perceived as a stable object whose size remains the same whether we are near to it or far away and whose shape remains unchanged regardless of our visual orientation. These constancies are not illusions; they reflect a genuine stability in the external world. The stability of persons is in some ways analogous. For we somehow manage to peer through a welter of ever-changing situations to perceive an individual's behavioral consistency. The constancy of personality is not as sturdy as that of chairs, but it has some reality even so.

To be sure, this constancy is far from perfect. We change from day to day; we're grouchy on Monday because of a headache, and cheery on Tuesday because of a sunny sky. We also change from year to year—with age, experience, and various shifts of fortune. A number of psychologists suspect that we underestimate the extent to which such changes occur. In observing others, we form a notion of their personality. In observing ourselves, we form a so-called *self-concept*—a set of ideas about who we ourselves are. (For more detail, see Chapters 12 and 18.) But in their view, our perception of the personality of others, as well as our own self-concept, are at bottom mental constructions and as such they are subject to error. One such error is the tendency to see more uniformity and coherence than is actually there, to exaggerate person constancy in others and in ourselves (Shweder, 1975; Nisbett and Wilson, 1977; Nisbett, 1980; Kihlstrom and Cantor, 1984).

But the fact that there are errors in our perception of persons, doesn't mean that their personality is entirely in our own eyes. After all, there are visual illusions, but their existence does not disprove the fact that by and large we see the world as it really is. What holds for the world of vision probably holds for person

*Person constancy and caricature*   Most artists have always believed that there is a constancy of behavioral as well as of bodily features, as illustrated in this 1743 print by William Hogarth. (Detail from "Characters and Caricaturas," subscription ticket for Marriage à la Mode; reproduced by courtesy of the Trustees of the British Museum)

perception as well, and this is probably why trait theory has continued to have so much appeal (Kenrick and Funder, 1988). Person constancy is a fact. Jane remains Jane whether she is at home or at the office, whether it is today or yesterday or the day after tomorrow. And at some level she is different from Carol and Margaret and five billion other humans alive today, for her personality—just like theirs—is unique.

## TRAITS AND BIOLOGY

To the extent that person constancy exists, we are probably justified in holding on to some version of the trait approach. People vary in their characteristic modes of behavior, and their variations can be described and assessed, however imperfectly, by the trait vocabulary. But how do such variations arise?

Thus far, we've talked about traits as if they were merely descriptive labels for broad groups of behavior patterns. But most trait theorists go further. In their view, traits are general predispositions to behave in one way or another that are ultimately rooted in the individual's biological makeup.

### Personality and Temperament

A number of modern investigators believe that personality traits grow out of the individual's *temperament,* a characteristic reaction pattern of the individual that is present from a rather early age. Like Hippocrates who coined the term some 2500 years ago, they believe that such temperamental patterns are largely genetic and constitutional in origin (though they obviously don't share his archaic ideas of their underlying humoral basis). Such characteristic behavior patterns may begin in the first few months of life. An example comes from a study of 141 children, observed for about a decade following birth:

> Donald exhibited an extremely high activity level almost from birth. At three months . . . he wriggled and moved about a great deal while asleep in his crib. At six months he "swam like a fish" while being bathed. At twelve months he still squirmed constantly while he was being dressed or washed. . . . At two years he was "constantly in motion, jumping and climbing." At three, he would "climb like a monkey and run like an unleashed puppy". . . . By the time he was seven, Donald was encountering difficulty in school because he was unable to sit still long enough to learn anything . . . (Thomas, Chess, and Birch, 1970, p. 104)

More recent investigators have tried to describe temperament within the framework of traditional trait classifications. An example is a temperament scale developed by Buss and Plomin that includes two major dimensions called sociability and emotionality (Buss and Plomin, 1984). According to Buss and Plomin, these two traits represent the core components of the main axes of Eysenck's system—extroversion and neuroticism/emotional stability. They feel that in young children, extroversion is best represented by sociability (which presumably affects the attachment bond between mother and child, reactions to strangers, and the like) while neuroticism/emotional instability is mainly represented by a greater tendency to be fearful (anxiety and guilt are reactions that come in later

# CHAPTER 18

# Personality II: Psychodynamic, Behavioral, and Humanistic Approaches

The preceding chapter has described many of the ways in which people differ in their characteristic modes of thought, desires, and behavior—that is, in their distinctive patterns of personality. Trait theorists try to understand these differences by reference to underlying trait dimensions, some of which may well be based on genetic predispositions. But there are several alternative approaches to personality that take another tack entirely. In this chapter, we will consider three of these alternatives: the *psychodynamic,* the *behavioral,* and the *humanistic.*

## THE PSYCHODYNAMIC APPROACH

Adherents of the psychodynamic approach do not deny that some people are more sociable than others, or more impulsive, or emotionally labile, or whatever. But they feel that explaining such tendencies as the expression of a personality trait is rather superficial. In their view, what people do and say—and even what they consciously think—is only the tip of the iceberg. As they see it, human acts and thoughts are just the outer expression of a whole set of motives and desires that are often derived from early childhood experiences, that lie buried underneath the surface, that are generally pitted against each other, and that are for the most part unknown to the person himself. They believe that to understand a per-

*Text and subtext   In many plays, what the characters leave unspoken (the subtext) is often more important than what they say (the text). (From a 1988 production of Anton Chekhov's* The Cherry Orchard, *directed by Peter Brook, starring Natasha Perry and Erland Josephson)*

*The dramatic presentation of inner conflicts   In some cases, actors play a character who is not fully aware of her own subtext, so she, like one of Freud's patients, is really lying to herself. An example is Blanche, in this scene from Tennessee Williams's play* A Streetcar Named Desire. *She is both sexually attracted and repelled by her brutal brother-in-law Stanley. (From the stage version of* A Streetcar Named Desire, *1947, with Marlon Brando and Jessica Tandy; photograph courtesy of the Museum of the City of New York)*

son is to understand these hidden psychological forces (often called ***dynamics***) that make him an individual divided against himself.

We've previously seen that the trait approach bears a certain similarity to dramatic forms that employ stock characters such as the comedies of the classical age. In such plays, everything was exactly what it appeared to be. Once the character entered, the audience knew pretty much what to expect. If he wore the mask of the cowardly soldier, he would brag and run away; if he wore the mask of the miserly old man, he would jealously guard his money. In contrast, the psychodynamic perspective is related to a more modern approach to drama in which nothing is quite what it seems. In playing a character, actors who follow this approach may pay more attention to the so-called *subtext* (the unspoken thoughts and musings that go through the character's head while he speaks his lines) than the *text* itself (the actual lines the playwright put into the character's mouth). And many actors are interested in a still deeper subtext, which consists of thoughts and wishes of which the character is generally unaware.

## Personality Structure and Development: The Freudian Account

All current versions of the psychodynamic approach are ultimately derived from the views of Sigmund Freud, the founder of psychoanalysis (1856–1939). We've already described Freud's general conceptions in a previous chapter (see Chapter 11), in which we saw that his theory of personality is a virtually all-embracing conception that encompasses phenomena as diverse as childhood development, neurotic symptoms, psychoanalytic therapy, myth, and art. Since our present concern is with differences in personalities, we will only present a brief review of psychodynamic conceptions that bear on this issue.

Freud's ideas grew out of studies of emotionally disturbed individuals whose symptoms seemed to reflect certain emotionally charged thoughts or wishes that these patients had shoved out of consciousness (or to use his term, ***repressed***). In his view, all human beings experience ***unconscious conflicts*** that originate in

*Acting with the subtext* Certain modern approaches to acting such as those developed by New York's Actor's Studio emphasize the importance of subtexts. The photo shows a scene from the film, Godfather PART II, featuring Lee Strasberg, the late head of the Actor's Studio, and Al Pacino, one of its illustrious graduates. In the scene, a gangster overlord plans a deadly double-cross of another, while telling him: "You're a wise and considerate young man." (From Godfather, PART II, *1974; courtesy the Kobal Collection*)

childhood and that influence later personality. He believed that many aspects of these conflicts are at bottom the same for us all.

Freud distinguished among three subsystems of the human personality that are usually locked in unconscious three-way combat: the *id,* a collection of blind instinctual strivings that scream out for immediate satisfaction; the *ego,* a set of partially conscious reaction patterns that try to mediate between the needs of the id and the realities of the actual world; and the *superego,* which corresponds to the internalized commands and prohibitions of the parents and punishes any transgressions with sharp pangs of guilt.

According to Freud, the fundamental principle of unconscious conflict is defense against anxiety. He believed that as parents reprimand the child for various forbidden thoughts or deeds, these thoughts or deeds become connected to anxiety. To ward off this unpleasant state, the child represses the thoughts, or memories, or desires that triggered the anxiety and shoves them out of consciousness. Repression is often supplemented by a number of other *defense mechanisms* against anxiety, including reaction formation, displacement, rationalization, and projection (see Chapter 11, pp. 433–34).

### PSYCHOSEXUAL DEVELOPMENT IN CHILDHOOD

Freud believed that all of us begin life as an id-derived collection of pleasure-seeking tendencies. This pleasure is obtained by the stimulation of the so-called *erogenous zones:* the mouth, anus, and the genitals. As the child develops, the relative importance of the three zones changes. Initially, there is the *oral stage,* during which the main focus is on the mouth and on the satisfactions of sucking, eating, and eventually biting, obtained in the course of feeding. Some time later, the emphasis shifts, and the child becomes concerned with matters related to toilet training during the *anal stage.*

At about four or five years of age, during the *phallic stage,* the primary stress is on the pleasure obtained from stimulation of the genitals and on the resolution of the Oedipus complex (see Chapter 11). At this point, the little boy directs his infantile sexual longings toward his mother, jealously hates his father, comes to fear his retribution, and finally shoves the entire set of conflicts out of consciousness and identifies with the father. (The little girl exhibits a symmetrical pattern: sexual desire for the father, rivalry and eventual identification with the mother.)

Following the furor of the Oedipal events, both girls and boys go through the six or seven years of the *latency period,* during which their sexuality lies dormant until it is reawakened beginning at puberty. With advancing adolescence, the last phase of psychosexual development brings the *genital stage,* in which the crude instinctual id-derived urges are transformed into mature sexual love, where the social and physical gratification of one's sexual partner plays a vital part.

### ADULT PERSONALITY DIFFERENCES AS REMNANTS OF CHILDHOOD PATTERNS

While the psychodynamic approach (and Freud's theory in particular) makes many assertions about the nature of human personality in general, it has rather less to say about the way in which people (especially "normal" people) differ from each other. One influential conception goes back to Freud: the idea that adult patterns can be understood and classified as remnants of reactions at one or another stage of childhood psychosexual development.

*The theory*    To develop, the child has to move from one stage to the next. But there are obstacles to smooth progression, for each change will necessarily produce some frustration as the child has to give up some earlier forms of gaining pleasure (for example, upon weaning). Certain reactions to the frustrations that occur at each changeover point may have lasting consequences. One such reaction is *fixation,* which refers to a lingering attachment to an earlier stage of pleasure seeking even after a new stage has been attained. Some remnants of the earlier pattern may hang on for a while, such as thumb-sucking in weaned infants.

Another mode of response to frustration during development is *reaction formation,* a mechanism of defense through which the forbidden impulse that was pushed out of consciousness is replaced by its very opposite. During toilet training, the child must not relax his sphincter, however much he would like to. Similarly for a whole set of related activities, such as being dirty, playing in the mud, and so on. His urge is to relax his sphincter. But given his parents' clearly expressed disapproval, this urge leads to anxiety. One means of dealing with the conflict is to do the exact opposite of what he really wants to. This reaction formation may manifest itself as constipation, or in a more general sense, by excessive neatness.

Freud believed that residues of early fixations and reaction formations continue into adulthood. The degree varies. Adult oral fixations might range from the common desire to give and receive oral caresses, to a fondness for sweets, to such extremes as compulsive orgies of overeating during periods of extreme anxiety.

Eventually Freud became convinced that what is really important in these stages is not just the particular anatomical region, whether mouth or anus, through which the child gains pleasure at the time. More crucial are certain ways of relating to other persons that are characteristic of a given stage and leave residues in adult behavior. According to one view, the degree to which the early social patterns persist is one important determinant in the shaping of adult personalities (Freud, 1940).

An example is the so-called *oral character,* which is said to go back to oral fixation. During the oral stage, the infant is utterly dependent upon the mother. He feels warm, well-fed, and protected, leading an idyllic existence in which all is given and nothing is asked for in return. According to Freud and his student Karl Abraham, certain adults are oral characters, whose relations to others recapitulate the passive dependency they enjoyed while suckling at the mother's breast (Abraham, 1927).

Freud and Abraham believed that there is also an *anal character,* whose personality derives from severe conflicts during toilet training (Freud, 1908; Abraham, 1927). Since toilet training often begins before the child is physically capable of voluntary sphincter control, it is a difficult task. One result may be considerable anxiety, which in turn leads to various defenses. One of these is a reaction formation in which the child inhibits rather than relaxes his bowels. This broadens and becomes manifest in more symbolic terms. The child becomes compulsively clean and orderly ("I must not soil myself").

Freud believed that there are several other such effects. One is obstinacy. The child asserts himself by holding back on his potty ("You can't make me if I don't want to"), a stubbornness which may soon become a more generalized "no." Another characteristic is stinginess. According to Freud, this is a general form of withholding, a refusal to part with what is one's own (that is, one's feces). This refusal generalizes, and the child becomes obsessed with property rights and jealously hoards his possessions. Freud believed that excessive conflicts during the anal stage may lead to an adult personality that displays the three symptomatic attributes of the anal character—compulsive orderliness, stubbornness, and stinginess.

*The evidence* What is the evidence on the role of early childhood events in producing differences in adult personality, in particular, the oral and anal characters? The verdict on the oral character is simple. There is little or no evidence that differences in the way the infant was fed have much of an effect (assuming adequate nutrition). Later adjustment and development appear to be much the same whether the infant was fed by breast or by bottle, was weaned early or weaned late (e.g., Sears, Maccoby, and Levin, 1957).

Studies directed at the concept of the "anal character" are more suggestive. There is evidence that the critical "anal traits"—neatness, obstinacy, and parsimony—do in fact correlate to a significant extent (Fisher and Greenberg, 1977). In one such study, a number of undergraduates were asked to rate their own and their friends' characteristics. Their ratings showed that the three critical traits do indeed form a coherent cluster. Those students who judged themselves (or were judged by others) to be obstinate were also those who tended to be orderly and a bit stingy. More important, the students with these "anal" characteristics tended to have mothers with similar attributes, as shown by questionnaires administered to the mothers. These results seem to vindicate Freud's theory, since it appears that anal children have anal mothers. But a further finding runs counter to the theory. The mothers were asked at what age they toilet-trained their children. There was no correlation whatever between this factor and the personality traits that define the anal character (Beloff, 1957).

This result fits in with other studies on the effects of toilet training. Some parents begin toilet training when their infant is as young as five months; others wait until the child is two years old. There are some slight indications that starting later makes the whole process simpler and may minimize certain childhood disorders of elimination such as bedwetting (Brazelton, 1962). But there is little evidence that shows any long-term effects growing out of toilet-training practices, either in our own or other cultures (Orlansky, 1949). For example, there seems to be no relation between the severity of toilet training in different cultures and the degree of hoarding or economic competition (Cohen, 1953). There is thus little evidence for Freud's claim that the toilet is a prep school for becoming a banker or a captain of industry.

But if so, what can we make of the fact that the three so-called "anal" traits form a cluster and seem to be transmitted from parent to child? Our best guess is that they are transmitted as part of a general pattern of middle-class values and attitudes, communicated by the general social atmosphere in which the child is raised and instilled as one facet of what the parents want the child to become. Seen in this light, obstinacy, orderliness, and parsimony may well be a result of the parents pushing their child toward independence and achievement. They are not by-products of getting the child out of diapers.

### Personality and Patterns of Defense: Psychoanalysis after Freud

A related approach to the description and analysis of personality differences is by reference to the dominant patterns of defense. Psychodynamic theorists believe that anxiety is an inevitable part of human existence and that some defenses against anxiety will therefore be found in everyone. What makes people different is the pattern of defenses they have erected. A number of authors have tried to describe some of the characteristic patterns observed in nineteenth-century Western society. Many of these theorists belong to a group of psychoanalytic dissidents often grouped together under the loose label *neo-Freudians.* By and large, the neo-Freudians accepted Freud's general views on internal conflicts but had different ideas as to what these conflicts were about. Their main argument with

***Self-destructive behavior*** *(From Kliban, B.* Luminous animals. *New York: Penguin Books, 1983. Copyright 1983, B. Kliban, Penguin Books)*

Freud was in their insistence that the description of our inner conflicts should be in social and interpersonal rather than biological terms (see Chapter 11).

### PATTERNS OF NEUROTIC CONFLICT

A major figure of the neo-Freudian movement was Karen Horney (1885–1952), who argued that many people in our society suffer from **basic anxiety**—an "all-pervading feeling of being alone and helpless in a hostile world" (Horney, 1937, p. 89). Horney believed that this anxious feeling should not be traced to childhood struggles with infantile sexual conflicts. She felt that instead its roots are in our culture, which often makes incompatible demands on the individual.

According to Karen Horney, the neurotics' basic anxiety leads them to the frantic pursuit of various goals, sought less for themselves than as a way to deaden this anxiety. Some neurotics try to assuage their anxiety by seeking love, others by seeking prestige or possessions, still others by withdrawing from any genuine emotional involvements, and yet others by deadening it with alcohol or drugs (Horney, 1937, 1945, 1950). Such efforts often fail, but they generally persist and harden into enduring patterns of personality. The question is why. Horney's answer is that the neurotic conflict creates a self-perpetuating **vicious circle.**

An example of such a vicious circle is the neurotic search for love. If a man needs a woman's love to deaden his sense of basic anxiety, his demands for affection will be unconditional and excessive. But if so, they can't possibly be fulfilled. The slightest failure to accede to his wishes will be interpreted as a rebuff and rejection. This will increase his feelings of anxiety, which will make him even more desperate for affectionate reassurance, which will further increase the chances of rebuff, and so on. Add the fact that such rebuffs—whether real or imagined— lead to hostility, which he can't possibly acknowledge lest he lose her altogether. Add the further fact that since his basic anxiety makes him devalue himself, he may well begin to devalue her. How could she be as wonderful as he thought at first, if she loves *him?* As Groucho Marx once said, "I wouldn't want to belong to any club that would accept me as a member." All of these further factors combine to enhance the love-seeking neurotic's sense of anxiety, which then refuels his desperate need for love and affection.

While vicious circles of this kind are a characteristic of deeply disturbed and unhappy persons, minor versions of such circular mechanisms are found in everyday life. A student has to write an important paper. The paper worries her so she puts it off. This makes her feel guilty, which makes her more anxious, which makes her put it off yet further, and so on (Hall, Lindzey, Loehlin, and Manosevitz, 1985). But as Horney points out, there are occasional "lucky circles." Some fortunate encounters in work or love may reverse the circle, by increasing self-confidence, which leads to appropriate further efforts and further successes. But all too often, the neurotic's own conflicts make her unable to recognize whatever luck may come her way. Put another way, neurotic conflicts tend to perpetuate themselves, which is one reason why at least some people try to break the pattern by seeking some form of psychotherapeutic help.

### COPING PATTERNS AND MENTAL HEALTH

The patterns we have just described characterize people with emotional conflicts that in some cases are quite serious. But can they help us understand normal persons? Psychodynamically oriented theorists would say that they can. For in their view, unconscious conflict and defense mechanisms are found in so-called normals as well as in persons with profound emotional disorders; what distinguishes the two is the extent to which those conflicts are appropriately resolved.

Several investigators have studied the characteristic patterns of defense using normal persons. Much of this work was influenced by an emerging new movement in psychoanalysis, called **ego psychology,** whose initial impetus probably came from Freud's daughter Anna Freud (1895–1982), and whose leaders include Heinz Hartmann (1894–1970), as well as Erik Erikson (1902–      ), whose work we've encountered in a previous chapter (see Chapter 15). Adherents of this position share the neo-Freudian concern with cultural factors and interpersonal factors. But they add a further element by stressing the healthy aspects of the self as it tries to *cope* with the world—to deal with reality as it is rather than to distort it or hide away from it (Freud, A., 1946; Hartmann, 1964).*

To find out how coping patterns are employed over the course of the life span, a number of investigators have performed **longitudinal studies,** that is, studies in which the same person is examined at different ages. Longitudinal studies that cover a span of twenty to thirty years represent an arduous undertaking; subjects drop out of the study for any number of reasons, and the investigators who begin the study are rarely the ones who finally complete it. In longitudinal studies of personality, the raw material is usually in the form of interview records conducted at different points in time. These records are later rated for various characteristics, such as certain personality traits, or the use of this or another mechanism of defense.

An example of such a longitudinal study is George Vaillant's analysis of the case reports of ninety-four male college graduates studied at different points in their life span. They were extensively interviewed at age nineteen and then again at thirty-one, and yet again at forty-seven. Vaillant studied the predominant patterns of defense—that is, ways of coping—each man used at these three ages. He classified these coping patterns according to their level of psychological maturity. At the bottom of the hierarchy were mechanisms that are often found in early childhood, and during serious psychiatric breakdown—for example, denial or gross distortions of external reality. Further up the ladder were patterns often seen in adolescence and in disturbed adults—for example, projection, hypochondria, and irrational, emotional outbursts, "acting out." Still higher were the mechanisms studied by Freud and seen in many adults—repression, isolation, reaction formation, and the like. At the top of the hierarchy were coping patterns that Vaillant had seen in "healthy" adolescents and adults—for example, humor, suppression (a conscious effort to push anxiety-evoking thoughts out of mind, at least for the time being, as opposed to repression, which is an unconscious process), and altruism (in which one tries to give to others what one might wish to receive oneself).

Vaillant's findings are simple enough. It's not particularly surprising (though certainly reassuring), that as his subjects grew older, their coping mechanisms generally became more mature. There was growth and change, but there was also some continuity; men whose coping patterns were better integrated at nineteen,

---

* A more recent and influential version of this ego-oriented position is **self psychology,** developed by Heinz Kohut (1913–1981) (Kohut, 1978).

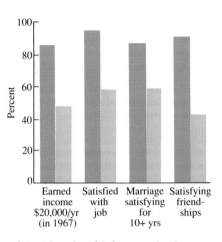

**18.1 Maturity of defense mechanisms and life adjustment** *Adult success at work and love, as shown by men with predominantly mature (blue) and immature (pink) adaptive styles. (After Vaillant, 1971)*

were—somewhat—more likely to have mature patterns in their forties, which then predicted various objective indices—satisfaction in marriage, rewarding friendships, more gratifying jobs, and better physical health (see Figure 18.1). As so often, it is by no means clear just what in those men's lives was cause and what was effect; but regardless of whether the mature coping defenses produced success in marriage and career or vice versa, it is worth knowing that the two tend to be correlated (Vaillant, 1974, 1976, 1977).

Similar results were obtained in a study by Jack Block that may be one of the most systematic longitudinal studies of personality ever undertaken. Block studied case records of some 250 men and women in junior high school, senior high school, and when they were in their thirties. A great deal of information had been gathered about each of these subjects at each time period, including lengthy interviews, tests of intelligence and personality, self-descriptions, life histories, and observations of actual behavior. In addition there were data about the family life of the subjects when they were around two, at which time both parents were interviewed and observed with the child in the home situation. All of this material was then given to (different) judges to rate along a number of personality categories (Block, 1971).

In many ways, the results were similar to those of Vaillant. Like Vaillant, Block found a general increase in overall personal adjustment. But he also found considerable evidence of continuity in characteristics such as grooming, enjoyment of social activities, self-assurance, and desire for achievement. In addition, he found a relation between the subjects' adjustment as adults and the family background from which they came. By and large, the well-adjusted adults were those that had a (psychologically) benign family atmosphere. Their mothers and fathers were active, self-assured, and warm, and took their parenting tasks seriously; they provided firm guidelines but were affectionate in doing so. In contrast, the subjects judged to be more poorly adjusted as adults came from less favorable family backgrounds. The parents were often at odds with each other, and they were either overinvolved with their child, or rejecting, dictatorial, or indifferent. As Block points out, these early histories differ widely; all that they have in common is that they are unfavorable. This is quite different from those of the more well-adjusted subjects, which tend to be much more alike. There are more ways to make a machine (or a human body, or a human personality) function badly than to make it work properly. As the Russian novelist Leo Tolstoy put it in *Anna Karenina,* "Happy families are all alike; every unhappy family is unhappy in its own way" (Tolstoy, 1875).

Block interprets these correlations in cause-and-effect terms. As he sees it, the parents provided a familial atmosphere that ultimately helped shape their child for good or ill by inducing healthy or unhealthy coping patterns. But as we saw in the previous chapter, this interpretation does not necessarily follow. One possibility is that the correlation was produced by a genetic similarity between child and parents. Another possibility is that the cause-and-effect relation is the reverse of the one proposed by Block; the child's own personality (in part, perhaps, based on genetic factors) may have influenced the way the parents treated her. No doubt there are other interpretations as well. Our present concern is merely to stress the enormous complexity of the issues. As yet, we have no easy solutions to the question of how any of us came to be the person we now are. (For further discussion, see Chapter 15, pp. 594–95.)

COPING AND THE UNCONSCIOUS

On the face of it, the preceding discussion of adaptive patterns may appear rather distant from the orientation of psychodynamic theorists, especially as represented by Freud. After all, Freud emphasized unconscious processes that operated in a murky underground of which we are unaware. In contrast, the coping responses of normal people seem much more ordinary, and they are at least sometimes in plain view. Is there any relation between these two?

Ego-oriented psychoanalysts—and most modern psychologists—would answer yes. For whatever their many differences, the defense mechanisms of the neurotic and the shoulder-shrugging reaction of the mature adult who refuses to worry about things he can't help anyway have one thing in common—they are both ways of trying to cope with and adapt to the strains and stresses of existence.

The fact that some of these adaptive reactions are fully conscious while others are not doesn't necessarily mean that there is a sharp break between them. For a number of psychologists have pointed out that what Freud called unconscious mechanisms may be regarded as ways of not attending (Erdelyi and Goldberg, 1979; Bowers, 1984; Erdelyi, 1985). The person who is in favor of a particular political candidate is much more likely to attend to arguments on his behalf than to arguments that favor his opponent. The first he will tend to remember; the second he is likely to forget. Similarly, the woman who has just suffered a painful divorce may prefer not to think about her ex-husband. When some topic comes up that starts to remind her about him, she will deliberately try to think about something else and may forget what it was that started the new train of thought. This method of turning away from one's own pain may not be as exotic as the complicated repressive maneuvers of Freud's patients, but it belongs to the same family.

Most of us physically avoid some situations we would rather not face; by the same token, some of us mentally avoid (that is, don't attend to) sights or thoughts or memories we find unpleasant or frightening. Seen in this light, the so-called unconscious mechanisms lose some of their mystery. They are just one more way of dealing with the world. (For further discussion, see Chapter 11, p. 448.)

## BEHAVIORAL APPROACHES TO PERSONALITY

Both trait theory and the psychodynamic approach try to explain the differences in what people do by reference to something that is within them: the one appeals to stable and perhaps built-in internal predispositions (that is, traits), the other to hidden conflicts and desires. The trait approach argues that people do what they do because of who they are: The jovial backslapper is the life of the party because he is an extreme extrovert. The psychodynamic approach argues that they do what they do because of what they want (even though they rarely know it): The backslapper clowns and laughs because he is covering up his own sense of emptiness (or his buried Oedipal conflicts or whatever). But there is an alternative view that takes issue with both trait theory and the psychodynamic orientation. This is the behavioral approach (which as we'll see, is a view with many shadings).

A       B       C

*Repertory roles*   *Lawrence Olivier is often regarded as the prototype of the repertory actor who could play any part. He once said that "in finding a character . . . I do it from the outside in," an approach quite different from that of the Actor's Studio. (A) As Hamlet (from the 1948 film he directed), (B) As Archie Rice, a cheap music hall entertainer (from the 1960 film,* The Entertainer*), (C) as the Mahdi, the fanatical leader of a 19th-century Sudanese sect (from the 1966 film* Khartoum*). (Courtesy Photofest)*

In contrast to trait and psychodynamic theory, the ***behavioral approach****\** asserts that human actions are determined from without: they are reactions to the external forces that impinge upon the person. This approach holds that people do what they do because of the situation in which they find themselves or in which they have found themselves on previous occasions. The life of the party acts his part precisely because he is *at* a party, a situation in which he will be reinforced for being outgoing and boisterous, as he has no doubt been reinforced on many previous occasions. This general view is obviously related to the situationist critique of trait theory we considered in the previous chapter (see Chapter 17, pp. 693–95). It is a position that is traditionally associated with ***behaviorism,*** a very influential theoretical outlook that dominated American psychology for the first half of this century, emphasizing the role of environment and of learning, and insisting that people, no less than animals, must be studied objectively— from the outside (see Chapter 4).

If the trait approach can be likened to dramatic productions with character types who wear one mask that defines them throughout, the behavioral view corresponds to the dramatic approach of a repertory company in which every member takes many parts. Today he plays one role, tomorrow he learns to play another, depending upon the play. Nor is the way he plays them determined by anything from inside. Actors of the behavioral school don't worry about inner motivations or subtle subtexts. If required to enact an emotion, they don't try to feel it themselves. They will instead pay a great deal of attention to its visible bodily manifestations; they will tremble or sway or clench their fists or breathe more rapidly, depending upon the particular emotion they want to enact. For in their view, all that matters is their outer behavior, because that's all the audience ever hears or sees. Here again, they are much like behavior theorists, who believe that the only way to understand people is by studying them objectively—from the outside.

---

\* This is sometimes called the *behavioral-cognitive* approach, since many recent adherents of the behavioral position assign increasing importance to cognitive factors such as expectations and beliefs.

***Radical behaviorism*** *(Drawing by W. Miller; © 1963, The New Yorker Magazine, Inc.)*

## Radical Behaviorism

Behaviorism comes in a number of different forms, some more "radical" than others. The most influential modern exponent of ***radical behaviorism*** is B.F. Skinner (1904–1990). To him, the subject matter of psychology is overt behavior and nothing else, without any reference to inferred, internal processes such as wishes, traits, or expectations. In Skinner's view, humans—no less than rats and pigeons—behave according to the way they are prompted by the external environment. This environment may be today's—people wear overcoats in the winter and polo shirts in the summer. But more often the relevant environment is yesterday's, when a particular situation led to learning.

In some cases, the relevant learning is by ***classical conditioning.*** Some hitherto neutral stimulus is paired with some motivationally significant event and will then elicit the same response; a dog salivates when it sees the food dish or a child cries when she sees the nurse who gave her a painful injection. In others, the learning is by ***operant (or instrumental) conditioning.*** A reinforcement is made contingent on some response, which will then be emitted in the future; a rat presses a lever for a food reward, or a four-year-old reverts to baby talk to get her parent's attention. In either case, what matters is the external environment that provides the conditions for learning. (For a review, see Chapter 4, p. 115.)

There is no doubt that Skinner's behaviorism represents a powerful and influential view of human—and, of course, of animal—nature. But can it account for the characteristic differences that we call differences in personality? Many behaviorists believe that it can. In their view, to say that people are different is just to say that they behave differently. Suppose Jane is generally sociable, while Anne is withdrawn, even when the external circumstances are the same. As Skinner sees it, there is little gained by attributing this difference to a difference in the trait of "sociability." He would instead assume that there is a difference in the two reinforcement histories. In the past, Jane was probably reinforced for amiable chatting, while Anne was offered little or no encouragement. Seen in this light, the so-called trait of sociability is just another case of operant learning (e.g., Skinner, 1969, 1971).

This line of argument brings up an immediate question. If reinforcement produces the difference between Jane and Anne, why do such differences often persist even when the reinforcements are changed? For persist they do. Jane will continue to smile and chatter even after her dinner party companions have become bored and stopped listening, while Anne will sit back in a corner despite everyone's best efforts to lure her out. Eventually, no doubt, both women will respond to the changed circumstances, but why does it generally take so long? Felix and Oscar of the *Odd Couple* will stay respectively fussy and sloppy no matter what, and Theophrastus's garrulous man will keep on talking and talking even though every citizen of Athens has repeatedly yawned in his face. It's just this persistence of characteristic behavior patterns that led to the idea that there are personality traits. How can Skinner (or any other behavior theorist) account for this persistence of characteristic behaviors?

The answer depends upon whether we are talking about behavior produced by operant or by classical conditioning. If the relevant behavior was developed by operant conditioning, the key to its persistence is the phenomenon of ***intermittent*** (sometimes called ***partial***) ***reinforcement.*** As we have seen in Chapter 4, resistance to extinction is markedly increased by intermittent reinforcement. Rats who are rewarded every time they run down an alley will stop running after a few trials if no more reward is obtained. But the situation is quite different when they are rewarded on only some proportion of the trials. Now they'll keep on running even when there is no reward, as if they've learned that if at first you don't succeed, it generally pays to try again.

According to Skinner and other behaviorists, what holds for rats, holds for people too. Many behavior patterns persist because they've been rewarded only sometimes. Gamblers keep on pulling slot machine levers because the machine pays off every once in a while, and children continue to throw temper tantrums because their parents did not ignore them—and thus extinguish them—all the time. Some people consistently whine and wheedle favors; others bully; still others sulk. Wheedling worked for the one, bullying for the other, and sulking for the third; not always, but sometimes, and that is precisely why each is still persisting in his characteristic behavior pattern. Similarly for Jane and Anne, who continue to smile or sit quietly because of previous intermittent reinforcement for these behavior patterns.

Behavior theorists offer a different explanation for the persistence of classically conditioned reactions based on fear. The reason is that avoidance learning is generally difficult to extinguish. Consider a little girl who became intensely afraid of dogs after she was accidentally knocked down by an overly playful Saint Bernard. Her fear was based on classical conditioning, with the dog as the conditioned stimulus and the pain as the unconditioned stimulus. Her fear generalized, so she avoided all dogs. As a result, she was never exposed to situations in which the presence of a dog was *not* followed by unpleasant consequences, so the fear never extinguished. The fear was self-perpetuating; it kept her from "testing reality" so she could never discover that it was—now—essentially groundless (see Chapters 4, p. 123, and 20, p. 811).

*Is personality coherent?* *Some early versions of the behavioral-cognitive approach argued that the consistency of personality is an illusion. (*Nude Descending a Staircase *by Marcel Duchamp, 1912; courtesy Philadelphia Museum of Art/Louise and Walter Arensberg Collection)*

## Social Learning Theory

While impressed with radical behaviorism's successes in achieving precise experimental control in some areas of behavior (especially in the animal laboratory), many authors have had misgivings over its ability to describe, let alone to explain, the more complex aspects of human personality. To be sure, people differ in their behavior—some brag, others sulk, still others tease—but can we define these subtle, interpersonal responses as readily as we can define the response of lever pressing in a rat? Nor is it clear that outer behavior is all that matters. Personality differences involve not only what people do but also what they generally think and believe and expect. The fact that Joe believes that women can't be trusted and that Carol expects to fail no matter how hard she tries are important aspects of their behavior. Such facts clearly go beyond the outwardly observable aspects of behavior, and as such they are difficult to describe in the language of radical behaviorism.

Such considerations gradually led to a liberalized behavioral approach to personality, which now accepts terms like "expectation" and "belief" as a matter of course. Those who subscribe to this modified approach to personality are often called *social learning theorists,* including such figures as Albert Bandura, Julian Rotter, and Walter Mischel.

At first glance, one might well think that social learning theorists would downplay the role of personality differences in predicting human behavior. For it was they (most prominently, Walter Mischel) who had attacked trait theory by arguing that differences between situations are more important than differences between persons in determining what people do. But by now, virtually everyone—whether trait or social learning theorist—has abandoned the extremes of the trait-situation controversy and agrees that both persons and situations matter, as well as the interaction between the two (see Chapter 17). Thus social learning theorists do accept the notion of personality differences after all. But what are the terms in which they express that notion?

In essence, they believe that many of the personal qualities that characterize different people are essentially cognitive: different ways of seeing the world, thinking about it, and interacting with it, acquired in the course of an individual's history. Mischel lists some of the cognitive qualities on which people may differ. One concerns the individual's *competencies*—the kinds of things a person can do and understand. Another concerns her *encoding strategies*—the way she tends to interpret situations. A third refers to her *expectancies*—her beliefs about what follows what: what acts will produce what outcomes, what events will lead to what consequences, and so on. A fourth difference concerns her *subjective values*—which outcomes she values. A final difference involves what Mischel calls *self-regulatory systems*—the way in which a person regulates her own behavior by various self-imposed goals and plans (Mischel, 1973, 1984).

***Loss of control*** *Patients in a Florida nursing home. (Photograph by Michael Heron, 1983/Woodfin Camp)*

CONTROL

We will consider only a few of the cognitive categories along which personalities may differ. One concerns a certain kind of expectancy: people's beliefs about the control they can exert on the world around them. But before discussing what different individuals *believe* about control, a few words are in order about the fact that just about all of them generally seem to *desire* it.

In a previous discussion, we saw that animals and babies behave as if they want to have a sense of control over their lives. Babies smile if an overhead mobile turns around because they made it turn; if it turns around regardless of what they do, they stop smiling. Dogs can cope with electric shocks if they can escape them; other dogs who get the same number of shocks no matter what they do, will suffer from learned helplessness (see Chapter 4). What holds for animals and babies also holds for human adults. They too prefer control.

A widely cited illustration is a series of studies of elderly persons in a nursing home. Patients on one floor of a nursing home were given small houseplants to take care of, and they were also asked to choose the time at which they wanted to participate in some of the nursing home activities (for example, visiting friends, watching television, planning social events). Patients on another floor were also given plants but with the understanding that they would be tended by the staff. They also participated in the same activities as the first group of patients, but at times chosen by the staff rather than by them. The results were clear-cut. According to both nurses and the patients' own report, the patients that were allowed to exert control were more active and felt better than the patients who lacked this control; this difference was still apparent a year later (Langer and Rodin, 1976; Rodin and Langer, 1977).

frustrated in the bargain) that they can continue to apply to more complex goal-directed efforts as they get older.

### SOCIAL LEARNING THEORY AND BEHAVIORISM

Looking back over our discussion, it's clear that social learning theorists have taken a considerable interest in relatively stable and generalized personal characteristics, as revealed by studies of locus of control, attributional style, and delay of gratification. But if so, how do they differ from trait theorists? They have also moved further and further away from radical behaviorism, having become increasingly interested in all kinds of cognitive processes, such as expectations, beliefs, and plans, none of which are directly observable from the outside. But if so, in what sense do they still regard themselves as behaviorists?

There are two answers. One has to do with the situation. By now, there is virtually no one who adheres to either extreme of the trait-situation controversy; but even so, social learning theorists, true to their behaviorist lineage, are more likely to stress the role of situational factors (or of a person-situation interaction) than trait theorists are. Thus Mischel found that delay of gratification is an index of a surprisingly stable personal attribute, but he was quick to point out that this index is strongly affected by the way the situation was set up (Was the reward visible?) and how it was construed (Did the child think about eating the reward?).

There is another answer that is even more important. For unlike trait theorists, who are generally inclined to believe that the major personality traits have a built-in, genetic basis, social learning theorists are more likely to assume that most such attributes are a result of learning. In this regard, social learning theory still shares the environmentalist bias that is a hallmark of American behaviorism. For both radical behaviorists and their social learning theory descendants hold to an empiricist world view, which in its extreme form asserts that virtually anyone can become anything by proper (or in some cases, improper) training. This view was well-expressed in a widely quoted pronouncement by the founder of American behaviorism, John B. Watson:

> Give me a dozen healthy infants, well-formed, and my own specified world to bring them up in and I'll guarantee to take any one at random and train him to become any type of specialist I might select—doctor, lawyer, artist, merchant-chief, and, yes even beggarman thief, regardless of his talents, penchants, tendencies, abilities, vocations, and race of his ancestors. (J.B. Watson, 1925)

This is just another way of climbing out to the most extreme pole of the nature-nurture controversy as it pertains to individual differences. Put in terms of our theatrical metaphor, it's a way of saying that any actor can take any part at all, put on any mask whatever, as long as he's properly coached.

Needless to say, such an extreme position is no longer held by anyone. As in most other areas of psychology, there is virtually no one who believes that behavior is determined by nature alone or by nurture alone. In this sense, the nature-nurture controversy is over. What's left are different biases. For different psychologists will still make different bets about which factors will be most illuminating in understanding this or another facet of a person—a built-in, genetic disposition, or its learning history. Trait theorists generally make one bet, and social learning theorists make the other. But sometimes, of course, there is no more room for betting, for the facts are already in.

## THE HUMANISTIC APPROACH

Some thirty years ago, a new perspective on human motivation and personality gained some prominence: the so-called *humanistic approach.* According to its adherents, neither trait theorists, psychodynamic theorists, or behaviorists have much to say about healthy, striving human beings. Psychoanalysts look at people as if they are all emotional cripples, behaviorists regard them as if they are blind, unthinking robots, and trait theorists see them as material to file in sterile pigeonholes. Humanistic psychologists believe that all of these views have lost sight of what is truly human about human beings. Healthy humans want to feel free to choose and determine their own lives rather than to exist as mere pawns pushed around by stimuli from without and unconscious impulses from within. They seek more than food and sex and safety, strive for more than mere adjustment—they want to grow, to develop their potentialities, to become *self-actualized.*

Returning to our theatrical analogy, the humanistic approach can be likened to certain modern movements in theater that emphasize spontaneity and improvisation. Actors who belong to this school insist that what is most important is genuine, authentic feeling. At least in principle (though rarely in actual practice), such actors might depart from the playwright's words and the director's stagings, to provide the audience and themselves with a sense of freedom and spontaneity. To the extent that this occurs, there is no mask left at all; the actor and the part have become one.

***Improvisation*** *Some actors are famed for their ability to improvise on the spur of the moment. An example is Robin Williams, who improvised many of his lines in the film* Good Morning Vietnam, *1987. (Courtesy the Kobal Collection)*

### The Major Features of the Humanistic Movement

According to Abraham Maslow (1908–1970), the humanistic movement represents a kind of "third force" in American psychology—the other two being behaviorism and psychoanalysis. For expositional purposes, we will begin by presenting some of the major features of this movement with a minimum of editorial comment before discussing them more critically.

#### A POSITIVE VIEW OF HUMAN MOTIVATION

A major contrast between humanistic psychologists and the behaviorists and psychoanalysts that they oppose is in their contrasting conception of human motivation. According to Maslow, behaviorists and psychoanalysts see human beings as engaged in a never-ending struggle to remove some internal tension or make up for some deficit. The result is an essentially pessimistic and negative conception of human nature. Seen in this light, people always want to get away from something (pain, hunger, sexual tension) rather than to gain something positive. This perspective necessarily led to an emphasis on the physiological needs—hunger, thirst, escape from pain, sex. Maslow called these *deficiency needs;* in all these cases, we experience a lack and want to fill it. According to Maslow, an analogous

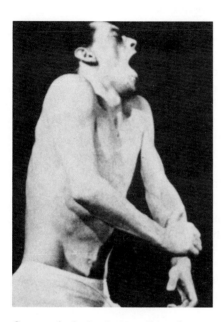

**Spontaneity in the theater** *Several modern movements emphasize spontaneity and creativity in the theater. An influential example is the theatrical school founded by the Polish director Jerzy Grotowski who requires his actors to perform in a kind of trance, to give themselves totally, in a confrontation with the play and the audience. The figure is taken from one of his productions,* The Constant Prince, *by Pedro Calderón de la Barca. (Reproduced by permission of Jerzy Grotowski)*

**18.3  Maslow's hierarchy of needs**
*People will strive for higher-order needs (esteem or artistic achievement) generally after lower-order needs (hunger, safety) have been satisfied. (After Maslow, 1954)*

deficiency sometimes underlies the so-called "social needs," such as the desire for prestige or security; an example is the woman who "hungers" for the admiration of all men around her and feels empty without it. But as Maslow pointed out, release from pain and tension does not account for everything we strive for. For we sometimes seek things for their own sake, as a positive goal in themselves rather than as a means to remove a noxious state. There is the joy of solving a puzzle, the exhilaration of galloping on a horse, the ecstasy of fulfilled love, the quiet rapture in the contemplation of great art and music or a beautiful sunrise. All of these are experiences that human beings seek, and it is these positive, enriching experiences—rather than the filled stomach or the sexual release at orgasm—that make us most distinctively human. A hungry rat and a sexually aroused monkey seek food and orgasmic release pretty much as we do, but the joy of Beethoven's Ninth Symphony is ours alone. Maslow insisted that to understand what is truly human, psychologists must consider motives that go beyond the deficiency needs (Maslow, 1968).

Maslow proposed that there is a ***hierarchy of needs,*** in which the lower-order physiological needs are at the bottom, safety needs are further up, the need for attachment and love is still higher, and the desire for esteem is yet higher. At the very top of the hierarchy is the striving for ***self-actualization***—the desire to realize oneself to the fullest (of which more later). (See Figure 18.3.)

Maslow believed that people will only strive for higher-order needs (say, seek esteem or artistic achievement) when lower-order needs (such as hunger) are satisfied. By and large this is plausible enough; the urge to write poetry generally takes a back place if one hasn't eaten for days. But as Maslow pointed out, there are exceptions. Some artists starve rather than give up their poetry or their paint-

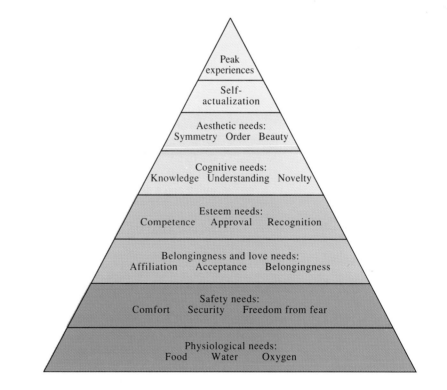

Peak experiences

Self-actualization

Aesthetic needs:
Symmetry  Order  Beauty

Cognitive needs:
Knowledge  Understanding  Novelty

Esteem needs:
Competence  Approval  Recognition

Belongingness and love needs:
Affiliation  Acceptance  Belongingness

Safety needs:
Comfort  Security  Freedom from fear

Physiological needs:
Food  Water  Oxygen

ing, and some martyrs proclaim their faith regardless of pain or suffering. But to the extent that Maslow's assumption holds, the motive at the very top of his hierarchy—that is, the drive toward self-actualization—will become a primary concern only when all the other needs beneath are satisfied.

### THE SELF IN HUMANISTIC PSYCHOLOGY

Before trying to describe what Maslow and other humanistic psychologists mean by self-actualization, we should say a word about the self that is (or is not) being actualized. We've previously encountered some issues related to the self; social psychologists study it under the headings of self-perception theory and self-presentation (pp. 471, 477–79), and Freud and Piaget treat it as a developmental matter since they believe that the "ego" emerges from an earlier diffuse state in which there is no self at all (pp. 431–32 and 549). To humanistic psychologists, the self is even more important, for one of their primary concerns is with subjective experience—with what the individual thinks and feels right here and now. According to Carl Rogers (1902–1987), who was a major figure in the humanistic movement, a crucial facet of this subjective experience is the *self* or *self-concept.* This self-concept is developed in early childhood and eventually comes to include one's sense of oneself as an agent who takes (or doesn't take) actions and makes (or doesn't make) decisions—the "I." It also includes one's sense of oneself as a kind of object that is seen and thought about and liked or disliked—the "me" (Rogers, 1959, 1961).

In the course of his work in clinical counseling, Rogers came to feel that an important condition for adult mental health is a solid sense of personal self-worth. Rogers believed that to achieve this the child requires ***unconditional positive regard***—the sense of being accepted and loved without condition or reservation. But such a prescription for child rearing is difficult to follow. For the parents can (and no doubt must) disapprove of some of the things the child does; they are unlikely to applaud when little Janie spills ketchup all over the new living room rug. They could still show Janie their unconditional positive regard by making it clear that while they certainly don't love *her behavior* they do and always will love *her.* But this is much easier said than done. Most parents probably do set some conditions on their love, no matter how subtly, indicating that they'll love her if she'll do well at school, or if she acts like a nice girl, or whatever. Rogers believed that the likely upshot is that the child will suppress some aspect of herself in order to feel loved and accepted. And this in turn may lead to a sense of confusion and disquiet, and a doubt of one's real self-worth.

### SELF-ACTUALIZATION

Given a reasonable sense of self-worth and the satisfaction of the lower-level needs, the stage is set for the motive at the very top of Maslow's hierarchy of needs, the desire for self-actualization. Maslow and other humanistic psychologists describe this as the desire to realize one's potentialities, to fulfill oneself, to become what one can become (Maslow, 1968, 1970). But exactly what does this mean?

Maslow gave some examples by presenting case histories of a number of persons that he and his collaborators regarded as "self-actualized." Some of them were actual persons that he had interviewed; others were historical figures (for ex-

*Self-actualization shown through self-portraits*  To actualize one's self may take a whole lifetime. Some great artists have given us a graphic record of the process at different points in their life, as in these self-portraits by Rembrandt. One was created at the age of 34, when he was very successful and saw himself as a Renaissance gentleman artist and virtuoso. The other was painted at about age 60, when he tried to reaffirm his identity through his art and portrayed himself as a painter holding the tools of his craft (Wright, 1982). (Left: Self-Portrait at the Age of 34; courtesy National Gallery. Right: Portrait of the Artist; courtesy English Heritage, The Iveagh Bequest)

ample, Thomas Jefferson and Ludwig van Beethoven) or recent luminaries (such as Eleanor Roosevelt and Albert Einstein), whose lives were studied by means of historical or other documents. Unlike most other investigators in the field, Maslow was not interested in these subjects' specific attributes or behavior patterns; all he looked for were some overall patterns that he felt were shared by them all. As Maslow saw it, these self-actualizers had many admirable characteristics. Among other things, they were realistically oriented, accepted themselves and others, were spontaneous, cared more about the problems they were working on than about themselves, had intimate relationships with a few people rather than superficial relationships with many, and had democratic values—all in all, an admirable list of human qualities (Maslow, 1968, 1970).

According to Maslow, one characteristic of self-actualized persons is that they are more likely to have so-called ***peak experiences*** than other people. Peak experiences are profound and deeply felt moments in a person's life, in which there is a "feeling of great ecstasy and awe . . . with the conviction that something extremely important and valuable had happened . . ." (Maslow, 1970, p. 164). Such moments might come while with a lover, or while watching the sea or a sunset, or while listening to music or watching a play—but regardless of when and where they occur, they seem to have some important and lasting effects on the individual who thereafter is likely to see himself and others in a more spontaneous and healthier way.

GROWTH

What happens to people whose self-regard is so low that the possibility of self-actualization doesn't arise? According to Rogers, some of these defects in one's sense of self could be healed by a special form of therapy in later life that provides a person with important growth experiences he lacked before. Rogers believed that new experiences in later life could provide some of the spontaneous warmth and positive regard that was lacking earlier. To that end, his therapy offered the client warmth and showed him that *his* feelings are accepted and that *he* is worthy of love (Rogers, 1980; for more details, see Chapter 20, p. 818).

Rogers's approach to therapy illustrates that he—and indeed most humanistic psychologists—regard the development of human personality as a kind of growth process. They believe that if given the appropriate conditions people will grow so as to realize their inherent potential. They further believe that in general this potential is for good rather than for evil. In this regard, their position is the very opposite of that held by such pessimists as Hobbes and Freud who insisted that Man cannot help but be a brute unless his baser instincts are tamed by civilization. In contrast, Rogers and Maslow felt that humans will only turn sour and ugly if they are somehow twisted and frustrated by the social conditions in which they live.

According to Rogers, people will attain a healthy sense of self if they are provided with the proper emotional climate. To grow into a healthy rose, the rose seedling needs water, sun, and soil. In the same vein, Rogers believed that humans will grow to be emotionally healthy if they are provided with warmth and acceptance, with what he called *empathic understanding* (where someone seems to understand what you feel, and so to speak "feels it with you"), and if they are with another person who is *genuine* (without a facade—open and trustworthy). His logic was simple. At bottom, people are good; given half a chance, they'll grow into their proper, good selves, just as the rose will bloom, given soil, water, and sunshine.

## Evaluating the Humanistic Approach

What can we say by way of evaluating the humanistic approach to personality? We should begin by asking about its empirical and conceptual foundations.

### EMPIRICAL AND CONCEPTUAL DIFFICULTIES

*"I'm quite fulfilled. I always wanted to be a chicken." (Drawing by Joseph Farris; © 1989, The New Yorker Magazine, Inc.)*

Consider Rogers's account of the origins of the feeling of self-worth. Is it really true that unconditional positive regard and empathic understanding are essential for the development of self-worth? We've previously noted the enormous difficulties in drawing any conclusions about the effects of child rearing on later personality development (see Chapter 15). Under the circumstances, Rogers's description of the parent-child relationships that lead to feelings of adequate or inadequate self-worth seems rather oversimplified. Nor is it clear that his form of therapy has all the beneficial effects that he claimed for it, though there is some evidence in his favor, especially for milder cases (Rogers, 1951; Rogers and Dymond, 1954).

Similar qualifications apply to a number of other assertions made by the proponents of the humanistic approach. How do we know that self-actualizers are in fact as Maslow described them to be—for example, realistically oriented, accepting of themselves and others, spontaneous, problem-centered, democratic, and so on? Or that peak experiences have lasting and often beneficial effects on later life? Or that self-actualizers have more such peak experiences than other people? As yet, there is no real evidence that would allow us to decide.

An even more serious criticism is the fact that many of the core conceptions of the humanistic approach are exceedingly unclear. Just what is meant by self-actualization, or by "letting yourself go and being yourself," or by unconditional positive regard, or by a peak experience? Since these terms are so vaguely defined, it is difficult to know how to evaluate any assertions about them.

Consider Maslow's study of self-actualizers. Maslow chose a number of persons as exemplars, including a number of prominent and historical figures. But by what criteria did he select them? Among the historical figures he chose were Thomas Jefferson, Abraham Lincoln (in his later years), Eleanor Roosevelt, and Albert Einstein. Most of us would agree that these were admirable and creative persons, and we can understand what is meant when someone says that they fulfilled their potentialities, and "actualized themselves." But why can't the same term be applied to many other individuals, some of whom are far from admirable and may be veritable monsters? What about Al Capone, or Napoleon, or even Adolf Hitler? It's very likely that these persons felt that they had become what they were meant to become (at least until Alcatraz, or St. Helena, or the final days in the Berlin bunker). But if so, why shouldn't we regard *them* as self-actualized? Given their belief that human growth has an inherent tendency toward good rather than evil, Maslow and Rogers would presumably rule out—by definition —moral monsters such as Capone or Hitler. But this line of reasoning can certainly be questioned. The development of personality may be a growth process, but this alone is not enough grounds for optimism. Given soil, sun, and water, a rose seedling will indeed become a rose. But if the seedling is a thistle, it may self-actualize and become a thistle.

### HUMANISTIC PSYCHOLOGY AS A PROTEST MOVEMENT

It appears that many of the major tenets of the humanistic approach to personality rest on rather shaky foundations. But if so, why should we take it seriously? One answer is that the humanistic approach is best considered as a protest movement. It reacts against both behaviorism and psychoanalysis because it regards them as representatives of a sterile mechanism that treats people as marionettes

*The theater of protest   The humanistic approach to personality is reminiscent of protest movements in the literary and political sphere. Examples are various modern dramatic productions that attack contemporary attitudes, as in Peter Weiss's play* Marat/Sade, *in which contemporary society is likened to an insane asylum. (From the 1966 filmed version of* Marat/Sade, *directed by Peter Brook; courtesy the Kobal Collection)*

**Romanticism in the arts**   *The romantic artists of the early 19th century stressed the full expression of the emotions. An example is this painting by Caspar David Friedrich. (*Man and Woman Gazing at the Moon; *courtesy Staatliche Museen Preussicher Kulturbesitz, Nationalgalerie, Berlin)*

pushed and pulled by forces from without and within. It reacts against trait psychology because it regards this approach as devoted to an endless cataloguing that reduces humans to mere ciphers. And it reacts against the general focus of much contemporary psychology, which it regards as narrow and pessimistic, oriented toward human sickness and deficiency rather than health and upward striving.

In some ways, the humanistic approach to personality is reminiscent of some prior movements in the political and literary spheres. Some two hundred years ago, the Romantic poets in England and Germany elevated feeling over reason, celebrated individualism and natural man, and deplored the effects of eighteenth-century science and technology. Some, such as William Blake and Samuel Coleridge, sought peak experiences in mystical visions or in opium dreams. Others railed against the cold, mechanical science that had left the universe dry and bare. An example is John Keats's lament that "Newton has destroyed all the poetry of the rainbow by reducing it to the prismatic colors" (Abrams, 1953, p. 303). And many of them agreed with the social philosopher Jean Jacques Rousseau (1712–1778), whose writings helped to shape the French and American Revolutions, that "man is by nature good, and . . . only our institutions have made him bad!" (in Durant and Durant, 1967, p. 19).

The similarity between these sentiments and many of the themes of the humanistic psychologists is clear enough. The Romantics protested against what they regarded as a cold, mechanical approach to nature and politics; the humanistic psychologists lodge similar complaints against contemporary approaches to psychology. This is not to say that the humanistic psychologists were directly influenced by Rousseau or the eighteenth-century Romantics, for they almost surely were not. The point is that by now Romanticism is a part of our cultural heritage that has provided a general vocabulary for many later protest movements. One example is the student revolution of the 1960s. Another is the humanistic movement in American psychology.

To be sure, the Romantic poets did much more than protest; they also made lasting contributions to literature. And Rousseau influenced the political landscape of Europe for a century after his death. Is there a corresponding positive contribution of humanistic psychology? Some critics feel that apart from Rogers's work on the practice and evaluation of psychotherapy, the humanists' concepts are as yet too vague and their assertions as yet too unproven to count as serious positive scientific accomplishments (e.g., Smith, 1950). Others argue that the humanists often serve as moral advocates rather than dispassionate scientists. They tell us what personality *should* be rather than what it *is*.

But there is one accomplishment of which we can be sure. The humanistic psychologists remind us of many phenomena that other approaches to the study of personality have largely ignored. People do strive for more than food and sex or prestige; they read poetry, listen to music, fall in love, have occasional peak experiences, try to actualize themselves. Whether the humanistic psychologists have really helped us to understand these elusive phenomena better than we did before is debatable. But there is no doubt that what they have done is to insist that these phenomena are there, that they constitute a vital aspect of what makes us human, and that they must not be ignored. By so insisting, they remind us of the unfinished tasks that a complete psychology of personality must ultimately deal with.

## TAKING STOCK

We've considered a number of approaches to personality. One is the trait approach, which tries to describe personality by reference to a few basic characteristics, many of which have a built-in basis. Another is the behavioral approach, which focuses on the individual's outwardly observable acts, and argues that these acts are produced by the situation that the individual faces now or has faced on previous occasions. Yet another is the psychodynamic approach, which centers on submerged feelings, unconscious conflicts and desires. And still another is the humanistic approach, which asks how people achieve their own selfhood and realize their human potentialities.

Today there are relatively few theorists who would espouse any of these approaches in their most extreme form. By now, most adherents of the behavioral approach have shifted to a more cognitive conception of the subject matter, most psychodynamic theorists see unconscious defenses and conscious coping mechanisms as parts of a continuum, and virtually everyone grants that what people do depends on both traits and situations.

But even so, some important differences in approach clearly remain. This is probably fortunate. For these different theoretical orientations reflect different perspectives on the same subject matter, each of which has some validity. Some aspects of personality are clearly built in (trait theory); others are learned (social learning theory); some reflect buried conflicts (psychodynamic theory); others reveal the need for self-actualization (humanistic approach). We cannot envisage what a complete theory of personality will look like in the year 2090, but it will surely have to describe all of these aspects of human functioning. For they are all there.

In this regard, the different perspectives on personality are again similar to different approaches to the presentation of character in literature or on stage. Is the human drama best described by the use of a number of stock types, perhaps designated by a few well-chosen masks, or by well-rounded characters that are like themselves alone and no others? There is no simple yes or no, for people are both similar to and different from each other. Is character best described by the Classicists, who stress human reason, or by the Romantics, who emphasize feeling? Again there is no answer, for both emotion and rationality are part of our very nature. Should actors portray the inner life and concentrate on what lies behind the mask, or should they focus on the outward mask since that is what the audience sees? Here too there is no answer, for we all have both an inner and an outer life.

We are similar to others but we are also different. We are pulled by outer and inner forces, but we are also free to make our own choices. We are rational, but we are also impelled by feeling. We are both the masks we wear and something else beneath. Each of the approaches to personality—and to dramatic character—focuses on one or another of these aspects of our nature. Each of these aspects exists. And to that extent each of the approaches is valid.

## SUMMARY

1. The *psychodynamic approach* is derived from Sigmund Freud's psychoanalytic theories, which emphasize *unconscious conflicts*. Many of these conflicts can be understood as defenses against *anxiety*. The fundamental defense is *repression*, often supplemented by other *defense mechanisms*, including reaction formation, displacement, rationalization, and projection. According to Freud, these conflicts have their origin during *psychosexual development* in early childhood, beginning with the *oral* and *anal* stages, continuing through the *phallic* stage and the accompanying turmoil of the *Oedipus complex*, and eventually culminating in the *genital* stage of adolescence and adulthood.

2. In Freud's view, differences in adult personality can be understood as residues of early *fixations* and *reaction formations*. An example is the *oral character*, whose nature he believed goes back to a powerful oral fixation. Another example is the *anal character*, whose attributes include compulsive neatness, obstinacy, and stinginess.

3. Later psychodynamic theorists take a *neo-Freudian* orientation. In contrast to Freud, they generally focus on interpersonal rather than biological forces in the individual, and are more interested in the individual's present situation rather than in his childhood past. An example is Karen Horney, who studied self-perpetuating vicious circles in adult neurotic conflicts.

4. Several modern psychodynamic theorists have studied characteristic patterns of defense and coping in normal persons, including patterns that are relatively immature and unhealthy (such as denial, projection, reaction formation) and patterns that are comparatively healthy and mature (e.g., humor, suppression). *Longitudinal studies* suggest that these patterns show considerable consistency over an individual's lifetime and indicate that, in later adulthood, those persons who used the more mature ways of coping in adolescence are likely to be more successful professionally and maritally, and will be in better physical health.

5. In contrast to the trait and psychodynamic approaches, the *behavioral approach* asserts that people do what they do because of the situation that they are in or have been in on

previous occasions. The most thoroughgoing version of this approach is the *radical behaviorism* of B.F. Skinner, who focuses on overt behavior and believes that differences in the ways people act are produced by differences in what they have learned through either *classical* or *operant conditioning.* The fact that characteristic behavior patterns persist even when the reinforcements that produced them are no longer there may reflect the effect of partial reinforcement on resistance to extinction.

6. *Social learning theory* is a more liberalized behavioral approach to personality. Unlike radical behaviorists, social learning theorists such as Albert Bandura, Julian Rotter, and Walter Mischel, are interested in what people think no less than in what they do, which is why their orientation is sometimes called the *behavioral-cognitive approach.* But like radical behaviorists, they emphasize the role of situational factors in determining behavior. Unlike trait theorists, who tend to believe that major personality traits have a built-in basis, social learning theorists also share the radical behaviorists' belief that most such attributes are the result of learning.

7. Social learning theorists are interested in various cognitive characteristics along which personalities may differ. One of these concerns the beliefs people have about the *control* they can exert on the world around them. One difference concerns their *perceived locus of control.* People with an internal perceived locus tend to believe that they are personally responsible for what happens to them; people with an external perceived locus feel that what happens to them is caused by forces outside of their own control. A related system of beliefs is a person's characteristic *attributional style*—the causes to which a person tends to attribute events that happen to her. Some of the interest in attributional style comes from its use in predicting depression. Being prone to depression is correlated with a tendency to attribute unfortunate events to internal, global, and stable causes.

8. While control refers to a person's ability to do what he wants to do, *self-control* refers to his ability to refrain from doing what he wants to do in order to get something he wants even more. There is evidence that four-year-olds who are able to tolerate delay of gratification for the sake of a more desirable reward show more social and academic competence in adolescence.

9. Another major orientation to personality is the *humanistic approach,* which maintains that what is most important about people is how they achieve their own selfhood and actualize their human potentialities. The humanistic approach emphasizes what it considers positive human motives such as *self-actualization* and positive personal events such as *peak experiences* rather than what it calls *deficiency needs.* According to Abraham Maslow, people will only strive for higher-order needs when lower-order needs are satisfied.

10. A major concern of humanistic psychologists is the *self.* According to Carl Rogers and other humanistic psychologists, its development is essentially based on *growth.* In their view, given the appropriate conditions, people will grow so as to realize their potential, which is for good rather than evil. Rogers believed that children will only achieve a solid sense of personal self-worth if they have experienced a sense of *unconditional positive regard.* Some defects in one's self can be healed in later life by providing the individual with important growth experiences he lacked before.

# CHAPTER 19

# Psychopathology

In the preceding chapter, we considered differences in human personality traits. We now turn to conditions in which such differences go beyond the range of normal functioning and take on the appearance of psychological disorder. The study of such disorders is the province of **psychopathology** or, as it is sometimes called, **abnormal psychology.** There is considerable debate about how the subject matter of abnormal psychology is to be defined. Is it simply a problem of statistical deviance, of behavior that is markedly different from the norm? Or should we take the term *psychopathology* more literally and regard its manifestations as something akin to illness? But if these manifestations are illnesses, of what kind are they? Are they caused by some bodily disorder, such as a defect in brain function or a biochemical imbalance? Or are they better conceived of as *mental* illnesses whose origin is psychological, such as a learned defense against anxiety?

As we shall see, there is no one answer to these questions. The reason is that the various conditions that are generally subsumed under the rubric of psychopathology are a very mixed lot. For some, the term *illness* seems quite appropriate; for others, this is not so clear. In any case, there is little doubt that many of the conditions that come to the attention of the psychopathologist—the psychiatrist, the clinical psychologist, or other mental-health specialists—often cause considerable anguish and and may seriously impair the afflicted person's functioning.

We will begin our discussion by considering some of the historical roots of our conceptions of what "madness" is and how it should be dealt with.

## DIFFERENT CONCEPTIONS OF MADNESS

Mental disorders existed for many millennia before psychiatrists appeared on the scene. Early mythological and religious writings are proof enough. The Greek

**An early example of mental disorder**
*King Nebuchadnezzar as depicted by William Blake (1795). (Courtesy the Tate Gallery, London)*

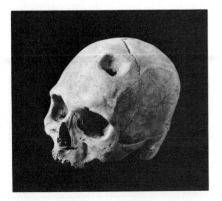

**19.1 Trephining** *A trephined prehistoric skull found in Peru. The patient apparently survived the operation for a while, for there is some evidence of bone healing. (Courtesy The American Museum of Natural History)*

hero, Ajax, slew a flock of sheep which he mistook for his enemies; King Saul of Judea alternated between bouts of murderous frenzy and suicidal depressions; and the Babylonian King Nebuchadnezzar walked on all fours in the belief that he was a wolf. Such phenomena were evidently not isolated instances. According to the Bible, young David feigned madness while seeking refuge from his enemies at the court of a Philistine king. This king had obviously encountered insanity before and upbraided his servants, "Do I lack madmen, that you have brought this fellow to play the madman in my presence?"

## Insanity as Demonic Possession

What leads to mental disorder? One of the earliest theories held that the afflicted person was possessed by evil spirits. It followed that the cure for the malady was to drive the devils out. If the patient was lucky, the exorcism procedures were fairly mild; the unruly demons were calmed by music or were chased away by prayers and religious rites. More often the techniques were less benign. One approach was to provide a physical escape hatch for the devils. According to some anthropologists, this may explain why Stone Age men sometimes cut large holes into their fellows' skulls; many such *trephined* skulls have been found, often with signs that the patient managed to survive the operation (Figure 19.1). The plausibility of this hypothesis is enhanced by the fact that trephining is still performed by some preliterate tribes, and for much the same reasons (Stewart, 1957). Yet another idea was to make things as uncomfortable for the devil as possible so as to induce him to escape. Accordingly, the patient was chained, immersed in boiling hot or ice-cold baths, or starved, flogged, or tortured. That such procedures usually drove the patient into worse and worse derangement is hardly surprising.

According to some medical historians, the demonological approach to mental disorder reached its culmination during the witch hunts of the sixteenth and sev-

**19.2 Witch hunts in sixteenth-century Europe** *Witches about to be burned at the stake. (Courtesy the Bettmann Archive)*

enteenth centuries (Zilboorg and Henry, 1941). This was a period marked by a host of social, political, and religious upheavals, of wars, famines, and pestilence, all of which triggered a search for scapegoats whose punishment might alleviate these ills. Persons accused of witchcraft were doomed to this role; according to most theological authorities of the times they had become possessed by striking a bargain with the devil, which gave them power to cause effects ranging from plagues and floods to sexual impotence and the souring of milk (Figure 19.2).

Since such people were clearly a menace to society, no measures were too stern to deal with them. As a result, there was an unrelenting series of witch hunts that involved most of Europe and whose bonfires claimed about 500,000 lives (Harris, 1974). Some of these unfortunates were undoubtedly deranged in one way or another; many were senile, some suffered from various delusions, from hysteria, or mania, and so on. Some may have experienced hallucinations under the influence of LSD-like drugs, taken either wittingly or by accident. Such hallucinogenic substances are now known to occur in grains that have been invaded by a certain fungus; it is quite possible that the girls whose visions sparked the Salem witchcraft trials had eaten bread made of such hallucinogenic rye (Caporael, 1976). But many of those accused of witchcraft seem not to have suffered from any mental disorder. Some may have participated in various local cults derived from pagan origins which orthodox Christianity condemned as a form of Satanism. Others probably fell prey to some neighbor's avarice, since a considerable proportion of a condemned person's property was awarded to his or her accuser (Kors and Peters, 1972).

### Insanity as a Disease

The demonological theory of mental disorder is a thing of the past. Even in its heyday there was an alternative view which held that such conditions were produced by natural causes and could be regarded as a kind of disease. But this belief did not necessarily lead to a more humane treatment of the afflicted. It might have done so if a ready cure had been available, but until recently, there was little hope of that. As a result, the "madmen" were treated with little sympathy, for they seemed to have no common bond with the rest of humanity, and there was little likelihood that they ever would have. They were seen as a nuisance at best and a menace at worst. In either case, the interests of society seemed best served by "putting them away."

To this end, a number of special hospitals were established throughout Europe. But until the beginning of the nineteenth century (and in some cases, much later still), most of these were hospitals in name only. Their real function was to serve as a place of confinement in which all kinds of social undesirables were segregated from the rest of humankind—criminals, idlers, old people, epileptics, incurables of all sorts, and the mentally disturbed (Rosen, 1966). After they had been in the "hospital" for a few years, it became hard to distinguish among them. Their treatment was barbaric. One author describes conditions in the major mental hospital for Parisian women at the end of the eighteenth century: "Madwomen seized by fits of violence are chained like dogs at their cell doors, and separated from keepers and visitors alike by a long corridor protected by an iron grille; through this grille is passed their food and the straw on which they sleep; by means of rakes, part of the filth that surrounds them is cleaned out" (Foucault, 1965, p. 72).

**19.3   The mentally disturbed on
exhibit**   *An eighteenth-century depiction
of a tour of Bedlam. (The Madhouse,
1735/1763, William Hogarth; courtesy the
Bettmann Archive)*

To most of their contemporaries, this treatment seemed only natural; after all,
the so-called madmen were like dangerous animals and had to be caged. But
since such animals are interesting to watch, some of the hospitals took on another
function—they became a zoo. At London's Bethlehem hospital (whose name was
slurred until it was popularly known as Bedlam), the patients were exhibited to
anyone curious enough to pay the required penny per visit. In 1814, there were
96,000 such visits (Figure 19.3).

A number of reformers gradually succeeded in eliminating the worst of these
practices. Historians have given much of the credit to the French physician,
Philippe Pinel (1745–1826), who was put in charge of the Parisian hospital system in 1793 when the Revolution was at its height. Pinel wanted to remove the
inmates' chains and fetters, but the government gave its permission only grudg-
ingly (Figure 19.4). A high functionary argued with Pinel, "Citizen, are you mad
yourself that you want to unchain these animals?" (Zilboorg and Henry, 1941, p.
322).

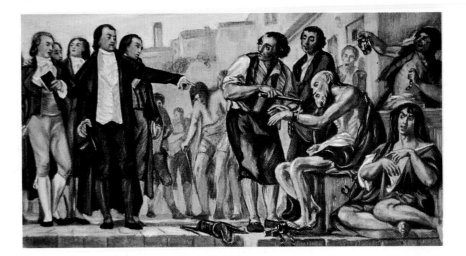

**19.4   Pinel ordering the removal of the
inmates' fetters**   *A nineteenth-century
painting by Charles Muller. (Courtesy the
Bettmann Archive)*

MENTAL DISORDER AS AN ORGANIC ILLNESS

Pinel and other reformers sounded one main theme: Madness is a disease. By this assertion, they transformed the inmates from prisoners to patients for whom a cure had to be found. To find such a cure, one first had to discover the cause of the disease (or rather, diseases, since it was already known that there were several varieties of mental disorder). Today, almost two hundred years after Pinel, we are still searching for the causes of most of them.

At least initially, the notion of mental disorder as an illness implied a bodily cause, most likely some disease of the brain. Proponents of this *somatogenic* hypothesis (from *soma,* "body") could point to such relevant discoveries as the effects of cerebral strokes in impairing speech (see Chapter 2). But the somatogenic position gained its greatest impetus at the end of the nineteenth century from the discovery of the organic cause of a once widely prevalent severe and debilitating disorder, *general paresis.* It is characterized by a general decline in physical and psychological functions, culminating in marked personality aberrations that may include childish delusions ("I am the Prince of Wales") or wild hypochondriacal depressions ("My heart has stopped beating"). Without treatment, there is increasing deterioration, progressive paralysis, and death within a few years (Dale, 1975).

By the end of the nineteenth century, the conviction had grown that general paresis has its roots in a syphilitic infection contracted many years prior to the appearance of overt symptoms. In some untreated syphilitics (according to recent estimates, perhaps 5 percent), the infection seems to be cured, but the spirochete that caused it remains, invading and damaging the nervous system. Experimental proof came in 1897. Several paretic patients were inoculated with matter taken from syphilitic sores, but none of them developed any of the earlier symptoms of syphilis.* This was a clear sign that they had contracted the disease previously. Once the cause of the disease was known, the discovery of its cure and prevention was just a matter of time. The preferred modern treatment is with penicillin. Its effectiveness is unquestioned. While general paresis at one time accounted for more than 10 percent of all admissions to mental hospitals; as of 1970, it accounted for less than 1 percent (Dale, 1975).

The conquest of general paresis reinforced the beliefs of somatogenicists that ultimately all mental disorders would be traced to some organic cause. They could point to some successes. Several psychoses had been explained as brain malfunctions. In the case of senile patients, the cause is atrophy of cortical cells; in the case of chronic alcoholics, the cause is a change in cerebral structures brought on by the dietary deficits that often accompany alcoholism. The question was whether this view could account for all mental disorders.

MENTAL DISORDER AS A PSYCHOLOGICAL ILLNESS

The achievements of the somatogenic approach were very impressive, but by the end of the nineteenth century it became clear that it could not include the full

---

* Modern medical and scientific practitioners are considerably more sensitive than our forebears to the ethical issues raised by this and similar studies. Today such a procedure would require the patients' informed consent.

**A**

**B**

*Psychogenically induced seizures   In late eighteenth-century France, a number of so-called hysterical patients suffered from psychogenically induced seizures that had a characteristic pattern. The illustrations below show some stages of this pattern, one of which resembled an epileptic seizure (A), another called the "clown period" (B). Some authors suspect that the behavior of these patients was caused by the fact that they were extremely suggestible: They could sense what their physicians expected them to do, and behaved appropriately. (Drawings by Paul Richter, 1885; published in Gilman, 1982)*

spectrum of mental disorders. One of the main stumbling blocks was a condition then known as ***hysteria,*** which we have already encountered in our discussion of psychoanalysis (see Chapter 11).

The story of hysteria (which is now called a ***conversion disorder,*** see p. 780) is part of the background that led to Freud's theories. For now, we will only reiterate the key discoveries. Hysteria featured a variety of symptoms that seemed to be organic but really were not; for example, paralyzed limbs that moved perfectly well during hypnosis. This suggested that hysteria is a ***psychogenic*** disorder; that is, a disorder whose origin is psychological rather than organic. A number of cases studied by French hypnotists of the nineteenth century seemed to have their origins in traumatic incidents. A patient trapped in a derailed railroad car developed hysterical paralysis of his legs; the legs were actually in perfect physical condition, but the patient's belief that they were crushed ultimately produced his hysterical symptoms. Freud's theories were cast in a similar psychogenic mold, but they were much more elaborate, focusing on repressed sexual fantasies in early childhood that threatened to break into consciousness and could only be held back by drastic defense maneuvers, of which the somatic symptom was one (see Chapter 11).

Exactly what produced the hysteria is not our present concern. The important point is that by the turn of the century most theorists had become convinced that the disorder was psychogenic. This was another way of saying that there are illnesses that have mental *causes* as well as mental *symptoms*.

EVALUATING THE SOMATOGENIC-PSYCHOGENIC DISTINCTION

The distinction between somatogenic and psychogenic disorders is sometimes criticized as artificial. The argument is that all behavior is ultimately based on organic processes in the nervous system. But if so, what remains of the distinction? Doesn't it then simply boil down to the difference between conditions whose organic basis has already been discovered and those for which it is as yet unknown?

The answer is no. There is no doubt that all psychological processes have a neurophysiological underpinning. But this doesn't necessarily mean that the proper scientific explanation of all psychological phenomena is necessarily at this neurophysiological level. As an example, consider two persons who can speak and see but who are unable to read. One of the two has a certain combination of brain lesions that disconnect the regions that control vision from those that handle language functions (see Chapter 2, pp. 58–59). The other person can't read because she was never taught. One can maintain that in a way both conditions are organically caused. In one case, the organic basis is the set of brain lesions; in the other, it consists of the failure to establish the various neurological changes that are brought about by learning to read. But it is perfectly obvious that while the organic account is a useful explanation in the one case, it provides no illumination in the other. This is not just because we don't yet know much of anything about the neurological basis of learning. Even if we did, to explain why someone is illiterate in terms of, say, a specification of millions of synaptic connections that were or were not formed is a much more cumbersome account than the simple statement that she can't read because she never learned.

The same analysis applies to the distinction between somatogenic and psychogenic disorders. To say that a disorder is somatogenic is to claim that the most direct explanation of the malfunction is at the organic level, as in the case of the syphilitic infection in general paresis. To say that the disorder is psychogenic is to assert that the most direct explanation of what ails the patient is at the psychological level, such as a learned mode of coping with anxiety in hysteria. This is not to deny that all psychological events are ultimately based on some underlying neurological processes. Of course they are, but for many purposes this fact is of little relevance.

## THE PATHOLOGY MODEL

Whatever their views about the somatogenic or psychogenic origins of mental disorders, most psychiatrists agree on one thing—these conditions are illnesses. They are called *mental* illnesses because their primary symptoms are psychological, but they are illnesses all the same, in some ways analogous to such nonpsychiatric illnesses as tuberculosis and diabetes. Given this assumption, it was only logical to propose that one should try to understand (and treat) such diseases according to the same broad set of rules by means of which we try to understand disease in general.

Just what are these rules? We will here class them together under a very general category that we'll call the ***pathology model.*** (Different practitioners subscribe to different subcategories of this model, of which more below.) According to the pathology model, various overt symptoms are produced by an underlying cause—the disease or pathology. The main object of the would-be healer is to remove the underlying pathology. After this is done, the symptoms will presumably disappear. As here used, the term *pathology model* makes no particular assumption about the kind of pathology that underlies a particular mental disorder. It might be somatogenic or psychogenic or perhaps a little of both.

### Subcategories of the Pathology Model

There are a number of different approaches to psychopathology, which can be regarded as subcategories of the pathology model. We will briefly present a few of these. As we will see, some of these models are probably more appropriate to some forms of mental disorder than to others.

#### THE MEDICAL MODEL

Some authors endorse the ***medical model,*** a particular version of the pathology model, which makes certain further assumptions. To begin with, it assumes that the underlying pathology is organic. Its practitioners therefore employ various forms of somatic therapy such as drugs. In addition, it takes for granted that the would-be healers are members of the medical profession (Siegler and Osmond, 1974).

Adherents of the *psychoanalytic model* follow the general conception of psychopathology developed by Sigmund Freud and other psychoanalysts. In their view, the symptoms of mental disorder are produced by psychogenic causes. The underlying pathology is a constellation of unconscious conflicts and various defenses against anxiety, often rooted in early childhood experience. Treatment is by some form of psychotherapy based on psychoanalytic principles, which allows the patient to gain insight into his own inner conflicts and thus removes the root of the pathology.

### THE LEARNING MODEL

The *learning model* tends to view mental disorders as the result of some form of maladaptive learning. According to some practitioners (usually called *behavior therapists*), these faulty learning patterns are best described and treated by the laws of classical and instrumental conditioning. According to others (often called *cognitive therapists*), they are more properly regarded as faulty modes of thinking that can be dealt with by changing the way in which the patient thinks about himself and his situation.

## Mental Disorder as Pathology

To get a better understanding of how mental disorder is viewed from the perspective of the general pathology model—in principle, regardless of subcategory—we must first ask what is meant by disease in general. A moment's reflection tells us that the concept of disease is both a scientific and an evaluative notion. To say that measles and rickets are diseases is to say something about the kinds of causes that produce such conditions—infections, dietary insufficiencies, and so on. But it also says that such conditions are undesirable. They produce pain and disability, and sometimes they lead to death. Speaking most generally, they are conditions that interfere with the organism's proper functioning as a biological system.

The extension of the disease concept to the psychological realm is based on certain parallels between the effects of psychopathology and those of nonpsychiatric, organic disorders. Where ordinary organic illnesses are often associated with physical pain, many mental disorders are accompanied by psychological distress in the form of anxiety or depression. (Some may lead to death, as in the case of suicidal depression.) But the most important criterion is the interference with proper psychological functioning. The mentally disordered person may be unable to form or maintain gratifying relationships with others. Or she may be unable to work effectively. Or she may be unable to relax and play. According to advocates of the pathology model of mental disorder, the inability to function properly in these psychological areas is the behavioral analogue of the malfunctions in such biological domains as respiration, circulation, digestion, and so on, that characterize ordinary organic illnesses.

Some special questions arise from the fact that the terms *psychopathology* and *abnormal psychology* are often used interchangeably. Does this mean that psychopathology necessarily involves behavior that deviates from some statistical

*Psychopathology is not defined by statistical abnormality*   *According to the psychopathology model, deviation from some statistical norm does not define psychopathology. The Black Death killed half to three-quarters of the population of many European countries during the fourteenth century, but that did not make it any less pathological. (Illustration from a fourteenth-century French manuscript,* Burying the plague victims at Tournai, *1349; Bibliotheque Royal Albert 1ᵉʳ, Brussels)*

norm? Advocates of the pathology model would answer no. They would concede that in actual practice mental disorder often involves aberrations from what people usually do in a given situation; the disordered person may hear voices, suffer from severe mood swings, or behave in ways that are clearly bizarre. It was surely for reasons of this sort that the term *abnormal* has become a near-synonym for *psychopathological.* But within the framework of the pathology model, deviation from a statistical norm is not what defines psychopathology. Consider the Black Death, which wiped out half of the population in the fourteenth century. At that time, having the plague may well have been statistically normal. But this did not change the plague's status as a disease. The same applies to behavior. Certain behavior patterns may be pathological no matter how common they are.

## Classifying Mental Disorders

The ways in which we decide what is and what is not a mental disorder are by no means settled. But no less controversial is the issue of classifying these disorders. How do we decide whether two patients have the same disorder or two different ones?

To answer this question, practitioners have tried to set up classificatory schemes for mental disorders analogous to the diagnostic systems in other branches of medicine. Here, as elsewhere in science, the purpose of a taxonomy is to bring some order into what at first seems a host of diverse phenomena. If the taxonomy is valid, then conditions that have been grouped together will turn out to have the same cause, and better yet, the same cure.

As in other branches of medicine, the diagnostic process begins with a consideration of the overt *symptoms.* In nonpsychiatric disorders, these might be such complaints as fever or chest pains. Examples of symptoms in psychopathology would be anxiety or a profound sense of worthlessness. The trouble is that an individual symptom is rarely enough for diagnosis; fever occurs in a multitude of organic illnesses, and anxiety is found in many different mental disorders. As a result, the diagnostician often looks for a pattern of symptoms that tend to go together, a so-called **syndrome.** An example of such a syndrome in psychopathology is a set of symptoms that includes disorganization of thinking, withdrawal from others, and hallucinations. This syndrome is characteristic of schizophrenia.

By groupings of this kind, psychiatrists have set up a taxonomy of mental disorders. The entire list covers an enormous range that includes mental deficiency, senile deterioration, schizophrenia, mood disorders such as bipolar disorder and depression, phobias, conversion disorders, and drug addiction, to mention only the most prominent.

Until about fifteen years ago, most psychiatrists believed that many of these conditions could be subsumed under two broad super-categories, **neurosis** and **psychosis.** They applied the term *neurosis* to any disorder whose main characteristic was thought to be anxiety or the defense against anxiety. Examples are the conditions now called phobia, panic disorder, obsessive-compulsive disorder, and dissociative disorders. Neurotic patients might be severely handicapped by their symptoms and were often in great distress, but they had not lost contact with reality no matter how miserable they might feel. In contrast, the term *psychosis* was applied to conditions such as schizophrenia and what was then called manic-depressive illness (and is now called bipolar disorder), in which the patients' thoughts, moods, and deeds were grossly disturbed and no longer met the demands of reality (DSM-II, 1968).

Today, the terms *psychosis* and *neurosis* are no longer widely used in psychiatric classification. A major reason for this change was the psychiatrists' desire to classify conditions by observable symptoms rather than by their inferred causes. The new taxonomy is embodied in the new diagnostic manual of their profession, DSM-III-R (1987). Both it and its immediate predecessor (DSM-III, 1980) depart from earlier manuals in a number of ways. The most important is a greater stress on the *description* of disorders rather than on theories about their underlying cause. As a result, a number of disorders that had formerly been grouped together because of a—psychoanalytically inspired—belief that they are at bottom alike, are now classified under different headings (for example, various conditions that

**Insanity as seen by an artist** *This painting undoubtedly shows aspects of what Francisco Goya saw when he visited an insane asylum in Spain, but it may also have been affected by the then current views of the classification of mental disorder. Most early descriptions included the raving maniac (here the nude men wrestling in the center), the hopeless melancholic (the despairing figures on the left), and those with grotesque delusions (the men with crowns demanding allegiance from their subjects). (*The Insane Asylum, c1810, Francisco Goya, Accademia S. Fernando, Madrid; courtesy Art Resource)

were once regarded as subcategories of neurosis; see pp. 773–83). One consequence of these changes in procedure has been a considerable increase in diagnostic reliability (Matarazzo, 1983; DSM-III-R, 1987).

Given these changes in official taxonomy, the terms *neurosis* and *psychosis* have become rather passé. But we will nevertheless use these two terms in the present account, at least in an informal way. To avoid them altogether is difficult, given the fact that they have by now become part of common parlance. The same holds for a number of other terms that are no longer used in official diagnosis, for example *sociopath, hysteria,* and some others.

### Explaining Disorder: Diathesis, Stress, and Pathology

Adherents of the pathology model believe that all—or at least many—mental disorders will ultimately prove to result from underlying causes, some organic and others psychological, that mirror the pathological processes found in other diseases. But since many of these pathologies are still unknown, how can we evaluate the assertion that they are actually there? One approach is to analyze a disease that is already well understood. This can then provide a standard against which the claims of the model's advocates can be judged. Our illustrative example will be an organic illness, diabetes.

The first step in the analysis of this, as of other medical disorders, is to look at the overt symptoms. In diabetes, these include declining strength, a marked increase in the quantity of urine passed, enormous thirst, and, in many cases, voracious appetite. The next step is to look for the underlying physiological pathology of which this syndrome is a manifestation. This pathology was discovered to be a disorder of carbohydrate metabolism which is produced by an insufficient secretion of insulin (see Chapter 3). These pathological conditions represent the immediate cause of the symptoms. But a full understanding of the disease requires a further step, an inquiry into the more remote causes that led to the present pathology.

When the causal chain is traced backward, two general factors emerge. One is a predisposition (technically called a ***diathesis***) toward the illness. The other is a set of environmental conditions which ***stress*** the system and precipitate the defective insulin mechanism; for example, obesity. In diabetes, the diathesis is based on genetic factors that create a marked susceptibility to the disease, which is then triggered by precipitating stress.

The treatment follows from the analysis of the cause-and-effect relations. Since the diabetic's pancreas does not secrete enough insulin, this substance must be supplied from the outside. Further control of the faulty metabolism is then imposed by an appropriate diet (Dolger and Seeman, 1985).

The preceding discussion illustrates the so-called ***diathesis-stress*** conception which has proved helpful in the understanding of many organic as well as mental disorders. Many of these conditions result from the interaction of a diathesis that makes the individual potentially vulnerable to a particular disorder, and some form of environmental stress that transforms the potentiality into actuality. Just what the diathesis is that creates the vulnerability depends on the particular disorder. In many cases, as in diabetes, it is based on genetic constitution. In others, it may be produced by various social and psychological factors, such as chronic feelings of worthlessness.

*Emil Kraepelin (1855–1925)    The major figure in psychiatric classification, Kraepelin distinguished between two groups of severe mental disorders, schizophrenia and manic-depressive psychosis (now called bipolar mood disorder). (Courtesy Historical Pictures Service)*

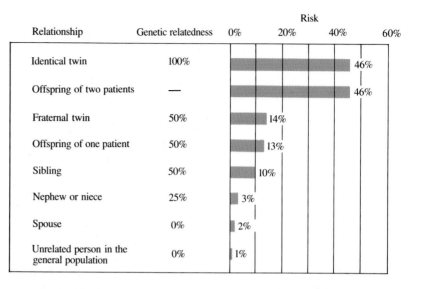

| Relationship | Genetic relatedness | Risk |
|---|---|---|
| Identical twin | 100% | 46% |
| Offspring of two patients | — | 46% |
| Fraternal twin | 50% | 14% |
| Offspring of one patient | 50% | 13% |
| Sibling | 50% | 10% |
| Nephew or niece | 25% | 3% |
| Spouse | 0% | 2% |
| Unrelated person in the general population | 0% | 1% |

**19.8   Genetic factors in schizophrenia**
*Risk estimates for schizophrenia as a function of relationship to a schizophrenic patient. (From Nicol and Gottesman, 1983, p. 399)*

of schizophrenia in the general population (Rosenthal, 1970). But again, as in the area of intelligence, such family resemblances don't settle anything about the nature-nurture issue, for they can be interpreted either way. For more conclusive evidence we have to turn to the familiar methodological standbys that are used to disentangle the contributions of heredity and environment—studies of twins and of adopted children. A widely used method focuses on twins, one of whom is schizophrenic. The question is whether the schizophrenic's twin is schizophrenic as well. The probability of this event, technically called *concordance,* is 44 percent if the twins are identical, compared to only 9 percent if they are fraternal (Gottesman and Shields, 1972, 1982; Gottesman, McGuffin, and Farmer, 1987; see Figure 19.8). Further evidence comes from adoption studies. Children born to schizophrenic mothers and placed in foster homes within a week or so after birth are more likely to become schizophrenic than persons in a matched control group of adoptees born to normal mothers (Heston, 1966; Kety, 1983; Kendler and Gruenberg, 1984).

### ENVIRONMENTAL STRESS

The preceding discussion indicates that schizophrenia has a genetic basis. But there is no doubt that environment also plays a role. One line of evidence comes from identical twins. Their concordance for schizophrenia is considerable, but is much less than 100 percent. Since identical twins have the same genotype, there must be some nongenetic factors that also have a say in the determination of who becomes schizophrenic and who does not.

What are these nongenetic factors? As yet, there is no consensus. We will consider a few lines of evidence that relate to various potentially stress-producing situations. Some involve the person's social class and economic condition; others concern his family. According to many modern investigators, these and other stress-producing environmental factors may bring out the latent pathology in a person with a genetic predisposition toward schizophrenia and will eventually precipitate the actual disorder, much as obesity or continued emotional stress

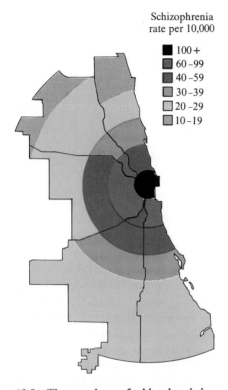

Schizophrenia
rate per 10,000

■ 100+
▨ 60–99
▨ 40–59
▨ 30–39
□ 20–29
□ 10–19

**19.9** *The prevalence of schizophrenia in different regions of a city* A map of Chicago (1922–1934) represented by a series of concentric zones. The center zone is the business and amusement area, which is without residents except for some transients and vagabonds. Surrounding this center is a slum region inhabited largely by unskilled laborers. Further out are more stable regions: a zone largely populated by skilled workers, followed by zones of middle- and upper-middle-class apartment dwellers and, furthest out, the upper-middle-class commuters. The map shows clearly that the incidence of schizophrenia increases the closer one gets to the city's center. (After Faris and Dunham, 1939)

precipitates diabetes. The stronger the diathesis, the less stress would presumably be required to convert the predisposition into actuality (Meehl, 1962; Gottesman and Shields, 1982).

*Social class* In searching for environmental causes, sociologically minded investigators have focused upon social class. They have found a sizable relationship. The proportion of schizophrenics is much higher at the bottom of the socioeconomic hierarchy than it is at the top. According to one study, the ratio is 9 to 1 (Hollingshead and Redlich, 1958). The prevalence of schizophrenia is highest in the poorest and most dilapidated areas of the city and diminishes progressively as one moves outward toward the higher status regions (Figure 19.9). This general relation between social class and schizophrenia has been found in city after city, from New York, Omaha, New Haven, and Milwaukee in the United States to Oslo, Helsinki, London, and Taiwan abroad (Kohn, 1968).

Some critics argue that this finding is an artifact. Incidence rates of schizophrenia are usually based on admissions to mental hospitals, and lower-class psychotics may be more likely to be hospitalized in such institutions than are psychotics from higher strata. To get around this problem, some investigators studied a representative sample of all persons in a community—whether inside a hospital or not—and had psychiatrically trained interviewers rate their mental health. The same general result was found; the poor are more likely to become schizophrenic than the rich.

One interpretation of this result is that poverty, inferior status, and low occupational rank lead to increased environmental stresses which sooner or later convert a genetic susceptibility toward schizophrenia into the actual disorder. According to this view, given the predisposition, one becomes a schizophrenic because one is at the lowest rung of the social ladder. But there is a theoretical alternative, for the causal direction may be reversed. Perhaps one falls to the bottom of the ladder because one is a schizophrenic. The evidence to date suggests that both factors play a role. If so, schizophrenia is an effect of lower socioeconomic status as well as a cause, although the issue is by no means settled (Kohn, 1968).

*Pathology in the family* A different emphasis pervades the work of more psychoanalytically oriented investigators. True to their general outlook, they have concentrated upon the schizophrenic's family. They paint a gloomy picture. As they describe them, schizophrenics' mothers are rejecting, cold, dominating, and prudish, while their fathers are detached, humorless, weak, and passive (Arieti, 1959). Later studies concentrated on the relationships within the family. In general, they found a high degree of instability. Many schizophrenics come from homes in which a parent was lost early in the patient's life through death or divorce. In homes with both parents, there is often serious discord. In many such families the children become directly involved in the marital schism, with each parent trying to undercut the other in continual attempts to enlist the child as an ally (Lidz, Cornelison, Fleck, and Terry, 1957).

Later critics argued that this family portrait of the schizophrenics is inaccurate. The descriptions of the parents were often sketched by the same psychiatrists who treated the children and who were probably guilty of partisanship, as they saw the parents through the patients' eyes. When these and other procedural flaws are eliminated, the schizophrenic's family doesn't appear to be quite as pathological as it did at first. But enough signs of pathology remain even so. Objective studies in which the families of schizophrenic patients are observed in discussions of various topics (such as "When should teenagers begin dating?") have shown more within-family conflicts than normal controls (Fontana, 1966).

*Disentangling cause and effect* Schizophrenics evidently come from a less benign family background than do normal children. But this does not prove that the familial environment is a *cause* of the patient's disorder. It may also be an *effect.* After all, having a schizophrenic in the family is surely quite disturbing. Several studies of parent-child interactions suggest that something of this sort may indeed play a role (Mishler and Waxler, 1968; Liem, 1974). In one of these studies, the investigators observed mothers who had both a schizophrenic and a healthy daughter (Mishler and Waxler, 1968). When observed with their schizophrenic daughters, the mothers seemed unresponsive and aloof. But when observed with their healthy daughters, the mothers behaved more normally. This suggests that their unresponsiveness was not a general characteristic of their personality (and thus perhaps a *cause* of their child's disorder), but it was instead a reaction to the schizophrenic daughter (and thus an *effect* of the child's disorder upon the mother's behavior).

All in all, there is clearly a relation between schizophrenia and various psychological characteristics of the family. This relationship is probably caused by three contributing factors. One is genetic—both the parents and their schizophrenic offspring share some pathological genes. A second factor is environmental—the parents' psychopathology may precipitate the disorder of the child. A third factor involves the reversed causal relation—having a schizophrenic child may produce psychopathological reactions in the rest of the family.

*Family environment as a factor in therapy and relapse* The preceding discussion suggests that poor familial relations may not cause the patient's illness. But some further findings show that they have much to do with keeping him from getting well. The evidence comes from studies of schizophrenic patients who had recovered well enough to be discharged from the hospital and who went back to live with their parents or spouses. The investigators interviewed these family members at the time of the patient's breakdown to determine how they felt about him: the extent to which they were critical, hostile, or emotionally overinvolved and manifested these negative feelings to the patient. The more intense the degree of these so-called "expressed emotions," the greater the chance that the patient would eventually relapse and have to be readmitted to the mental hospital (Hooley, 1985). On reflection, this is hardly surprising. Parents or spouses who tell an interviewer "He is stupid. . . . The farther I am away from him the better" or [on hearing that it was a *mental* hospital] "I thought *I'd* have to go there myself from the shock" will probably say something quite similar to the patient when he returns from the hospital, which is unlikely to aid his ultimate recovery. Some grounds for encouragement come from the finding that family members can be taught to reduce the level of their expressed emotion by an educational program in which they learn some facts about schizophrenia and have sessions in which they can talk about their problems. Patients whose families had participated in such a program were much less likely to suffer a relapse than patients whose families had not (Leff, Kuippers, Berkowitz, Eberlein-Vries, and Sturgeon, 1982).

## The Pathology Model and Schizophrenia

We have considered schizophrenia under the same headings that are used to analyze nonpsychiatric illnesses—the symptom patterns, the underlying pathology, the role of more remote causes such as genetic predisposition, and precipitating factors. What can we conclude? To guide our evaluation, we will refer to a schematic diagram of the main factors in the schizophrenic disorder that is analogous to the one we used to analyze diabetes (Figure 19.10).

It appears that the main symptoms of schizophrenia can be regarded as the manifestations of an underlying psychological deficit, perhaps a defect in the ability to focus in space and time. The best guess is that this psychological malfunction reflects an underlying organic pathology whose exact nature is still unknown. Most investigators believe that this organic pathology has two sources: one is a biochemical defect, most likely one that involves some neurotransmitter system. The other is a loss of brain tissue, perhaps through atrophy. The pathology that represents the immediate cause of the disorder is in turn produced by more remote causes. One is a hereditary diathesis. Another is a set of environmental stresses, including socioeconomic and familial pressures, which trigger the pathological process in persons with the initial diathesis.

A final word. Schizophrenia varies in severity. In describing it, we have concentrated on the most clear-cut examples, and these tend to be quite severe. But this should not blind us to the fact that there are some schizophrenics whose affliction is relatively mild and who may be able to function reasonably well in the ordinary world. There are also cases in which the symptoms are present mostly during acute psychotic episodes; at other times, the patient may be nearly symptom free. Total disability is relatively rare (Bernheim and Lewine, 1979).

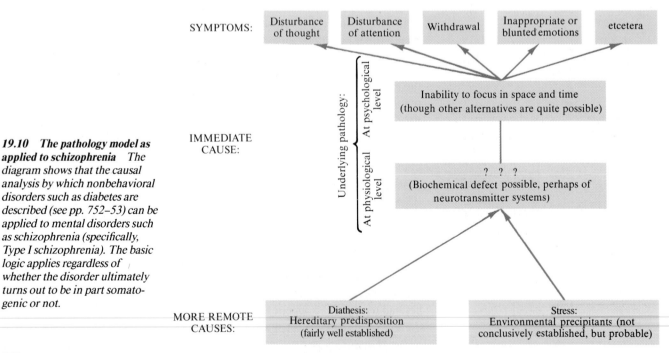

*19.10   The pathology model as applied to schizophrenia   The diagram shows that the causal analysis by which nonbehavioral disorders such as diabetes are described (see pp. 752–53) can be applied to mental disorders such as schizophrenia (specifically, Type I schizophrenia). The basic logic applies regardless of whether the disorder ultimately turns out to be in part somatogenic or not.*

SYMPTOMS:   | Disturbance of thought | Disturbance of attention | Withdrawal | Inappropriate or blunted emotions | etcetera |

Underlying pathology:
At psychological level

IMMEDIATE CAUSE:

Inability to focus in space and time (though other alternatives are quite possible)

At physiological level

?  ?  ?
(Biochemical defect possible, perhaps of neurotransmitter systems)

MORE REMOTE CAUSES:

Diathesis:
Hereditary predisposition (fairly well established)

Stress:
Environmental precipitants (not conclusively established, but probable)

*Depression and despair* Edward Adamson, a professional artist, founded a studio in a British mental hospital for the use of the institutionalized patients. Many of their works forcefully express these patients' depression and despair, as in the case of this painting entitled Cri de Coeur or "Cry from the heart." (Cri de Coeur, by Martha Smith; reproduced from Adamson, 1984)

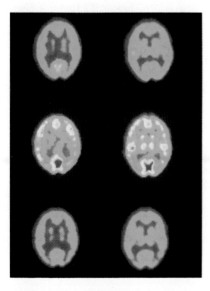

*PET scan of a rapid-cycling bipolar patient* The top and bottom row are scans obtained on days in which the patient was depressed; the middle row on a day in which he was mildly manic. Reds and yellows indicate a high rate of metabolic activity; blues and greens indicate low rates. (Courtesy Dr. John Mazziotta)

## MOOD DISORDERS

While schizophrenia can be regarded as essentially a disorder of thought, in another group of disorders the dominant disturbance is one of *mood.* These are the ***mood disorders*** (formerly called ***affective disorders***), which are characterized by two emotional extremes—the vehement energy of mania, the despair and lethargy of depression, or both.

### The Symptom Pattern

An initial distinction is that between ***bipolar disorder*** (essentially equivalent to what was formerly called ***manic-depressive psychosis***) and ***major depression.*** In bipolar disorder, the patient swings from one emotional extreme to the other, sometimes with intermittent periods of normalcy, and experiences both manic and depressive episodes that may be as short as one or two days and as long as several months or more. Bipolar disorders occur in about 1 percent of the population. Much more frequent are cases of major depression (sometimes called ***unipolar disorder,*** since the mood extreme is of one kind only). According to several estimates, about 10 percent of all men and over 20 percent of all women in America will suffer from a major depressive episode (defined as one that lasts for at least two weeks) at some time during their lives (Hirschfeld and Cross, 1981; Weissman and Boyd, 1985).

MANIA

In their milder form, manic states are often hard to distinguish from normal high spirits. The person seems to have shifted into some form of mental high gear: she is more lively and infectiously merry, is extremely talkative and always on the go, is charming, utterly self-confident, and indefatigable. It is hard to see that something is wrong unless one notices that she jumps from one plan to another, seems unable to sit still for a moment, and quickly shifts from unbounded elation to intense irritation if she meets even the smallest frustration. These pathological signs become greatly intensified as the manic episode becomes more severe (***acute mania***). Now the motor is racing and all brakes are off. There is an endless stream of talk that runs from one topic to another and knows no inhibitions of social or personal (or for that matter, sexual) propriety. Patients are incessantly busy. They rarely sleep, burst into shouts of song, smash furniture out of sheer overabundance of energy, do exercises, conceive grandiose plans for rebuilding the hospital or redirecting the nation's foreign policy or making millions in the stock market —a ceaseless torrent of activity that continues unabated over many days and sleepless nights and will eventually sap the patients' health (and that of those around them) if they are not sedated.

An example of a manic episode is described in an autobiography by Clifford Beers, a man who lived through three years of a severe bipolar disorder, recovered, and went on to become a crusader for mental hospital reform. Beers started to write letters about everything that was happening to him. He soon ran out of stationery so he obtained large rolls of wrapping paper which he cut into one-foot strips and pasted together into long rolls, writing letters that were twenty to thirty feet long, and continuing to write at the rate of twelve feet per hour. He eventually tried to take charge of the hospital, was put in a small cell, and soon tried his hand at inventions. He decided to overcome the force of gravity. He tore a carpet into strips and used the makeshift ropes to suspend his bed (with himself in it) off the floor. "So epoch-making did this discovery appear to me that I noted the exact position of the bed so that a wondering posterity might ever afterward view and revere the exact spot on the earth's surface whence one of man's greatest thoughts had winged its way to immortality" (quoted in White and Watt, 1973).

DEPRESSION

In many ways, depression is the polar opposite of mania. The patient's mood is utterly dejected, his outlook is hopeless; he has lost his interest in other people and regards himself as completely worthless. In many cases, both thought and action slow down to a crawl:

> The patient appears dejected and cheerless; everything he says and does is with effort. . . . He speaks only in response to questions and even then answers in a word, not a sentence. . . . He speaks in such a low tone that one finds oneself moving close to him and speaking more loudly as if he were the one who could not hear. He says that everything is hopeless, that he is a disgrace to his family; he recalls that when he was a boy he took a paper from the newsstand and did not pay for it. (Cohen, 1975, p. 1019)

In severe cases, there may be delusions or even hallucinations. Most are variations on the same theme of personal worthlessness: "I must weep myself to death. I cannot live. I cannot die. I have failed so. It would be better if I had not been born. . . . I am the most inferior person in the world. . . . I am subhuman" (Beck, 1967, p. 38).

In addition there are various physical symptoms. There is a loss of appetite, weakness, fatigue, poor bowel functioning, disturbance of sleep, and little if any interest in sex. It is as if both bodily and psychic batteries have run down completely.

*Depression and suicide*   Depression can be lethal. Given the depressive's bottomless despair it is not surprising that suicide is a very real risk. Probably no patient in real life has described his preoccupation with death, suicide, and dissolution as eloquently as that greatest depressive in all of English literature, Prince Hamlet:

> O that this too too sullied* flesh would melt,
> Thaw, and resolve itself into a dew,
> Or that the Everlasting had not fixed
> His canon 'gainst self-slaughter. O God, God,
> How weary, stale, flat, and unprofitable
> Seem to me all the uses of this world!
> Fie on 't, ah fie, 'tis an unweeded garden
> That grows to seed.
>
> (*Hamlet,* Act I, Scene ii)

***Depression***   *(Photograph by Rhoda Sydney, Leo de Wys)*

---

* While Shakespeare scholars are divided on whether the correct text of the first line is "*solid* flesh" or "*sullied* flesh," most lean toward the second reading, which certainly fits in well with the depressive's characteristic self-hatred.

Like Hamlet, many depressives think of suicide. Some attempt the act, and more than a few succeed.

According to the official statistics, the annual suicide rate in the United States is 25,000 per year. Since many suicides are misreported as accidents, the real figure is sometimes thought to be as large as 100,000. The large majority of them suffered from depression. For every actual suicide, there are about ten times as many unsuccessful attempts. Of these persons, a large number suffered from depression. Women are more likely to attempt suicide than men are; but when men make the attempt, they are much more likely to succeed. One reason for the difference is in the choice of methods. The methods that women tend to use don't have the absolute finality of those generally used by men. While women are more likely to cut their wrists or swallow a bottle of sleeping pills, men tend to use methods that are irreversible, such as shooting themselves or jumping off a rooftop (Rosenhan and Seligman, 1989).

Contrary to what one might expect, the risk of suicide is relatively low while the patient is still in the trough of the depressive phase. At that point his gloom is deepest, but so is his apathy. The risk increases as the patient begins to come out of the worst phase of his depression. Suicide rates are greatest during weekend leaves from the hospital and shortly after discharge (Beck, 1967). Then the patient's mood may still be black, but he has regained some of his energy and ability to act. He has recovered just enough to do the one thing that will prevent all further recovery.

### SEASONAL AFFECTIVE DISORDER

In recent years, clinical workers have become aware that certain mood disorders have a seasonal pattern. Patients with this disorder have depressions that start in late fall when the days become shorter and end—or even switch to mania—when the days lengthen in March or April. Such *seasonal affective disorders* are evidently linked to the amount of sunlight the patients are exposed to (see Figure 19.11). When they travel south in the winter, their depression lifts within a few days; when they travel north in the fall or winter, their depression gets worse. Given these findings, it was only natural to attempt a treatment using bright artificial lights to lighten the "days." According to several studies, the treatment relieves the depressive symptoms. It's probably not surprising that one of the first regions of the country in which this therapy was used was Alaska (Rosenthal et

**19.11 Seasonal affective disorder and day length** (A) Percentage of patients with seasonal affective disorder who report being depressed in any given month. (B) Mean minutes of daylight per month. (From Rosenthal et al, 1984)

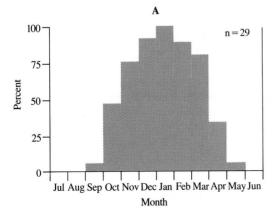

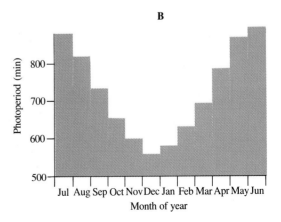

al., 1984; Rosenthal et al., 1986; Hellekson, Kline, and Rosenthal, 1986; Lewy, Sack, Miller, and Hoban, 1987).

What might account for this striking effect of light on mood in persons with seasonal affective disorder? As yet, we don't know. One possibility is that the effect is somehow connected with the sleep cycle (which is in turn affected by the light). There is some evidence that some depressed persons show disturbances in their sleep rhythms, including overly quick onset of REM sleep (Kupfer, Foster, and Reich, 1976). Whether these are also persons whose depression is seasonal is as yet unknown.

## Organic Factors

What produces the mood extremes of bipolar disorder and depression? According to one view, some of these conditions—especially the bipolar variety—are produced by some internal, organic pathology.

### GENETIC COMPONENTS

The belief that such an organic pathology exists is based on several considerations. We'll see that as in schizophrenia, there are the rather specific therapeutic effects of certain drugs. And again, as in schizophrenia, there is good reason to suppose that at least some of the mood disorders have an important hereditary component. This is almost certainly true of the bipolar condition. Concordances for identical twins with this affliction have been found to be some four times higher than those for fraternal twins, and the biological parents of bipolar patients are about three times more likely to suffer from some mood disorder (whether bipolar or unipolar) than are their adoptive parents. While there is evidence that genetic factors play a role in unipolar cases as well, their contribution is probably not as powerful as it is in the bipolar condition (Allen, 1976; Mendlewicz and Rainer, 1977; Gershon, Nurnberger, Berrettini, and Goldin, 1985; Torgersen, 1986; Wender, Kety, Rosenthal, Schulsinger, and Ortmann, 1986).

The most convincing demonstration of the genetic basis of bipolar disorder comes from a recent genealogical study of the Amish, a very conservative Protestant sect in Southern Pennsylvania. In this fairly small and very tight-knit community of some 12,000 persons, it was possible to identify thirty-two current cases of bipolar disorder and to construct a family tree of this condition. In each case, the investigators found evidence for ancestors with the disorder going back for several generations. Since 1880, there have been twenty-six documented cases of suicide; all were traced back to just four families. The final step was the discovery of the gene that led to the susceptibility to the disorder. By analyzing the genetic material in the blood cells of the afflicted persons, the investigators found a gene defect at a particular location of one particular chromosome. This gene defect did not guarantee that a person would have a mood disorder, but it made it very likely; 63 percent of the persons who had it showed at least minimal signs of the bipolar condition (Egeland et al., 1987).

### BIOCHEMICAL HYPOTHESES

The genetic evidence is a strong argument for the view that there is some biological factor that underlies mood disorders (perhaps especially the bipolar ones).

This view is further bolstered by the fact that in bipolars the switch from one mood to another is often quite divorced from external circumstances. The most plausible interpretation is that there is some internal, biological switch.

A widely held hypothesis is that many of the mood disorders are based on a biochemical defect that involves the supply of some important neurotransmitters at certain critical sites of the brain. When there is a shortage, there is depression. Some investigators believe that this transmitter is **norepinephrine;** others feel that it is **serotonin;** still others suspect that both of these substances are involved (Schildkraut, 1965; Schildkraut, Green, and Mooney, 1985).

One line of evidence for the role of these neurotransmitters came from an analysis of the metabolic breakdown of these substances in the spinal fluid or the urine. If the level of these by-products is low, there should be a correspondingly low supply of the neurotransmitters from which they are derived. Just as predicted, the relevant metabolic by-products were in fact lower in at least some depressed patients than in controls. In addition, the norepinephrine levels in bipolar patients were below average when the patients were depressed and increased when the patients became manic (Muscettola, Potter, Pickar, and Goodwin, 1984; Schildkraut, Green, and Mooney, 1985).

Further confirmation comes from the effect of two kinds of **antidepressant drugs:** the **tricyclics** and the **monoamine oxidase (MAO) inhibitors.** Both of these drugs have some success in relieving depression, and both increase the amount of norepinephrine and serotonin available for synaptic transmission.

In recent years, some further findings have complicated the picture. One problem is the time course of the drug effects. While the antidepressant drugs lead to an almost immediate increase in the amounts of available norepinephrine or serotonin, this increase is short-lived; within a few days, the transmitter levels subside to what they had been before the drug was first administered. But the effect of the drugs in relieving the depression doesn't begin until one or two weeks after the drug therapy has been started. This means that the antidepressants don't exert their effect by increasing the supply of neurotransmitters. But if so, how do they accomplish their mission? Some recent studies indicate that instead of increasing the supply of the neurotransmitters, the antidepressant drugs make the relevant neurons more sensitive to them (e.g., Schildkraut, Green, and Mooney, 1985).

## Psychogenic Factors

The organic pathology—whatever it may turn out to be—might account for the extremes of some patients' moods, the fact that they are speeded up or slowed down in virtually all respects. But can it explain *what* the patient thinks or does, the manic's glow of overweening satisfaction and the depressive's hopeless despair and self-loathing? How does an inadequate supply of norepinephrine or serotonin lead to the belief that one is the "most inferior person in the world"?

### MOOD OR COGNITION?

What comes first, mood or cognition? The question is again one of cause and effect. Theorists who regard the disorder as primarily somatogenic believe that what the patient thinks *follows* from her mood. If a transmitter insufficiency (or some other biochemical state) makes her feel sluggish and gloomy, she looks for reasons to explain her own mood. Eventually she will find them; the world is no good and neither is she. The end result is that her cognitions match her feelings. (For an analogous approach to the nature of emotional feelings in normals, see Chapter 12.)

Does this approach really do justice to the phenomenon? Theorists who believe in a psychogenic explanation think not. They grant that mood disorders—especially those that are bipolar—may involve a constitutional predisposition toward mood excess, but they insist that psychological factors play a vital role in at least some cases of depression. In their view, the patient's view that she and the world are no good comes first and her depression comes second—as an *effect* of these cognitions rather than as their cause.

*Sorrow   (Vincent Van Gogh, 1882; courtesy Vincent Van Gogh Foundation/ National Museum Vincent Van Gogh, Amsterdam)*

### BECK'S COGNITIVE THEORY OF DEPRESSION

This cognitive view underlies a very influential approach to the understanding and treatment of depression developed by Aaron Beck (Beck, 1967, 1976). Beck believes that the patient's condition can be traced to a trio of intensely negative and irrational beliefs about himself, about his future, and about the world around him: that he is worthless, that his future is bleak, and that whatever happens around him is sure to turn out to be for the worst. According to Beck, these beliefs form the core of a negative cognitive schema in terms of which the patient interprets whatever happens to him. Facing minor setbacks, the depressive makes mountains out of molehills (insisting that he has ruined his car when he's only scratched a fender); facing major accomplishments he makes molehills out of mountains (insisting that he's inept even though he's just won an important professional prize). These negative schemas are ultimately derived from a succession of unfortunate experiences in earlier life: a harshly critical attitude in the home or in school, the loss of a parent, rejection by peers, and so on. But whatever their origins, such negative schemas become self-fulfilling; expecting defeat, the depressive eventually will be defeated. To counteract this system of essentially irrational beliefs, Beck has developed a psychological treatment called **cognitive therapy** by means of which the patients are made to confront and overcome the essential irrationality of their beliefs, which we will discuss in a later section (Beck, 1967; Beck, Rush, Shaw, and Emery, 1979; see Chapter 20).

### LEARNED HELPLESSNESS AND DEPRESSIVE ATTRIBUTIONS

Where Beck's cognitive theory grew out of clinical observations of depressed patients, a related cognitive account, proposed by Martin Seligman, had its source in studies of animal learning. The initial findings that led to Seligman's approach concerned **learned helplessness,** first observed in the animal laboratory (Seligman, 1975; see Chapter 4).

*Learned helplessness and depression*   When normal dogs are placed in a shuttlebox in which they have to jump from one compartment to another in order to escape an electric shock, they learn to do so with little difficulty. This is in contrast with a second group of dogs who have first been exposed to a series of painful shocks about which they could do absolutely nothing. When this second group was later placed in the shuttlebox, their performance was drastically different from that of normal dogs. They did not look for some means of escape. Nor did they ever find the correct response—jumping over the hurdle. Instead, they simply gave up; they lay down, whimpered, and passively accepted their fate. They had learned to become helpless (Seligman, Maier, and Solomon, 1971).

Seligman argued that learned helplessness in animals is in many ways similar to at least some forms of depression. Like the helpless dogs, depressed patients have given up. They just sit there, passively, unable to take any initiative that might help them cope. Some further similarities concern the effects of antidepressant drugs. As we've seen, these drugs alleviate the symptoms of many depressed patients. It turns out that they have a similar effect on animals rendered helpless; the helplessness disappears, and the animals behave much like normals (Porsolt, LePichon, and Jalfre, 1977).

Seligman supposed that the essential similarity between the helpless dogs and the depressed people is the expectation that one's own acts are of no avail. In dogs, the cause was a series of inescapable shocks that the animals could do nothing about. In humans, the precipitating factor may be some personal catastrophe —rejection, bankruptcy, physical disease, the death of a loved one. In some persons, this may lead to a generalized sense of impotence, a belief that there is nothing one can do to shape one's own destiny, that one is a passive victim with no control over events—that one is helpless.

*Attributional style and depression* The helplessness interpretation of depression runs into a number of problems. To begin with, it can't explain why being helpless doesn't necessarily lead to depression. People who are about to undergo an operation are helpless in the sense of being utterly dependent on their surgeons, but if they believe they will recover they will generally not become depressed. A further problem is the depressive's self-hatred. If he thinks that he is helpless, then why does he blame himself? (Abramson and Sackheim, 1977). Considerations of this sort led to a revised version of the helplessness theory, which proposed that what really matters is the individual's **attributional style,** the way in which he habitually tries to explain events—especially bad events—that happen to him (see also Chapter 18, pp. 728–29). Does he attribute unfortunate events to internal, global, and stable causes—that is, to causes that refer to something within himself, that will generalize to other situations, and that will continue over time (for example, being unattractive or unintelligent)? If so, he has an attributional style that will predispose him to depression (Abramson, Seligman, and Teasdale, 1978). There is good evidence that this despondent explanatory style is indeed characteristic of depressed persons (as shown by results with the Attributional Style Questionnaire described in Chapter 18, p. 728; Peterson and Seligman, 1984).

A number of critics have argued that this and other cognitive theories of depression (including Beck's) confuse the symptom with the cause (Coyne and Gotlib, 1983; Lewinsohn, Hoberman, Teri, and Hautzinger, 1985). After all, hopelessness, helplessness, and unmitigated self-blame are among the symptoms of the condition we call depression. To say they are the cause is a bit like saying that someone has a cold *because* he sneezes. In contrast, cognitive theorists believe that the attributional style (or the negative cognitive schema) is a predisposing condition; given this style, the depression will then be precipitated by some environmental stress. If so the cognitive patterns should *precede* the depressive episode.

Evidence that this may well be so comes from studies which show that persons who are not currently depressed but who exhibit the despondent explanatory style are more likely to *become* depressed when faced with failure or stress. Thus college students who manifested this style at the start of the semester were more likely to become depressed on learning that they received a poor grade on an examination; prison inmates who displayed it at the start of their term were more likely to become depressed after some months of imprisonment; pregnant mothers who showed it in their second trimester were more likely to become depressed three months after childbirth (Peterson and Seligman, 1984). The issue is by no means settled, for there are a number of contradictory findings. But taken as a whole, there is reason to believe that the cognitive account fits some individuals, and that certain habitual ways of interpreting the world are among the factors that predispose an individual toward depression. (For some contrary evidence, see Lewinsohn, Steinmetz, Larson, and Franklin, 1981.)

A recent extension of this general approach focuses on hopelessness. Its main point is that in some cases of depression, hopelessness is a major cause rather than a symptom. If the patient believes that he has absolutely nothing to look forward to and that the future is utterly bleak, he will probably start a downward spiral that will eventually have bodily manifestations and end in a full-fledged depression. The precise differences between this and related psychogenic views (such as Beck's and other offshoots of the learned helplessness approach) are still being spelled out (Alloy, Hartlage, and Abramson, 1988; Abramson, Metalsky, and Alloy, 1989).

*The male-female ratio in depression*   Conceptions derived from the learned helplessness theory and related views may help us understand an important fact about major depressions. They are about twice as common in women than in men, even when incomes and socioeconomic levels are held constant. What accounts for this difference? While hormonal factors, such as drops in estrogen and progesterone levels during the premenstrual period, the postpartum period, and menopause may play a role, they are at best only part of the picture. The best guess is that the sex ratio is produced by culturally produced differences in the way men and women are taught to cope with difficult life situations. The culture expects men to be self-reliant and active while women are supposed to be more passive and dependent. To the extent that this is true, men learn that they have control over their fate, while women gradually feel much less able to determine what happens to them—the very condition that presumably leads to learned helplessness and depression. A further factor may be a difference in the way the culture determines how men and women deal with their own moods. According to a recent study, when men are depressed, they try to distract themselves: "I avoid thinking of reasons why I'm depressed," or "I do something physical." In contrast, women who are depressed seem to dwell on their despondency: "I try to determine why I'm depressed," "I talk to other people about my feelings," and "I cry to relieve the tension." The result of these different ways of dealing with one's own feelings is that the initial depression is more likely to escalate and last longer in women than in men (Nolen-Hoeksema, 1987).

**Depression in women**   *Major depressions are about twice as common in women as in men. (Photograph by Mark Antman/ The Image Works)*

## Mood Disorders and the Diathesis-Stress Conception

Mood disorders are often preceded by some stressful event—marital difficulties, difficulties at work, serious physical illness, or a death in the family (Leff,

Roatsch, and Bunney, 1970; Paykel, 1982). But it's clear that environmental stress cannot be the whole story. After all, there are many people who suffer major setbacks and serious losses but who don't fall into a depressive collapse. There is evidently a diathesis—some people are more prone to mood disorders than others—and the stressful event precipitates it. This diathesis may be based on biological factors—such as an insufficiency of available norepinephrine or serotonin. But the predisposition may well be psychological in nature—such as a negative view of oneself or the world or a depressive attributional style. In either case, the diathesis makes the individual more vulnerable to later stress.

Seen in this light, psychological and biological factors are intermingled, so that the distinction between somatogenic and psychogenic origins becomes somewhat blurred. Negative cognitions and learned helplessness can produce a depletion of norepinephrine and serotonin, but the causal chain can also run the other way around. Either way, there will be a predisposition for later depression, which will be manifested in both behavior and in biochemistry.

## ANXIETY DISORDERS

In major depressions, the primary symptom is a profoundly dejected mood: the patient believes that his condition *is* awful and that there is no hope that it will ever get better. In another group of conditions, the **anxiety disorders,** the primary symptoms are anxiety or defenses against anxiety: the patient fears that something awful *will* happen to him. While such symptoms often cause serious distress and impair the person's functioning, they generally do not render him incapable of coping with external reality. In the terms of an earlier nomenclature, he is a neurotic, not a psychotic.*

### Phobias

A relatively common anxiety disorder is a **phobia,** which is characterized by an intense and irrational fear of some object or situation. During the nineteenth century, some of these irrational fears were catalogued and assigned high-sounding Greek or Latin names. Examples are fear of high places (acrophobia), or open places (agoraphobia), or enclosed places (claustrophobia), or of crowds (ocholophobia), or germs (mysophobia), or cats (ailurophobia)—the list is potentially endless. The crucial point in the definition is that the fear must be *irrational,* that there really is no danger or that the danger is exaggerated out of all proportion. An African villager who lives at the outskirts of the jungle and is worried about leopards has an understandable fear; a San Francisco apartment dweller with a similar fear has a phobia. In many cases, this irrationality is quite apparent to the sufferer, who knows that the fear is groundless but continues to be afraid all the same.

---

* In the psychiatric classification system prior to DSM-III and DSM-III-R, anxiety disorders were listed under the general rubric *neurosis* because of a belief that these conditions, along with a number of others such as conversion disorders and dissociative states, could all be understood as the manifestation of unconscious defenses against anxiety.

A  B

**Phobias**  *An artist's conception of (A) the fear of dirt, and (B) the fear of open spaces. (Paintings by Vassos)*

In phobia, the irrational fear exerts an enormous effect on every aspect of the sufferer's life, for he is always preoccupied with his phobia. On the face of it, it is not entirely clear why this should be so. Why can't the phobic simply avoid the situations that frighten him? If he is afraid of leopards and snakes, he should stay away from the zoo; if he is terrified of heights, he should refrain from visits to the top of the Sears Tower. Some phobias may be minor enough to be handled this easily, but most cannot. In many cases this is because the phobia tends to expand. The fear of leopards becomes a fear of the part of the city where the zoo is located, of all cats and catlike things, or of all spotted objects, and so on. Other phobias may be more wide-ranging to begin with. An example is ***agoraphobia*** (from a Greek word meaning "fear of the marketplace"), which is sometimes described as a fear of open places but is essentially a fear of being in places from which escape would be difficult.*

THE CONDITIONING ACCOUNT OF PHOBIAS

What is the mechanism that underlies phobias? One notion goes back to John Locke who believed that such fears are produced by a chance association of ideas, as when a child is told stories about goblins that come by night and is forever after terrified of the dark (Locke, 1690). Several modern authors express much the same idea in the language of conditioning theory. In their view, phobias result from classical conditioning; the conditioned stimulus is the feared object (e.g., cats) and the response is the autonomic upheaval (increased heart rate, cold sweat, and so on) characteristic of fear (Wolpe, 1958).

A number of phobias may indeed develop in just this fashion. Examples include fear of dogs after dog bites, fear of heights after a fall down a flight of stairs, and fear of cars or driving after a serious automobile accident (Marks, 1969). Conditioning theorists can readily explain why phobias acquired in this manner expand and spread to new stimuli. The fear response is initially conditioned to a

* In many cases, agoraphobia accompanies panic disorder (see p. 777).

particular stimulus. If this stimulus subsequently occurs in a new context, the fear will be evoked and thus conditioned to a whole set of new stimuli. An example is a woman who developed a fear of anesthetic masks after experiencing a terrifying sensation of suffocation while being anesthetized. This same sense of suffocation reoccurred later when she was in a stuffy, crowded elevator. This in turn led to a dread of elevators, whether empty or crowded. The phobia generalized to any and all situations in which she could not leave at will, even playing cards (Wolpe, 1958, p. 98).

### PHOBIAS AND PREPAREDNESS

There is an odd fact about phobias that is not easy to reconcile with a simple conditioning account. By and large, phobic patients are afraid of a rather limited class of stimuli, such as snakes, spiders, and heights. On the other hand, fears of hammers, knives, frying pans, and electrical outlets are extremely rare. If phobias were produced by the mere association of a traumatic event with whatever stimuli happened to be around at the time, then the class of fear-arousing objects should be much larger than it is. After all, there's little doubt that in urban America more children have been shocked by an open outlet or been burned by hot grease from a frying pan than have been bitten by a snake or by a tarantula. But if so, why the disproportionate number of snake and spider phobias? A suggestion comes from the study of acquired taste aversions, which indicates that the organism is "prepared" to learn some associations more readily than others. Rats are very quick to associate tastes with illness, but are unlikely to associate illness with tones or lights (see Chapter 4). According to the ***preparedness theory of phobias,*** a similar account applies to phobias. Snakes, spiders, and a number of other stimuli were exceedingly dangerous to our primate ancestors; since this is so, evolution favored animals who had a built-in predisposition (that is, preparedness) to come to fear such stimuli very quickly (Seligman, 1971).

Some evidence for the preparedness theory of phobias comes from fear-conditioning experiments on normal (that is, non-phobic) subjects in which pictures of various objects were paired with electric shock. Pictures of snakes and spiders were considerably more effective as conditioned stimuli than were pictures of flowers and mushrooms (Öhman, Eriksson, and Olofsson, 1975; Öhman, Dimberg, and Öst, 1985). These studies have come in for some criticism (e.g., McNally, 1987). One problem is that there is no way of knowing what prior fears and associations the subjects may have had before they entered the laboratory. These may have developed through contacts with other people's fears and various cultural traditions such as folklore, legends, and the like. To control such factors, one group of investigators turned to nonhuman primates. The subjects were laboratory-reared rhesus monkeys who were exposed to videotapes of other monkeys that served as fear-inducing models. These models were clearly frightened; they screamed, or grimaced, or retreated to the back of the cage and clutched at its wall (see Figure 19.12). The videotapes were edited so that some showed the models reacting fearfully to a toy snake, while others showed them being just as frightened by a bunch of artificial flowers. The monkeys who watched these videotapes had never seen a snake or a flower in their lives. When they first encountered the snake or the flowers, they were quite indifferent to both. But after they saw the videotaped models becoming frightened of the toy snake, they quickly became frightened also. In contrast, there was no such effect when the models

**19.12 Prepared fears of snakes in monkeys** *The sight of the snake in the foreground leads to a characteristic fear grimace in the monkey, accompanied by a quick retreat to the rear of its cage while leaving its food untouched. (Courtesy of Susan Mineka)*

showed fear of the flowers. This is in line with the preparedness theory. We—and our primate ancestors—come to fear some stimuli much more readily than others (Cook and Mineka, 1989).

## Obsessive-Compulsive Disorders

In phobias, anxiety is aroused by external objects or situations. In contrast, anxiety in *obsessive-compulsive disorders* is produced by internal events—persistent thoughts or wishes that intrude into consciousness and cannot be stopped. An example of such an *obsession* is a mother who has recurrent thoughts of strangling her children. To ward off the anxiety produced by such obsessions, the patient often feels compelled to perform a variety of ritualistic acts. Such *compulsions* are attempts to counteract the anxiety-producing impulse that underlies the obsessive thought; in Freud's terms, a way of *undoing* what should not have been done. Examples of such compulsions are ritualistic cleaning, handwashing, and incessant counting. The mother with uncontrollable thoughts of committing infanticide might feel compelled to count her children over and over again, as if to check that they are all there, that she hasn't done away with any. The obsessive-compulsive patient is aware that his behavior is irrational but he can't help himself even so. Lady Macbeth knew that "what's done cannot be undone," but she nevertheless continued to wash the invisible blood off her hands.

Minor and momentary obsessional thoughts or compulsions are commonplace. After all, most people have had the occasional feeling that they ought to check whether the door is locked even when they are perfectly sure that it is. But in obsessive-compulsive disorders, such thoughts and acts are the patient's major preoccupation and are crippling:

*Compulsive hand washing in literature*    A scene from the Old Vic's 1956 production of Macbeth *with Coral Browne. It shows Lady Macbeth walking in her sleep and scrubbing imaginary blood off her hands, as she relives the night in which she and her husband murdered the king. (Courtesy of the Performing Arts Research Center, The New York Public Library)*

> A man in his 30's, fearing lest he push a stranger off the subway platform in the path of an oncoming train, was compelled to keep his arms and hands glued rigidly to his sides. . . . [He] was on one occasion obsessed with the idea that, despite his stringent precautions, he had, after all, inadvertently knocked someone off the subway platform. He struggled with himself for weeks to dispel what he rationally knew was a foolish notion but was at length compelled to call the transport authority to reassure himself that there had not in fact been any such accident. The same patient was for a time preoccupied with the concern that, when he walked on the streets, he was dislodging manhole covers so that strangers passing by would fall into the sewer and be injured. Whenever he passed a manhole in the company of friends, he would be compelled to count his companions to make sure that none was missing. (Nemiah, 1985, p. 913)

## Generalized Anxiety Disorders

In the anxiety disorders we have discussed thus far, anxiety is relatively focused, for it occurs in response to a fairly specific condition. In phobia, anxiety is aroused by the feared object; in obsessive-compulsive disorder, it is aroused by a thought or the belief that one hasn't performed some important act. In contrast, there are several conditions in which anxiety is not related to anything in particular, but isn't any less upsetting for all that.

not face the idea of being a coward may become hysterically paralyzed. This allows him to give in to his impulse of refusing to march. But it also lets him do so without guilt or shame—he is not marching because he *cannot* march.

We will not describe the symptom pattern of conversion conditions in any detail since we already did so in a previous chapter (see Chapter 11). We will, however, comment on some interesting oddities in the incidence of the disorder. A century ago, such cases were fairly common, but today they account for a much smaller fraction of mental disorders. How can we explain this changing fashion in psychopathological conditions? Some authors believe that this is due to a less restrictive family atmosphere and more permissive child rearing, especially in the sexual sphere, with a resulting decline in symptoms produced by repressed sexual and aggressive thoughts and memories (Chodoff, 1954). Other investigators suggest that the cause is a general increase in the medical sophistication of the population at large. In modern Western society, there are fewer people who believe that one can be suddenly struck blind or become paralyzed without some other accompanying bodily signs (say, of a stroke). But if so, hysterical blindness or paralysis would be rather transparent as psychological defenses and thus much less acceptable to both the patient and those around him. Some evidence that can fit either of these views is the fact that the frequency of such disorders is greater in just those geographical areas in which one would expect a less permissive family atmosphere as well as lesser medical know-how: in backward rural regions of America rather than urban centers and in less industrialized rather than in more industrialized nations (Watson and Buranen, 1979).

An additional problem is posed by the sheer difficulty in making the diagnosis of conversion disorder. How can we be sure that the patient's ailment is not organic after all? To be sure, the patient may inadvertently "give himself away" by showing up with a symptom that makes no anatomical sense, such as the glove anesthesias we described in a previous chapter (see Chapter 11, p. 424). But patients rarely make the doctor's job as easy as that. Since this is so, how can we be sure there is no subtle organic disorder (say, a neurological defect) that produces the effect? The diagnosis "conversion disorder" (or, to use layman's language, "it's just psychological") may reflect medical ignorance rather than psychiatric wisdom. This possibility certainly fits in with changes in the frequency with which this diagnosis is given. Medical knowledge has grown immensely since Freud's time and tends to be greater in urban than in backward rural areas, and greater in industrial than in less industrial nations. Further support comes from follow-up studies of patients whose symptoms were diagnosed as conversions. A fair proportion of these patients were later found to have had organic disorders after all, many of which involved neurological damage (Slater and Glithero, 1965; Watson and Buranen, 1979). This suggests that the decision that a patient suffers from a conversion disorder is sometimes a diagnosis by default. No organic cause was found, so the disorder had to be a conversion! In some of these cases, such organic conditions were present after all and were eventually recognized as such.

## Dissociative Disorders

Another way in which a person can deny responsibility for some acts (or thoughts or wishes) is by insisting that they were never committed, or at least not by him. This approach is characteristic of **dissociative reactions.** In these disorders, a

***A movie recreation of a case of multiple personality***  *Joanne Woodward in* The Three Faces of Eve *portraying Eve White (above) and Eve Black (below). (Courtesy the Museum of Modern Art/Film Stills Archive)*

whole set of mental events—acts, thoughts, feelings, memories—is shoved out of ordinary consciousness. One example is psychogenic ***amnesia*** in which the individual is unable to remember some period of his life, or sometimes all events prior to the onset of the amnesia, including his own identity. In other cases, the dissociation involves a ***fugue state,*** in which the individual wanders away from home, and then, days, weeks, or even years thereafter, suddenly realizes that he is in a strange place, doesn't know how he got there, and has total amnesia for the entire period.

Still more drastic are cases of ***multiple personality.*** Here the dissociation is so massive that it results in two or more separate personalities. The second—and sometimes third or fourth—personality is built upon a nucleus of memories that already had some prior separate status. An example is a shy and inhibited person who has had fantasies of being carefree and outgoing from childhood on. These memories eventually take on the characteristics of a separate self. Once formed, the new self may appear quite suddenly, as in the famous case of Eve White:

> After a tense moment of silence, her hands dropped. There was a quick, reckless smile and, in a bright voice that sparkled, she said, "Hi there, Doc." . . . There was in the newcomer a childishly daredevil air, an erotically mischievous glance, a face marvelously free from the habitual signs of care, seriousness, and underlying distress, so long familiar in her predecessor. This new and apparently carefree girl spoke casually of Eve White and her problems, always using *she* or *her* in every reference, always respecting the strict bounds of a separate identity. When asked her own name she immediately replied, "Oh, I'm Eve Black." (Thigpen and Cleckley, 1957, as described in Coleman, 1972, p. 246)

### Factors That Underlie Conversions and Dissociative Conditions

The cause of conversion and dissociative symptoms is still obscure. Freud believed that such symptoms are a defense against anxiety. Conditioning theorists hold a similar position, translated into their own conceptual framework. But this anxiety hypothesis only accounts for the patient's motives. It may explain why he wants not to see or not to walk or to develop an alternate personality; it does not explain how he accomplishes these feats, especially the wholesale alterations of consciousness that characterize dissociations.

Some authors suggest that such phenomena may represent an unusual form of self-dramatization in which the person acts *as if* she were blind or *as if* she were Eve Black without any consciousness that any playacting is going on (Ziegler, Imboden, and Rodgers, 1963; Sarbin and Allen, 1968). According to this view, the patient is like an actor who becomes so involved in his role that he is no longer aware that he is on stage. In actuality, of course, no actor ever completely forgets that he is playing a part; if he did, he would be unable to leave the stage when the play calls for his exit. But by the same token, no patient is ever completely paralyzed or blind and so on; his "paralyzed" leg still responds to reflex stimulation and will probably serve quite well in emergencies such as a fire.

Much the same kind of as-if behavior characterizes a deeply hypnotized patient who is given a suggestion, say, not to see a chair in the middle of the room. When asked whether she sees it, she answers no; but when she walks across the room, she somehow never bumps into it; she manages to circle around it, as if to see it so as not to see it. The important point is that the patient, the hypnotized person, and—to a lesser extent—the deeply involved actor, are not aware of what they are aware of.

Whether dissociations and conversion reactions are a defense against anxiety or an unconscious kind of playacting, most investigators suspect that they have roots in earlier patterns of behavior that set the stage for the full-blown disorder under later conditions of stress. An example is provided by cases of multiple personality. Those with this disorder often seem to have histories of severe abuse in childhood (Bliss, 1980; Putnam, Guroff, Silberman, Barban, and Post, 1986). According to one investigator, such patients were unusually adept at self-hypnosis during early childhood and created a new personality during their hypnotic trance as a form of escape from the threatening traumatic event (Bliss, 1980).

## PSYCHOPHYSIOLOGICAL DISORDERS

Thus far, our concern has been with psychopathological disorders whose primary symptoms are psychological. But certain other conditions can lead to genuine organic damage. For example, peptic ulcer or asthma may be produced by organic causes, as in the case of an asthmatic allergic reaction. Yet they may also be produced (or aggravated) by emotional factors. If so, they are called *psychophysiological conditions* (or, to use an older term, *psychosomatic disorders*).* But whether their origin is organic or mental makes no difference to the victim: they are equally real in either case.

In this regard, the symptoms of a psychophysiological condition are quite different from the somatic complaints of a patient with a conversion disorder. That patient's paralysis of the legs may disappear after his underlying conflict is resolved; after all, his locomotor machinery is still intact. But the patient with a psychophysiological ulcer (or asthma, or high blood pressure) has a disorder that plays for keeps. His ulcer will bleed and hurt just as much as an ulcer caused by a gastric disease, and if it perforates his stomach wall he will suffer the same case of peritonitis and, if he dies, his death will be no less final.

### Essential Hypertension

Several psychophysiological disorders involve the circulatory system. One is *essential hypertension.* This is a chronic elevation of blood pressure that can lead to serious disability and premature death. While some cases of hypertension result from various organic pathologies, essential hypertension is at least partially psychogenic (Lipowski, 1975; Harrell, 1980).

#### THE EFFECT OF CONTINUED AUTONOMIC AROUSAL

*Blood pressure* is the pressure exerted by the blood as the heart pumps it through the body's arteries. One way in which this pressure can rise is by the constriction of the arteries. This occurs in fight-or-flight emergencies, as when a zebra suddenly sees a hungry lion (see Chapter 3). The sympathetic branch of the auto-

---

* In DSM-III-R, they are listed under "psychological factors affecting physical conditions."

nomic nervous system is aroused and, among other things, this leads to the contraction of the muscles of the arterial walls. The effect is much like squeezing on a water hose. There is an immediate increase in the force of the liquid spurting out. As a result, the skeletal muscle, and the heart muscles themselves, get blood more quickly—a vital necessity in life-or-death situations which call for sudden, violent exertions.

Such extraordinary measures are all very well for zebras trying to get away from lions. The emergency really does call for increased muscular effort; when it is over, the muscles inform the nervous system that they no longer need the same supply of food. When this happens, the circulatory system soon returns to normal. The situation is quite different for us today. We rarely encounter emergencies that call for violent muscular effort. But our lives are filled with any number of fear- and anger-producing situations. An unfair grade, a neighbor's snub, a near-miss on the superhighway—all these trigger the sympathetic emergency reaction, even though a sudden spurt of muscular energy is of no avail. But our autonomic nervous system doesn't know that. And so we are put on an emergency basis, some of us more than others, but all to some extent. As a result, our blood pressure goes up, again and again, in the daily stress of living. Since the emergency does not lead to any extra muscular effort, the autonomic nervous system never gets the proper message that signals the end of the emergency. As a result, the blood pressure remains up for a while after the incident has passed.

In some people, continued autonomic overactivity eventually takes its toll—the elevated blood pressure no longer comes down to normal. One reason is a gradual thickening of the arterial muscle walls. This, together with an increased sensitivity to stimulation, makes these muscles overreact to normal neural impulses. As a result, they are in an almost continual state of constriction. The more constricted they are, the thicker and more sensitive they get. The ultimate effect of this vicious cycle is *hypertension,* a condition that afflicts twenty-three million Americans and represents a major public health problem. Among its relatively minor symptoms are headaches and dizziness. If serious and prolonged, the disorder leads to lesions in the arteries that supply the kidneys, the brain, and the heart. The final results include kidney failure, cerebral stroke, coronary disease, and heart attacks (Lipowski, 1975).

### HYPERTENSION AND EMOTIONAL STRESS

Hypertension is evidently a residue of continued sympathetic arousal. Thus, we would expect its incidence to go up with increasing emotional stress. This is indeed the case. For example, there was a marked increase in the rate of hypertension among the inhabitants of Leningrad during the siege and bombardment of that city during World War II (Henry and Cassel, 1969). Similar effects are produced by socioeconomic stress. Hypertension is much more common among blacks than whites in the United States; and it is especially prevalent in metropolitan regions marked by high population density, poverty, and crime (Lipowski, 1975). Still other studies show that hypertension is more prevalent among persons whose occupations impose unusual emotional stress. An example is provided by air-traffic controllers, especially those who work in airports in which traffic density is high (Cobb and Rose, 1973; Rose, Jenkins, and Hurst, 1978).

In all of these cases, the critical element is not environmental stress as such, but rather the individual's reaction to it. What the besieged citizen of Leningrad, the

poor more often than the well-to-do. The mental patient whose family can keep him at home or put him in a private hospital is less likely to be legally committed (Kittrie, 1971). A number of recent patients' rights campaigns have led to the establishment of more stringent safeguards on commitment procedures. But while such measures have curbed some abuses, they have not changed the fact that mentally disturbed people are still more or less banished and live under a social stigma that is hard to remove. In retrospect, it is ironic that some of the first mental asylums in Europe were set up in former leper houses that had become empty. Leprosy had disappeared, so now the "madman" took over the part of the pariah that the leper had played in former times (Foucault, 1965).

## Whom Does Society Call Mad?

The treatment society metes out to mentally disordered persons is grim even with enlightened attitudes. The sociological critics of the pathology model ask who the people are who are treated in this way. To the mental health practitioner, the answer is obvious: Those who demonstrate mental illness by a variety of signs and symptoms. The sociological critics reply that in many ways the causal chain works in reverse; sometimes the label creates the symptoms. The fact that a person is called mentally ill makes others see and treat him differently. Eventually, the labeled individual may change his own self-perception; then he and others will behave so as to make the label fit more and more.

To the extent that this is true, it is a demonstration of a self-fulfilling prophecy. This sometimes has paradoxical effects. To the hospital authorities—attendants, nurses, psychiatrists—the very fact that a person is an inmate is virtual proof that there must be something wrong with her. If a mental patient proclaims her sanity, this is merely evidence that she is even more deranged than anyone had suspected; she doesn't even "have insight." The patient has a better chance of getting discharged if she first admits that she is sick. She can then announce that she is getting better; now the authorities will tend to look at her more kindly, for she is obviously "responding to treatment" (Goffman, 1961).

*Are those whom society calls mad merely those of whom society disapproves?* *The film* One Flew over the Cuckoo's Nest *with Jack Nicholson dramatizes this question. (Courtesy the Museum of Modern Art/Film Stills Archives)*

## MENTAL ILLNESS AS A MYTH

Some critics maintain that the key to mental disorder is the label; without this, there would be no disorder at all. A prominent exponent of this position is psychiatrist Thomas Szasz. According to Szasz, mental illness is a myth (Szasz, 1974). He and other critics charge that it is merely a term by which we designate people whose behavior deviates from the norms of their society but does not fall into any of the recognized categories of nonconformity. They are neither criminals, nor prostitutes, nor heretics, nor revolutionaries, and so on. To account for their deviance, only one explanation is left—they are mentally ill (Scheff, 1966). Seen in this light, mental disorder is not a condition that is inherent in the individual; instead, it depends upon how the individual is seen by others. According to this position, madness (like beauty) is in the eye of the beholder.

## THE EVIDENCE ON THE ROLE OF LABELING

*Cross-cultural comparisons*   What evidence supports the labeling theory? One line of argument comes from the study of different cultures. There is no doubt that what is deviant in one culture is not necessarily deviant in another. The Kwakiutl Indian who burns valuable blankets at a special ceremony to shame his rivals is honored by his fellow chiefs; the Los Angeles executive who decides to dynamite his speedboat and swimming pool to prove that he can afford to do so is quietly sent off to a private sanitarium. To labeling theorists this suggests that what is meant by *mental disorder* is relative to the culture and is therefore essentially arbitrary.

This point does not follow. Even if it were true that all mental disorders are culturally determined, this would not prove that these disorders are caused by labeling. Such a result might support the notion that the disorders are psychogenic and are somehow caused by the cultural pattern. But this is quite different from the statement that the disorder does not really exist except as a label attached by others.

In any case, there is good evidence that shows that there is less cultural relativism in psychiatric matters than labeling theorists suppose. To be sure, some kinds of disorders may be more prevalent in one culture than another; conversion cases may be an illustration. But the fact that some disorders may be culturally determined doesn't prove that all disorders are. The best evidence suggests that schizophrenia is found throughout the world. One investigator studied Eskimo villagers on an Arctic island and a group of Yorubas, a tribe in West Africa. Both groups have a word for "being crazy." The Yoruba call a person *were* if he hears voices where there are none, laughs when there is nothing to laugh at, talks all the time, tears off his clothes, defecates in public, or suddenly attacks others with a weapon. Similar patterns of behavior characterize people that the Eskimos call *nuthkavihak.* Interestingly enough, the prevalence of such conditions is roughly comparable to that found in Western societies. Among samples collected in Canadian and Swedish villages, the rate of schizophrenia was 5.6 per 1,000. Among the Yorubas, 6.8 out of 1,000 people were described as *were;* among the Eskimos 4.4 per 1,000 were said to be *nuthkavihak.* The fact that a disorder that resembles schizophrenia is found in many cultures and occurs with about the same rate of incidence in them makes it hard to believe that this condition is a result of labeling (Murphy, 1976).

**Madness as label**   *The influential physician-anatomist Sir Charles Bell made this drawing after a visit to Bedlam in 1805 to illustrate the nature of "madness." The drawing reflects the then prevailing concept of the "madman" as a wild and ferocious being, reduced to the state of a lower animal. (Charles Bell's "Madness" from his* Essays on the Anatomy of Expression in Painting, *1806)*

wither away by themselves. In effect, Freud's prescription for the neuroses is the victory of reason over passion: "Where id was, there shall ego be."

### THE RECOVERY OF UNCONSCIOUS MEMORIES

*Free association* The origin of psychoanalytic technique dates back to Freud's attempts to treat hysteria by helping the patient recover some emotionally charged memories (see Chapter 11). Initially, Freud and his then collaborator, Josef Breuer, probed for these memories while their patients were hypnotized. Later on it became clear that such memories could be dug up even in the normal waking state by the method of *free association.* The patient was asked to say whatever came into his mind, and sooner or later the relevant memory was likely to emerge. Various forms of *resistance,* usually unconscious, by which the patient tried to derail a given train of thought—by changing the topic, forgetting what he was about to say, and so on—often gave important clues that the patient was about to remember something he had previously tried to forget.

In popularized movie or TV versions, this dredging up of forgotten memories is often presented as the essence of psychoanalysis. The distraught heroine finally remembers a childhood scene in which she was spanked for a little sister's misdeed, suddenly a weight lifts from her shoulders, she rises from the couch reborn, is ready to face life and love serenely, and will live happily—or at least unneurotically—ever after. But as Freud described it, what actually happens is much less dramatic. The discovery of the patient's unconscious conflicts comes bit by bit, as a memory surfaces here, a dream or a slip of the tongue suggests a meaning there, and as the analyst offers an occasional interpretation of the resistances that crop up in a given session. To help the patient see how all of these strands of her mental life are woven together is one of the analyst's main tasks.

*Interpretation* How does one decide whether a particular interpretation is correct? According to Freud, the best test is the patient's reaction. If she genuinely

**A picture of Freud's consultation room**
*In classical psychoanalysis, the patient reclines on the couch while the analyst sits behind him, out of sight. Freud adopted this method to avoid influencing the patient's flow of associations by his own facial expressions. He also had a personal motive: "I cannot bear to be gazed at for eight hours a day." (Freud, 1913; photograph by Edmund Engelman)*

accepts it, perhaps with a sense of "Aha!" the interpretation is probably right. But many psychoanalysts contend that an interpretation is not necessarily wrong even if the patient rejects it; her "No" may simply be a sign of resistance and the very vehemence of her denial a hint that the analyst's assertion is really true. Given this "Heads, I win; tails, you lose" style of argument, how can we possibly decide?

Freud felt that there was a way. In his view, psychoanalysis is a bit like solving a jigsaw puzzle. By the time the puzzle is completed, each piece can fit into one and only one place. In a similar way, one can judge the correctness of an interpretation by noting how it fits into the overall picture (Fenichel, 1945). This analogy is interesting but not altogether convincing. Is it really true that the dreams, memories, and thoughts of a patient will make sense in one and only one arrangement?

### EMOTIONAL INSIGHT

Psychoanalysts want their patients to attain insight into the motives of which they were formerly unaware, but they don't want that insight to be merely intellectual. The patient must regain access, not just to various repressed thoughts and memories, but also and more importantly, to the feelings that go along with them. Freud was emphatic that recollections without emotions have little therapeutic effect. Genuine self-discovery is only achieved when the patient rids himself of the repressive forces that had kept the insights from him, and this typically requires a good deal of emotional involvement. Without this involvement, the psychoanalytic process is an intellectual exercise rather than a therapy (Freud, 1913).

*Catharsis* What would produce the necessary emotional involvement? Originally, Freud put his faith in the **catharsis** that accompanied the recovery of certain long-lost memories. When these surfaced, a host of associated emotions followed in their wake and were explosively discharged in fits of sobbing or in bursts of sharp anger. Such an emotional release is generally experienced as a kind of relief. It turned out, however, that dramatic reactions of this kind were fairly rare. Moreover, even when they did occur, their benefits proved rather short-lived; after a while, the symptoms reappeared. If emotions are a necessary ingredient of analytic therapy, they have to be evoked by another means.

It is worth noting that it is by no means clear why catharsis should be therapeutic (or whether it always is). But right or wrong, the notion that catharsis helps goes back to antiquity. The Greeks used the term to describe both the purging of the body (by an emetic or strong laxative) and the purification of the emotions (by watching a deeply moving event, as in a tragedy on stage). In effect, they drew an analogy between indigestible foods and troubling, unexpressed emotions. They evidently believed that both ought to be expelled, as if voiding and vomiting were to the body as weeping is to the soul.

*Transference* Freud believed that the major means for providing the necessary emotional component is the **transference** relationship in which the patient responds to the analyst in increasingly personal terms (see Chapter 11). He reacts to him as he had reacted to the major figures in his own life, and he will therefore love or hate the analyst as he had loved or hated his mother, father, siblings and, more recently, his lovers and friends. All of these feelings are transferred to the

1961). Perhaps this is just a modern restatement of the old idea that love can redeem us all.*

EXISTENTIAL THERAPY

Rogers's approach to therapy is distinctively American in its optimistic faith in an almost limitless human capacity for growth and self-improvement. Another humanistic approach to therapy originates in Europe and takes a more somber view. This is *existential therapy,* a movement that echoes some of the major themes sounded by a group of philosophers called *existentialists.* Existential therapists are primarily concerned with what they regard as the major emotional sickness of our times, an inability to endow life with meaning. In their view, this condition is a by-product of the rootless, restless anonymity of twentieth-century Western life; it is especially prevalent in modern Europe, in the wake of the despair that followed two bloody world wars and the Nazi terror. It is marked by a sense that one is alienated, lost, and dehumanized; that one is nothing but a cog in a huge, impersonal machine; and that one's existence is meaningless. According to existential therapists, this feeling that everything is pointless is a common facet of many modern emotional disorders. It is this, rather than the specific symptoms of the disorders —the phobias, the obsessions, and the like—that they want to rectify (Ofman, 1985).

In essence, existential therapists try to help people achieve a personal outlook that gives meaning to their lives. How do they do this? It turns out that most existential therapists have no distinctive technique. Some use the couch and ask the patient to free associate, while others sit face to face and have lengthy philosophical discussions. What is distinctive about them is their underlying attitude. They try to make their patients aware of the importance of free choice. They insist that people are persons and not objects, that human acts spring from within rather than being imposed from without, that there are always choices—even in jail, even in a concentration camp—and that what one is is ultimately what one chooses to do. The therapist's job is to help the patient realize that the responsibility for finding and for making her life's choices is hers and hers alone. If and when the patient accepts this responsibility, she will no longer be plagued by the vacuum of her own existence but will begin to feel "authentic."

Like practitioners of most other schools, existential therapists stress the role of the therapeutic relationship in affecting the changes they want to bring about. In their view, the key element of this relationship is what they call the *encounter,* in which two individuals meet as genuine persons of whose independent human existence neither has any doubt. According to existential therapists, the experience derived from this encounter will ultimately transfer to the way in which the patient sees himself and others (May, 1958).

In the past, the task that existential therapists set themselves was generally held to be the province of clergymen. It was priests and parsons and rabbis who tried to help people find some meaning in their existence. They did so within a reli-

***Existential therapy*** *(Hand with Reflecting Sphere, 1935, by M. C. Escher; © M. C. Escher Heirs, c/o Cordon Art, Baarn, Holland)*

---

* Rogers's humanistic approach has often been attacked by behavior therapists who regard him as "antiscientific." Under the circumstances, it is somewhat ironic that Rogers was one of the pioneers of psychotherapy evaluation, the first major figure in the field of psychotherapy who looked for evidence that his techniques were actually having some effect.

gious framework that defined the spiritual dimension of human life. As religious values have eroded, other social institutions have stepped in and have tried to take the clergy's place. One of these is modern humanistic psychotherapy, especially the existentialist school. It is no accident that an influential book by a prominent existential therapist bears the title *The Doctor and the Soul* (Frankl, 1966).

## Some Common Themes

The various forms of psychotherapy differ in some important regards in what they try to do. The psychoanalytically oriented therapists' primary focus is on *understanding.* Their aim is to help the patient realize what is behind his thoughts and actions so that he can face his unconscious conflicts and overcome them. Behavior therapists emphasize *doing.* They try to help their patients eliminate undesirable responses and extinguish irrational fears. Cognitive-behavioral therapists are most concerned with *thinking.* They want to enable their patients to overcome patterns of irrational and self-defeating thoughts. Humanistic therapists stress *feeling.* Their hope is to help their clients come to terms with who they really are by accepting what they want and feel in the here-and-now.

These differences among the various therapeutic schools are real enough. But of late there have been trends toward a rapprochement between the different schools of therapy. Thus, some psychoanalytically oriented practitioners have come to use techniques that were formerly the exclusive preserve of behavior therapists; for example, modeling and "homework" assignments (Wachtel, 1977, 1982). And on the other side, many behavior therapists have come to realize that the client-therapist relation is an important part of treatment, that something like Freud's "transference" comes into play even in therapies such as flooding or desensitization, which are based on classical conditioning concepts (Lazarus, 1971, 1981).

But quite apart from such trends toward an eclectic approach to therapy, there are some underlying common themes that run through the beliefs and practices of all the contending schools, despite all of their divergences.

### EMOTIONAL DEFUSING

All psychotherapies aim at some kind of emotional reeducation. They try to help the patient rid himself of various intense and unrealistic fears. To this end, these fears, and other strong emotions such as anger, are evoked during the therapeutic session. Since this happens in the presence of an accepting, noncondemning therapist, the fear is weakened.

### INTERPERSONAL LEARNING

All major schools stress the importance of interpersonal learning and follow Freud in believing that the therapeutic relationship is an important tool in bringing this about. This relationship shows the patient how she generally reacts to others and also provides a vehicle through which she can discover and rehearse new and better ways for doing so.

A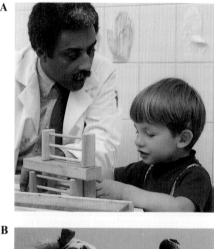

B

*Play therapy, an extension of psychotherapy adapted for children* (A) In play therapy, the therapist tries to help the child understand and express his feelings about his parents and other family members through play with various toys. (B) Puppets are sometimes used to act out problems, as in this example of a therapy session with victims of child abuse. (Top: photograph by Michal Heron, 1979/ Monkmeyer Press. Bottom: photograph by Bart Bartholomew, 1984/Black Star)

### INSIGHT

Most psychotherapists try to help their patients achieve greater self-knowledge, though different therapeutic schools differ in what kind of self-knowledge they try to bring about. For psychoanalysts, the crucial emotional insights the patient must acquire refer to his own past; for Rogerians, they concern one's feelings in the present; for behavior therapists, the relevant self-understanding is the correct identification of the stimuli to which fear has been conditioned.

### THERAPY AS A STEP-BY-STEP PROCESS

There is general agreement that therapy is a gradual affair and that this is so regardless of whether the therapy emphasizes cognitive insight, feelings, or behaviors. There are few sudden flashes of insight or emotional understanding which change a patient overnight. Instead, each newfound insight and freshly acquired skill must be laboriously applied in one life situation after another before the patient can call it her own.

### THERAPY AS A SOCIALLY ACCEPTED PRACTICE

Most psychotherapists operate within a social context that gives them the status of officially designated healers for emotional ills. As a result, the stage is set for a number of nonspecific gains of psychotherapy. One is an intimate, confiding relation with another person. This alone may be a boon to some persons who have no close bonds to anyone and for whom psychotherapy may amount to what one author calls "the purchase of friendship" (Schofield, 1964). Another nonspecific gain is the hope that one will get better. This may lead the patient to think better of himself, which may lead to small successes in the outside world, which may fuel further hope, and increase the chances of yet other successes.

*Psychotherapy—the purchase of friendship?* *(© 1950, 1952 United Feature Syndicate Inc.)*

## EVALUATING THERAPEUTIC OUTCOME

We have just surveyed what different kinds of therapists do. We now ask whether what they do does any good. This question often arouses indignant protests from therapists and patients alike. For many of them feel utterly certain that they help or have been helped; they therefore see no point in questioning what to them is obvious. But their testimonials alone are not convincing. For one thing, both patients and therapists have a serious stake in believing that psychotherapy works. If it doesn't, the patient has wasted his money and the therapist has wasted his time. Under the circumstances, neither may be the most objective judge in assessing whether there was a significant change. But even granting that change occurred, what caused this change? Was it produced by the therapeutic situation, or would it have come about in any case? And, assuming that the therapy did play a role, was the improvement caused by the therapy as such or was it produced by nonspecific, placebo-like factors such as hope, expectations of cure, and the decision to "turn a new leaf"?

## Does Psychotherapy Work?

Much of the impetus for discussions of psychotherapeutic outcomes came from a sharp attack on the efficacy of psychoanalysis and similar "insight therapies" launched by the British psychologist Hans Eysenck (Eysenck, 1961). Eysenck surveyed some two dozen articles that reported the number of neurotic patients who improved or failed to improve after psychotherapy. Overall, about 60 percent improved, a result that might be considered fairly encouraging. But Eysenck argued that there was really nothing to cheer about. According to Eysenck's analysis, the spontaneous recovery rate in neurotics who received *no* treatment was, if anything, even higher—about 70 percent. If so, psychotherapy apparently has no curative effects.

In retrospect, it appears that Eysenck's appraisal was unduly harsh. In particular, he evidently overestimated the rate of spontaneous improvement. According to one review, the median rate of patients who get better without therapy is around 30 percent compared to an average improvement rate of 60 percent for neurotic patients who received psychotherapy, a difference that constitutes what the author called "some modest evidence that psychotherapy 'works'" (Bergin, 1971, p. 229; see also Luborsky, Singer, and Luborsky, 1975).

### META-ANALYSES OF THERAPY OUTCOME

More recent analyses of the research literature provide an even more optimistic picture. For the most part, they are based on a new statistical technique called **meta-analysis** by means of which the results of many different studies can be combined. In the most comprehensive analysis of this kind, Smith, Glass, and Miller reviewed 475 different studies, comprising 25,000 patients in all (Smith, Glass, and Miller, 1980). In each of these studies, patients who received some kind of psychotherapy were compared with a reasonably comparable group of patients who did not. The studies differed in many respects. One factor that varied was the particular brand of psychotherapy. In some studies, the therapy was psychodynamic, in others, it was humanistic, or behavioral, or cognitive. Another factor that varied was the criterion of improvement. In some cases, it was focused on a symptom: Did a snake phobic show less fear when shown a snake, did the compulsive washer wash less frequently, and so on. In others, it was based on an improvement in functioning, such as a rise in a disturbed student's grade point average. In still others, such as studies on depressed patients, it was concerned with an improvement in mood, as rated by scales filled out by the patient himself or by knowledgeable outsiders such as spouse and children. Given all these differences between the studies, is there any way to combine the results? Meta-analysis provides a method.

Consider two hypothetical studies, *A* and *B*. Let's say that Study *A* shows that after treatment the average snake phobic can approach a snake more closely than a group of patients who received no treatment. Let's assume that Study *B* found that depressed students who received psychotherapy show a greater increase in grade point average (GPA) than do equivalent students in an untreated control group. On the face of it, there's no way to average the results of the two studies, for they are measured in completely different units. In the first case, the average effect of therapy—that is, the difference between the group that received treatment and the one that did not—is measured in feet (how near to the snake the patient will go); in the second, it is counted in GPA points. But meta-analysis provides a way. The trick is to determine the percentage of persons in the untreated group whose improvement score is below the average improvement score of the treated group. Let's suppose we find that in Study *A,* 85 percent of the patients are able to approach the snake more closely than the average untreated patient can. Let's further suppose that in Study *B,* 75 percent of the students who received psychotherapy get a GPA that's higher than the average GPA of the untreated students. Now we can average the scores. To be sure, feet and GPA points are like apples and oranges and cannot be compared. But the ***percentage relationships***—in our case, 85 and 75—are comparable. Since this is so, they can be averaged across different studies.

By averaging across the 475 studies reviewed in their analysis, Smith, Glass, and Miller concluded that the "average person who receives therapy is better off at the end of it than 80 percent of the persons who do not" (Smith, Glass, and Miller, 1980, p. 87). Later analyses that used somewhat more stringent criteria in eliminating studies that were methodologically suspect yielded similar results (e.g., Andrews and Harvey, 1981; Shapiro and Shapiro, 1982). Further studies have shown that these improvements are still found when patients are studied months or years after treatment (Nicholson and Berman, 1983).

DETERIORATION EFFECTS

It appears that, speaking overall, patients who received psychotherapy are better off than patients who did not. But this statement applies to averages. When we look at individuals, we find that while psychotherapy has an effect, this effect is not always for the better. A certain proportion of patients seem to get worse. Some evidence that this is so came from an inspection of the variability of post-treatment test scores (for example, self-ratings). After psychotherapy, the scores on such tests are more spread out than the scores of an untreated control group. This suggests that while some patients are improving, some others—fortunately, a smaller number—become worse than they were to start with (Bergin, 1967).

One possible cause of this so-called ***deterioration effect*** is that psychotherapy sometimes disturbs an unstable neurotic equilibrium without supplying an appropriate substitute (Bergin, 1967). There is some evidence that certain therapists are more likely to produce such negative effects than others. It is probably not too surprising that these therapists are people who are rather unappealing. They tend to be (or at least, appear to be) overly aggressive, intrusive, impatient, not particularly warm and friendly, and in some cases, downright nasty (Rosenhan and Seligman, 1989).

## Comparing Different Therapies

The preceding discussion indicates that patients who receive psychotherapy will —on the average—be better off than patients who do not. To the extent that this is so, psychotherapy works. But as we've seen, there are any number of different psychotherapies: psychodynamic, humanistic, behavioral, cognitive, and so on. Do any of them get better results than the others?

### THE DODO BIRD VERDICT

Which form of psychotherapy works better than the others? This question has been asked by several investigators. Their answer is unlikely to provide comfort for the adherents of any one school of psychotherapy. Most studies of psychotherapeutic outcomes suggest that the differences in the effectiveness of the various psychotherapies are slight or nonexistent. This view is sometimes called the **_Dodo Bird verdict_** after the Dodo Bird in _Alice in Wonderland_ who organized a race between various Wonderland creatures and concluded that "Everyone has won and all must have prizes" (Luborsky, Singer, and Luborsky, 1975). While a few reviewers feel that the behavioral and cognitive therapies have a slight advantage (e.g., Shapiro and Shapiro, 1982), many others judge that the outcome similarities far outweigh the differences (e.g., Smith, Glass, and Miller, 1980; Sloane, Staples, Cristol, Yorkston, and Whipple, 1975).

### PLACEBO EFFECTS

How can we explain the Dodo Bird effect? One possibility is that psychotherapy generates a placebo effect. According to this view, the patients got better because they expected to get better, in a manner quite analogous to what happens when patients ingest little blue sugar pills in the belief that they are swallowing a potent medicine (see pp. 801–802). We wouldn't expect blue sugar pills to be more helpful than red or green sugar pills; analogously, we shouldn't expect psychodynamic therapies to be more (or less) effective than, say, humanistic therapies. Whether we're dealing with sugar pills or with psychotherapies, in this view, all that matters is the patients' belief. An ingenious demonstration of a placebo effect in psychotherapy was provided in a classic study by Gordon Paul in which students who suffered from severe anxiety when they had to talk in front of others were given five sessions of a bogus treatment. During each session, they took what they thought was a potent tranquilizer (it actually was a capsule of bicarbonate) and performed a boring discrimination task. They were told that this task was ordinarily very stressful but would not be so for them because of the "tranquilizer." If repeated often enough, this experience would then inoculate them against anxiety-provoking situations in real life. Needless to say, all of this was a ruse, but the subjects accepted it and believed that the treatment would help them. When later tested for speech anxiety, these subjects improved considerably more than an untreated control group, providing a powerful demonstration of a psychotherapeutic placebo effect (Paul, 1966).

The mere expectation of getting better seems to help. But is that all there is to psychotherapy? The bulk of the evidence argues otherwise. Several meta-analytic studies have compared the effect of placebo treatments (such as Paul's) to the effect of genuine psychotherapies. By and large, genuine psychotherapy led to more improvement than placebo treatments (Smith, Glass, and Miller, 1980, p. 91; Andrews and Harvey, 1981; for a contrary view and discussion, see Prioleau, Murdock, and Brody, 1983).

## COMMON FACTORS

Placebo effects are evidently smaller than the benefits produced by genuine psychotherapy. But if so, we are still left with the problem of explaining the Dodo Bird effect.

The best guess is that despite all of their apparent divergences, the various psychotherapies have many things in common. We've previously described some of the shared themes that underlie many of the beliefs and practices of the various schools, such as attempts at emotional defusing, efforts to provide interpersonal learning, and an empathic relationship with another human being conducted within an accepted social framework (see pp. 820–21). To the extent that these features are indeed therapeutic and are common to the various schools, we would expect that they (together with some shared psychological placebo effects) will exert similar beneficial effects.

### ARE THERE ANY SPECIFIC FACTORS?

The Dodo Bird verdict asserts that at bottom all psychotherapies are equally effective, regardless of the banner under which they are practiced. But there may well be some differences that are not so readily picked up by the studies (for the most part, meta-analytic) that we've discussed thus far. The real issue may not be which therapy is most effective, but rather what treatment is *specific* for which condition; that is, which treatment is most effective for which patient under which set of circumstances (Paul, 1967). Meta-analysis may not be the best way to answer this question, for it tends to lump different disorders together. But if so, it may not uncover specific differences even if they do exist.

Is there any indication that certain psychotherapies are specific for particular conditions? While the complete evidence is not yet in, many practitioners believe that some specific therapies do exist, and argue that for at least some mental disorders—specifically, phobias, panic disorders, compulsions, and depression—certain psychotherapeutic procedures are the therapy of choice. For example, it is widely believed that phobias and related anxiety conditions are best treated by any of the behavior therapies that try to eliminate fear, specifically, systematic desensitization, flooding, and implosion, especially if conducted in vivo (Emmelkamp, 1986). Similar techniques have proved useful in dealing with panic conditions, although recent evidence suggests that cognitive therapy (especially in conjunction with appropriate drug treatment) is even more effective (Clark, 1988). In cases of depression, cognitive therapy is the psychotherapy of choice. While it seems to produce about the same degree of improvement as do antidepressants, its results are more long-lasting, for it leads to lower relapse rates than do the drug therapies. The best evidence suggests that a combination of the two therapies works better than either alone (Hollon and Beck, 1986; DeRubeis, Hollon, Evans, and Bernis, 1982; Hollon et al., 1990).

## EXTENSIONS OF PSYCHOTHERAPY

In Freud's time, psychotherapy was still considered a somewhat arcane art, practiced by a few initiates and limited to a selected group of well-educated adult patients. Since then, psychotherapy has been broadened and extended to cover increasingly more terrain. One set of extensions widened the patient population to include children, retarded persons, various kinds of sociopaths, and psychotics. Another extension was a shift from the original one-therapist, one-patient formula to various modes of ***group therapy*** that feature all conceivable permutations: one therapist and several patients, several therapists and several patients, several patients and no therapist, and so on.

## Group Therapy

One reason for treating patients in groups is that there simply aren't enough trained therapists for all the people who want their services; seeing clients in groups is one way of making the supply fit the demand. But the appeal of group therapy may have some deeper reasons as well. For instance, the new therapeutic groups seem to fill a void, at least temporarily, left by the weakening of family and religious ties in modern urbanized society.

### SHARED-PROBLEM GROUPS

One approach is to organize a group of people all of whom have the same problem. They may all be alcoholics, or drug addicts, or ex-convicts. The members meet, share relevant advice and information, help newcomers along, exhort and support each other in their resolve to overcome their handicaps. The classic example is ***Alcoholics Anonymous,*** which provides the alcoholic with a sense that he

*(Drawing by Whitney Darrow, Jr.; ©
1976, The New Yorker Magazine, Inc.)*

*"When Jud accuses Zack, here, of hostility toward his daughter, like he seems to every session, why, it's plain to me he's only rationalizing his own lack of gumption in standing up to a stepson who's usurping the loyalty of his second wife. The way he lit into him just now shows he's got this here guilt identification with Zack's present family constellation. Calling Zack egotistical ain't nothing but a disguise mechanism for concealing his secret envy of Zack's grit and all-around starch, and shows mighty poor ego boundaries of his own, it appears to me."*

is not alone and helps him weather crises without suffering a relapse. In such we-are-all-in-the-same-boat groups, the primary aim of the group is to *manage* the problem that all members share. No specific therapy is provided for emotional problems that are unique to any one individual.

### THERAPY GROUPS

The rules of the game are very different in groups explicitly organized for the purpose of ***group therapy.*** Here, a group of selected patients, usually around ten, are treated together under the guidance of a trained therapist. This form of therapy may have some advantages that individual treatment lacks. According to its proponents, in group therapy the therapist does not really treat the members of the group; instead, he helps them to treat each other. The specific techniques of the therapist may vary from psychoanalytically oriented insight therapy to various forms of behavior therapy to Rogerian client-centered approaches. But whatever techniques the therapist favors, the treatment of each group member really begins as he realizes that he is not all that different from the others. He learns that there are other people who are painfully shy, who have hostile fantasies about their parents, or whatever. Further benefits come from a sense of group belongingness, of support, and of encouragement. But most important of all is the fact that the group provides a ready-made laboratory in interpersonal relations. The patient can discover just what he does that rubs others the wrong way, how he can relate to certain kinds of people more effectively, and so on (Sadock, 1975).

## Marital and Family Therapy

In the therapy groups we've considered thus far, the members are almost always strangers before the sessions begin. This is in marked contrast to what happens in ***marital and family therapy.*** Here the persons seeking help have known each other very well (sometimes only too well) before they enter therapy.

In recent years, family therapy has become a major therapeutic movement (Satir, 1967; Minuchin, 1974; Kerr and Bowen, 1988). It is probably no coincidence that this growth has occurred during a time of turmoil in American families, evidenced by spiraling divorce rates and increasing numbers of single-parent households.

Family and marital therapists regard the family as an emotional unit that can influence the onset and continuing symptoms of many mental disorders and social problems. Seen from this perspective, the key to marital and family distress is not necessarily in the pathology of any individual spouse or family member. It is rather in the relationships within the family system: between the husband and wife, or the various members of the family. In a dislocated shoulder, both the upper arm and shoulder socket may be perfectly sound, but until their mutual relationship is appropriately readjusted, there will necessarily be pain and the shoulder won't be able to function. Many marital (or couple) and family therapists feel that their task is in principle similar to that of the orthopedist who resets the dislocated shoulder: They try to help the couple or the family readjust their interrelations.

Many family therapists prefer to see the members of the couple or family together rather than individually. In such joint sessions, the therapist can act as an

*"We're not living happily ever after."*
*(Drawing by Chas. Addams; © 1959, 1987,*
*The New Yorker Magazine, Inc.)*

emotional translator who can help the spouses or family members to understand each other better. An example is this exchange between therapist (T), husband (H), and wife (W):

H:  She never comes up to me and kisses me. I am always the one to make the overtures.
T:  (to wife): Is this the way you see yourself behaving with your husband?
W:  Yes, I would say he is the demonstrative one. I didn't know he wanted me to make the overtures.
T:  Have you told your wife that you would like this from her—more open demonstration of affection?
H:  Well, no, you'd think she'd know.
W:  No. How would I know? You always said you don't like aggressive women.
H:  I don't. I don't like *dominating* women.
W:  Well, I thought you meant women who make the overtures. How am I to know what you want?
T:  You'd have a better idea if he had been able to *tell* you.

(From Satir, 1967, pp. 72–73)

Some reviewers believe that this approach achieves therapeutic results, especially when the spouses or family members are seen together rather than individually (Gurman and Kniskern, 1981; Hazelrigg, Cooper, and Borduin, 1987). But this conclusion can be questioned on various methodological grounds. For example, the superiority of conjoint to individual therapy may reflect a difference in who chooses what treatment. Perhaps the Smiths who refuse to see a therapist together are more at odds with each other than the Browns who decide to see him jointly. To achieve the appropriate controls for outcome evaluation may be even more difficult in this area than in the field of individual therapy.

### The Expansion of Therapeutic Goals

Group methods and other extensions made psychotherapy available to a much larger number of people. But did all of them really need it? The answer depends on what one believes the goals of therapy to be.

To Freud, the matter was simple. Most of the neurotics he saw were incapable of any kind of healthy life. They were crippled by terrorizing phobias or all-consuming compulsions and were thus unable to work and love. Freud wanted to cure these pathologies so that his patients could once again deal with their everyday existence. But he never regarded this cure as equivalent to happiness or fulfillment or the discovery of a meaning in life. These the patients had to find for themselves, and they might very well fail to do so even when no longer saddled with their neuroses.

Later therapists broadened the treatment goals. This is especially true of humanistic therapists such as Rogers. To be sure, Rogerian therapists try to remove or alleviate their clients' distress. But their ambitions go further. They aim at more than a cure (the goal of psychoanalysts, at least in their early days) and at more than the modification of unwanted behavior patterns (the goal of behavior therapists). Their ultimate object is to help their clients to "grow" and to "realize their human potentialities." But with this expansion of the therapeutic goal, there is a concomitant widening of the group to which the therapeutic enterprise may be said to apply. Now therapy can be appropriate for just about anyone, regardless of whether he suffers some form of psychopathology or does not (Orne, 1975). After all, who among us can claim to have achieved his full potential?

## A CENTURY OF THERAPY

Where does all of this leave us? What can we say today about the treatment of mental disorder about a hundred years after the discovery that general paresis is caused by syphilis and after Freud and Breuer conducted their classic studies of hysteria?

All in all, we can say that the last century has shown a great deal of progress.

Let's begin with psychotherapy. The first thing to say is that there is little doubt that psychotherapy produces some nonspecific benefits. It helps people by providing someone in whom they can confide, who can give advice about troubling matters, who listens to them, and who instills new hope and the expectation that they will get better. The critic may reply that such gains merely reflect placebo effects and similar matters. According to this view, the benefits are not produced by any specific psychotherapeutic technique but might just as easily have been provided by a wise uncle or an understanding family doctor. Even if this were true—and it is certainly not the whole story—the point may not be relevant. For wise uncles are in short supply today. The extended family in which uncles, nieces, and grandparents lived in close proximity is largely a thing of the past. The same is true of the family doctor, who has vanished from the scene, together with his bedside manner. All of this suggests that psychotherapy has come to fill a social vacuum. Some of its effect may well be placebo-like, but a placebo may be better than nothing. And for the present, the psychotherapeutic professions seem to be the officially designated dispensers of such placebos.

But this is by no means all. For over and above placebos there are some genuine specific psychotherapeutic effects that produce improvement, though rarely a complete cure. The specific ingredients that bring these effects about have not been identified with certainty but they probably include emotional defusing, interpersonal learning, and some insight—all acquired within the therapeutic situation and somehow transferred to the patient's life beyond.

How about somatic therapies? Here too there has been progress. The antipsychotic drugs alleviate some of the worst symptoms of schizophrenia, the antidepressants (and where appropriate, electroconvulsive therapy) do the same for depression, and lithium salts do a good job in controlling manic episodes in bipolar disorder. These advances are far from what one might wish. The drugs don't begin to effect a cure and generally have side effects. But we're farther along than we were a hundred years ago.

How far is far? As so often, it depends on where we look. If we look back and compare our current practices with those at the time of the American Revolution when Benjamin Rush dunked his patients into ice cold water or whirled them around until they were unconscious, we've come a long way. But if we look ahead to some diagnostic manual of the future in which schizophrenia, mood disorders, anxiety states, and all the rest of the current DSM-III-R entries have neatly catalogued therapies that are sure to work, we must recognize that we have a much longer way to go. But considering how much progress was made in the last hundred years, there is certainly room for hope.

## SUMMARY

1. One major form of treatment of mental disorder is by *somatic therapies.* Of these, the most widely used are *drug therapies. Antipsychotic drugs* such as *phenothiazines* are helpful in alleviating the major symptoms of schizophrenia; *antidepressants,* including the *MAO inhibitors* and *tricyclics,* counteract depression; and *lithium carbonate* is useful in cases of bipolar mood disorders, especially in forestalling manic episodes.

2. The effectiveness of drug treatment—as indeed of all therapies—requires careful evaluation procedures that control for *spontaneous improvement* and *placebo effects,* and that also guard against both the physicians' and the patients' expectations by use of *double-blind techniques.* Such studies have demonstrated genuine effects of certain psychiatric drugs, some of which are quite specific to a particular disorder. But thus far these drugs have not produced complete cures, especially in schizophrenia. Without a *maintenance dose,* a discharged patient may relapse; even with it, his adjustment may be only marginal.

3. Other somatic therapies include *frontal lobotomy,* a procedure now widely suspect, and *electroconvulsive shock treatment (ECT)* in cases of severe and potentially suicidal depression.

4. Another approach to mental disorder, *psychotherapy,* relies on psychological means alone. It derives from *classical psychoanalysis.* Psychoanalysts try to help their patients to recover repressed memories and wishes so that they can overcome crippling internal conflicts. Their tools are *free association* and the *interpretation* of the patient's *resistance.* The goal is emotional rather than mere intellectual insight, an achievement made possible by an analysis of the *transference* relationship between analyst and patient.

5. Many modern psychoanalysts practice modified variants of Freud's technique. They generally place greater emphasis on interpersonal and social problems in the present than on psychosexual matters in the past. They also tend to take a more active role in helping the patient extend the therapeutic experience to the world outside.

6. A different approach is taken by *behavior therapists* whose concern is with unwanted, overt behaviors rather than with hypothetical underlying causes. Many of the behavior therapists' techniques are derived from the principles of classical and instrumental conditioning. Therapies based on classical conditioning include *flooding and implosion,* which attempt to extinguish the patient's fear by evoking the fear response in full force. Others are *systematic desensitization,* which tries to *countercondition* the patient's fear by a policy of gradualism. Yet another is *aversion therapy,* in which undesirable behaviors, thoughts, and desires are coupled with unpleasant stimuli. Therapies based on operant conditioning principles include the use of *token economies,* in which patients are systematically reinforced for desirable behaviors.

7. Some recent offshoots of behavior therapy share its concrete and *directive* orientation but not its emphasis on conditioning. One example is *cognitive therapy,* which tries to change the way the patient thinks about his situation. Others include various attempts to advance the patient's social education, using techniques such as *graded task assignments, modeling,* and *role playing.*

8. Another group of practitioners, the *humanistic therapists,* charge that both behavior therapy and psychoanalysis are too mechanistic and manipulative and that they fail to deal with their patients as "whole persons." An example of such a humanistic approach is Rogers's *client-centered therapy,* which is largely *nondirective,* and is based on the idea that therapy is a personal growth process. A related approach is *existential therapy,* whose goal is to help patients recognize the importance of personal responsibility and free choice, and to assist them in discovering some meaning in life.

9. In recent years, many investigators have assessed the effectiveness of psychotherapies through a statistical technique called *meta-analysis,* by means of which the results of many different studies can be combined. The results of such analyses indicate that the various psychotherapies are more effective than *placebo treatments,* which in turn are better than no treatment at all. Comparing the effect of different psychotherapies is enormously difficult. Some authors believe that the evidence indicates that all therapies are fairly effective, and that they are effective to about the same extent (the *Dodo Bird verdict*).

10. The last few decades have seen an enormous extension of psychotherapy. One extension is of method. An example is *group therapy,* in which patients are treated in groups rather than individually. Another example is *family (and marital) therapy,* whose practitioners believe that family distress is not in the pathology of any one individual but in the relationships within the family system, and who therefore try to rectify these faulty relationships. Another extension concerns the *therapeutic goals.* While the original purpose of psychotherapy was to cure pathology, some practitioners gradually broadened this goal to include personal growth and the discovery of meaning in life.

# Epilogue

We have come to the end of our journey. We have traveled through the sprawling fields of psychology, a loosely federated intellectual empire that stretches from the domains of the biological sciences on one border to those of the social sciences on the other. We have gone from one end of psychology to another. What have we learned?

In looking back over our journey, there is little doubt that we have encountered many more questions than answers. To be sure, very much more is known today about mind and behavior than was known in the days of, say, Thorndike and Köhler, let alone those of Descartes, Locke, and Kant. For by now, psychology has assuredly become a science, and in fact, a science of quite respectable accomplishments. But this does not change the fact that what we know today is just a small clearing in a vast jungle of ignorance. As we come to know more, the clearing expands, but so does the circumference that borders on the uncharted wildness.

What can we say? We can point at what we know and congratulate ourselves. Or we can consider what we do not know and bemoan our ignorance. Perhaps a wiser course is one recommended by Sigmund Freud on thinking about some aspects of human intellectual history (Freud, 1917).

Freud suggested a parallel between the psychological growth of each human child and the intellectual progress of humanity as a whole. As he saw it, the infant is initially possessed by an all-prevading sense of his own power and importance. He cries and his parents come to change or feed or rock him and so he feels that he is the cause of whatever happens around him, the sole center of a world that revolves around him alone. But this happy delusion of his own omnipotence cannot last forever. Eventually the growing infant discovers that he is not the hub of the universe. This recognition may come as a cruel blow, but he will ultimately be the better for it. For the child cannot become strong and capable without some

meaningful—not arbitrary, as in the case of categorical scales. If individuals are asked to list the ten people they most admire, the number 1 can be assigned to the most admired person, 2 to the runner-up, and so on. The smaller the number assigned, the more the person is admired. Notice that no such statement can be made of television channels: Channel 4 is not more anything than channel 2, just different from it.

Scores which are ordinally scaled cannot, however, be added or subtracted. The first two persons on the most-admired list differ in admirability by 1; so do the last two. Yet the individual who has done the ranking may admire the first person far more than the other nine, all of whom might be very similar in admirability; in other words, given an ordinal scale, differences of 1 are not necessarily equal psychologically. Imagine a child who, given this task, lists his mother first, followed by the starting lineup of the Chicago Cubs baseball team. In this example, the difference of 8 between person 2 and person 10 probably represents a smaller difference in judged admirability than the difference of 1 obtained between persons 1 and 2 (at least so the mother hopes).

## Interval Scales

Scales in which equal differences between scores, or intervals, *can* be treated as equal units are called *interval scales.* Reaction time is a common psychological variable which is usually treated as an interval scale. In some memory experiments, a subject must respond as quickly as possible to each of several words, some of which he has seen earlier in the experiment; the task is to indicate whether each word has appeared before by pressing one of two buttons. An unknown, but possibly constant, part of the reaction time is simply the time required to press the response button; the rest is the time required for the decision-making process:

$$\text{reaction time} = \text{decision time} + \text{button-press time} \qquad (1)$$

Suppose a subject requires an average of 2 seconds to respond to nouns, 3 seconds for verbs, and 4 seconds for adjectives. The difference in decision time between nouns and verbs ($3 - 2 = 1$ second) is the same as the difference in decision time between verbs and adjectives ($4 - 3 = 1$ second). We can make this statement—which in turn suggests various hypotheses about the factors that underlie such differences—precisely because reaction time can be regarded as an interval scale.

## Ratio Scales

Scores based on an interval scale allow subtraction and addition. But they do not necessarily allow multiplication and division. Consider the centigrade scale of temperature. There is no doubt that the difference between 10 and 20 degrees centigrade is equal to that between 30 and 40 degrees centigrade. But can one say that 20 degrees centigrade is *twice* as high a temperature as 10 degrees centigrade? The answer is no, for the centigrade scale of temperature is only an interval scale. It is not a *ratio scale* which allows statements such as 10 feet is 1/5 as long as 50 feet, or 15 pounds is 3 times as heavy as 5 pounds. To make such statements one needs a true zero point. Such a ratio scale with a zero point does exist for temperature—the Kelvin absolute temperature scale, whose zero point is about $-273$ degrees centigrade.

Some psychological variables can be described by a ratio scale. This is true of various forms of sensory intensity—brightness, loudness, and so on. For example, it makes sense to say that the rock music emanating from your neighbor's apartment is four times as loud as your roommate singing in the shower. But there are many psychological variables which cannot be so readily described in ratio terms. Let's go back to reaction time. This cannot be considered a ratio scale for the decision process. In our previous example we saw that the reaction time for adjectives was 4 seconds, while that for nouns was 2 seconds. But we cannot say that the 4-second response represents twice as much *decision* time as the 2-second response, because of the unknown time required to press the response button. Since this time is unknown, we have no zero point.

The fact that very few variables are ratio scaled does not, of course, prevent people from describing ordinal- or interval-scaled variables in ratio terms. A claim by an advertiser that drug $A$ is "twice as effective" as drug $B$ may mean that $A$ works twice as fast, or for twice the time, or is successful on twice as many people, or requires only half the dose. A potential consumer needs to know the advertiser's meaning of "effective" to evaluate the claim. Similarly, a 4-second reaction time in the word-recognition experiment is certainly twice as long as a 2-second reaction time; there is no harm in saying so, as long as it is understood that we are not talking about the decision time but rather about the total reaction time.

## COLLECTING THE DATA

The kinds of scales we have just discussed concern the ways in which psychological variables are described in numerical terms. The point of most psychological investigations is to see how such variables are related to various factors that may produce them. Psychologists—and most other scientists—employ three major methodological tools to achieve this end: the experiment, the observational study, and the case study.

### The Experiment

An *experiment* is a study in which the experimenter deliberately manipulates one or more variables to determine the effect of this manipulation on another variable. As an example, consider an experiment conducted to determine whether visual imagery aids memory. Participants in the experiment listen to a list of words, which they are instructed to memorize; later they are asked to recall as many words as possible. Two groups of subjects are chosen. One is the *experimental group;* this is the group to which the experimenter's manipulation is applied. It consists of subjects who are instructed to form visual images that connect each word to the preceding word. Other subjects form the *control group,* a group to which the experimenter's manipulation is not applied. These control subjects are not given imagery instructions. Many experiments have more than one experimental group (in this example, different groups might be told to do their visual

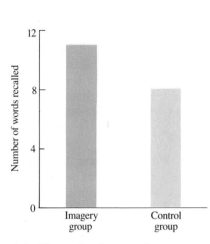

Number of words recalled

12

8

4

0

Imagery group     Control group

**A.1   The results of an experiment on memorizing**   *Subjects in the imagery group, who formed visual images of the words they were to memorize, recalled an average of 11 words. Subjects in the control group, who received no special instructions, recalled an average of 8 words.*

imagining in different ways), or more than one control group (here, a second control group might be instructed to rehearse by repeating each word over and over).

Like many other experiments, this one can be thought of as a situation in which the experimenter varies something (here the instructions given to the subjects) and observes the effect of this variation on certain responses of the subjects (the number of words they correctly recall). The variable which is manipulated by the experimenter (imagery instructions) is called the ***independent variable.*** The subject's response (number of words recalled) is called the ***dependent variable,*** since the investigator wants to know whether it is dependent upon his manipulation of the independent variable. Speaking loosely, independent variables are sometimes regarded as causes, dependent variables as effects.

The results of our experiment are graphically presented in Figure A.1. The values of the independent variable are indicated on the horizontal, or *x*-axis, and the values of the dependent variable on the vertical, or *y*-axis. The figure displays the average number of items recalled for subjects who used visual imagery in memorizing and for those who did not. We will have more to say about this experiment presently.

## Observational Studies

Much psychological research departs from the experimental method in that investigators do not produce the effects directly, but only observe them. They do not so much design the experiment as discover it. Such an investigation is called an ***observational study.*** Consider the question "What is the effect of prenatal malnutrition on IQ?" This question can only be answered by locating children whose mothers were malnourished during pregnancy and measuring their IQs; to deliberately provide pregnant women with inadequate diets is obviously worse than unethical. But even though the investigators do not manipulate the mother's diet (or indeed, anything else), some of the methodological terms used before can still be applied. We can consider the mother's diet as the independent variable, and the child's IQ as the dependent variable. A group analogous to the experimental group would consist of children whose mothers were malnourished during pregnancy. An analogue to the control group is a group of children whose mothers' diet was adequate.

Observational studies like this one are sometimes called "experiments of nature." Because nature does not always provide exactly those control groups which the investigator might have wished for, observational studies can be difficult to interpret. For example, children whose mothers were malnourished during pregnancy are often born into environments which might also be expected to have negative effects on IQ. Women whose diet is inadequate during pregnancy are likely to be poor; they are therefore less likely to provide some of the physical advantages (like good food and health care) and educational advantages (like books and nursery schools) which may well be helpful in developing intelligence.

## The Case Study

In many areas of psychology, conclusions are based on only one person who is studied intensively. Such an investigation is called a ***case study.*** Individuals who display unusual psychological or physiological characteristics, such as rare forms of color blindness, exceptionally good or poor memory, or brain injuries, can sometimes provide information about normal vision, memory, or brain function that would be difficult or impossible to obtain from normal individuals. Take the patient known as H.M., who suffered severe amnesia after brain surgery (see Chapter 7). Before the operation his memory was normal; afterward he could remember virtually nothing about events that occurred after the operation. This patient has been extensively studied because of his unusual memory disorder. Since his amnesia is apparently the result of the destruction of a particular structure in the brain, the hippocampus, a comparison of H.M.'s performance with that of normal individuals allows us to make inferences about the role of the hippocampus in normal memory.

Some of the most famous case studies in psychology are those described by Sigmund Freud, whose extensive psychoanalytic interviews of his patients led him to develop theories of dreams, defense mechanisms, and other psychological processes (see Chapter 12).

## SELECTING THE SUBJECTS

How does one select the subjects for a psychological study? To answer this question, we have to consider the difference between a population and a sample.

### Sample and Population

Psychologists—again like other scientists—usually want to make statements about a larger group of persons (or animals) than the particular subjects they happen to use in their study. They want their conclusions to apply to a given *population:* all members of a given group—say, all three-year-old boys, all schizophrenic patients, all U.S. voters, and in some cases, all humans. But they obviously can't study all members of the population. As a result, they have to select a *sample,* that is, a subset of the population they are interested in. Their hope is that the results found in the sample can be generalized to the population from which the sample is drawn.

It is important to realize that generalizations from a given sample to a particular population can only be made if the sample is representative (that is, typical) of the population to which one wants to generalize. Suppose one does a study on memory by using college students. Can one generalize the results to adults in general? Strictly speaking one cannot, for college students are on the average younger than the population at large and are more accustomed to memorizing things. Under the circumstances, the safest course may be to restrict one's generalizations to the population of college students.

Most experimenters would probably argue that college students don't differ too greatly from the general population (at least in memory skills), so that results obtained with them do apply in general, at least approximately. But there are many cases in which inadequate sampling leads to gross blunders. The classic example is a 1936 poll which predicted that Franklin D. Roosevelt would lose the presidential election. In fact, he won by a landslide. This massive error was produced by a *biased sample*—all persons polled were selected from telephone directories. But in 1936 having a telephone was much more likely among persons of higher than of lower socioeconomic status. As a result, the sample was not representative of the voting population as a whole. Since socioeconomic level affected voting preference, the poll predicted falsely.

### Random and Stratified Samples

To ensure that one can generalize from sample to population, investigators use a *random sample.* This is a sample in which every member of the population has an equal chance of being picked—as in a jury drawn by lot from all the voters of a given district (if none are disqualified or excuse themselves). The random sampling procedure applies with special force to the assignment of subjects in an experiment. Here every effort has to be made to assign subjects randomly to the various experimental or control groups.

For some purposes, even a random sample may not be good enough. While every member of the population has an equal chance of being selected, the sample may still turn out to be atypical by chance alone. This danger of chance error becomes less and less the greater the size of the sample. But if one is forced to use a small sample (and one often is because of lack of time or money), other sampling procedures may be necessary. Suppose we want to take a poll to determine the attitudes of American voters toward legalized abortion. We can expect peoples' attitudes to differ depending on (at least) their age, sex, and religion. If the sample is fairly small, it is important that each subgroup of the population be (randomly) sampled in proportion to its size. This procedure is called *stratified sampling,* and is common in studying psychological traits or attitudes which vary greatly among different subgroups of the population.

### Sampling Responses

The distinction between sample and population does not only apply to subjects. It also applies to the subjects' responses. Consider the investigators who studied aggressive behavior in 50 three-year-old boys. Each of these boys was observed on 10 occasions. Those 10 occasions can be regarded as a sample of all such occasions, just as the 50 boys can be regarded as a sample of all three-year-old boys (or at least of all middle-class U.S. boys). The investigators will surely want to generalize from this sample of occasions to the population of all such occasions. To make sure that such a generalization is warranted, one has to see to it that the occasions are not atypical—that the child isn't especially tired, or sick, and so on.

## ORGANIZING THE DATA: DESCRIPTIVE STATISTICS

We have considered the ways in which psychologists describe the data provided by their subjects by assigning numbers to them (scaling) and the ways in which they collect these data in the first place (experiments, observational studies, case studies). Our next task is to see how these data are organized.

## The Frequency Distribution

Suppose we have designed and performed an experiment such as the imagery study described previously. The data will not automatically arrange themselves in the form shown in Figure A.1. Instead, investigators will first be faced with a list of numbers, the scores (number of words recalled correctly) for each subject in a given group. For example, if there were 10 subjects in the control group, their scores (in words correct) might have been

$$8, 11, 6, 7, 5, 9, 5, 9, 9, 11$$

A first step in organizing the data is to list all the possible scores and the frequency with which they occurred, as shown in Table A.1. Such an arrangement is called a *frequency distribution.*

Table A.1    FREQUENCY DISTRIBUTION

| Score | Frequency |
| --- | --- |
| 11 | 2 |
| 10 | 0 |
| 9 | 3 |
| 8 | 1 |
| 7 | 1 |
| 6 | 1 |
| 5 | 2 |

The frequency distribution can be expressed graphically. A common means for doing this is a *histogram* which depicts the frequency distribution by a series of contiguous rectangles (Figure A.2). The values of the dependent variable (here, number of words recalled) are shown by the location of each rectangle on the horizontal or *x*-axis. The frequency of each score is shown on the vertical or *y*-axis, that is, by the height of each rectangle. This is simple enough for our example, but in practice graphic presentation often requires a further step. The number of possible values the dependent variable can assume is often very large. As a result, exactly equal values rarely occur, as when reaction times are measured to the nearest millisecond (thousandth of a second). To get around this, the scores are generally grouped by intervals for purposes of graphic display. The histogram might then plot the frequency of all reaction times between, say, 200 and 225 milliseconds, between 226 and 250 milliseconds, and so on.

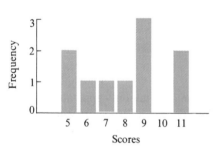

**A.2   Histogram** *In a histogram, a frequency distribution is graphically represented by a series of rectangles. The location of each rectangle on the x-axis indicates a score value, while its height shows how often that score value occurred.*

## Measures of Central Tendency

A frequency distribution is a more concise description of the result of the experiment than the raw list of scores from which it was derived, but for many purposes we may want a description that is even more concise. We often wish to summarize an entire distribution by a single, central score; such a score is called a *measure of central tendency.* Three measures of central tendency are commonly used to express this central point of a distribution: the mode, the median, and the mean.

The *mode* is simply the score that occurs most frequently. In our example, the

## DESCRIBING THE RELATION BETWEEN TWO VARIABLES: CORRELATION

The basic problem facing psychological investigators is to account for observed differences in some variable they are interested in. Why, for example, do some people display better memory than others? The experimental approach to the problem, described earlier, is to ask whether changes in an independent variable produce systematic changes in the dependent variable. In the memory experiment, we asked whether subjects using visual imagery as an aid to memorizing would recall more words on the average than those who did not. In an observational study, however, our approach must be different, for in such a study we do not manipulate the variables. What is often done here is to observe the relationship between two—sometimes more—variables as they occur naturally, in the hope that differences in one variable can be attributed to differences in a second.

### Positive and Negative Correlation

Imagine that a taxicab company wants to identify drivers who will earn relatively large amounts of money (for themselves and, of course, for the company). The company's officers make the plausible guess that one relevant factor is the driver's knowledge of the local geography, so they devise an appropriate test of street names, routes from place to place, and so on, and administer the test to each driver. The question is whether this test score is related to the driver's job performance as measured by his weekly earnings. To decide, one has to find out whether the test score and the earnings are **correlated**—that is, whether they tend to vary together.

In the taxicab example, the two variables will probably be **positively correlated** —as one variable (test score) increases, the other (earnings) will generally increase too. But other variables may be **negatively correlated**—when one increases, the other will tend to decrease. An example is a phenomenon called Zipf's law, which states that words that occur frequently in a language tend to be relatively short. The two variables word length and word frequency are negatively correlated, since one variable tends to increase as the other decreases.

Correlational data are often displayed in a **scatter plot** (or scatter diagram), in which values of one variable are shown on the horizontal axis and variables of the other on the vertical axis. Figure A.5A is a scatter plot of word frequency versus word length for the words in this sentence.* Each word is represented by a single point. An example is provided by the word *plot,* which is 4 letters long and occurs with a frequency of 37 times per million words of English text (and is represented by the circled dot). The points on the graph display a tendency to decrease on one variable as they increase on the other, although the relation is by no means perfect. It is helpful to draw a straight line through the various points in a scatter plot which comes as close as possible to all of them (Figure A.5B). The line is called a *line of best fit,* and it indicates the general trend of the data. Here, the line slopes downward because the correlation between the variables is negative.

---

* There is no point for the "word" A.5A in this sentence. The frequencies of the other words are taken from H. Kucera and W. N. Francis, *Computational Analysis of Present-Day American English* (Providence, R. I.: Brown University Press, 1967).

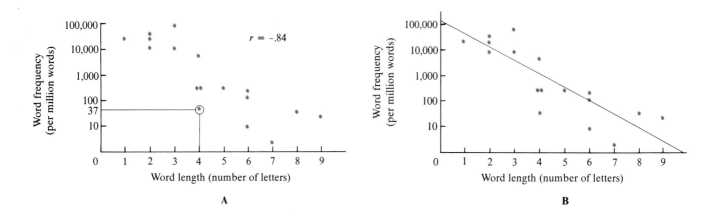

**A.5   Scatter plot of a negative correlation between word length and word frequency**

The three panels of Figure A.6 are scatter plots showing the relation between other pairs of variables. In Figure A.6*A* hypothetical data from the taxicab example show that there is a positive correlation between test score and earnings (since the line of best fit slopes upward), but that test score is not a perfect predictor of on-the-job performance (since the points are fairly widely scattered around the line). Points above the line represent individuals who earn more than their test score would lead one to predict, points below the line individuals who earn less.

The examples in Figures A.5 and A.6*A* each illustrate moderate correlations; panels *B* and *C* of Figure A.6 are extreme cases. Figure A.6*B* shows data from a hypothetical experiment conducted in a fourth-grade class to illustrate the relation between metric and English units of length. The heights of five children are measured twice, once in inches and once in centimeters; each point on the scatter plot gives the two height measurements for one child. All the points in the figure fall on the line of best fit, because height in centimeters always equals 2.54 times height in inches. The two variables, height in centimeters and height in inches, are perfectly correlated—one can be perfectly predicted from the other. Once you know your height in inches, there is no information to be gained by measuring yourself with a meterstick.

Figure A.6*C* presents a relation between IQ and shoe size. These variables are unrelated to each other; people with large shoes have neither a higher nor a lower IQ than people with small ones. The line of best fit is therefore horizontal, because the best guess of an individual's IQ is the same no matter what his or her shoe size—it is the mean IQ of the population.

## The Correlation Coefficient

Correlations are often described by a ***correlation coefficient,*** denoted *r,* a number that can vary from $+1.00$ to $-1.00$ which expresses the strength and the direction of the correlation. For positive correlations, *r* is positive; for negative correlations, it is negative; for variables which are completely uncorrelated, $r = 0$. The largest positive value *r* can have is $+1.00$, which represents a perfect correlation (as in Figure A.6*B*); the largest possible negative value is $-1.00$, which is also a perfect correlation. The closer the points in a scatter plot come to falling on the line of best fit, the nearer *r* will be to $+1.00$ or $-1.00$, and the more confident we

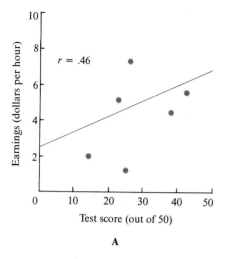

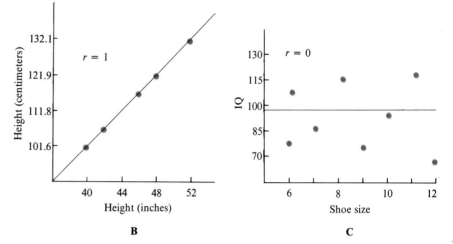

A

B

C

**A.6 Scatter plots of various correlations** *(A) The scatter plot and line of best fit show a positive correlation between a taxi-driving test and earnings. (B) A perfect positive correlation. The line of best fit passes through all the points. (C) A correlation of zero. The line of best fit is horizontal.*

can be in predicting scores on one variable from scores on the other. The values of $r$ for the scatter plots in Figures A.5 and A.6A are given on the figures.

The method for calculating $r$ between two variables, $X$ and $Y$, is shown in Table A.5. The formula is

$$r = \frac{\text{sum } (z_x z_y)}{N} \qquad (4)$$

The variable $z_x$ is the z-score corresponding to $X$; $z_y$ is the z-score corresponding to $Y$. To find $r$, each $X$ and $Y$ score must first be converted to a z-score by subtracting the mean and then dividing by the standard deviation. Then the product of $z_x$ and $z_y$ is found for each pair of scores. The average of these products (the sum of the products divided by $N$, the number of pairs of scores) is the correlation coefficient $r$.

Figure A.7 illustrates why this procedure yields positive values of $r$ for posi-

**A.7 Correlation coefficients** *(A) Two positively correlated variables. Most of the points lie in the upper right and lower left quadrants, where $z_x z_y$ is positive, so r is positive. (B) Two negatively correlated variables. Most of the points lie in the upper left and lower right quadrants, where $z_x z_y$ is negative, so r is negative.*

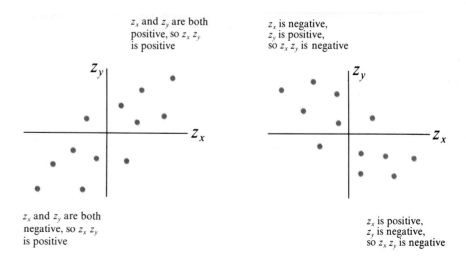

Table A.5   CALCULATION OF THE CORRELATION COEFFICIENT

1. Data (from Figure A.6A).

| Test score (X) | Earnings (Y) |
|:---:|:---:|
| 45 | 6 |
| 25 | 2 |
| 15 | 3 |
| 40 | 5 |
| 25 | 6 |
| 30 | 8 |

2. Find the mean and standard deviation for $X$ and $Y$.

For $X$, mean = 30, standard deviation = 10
For $Y$, mean =  5, standard deviation = 2

3. Convert each $X$ and each $Y$ to a $z$-score, using $z = \dfrac{(\text{score} - M)}{SD}$

| X | Y | z-score for X ($z_x$) | z-score for Y ($z_y$) | $z_x z_y$ |
|:---:|:---:|:---:|:---:|:---:|
| 45 | 6 | 1.5 | 0.5 | 0.75 |
| 25 | 2 | −0.5 | −1.5 | 0.75 |
| 15 | 3 | −1.5 | −1.0 | 1.50 |
| 40 | 5 | 1.0 | 0.0 | 0.00 |
| 25 | 6 | −0.5 | 0.5 | −0.25 |
| 30 | 8 | 0.0 | 1.5 | 0.00 |
|  |  |  |  | 2.75 |

4. Find the product $z_x z_y$ for each pair of scores.

5. $r = \dfrac{\text{sum } (z_x z_y)}{N} = \dfrac{2.75}{6} = .46$

tively related variables and negative values of $r$ for negatively related variables. For positively correlated variables, most points are either above or below the mean on both variables. If they are above the mean, both $z_x$ and $z_y$ will be positive; if they are below, both $z_x$ and $z_y$ will be negative. (This follows from the definition of a $z$-score.) In either case the product $z_x z_y$ will be positive, so $r$ will be positive. For negatively correlated variables, most points which are above the mean on one variable are below the mean on the other—either $z_x$ is positive and $z_y$ is negative, or vice versa. The product $z_x z_y$ is therefore negative, and so is $r$.

## Interpreting and Misinterpreting Correlations

It is tempting, but false, to assume that if two variables are correlated, one is the cause of the other. There is a positive correlation between years of education and annual income in the population of North American adults; many people, including some educators, argue from these data that students should stay in school as long as possible in order to increase their eventual earning power. The difficulty with this reasoning is not the existence of counterexamples (such as Andrew

ing the hypothesis that the score in question comes from the distribution of neutral responses. Put another way, we don't feel justified in accusing the person of lying. Our feelings might be different if the score were 70 or above. For now the $z$-score is $(70 - 50)/10$, or 2 standard deviations above the mean of the neutral distribution. The chances that a score this high or higher is from a sample drawn from the population of neutral responses is only 2 in a 100. We might now feel more comfortable in rejecting the hypothesis that this score is simply a chance event. We are more likely to assume that it is drawn from another distribution—in short, that the person is lying.

In this example we had to decide between two hypotheses. We look at a given score (or a set of scores) obtained under a particular experimental condition (in this case, a loaded question). One hypothesis is that the experimental condition has no effect, that the score is merely a reflection of the ordinary variability around the mean of a control condition (in this case, neutral questions). This is the so-called **null hypothesis,** the hypothesis that there really is no effect. The **alternative hypothesis** is that the null hypothesis is false, that the score is far enough away from the control mean so that we can assume that the same experimental condition has some effect. To decide between these two hypotheses, the data are expressed as a $z$-score, which in the context of hypothesis testing is called a **critical ratio.** Behavioral scientists generally accept a critical ratio of 2 as a cutting point. If this ratio is 2 or greater, they generally reject the null hypothesis and assume there is an effect of the experimental condition. (Such critical ratios of 2 or more are said to be **statistically significant,** which is just another way of saying that the null hypothesis can be rejected.) Critical ratios of less than 2 are considered too small to allow the rejection of the null hypothesis.

This general procedure is not foolproof. It is certainly possible for a subject in the lie-detection example to have an arousal score of 70 (a critical ratio of 2) or higher even though he is telling the truth. According to Figure A.3, this will happen about 2 percent of the time, and the person administering the test will erroneously "detect" a lie. Raising the cutoff value to the critical ratio of 3 or 4 would make such errors less common, but would not eliminate them entirely; furthermore, such a high critical value might mean failure to discover any lies the subject does utter. One of the important consequences of the variability in psychological data can be seen here: the investigator who has to decide between two interpretations of the data (the null hypothesis and the alternative hypothesis) cannot be correct all the time.

TESTING HYPOTHESES ABOUT MEANS

In the preceding discussion, our concern was with hypotheses about single scores. We now turn to the more commonly encountered problems in which the hypotheses involve means.

In many experiments, the investigator compares two or more groups—subjects tested with or without a drug, with or without imagery instructions, and so on. Suppose we get a difference between the two groups. How do we decide whether the difference is genuine rather than a mere chance fluctuation?

Let us return to the experiment in which memory for words was tested with and without instructions to imagine the items visually. To simplify the exposition, we will here consider a modified version of the experiment in which the same subjects serve in both the imagery and the nonimagery conditions. Each subject memorizes a list of 20 words without instructions, then memorizes a second list of 20 words under instructions to visualize. What we want to know is whether the subjects show any improvement with imagery instructions. There is no separate control group in this experiment, but, because a subject's score in the imagery condition can be compared with his score in the uninstructed condition, each subject provides his own control.

Table A.6 gives data for the 10 subjects in the experiment. For each subject, the table lists the number of words recalled without imagery instructions, the number recalled with such instructions, and the improvement (the difference between the two scores). The mean improvement overall is 3 words, from a mean of 8 words recalled without imagery to a mean of 11 words with imagery. But note that this does not hold for all subjects. For example, for Fred and Hortense, the "improvement" is negative—they both do better without imagery instructions. The question is whether we can conclude that there is an imagery facilitation effect overall. Put in other words, is the difference between the two conditions statistically significant?

Table A.6  NUMBER OF ITEMS RECALLED WITH AND WITHOUT IMAGERY
INSTRUCTION, FOR 10 SUBJECTS

| Subject | Score with imagery | Score without imagery | Improvement |
|---|---|---|---|
| Alphonse | 11 | 5 | 6 |
| Betsy | 15 | 9 | 6 |
| Cheryl | 11 | 5 | 6 |
| Davis | 9 | 9 | 0 |
| Earl | 13 | 6 | 7 |
| Fred | 10 | 11 | −1 |
| Germaine | 11 | 8 | 3 |
| Hortense | 10 | 11 | −1 |
| Imogene | 8 | 7 | 1 |
| Jerry | 12 | 9 | 3 |
| Mean | 11 | 8 | 3 |

$$\text{Variance of improvement scores} = \frac{\text{sum of (score} - 3)^2}{10} = 8.8$$

$$\text{Standard deviation of improvement scores} = \sqrt{8.8} = 2.97$$

To show how this question is answered, we will follow much the same logic as that used in the analysis of the lie-detection problem. We have a mean—the average difference score of 10 subjects. What we must realize is that this mean—3—is really a sample based on the one experiment with 10 subjects we have just run. Suppose we had run the experiment again, with another set of 10 subjects—not just once, but many times. Each such repetition of the experiment would yield its own mean. And each of these means would constitute another sample. But what is the population to which these samples refer? It is the set of all of these means— the average differences between imagery and nonimagery instructions obtained in each of the many repetitions of the experiment we might possibly perform. And the mean of these means—a kind of grand mean—is the mean of the population. Any conclusions we want to draw from our experiment are really assertions about this population mean. If we say that the difference we found is statistically significant, we are asserting that the population mean is a difference score which is greater than zero (and in the same direction as in the sample). Put another way, we are asserting that the difference we found is not just a fluke but is real and would be obtained again and again if we repeated the experiment, thus rejecting the null hypothesis.

The null hypothesis amounts to the claim that the mean we actually obtained could have been drawn by chance from a distribution of sample means (that is, the many means of the possible repetitions of our experiment) around a population mean of zero. To test this claim, we have to compute a critical ratio that can tell us how far from zero our own mean actually is. Like all critical ratios, this is a $z$-score which expresses the distance of a score from a mean in units of the standard deviation (the SD). Thus, $z = (\text{score} - M)/SD$. In our present case, the score is our obtained mean (that is, 3); the mean is the hypothetical population mean of zero (assumed by the null hypothesis). But what is the denominator? It is the standard deviation of the distribution of sample means, the means of the many experiments we might have done.

The standard deviation of such a distribution of sample means is called the **standard error** of the mean **(SE).** Its value is determined by two factors: the standard deviation of the sample and the size of that sample. Specifically,

$$SE = \frac{SD}{\sqrt{N-1}} \tag{5}$$

It is clear that the variability of a mean (and this is what the standard error measures) goes down with the increasing sample size. (Why this factor turns out to be $\sqrt{N-1}$ is beyond the scope of this discussion.) A clue as to why comes from the consideration of the effects of an atypical score. Purely by chance, a sample may include an extreme case. But the larger the size of that sample, the less the effect of on extreme case on the average. If a sample of 3 persons includes a midget, the average height will be unusually far from the population mean. But in a sample of 3,000, one midget will not affect the average very markedly.

We can now conclude our analysis of the results of the memorization experiment. The critical ratio to be evaluated is:

$$\text{Critical Ratio} = \frac{\text{obtained sample mean} - \text{population mean}}{SE}$$

Since the population mean is assumed to be zero (by the null hypothesis), this expression becomes:

$$\text{Critical Ratio} = \frac{\text{obtained sample mean}}{SE} \tag{6}$$

This critical ratio expresses the mean difference between the two experimental conditions in units of the variability of the sample mean, that is, the standard error.* To compute the standard error, we first find the standard deviation of the

---

* There are several simplifications in this account. One is that the critical ratio described here does not have an exactly normal distribution. When the sample size is large, this effect is unimportant, but for small samples (like the one in the example) they can be material. To deal with these and related problems, statisticians often utilize measures that refer to distributions other than the normal one. An example is the $t$-test, a kind of critical ratio based on the so-called $t$-distribution.

improvement scores; this turns out to be 2.97, as shown in Table A.6. Then equation (5) tells us

$$SE = \frac{SD}{\sqrt{N-1}} = \frac{2.97}{\sqrt{10-1}} = .99$$

The critical ratio is now the obtained mean difference divided by the standard error, or $3/.99 = 3.03$. This is clearly larger than 2.0, so we conclude that the observed difference in memory between the imagery and control conditions is much too great to be attributed to chance factors. Thus using visual imagery evidently does improve recall.

CONFIDENCE INTERVALS

In statistical hypothesis testing we ask whether a certain sample mean could be drawn by chance from a distribution of sample means around some assumed population mean. (When testing the null hypothesis, this assumed population mean is zero.) But there is another way of phrasing this question. Can we be reasonably confident that the mean of the population falls within a certain specified interval? If we know the standard error of the mean, the answer is yes. We have already seen that about 2 percent of the scores in a normal distribution are more than two standard deviations above, and about 2 percent are lower than two standard deviations below the mean of that distribution. Since this is so, we can conclude that the chances are roughly 4 in 100 that the population mean is within an interval whose largest value is two standard errors above the sample mean and whose lowest value is two standard errors below. Because we can be fairly (96 percent) confident that the actual population mean will fall within this specified range, it is often called the *confidence interval.*

As an example, consider the prediction of political elections. During election campaigns, polling organizations report the current standing of various candidates by statements such as the following: "In a poll of 1,000 registered voters, 57 percent favored candidate Smith; the margin of error was 3 percent." This margin of error is the confidence interval around the proportion (that is, $\pm 3$ percent).

To determine this confidence interval, the pollsters compute the standard error of the proportion they found. (In this case, .57). This standard error is analogous to the standard error of a mean we discussed in the previous section. Given an N of 1,000, this standard error happens to be .015.* Since $2 \times .015$ is .03 or 3 percent, the appropriate confidence interval for our example is the interval from 54 to 60 percent. Under the circumstances, candidate Smith can be fairly confident

---

* The standard error of a proportion (e.g., the proportion of polled voters who express pro-X sentiments) is analogous to the standard error of the mean, and measures the precision with which our sample proportion estimates the population proportion. The formula for the standard error of a proportion p is:

$$SE_P = \sqrt{\frac{p \times (1-p)}{N}} \tag{7}$$

In our example, $p = .57$ and $N = 1,000$, so $SE_P = .015$.

that she has the support of at least 50 percent of the electorate since 50 percent is well *below* the poll's confidence interval (see Figure A.10).

## Some Implications of Statistical Inference

The methods of testing hypotheses and estimating confidence intervals which we have just described are routinely employed in evaluating the results of psychological research. But they have several characteristics that necessarily affect the interpretation of all such results.

### THE PROBABILISTIC NATURE OF HYPOTHESIS TESTING AND CONFIDENCE INTERVALS

Since there is always some unexplained variance in any psychological study, there is always some probability that the conclusions are wrong as applied to the population. If we use a confidence interval of $\pm 2$ SE, the chances that the population mean (or proportion, or whatever) falls outside of that interval are less than 4 or 5 in 100. Do we want to be more confident than this? If so, we might use a confidence interval of $\pm 3$ SE where the equivalent chance is only 1 in 1,000. The same holds for critical ratios. We can say that a critical ratio of 2 means that a difference is statistically significant, but that only means that the chances are less than 2 in 100 that the difference as large or larger than this arose by chance. If we want to be more certain than this, we must insist that the critical ratio be larger—perhaps 3 (a chance factor of 1 in 2,000) or 4 (5 in 100,000), and so on. As long as there is some unexplained variance, there is some chance of error.

The probabilistic nature of statistical reasoning has another consequence. Even if we can come to a correct conclusion about the mean of a population (or a proportion, as in polls), we cannot generalize to individuals. Thus a study which shows that men have higher scores than women on spatial relations tests is not inconsistent with the existence of brilliant female artists or architects. Sample means for the two groups can differ significantly, even though there is considerable overlap in the two distributions of scores.

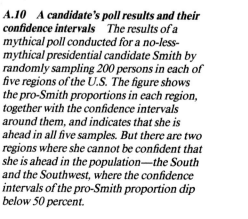

*A.10   A candidate's poll results and their confidence intervals   The results of a mythical poll conducted for a no-less-mythical presidential candidate Smith by randomly sampling 200 persons in each of five regions of the U.S. The figure shows the pro-Smith proportions in each region, together with the confidence intervals around them, and indicates that she is ahead in all five samples. But there are two regions where she cannot be confident that she is ahead in the population—the South and the Southwest, where the confidence intervals of the pro-Smith proportion dip below 50 percent.*

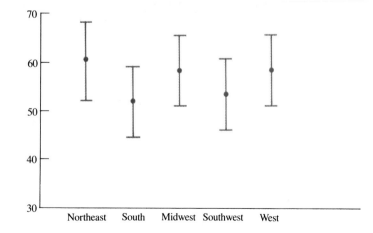

THE CONSERVATIVE NATURE OF HYPOTHESIS TESTING

Another characteristic of statistical hypothesis testing is that it is essentially conservative. This is because of the great stress placed on the null hypothesis in reaching a decision: one has to be quite sure that the null hypothesis is false before one entertains the alternative hypothesis. There are other imaginable strategies for reaching statistical decisions, but the conservative one has a perfectly rational basis. Let's suppose that some independent variable *does* produce a difference between two groups that is quite genuine and not the result of chance, but that the critical ratio is too low to reject the null hypothesis. If so, we will have falsely concluded that no difference exists in the population. As a result, we will have failed to discover a small effect. But what of it? If the effect is interesting enough, someone else may well attempt a similar experiment and manage to find the difference we didn't uncover. On the other hand, suppose we "discover" that some independent variable has an effect when it actually does not (that is, the null hypothesis is true). By falsely rejecting the null hypothesis, we will have added an inaccurate "fact" to the store of scientific knowledge, and run the risk of leading other investigators into a blind alley.

THE ROLE OF SAMPLE SIZE

A last point concerns the role of sample size in affecting the interpretations of results. The larger the sample, the smaller the standard error and the smaller the confidence interval around the mean or the proportion. This can have major effects on hypothesis testing.

Suppose that, in the population, a certain independent variable produces a very small difference. As an example, suppose that the population difference between men and women on a certain test of spatial relations is 1 percent. We would probably be unable to reject the null hypothesis (that there is no sex difference on the test) with samples of moderate size. But if the sample size were sufficiently increased, we could reject the null hypothesis. For such a sizable increase in N would lead to a decrease in the standard errors of the sample means, which in turn would lead to an increase in the critical ratio. Someone who read a report of this experiment would now learn that, by using thousands of subjects, we had discovered a "significant" difference of 1 percent. A fair reaction to this bit of intelligence would be that the null hypothesis can indeed be rejected, but that the *psychological* significance of this finding is rather slight. The moral is simple. Statistical significance is required before a result can be considered reliable, but this statistical significance does not guarantee that the effect discovered is of psychological significance or of any practical importance.

## SUMMARY

1. Statistical methods concern the ways in which investigators describe, gather, organize, and interpret collections of numerical data. A crucial concern of statistical endeavors is to deal with the variability that is encountered in all research.

2. An early step in the process is *scaling,* a procedure for assigning numbers to psychological responses. Scales can be *categorical, ordinal, interval,* or *ratio scales.* These differ in the degree to which they can be subjected to arithmetical operations.

3. There are three main methods for conducting psychological research: by means of an *experiment,* an *observational study,* and a *case study.* In an experiment, the investigator manipulates one variable, the *independent variable,* to see how it affects the subject's response, the *dependent variable.* In an observational study, the investigator does not manipulate any variables directly but rather observes them as they occur naturally. A case study is an investigation in which one person is studied in depth.

4. An important distinction in psychological research is that between *sample* and *population.* The population is the entire group about which the investigator wants to draw conclusions. The sample is the subset (usually small) of that population that is actually tested. Generalizations from sample to population are only possible if the one is representative of the other. This requires the use of *random samples.* In some cases a special version of the random sample, the *stratified sample,* may be employed.

5. A first step in organizing the data is to arrange them in a *frequency distribution,* often displayed in graphic form, as in a *histogram.* Frequency distributions are characterized by a *central tendency* and by *variability* around this central tendency. The common measure of central tendency is the *mean,* though sometimes another measure, the *median,* may be preferable, as in cases when the distribution is *skewed.* Important measures of variability are the *variance* and the *standard deviation.*

6. One way of comparing two scores drawn from different distributions is to convert both into *percentile ranks.* Another is to transform them into *z-scores,* which express the distance of a score from its mean in standard deviation units. The percentile rank of a *z*-score can be computed if the shape of that score's distribution is known. An important example is the *normal distribution,* graphically displayed by the *normal curve* which describes the distribution of many psychological variables and is basic to much of statistical reasoning.

7. In observational studies, the relation between variables is often expressed in the form of a *correlation* which may be positive or negative. It is measured by the *correlation coefficient,* a number that can vary from $+1.00$ to $-1.00$. While correlations reflect the extent to which two variables vary together, they do not necessarily indicate that one of them causes the other.

8. A major task of any investigator is to explain the variability of some dependent variable, usually measured by the variance. One means for doing so is to see whether that variance is reduced when a certain independent variable is controlled. If so, this independent variable is said to account for some of the variability of the dependent variable.

9. One of the main functions of statistical methods is to help test hypotheses about population given information about the sample. An important example is the difference between mean scores obtained under two different conditions. Here the investigator has to decide between the *null hypothesis* which asserts that the difference was obtained by chance, and the *alternative hypothesis* which asserts that the difference is genuine and exists in the population. The decision is made by dividing the obtained mean difference by the *standard error,* a measure of the variability of that mean difference. If the resulting ratio, called the *critical ratio,* is large enough, the null hypothesis is rejected, the alternative hypothesis is accepted, and the difference is said to be *statistically significant.* A related way of making statistical decisions is by using a *confidence interval,* or margin of error. This is based on the variability of the scores from a sample and determines the interval within which the population mean or proportion probably falls.

# Glossary

**absolute threshold**  The lowest intensity of some stimulus that produces a response.

**accommodation**  (1) The process by which the lens is thickened or flattened to focus on an object. (2) In Piaget's theory of development, one of the twin processes that underlies cognitive development. *See* assimilation and accommodation.

**accommodative distortion**  Retrospective alterations of memory to fit a schema. *See also* schema.

**acetylcholine**  A neurotransmitter found in many parts of the nervous system. Among many other functions, it serves as an excitatory transmitter at the synaptic junctions between muscle fibers and motor neurons.

**across-fiber theory**  The theory that a certain sensory quality is signaled by the pattern of neural activity across a number of different nerve fibers.

**action potential**  A brief change in the electrical potential of an axon which is the physical basis of the nervous impulse.

**active memory**  *See* short-term memory.

**active sleep (or REM sleep)**  A stage of sleep during which the EEG is similar to that of waking, during which there are rapid eye movements (REMs), and during which dreams occur.

**actor-observer difference**  The difference in attributions made by actors who describe their own actions and observers who describe another person's. The former emphasizes external, situational causes; the latter, internal, dispositional factors. *See also* attribution theory, fundamental attribution error, self-serving bias.

**adaptive value**  In biological terms, the extent to which an attribute increases the likelihood of viable offspring. Also, the unit of inheritance.

**additive color mixture**  Mixing colors by stimulating the eye with two sets of wavelengths simultaneously (e.g., by focusing filtered light from two projectors on the same spot). *See also* subtractive color mixture.

**adrenaline**  *See* epinephrine.

**affective disorders**  *See* mood disorders.

**afferent nerves**  Sensory nerves that carry messages to the brain.

**agnosia**  A serious disturbance in the organization of sensory information produced by lesions in certain cortical association areas. An example is visual agnosia, in which the patient can see, but often does not recognize what it is that he sees.

**alarm call**  Special, genetically pre-programmed cry that impels members of a given species to seek cover. A biological puzzle, since it suggests a form of altruism in which the individual appears to endanger his own survival. *See also* altruism.

**algorithm**  In computer problem solving, a procedure in which all of the operations are specified step-by-step. *See also* heuristics.

**all-or-none law**  Describes the fact that once a stimulus exceeds threshold, further increases do not increase the amplitude of the action potential.

**alpha blocking**  The disruption of the alpha rhythm by visual stimulation or by active thought with the eyes closed.

**alpha waves**  Fairly regular EEG waves, between eight to twelve per second, characteristic of a relaxed, waking state, usually with eyes closed.

**alternative hypothesis**  In statistics, the hypothesis that the null hypothesis is false; that an obtained difference is so far from zero that one has to assume that the mean difference in the population is greater than zero and that the experimental condition has some effect. *See also* null hypothesis.

**altruism**  (1) Acting so as to elevate the interests and welfare of others above one's own. (2) As used by sociobiologists, any behavior pattern that benefits individuals who are not one's own offspring (e.g., an alarm call). According to the kin-selection hypothesis, such altruism has biological survival value because the altruist's beneficiaries tend to be close relatives who carry a high proportion of his or her own genes. According to the reciprocal altruism hypothesis, altruism is based on the expectation that today's giver will be tomorrow's taker. *See also* alarm call.

**Alzheimer's disease**  A degenerative brain disorder characterized by increasing memory loss followed by increasing disorientation culminating in total physical and mental helplessness and death. One of the major sites of the destruction is a pathway of acetylcholine-releasing cells leading from the base of the forebrain to the cortex and hippocampus. *See also* acetylcholine.

**ambiguity** (in sentence meaning) The case in which a sentence (i.e., one surface structure) has two meanings (i.e., two underlying structures). (For example, "These missionaries are ready to eat" overheard in a conversation between two cannibals.)

**American Sign Language (ASL)** The manual-visual language system of deaf persons in America.

**anal character** According to Freud, a personality type that derives from serious conflicts during the anal stage and is distinguished by three symptomatic traits: compulsive orderliness, stubbornness, and stinginess. *See also* anal stage.

**anal stage** In psychoanalytic theory, the stage of psychosexual development during which the focus of pleasure is on activities related to elimination.

**androgen** Any male sex hormone.

**anorexia nervosa** An eating disorder that primarily afflicts young women and that is characterized by an exaggerated concern with being overweight, and by compulsive dieting, sometimes to the point of self-starvation. *See also* bulimia and obesity.

**anterograde amnesia** A memory deficit suffered after some brain damage. It is an inability to learn and remember any information imparted after the injury, with little effect on memory for information acquired previously. *See also* retrograde amnesia.

**antidepressant drugs** Drugs that alleviate depressive symptoms, presumably because they increase the availability of certain neurotransmitters (especially norepinephrine and serotonin) at synaptic junctions. The two major classes are monoamine oxidase (MAO) inhibitors and tricyclics. Of these, the tricyclics, such as imipramine, are the most widely used.

**antidiuretic hormone (ADH)** A hormone secreted by one of the parts of the pituitary gland. This hormone instructs the kidneys to reabsorb more of the water that passes through them. *See also* pituitary gland.

**antisocial personality** Also called psychopath or sociopath. The term describes persons who get into continual trouble with society, are indifferent to others, impulsive, with little concern for the future or remorse about the past.

**anxiety** An emotional state akin to fear. According to Freud, many mental illnesses center around anxiety and on attempts to ward it off by various unconscious mechanisms.

**anxiety disorders** *See* phobia, generalized anxiety disorder, obsessive-compulsive disorders.

**anxiety hierarchy** *See* systematic desensitization.

**aphagia** Refusal to eat (and in an extreme version, to drink) brought about by lesion of the lateral hypothalamus.

**aphasia** A disorder of language produced by lesions in certain association areas of the cortex. A lesion in Broca's area leads to expressive aphasia, one in Wernicke's area to receptive aphasia.

**apparent movement** The perception of movement produced by stimuli that are stationary but flash on and off at appropriate time intervals.

**apraxia** A serious disturbance in the organization of voluntary action produced by lesions in certain cortical association areas, often in the frontal lobes.

**artificial intelligence** A field that draws on concepts from both cognitive psychology and computer science to develop artificial systems that display some aspects of human-like intelligence. Examples are computer programs that recognize patterns or solve certain kinds of problems.

**assimilation and accommodation** In Piaget's theory, the twin processes by means of which cognitive development proceeds. Assimilation is the process whereby the environment is interpreted in terms of the schemas the child has at the time. Accommodation is the way the child changes his schemas as he continues to interact with the environment.

**association areas** Regions of the cortex that are not projection areas. They tend to be involved in the integration of sensory information or of motor commands.

**association** A linkage between two psychological processes as a result of past experience in which the two have occurred together. A broad term that subsumes conditioning and association of ideas among others.

**attachment** The tendency of the young of many species to stay in close proximity to an adult, usually their mother. *See also* imprinting.

**attention** A collective label for all the processes by which we perceive selectively.

**attitude** A fairly stable, evaluative disposition that makes a person think, feel, or behave positively or negatively about some person, group, or social issue.

**attribution theory** A theory about the process by which we try to explain a person's behavior, attributing it to situational factors or to inferred dispositional qualities or both.

**attributional style** The characteristic manner in which a person explains good or bad fortunes that befall him. A particular attributional style in which bad fortunes are generally attributed to internal, global, and stable causes may create a predisposition that makes a person vulnerable to depression. *See also* depression.

**authoritarian personality** A cluster of personal attributes (e.g., submission to persons above and harshness to those below) and social attitudes (e.g., prejudice against minority groups), which is sometimes held to constitute a distinct personality.

**automatization** A process whereby components of a skilled activity become subsumed under a higher-order organization and are run off automatically.

**autonomic nervous system (ANS)** A part of the nervous system that controls the internal organs, usually not under voluntary control.

**availability heuristic** A rule of thumb often used to make probability estimates, which depends on the frequency with which certain events readily come to mind. This can lead to errors since very vivid events will be remembered out of proportion to their actual frequency of occurrence.

**aversion therapy** A form of behavior therapy in which the undesirable response leads to an aversive stimulus (e.g., the patient shocks himself every time he reaches for a cigarette).

**avoidance learning** Instrumental learning in which the response averts an aversive stimulus before it occurs. This poses a problem: What is the reinforcement for this kind of learning? *See also* punishment training, escape learning.

**axon** Part of a neuron which transmits impulses to other neurons or effectors.

**backward pairing** A classical conditioning procedure in which the conditioned stimulus (CS) follows the unconditioned stimulus (US). *See also* forward pairing, simultaneous pairing.

**Barnum effect** Describes the fact that a properly worded description of one's personality will often be uncritically accepted as valid if it is stated in sufficiently broad and general terms.

**base rate** *See* representativeness heuristic.

**basilar membrane** *See* cochlea.

**behavior therapy** A general approach to psychological treatment which (1) holds that the disorders to which it addresses itself are produced by maladaptive learning and must be remedied by reeducation, (2) proposes techniques for this reeducation based on principles of learning and conditioning, (3) focuses on the maladaptive behaviors as such rather than on hypothetical unconscious processes of which they may be expressions.

**behavioral-cognitive approach to personality** An approach that defines personality differences by the way in which different people act and think about their actions. It tends to emphasize situational determinants and prior learning in trying to explain how such differences come about.

**belongingness in learning** The fact that the ease with which associations are formed depends upon the items to be associated. This holds for classical conditioning in which some CS-US combinations are more effective than others (e.g., learned taste aversions) and for instrumental conditioning in which some response-reinforcer combinations work more easily than others (e.g., specific defense reactions in avoidance conditioning of species).

**between-family differences** A term often used in the discussion of the role of environment. It describes environmental differences that apply to entire families, such as differences in socioeconomic status, religion, or child-rearing attitudes. For personality attributes, these seem to be less important than within-family differences. *See also* within-family differences.

**between-group heritability** The extent to which variation between groups (as in the difference between the mean IQs of U.S. whites and blacks) is attributable to genetic factors. *See also* heritability, within-group heritability.

**bidirectional activation models** Models of pattern recognition in which elements are activated as well as inhibited from both lower levels (bottom-up processing) and higher levels (top-down processing).

**bipolar disorder** Affective disorder in which the patient swings from one emotional extreme to another, experiencing both manic and depressive episodes. Formerly called manic-depressive psychosis.

**blocking** An effect produced when two conditioned stimuli, *A* and *B*, are both presented together with the unconditioned stimulus (US). If stimulus *A* has previously been associated with the unconditioned stimulus while *B* has not, the formation of an association between stimulus *B* and the US will be impaired (that is, blocked).

**bottom-up processes** *See* top-down processes.

**brightness** A perceived dimension of visual stimuli—the extent to which they appear light or dark.

**brightness contrast** The perceiver's tendency to exaggerate the physical difference in the light intensities of two adjacent regions. As a result, a gray patch looks brighter on a black background, darker on a white background.

**brightness ratio** The ratio between the light reflected by a region and the light reflected by the area that surrounds it. According to one theory, perceived brightness is determined by this ratio.

**British empiricism** A school of thought that holds that all knowledge comes by way of empirical experience, that is, through the senses.

**Broca's area** *See* aphasia.

**bulimia** A milder form of eating disorder characterized by repeated binge-and purge bouts. In contrast to anorexics, bulimics tend to be of roughly normal weight. *See also* anorexia nervosa, obesity.

**bystander effect** The phenomenon that underlies many examples of failing to help strangers in distress: The larger the group a person is in (or thinks he is in), the less likely he is to come to the stranger's assistance. One reason is diffusion of responsibility (no one thinks it is *his* responsibility to act).

**case study** An observational study in which one person is studied intensively.

**CAT scan (Computerized Axial Tomography)** A technique for examining brain structure in living humans by constructing a composite X-ray picture based on views from all different angles.

**catatonic schizophrenia** A subcategory of schizophrenia. Its main symptoms are peculiar motor patterns such as periods in which the patient is immobile and maintains strange positions for hours on end.

**catecholamines** A family of neurotransmitters that have an activating function, including epinephrine, norepinephrine, and dopamine.

**categorical scale** A scale that divides the responses into categories that are not numerically related. *See also* interval scale, ordinal scale, ratio scale.

**catharsis** An explosive release of hitherto dammed-up emotions that is sometimes believed to have therapeutic effects.

**censorship in dreams** *See* Freud's theory of dreams.

**central nervous system (CNS)** The brain and spinal cord.

**central route to persuasion** *See* elaboration-likelihood model of persuasion.

**central tendency** The tendency of scores in a frequency distribution to cluster around a central value. *See also* median, mean, and variability.

**central trait** A trait that is associated with many other attributes of the person who is being judged. Warm and cold are central because they are important in determining overall impressions.

**cerebellum** Two small hemispheres that form part of the hindbrain and control muscular coordination and equilibrium.

**cerebral cortex** The outermost layer of the gray matter of the cerebral hemispheres.

**cerebral hemispheres** Two hemispherical structures that comprise the major part of the forebrain in mammals and serve as the main coordinating center of the nervous system.

**childhood amnesia** The failure to remember the events of our very early childhood. This is sometimes ascribed to massive change in retrieval cues, sometimes to different ways of encoding memories in early childhood.

**chlorpromazine** *See* phenothiazines.

**chromosomes** Structures in the nucleus of each cell which contain the genes, the units of hereditary transmission. A human cell has 46 chromosomes, arranged in 23 pairs. One of these pairs consists of the sex chromosomes. In males, one member of the pair is an X-chromosome, the other a Y-chromosome. In females, both members are X-chromosomes. *See also* gene.

**chunking** A process of reorganizing (or recoding) materials in memory which permits a number of items to be packed into a larger unit.

**classical conditioning** A form of learning in which a hitherto neutral stimulus, the conditioned stimulus (CS) is paired with an unconditioned stimulus (US) regardless of what the animal does. In effect, what has to be learned is the relation between these two stimuli. *See also* instrumental conditioning.

**client-centered therapy**   A humanistic psychotherapy developed by Carl Rogers. *See also* humanistic therapies.

**closed-class morphemes**   Consists of all the "little" words and morphemes whose function is grammatical (e.g., *the, and, who, -ed, -s,* etc.). This is in contrast to the open-class morphemes, which consist of all the nouns, adjectives, verbs, and adverbs of the language, and which carry the major meanings in sentences.

**closure**   A factor in visual grouping. The perceptual tendency to fill in gaps in a figure so that it looks closed.

**cochlea**   Coiled structure in the inner ear which contains the basilar membrane whose deformation by sound-produced pressure stimulates the auditory receptors.

**cognitive dissonance**   An inconsistency among some experiences, beliefs, attitudes, or feelings. According to dissonance theory, this sets up an unpleasant state that people try to reduce by reinterpreting some part of their experiences to make them consistent with the others.

**cognitive interpretation theory of emotions**   A theory proposed by Schachter and Singer which asserts that emotions are an interpretation of our own autonomic arousal in the light of the situation to which we attribute it. *See also* attribution theory.

**cognitive map**   *See* cognitive theory.

**cognitive theory**   A conception of human and animal learning which holds that both humans and animals acquire items of knowledge (cognitions) such as what is where (cognitive map) or what leads to what (expectancy). This contrasts with theories of instrumental learning such as Thorndike's or Skinner's which assert that learning consists of the strengthening or weakening of particular response tendencies.

**cognitive therapy**   An approach to therapy that tries to change some of the patient's habitual modes of thinking. It is related to behavior therapy because it regards such thought patterns as a form of behavior.

**common sense**   As used in the discussion of artificial intelligence, the term refers to an understanding of what is relevant to a problem and what is not.

**complementary colors**   Two colors that, when additively mixed with each other in the right proportions, produce the sensation of gray.

**compulsions**   *See* obsessive-compulsive disorders.

**concept**   A class or category that subsumes a number of individual instances. An important way of relating concepts is through propositions, which make some assertion that relates a subject (e.g., *chickens*) and a predicate (e.g., *lay eggs*).

**concordance**   The probability that a person who stands in a particular family relationship to a patient (e.g., an identical twin) has the same disorder as the patient.

**concrete operational period**   In Piaget's theory, the period from ages six or seven to about eleven. At this time, the child has acquired mental operations that allow her to abstract some essential attributes of reality such as number and substance; but these operations are as yet applicable only to concrete events and cannot be considered entirely in the abstract.

**conditional statement**   A construction of the form *If A, then B*. These can be tested by applying either a positive (If *A* is true, then *B* must be true) or a negative rule (If *B* is false, then *A* must be false) of if-then inference. The negative rule is considerably more difficult to apply than the negative rule as shown by the results of Wason's card selection task.

**conditioned reflex**   *See* conditioned response.

**conditioned reinforcer**   An initially neutral stimulus that acquires reinforcing properties through pairing with another stimulus that is already reinforcing.

**conditioned response (CR)**   A response elicited by some initially neutral stimulus, the conditioned stimulus (CS), as a result of pairings between that CS and an unconditioned stimulus (US). This CR is typically not identical with the unconditioned response though it often is similar to it. *See also* conditioned stimulus, unconditioned response, unconditioned stimulus.

**conditioned stimulus (CS)**   In classical conditioning, the stimulus which comes to elicit a new response by virtue of pairings with the unconditioned stimulus. *See also* conditioned response, unconditioned response, unconditioned stimulus.

**cones**   Visual receptors that respond to greater light intensities and give rise to chromatic (color) sensations.

**confidence interval**   An interval around a sample mean or proportion within which the population mean or proportion is likely to fall. In common practice, the largest value of the interval is 2 standard errors above the mean or proportion, and the smallest value is 2 standard errors below it.

**confirmation bias**   The tendency to seek evidence to confirm one's hypothesis rather than to look for evidence to see whether the hypothesis is false.

**conservation**   In Piaget's theory, the understanding that certain attributes such as substance and number remain unchanged despite various transformations (e.g., liquid conservation, the realization that the amount of liquid remains the same when poured from a tall, thin beaker into a wide jar).

**construct validity**   The extent to which performance on a test fits into a theoretical scheme about the attribute the test tries to measure.

**content morphemes**   Morphemes that carry the main burden of meaning (e.g., *strange*). This is in contrast to function morphemes that add details to the meaning but also serve various grammatical purposes (e.g., the suffixes *s* and *er*, the connecting words *and, or, if,* and so on).

**context effects**   *See* top-down processes.

**contiguity**   The togetherness in time of two events, which is sometimes regarded as the condition that leads to association.

**contingency**   A relation between two events in which one is dependent upon another. If the contingency is greater than zero, then the probability of event *A* will be greater when event *B* is present than when it is absent.

**convergence**   The movement of the eyes as they swivel toward each other to focus upon an object.

**conversion disorders**   Formerly called conversion hysteria. A condition in which there are physical symptoms that seem to have no physical basis. They instead appear to be linked to psychological factors and are often believed to serve as a means of reducing anxiety. *See also* hysteria.

**conversion hysteria**   *See* conversion disorders.

**corpus callosum**   A bundle of fibers that connects the two cerebral hemispheres.

**correlation**   The tendency of two variables to vary together. If one goes up as the other goes up, the correlation is positive; if one goes up as the other goes down, the correlation is negative.

**correlation coefficient**   A number, referred to as *r*, that expresses

both the size and the direction of a correlation, varying from +1.00 (perfect positive correlation) through 0.00 (absence of any correlation) to −1.00 (perfect negative correlation).

**counterconditioning** A procedure for weakening a classically conditioned CR by connecting the stimuli that presently evoke it to a new response that is incompatible with the CR.

**criterion groups** Groups whose test performance sets the validity criterion for certain tests (e.g., the Minnesota Multiphasic Personality Inventory, MMPI, which uses several psychiatric criterion groups to define most of its subscales).

**critical period** Period in the development of an organism when it is particularly sensitive to certain environmental influences. Outside of this period, the same environmental influences have little effect (e.g., the period during which a duckling can be imprinted). After embryonic development, this phenomenon is rarely all-or-none. As a result, most developmental psychologists prefer the term *sensitive period.*

**critical ratio** A *z*-score used for testing the null hypothesis. It is obtained by dividing an obtained mean difference by the standard error *(SE)* so that critical ratio = obtained mean difference/*SE*. If this ratio is large enough, the null hypothesis is rejected and the difference is said to be statistically significant. *See also* standard error of the mean.

**crystallized intelligence** The repertoire of information, cognitive skills, and strategies acquired by the application of fluid intelligence to various fields. This is said to increase with age, in some cases into old age. *See also* fluid intelligence.

**cultural anthropology** A branch of anthropology that compares the similarities and differences among human cultures.

**culture fairness of a test** The extent to which test performance does not depend upon information or skills provided by one culture but not another.

**curare** A drug that completely paralyzes the skeletal musculature but does not affect visceral reactions.

**cutoff score** A score on a test used for selection below which no individual is accepted.

**decay** A possible factor in forgetting, producing some loss of the stored information through erosion by some as yet unknown physiological process

**decision making** The process of forming probability estimates of events and utilizing them to choose between different courses of action.

**declarative knowledge** Knowing "that" (e.g., someone's name) as contrasted with procedural knowledge, which is knowing "how" (e.g., riding a bicycle).

**deductive reasoning** Reasoning in which one tries to determine whether some statement logically follows from certain premises, as in the analysis of syllogisms. This is in contrast with inductive reasoning in which one observes a number of particular instances and tries to determine a general rule that covers them all.

**defense mechanism** In psychoanalytic theory, a collective term for a number of reactions that try to ward off or lessen anxiety by various unconscious means. *See also* displacement, projection, rationalization, reaction formation, repression.

**definition** (of a word) A set of necessary and sufficient features shared by all members of a category which are the criteria for membership in that category.

**deindividuation** A weakened sense of personal identity in which self-awareness is merged in the collective goals of a group.

**delay of gratification** The postponement of immediate satisfaction in order to achieve a more important reward later on, a process that plays an important role in some behavioral-cognitive approaches to personality.

**delusion** Systematized false beliefs, often of grandeur or persecution.

**demand characteristics** (of an experiment) The cues that tell a subject what the experimenter expects of him.

**dendrites** A typically highly branched part of a neuron that receives impulses from receptors or other neurons and conducts them toward the cell body and axon.

**dependent variable** *See* experiment.

**depolarization** A drop of the membrane potential of a neuron from its resting potential. The basis of neural excitation.

**depression** A state of deep and pervasive dejection and hopelessness, accompanied by apathy and a feeling of personal worthlessness.

**depth-of-processing approach** An approach to memory that stresses the nature of encoding at the time of acquisition. It argues that deeper levels of processing (for example, attending to a word's meaning) lead to better retention and retrieval than shallower levels of processing (for example, attending to the word's sound). Thus maintenance rehearsal leads to much poorer retrieval than elaborative rehearsal. *See also* encoding, elaborative rehearsal, maintenance rehearsal.

**descriptive rules** *See* prescriptive rules.

**deviation IQ** A measure of intelligence test performance based on an individual's standing relative to his own age-mates (e.g., an IQ of 100 is average and IQs of 70 and 130 correspond to percentile ranks of 2 and 98 respectively). *See also* Intelligence Quotient.

**diathesis** *See* diathesis-stress conception.

**diathesis-stress conception** The belief that many organic and mental disorders arise from an interaction between a diathesis (a predisposition toward the illness) and some form of precipitating environmental stress.

**dichotic listening** A procedure by which each ear receives a different message while the listener is asked to attend to one.

**difference threshold** The amount by which a given stimulus must be increased or decreased so that the subject can perceive a just noticeable difference (j.n.d.).

**differentiation** A progressive change from the general to the particular and from the simpler to the more complex which characterizes embryological development. According to some theorists, the same pattern holds for the development of behavior after birth.

**diffusion of responsibility** *See* bystander effect.

**diminishing returns principle** Applied to the perceived value of money, the principle states that the increase in the subjective value produced by every additional dollar decreases the more dollars the person has already. The same principle applies to the subjective value of other gains and losses. It also applies to the psychological magnitude of sensory qualities, as in the case of Weber's law.

**directed thinking** Thinking that is aimed at the solution of a problem.

**discrimination** A process of learning to respond to certain stimuli that are reinforced and not to others that are unreinforced.

**disinhibition** An increase of some reaction tendency by the removal of some inhibiting influence upon it (e.g., the increased strength of a frog's spinal reflexes after decapitation).

**disorganized type of schizophrenia** A subtype of schizophrenia for-

merly called hebephrenia in which the predominant symptoms are extreme incoherence of thought and marked inappropriateness of behavior and affect.

**displacement**   In psychoanalytic theory, a redirection of an impulse from a channel that is blocked into another, more available outlet (e.g., displaced aggression, as in a child who hits a sibling when punished by her parents).

**display**   Term used by ethologists to describe genetically preprogrammed responses that serve as stimuli for the reaction of others of the same species, and thus serve as the basis of a communication system (e.g., mating rituals).

**dissociative disorders**   Disorders in which a whole set of mental events is stored out of ordinary consciousness. These include psychogenic amnesia, fugue states and, very rarely, cases of multiple personality.

**dissonance theory**   *See* cognitive dissonance.

**distal stimulus**   An object or event outside (e.g., a tree) as contrasted to the proximal stimulus (e.g., the retinal image of the tree), which is the pattern of physical energies that originates from the distal stimulus and impinges on a sense organ.

**doctrine of specific nerve energies**   The assertion that qualitative differences in sensory experience are not attributable to the differences in the stimuli that correspond to different sense modalities (e.g., light versus sound) but rather to the fact that these stimuli excite different nervous structures.

**dominant gene**   *See* gene.

**dopamine (DA)**   A neurotransmitter involved in various brain structures, including those that control motor action. Some authors believe that one subtype of schizophrenia is produced by an oversensitivity to dopamine in some parts of the brain.

**dopamine hypothesis of schizophrenia**   Asserts that schizophrenics are oversensitive to the neurotransmitter dopamine and are therefore in a state of overarousal. Evidence for this view comes from the fact that the phenothiazines, which alleviate schizophrenic symptoms, block dopamine transmission. *See also* phenothiazines.

**double-blind technique**   A technique for evaluating drug effects independent of the effects produced by the expectations of patients (placebo effects) and of physicians. This is done by assigning patients to a drug group or a placebo group with both patients and staff members in ignorance of who is assigned to which group. *See also* placebo effect.

**drive-reduction theory**   A theory that claims that all built-in rewards are at bottom reductions of some noxious bodily state. The theory has difficulty in explaining motives in which one seeks stimulation, such as sex and curiosity.

**DSM-III**   The diagnostic manual of the American Psychiatric Association adopted in 1980. A major distinction between it and its predecessor is that it categorizes mental disorders by their descriptive characteristics rather than by theories about their underlying cause. Thus a number of disorders that were formerly grouped together under the general heading "neurosis" (e.g., phobias, conversion disorders) are now classified under separate headings. *See also* conversion disorders, neurosis, phobia.

**DSM-III-R**   The current diagnostic manual of the American Psychiatric Association adopted in 1987, a relatively minor revision of its predecessor, DSM-III.

**effectors**   Organs of action; in humans, muscles and glands.

**efferent nerves**   Nerves that carry messages to the effectors.

**ego**   In Freud's theory, a set of reactions that try to reconcile the id's blind pleasure strivings with the demands of reality. These lead to the emergence of various skills and capacities that eventually become a system that can look at itself—an "I." *See also* id and superego.

**egocentrism**   In Piaget's theory, a characteristic of preoperational children, an inability to see another person's point of view.

**eidetic memory**   A relatively rare kind of memory characterized by relatively long-lasting and detailed images of scenes that can be scanned as if they were physically present.

**elaboration-likelihood model of persuasion**   A theory that asserts that the factors that make for persuasion depend on the extent to which the arguments of the persuasive message are thought about (elaborated). If they are seriously thought about, the central route to persuasion will be used, and attitude change will depend on the nature of the arguments. If they are not seriously considered, the peripheral route to persuasion will be used, and attitude change will depend on more peripheral factors.

**elaborative rehearsal**   Rehearsal in which material is actively reorganized and elaborated while being held in short-term memory. In contrast to maintenance rehearsal, this confers considerable benefit. *See also* maintenance rehearsal.

**Electra complex**   *See* Oedipus complex.

**electroconvulsive shock treatment (ECT)**   A somatic treatment, mostly used for cases of severe depression, in which a brief electric current is passed through the brain to produce a convulsive seizure.

**electroencephalogram (EEG)**   A record of the summed activity of cortical cells picked up by wires placed on the skull.

**embryo**   The earliest stage in a developing animal. In humans, up to about eight weeks after conception.

**empathic concern**   A feeling of sympathy and concern for the sufferings of another coupled with the desire to relieve this suffering. *See also* vicarious distress.

**encoding**   The form in which some information is stored.

**encoding specificity principle**   The hypothesis that retrieval is most likely if the context at the time of recall approximates that during the original encoding.

**endocrine system**   The system of ductless glands whose secretions are released directly into the bloodstream and affect organs elsewhere in the body (e.g., adrenal gland).

**endorphin**   A drug produced within the brain itself whose effects and chemical composition are similar to such pain-relieving opiates as morphine.

**epinephrine** (adrenaline)   A neurotransmitter released into the bloodstream by the adrenal medulla whose effects are similar to those of sympathetic activation (e.g., racing heart).

**episodic memory**   Memory for particular events in one's own life (e.g., I missed the train this morning). *See also* generic memory.

**erogenous zones**   In psychoanalytic theory, the mouth, anus, and genitals. These regions are particularly sensitive to touch. According to Freud, the various pleasures associated with each of them have a common element, which is sexual.

**escape learning**   Instrumental learning in which reinforcement consists of the reduction or cessation of an aversive stimulus (e.g., electric shock). *See also* punishment training, avoidance learning.

**essential hypertension**   *See* psychophysiological disorders.

**estrogen**   A female sex hormone that dominates the first half of the

female cycle through ovulation; in animals, estrus performs this function.

**estrus** In mammalian animals, the period in the cycle when the female is sexually receptive (in heat).

**ethology** A branch of biology that studies the behavior of animals under natural conditions.

**excitation transfer effects** The transfer of autonomic arousal from one situation to another, as when strenuous exercise leads to an increased arousal when presented with aggression-arousing or erotic stimuli.

**existential therapy** A humanistic therapy that emphasizes people's free will and tries to help them achieve a personal outlook to give meaning to their lives.

**expectancy** *See* cognitive theory.

**experiment** A study in which the investigator manipulates one (or more than one) variable (the independent variable) to determine its effect on the subject's response (the dependent variable).

**expert systems** Computer problem-solving programs with a very narrow scope which only deal with problems in a limited domain of knowledge (e.g., the diagnosis of infectious diseases).

**explicit memory** Memory retrieval in which there is awareness of remembering at the time of retrieval. *See also* implicit memory.

**expressive movements** Movements of the face and body in animals and humans that seem to express emotion. They are usually regarded as built-in social displays.

**externality hypothesis** The hypothesis that some and perhaps all obese people are relatively unresponsive to their own internal hunger state but are much more susceptible to signals from without.

**extinction** In classical conditioning, the weakening of the tendency of CS to elicit CR by unreinforced presentations of CS. In instrumental conditioning, a decline in the tendency to perform the instrumental response brought about by unreinforced occurrences of that response.

**extroversion-introversion** In Eysenck's system, a trait dimension that refers to the main direction of a person's energies; toward the outer world of objects and other people (extroversion) or toward the inner world of one's own thoughts and feelings (introversion).

**facial feedback hypothesis** The hypothesis that sensory feedback from the facial muscles will lead to subjective feelings of emotion that correspond to the particular facial pattern. *See* fundamental emotions.

**factor analysis** A statistical method for studying the interrelations among various tests, the object of which is to discover what the tests have in common and whether these communalities can be ascribed to one or several factors that run through all or some of these tests.

**false alarm** *See* payoff matrix.

**familiarity effect** The fact that increased exposure to a stimulus tends to make that stimulus more likable.

**family resemblance structure** Overlap of features among members of a category of meaning such that no members of the category have all of the features but all members have some of them.

**family therapy** A general term for a number of therapies that treat the family (or a couple), operating on the assumption that the key to family or marital distress is not necessarily in the pathology of any individual spouse or family member but is rather in the interrelationships within the family or marriage system.

**feature detectors** Neurons in the retina or brain that respond to specific features of the stimulus such as movement, orientation, and so on.

**Fechner's law** The assertion that the strength of a sensation is proportional to the logarithm of physical stimulus intensity.

**feedback system** A system in which some action produces a consequence that affects (feeds back on) the action. In negative feedback, the consequence stops or reverses the action (e.g., thermostat-controlled furnace). In positive feedback, the consequence strengthens the action (e.g., rocket that homes in on airplanes).

**fetus** A later stage in embryonic development. In humans, from about eight weeks until birth.

**figure-ground organization** The segregation of the visual field into a part (the figure) which stands out against the rest (the ground).

**fixed-action patterns** Term used by ethologists to describe stereotyped, species-specific behaviors triggered by genetically pre-programmed releasing stimuli.

**flashbulb memories** Vivid, detailed, and apparently accurate memories said to be produced by unexpected and emotionally important events.

**flooding** A form of behavior therapy based on concepts derived from classical conditioning, in which the patient exposes himself to whatever he is afraid of, thus extinguishing his fear. *See also* implosion therapy.

**fluid intelligence** The ability, which is said to decline with age, to deal with essentially new problems. *See also* crystallized intelligence.

**forced compliance effect** An individual forced to act or speak publicly in a manner contrary to his own beliefs may change his own views in the direction of the public action. But this will happen only if his reward for the false public pronouncement is relatively small. If the reward is large, there is no dissonance and hence no attitude change. *See also* cognitive dissonance.

**forebrain** In mammals, the bulk of the brain. Its foremost region includes the cerebral hemispheres; its rear includes the thalamus and hypothalamus.

**forward pairing** A classical conditioning procedure in which the conditioned stimulus (CS) precedes the unconditioned stimulus (US). This contrasts with simultaneous pairing, in which CS and US are presented simultaneously, and backward pairing, in which CS follows US. *See also* classical conditioning, conditioned stimulus, unconditioned stimulus.

**framing** A heuristic that affects the subjective desirability of an event by changing the standard of reference for judging the desirability of that event.

**fraternal twins** Twins that arise from two different eggs that are (simultaneously) fertilized by different sperm cells. Their genetic similarity is no different than that between ordinary siblings. *See also* identical twins.

**free association** Method used in psychoanalytic therapy in which the patient is to say anything that comes to her mind, no matter how apparently trivial, unrelated, or embarrassing.

**free recall** A test of memory that asks for as many items in a list as a subject can recall regardless of order.

**frequency distribution** An arrangement in which scores are tabulated by the frequency in which they occur.

**Freud's theory of dreams** A theory that holds that at bottom all dreams are attempts to fulfill a wish. The wish fulfillment is in the latent dream, which represents the sleeper's hidden desires. This latent

dream is censored and reinterpreted to avoid anxiety. It reemerges in more acceptable form as the manifest dream, the dream the sleeper remembers upon awakening.

**frontal lobe**   A lobe in each cerebral hemisphere which includes the motor projection area.

**function morphemes**   *See* content morphemes.

**functional fixedness**   A set to think of objects in terms of their normal function.

**fundamental attribution error**   The tendency to attribute behaviors to dispositional qualities while underrating the role of the situation. *See also* actor-observer difference, attribution theory, self-serving bias.

**fundamental emotions**   According to some theorists, a small set of elemental, built-in emotions revealed by distinctive patterns of facial expression. *See also* facial feedback hypothesis.

**galvanic skin response (GSR)**   A drop in the electrical resistance of the skin, widely used as an index of autonomic reaction.

**gender constancy**   The recognition that being male or female is to all intents and purposes irrevocable.

**gender identity**   The inner sense of being male or female. *See also* gender role, sexual orientation.

**gender role**   The set of external behavior patterns a given culture deems appropriate for each sex. *See also* gender identity and sexual orientation.

**gene**   The unit of hereditary transmission, located at a particular place in a given chromosome. Both members of each chromosome pair have corresponding locations at which there are genes that carry instructions about the same characteristic (e.g., eye color). If one member of a gene pair is dominant and the other is recessive, the dominant gene will exert its effect regardless of what the recessive gene calls for. The characteristic called for by the recessive gene will only be expressed if the other member of the gene pair is also recessive. *See also* chromosomes.

**general paresis**   A psychosis characterized by progressive decline in cognitive and motor function culminating in death, reflecting a deteriorating brain condition produced by syphilitic infection.

**generalization gradient**   The curve that shows the relationship between the tendency to respond to a new stimulus and its similarity to the original conditioned stimulus (CS).

**generalized anxiety disorder**   A mental disorder (formerly called anxiety neurosis) whose primary characteristic is an all-pervasive, "free-floating" anxiety. A member of the diagnostic category "anxiety disorders," which also includes phobias and obsessive-compulsive disorders. *See also* phobia, obsessive-compulsive disorders.

**generic memory**   Memory for items of knowledge as such (e.g., The capital of France is Paris), independent of the occasion on which they are learned. *See also* episodic memory.

**genital stage**   In psychoanalytic theory, the stage of psychosexual development reached in adult sexuality in which sexual pleasure involves not only one's own gratification but also the social and bodily satisfaction brought to another person.

**genotype**   The genetic blueprint of an organism which may or may not be overtly expressed by its phenotype. *See also* phenotype.

**Gestalt**   An organized whole such as a visual form or a melody.

**Gestalt psychology**   A theoretical approach that emphasizes the role of organized wholes (Gestalten) in perception and other psychological processes.

**glove anesthesia**   A condition sometimes seen in conversion disorders, in which there is an anesthesia of the entire hand with no loss of feeling above the wrist. This symptom makes no organic sense given the anatomical arrangement of the nerve trunks and indicates that the condition has a psychological basis.

**glucose**   A form of sugar which is the major source of energy for most bodily tissues. If plentiful, much of it is converted into glycogen and stored away.

**glycogen**   A stored form of metabolic energy derived from glucose. To be used, it must first be converted back into glucose.

**good continuation**   A factor in visual grouping. Contours tend to be seen in such a way that their direction is altered as little as possible.

**gradient of reinforcement**   The curve that describes the declining effectiveness of reinforcement, with increasing delay between the response and the reinforcer.

**group-factor theory of intelligence**   A factor-analytic approach to intelligence test performance which argues that intelligence is the composite of separate abilities (group factors such as verbal ability, spatial ability, etc.) without a sovereign capacity that enters into each. *See also* factor analysis, Spearman's theory of general intelligence.

**group therapy**   Psychotherapy of several persons at one time.

**habituation**   A decline in the tendency to respond to stimuli that have become familiar. While short-term habituation dissipates in a matter of minutes, long-term habituation may persist for days or weeks.

**habituation procedure**   A widely used method for studying infant perception. After some exposure to a visual stimulus, an infant becomes habituated and stops looking at it. The extent to which a new stimulus leads to renewed interest and resumption of looking is taken as a measure of the extent to which the infant regards this new stimulus as different from the old one to which she became habituated.

**hallucination**   Perceived experiences that occur in the absence of actual sensory stimulation.

**heritability**   As measured by *H,* the heritability ratio, this refers to the relative importance of heredity and environment in determining the variation of a particular trait. More specifically, *H* is the proportion of the variance of the trait in a given population that is attributable to genetic factors.

**hermaphrodite**   A person whose reproductive organs are anatomically ambiguous so that they are not exclusively male or female.

**heterosexuality**   A sexual orientation leading to a choice of sexual partners of the opposite sex.

**heuristics**   In computer problem solving, a procedure that has often worked in the past and is likely, but not certain, to work again. *See also* algorithm.

**hierarchical organization**   Organization in which narrower categories are subsumed under broader ones, which are subsumed under still broader ones, and so on. Often expressed in the form of a tree diagram.

**hierarchy of needs**   According to Maslow and other adherents of the humanistic approach, human needs are arranged in a hierarchy with physiological needs such as hunger at the bottom, safety needs further up, the need for attachment and love still higher, and the desire for esteem yet higher. At the very top of the hierarchy is the striving for self-actualization. By and large, people will only strive for the higher-order needs when the lower ones are fulfilled. *See* self-actualization.

**higher-order conditioning** In classical conditioning, a procedure by which a new stimulus comes to elicit the conditioned response (CR) by virtue of being paired with an effective conditioned stimulus (CS) (e.g., first pairings of tone and food, then pairings of bell and tone, until finally the bell elicits salivation by itself).

**hindbrain** The most primitive portion of the brain, which includes the medulla and the cerebellum.

**hippocampus** A structure in the temporal lobe that constitutes an important part of the limbic system. One of its functions seems to involve memory.

**histogram** A graphic rendering of a frequency distribution which depicts the distribution by a series of contiguous rectangles. *See also* frequency distribution.

**homeostasis** The body's tendency to maintain the conditions of its internal environment by various forms of self-regulation.

**homogamy** The tendency of like to marry like.

**homosexuality** A sexual orientation leading to a choice of partners of the same sex.

**hue** A perceived dimension of visual stimuli whose meaning is close to the term *color* (e.g., red, blue).

**humanistic approach to personality** Asserts that what is most important about people is how they achieve their selfhood and actualize their potentialities. *See also* behavioral-cognitive approach, psychodynamic approach, trait theory.

**humanistic therapies** Methods of treatment that emphasize personal growth and self-fulfillment. They try to be relatively nondirective since their emphasis is on helping the clients achieve the capacity for making their own choices. *See also* nondirective techniques.

**hyperphagia** Voracious, chronic overeating brought about by lesion of the ventromedial region of the hypothalamus.

**hyperpolarization** A rise of the membrane potential of a neuron from its resting potential. The basis of neural inhibition. *See also* depolarization.

**hypnosis** A temporary, trancelike state that can be induced in normal persons. During hypnosis, various hypnotic or posthypnotic suggestions sometimes produce effects that resemble some of the symptoms of conversion disorders. *See also* conversion disorders.

**hypothalamus** A small structure at the base of the brain which plays a vital role in the control of the autonomic nervous system, of the endocrine system, and of the major biological drives.

**hysteria** An older term for a group of presumably psychogenic disorders that included conversion disorders and dissociative disorders. Since DSM-III, it is no longer used as a diagnostic category, in part because of an erroneous implication that the condition is more prevalent in women (Greek *hystera*—womb). *See also* conversion disorders, dissociative disorders, glove anesthesia.

**id** In Freud's theory, a term for the most primitive reactions of human personality, consisting of blind strivings for immediate biological satisfaction regardless of cost. *See also* ego and superego.

**ideas of reference** A characteristic of some mental disorders, notably schizophrenia, in which the patient begins to think that external events are specially related to him personally (e.g., "People walk by and follow me").

**identical twins** Twins that originate from a single fertilized egg that then splits into two exact replicas that develop into two genetically identical individuals. *See also* fraternal twins.

**identification** In psychoanalytic theory, a mechanism whereby a child models himself or herself (typically) on the same-sex parent in an effort to become like him or her.

**idiot savant** A mentally retarded person who has some remarkable talent that seems out of keeping with his or her low level of general intelligence.

**ill-defined problems** *See* well-defined problems.

**imipramine** *See* antidepressant drugs.

**implicit memory** Memory retrieval in which there is no awareness of remembering at the time of retrieval. *See also* explicit memory.

**implicit theories of personality** Beliefs about the way in which different patterns of behavior of people hang together and why they do so.

**implosion therapy** A form of behavior therapy related to flooding in which the patient exposes herself to whatever she is afraid of, in its most extreme form, but does so in imagination rather than in real life (e.g., a person afraid of dogs has to imagine herself surrounded by a dozen snarling Dobermans). *See* flooding.

**impossible figure** A figure that appears acceptable when looked at locally but poses unresolvable visual contradictions when seen as a whole.

**imprinting** A learned attachment that is formed at a particular period in life (the critical period) and is difficult to reverse (e.g., the duckling's acquired tendency to follow whatever moving stimulus it encounters twelve to twenty-four hours after hatching).

**incidental learning** Learning without trying to learn (e.g, as in a study in which subjects judge a speaker's vocal quality when she recites a list of words and are later asked to produce as many of the words as they can recall). *See also* intentional learning.

**incremental validity** The extent to which a test adds to the predictive validity already provided by other measures (e.g., the extent to which a projective technique adds to what is already known through an ordinary interview).

**independent variable** *See* experiment.

**induced movement** Perceived movement of an objectively stationary stimulus that is enclosed by a moving framework.

**inductive reasoning** Reasoning in which one observes a number of particular instances and tries to determine a general rule that covers them all.

**information processing** A general term for the presumed operations whereby the crude raw materials provided by the senses are refashioned into items of knowledge. Among these operations are perceptual organization, comparison with items stored in memory, and so on.

**insightful learning** Learning by understanding the relations between components of the problem; often contrasted with "blind trial and error" and documented by wide and appropriate transfer if tested in a new situation.

**instrumental conditioning** Also called operant conditioning. A form of learning in which a reinforcer (e.g., food) is given only if the animal performs the instrumental response (e.g., pressing a lever). In effect, what has to be learned is the relationship between the response and the reinforcer. *See* classical conditioning.

**insulin** A hormone with a crucial role in utilization of nutrients. One of its functions is to help promote the conversion of glucose into glycogen.

**Intelligence Quotient (IQ)** A ratio measure to indicate whether a child's mental age (MA) is ahead or behind her chronological age

(CA); specifically IQ = 100 × MA/CA. *See also* deviation IQ, mental age.

**intentional learning**   Learning when informed that there will be a later test of learning. *See also* incidental learning.

**interference theory of forgetting**   The assertion that items are forgotten because they are somehow interfered with by other items learned before or after.

**internalization**   The process whereby moral codes are adopted by the child so that they control his behavior even where there are no external rewards or punishments.

**interneurons**   Neurons that receive impulses and transmit them to other neurons.

**interval scale**   A scale in which equal differences between scores can be treated as equal so that the scores can be added or subtracted. *See also* categorical scale, ordinal scale, ratio scale.

**introversion**   *See* extroversion-introversion.

**invariant**   Some aspect of the proximal stimulus pattern that remains unchanged despite various transformations of the stimulus.

**isolation**   A mechanism of defense in which anxiety arousing memories are retained but without the emotion that accompanied them.


**James-Lange theory of emotions**   A theory that asserts that the subjective experience of emotion is the awareness of one's own bodily reactions in the presence of certain arousing stimuli.

**just noticeable difference (j.n.d.)**   *See* difference threshold.


**kin-selection hypothesis**   *See* altruism.

**kinesthesis**   A general term for sensory information generated by receptors in the muscles, tendons, and joints which informs us of our skeletal movement.

**Korsakoff syndrome**   A brain disorder characterized by serious memory disturbances. The most common cause is extreme and chronic alcohol use.


**labeling theory of mental disorders**   The assertion that the label "mental illness" acts as a self-fulfilling prophecy that perpetuates the condition once the label has been applied. In its extreme form, it asserts that the concept is a myth, mental illness being merely the term by which we designate social deviance that does not fall into other, recognized categories of deviance.

**latency**   General term for the interval before some reaction occurs.

**latency period**   In psychoanalytic theory, a stage in psychosexual development in which sexuality lies essentially dormant, roughly from ages five to twelve.

**latent dream**   *See* Freud's theory of dreams.

**latent learning**   Learning that occurs without being manifested by performance.

**lateral hypothalamus**   A region of the hypothalamus which is said to be a "hunger center" and to be in an antagonistic relation to a supposed "satiety center," the ventromedial region of the hypothalamus.

**lateral inhibition**   The tendency of adjacent neural elements of the visual system to inhibit each other; it underlies brightness contrast and the accentuation of contours. *See also* brightness contrast.

**lateralization**   An asymmetry of function of the two cerebral hemispheres. In most right-handers, the left hemisphere is specialized for language functions, while the right hemisphere is better at various visual and spatial tasks.

**law of effect**   A theory that asserts that the tendency of a stimulus to evoke a response is strengthened if the response is followed by reward and is weakened if the response is not followed by reward. Applied to instrumental learning, this theory states that as trials proceed, incorrect bonds will weaken while the correct bond will be strengthened.

**learned helplessness**   A condition created by exposure to inescapable aversive events. This retards or prevents learning in subsequent situations in which escape or avoidance is possible.

**learned helplessness theory of depression**   The theory that depression is analogous to learned helplessness effects produced in the laboratory by exposing subjects to uncontrollable aversive events.

**learning curve**   A curve in which some index of learning (e.g., the number of drops of saliva in Pavlov's classical conditioning experiment) is plotted against trials or sessions.

**learning model**   As defined in the text, a subcategory of the pathology model that (1) views mental disorders as the result of some form of faulty learning, and (2) believes that these should be treated by behavior therapists according to the laws of classical and instrumental conditioning, or by cognitive therapists who try to affect faulty modes of thinking. *See also* behavior therapy, cognitive therapy, medical model, pathology model, psychoanalytic model.

**learning set**   The increased ability to solve various problems, especially in discrimination learning, as a result of previous experience with problems of a similar kind.

**lexical access**   The process of recognizing and understanding a word, which is presumably achieved by making contact (accessing) with the word in the mental lexicon.

**lightness constancy**   The tendency to perceive the lightness of an object as more or less the same despite the fact that the light reflected from these objects changes with the illumination that falls upon them.

**limbic system**   A set of brain structures including a relatively primitive portion of the cerebral cortex and parts of the thalamus and hypothalamus; it is believed to be involved in the control of emotional behavior and motivation.

**line of best fit**   A line drawn through the points in a scatter diagram; it yields the best prediction of one variable when given the value of the other variable.

**lithium carbonate**   A drug used in the treatment of mania and bipolar disorders.

**lobotomy**   *See* prefrontal lobotomy.

**long-term habituation**   *See* habituation.

**long-term memory**   Also called secondary memory. Those parts of the memory system that are currently dormant and inactive, but have enormous storage capacity. According to the stage theory of memory, information can only enter into the long-term store if it first passes through short-term memory and remains in it for some period of time. *See also* short-term memory, stage theory of memory.

**longitudinal study**   A developmental study in which the same person is tested at various ages.

**maintenance rehearsal**   Rehearsal in which material is merely held in short-term memory for a while. In contrast to elaborative rehearsal, this confers little benefit. *See also* elaborative rehearsal.

**mania**   Hyperactive state with marked impairment of judgment, usually accompanied by intense euphoria.

**manifest dream**   *See* Freud's theory of dreams.

**marital therapy**   *See* family therapy.

**matching hypothesis**   The hypothesis that persons of a given level of physical attractiveness will seek out partners of a roughly similar level.

**matching to sample**   A procedure in which an organism has to choose one of two alternative stimuli which is the same as a third sample stimulus.

**maturation**   A pre-programmed growth process based on changes in underlying neural structures that are relatively unaffected by environmental conditions (e.g., flying in sparrows and walking in humans).

**maximum likelihood principle**   The assertion that we interpret the proximal stimulus pattern as that external stimulus object that most probably produced it.

**mean (M)**   The most commonly used measure of the central tendency of a frequency distribution. It is the arithmetical average of all the scores. If $M$ is the mean and $N$ the number of cases, then $M =$ sum of the scores/$N$. *See also* central tendency, median.

**medial forebrain bundle (MFB)**   A bundle of fibers that runs through the base of the forebrain and parts of the hypothalamus. Electric stimulation of this bundle is usually rewarding.

**median**   A measure of the central tendency of a frequency distribution. It is the point that divides the distribution into two equal halves when the scores are arranged in ascending order. *See also* central tendency and mean.

**medical model**   As defined in the text, a subcategory of the pathology model that (1) holds that the underlying pathology is organic, and that (2) the treatment should be conducted by physicians. *See also* learning model, pathology model, psychoanalytic model.

**medulla**   The rearmost portion of the brain, just adjacent to the spinal cord. It includes centers that help to control respiration and muscle tone.

**memory span**   The number of items a person can recall after just one presentation.

**memory trace**   The change in the nervous system left by an experience which is the physical basis of its retention in memory. What this change is, is still unknown.

**mental age (MA)**   A score devised by Binet to represent a child's test performance. It indicates the chronological age at which 50 percent of the children in that age group will perform. If the child's MA is greater than his chronological age (CA), he is ahead of his age mentally; if his MA is lower than his CA, he lags behind.

**mental retardation**   Usually defined as an IQ of 70 and below.

**mental set**   The predisposition to perceive (or remember or think of) one thing rather than another.

**meta-analysis**   A statistical technique by means of which the results of many different techniques can be combined. Has been useful in studies on the outcome of psychotherapy.

**metacognition**   A general term for knowledge about knowledge, as in knowing that we do or don't remember something.

**midbrain**   Part of the brain which includes some lower centers for sensory-motor integration (e.g., eye movements) and part of the reticular formation.

**middle ear**   An antechamber to the inner ear which amplifies sound-produced vibrations of the eardrum and imparts them to the cochlea. *See also* cochlea.

**Minnesota Multiphasic Personality Inventory (MMPI)**   *See* criterion groups.

**mnemonics**   Deliberate devices for helping memory. Many of them utilize imagery such as the method of pegs and method of loci.

**monoamine oxidase (MAO) inhibitors**   *See* antidepressant drugs.

**monocular depth cues**   Various features of the visual stimulus which indicate depth, even when viewed with one eye (e.g., linear perspective and motion parallax).

**mood disorders**   A group of disorders (formerly called affective disorders) whose primary characteristic is a disturbance of mood, and which is characterized by two emotional extremes—the energy of mania, or the despair or lethargy of depression, or both. *See also* bipolar disorder, depression, mania, unipolar disorder.

**morpheme**   The smallest significant unit of meaning in a language (e.g., the word *boys* has two morphemes, *boy* and *s*).

**Motherese**   A whimsical term for the speech pattern that mothers and other adults generally employ when talking to infants.

**motor projection areas**   *See* projection areas.

**nalaxone**   A drug that inhibits the effect of morphine and similar opiates and blocks the pain alleviation ascribed to endorphins.

**nativism**   The view that some important aspects of perception and of other cognitive processes are innate.

**natural selection**   The explanatory principle that underlies Darwin's theory of evolution. Some organisms produce offspring that are able to survive and reproduce while other organisms of the same species do not. Thus organisms with these hereditary attributes will eventually outnumber organisms who lack these attributes.

**negative rule of if-then inference**   *See* conditional statement.

**negative feedback**   *See* feedback system.

**negative symptoms of schizophrenia**   Symptoms that involve a lack of normal functioning, such as apathy, poverty of speech, and emotional blunting. *See* positive symptoms of schizophrenia.

**neo-Freudians**   A group of theorists who accept the psychoanalytic conception of unconscious conflict but who differ with Freud in (1) describing these conflicts in social terms rather than in terms of particular bodily pleasures or frustrations, and (2) maintaining that many of these conflicts arise from the specific cultural conditions under which the child was reared rather than being biologically preordained.

**neophobia**   A term used in the study of food selection, where it refers to an animal's tendency to refuse new foods.

**nerve impulse**   *See* action potential.

**network model**   Theories of cognitive organization, especially of semantic memory, that assert that items of information are represented by a system of nodes linked through associative connections. *See also* node.

**neuron**   A nerve cell.

**neurosis**   In psychoanalytic theory, a broad term for mental disorders whose primary symptoms are anxiety or what seem to be defenses against anxiety. Since the adoption of DSM-III, the term has been dropped as the broad diagnostic label it once was. Various disorders that were once diagnosed as subcategories of neurosis (e.g., phobia, conversion disorders, dissociative disorders) are now classified as separate disorders.

**neuroticism**   A trait dimension that refers to emotional instability and maladjustment.

**neurotransmitters**   Chemicals liberated at the terminal end of an

axon which travel across the synapse and have an excitatory or inhibitory effect on an adjacent neuron (e.g., norepinephrine).

**node** A point in a network on which a number of connections converge.

**nondirective techniques** A set of techniques for psychological treatment developed by Carl Rogers. As far as possible, the counselor refrains from offering advice or interpretation but only tries to clarify the patient's own feelings by echoing him or restating what he says.

**nonsense syllable** Two consonants with a vowel between that do not form a word. Used to study associations between relatively meaningless items.

**norepinephrine (NE)** The neurotransmitter by means of which the sympathetic fibers exert their effect on internal organs. It is also the neurotransmitter of various arousing systems in the brain.

**normal curve** A symmetrical, bell-shaped curve that describes the probability of obtaining various combinations of chance events. It describes the frequency distributions of many physical and psychological attributes of humans and animals.

**normal distribution** A frequency distribution whose graphic representation has a symmetric, bell-shaped form—the normal curve. Its characteristics are often referred to when investigators test statistical hypotheses and make inferences about the population from a given sample.

**null hypothesis** The hypothesis that an obtained difference is merely a chance fluctuation from a population in which the true mean difference is zero. *See also* alternative hypothesis.

**obesity** A condition of marked overweight in animals and humans; it is produced by a large variety of factors including metabolic factors (oversecretion of insulin) and behavioral conditions (overeating, perhaps produced by nonresponsiveness to one's own internal state).

**object permanence** The conviction that an object remains perceptually constant over time and exists even when it is out of sight. According to Piaget, this does not develop until infants are age eight months or more.

**observational study** A study in which the investigator does not manipulate any of the variables but simply observes their relationship as they occur naturally.

**obsessions** *See* obsessive-compulsive disorders.

**obsessive-compulsive disorders** A disorder whose symptoms are obsessions (persistent and irrational thoughts or wishes) and compulsions (uncontrollable, repetitive acts), which seem to be defenses against anxiety. A member of a diagnostic category called anxiety disorders, which also includes generalized anxiety disorder and phobias. *See also* generalized anxiety disorder and phobia.

**occipital lobe** A lobe in each cerebral hemisphere which includes the visual projection area.

**Oedipus complex** In psychoanalytic theory, a general term for a whole cluster of impulses and conflicts which occur during the phallic phase, at around age five. In boys, a fantasied form of intense sexual love is directed at the mother, which is soon followed by hate and fear of the father. As the fear mounts, the sexual feelings are pushed underground and the boy identifies with the father. An equivalent process in girls is called the Electra complex.

**open-class morphemes** *See* closed-class morphemes.

**operant conditioning** *See* instrumental conditioning.

**operant** In Skinner's system, an instrumental response. *See also* instrumental conditioning.

**opponent-process theory of color vision** A theory of color vision that asserts that there are three pairs of color antagonists: red-green, blue-yellow, and white-black. Excitation of one member of a pair automatically inhibits the other member.

**opponent-process theory of motivation** A theory that asserts that the nervous system has the general tendency to counteract any deviation from the neutral point of the pain-pleasure dimension. If the original stimulus is maintained, there is an attenuation of the emotional state one is in; if it is withdrawn, the opponent process reveals itself, and the emotional state swings sharply in the opposite direction.

**oral character** According to Freud, a personality type based on a fixation at the oral stage of development whose symptomatic attribute is passive dependency. *See also* oral stage.

**oral stage** In psychoanalytic theory, the earliest stage of psychosexual development during which the primary source of bodily pleasure is stimulation of the mouth and lips, as in sucking at the breast.

**ordinal scale** A scale in which responses are rank-ordered by relative magnitude but in which the intervals between successive ranks are not necessarily equal. *See also* categorical scale, interval scale, ratio scale.

**orienting response** In classical conditioning, an animal's initial reaction to a new stimulus (e.g., turning toward it and looking attentive).

**osmoreceptors** Receptors that help to control water intake by responding to the concentrations of body fluids. *See also* volume receptors.

**paired-associate method** A procedure in which subjects learn to provide particular response terms to various stimulus items.

**panic disorder** A disorder characterized by sudden anxiety attacks in which there are bodily symptoms such as choking, dizziness, trembling, and chest pains, accompanied by feelings of intense apprehension, terror, and a sense of impending doom.

**parallel search** The simultaneous comparison of a target stimulus to several items in memory. *See also* serial search.

**paranoid schizophrenia** A subcategory of schizophrenia. Its dominant symptom is a set of delusions which are often elaborately systematized, usually of grandeur or persecution.

**paraphrase** The relation between two sentences whose meanings (underlying structures) are the same but whose surface structures differ (e.g., *The boy hit the ball / The ball was hit by the boy*).

**parasympathetic overshoot** A rebound effect in which the parasympathetic system responds above its normal level after the inhibition from its sympathetic antagonist is suddenly lifted (e.g., weeping).

**parasympathetic system** A division of the autonomic nervous system which serves vegetative functions and conserves bodily energies (e.g., slowing heart rate). Its action is antagonistic to that of the sympathetic system.

**parietal lobe** A lobe in each cerebral hemisphere which includes the somatosensory projection area.

**Parkinson's disease** A degenerative neurological disorder characterized by various difficulties of movement. Produced by degeneration of dopamine-releasing neurons in a pathway of the brain crucial for motor control.

**partial reinforcement** A condition in which a response is reinforced only some of the time.

**partial-reinforcement effect** The fact that a response is much harder to extinguish if it was acquired during partial rather than continuous reinforcement.

**pathology model**  A term adopted in the text to describe a general conception of mental disorders which holds that (1) one can generally distinguish between symptoms and underlying causes, and (2) these causes may be regarded as a form of pathology. *See also* learning model, medical model, psychoanalytic model.

**pattern recognition**  The process by which the perceptual system matches the form of a figure against a figure stored in memory.

**payoff matrix**  (1) In a detection experiment, a table that shows the costs and benefits for each of the four possible outcomes: a hit, reporting the stimulus when it is present; a correct negative, reporting it as absent when it is in fact absent; a miss, failing to report it when it is present; and a false alarm, reporting it as present when it is not. (2) In the context of the use of tests for selection an analogous table that shows the costs and benefits of correct and incorrect acceptances and rejections respectively.

**peak experience**  Profound and deeply felt moments in a person's life, sometimes said to be more common in self-actualized persons than in others. *See* self-actualization.

**perceived locus of control**  A person's belief about the source of outcomes that befall him. That perceived source (locus) may be internal, the result of something he did, or external, the result of forces outside of his own control.

**percentile rank**  The percentage of all the scores in a distribution that lie below a given score.

**perceptual adaptation**  The gradual adjustment to various distortions of the perceptual world, as in wearing prisms that tilt the entire visual world in one direction.

**perceptual defense**  The tendency to perceive anxiety-related stimuli less readily than neutral stimuli.

**perceptual differentiation**  Learning to perceive features of stimulus patterns that were not perceptible at first. A phenomenon central to the theory of perceptual learning proposed by J. J. Gibson and E. J. Gibson.

**perceptual parsing**  The process of grouping the various visual elements of a scene appropriately, deciding which elements go together and which do not.

**period of formal operations**  In Piaget's theory, the period from about age eleven on, when genuinely abstract mental operations can be undertaken (e.g., the ability to entertain hypothetical possibilities).

**peripheral route to persuasion**  *See* elaboration-likelihood model of persuasion.

**person-by-situation interaction**  The fact that the effect of a situational variable may depend on the person. Thus some people may on average be equally fearful, but while one is afraid of meeting people but unafraid of large animals, another may be afraid of large animals but be unafraid of meeting people. *See also* reciprocal interaction, situationism.

**personality inventories**  Paper-and-pencil tests of personality that ask questions about feelings or customary behavior. *See also* projective techniques.

**PET scan (Positron Emission Tomography)**  A technique for examining brain structure and function in intact humans by recording the degree of metabolic activity of different regions of the brain.

**phallic stage**  In psychoanalytic theory, the stage of psychosexual development during which the child begins to regard his genitals as a major source of gratification.

**phenothiazines**  A group of drugs, including chlorpromazine, that seem to be effective in alleviating the major symptoms of schizophrenia.

**phenotype**  The overt appearance and behavior of an organism, regardless of its genetic blueprint. *See also* genotype.

**phenylketonuria (PKU)**  A severe form of mental retardation determined by a single gene. This disorder can be treated by means of a special diet (if detected early enough), despite the fact that the disorder is genetic.

**pheromones**  Special chemicals secreted by many animals which trigger particular reactions in members of the same species.

**phobia**  One of a group of mental disorders called anxiety disorders which is characterized by an intense and, at least on the surface, irrational fear. *See also* generalized anxiety disorder, obsessive-compulsive disorders.

**phoneme**  The smallest significant unit of sound in a language. In English, it corresponds roughly to a letter of the alphabet (e.g., *apt, tap,* and *pat* are all made up of the same phonemes).

**phonology**  The rules in a language that govern the sequence in which phonemes can be arranged.

**phrase**  A sequence of words within a sentence that function as a unit (e.g., *The ball/rolled/down the hill*).

**phrase structure**  The organization of sentences into phrases. Surface structure is the phrase organization of sentences as they are spoken or written. Underlying structure is the phrase organization that describes the meaning of parts of the sentence, such as doer, action, and done-to.

**pituitary gland**  An endocrine gland heavily influenced by the hypothalamus. A master gland because many of its secretions trigger hormone secretions in other glands.

**placebo**  In medical practice, a term for a chemically inert substance that the patient believes will help him.

**placebo effect**  A beneficial effect of a treatment administered to a patient who believes it has therapeutic powers even though it has none.

**pluralistic ignorance**  A situation in which individuals in a group don't know that there are others in the group who share their feelings.

**polyandry**  A mating system in which one female monopolizes the reproductive efforts of several males.

**polygenic inheritance**  Inheritance of an attribute whose expression is controlled not by one but by many gene pairs.

**polygyny**  A mating system in which one male monopolizes the reproductive efforts of several females.

**population**  The entire group of subjects (or test trials) about which the investigator wants to draw conclusions. *See also* sample.

**positive feedback**  *See* feedback system.

**positive rule of if-then inference**  *See* conditional statement.

**positive symptoms of schizophrenia**  Symptoms that center on what these patients do (or think or perceive) that normals don't, for example, hallucinations, delusions, and bizarre behaviors. *See* negative symptoms of schizophrenia.

**predicate**  *See* concept.

**predictive validity**  A measure of a test's validity based on the correlation between the test score and some criterion of behavior the test predicted (e.g., a correlation between a scholastic aptitude test and college grades).

**prefrontal lobotomy**  A somatic treatment for severe mental disorders which surgically cuts the connections between the thalamus and the frontal lobes.

**preoperational period** In Piaget's theory, the period from about ages two to six during which children come to represent actions and objects internally but cannot systematically manipulate these representations or relate them to each other; the child is therefore unable to conserve quantity across perceptual transformations and also is unable to take points of view other than her own.

**preparedness theory of phobias** The theory that phobias grow out of a built-in predisposition (preparedness) to learn to fear certain stimuli (e.g., snakes and spiders) that may have posed serious dangers to our primate ancestors.

**prescriptive rules** Rules prescribed by "authorities" about how people *ought* to speak and write that often fail to conform to the facts about natural talking and understanding. This is in contrast to the structural principles of a language which describe (rather than prescribe) the principles according to which native speakers of a language actually arrange their words into sentences. Sentences formed according to these principles are called well-formed or grammatical.

**prestige suggestion** Approving some statement because a high-prestige person has approved it.

**primacy effect** (1) In free recall, the superiority of the items in the first part of a list compared to those in the middle. (2) In forming an impression of another person, the phenomenon whereby attributes first noted carry a greater weight than attributes noted later on. *See* recency effect.

**primary memory** *See* short-term memory.

**prisoner's dilemma** A particular arrangement of payoffs in a two-person situation in which each individual has to choose between two alternatives without knowing the other's choice. The payoff structure is so arranged that the optimal strategy for each person depends upon whether he can trust the other or not. If trust is possible, the payoffs for each will be considerably higher than if there is no trust.

**proactive inhibition** Disturbance of recall of some material by other material learned previously. *See* retroactive inhibition.

**procedural knowledge** *See* declarative knowledge.

**progesterone** A female sex hormone that dominates the latter phase of the female cycle during which the uterus walls thicken to receive the embryo.

**projection** In psychoanalytic theory, a mechanism of defense in which various forbidden thoughts and impulses are attributed to another person rather than the self, thus warding off some anxiety (e.g., "I hate you" becomes "You hate me").

**projection areas** Regions of the cortex that serve as receiving stations for sensory information or as dispatching stations for motor commands.

**projective techniques** Devices for assessing personality by presenting relatively unstructured stimuli that elicit subjective responses of various kinds. Their advocates believe that such tasks allow the person to "project" her own personality into her reactions (e.g., the TAT and the Rorschach inkblot test). *See also* personality inventories.

**proposition** *See* concept.

**prosopagnosia** The inability to recognize faces produced by a brain lesion.

**prototype** The typical example of a category of meaning (e.g., robin is a prototypical bird).

**proximal stimulus** *See* distal stimulus.

**psychoanalysis** (1) A theory of human personality formulated by Freud whose key assertions include unconscious conflict and psychosexual development. (2) A method of therapy that draws heavily on this theory of personality. Its main aim is to have the patient gain insight into his own, presently unconscious, thoughts and feelings. Therapeutic tools employed toward this end include free association, interpretation, and the appropriate use of the transference relationship between patient and analyst. *See also* free association, transference.

**psychoanalytic model** As defined in the text, a subcategory of the pathology model which holds that (1) the underlying pathology is a constellation of unconscious conflicts and defenses against anxiety, usually rooted in early childhood, and (2) treatment should be by some form of psychotherapy based on psychoanalytic principles.

**psychodynamic approach of personality** An approach to personality originally derived from psychoanalytic theory that asserts that personality differences are based on unconscious (dynamic) conflicts within the individual.

**psychogenic disorders** Disorders whose origins are psychological rather than organic (e.g., phobias). *See also* somatogenic mental disorders.

**psychometric approach to intelligence** An attempt to understand the nature of intelligence by studying the pattern of results obtained on intelligence tests.

**psychopath** *See* antisocial personality.

**psychopathology** The study of psychological disorders.

**psychophysics** The field that tries to relate the characteristics of physical stimuli to the sensory experience they produce.

**psychophysiological disorders** In these disorders (formerly called psychosomatic), the primary symptoms involve genuine organic damage whose ultimate cause is psychological (e.g., essential hypertension, a condition of chronic high blood pressure brought about by the bodily concomitant of chronic emotional stress).

**psychosexual development** In psychoanalytic theory, the description of the progressive stages in the way the child gains his main source of pleasure as he grows into adulthood, defined by the zone of the body through which this pleasure is derived (oral, anal, genital) and by the object toward which this pleasurable feeling is directed (mother, father, adult sexual partner). *See also* anal stage, genital stage, oral stage, phallic stage.

**psychosis** A broad category that describes some of the more severe mental disorders in which the patient's thoughts and deeds no longer meet the demands of reality.

**psychosocial crises** In Erik Erikson's theory, a series of crises through which all persons must pass as they go through their life cycle (e.g., the identity crisis during which adolescents or young adults try to establish the separation between themselves and their parents).

**psychotherapy** As used here, a collective term for all forms of treatment that use psychological rather than somatic means.

**punishment training** An instrumental training procedure in which a response is suppressed by having its occurrence followed by an aversive event. *See also* avoidance learning, escape learning.

**quiet sleep** Stages 2 to 4 of sleep during which there are no rapid eye movements and during which the EEG shows progressively less cortical arousal. Also known as non-REM sleep.

**radical behaviorism** An approach usually associated with B. F. Skinner that asserts that the subject matter of psychology is overt behavior, without reference to inferred, internal processes such as wishes, traits, or expectations.

**random sample**   *See* sample.

**ratio scale**   An interval scale in which there is a true zero point, thus allowing ratio statements (e.g., this sound is twice as loud as the other). *See also* categorical scale, interval scale, ordinal scale.

**ratio schedule**   A schedule of reinforcement in which reinforcement is delivered after a certain number of responses. In a fixed-ratio schedule, the subject has to produce a specified number of responses for every reinforcement; in a variable-ratio schedule this number varies irregularly.

**rationalization**   In psychoanalytic theory, a mechanism of defense by means of which unacceptable thoughts or impulses are reinterpreted in more acceptable and thus less anxiety-arousing terms (e.g., the jilted lover who convinces himself he never loved her anyway).

**reaction formation**   In psychoanalytic theory, a mechanism of defense in which a forbidden impulse is turned into its opposite (e.g., hate toward a sibling becomes exaggerated love).

**reaction time**   The interval between the presentation of a signal and the observer's response to that signal.

**recall**   A task in which some item must be produced from memory. *See* recognition.

**recency effect**   In free recall, the recall superiority of the items at the end of the list compared to those in the middle. *See* primacy effect (in recall).

**receptive field**   The retinal area in which visual stimulation affects a particular cell's firing rate.

**receptors**   A specialized cell that can respond to various physical stimuli and transduce them.

**recessive gene**   *See* gene.

**reciprocal altruism**   *See* altruism.

**reciprocal inhibition**   The arrangement by which excitation of some neural system is accompanied by inhibition of that system's antagonist (as in antagonistic muscles).

**reciprocal interaction**   The fact that different people seek out different situations.

**reciprocity principle**   A basic rule of many social interactions that decrees that one must repay whatever one has been given.

**recoding**   Changing the form in which some information is stored.

**recognition**   A task in which a stimulus has to be identified as having been previously encountered in some context or not. *See also* recall.

**reference**   The relations between words or sentences and objects or events in the world (e.g., "ball" refers to ball).

**reflex**   A simple, stereotyped reaction in response to some stimulus (e.g., limb flexion in withdrawal from pain).

**rehearsal**   *See* elaborative rehearsal, maintenance rehearsal.

**reinforced trial**   In classical conditioning, a trial on which the CS is accompanied by the US. In instrumental conditioning, a trial in which the instrumental response is followed by reward, cessation of punishment, or other reinforcement.

**reinforcement**   In classical conditioning, the procedure by which the US is made contingent on the CS. In instrumental conditioning, the procedure by which the instrumental response is made contingent upon some sought-after outcome.

**releasing stimulus**   Term used by ethologists to describe a stimulus which is genetically pre-programmed to elicit a fixed-action pattern (e.g., a long, thin, red-tipped beak which elicits a herring gull chick's begging response). *See also* fixed-action patterns.

**reliability**   The consistency with which a test measures what it measures, as assessed, for example, by the test-retest method.

**REM sleep**   *See* active sleep.

**repetition priming**   An increase in the likelihood that an item word is identified, recognized, or recalled by recent exposure to that item which may occur without explicit awareness.

**representational thought**   In Piaget's theory, thought that is internalized and includes mental representations of prior experiences with objects and events.

**representativeness heuristic**   A rule of thumb in estimating the probability that an object (or event) belongs to a certain category based on the extent to which it resembles the prototype of that category regardless of the base rate at which it occurs. *See also* prototype.

**repression**   In psychoanalytic theory, a mechanism of defense by means of which thoughts, impulses, or memories that give rise to anxiety are pushed out of consciousness.

**resistance**   In psychoanalysis, a collective term for the patient's failures to associate freely and say whatever enters his head.

**response bias**   A preference for one or another response in a psychophysical experiment, independent of the stimulus situation.

**response suppression**   The inhibition of a conditioned response by conditioned fear.

**restrained-eating hypothesis**   The hypothesis that the oversensitivity of obese persons to external cues is caused by the disinhibition of conscious restraints on eating. *See also* externality hypothesis, setpoint hypothesis.

**restructuring**   A reorganization of a problem, often rather sudden, which seems to be a characteristic of creative thought.

**retention**   The survival of the memory trace over some interval of time.

**reticular activating system (RAS)**   A system that includes the upper portion of the reticular formation and its ascending branches to much of the brain. Its effect is to arouse the brain.

**reticular formation**   A network of neurons extending throughout the midbrain with ramifications to higher parts of the brain. This plays an important role in sleep and arousal.

**retina**   The structure that contains the visual receptors and several layers of neurons further up along the pathway to the brain.

**retinal image**   The image of an object that is projected on the retina. Its size increases with the size of that object and decreases with its distance from the eye.

**retrieval**   The process of searching for some item in memory and of finding it. If retrieval fails, this may or may not mean that the relevant memory trace is not present; it simply may be inaccessible.

**retrieval cue**   A stimulus that helps to retrieve a memory trace.

**retroactive inhibition**   Disturbance of recall of some material by other material learned subsequently. *See also* proactive inhibition.

**retrograde amnesia**   A memory deficit suffered after head injury or concussion in which the patient loses memory of some period prior to the injury. *See also* anterograde amnesia.

**reuptake**   A mechanism by which a neurotransmitter is drawn back into the presynaptic terminal that released it.

**ROC curve**   A curve that shows the relationship between hits and false alarms in a detection experiment.

**rods**   Visual receptors that respond to lower light intensities and give rise to achromatic (colorless) sensations.

**Rorschach inkblot test** A projective technique that requires the person to look at inkblots and say what she sees in them.

**safety signal** A stimulus that has been contingent on the absence of an electric shock (or another negative reinforcer) in a situation in which such shocks are sometimes delivered. *See also* contingency.

**sample** A subset of a population selected by the investigator for study. A random sample is one so constructed that each member of the population has an equal chance to be picked. A stratified sample is one so constructed that every relevant subgroup of the population is randomly sampled in proportion to its size. *See also* population.

**saturation** A perceived dimension of visual stimuli that describes the "purity" of a color—the extent to which it is rich in hue (e.g., green rather than olive).

**scaling** A procedure for assigning numbers to a subject's responses. *See also* categorical scale, interval scale, ordinal scale, ratio scale.

**schedule of reinforcement** A rule that determines the occasions when a response is reinforced. Examples are ratio and interval schedules.

**schema** (1) In theories of memory and thinking, a term that refers to a general cognitive structure in terms of which information can be organized. (2) In Piaget's theory of development, a mental pattern.

**schizophrenia** A group of severe mental disorders characterized by at least some of the following: marked disturbance of thought, withdrawal, inappropriate or flat emotions, delusions, and hallucinations. *See also* catatonic schizophrenia, paranoid schizophrenia.

**score profile** *See* test profile.

**script** A subcase of a schema, which describes a characteristic scenario of behaviors in a particular setting, such as a restaurant script. *See also* schema.

**seasonal depressive disorder** A mood disorder with a seasonal pattern, with depressions that start in the late fall when the days become shorter and end when the days lengthen in the spring.

**secondary memory** *See* long-term memory.

**self-perception theory** The assertion that we don't know ourselves directly but rather infer our own states and dispositions by an attribution process analogous to that which we use when we try to explain the behavior of other persons. *See also* attribution theory.

**self-actualization** A major concern of Maslow and other adherents of the humanistic approach, it is the realization of one's potentialities so that one becomes what one can become. *See also* hierarchy of needs, peak experience.

**self-monitoring** Monitoring one's own behavior so that it fits the situation.

**self-perception theory** A theory that asserts that we do not know our own attitudes and feelings directly but must infer them by observing our own behavior and then performing much the same attribution processes that we employ when trying to understand the behavior of others.

**self-serving bias** The tendency to deny responsibility for failures but take credit for successes. *See also* attribution theory, fundamental attribution error, actor-observer difference.

**semantic feature** The smallest significant unit of meaning within a word (e.g., male, human, and adult are semantic features of the word "man").

**semantic memory** The component of generic memory that concerns the meaning of words and concepts.

**semantics** The organization of meaning in language.

**sensation** According to the British empiricists, the primitive experiences that the senses give us (e.g., green, bitter).

**sensation seeking** The tendency to seek novel experiences, look for thrills and adventure, and be highly susceptible to boredom.

**sensitive period** *See* critical period.

**sensory adaptation** The decline in sensitivity found in most sensory systems after continuous exposure to the same stimulus.

**sensory code** The rule (code) by which the nervous system represents sensory characteristics of the stimulus. An example is firing frequency, which is the general code for increased stimulus intensity.

**sensory coding** The process by which the nervous system translates various aspects of the stimulus into dimensions of our sensory experience.

**sensory-motor intelligence** In Piaget's theory, intelligence during the first two years of life which consists mainly of sensations and motor impulses with, at first, little in the way of internalized representations.

**sensory projection areas** *See* projection areas.

**Sentence Analyzing Machinery (SAM)** A set of procedures by which listeners comprehend sentences.

**serial search** The successive comparison of a target stimulus to different items in memory. *See also* parallel search.

**serotonin (5HT)** A neurotransmitter involved in many of the mechanisms of sleep and emotional arousal.

**set** *See* mental set.

**setpoint** A general term for the level at which negative feedback tries to maintain the system. An example is the setting of a thermostat. *See also* setpoint hypothesis.

**setpoint hypothesis** The hypothesis that different persons have different setpoints for weight. *See also* setpoint.

**sexual orientation** The direction of a person's choice of a sexual partner, which may be heterosexual or homosexual. *See also* gender identity, gender role.

**sexual dimorphism** A condition that describes a species in which there is a marked difference in the size and/or form of the two sexes as in the case of deer (antlers) or peacocks (long tail feathers).

**shape constancy** The tendency to perceive the shape of objects as more or less the same despite the fact that the retinal image of these objects changes its shape as we change the angle of orientation from which we view them.

**shaping** An instrumental learning procedure through which an animal (or human) is trained to perform a rather difficult response by reinforcing successive approximations to that response.

**short-term memory** Also called primary memory, active memory, and working memory. A part of the memory system that is currently activated, but has relatively little cognitive capacity. According to the stage theory of memory, information can only enter into the long-term store if it first passes through short-term memory and remains in it for some period of time. *See also* short-term memory, stage theory of memory.

**short-term habituation** *See* habituation.

**signal-detection theory** A theory that asserts that observers who are asked to detect the presence or absence of a stimulus try to decide whether an internal sensory experience should be attributed to background noise or to a signal added to background noise.

**simultaneous pairing**  A classical conditioning procedure in which the conditioned stimulus (CS) and the unconditioned stimulus (US) are presented simultaneously. *See also* backward pairing, forward pairing.

**situational factors**  *See* attribution theory.

**situationism**  The view that human behavior is largely determined by the characteristics of the situation rather than those of the person. *See also* trait theory.

**size constancy**  The tendency to perceive the size of objects as more or less the same despite the fact that the retinal image of these objects changes in size whenever we change the distance from which we view them.

**social comparison**  A process of reducing uncertainty about one's own beliefs and attitudes by comparing them to those of others.

**social exchange theory**  A theory that asserts that each partner in a social relationship gives something to the other and expects to get something in return.

**social facilitation**  The tendency to perform better in the presence of others than when alone. This facilitating effect works primarily for simple and/or well-practiced tasks.

**social impact theory**  A theory that asserts that the influence others exert on an individual increases with their number, their immediacy, and their strength (e.g., status).

**social learning theory**  A theoretical approach to socialization and personality that is midway between behavior theories such as Skinner's and cognitive approaches. It stresses learning by observing others who serve as models for the child's behavior. The effect of the model may be to allow learning by imitation and also may be to show the child whether a response he already knows should or should not be performed.

**socialization**  The process whereby the child acquires the patterns of behavior characteristic of her society.

**sociobiology**  A recent theoretical movement in biology that tries to trace social behavior to genetically based predispositions; an approach that has led to some controversy when extended to humans.

**sociopath**  *See* antisocial personality.

**somatic therapies**  A collective term for any treatment of mental disorders by means of some organic manipulation. This includes drug administration, any form of surgery, convulsive treatments, etc.

**somatogenic mental disorders**  Mental disorders that are produced by an organic cause. This is the case for some disorders (e.g., general paresis) but almost surely not for all (e.g., phobias). *See also* psychogenic disorders.

**sound waves**  Successive pressure variations in the air which vary in amplitude and wave length.

**Spearman's theory of general intelligence (g)**  Spearman's account, based on factor analytic studies, ascribes intelligence test performance to one underlying factor, general intelligence *(g)* which is tapped by all subtests, and a large number of specific skills *(s's)* which depend on abilities specific to each subtest. *See also* factor analysis, group-factor theory.

**specificity theory**  The theory that different sensory qualities are signaled by the action of specific nerve fibers.

**split brain**  A condition in which the corpus callosum and some other fibers are cut so that the two cerebral hemispheres are isolated.

**spontaneous recovery**  An increase in the tendency to perform an ex-
tinguished response after a time interval in which neither conditioned stimulus (CS) nor unconditioned stimulus (US) are presented.

**spreading activation model**  A memory model that assumes that elements in a semantic memory network are activated the smaller the distance between them.

**stabilized image technique**  A procedure by which the retina receives a stationary image even though the eye is moving.

**stage theory of memory**  A theoretical approach that asserts that there are several memory stores. One is short-term memory, which holds information for fairly short intervals and has a small capacity; another is long-term memory, which holds information for very long periods and has a vast capacity. According to the theory, information will only enter into long-term memory if it has been in short-term memory for a while. *See also* long-term memory, short-term memory.

**standard deviation (SD)**  A measure of the variability of a frequency distribution which is the square root of the variance. If $V$ is the variance and $SD$ the standard deviation, then $SD = \sqrt{V}$. *See also* variance.

**standard error of the mean**  A measure of the variability of the mean whose value depends both on the standard deviation *(SD)* of the distribution and the number of cases in the sample *(N)*. If $SE$ is the standard error, then $SE = SD/\sqrt{N-1}$.

**standard score (z-score)**  A score that is expressed as a deviation from the mean in standard deviation units, which allows a comparison of scores drawn from different distributions. If $M$ is the mean and $SD$ the standard deviation, then $z = (\text{score} - M)/SD$.

**standardization group**  The group against which an individual's test score is evaluated.

**stimulus**  Anything in the environment which the organism can detect and respond to.

**stimulus generalization**  In classical conditioning, the tendency to respond to stimuli other than the original conditioned stimulus (CS). The greater the similarity between the CS and the new stimulus, the greater this tendency will be. An analogous phenomenon in instrumental conditioning is a response to stimuli other than the original discriminative stimulus.

**Stroop effect**  A marked decrease in the speed of naming the colors in which various color names (such as green, red, etc.) are printed when the colors and the names are different. An important example of automatization.

**structural principles (of language)**  *See* prescriptive rules.

**subtractive color mixture**  Mixing colors by subtracting one set of wavelengths from another set (as in mixing colors on a palette or superimposing two colored filters). *See also* additive color mixture.

**superego**  In Freud's theory, a set of reaction patterns within the ego that represent the internalized rules of society and that control the ego by punishing with guilt. *See also* ego and id.

**surface structure**  *See* phrase structure.

**sympathetic system**  A division of the autonomic nervous system which mobilizes the body's energies for emergencies (e.g., increasing heart rate). Its action is antagonistic to that of the parasympathetic system.

**symptoms**  The outward manifestations of an underlying pathology.

**synapse**  The juncture between the axon of one neuron and the dendrite or cell body of another.

**syndrome**  A pattern of symptoms that tend to go together.

**systematic desensitization**  A behavior therapy that tries to remove anxiety connected to various stimuli by a gradual process of counter-conditioning to a response incompatible with fear, usually muscular relaxation. The stimuli are usually evoked as mental images according to an anxiety hierarchy whereby the less frightening stimuli are counterconditioned before the more frightening ones.

**taste buds**  The receptor organs for taste.

**taxonomy**  A classification system.

**temperament**  In modern usage, a characteristic level of reactivity and energy, often thought to be based on constitutional factors.

**temporal lobe**  A lobe in each cerebral hemisphere which includes the auditory projection area.

**territory**  Term used by ethologists to describe a region a particular animal stakes out as its own. The territory holder is usually a male, but in some species the territory is held by a mating pair or by a group.

**test profile**  A graphic indication of an individual's performance on several components of a test. This is often useful for guidance or clinical evaluation because it indicates which abilities or traits are relatively high or low in that person.

**testosterone**  The principal male sex hormone (androgen) in mammals.

**texture gradient**  A distance cue based on changes in surface texture which depend on the distance of the observer.

**thalamus**  A part of the lower portion of the forebrain which serves as a major relay and integration center for sensory information.

**Thematic Apperception Test (TAT)**  A projective technique in which persons are shown a set of pictures and asked to write a story about each.

**threshold**  Some value a stimulus must reach to produce a response.

**tip-of-the-tongue phenomenon**  The condition in which one keeps on feeling on the verge of retrieving a word or name but continues to be unsuccessful even so.

**token economy**  An arrangement for operant behavior modification in hospital settings. Certain responses (e.g., talking to others) are reinforced with tokens which can be exchanged for desirable items.

**tolerance**  *See* opponent-process theory of motivation.

**top-down processes**  Processes in form recognition, which begin with higher units and then work down to smaller units (e.g., from phrases to words to letters). This is in contrast to bottom-up processes, which start with smaller component parts and then gradually build up to the higher units on top (e.g., from letters to words to phrases). One demonstration of top-down processing is provided by context effects in which knowledge or expectations affect what one sees.

**trace consolidation hypothesis**  The hypothesis that newly acquired traces undergo a gradual change that makes them more and more resistant to any disturbance.

**trait**  *See* trait theory.

**trait theory**  The view that people differ in regard to a number of underlying attributes (traits) that partially determine behavior and that are presumed to be essentially consistent from time to time and situation to situation. It tends toward the view that many such traits are based on genetic predispositions. *See also* behavioral-cognitive approach, humanistic approach, psychodynamic approach, situationism.

**transduction**  The process by which a receptor translates some physical stimulus (e.g., light or pressure) to give rise to an action potential in another neuron.

**transfer of training**  The effect of having learned one task on learning another. If the transfer of the first task helps in learning the second, the transfer is called positive. If it impedes in learning the second, the transfer is said to be negative.

**transference**  In psychoanalysis, the patient's tendency to transfer emotional reactions that were originally directed to one's own parents (or other crucial figures in one's early life) and redirect them toward the analyst.

**transposition**  The phenomenon whereby visual and auditory patterns (i.e., figures and melodies) remain the same even though the parts of which they are composed are changed.

**tricyclics**  *See* antidepressant drugs.

**two-syndrome hypothesis of schizophrenia**  The hypothesis that schizophrenia is a composite of two different syndromes, Type I and Type II. According to the hypothesis, Type I is produced by a malfunction of transmitters, especially dopamine, and produces primarily positive symptoms, while Type II is caused by cerebral damage and atrophy and leads to negative symptoms.

**Type A personality**  A personality type characterized by extreme impatience, competitiveness, and vehement aggressiveness when thwarted. *See also* Type B personality.

**Type B personality**  In contrast to the Type A personality, characterized by a more easygoing, less hurried, less competitive, and friendlier behavior pattern. *See also* Type A personality.

**unconditioned reflex**  *See* unconditioned response.

**unconditioned response (UR)**  In classical conditioning, the response that is elicited by the unconditioned stimulus without prior training. *See* conditioned response, conditioned stimulus, unconditioned stimulus.

**unconditioned stimulus (US)**  In classical conditioning, the stimulus that elicits the unconditioned response and the presentation of which acts as reinforcement. *See* conditioned response, conditioned stimulus, unconditioned response.

**unconscious inference**  A process postulated by Helmholtz to explain certain perceptual phenomena such as size constancy. An object is perceived to be in the distance and is therefore unconsciously perceived or inferred to be larger than it appears to be retinally. *See also* size constancy.

**underlying structure**  *See* phrase structure.

**unipolar disorder**  Mood disorder (usually depression) in which there is no back-and-forth swing between the two emotional extremes.

**validity**  The extent to which a test measures what it is supposed to measure. *See also* construct validity, incremental validity, predictive validity.

**variability**  The tendency of scores in a frequency distribution to scatter away from the central value. *See also* central tendency, standard deviation, variance.

**variance (V)**  A measure of the variability of a frequency distribution. It is computed by finding the difference between each score and the mean, squaring the result, adding all the squared deviations obtained in this manner and dividing it by the number of cases. If $V$ is

the variance, $M$ the mean, and $N$ the number of scores, then $V = $ sum of (score $- M)^2 / N$.

**vasoconstriction** The constriction of the capillaries brought on by activation of the sympathetic division of the autonomic nervous system in response to excessive cold.

**vasodilatation** The dilating of the capillaries brought on by activation of the parasympathetic division of the autonomic nervous system in response to excessive heat.

**ventromedial region of the hypothalamus** An area in the hypothalamus that is said to be a "satiety center" and in an antagonistic relation to a supposed "hunger center," the lateral hypothalamus.

**vestibular senses** A set of receptors that provide information about the orientation and movements of the head, located in the semicircular canals and the vestibular sacs of the inner ear.

**vicarious distress** The distress produced by witnessing the suffering of another. This is a less reliable motive for helping that person than empathic concern. *See also* empathic concern.

**vicarious reinforcement** According to social learning theorists, a form of reinforcement said to occur when someone watches a model being rewarded or punished.

**visual cliff** A device for assessing depth perception in young organisms; it consists of a glass surface that extends over an apparently deep side (the cliff) and an apparently shallow side.

**volume receptors** Receptors that help to control water intake by responding to the total volume of fluids in the body. *See also* osmoreceptors.

**Weber's law** The observation that the size of the difference threshold is proportional to the intensity of the standard stimulus.

**well-defined problems** Problems in which there is a clear-cut way for deciding whether a proposed solution is correct. This is in contrast to ill-defined problems in which it is not clear what a correct solution might be.

**Wernicke's area** *See* aphasia.

**wish fulfillment in dreams** *See* Freud's theory of dreams.

**withdrawal effects** *See* opponent-process theory of motivation.

**within-family differences** A term often used in the discussion of the role of environment. It describes differences in the environment of different members of the same family (e.g., different schools) For personality attributes, these seem to be more important than between-family differences. *See also* between-family differences.

**within-group heritability** The extent to which variation within groups (e.g., among U.S. whites) is attributable to genetic factors. *See also* between-group heritability, heritability.

**working memory** *See* short-term memory.

**z-score** *See* standard score.

# References

ABRAHAM, K. 1927. The influence of oral eroticism on character formation. In Abraham, K., *Selected papers,* pp. 393–406. London: Hogarth Press.

ABRAMS, M. H. 1953. *The mirror and the lamp: Romantic theory and the critical tradition.* New York: Oxford University Press.

ABRAMSON, L. Y.; METALSKY, G. I.; AND ALLOY, L. B. 1989. Hopelessness depression: A theory-based subtype of depression. *Psychological Review* 96:358–72.

ABRAMSON, L. Y.; SELIGMAN, M. E. P.; AND TEASDALE, J. D. 1978. Learned helplessness in humans: Critique and reformulation. *Journal of Abnormal Psychology* 87:49–74.

ABRAMSON, L. Y., AND SACKHEIM, H. A. 1977. A paradox in depression: Uncontrollability and self-blame. *Psychological Bulletin* 84: 835–51.

ADAMSON, E. 1984. *Art as healing.* London: Coventure Ltd.

ADLER, N. 1969. Effects of the male's copulatory behavior on successful pregnancy of the female rat. *Journal of Comparative and Physiological Psychology* 69:613–22.

ADOLPH, E. F. 1947. Urges to eat and drink in rats. *American Journal of Physiology* 151:110–25.

ADORNO, T. W.; FRENKEL-BRUNSWIK, E.; LEVINSON, D. J.; AND SANFORD, R. N. 1950. *The authoritarian personality.* New York: Harper & Row.

AINSWORTH, M. D. S., AND BELL, S. M. 1970. Attachment, exploration, and separation: Illustrated by the behavior of one-year-olds in a strange situation. *Child Development* 41:49–67.

AINSWORTH, M. D. S.; BLEHAR, M. C.; WATERS, E.; AND WALL, S. 1978. *Patterns of attachment.* Hillsdale, N.J.: Erlbaum.

ALBA, J. W., AND HASHER, W. 1983. Is memory schematic? *Psychological Bulletin* 93:203–31.

ALBERT, M. S.; BUTTERS, N.; AND LEVIN, J. 1979. Temporal gradients in the retrograde amnesia of patients with alcoholic Korsakoff's disease. *Archives of Neurology* 36:211–16.

ALEXANDER, B. K., AND HADAWAY, B. F. 1982. Opiate addiction: The case for an adaptive orientation. *Psychological Bulletin* 92:367–81.

ALEXANDER, F., AND FRENCH, T. 1946. *Psychoanalytic theory.* New York: Ronald Press.

ALLARD, F.; GRAHAM, S.; AND PAARSALU, M. E. 1980. Perception in sport: Basketball. *Journal of Sport Psychology* 2:14–21.

ALLEN, M. 1976. Twin studies of affective illness. *Archives of General Psychiatry* 33:1476–78.

ALLEN, V. L. 1975. Social support for non-conformity. In L. Berkowitz (Ed.), *Advances in experimental social psychology,* vol. 8. New York: Academic Press.

ALLEN, V. L., AND LEVINE, J. M. 1969. Consensus and conformity. *Journal of Experimental Social Psychology* 5:389.

ALLEN, V. L., AND LEVINE, J. M. 1971. Social support and conformity: The role of independent assessment. *Journal of Experimental Social Psychology* 7:48–58.

ALLOY, L. B.; HARTLAGE, S.; AND ABRAMSON, L. Y. 1988. Testing the cognitive-diathesis stress theories of depression: Issues of research design, conceptualization, and assessment. In Alloy, L. B. (Ed.), *Cognitive processes in depression.* New York: Guilford.

ALLPORT, F. 1920. The influence of the group upon association and thought. *Journal of Experimental Psychology* 3:159–82.

ALLPORT, G. W. 1937. *Personality: A psychological interpretation.* New York: Henry Holt.

ALLPORT, G. W., AND ODBERT, H. S. 1936. Trait-names: A psychological study. *Psychological Monographs* 47(Whole No. 211).

AMOORE, J. E.; JOHNSON, J. W., JR.; AND RUBIN, M. 1964. The sterochemical theory of odor. *Scientific American* 210:42–49.

ANASTASI, A. 1958. *Differential psychology,* 3rd ed. New York: Macmillan.

ANASTASI, A. 1971. More on heritability: Addendum to the Hebb and Jensen interchange. *American Psychologist* 26:1036–37.

ANASTASI, A. 1984. The K-ABC in historical perspective. *Journal of Special Education* 18:357–66.

ANASTASI, A. 1985. Review of Kaufman's Assessment Battery for Children. *Ninth Mental Measurements Yearbook,* vol. 1, pp. 769–71.

ANASTASI, A. 1988. *Psychological testing,* 6th ed. New York: Macmillan.

ANDERSON, J. R. 1990. *Cognitive psychology and its implications,* 3rd ed. San Francisco: Freeman.

ANDERSON, N. H. 1965. Averaging versus adding as a stimulus-combination rule in impression formation. *Journal of Experimental Psychology* 70:394–400.

ANDERSON, R. C., AND PICHERT, J. 1978. Recall of previously unrecallable information following a shift in perspective. *Journal of*

*Verbal Learning and Verbal Behavior* 17:1–12.

ANDREASEN, N. C. 1985. Positive vs. negative schizophrenia: A critical evaluation. *Schizophrenia Bulletin* 1985:380–89.

ANDREASEN, N. C.; NASRALLAH, H. A.; DUNN, V.; OLSEN, S. C.; GROVE, W. M.; EHRHARDT, J. C.; COFFMAN, J. A.; AND CROSSETT, I. H. W. 1986. Structural abnormalities in the frontal system in schizophrenia: A magnetic resonance imaging study. *Archives of General Psychiatry* 43:136–44.

ANDRES, R. 1980. Influence of obesity on longevity in the aged. In Borek, C.; Fenoglio, C. M.; and King, D. W. (Eds.), *Aging, cancer, and cell membranes,* pp. 230–46. New York: Thieme-Stratton.

ANDREWS, G., AND HARVEY, R. 1981. Does psychotherapy benefit neurotic patients? A reanalysis of the Smith, Glass, and Miller data. *Archives of General Psychiatry* 38:1203–1208.

ANGLIN, J. M. 1975. The child's first terms of reference. In Ehrlich, S., and Tulving, E. (Eds.), *Bulletin de Psychologie,* special issue on semantic memory.

ANGRIST, B.; SATHANANTHAN, G.; WILK, S.; AND GERSHON, S. 1974. Amphetamine psychosis: Behavioral and biochemical aspects. *Journal of Psychiatric Research* 11:13–24.

ANSTIS, S. M. 1975. What does visual perception tell us about visual coding? In Gazzaniga, M. S., and Blakemore, C. (Eds.), *Handbook of psychobiology.* New York: Academic Press.

APPEL, L. F.; COOPER, R. G.; McCARRELL, N.; SIMS-KNIGHT, J.; YUSSEN, S. R.; AND FLAVELL, J. H. 1972. The development of the distinction between perceiving and memorizing. *Child Development* 43:1365–81.

ARANOFF, M. 1976. *Word-formation in generative grammar* (Linguistic Inquiry Monograph 1). Cambridge, Mass.: MIT Press.

ARBIB, M. A. 1972. *The metaphorical brain.* New York: Wiley.

ARDREY, R. 1966. *The territorial imperative.* New York: Dell.

ARENDT, H. 1965. *Eichmann in Jerusalem: A report on the banality of evil.* New York: Viking Press.

ARIETI, S. 1959. Schizophrenia: The manifest symptomatology, the psychodynamic and formal mechanisms. In Arieti, S. (Ed.), *American handbook of psychiatry,* vol. 1, pp. 455–84. New York: Basic Books.

ARISTOTLE. CA. 330 B.C. On sleep and waking; On dreams; On prophesy in sleep. In *The works of Aristotle,* vol. 3. London: Oxford University Press, 1931.

ARMSTRONG, S. L.; GLEITMAN, L. R.; AND GLEITMAN, H. 1983. What some concepts might not be. *Cognition* 13:263–308.

ARNOLD, M. B. 1970. Perennial problems in the field of emotion. In Arnold, M. B. (Ed.), *Feelings and emotion: The Loyola symposium.* New York: Academic Press.

ARONFREED, J. 1968. *Conduct and conscience.* New York: Academic Press.

ARONFREED, J. 1969. The problem of imitation. In Lipsett, L. P., and Reese, H. W. (Eds.), *Advances in child development and behavior,* vol. 4. New York: Academic Press.

ARONSON, E. 1969. The theory of cognitive dissonance: A current perspective. In Berkowitz, L. (Ed.), *Advances in experimental social psychology,* vol. 4, pp. 1–34. New York: Academic Press.

ARONSON, E., AND CARLSMITH, J. M. 1963. The effect of the severity of threat on the devaluation of forbidden behavior. *Journal of Abnormal and Social Psychology* 66:584–88.

ARONSON, E., AND MILLS, J. 1959. The effect of severity of initiation on liking for a group. *Journal of Abnormal and Social Psychology* 59:177–81.

ARONSON, E.; TURNER, J. A.; AND CARLSMITH, J. M. 1963. Communicator credibility and communication discrepancy as determinants of opinion change. *Journal of Abnormal and Social Psychology* 67:31–36.

ASCH, S. E. 1946. Forming impressions of personality. *Journal of Abnormal and Social Psychology* 41:258–90.

ASCH, S. E. 1952. *Social psychology.* New York: Prentice-Hall.

ASCH, S. E. 1955. Opinions and social pressure. *Scientific American* 193:31–35.

ASCH, S. E. 1956. Studies of independence and conformity: A minority of one against a unanimous majority. *Psychological Monographs* 70 (9, Whole No. 416).

ASCH, S. E., AND GLEITMAN, H. 1953. Yielding to social pressure as a function of public or private commitment. Unpublished manuscript.

ASHER, E. J. 1935. The inadequacy of current intelligence tests for testing Kentucky Mountain children. *Journal of Genetic Psychology* 46:480–86.

ASLIN, R. N. 1987. Visual and auditory development in infancy. In Osofksy, J. D. (Ed.), *Handbook of infant development,* 2nd ed., pp. 5–97. New York: Wiley.

ATKINSON, J. W., AND McCLELLAND, D. C. 1948. The projective expression of needs. II. The effect of different intensities of the hunger drive on thematic apperception. *Journal of Experimental Psychology* 38:643–58.

ATKINSON, R. C., AND SHIFFRIN, R. M. 1968. Human memory: A proposed system and its control. In Spence, K. W., and Spence, J. T. (Eds.), *The psychology of learning and motivation,* vol. 2, pp. 89–105. New York: Academic Press.

ATTNEAVE, F. 1971. Multistability in perception. *Scientific American* 225:62–71.

AUGUSTINE. 397 A.D. *The confessions.* Translated and annotated by Pilkington, J. G. P. Cleveland: Fine Editions Press, 1876.

AUSTIN, J. 1962. *How to do things with words.* Oxford: Clarendon Press.

AVERILL, J. R. 1978. Anger. In Howe, H., and Dienstbier (Eds.), *Nebraska Symposium on Motivation.* Lincoln, Neb.: University of Nebraska Press.

AX, A. F. 1953. The physiological differentiation of fear and anger in humans. *Psychosomatic Medicine* 15:433–42.

AYLLON, T., AND AZRIN, N. H. 1968. *The token economy: A motivational system for therapy and rehabilitation.* New York: Appleton-Century-Crofts.

BABIGIAN, H. M. 1975. Schizophrenia: Epidemiology. In Freedman, A. M.; Kaplan, H. I.; and Sadock, B. J. (Eds.), *Comprehensive textbook of psychiatry—II,* vol. 1, pp. 860–66. Baltimore: Williams & Wilkins.

BADDELEY, A. D. 1976. *The psychology of human memory.* New York: Basic Books.

BADDELEY, A. D. 1978. The trouble with levels: A reexamination of Craik and Lockhart's framework for memory research. *Psychological Review* 85:139–52.

BADDELEY, A. D. 1986. *Working memory.* Oxford: Clarendon Press.

BAHRICK, H. P. 1984. Semantic memory content in permastore:50 years of memory for Spanish learned in school. *Journal of Experimental Psychology: General* 113:1–29.

BAILLARGEON, R. 1987a. Object permanence in 3½- and 4½-month-old infants. *Developmental Psychology* 23:655–664.

BAILLARGEON, R. 1987b. Young infants' reasoning about the physical and spatial properties of a hidden object. *Cognitive Development* 2:179–200.

BAILLARGEON, R., AND GRABER, M. 1987. Where is the rabbit? 5½-month-old infants' representation of the height of hidden objects. *Cognitive Development* 2:375–92.

BAILLARGEON, R.; SPELKE, E. S.; AND WASSERMAN, S. 1985. Object permanence in five-month-old infants. *Cognition* 20: 191–208.

BAKER, C., AND McCARTHY, J. (EDS.). 1981. *The logical problem of language acquisition.* Cambridge, Mass.: MIT Press.

BALL, W., AND TRONICK, E. 1971. Infant responses to impending collision: optical and real. *Science* 171:818–20.

BALOGH, R. D., AND PORTER, R. H. 1986. Olfactory preferences resulting from mere exposure in human neonates. *Infant Behavior and Development* 9:395–401.

BALTES, P. B.; REESE, H. W.; AND LIPSITT, L. P. 1980. Life-span developmental psychology. In Rosenzweig, M. R., and Porter, L. W. (Eds.), *Annual Review of Psychology* 31:65–110.

BALTES, P. B., AND SCHAIE, K. W. 1976. On the plasticity of intelligence in adulthood and old age. *American Psychologist* 31: 720–25.

BANCROFT, J. 1986. The roles of hormones in female sexuality. In Dennerstein and Fraser (Eds.), *Hormones and behavior* pp. 551–60. Amsterdam: International Society of Psychosomatic Obstetrics and Gynecology, Elsevier.

BANDURA, A. 1965. Influence of models' reinforcement contingencies on the acquisition of imitative responses. *Journal of Personality and Social Psychology* 1:589–95.

BANDURA, A.; ROSS, D.; AND ROSS, S. A. 1963. Imitation of film-mediated aggressive models. *Journal of Abnormal and Social Psychology* 66:3–11.

BANDURA, A., AND WALTERS, R. H. 1963. *Social learning and personality development*. New York: Holt, Rinehart & Winston.

BARASH, D. P. 1982. *Sociobiology and behavior*, 2nd ed. New York: Elsevier.

BARBER, T. X. 1969. *Hypnosis: A scientific approach*. New York: Van Nostrand Reinhold.

BARD AND RIOCH, 1937. Quoted in Gallistel, R. C., 1980. *The organization of action*. Hillsdale, N.J.: Erlbaum.

BAREFOOT, J. C.; DODGE, K. A.; PETERSON, B. L.; DAHLSTROM, W. G.; AND WILLIAMS, R. B. 1989. The Cook-Medley Hostility Scale: Item content and ability to predict survival. *Psychosomatic Medicine* 51:46–57.

BARLOW, H. B., AND HILL, R. M. 1963. Evidence for a physiological explanation of the waterfall illusion and figural after-effects. *Nature* 200:1345–47.

BARNETT, S. A. 1963. *The rat: A study in behavior*. Chicago: Aldine.

BARNOUW, V. 1963. *Culture and personality*. Homewood, Ill.: Dorsey Press.

BARON, J. 1985. What kinds of intelligence components are fundamental? In Chipman, S. F.; Segal, J. W.; and Glaser, R. (Eds.), *Thinking and learning skills. Vol. 2: Research and open questions*. Hillsdale, N.J.: Erlbaum.

BARON, J. 1988. *Thinking and deciding*. New York: Cambridge University Press.

BARRERA, M. E., AND MAURER, D. 1981. Recognition of mother's photographed face by the three-month-old infant. *Child Development* 52:714–16.

BARRY, H., III; CHILD, I. L.; AND BACON, M. K. 1959. Relation of child training to subsistence economy. *American Anthropologist* 61:51–63.

BARTLETT, F. C. 1932. *Remembering: A study in experimental and social psychology*. Cambridge, England: Cambridge University Press.

BARTOL, C. R., AND COSTELLO, N. 1976. Extraversion as a function of temporal duration of electric shock: An exploratory study. *Perceptual and Motor Skills* 42:1174.

BARTOSHUK, L. 1988. Taste. In Atkinson, R. C.; Herrnstein, R. J.; Lindzey, G.; and Luce, R. D. (Eds.), *Stevens' handbook of experimental psychology: Vol. 1. Perception and motivation*, rev. ed., pp. 461–502. New York: Wiley.

BASSO, A.; SPINNLER, H.; VALLAR, G.; AND ZANOBIO, E. 1982. Left hemisphere damage and selective impairment of auditory verbal short-term memory. *Neuropsychologia* 20:263–74.

BATES, E. 1976. *Language and context: The acquisition of pragmatics*. New York: Academic Press.

BATES, E., AND MACWHINNEY, B. 1982. Functionalist approaches to grammar. In Wanner, E., and Gleitman, L. (Eds.), *Language acquisition: State of the art*. New York: Cambridge University Press.

BATESON, P. P. G. 1984. The neural basis of imprinting. In Marler, P., and Terrace, H. S. (Eds.), *The biological basis of learning*, pp. 325–39. Dahlem-Konferenzen. Berlin: Springer.

BAUM, W. M. 1970. Extinction of avoidance response following response prevention. *Psychological Bulletin* 74:276–84.

BAUMRIND, D. 1967. Child care practices anteceding three patterns of preschool behavior. *Genetic Psychology Monographs* 75: 43–88.

BAUMRIND, D. 1971. Current patterns of parental authority. *Genetic Psychology Monographs* 1.

BAUMRIND, D. 1977. *Socialization determinants of personal agency*. Paper presented at the biennial meetings of the Society for Research in Child Development, New Orleans. (Cited in Maccoby, E. E. 1980. *Social development*. New York: Harcourt Brace Jovanovich.)

BAUMRIND, D. 1986. Sex differences in moral reasoning: Response to Walker's (1984) conclusion that there are none. *Child Development* 57:511–21.

BAYER, E. 1929. Beitrge zur Zweikomponententheorie des Hungers. *Zeitschrift der Psychologie* 112:1–54.

BAYLEY, N. 1970. Development of mental abilities. In Mussen, P. H. (Ed.), *Carmichael's manual of child psychology*, 3rd ed., pp. 1163–1209. New York: Wiley.

BECK, A. T. 1967. *Depression: Causes and treatment*. Philadelphia: University of Pennsylvania Press.

BECK, A. T. 1976. *Cognitive therapy and the emotional disorders*. New York: International Universities Press.

BECK, A. T. 1985. Cognitive therapy. In Kaplan, H. I., and Sadock, J. (Eds.), *Comprehensive textbook of psychiatry*, 4th ed. Baltimore: Williams & Wilkins.

BECK, A. T. 1988. Cognitive approaches to panic disorders: Theory and therapy. In Rachman, S., and Maser, J. D. (Eds.), *Panic: psychological perspectives*. Hillsdale, N.J.: Erlbaum.

BECK, A. T.; RUSH, A. J.; SHAW, B. F.; AND EMERY, G. 1979. *Cognitive therapy of depression*. New York: Guilford Press.

BECK, J. 1966. Effect of orientation and of shape similarity on perceptual grouping. *Perception and Psychophysics* 1:300–302.

BECK, J. 1982. Textural segmentation. In Beck, J. (Ed.), *Organization and representation in perception*, pp. 285–318. Hillsdale, N.J.: Erlbaum.

BÉKÉSY, G. VON. 1957. The ear. *Scientific American* 197:66–78.

BELL, A. P.; WEINBERG, M. S.; AND HAMMERSMITH, S. K. 1981. *Sexual preference: Its development in men and women*. Bloomington, Ind.: Indiana University Press.

BELL, R. Q. 1968. A reinterpretation of the direction of effects in studies of socialization. *Psychological Review* 75:81–95.

BELL, R. Q., AND HARPER, L. V. 1977. *Child effects on adults*. Hillsdale, N.J.: Erlbaum.

BELLAK, L. 1986. *The thematic apperception test, the children's apperception test, and the senior apperception test in clinical use*, 4th ed. Orlando, Fla.: Academic Press.

BELLI, R. F. 1989. Influences of misleading postevent information: Misinformation interference and acceptance. *Journal of Experimental Psychology: General* 118:72–85.

BELLUGI, U. 1971. Simplification in children's language. In Huxley, R., and Ingram, E., (Eds.), *Language acquisition: Models and methods*. New York: Academic Press.

BELLUGI, U.; POIZNER, H.; AND KLIMA, E. S. 1983. Brain organization for language: Clues from sign aphasia. *Human Neurobiology* 2:155–71.

BELOFF, H. 1957. The structure and origin of the anal character. *Genetic Psychology Monographs* 55:141–72.

BEM, D. J. 1967. Self-perception: An alternative interpretation of cognitive dissonance phenomena. *Psychological Review* 74:183–200.

BEM, D. J. 1972. Self-perception theory. In Berkowitz, L. (Ed.), *Advances in experimental social psychology,* vol. 6, pp. 2–62. New York: Academic Press.

BEM, D. J., AND ALLEN, A. 1974. On predicting some of the people some of the time: The search for cross-situational consistencies in behavior. *Psychological Review* 81:506–20.

BEM, S. L. 1984. Androgyny and gender schema theory: A conceptual and empirical integration. In Sondregger, T. B. (Ed.), *Nebraska Symposium on Motivation.* Lincoln, Neb.: University of Nebraska Press.

BENBOW, C. P. 1988. Sex differences in mathematical reasoning ability in intellectually talented preadolescents: Their nature, effects, and possible causes. *Behavior and Brain Sciences* 11:169–232.

BENBOW, C. P., AND STANLEY, J. C. 1983. Sex differences in mathematical reasoning: More facts. *Science* 222:1029–31.

BENTLEY, E. 1983. *The life of the drama.* New York: Atheneum.

BERGIN, A. E. 1967. An empirical analysis of therapeutic issues. In Arbuckle, D. (Ed.), *Counseling and psychotherapy: An overview,* pp. 175–208. New York: McGraw-Hill.

BERGIN, A. 1971. The evaluation of therapeutic outcomes. In Bergin, A. E. and Garfield, S. L. (Eds.), *Handbook of psychotherapy and behavior change: An empirical analysis.* New York: Wiley.

BERMANT, G., AND DAVIDSON, J. M. 1974. *Biological bases of sexual behavior.* New York: Harper & Row.

BERNARD, V. W.; OTTENBERG, P.; AND REDL, F. 1965. Dehumanization: A composite psychological defense in relation to modern war. In Schwebel, M. (Ed.), *Behavioral science and human survival,* pp. 64–82. Palo Alto, Calif.: Science and Behavior Books.

BERNHEIM, K. W., AND LEWINE, R. R. J. 1979. *Schizophrenia: Symptoms, causes, treatments.* New York: Norton.

BERSCHEID, E. 1985. Interpersonal attraction. In Lindzey, G., and Aronson, E. (Eds.), *Handbook of social psychology,* vol. 2, pp. 413–84. New York: Academic Press.

BERSCHEID, E.; DION, K.; WALSTER, E.; AND WALSTER, G. W. 1971. Physical attractiveness and dating choice: A test of the matching hypothesis. *Journal of Experimental Social Psychology* 7:173–89.

BERSCHEID, E., AND WALSTER, E. 1974. Physical attractiveness. In Berkowitz, L. (Ed.), *Advances in experimental social psychology,* vol. 7. New York: Academic Press.

BERSCHEID, E., AND WALSTER, E. H. 1978. *Interpersonal attraction,* 2nd ed. Reading, Mass.: Addison-Wesley.

BEST, D. L.; WILLIAMS, J. E.; CLOUD, J. M.; DAVIS, S. W.; ROBERTSON, L. S.; EDWARDS, J. R.; GILES, E.; AND FOWLES, J. 1977. Development of sex-trait stereotypes among young children in the United States, England, and Ireland. *Child Development* 48:1375–84.

BEVER, T. G. 1970. The cognitive basis for linguistic structures. In Hayes, J. R. (Ed.), *Cognition and the development of language,* pp. 279–362. New York: Wiley.

BICKMAN, L. 1971. The effect of another bystander's ability to help on bystander intervention in an emergency. *Journal of Experimental Social Psychology* 7:369–79.

BIEBER, I. 1965. Clinical aspects of male homosexuality. In Marmor, J. (Ed.), *Sexual inversion,* pp. 248–67. New York: Basic Books.

BIEBER, I.; DAIN, H. J.; DINCE, P. R.; DRELLICH, M. G.; GRAND, H. G.; GUNDLACH, R. H.; KREMER, M. W.; RIFKIN, A. H.; WILBUR, C. B.; AND BIEBER, T. B. 1962. *Homosexuality: A psychoanalytic study.* New York: Basic Books.

BIEDERMAN, I. 1985. Human image understanding: Recent experiments and a theory. *Computer Vision, Graphics, and Image Processing* 32:29–73.

BIEDERMAN, I. 1987. Recognition-by-components: A theory of human image understanding. *Psychological Review:* 94:115–47.

BIGELOW, A. 1987. Early words of blind children. *Journal of Child Language* 14(1):1–22.

BILSKY, L.; EVANS, R. A.; AND GILBERT, L. 1972. Generalization of associative clustering tendencies in mentally retarded adoles-cents: Effects of novel stimuli. *American Journal of Mental Deficiency* 77:77–84.

BIRCH, H. G.; PIÑEIRO, C.; ALCADE, E.; TOCA, T.; AND CRAVIOTA, J. 1971. Relation of *kwashiokor* in early childhood and intelligence at school age. *Pediatric Research* 5:579–92.

BJORK, R. A. 1970. Positive forgetting: The noninterference of items intentionally forgotten. *Journal of Verbal Learning and Verbal Behavior* 9:255–68.

BJÖRKLUND, A., AND STENEVI, U. 1984. Intracerebral implants: Neuronal replacement and reconstruction of damaged circuitries. *Annual Review of Neuroscience* 7:279–308.

BJÖRKLUND, A.; STENEVI, U.; SCHMIDT, R. H.; DUNNETT, S. B.; AND GAGE, F. H. 1983. Intracerebral grafting of neuronal suspensions I. Introduction and general methods of preparation. *Acta Physiologica Scandinavica Supplement* 522:1–8.

BLAKEMORE, C. 1977. *Mechanics of the mind.* New York: Cambridge University Press.

BLANK, M. A., AND FOSS, D. J. 1978. Semantic facilitation and lexical access during sentence processing. *Memory and Cognition* 6:644–52.

BLASI, A. 1980. Bridging moral cognition and moral action: A critical review of the literature. *Psychological Bulletin* 88:1–45.

BLASI, A. 1984. Moral identity: Its role in moral functioning. In Kurtines, W. M., and Gewirtz, L. (Eds.), *Morality, moral behavior, and moral development,* pp. 128–39. New York: Wiley.

BLASS, E. M., AND EPSTEIN, A. N. 1971. A lateral preoptic osmosensitive zone for thirst in the rat. *Journal of Comparative and Physiological Psychology* 76:378–94.

BLEULER, E. 1911. *Dementia praecox, or the group of schizophrenias.* English translation by Zinkin, J., and Lewis, N. D. C. New York: International Universities Press, 1950.

BLISS, E. L. 1980. Multiple personalities: Report of fourteen cases with implications for schizophrenia and hysteria. *Archives of General Psychiatry* 37:1388–97.

BLOCK, J. 1971. *Lives through time.* Berkeley, Calif.: Bancroft Books.

BLOCK, J. 1977. Advancing the psychology of personality: Paradigmatic shift or improving the quality of research. In Magnusson, D., and Endler, N. S. (Eds.), *Personality at the crossroads,* pp. 37–64. New York: Wiley.

BLOCK, N.J., AND DWORKIN, G. 1976. *The IQ controversy: Critical readings.* New York: Pantheon.

BLOOM, F. E. 1983. The endorphins: A growing family of pharmacologically pertinent peptides. *Annual Review of Pharmacology and Toxicology* 23:151–70.

BLOOM, F. E.; LAZERSON, A.; AND HOFSTADTER, L. 1988. *Brain, mind, and behavior.* New York: Freeman.

BLOOM, K. 1988. Quality of adult vocalizations affects the quality of infant vocalizations. *Journal of Child Language* 15(1):469–80.

BLOOM, L. 1970. *Language development: Form and function in emerging grammars.* Cambridge, Mass.: MIT Press.

BLOOM, P. 1990. Syntactic distinctions in child language. *Journal of Child Language* 17(2):343–56.

BLUM, G. S. 1949. A study of the psychoanalytic theory of psychosexual development. *Genetic Psychology Monographs* 39:3–99.

BLUM, G. S. 1950. *The Blacky pictures.* New York: Psychological Corporation.

BLUM, J. E.; JARVIK, L. F.; AND CLARK, E. T. 1970. Rate of change on selective tests of intelligence: A twenty-year longitudinal study. *Journal of Gerontology* 25:171–76.

BLURTON-JONES, N., AND KONNER, M. J. 1976. !Kung knowledge of animal behavior. In Lee, B., and DeVore, I. (Eds.), *Kalahari hunter-gatherers.* Cambridge, Mass: Harvard University Press.

BODEN, M. 1977. *Artificial intelligence and natural man.* New York: Basic Books.

BODNAR, R. J.; KELLY, D. D.; BRUTUS, M.; AND GLUSMAN, M.

1980. Stress-induced analgesia: Neural and hormonal determinants. *Neuroscience and biobehavioral reviews* 4:87–100.

BOGEN, J. E. 1969. The other side of the brain II: An appositional mind. *Bulletin of the Los Angeles Neurological Societies* 34:135–62.

BOGEN, J. E.; FISHER, E. D.; AND VOGEL, P. J. 1965. Cerebral commissurotomy: A second case report. *Journal of the American Medical Association* 194:1328–29.

BOLLES, R. C. 1970. Species-specific defense reactions and avoidance learning. *Psychological Review* 77:32–48.

BOLLES, R. C., AND FANSELOW, M. S. 1982. Endorphins and behavior. *Annual Review of Psychology* 33:87–102.

BOOTH, D. A. 1980. Acquired behavior controlling energy and output. In Stunkard, A. J. (Ed.), *Obesity,* pp. 101–43. Philadelphia: Saunders.

BORDEN, R. J. 1980. Audience influence. In Paulus, P. B. (Ed.), *Psychology of group influence,* pp. 99–132. Hillsdale, N.J.: Erlbaum.

BORER, H., AND WEXLER, K. 1987. The maturation of syntax. In Roeper, T., and Williams, E. (Eds.), *Parameter setting and language acquisition.* Dordrecht, Netherlands: Reidel.

BORG, G.; DIAMANT, H.; STROM, C.; AND ZOTTERMAN, Y. 1967. The relation between neural and perceptual intensity: A comparative study of neural and psychophysical responses to taste stimuli. *Journal of Physiology* 192:13–20.

BORING, E. G. 1930. A new ambiguous figure. *American Journal of Psychology* 42:444–45.

BORING, E. G. 1942. *Sensation and perception in the history of experimental psychology.* New York: Appleton-Century-Crofts.

BORING, E. G. 1964. Size constancy in a picture. *American Journal of Psychology* 77:494–98.

BORING, E. G.; LANGFELD, H. S.; AND WELD, H. P. 1939. *Introduction to psychology.* New York: Wiley.

BORKE, H. 1975. Piaget's mountains revisited: Changes in the egocentric landscape. *Developmental Psychology* 11:240–43.

BORNSTEIN, M. H. 1985. Perceptual development. In Bornstein, M. H., and Lamb, M. E. (Eds.), *Developmental psychology: An advanced textbook,* pp. 81–132. Hillsdale, N.J.: Erlbaum.

BOTVIN, G. J., AND MURRAY, F. B. 1975. The efficacy of peer modelling and social conflict in the acquisition of conservation. *Child Development* 46:796–97.

BOUCHARD, C.; TREMBLAY, A.; DESPRÈS, J-P.; NADEAU, A.; LUPIEN, P. L.; THÈRIAULT, G.; DUSSAULT, J.; MOORJANI, S.; PINAULT, S. M.; AND FOURNIER, G. 1990. The response to long-term overfeeding in identical twins. *New England Journal of Medicine* 322:1477–82.

BOUCHARD, T. J., JR., AND McGUE, M. 1981. Familial studies of intelligence: A review. *Science* 212:1055–59.

BOUCHARD, T. J., JR. 1984. Twins reared apart and together: What they tell us about human diversity. In Fox, S. (Ed.), *The chemical and biological bases of individuality,* pp. 147–84. New York: Plenum.

BOWER, G. H. 1970. Analysis of a mnemonic device. *American Scientist* 58:496–510.

BOWER, G. H.; BLACK, J. B.; AND TURNER, T. J. 1979. Scripts in memory for text. *Cognitive Psychology* 11:177–220.

BOWER, T. G. R. 1966. Slant perception and shape constancy in infants. *Science* 151:832–34.

BOWERMAN, M. 1982. Reorganizational processes in language development. In Wanner, E., and Gleitman, L. R. (Eds.), *Language development: State of the art.* New York: Cambridge University Press.

BOWERS, K. S. 1984. On being unconsciously influenced and informed. In Bowers, K. S., and Meichenbaum, D. (Eds.), *The unconscious reconsidered.* New York: Wiley.

BOWLBY, J. 1969. *Attachment and loss: Vol. 1. Attachment.* New York: Basic Books.

BOWLBY, J. 1973. *Separation and loss.* New York: Basic Books.

BOWMAKER, J. K., AND DARTNALL, H. J. A. 1980. Visual pigments and rods and cones in a human retina. *Journal of Physiology*

298:501–11.

BRABECK, M. 1983. Moral judgement: Theory and research on differences between males and females. *Developmental Review* 3:274–91.

BRADLEY, D. C.; GARRETT, M. F.; AND ZURIF, E. G. 1979. Syntactic deficits in Broca's aphasia. In Caplan, D., (Ed.), *Biological studies of mental processes.* Cambridge, Mass.: MIT Press.

BRADLEY, G. W. 1978. Self-serving biases in the attribution process: A reexamination of the fact or fiction question. *Journal of Personality and Social Psychology* 13:420–32.

BRADY, I. 1983. Special section. Speaking in the name of the real: Freeman and Mead on Samoa. *American Anthropologist* 85:908–47.

BRADY, J. P. 1985. Behavior therapy. In Kaplan, H. I., and Sadock, J. (Eds.), *Comprehensive textbook of psychiatry,* 4th ed, pp. 1365–73. Baltimore: Williams & Wilkins.

BRAIN, L. 1965. *Speech disorders: Aphasia, apraxia, and agnosia.* London: Butterworth.

BRAINE, M. D. S. 1963. The ontogeny of English phrase structure: The first phase. *Language* 39:3–13.

BRAINE, M. D. S. 1976. Children's first word combinations. *Monographs of the Society for Research in Child Development* 41(1, Serial No. 164).

BRAINERD, C. J. 1978. The stage question in cognitive development. *Behavioral and Brain Sciences* 2:173–213.

BRANSFORD, J. D., AND JOHNSON, M. K. 1972. Contextual prerequisites for understanding. *Journal of Verbal Learning and Verbal Behavior* 11:717–26.

BRAZELTON, T. B. 1972. Implications of infant development among the Mayan Indians of Mexico. *Human Development* 15: 90–111.

BRAZELTON, T. B. 1962. A child-oriented approach to toilet training. *Pediatrics* 29:121–28.

BREGER, L.; HUNTER, I.; AND LANE, R. W. 1971. The effect of stress on dreams. *Psychological Issues* 7(3, Monograph 27):1–213.

BREGGIN, P. R. 1979. *Electroshock: Its brain-disabling effects.* New York: Springer.

BREHM, J. W. 1956. Post-decision changes in desirability of alternatives. *Journal of Abnormal and Social Psychology* 52:384–89.

BRELAND, K., AND BRELAND, M. 1951. A field of applied animal psychology. *American Psychologist* 6:202–204.

BRELAND, K., AND BRELAND, M. 1961. *American Psychologist* 16:681–84.

BRETHERTON, I.; McNEW, S.; AND BEEGHLY-SMITH, M. 1981. Early person knowledge as expressed in gestural and verbal communications. When do infants acquire a "theory of mind"? In Lamb, M. E., and Sherrod, L. R. (Eds.), *Infant social cognition.* Hillsdale, N.J.: Erlbaum.

BRICKMAN, J. C., AND D'AMATO, B. 1975. Exposure effects in a free-choice situation. *Journal of Personality and Social Psychology* 32:415–20.

BRIDGES, K. M. B. 1932. Emotional development in early infancy. *Child Development* 3:324–41.

BROADBENT, D. E. 1958. *Perception and communication.* London: Pergamon Press.

BRODIE, H. K. H.; GARTRELL, N.; DOERING, C.; AND RHUE, T. 1974. Plasma testosterone levels in heterosexual and homosexual men. *American Journal of Psychiatry* 131:82–83.

BRODY, E. B., AND BRODY, N. 1976. *Intelligence: Nature, determinants, and consequences.* New York: Academic Press.

BRODY, N. 1988. *Personality.* New York: Academic Press.

BROEN, W. E., JR. 1968. *Schizophrenia: Research and theory.* New York: Academic Press.

BRONFENBRENNER, U. 1975. Is early intervention effective? In Guttentag, M., and Struening, E. L. (Eds.), *Handbook of evaluation research,* vol. 2. Beverly Hills, Calif.: Sage.

BRONSON, W. C. 1966. Central orientations. A study of behavior

organization from childhood to adolescence. *Child Development* 37: 125–55.

BRONSON, W. C. 1967. Adult derivatives of emotional expressiveness and reactivity control: Developmental continuities from childhood to adulthood. *Child Development* 38:801–17.

BROWN. A. L. 1974. The role of strategic memory in retardate-memory. In Ellis, N. R. (Ed.), *International review of research in mental retardation*, vol. 7, pp. 55–108. New York: Academic Press.

BROWN, A. L.; BRANSFORD, J. D.; FERRARA, R. A.; AND CAMPIONE, J. C. 1983. Learning, remembering, and understanding. In Mussen, P. (Ed.), *Carmichael's manual of child psychology: Vol. 3. Cognitive development* (Markman, E. M., and Flavell, J. H., volume editors). New York: Wiley.

BROWN, A. L.; CAMPIONE, J. C.; BRAY, N. W.; AND WILCOX, B. L. 1973. Keeping track of changing variables: Effects of rehearsal training and rehearsal prevention in normal and retarded adolescents. *Journal of Experimental Psychology* 101:123–31.

BROWN, A. L.; CAMPIONE, J. C.; AND DAY, J. D. 1981. Learning to learn: On training students to learn from texts. *Educational Researcher* 10:14–21.

BROWN, J. F. 1940. *The psychodynamics of abnormal behavior.* New York: McGraw-Hill.

BROWN, J. W. 1972. *Aphasia, apraxia, and agnosia.* Springfield, Ill.: Thomas.

BROWN, R. 1954. Mass phenomena. In Lindzey, G. (Ed.), *Handbook of social psychology*, vol. 2, pp. 833–76. Reading, Mass.: Addison-Wesley.

BROWN, R. 1957. Linguistic determinism and parts of speech. *Journal of Abnormal and Social Psychology* 55:1–5.

BROWN, R. 1958. *Words and things.* New York: Free Press, Macmillan.

BROWN, R. 1965. *Social psychology.* New York: Free Press, Macmillan.

BROWN, R., AND BELLUGI, U. 1964. Three processes in the child's acquisition of syntax. *Harvard Educational Review* 34:133–51.

BROWN, R. 1973. *A first language: The early stages.* Cambridge, Mass.: Harvard University Press.

BROWN, R.; CAZDEN, C.; AND BELLUGI-KLIMA, U. 1969. The child's grammar from 1 to 11. In Hill, J. P. (Ed.), *Minnesota Symposium on Child Psychology*, vol. 2, pp. 28–73. Minneapolis: University of Minnesota Press.

BROWN, R., AND HANLON, C. 1970. Derivational complexity and order of acquisition in child speech. In Hayes, J. R. (Ed.), *Cognition and the development of language*, pp. 11–53. New York: Wiley.

BROWN, R., AND KULIK, J. 1977. Flashbulb memories. *Cognition* 5:73–99.

BROWN, R., AND MCNEILL, D. 1966. The tip of the tongue phenomenon. *Journal of Verbal Learning and Verbal Behavior* 5:325–27.

BRUCE, V., AND GREEN, P. 1985. *Visual perception: Physiology, psychology, and ecology.* Hillsdale, N.J.: Erlbaum.

BRUCH, H. 1973. *Eating disorders.* New York: Basic Books.

BRUNER, J. S. 1974/1975. From communication to language—a psychological perspective. *Cognition* 3:255–78.

BRUNER, J. S., AND TAGIURI, R. 1954. The perception of people. In Lindzey, G. (Ed.), *Handbook of social psychology*, vol. 2. Reading, Mass.: Addison-Wesley.

BRYAN, W. L., AND HARTER, N. 1897. Studies in the physiology and psychology of telegraphic language. *Psychological Review* 4:27–53.

BRYAN, W. L., AND HARTER, N. 1899. Studies on the telegraphic language: The acquisition of a hierarchy of habits. *Psychological Review* 6:345–75.

BUCHANAN, B. G., AND SHORTLIFFE, E. H. (Eds.). 1985. *Rule-based expert systems: The MYCIN experiments of the Stanford Heuristics Programming Project.* Reading, Mass: Addison-Wesley.

BUGELSKI, B. R., AND ALAMPAY, D. A. 1961. The role of fre-

quency in developing perceptual sets. *Canadian Journal of Psychology* 15:205–11.

BULLOUGH, E. 1912. "Psychical distance" as a factor in art and an aesthetic principle. *British Journal of Psychology* 5:87–118.

BURGESS, E. W., AND WALLIN, P. 1943. Homogamy in social characteristics. *American Journal of Sociology* 49:109–24.

BURNETT, S. A.; LANE, D. M.; AND DRATT, L. M. 1979. Spatial differences and sex differences in quantitative ability. *Intelligence* 3:345–54.

BURTON, R. V. 1963. Generality of honesty reconsidered. *Psychological Review* 70:481–99.

BURTON, R. V., AND WHITING, J. W. M. 1961. The absent father and cross-sex identity. *Merrill-Palmer Quarterly* 7:85–95.

BURY, J. B. 1932. *The idea of progress.* New York: Macmillan.

BUSS, A. H., AND PLOMIN, R. 1975. *A temperament theory of personality development.* New York:Wiley.

BUSS, A. H., AND PLOMIN, R. 1984. *Temperament: Early developing personality traits.* Hillsdale, N.J.: Erlbaum.

BUSS, D. M., AND CRAIK, K. H. 1983. Dispositional analysis of everyday conduct. *Journal of Personality* 51:393–412.

BUTTERS, N., AND ALBERT, M. S. 1982. Processes underlying failures to recall remote events. In Cermak, L. S. (Ed.), *Human memory and amnesia*, pp. 257–74. Hillsdale, N.J.: Erlbaum.

BYRNE, R. 1989. Chess-playing computer closing in on champions. *New York Times*, September 26, 1989, C1 and 12.

CAIN, W. S. 1977. Differential sensitivity for smell: "Noise" at the nose. *Science* 195:796–98.

CAIN, W. S. 1988. Olfaction. In Atkinson, R. C.; Herrnstein, R. J.; Lindzey, G.; and Luce, R. D. (Eds.), *Stevens' handbook of experimental psychology: Vol. 1. Perception and motivation*, rev. ed., pp. 409–59. New York: Wiley.

CAIRNS, R. B. 1984. Research in language comprehension. In R. C. Naremore (Ed.), *Language science.* San Diego: College-Hill Press.

CAMPBELL, J. B., AND HAWLEY, C. W. 1982. Study habits and Eysenck's theory of extraversion-introversion. *Journal of Research in Personality* 16:139–46.

CAMPBELL, J. D.; TESSER, A., AND FAIREY, P. J. 1986. Conformity and attention to the stimulus: Some temporal and contextual dynamics. *Journal of Personality and Social Psychology* 51:315–24.

CAMPIONE, J. C., AND BROWN, A. L. 1977. Memory and metamemory development in educable retarded children. In Kail, R. V., Jr., and Hagen, J. W. (Eds.), *Perspectives on the development of memory and cognition.* Hillsdale, N.J.: Erlbaum.

CAMPIONE, J. C.; BROWN, A. L.; AND FERRARA, R. A. 1982. Mental retardation and intelligence. In Sternberg, R. J. (Ed.), *Handbook of human intelligence*, pp. 392–492. New York: Cambridge University Press.

CAMPOS, J. J.; BARRETT, K. C.; LAMB, M. E.; GOLDSMITH, H. H.; AND STERNBERG, C. 1983. Socioemotional development. In Mussen, P. E. (Ed.), *Carmichael's manual of child psychology: Vol. 2. Infancy and developmental psychobiology* (Haith, M. M., and Campos, J. J., volume editor), pp. 783–916. New York: Wiley.

CANNON, W. B. 1927. The James-Lange theory of emotions: A critical examination and an alternative theory. *American Journal of Psychology* 39:106–24.

CANNON, W. B. 1929. *Bodily changes in pain, hunger, fear and rage*, rev. ed. New York: Appleton-Century.

CANNON, W. B. 1932 and 1960 (revised and enlarged). *The wisdom of the body.* New York: Norton.

CANTOR, J. R.; ZILLMAN, D.; AND BRYANT, J. 1975. Enhancement of experienced sexual arousal in response to erotic stimuli through misattribution of unrelated residual excitation. *Journal of Personality and Social Psychology* 32:69–75.

CANTOR, N., AND MISCHEL, W. 1977. Traits as prototypes: Ef-

fects on recognition memory. *Journal of Personality and Social Psychology* 35:38–48.

CANTOR, N., AND MISCHEL, W. 1979. Prototypes in person perception. In L. Berkowitz (Ed.), *Advances in experimental social psychology,* vol. 12. New York: Academic Press.

CAPORAEL, L. 1976. Satanism: The satan loosed in Salem? *Science* 192:21–26.

CAREY, G., AND GOTTESMAN, I. I. 1981. Twin and family studies of anxiety, phobic, and obsessive disorders. In Klein, D. F., and Rabkin, J. (Eds.), *Anxiety: New research and changing concepts,* pp. 117–36. New York: Raven Press.

CAREY, S. 1982. Semantic development: State of the art. In Wanner, E., and Gleitman, L. R. (Eds.), *Language acquisition: State of the art.* New York: Cambridge University Press.

CAREY, S. 1985. *Conceptual change in childhood.* Cambridge, Mass.: MIT Press.

CARLSON, G., AND TANENHAUS, M. 1988. Thematic roles and language comprehension. In W. Wilkins (Ed.), *Syntax and semantics: Vol. 21. Thematic relations.* San Diego: Academic Press.

CARLSON, N. R. 1986. *Physiology of behavior,* 3rd ed. Boston: Allyn and Bacon.

CARON, A. J.; CARON, R. F.; AND CARLSON, V. R. 1979. Infant perception of the invariant shape of objects varying in slant. *Child Development* 50:716–21.

CARR, D.; BULLEN, B.; KRINAR, G.; ARNOLD, M.; ROSENBLATT, M.; BEITINS, I. Z.; MARTIN, J. B.; AND McARTHUR, J. W. 1981. Physical conditioning facilitates the exercise-induced secretion of beta-endorphin and beta-lipopotrin in women. *New England Journal of Medicine* 305:560–63.

CARRINGTON, P. 1972. Dreams and schizophrenia. *Archives of General Psychiatry* 26:343–50.

CARROLL, L. 1865. *Alice in wonderland.* Abridged by Frank, J. and illustrated by Torrey, M. M. New York: Random House, 1969.

CARROLL, L. 1871. *Through the looking glass and what Alice found there.* Illustrated by John Tenniel, colored by Fritz Kredel. New York: Random House, 1946.

CARTWRIGHT, R. D. 1977. *Night life: Explorations in dreaming.* Englewood Cliffs, N.J.: Prentice-Hall.

CASE, R. 1978. Intellectual development from birth to adulthood: A neo-Piagetian interpretation. In Siegler, R. S. (Ed.), *Children's thinking: What develops?,* pp. 37–72. Hillsdale, N.J.: Erlbaum.

CASE, R. 1985. *Intellectual development: Birth to adulthood.* New York: Academic Press.

CATEL, J. 1953. Ein Beitrag zur Frage von Hirnenentwicklung unter Menschwerdung. *Klinische Weisschriften* 31:473–75.

CATTELL, R. B. 1957. *Personality and motivation structure and measurement.* New York: Harcourt, Brace and World.

CATTELL, R. B. 1963. Theory of fluid and crystallized intelligence: A critical experiment. *J. of Educational Psychology* 54: 1–22.

CATTELL, R. B. 1966. *The scientific analysis of personality.* Chicago: Aldine.

CATTELL, R. B., AND NESSLEROADE, J. R. 1967. Likeness and completeness theories examined by sixteen personality factor measures on stably and unstably married couples. *Journal of Personality and Social Psychology* 7:351–61.

CAZDEN, U. 1968. The acquisition of noun and verb inflections. *Child Development* 39:433–48.

CERMAK, L. S. (Ed.). 1982. *Human memory and amnesia.* Hillsdale, N.J.: Erlbaum.

CERNOCH, J. M., AND PORTER, R. H. 1985. Recognition of maternal axillary odors by infants. *Child Development* 56:1593–98.

CHAIKEN, S. 1987. The heuristic model of persuasion. In Zanna, M. P.; Olson, J. M.; and Herman, C. P. (Eds.), *Social influence: The Ontario symposium,* vol. 5, pp. 3–40. Hillsdale, N.J.: Erlbaum.

CHAMBERS, D., AND REISBERG, D. 1985. Can mental images be ambiguous? *Journal of Experimental Psychology: Human Perception and Performance* 11:317–28.

CHAPLIN, W. F., AND GOLDBERG, L. R. 1984. A failure to replicate the Bem and Allen study of individual differences in cross-situational consistency. *J. of Person. and Social Psychology* 47:1074–90.

CHAPMAN, L. J., AND CHAPMAN, J. P. 1973. *Disordered thought in schizophrenia.* New York: Appleton-Century-Crofts.

CHARNESS, N. 1981. Search in chess: Age and skill differences. *Journal of General Psychology: General* 110:21–38.

CHASE, W. G., AND SIMON, H. A. 1973a. Perception in chess. *Cognitive Psychology* 4:55–81.

CHASE, W. G., AND SIMON, H. A. 1973b. The mind's eye in chess. In Chase, W. G., *Visual information processing.* New York: Academic Press.

CHENEY, D. L., AND WRANGHAM, R. W. 1986. Predation. In Smuts, B. B.; Cheney, D. L.; Seyfarth, R. M.; Wrangham, R. W.; and Struhsaker, T. T., *Primate societies.* Chicago: Univ. of Chicago Press.

CHENG, P. W., AND HOLYOAK, K. J. 1985. Pragmatic reasoning schemas. *Cognitive Psychology* 17:391–416.

CHENG, P. W.; HOLYOAK, K. J.; NISBETT, R. E.; AND OLIVER, L. M. 1986. Pragmatic versus syntactic approaches to training deductive reasoning. *Cognitive Psychology* 18:293–328.

CHERRY, E. C. 1953. Some experiments upon the recognition of speech, with one and with two ears. *Journal of the Acoustical Society of America* 25:975–79.

CHESS, S. 1987. Let us consider the roles of temperament and of fortuitous events. Peer commentary on Plomin, R., and Daniels, D. 1987. Why are children from the same family so different from one another? *Behavioral and Brain Sciences* 10:38–39.

CHEVRIER, J., AND DELORME, A. 1983. Depth perception in Pandora's box and size illusion: Evolution with age. *Perception* 12:177–85.

CHI, M. T. H. 1978. Knowledge structures and memory development. In Siegler, R. S. (Ed.), *Children's thinking: What develops?,* pp. 73–96. Hillsdale, N.J.: Erlbaum.

CHI, M. T. H. 1985. Changing conceptions of sources of memory development. *Human Development* 28:50–56.

CHI, M. T. H.; FELTOVICH, P. J.; AND GLASER, R. 1981. Categorization and representation of physics problems by experts and novices. *Cognitive Science* 5:121–52.

CHI, M. T. H.; GLAZER, R.; AND REES, E. 1982. Expertise in problem solving. In R. Sternberg (Ed.), *Advances in the psychology of human intelligence,* vol. 1. Hillsdale, N.J.: Erlbaum.

CHLOPAN, B. E.; McCAIN, M. L.; CARBONELL, J. L.; AND HAGEN, R. L. 1985. Empathy: Review of available measures. *Journal of Personality and Social Psychology* 48:635–53.

CHODOFF, P. 1954. A reexamination of some aspects of conversion hysteria. *Psychiatry* 17:75–81.

CHOMSKY, N. 1957. *Syntactic structures.* The Hague: Mouton.

CHOMSKY, N. 1965. *Aspects of the theory of syntax.* Cambridge, Mass.: MIT Press.

CHOMSKY, N. 1975. *Reflections on language.* New York: Pantheon.

CHOMSKY, N. 1980. *Rules and representations.* New York: Columbia University Press.

CHOMSKY, C. 1984. From hand to mouth: A study of speech and language through touch (manuscript, Harvard University).

CHOMSKY, N. 1987. *Knowledge of language: Its nature, origin, and use.* New York: Praeger.

CHOMSKY, N., AND HALLE, M. 1968. *The sound patterns of English.* New York: Harper & Row.

CHRISTIE, R. 1954. Authoritarianism re-examined. In Christie, R., and Jahoda, M. (Eds.), *Studies in the scope and method of "The authoritarian personality."* New York: Free Press, Macmillan.

CIALDINI, R. B. 1984. *Influence: How and why people agree to do things.* New York: Quill.

CIALDINI, R. B.; PETTY, R. E.; AND CACIOPPO, J. T. 1981. Atti-

tude and attitude change. In Rosenzweig, M. R., and Porter, L. W. (Eds.), *Annual Review of Psychology* 32:357–404.

CIALDINI, R. R.; VINCENT, J. E.; LEWIS, S. K.; CATALAN, J.; WHEELER, D.; AND DARBY, L. 1975. Reciprocal concession procedure for inducing compliance: The door-in-the-face technique. *Journal of Personality and Social Psychology* 31:206–15.

CLARIDGE, D. 1983. The Eysenck psychoticism scale. In Butcher, J. N., and Spielberger, C. (Eds.), *Advances in personality assessment*, vol. 2, pp. 71–114. Hillsdale, N.J.: Erlbaum.

CLARK, D. M. 1986. A cognitive approach to panic. *Behavior Research and Therapy* 24:461–70.

CLARK, D. M. 1988. A cognitive model of panic attacks. In Rachman, S., and Maser, J. D. (Eds.), *Panic: Psychological perspectives.* Hillsdale, N.J.: Erlbaum.

CLARK, E. V. 1973. What's in a word?: On the child's acquisition of semantics in his first language. In Moore, T. E. (Ed.), *Cognitive development and the acquisition of language.* New York: Academic Press.

CLARK, E. V. 1982. The young word-maker: A case study of innovation in the child's lexicon. In Wanner, E., and Gleitman, L. R. (Eds.), *Language acquisition: State of the art.* New York: Cambridge University Press.

CLARK, E. V. 1987. The Principle of contrast: A constraint on acquisition. In MacWhinney, B. (Ed.), *Mechanisms of language acquisition,* Hillsdale, N.J.: Erlbaum.

CLARK, H. H. 1978. Inferring what is meant. In Levelt, W., and Flores d'Arcais, G.(Eds.), *Studies in the perception of language.* Chichester: Wiley.

CLARK, H. H. 1979. Responding to indirect speech acts. *Cognitive Psychology* 11:430–77.

CLARK, H. H., AND CLARK, E. V. 1977. *Psychology and language: An introduction to psycholinguistics.* New York: Harcourt Brace Jovanovich.

CLARKE, A. C. 1952. An examination of the operation of residual propinquity as a factor in mate selection. *American Sociological Review* 27:17–22.

CLARKE-STEWART, K. A. 1978. And daddy makes three: The father's impact on mother and young child. *Child Development* 49:466–78.

CLARKE-STEWART, A.; PERLMUTTER, M.; AND FRIEDMAN, S. 1988. *Lifelong human development.* New York: Wiley.

CLECKLEY, J. 1976. *The mask of sanity,* 5th ed. St. Louis: Mosby.

CLEMENTE, C. D., AND CHASE, M. H. 1973. Neurological substrates of aggressive behavior. *Annual Review of Physiology* 35: 329–56.

COBB, S. 1941. *Foundations of neuropsychiatry.* Baltimore: Williams & Wilkins.

COBB, S., AND ROSE, R. M. 1973. Hypertension, peptic ulcer and diabetes in air traffic controllers. *Journal of the American Medical Association* 224:489–92.

COFFMAN, C. E. 1985. Review of Kaufman's Assessment Battery for Children. *Ninth Mental Measurements Yearbook,* vol. 1. pp. 771–73.

COHEN, D. B., AND WOLFE, G. 1973. Dream recall and repression: Evidence for an alternative hypothesis. *Journal of Consulting and Clinical Psychology* 41:349–55.

COHEN, H. 1972. Active (REM) sleep deprivation. In Chase, M. H. (Ed.), *The sleeping brain: Perspectives in the brain sciences,* vol. 1, pp. 343–47. Los Angeles: Brain Research Institute, University of California.

COHEN, N.J., AND SQUIRE, L. R. 1980. Preserved learning and retention of pattern-analyzing skill in amnesia: Dissociation of knowing how and knowing what. *Science* 210:207–10.

COHEN, R. A. 1975. Manic-depressive illness. In Freedman, A. M.; Kaplan, H. I.; and Sadock, B. J. (Eds.), *Comprehensive textbook of psychiatry—II,* vol. 1, pp. 1012–24. Baltimore: Williams & Wilkins.

COHEN, Y. A. 1953. A study of interpersonal relations in a Jamaican community. Unpublished doctoral dissertation, Yale University.

COLARUSSO, C. A., AND NEMIROFF, R. A. 1981. *Adult development: A new dimension in psychodynamic theory and practice.* New York: Plenum Press.

COLBY, A., AND KOHLBERG, L. 1986. *The measurement of moral judgment.* New York: Cambridge University Press.

COLBY, A.; KOHLBERG, L.; GIBBS, J.; AND LIEBERMAN, M. 1983. A longitudinal study of moral judgment. *Monographs of the Society for Research in Child Development* 48 (1, Serial No. 200).

COLE, J. O., AND DAVIS, J. M. 1975. Antidepressant drugs. In Freedman, A. M.; Kaplan, H. I.; and Sadock, B. J. (Eds.), *Comprehensive textbook of psychiatry,* vol 2. pp. 1941–56. Baltimore: Williams & Wilkins.

COLE, M. 1975. An ethnographic psychology of cognition. In Brislin, R. W.; Bochner, S.; and Lonner, W. J. (Eds.), *Cross-cultural perspectives on learning.* New York: Wiley.

COLE, M.; GAY J.; GLICK J. A.; AND SHARP, D. W. 1971. *The cultural context of learning and thinking.* New York: Basic Books.

COLE, M., AND SCRIBNER, S. 1974. *Culture and thought: A psychological introduction.* New York: Wiley.

COLEMAN, J.C. 1972. *Abnormal psychology and modern life,* 4th ed. Glenview, Ill.: Scott, Foresman.

COLEMAN, J. C.; BUTCHER, J. N.; AND CARSON, R. C. 1984. *Abnormal psychology and modern life,* 7th ed. Glenview, Ill.: Scott, Foresman.

COLEMAN, J. S.; CAMPBELL, E. Q.; HOBSON, C. J.; McPARTLAND, J.; MOOD, A.; WEINFELD, F. D.; AND YORK, R. L. 1966. *Equality of educational opportunity.* Washington, D. C.: U. S. Government Printing Office.

COLLINS, A. M., AND LOFTUS, E. F. 1975. A spreading activation theory of semantic processing. *Psychological Review* 82:407–28.

COLLINS, A. M., AND QUILLIAN, M. R. 1969. Retrieval time from semantic memory. *Journal of Verbal Learning and Verbal Behavior* 8:240–47.

COLLINS, R. L., AND FULLER, J. L. 1968. Audiogenic seizure prone (ASP): A gene affecting behavior in linkage group VIII of the mouse. *Science* 162:1137–39.

COLLIS, G. 1975. The integration of gaze and vocal behavior in the mother-infant dyad. Paper presented at Third International Child Language Symposium, London.

COLWILL, R. M., AND RESCORLA, R. A. 1985. Postconditioning devaluation of a reinforcer affects instrumental responding. *Journal of Experimental Psychology: Animal Behavior Processes* 11:120–32.

COMRIE, B. 1987. Introduction. In Comrie, B. (Ed.), *The world's major languages.* New York: Oxford University Press.

CONEL, J. L. 1939. *The postnatal development of the human cortex,* vol. 1. Cambridge, Mass.: Harvard University Press.

CONEL, J. L. 1947. *The postnatal development of the human cortex,* vol. 3. Cambridge, Mass.: Harvard University Press.

CONEL, J. L. 1955. *The postnatal development of the human cortex,* vol. 5. Cambridge, Mass.: Harvard University Press.

CONRAD, C. 1972. Cognitive economy in semantic memory. *Journal of Experimental Psychology* 92:149–54.

COOK, M., AND BIRCH, R. 1984. Infant perception of the shapes of tilted plane forms. *Infant Behavior and Development* 7:389–402.

COOK, M., AND MINEKA, S. 1989. Observational conditioning of fear to fear-relevant versus fear-irrelevant stimuli in rhesus monkeys. *Journal of Abnormal Psychology* 98:448–59.

COOLEY, C. H. 1902. *Human nature and the social order.* New York: Scribner's.

COOPER, J., AND FAZIO, R. H. 1984. A new look at dissonance theory. In Berkowitz, L. (Ed.), *Advances in experimental social psychology,* vol. 17. New York: Academic Press.

COOPER, J.; ZANNA, M. P.; AND GOETHALS, G. R. 1974. Mistreatment of an esteemed other as a consequence affecting dissonance reduction. *Journal of Experimental Social Psychology* 10:224–33.

COOPER, L. A., AND SHEPARD, R. N. 1973. The time required to prepare for a rotated stimulus. *Memory and Cognition* 1:246–50.

COREN, S., AND GIRGUS, J. S. 1978. *Seeing is deceiving: The psychology of visual illusions.* Hillsdale, N.J.: Erlbaum.

COREN, S.; PORAC, C.; AND WARD, L.M. 1978, 1984. *Sensation and perception.* New York: Academic Press.

COREN, S., AND WARD, L. M. 1989. *Sensation and perception,* 3rd ed. San Diego, Calif.: Harcourt Brace Jovanovich.

CORKIN, S. 1965. Tactually-guided maze-learning in man: Effects of unilateral cortical excisions and bilateral hippocampal lesions. *Neuropsychologia* 3:339–51.

CORKIN, S. 1984. Lasting consequences of bilateral medial temporal lobectomy: Clinical course and experimental findings in H. M. *Semin. Neurology* 4:249–59.

CORNSWEET, T. M. 1970. *Visual perception.* New York: Academic Press.

CORY, T. L.; ORMISTON, D. W.; SIMMEL, E.; AND DAINOFF, M. 1975. Predicting the frequency of dream recall. *Journal of Abnormal Psychology* 84:261–66.

COSTA, P. T., JR.; MCCRAE, R. R.; AND ARENBERG, D. 1980. Enduring dispositions in adult males. *Journal of Personality and Social Psychology* 38:793–800.

COWLES, J. T. 1937. Food-tokens as incentives for learning by chimpanzees. *Comparative Psychology Monographs* 14 (5, Serial No. 71).

COYLE, J. T.; PRICE, D.; AND DELONG, M. R. 1983. Alzheimer's disease: A disorder of cholinergic innervation. *Science* 219:1184–90.

COYNE, J. C., AND GOTLIB, I. H. 1983. The role of cognition in depression: A critical appraisal. *Psychological Bulletin* 94:472–505.

CRAIK, F. I. M., AND LOCKHART, R. S. 1972. Levels of processing: A framework for memory research. *Journal of Verbal Learning and Verbal Behavior* 11:671–84.

CRAIK, F. I. M., AND TULVING, E. 1975. Depth of processing and the retention of words in episodic memory. *Journal of Experimental Psychology: General* 104:268–94.

CRAIK, F. I. M., AND WATKINS, M. J. 1973. The role of rehearsal in short-term memory. *Journal of Verbal Learning and Verbal Behavior* 12:599–607.

CRAIN, S., AND FODOR, J. D. 1985. How can grammars help parsers? In Dowty, D.; Kartunnen, L.; and Zwicky, A. (Eds.), *Natural language parsing: Psychological, computational, and theoretical perspectives.* Cambridge: Cambridge University Press.

CRAIN, S., AND STEEDMAN, M. 1985. On not being led up the garden path: The use of context by the psychological syntax parser. In Dowty, D.; Kartunnen, L.; and Zwicky, A. (Eds.), *Natural language parsing.* Cambridge: Cambridge University Press.

CRONBACH, L. J. 1970a. *Essentials of psychology testing,* 3rd ed. New York: Harper & Row.

CRONBACH, L. J. 1970b. Test validation. In Thorndike, R. L. (Ed.), *Educational measurement.* Washington, D.C.: American Council on Education.

CRONBACH, L. J. 1975. Beyond the two disciplines of scientific psychology. *American Psychologist* 30:116–27.

CRONBACH, L. J. 1984. *Essentials of psychological testing,* 4th ed. New York: Harper & Row.

CRONBACH, L. J., AND MEEHL, P. E. 1955. Construct validity in psychological tests. *Psychological Bulletin* 52:281–302.

CROOK, C. 1987. Taste and olfaction. In Salapatek, P., and Cohen, L. (Eds.), *Handbook of infant perception: From perception to cognition,* vol. 2, pp. 237–64. Orlando, Fla.: Academic Press.

CROW, T. J. 1980. Molecular pathology of schizophrenia: More than one disease process? *British Medical Journal* 280:66–68.

CROW, T. J. 1982. Two dimensions of pathology in schizophrenia: Dopaminergic and non-dopaminergic. *Psychopharmacology Bulletin* 18:22–29.

CROW, T. J. 1985. The two-syndrome concept: Origins and current status. *Schizophrenia Bulletin* 11:471–86.

CROWDER, R. G. 1976. *Principles of learning and memory.* Hillsdale, N.J.: Erlbaum.

CROWDER, R. G. 1982. The demise of short-term memory. *Acta Psychologica* 50:291–323.

CROWDER, R. G. 1985. On access and the forms of memory. In Weinberger, N. M.; McGaugh, J. L.; and Lynch, G. (Eds.), *Memory systems of the brain,* pp. 442–51. New York: Guilford Press.

CRUTCHFIELD, R. S. 1955. Conformity and character. *American Psychologist* 10:191–99.

CUNNINGHAM, M. R. 1986. Measuring the physical in physical attraction: Quasi-experiments on the sociobiology of female beauty. *Journal of Personality and Social Psychology* 50:925–35.

CURTISS, S. 1977. *Genie: A linguistic study of a modern-day "wild child."* New York: Academic Press.

DALE, A. J. D. 1975. Organic brain syndromes associated with infections. In Freedman, A. M.; Kaplan, H. I.; and Sadock, B. J. (Eds.), *Comprehensive textbook of psychiatry—II,* vol. 1, pp. 1121–30. Baltimore: Williams & Wilkins.

DARLEY, J. M., AND BATSON, C. D. 1973. "From Jerusalem to Jericho": A study of situational and dispositional variables in helping behavior. *Journal of Personality and Social Psychology* 27:100–108.

DARLEY, J., AND LATANÉ, B. 1968. Bystander intervention in emergencies: Diffusion of responsibility. *Journal of Personality and Social Psychology* 10:202–14.

DARNTON, R. 1984. The meaning of Mother Goose. *New York Review of Books,* February 2, 1984, 41–47.

DARWIN, C. 1872a. *The origin of species.* New York: Macmillan, 6th ed., 1962.

DARWIN, C. 1872b. *The expression of the emotions in man and animals.* London: Appleton.

DARWIN, C. 1877. A biographical sketch of a young child. *Kosmos* 1:367–76 (as cited in Bornstein, M. H. 1978. Chromatic vision in infancy. In Reese, H., and Lipsitt, L. (Eds.), *Advances in child development and behavior,* vol. 12. New York: Academic Press).

DAVIDSON, A. R., AND JACCARD, J. J. 1979. Variables that moderate the attitude-behavior relation: Results of a longitudinal survey. *Journal of Personality and Social Psychology* 37:1364–76.

DAVIDSON, J. M. 1969. Hormonal control of sexual behavior in adult rats. In Rasp, G. (Ed.), *Advances in bioscience,* vol. 1, pp. 119–69. New York: Pergamon.

DAVIDSON, J. M. 1986. Androgen replacement therapy in a wider context: Clinical and basic aspects. In Dennerstein and Fraser (Eds.), *Hormones and behavior,* pp. 433–40. Amsterdam: International Society of Psychosomatic Obstetrics and Gynecology, Elsevier.

DAVIS, D. E. 1964. The physiological analysis of aggressive behavior. In Etkin, W. (Ed.), *Social behavior and organization among vertebrates.* Chicago: University of Chicago Press.

DAVIS, J. M. 1974. A two-factor theory of schizophrenia. *Journal of Psychiatric Research* 11:25–30.

DAVIS, J. M. 1978. Dopamine theory of schizophrenia: A two-factor theory. In Wynne, L. C.; Cromwell, R. L.; and Matthysse, S. (Eds.), *The nature of schizophrenia.* New York: Wiley.

DAVIS, J. M. 1985a. Antipsychotic drugs. In Kaplan, H. I., and Sadock, J. (Eds.), *Comprehensive textbook of psychiatry,* 4th ed., pp. 1481–1513. Baltimore: Williams & Wilkins.

DAVIS, J. M. 1985b. Antidepressant drugs. In Kaplan, H. I., and Sadock, J. (Eds.), *Comprehensive textbook of psychiatry,* 4th ed., pp. 1513–37. Baltimore: Williams & Wilkins.

DAVIS, K. 1947. Final note on a case of extreme social isolation. *American Journal of Sociology* 52:432–37.

DAVIS, W. L., AND PHARES, E. J. 1969. Parental antecedents of internal-external control of reinforcement. *Psychological Reports* 24:427–36.

DAVISON, G. C. 1968. Systematic desensitization as a counter-

conditioning process. *Journal of Abnormal Psychology* 73:84–90.

DAVISON, G. C., AND NEALE, J. M. 1986. *Abnormal psychology,* 4th ed. New York: Wiley.

DAWES, R. M. 1988. *Rational choice in an uncertain world.* New York: Harcourt Brace Jovanovich.

DAY, R. H., AND MCKENZIE, B. E. 1981. Infant perception of the invariant size of approaching and receding objects. *Developmental Psychology* 17:670–77.

DAY, R. H.; STUART, G. W.; AND DICKINSON, R. G. 1980. Size constancy does not fail below half a degree. *Perception and Psychophysics* 28:263–65.

DECASPER, A. J., AND FIFER, W. P. 1980. Of human bonding: Newborns prefer their mothers' voices. *Science* 208:1174–76.

DE GROOT, A. D. 1965. *Thought and choice in chess.* The Hague: Mouton.

DE ROUGEMONT, D. 1940. *Love in the Western world.* New York: Harcourt Brace Jovanovich.

DE VALOIS, R. L. 1965. Behavioral and electrophysiological studies of primate vision. In Neff, W. D. (Ed.), *Contributions of sensory physiology,* vol. 1. New York: Academic Press.

DE VALOIS, R. L., AND DE VALOIS, K. K. 1975. Neural coding of color. In Carterette, E. C., and Friedman, M. P. (Eds.), *Handbook of perception,* vol. 5, pp. 117–62. New York: Academic Press.

DE VILLIERS, J. G. 1980. The process of rule learning in child speech: A new look. In Nelson, K. (Ed.), *Child language,* vol. 2. New York: Gardner Press.

DE VILLIERS, J. G., AND DE VILLIERS, P. A. 1973. Development of the use of word order in comprehension. *Journal of Psycholinguistic Research* 2:331–41.

DELL, G. S. 1986. A spreading activation theory of retrieval in sentence-production. *Psychological Review* 93:283–321.

DEMENT, W. C. 1974. *Some must watch while some must sleep.* San Francisco: Freeman.

DEMENT, W. C., AND KLEITMAN, N. 1957. The relation of eye movements during sleep to dream activity: An objective method for the study of dreaming. *Journal of Experimental Psychology* 53:339–46.

DEMENT, W. C., AND WOLPERT, E. A. 1958. The relationship of eye-movements, body motility, and external stimuli to dream content. *Journal of Experimental Psychology* 55:543–53.

DENNIS, W. 1940. Does culture appreciably affect patterns of infant behavior? *Journal of Social Psychology* 12:305–17.

DERUBEIS, R. J.; HOLLON, S. D.; EVANS, M. D.; AND BERNIS, K. M. 1982. Can psychotherapies for depression be discriminated? A systematic investigation of cognitive therapy and interpersonal therapy. *Journal of Consulting and Clinical Psychology* 50:744–56.

DESCARTES, R. 1662. *Trait de l'homme.* Translated by Haldane, E. S., and Ross, G. R. T. Cambridge, England: Cambridge University Press, 1911.

DEUTSCH, A. 1948. *The shame of the states.* New York: Harcourt and Brace. (Reprint edition, New York: Arno Press, 1973.)

DEUTSCH, J. A. 1960. *The structural basis of behavior.* Chicago: University of Chicago Press.

DEUTSCH, J. A.; ADAMS, D. W.; AND METZNER, R. J. 1964. Choice of intracranial stimulation as a function of the delay between stimulations and competing drive. *Journal of Comparative and Physiological Psychology* 57:241–43.

DEUTSCH, J. A.; PUERTO, A.; AND WANG, M. L. 1978. The stomach signals satiety. *Science* 201:165–67.

DI VESTA, F. J.; INGERSOLL, G.; AND SUNSHINE, P. 1971. A factor analysis of imagery tests. *Journal of Verbal Learning and Verbal Behavior* 10:471–79.

*Diagnostic and statistical manual of mental disorders,* 2nd ed. Washington, D.C.: American Psychiatric Association, 1968.

*Diagnostic and statistical manual of mental disorders,* 3rd ed. Washington, D.C.: American Psychiatric Association, 1980.

*Diagnostic and statistical manual of mental disorders,* 3rd ed., Revised (DSM-III-R). Washington, D. C.: American Psychiatric Association, 1987.

DIAMOND, A. 1988. The abilities and neural mechanisms underlying A-not-B performance. *Child Development* 59:523–27.

DIAMOND, A. 1989. Developmental progression in human infants and infant monkeys, and the neural bases of A-not-B and delayed response performance. Paper presented at a meeting on "The development and neural bases of higher cognitive functions," Philadelphia, Pa., May 20–24, 1989.

DIAMOND, A., AND GOLDMAN-RAKIC, P. S. 1989. Comparative development of human infants and rhesus monkeys on Piaget's A-not-B task: Evidence for dependence on dorsolateral prefrontal cortex. *Experimental Brain Research* 74:24–40.

DIAMOND, M. 1982. Sexual identity, monozygotic twins reared in discordant sex roles, and a BBC follow-up. *Archives of Sexual Behavior* 11:181–86.

DIAMOND, R., AND ROZIN, P. 1984. Activation of existing memories in the amnesic syndrome. *Journal of Abnormal Psychology* 93:98–105.

DICKINSON, A. 1987. Animal conditioning and learning theory. In Eysenck, H. J., and Martin, I. (Eds.), *Theoretical Foundations of Behavior Theory.* New York: Plenum.

DICKS, H. V. 1972. *Licensed mass murder: A sociopsychological study of some S. S. killers.* New York: Basic Books.

DICKSON, D. H., AND KELLY, I. W. 1985. The "Barnum effect" in personality assessment: A review of the literature. *Psychological Reports* 57:367–82.

DIENER, F. 1977. Deindividuation: Causes and consequences. *Social Behavior and Personality* 5:143–55.

DIENER, E. 1979. Deindividuation: The absence of self-awareness and self-regulation in group members. In Paulus, P. (Ed.), *The psychology of group influence,* pp. 209–42. Hillsdale, N.J.: Erlbaum.

DIENER, F.; FRASER, S. C.; BEAMAN, A. L.; AND KELEM, Z. R. T. 1976. Effects of deindividuation variables on stealing among Halloween trick-or-treaters. *Journal of Personality and Social Psychology* 5:143–55.

DILGER, W. C. 1962. The behavior of lovebirds. *Scientific American* 206:88–98.

DODD, B. 1979. Lip reading in infants: Attention to speech presented in- and out-of-synchrony. *Cognitive Psychology* 11:478–84.

DOLGER, H., AND SEEMAN, B. 1985. *How to live with diabetes,* 5th ed. New York: Norton.

DOMJAN, M. 1983. Biological constraints on instrumental and classical conditioning: Implications for general process theory. In Bower, G. H. (Ed.), *The psychology of learning and motivation,* vol. 17. New York: Academic Press.

DOUVAN, E., AND ADELSON, J. 1958. The psychodynamics of social mobility in adolescent boys. *Journal of Abnormal and Social Psychology* 56:31–44.

DRISCOLL, R.; DAVIS, K. E.; AND LIPITZ. 1972. Parental interference and romantic love: The Romeo and Juliet effect. *Journal of Personality and Social Psychology* 24:1–10.

DUDA, R. O., AND SHORTLIFFE, E. H. 1983. Expert systems research. *Science* 220:261–68.

DUNCKER, K. 1929. Über induzierte Bewegung. *Psychologische Forschung* 12:180–259.

DUNCKER, K. 1945. On problem solving. *Psychological Monographs* (Whole No. 270):1–113.

DURANT, W., AND DURANT, A. 1967. *The story of civilization: Part X. Rousseau and Revolution.* New York: Simon and Schuster.

DUTTON, D. G., AND ARON, A. P. 1974. Some evidence for heightened sexual attraction under conditions of high anxiety. *Journal of Personality and Social Psychology* 30:510–17.

DYMOND, R. 1954. Interpersonal perception and marital happiness. *Canadian Journal of Psychology* 8:164–71.

EAGLY, A. H., AND CHAIKIN, S. 1984. Cognitive theories of persuasion. In Berkowitz, L. (Ed.), *Advances in experimental social psychology,* vol. 17. New York: Academic Press.

EBBINGHAUS, H. 1885. *Memory.* New York: Teacher's College, Columbia University, 1913. (Reprint edition, New York: Dover, 1964.)

ECCLES, J. 1973. *The understanding of the brain.* New York: McGraw-Hill.

ECCLES, J. C. 1982. The synapse: From electrical to chemical transmission. *Annual Review of Neuroscience* 5:325–39.

EDGERTON, R. B. 1979. *Mental retardation.* Cambridge, Mass.: Harvard University Press.

EDMONDS, J. M., ed. and trans. 1929. *The characters of Theophrastus.* Cambridge, Mass.: Harvard University Press.

EGELAND, J. A.; GERHARD, D. S.; PAULS, D. L.; SUSSEX, J. N.; KIDD, K. K.; ALLEN, C. R.; HOSTETTER, A. M.; AND HOUSMAN, D. E. 1987. Bipolar affective disorders linked to DNA markers on chromosome 11. *Nature* 325:783–87.

EGETH, H.; JONIDES, J.; AND WALL, S. 1972. Parallel processing of multielement displays. *Cognitive Psychology* 3:674–98.

EGGER, M. D., AND FLYNN, J. P. 1963. Effect of electrical stimulation of the amygdala on hypothalamically elicited behavior in cats. *Journal of Neurophysiology* 26:705–20.

EHRHARDT, A. A. 1984. Gender differences: A biological perspective. In Dienstbier, R. A., and Sonderegger, T. B. (Eds.), *Nebraska Symposium on Motivation,* pp. 37–58. Lincoln, Neb.: University of Nebraska.

EICH, J. E. 1980. The cue-dependent nature of state-dependent retrieval. *Memory and Cognition* 8:157–73.

EIKELBOOM, R., AND STEWART, J. 1982. Conditioning of drug-induced physiological responses. *Psychological Review* 89:507–28.

EIMAS, P. D.; SIQUELAND, E. R.; JUSCZYK, P.; AND VIGORITO, J. 1971. Speech perception in infants. *Science* 171:303–306.

EKMAN, P. 1971. Universals and cultural differences in facial expression. In Cole, J. K. (Ed.), *Nebraska Symposium on Motivation,* pp. 207–84. Lincoln, Neb.: University of Nebraska Press.

EKMAN, P. 1973. Cross-cultural studies of facial expression. In Ekman, P. (Ed.), *Darwin and facial expression,* pp. 169–222. New York: Academic Press.

EKMAN, P. 1977. Biological and cultural contributions to body and facial movement. In Blacking, J. (Ed.), *The anthropology of the body.* A. S. A. Monograph 15. London: Academic Press.

EKMAN, P. 1984. Expression and the nature of emotion. In Ekman, P., and Scherer, K. (Eds.), *Approaches to emotion,* pp. 319–43. Hillsdale, N.J.: Erlbaum.

EKMAN, P. 1985. *Telling lies.* New York: Norton.

EKMAN, P., AND FRIESEN, W. V. 1975. *Unmasking the face.* Englewood Cliffs, N.J.: Prentice-Hall.

EKMAN, P., AND OSTER, H. 1979. Facial expression of emotion. *Annual Review of Psychology* 30:527–54.

EKSTRAND, B. R. 1972. To sleep, perchance to dream (about why we forget) In Duncan, C. P.; Sechrest, L.; and Melton, A. W. (Eds.), *Human memory: Festschrift for Benton J. Underwood,* pp. 59–82. New York: Appleton-Century-Crofts.

EKSTRAND, B. R.; BARRETT, T. R.; WEST, J. M.; AND MAIER, W. G. 1977. The effect of sleep on human memory. In Drucker-Colin, R., and McGaugh, J. L. (Eds.), *Neurobiology of sleep and memory.* New York: Academic Press.

ELDER, G. H., JR. 1980. Adolescence in historical perspective. In Adelson, J. (Ed.), *Handbook of adolescent psychology.* New York: Wiley.

ELLENBERGER, H. F. 1970. *The discovery of the unconscious.* New York: Basic Books.

ELLIS, A. 1962. *Reason and emotion in psychotherapy.* Secaucus, N.J.: Lyle Stuart.

ELLIS, L.; AND AMES, M. A. 1987. Neurohormonal functioning and sexual orientation: A theory of homosexuality-heterosexuality. *Psychological Bulletin* 101:233–58.

ELLIS, L.; AMES, M. A.; PECKHAM, W.; AND BURKE, D. 1988. Sexual orientation of offspring may be altered by severe maternal stress during pregnancy. *Journal of Sex Research* 25:152–57.

ELLSWORTH, P. C., AND TOURANGEAU, R. 1981. On our failure to disconfirm what nobody ever said. *Journal of Personality and Social Psychology* 40:363–69.

ELMS, A. C., AND MILGRAM, S. 1966. Personality characteristics associated with obedience and defiance toward authoritative command. *Journal of Experimental Research in Personality* 1:282–89.

EMMELKAMP, P. M. G. 1986. Behavior therapy with adults. In Garfield, S. L., and Bergin, A. E. (Eds.), *Handbook of psychotherapy and behavior change,* 3rd ed. New York: Wiley.

EMMELKAMP, P. M. G., AND WESSELS, H. 1975. Flooding in imagination vs. flooding in vivo: A comparison with agoraphobics. *Behavior Research and Therapy* 13:7–15.

EMMERICH, W. 1966. Continuity and stability in early social development, II. Teacher ratings. *Child Development* 37:17–27.

ENDLER, N. S. 1982. Interactionism comes of age. In Zanna, M. P.; Higgins, E. T.; and Herman, C. P. (Eds.), *Consistency in social behavior. The Ontario Symposium,* vol. 2. Hillsdale, N.J.: Erlbaum.

ENDLER, N. S., AND HUNT, J. M. 1969. Generalization of contributions from sources of variance in the S-R inventories of anxiousness. *Journal of Personality* 37:1–24.

EPSTEIN, A. N.; FITZSIMONS, J. T.; AND ROLLS, B. J. 1970. Drinking induced by injection of angiotensin into the brain of the rat. *Journal of Physiology* 210:457–74.

EPSTEIN, A. W., AND TEITELBAUM, P. 1962. Regulation of food intake in the absence of taste, smell, and other oropharyngeal sensations. *Journal of Comparative and Physiological Psychology* 55:753–59.

EPSTEIN, S. 1979. The stability of behavior: I. On predicting most of the people much of the time. *Journal of Personality and Social Psychology* 37:1097–1126.

EPSTEIN, S. 1980. The stability of behavior. II. Implications for psychological research. *American Psychologist* 35:790–806.

EPSTEIN, S. 1983. The stability of confusion: A reply to Mischel and Peak. *Psychological Review* 90:179–84.

EPSTEIN, W. 1961. The influence of syntactical structure on learning. *American Journal of Psychology* 74:80–85.

ERDELYI, M. H. 1985. *Psychoanalysis: Freud's cognitive psychology.* New York: Freeman.

ERDELYI, M. H., AND GOLDBERG, B. 1979. Let's not sweep repression under the rug. In Kihlstrom, J. F., and Evans, F. J. (Eds.), *Functional disorders of memory,* pp. 355–402. Hillsdale, N.J.: Erlbaum.

ERICSSON, K. A.; CHASE, W. G.; AND FALOON, S. 1980. Acquisition of a memory skill. *Science* 208:1181–82.

ERIKSEN, C. W., AND HOFFMAN, J. E. 1972. Temporal and spatial characteristics of selective encoding from multielement displays. *Perception and Psychophysics* 12:201–204.

ERIKSEN, C. W., AND PIERCE, J. 1968. Defense mechanisms. In Borgatta, E. F., and Lambert, W. W. (Eds.), *Handbook of personality theory and research,* pp. 1007–40. Chicago: Rand McNally.

ERIKSON, E. H. 1963. *Childhood and society.* New York: Norton.

ERIKSON, E. H. 1974. *Dimensions of a new identity: The Jefferson lectures in the humanities.* New York: Norton.

ERON, L. D. 1950. A normative study of the thematic apperception test. *Psychological Monographs* 64 (Whole No. 315).

ERVIN, S. 1964. Imitation and structural change in children's language. In Lenneberg, E. H. (Ed.), *New directions in the study of language.* Cambridge, Mass.: MIT Press.

ESSOCK-VITALE, S. M., AND McGUIRE, M. T. 1985. Women's lives viewed from an evolutionary perspective: II. Patterns of helping. *Ethology and Sociobiology* 6:155–73.

ESTES, W. K., AND SKINNER, B. F. 1941. Some quantitative properties of anxiety. *Journal of Experimental Psychology* 29: 390–400.

ETKIN, W. 1964. Reproductive behaviors. In Etkin, W. (Ed.), *Social behavior and organization among vertebrates,* pp. 75–116. Chicago: University of Chicago Press.

EXNER, J. E. 1974. The Rorschach system. New York: Grune and Stratton.

EXNER, J. E. 1978. *A comprehensive system: Current research and advanced interpretation,* vol. 2. New York: Wiley Interscience.

EXNER, J. E., AND CLARK, B. 1978. The Rorschach. In Wolman, B. B. *Clinical diagnosis of mental disorders.* New York: Plenum.

EYFERTH, K. 1961. Leistungen verschiedener Gruppen von Besatzungskindern im Hamburg-Wechsler Intelligenz Test für Kinder (HAWIK). *Archiv für die gesamte Psychologie* 113:222–41.

EYSENCK, H. J. 1961. The effects of psychotherapy. In Eysenck, H. J. (Ed.), *Handbook of abnormal psychology,* pp. 697–725. New York: Basic Books.

EYSENCK, H. J., AND EYSENCK, S. B. G. 1975. *Psychoticism as a dimension of personality.* London: Hodder and Stoughton.

EYSENCK, H. J., AND EYSENCK, S. B. G. 1983. Recent advances: The cross-cultural study of personality. In Butcher, J. N., and Spielberger, C. D. (Eds.), *Advances in personality assessment,* vol. 2, pp. 41–72. Hillsdale, N.J.: Erlbaum.

EYSENCK, H. J. VERSUS KAMIN, L. 1981. *The intelligence controversy.* New York: Wiley.

EYSENCK, H. J., AND RACHMAN, S. 1965. *The causes and cures of neurosis.* San Diego, Calif.: Robert E. Knapp.

FAGAN, J. F. 1976. Infants' recognition of invariant features of faces. *Child Development* 47:627–38.

FAGAN, J. F. 1984. The intelligent infant: Theoretical implications. *Intelligence* 8:1–9.

FAGAN, J. F. 1985. A new look at infant intelligence. In Detterman, D. K. (Ed.), *Current topics in human intelligence. Vol. 1: Research Methodology.* Norwood, N.J.: Ablex.

FALLON, A. E., AND ROZIN, P. 1985. Sex differences in perceptions of desirable body shape. *Journal of Abnormal Psychology* 94:102–105.

FANCHER, R. E. 1987. *The intelligence men: Makers of the IQ controversy.* New York: Norton.

FANT, L. G. 1972. *Ameslan: An introduction to American Sign Language.* Silver Springs, Md.: National Association of the Deaf.

FANTZ, R. L. 1957. Form preferences in newly hatched chicks. *Journal of Comparative and Physiological Psychology* 50:422–30.

FANTZ, R. L. 1961. The origin of form perception. *Scientific American* 204:66–72.

FANTZ, R. L. 1970. Visual perception and experience in infancy: Issues and approaches. In National Academy of Science, *Early experience and visual information processing in perceptual and reading disorders,* pp. 351–81. New York: National Academy of Science.

FARIS, R. E. L., AND DUNHAM, H. W. 1939. *Mental disorders in urban areas.* Chicago: University of Chicago Press.

FEARING, F. 1930. *Reflex action: A study in the history of physiological psychology.* Baltimore: Williams & Wilkins.

FEDER, H. H. 1984. Hormones and sexual behavior. *Annual Review of Psychology* 35:165–200.

FELDMAN, H.; GOLDIN-MEADOW, S.; AND GLEITMAN, L. R. 1978. Beyond Herodotus: The creation of language by linguistically deprived deaf children. In Lock, A. (Ed.), *Action, gesture, and symbol: The emergence of language.* London: Academic Press.

FELDMAN, N. S.; KLOSSON, E. C.; PARSONS, J. E.; RHOLES, W. S.; AND RUBLE, D. N. 1976. Order of information presentation and children's moral judgments. *Child Development* 47:556–59.

FELIPE, N.J., AND SOMMER, R. 1966. Invasions of personal space. *Social Problems* 14:206–14.

FENICHEL, O. 1945. *The psychoanalytic theory of neurosis.* New York: Norton.

FERNALD, A. 1984. The perceptual and affective salience of mothers' speech to infants. In Feagans, L.; Garvey, C.; and Golinkoff, R. (Eds.), *The origins and growth of communication.* New Brunswick: Ablex.

FERNALD, A. AND KUHL, P. 1987. Acoustic determinants of infant preference for motherese speech. *Infant Behavior and Development* 10:279–93.

FERNALD, A., AND SIMON, T. 1984. Expanded intonation contours in mothers' speech to newborns. *Developmental Psychology* 20:104–13.

FERNALD, A.; TAESCHNER, T.; DUNN, J.; PAPOUSEK, M.; DE BOYSSON-BARDIES, B.; AND FUKUI, I. 1989. A cross-linguistic study of prosodic modifications in mothers' and fathers' speech to preverbal infants. *Journal of Child Language* 16(3):477–502.

FERSTER, C. B., AND SKINNER, B. F. 1957. *Schedules of reinforcement.* New York: Appleton-Century-Crofts.

FERSTER, D. 1981. A comparison of binocular depth mechanisms in areas 17 and 18 of the cat visual cortex. *Journal of Physiology* 311:623–55.

FESHBACH, N., AND ROE, K. 1968. Empathy in six- and seven-year-olds. *Child Development* 39:133–45.

FESHBACH, S. 1970. Aggression. In Mussen, P. H. (Ed.), *Carmichael's manual of child psychology,* 3rd ed., pp. 159–260. New York: Wiley.

FESTINGER, L. 1954. A theory of social comparison processes. *Human Relations* 7:117–40.

FESTINGER, L. 1957. *A theory of cognitive dissonance.* Evanston, Ill.: Row, Peterson.

FESTINGER, L., AND CARLSMITH, J. M. 1959. Cognitive consequences of forced compliance. *Journal of Abnormal and Social Psychology* 58:203–10.

FESTINGER, L.; PEPITONE, A.; AND NEWCOMB, T. 1952. Some consequences of deindividuation in a group. *Journal of Abnormal and Social Psychology* 47:387–89.

FESTINGER, L.; RIECKEN, H.; AND SCHACHTER, S. 1956. *When prophecy fails.* Minneapolis: University of Minnesota Press.

FIELD, T. 1978. Interaction behaviors of primary versus secondary caretaker fathers. *Developmental Psychology* 14:183–84.

FIEVE, R. R. 1975. Lithium (antimanic) therapy. In Freedman, A. M.; Kaplan, H. I.; and Sadock, B. J. (Eds.), *Comprehensive textbook of psychiatry,* vol. 2, pp. 1982–87. Baltimore: Williams & Wilkins.

FIGLER, M. 1972. The relation between eliciting stimulus strength and habituation of the threat display in male Siamese fighting fish, *Betta splendens. Behavior* 42:63–96.

FILLMORE, C. 1968. The case for case. In Bach, E., and Harms, R. (Eds.), *Universals in linguistic theory.* New York: Holt, Rinehart and Winston.

FINDLEY, M. J., AND COOPER, H. M. 1983. Locus of control and academic achievement: A literature review. *Journal of Personality and Social Psychology* 44:419–27.

FINE, A. 1986. Transplantation in the central nervous system. *Scientific American* (August issue, pp. 52–58).

FINKE, R. A.; PINKER, S.; AND FARAH, M. J. 1989. Reinterpreting visual patterns in imagery. *Cognitive Science* 13:51–78.

FISHER, C., GLEITMAN, H., AND GLEITMAN, L. 1991. On the semantic content of subcategorization frames. *Cognitive Psychology,* in press.

FISHER, S., AND GREENBERG, R. P. 1977. *The scientific credibility of Freud's theory and therapy.* New York: Basic Books.

FITZGERALD, F. T. 1981. The problem of obesity. *Annual Review of Medicine* 32:221–31.

FITZSIMONS, J. T., AND MOORE-GILLOW, M. J. 1980. Drinking and antidiuresis in response to reductions in venous return in the

dog: Neural and endocrine mechanisms. *Journal of Physiology* 307:403–16.

FLANAGAN, J. C. 1947. Scientific development of the use of human resources: Progress in the Army Air Forces. *Science* 105:57–60.

FLAVELL, J. H. 1970. Developmental studies of mediated memory. In Reese, H. W., and Lipsitt, L. P. (Eds.), *Advances in child development and behavior,* vol. 5. New York: Academic Press.

FLAVELL, J. H. 1977. *Cognitive development.* Englewood Cliffs, N.J.: Prentice-Hall.

FLAVELL, J. H. 1985. *Cognitive development,* 2nd ed. Englewood Cliffs, N.J.: Prentice-Hall.

FLAVELL, J. H.; BEACH, D. H.; AND CHINSKY, J. M. 1966. Spontaneous verbal rehearsal in a memory task as a function of age. *Child Development* 37:283–99.

FLAVELL, J. H.; FLAVELL, E. R.; AND GREEN, F. L. 1983. Development of the appearance-reality distinction. *Cognitive Psychology* 15:95–120.

FLAVELL, J. H., AND WELLMAN, H. M. 1977. Metamemory. In Kail, R. V., Jr., and Hagen, J. W. (Eds.), *Perspectives on the development of memory and cognition,* pp. 3–34. Hillsdale, N.J.: Erlbaum.

FLODERUS-MYRHED, B.; PEDERSEN, N.; AND RASMUSON, L. 1980. Assessment of heritability for personality, based on a short form of the Eysenck Personality Inventory: A study of 12,898 twin pairs. *Behavior Genetics* 10:153–62.

FLYNN, J.; VANEGAS, H.; FOOTE, W.; AND EDWARDS, S. 1970. Neural mechanisms involved in a cat's attack on a rat. In Whalen, R. F.; Thompson, M.; Verzeano, M.; and Weinberger, N. (Eds.), *The neural control of behavior.* New York: Academic Press.

FLYNN, S. 1987. *A parameter-setting model of L2 acquisition: Experimental studies in anaphora.* Dordrecht: Reidel.

FOARD, C. F. 1975. *Recall subsequent to tip-of-the-tongue experience.* Unpublished first-year graduate research paper, University of Pennsylvania, Philadelphia.

FOCH, T. T., AND McCLEARN, G. E. 1980. Genetics, body weight, and obesity. In Stunkard, A. J. (Ed.), *Obesity,* pp. 48–71. Philadelphia: Saunders.

FODOR, J. A. 1972. Some reflections on L. S. Vygotsky's *Thought and language. Cognition* 1:83–95.

FODOR, J. A. 1975. *The language of thought.* New York: Crowell.

FODOR, J. A. 1983. *The modularity of mind.* Cambridge, Mass.: MIT Press, Bradford Books.

FODOR, J. A. 1988. *Psychosemantics.* Cambridge, Mass.: MIT Press.

FOLKOW, B., AND RUBENSTEIN, E. H. 1966. Cardiovascular effects of acute and chronic stimulations of the hypothalamic defense area in the rat. *Acta Physiologica Scandinavica* 68:48–57.

FONTANA, A. F. 1966. Familial etiology of schizophrenia: Is a scientific methodology possible? *Psychological Bulletin* 66:214–77.

FORD, C. S., AND BEACH, F. A. 1951. *Patterns of sexual behavior.* New York: Harper & Row.

FORER, B. R. 1949. The fallacy of personal validation: A classroom demonstration of gullibility. *Journal of Abnormal and Social Psychology* 44:118–23.

FORSTER, E. M. 1927. *Aspects of the novel.* New York: Harcourt, Brace, and World.

FOUCAULT, M. 1965. *Madness and civilization.* New York: Random House.

FOULKE, E., AND STICHT, T. G. 1969. Review of research on the intelligibility and compression of accelerated speech. *Psychological Bulletin* 72:50–62.

FOUTS, R. S. 1972. Use of guidance in teaching sign language to a chimpanzee *(Pantroglodytes). Journal of Comparative and Physiological Psychology* 80:515–22.

FOUTS, R. S.; HIRSCH, A. D.; AND FOUTS, D. H. 1982. Cultural transmission of a human language in a chimpanzee mother-infant re-

lationship. In Fitzgerald, H. E.; Mullins, J. A.; and Gage, P. (Eds.), *Child nurturance: Vol. 3, Studies of development in nonhuman primates,* pp. 159–69. New York: Plenum.

FOWLER, A. 1986. Language acquisition in Down's Syndrome children. In Cichette, D., and Beeghley, M. (Eds.), *Down's Syndrome: The developmental perspective.* New York: Cambridge University Press.

FOWLER, A. 1989. Language acquisition in Down's Syndrome children: Syntax and morphology. In Cicchetti, D., and Beeghly, M., *Down's Syndrome: The developmental perspective,* 2nd ed. New York: Cambridge University Press.

FRANK, M. 1973. An analysis of hamster afferent taste nerve response functions. *Journal of General Physiology* 61:588–618.

FRANKL, V. E. 1966. *The doctor and the soul.* New York: Knopf.

FRAZIER, L., AND FODOR, J. D. 1978. The sausage machine: A new two-stage parsing model. *Cognition* 6:291–325.

FREED, W. J.; DE MEDICACELLI, L.; AND WYATT, R. J. 1985. Promoting functional plasticity in the damaged nervous system. *Science* 227:1544–52.

FREEDMAN, D. G. 1971. Behavioral assessment in infancy. In Stoeling, G. B. A., and Van Der Weoff Ten Bosch, J. J. (Eds.), *Normal and abnormal development of brain and behavior,* pp. 92–103. Leiden: Leiden University Press.

FREEDMAN, J. L., AND FRASER, S. C. 1966. Compliance without pressure: The foot-in-the-door technique. *Journal of Personality and Social Psychology* 4:195–202.

FREEDMAN, J. L.; SEARS, D. O.; AND CARLSMITH, J. M. 1981. *Social psychology,* 4th ed. Englewood Cliffs, N.J.: Prentice-Hall.

FREEMAN, D. 1983. *Margaret Mead and Samoa: The making and unmaking of an anthropological myth.* Canberra: Australian National University Press.

FREEMAN, D. 1986. Rejoinder to Patience and Smith. *American Anthropologist* 88:161–67.

FREGE, G. (1892/1952). On sense and reference, In Geach, P., and Black, M. (Eds.), *Philosophical writings of Gottlob Frege.* Oxford: Oxford University Press.

FRENCH, J. D. 1957. The reticular formation. *Scientific American* 196:54–60.

FREUD, A. 1946. The ego and the mechanisms of defense. London: Hogarth Press.

FREUD, S. 1900. The interpretation of dreams. In Strachey, J., trans. and ed., *The complete psychological works,* vols. 4–5. New York: Norton, 1976.

FREUD, S. 1901. The psychopathology of everyday life. Translated by Tyson, A. New York: Norton, 1971.

FREUD, S. 1905. Three essays on the theory of sexuality. In Strachey, J., trans. and ed., *The complete psychological works,* vol. 7. New York: Norton, 1976.

FREUD, S. 1908. Character and anal eroticism. In Rieff, P. (Ed.), *Collected papers of Sigmund Freud: Character and culture.* New York: Collier Books, 1963.

FREUD, S. 1911. Psychoanalytic notes upon an autobiographical account of a case of paranoia (dementia paranoides). In Strachey, J., trans. and ed., *The complete psychological works,* vol. 12. New York: Norton, 1976.

FREUD, S. 1913. *Further recommendations in the technique of psychoanalysis.* In Strachey, J., trans. and ed., *The complete psychological works,* vol. 12. New York: Norton, 1976.

FREUD, S. 1917. *A general introduction to psychoanalysis.* Translated by Riviere, J. New York: Washington Square Press, 1952.

FREUD, S. 1923. *The ego and the id.* Translated by Riviere, J. New York: Norton, 1962.

FREUD, S. 1925. Some psychical consequences of the anatomical distinction between the sexes. In Strachey, J., trans. and ed., *The complete psychological works,* vol. 19. New York: Norton, 1976.

FREUD, S. 1930. *Civilization and its discontents.* Translated by

Strachey, J. New York: Norton, 1961.

FREUD, S. 1940. *An outline of psychoanalysis.* Translated by Strachey, J. New York: Norton, 1970.

FREUD, S., AND BREUER, J. 1895. Studies on hysteria. In Strachey, J., trans. and ed., *The complete psychological works,* vol. 2. New York: Norton, 1976.

FRIDLUND, A. J. 1990. Evolution and facial action in reflex, social motive, and paralanguage. In Ackles, P. K.; Jennings, J. R.; and Coles, M. G. H. (Eds.), *Advances in psychophysiology,* vol. 4. Greenwich, Conn.: JAI Press.

FRIDLUND, A. J.; EKMAN, P.; AND OSTER, H. 1983. Facial expression of emotion: Review of literature, 1970–1983. In Siegman, A. (Ed.), *Nonverbal behavior and communication.* Hillsdale, N.J.: Erlbaum.

FRIEDMAN, M., AND ROSENMAN, R. H. 1974. *Type A behavior.* New York: Knopf.

FRIEDMAN, M. I., AND STRICKER, E. M. 1976. The physiological psychology of hunger: A physiological perspective. *Psychological Review* 83:409–31.

FRISBY, J. P. 1980. *Seeing: Illusion, brain and mind.* New York: Oxford University Press.

FRISHBERG, N. 1975. Arbitrariness and iconicity: Historical change in American Sign Language. *Language* 51:696–719.

FROMKIN, V.; KRASHEN, S.; CURTISS, S.; RIGLER, D.; AND RIGLER, M. 1974. The development of language in Genie: A case of language acquisition beyond the "critical period." *Brain and Language* 1:81–107.

FULTZ, J.; BATSON, C. D.; FORTENBACH, V. A.; MCCARTHY, P. M.; AND VARNEY, L. L. 1986. Social evaluation and the empathy-altruism hypothesis. *Journal of Personality and Social Psychology* 50:761–69.

FUNKENSTEIN, D. H. 1956. Norepinephrine-like and epinephrine-like substances in relation to human behavior. *Journal of Mental Diseases* 124:58–68.

GAGE, F. H., AND BJÖRKLUND, A. 1986. Cholinergic septal grafts into the hippocampal formation improve spatial learning and memory in aged rats by an atropine-sensitive mechanism. *Journal of Neuroscience* 6:2837–47.

GAGNON, J. H., AND SIMON, W. 1973. *Sexual conduct.* Chicago: Aldine.

GALLAGAN, R. 1987. Intonation with single words: purposive and grammatical use. *Journal of Child Language* 14:1–22.

GALLISTEL, C. R. 1973. Self-stimulation: The neurophysiology of reward and motivation. In Deutsch, J. A. (Ed.), *The physiological basis of memory,* pp. 175–267. New York: Academic Press.

GALLISTEL, C. R. 1980. *The organization of action.* Hillsdale, N.J.: Erlbaum.

GALLISTEL, C. R. 1983. Self-stimulation. In Deutsch, J. A. (Ed.), *The physiological basis of memory,* pp. 269–349. New York: Academic Press.

GALLISTEL, C. R. 1986. The role of the dopaminergic projections in MFB self-stimulation. *Behavior and Brain Research* 20:313–21.

GALLISTEL, C. R.; SHIZGAL, P.; AND YEOMANS, J. 1981. A portrait of the substrate for self-stimulation. *Psychological Review* 88:228–73.

GALTON, F. 1869. *Hereditary genius: An inquiry into its laws and consequences.* London: Macmillan.

GALTON, F. 1883. *Inquiries into human faculty and its development.* London: Macmillan.

GARBER, H., AND HEBER, R. 1982. Modification of predicted cognitive development in high-risk children through early intervention. In Detterman, D. K., and Sternberg, R. J. (Eds.), *How and how much can intelligence be increased?,* pp. 121–40. Norwood, N.J.: Ablex.

GARCIA, J.; ERVIN, F. R.; AND KOELLING, R. A. 1966. Learning with prolonged delay of reinforcement. *Psychonomic Science* 5:121–22.

GARCIA, J., AND KOELLING, R. A. 1966. The relation of cue to consequence in avoidance learning. *Psychonomic Science* 4:123–24.

GARDNER, H. 1975. *The shattered mind.* New York: Vintage Press.

GARDNER, H. 1983. *Frames of mind: The theory of multiple intelligences.* New York: Basic Books.

GARDNER, R. A., AND GARDNER, B. T. 1969. Teaching sign language to a chimpanzee. *Science* 165:664–72.

GARDNER, R. A., AND GARDNER, B. T. 1975. Early signs of language in child and chimpanzee. *Science* 187:752–53.

GARDNER, R. A., AND GARDNER, B. T. 1978. Comparative psychology and language acquisition. *Annals of the New York Academy of Science* 309:37–76.

GATHERCOLE, V. C. 1987. The contrastive hypothesis for the acquisition of word meaning: A reconsideration of the theory. *Journal of Child Language* 14(3):493–532.

GAZZANIGA, M. S. 1967. The split brain in man. *Scientific American* 217:24–29.

GAZZANIGA, M. S. 1970. *The bisected brain.* New York: Appleton-Century-Crofts.

GAZZANIGA, M. S. 1983. Right hemisphere language following brain bisection: A 20-year perspective. *American Psychologist* 38:525–37.

GEFFEN, G.; BRADSHAW, J. L.; AND WALLACE, G. 1971. Interhemispheric effects on reaction time to verbal and nonverbal visual stimuli. *Journal of Experimental Psychology* 87:415–22.

GELDARD, F. A. 1972. *The human senses.* New York: Wiley.

GELMAN, R. 1972. Logical capacity of very young children: Number invariance rules. *Child Development* 43:75–90.

GELMAN, R. 1978. Cognitive development. *Annual Review of Psychology* 29:297–332.

GELMAN, R., AND BAILLARGEON, R. 1983. A review of some Piagetian concepts. In Mussen, P. (Ed.), *Carmichael's manual of child psychology: Vol 3. Cognitive development* (Markman, E. M., and Flavell, J. H., volume editors), pp. 167–230. New York: Wiley.

GELMAN, R., AND GALLISTEL, C. R. 1978. *The young child's understanding of number: A window on early cognitive development.* Cambridge, Mass.: Harvard University Press.

GEORGOTAS, A. 1985. Affective disorders: Pharmacotherapy. In Kaplan, H. I., and Sadock, J. (Eds.), *Comprehensive textbook of psychiatry,* 4th ed. Baltimore: Williams & Wilkins.

GERARD, H. B., AND MATHEWSON, G. C. 1966. The effects of severity of initiation on liking for a group: A replication. *Journal of Experimental Social Psychology* 2:278–87.

GERARD, H. B.; WILHELMY, R. A.; AND CONOLLEY, E. S. 1968. Conformity and group size. *Journal of Personality and Social Psychology* 8:79–82.

GERBINO, L.; OLESHANSKY, M.; AND GERSHON, S. 1978. Clinical use and mode of action of lithium. In Killiam, F. K. (Ed.), *Psychopharmacology: A generation of progress,* pp. 1261–75. New York: Raven.

GERGEN, K. 1973. Social psychology as history. *Journal of Personality and Social Psychology* 26:309–20.

GERKEN, L.; LANDAU, B.; AND REMEZ, R. 1990. Function morphemes in young children's speech perception and production. *Developmental Psychology* 26(2):204–16.

GERSHON, E. S.; NURNBERGER, J. I., JR.; BERRETTINI, W. H.; AND GOLDIN, L. R. 1985. Affective disorders: Genetics. In Kaplan, H. I., and Sadock, J. (Eds.), *Modern synopsis of comprehensive textbook of psychiatry,* 4th ed. Baltimore: Williams & Wilkins.

GESCHWIND, N. 1970. The organization of language and the brain. *Science* 170:940–44.

GESCHWIND, N. 1972. Language and the brain. *Scientific American* 226:76–83.

GESCHWIND, N. 1975. The apraxias: Neural mechanisms of disorders of learned movement. *American Scientist* 63:188–95.

GESELL, A. L., AND THOMPSON, H. 1929. Learning and growth in identical twins: An experimental study by the method of co-twin control. *Genetic Psychology Monographs,* vol. 6.

GIBBS, J., AND SMITH, G. P. 1984. The neuroendocrinology of postprandial satiety. In Martini, L., and Ganong, W. F. (Eds.), *Frontiers in neuroendocrinology,* vol. 8. New York: Raven.

GIBBS, J. C.; CLARK, P. M.; JOSEPH, J. A.; GREEN, J. L.; GOODRICK, T. S.; AND MAKOWSKI, D. G. 1986. Relations between moral judgment, moral courage, and field independence. *Child Development* 57:1040–43.

GIBSON, E. J. 1969. *Principles of perceptual learning and development.* New York: Appleton-Century-Crofts.

GIBSON, J. J. 1950. *The perception of the visual world.* Boston: Houghton Mifflin.

GIBSON, J. J. 1966. *The senses considered as perceptual systems.* Boston: Houghton Mifflin.

GIBSON, J. J. 1979. *The ecological approach to visual perception.* Boston: Houghton Mifflin.

GICK, M. L., AND HOLYOAK, K. J. 1980. Analogical problem solving. *Cognitive Psychology* 12:306–55.

GICK, M. L., AND HOLYOAK, K. J. 1983. Schema induction and analogical transfer. *Cognitive Psychology* 15:1–38.

GILLIGAN, C. 1982. *In a different voice: Psychological theory and women's development.* Cambridge, Mass.: Harvard University Press.

GILLIGAN, C. 1986. Profile of Carol Gilligan. In Scarr, S.; Weinberg, R. A.; and Levine, A. 1986. *Understanding development,* pp. 488–91. New York: Harcourt Brace Jovanovich.

GILMAN, S. 1982. *Seeing the insane.* New York: Wiley.

GINZBERG, L. 1909. *The legends of the Jews,* vol. 1. Translated by Szold, H. Philadelphia: Jewish Publication Society of America.

GLADUE, B. A.; GREEN, R.; AND HELLMAN, R. E. 1984. Neuroendocrine responses to estrogen and sexual orientation. *Science* 225:1496–98.

GLADWIN, T. 1970. *East is a Big Bird.* Cambridge, Mass.: Belknap Press.

GLANZER, M., AND CUNITZ, A. 1966. Two storage mechanisms in free recall. *Journal of Verbal Learning and Verbal Behavior* 5:531–60.

GLEITMAN, H. 1963. Place-learning. *Scientific American* 209:116–22.

GLEITMAN, H. 1971. Forgetting of long-term memories in animals. In Honig, W. K., and James, P. H. R. (Eds.), *Animal memory,* pp. 2–46. New York: Academic Press.

GLEITMAN, H. 1985. Some trends in the study of cognition. In Koch, S., and Leary, D. E. (Eds.), *A century of psychology as science,* pp. 420–36. New York: McGraw-Hill.

GLEITMAN, H. 1990. Some reflections on drama and the dramatic experience. In Rock, I. (Ed.), *The legacy of Solomon Asch: Essays in cognition and social psychology.* Hillsdale, N.J.: Erlbaum.

GLEITMAN, L. R. 1986. Biological dispositions to learn language. In Demopolous, W., and Marras, A. (Eds.), *Language learning and concept acquisition.* Norwood, N.J.: Ablex.

GLEITMAN, L. R. 1990. Structural sources of verb learning. *Language Acquisition* 1:1–54.

GLEITMAN, L. R.; GLEITMAN, H.; LANDAU, B.; AND WANNER, E. 1988. Where learning begins: Initial representations for language learning. In Newmeyer, F. (Ed.), *Linguistics: The Cambridge survey: Vol. III. Language: Psychological and biological aspects.* Cambridge: Cambridge University Press.

GLEITMAN, L. R.; GLEITMAN, H.; AND SHIPLEY, E. F. 1972. The emergence of the child as grammarian. *Cognition* 1(2):137–64.

GLEITMAN, L. R.; AND ROZIN, P. 1977. The structure and acquisition of reading. I: Relations between orthographies and the structure of language. In Reber, A., and Scarborough, D. (Eds.), *Toward a psy-chology of reading.* Hillsdale, N.J.: Erlbaum.

GLEITMAN, L. R., AND WANNER, E. 1982. Language acquisition: The state of the art. In Wanner, E., and Gleitman, L. (Eds.), *Language acquisition: The state of the art.* New York: Cambridge University Press.

GLICK, J. 1975. Cognitive development in cross-cultural perspective. In Horowitz, F. G. (Ed.), *Review of child development research,* vol. 4. Chicago: University of Chicago Press.

GLUCKSBERG, S. 1962. The influence of strength of drive on functional fixedness and perceptual recognition. *Journal of Experimental Psychology* 63:36–41.

GODDEN, D. R., AND BADDELEY, A. D. 1975. Context-dependent memory in two natural environments: On land and underwater. *British Journal of Psychology* 66:325–31.

GOFFMAN, E. 1959. *The presentation of self in everyday life.* Garden City, N.Y.: Anchor Books, Doubleday.

GOFFMAN, E. 1961. *Asylums.* Chicago: Aldine.

GOLANI, I.; WOLGIN, D. L.; AND TEITELBAUM, P. 1979. A proposed natural geometry of recovery from akinesia in the lateral hypothalamic rat. *Brain Research* 164:237–67.

GOLD, R. 1978. On the meaning of nonconservation. In Lesgold, A. M.; Pellegrino, J. W.; Fokkema, S. D.; and Glaser, R. (Eds.), *Cognitive psychology and instruction.* New York: Plenum.

GOLDBERG, L. R. 1981a. Developing a taxonomy of trait-descriptive terms. In Fiske, D. W. (Ed.), *Problems with language imprecision,* pp. 43–66. San Francisco: Jossey-Bass.

GOLDBERG, L. R. 1981b. Language and individual differences: The search for universals in personality lexicons. In Wheeler, L. (Ed.), *Review of Personality and Social Psychology* 2:141–65.

GOLDBERG, L. R. 1982. From ace to zombie: Some explorations in the language of personality. In Spielberger, C., and Butcher, J. N. (Eds.), *Advances in personality assessment,* vol. 1. Hillsdale, N.J.: Erlbaum.

GOLDEN, T. 1990. Ill, possibly violent, and no place to go. *New York Times,* Monday, April 2, 1990, pp. A1 and B4.

GOLDFARB, W. 1955. Emotional and intellectual consequences of psychological deprivation in infancy: A reevaluation. In Hock, P. H., and Zubin, J. (Eds.), *Psychopathology of childhood.* New York: Grune and Stratton.

GOLDIN-MEADOW, S. 1982. Fragile and resilient properties of language learning. In Wanner, E., and Gleitman, L. R. (Eds.), *Language acquisition: State of the art.* New York: Cambridge University Press.

GOLDIN-MEADOW, S., AND MYLANDER, C. 1983. Gestural communication in deaf children: The non-effects of parental input. *Science* 221:372–74.

GOLDSTEIN, E. B. 1984. *Sensation and perception,* 2nd ed. Belmont, Calif.: Wadsworth.

GOLDSTEIN, E. B. 1989. *Sensation and perception,* 3rd ed. Belmont, Calif.: Wadsworth.

GOMBRICH, E. H. 1961. *Art and illusion.* Princeton, N.J.: Bollingen Series, Princeton University Press.

GOODE, E., AND HUBER, L. 1977. Sexual correlates of homosexual experience: An exploratory study of college women. *Journal of Sex Research* 13:12–21.

GOODMAN, J. F. 1990. Infant intelligence: Do we, can we, should we assess it? In Reynolds, C. R., and Kamphaus, R. (Eds.), *Handbook of psychological and educational assessment.* New York: Guilford.

GORDON, H. 1923. Mental and scholastic tests among retarded children. *Educational Pamphlet,* no. 44. London: Board of Education.

GOTTESMAN, I. I.; McGUFFIN, P.; AND FARMER, A. 1987. Clinical genetics as clues to the "real" genetics of schizophrenia (a decade of modest gains while playing for time). *Schizophrenia Bulletin* 13:23–47.

GOTTESMAN, I. I., AND SHIELDS, J. 1972. *Schizophrenia and genetics: A twin study vantage point.* New York: Academic Press.

GOTTESMAN, I. I., AND SHIELDS, J. 1982. *Schizophrenia: The epigenetic puzzle.* New York: Cambridge University Press.

GOTTLIEB, G. 1961. Developmental age as a baseline for determination of the critical period for imprinting. *Journal of Comparative and Physiological Psychology* 54:422–27.

GOTTLIEB, G. 1976. The role of experience in the development of behavior and the nervous system. In Gottlieb, G. (Ed.), *Neural and behavioral specificity,* pp. 25–56. New York: Academic Press.

GOUGH, H. G. 1975. *California psychological inventory: Manual,* rev. ed. Palo Alto, Calif.: Consulting Psychologists Press (original edition, 1957).

GOULD, S. J. 1977. *Ontogeny and phylogeny.* Cambridge, Mass.: Harvard University Press.

GOULD, S. J. 1978. Sociobiology: The art of storytelling. *New Scientist* 80:530–33.

GOULDNER, A. W. 1960. The norm of reciprocity: A preliminary statement. *American Sociological Review* 25:161–79.

GOY, R. W. 1968. Organizing effect of androgen on the behavior of rhesus monkeys. In Michael, R. P. (Ed.), *Endocrinology and human behavior.* London: Oxford University Press.

GRAF, P., AND MANDLER, G. 1984. Activation makes words more accessible, but not necessarily more retrievable. *Journal of Verbal Learning and Verbal Behavior* 23:553–68.

GRAF, P.; MANDLER, G.; AND HADEN, P. 1982. Simulating amnesic symptoms in normal subjects. *Science* 218:1243–44.

GRAF, P.; MANDLER, G.; AND SQUIRE, L. R. 1984. The information that amnesic patients don't forget. *Journal of Experimental Psychology: Learning, Memory, and Cognition* 10:164–78.

GRAF, P., AND SCHACTER, D. L. 1985. Implicit and explicit memory for new associations in normal and amnesic subjects. *Journal of Experimental Psychology: Learning, Memory, and Cognition* 11:501–18.

GRAHAM, C. H., AND HSIA, Y. 1954. Luminosity curves for normal and dichromatic subjects including a case of unilateral color blindness. *Science* 120:780.

GRANT, V. W. 1976. *Falling in love.* New York: Springer.

GRAY, G. W. 1948. The great ravelled knot. *Scientific American* 179:26–38.

GRAY, S. 1977. Social aspects of body image: Perception of normalcy of weight and affect of college undergraduates. *Perceptual and Motor Skills* 45:1035–40.

GREEN, D. M. 1976. *An introduction to hearing.* New York: Academic Press.

GREEN, D. M., AND SWETS, J. A. 1966. *Signal detection theory and psychophysics.* New York: Wiley.

GREEN, P., AND PRESTON, M. 1981. Reinforcement of vocal correlates of auditory hallucinations by auditory feedback: A case study. *British Journal of Psychiatry* 139:204–208.

GREEN, R. 1969. Age-intelligence relationships between ages sixteen and sixty-four: A rising trend. *Developmental Psychology* 1:618–27.

GREEN, R. 1979. Childhood cross-gender behavior and subsequent sexual preference. *American Journal of Psychiatry* 136:106–108.

GREEN, S. K.; BUCHANAN, D. R.; AND HEUER, S. K. 1984. Winners, losers, and choosers: A field investigation of dating initiation. *Personality and Social Psychology Bulletin* 10:502–11.

GREENBERG, J.; PYSZCZYNSKI, T.; AND SOLOMON, S. 1982. The self-serving attributional bias: Beyond self-presentation. *Journal of Experimental Social Psychology* 18:56–67.

GREENFIELD, P. M. 1966. On culture and conservation. In Bruner, R. R.; Olver, R. R.; and Greenfield, P. M. (Eds.), *Studies in cognitive growth.* New York: Wiley.

GREENFIELD, P. M. 1976. Cross-cultural research and Piagetian theory: Paradox and progress. In Riegel, K., and Meacham, J. (Eds.), *The developing individual in a changing world,* vol. 1. The Hague: Mouton.

GREENFIELD, P. M., AND SMITH, J. H. 1976. *The structure of communication in early language development.* New York: Academic Press.

GREGORY, R. L. 1963. Distortion of visual space as inappropriate constancy scaling. *Nature* 199:678–80.

GREGORY, R. L. 1966. Visual illusions. In Foss, B. (Ed.), *New horizons in psychology.* Baltimore: Penguin Books.

GREGORY, R. L. 1974. Choosing a paradigm for perception. In Carterette, E. C., and Friedman, M. P. (Eds.), *Handbook of perception: Vol. 1. Historical and philosophical roots of perception.* New York: Academic Press.

GREVEN, P. J., JR. 1970. *Four generations: Population, land, and family in colonial Andover, Massachusetts.* Ithaca: N.Y.: Cornell University Press.

GREVERT, P., AND GOLDSTEIN, A. 1985. Placebo analgesia, naloxone, and the role of endogenous opioids. In White, L.; Turks, B.; and Schwartz, G. E. (Eds.), *Placebo,* pp. 332–51. New York: Guilford.

GRICE, H. P. 1968. Utterer's meaning, sentence-meaning and word-meaning. *Foundations of Language* 4:225–42.

GRICE, P. 1975. Logic and conversation. In Cole, P., and Morgan, J. (Eds.), *Syntax and semantics,* vol. 3. New York: Academic Press.

GRIGGS, R. A., AND COX, J. R. 1982. The elusive thematic-materials effect in Wason's selection task. *British Journal of Psychology* 73:407–20.

GRILL, H. J., AND BERRIDGE, K. C. 1985. Taste reactivity as a measure of the neural control of palatability. *Progress in psychobiology and physiological psychology,* vol. 11, pp. 1–61. New York: Academic Press.

GRIMSHAW, J. 1981. Form, function, and the language acquisition device. In Baker, C., and McCarthy, J. (Eds.), *The logical problem of language acquisition.* Cambridge, Mass.: MIT Press.

GROSSMAN, H. J. (Ed.). 1983. *Manual on terminology and classification in mental retardation,* rev. ed. Washington, D. C.: American Association for Mental Deficiency.

GROVES, P. M., AND REBEC, G. V. 1988. *Introduction to biological psychology,* 3rd ed. Dubuque, Iowa: W. C. Brown.

GRÜNBAUM, A. 1984. *The foundations of psychoanalysis: A philosophical inquiry.* Berkeley, Calif.: University of California Press.

GUILFORD, J. P. 1967. *The nature of human intelligence.* New York: McGraw-Hill.

GURMAN, A. S., AND KNISKERN, D. P. 1981. Family therapy outcome research. In Gurman, A. S., and Kniskern, D. P. (Eds.), *Handbook of family therapy.* New York: Brunner/Mazel.

GUTTMAN, N., AND KALISH, H. I. 1956. Discriminability and stimulus generalization. *Journal of Experimental Psychology* 51:79–88.

GUYTON, A. C. 1981. *Textbook of medical physiology.* Philadelphia: Saunders.

HABER, R. N. 1969. Eidetic images. *Scientific American* 220:36–44.

HABER, R. N. 1983. The impending demise of the icon: A critique of the concept of iconic storage in visual information processing. *The Behavioral and Brain Sciences* 6:1–54.

HAILMAN, J. P. 1967. The ontogeny of an instinct. *Behavior Supplements* 15:1–159.

HALL, C. S. 1953. A cognitive theory of dream symbols. *Journal of General Psychology* 48:169–86.

HALL, C. S. 1966. *The meaning of dreams.* New York: McGraw-Hill.

HALL, C. S.; LINDZEY, G.; LOEHLIN, J. C.; AND MANOSEVITZ, M. 1985. *Introduction to theories of personality.* New York: Wiley.

HALL, C. S., AND VAN DE CASTLE, R. 1966. *The content analysis of dreams.* New York: Appleton-Century-Crofts.

HALL, E. T. 1959. *The silent language.* New York: Doubleday.

HALL, J. A., AND TAYLOR, S. E. 1976. When love is blind: Main-

taining idealized images of one's spouse. *Human Relations* 29:751–61.

HALPERN, D. F. 1986. *Sex differences in cognitive abilities.* Hillsdale, N.J.: Erlbaum

HALVERSON, H. M. 1931. An experimental study of prehension infants by means of systematic cinema records. *Genetic Psychology Monographs* 47:47–63.

HAMBURG, D. A.; MOOS, R. H.; AND YALOM, I. D. 1968. Studies of distress in the menstrual cycle and the postpartum period. In Michael, R. P. (Ed.), *Endocrinology and human behavior,* pp. 94–116. London: Oxford University Press.

HAMILTON, D. L., AND ROSE, T. L. 1980. Illusory correlation and the maintenance of stereotypic beliefs. *Journal of Personality and Social Psychology* 39:832–45.

HAMILTON, W. D. 1964. The genetical evolution of social behavior. *Journal of Theoretical Biology* 7:1–51.

HARDY, J. D., AND SMITH, T. W. 1988. Cynical hostility and vulnerability to disease: Social support, life stress, and physiological response to conflict. *Health Psychology* 7:447–59.

HARE, R. D. 1965. Temporal gradients of fear arousal in psychopaths. *Journal of Abnormal Psychology* 70:422–45.

HARE, R. D. 1978. A research scale for the assessment of psychopathy in criminal populations. *Personality and Individual Differences* 1:111–19.

HAREVEN, T. K. 1978. The last stage: Historical adulthood and old age. In Erikson, E. H. (Ed.), *Adulthood,* pp. 201–16. New York: Norton.

HARKINS, S., AND GREEN, R. G. 1975. Discriminability and criterion differences between extraverts and introverts during vigilance. *Journal of Research in Personality* 9:335–40.

HARLOW, H. F. 1949. The formation of learning sets. *Psychological Review* 56:51–65.

HARLOW, H. F. 1950. Learning and satiation of response in intrinsically motivated complex puzzle performance in monkeys. *Journal of Comparative and Physiological Psychology* 43:289–94.

HARLOW, H. F. 1958. The nature of love. *American Psychologist* 13:673–85.

HARLOW, H. F. 1959. Learning set and error factor theory. In Koch, S. (Ed.), *Psychology: A study of a science,* vol. 2, pp. 492–537. New York: McGraw-Hill.

HARLOW, H. F. 1962. The heterosexual affectional system in monkeys. *American Psychologist* 17:1–9.

HARLOW, H. F., AND HARLOW, M. K, 1972. The young monkeys. *Readings in Psychology Today,* 2nd ed. Albany, N.Y.: Delmar Publishers, CRM Books.

HARLOW, H. F., AND NOVAK, M. A. 1973. Psychopathological perspectives. *Perspectives in Biology and Medicine* 16:461–78.

HARRELL, J. P. 1980. Psychological factors and hypertension: A status report. *Psychological Bulletin* 87:482–501.

HARRIS, G. W., AND MICHAEL, R. P. 1964. The activation of sexual behavior by hypothalamic implants of estrogen. *Journal of Physiology* 171:275–301.

HARRIS, M. 1974. *Cows, pigs, wars, and witches.* New York: Random House.

HARRIS, P. L. 1983. Infant cognition. In Mussen, P. (Ed.), *Carmichael's manual of child psychology: Vol. 2. Infancy and developmental psychobiology* (Haith, M. M., and Campos, J. J., volume editors), pp. 689–782. New York: Wiley.

HARRIS, P. L. 1987. The development of search. In Salapatek, P., and Cohen, L. (Eds.), *Handbook of infant perception,* pp. 155–208. New York: Academic Press.

HARTMANN, E. 1973. *The functions of sleep.* New Haven: Yale University Press.

HARTMANN, H. 1964. *Essays on ego psychology: Selected problems in psychoanalytic theory.* New York: International Universities Press.

HARTSHORNE, H., AND MAY, M. A. 1928. *Studies in the nature*

*of character,* vol. 1. New York: Macmillan.

HARVEY, L. O., JR., AND LEIBOWITZ, H. 1967. Effects of exposure duration, cue reduction, and temporary monocularity on size matching at short distances. *Journal of the Optical Society of America* 57:249–53.

HASE, H. D., AND GOLDBERG, L. R. 1967. Comparative validities of different strategies of constructing personality inventory scales. *Psychological Bulletin* 67:231–48.

HAYNES, S. G.; FEINLEIB, M.; AND KANNEL, W. B. 1980. The relationship of psychosocial factors to coronary heart disease in the Framingham study: Eight years incidence in coronary heart disease. *American Journal of Epidemiology* 3:37–85.

HAYES, C. 1952. *The ape in our house.* London: Gollacz.

HAZELRIGG, M. D.; COOPER, H. M.; AND BORDUIN, C. M. 1987. Evaluating the effectiveness of family therapies: An integrative review and analysis. *Psychological Bulletin* 101:428–42.

HEALY, A. F., AND MILLER, G. A. 1970. The verb as the main determinant of sentence meaning. *Psychonomic Science* 20:372.

HEARST, E. 1972. Psychology across the chessboard. In *Readings in Psychology Today,* 2nd ed. Albany, N.Y.: Delmar Publishers, CRM Books.

HEATH, R. 1964. Pleasure response of human subjects to direct stimulation of the brain: Physiologic and psychodynamic considerations. In Heath, R. (Ed.), *The role of pleasure in behavior,* pp. 219–43. New York: Harper & Row.

HEBB, D. O. 1949. *The organization of behavior: A neuropsychological theory.* New York: Wiley.

HEDIGER, H. 1968. *The psychology and behavior of animals in zoos and circuses.* New York: Dover.

HEIDBREDER, E. 1933. *Seven psychologies.* New York: Appleton-Century-Crofts.

HEIDER, F. 1958. *The psychology of interpersonal relationships.* New York: Wiley.

HEILMAN, K. M., AND WATSON, R. T. 1977. The neglect syndrome—a unilateral defect of the orienting response. In Harnard, S.; Doty, R. W.; Goldstein, J.; and Krauthamer, G. (Eds.), *Lateralization in the nervous system.* New York: Academic Press.

HEINICKE, C., AND WESTHEIMER, I. 1966. *Brief separations.* London: Longmans, Green.

HELLEKSON, C. J.; KLINE, J. A.; AND ROSENTHAL, N. E. 1986. Phototherapy for seasonal affective disorder in Alaska. *American Journal of Psychiatry* 143:1035–37.

HELLER, H. C.; CRANSHAW, L. I.; AND HAMMEL, H. T. 1978. The thermostat of vertebrate animals. *Scientific American* 239:102–13.

HELMHOLTZ, H. 1909. *Wissenschaftliche Abhandlungen, II,* pp. 764–843.

HELMHOLTZ, H. 1910. *Treatise on physiological optics,* vols. 2 and 3. Trans. and ed. from the 3rd German ed. Southall, J. P. Rochester, N.Y.: Optical Society of America.

HENLE, M. 1962. On the relation between logic and thinking. *Psychological Review* 69:366–78.

HENRY, J. P., AND CASSEL, J. C. 1969. Psychosocial factors in essential hypertension. *American Journal of Epidemiology* 90:171.

HERING, E. 1920. *Outlines of a theory of the light sense,* pp. 150–51. Edited by Hurvich, L. M., and Jameson, D. Cambridge, Mass.: Harvard University Press.

HERMAN, C. P., AND POLIVY, J. 1980. Restrained eating. In Stunkard, A. J. (Ed.), *Obesity,* pp. 208–25. Philadelphia: Saunders.

HERMAN, C. P., AND MACK, D. 1975. Restrained and unrestrained eating. *Journal of Personality* 43:647–60.

HESS, E. H. 1958. "Imprinting" in animals. *Scientific American* 198:82.

HESS, E. H. 1959. Imprinting. *Science* 130:133–41.

HESS, E. H. 1973. *Imprinting: Early experience and the developmental psychobiology of attachment.* New York: Van Nostrand.

HESS, R. D. 1970. Social class and ethnic influences on socializa-

tion. In Mussen, P. H. (Ed.), *Carmichael's manual of child psychology,* 3rd ed., vol. 2, pp. 457–558. New York: Wiley.

HESTON, L. L. 1966. Psychiatric disorders in foster home reared children of schizophrenic mothers. *British Journal of Psychiatry* 112:819–25.

HILGARD, E. R. 1977. *Divided consciousness: Multiple controls in human thought and action.* New York: Wiley.

HILL, A. L. 1978. Savants: Mentally retarded individuals with specific skills. In N. R. Ellis (Ed.), *International Review of Research in Mental Retardation,* vol. 9. New York: Academic Press.

HILL, C. T.; RUBIN, L.; AND PEPLAU, L. A. 1976. Breakups before marriage: The end of 103 affairs. *Journal of Social Issues* 32:147–68.

HINELINE, P. N., AND RACHLIN, H. 1969. Escape and avoidance of shock by pigeons pecking a key. *Journal of the Experimental Analysis of Behavior* 12:533–38.

HIRSCH, J., AND KNITTLE, J. L. 1970. Cellularity of obese and nonobese human adipose tissue. *Federation of American Societies for Experimental Biology: Federation Proceedings* 29:1516–21.

HIRSCHFELD, AND CROSS, C. K. 1981. Epidemiology of affective disorders. *Archives of General Psychiatry* 39:3546

HIRSH-PASEK, K.; GOLINKOFF, R.; FLETCHER; DEGASPE-BEAUBIEN; AND CAULEY. 1985. In the beginning: one-word speakers comprehend word order. Paper presented at Boston Child Language Conference, October, 1985.

HIRSH-PASEK, K.; KEMLER-NELSON, D.; JUSCZYK, P.; CASSIDY, K.; DRUSS, B.; AND KENNEDY, L. 1987. Clauses are perceptual units for young infants. *Cognition* 26:269–86.

HIRTH, D. H., AND MCCULLOUGH, D. R. 1977. Evolution of alarm signals in ungulates with special reference to white-tailed deer. *American Naturalist* 111:31–42.

HOBBES, T. 1651. *Leviathan.* Baltimore: Penguin Books, 1968.

HOBSON, J. A. 1988. *The dreaming brain.* New York: Basic Books.

HOCHBERG, J. E. 1970. Attention, organization and consciousness. In Mostofsky, D. I. (Ed.), *Attention: Contemporary theory and analysis,* pp. 99–124. New York: Appleton-Century-Crofts.

HOCHBERG, J. E. 1978a. *Perception,* 2nd ed. Englewood Cliffs, N.J.: Prentice-Hall.

HOCHBERG, J. E. 1978b. Art and perception. In Carterette, E. C., and Friedman, M. P. (Eds.), *Handbook of perception,* vol. 10, pp. 225–55. New York: Academic Press.

HOCHBERG, J. E. 1980. Pictorial functions and perceptual structures. In Hagen, M. A. (Ed.), *The perception of pictures,* vol. 2, pp. 47–93. New York: Academic Press.

HOCHBERG, J. 1981. On cognition in perception: Perceptual coupling and unconscious inference. *Cognition* 10:127–34.

HOCHBERG, J. 1988. Visual perception. In Atkinson, R. C.; Herrnstein, R. J.; Lindzey, G.; and Luce, R. D. (Eds.), *Stevens' handbook of experimental psychology: Vol. 1. Perception and motivation,* rev. ed., pp. 195–276. New York: Wiley.

HODGKIN, A. L., AND HUXLEY, A. F. 1939. Action potentials recorded from inside nerve fiber. *Nature* 144:710–11.

HOFFMAN, H. S. 1978. Experimental analysis of imprinting and its behavioral effects. *The Psychology of Learning and Motivation* 12:137.

HOFFMAN, H. S., AND FLESHLER, M. 1964. An apparatus for the measurement of the startle response in the rat. *American Journal of Psychology* 77:307–308.

HOFFMAN, M. L. 1970. Moral development. In Mussen, P. H., (Ed.), *Carmichael's manual of child psychology,* 3rd. ed., vol. 2, pp. 457–558. New York: Wiley.

HOFFMAN, L. W. 1974. Effects of maternal employment on the child. A review of the research. *Developmental Psychology* 10:204–28.

HOFFMAN, M. L. 1975a. Altruistic behavior and the parent-child relationship. *Journal of Personality and Social Psychology* 31:937–43.

HOFFMAN, M. L. 1977a. Empathy, its development and proso-

cial implications. In Keasey, C. B. (Ed.), *Nebraska Symposium on Motivation* 25:169–217.

HOFFMAN, M. L. 1977b. Sex differences in empathy and related behaviors. *Psychological Bulletin* 84:712–22.

HOFFMAN, M. L. 1979. Development of moral thought, feeling, and behavior. *American Psychologist* 34:295–318.

HOFFMAN, M. L. 1984. Empathy, its limitations, and its role in a comprehensive moral theory. In Kurtines, W. M., and Gewirtz, L. (Eds.), *Morality, moral behavior, and moral development,* pp. 283–302. New York: Wiley.

HÖHN, E. O. 1969. The phalarope. *Scientific American* 220:104.

HOLDING, D. H. 1985. *The psychology of chess skill.* Hillsdale, N.J.: Erlbaum.

HOLDING, D. H., AND REYNOLDS, R. I. 1982. Recall or evaluation of chess positions as determinants of chess skill. *Memory and Cognition* 10:237–42.

HOLLAND, P. 1984. Origins of behavior in Pavlovian conditioning. *Psychology of Learning and Motivation* 18:129–174.

HOLLINGSHEAD, A. B., AND REDLICH, F. C. 1958. *Social class and mental illness: A community study.* New York: Wiley.

HOLLIS, K. I. 1982. Pavlovian conditioning of signal-centered action patterns and autonomic behavior: A biological analysis of function. In Rosenblatt, J. S.; Hinde, R. A.; Beer, C.; and Busnel, M. (Eds.), *Advances in the study of behavior,* vol. 12, pp. 1–64. New York: Academic Press.

HOLLIS, K. L. 1984. The biological function of Pavlovian conditioning: The best defense is a good offense. *Journal of Experimental Psychology: Animal Learning and Behavior* 10:413–25.

HOLLON, S., AND BECK, A. T. 1986. Cognitive and cognitive-behavioral therapies. *Handbook of psychotherapy and behavior change,* 3rd ed. New York: Wiley.

HOLLON, S. D.; DERUBEIS, R. J.; EVANS, M. D.; WIEMER, M. J.; GARVEY, M. J.; GROVE, W.; AND TUASON, V. B. 1990. *Cognitive therapy, pharmacotherapy and combined cognitive-pharmacotherapy in the treatment of depression.* Unpublished manuscript, University of Minnesota and the St. Paul-Ramsey Medical Center, Minneapolis-St. Paul, Minn.

HOLT, R. R. 1978. *Methods in clinical psychology: Vol. 1. Projective assessment.* New York: Plenum.

HOLTZWORTH-MUNROE, A., AND JACOBSON, N. S. 1985. Causal attributions of married couples: When do they search for causes? What do they conclude when they do? *Journal of Personality and Social Psychology* 48:1398–1412.

HOLWAY, A. F., AND BORING, E. G. 1947. Determinants of apparent visual size with distance variant. *American Journal of Psychology* 54:21–37.

HOOKER, E. 1957. The adjustment of the male overt homosexual. *Journal of Projective Techniques* 21:18–31.

HOOKER, E. 1965. Male homosexuals and their "worlds." In Marmor, J. (Ed.), *Sexual inversion,* pp. 83–107. New York: Basic Books.

HOOLEY, J. M. 1985. Expressed emotion: A review of the critical literature. *Clinical Psychology Review* 5:119–39.

HORN, J. L., AND CATTELL, R. B. 1967. Age differences in fluid and crystallized intelligence. *Acta Psychologica* 26:107–29.

HORN, J. L., AND DONALDSON, G. 1976. On the myth of intellectual decline in adulthood. *American Psychologist* 31:701–19.

HORN, J. M. 1983. The Texas Adoption Project: Adopted children and their biological and adoptive parents. *Child Development* 54:268–75.

HORN, J. M.; LOEHLIN, J. C.; AND WILLERMAN, L. 1975. Preliminary report of Texas Adoption Project. In Munsinger, H., The adopted child's IQ: A critical review. *Psychological Bulletin* 82:623–59.

HORN, J. M.; LOEHLIN, J. C.; AND WILLERMAN, L. 1979. Intellectual resemblance among adoptive and biological relatives: The Texas Adoption Project. *Behavior Genetics* 13:459–71.

HORN, J. M.; LOEHLIN, J. C.; AND WILLERMAN, L. 1982. Aspects of the inheritance of intellectual abilities. *Behavior Genetics* 12:479–516.

HORNE, J. 1988. *Why we sleep: The functions of sleep in humans and other mammals.* New York: Oxford University Press.

HORNE, R. L., AND PICARD, R. S. 1979. Psychosocial risk factors for lung cancer. *Psychosomatic Medicine* 41:503–14.

HORNEY, K. 1937. *The neurotic personality of our time.* New York: Norton.

HORNEY, K. 1945. *Our inner conflicts.* New York: Norton.

HORNEY, K. 1950. *New ways in psychoanalysis.* New York: Norton.

HOVLAND, C. I., AND WEISS, W. 1952. The influence of source credibility on communication effectiveness. *Public Opinion Quarterly* 15:635–50.

HOWARD, D. V. 1983. *Cognitive psychology.* New York: Macmillan.

HRDY, S. B. 1988. The primate origins of sexuality. In Smith, M. S.; Hamilton, W. D.; Margulis, L.; Hrdy, S. B.; Raven, P. H.; and Hefner, P. J. (Eds.), *The evolution of sex.* San Francisco: Harper & Row.

HRDY, S. B., AND WILLIAMS, G. C. 1983. Behavioral biology and the double standard. In Wasser, S. K., (Ed.), *The social behavior of female vertebrates,* pp. 3–17. New York: Academic Press.

HUBEL, D. H. 1963. The visual cortex of the brain. *Scientific American* 209:54–62.

HUBEL, D. H., AND WIESEL, T. N. 1959. Receptive fields of single neurons in the cat's visual cortex. *Journal of Physiology* 148:574–91.

HUBEL, D. H., AND WIESEL, T. N. 1970. Stereoscopic vision in the macaque monkey. Nature 225:41–42.

HUBEL, D. H., AND WIESEL, T. N. 1979. Brain mechanisms of vision. *Scientific American* 241:150–68.

HULL, C. L. 1943. *Principles of behavior.* New York: Appleton-Century-Crofts.

HUMPHREY, G. 1951. *Thinking: An introduction to its experimental psychology.* New York: Wiley.

HUMPHREYS, L. G. 1939. The effect of random alternation of reinforcement on the acquisition and extinction of conditioned eyelid reactions. *Journal of Experimental Psychology* 25:141–58.

HUNT, E. 1976. Varieties of cognitive power. In Resnick, L. B. (Ed.), *The nature of intelligence.* Hillsdale, N.J.: Erlbaum.

HUNT, E. 1978. Mechanics of verbal ability. *Psychological Review* 85:109–30.

HUNT, E. 1985a. The correlates of intelligence. In D. K. Detterman (Ed.), *Current topics in human intelligence,* vol. 1. Norwood, N.J.: Ablex.

HUNT, E. 1985b. Verbal ability. In Sternberg, R. J. (Ed.), *Human abilities: An information processing approach,* pp. 31–58. New York: Freeman.

HUNT, E.; LUNNEBORG, C.; AND LEWIS, J. 1975. What does it mean to be high verbal? *Cognitive Psychology* 7:194–227.

HUNT, J. M. 1961. *Intelligence and experience.* New York: Ronald Press.

HUNT, M. M. 1959. *The natural history of love.* New York: Knopf.

HUNT, P., AND HILLERY, J. M. 1973. Social facilitation in a coaction setting: An examination of the effects over learning trials. *Journal of Experimental Social Psychology* 9:563–71.

HURVICH, L. M. 1981. *Color vision.* Sunderland, Mass.: Sinauer Assoc.

HURVICH, L. M., AND JAMESON, D. 1957. An opponent-process theory of color vision. *Psychological Review* 64:384–404.

HURVICH, L. M., AND JAMESON, D. 1974. Opponent processes as a model of neural organization. *American Psychologist* 29:88–102.

HUSTON, A. C. 1983. Sex-typing. In Mussen, P. (Ed.), *Carmichael's manual of child psychology: Vol. 4. Socialization, personality, and social development,* pp. 387–468. (Hetherington, E. M., volume editor). New York: Wiley.

HUSTON, T. L.; RUGGIERO, M.; CONNER, R.; AND GEIS, G. 1981. Bystander intervention into crime: A study based on naturally occurring episodes. *Social Psychology Quarterly* 44:14–23.

HUTCHINSON, R. R., AND RENFREW, J. W. 1966. Stalking attack and eating behaviors elicited from the same sites in the hypothalamus. *Journal of Comparative and Physiological Psychology* 61:360–67.

HUTTENLOCHER, J.; SMILEY, P.; AND CHARNEY, R. 1983. Emergence of action categories in the child: Evidence from verb meanings. *Psychological Review* 90:72–93.

HUTTENLOCHER, P. R. 1979. Synaptic density in human frontal cortex—developmental changes and effects of aging. *Brain Research* 163:195–205.

HYAMS, N. 1986. *Language acquisition and the theory of parameters.* Dordrecht: Reidel.

HYDE, D. M. 1959. An investigation of Piaget's theories of the development of the concept of number. Unpublished doctoral dissertation. University of London. (Quoted in Flavell, J. H., *The developmental psychology of Jean Piaget,* p. 383. New York: Van Nostrand Reinhold).

HYDE, J. S. 1981. How large are cognitive gender differences? A meta-analysis using $w^2$ and d. *American Psychologist* 36:892–901.

HYDE, J. S., AND LYNN, M. C. 1988. Gender differences in verbal ability: A meta-analysis. *Psychological Bulletin* 104:53–69.

ILYIN, N. A., AND ILYIN, V. N. 1930. Temperature effects on the color of the Siamese cat. *Journal of Heredity* 21:309–18.

IMPERATO-McGINLEY, J.; GUERRERO, L.; GAUTIER, T.; AND PETERSON, R. E. 1974. Steroid 5-alpha reductase deficiency in man: An inherited form of male pseudohermaphroditism. *Science* 186:1213–15.

IMPERATO-McGINLEY, J.; PETERSON, R. E.; GAUTIER, T.; AND STURLA, E. 1979. Androgens and the evolution of male-gender identity among male pseudohermaphrodites with 5-alpha reductase deficiency. *The New England Journal of Medicine* 300:1233–37.

INBAU, F. E., AND REID, J. E. 1953. *Truth and deception: The polygraph ("lie detector") technique.* Baltimore: Williams & Wilkins.

INGLIS, J. 1969. Electrode placement and the effect of ECT on mood and memory in depression. *Canadian Psychiatric Association Journal* 14:463–471.

INGVAR, D. H., AND LASSEN, N. A. 1979. Activity distribution in the cerebral cortex in organic dementia as revealed by measurements of regional cerebral blood flow. *Bayer Symposium VII. Brain function in old age,* 268–77.

IZARD, C. E. 1971. *The face of emotion.* New York: Appleton-Century-Crofts.

IZARD, C. E. 1977. *Human emotions.* New York: Plenum.

IZARD, C. E. 1981. Differential emotions theory and the facial feedback hypothesis of emotion activation: Comments on Tourangeau and Ellsworth's "The role of facial response in the experience of emotion." *Journal of Personality and Social Psychology* 40:350–54.

IZZETT, R. 1971. Authoritarianism and attitudes toward the Vietnam War as reflected in behavioral and self-report measures. *Journal of Personality and Social Psychology* 17:145–48.

JACKENDOFF, R. 1987. The status of thematic relations in linguistic theory. *Linguistic Inquiry* 18(3):369–411.

JACKSON, J. M., AND LATANÉ, B. 1981. All alone in front of all those people: Stage fright as a function of the number and type of coperformers and audience. *Journal of Personality and Social Psychology* 40:73–85.

JACKSON, M., AND McCLELLAND, J. L. 1975. Sensory and cognitive determinants of reading speed. *Journal of Verbal Learning and Verbal Behavior* 14:565–74.

JACKSON, M. D., AND McCLELLAND, J. L. 1979. Processing de-

terminants of reading speed. *Journal of Experimental Psychology: Experimental* 108:151–58.

JACOBS, A. 1955. Formation of new associations to words selected on the basis of reaction-time-GSR combinations. *Journal of Abnormal and Social Psychology* 51:371–77.

JACOBY, L. L., AND DALLAS, M. 1981. On the relationship between autobiographical memory and perceptual learning. *Journal of Experimental Psychology: General* 3:306–40.

JACOBY, L. L., AND WITHERSPOON, D. 1982. Remembering without awareness. *Canadian Journal of Psychology* 36:300–24.

JAHODA, G. 1979. A cross-cultural perspective on experimental social psychology. *Person. and Social Psych. Bulletin* 5:142–48.

JAMES, W. 1890. *Principles of psychology.* New York: Henry Holt.

JAMES, W. T. 1941. Morphological form and its relation to behavior. In Stockard, C. R., *The genetic and endocrinic basis for differences in form and behavior,* pp. 525–643. Philadelphia: Wistar Institute.

JAMESON, D. 1975. From contrast to assimilation in art and in the eye. *Leonardo* 8:125–31.

JAMESON, D., AND HURVICH, L. M.. 1975. From contrast to assimilation: In art and in the eye. *Leonardo* 8:125–31.

JANICAK, P. G.; DAVIS, J. M.; GIBBONS, R. D.; ERICKSEN, S.; CHANG, S.; AND GALLAGHER, P. 1985. Efficacy of ECT: A meta-analysis. *American Journal of Psychiatry* 142:297–302.

JANIS, I. L.; MAHL, G. G.; KAGAN, J.; AND HOLT, R. R. 1969. *Personality: Dynamics, development and assessment.* New York: Harcourt, Brace and World.

JENCKS, C.; SMITH, M.; ACLAND, H.; BANE, M. J.; COHEN, D.; GINTIS, H.; HEYNS, B.; AND MICHELSON, S. 1972. *Inequality: A reassessment of the effect of family and schooling in America.* New York: Basic Books.

JENKINS, C. D.; ROSENMAN, R. H.; AND FRIEDMAN, M. 1967. Development of an objective psychological test for the determination of the coronary prone behavior pattern in employed men. *Journal of Chronic Disease* 20:371–79.

JENKINS, H. M., AND MOORE, B. R. 1973. The form of the auto-shaped response with food or water reinforcers. *Journal of the Experimental Analysis of Behavior* 20:163–81.

JENKINS, J. G., AND DALLENBACH, K. M. 1924. Oblivescence during sleep and waking. *American Journal of Psychology* 35:605–12.

JENSEN, A. R. 1965. Scoring the Stroop test. *Acta Psychologica* 24:398–408.

JENSEN, A. R. 1969. How much can we boost I. Q. and scholastic achievement? *Harvard Educational Review* 39:1–123.

JENSEN, A. R. 1973. *Educability and group differences.* New York: Harper & Row.

JENSEN, A. R. 1985. The nature of the black-white difference on various psychometric tests: Spearman's hypothesis. *Behavioral and Brain Sciences* 8:193–263.

JOHNSON, B. L. & KILMANN, P. R. 1975. The relationship between recalled parental attitudes and internal-external control. *Journal of Clinical Psychology* 31:40–42.

JOHNSON, J., AND NEWPORT, E. 1989. Critical period efforts in second-language learning: The influence of maturational state on the acquisition of English as a second language. *Cognitive Psychology* 21:60–90.

JOHNSON, N. F. 1965. The psychological reality of phrase structure rules. *Journal of Verbal Learning and Verbal Behavior* 5:469–75.

JOHNSON, R. E. 1979. *Juvenile delinquency and its origins.* New York: Cambridge University Press.

JOHNSON, S. 1765. Shakespeare criticism. In Danziger, M. K. (Ed.), *Samuel Johnson on literature.* New York: Ungar, 1979.

JONES, E. 1954. *Hamlet and Oedipus.* New York: Doubleday.

JONES, E. E.; DAVIS, K. E.; AND GERGEN, K. J. 1961. Role playing variations and their informational value for person perception. *Journal of Abnormal and Social Psychology* 63:302–10.

JONES, E. E., AND HARRIS, V. A. 1967. The attribution of attitudes. *Journal of Experimental Social Psychology* 3:1–24.

JONES, E. E., AND NISBETT, R. E. 1972. The actor and the observer: Divergent perceptions of the cause of behavior. In Jones, E. E.; Karouse, D. E.; Kelley, H. H.; Nisbett, R. E.; Valins, S.; and Weiner, B. (Eds.), *Attribution: Perceiving the causes of behavior.* Morristown, N.J.: General Learning Press.

JONES, H. E., AND KAPLAN, O. J. 1945. Psychological aspects of mental disorders in later life. In Kaplan, O. J. (Ed.), *Mental disorders in later life,* pp. 69–115. Stanford, Calif.: Stanford University Press.

JONES, R. E. 1983. Street people and psychiatry: An introduction. *Hospital Community Psychiatry* 34:807–11.

JONIDES, J. 1980. Toward a model of the mind's eye's movement. *Canadian Journal of Psychology* 34:103–12.

JONIDES, J. 1983. Further toward a model of the mind's eye's movement. *Bulletin of the Psychonomic Society* 21:247–50.

JONIDES, J., AND BAUM, D. R. 1978. Cognitive maps as revealed by distance estimates. Paper presented at the 18th annual meeting of the Psychonomic Society. Washington, D.C.

JORGENSEN, B. W., AND CERVONE, J. C. 1978. Affect enhancement in the pseudo recognition task. *Personality and Social Psychology Bulletin* 4:285–88.

JOSHI, A. K. 1983. Varieties of cooperative responses in question-answer systems. In Keifer, F. (Ed.), *Questions and answers,* pp. 229–40. Amsterdam: D. Reidel Publishing Co.

JOSSELSON, R. 1980. Ego development in adolescence. In Adelson, J. (Ed.), *Handbook of adolescent psychology,* pp. 188–211. New York: Wiley.

JOUVET, M. 1967. The stages of sleep. *Scientific American* 216:62–72.

JULESZ, B. 1978. Perceptual limits of texture discrimination and their implications to figure-ground separation. In Leeuwenberg, E. and Buffart, H. (Eds.), *Formal theories of perception,* pp. 205–16. New York: Wiley.

JULIEN, R. M. 1985. *A primer of drug action,* 4th ed. New York: Freeman.

JUSCZYK, P. 1985. On characterizing the development of speech perception. In Mehler, J., and Fox, R. (Eds.), *Neonate cognition: Beyond the blooming buzzing confusion.* Hillsdale, N.J.: Erlbaum.

KAGAN, J. 1976. Emergent themes in human development. *American Scientist* 64:186–96.

KAGAN, J. 1984. *The nature of the child.* New York: Basic Books.

KAGAN, J. 1989. Commentary. *Human Development* (Special Topic: Continuity in early cognitive development—conceptual and methodological challenges) 32:172–76.

KAGAN, J.; KEARSLEY, R. B.; AND ZELAZO, P. R. 1978. *Infancy: Its place in human development.* Cambridge,: Harvard Univ. Press.

KAGAN, J., AND MOSS, H. A. 1962. *Birth to maturity: The Fels study of psychological development.* New York: Wiley.

KAHNEMAN, D., AND MILLER, D. T. 1986. Norm theory: Comparing reality to its alternatives. *Psychological Review* 93:136–53.

KAHNEMAN, D., AND TVERSKY, A. 1972. Subjective probability: A judgment of representativeness. *Cognitive Psychology* 3:430–54.

KAHNEMAN, D., AND TVERSKY, A. 1973. On the psychology of prediction. *Psychological Review* 80:237–51.

KAHNEMAN, D., AND TVERSKY, A. 1982. The simulation heuristic. In Kahneman, D.; Slovic, P.; and Tversky, A. (Eds.), *Judgment under uncertainty.* New York: Cambridge University Press.

KAHNEMAN, D., AND TVERSKY, A. 1984. Choices, values, and frames. *American Psychologist* 39:341–50.

KALAT, J. W. 1984. *Biological psychology,* 2nd ed. Belmont, Calif.: Wadsworth.

KALLMAN, F. J. 1952. Comparative twin study of genetic aspects of male homosexuality. *Journal of Mental and Nervous Diseases* 15:283–98.

KAMIN, L. J. 1965. Temporal and intensity characteristics of the conditioned stimulus. In Prokasy, W. F. (Ed.), *Classical conditioning.* New York: Appleton-Century-Crofts.

KAMIN, L. J. 1968. "Attention-like" processes in classical conditioning. In Jones, M. R. (Ed.), *Miami symposium on the prediction of behavior: Aversive stimuli.* Miami: University of Miami Press.

KAMIN, L. J. 1969. Predictability, surprise, attention and conditioning. In Campbell, B. A., and Church, R. M. (Eds.), *Punishment and aversive behavior,* pp. 279–96. New York: Appleton-Century-Crofts.

KAMIN, L. J. 1974. *The science and politics of I. Q.* New York: Wiley.

KANDEL, D. 1978. Similarity in real-life adolescent friendship pairs. *Journal of Personality and Social Psychology* 36:306–12.

KANIZSA, G. 1976. Subjective contours. *Scientific American* 234:48–52.

KATKOWSKI, W., CRANDALL, V. C.; AND GOOD, S. 1967. Parental antecedents of children's beliefs in intellectual achievement situations. *Child Development* 28:765–76.

KATZ, B. 1952. The nerve impulse. *Scientific American* 187:55–64.

KATZ, J. J. 1972. *Semantic theory.* New York: Harper & Row.

KATZ, J. J., AND FODOR, J. A. 1963. The structure of a semantic theory. *Language* 39:170–210.

KATZ, N.; BAKER, E.; AND MacNAMARA, J. 1974. What's in a name? A study of how children learn common and proper names. *Child Development* 45:469–73.

KAUFMAN, A. S.; KAMPHAUS; R. W.; AND KAUFMAN, N. L. 1985. The Kaufman Assessment Battery for Children (K-ABC). In Newmark, C. S. (Ed.), *Major psychological assessment instruments.* Boston: Allyn and Bacon.

KAUFMAN, L., AND ROCK, I. 1962. The moon illusion. *Scientific American* 207:120–30.

KEELE, S. W. 1982. Learning and control of coordinated motor patterns: The programming perspective. In Kelso, J. A. S. (Ed.), *Human motor behavior;* pp. 143–60. Hillsdale, N.J.: Erlbaum.

KEESEY, R. E., AND PAWLEY, T. L. 1986. The regulation of body weight. *Annual Review of Psychology* 37:109–34.

KEETON, W. T. 1972 AND 1980. *Biological science,* 2nd and 3rd eds. New York: Norton.

KEETON, W. T., AND GOULD, J. L. 1986. *Biological science,* 4th ed. New York: Norton.

KEIL, F. C. 1979. *Semantic and conceptual development: An ontological perspective.* Cambridge, Mass.: Harvard University Press.

KEIL, F. C., AND BATTERMAN, N. 1984. A characteristic-to-defining shift in the development of word meaning. *Journal of Verbal Learning and Verbal Behavior* 23:221–36.

KELLER, H. 1985. *Teacher: Anne Sullivan Macy.* Westport, Conn.: Greenwood Press.

KELLEY, H. H. 1967. Attribution theory in social psychology. In Levine, D. (Ed.), *Nebraska Symposium on Motivation,* pp. 192–238. Lincoln, Neb.: University of Nebraska Press.

KELLEY, H. H., AND MICHELA, J. L. 1980. Attribution theory and research. *Annual Review of Psychology* 31:457–501.

KELLEY, H., AND THIBAUT, J. W. 1978. *Interpersonal relations: A theory of interdependence.* New York: Wiley-Interscience.

KELLEY, S., AND MIRER, T. W. 1974. The simple act of voting. *American Political Science Review* 68:572–91.

KELLMAN, P. J., AND SPELKE, E. S. 1983. Perception of partially occluded objects in infancy. *Cognitive Psychology* 15:483–524.

KELLMAN, P. J.; SPELKE, E. S.; AND SHORT, K. R. 1986. Infant perception of object unity from translatory motion in depth and vertical translation. *Child Development* 57:72–86.

KENDLER, K. S., AND GRUENBERG, A. M. 1984. An independent analysis of the Danish adoption study of schizophrenia: VI. The relationship between psychiatric disorders as defined by DSM-III in the relatives and adoptees. *Archives of General Psychiatry* 41:555–64.

KENRICK, D. T., AND CIALDINI, R. B. 1977. Romantic attraction: Misattribution versus reinforcement explanations. *Journal of Personality and Social Psychology* 35:381–91.

KENRICK, D. T.; CIALDINI, R. B.; AND LINDER, D. E. 1979. Misattribution under fear-producing circumstances: Four failures to replicate. *Personality and Social Psychology Bulletin* 5:329–34.

KENRICK, D. T., AND FUNDER, D. C. 1988. Profiting from controversy: Lessons from the person-situation debate. *American Psychologist* 43:23–34.

KERR, M. E., AND BOWEN, M. 1988. *Family evaluation.* New York: Norton.

KESSEL, E. L. 1955. The mating activities of balloon flies. *Systematic Zoology* 4:97–104.

KETY, S. S. 1983. Mental illness in the biological and adoptive relatives of schizophrenic adoptees: Findings relevant to genetic and environmental factors in etiology. *Journal of American Psychiatry* 140:720–27.

KIHLSTROM, J. F., AND CANTOR, N. 1984. Mental representations of the self. In Berkowitz, L. (Ed.), *Advances in experimental social psychology,* vol. 17, pp. 1–47. New York: Academic Press.

KILHAM, W., AND MANN, L. 1974. Level of destructive obedience as a function of transmitter and executant roles in the Milgram obedience paradigm. *Journal of Personality and Social Psychology* 29:696–702.

KIMBALL, J. 1973. Seven principles of surface structure parsing in natural language. *Cognition* 2:15–47.

KIMBLE, G. A. 1961. *Hilgard and Marquis' conditioning and learning.* New York: Appleton-Century-Crofts.

KING, H. E. 1961. Psychological effects of excitation in the limbic system. In Sheer, D. E. (Ed.), *Electrical stimulation of the brain.* Austin: University of Texas Press.

KINSEY, A. C.; POMEROY, W. B.; AND MARTIN, C. E. 1948. *Sexual behavior in the human male.* Philadelphia: Saunders.

KINSEY, A.; POMEROY, W.; MARTIN, C.; AND GEBHARD, P. 1953. *Sexual behavior in the human female.* Philadelphia: Saunders.

KINTSCH, W., AND van DIJK, T. 1977. Toward a model of text comprehension and production. *Psychological Review* 85:63–94.

KITCHER, P. 1985. *Vaulting ambition: Sociobiology and the quest for human nature.* Cambridge, Mass: M. I. T. Press.

KITCHER, P. 1987. Précis of *Vaulting ambition: Sociobiology and the quest for human nature* (and open peer commentary). *Behavioral and Brain Sciences* 10:61–100.

KITTRIE, N. N. 1971. *The right to be different: Deviance and enforced therapy.* Baltimore: Penguin Books.

KLEINMUNTZ, B. 1982. *Personality and psychological assessment.* New York: St. Martin's Press.

KLEITMAN, N. 1960. Patterns of dreaming. *Scientific American* 203:82–88.

KLIMA, E.; AND BELLUGI, U.; WITH BATTISON, R.; BOYES-BRAEM, P.; FISCHER, S.; FRISHBERG, N.; LANE, H.; LENTZ, E. M.; NEWKIRK, D.; NEWPORT, E.; PEDERSEN, C.; AND SIPLE, P. 1979. *The signs of language.* Cambridge, Mass.: Harvard University Press.

KLINEBERG, O. 1940. *Social psychology.* New York: Henry Holt.

KLOPFER, B.; AINSWORTH, M.; KLOPFER, W. G.; AND HOLT, R. R. 1954. *Developments in the Rorschach technique.* Yonkers, N.Y.: World Book.

KLOPFER, P. H. 1974. *An introduction to animal behavior: Ethology's first century.* Englewood Cliffs, N.J.: Prentice-Hall.

KNITTLE, J. L., AND HIRSCH, J. 1968. Effect of early nutrition on the development of the rat epididymal fat pads: Cellularity and metabolism. *Journal of Clinical Investigations* 47:2091.

KNOX, R. E., AND INKSTER, J. A. 1968. Postdecision dissonance at post-time. *Journal of Personality and Social Psychology* 8:319–23.

KOHLBERG, L. 1963. Development of children's orientations toward a moral order. *Vita Humana* 6:11–36.

KOHLBERG, L. 1966. A cognitive developmental analysis of children's sex-role concepts and attitudes. In Maccoby, E. E. (Ed.), *The development of sex differences,* pp. 82–171. Stanford, Calif.: Stanford University Press.

KOHLBERG, L. 1969. Stage and sequence: The cognitive developmental approach to socialization. In Goslin, D. A. (Ed.), *Handbook of socialization theory of research,* pp. 347–480. Chicago: Rand McNally.

KOHLBERG, L. AND CANDEE, D. 1984. The relationship of moral judgment to moral action. In Kurtines, W. M., and Gewirtz, L. (Eds.), *Morality, moral behavior, and moral development,* pp. 52–73. New York: Wiley.

KOHLBERG, L.; LEVINE, C.; AND HEWER, A. 1984. Synopses and detailed replies to critics. In Kohlberg, L. (Ed.), *The psychology of moral development: The nature and validity of moral stages,* pp. 320–86. San Francisco: Harper & Row.

KÖHLER, W. 1925. *The mentality of apes.* New York: Harcourt Brace and World.

KÖHLER, W. 1947. *Gestalt psychology.* New York: Liveright.

KOHN, M. L. 1968. Social class and schizophrenia: A critical review. In Rosenthal, D., and Kety, S. S. (Eds.), *The transmission of schizophrenia,* pp. 155–74. London: Pergamon.

KOHN, M. L. 1969. *Class and conformity: A study in values.* Chicago: University of Chicago Press.

KOHUT, H. 1978. *The psychology of the self: A case book.* New York: International Universities Press.

KOLB, B., AND MILNER, B. 1981. Performance of complex art and facial movements after focal brain lesions. *Neuropsychologia* 19:491–503.

KOLB, B., AND WHISHAW, I. Q. 1980. *Fundamentals of human neuropsychology.* San Francisco: Freeman.

KOLB, B., AND WHISHAW, I. 1990. *Fundamentals of human neuropsychology,* 3rd ed. San Francisco: Freeman.

KOLERS, P. A. 1972. *Aspects of motion perception.* New York: Pergamon.

KOLERS, P. A., AND POMERANTZ, J. R. 1971. Figural change in apparent motion. *Journal of Experimental Psychology* 87:99–108.

KOLODNY, R.; MASTERS, W.; HENDRYX, J.; AND TORO, G. 1971. Plasma testosterone and semen analysis in male homosexuals. *New England Journal of Medicine* 285:1170–74.

KORIAT, A., AND LIEBLICH, I. 1974. What does a person in a TOT state know that a person in a "Don't Know" state doesn't know? *Memory and Cognition* 2:647–55.

KORS, A. C., AND PETERS, E. 1972. *Witchcraft in Europe:1100–1700. A documentary history.* Philadelphia: University of Pennsylvania Press.

KOSSLYN, S. M. 1980. *Image and mind.* Cambridge, Mass.: Harvard University Press.

KOSSLYN, S. M. 1984. *Ghosts in the mind's machine.* New York: Norton.

KOSSLYN, S. M.; BALL, T. M.; AND REISSER, B. J. 1978. Visual images preserve metric spatial information: Evidence from studies of image scanning. *Journal of Experimental Psychology: Human Perception and Performance* 4:1–20.

KOSTLAN, A. 1954. A method for the empirical study of psychodiagnosis. *Journal of Consulting Psychology* 18:83–88.

KOTELCHUK, M. 1976. The infant's relationship to the father: Some experimental evidence. In Lamb, M. (Ed.), *The role of the father in child development.* New York: Wiley.

KOULACK, D., AND GOODENOUGH, D. R. 1976. Dream recall and dream recall failure: An arousal-retrieval model. *Psychological Bulletin* 83:975–84.

KRANTZ, D. S.; CONTRADA, R. J.; HILL, D. R.; AND FRIEDLER, E. 1988. Environmental stress and behavioral antecedents of coronary heart disease. *Journal of Consulting and Clinical Psychology* 56: 333–41.

KRASHEN, S. 1981. Second language acquisition and second language learning. London: Pergamon Press.

KREBS, J. R. 1982. Territorial defence in the great tit. *Parus Major L. Ecology* 52:2–22.

KREBS, J. R., AND DAVIES, N. B. 1987. *An introduction to behavioral ecology,* 2nd ed. Boston: Blackwell Scientific Publications.

KRECH, D., AND CRUTCHFIELD, R. 1958. *Elements of psychology.* New York: Knopf.

KUCZAJ, S. A. 1977. The acquisition of regular and irregular past tense forms. *Journal of Verbal Learning and Verbal Behavior* 16: 589–600.

KUFFLER, S. W. 1953. Discharge pattern and functional organization of mammalian retina. *Journal of Neurophysiology* 16:37–68.

KUPFER, D. J.; FOSTER, F. G.; AND REICH, L. 1976. EEG sleep changes as predictors in depression. *American Journal of Psychiatry* 133:622.

KUZNICKI, J. T., AND MCCUTCHEON, N. B. 1979. Cross enhancement of the sour taste of single human taste papillae. *Journal of Experimental Psychology* 198:68–89.

LA BERGE, D. 1975. Acquisition of automatic processing in perceptual and associative learning. In Rabbitt, P. M. A., and Dormic, S. (Eds.), *Attention and performance,* vol. 5. London: Academic Press.

LABOV, W. 1970. The logic of nonstandard English. In Williams, F. (Ed.), *Language and poverty: Perspectives on a theme,* pp. 153–89. Chicago: Markham.

LACK, D. 1953. Darwin's finches. *Scientific American* 188: 66–72.

LAIRD, J. D. 1974. Self-attribution of emotion: The effects of expressive behavior on the quality of emotional experience. *Journal of Personality and Social Psychology* 29:475–86.

LAKOFF, G., AND JOHNSON, M. 1980. *Metaphors we live by.* Chicago: University of Chicago Press.

LAMB, H. R. 1984. Deinstitutionalization and the homeless mentally ill. *Hospital Community Psychiatry* 35:899–907.

LAMB, M. E. 1977. Father-infant and mother-infant interaction in the first year of life. *Child Development* 48:167–81.

LAMB, M. E.; THOMPSON, R. M.; GARDNER, W.; CHARNOV, E. L.; AND ESTES, D. 1985. *Infant-mother attachment.* Hillsdale, N.J.: Erlbaum.

LANDAU, B. 1982. Will the real grandmother please stand up? The psychological reality of dual meaning representations. *Journal of Psycholinguistic Research* 11:47–62.

LANDAU, B., AND GLEITMAN, L. R. 1985. *Language and experience: Evidence from the blind child.* Cambridge, Mass.: Harvard University Press.

LANDAU, B.; GLEITMAN, H.; AND SPELKE, E. 1981. Spatial knowledge and geometric representation in a child blind from birth. *Science* 213:1275–78.

LANDAU, B.; SMITH, L.; AND JONES, S. 1988. The importance of shape in early lexical learning. *Cognitive Development* 3:299–321.

LANDAU, B.; SPELKE, E.; AND GLEITMAN, H. 1984. Spatial knowledge in a young blind child. *Cognition* 16:225–60.

LANDIS, C., AND HUNT, W. A. 1932. Adrenalin and emotion. *Psychological Review* 39:467–85.

LANGER, E. J., AND RODIN, J. 1976. The effects of choice and enhanced personal responsibility for the aged: A field experiment in an institutional setting. *Journal of Personality and Social Psychology* 34: 191–98.

LANGLOIS, J. H., AND DOWNS, A. C. 1980. Mothers, fathers, and peers as socialization agents of sex-typed play behaviors in young children. *Child Development* 51:1237–1347.

LANYON, R. I., AND GOLDSTEIN, L. D. 1971. *Personality assessment.* New York: Wiley.

LANYON, R. I., AND GOLDSTEIN, L. D. 1982. *Personality assessment.* 2nd ed. New York: Wiley.

LAPIERE, R. 1934. Attitudes versus actions. *Social Forces* 13:230–37.

LARKIN, J.; MCDERMOTT, J.; SIMON, D. P.; AND SIMON, H. A. 1980. Expert and novice performance in solving physics problems. *Science* 208:1335–42.

LASH, J. P. 1980. *Helen and Teacher: The story of Helen Keller and Anne Sullivan Macy.* New York: Delacorte Press.

LASHLEY, K. S. 1930. The mechanism of vision:1. A method for rapid analysis of pattern-vision in the rat. *Journal of Genetic Psychology* 37:453–60.

LASHLEY, K. S. 1951. The problem of serial order in behavior. In Jeffress, L. A. (Ed.), *Cerebral mechanisms in behavior, the Hixon Symposium.* New York: Wiley.

LASKY, J. J.; HOVER, G. L.; SMITH, P. A.; BOSTIAN, D. W.; DUF-FENDECK, S. C.; AND NORD, C. L. 1959. Post-hospital adjustment as predicted by psychiatric patients and by their staff. *Journal of Consulting Psychology* 23:213–18.

LASSEN, N. A.; INGVAR, D. H.; AND SKINHOJ, E. 1978. Brain function and blood flow. *Scientific American* 239:62–71.

LATANÉ, B. 1981. The psychology of social impact. *American Psychologist* 36:343–56.

LATANÉ, B., AND DARLEY, J. M. 1968. Group inhibition of bystander intervention in emergencies. *Journal of Personality and Social Psychology* 10:215–21.

LATANÉ, B., AND HARKINS, S. 1976. Cross-modality matches suggest anticipated stage fright as a multiplicative power function of audience size and status. *Perception and Psychophysics* 20:482–88.

LATANÉ, B., AND NIDA, S. 1981. Group size and helping. *Psychological Bulletin* 89:308–24.

LATANÉ, B.; NIDA, S. A.; AND WILSON, D. W. 1981. The effects of group size on helping behavior. In Rushton, J. P., and Sorrentino, R. M. (Eds.), *Altruism and helping behavior: Social, personality, and developmental perspectives.* Hillsdale, N.J.: Erlbaum.

LATANÉ, B., AND RODIN, J. 1969. A lady in distress: Inhibiting effects of friends and strangers on bystander intervention. *Journal of Experimental Social Psychology.* 5:189–202.

LATANÉ, B.; WILLIAMS, K.; AND HARKINS, S. 1979. Many hands make light the work: The causes and consequences of social loafing. *Journal of Personality and Social Psychology* 37:822–32.

LAU, R. R., AND RUSSELL, D. 1980. Attributions in the sports pages. *Journal of Personality and Social Psychology* 39:29–38.

LAYZER, D. 1972. Science or superstition: A physical scientist looks at the I. Q. controversy. *Cognition* 1:265–300.

LAZAR, I. AND DARLINGTON, R. 1982. Lasting effects of early education: A report from the Consortium for Longitudinal Studies. *Monographs of the Society for Research in Child Development* 47 (2–3, Serial No. 195).

LAZARUS, A. A. 1971. *Behavior therapy and beyond.* New York: McGraw-Hill.

LAZARUS, A. A. 1981. *The practice of multi-modal therapy.* New York: McGraw-Hill.

LE BON, G. 1895. *The crowd.* New York: Viking Press, 1960.

LEASK, J.; HABER, R. N.; AND HABER, R. B. 1969. Eidetic imagery in children: II. Longitudinal and experimental results. *Psychonomic Monograph Supplements* 3(Whole No. 35):25–48.

LEATON, R. N. 1976. Long-term retention of the habituation of lick suppression and startle response produced by a single auditory stimulus. *Journal of Experimental Psychology: Animal Behavior Processes* 2:248–59.

LEEPER, R. W. 1935. A study of a neglected portion of the field of learning: The development of sensory organization. *Journal of Genetic Psychology* 46:41–75.

LEFCOURT, H. M. 1976. *Locus of control: Current trends in theory and research.* New York: Erlbaum.

LEFF, J.; KUIPPERS, L.; BERKOWITZ, R.; EBERLEIN-VRIES, R.; AND STURGEON, D. 1982. A controlled trial of social intervention in the families of schizophrenic persons. *British Journal of Psychiatry* 141:121–34.

LEFF, M. J.; ROATSCH, J. F.; AND BUNNEY, W. E., JR. 1970. Environmental factors preceding the onset of severe depressions. *Psychiatry* 33:298–311.

LEFKOWITZ, M. M.; BLAKE, R. R.; AND MOUTON, J. S. 1955. Status factors in pedestrian violation of traffic signals. *Journal of Abnormal and Social Psychology* 51:704–706.

LEIBOWITZ, H.; BRISLIN, R.; PERLMUTTER, L.; AND HENNESSY, R. 1969. Ponzo perspective illusion as a manifestation of space perception. *Science* 166:1174–76.

LEMPERS, J. S.; FLAVELL, E. R.; AND FLAVELL, J. H. 1977. The development in very young children of tacit knowledge concerning visual perception. *Genetic Psychology Monographs* 95:3–53.

LENNEBERG, E. H. 1967. *Biological foundations of language.* New York: Wiley.

LEPPER, M. R. 1983. Social control processes, attributions of motivation, and the internalization of social values. In Higgins, E. T.; Ruble, D. N.; and Hartup, W. W. (Eds.), *Social cognition and social behavior: Developmental perspectives.* New York: Cambridge University Press.

LERNER, M. J. 1971. Observer's evaluation of a victim: Justice, guilt and veridical perception. *Journal of Personality and Social Psychology* 20:127–35.

LEVELT, W. 1970. A scaling approach to the study of syntactic relations. In Flores d'Arcais, G., and Levelt, W. (Eds.), *Advances in psycholinguistics.* Amsterdam: North-Holland.

LEVELT, W. J. M. 1989. *Speaking: From intention to articulation.* Cambridge, Mass.: MIT Press.

LEVENTHAL, H. 1984. A perceptual-motor theory of emotion. In L. Berkowitz (Ed.), *Advances in experimental social psychology,* vol. 13. New York: Academic Press.

LEVINE, J. D.; GORDON, N. C.; AND FIELDS, H. L. 1979. The role of endorphins in placebo analgesia. In Bonica, J. J.; Liebesking, J. C.; and Albe-Fessard, D. (Eds.), *Advances in pain research and therapy,* vol. 3. New York: Raven.

LEVINGER, G. 1983. Development and change. In Kelley, H. H.; Berscheid, E.; Christensen, A.; Harvey, J.; Huston, T. L.; Levinger, G.; McClintock, E.; Peplau, A.; and Peterson, D. R. (Eds.), *Close relationships.* San Francisco: Freeman.

LEVINSON, D. J. 1978. *The seasons of a man's life.* New York: Knopf.

LEVY, J. 1974. Psychobiological implications of bilateral asymmetry. In Dimond, S. J., and Beaumont, J. G. (Eds.), *Hemisphere function in the human brain,* pp. 121–83. New York: Wiley.

LEVY, J. 1979. Personal communication.

LEVY, J. 1983. Language, cognition, and the right hemisphere: A response to Gazzaniga. *American Psychologist* 38:538–41.

LEVY, J. 1985. Right brain, left brain: Facts and fiction. *Psychology Today* 19:38–44.

LEVY, J.; TREVARTHEN, C.; AND SPERRY, R. W. 1972. Perception of bilateral chimeric figures following hemispheric deconnexion. *Brain* 95:61–78.

LEWANDOWSKY, S.; DUNN, J. C.; AND KIRSNER, K. (Eds.). 1989. *Implicit memory: Theoretical issues.* Hillsdale, N.J.: Erlbaum.

LEWINSOHN, P. M.; HOBERMAN, H.; TERI, L.; AND HAUT-ZINGER, M. 1985. An integrative theory of depression. In Reiss, S., and Bootzin, R. (Eds.), *Theoretical issues in behavior therapy.* Orlando, Fla.: Academic Press.

LEWINSOHN, P. M.; STEINMETZ, J. L.; LARSON, D. W.; AND FRANKLIN, J. 1981. Depression-related cognitions: Antecedents or consequences? *Journal of Abnormal Psychology* 79:213–19.

LEWIS, E. R. et al. 1969. Study of neural organization in aplysia with the scanning electron microscope. *Science* 165:1140–43.

LEWONTIN, R. C. 1976. Race and intelligence. In Block, N. J., and Dworkin, G. (Eds.), *The IQ controversy,* pp. 78–92. New York: Pantheon.

LEWONTIN, R. C.; ROSE, S.; AND KAMIN, L. J. 1984. *Not in our genes: Biology, ideology, and human nature.* New York: Random House.

LEWY, A.; SACK, L.; MILLER, S.; AND HOBAN, T. M. 1987. Antidepressant and circadian-phase shifting effects of light. *Science* 235: 352–54.

LIBERMAN, A. M. 1970. The grammars of speech and language. *Cognitive Psychology* 1:301–23.

LICKLEY, J. D. 1919. *The nervous system.* New York: Longman.

LIDZ, T.; CORNELISON, A.; FLECK, S.; AND TERRY, D. 1957. The intrafamilial environment of schizophrenic patients: II. Marital schism and marital skew. *American Journal of Psychiatry* 114:241–48.

LIEBERMAN, P. L. 1975. *On the origins of language.* New York: Macmillan.

LIEBERMAN, S. 1956. The effects of changes in roles on the attitudes of role occupants. *Human Relations* 9:385–402.

LIEBERT, R. M.; POULOS, R. W.; AND STRAUSS, G. D. 1974. *Developmental psychology.* Englewood Cliffs, N.J.: Prentice-Hall.

LIEM, J. H. 1974. Effects of verbal communications of parents and children: A comparison of normal and schizophrenic parents. *Journal of Consulting and Clinical Psychology* 42:438–50.

LINDSAY, P. H., AND NORMAN, D. A. 1977. *Human information processing,* 2nd ed. New York: Academic Press.

LINDSLEY, D. B. 1960. Attention, consciousness, sleep, and wakefulness. In *Handbook of physiology: vol. 3, sect. 1, Neurophysiology.* Washington, D. C.: American Physiological Society.

LINDSLEY, D. B.; SCHREINER, L. H.; KNOWLES, W. B.; AND MAGOUN, H. W. 1950. Behavioral and EEG changes following chronic brain stem lesions in the cat. *Electroencephalography and Clinical Neurophysiology* 2:483–98.

LIPOWSKI, Z. J. 1975. Psychophysiological cardiovascular disorders. In Freedman, A. M.; Kaplan, H. I.; and Sadock, B. J. (Eds.), *Comprehensive textbook of psychiatry,* vol. 2, pp. 1660–68. Baltimore: Williams & Wilkins.

LIPPERT, W. W., AND SENTER, R. J. 1966. Electrodermal responses in the sociopath. *Psychonomic Science* 4:25–26.

LISKE, E., AND DAVIS, W. J. 1984. Sexual behavior of the Chinese praying mantis. *Animal Behavior* 32:916.

LITTLE, K. B., AND SHNEIDMAN, E. S. 1959. Congruencies among interpretations of psychological test and anamnestic data. *Psychological Monographs* 73 (Whole No. 476).

LOCKE, J. 1690. *An essay concerning human understanding.* Edited by A. D. Woozley. Cleveland: Meridian Books, 1964.

LOEHLIN, J. C. 1982. Are personality traits differentially heritable. *Behavior Genetics* 12:417–28.

LOEHLIN, J. C.; LINDZEY, G.; AND SPUHLER, J. N. 1975. *Race difference in intelligence.* San Francisco: Freeman.

LOEHLIN, J. C., AND NICHOLS, R. C. 1976. *Heredity, environment and personality: A study of 850 sets of twins.* Austin: University of Texas Press.

LOEVINGER, J., AND KNOLL, E. 1983. Personality: Stages, traits, and the self. In Rosenzweig, M. R., and Porter, L. W. (Eds.), *Annual Review of Psychology* 34:195–222.

LOEWI, O. 1960. An autobiographical sketch. *Perspectives in Biological Medicine* 4:2–35.

LOFTUS, E. F. 1973. Activation of semantic memory. *American Journal of Psychology* 86:331–37.

LOFTUS, E. F. 1975. Leading questions and the eyewitness report. *Cognitive Psychology* 7:560–72.

LOFTUS, E. F., AND HOFFMAN. 1989. Misinformation and memory: The creation of new memories. *Journal of Experimental Psychology: General* 118:100–104.

LOFTUS, E. F., AND LOFTUS, G. R. 1980. On the permanence of stored information in the human brain. *American Psychologist* 35: 409–20.

LOFTUS, E. F., AND PALMER, J. C. 1974. Reconstruction of automobile destruction: An example of the interaction between language and memory. *Journal of Verbal Learning and Verbal Behavior* 13: 585–89.

LOFTUS, E. F., AND ZANNI, G. 1975. Eyewitness testimony: The influence of the wording of a question. *Bulletin of the Psychonomic Society* 5:86–88.

LOGAN, G. D. 1988. Toward an instance theory of automatization. *Psychological Review* 95:492–527.

LOGUE, A. W. 1979. Taste aversion and the generality of the laws of learning. *Psychological Bulletin* 86:276–96.

LOGUE, A. W. 1986. *The psychology of eating and drinking.* New York: Freeman.

LONDON, P. 1964. *The modes and morals of psychotherapy.* New York: Holt, Rinehart & Winston.

LONDON, P. 1970. The rescuers: Motivational hypotheses about Christians who saved Jews from the Nazis. In Macauley, J., and Berkowitz, L. (Eds.), *Altruism and helping behvaior.* New York: Academic Press.

LORENZ, K. Z. 1952. *King Solomon's ring.* New York: Crowell.

LORENZ, K. Z. 1966. *On aggression.* London: Methuen.

LUBORSKY, L. 1973. Forgetting and remembering (momentary forgetting) during psychotherapy: A new sample. *Psychological Issues* 8(20):29–55.

LUBORSKY, L.; SACKHEIM, H.; AND CHRISTOPH, P. 1979. The state conducive to momentary forgetting. In Kihlstrom, J. F., and Evans, F. J. (Eds.), *Functional disorders of memory,* pp. 325–54. Hillsdale, N.J.: Erlbaum.

LUBORSKY, L. I.; SINGER, B.; AND LUBORSKY, L. 1985. Comparative studies of psychotherapies. *Archives of General Psychiatry* 20:84–88.

LUCE, R. D., AND RAIFFA, H. 1957. *Games and decisions.* New York: Wiley.

LUCHINS, A. S. 1942. Mechanization in problem-solving: The effect of Einstellung. *Psychological Monographs* 54 (Whole No. 248).

LUCHINS, A. S. 1957. Primacy-recency in impression formation: The effect of Einstellung. In Hovland, C. (Ed.), *The order of presentation in persuasion.* New Haven: Yale University Press.

LUGINBUHL, J. E. R.; CROWE, D. H.; AND KAHAN, J. P. 1975. Causal attributions for success and failure. *Journal of Personality and Social Psychology* 31:86–93.

LURIA, A. R. 1966. *Higher cortical functions in man.* New York: Basic Books.

LURIA, A. R. 1971. *International Journal of Psychology* 6: p. 259 ff. (cited in Scribner, S. & Cole, M. 1973. Cognitive consequences of formal and informal education. *Science* 182:553–59).

LUST, B. 1987. *Studies in the acquisition of anaphora.* Dordrecht: Reidel.

LYKKEN, D. T. 1979. The detection of deception. *Psychological Bulletin* 86:47–53.


MAASS, A., AND CLARK, R. D., III. 1984. Hidden impact of minorities: Fifteen years of research on minority influence research. *Psychological Bulletin* 95:428–55.

MACCOBY, E. E. 1980. *Social development.* New York: Harcourt Brace Jovanovich.

MACCOBY, E. E., AND JACKLIN, C. N. 1974. *The psychology of sex differences.* Stanford, Calif.: Stanford University Press.

MACCOBY, E. E., AND JACKLIN, C. N. 1980. Sex differences in aggression: A rejoinder and reprise. *Child Development* 51:964–80.

MACCOBY, E. E., AND MARTIN, J. A. 1983. Socialization in the context of the family: Parent-child interaction. In Mussen, P. H. (Ed.), *Carmichael's manual of child psychology: Vol. 4. Socialization, per-*

*sonality and social development* (Hetherington, M. E., volume editor), pp. 1–102. New York: Wiley.

MacFarlane, A. 1975. Olfaction in the development of social preferences in the human neonate. *Parent-infant interaction.* Amsterdam: CIBA Foundation Symposium.

MacKenzie, N. 1965. *Dreams and dreaming.* London: Aldus Books.

Mackintosh, N. J. 1983. *Conditioning and associative learning.* Oxford, England: Oxford University Press.

MacNeilage, P. 1972. Speech physiology. In Gilbert, J. (Ed.), *Speech and cortical functioning.* New York: Academic Press.

MacNichol, E. F., Jr. 1964. Three-pigment color vision: *Scientific American* 211:48–56.

MacNichol, E. F. Jr. 1986. A unifying presentation of photopigment spectra. *Vision Research* 29:543–46.

Magnus, O., and Lammers, J. 1956. The amygdaloid-nuclear complex. *Folia Psychiatrica Neurologica et Neurochirurgico Neerlandica* 59:552–82.

Magnusson, D., and Endler, N. S. 1977. Interactional psychology: Present status and future prospects. In Magnusson, D., and Endler, N. S. (Eds.), *Personality at the crossroads,* pp. 3–31. New York: Wiley.

Magoun, H. W.; Harrison, F.; Brobeck, J. R.; and Ranson, S. W. 1938. Activation of heat loss mechanisms by local heating of the brain. *Journal of Neurophysiology* 1:101–14.

Maher, B. A. 1966. *Principles of psychopathology.* New York: McGraw-Hill.

Mahoney, M. J. 1976. *Scientist as subject: The psychological imperative.* Cambridge, Mass.: Ballinger.

Maier, S. F.; Laudenslager, M. L.; and Ryan, S. M. 1985. Stressor controllability, immune function, and endogenous opiates. In Bush, F., and Overmier, J. B. (Eds.), *Affect, conditioning, and cognition.* Hillsdale, N.J.: Erlbaum.

Maier, S. F.; Seligman, M. E. P.; and Solomon, R. L. 1969. Pavlovian fear conditioning and learned helplessness: Effects on escape and avoidance behavior of (a) the CS-US contingency and (b) the independence of the US and voluntary responding. In Campbell, B. A., and Church, R. M. (Eds.), *Punishment and aversive behavior,* pp. 299–342. New York: Appleton-Century-Crofts.

Malan, H. 1963. *A study of brief psychotherapy.* Philadelphia: Lippincott.

Malinowski, B. 1926. *Crime and custom in savage society.* London: Paul, Trench, and Trubner.

Malinowski, B. 1927. *Sex and repression in savage society.* New York: Meridian, 1955.

Mandler, G. 1975. *Mind and emotion.* New York: Wiley.

Mandler, G. 1984. *Mind and body: Psychology of emotion and stress.* New York: Norton.

Mann, F.; Bowsher, D.; Mumford, J.; Lipton, S.; and Miles, J. 1973. Treatment of intractable pain by acupuncture. *Lancet* 2:57–60.

Mann, L. 1981. The baiting crowd in episodes of threatened suicide. *Journal of Personality and Social Psychology* 41:703–709.

Markman, E. M., and Hutchinson, J. E. 1984. Children's sensitivity to constraints on word meaning: Taxonomic vs. thematic relations. *Cognitive Psychology* 16:1–27.

Markman, E. M., and Wachtel, G. A. 1988. Children's use of mutual exclusivity to constrain the meaning of words. *Cognitive Psychology* 20:121–57.

Marks, I. M. 1969. *Fears and phobias.* New York: Academic Press.

Marler, P. R. 1970. A comparative approach to vocal learning: Song development in white-crowned sparrows. *Journal of Comparative and Physiological Psychology Monographs* 71(No. 2, Part 2):1–25.

Marmor, J. 1975. Homosexuality and sexual orientation disturbances. In Freedman, A. M.; Kaplan, H. I.; and Sadock, B. J. (Eds.),

*Comprehensive textbook of psychiatry—II,* vol. 2, pp. 1510–19. Baltimore: Williams & Wilkins.

Marr, D. 1976. Early processing of visual information. *Philosophical Transactions of the Royal Society of London,* Series B, 275:483–524.

Marr, D. 1982. *Vision.* San Francisco: Freeman.

Marsden, C. D. 1985. Defects of movement in Parkinson's disease. In Delwaide, P. J., and Agnoli, A. (Eds.), *Clinical neurophysiology in Parkinsonism.* Amsterdam: Elsevier.

Marshall, D. A., and Moulton, D. G. 1981. Olfactory sensitivity to α-ionine in humans and dogs. *Chemical Senses* 6:53–61.

Marshall, G. D., and Zimbardo, P. G. 1979. Affective consequences of inadequately explained physiological arousal. *Journal of Personality and Social Psychology* 37:970–88.

Marslen-Wilson, W. 1975. Sentence perception as an interactive parallel process. *Science* 189:226–28.

Marslen-Wilson, W. D., and Teuber, H. L. 1975. Memory for remote events in anterograde amnesia: Recognition of public figures from news photographs. *Neuropsychologia* 13:353–64.

Maslach, C. 1979. Negative emotional biasing of unexplained physiological arousal. *Journal of Personality and Social Psychology* 37:953–69.

Maslow, A. H. 1954. *Motivation and personality.* New York: Harper & Row.

Maslow, A. H. 1968. *Toward a psychology of being,* 2nd ed. Princeton, N.J.: Van Nostrand.

Maslow, A. H. 1970. *Motivation and personality,* 2nd ed. New York: Harper.

Matarazzo, J. D. 1983. The reliability of psychiatric and psychological diagnosis. *Clinical Psychology Review* 3:103–45.

Mathews, K. A. 1982. Psychological perspectives on the type A behavior pattern. *Psychological Bulletin* 91:293–323.

Matsumoto, D., and Ekman, P. 1989. Japanese and Caucasian Facial Expressions of Emotion. JACFEE.

Maugh, T. M. 1981. Biochemical markers identify mental states. *Science* 214:39–41.

May, R. 1958. Contributions of existential psychotherapy. In May, R.; Angel, E.; and Ellenberger, H. F. (Eds.), *Existence,* pp. 37–91. New York: Basic Books.

Mayer, D. J.; Price, D. D.; Rafii, A.; and Barber, J. 1976. Acupuncture hypalgesia: Evidence for activation of a central control system as a mechanism of action. In Bonica, J. J., and Albe-Fessard, D. (Eds.), *Advances in pain research and therapy,* vol. 1. New York: Raven Press.

Mayer, D. J. 1979. Endogenous analgesia systems: Neural and behavioral mechanisms. In Bonica, J. J. et al. (Eds.), *Advances in pain research and therapy,* vol. 3. New York: Raven.

Mayer, J. 1955. Regulation of energy intake and body weight: The glucostatic theory and the lipostatic hypothesis. *Annals of the New York Academy of Sciences* 63:15–43.

Mayes, A. R. 1988. *Human organic memory disorders.* New York: Cambridge University Press.

Maynard-Smith, J. 1965. The evolution of alarm calls. *American Naturalist* 100:637–50.

McBurney, D. H.; Levine, J. M.; and Cavanaugh, P. H. 1977. Psychophysical and social ratings of human body odor. *Personality and Social Psychology Bulletin* 3:135–38.

McBurney, D. H., and Shick, T. R. 1971. Taste and water taste of twenty-six compounds for man. *Perception and Psychophysics* 10:249–52.

McCall, R. B. 1979. The development of intellectual functioning in infancy and the prediction of later I. Q. In Osofsky, S. D. (Ed.), *The Handbook of infant development,* pp. 707–41. New York: Wiley.

McCall, R. B. 1989. Commentary. *Human Development* (Special Topic: Continuity in early cognitive development—Conceptual and methodological challenges) 32:177–86.

McClearn, G. E., and DeFries, J. C. 1973. *Introduction to behavioral genetics*. San Francisco: Freeman.

McClelland, D. C. 1975. *Power: The inner experience*. New York: Irvington.

McClelland, D. C.; Atkinson, J. W.; Clark, R. A.; and Lowell, E. L. 1953. *The achievement motive*. New York: Appleton.

McClelland, J., and Kawamoto, A. 1986. Mechanisms of sentence processing: Assigning roles to constituents of sentences. In McClelland, J.; Rumelhart, D.; and the PDP Research Group (Eds.), *Parallel distributed processing: Explorations in the microstructure of cognition*, vol. 1. Cambridge, Mass.: MIT Press.

McClelland, J. L.; Rumelhart, D. E.; and Hinton, G. E. 1986. The appeal of parallel distributed processing. In Rumelhart, D. E.; McClelland, J. L.; and the PDP Research Group, *Parallel distributed processing: Vol. 1. Foundations*, pp. 3–44. Cambridge, Mass.: MIT Press.

McClintock, M. K. 1971. Menstrual synchrony and suppression. *Nature* 229:244–45.

McClintock, M. K., and Adler, N. T. 1978. The role of the female during copulation in wild and domestic Norway rats *(Rattus Norvegicus)*. *Behaviour* 67:67–96.

McCloskey, M.; Wible, C. G.; and Cohen, N. J. 1988. Is there a special flashbulb-memory mechanism? *Journal of Experimental Psychology: General* 117:171–81.

McConaghy, M. J. 1979. Gender constancy and the genital basis of gender: Stages in the development of constancy by gender identity. *Child Development* 50:1223–26.

McCord, W., and McCord, J. 1964. *The psychopath: An essay on the criminal mind*. New York: Van Nostrand.

McEwen, B. S.; Biegon, A.; Davis, P. G.; Krey, L. C.; Luine, V. N.; McGinnis, M.; Paden, C. M.; Parsons, B.; and Rainbow, T. C. 1982. Steroid hormones: Humoral signals which alter brain cell properties and functions. *Recent Progress in Brain Research* 38:41–83.

McGhie, A., and Chapman, J. 1961. Disorders of attention and perception in early schizophrenia. *British Journal of Medical Psychology* 34:103–16.

McGraw, M. B. 1935. *Growth: A study of Johnny and Jimmy*. New York: Appleton-Century.

McGuigan, F. J. 1966. Covert oral behavior and auditory hallucinations. *Psychophysiology* 3:421–28.

McGuire, W. J. 1985. The nature of attitude and attitude change. In Lindzey, G., and Aronson, E. (Eds.), *Handbook of social psychology*, 3rd ed., vol. 2. New York: Random House.

McKay, D. G. 1973. Aspects of the theory of comprehension, memory and attention. *Quarterly Journal of Experimental Psychology* 25:22–40.

McKay, H.; Sinisterra, L.; McKay, A., Gomez, H.; and Lloreda, P. 1978. Improving cognitive ability in chronically deprived children. *Science* 200:270–78.

McKenzie, B. E.; Tootell, H. E.; and Day, R. H. 1980. Development of size constancy during the 1st year of human infancy. *Developmental Psychology* 16:163–74.

McKoon, G., and Ratcliff, R. 1979. Priming in episodic and semantic memory. *Journal of Verbal Learning and Verbal Behavior* 18:463–80.

McNally, J. 1987. Preparedness and phobia: A review. *Psychological Bulletin* 101:283–303.

Mead, G. H. 1934. *Mind, self, and society*. Chicago: University of Chicago Press.

Mead, M. 1935. *Sex and temperament in three primitive societies*. New York: Morrow.

Mead, M. 1937. *Cooperation and competition among primitive peoples*. New York: McGraw-Hill.

Mead, M. 1939. *From the South Seas: Studies of adolescence and sex in primitive societies*. New York: Morrow.

Meehl, P. E. 1959. Some ruminations on the validation of clinical procedures. *Canadian Journal of Psychology* 13:102–28.

Meehl, P. E. 1956. Profile analysis of the MMPI in differential diagnosis. In Welsh, G. S., and Dahlstrom, W. G. (Eds.), *Basic readings on the MMPI in psychology and medicine*, pp. 291–97. Minneapolis: University of Minnesota Press.

Meehl, P. D. 1962. Schizotaxia, schizotypy, schizophrenia. *American Psychologist* 17:827–38.

Mellor, C. S. 1970. First rank symptoms of schizophrenia. *British Journal of Psychiatry* 117:15–23.

Meltzer, H. Y. 1987. Biological studies in schizophrenia. *Schizophrenia Bulletin* 13:77–111.

Meltzoff, A. N., and Borton, R. W. 1979. Intermodal matching by human neonates. *Nature* 282:403–404.

Melzack, R. 1973. *The puzzle of pain*. New York: Basic Books.

Mendlewicz, J., and Rainer, J. D. 1977. Adoption study supporting genetic transmission in manic-depressive illness. *Nature* 268:327–29.

Menyuk, P. 1977. *Language and maturation*. Cambridge, Mass.: MIT Press.

Menzel, E. W. 1973. Chimpanzee spatial memory organization. *Science* 182:943–45.

Menzel, E. W. 1978. Cognitive maps in chimpanzees. In Hulse, S. H.; Fowler, H.; and Honig, W. K. (Eds.), *Cognitive processes in animal behavior*, pp. 375–422. Hillsdale, N.J.: Erlbaum.

Mercer, J. 1973. *Labelling the mentally retarded*. Berkeley, Calif.: University of California Press.

Mervis, C. B., and Crisafi, M. 1978. Order acquisition of subordinate, basic, and superordinate level categories. *Child Development* 49:988–98.

Metalsky, G. I.; Abramson, L. Y.; Seligman, M. E. P.; Semmel; and Peterson, C. 1982. Attributional style and life events in the classroom: Vulnerability and invulnerability to depressive mood reactions. *Journal of Personality and Social Psychology* 43:612–17.

Metalsky. G. I.; Halberstadt, L. J.; and Abramson, L. Y. 1987. Vulnerability to depressive mood reactions: Toward a more powerful test of the diathesis-stress and causal mediation components of the reformulated theory of depression. *Journal of Personality and Social Psychology* 52:386–93.

Meyer, J. P., and Mulherin, A. 1980. From attribution to helping: An analysis of the mediating effects of affect and expectancy. *Journal of Personality and Social Psychology* 39:201–10.

Meyer, D. E., and Schvaneveldt, R. W. 1971. Facilitation in recognizing pairs of words: Evidence of a dependence between retrieval operations. *Journal of Experimental Psychology* 90:227–34.

Michael, R. P., and Keverne, E. B. 1968. Pheromones in the communication of sexual status in primates. *Nature* 218:746–49.

Michaels, J. W.; Blommel, J. M.; Brocato, R. M.; Linkous, R. A.; and Rowe, J. S. 1982. Social facilitation and inhibition in a natural setting. *Replications in Social Psychology* 2:21–24.

Milgram, S. 1963. Behavioral study of obedience. *Journal of Abnormal and Social Psychology* 67:371–78.

Milgram, S. 1965. Some conditions of obedience and disobedience to authority. *Human Relations* 18:57–76.

Milgram, S. 1974. *Obedience to authority*. New York: Harper & Row.

Milgram, S.; Bickman, I.; and Berkowitz, L. 1969. Note on the drawing power of crowds of different size. *Journal of Personality and Social Psychology* 13:79–82.

Mill, J. S. 1865. *An examination of Sir William Hamilton's philosophy*. London: Longman, Green, Longman, Roberts & Green.

Miller, A. G. 1986. *The obedience experiments: A case study of controversy in social science*. New York: Praeger.

Miller, D. T. 1976. Ego involvement and attribution for success and failure. *Journal of Personality and Social Psychology* 34:901–906.

MILLER, D. T., AND ROSS, M. 1975. Self-serving bias in the attribution of causality. Fact or fiction? *Psychological Bulletin* 82:213–25.

MILLER, G. A. 1956. The magical number seven plus or minus two: Some limits in our capacity for processing information. *Psychological Review* 63:81–97.

MILLER, G. A.; GALANTER, E.; AND PRIBRAM, K. H. 1960. *Plans and the structure of behavior.* New York: Holt, Rinehart & Winston.

MILLER, G., AND GILDEA, P. 1987. How children learn words. *Scientific American* 257:94–99.

MILLER, G., AND JOHNSON-LAIRD, P. 1976. *Language and perception.* Cambridge, Mass.: Harvard University Press.

MILLER, N. E. 1978. Biofeedback and visceral learning. *Annual Review of Psychology* 29:373–404.

MILLER, N. E.; BAILEY, C. J.; AND STEVENSON, J. A. F. 1950. Decreased "hunger" but increased food intake resulting from hypothalamic lesions. *Science* 112:256–59.

MILLON, T. 1969. *Modern psychopathology.* Philadelphia: Saunders.

MILNER, B. 1966. Amnesia following operation on the temporal lobes. In Whitty, C. W. M., and Zangwill, O. L. (Eds.), *Amnesia,* pp. 109–33. London: Butterworth.

MILNER, B.; CORKIN, S.; AND TEUBER, H. L. 1968. Further analysis of the hippocampal syndrome: 14-year follow-up study of H. M. *Neuropsychologia* 6:215–34.

MINEKA, S. 1979. The role of fear in theories of avoidance learning, flooding, and extinction. *Psychological Bulletin* 86:985–1010.

MINUCHIN, S. 1974. *Families and family therapy.* Cambridge, Mass.: Harvard University Press.

MISCHEL, W. 1968. *Personality and assessment.* New York: Wiley.

MISCHEL, W. 1970. Sex-typing and socialization. In Mussen, P. H. (Ed.), *Carmichael's manual of child development,* vol. 1. New York: Wiley.

MISCHEL, W. 1973. Towards a cognitive social learning reconceptualization of personality. *Psychological Review* 80:252–83.

MISCHEL, W. 1974. Processes in delay of gratification. In Berkowitz, L. (Ed.), *Advances in experimental social psychology,* vol. 7. New York: Academic Press.

MISCHEL, W. 1979. On the interface of cognition and personality: Beyond the person-situation debate. *American Psychologist* 34:740–54.

MISCHEL, W. 1984. Convergences and challenges in the search for consistency. *American Psychologist* 39:351–64.

MISCHEL, W. 1986. *Introduction to personality,* 4th ed. New York: Holt, Rinehart & Winston.

MISCHEL, W., AND BAKER, N. 1975. Cognitive appraisals and transformations in delay behavior. *Journal of Personality and Social Psychology* 31:254–61.

MISCHEL, W.; EBBESEN, E. B.; AND ZEISS, A. R. 1972. Cognitive and attentional mechanisms in delay of gratification. *Journal of Personality and Social Psychology* 21:204–18.

MISCHEL, W., AND MISCHEL, H. N. 1983. Development of children's knowledge of self-control strategies. *Child Development* 54:603–19.

MISCHEL, W., AND PEAKE, P. K. 1983. Some facets of consistency. Replies to Epstein, Funder and Bem. *Psychological Review* 90:394–402.

MISCHEL, W.; SHODA, Y.; AND PEAKE, P. K. 1988. The nature of adolescent competencies predicted by preschool delay of gratification. *Journal of Personality and Social Psychology* 54:687–96.

MISCHEL, W., AND MOORE, B. 1980. The role of ideation in voluntary delay for symbolically presented awards. *Cognitive Therapy and Research* 4:211–21.

MISELIS, R. R., AND EPSTEIN, A. N. 1970. Feeding induced by 2-deoxy-D-glucose injections into the lateral ventrical of the rat. *The Physiologist* 13:262.

MISHKIN, M., AND APPENZELLER, T. 1987. The anatomy of memory. *Scientific American* 256:80–89.

MISHLER, E. G., AND WAXLER, N. E. 1968. Family interaction and schizophrenia: Alternative frameworks of interpretation. In Rosenthal, D., and Kety, S. S. (Eds.), *The transmission of schizophrenia,* pp. 213–22. New York: Pergamon.

MITA, T. H.; DERMER, M.; AND KNIGHT, J. 1977. Reversed facial images and the mere exposure hypothesis. *Journal of Personality and Social Psychology* 35:597–601.

MITCHELL, D. E.; REARDON, J.; AND MUIR, D. W. 1975. Interocular transfer of the motion after-effect in normal and stereoblind observers. *Experimental Brain Research* 22:163–73.

MITROFF, I. I. 1974. *The subjective side of science.* Amsterdam: Elsevier.

MONEY, J. 1980. *Love and love sickness.* Baltimore: Johns Hopkins University Press.

MONEY, J., AND EHRHARDT, A. A. 1972. *Man and woman, boy and girl.* Baltimore: Johns Hopkins University Press.

MONEY, J., AND TUCKER, P. 1975. *Sexual signatures: On being a man or a woman.* Boston: Little, Brown.

MONSON, T. C.; HESLEY, J. W.; AND CHERNICK, L. 1982. Specifying when personality traits can and cannot predict behavior: An alternative to abandoning the attempt to predict single-act criteria. *Journal of Personality and Social Psychology* 43:385–99.

MOORE, J. W. 1972. Stimulus control: Studies of auditory generalization in rabbits. In Black, A. H., and Prokasy, W. F. (Eds.), *Classical conditioning II: Current research and theory,* pp. 206–30. New York: Appleton-Century-Crofts.

MOOS, R. H. 1969. Sources of variance in responses to questionnaires and in behavior. *Journal of Abnormal Psychology* 74:405–12.

MORA, G. 1975. Historical and theoretical trends in psychiatry. In Freedman, A. M.; Kaplan, H. I.; and Sadock, B. J. (Eds.), *Comprehensive textbook of psychiatry,* vol. 1, pp. 1–75. Baltimore: Williams & Wilkins.

MORA, F.; ROLLS, E. T.; AND BURTON, M. J. 1976. Modulation during learning of the responses of neurons in the lateral hypothalamus to the sight of food. *Experimental Neurology* 53:508–19.

MORAY, N. 1959. Attention in dichotic listening: Affective cues and the influence of instructions. *Quarterly Journal of Experimental Psychology* 11:56–60.

MORELAND, R. L., AND ZAJONC, R. B. 1982. Exposure effects in person perception: Familiarity, similarity, and attraction. *Journal of Experimental Social Psychology* 18:395–415.

MORGAN, C. D., AND MURRAY, H. A. 1935. A method for investigating fantasies: The thematic apperception test. *Archives of Neurological Psychiatry* 34:289–306.

MORGAN, J. 1986. *From simple input to complex grammar,* Cambridge, Mass.: MIT Press.

MORGAN, J., AND NEWPORT, E. 1981. The role of constituent structure in the induction of an artificial language. *Journal of Verbal Learning and Verbal Behavior* 20:67–85.

MORGAN, J., AND TRAVIS, L. 1989. Limits on negative information in language input. *Journal of Child Language* 16(3):531–52.

MORRIS, D. 1967. *The naked ape.* New York: McGraw-Hill.

MORTON, J. 1969. Interaction of information in word recognition. *Psychological Review* 76:165–78.

MOSCOVICI, S. 1985. Social influence and conformity. In Lindzey, G., and Aronson, E. (Ed.), *Handbook of social psychology,* 3rd ed., vol 2, pp. 347–412. New York: Random House.

MOSCOVITCH, M. 1972. Choice reaction-time study assessing the verbal behavior of the minor hemisphere in normal adults. *Journal of Comparative and Physiological Psychology* 80:66–74.

MOSCOVITCH, M. 1979. Information processing and the cerebral hemispheres. In Gazzaniga, M. S., *Handbook of behavioral neurobiology,* vol. 2, pp. 379–446. New York: Plenum.

MOSCOVITCH, M., AND ROZIN, P. 1989. Disorders of the nervous system and psychopathology. In Rosenhan, D. L., and Seligman, M. E. P. *Abnormal psychology,* 2nd ed., pp. 558–602. New York: Norton.

MOSKOWITZ, D. W. 1982. Coherence and cross-situational generality in personality: A new analysis of old problems. *Journal of Personality and Social Psychology* 43:754–68.

MULFORD, R. 1986. First words of the blind child. In Smith, M., and Locke, J. (Eds.), *The emergent lexicon: The child's development of a linguistic vocabulary.* New York: Academic Press.

MURDOCK, B. 1962. The serial position effect of free recall. *Journal of Experimental Psychology* 64:482–88.

MURPHY, J. M. 1976. Psychiatric labelling in cross-cultural perspective. *Science* 191:1019–28.

MURRAY, F. B. 1978. Teaching strategies and conservation training. In Lesgold, A. M.; Pellegrino, J. W.; Fekkeman, D.; and Glaser, R. (Eds.), *Cognitive psychology and instruction,* vol. 1. New York: Plenum.

MUSCETTOLA, G.; POTTER, W. Z.; PICKAR, D.; AND GOODWIN, F. K. 1984. Urinary 3-methoxy-4-hydroxyphenylglycol and major affective disorders. *Archives of General Psychiatry* 41:337–42.

MUUSS, R. E. 1970. Puberty rites in primitive and modern societies. *Adolescence* 5:109–28.

MYERS, J. K.; WEISSMAN, M. M.; TISCHLERM, G. L.; HOLZER, C. E.; LEAF, P. J.; ORVASCHEL, H. A.; ANTHONY, J. C.; BOYD, J. H.; BURKE, J. D.; KRAMER, M.; AND STOLTZMAN, R. 1984. Six-month prevalance of psychiatric disorders in three communities:1980–1982. *Archives of General Psychiatry* 41:959–67.

NAUTA, W. J. H., AND FEIRTAG, M. 1986. *Fundamental neuroanatomy.* New York: Freeman.

NEAL, P. 1988. *As I am.* New York: Simon and Schuster.

NEISSER, U. 1963. The imitation of man by machine. *Science* 139:193–97.

NEISSER, U. 1967. *Cognitive psychology.* New York: Appleton-Century-Crofts.

NEISSER, U. 1982a. *Memory observed.* San Francisco: Freeman.

NEISSER, U. 1982b. *On the trail of the tape-recorder fallacy.* Paper presented at a symposium on "The influence of hypnosis and related states on memory: Forensic implications" at the meetings of the American Association for the Advancement of Science, Washington, D. C., in January 1982.

NEISSER, U. 1986. Remembering Pearl Harbor: Reply to Thompson and Cowan. *Cognition* 23:285–86.

NEISSER, U. 1989. Domains of memory. In Solomon, P. R.; Goethals, G. R.; Kelley, C. M.; and Stephens, B. R. (Eds.), *Memory: Interdisciplinary approaches,* pp. 67–83. New York: Springer Verlag.

NELSON, K. 1973. Structure and strategy in learning to talk. *Monographs of the Society for Research in Child Development* 38: (1–2, Serial No. 149).

NEMIAH, J. C. 1985. Obsessive-compulsive disorder (Obsessive-compulsive neurosis). In Kaplan, H. I., and Sadock, J. (Eds.), *Comprehensive textbook of psychiatry,* 4th ed. Baltimore: Williams & Wilkins.

NESSE, F. M.; CAMERON, O. G.; CURTIS, G. C.; McCANN, D. S.; AND HUBER-SMITH, M. J. 1984. Adrenergic function in patients with panic anxiety. *Archives of General Psychiatry* 41:771–76.

NEWELL, A.; SHAW, J. C.; AND SIMON, H. A. 1958. Elements of a theory of human problem solving. *Psychological Review* 65:151–66.

NEWELL, A., AND SIMON, H. A. 1972. *Human problem solving.* Englewood Cliffs, N.J.: Prentice-Hall.

NEWELL, A., AND ROSENBLOOM, P. S. 1981. Mechanisms of skill acquisition and the law of practice. In Anderson, J. R. (Ed.), *Cognitive skills and their acquisition,* pp. 1–55. Hillsdale, N.J.: Erlbaum.

NEWMEYER, F. 1983. *Linguistic theory in America,* New York: Academic Press.

NEWPORT, E. L. 1984. Constraints on learning: Studies in the acquisition of American Sign Language. *Papers and Reports on Child Language Development* 23:1–22. Stanford, Calif.: Stanford University Press.

NEWPORT, E. 1990. Maturational constraints on language learning. *Cognitive Science* 14:11–28.

NEWPORT, E. L., AND ASHBROOK, E. F. 1977. The emergence of semantic relations in American Sign Language. *Papers and Reports in Child Language Development* 13.

NEWPORT, E., GLEITMAN, H., AND GLEITMAN, L. 1977. Mother, I'd rather do it myself: Some effects and non-effects of maternal speech style. In Snow, C., and Ferguson, C. (Eds.), *Talking to children: Language input and acquisition.* New York: Cambridge University Press.

NICHOLSON, R. A., AND BERMAN, J. S. 1983. Is follow-up necessary in evaluating psychotherapy? *Psychological Bulletin* 93:261–78.

NICOL, S. E., AND GOTTESMAN, I. I. 1983. Clues to the genetics and neurobiology of schizophrenia. *American Scientist* 71:398–404.

NILSSON, L. 1974. *Behold man.* Boston: Little, Brown.

NISBETT, R. E. 1968. Taste, deprivation, and weight determinants of eating behavior. *Journal of Personality and Social Psychology* 10:107–16.

NISBETT, R. E. 1972. Eating behavior and obesity in man and animals. *Advances in Psychosomatic Medicine* 7:173–93.

NISBETT, R. E. 1977. Interaction versus main effects as goals of personality research. In Magnusson, D., and Endler, L. (Eds.), *Personality at the crossroads: Current issues in interactional psychology,* pp. 235–41. Hillsdale, N.J.: Erlbaum.

NISBETT, R. E. 1980. The trait construct in lay and professional psychology. In Festinger, L. (Ed.), *Retrospections on social psychology,* pp. 109–30. New York: Oxford University Press.

NISBETT, R. E.; CAPUTO, C.; LEGANT, P.; AND MARACEK, J. 1973. Behavior as seen by the actor and as seen by the observer. *Journal of Personality and Social Psychology* 27:154–64.

NISBETT, R., AND ROSS, L. 1980. *Human inference: Strategies and shortcomings of social judgment.* Englewood Cliffs, N.J.: Prentice-Hall.

NISBETT, R. E., AND WILSON, T. D. 1977. Telling more than we can know: Verbal reports on mental processes. *Psychological Review* 84:231–59.

NOLEN-HOEKSEMA, S. 1987. Sex differences in unipolar depression: Evidence and theory. *Psychological Bulletin* 101:259–82.

NORMAN, W. T. 1963. Toward an adequate taxonomy of personality attributes: Replicated factor structure in peer nomination personality ratings. *Journal of Abnormal and Social Psychology* 66: 574–83.

NOTTEBOHM, F. 1987. Plasticity in adult avian central nervous system: Possible relations between hormones, learning, and brain repair. In Plum, F. (Ed.), *Higher functions of the nervous system: Section I, Vol. 5. Handbook of physiology.* Washington, D. C.: American Physiological Society.

NOVAK, M. A., AND HARLOW, H. F. 1975. Social recovery of monkeys isolated for the first year of life: I. Rehabilitation and therapy. *Developmental Psychology* 11:453–65.

NOWLIS, G. H., AND FRANK, M. E. 1981. Quality coding in gustatory systems of rats and hamsters. In Norris, D. M. (Ed.), *Perception of behavioral chemicals,* pp. 58–80. Amsterdam: Elsevier.

O'KEEFE, J., AND NADEL, L. 1978. *The hippocampus as a cognitive map.* Oxford: Clarendon Press.

ODIORNE, J. M. 1957. Color changes. In Brown, M. E. (Ed.), *The physiology of fishes,* vol. 2. New York: Academic Press.

OFMAN, W. V. 1985. Existential psychotherapy. In Kaplan, H. I., and Sadock, J. (Eds.), *Comprehensive textbook of psychiatry,* 4th ed, pp. 1438–43. Baltimore: Williams & Wilkins.

OHANIAN, H. C. 1985. *Physics.* New York: Norton.

ÖHMAN, A.; DIMBERG, U.; AND ÖST, L. G. 1985. Biological constraints on the fear response. In Reiss, S. and Bootsin, R. (Eds.), *Theoretical issues in behavior therapy*, pp. 123–75. New York: Academic Press.

ÖHMAN, A.; ERIKSSON, A.; AND OLOFSSON, 1975. One-trial learning and superior resistance to extinction of autonomic responses conditioned to potentially phobic stimuli. *Journal of Comparative and Physiological Psychology* 88:619–27.

OLDS, J., AND MILNER, P. 1954. Positive reinforcement produced by electrical stimulation of septal areas and other regions of rat brains. *Journal of Comparative and Physiological Psychology* 47:419–27.

OLDS, M. E., AND FOBES, T. 1981. The central basis of motivation: Intracranial self-stimulation. *Annual Review of Psychology* 32:523–74.

OLTON, D. S. 1978. Characteristics of spatial memory. In Hulse, S. H., Fowler, H., and Honig, W. K. (Eds.), *Cognitive processes in animal behavior*, pp. 341–73. Hillsdale, N.J.: Erlbaum.

OLTON, D. S. 1979. Mazes, maps, and memory. *American Psychologist* 34:583–96.

OLTON, D. S., AND SAMUELSON, R. J. 1976. Remembrance of places passed: Spatial memory in rats. *Journal of Experimental Psychology: Animal Behavior Processes* 2:97–116.

OLWEUS, D. 1980. Familial and temperamental determinants of aggressive behavior in adolescent boys: A causal analysis. *Developmental Psychology* 16:644–66.

OPLER, L. A.; KAY, S. R.; ROSADO, V.; AND LINDENMAYER, J. P. 1984. Positive and negative symptoms in chronic schizophrenic patients. *Journal of Nervous and Mental Diseases* 172:317–25.

ORLANSKY, H. 1949. Infant care and personality. *Psychological Bulletin* 46:1–48.

ORNE, M. T. 1951. The mechanisms of hypnotic age regression: An experimental study. *Journal of Abnormal and Social Psychology* 58:277–99.

ORNE, M. T. 1975. Psychotherapy in contemporary America: Its development and context. In Arieti, S. (Ed.), *American handbook of psychiatry*, 2nd ed., vol. 5, pp. 1–33. New York: Basic Books.

ORNE, M. T. 1979. The use and misuse of hypnosis in court. *The International Journal of Clinical and Experimental Hypnosis* 27:311–41.

ORNE, M. T., AND HAMMER, A. G. 1974. Hypnosis. in *Encyclopaedia Brittannica*, 5th ed., pp. 133–40. Chicago: Encyclopaedia Brittannica.

ORNSTEIN, R. 1977. *The psychology of consciousness* 2nd ed. New York: Harcourt Brace Jovanovich.

OSOFSKY, J. D., AND DANZGER, B. 1974. Relationships between neo-natal characteristics and mother-infant characteristics. *Developmental Psychology* 10:124–30.

OSTROM, T. M. 1977. Between-theory and within-theory conflict in explaining context effects in impression formation. *Journal of Experimental Social Psychology* 13:492–503.


PACKER, C. 1977. Reciprocal altruism in olive baboons. *Nature* 265:441–43.

PAGE, E. B. 1985. Review of Kaufman's Assessment Battery for Children. *Ninth mental measurements yearbook*, vol. 1., pp. 773–77.

PAI, M. N. 1946. Sleep-walking and sleep activities. *Journal of Mental Science* 92:756–65.

PARKE, R. D. 1981. *Fathers.* Cambridge, Mass.: Harvard University Press.

PARKE, R. D., AND SLABY, R. G. 1983. The development of aggression. In Mussen, P. H. (Ed.), *Carmichael's manual of child psychology: Vol. 4. Socialization, personality and social development* (Hetherington, M. E., volume editor), pp. 547–642. New York: Wiley.

PASCALE-LEONE, J. 1978. Compounds, confounds and models in developmental information processing: A reply to Trabasso and Foel-

linger. *Journal of Experimental Child Psychology* 26:18–40.

PATIENCE, A., AND SMITH, J. W. 1986. Derek Freeman and Samoa: The making and unmaking of a biobehavioral myth. *American Anthropologist* 88:157–61.

PATTERSON, T.; SPOHN, H. E.; BOGIA, D. P.; AND HAYES, K. 1986. Thought disorder in schizophrenia: Cognitive and neuroscience approaches. *Schizophrenia Bulletin* 12:460–72.

PAUL, G. L. 1966. *Insight vs. desensitization in psychotherapy: An experiment in anxiety reduction.* Stanford, Calif.: Stanford University Press.

PAUL, G. L. 1967. Insight versus desensitization in psychotherapy two years after termination. *Journal of Consulting Psychology* 31:333–48.

PAVLOV, I. 1927. *Conditioned reflexes.* Oxford, England: Oxford University Press.

PAVLOV, I. 1928. *Lectures on conditioned reflexes,* vol 1. New York: International Publishers Co., Inc.

PAYKEL, E. S. 1982. Life events and early environment. In Paykel, E. S. (Ed.), *Handbook of affective disorders.* New York: Guilford.

PEEKE, H. V. S. 1984. Habituation and the maintenance of territorial boundaries. In Peeke, H. V. S., and Petrinovich, L. (Eds.), *Habituation, sensitization and behavior,* pp. 393–422. New York: Academic Press.

PENFIELD, W. 1975. *The mystery of the mind.* Princeton, N.J.: Princeton University Press.

PENFIELD, W., AND RASMUSSEN, T. 1950. *The cerebral cortex of man.* New York: Macmillan.

PENFIELD, W., AND ROBERTS, L. 1959. *Speech and brain mechanisms.* Princeton, N.J.: Princeton University Press.

PENROSE, L. S., AND PENROSE, R. 1958. Impossible objects: A special type of visual illusion. *British Journal of Psychology* 49:31–33.

PERIN, C. T. 1943. A quantitative investigation of the delay of reinforcement gradient. *Journal of Experimental Psychology* 32:37–51.

PETERSON, C.; SEMMEL, A.; VON BAEYER, C.; ABRAMSON, L. Y.; METALSKY, G. I.; AND SELIGMAN, M. E. P. 1982. The Attributional Style Questionnaire. *Cognitive Therapy and Research* 6:287–99.

PETERSON, C., AND SELIGMAN, M. E. P. 1984. Causal explanations as a risk factor for depression: Theory and evidence. *Psychological Review* 91:341–74.

PETTY, R. E., AND CACIOPPO, J. T. 1985. The elaboration likelihood model of persuasion. In Berkowitz, L. (Ed.), *Advances in experimental social psychology*, vol. 19. New York: Academic Press.

PETTY, R. E.; WELLS, G. L.; AND BROCK, T. C. 1976. Distraction can enhance or reduce yielding to propaganda: Thought disruption versus effort justification. *Journal of Personality and Social Psychology* 34:874–84.

PHARES, E. J. 1976. *Locus of control in personality.* Morristown, N.J.: General Learning Press.

PIAGET, J. 1932. *The moral judgment of the child.* London: Kegan Paul.

PIAGET, J. 1951. *Play, dreams and imitation in childhood.* New York: Norton.

PIAGET, J. 1952. *The origins of intelligence in children.* New York: International University Press.

PIAGET, J. 1954. *The construction of reality in the child.* New York: Basic Books.

PIAGET, J. 1972. *The child's conception of the world.* Totowa, N.J.: Littlefield, Adams.

PIAGET, J., AND INHELDER, B. 1956. *The child's conception of space.* London: Routledge and Kegan Paul.

PIAGET, J., AND INHELDER, B. 1967. *The child's conception of space.* New York: Norton.

PILIAVIN, J. A., AND PILIAVIN, I. M. 1972. Effect of blood on reaction to a victim. *Journal of Personality and Social Psychology* 23:353–61.

PILLARD, R. C., AND WEINREICH, J. D. 1986. Evidence of familial nature of male homosexuality. *Archives of General Psychiatry* 43:808–12.

PILLEMER, D. B. 1984. Flashbulb memories of the assassination attempt on President Reagan. *Cognition* 16:63–80.

PINKER, S. 1984. *Language learnability and language development.* Cambridge, Mass: Harvard University Press.

PINKER, S. 1989. *Learnability and cognition: The acquisition of argument structure.* Cambridge, Mass: MIT Press.

PINKER, S., AND PRINCE, A. 1988. On language and connectionism: Analysis of a parallel distributed processing model of language acquisition. *Cognition* 28(1):73–194.

PLECK, J. H. 1985. *Working wives/working husbands.* Beverly Hills, Calif: Sage.

PLOMIN, R., AND DANIELS, D. 1987. Why are children from the same family so different from one another? *Behavioral and Brain Sciences* 10:1–16.

PLUTCHIK, R. 1970. Emotions, evolution, and adaptive processes. In Arnold, M. B. (Ed.), *Feelings and emotions: The Loyola symposium.* New York: Academic Press.

PLUTCHIK, R. 1980. The evolutionary context. In Plutchik, R., and Kellerman, H. (Eds.), *Emotion: Theory, research and experience,* vol. 1. New York: Academic Press.

PLUTCHIK, R. 1984. Emotions: A general psychoevolutionary approach. In Scherer, K., and Ekman, P. *Approaches to emotion.* Hillsdale, N.J.: Erlbaum.

PODLESNY, J. A., AND RASKIN, D. C. 1977. Physiological measures and the detection of deception. *Psychological Bulletin,* 84:782–99.

POGGIO, G. F., AND FISCHER, B. 1978. Binocular interaction and depth sensitivity in striate and prestriate cortex of behaving rhesus monkey. *Journal of Neurophysiology* 40:1392–1405.

POGUE-GEILE, M. F., AND ROSE, R. J. 1985. Developmental genetic studies of adult personality. *Developmental Psychology* 21:547–57.

POLEY, W. 1974. Dimensionality in the measurement of authoritarian and political attitudes. *Canadian Journal of Behavioral Science* 6:83–94.

POMERANTZ, J. R., AND KUBOVY, M. 1986. Theoretical approaches to perceptual organization. In Boff, K. R.; Kauffman, L.; and Thomas, J. P. (Eds.), *Handbook of perception and human performance: Vol. 2. Cognitive processes and performance,* pp. 1–46. New York: Wiley.

PORSOLT, R. D.; LePICHON, M.; AND JALFRE, M. 1977. Depression: A new animal model sensitive to antidepressant treatments. *Nature* 266:730–32.

POSTAL, P. M. 1968. Epilogue. In Jacobs, R. A., and Rosenbaum, P. S., *English transformational grammar,* pp. 253–89. Waltham, Mass.: Blaisdell.

PREMACK, D. 1976. *Intelligence in ape and man.* Hillsdale, N.J.: Erlbaum.

PREMACK, D. 1978. On the abstractness of human concepts: Why it would be difficult to talk to a pigeon. In Hulse, S. H.; Fowler, H.; and Honig, W. K. (Eds.), *Cognitive processes in animal behavior.* Hillsdale, N.J.: Erlbaum.

PREMACK, A., AND PREMACK, D. 1983. *The mind of an ape.* New York: Norton.

PREMACK, D., AND WOODRUFF, G. 1978. Does the chimpanzee have a theory of mind? *The Behavioral and Brain Sciences* 4:515–26.

PRICE, R. H., AND BOUFFARD, B. L. 1974. Behavioral appropriateness and situational constraint. *Journal of Personality and Social Psychology* 30:579–86.

PRICE-WILLIAMS, D. R. 1981. Concrete and formal operations. In Munroe, R. H.; Munroe, R. L.; and Whiting, B. B. (Eds.), *Handbook of cross-cultural development,* pp. 403–22. New York: Garland.

PRICE-WILLIAMS, D. R. 1985. Cultural psychology. In Lindzey, G., and Aronson, E. (Eds.), *Handbook of social psychology,* vol. 2, pp. 993–1042. New York: Academic Press.

PRICE-WILLIAMS, D., GORDON, W., AND RAMIREZ, M. 1969. Skill and conservation: A study of pottery-making children. *Developmental Psychology* 1:769.

PRINCE, E. 1981. Toward a taxonomy of given-new information. In P. Cole (Ed.), *Syntax and semantics 9 Pragmatics.* New York: Academic Press.

PRINCE, G. 1978. Putting the other half of the brain to work. *Training: The Magazine of Human Resources Development* 15:57–61.

PRINZHORN, H. 1972. *Artistry of the mentally ill.* New York: Springer-Verlag.

PRIOLEAU, L.; MURDOCK, M.; AND BRODY, N. 1983. An analysis of psychotherapy versus placebo studies. *The Behavioral and Brain Sciences* 6:275–310.

PRITCHARD, R. M. 1961. Stabilized images on the retina. *Scientific American* 204:72–78.

PROVENCE, S., AND LIPTON, R. C. 1962. *Infants in institutions.* New York: International Universities Press.

PUTNAM, F. W.; GUROFF, J. J.; SILBERMAN, E. K.; BARBAN, L.; AND POST, R. M. 1986. The clinical phenomenology of multiple personality disorder: Review of 100 recent cases. *Journal of Clinical Psychiatry* 47:285–93.

PUTNAM, H. 1975. The meaning of "meaning." In Gunderson, K. (Ed.), *Language, mind, and knowledge.* Minneapolis: University of Minnesota Press.

PUTNAM, K. E. 1979. Hypnosis and distortions in eye witness memory. *International Journal of Clinical and Experimental Hypnosis* 27:437–48.

QUAY, H. C. 1965. Psychopathic personality as pathological stimulation seeking. *American Journal of Psychiatry* 122:180–83.

QUAY, L. C. 1971. Language, dialect, reinforcement, and the intelligence test performance of Negro children. *Child Development* 42:5–15.

RACHMAN, S. J., AND TEASDALE, J. 1969. Aversion therapy: An appraisal. In Franks, C. M. (Ed.), *Behavior therapy: Appraisal and status,* pp. 279–320. New York: McGraw-Hill.

RADFORD, A. 1988. *Transformational grammar: A first course* New York: Cambridge University Press.

RADKE-YARROW, M.; ZAHN-WAXLER, C.; AND CHAPMAN, M. 1983. Children's prosocial dispositions and behavior. In Mussen, P. E. (Ed.), *Carmichael's manual of child psychology: Vol. 4. Socialization, personality, and social development* (Hetherington, E. M., volume editor), pp. 469–546. New York: Wiley.

RAINER, J. D.; MESNIKOFF, A.; KOLB, L. C.; AND CARR, A. 1960. Homosexuality and heterosexuality in identical twins. *Psychosomatic Medicine* 22:251–58.

RAPPAPORT, M., AND LEVIN, B. 1988. What to do with roles. In W. Wilkins (Ed), *Syntax and semantics: Vol. 21. Thematic relations.* San Diego: Academic Press.

RAVEN, B. H., AND RUBIN, J. Z. 1976. *Social psychology: People in groups.* New York: Wiley.

RAYNER, K. 1978. Eye movements in reading and information processing. *Psychological Bulletin* 85:618–60.

READ, C., AND SCHREIBER, P. 1982. Why short subjects are harder to find than long ones. In Wanner, E., and Gleitman, L. R. (Eds.), *Language acquisition: The state of the art.* New York: Cambridge University Press.

REBER, A. S. 1985. *The Penguin dictionary of psychology.* New York: Viking Penguin.

REDL, F. 1973. The superego in uniform. In Sanford, N., and Comstock, C. (Eds.), *Sanctions for evil.* San Francisco: Jossey-Bass.

REDLICH, F. C., AND FREEDMAN, D. X. 1966. *The theory and practice of psychiatry.* New York: Basic Books.

REISBERG, D., AND CHAMBERS, D. 1990. Neither pictures nor

propositions: What we can learn from a mental image. *Canadian Journal of Psychology*, in press.

REISENZEIN, R. 1983. The Schachter theory of emotions: Two decades later. *Psychological Bulletin* 94:239–64.

RENNER, M. J., AND ROSENZWEIG, M. R. 1987. *Enriched and impoverished environments: Effects on brain and behavior.* New York: Springer.

RESCORLA, R. A. 1966. Predictability and number of pairings in Pavlovian fear conditioning. *Psychonomic Science* 4:383–84.

RESCORLA, R. A. 1967. Pavlovian conditioning and its proper control procedures. *Psychological Review* 74:71–80.

RESCORLA, R. A. 1980. *Pavlovian second-order conditioning.* Hillsdale, N.J.: Erlbaum.

RESCORLA, R. A. 1988. Behavioral studies of Pavlovian conditioning. *Annual Review of Neuroscience* 11:329–52.

RESCORLA, R. A., AND HOLLAND, P. C. 1982. Behavioral studies of associative learning in animals. *Annual Reviews of Psychology* 33:265–308.

RESCORLA, R. A., AND WAGNER, A. R. 1972. A theory of Pavlovian conditioning: Variations in the effectiveness of reinforcement and non-reinforcement. In Black, A. H., and Prokasy, W. F. (Eds.), *Classical conditioning II.* New York: Appleton-Century-Crofts.

REST, J. R. 1983. Morality. In Mussen, P. E. (Ed.), *Carmichael's manual of child psychology: Vol. 4. Socialization, personality, and social development* (Hetherington, E. M., volume editor). New York: Wiley.

REST, J. R. 1984. The major components of morality. In Kurtines, W. M., and Gewirtz, L. (Eds.), *Morality, moral behavior, and moral development.* New York: Wiley.

REVLIN, R., AND LEIRER, V. O. 1980. Understanding quantified categorical expressions. *Memory and Cognition* 8:447–58.

REVUSKY, S. H. 1971. The role of interference in association over a delay. In Honig, W. K., and James, H. R. (Eds.), *Animal memory.* New York: Academic Press.

REVUSKY, S. 1977. Learning as a general process with an emphasis on data from feeding experiments. In Milgram, N. W.; Krames, L.; and Alloway, T. H. (Eds.), *Food aversion learning,* pp. 1–51. New York: Plenum.

REYNOLDS, G. S. 1968. *A primer of operant conditioning.* Glenview, Ill.: Scott, Foresman.

RHEINGOLD, H. L.; HAY, D. F.; AND WEST, M. J. 1976. Sharing in the second year of life. *Child Development* 47:1148–58.

RICHARDS, W. 1977. Lessons in constancy from neurophysiology. In Epstein, W. W. (Ed.), *Stability and constancy in visual perception: Mechanisms and processes,* pp. 421–36. New York: Wiley.

RICKS, S. S. 1985. Father-infant interactions: A review of empirical research. *Family Relations* 34:505–11.

RIGGS, L. A.; RATLIFF, F.; CORNSWEET, J. C.; AND CORNSWEET, T. N. 1953. The disappearance of steadily fixated visual test objects. *Journal of the Optical Society of America* 43:495–501.

RIPS, L. J.; SHOBEN, E. J.; AND SMITH, E. E. 1973. Semantic distance and the verification of semantic relations. *Journal of Verbal Learning and Verbal Behavior* 12:1–20.

RIPS, L. J.; SMITH, E. E.; AND SHOBEN, E. J. 1978. Semantic composition in sentence verification. *Journal of Verbal Learning and Verbal Behavior* 19:705–21.

ROBBIN, A. A. 1958. A controlled study of the effects of leucotomy. *Journal of Neurology, Neurosurgery and Psychiatry* 21:262–69.

ROBBINS, S. J. 1990. Mechanisms underlying spontaneous recovery in autoshaping. *Journal of Experimental Psychology: Animal Behavior Processes* 16:235–49.

ROBINS, L. R. 1966. *Deviant children grown up: A sociological and psychiatric study of sociopathic personality.* Baltimore: Williams & Wilkins.

ROCK, I. 1973. *Orientation and form.* New York: Academic Press.

ROCK, I. 1975. *An introduction to perception.* New York: Macmillan.

ROCK, I. 1977. In defense of unconscious inference. In Epstein, W. W. (Ed.), *Stability and constancy in visual perception: Mechanisms and processes,* pp. 321–74. New York: Wiley.

ROCK. I. 1983. *The logic of perception.* Cambridge, Mass.: MIT Press.

ROCK, I. 1986. The description and analysis of object and event perception. In Boff, K. R.; Kauffman, L.; and Thomas, J. P. (Eds.), *Handbook of perception and human performance: Vol. 2. Cognitive processes and performance,* pp. 1–71. New York: Wiley.

ROCK. I., AND KAUFMAN, L. 1962. The moon illusion, II. *Science* 136:1023–31.

RODIN, J. 1980. The externality theory today. In Stunkard, A. J. (Ed.), *Obesity,* pp. 226–39. Philadelphia: Saunders.

RODIN, J. 1981. Current status of the internal-external hypothesis for obesity. What went wrong? *American Psychologist* 36:361–72.

RODIN, J., AND LANGER, E. J. 1977. Long-term effects of a control-relevant intervention with the institutionalized aged. *Journal of Personality and Social Psychology* 35:897–902.

ROEDER, K. D. 1935. An experimental analysis of the sexual behavior of the praying mantis. *Biological Bulletin* 69:203–20.

ROEDER, L. 1967. *Nerve cells and insect behavior.* Cambridge, Mass.: Harvard University Press.

ROEPER, T., AND WILLIAMS, E. (Eds.). 1987. *Parameter setting.* Dordrecht: Reidel.

ROGERS, C. R. 1942. *Counseling and psychotherapy: New concepts in practice.* Boston: Houghton Mifflin.

ROGERS, C. R. 1951 and 1970. *Client-centered therapy: Its current practice, implications, and theory,* 1st and 2nd eds. Boston: Houghton Mifflin.

ROGERS, C. R. 1959. A theory of therapy, personality, and interpersonal relationships as developed in the client-centered framework. In Koch, S. (Ed.), *Psychology: A study of a science,* vol. 3. New York: McGraw-Hill.

ROGERS, C. R. 1961. *On becoming a person: A therapist's view of psychotherapy.* Boston: Houghton Mifflin.

ROGERS, C. R. 1980. *A way of being.* Boston: Houghton Mifflin.

ROGERS, C. R., AND DYMOND, R. F. 1954. *Psychotherapy and personality change: Coordinated studies in the client-centered approach.* Chicago: University of Chicago Press.

ROGOFF, B.; GAUVAIN, M.; AND ELLIS, S. 1984. Development viewed in its cultural context. In Bornstein, M. H., and Lamb, M. E. (Eds.), *Developmental psychology: An advanced textbook.* Hillsdale, N.J.: Erlbaum.

ROLLS, B. J., AND ROLLS, E. T. 1982. *Thirst.* New York: Cambridge University Press.

ROLLS, E. J. 1978. Neurophysiology of feeding. *Trends in Neurosciences* 1:1–3.

ROLLS, E. T. 1975. *The brain and reward.* New York: Pergamon.

ROMANES, G. J. 1882. *Animal intelligence.* London: Kegan Paul.

RORER, L. G., AND WIDIGER, T. A. 1983. Personality structure and assessment. In Rosenzweig, M. R., and Porter, L. W. (Eds.), *Annual Review of Psychology* 34:431–63.

ROSCH, E. H. 1973a. Natural categories. *Cognitive Psychology* 4:328–50.

ROSCH, E. H. 1973b. On the internal structure of perceptual and semantic categories. In Moore, T. E. (Ed.), *Cognitive development and the acquisition of language.* New York: Academic Press.

ROSCH, E. H. 1978. Principles of categorization. In Rosch, E., and Lloyd (Eds.), *Cognition and categorization.* Hillsdale, N.J.: Erlbaum.

ROSCH, E. H., AND MERVIS, C. B. 1975. Family resemblances: Studies in the internal structure of categories. *Cognitive Psychology* 7:573–605.

ROSCH, E. H.; MERVIS, C. B.; GRAY, W. D.; JOHNSON, D. M.; AND BOYES-BRAEM, P. 1976. Basic objects in natural categories. *Cognitive Psychology* 8:382–439.

ROSE, R. M.; JENKINS, C. D.; AND HURST, M. W. 1978. *Air traf-*

*fic controller health change study.* Report to the Federal Aviation Administration. Cited in Davison and Neale, 1986.

ROSEN, G. 1966. *Madness in society.* Chicago: University of Chicago Press.

ROSENFELD, P.; GIACALONE, R. A.; AND TEDESCHI, J. T. 1984. Cognitive dissonance and impression management explanations for effort justification. *Personality and Social Psychology Bulletin* 10: 394–401.

ROSENHAN, D. L. 1973. On being sane in insane places. *Science* 179:250–58.

ROSENHAN, D. L., AND SELIGMAN, M. E. P. 1989. *Abnormal Psychology,* 2nd ed. New York: Norton.

ROSENMAN, R. H. 1978. The interview method of assessment of the coronary-prone behavior pattern. In Dembrowski, T. M.; Weiss, S. M.; Shields, J. L. et al. (Eds.), *Coronary-prone behavior.* New York: Springer.

ROSENMAN, R. H.; BRAND, R. J.; JENKINS, C. D.; FRIEDMAN, M.; AND STRAUS, R. 1975. Coronary heart disease in the Western Collaborative Group Study: Final follow-up experience of 8½ years. *Journal of the American Medical Association* 233:872–77.

ROSENTHAL, A. M. 1964. *Thirty-eight witnesses.* New York: McGraw-Hill.

ROSENTHAL, D. 1970. *Genetic theory and abnormal behavior.* New York: McGraw-Hill.

ROSENTHAL, N. E.; CARPENTER, C. J.; JAMES, S. P.; PARRY, B. L.; ROGERS, S. L. B.; AND WEHER, T. A. 1986. Seasonal affective disorder in children and adolescents. *American Journal of Psychiatry* 143:356–58.

ROSENTHAL, N. E.; SACK, D. A.; GILLIN, J. C.; LEWY, A. J.; GOODWIN, F. K.; DAVENPORT, Y.; MUELLER, P. S.; NEWSOME, D. A.; AND WEHR, T. A. 1984. Seasonal affective disorder: A description of the syndrome and preliminary findings with light therapy. *Archives of General Psychiatry* 41:72–80.

ROSENZWEIG, M. R., AND BENNETT. 1972. Cerebral changes in rats exposed individually to an enriched environment. *Journal of Comparative and Physiological Psychology* 80:304–13.

ROSENZWEIG, M. R., AND LEIMAN, A. L. 1982. *Physiological psychology.* Lexington, Mass.: Heath.

ROSENZWEIG, M. R., AND LEIMAN, A. L. 1989. *Physiological psychology,* 2nd ed. New York: Random House.

ROSS, J., AND LAWRENCE, K. Q. 1968. Some observations on memory artifice. *Psychonomic Science* 13:107–108.

ROSS, L. 1977. The intuitive psychologist and his shortcomings: Distortions in the attribution process. In Berkowitz, L. (Ed.), *Advances in experimental social psychology,* vol. 10. New York: Academic Press.

ROSS, L.; AMABILE, T. M.; AND STEINMETZ, J. L. 1977. Social roles, social control, and biases in social perception processes. *Journal of Experimental Social Psychology* 35:817–29.

ROTTER, J. B. 1966. Generalized expectancies for internal versus external control of reinforcement. *Psychological Monographs* 80 (1, Whole Number 609).

ROTTER, J. B. 1975. Some problems and misconceptions related to the construct of internal versus external control of reinforcement. *Journal of Consulting and Clinical Psychology* 43:56–67.

ROZIN, P. 1976a. The evolution of intelligence and access to the cognitive unconscious. In Stellar, E., and Sprague, J. M. (Eds.), *Progress in psychobiology and physiological psychology,* vol. 6. New York: Academic Press.

ROZIN, P. 1976b. The psychobiological approach to human memory. In Rosenzweig, M. R., and Bennett, E. L., *Neural mechanisms of learning and memory,* pp. 3–48. Cambridge, Mass.: MIT Press.

ROZIN, P. 1976c. The selection of foods by rats, humans and other animals. *Advances in the study of behavior,* vol. 6, pp. 21–76. New York: Academic Press.

ROZIN, P. 1982. Human food selection: The interaction of biology, culture, and individual experience. In Barker, L. M. (Ed.), *The psychology of human food selection,* pp. 225–54. Westport, Conn.: AVI Publ. Co.

ROZIN, P., AND KALAT, J. W. 1971. Specific hungers and poison avoidance as adaptive specializations of learning. *Psychological Review* 78:459–86.

RUBLE, D. N. 1984. Sex-role development. In Bornstein, M. H., and Lamb, M. E. (Eds.), *Developmental psychology: An advanced textbook.* Hillsdale, N.J.: Erlbaum.

RUMBAUGH, D. M. (Ed.). 1977. *Language learning by a chimpanzee: The Lana Project.* New York: Academic Press.

RUMELHART, D., AND MCCLELLAND, J. 1986. On learning the past tenses of English verbs. In McClelland, J.; Rumelhart, D.; and the PDP Research Group (Eds.), *Parallel distributed processing: Explorations in the microstructure of cognition,* vol. I. Cambridge, Mass: MIT Press.

RUNDUS, D. 1977. Maintenance rehearsal and single-level processing. *Journal of Verbal Learning and Verbal Behavior* 16:665–82.

RUSHTON, J. P.; FULKER, D. W.; NEALE, M. C.; NIAS, D. K. B.; EYSENCK, H. J. 1986. Altruism and aggression: The heritability of individual differences. *Journal of Personality and Social Psychology* 50:1192–98.

RUSSEK, M. 1971. Hepatic receptors and the neurophysiological mechanisms controlling feeding behavior. In Ehrenpreis, S. (Ed.), *Neurosciences research,* vol. 4. New York: Academic Press.

RUSSELL, G. V. 1961. Interrelationship within the limbic and centrencephalic systems. In Sheer, D. E. (Ed.), *Electrical stimulation of the brain,* pp. 167–81. Austin, Tex.: University of Texas Press.

RUSSELL, M. J. 1976. Human olfactory communication. *Nature* 260:520–22.

RUSSELL, M. J.; SWITZ, G. M.; AND THOMPSON, K. 1980. Olfactory influence on the human menstrual cycle. *Pharmacology, Biochemistry, and Behavior* 13:737–38.

SABINI, J. 1992. *Social psychology.* New York: Norton, in press.

SABINI, J., AND SILVER, M. 1982. *Moralities of everyday life.* New York: Oxford University Press.

SACHS, J. 1967. Recognition memory for syntactic and semantic aspects of connected discourse. *Perception and Psychophysics* 2:437–42.

SACHS, J., AND TRUSWELL, L. 1978. Comprehension of two-word instructions by children in the one-word stage. *Journal of Child Language* 5:17–24.

SACKS, O. 1985. *The man who mistook his wife for a hat.* New York: Harper & Row.

SADLER, H. H.; DAVISON, L.; CARROLL, C.; AND KOUNTZ, S. L. 1971. The living, genetically unrelated, kidney donor. *Seminars in Psychiatry* 3:86–101.

SADOCK, B. J. 1975. Group psychotherapy. In Freedman, A. M.; Kaplan, H. I.; and Sadock, B. J. (Eds.), *Comprehensive textbook of psychiatry,* vol. 2, pp. 1850–76. Baltimore: Williams & Wilkins.

SAGHIR, M. T., AND ROBINS, E. 1973. *Male and female homosexuality.* Baltimore: Williams & Wilkins.

SAGI, A., AND HOFFMAN, M. L. 1976. Empathic distress in the newborn. *Developmental Psychology* 12:175–76.

SAHLINS, M. 1976. *The use and abuse of biology.* Ann Arbor, Mich.: University of Michigan Press.

SALAPATEK, P. 1975. Pattern perception in early infancy. In Cohen, L. B., and Salapatek, P. (Eds.), *Infant perception: From sensation to cognition,* vol. 1, pp. 133–248. New York: Academic Press.

SALAPATEK, P., AND KESSEN, W. 1966. Visual scanning of triangles by the human newborn. *Journal of Experimental Child Psychology* 3:113–22.

SARASON, S. B. 1973. Jewishness, blackness, and the nature-nurture controversy. *American Psychologist* 28:926–71.

SARBIN, T. R., AND ALLEN, V. L. 1968. Role theory. In Lindzey, G., and Aronson, E. (Eds.), *The handbook of social psychology,* 2nd ed., vol. 1, pp. 488–567. Reading, Mass.: Addison-Wesley.

SARNOFF, C. 1957. *Medical aspects of flying motivation—a fear-of-flying case book.* Randolph Air Force Base, Texas: U. S. Air Force, Air University, School of Aviation Medicine.

SATINOFF, E. 1964. Behavioral thermoregulation in response to local cooling of the rat brain. *American Journal of Physiology* 206:1389–94.

SATINOFF, E. 1978. Neural organization and evolution of thermal regulation in mammals. *Science* 201:16–22.

SATINOFF, E. AND RUTSTEIN, 1970. Behavioral thermoregulation in rats with anterior hypothalamic lesions. *Journal of Comparative and Physiological Psychology* 71:77–82.

SATINOFF, E., AND SHAN, 1971. Loss of behavioral thermoregulation after anterior hypothalamic lesions in rats. *Journal of Comparative and Physiological Psychology* 77:302–12.

SATIR, V. 1967. *Conjoint family therapy,* rev. ed. Palo Alto, Calif.: Science and Behavior Books.

SAVAGE-RUMBAUGH, E.; McDONALD, D.; SEVCIK, R.; HOPKINS, W.; AND RUPERT, E. 1986. Spontaneous symbol acquisition and communicative use by pygmie chimpanzees. *Journal of Experimental Psychology: General* 115:211–235.

SAVAGE-RUMBAUGH, E.; RUMBAUGH, D.; SMITH, S.; AND LAWSON, J. 1980. Reference: The linguistic essential. *Science* 210:922–25.

SAVAGE-RUMBAUGH, S. 1987. A new look at ape language: Comprehension of vocal speech and syntax. *Nebraska Symposium on Motivation* 35:201–55.

SAWREY, W. L.; CONGER, J. J.; AND TURRELL, E. S. 1956. An experimental investigation of the role of psychological factors in the production of gastric ulcers in the rat. *Journal of Comparative and Physiological Psychology* 49:457–61.

SCARR, S. 1987. Distinctive environments depend on genotypes. Peer commentary to article by Plomin, R., and Daniels, D. Why are children from the same family so different from one another? *Behavioral and Brain Sciences* 10:38–39.

SCARR, S., AND CARTER-SALTZMAN, L. 1979. Twin method: Defense of a critical assumption. *Behavior Genetics* 9:527–42.

SCARR, S., AND CARTER-SALTZMAN, L. 1982. Genetics and intelligence. In Sternberg, R. J. (Ed.), *Handbook of human intelligence,* pp. 792–896. New York: Cambridge University Press.

SCARR, S., AND McCARTNEY, K. 1983. How people make their own environments: A theory of genotype-environment effects. *Child Development* 54:424–35.

SCARR, S., AND WEINBERG, R. A. 1976. IQ test performance of black children adopted by white families. *American Psychologist* 31:726–39.

SCARR, S., AND WEINBERG, R. A. 1983. The Minnesota adoption studies genetic differences and malleability. *Child Development* 54:260–67.

SCHACHER, S. 1981. Determination and differentiation in the development of the nervous system. In Kandel, E. R., and Schwartz, J. H. (Eds.), *Principles of neural science.* New York: Elsevier North Holland.

SCHACHTEL, E. G. 1947. On memory and childhood amnesia. *Psychiatry* 10:1–26.

SCHACHTER, S. 1964. The interaction of cognitive and physiological determinants of emotional state. In Berkowitz, L. (Ed.), *Advances in Experimental Social Psychology,* pp. 49–80. New York: Academic Press.

SCHACHTER, S. 1971. Some extraordinary facts about obese humans and rats. *American Psychologist* 26:129–44.

SCHACHTER, S., AND RODIN, J. 1974. *Obese humans and rats.* Washington, D. C.: Erlbaum-Halstead.

SCHACHTER, S., AND SINGER, J. 1962. Cognitive, social and physiological determinants of emotional state. *Psychological Review* 69:379–99.

SCHACHTER, S., AND SINGER, J. E. 1979. Comments on the Maslach and Marshall-Zimbardo experiments. *Journal of Personality and Social Psychology* 37:989–95.

SCHACTER, D. L. 1987. Implicit memory: History and current status. *Journal of Experimental Psychology: Learning, Memory, and Cognition* 13:501–18.

SCHÄFER, S. 1977. Sociosexual behavior in male and female homosexuals: A study in sex differences. *Archives of Sexual Behavior* 6:355–64.

SCHAFFER, H. R., AND CALLENDER, W. M. 1959. Psychological effects of hospitalization in infancy. *Pediatrics* 24:528–39.

SCHAIE, K. W. 1979. The primary mental abilities in adulthood: An exploration in the development of psychometric intelligence. In Baltes, P. B., and Brim, O. G., Jr. (Eds.), *Life-span development and behavior,* vol. 2. New York: Academic Press.

SCHAIE, K., AND STROTHER, C. 1968. A cross-sequential study of age changes in cognitive behavior. *Psychological Bulletin* 70:671–80.

SCHANK, R. C., AND ABELSON, R. 1977. *Scripts, plans, goals, and understanding.* Hillsdale, N.J.: Erlbaum.

SCHAPIRO, S., AND VUKOVICH, K. R. 1976. Early experience effects on cortical dendrites: A proposed model for development. *Science* 167:292–94.

SCHEERER, M. 1963. Problem solving. *Scientific American* 208: 118–28.

SCHEERER, M.; GOLDSTEIN, K.; AND BORING, E. G. 1941. A demonstration of insight: The horse-rider puzzle. *American Journal of Psychology* 54:437–38.

SCHEFF, S. W., AND COTMAN, C. W. 1977. Recovery of spontaneous alternation following lesions of the entorhinal cortex in adult rats: Possible correlation to axon sprouting. *Behavioral Biology* 21: 286–93.

SCHEFF, T. 1966. *Being mentally ill: A sociological theory.* Chicago: Aldine.

SCHIFF, M.; DUYME, M.; DUMARET, A.; AND TOMKIEWICZ, S. 1982. How much *could* we boost scholastic achievement and IQ scores? A direct answer from a French adoption study. *Cognition* 12: 165–96.

SCHIFF, W. 1965. Perception of impending collision. *Psychological Monographs* 79:1–26.

SCHIFFMAN, H. R. 1976. *Sensation and perception: An integrated approach.* New York: Wiley.

SCHIFFRIN, D. 1988. Conversational analysis. In F. Newmeyer (Ed.), *Linguistics: The Cambridge survey: Vol. IV. The socio-cultural context.* Cambridge: Cambridge University Press.

SCHILDKRAUT, J. J. 1965. The catecholamine hypothesis of affective disorders: A review of supporting evidence. *American Journal of Psychiatry* 122:509–22.

SCHILDKRAUT, J. J.; GREEN, A. I.; AND MOONEY, J. J. 1985. Affective disorders: Biochemical aspects. In Kaplan, H. I.; and Sadock, J. (Eds.), *Comprehensive textbook of psychiatry,* 4th ed. Baltimore: Williams & Wilkins.

SCHLEIDT, W. M. 1961. Ueber die Aufloesung der Flucht bor Raubvoeglns bei Truthuenern. *Naturwissenschaften* 48:141–42.

SCHLENKER, R. B. 1980. *Impression management: The self-concept, social identity and interpersonal relations.* Monterey, Calif.: Brooks/Cole.

SCHLENKER, R. B.; HALLAM, J. R.; AND McCOWN, N. E. 1983. Motives and social evaluation: Actor-observer differences in the delineation of motives for a beneficial act. *Journal of Experimental Social Psychology* 19:254–73.

SCHNEIDER, D. J. 1973. Implicit personality theory: A review. *Psychological Bulletin* 79:294–309.

SCHNEIDER, D. J.; HASTORF, A. H.; AND ELLSWORTH, P. C. 1979. *Person perception,* 2nd ed. Reading, Mass.: Addison-Wesley.

SCHOFIELD, W. 1964. *Psychotherapy: The purchase of friendship.* Englewood Cliffs, N.J.: Prentice-Hall.

SCHOPLER, J., AND COMPERE, J. S. 1971. Effects of being kind or harsh to another on liking. *Journal of Personality and Social Psychology* 20:155–59.

SCHULL, J. 1979. A conditioned opponent theory of Pavlovian conditioning and habituation. In Bower, G. (Ed.), *The psychology of learning and motivation,* vol. 13. New York: Academic Press.

SCHWAB, E. C., AND NUSBAUM, H. C. (Eds.). 1986. *Pattern recognition by humans and machines,* vol. 2. New York: Academic Press.

SCHWARTZ, B. 1974. On going back to nature: A review of Seligman and Hager's *Biological boundaries of learning. Journal of the Experimental Analysis of Behavior* 21:183–98.

SCHWARTZ, B. 1989. *Psychology of learning and behavior,* 3rd ed. New York: Norton.

SCHWARTZ, B., AND GAMZU, E. 1977. Pavlovian control of operant behavior. In Honig, W. K., and Staddon, J. E. R. (Eds.), *Handbook of operant behavior.* Englewood Cliffs, N.J.: Prentice-Hall.

SCHWARTZ, B., AND REISBERG, D. 1991. *Psychology of learning and memory.* New York: Norton.

SCHWARTZ, G. E.; WEINBERGER, D. A.; AND SINGER, J. A. 1981. Cardiovascular differentiation of happiness, sadness, anger, and fear following imagery and exercise. *Psychosomatic Medicine* 43:343–64.

SCHWARTZ, S. H., AND CLAUSEN, G. 1970. Responsibility, norms, and helping in an emergency. *Journal of Personality and Social Psychology* 16:299–310.

SCOTT, J. P., AND FULLER, J. L. 1965. *Genetics and the social behavior of the dog.* Chicago: University of Chicago Press.

SCRIBNER, S., AND COLE, M. 1973. Cognitive consequences of formal and informal education. *Science* 182:553–59.

SEARLE, J. R. 1969. *Speech acts: An essay in the philosophy of language.* New York: Cambridge University Press.

SEARS, R. R.; MACCOBY, E. E.; AND LEVIN, H. 1957. *Patterns of child rearing.* Evanston, Ill.: Row, Peterson.

SEAY, B.; ALEXANDER, B. K.; AND HARLOW, H. F. 1964. Maternal behavior of socially deprived rhesus monkeys. *Journal of Abnormal and Social Psychology* 69:345–54.

SEIDENBERG, M. S., AND PETITTO, L. A. 1979. Signing behavior in apes: A critical review. *Cognition* 7:177–215.

SELFE, L. 1977. *Nadia: A case of extraordinary drawing ability in an autistic child.* New York: Academic Press.

SELFRIDGE, O. G. 1955. Pattern recognition and modern computers. In *Proceedings of Western Joint Computer Conference,* Los Angeles, Calif.

SELFRIDGE, O. G. 1959. Pandemonium: A paradigm for learning. In Blake, D. V., and Uttley, A. M. (Eds.), *Proceedings of the Symposium on the Mechanisation of Thought Processes.* London: HM Stationary Office.

SELIGMAN, M. E. P. 1968. Chronic fear produced by unpredictable electric shock. *Journal of Comparative and Physiological Psychology* 66:402–11.

SELIGMAN, M. E. P. 1970. On the generality of the laws of learning. *Psychological Review* 77:406–18.

SELIGMAN, M. 1971. Phobias and preparedness. *Behavior Therapy* 2:307–20.

SELIGMAN, M. E. P. 1975. *Helplessness: On depression, development, and death.* San Francisco: Freeman.

SELIGMAN, M. E. P.; KLEIN, D. C.; AND MILLER, W. R. 1976. Depression. In Leitenberg, H. (Ed.), *Handbook of behavior modification and behavior therapy.* Englewood Cliffs, N.J.: Prentice-Hall.

SELIGMAN, M. E. P., AND MAIER, S. F. 1967. Failure to escape traumatic shock. *Journal of Experimental Psychology* 74:1–9.

SELIGMAN, M. E. P.; MAIER, S. F.; AND SOLOMON, R. L. 1971. Unpredictable and uncontrollable aversive events. In Brush, F. R. (Ed.), *Aversive conditioning and learning.* New York: Academic Press.

SELLS, P. 1985. *Lectures on contemporary syntactic theories.* Stanford, Calif.: Center for the Study of Language and Information.

SENDAK, M. 1963. *Where the wild things are.* New York: Harper & Row.

SENDAK, M. 1979. *Higglety pigglety pop! or There must be more to life.* New York: Harper & Row.

SEYFARTH, R. 1978. Social relations among adult male and female baboons. I. Behavior during sexual consortship. *Behavior* 64:204–26.

SHALLICE, T., AND WARRINGTON, E. K. 1970. Independent functioning of verbal memory stores: A neuropsychological study. *Quarterly Journal of Experimental Psychology* 22:261–73.

SHALTER, M. D. 1984. Predator-prey behavior and habituation. In Peeke, H. V. S., and Petrinovich, L. (Eds.), *Habituation, sensitization and behavior,* pp. 423–58. New York: Academic Press.

SHAPIRO, A. K. 1971. Placebo effects in medicine, psychotherapy, and psychoanalysis. In Bergin, A. E., and Garfield, S. L. (Eds.), *Handbook of psychotherapy and behavior change,* pp. 439–73. New York: Wiley.

SHAPIRO, C. M.; BORTZ, R.; MITCHELL, D.; BARTELL, P.; AND JOOSTE, P. 1981. Slow wave sleep: A recovery period after exercise. *Science* 214:1253–54.

SHAPIRO, D. A., AND SHAPIRO, D. 1982. Meta-analysis of comparative therapy outcome studies: A replication and refinement. *Psychological Bulletin* 92:581–604.

SHEEAN, D. 1985. Monoamine oxidase inhibitors and alprazolam in the treatment of panic disorder and agoraphobia. *Psychiatric Clinics of North America* 8:49–82.

SHEFFIELD, F. D., AND ROBY, T. B. 1950. Reward value of a nonnutritive sweet taste. *Journal of Comparative and Physiological Psychology* 43:471–81.

SHEFFIELD, F. D.; WULFF, J. J.; AND BACKER, R. 1951. Reward value of copulation without sex drive reduction. *Journal of Comparative and Physiological Psychology* 44:3–8.

SHEINGOLD, K., AND TENNEY, Y. J. 1982. Memory for a salient childhood event. In Neisser, U. (Ed.), *Memory observed,* pp. 201–12. San Francisco: Freeman.

SHEKELLE, R. B.; RAYNOR, W. J.; OSTFELD, A. M.; GARRON, D. C.; BIELIAVSKAS, L. A.; LIV, S. C.; MALIZA, C.; AND PAUL, O. 1981. Psychological depression and the 17-year risk of cancer. *Psychosomatic Medicine* 43:117–25.

SHEPARD, R. N., AND COOPER, L. A. 1982. *Mental images and their transformations.* Cambridge, Mass.: MIT Press.

SHERMAN, P. W. 1977. Nepotism and the evolution of alarm calls. *Science* 197:1246–54.

SHERRICK, C. E., AND CHOLEWIAK, R. W. 1986. Cutaneous sensitivity. In Boff, K. R.; Kaufman, L.; and Thomas, J. P. (Eds.), *Handbook of perception and human performance,* Chapter 12. New York: Wiley.

SHERRINGTON, C. S. 1906. *The integrative action of the nervous system,* 2nd ed. New Haven, Conn.: Yale University Press, 1947.

SHETTLEWORTH, S. J. 1972. Constraints on learning. In Lehrman, D. S.; Hinde, R. A.; and Shaw, E. (Eds.), *Advances in the study of behavior,* vol. 4. New York: Academic Press.

SHIFFRIN, R. M., AND SCHNEIDER, W. 1977. Controlled and automatic human information processing: II. Perceptual learning, automatic attending, and a general theory. *Psychological Review* 84:127–90.

SHIMBERG, M. E. 1929. An investigation into the validity of norms with special reference to urban and rural groups. In *Archives of Psychology,* No. 104.

SHIPLEY, E. F., AND KUHN, I. F. 1983. A constraint on comparisons: Equally detailed alternatives. *Journal of Experimental Child Psychology* 35:195–222.

SHIPLEY, E. F.; KUHN, I. F.; AND MADDEN, E. C. 1983. Mothers' use of superordinate terms. *Journal of Child Language* 10:571–88.

SHIPLEY, E. F.; SMITH, C. S.; AND GLEITMAN, L. R. 1969. A

study in the acquisition of language: Free responses to commands. *Language* 45:322–42.

SHIRLEY, M. M. 1961. *The first two years: A study of twenty-five babies.* Minneapolis: University of Minnesota Press.

SHORTLIFFE, E. H.; AXLINE, S. G.; BUCHANAN, B. G.; MERIGAN, T. C.; AND COHEN, N. S. 1973. An artificial intelligence program to advise physicians regarding antimicrobial therapy. *Computers and Biomedical Research* 6:544–60.

SHUEY, A. 1966. *The testing of Negro intelligence.* New York: Social Science Press.

SHWEDER, R. A. 1975. How relevant is an individual difference theory of personality? *Journal of Personality* 43:455–85.

SICOLY, F., AND ROSS, M. 1977. Facilitation of ego-biased attributions by means of self-serving observer feedback. *Journal of Personality and Social Psychology* 35:734–41.

SIEGEL, R. K. 1984. Changing patterns of cocaine use: Longitudinal observations, consequences, and treatment. In Grabowski, J. (Ed.), *Cocaine: Pharmacology, effects, and treatment of abuse,* pp. 92–110. NIDA Research Monograph 50.

SIEGEL, S. 1977. Morphine tolerance acquisition as an associative process. *Journal of Experimental Psychology: Animal Behavior Processes* 3:1–13.

SIEGEL, S. 1979. The role of conditioning in drug tolerance and addiction. In Keehn, J. D. (Ed.), *Psychopathology in animals: Research and treatment implications.* New York: Academic Press.

SIEGEL, S. 1983. Classical conditioning, drug tolerance, and drug dependence. In Israel, Y.; Glaser, F. B.; Kalant, H.; Popham, R. E.; Schmidt, W.; and Smart, R. G. (Eds.), *Research advances in alcohol and drug problems,* vol. 7. New York: Plenum.

SIEGEL, S.; HINSON, R. E.; KRANK, M. D.; AND MCCULLY, J. 1982. Heroin "overdose" death: Contribution of drug-associated environmental cues. *Science* 216:436–37.

SIEGLER, R. S. 1983. Information processing approaches to child development. In Mussen, P. H., *Handbook of child psychology: Vol. 1. History, theory, and methods* (Kessen, W., volume editor). New York: Wiley.

SIEGLER, R. S. 1989. Mechanisms of cognitive development. In Rosenzweig, M. R., and Porter, L. W. (Eds.), *Annual Review of Psychology* 40:353–79.

SIEGLER, M., AND OSMOND, H. 1974. *Models of madness, models of medicine.* New York: Harper & Row.

SILK, J. B. 1986. Social behavior in evolutionary perspective. In Smuts, B. B.; Cheney, D. L.; Seyfarth, R. M.; Wrangham, R. W.; and Struhsaker, T. T. (Eds.), *Primate societies.* Chicago: University of Chicago Press.

SILVERMAN, I. 1971. Physical attractiveness and courtship. Cited in Hatfield, E., and Walster, G. W. *A new look at love.* Reading, Mass.: Addison-Wesley, 1981.

SIMMEL, G. 1911. *On individuality and social form.* Levine, D. N. (editor of 1971 edition). Chicago, Ill.: University of Chicago Press.

SIMNER, M. L. 1971. Newborn's response to the cry of another infant. *Developmental Psychology* 5:136–50.

SIMON, H. A. 1956. Rational choice and the structure of the environment. *Psychological Review* 63:129–38.

SIMS, E. A. 1986. Energy balance in human beings: The problems of plentitude. *Vitamins and hormones: Research and applications* 43:1–101.

SINCLAIR, H. 1970. The transition from sensory-motor behavior to symbolic activity. *Interchange* 1:119–26.

SINCLAIR, H. 1973. Language acquisition and cognitive development. In Moore, T. E. (Ed.), *Cognitive development and the acquisition of language.* New York: Academic Press.

SJÖSTRÖM, L. 1980. Fat cells and body weight. In Stunkard, A. J. (Ed.), *Obesity.* pp. 72–100. Philadelphia: Saunders.

SKEELS, H. 1966. Adult status of children with contrasting early life experiences. *Monograph of the Society for Research in Child Development* 31 (No. 3).

SKINNER, B. F. 1938. *The behavior of organisms.* New York: Appleton-Century-Crofts.

SKINNER, B. F. 1969. *Contingencies of reinforcement: A theoretical analysis.* New York: Appleton-Century-Crofts.

SKINNER, B. F. 1971. *Beyond freedom and dignity.* New York: Alfred Knopf.

SKODAK, M., AND SKEELS, H. M. 1945. A follow-up study of children in adoptive homes. *Journal of Genetic Psychology* 66:21–58.

SKODAK, M., AND SKEELS, H. M. 1947. A follow-up study of the development of one-hundred adopted children in Iowa. *American Psychologist* 2:278.

SKODAK, M., AND SKEELS, H. M. 1949. A final follow-up study of children in adoptive homes. *Journal of Genetic Psychology* 75:85–125.

SLATER, E. 1943. The neurotic constitution. *Journal of Neurological Psychiatry* 6:1–16.

SLATER, E., AND GLITHERO, E. 1965. A follow-up of patients diagnosed as suffering from hysteria. *Journal of Psychosomatic Research* 9:9–13.

SLOANE, R. B.; STAPLES, F. R.; CRISTOL, A. H.; YORKSTON, N.J.; AND WHIPPLE, K. 1975. *Psychotherapy vs. behavior therapy.* Cambridge, Mass.: Harvard University Press.

SLOBIN, D. I. 1966. Grammatical transformations and sentence comprehension in childhood and adulthood. *Journal of Verbal Learning and Verbal Behavior* 5:219–27.

SMEDSLUND, J. 1961. The acquisition of conservation of substance and weight in children. *Scandinavia Journal of Psychology* 2:11–20.

SMELSER, N. J. 1963. *Theory of collective behavior.* New York: Free Press, Macmillan.

SMITH, B. M. 1967. The polygraph. *Scientific American* 216:25–31.

SMITH, C., AND LLOYD, B. 1978. Maternal behavior and perceived sex of infant: Revisited. *Child Development* 49:1263–65.

SMITH, D. G. 1981. The association between rank and reproductive success of male rhesus monkeys. *American Journal of Primatology* 1:83–90.

SMITH, E. E., AND MEDIN, D. L. 1981. *Categories and concepts.* Cambridge, Mass.: Harvard University Press.

SMITH, M. B. 1950. The phenomenological approach in personality theory: Some critical remarks. *Journal of Abnormal and Social Psychology* 45:516–22.

SMITH, M. L.; GLASS, G. V.; AND MILLER, R. L. 1980. *The benefits of psychotherapy.* Baltimore: Johns Hopkins Press.

SMITH, S. M. 1979. Remembering in and out of context. *Journal of Experimental Psychology: Human Learning and Memory* 5:460–71.

SNOW, C., AND HOEFNAGEL-HOHLE, M. 1978. The critical period for language acquisition: Evidence from second language learning. *Child Development* 49:1114–28.

SNYDER, C. R.; SHENKEL, R. J.; AND LOWERY, C. R. 1977. Acceptance of personality interpretations: The "Barnum" effect and beyond. *Journal of Consulting and Clinical Psychology* 45:104–14.

SNYDER, M. 1981. On the influence of individuals on situations. In Cantor, N., and Kihlstrom, J. F. (Eds.), *Personality, cognition, and social interaction.* Hillsdale, N.J.: Erlbaum.

SNYDER, M. 1987. *Public appearances/private realities.* New York: Freeman.

SNYDER, M., AND CUNNINGHAM, M. R. 1975. To comply or not comply: Testing the self-perception explanation of the "foot-in-the-door" phenomenon. *Journal of Personality and Social Psychology* 31:64–67.

SNYDER, M., AND ICKES, W. 1985. Personality and social behavior. In Lindzey, G., and Aronson, E. (Eds.), *Handbook of Social Psy-*

*chology,* 3rd ed., vol. 2. New York: Random House.

SNYDER, M. L.; STEPHAN, W. G.; AND ROSENFIELD, D. 1976. Egotism and attribution. *Journal of Personality and Social Psychology* 33:435–41.

SNYDER, M.; TANKE, E. D.; AND BERSCHEID, E. 1977. Social perception and interpersonal behavior: On the self-fulfilling nature of social stereotypes. *Journal of Personality and Social Psychology* 35:656–66.

SNYDER, S. H. 1976. The dopamine hypothesis of schizophrenia. *American Journal of Psychiatry* 133:197–202.

SNYDER, S. H., AND CHILDERS, S. R. 1979. Opiate receptors and opioid peptides. *Annual Review of Neuroscience* 2:35–64.

SOLOMON, R. C. 1981. The love lost in clichés. *Psychology Today,* October 1981, pp. 83–85, 87–88.

SOLOMON, R. L. 1980. The opponent-process theory of acquired motivation: The costs of pleasure and the benefits of pain. *American Psychologist* 35:691–712.

SOLOMON, R. L., AND CORBIT, J. D. 1974. An opponent-process theory of motivation: I. Temporal dynamics of affect. *Psychological Review* 81:119–45.

SOLOMON, R. L., AND WYNNE, L. C. 1953. Traumatic avoidance learning: Acquisition in normal dogs. *Psychological Monographs* 67 (Whole No. 354).

SPEARMAN, C. 1927. *The abilities of man.* London: Macmillan.

SPELKE, E. S. 1976. Infants' intermodal perception of events. *Cognitive Psychology* 8:553–60.

SPELKE, E. S. 1981. The development of intermodal perception. In Cohen, L. B., and Salapatek, P. (Eds.), *Handbook of infant perception.* New York: Academic Press.

SPELKE, E. S. 1983. Perception of unity, persistence, and identity: Thoughts on infants' conceptions of objects. In Meehler, J. (Ed.), *Infant and neonate cognition.* Hillsdale, N.J.: Erlbaum.

SPELKE, E. S. 1987. The development of intermodal perception. In Salapatek, P., and Cohen, L. (Eds.), *Handbook of infant perception,* pp. 233–74. New York: Academic Press.

SPEMANN, H. 1967. *Embryonic development and induction.* New York: Hafner Publishing Company.

SPENCE, J. T., AND SPENCE, K. W. 1966. The motivational components of manifest anxiety: Drive and drive stimuli. In Spielberger, C. D. (Ed.), *Anxiety and behavior.* New York: Academic Press.

SPERBER, D., AND WILSON, D. 1986. *Relevance: Communication and cognition.* Oxford: Blackwell.

SPERLING, G. 1960. The information available in brief visual presentations. *Psychological Monographs* 74 (Whole No. 11).

SPERRY, R. W. 1974. Lateral specialization in the surgically separated hemispheres. In Schmitt, F. O., and Worden, F. G. (Eds.), *The Neuroscience Third Study Program.* Cambridge, Mass.: MIT Press.

SPERRY, R. W. 1982. Some effects of disconnecting the cerebral hemispheres. *Science* 217:1223–26.

SPIES, G. 1965. Food versus intracranial self-stimulation reinforcement in food deprived rats. *Journal of Comparative and Physiological Psychology* 60:153–57.

SPILICH, G. S.; VESONDER, G. T.; CHIESI, H. L.; AND VOSS, J. F. 1979. Text processing of domain-related information for individuals with high and low domain knowledge. *Journal of Verbal Learning and Verbal Behavior* 18:275–90.

SPIRO, R. J. 1980. Accommodative reconstruction in prose recall. *Journal of Verbal Learning and Verbal Behavior* 19:84–95.

SPITZER, R. L. 1976. More on pseudoscience in science and the case for psychiatric diagnosis. *Archives of General Psychiatry* 33:459–70.

SPOONER, A., AND KELLOGG, W. N. 1947. The backward conditioning curve. *American Journal of Psychology* 60:321–34.

SPRINGER, S. P., AND DEUTSCH, G. 1981. *Left brain, right brain.* San Francisco: Freeman.

SQUIRE L. R. 1977. ECT and memory loss. *American Journal of Psychiatry* 134:997–1001.

SQUIRE, L. R. 1986. Mechanisms of memory. *Science* 232:1612–19.

SQUIRE, L. R. 1987. *Memory and brain.* New York: Oxford University.

SQUIRE, L. R., AND COHEN, N. J. 1979. Memory and amnesia: Resistance to disruption develops for years after learning. *Behavioral Biology and Neurology* 25:115–25.

SQUIRE, L. R., AND COHEN, N. J. 1982. Remote memory, retrograde amnesia, and the neuropsychology of memory. In Cermak, L. S. (Ed.), *Human memory and amnesia,* pp. 275–304. Hillsdale, N.J.: Erlbaum.

SQUIRE, L. R., AND COHEN, N. J. 1984. Human memory and amnesia. In McGaugh, J.; Lynch, G.; and Weinberger, N. *Neurobiology of learning and memory.* New York: Guilford.

SQUIRE, L. R., AND ZOUZOUNIS, J. A. 1986. ECT and memory: Brief pulse versus sine wave. *American Journal of Psychiatry* 143: 596–601.

SROUFE, L. A. 1979. The coherence of individual development: Early care, attachment, and subsequent developmental issues. *American Psychologist* 34:834–41.

STACHER, G.; BAUER, H.; AND STEINRINGER, H. 1979. Cholecystokinin decreases appetite and activation evoked by stimuli arising from preparation of a meal in man. *Physiology and Behavior* 23:325–31.

STAMPFL, T. G. 1975. Implosive therapy: Staring down your nightmares. *Psychology Today* 8:66–68.

STAMPFL, T. G., AND LEVIS, D. J. 1967. Essentials of implosive therapy: A learning-theory-based psychodynamic behavior therapy. *Journal of Abnormal Psychology* 72:496–503.

STARK, L., AND ELLIS, S. 1981. Scanpaths revisited: Cognitive models direct active looking. In Fisher, D.; Monty, R.; and Senders, I. (Eds.), *Eye movements: Cognition and visual perception,* pp. 193–226. Hillsdale, N.J.: Erlbaum.

STARR, C., AND TAGGART, R. 1989. *Biology: The unity and diversity of life,* 5th ed. Belmont, CA: Wadsworth.

STAUB, E. A. 1970. The influence of age and number of witnesses on children's attempts to help. *Journal of Personality and Social Psychology* 14:130–40.

STEELE, C. M., AND LIU, T. J. 1983. Dissonance processes as self-affirmation. *Journal of Personality and Social Psychology* 45:5–19.

STEINER, J. E. 1974. The gustafacial response: Observation on normal and anencephalic newborn infants. In Bosma, F. J. (Ed.), *Fourth symposium on oral sensation and perception: Development in the fetus and infant* (DHEW Publication No. NIH 73–546). Washington, D. C.: U. S. Government Printing Office.

STEINER, J. E. 1977. Facial expressions of the neonate infant indicating the hedonics of food-related chemical stimuli. In Weiffenbach, J. M. (Ed.), *Taste and development: The genesis of sweet preference* (DHEW Publication No. NIH 77–1068), pp. 173–88. Washington, D. C.: U. S. Government Printing Office.

STELLAR, E. 1954. The physiology of motivation. *Psychological Review* 61:5–22.

STELLAR, J. R., AND STELLAR, E. 1985. *The neurobiology of motivation and reward.* New York: Springer Verlag.

STERNBACH, R. A. 1963. Congenital insensitivity to pain: A review. *Psychological Bulletin* 60:252–64.

STERNBERG, R. J. 1977. *Intelligence, information processing, and analogical reasoning: The componential analysis of human abilities.* Hillsdale, N.J.: Erlbaum.

STERNBERG, R. J. 1982. Reasoning, problem solving, and intelligence. In Sternberg, R. J. (Ed.), *Handbook of human intelligence,* pp. 225–307. New York: Cambridge University Press.

STERNBERG, R. J. 1985. General intellectual ability. In Sternberg, R. *Human abilities: An information processing approach.* New York: Freeman.

STERNBERG, R. J. 1986. A triangular theory of love. *Psychological Review* 93:119–35.

STERNBERG, R. J. 1988. *The triangle of love: Intimacy, passion, commitment.* New York: Basic Books.

STERNBERG, R. J., AND DAVIDSON, J. E. 1983. Insight in the gifted. *Educational Psychologist* 18:51–57.

STERNBERG, R. J., AND GARDNER, M. K. 1983. Unities in inductive reasoning. *Journal of Experimental Psychology: General* 112:80–116.

STERNBERG, S. 1969. Memory-scanning: Mental processes revealed by reaction-time experiments. *American Scientist* 57:421–57.

STERNBERG, S. 1970. Memory-scanning: Mental processes revealed by reaction time experiments. In Antrobus, J. S., *Cognition and affect,* pp. 13–58. Boston: Little, Brown.

STERNBERG, S. 1975. Memory scanning: New findings and current controversies. *Quarterly Journal of Experimental Psychology* 27:1–32.

STEVENS, A., AND COUPE, P. 1978. Distortions in judged spatial relations. *Cognitive Psychology* 10:422–37.

STEVENS, L., AND JONES, E. E. 1976. Defensive attributions and the Kelley cube. *Journal of Personality and Social Psychology* 34:809–20.

STEVENS, S. S. 1955. The measurement of loudness. *Journal of the Acoustical Society of America* 27:815–19.

STEWART, K. 1951. Dream theory in Malaya. *Complex* 6:21–34.

STEWART, T. D. 1957. Stone age surgery: A general review, with emphasis on the New World. *Annual Review of the Smithsonian Institution.* Washington, D. C.: Smithsonian Institute.

STOCH, M. B.; SMYTHE, P. M.; MOODIE, A. D.; AND BRADSHAW, D. 1982. Psychosocial outcome and CT findings after gross undernourishment during infancy: A 20-year developmental study. *Developmental Medicine and Child Neurology* 24:419–36.

STOKOE, W. C., JR. 1960. Sign language structure: An outline of the visual communication systems. *Studies in Linguistics Occasional Papers* 8.

STOLLER, R. J. 1968. *Sex and gender: On the development of masculinity and femininity.* New York: Science House.

STONE, A. 1975. *Mental health and law: A system in transition.* (DHEW Publication No. 75176). Washington, D.C.: U. S. Government Printing Office.

STORMS, M. D. 1973. Videotape and the attribution process: Reversing actors' and observers' points of view. *Journal of Personality and Social Psychology* 27:165–75.

STORMS, M. D. 1981. A theory of erotic orientation development. *Psychological Review* 88:340–53.

STOTLAND, E.; MATHEWS, K. E., JR.; SHERMAN, S. E.; HANSSON, R. O.; AND RICHARDSON, B. Z. 1978. *Empathy, fantasy, and helping.* Sage Library of Social Research, vol. 65. Beverly Hills, Calif.: Sage Publications.

STOWE, L. 1987. Thematic structures and sentence comprehension. In Carlson, G., and Tanenhaus, M. (Eds.), *Linguistic structure in language processing.* Dordrecht: Reidel.

STREET, R. F. 1931. *A Gestalt completion test.* New York: Teachers College Press, Columbia University.

STRICKER, E. M., AND ZIGMOND, M. J. 1976. Recovery of function after damage to catecholamine-containing neurons: A neurochemical model for the lateral hypothalamic syndrome. In Sprague, J. M., and Epstein, A. N. (Eds.), *Progress in psychobiology and physiological psychology,* vol. 6, pp. 121–88. New York: Academic Press.

STROOP, J. R. 1935. Studies of interference in serial verbal reactions. *Journal of Experimental Psychology* 18:643–62.

STRUPP, H. H., AND BINDER, J. L. 1984. *Psychotherapy in a new key: A guide to time-limited dynamic psychotherapy.* New York: Basic Books.

STUART, R. B., AND MITCHELL, C. 1980. Self-help groups in the control of body weight. In Stunkard, A. J. (Ed.), *Obesity,* pp. 354–55. Philadelphia: Saunders.

STUNKARD, A. J. 1975. Obesity. In Freedman, A. M.; Kaplan, H. I.; and Sadock, B. J. (Eds.), *Comprehensive textbook of psychiatry*

—*II,* vol. 2, pp. 1648–54. Baltimore: Williams & Wilkins.

STUNKARD, A. 1980. Psychoanalysis and psychotherapy. In Stunkard, A. J. (Ed.), *Obesity,* pp. 355–68. Philadelphia: Saunders.

SULS, J. M. 1972. A two-stage model for the appreciation of jokes and cartoons: An information processing analysis. In Goldstein, J. H., and McGhee, P. E. (Eds.), *The psychology of humor,* pp. 81–100. New York: Academic Press.

SULS, J. M. 1983. Cognitive processes in humor appreciation. In McGhee, P. E., and Goldstein, J. H. (Eds.), *Handbook of humor research,* vol. 1, pp. 39–58. New York: Springer.

SULS, J. M., AND MILLER, R. L. (Eds.). 1977. *Social comparison processes: Theoretical and empirical perspectives.* New York: Washington Hemisphere Publishing Co.

SUOMI, S. J. 1989. Personal communication.

SUOMI, S. J., AND HARLOW, H. F. 1971. Abnormal social behavior in young monkeys. In Helmuth, J. (Ed.), *Exceptional infant: Studies in abnormalities,* vol. 2, pp. 483–529. New York: Brunner/Mazel.

SUOMI, S., AND HARLOW, H. 1972. Social rehabilitation of isolate-reared monkeys. *Developmental Psychology* 6:487–96.

SUPALLA, T. 1986. The classifier system in American Sign Language. In Craig, C. (Ed.), *Noun classes and categorization: Typological studies in language,* vol. 7. Amsterdam: John Benjamins.

SUPALLA, I., AND NEWPORT, E. L. 1978. How many seats in a chair? The derivation of nouns and verbs in American Sign Language. In Siple, P. (Ed.), *Understanding language through sign language research.* New York: Academic Press.

SUPER, C. M. 1976. Environmental effects on motor development. *Developmental Medicine and Child Neurology* 18:561–67.

SYMONS, D. 1979. *The evolution of human sexuality.* New York: Oxford University Press.

SZASZ, T. S. 1974. *The myth of mental illness: Foundations of a theory of personal conduct,* rev. ed. New York: Harper & Row.

TAKAHASHI, Y. 1979. Growth hormone secretion related to the sleep waking rhythm. In Drucker-Colín, R.; Shkurovich, M.; and Sterman, M. B. (Eds.), *The functions of sleep.* New York: Academic Press.

TANENHAUS, M. 1988. Psycholinguistics: An overview. In Newmeyer, F. (Ed.), *Linguistics: The Cambridge survey, Vol. III, Language: Psychological and biological aspects.* Cambridge: Cambridge University Press.

TANNER, J. M. 1970. Physical growth. In Mussen, P. H. (Ed.), *Carmichael's manual of child psychology,* 3rd ed., pp. 77–105. New York: Wiley.

TAPLIN, J., AND STAUDENMAYER, H. 1973. Interpretation of abstract conditional sentences in deductive reasoning. *Journal of Verbal Learning and Verbal Behavior* 12:530–42.

TAYLOR, S. E., AND FISKE, S. T. 1975. Point of view and perceptions of causality. *Journal of Personality and Social Psychology* 32:439–45.

TEACH, R. L., AND SHORTLIFFE, E. H. 1985. An analysis of physicians' attitudes. In Buchanan, B. G., and Shortliffe, E. H. (Eds.), *Rule-based expert systems: The MYCIN experiments of the Stanford Heuristics Programming Project.* Reading, Mass: Addison-Wesley.

TEGHTSOONIAN, R. 1971. On the exponent in Stevens' Law and the constant in Ekman's Law. *Psychological Review* 78:71–80.

TEITELBAUM, P. 1955. Sensory control of hypothalamic hyperphagia. *Journal of Comparative and Physiological Psychology* 48:156–63.

TEITELBAUM, P. 1961. Disturbances in feeding and drinking behavior after hypothalamic lesions. In Jones, M. R. (Ed.), *Nebraska Symposium on Motivation,* pp. 39–65. Lincoln, Neb.: University of Nebraska Press.

TEITELBAUM, P., AND EPSTEIN, A. N. 1962. The lateral hypothalamic syndrome: Recovery of feeding and drinking after lateral hypothalamic lesions. *Psychological Review* 69:74–90.

TEITELBAUM, P., AND STELLAR, E. 1954. Recovery from failure to eat produced by hypothalamic lesions. *Science* 120:894–95.

TELLEGEN, A.; LYKKEN, D. T.; BOUCHARD, T. J.; WILCOX, K. J.; SEGAL, N. L.; AND RICH, S. 1988. Personality of twins reared apart and together. *Journal of Personality and Social Psychology* 54:1031–39.

TERMAN, L. M., AND MERRILL, M. A. 1973. *Stanford-Binet intelligence scale—manual for the third revision,* Form L-M. Boston: Houghton Mifflin.

TERRACE, H. S. 1979. *Nim.* New York: Knopf.

TERRACE, H. S.; PETITTO, L. A.; SANDERS, D. L.; AND BEVER, T. G. 1979. Can an ape create a sentence? *Science* 206:891–902.

TERVOORT, B. T. 1961. Esoteric symbolism in the communication behavior of young deaf children. *American Annals of the Deaf* 106:436–80.

TESSER, A.; CAMPBELL, J.; AND SMITH, M. 1984. Friendship choice and performance: Self-evaluation maintenance in children. *Journal of Personality and Social Psychology* 46:561–74.

THEOPHRASTUS. 319 B.C. *The characters.* Translated by Edmonds, J. M. Cambridge, Mass.: Harvard University Press, 1929.

THIGPEN, C. H., AND CLECKLEY, H. M. 1957. *The three faces of Eve.* New York: McGraw-Hill.

THOMAS, A.; CHESS, S.; AND BIRCH, H. G. 1970. The origin of personality. *Scientific American* 223:102–109.

THOMPSON, C. P., AND COWAN, T. 1986. Flashbulb memories: A nicer recollection of a Neisser recollection. *Cognition* 22:199–200.

THOMPSON, N. L.; McCANDLESS, B. R.; AND STRICKLAND, B. R. 1971. Personal adjustment of male and female homosexuals and heterosexuals. *Journal of Abnormal and Social Psychology* 78:237–40.

THOMPSON, R. F. 1973. *Introduction to biopsychology.* San Francisco: Albion Publishing Co.

THORNDIKE, E. L. 1898. Animal intelligence: An experimental study of the associative processes in animals. *Psychological Monographs* 2 (Whole No. 8).

THORNDIKE, E. L. 1899. The associative processes in animals. *Biological lectures from the Marine Biological Laboratory at Woods Hole.* Boston: Atheneum.

THORNDIKE, E. L. 1911. *Animal intelligence: Experimental studies.* New York: Macmillan.

THORNDIKE, E. L. 1924. The measurement of intelligence: Present status. *Psychological Review* 31:219–52.

THURSTONE, L. L. 1938. Primary mental abilities. *Psychometric Monographs* No. 1.

TINBERGEN, N. 1951. *The study of instinct.* Oxford, England: Clarendon.

TIZARD, B., AND HODGES, J. 1978. The effect of early institutional rearing on the development of eight-year-old children. *Journal of Child Psychology and Psychiatry* 19:98–118.

TOLMAN, E. C. 1932. *Purposive behavior in animals and men.* New York: Appleton-Century-Crofts.

TOLMAN, E. C. 1948. Cognitive maps in rats and men. *Psychological Review* 55:189–208.

TOLMAN, E. C., AND GLEITMAN, H. 1949. Studies in learning and motivation: I. Equal reinforcements in both end-boxes, followed by shock in one end-box. *Journal of Experimental Psychology* 39:810–19.

TOLMAN, E. C., AND HONZIK, C. H. 1930. Introduction and removal of reward, and maze performance in rats. *University of California Publications in Psychology* 4:257–75.

TOLSTOY, L. *Anna Karenina.* 1875. Trans. C. Garnett. New York: Random House, 1939.

TOMKINS, S. S. 1981. The role of facial response in the experience of emotion: A reply to Tourangeau and Ellsworth. *Journal of Personality and Social Psychology* 40:355–57.

TORGERSEN, S. 1983. Genetic factors in anxiety disorders. *Archives of General Psychiatry* 40:1085–89.

TORGERSEN, S. 1986. Genetic factors in moderately severe and mild affective disorders. *Archives of General Psychiatry* 43:222–26.

TOURANGEAU, R., AND ELLSWORTH, P. C. 1979. The role of facial response in the experience of emotion. *Journal of Personality and Social Psychology* 37:1519–31.

TOWNSEND, J. T. 1971. A note on the identifiability of parallel and serial processes. *Perception and Psychophysics* 10:161–63.

TREISMAN, A. M. 1964. Selective attention in man. *British Medical Bulletin* 20:12–16.

TRIVERS, R. L. 1971. The evolution of reciprocal altruism. *Quarterly Review of Biology* 46:35–57.

TRIVERS, R. L. 1972. Parental investment and sexual selection. In Campbell, B. (Ed.), *Sexual selection and the descent of man,* pp. 139–79. Chicago: Aldine.

TULVING, E. 1972. Episodic and semantic memory. In Tulving, E., and Donaldson, W. (Eds.), *Organization and memory.* New York: Academic Press.

TULVING, E., AND OSLER, S. 1968. Effectiveness of retrieval cues in memory for words. *Journal of Experimental Psychology* 77:593–601.

TULVING, E., AND PEARLSTONE, Z. 1966. Availability versus accessability of information in memory for words. *Journal of Verbal Learning and Verbal Behavior* 5:381–91.

TULVING, E.; SCHACTER, D. L.; AND STARK, H. A. 1982. Priming effects in word-fragment completion are independent of recognition memory. *Journal of Experimental Psychology: Learning, Memory, and Cognition* 8:336–42.

TULVING, E., AND THOMSON, D. M. 1973. Encoding specificity and retrieval processes in episodic memory. *Psychological Review* 80:352–73.

TURING, A. M. 1950. Computing machinery and intelligence. *Mind* 59:433–60.

TURNER, A. M., AND GREENOUGH, W. T. 1985. Differential rearing effects on rat visual cortex synapses. I. Synaptic and neuronal density and synapses per neuron. *Brain Research* 329:195–203.

TVERSKY, A., AND KAHNEMAN, D. 1973. Availability: A heuristic for judging frequency and probability. *Cognitive Psychology* 5:207–32.

TVERSKY, A., AND KAHNEMAN, D. 1974. Judgment under uncertainty: Heuristics and biases. *Science* 125:1124–31.

TVERSKY, A. AND KAHNEMAN, D. 1981. The framing of decisions and the psychology of choice. *Science* 211:453–58.

TVERSKY, A., AND KAHNEMAN, D. 1983. Extensional vs. intuitive reasoning: The conjunction fallacy in probability judgment. *Psychological Review* 90:293–315.

TVERSKY, B., AND TUCHIN, M. 1989. A reconciliation of the evidence on eyewitness testimony: Comments on McCloskey and Zaragoza(1985). *Journal of Experimental Psychology: General* 118:86–91.

TYLER, L. E. 1965. *The psychology of human differences.* New York: Appleton-Century-Crofts.

TZENG, O., AND WANG, W. Y. S. 1984. Search for a common neurocognitive mechanism for language and movements. *American Journal of Physiology* 246:904–11.


U. S. PUBLIC HEALTH SERVICE, DIVISION OF CHRONIC DISEASES. 1966. *Obesity and health* (Public Health Service Publication No. 1485). Washington, D.C.: U. S. Government Printing Office.

UNGERSTEDT, U., AND LJUNGBERG, T. 1974. Central dopamine neurons and sensory processing. *Journal of Psychiatry Research* 11:149–50.

URWIN, C. 1983. Dialogue and cognitive functioning in the early language development of three blind children. In Mills, A. E. (Ed.), *Language acquisition in the blind child.* London: Croom Helm.


VAILLANT, G. E. 1971. Theoretical hierarchy of adaptive ego mechanisms. *Archives of General Psychiatry* 24:107–18.

VAILLANT, G. E. 1974. Natural history of male psychological health. II. Some antecedents of health adult adjustment. *Archives of General Psychiatry* 31:15–22.

VAILLANT, G. E. 1976. Natural history of male psychological health. V: Relation of choice of ego mechanisms of defense to adult adjustment. *Archives of General Psychiatry* 33:535–45.

VAILLANT, G. E. 1977. *Adaptation to life*. Boston: Little, Brown & Co.

VALENTA, J. G., AND RIGBY, M. K. 1968. Discrimination of the odor of stressed rats. *Science* 161:599–601.

VALINS, S. 1966. Cognitive effects of false heart-rate feedback. *Journal of Personality and Social Psychology* 4:400–408.

VALLAR, G., AND BADDELEY, A. D. 1984. Phonological short-term store, phonological processing and sentence comprehension: A neuropsychological case study. *Cognitive Neuropsychology* 1:121–41.

VAN CANTFORT, E., AND RIMPAU, J. 1982. Sign language studies with children and chimpanzees. *Sign Language Studies* 34:15–72.

VANDELL, D. L.; HENDERSON, V. K.; AND WILSON, K. S. 1988. A longitudinal study of children with day care experiences of varying quality. *Child Development* 59:1286–92.

VAN ZOEREN, J. G., AND STRICKER, E. M. 1977. Effects of preoptic, lateral hypothalamic, or dopamine-depleting lesions on behavioral thermoregulations in rats exposed to the cold. *Journal of Comparative and Physiological Psychology* 91:989.

VAULTIN, R. G., AND BERKELEY, M. A. 1977. Responses of single cells in cat visual cortex to prolonged stimulus movement: Neural correlates of visual aftereffects. *Journal of Neurophysiology* 40:1051–65.

VERAA, R. P., AND GRAFSTEIN, B. 1981. Cellular mechanisms for recovery from nervous system injury: A conference report. *Experimental Neurology* 71:6–75.

VERY, P. S. 1967. Differential factor structure in mathematical ability. *Genetic Psychology Monographs* 75:169–208.

VISCOTT, D. S. 1979. A musical idiot savant: A psychodynamic study, and some speculations on the creative process. *Psychiatry* 33:494–515.

VISINTAINER, M.; VOLPICELLI, J. R.; AND SELIGMAN, M. E. P. 1982. Tumor rejection in rats after inescapable or escapable shock. *Science* 216:437–39.

VOLPICELLI, J. 1989. Psychoactive substance use disorders. In Rosenhan, D. L., and Seligman, M. E. P. *Abnormal psychology*, 2nd ed. New York: Norton.

VON DOMARUS, E. 1944. The specific laws of logic in schizophrenia. In Kasanin, J. (Ed.), *Language and thought in schizophrenia*. Berkeley, Calif.: University of California Press.


WABER, D. P. 1977. Sex differences in mental abilities, hemispheric lateralization, and rate of physical growth at adolescence. *Developmental Psychology* 13:29–38.

WABER, D. P. 1979. Cognitive abilities and sex-related variations in the maturation of cerebral cortical functions. In Wittig, M. A., and Petersen, A. C. (Eds.), *Sex-related differences in cognitive functioning*, pp. 161–89. New York: Academic Press.

WACHTEL, P. 1973. Psychodynamics, behavior therapy and the implacable experimenter: An inquiry into the consistency of personality. *Journal of Abnormal Psychology* 82:324–34.

WACHTEL, P. L. 1977. *Psychoanalysis and behavior therapy: Toward an integration*. New York: Basic Books.

WACHTEL, P. L. 1982. What can dynamic therapies contribute to behavior therapy? *Behavior Therapy* 13:594–609.

WAGNER, A. R. 1979. Habituation and memory. In Dickinson, A., and Boakes, R. A. (Eds.), *Mechanisms of learning and memory: A memorial to Jerzy Konorski*, pp. 53–82. Hillsdale, N.J.: Erlbaum.

WAGNER, D. A. 1974. The development of short-term and incidental memory: A cross-cultural study. *Child Development* 45:389–96.

WAGNER, D. A. 1978. Memories of Morocco: The influence of age, schooling, and environment on memory. *Cognitive Psychology* 10:1–28.

WALD, G. 1950. Eye and camera. *Scientific American* 183:32–41.

WALDFOGEL, S. 1948. The frequency and affective character of childhood memories. *Psychological Monographs,* vol. 62 (Whole No. 291).

WALK, R. 1978. Depth perception and experience. In Walk, R., and Pick, H. (Eds.), *Perception and experience*. New York: Plenum.

WALK, R. D., AND GIBSON, E. J. 1961. A comparative and analytical study of visual depth perception. *Psychological Monographs* 75 (Whole No. 519).

WALKER, L. J. 1984. Sex differences in the development of moral reasoning: A critical review. *Child Development* 55:677–91.

WALL, P. D. 1980. Mechanisms of plasticity of connection following damage of adult mammalian nervous system. In Bach-y-Rita, P. (Ed.), *Recovery of function: Theoretical considerations for brain injury rehabilitation*. Bern: Hans Huber.

WALLACH, H. 1948. Brightness constancy and the nature of achromatic colors. *Journal of Experimental Psychology* 38:310–24.

WALSTER, E.; ARONSON, E.; AND ABRAHAMS, D. 1966. On increasing the persuasiveness of a low prestige communicator. *Journal of Experimental Social Psychology* 2:325–42.

WALSTER, E.; ARONSON, E.; ABRAHAMS, D.; AND ROTTMAN, L. 1966. The importance of physical attractiveness in dating behavior. *Journal of Personality and Social Psychology* 4:508–16.

WALSTER, E., AND BERSCHEID, E. 1974. A little bit about love: A minor essay on a major topic. In Huston, T. L. (Ed.), *Foundations of interpersonal attraction*. New York: Academic Press.

WALSTER (HATFIELD), E., AND WALSTER, G. W. 1978. *A new look at love*. Reading, Mass.: Addison-Wesley.

WALTERS, J. R., AND SEYFARTH, R. M. 1986. Conflict and cooperation. In Smuts, B. B.; Cheney, D. L.; Seyfarth, R. M.; Wrangham, R. W.; and Struhsaker, T. T. (Eds.), *Primate societies*. Chicago: University of Chicago Press.

WANNER, E., AND MARATSOS, M. 1978. An ATN approach to comprehension. In Halle, M.; Bresnan, J.; and Miller, G. A. (Eds.), *Linguistic theory and psychological reality*. Cambridge, Mass.: MIT Press.

WAPNER, W. T.; JUDD, T.; AND GARDNER, H. 1978. Visual agnosia in an artist. *Cortex* 14:343–64.

WARD, I. L. 1984. The prenatal stress syndrome: Current status. *Psychoneuroendocrinology* 9:3–11.

WARREN, R. M. 1970. Perceptual restorations of missing speech sounds. *Science* 167:392–93.

WARRINGTON, E. K., AND WEISKRANTZ, L. 1978. Further analysis of the prior learning effect in amnesic patients. *Neuropsychologia* 16:169–76.

WASMAN, M., AND FLYNN, J. P. 1962. Directed attack elicited from the hypothalamus. *Archives of Neurology* 6:220–27.

WASON, P. C. 1960. On the failure to eliminate hypotheses in a conceptual task. *Quarterly Journal of Experimental Psychology* 12:129–40.

WASON, P. C. 1966. Reasoning. In Foss, B. M. (Ed.), *New horizons in psychology*, vol. 1., pp. 135–51. Harmondsworth, England: Penguin Books.

WASON, P. C. 1968. On the failure to eliminate hypotheses—A second look. In Wason, P. C., and Johnson-Laird, P. N. (Eds.), *Thinking and reasoning*. Harmondsworth, England: Penguin Books.

WASON, P. C., AND JOHNSON-LAIRD, P. N. 1972. *Psychology of reasoning*. London: B. T. Batsford, Ltd.

WASSERMAN, E. M.; GOMITA, Y.; AND GALLISTEL, C. R. 1982. Pimozide blocks reinforcement but not priming from MFB stimulation in the rat. *Pharmacology Biochemistry and Behavior* 17:783–87.

WATERS, E. 1978. The reliability and stability of individual differences in infant-mother attachment. *Child Development* 49:483–94.

WATERS, E.; WIPPMAN, J.; AND SROUFE, L. A. 1979. Attachment, positive affect, and competence in the peer group: Two studies in construct validation. *Child Development* 50:821–29.

WATKINS, L. R., AND MAYER, D. J. 1982. Organization of endogenous opiate and nonopiate pain control systems. *Science* 216:1185–92.

WATSON, C. G., AND BURANEN, C. 1979. The frequency of conversion reaction. *Journal of Abnormal Psychology* 88:209–11.

WATSON, D. 1982. The actor and the observer: How are their perceptions of causality different? *Psychological Bulletin* 92:682–700.

WATSON, J. B. 1925. *Behaviorism.* New York: Norton.

WATSON, J. S. 1967. Memory and "contingency analysis" in infant learning. *Merrill-Palmer Quarterly* 13:55–76.

WATSON, R. I. 1973. Investigation into deindividuation using cross-cultural techniques. *Journal of Personality and Social Psychology* 25:342–45.

WAUGH, N. C., AND NORMAN, D. A. 1965. Primary memory. *Psychological Review* 72:89–104.

WEBB, W. B. 1972. Sleep deprivation: Total, partial, and selective. In Chase, M. H. (Ed.), *The sleeping brain,* pp. 323–62. Los Angeles: Brain Information Service, Brain Research Institute.

WEBB, W. B. 1974. Sleep as an adaptive process. *Perceptual and Motor Skills* 38:1023–27.

WEBB, W. B. 1979. Theories of sleep functions and some clinical implications. In Drucker-Colin, R.; Shkurovich, M.; and Sterman, M. B. (Eds.), *The functions of sleep,* pp. 19–36. New York: Academic Press.

WEBB, W. B. 1982. Some theories about sleep and their clinical implications. *Psychiatric Annals* 11:415–22.

WECHSLER, D. 1958. *The measurement and appraisal of adult intelligence,* 4th ed. Baltimore: Williams & Wilkins.

WEIGEL, R. H.; VERNON, D. T. A.; AND TOGNACCI, L. N. 1974. Specificity of the attitude as a determinant of attitude-behavior congruence. *Journal of Personality and Social Psychology* 30:724–28.

WEINER, B. 1982. The emotional consequences of causal attributions. In Clark, M. S., and Fiske, S. T. (Eds.), *Affect and cognition: The 17th annual Carnegie symposium on cognition.* Hillsdale, N.J.: Erlbaum.

WEINER, H.; THALER, M.; REISER, M. F.; AND MIRSKY, I. A. 1957. Etiology of duodenal ulcer: I. Relation of specific psychological characteristics to rate of gastric secretion. *Psychosomatic Medicine* 19:1–10.

WEINER, R. D. 1984a. Does electroconvulsive therapy cause brain damage? (with peer commentary). *The Behavioral and Brain Sciences* 7:1–54.

WEINER, R. D. 1984b. Convulsive therapy: 50 years later. *American Journal of Psychiatry* 141:1078–79.

WEINER, R. D. 1985. Convulsive therapies. In Kaplan, H. I., and Sadock, J. (Eds.), *Comprehensive textbook of psychiatry,* 4th ed. Baltimore: Williams & Wilkins.

WEINGARTNER, H., AND PARKER, E. S. (Eds.). 1984. *Memory consolidation: Psychobiology of cognition.* Hillsdale, N.J.: Erlbaum.

WEINSTOCK, S. 1954. Resistance to extinction of a running response following partial reinforcement under widely spaced trials. *Journal of Comparative and Physiological Psychology* 47:318–22.

WEISBERG, R. W., AND ALBA, J. W., 1981. An examination of the alleged role of "fixation" in the solution of several "insight" problems. *Journal of Experimental Psychology: General* 110:169–92.

WEISKRANTZ, L., AND WARRINGTON, E. K. 1979. Conditioning in amnesic patients. *Neuropsychologia* 18:177–84.

WEISS, J. M. 1970. Somatic effects of predictable and unpredictable shock. *Psychosomatic Medicine* 32:397–408.

WEISS, J. M. 1977. Psychological and behavioral influences on gastrointestinal lesions in animal models. In Maser, J. D., and Seligman, M. E. P. (Eds.), *Psychopathology: Experimental models,* pp. 232–69. San Francisco: Freeman.

WEISS, B., AND LATIES, V. G. 1961. Behavioral thermoregulation. *Science* 133:1338–44.

WEISSMAN, M., AND BOYD, J. H. 1985. Affective disorders: Epidemiology. In Kaplan, H. I., and Sadock, J. (Eds.), *Modern synopsis of comprehensive textbook of psychiatry,* 4th ed. Baltimore: Williams & Wilkins.

WEISSTEIN, N., AND WONG, E. 1986. Figure-ground organization and the spatial and temporal responses of the visual system. In Schwab, E. C., and Nusbaum, H. C. (Eds.), *Pattern recognition by humans and machines,* vol. 2. New York: Academic Press.

WELCH, C. A.; WEINER, R. D.; WEIR, D.; CAHILL, J. F.; ROGERS, H. J.; DAVIDSON, J.; MILLER, R. D.; AND MANDEL, M. R. 1982. Efficacy of ECT in the treatment of depression: Wave form and electrode placement considerations. *Psychopharmacological Bulletin* 18:31–34.

WELKER, W. I.; JOHNSON, J. I.; AND PUBOLS, B. H. 1964. Some morphological and physiological characteristics of the somatic sensory system in raccoons. *American Zoologist* 4:75–94.

WELLMAN, H. M.; RITTER, K.; AND FLAVELL, J. H. 1975. Deliberate memory behavior in the delayed reactions of very young children. *Developmental Psychology* 11:780–87.

WENDER, P. H.; KETY, S. S.; ROSENTHAL, D.; SCHULSINGER, F.; AND ORTMANN, J. 1986. Psychiatric disorders in the biological relatives of adopted individuals with affective disorders. *Archives of General Psychiatry* 43:923–29.

WERKER, J., AND TEES, R. 1984. Cross-language speech perception: Evidence for perceptual reorganization during the first year of life. *Infant Behavior and Development* 7:49–63.

WERTHEIMER, M. 1912. Experimentelle Studien über das Gesehen von Bewegung. *Zeitschrift fr Psychologie* 61:161–265.

WERTHEIMER, M. 1923. Untersuchungen zur Lehre von der Gestalt, II. *Psychologische Forschung* 4:301–50.

WERTHEIMER, M. 1945. *Productive thinking.* New York: Harper.

WERTHEIMER, M. 1961. Psychomotor coordination of auditory and visual space at birth. *Science* 134:1692.

WEST, S. G.; WHITNEY, G.; AND SCHNEDLER, R. 1975. Helping a motorist in distress: The effects of sex, race, and neighborhood. *Journal of Personality and Social Psychology,* 31:691–98.

WESTERMEYER, J. 1987. Public health and chronic mental illness. *American Journal of Public Health* 77:667–68.

WETZEL, M., AND STUART, D. G. 1976. Ensemble characteristics of cat locomotion and its neural control. *Progress in Neurobiology* 7:1–98.

WEXLER, K. AND CULICOVER, P. 1980. *Formal principles of language acquisition.* Cambridge, Mass.: MIT Press.

WHEELER, L. R. 1942. A comparative study of the intelligence of East Tennessee mountain children. *Journal of Educational Psychology* 33:321–34.

WHITE, G. L. 1980. Physical attractiveness and courtship progress. *Journal of Personality and Social Psychology* 39:660–68.

WHITE, R. W., AND WATT, N. F. 1973. *The abnormal personality,* 4th ed. New York: Ronald Press.

WHITE, S. H., AND PILLEMER, D. B. 1979. Childhood amnesia and the development of a functionally accessible memory system. In Kihlstrom, J. F., and Evans, F. J. (Eds.), *Functional disorders of memory.* Hillsdale, N.J.: Erlbaum.

WHITING, J. W. M., AND WHITING, B. B. 1975. *Children of six cultures: A psychocultural analysis.* Cambridge, Mass.: Harvard University Press.

WHITLOW, J. W., JR., AND WAGNER, A. R. 1984. Memory and habituation. In Peeke, H. V. S., and Petrinovich, L. (Eds.), *Habituation, sensitization, and behavior,* pp. 103–53. New York: Academic Press.

WICKELGREN, W. A. 1974. *How to solve problems.* San Francisco: Freeman.

WICKER, A. W. 1969. Attitudes versus action: The relationship of verbal and overt behavioral responses to attitude objects. *Journal of Social Issues* 25:41–78.

WIENS, A. N., AND MENUSTIK, C. E. 1983. Treatment outcome and patient characteristics in an aversion therapy program for alcoholism. *American Psychologist* 38:1089–96.

WIESENTHAL, D. L.; ENDLER, N. S.; COWARD, T. R.; AND EDWARDS, J. 1976. Reversibility of relative competence as a determinant of conformity across different perceptual tasks. *Representative Research in Social Psychology* 7:319–42.

WILCOXIN, H. C.; DRAGOIN, W. B.; AND KRAL, P. A. 1971. Illness-induced aversions in rat and quail: Relative salience of visual and gustatory cues. *Science* 171:826–28.

WILLIAMS, C. D. 1959. The elimination of tantrum behavior by extinction procedures. *Journal of Abnormal and Social Psychology* 59:269.

WILLIAMS, G. C. 1966. *Adaptation and natural selection.* Princeton, N.J.: Princeton University Press.

WILLIAMS, H. L.; TEPAS, D. I.; AND MORLOCK, H. C. 1962. Evoked responses to clicks and electroencephalographic stages of sleep in man. *Science* 138:685–86.

WILLIAMS, D. R., AND WILLIAMS, H. 1969. Auto maintenance in the pigeon: Sustained pecking despite contingent non-reinforcement. *Journal of the Experimental Analysis of Behavior* 12:511–20.

WILLIAMS, K., HARKINS, S., AND LATANÉ, B. 1981. Identifiability as a deterrent to social loafing: Two cheering experiments. *Journal of Personality and Social Psychology* 40:303–11.

WILLIAMS, M. D., AND HOLLAN, J. D. 1982. The process of retrieval from very long-term memory. *Cognitive Science* 5:87–119.

WILLIAMS, R. B. 1987. Psychological factors in coronary artery disease: Epidemiological evidence. *Circulation* 76 (suppl I) 117–23.

WILSON, D. H.; REEVES, A. G.; GAZZANIGA, M. S.; AND CULVER, C. 1977. Cerebral commissurotomy for the control of intractable seizures. *Neurology* 27:708–15.

WILSON, E. O. 1978. *On human nature.* Cambridge, Mass; Harvard University Press.

WILSON, E. O. 1975. *Sociobiology.* Cambridge, Mass.: Harvard University Press.

WILSON, G. 1978. Introversion/extraversion. In London, H., and Exner, J. (Eds.), *Dimensions of personality.* New York: Wiley.

WILSON, G. 1985. *The psychology of the performing arts.* London and Sydney: Croom Helm.

WILSON, G. T. 1980. Behavior modification and the treatment of obesity. In Stunkard, A. J. (Ed.), *Obesity,* pp. 325–44. Philadelphia: Saunders.

WINCH, R. F., AND MORE, D. M. 1956. Does TAT add information to interviews? Statistical analysis of the increment. *Journal of Clinical Psychology* 12:316–21.

WINKLER, J. & TAYLOR, S. E. 1979. Preference, expectation, and attributional bias: Two field experiments. *Journal of Applied Social Psychology* 2:183–97.

WINTER, R. 1976. *The smell book: Scents, sex, and society.* Philadelphia: Lippincott.

WINTON, W. M. 1986. The role of facial response in self-reports of emotion: A critique of Laird. *Journal of Personality and Social Psychology* 50:808–12.

WISE, R. A. 1987. The role of reward pathways in the development of drug dependence. *Pharmacological Therapy* 35:227–63.

WISE, R. A., AND BOZARTH, M. A. 1987. A psychomotor stimulant theory of addiction. *Psychological Review* 94:469–92.

WISE, R. A., AND ROMPRE, P. P. 1989. Brain dopamine and reward. *Annual Review of Psychology* 40:191–226.

WISHNER, J. 1960. Reanalysis of "impressions of personality." *Psychological Review* 67:96–112.

WISHNER, J. 1974. *Psychopathology: Defective concept or defective practice?* Invited address delivered at the XVIII International Congress of Applied Psychology, Montreal, Canada.

WITTGENSTEIN, L. 1953. *Philosophical investigations.* Trans. by Anscombe, G. E. M. Oxford, England: Blackwell.

WOHLWILL, J. H. 1973. *The study of behavioral development.* New York: Academic Press.

WOLF, S. 1971. Psychosocial influences in gastrointestinal function. In Levi, L. (Ed.), *The psychosocial environment and psychosomatic disease,* vol. 1, pp. 362–68. London: Oxford University Press.

WOLLEN, K. A.; WEBER, A.; AND LOWRY, D. 1972. Bizarreness versus interaction of mental images as determinants of learning. *Cognitive Psychology* 3:518–23.

WOLPE, J. 1958. *Psychotherapy by reciprocal inhibition.* Stanford, Calif.: Stanford University Press.

WOLPE, J., AND LAZARUS, A. A. 1966. *Behavior therapy techniques: A guide to the treatment of neuroses.* Elmsford, N.Y.: Pergamon.

WOLPERT, E. A., AND TROSMAN, H. 1958. Studies in psychophysiology of dreams: I. Experimental evocation of sequential dream episodes. *Archives of Neurology and Psychiatry* 79:603–606.

WOODS, B. T., AND TEUBER, H. L. 1978. Changing patterns of childhood aphasia. *Archives of Neurology* 3:273–80.

WOODS, R. L. 1947. *The world of dreams: An anthology.* New York: Random House.

WOODWORTH, R. S. 1938. *Experimental psychology.* New York: Holt.

WRIGHT, C. 1982. Rembrandt: Self-portraits. London: Gordon Fraser.

WYERS, E. J.; PEEKE, H. V. S.; AND HERZ, M. J. 1973. Behavioral habituation in invertebrates. In Peeke, H. V. S., and Herz, M. J. (Eds.), *Habituation: Vol. 1. Behavioral studies.* New York: Academic Press.

YANDO, R.; SEITZ, V.; AND ZIGLER, E. 1978. *Imitation: A developmental perspective.* Hillsdale, N.J.: Erlbaum.

YARBUS, A. L. 1967. Eye movements and vision. Trans. by Riggs, L. A. New York: Plenum Press.

YARROW, L. J. 1961. Maternal deprivation: Toward an empirical and conceptual reevaluation. *Psychological Bulletin* 58:459–90.

YARROW, L. J., AND GOODWIN, M. S. 1973. The immediate impact of separation reactions of infants to a change in mother figures. In Stone, L. J.; Smith, T. J.; and Murphy, L. B. (Eds.), *The competent infant.* New York: Basic Books.

YERKES, R. M., AND MORGULIS, S. 1909. Method of Pavlov in animal psychology. *Psychological Bulletin* 6:264.

YONAS, A. 1981. Infants' response to optical information for collision. In Aslin, R. N.; Alberts, J. R.; and Petersen, M. R. (Eds.), *Development of perception,* pp. 313–34. New York: Academic Press.

YUSSEN, S. R., AND LEVY, V. M. 1975. Developmental changes in predicting one's own span of memory. *Journal of Experimental Child Psychology* 19:502–508.

ZAIDEL, E. 1976. Auditory vocabulary of the right hemisphere following brain bisection or hemidecortication. *Cortex* 12:191–211.

ZAIDEL, E. 1983. A response to Gazzaniga: Language in the right hemisphere. *American Psychologist* 38:542–46.

ZAJONC, R. B. 1965. Social facilitation. *Science* 149:269–74.

ZAJONC, R. B. 1968. Attitudinal effects of mere exposure. *Journal of Personality and Social Psychology Monograph Supplement* 9:1–27.

ZAJONC, R. B. 1980. Copresence. In Paulus, P. (Ed.), *The psychology of group influence.* Hillsdale, N.J.: Erlbaum.

ZAJONC, R. B., HEINGERTNER, A.; AND HERMAN, E. M. 1969. Social enhancement and impairment of performance in the cockroach. *Journal of Personality and Social Psychology* 13:83–92.

ZARAGOZA, M. S., AND McCLOSKEY, M. 1989. Misleading postevent information and the memory impairment hypothesis: Comment on Belli and reply to Tversky and Tuchin. *Journal of Experimental Psychology: General* 118:92–99.

ZEIGLER, H. P., AND LEIBOWITZ, H. 1957. Apparent visual size as a function of distance for children and adults. *American Journal of Psychology* 70:106–109.

ZENER, K. 1937. The significance of behavior accompanying conditioned salivary secretion for theories of the conditioned response. *American Journal of Psychology* 50:384–403.

ZENTALL, T., AND HOGAN, D. 1974. Abstract concept learning in the pigeon. *Journal of Experimental Psychology* 102:393–98.

ZIEGLER, F. J.; IMBODEN, J. B.; AND RODGERS, D. A. 1963. Contemporary conversion reactions: III. Diagnostic considerations. *Journal of the American Medical Association* 186:307–11.

ZIGLER, E., AND BERMAN, W. 1983. Discerning the future of early childhood intervention. *American Psychologist* 38:894–906.

ZIGLER, E., AND CHILD, I. L. 1969. Socialization. In Lindzey, G., and Aronson, E. (Eds.), *The handbook of social psychology*, vol. 3, pp. 450–589. Reading, Mass.: Addison-Wesley.

ZIGLER, E. F.; LAMB, M. E.; AND CHILD, I. L. 1982. *Socialization and personality development*, 2nd ed. New York: Oxford University Press.

ZILBOORG, G., AND HENRY, G. W. 1941. *A history of medical psychology*. New York: Norton.

ZILLMAN, D. 1983. Transfer of excitation in emotional behavior. In Cacioppo, J. T., and Petty, R. E. (Eds.), *Social psychophysiology: A sourcebook*, pp. 215–40. New York: Guilford.

ZILLMAN, D.; KATCHER, A. H.; AND MILAVSKY, B. 1972. Excitation transfer from physical exercise to subsequent aggressive behavior. *Journal of Experimental Social Psychology* 8:247–59.

ZIMBARDO, P. G. 1969. The human choice: Individuation, reason, and order versus deindividuation, impulse and chaos. In Arnold, W. J. and Levine, E. (Eds.), *Nebraska Symposium on Motivation*, pp. 237–308. Lincoln, Neb.: University of Nebraska Press.

ZUBIN, J.; ERON, L. D.; AND SHUMER, F. 1965. *An experimental approach to projective techniques*. New York: Wiley.

ZUCKERMAN, M. 1979. *Sensation seeking: Beyond the optimum level of arousal*. Hillsdale, N.J.: Erlbaum.

ZUCKERMAN, M. 1983. A biological theory of sensation seeking. In Zuckerman, M. (Ed.), *Biological bases of sensation seeking, impulsivity, and anxiety*. Hillsdale, N.J.: Erlbaum.

ZUCKERMAN, M. 1987. All parents are environmentalists until they have their second child. Peer commentary on Plomin, R., and Daniels, D. Why are children from the same family so different from one another? *Behavioral and Brain Sciences* 10:38–39.

ZUCKERMAN, M.; BALLENGER, J. C.; JIMERSON, D. C.; MURPHY, D. L.; AND POST, R. M. 1983. A correlational test in humans of the biological models of sensation seeking and anxiety. In Zuckerman, M. (Ed.), *Biological bases of sensation seeking, impulsivity, and anxiety*, pp. 229–48. Hillsdale, N.J.: Erlbaum.

ZUCKERMAN, M.; KLORMAN, R.; LARRANCE, D.; AND SPIEGEL, N. H. 1981. Facial, autonomic, and subjective components of emotion: The facial feedback hypothesis versus the externalizer-internalizer distinction. *Journal of Personality and Social Psychology* 41:929–44.

ZUGER, B. 1984. Early effeminate behavior in boys. *Journal of Nervous and Mental Disease* 172:90–96.

# Acknowledgments and Copyrights

## FIGURES

**1.1** Courtesy of Kaiser Porcelain Ltd. **1.2 A,B,C** Bugelski, B. R., and Alampay, D. A., The role of frequency in developing perceptual sets, *Canadian Journal of Psychology* 15 (1961):205–11. Adapted by permission of the Canadian Psychological Association. **1.3A** Courtesy of Richard D. Walk. **1.3B** Courtesy of William Vandivert. **1.4A** Photograph by Keith Gunnar/Bruce Coleman. **1.4B** Photograph by B. Caster/Bruce Coleman. **1.4C** Photograph by William E. Ferguson. **1.5A** Photograph by George H. Harrison/Grant Heilman. **1.5B** Photograph by Suzanne Szasz. **1.6** Collection of Robert H. Helmick; courtesy Brooke Alexander, New York. **1.7** Dement, W. C., *Some Must Watch While Some Must Sleep.* New York: W. W. Norton & Company, Inc. Copyright © 1972, 1974, 1976 by William C. Dement. **1.8** Courtesy of William C. Dement. **1.9** Courtesy of the Smithsonian Institution. **1.10** Courtesy the Museum of Modern Art/Film Stills Archive.

**2.1** Photograph by Michael Abbey/Photo Researchers. **2.2B** Photograph by Dr. John Mazziotta, UCLA School of Medicine/ Science Photo Library/Photo Researchers. **2.4B** Nilsson, Lennart, *Behold Man.* Boston: Little, Brown & Company, 1974. Reproduced by permission of the publisher. **2.5C** © Guigoz/Dr. A. Privat/Petit Format/Science Source/Photo Researchers. **2.9** From *Biology: The Unity and Diversity of Life,* Fifth Edition, by Cecie Starr and Ralph Taggart, © 1989 by Wadsworth, Inc. Reprinted by permission of the publisher. **2.10** Eccles, J. C., *The Understanding of the Brain.* New York: McGraw-Hill, 1973. Adapted by permission of McGraw-Hill, Inc. **2.14** Roeder, K., *Nerve Cells and Insect Behavior.* Cambridge, Mass.: Harvard University Press, 1972, p. 198. Adapted by permission of Harvard University Press. **2.15** Lewis, E. R., Everhart, T. E., and Zeevi, Y. Y., Studying neural organization in aplysia with the scanning electron microscope, *Science* 165 (12 September 1969): 1140–43. Copyright 1969 by the American Association for the Advancement of Science. Reprinted by permission of the publisher and the author. **2.17** Bloom, F. E., Lazerson, A., and Hofstadter, L., *Brain, Mind and Behavior.* New York: Freeman, 1988. Adapted by permission of WNET/Thirteen. **2.18** *Physiological Psychology,* 2nd ed., by Mark Rosenzweig and Arnold Leiman. Copyright © 1989 by Random House. Reprinted by permission of McGraw-Hill. **2.19** Blakemore, C., *Mechanics of the Mind,* p. 42. New York: Cambridge University Press, 1977. Reprinted by permission of the publisher. **2.22** Bloom, F. E., Lazerson, A., and Hofstadter, L., *Brain, Mind, and Behavior.* New York: Freeman, 1988. Adapted by permission of WNET/Thirteen. **2.23** Lickley, J. D., *The Nervous System.* Essex, England: Longman, 1919. Reprinted by permission of the publisher. **2.24A** Photograph by Biophoto Associates/Photo Researchers. **2.24B** Keeton, W. T., *Biological Science,* 3rd ed. New York: W. W. Norton & Company, Inc., 1980. Copyright © 1980, 1979, 1972, 1967 by W. W. Norton & Company, Inc. Used with permission. **2.27** Bloom, F. E., Lazerson, A., and Hofstadter, L., *Brain, Mind, and Behavior.* New York: Freeman, 1988. Adapted by permission of WNET/Thirteen. **2.28** Adapted with permission of Macmillan Publishing Co., Inc., from *The Cerebral Cortex of Man* by Wilder Penfield and Theodore Rasmussen. Copyright © 1950 by Macmillan Publishing Co., Inc., renewed 1978 by Theodore Rasmussen. **2.29** Cobb, S., *Foundations of Neuropsychiatry.* Baltimore, Md.: William & Wilkins, 1941. © 1941, the Williams & Wilkins Co., Baltimore. Adapted by permission of the publisher. **2.30A** Radiography Department, Royal Victoria Infirmary, Newcastle-upon-Tyne. Photo by Simon Fraser/Science Photo Library/Photo Researchers, Inc. **2.30B** © 1988 Grant LeDuc/Monkmeyer. **2.31** NIH/SPL/Photo Researchers, Inc. **2.32** Photograph by Dr. John Mazziotta et al./Photo Researchers. **2.33** From *Higher Cortical Functions in Man* by Aleksandr Romanovich Luria. Copyright © 1966, 1979 Consultants Bureau Enterprises, Inc., and Basic Books, Inc. Reprinted by permission of Basic Books, Inc., Publishers, New York. **2.34** *Physiological Psychology,* 2nd ed., by Mark Rosenzweig and Arnold Leiman. Copyright © 1989 by Random House. Reprinted by permission of McGraw-Hill. **2.35** Photograph by M. Sakka, Courtesy Musée de l'Homme et Musée Depuytren, Paris. **2.38** Gazzaniga, M. S., The split brain in man, *Scientific American* 217 (August 1967):25. Copyright © 1967 by Scientific American, Inc. All rights reserved. **2.40** Levy, J., Trevarthen, C. and Sperry, R. W., Perception of chimerical figures following hemispheric disconnection, *Brain* 95 (1972):70. Adapted by permission of Oxford University Press. **2.41** Courtesy of Niels A. Lassen. **2.42** After figure "Space Relations" (p. 354) from *Essentials of Psychological Testing,* 3rd edition, by Lee J. Cronbach. Copyright © 1949 by Harper & Row, Publishers, Inc. Copyright © 1960, 1970 by Lee J. Cronbach. Reprinted by permission of HarperCollins Publishers. **2.43** Adapted from Björklund, A., Stenevi, U., Schmidt, R. H., Dunnett, S. B., and Gage, F. H., Intracerebral grafting of neuronal suspensions I: Induction and general methods of preparation, *Acta Physiologica Scandinavica Supplement* 522 (1983):1–7. Reproduced by permission of Acta Physiologica Scandinavica. **2.44** Adapted from Coyle, J. T., Price, D., and Delong, M. R., Alzheimer's disease: A disorder of cholinergic innervation, *Science* 219 (1983):1184–90. Copyright 1983 by the American Association for the Advancement of Science (AAAS). Reproduced by permission of the AAAS and the author. **2.45** Patricia Neal's collection/Globe Photos.

**3.3** Keeton, W. T., and Gould, J. L., *Biological Science,* 4th edition. New York: W. W. Norton & Company, Inc., 1986. Copyright © 1986, 1980, 1979, 1972, 1967 by W. W. Norton & Company, Inc. **3.4** Weiss, B., and Laties, V. G., Behavioral thermoregulation, *Science* 133 (28 April 1961):1338–44, Fig. 1. Copyright 1961 by the American Association for the Advancement of Science. Reproduced by permission of the AAAS and the author. **3.7B** Courtesy Neal E. Miller, Rockefeller University. **3.8** Photographs courtesy of Jacob Steiner. **3.9** *Left* Laura Riley/Bruce Coleman. *Center* Joanne Zembal/Black Star. *Right* Helen Williams/Photo Researchers. **3.10** Adapted from Bouchard, C., Tremblay, A., Desprès, J.-P., Nadeau, A., Lupien, P. L., Thèriault, G., Dussault, J., Moorjani, S., Pinault, S. M., and Fournier, G., The response to long-term overfeeding in identical twins, *New England Journal of Medicine* 322 (1990):1477–82. Reprinted by permission of the New England Journal of Medicine. **3.11** Adapted from Nisbett, R. E., Taste, deprivation and weight determinants of eating behavior, *Journal of Personality and Social Psychology* 10 (1968):107–16. Copyright 1968 by the American Psychological Association. Adapted by permission of the author. **3.12** Herman, H. C., and Mack, D., Restrained and unrestrained eating, *Journal of Personality* 43 (1975):647–60. Adapted by permission of Duke University Press. **3.13** Andres, R., Influence of obesity on longevity in the aged, in Borek, C., Fenoglio, C. M., and King, D. W. (Eds.), *Aging, Cancer, and Cell Membranes,* pp. 230–46. New York: Thieme-Stratton, 1980. **3.14** Reprinted by permission of Hawthorne Properties (Elsevier-Dutton Publishing Co., Inc.) from *Bodily Changes in Pain, Hunger, Fear and Rage* by W. B. Cannon. Copyright © 1929 by Appleton-Century-Co.; 1957 by W. B. Cannon. **3.15** Photograph by Walter Chandoha, 1990. **3.16A** Photograph by Mary Shuford. **3.16B** Inbau, F. E., and Reid, J. E., *The Polygraph ("Lie Detector") Technique,* 2nd ed. Baltimore, Md.: Williams & Wilkins, 1977. © Professor Fred E. Inbau. **3.17** Adapted from Keeton, W. T., and Gould, J. L., *Biological Science,* 4th ed. New York: Norton, 1986. Copyright © 1986, 1980, 1979, 1972, 1967 by W. W. Norton & Company, Inc. used with permission. **3.18** Adapted from Bloom, F. E., Lazerson, A., and Hofstadter, L., *Brain, Mind, and Behavior.* New York: Freeman, 1988. Adapted by permission of WNET/Thirteen. **3.22** Courtesy of William C. Dement. **3.23** Adapted from Kleitman, N., Patterns of dreaming, *Scientific American* 203 (November 1960):82–88. Copyright © 1960 by Scientific American, Inc. All rights reserved. **3.25** Photograph courtesy of the University of Wisconsin Primate Laboratory. **3.26** Courtesy of Dr. M. E. Olds. **3.27** Adapted from *Physiological Psychology,* 2nd ed., by Mark Rosenzweig and Arnold Leiman. Copyright © 1989 by Random House. Reprinted by permission of McGraw-Hill.

**4.2** Hoffman, H. S., and Fleshler, M., An apparatus for measurement of the startle response in the rat, *American Journal of Psychology* 77 (1964):307–308. Copyright © 1964 by the Board of Trustees of the University of Illinois. Used with permission of the University of Illinois Press. **4.6** Pavlov, I. P., *Lectures on Conditioned Reflexes,* vol. I. New York: International Publishers Co., Inc., 1928. Adapted by permission of International Publishers Co., Inc. **4.7** Moore, J. W., Stimulus control: Studies of auditory generalization in rabbits, in Black, A. H., and Prokasy, W. F. (Eds.), *Classical Conditioning II: Current Theory and Research.* © 1972. Adapted by permission of Prentice-Hall, Inc., Englewood Cliffs, N.J. **4.12A** Photograph by Mike Salisbury. **4.12B** Courtesy Susan M. Hogue. **4.14** From *A Primer of Operant Conditioning* by G. S. Reynolds. Copyright © 1968 by Scott, Foresman & Co. Reprinted by permission. **4.15** Photographs courtesy of Animal Behavior Enterprises, Inc. **4.16** Courtesy Yerkes Regional Primate Research Center of Emory University. **4.18, 4.19, 4.20** Ferster, C. B., and Skinner, B. F., *Schedules of Reinforcement.* © 1957, pp. 56, 399. Englewood Cliffs, N.J.: Prentice-Hall, Inc., 1957. Adapted by permis-sion of the author. **4.25** Spooner, A., and Kellogg, W. N., The backward conditioning curve, *American Journal of Psychology* 60 (1947):321–34. Copyright © 1947 by Board of Trustees of the University of Illinois. Used with permission of the publisher, The University of Illinois Press. **4.26** Rescorla, R. A. 1966. Predictability and number of pairings in Pavlovian fear conditioning. *Psychonomic Science* 4:383–84. **4.27** Kamin, L. J., Predictability, surprise, and conditioning, in Campbell, B. A., and Church, R. M. (Eds.), *Punishment and Aversive Behavior,* 1969. Used with permission of Prentice-Hall, Inc., Englewood Cliffs, N.J. **4.29** Colwill, R. M., and Rescorla, R. A., Postconditioning devaluation of a reinforcer affects instrumental responding, *Journal of Experimental Psychology: Animal Behavior Processes* 11 (1985):120–32. Copyright 1985 by the American Psychological Association. Adapted by permission of the American Psychological Association and the authors. **4.31** Maier, S. F., Seligman, M. E. P., and Solomon, R. L., Pavlovian fear conditioning and learned helplessness: Effects on escape and avoidance behavior of (a) the CS-US contingency and (b) the independence of the US and voluntary responding, in Campbell, B. A., and Church, R. M. (Eds.), *Punishment and Aversive Behavior,* © 1969, p. 328. Adapted by permission of Prentice-Hall, Inc., Englewood Cliffs, N.J. **4.33** Photographs by Bruce Moore. **4.34** Olton, D. S., and Samuelson, R. J., Remembrance of places passed: Spatial memory in rats, *Journal of Experimental Psychology: Animal Behavior Processes* 2 (1976):97–116. Copyright 1976 by the American Psychological Association. Reprinted by permission. **4.40** Figure adapted from *Why Chimps Can Read* by A. J. Premack. Copyright © 1976 by Ann J. Premack. Reprinted by permission of HarperCollins Publishers. **4.41** Premack, D., and Woodruff, G., Chimpanzee problem-solving: A test for comprehension, *Science* 202 (3 November 1978):533–34. Copyright 1978 by the American Association for the Advancement of Science.

**5.2** *The School of Athens* by Raphael, 1505; Stanza della Segnatura, Vatican; courtesy Scala/Art Resource, New York. **5.6A** Krech, D., and Crutchfield, R., *Elements of Psychology.* New York: Knopf, Inc., 1958. Adapted by permission of Hilda Krech. **5.6B** Adapted from *Biological Psychology,* 2nd ed., by James W. Kalat. © 1984 by Wadsworth, Inc. **5.7** Adapted from Carlson, N. R., *Physiology of Behavior,* 3rd ed. Boston: Allyn and Bacon, 1986. Reproduced by permission of the publisher. **5.8** Frank, M., An analysis of hamster afferent taste nerve response functions. *Journal of General Physiology* 61 (1973):588–618. Reproduced by permission of the Rockefeller University Press. **5.10** Gibson, James J., *The Senses Considered as Perceptual Systems,* p. 80, Fig. 5.4. Boston: Houghton Mifflin Company, 1966. Reprinted by permission of the publisher. **5.11** Thompson, R. F., *Introduction to Biopsychology.* San Rafael, Calif.: Albion Publishing Company, 1973. Adapted by permission of the publisher. **5.13, 5.14A, 5.15A** Lindsay, P. H., and Norman, D. A., *Human Information Processing,* 2nd edition, pp. 126, 133, and 136. New York: Academic Press, 1977. Adapted by permission of the author and Harcourt Brace Jovanovich. **5.14B, 5.15B, 5.17** Coren, S., and Ward, L. M., *Sensation and Perception,* 3rd ed. San Diego: Harcourt Brace Jovanovich, 1989. Adapted by permission of the author and publisher. **5.16** Wald, G., Eye and camera, *Scientific American* 183 (August 1950):33. Copyright © 1950 by Scientific American, Inc. All rights reserved. **5.18, 5.19, 5.20** Cornsweet, T. M., *Visual Perception.* New York: Academic Press, 1970. Adapted by permission of the author and Harcourt Brace Jovanovich. **5.23** Hering, E., *Outlines of a Theory of the Light Sense,* 1920 (translated by Hurvich, L. M., and Jameson, D., 1964), pp. 150–51. Cambridge, Mass.: Harvard University Press, 1964. Adapted by permission of Harvard University Press. **5.24A** *Arcturus* by Victor Vasarely (© ADAGP, Paris, 1981). **5.25** Coren, S., Porac, C., and Ward, L. M., *Sensation and Perception,* p. 155. New York: Academic Press, 1978. Adapted by permission of the author and Harcourt Brace Jovanovich. Also **5.25** Cornsweet, T. M., *Visual Perception,* p. 276.

New York: Academic Press, 1970. Adapted by permission of the author and Harcourt Brace Jovanovich. **5.26** Schiffman, H., *Sensation and Perception.* New York: John Wiley and Sons, Inc., 1976. Adapted by permission of the publisher. **5.27** Adapted from Kuffler, S. W., Discharge pattern and functional organization of mammalian retina, *Journal of Neurophysiology* 16 (1953):37–68. **5.31** Hurvich, L. M., *Color Vision.* Sunderland, Mass.: Sinauer Associates, Publications, 1981. Reproduced by permission of Sinauer Associates. **5.33 and 5.34** Courtesy of Munsell Color, 2441 N. Calvert Street, Baltimore, MD 21218 USA. **5.37** Detail and full use of Georges Seurat's *The Channel of Gravelines* (Petit Fort Philippe), 1890, oil on canvas, 45.195. © Indianapolis Museum of Art, gift of Mrs. James W. Fesler in memory of Daniel W. and Elizabeth C. Marmon. **5.42** Hurvich, L. M., and Jameson, D., An opponent-process theory of color vision, *Psychological Review* 64 (1957):384–404. Copyright 1957 by the American Psychological Association. Adapted by permission of the author. **5.44** DeValois, R. L., and DeValois, K. K., *Neural Coding of Color,* in Carterette, E. C., and Friedman, M. P., (Eds.), *Handbook of Perception,* vol. 5. New York: Academic Press, 1975. Adapted by permission of the publisher.

**6.1** Julian Hochberg, *Perception,* 2nd ed., © 1978, p. 56. Adapted by permission of Prentice-Hall, Inc., Englewood Cliffs, N.J. **6.3** Photograph by Roberta Intrater. **6.5** Photographs by Hans Wallach and Robert Gillmor. **6.6** Figures 40 and 41 from *The Perception of the Visual World* by James J. Gibson. Copyright © 1978, 1950 by Houghton Mifflin Company. Used with permission. **6.7** Coren, S., and Ward, L. M., *Sensation and Perception,* 3rd ed. San Diego: Harcourt Brace Jovanovich. Adapted by permission of the author and Harcourt Brace Jovanovich. **6.8A** Bruce, V., and Green, P., *Visual Perception: Physiology, Psychology, and Ecology.* Hillsdale, N.J.: Erlbaum, 1985. Reprinted by permission of Lawrence Erlbaum Associates, Inc. **6.8B** Adapted from Figure 56 from *The Perception of the Visual World* by James J. Gibson. Copyright © 1978, 1950 by Houghton Mifflin Company. Used with permission. **6.9** Photograph by Richard D. Walk. **6.11** Duncker, K., Uber induzierte Bewegung, *Psychologische Forschung* 12 (1929):180–259. Adapted by permission of Springer-Verlag, Inc., Heidelberg. **6.13** Fagan, J. F., Infants' recognition of invariant features of faces, *Child Development* 47 (1976):627–38. © The Society for Research in Child Development, Inc. **6.14** Hubel, D. H., The visual cortex of the brain, *Scientific American* 209 (November 1963): 54–58. Copyright © 1963 by Scientific American, Inc. All rights reserved. **6.16** Photograph by Jeffery Grosscup. **6.19** Salvador Dali's *The Trojan War;* courtesy Esquire. **6.21** Beck, J., Effect of orientation and shape similarity on perceptual grouping, *Perception and Psychophysics* 1 (1966):300–302. Reprinted by permission of the Psychonomic Society, Inc. **6.23** Köhler, W., *Gestalt Psychology.* New York: Liveright Publishing Company, 1947. Adapted by permission of the publisher. **6.24A** Courtesy U.S. Government. **6.24B** Ferrell Grehan/ Photo Researchers. **6.26** Kanizsa, G., Subjective contours, *Scientific American* 234 (1976):48–52. Copyright © 1976 by Scientific American, Inc. All rights reserved. **6.28** Marr, D., Early processing of visual information, *Philosophical Transactions of the Royal Society of London,* Series B, 275 (1976):483–524. Reproduced by permission of The Royal Society. **6.30** Rock, I. *Orientation and Form.* New York: Academic Press, 1973. Reprinted by permission of the publisher and author. **6.31** Adapted from *Sensation and Perception,* 2nd edition, by E. Bruce Goldstein. © 1984 by Wadsworth Inc. Reprinted by permission of the publisher. **6.32** Biederman, I., Recognition-by-components: A theory of human image understanding, *Psychological Review* 94 (1987):115–47. Copyright 1987 by the American Psychological Association. Reprinted by permission of the American Psychological Association and the author. **6.33** Selfridge, O. G., Pattern recognition and modern computers, in *Proceedings of Western Joint Computer Conference,* Los Angeles, Calif., 1955. **6.34** Boring, E. G., A new ambiguous

figure, *American Journal of Psychology* 42 (1930):444–45; and Leeper, R. W. A study of a neglected portion of the field of learning: The development of sensory organization. *Journal of Genetic Psychology* 46 (1935):41–75. Reproduced by permission of Lucy D. Boring. **6.36** Roy F. Street, *A Gestalt Completion Test,* 1931. Teacher's College dissertation. **6.37** Photograph by Ronald James. **6.38** Reprinted with permission from Kolers, P. A., *Aspects of Motion Perception.* Copyright 1972, Pergamon Press PLC. **6.39** Kolers, P. A., and Pomerantz, J. R. Figural change in apparent motion, *Journal of Experimental Psychology* 87 (1971):99–108. Adapted by permission of the author. **6.40** Penrose, L. S., and Penrose, R., Impossible objects: A special type of visual illusion, *British Journal of Psychology* 49 (1958):31–33. Reprinted by permission of the British Psychological Society. **6.41 and 6.42** Yarbus, A. L., *Eye Movements and Vision,* pp. 179–85. Translated by Riggs, R. A. New York: Plenum Press, 1967. Copyright 1967 by Plenum Press. Reprinted by permission of the publisher. **6.43 and 6.44** Photographs by Jeffrey Grosscup. **6.45** Adapted with permission of Macmillan Publishing Co., Inc., from *An Introduction to Perception* by Irvin Rock. Copyright © 1975 by Irvin Rock. **6.47** Gibson, James J., *The Perception of the Visual World.* Copyright © 1978, 1950 by Houghton Mifflin Company. Used with permission. **6.49A** Rock, I., and Kaufman, L., The moon illusion, II, *Science* 136 (June 1962):1023–31, Figure 22. Copyright 1962 by the American Association for the Advancement of Science. Reprinted by permission of the publisher. **6.49B** Drawings by Debra Mackay. **6.50** Coren, S., and Girgus, J. S., 1978. *Seeing Is Deceiving.* Hillsdale, N.J.: Lawrence Erlbaum Associates, Inc. Reprinted with permission of the publisher. **6.52** Courtesy The Egyptian Museum, Cairo. **6.53** *The Annunciation* by Crivelli; courtesy the National Gallery, London. **6.54** *Bend in the Epte River, near Giverny* by Claude Monet; courtesy Philadelphia Museum of Art; the William L. Elkins Collection. **6.55** Picasso, Pablo. *Violin and Grapes.* Céret and Sorgues (spring-early fall 1912), oil on canvas, 20″ x 24″; collection, The Museum of Modern Art, New York. Mrs. David M. Levy Bequest. **6.56** Private Collection, U.S.A.

**7.1** Adapted from Waugh, N. C., and Norman, D. A., Primary memory, *Psychological Review* 72 (1965):89–104. Copyright 1965 by the American Psychological Association. **7.2 and 7.4** Adapted from Murdock, B., The serial position effect of free recall. *Journal of Experimental Psychology* 64 (1962):482–88. Copyright 1962 by the American Psychological Association. Reprinted by permission of the American Psychological Association and the author. **7.3** Glanzer, M., and Cunitz, A., Two storage mechanisms in free recall, *Journal of Verbal Learning and Verbal Behavior* 5 (1966):351–60. Adapted by permission of the author and Academic Press, Inc. **7.6** Adapted from Ericsson, K. A., Chase, W. G., and Faloon, S., Acquisition of a memory skill, *Science* 208 (June 1980):1181–82. Copyright 1980 by the American Association for the Advancement of Science. Used with permission of the author and publisher. **7.7** Adapted from Bower, G. H., Analysis of a mnemonic device, *American Scientist* 58 (1970):496–510. Reprinted by permission of *American Scientist,* journal of Sigma Xi, The Scientific Research Society. **7.8** Godden, D. R., and Baddeley, A. D., Context-dependent memory in two natural environments: On land and underwater, *British Journal of Psychology* 66 (1975):325–31. Used by permission of the British Psychological Society and the author. **7.12** Sternberg, S., Memory scanning: Mental processes revealed by reaction time experiments, in Antrobus, J. S., *Cognition and Affect,* pp. 13–58. Boston: Little, Brown & Company, 1970. Adapted by permission of Saul Sternberg. **7.13** Bartlett, F. C., *Remembering,* p. 180. Cambridge, England: Cambridge University Press, 1932. Adapted by permission of the publisher. **7.14** Orne, M. T., The mechanisms of hypnotic age regression: An experimental study, *Journal of Abnormal and Social Psychology* 58 (1951):277–99. Copyright 1951 by the American Psychological Association. **7.17**

Collins, A. M., and Loftus, E. F., A spreading activation theory of semantic processing. *Psychological Review* 82 (1975):407–28. Copyright 1975 by the American Psychological Association. **7.18** Illustration by Marjorie Torrey; from Lewis Carroll's *Alice in Wonderland,* illustrated by Marjorie Torrey. Copyright © 1955 by Random House, Inc. Reprinted by permission of Random House, Inc. **7.20** Adapted from Kosslyn, S. M., Ball, T. M., and Reisser, V. J., Visual images preserve metric spatial information: Evidence from studies of image scanning, *Journal of Experimental Psychology: Human Perception and Performance* 4 (1978):47–60. Copyright 1978 by the American Psychological Association. **7.24** Adapted from Bahrick, H. P., Semantic memory content in permastore: Fifty years of memory for Spanish learned in school, *Journal of Experimental Psychology: General* 113 (1984):1–35. Copyright 1984 by the American Psychological Association. Used by permission of the American Psychological Association and the author. **7.25A** Top to bottom: *1940s* Douglas MacArthur (Courtesy of AP/Wide World Photos); Betty Grable (Courtesy of AP/Wide World Photos); Joe DiMaggio (Photograph by Calvin D. Campbell/ Black Star). *1950s* Mamie Eisenhower (Courtesy of Photoworld); Joe McCarthy (Courtesy of AP/Wide World Photos); Adlai Stevenson (Courtesy of UPI/Bettmann Newsphotos). *1960s* Nikita Khrushchev (Courtesy of AP/Wide World Photos); Coretta Scott King (Photograph by Bob Fitch/Black Star); Golda Meir (Photograph by Fred Ward/Black Star). *1970s* Anwar El-Sadat (Courtesy of United Nations/M. Tzovaras); Betty Ford (Reproduced from The Collection of the Library of Congress); Patty Hearst (Photograph by Owen D. B./ Black Star). *1980s* Robert Bork (Courtesy AP/Wide World Photos); Geraldine Ferrara (Courtesy of AP/Wide World Photos); Bjorn Borg (Courtesy AP/Wide World Photos). **7.25B** Marslan-Wilson, W. D., and Teuber, H. L., Memory for remote events in anterograde amnesia: Recognition of public figures from news photographs, *Neuropsychologia* 13 (1975):353–64. **7.26A** From *Fundamentals of Human Neuropsychology,* 2nd ed., by B. Kolb and I. Q. Whishaw, Figure 20–5, p. 485. San Francisco: W. H. Freeman and Company. Copyright © 1980, 1985. **7.26B** Milner, B., Corkin, S., and Teuber, H. L., Further analysis of the hippocampal amnesic syndrome: Fourteen-year follow-up of H. M., *Psychologia* 6 (1968):215–34.

**8.8** Adapted from Duncker, K., On problem solving, *Psychological Monographs,* Whole No. 270 (1945):1–113. **8.9** Adapted from E. Hearst, Psychology across the chessboard, in *Readings in Psychology Today,* 2nd ed., p. 24. DelMar, Calif.: CRM Books, 1972. Reprinted by permission of McGraw-Hill, Inc. **8.10** After Figure 73 (p. 109) from *Productive Thinking,* enlarged edition, edited by Max Wertheimer and Michael Wertheimer. Copyright © 1945, 1959, by Valentin Wertheimer. Reprinted by permission of HarperCollins Publishers. **8.15, 8.20** Scheerer, M., Goldstein, K., and Boring, E. G., A demonstration of insight: The horse-rider puzzle, *American Journal of Psychology* 54 (1941):437–38. Copyright © 1941 by Board of Trustees of the University of Illinois, used with permission of the University of Illinois Press. **8.16** Photographs by Jeffrey Grosscup. **8.18** Wickelgren, W. A., *How to Solve Problems.* San Francisco: Freeman, 1974. Reproduced by permission of W. H. Freeman. **8.21** Engraving by Walter H. Ruff; courtesy The Granger Collection. **8.22** Adapted from Suls, J. M., A two-stage model for the appreciation of jokes and cartoons, in Goldstein, J. H., and McGhee, P. E. (Eds.), *The Psychology of Humor.* New York: Academic Press, 1972, p. 85. Reprinted by permission of the publisher and the author. **8.24** Photograph by Bruce Helm, U.S. Chess Federation. **8.27** Reproduced from Lewis Carroll's *Alice in Wonderland,* original illustrations by John Tenniel; in color for this edition by Martina Selway. Secaucus, N.J.: Castle Books. **8.28** Photograph by Owen Franken/Stock, Boston. **8.29** Adapted from Kahneman, D., and Tversky, A., Choices, values, and frames. *American Psychologist* 39 (1984):341–50. Copyright 1984 by the American Psychological Association.

**9.3** Reproduced from Lewis Carroll's *Alice in Wonderland,* original illustrations by John Tenniel; in color for this edition by Martina Selway. Secaucus, N.J.: Castle Books. **9.4** Courtesy Sharon Armstrong. **9.13** Adapted from Slobin, D. I., Grammatical transformation and sentence comprehension in childhood and adulthood, *Journal of Verbal Learning and Verbal Behavior* 5 (1966):219–27. Used by permission of Academic Press. **9.16A** Photograph by Philip Morse, University of Wisconsin. **9.16B** Eimas, P. D., Siqueland, E. R., Jusczyk, P., and Vigorito, J., Speech perception in infants, *Science* 171 (1971):303–306. Copyright 1971 by the American Association for the Advancement of Science. **9.18** Courtesy of Roberta Golinkoff. **9.20** Reproduced from *Higglety Pigglety Pop! or There Must Be More to Life* by Maurice Sendak, New York: HarperCollins. Copyright M. Sendak. **9.22** Brown, R., Cazden, C., and Bellugi-Klima, U., The child's grammar from 1 to 3, in Hill, J. P. (Ed.), *Minnesota Symposium on Child Psychology* by The university of Minnesota Press, Minneapolis. Copyright © 1969 by the University of Minnesota. **9.24** Photographs courtesy AP/Wide World Photos. **9.25** Frishberg, N., Arbitrariness and iconicity: Historical change in American Sign Language, *Language* 51 (1975):696–719. **9.26** Drawings courtesy Noel Yovovich. **9.27** Drawings courtesy Robert Thacker. **9.29** Marler, P. R., A comparative approach to vocal learning: Song development in white crowned sparrows, *Journal of Comparative and Physiological Psychology Monograph* 71 (May 1970):(No. 2, Part 2), pp. 1–25. Copyright 1970 by the American Psychological Association. Reprinted by permission of the author. **9.30** Adapted from Johnson, J., and Newport, E., Critical period effects in second language learning: The influence of maturational state on the acquisition of English as a second language, *Cognitive Psychology* 21 (1989):60–99. Copyright 1989 by Academic Press, Inc. Reprinted by permission of the publisher and authors. **9.31** Adapted from Newport, E., Maturational constraints on language learning, *Cognitive Science* 14:11–28. **9.32** Photographs courtesy of David Premack.

**10.1** Adapted from Keeton, W. T., and Gould, J. L., *Biological Science,* 4th ed. New York: Norton, 1986. Copyright © 1986, 1980, 1979, 1972, 1967 by W. W. Norton & Company, Inc. Used with permission. **10.2** Photograph by Jen and Des Bartlett/Bruce Coleman. **10.3** Barnett, S. A., 1963. *The Rat: A Study in Behavior,* Chicago: The University of Chicago Press. Reprinted by permission of the University of Chicago Press. **10.4** Photographs by Leonard Lee Rue III/Bruce Coleman. **10.5A** Photograph by Joseph T. Collins/Photo Researchers. **10.5B** Photograph by Wolfgang Bayer/Bruce Coleman. **10.6A** Courtesy L. T. Nash, Arizona State University. **10.6B** Courtesy of Bruce Coleman. **10.7A** © 1978 Allan D. Cruickshank/Photo Researchers. **10.7B** © J. Masserschmidt/Bruce Coleman. **10.8** Photograph by Mitch Reardon/Photo Researchers. **10.9** © 1987 Garry D. McMichael/Photo Researchers. **10.10A** Photograph by Philip Green. **10.10B** Photograph by Bob and Clara Calhoun/Bruce Coleman. **10.10C** Photograph by Jeff Foott/Bruce Coleman. **10.11** Peter H. Klopfer, *An Introduction to Animal Behavior: Ethology's First Century,* 2nd ed., © 1974, p. 208. Adapted by permission of Prentice-Hall, Inc., Englewood Cliffs, N.J. **10.12** Hohn, E. O., The phalarope, *Scientific American* 220 (June 1969):104. Copyright © 1969 by Scientific American, Inc. All rights reserved. **10.13** Adapted from Keeton, W. T., and Gould, J. L., *Biological Science,* 4th ed. New York: W. W. Norton & Company, Inc., 1986. Copyright © 1986, 1980, 1979, 1972, 1967 by W. W. Norton & Company, Inc. **10.14** Bermant, G., and Davidson, J. M., *Biological Bases of Sexual Behavior.* New York: Harper & Row, 1974. In turn adapted from data of Davidson, J. M., Rodgers, C. H., Smith, E. R., and Bloch, G. J., Relative thresholds of behavioral and somatic responses to estrogen, *Physiology and Behavior* 3 (1968):227–29. Copyright 1968, Pergamon Press, PLC. **10.15A** © Pat and Tom Leeson/Photo Researchers. **10.15B** Nina Leen/Life Magazine, © Time Warner, Inc. **10.16** Photographs courtesy of Ian Wyllie,

Monks Wood Experiment Station. **10.17A** Lorenz, K., Die angeborenen Formen moeglicher Erfahrung. *Zeitschrift Für Tierpsychologie* 5 (1943):276. Adapted by permission of Paul Parey Verlagsbuchhandlung, Hamburg and Berlin. **10.17B** Photograph by Michael S. Renner/Bruce Coleman. **10.18** © Paul Ekman, 1971. **10.19** Courtesy I. Eibl-Eibesfeldt. **10.20** Ekman, P., and Friesen, W. V., *Unmasking the Face.* Englewood Cliffs, N.J.: Prentice-Hall, 1975. Reprinted by permission of the author. **10.21** Photograph by Wayne Lankinen/Bruce Coleman. **10.22** Photograph by George D. Lepp/Bio-Tec Images.

**12.1** Asch, S. E., Studies of independence and conformity: A minority of one against a unanimous majority, *Psychological Monographs* 70 (9, Whole No. 416), 1956. Copyright 1956 by the American Psychological Association. **12.2** Photographs by William Vandivert. **12.4** Festinger, L., and Carlsmith, J. M., Cognitive consequences of forced compliance, *Journal of Abnormal and Social Psychology* 58 (1959):203–10. Copyright 1959 by the American Psychological Association. Reprinted by permission of the author.

**13.4** Leonardo da Vinci's *La Jaconde* (Mona Lisa), Louvre, Paris; photograph courtesy of Service Photographique de la Reunion des Musées Nationaux. **13.5 and 13.6** Copyright 1965 by Stanley Milgram. From the film *Obedience,* distributed by the Pennsylvania State University, PCR.

**14.1** Reproduced from Keeton, W. T., and Gould, J. L., *Biological Science,* 4th ed. New York: Norton, 1986. Copyright © 1986, 1980, 1979, 1972, 1967 by W. W. Norton & Company, Inc. Used with permission. **14.2** Liebert, R. M., Poulos, R. W., and Strauss, G. D., *Developmental Psychology,* Fig. III–10, p. 81. Englewood Cliffs, N.J.: Prentice-Hall, Inc., 1974. Originally adapted from H. M. Halverston, printed by The Journal Press, 1931. Photographs by Kathy Hirsh-Pasek. **14.3** Nilsson, Lennart, *Behold Man.* Boston: Little, Brown, and Company, 1974. **14.4** Tanner, J. M., Physical growth, in *Carmichael's Manual of Child Psychology,* 3rd ed., vol. 1, Mussen, P. H., ed., Fig. 6, p. 85. New York: John Wiley & Sons, 1970. Copyright 1970 by John Wiley & Sons. **14.5** Conel, J. L., *The Postnatal Development of the Human Cortex,* vols. 1, 3, 5. Cambridge, Mass.: Harvard University Press, 1939, 1947, 1955. **14.6** Shirley, M. M., *The First Two Years: A Study of Twenty-five Babies,* vol. II. University of Minnesota Press, Minneapolis. © 1933, 1961, University of Minnesota Press. **14.7** Photograph courtesy of M. M. Grumbach. **14.9** Reproduced from Keeton, W. T., and Gould, J. L., *Biological Science,* 4th ed. New York: Norton, 1986. Copyright © 1986, 1980, 1979, 1972, 1967 by W. W. Norton & Company, Inc. Used with permission. **14.10** Photograph by Victor Englebert/Photo Researchers. **14.11** Courtesy Dr. Mark Rosenzweig. **14.12** Photographs by Doug Goodman 1986/Monkmeyer. **14.13, 14.14, and 14.15** Photographs by Chris Massey. **14.16** Piaget, J., and Inhelder, B., *The Child's Conception of Space.* Humanities Press International Inc., Atlantic Highlands, N.J., 1967. Adapted by permission of the publisher and Routledge & Kegan Paul Ltd. **14.19** Photographs by Phillip Kellman. **14.20** Kellman, P. J., and Spelke, E. S., Perception of partially occluded objects in infancy, *Cognitive Psychology* 15 (1983):483–524. Copyright 1983 by the American Psychological Association. Adapted by permission of the author. **14.21** Adapted from Baillargeon, R., Object permanence in 3½- and 4½-month-old infants. *Developmental Psychology* 23 (1987):655–64. Used by permission of the author. **14.22** Adapted from Baillargeon, R., and Graber, M., Where is the rabbit? 5½-month-old infants' representation of the height of hidden objects. *Cognitive Development* 2 (1988):375–92. **14.23** Photographs courtesy of Adele Diamond. **14.24** Photographs courtesy of Helene Borke. Borke, H., Piaget's mountains revisited: Changes in the egocentric landscape. *Developmental Psychology* 11 (1975):240–43. **14.25** Photographs courtesy of Hilary Schmidt. **14.26A** Photograph by Pat Lynch/Photo Researchers. **14.26B** Photograph by Ray Ellis/Photo Researchers. **14.26C** Photograph by Chris Massey. **14.27** Case, R. 1978. Intellectual development from birth to adulthood: A neo-Piagetian interpretation, in Siegler, R., ed., *Children's Thinking: What Develops.* Hillsdale, N.J.: Lawrence Erlbaum Associates, Inc. Reproduced by permission of Lawrence Erlbaum Associates, Inc.

**15.1** Photograph by Martin Rogers/Stock, Boston. **15.2** Photograph by Suzanne Szasz. **15.4A** Photograph by Jane von Lawick-Goodall. **15.4B** Courtesy Barnardo Photographic Archive. **15.5** Ainsworth, M., Blehar, M., Waters, E., and Wall, S. 1978. *Patterns of Attachment,* p. 34. Hillsdale, N.J.: Lawrence Erlbaum Associates, Inc. Reproduced by permission of Lawrence Erlbaum Associates, Inc. **15.6** Photographs by Kathy Hirsh-Pasek. **15.7, 15.8, and 15.9** Courtesy Harry Harlow, University of Wisconsin Primate Laboratory. **15.10** Photograph by Michael Heron/Woodfin Camp. **15.11** Bandura, A., Ross, D., and Ross, S. A., Imitation of film-mediated aggressive models, *Journal of Abnormal and Social Psychology* 66 (1963):8. Copyright 1963 by the American Psychological Association. Reprinted by permission of the author. **15.12** Feshbach, N., and Roe, K., Empathy in six- and seven-year-olds, *Child Development* 39 (1968):133–45. Reprinted by permission of The Society for Research in Child Development, Inc. **15.13** Kohlberg, L., Development of children's orientation towards a moral order in sequence in the development of moral thought, *Vita Humana* 6 (1963):11–36. Adapted by permission of S. Karger AG, Basel. **15.17** Tanner, J. M., Physical growth, in Mussen, P. H., (Ed.), *Carmichael's Manual of Child Psychology,* 3rd ed., vol. 1, Fig. 6, p. 85. New York: John Wiley & Sons, 1970. Reprinted by permission of the publisher. **15.18A** Photograph by Blair Seitz, 1986/Photo Researchers. **15.18B** Photograph by Thomas D. W. Friedmann/Photo Researchers. **15.19A** AP/Wide World Photos. **15.19B** © Jerry Howard/Positive Images, 1982.

**16.1** Reprinted with permission of Macmillan Publishing Co., Inc. from *Differential Psychology,* 3rd ed., p. 57, by Ann Anastasi. Copyright © 1958 by Macmillan Publishing Co., Inc. **16.6** Test item from Horn Art Aptitude Inventory, 1953. Courtesy Stoelting Co., Chicago. **16.7** Sample item from the Bennett Test of Mechanical Comprehension. Copyright © 1967, 1968 by The Psychological Corporation. Reproduced by permission. All rights reserved. **16.8** Figure 13.7 (p. 432) from *Essentials of Psychological Testing,* 3rd ed., by Lee J. Cronbach. Copyright © 1949 by Harper & Row, Publishers, Inc. Copyright © 1960, 1970 by Lee J. Cronbach. Reprinted by permission of HarperCollins Publishers. **16.10** Adapted by permission from the *Wechsler Adult Intelligence Scale—Revised.* Copyright © 1955, 1981 by The Psychological Corporation. All rights reserved. **16.11** SAT questions selected from *10 SAT's,* College Entrance Examinations Board (1983). Reprinted by permission of Educational Testing Service, the copyright owner of the test questions. **16.12** From the Raven Standard Progressive Matrices, by permission of J. C. Raven Limited. **16.13** Guilford, J. P., *Psychometric Methods,* p. 38. New York: McGraw-Hill, 1954. Reproduced with permission of McGraw-Hill, Inc. **16.14** Selfe, S. *Nadia: A Case of Extraordinary Drawing Ability in an Autistic Child.* New York: Academic Press, 1977. Reproduced by permission of Academic Press and Lorna Selfe. **16.15** Courtesy Photofest. **16.16** Jones, H. E., and Kaplan, O. J., Psychological aspects of mental disorders in later life, in Kaplan, O. J. (Ed.), *Mental Disorders in Later Life,* 72. Stanford, Calif.: Stanford University Press, 1945. Adapted by permission of Stanford University Press. **16.17** Schaie, K., and Strother, C., A cross-sequential study of age changes in cognitive behavior, *Psychological Bulletin* 70 (1968):671–80. Copyright 1968 by the American Psychological Association. Reprinted by permission of the author. **16.18** Photographs courtesy of Dr. Franklin A. Bryan.

**17.1** Lanyon, R. I., and Goodstein, L. D., *Personality Assessment,* p. 79. New York: John Wiley & Sons, Inc., 1971. Copyright © 1971 John Wiley & Sons, Inc. Adapted by permission of John Wiley & Sons, Inc. **17.5** Courtesy Leopold Bellak; reproduced by permission of C. P. S., Inc., Box 83, Larchmont, NY 10538, from The Children's Apperception Test (C.A.T.). **17.6** Courtesy Dr. Gerald S. Blum and Psychodynamic Instruments, Ann Arbor, Michigan. **17.7** Eysnck, H. J., and Rachman, S., *The causes and cures of neurosis,* p. 16. San Diego, Calif.: Robert R. Knapp, 1965. **17.8** Courtesy The Bettmann Archive. **17.9A** Photograph by Wilfong Photographic/Leo de Wys, Inc. **17.9B and C** Photographs by H. Reinhard/Bruce Coleman.

**18.3** "Hierarchy of Needs" from *Motivation and Personality* by Abraham H. Maslow. Copyright 1954 by Harper & Row, Publishers, Inc. Copyright © 1970 by Abraham H. Maslow. Reprinted by permission of HarperCollins Publishers.

**19.1** Negative #31568. Courtesy Department of Library Services, The American Museum of Natural History. **19.2** Courtesy The Bettmann Archive. **19.3** William Hogarth's *The Madhouse,* 1735/1763; courtesy The Bettmann Archive. **19.4** Charles's Muller's *Pinel Ordering the Removal of the Inmates' Fetters;* courtesy The Bettmann Archive. **19.6** Photograph by Bill Bridges/Globe Photos. **19.8** Nicol, S. E., and Gottesman, I. I., Clues to the genetics and neurobiology of schizophrenia, *American Scientist,* 71 (1983):398–404. Reprinted by permission of *American Scientist,* journal of Sigma Xi, The Scientific Research Society. **19.9** Data from Faris, R. E. L., and Dunham, H. W., *Mental Disorders in Urban Areas.* Chicago: University of Chicago Press, 1939. Adapted by permission of the author. **19.11** Rosenthal, N. E., Sack, D. A., Gillin, J. C., Lewy, A. J., Goodwin, F. K., Davenport, Y., Mueller, P. S., Newsome, D. A., and Wehr, T. A., Seasonal affective disorder: A description of the syndrome and preliminary findings with light therapy. *Archives of General Psychiatry* 41 (1984):72–80. Copyright 1984, American Medical Association. **19.12** Photograph courtesy of Susan Mineka. **19.13** Folkow, B., and Rubenstein, E. H., Cardiovascular effects of acute and chronic stimulations of the hypothalamic defense area in the rat, *Acta Physiologica Scandinavica* 68 (1966):48–57. Adapted by permission of Acta Physiologica Scandinavica. **19.14A** Photographs by Jerry Cooke/Life Magazine, © Time Warner, Inc. **19.14B and C** Photographs by Ken Heyman/Life Magazine, © Time Warner, Inc. **19.15** Stone, A., Mental health and law: A system in transition, U.S. Department of Health, Education and Welfare, #75176, p. 7, 1975. **19.16** Hare, R. D., Temporal gradient of fear arousal in psychopaths, *Journal of Abnormal Psychology* 70 (1965):442–45. Copyright 1965 by the American Psychological Association. Reprinted by permission of the author.

**20.1A** Courtesy Historical Pictures Service. **20.1B** Courtesy National Library of Medicine. **20.1C** Courtesy Culver Pictures. **20.5** Photograph by James D. Wilson/Woodfin Camp.

## TABLES

**14.1** Lenneberg, E. H., *Biological Foundations of Language.* New York: John Wiley & Sons, 1967. Copyright 1967 by John Wiley & Sons, Inc. Reprinted by permission of John Wiley & Sons, Inc. **15.1** Adapted from Kohlberg, L., Classification of moral judgment into levels and stages of development, in Sizer, Theodore R., *Religion and Public Education,* pp. 171–73. Copyright © 1967 Houghton Mifflin Company. Used with permission. **15.2** Erikson, E. H., *Childhood and society.* New York: W. W. Norton & Company, Inc., 1963. Adapted by permission. **16.3** Terman, L. M., and Merrill,

M. A., *Stanford-Binet Intelligence Scale-Manual for the Third Revision,* form L-M. Copyright © 1973, reproduced with the permission of The Riverside Publishing Company. **16.4** Grossman, H. J. (Ed.), *Manual on Terminology and Classification in Mental Retardation,* revised edition. Washington, D.C.: American Association on Mental Deficiency, 1983. Used with permission. **16.5** Wechsler, D., *The Measurement and Appraisal of Adult Intelligence,* 4th ed. Baltimore, Md.: The Williams & Wilkins Co., 1958. © 1958 David Wechsler. Used by permission of Ruth Wechsler, executor David Wechsler estate. Table adapted from the Manual for the Wechsler Adult Intelligence Scale. Copyright © 1955 by The Psychological Corporation. **16.7** Bayley, N., Mental growth during the first three years, *Genetic Psychology Monographs* 14 (1933):1–92. **17.3** Norman, W. T., Toward an adequate taxonomy of personality attributes: Replicated factor structure in peer nomination personality ratings, *Journal of Abnormal and Social Psychology* 66 (1963):577. Copyright 1963 by the American Psychological Association. Adapted by permission of the author. **18.1** Rotter, J. B., Generalized expectancies for internal versus external control of reinforcement. *Psychological Monographs* 80 (1966):1, Whole Number 609. Copyright 1966 by the American Psychological Association.

## UNNUMBERED PHOTOS AND ART

**6** Salvador Dali's *The Grand Paranoic,* 1936, oil on panel, 62 x 62 cm.; collection Museum Boymans-van-Beuningen, Rotterdam. **11** Two illustrations from *Where the Wild Things Are,* written and illustrated by Maurice Sendak. Copyright 1963 by Maurice Sendak. Reprinted by permission of HarperCollins Publishers. **12** *Top* Courtesy Historical Pictures Service, Chicago. *Bottom* Courtesy The Warder Collection. **15** *(Part opener I)* Detail from Peter Paul Rubens's *Löwenjagd (Lion Hunt),* Alte Pinakothek, München; photograph by Joachim Blauel/Artothek. **18** Courtesy National Library of Medicine. **25** Nilsson, Lennart, *Behold Man.* Boston: Little Brown & Company, 1974. Reproduced by permission of the publisher. **26** Courtesy National Library of Medicine. **33** Photograph by Borys Malkin/Anthro Photo. **63** Theodore Gericault's *The Raft of the Medusa,* 1818–19, The Louvre; © Photo R. M. N. (Service Photographique de la Réunion des Musées Nationaux). **68** Scene from *Mutiny on the Bounty,* 1935; courtesy Photofest. **72** Pieter Bruegel The Elder's *Peasant Wedding Feast.* Courtesy Kunsthistorisches Museum, Vienna. **76** Photograph by Suzanne Szasz. **80** *Left The Venus of Willendorf;* courtesy Naturhistorisches Museum, Wien. *Center* Peter Paul Rubens's *The Three Graces;* © Museo del Prado, Madrid. *Right* Photograph by Mauro Carraro/Gamma Liaison Network. **88** Photograph courtesy of National Library of Medicine. **88** Photograph by Grant Leduc/Monkmeyer. **91** *Jacob's Ladder,* from the Lambeth Bible; courtesy the Archbishop of Canterbury and the Trustees of Lambeth Palace Library. **93** *Left* Georg Gerster/Comstock. *Center* Guy Sauvage, Agence Vandystadt/Photo Researchers. *Right* Courtesy The Kobal Collection. **103** Photograph by Toni Angermayer/Photo Researchers. **105** Courtesy Sovfoto. **111** Courtesy of the Museum of the City of New York. **112** Courtesy The Granger Collection. **115** Photograph by Nina Leen/Life Magazine, © Time Warner, Inc. **116** Photograph by Patrick Donehue/Photo Researchers. **122** Photograph by Erika Stone. **124** Courtesy Psychology Department, University of California, Berkeley. **135** Courtesy Animal Behavior Enterprises, Inc. **136** Photograph by Lincoln P. Brower. **139** Photographs courtesy of Animal Behavior Enterprises, Inc. **141** Courtesy The Warder Collection. **149** *(Part opener II)* Detail from Raphael's *School of Athens,* 1505, Stanza della Segnatura, Vatican; courtesy Scala/Art Resource, New York. **151** Courtesy National Library of Medicine. **152** Detail from *The Bermuda*

*Group* by John Smibert; courtesy Yale University Art Gallery; gift of Isaac Lothrop of Plymouth, Mass. **154** Courtesy National Library of Medicine. **156** Courtesy National Library of Medicine. **157** Courtesy National Library of Medicine. **174** Courtesy Nobel Stiftelsen. **175** Courtesy National Library of Medicine. **189** Photographs by Fritz Goro. **200** Claude Monet's *Terrace at Sainte-Adresse,* oil on canvas, 38⅝ x 51⅛″; reproduced by permission of the Metropolitan Museum of Art, New York; purchased with special contributions and purchase funds given or bequeathed by friends of the Museum, 1967. **210** Photograph courtesy Omikron. **245** Salvador Dali's *The Persistence of Memory,* 1931, oil on canvas, 9½ x 13″; Collection, The Museum of Modern Art, New York; given anonymously. **246** Photograph courtesy of Kathy Hirsh-Pasek. **248** Photograph courtesy of The Kobal Collection. **252** Detail of *Netherlandish Proverbs* by Pieter Brueghel, 1559; courtesy of Gemaldegalerie, Staatliche Museen Preußischer Kulturbesitz, Berlin. **254** Paul Cezanne's *The Cardplayers;* courtesy Metropolitan Museum of Art, bequest of Stephen C. Clark, 1960. **260** Photograph courtesy of The Kobal Collection. **261** Photograph by Nina Leen/Life Magazine, © Time Warner, Inc. **280** Photograph by Suzanne Szasz. **281** Marc Chagall's *I and the Village,* 1911, oil on canvas, 63⅝″ x 59⅝″ (192.1 x 151.4 cm); collection, The Museum of Modern Art, New York, Mrs. Simon Guggenheim Fund. **283** Photographs courtesy of The Bettmann Archive. **291** Rembrandt's *Aristotle with a Bust of Homer,* oil on canvas, 56½″ x 53¾″; courtesy The Metropolitan Museum of Art, purchased with special funds and gifts of friends of the Museum, 1961. **292** Pablo Picasso's *Portrait of Amboise Vollard,* 1909, Puskin Museum, Moscow; courtesy Scala/Art Resource, New York. **308** Courtesy Melvin L. Prueitt, C-6, Los Alamos National Laboratory. **321** From a British National Theatre production of *Galileo* by Bertolt Brecht; photograph by Zoe Dominic. **334** Pieter Brueghel the Elder, *Turmbau zu Babel (Tower of Babel);* courtesy Kunsthistorisches Museum, Vienna. **335** *My Fair Lady;* photograph by Leonard McCombe/Life Magazine, © Time Warner, Inc. **336** William Blake's *Adam Naming the Beasts,* courtesy The Stirling Maxwell Collection, Pollak House, Glasgow Museums & Art Galleries. **337** Henri Rousseau's *The Sleeping Gypsy,* 1897, oil on canvas, 51″ x 6′7″; collection, The Museum of Modern Art, New York. Gift of Mrs. Simon Guggenheim. **342** By permission. From *Webster's Ninth New Collegiate Dictionary.* © 1990 by Merriam-Webster Inc., publisher of the Merriam-Webster® dictionaries. **343** Reproduced from Lewis Carroll's *Alice in Wonderland,* original illustrations by John Tenniel; in color for this edition by Martina Selway. Secaucus, N.J.: Castle Books. **215** Photographs by Joseph Van Wormer/Bruce Coleman and M. P. Kahl/Bruce Coleman. **346** Reproduced from Lewis Carroll's *Alice in Wonderland,* original drawings by John Tenniel; in color for this edition by Martina Selway. Secaucus, N.J.: Castle Books. **358** Lewis Carroll's *Through the Looking Glass,* illustration by Tenniel, courtesy of General Research Division, The New York Public Library, Astor, Lenox, and Tilden Foundations. **360** Photograph by Erika Stone. **363** Photograph by Erika Stone. **369** Photograph by Roberta Grobel Intrater. **374** Courtesy New York School for the Deaf. **375** Courtesy American Foundation for the Blind, New York. **376** Photograph by Larry Morris/New York Times Photography; courtesy American Foundation for the Blind, New York. **385** Photographs courtesy of Herbert Terrace. **389** *(Part opener III)* Detail from Auguste Renoir's *Le Moulin de la Galette,* 1876, Louvre, Paris; photograph courtesy Service Photographique, La Reunion des Musées Nationaux. **391** Painting by John Michael Wright; courtesy The Granger Collection. **392** Painting by J. Collier; courtesy of The National Portrait Gallery, London. **393** *Top* Photograph by G. K. Brown/Ardea London Ltd. *Bottom* Photograph by Brian M. Rogers/Biophotos. **394** Photographs by Nina Leen. **397** *Top* Stouffer Productions/Animals Animals. *Bottom* Robert W. Hernández/Photo Researchers. **408** © Photograph by Robert W. Hernández/Photo Researchers. **409** © Carol Rosegg/Martha Swope Photography, Inc. **411** Photograph by Roy P. Fontaine. **413** *Left* © 1976 George Holton/Photo Researchers. *Right* © 1988 James Sugar/Black Star. **416** Photograph by Benny Ortiz. **420** Courtesy of Photofest. **421** Francisco de Zurbarán's *St. Serapion,* 1628, oil on canvas, 47 9/16 x 41 in.; courtesy of Wadsworth Atheneum, Hartford. The Ella Gallup Sumner and Mary Caitlin Sumner Collection. **425** Courtesy National Library of Medicine. **426** Courtesy National Library of Medicine. **428** Gravure's *Jean M. Charcot—A Clinical Lecture at the Salpetriere;* courtesy The Bettmann Archive. **432** Photograph by Nobby Clark. **434** Reproduced from Walter Crane's *The Baby's Own Aesop,* engraved and printed by Edmund Evans; reproduced from the Print Collection, Miriam & Ira D. Wallach Division of Art, Prints and Photographs, The New York Public Library, Astor, Lenox, and Tilden Foundations. **435** Pavel Tchelitchew's *Hide-and-Seek,* 1940–42, oil on canvas, 6′6½″ x 7′¾″; collection, The Museum of Modern Art, New York, Mrs. Simon Guggenheim Fund. **436** Courtesy Billy Rose Theatre Collection, The New York Public Library at Lincoln Center, Astor, Lenox, and Tilden Foundations. **439** Courtesy The Museum of Modern Art/Film Stills Archive. **440** Frontispiece of *Les rêves et les moyens de les diriger* by the Marquis d'Harvey de Saint Denis, 1867. **441** Courtesy The Museum of Modern Art/Film Stills Archive. **442** From *The Subject Was Children,* ed. by Gene Mitchell, New York: Dutton, 1979; illustration by Jesse Wilcox Smith; courtesy Michael Larsen/Larsen-Pomada Literary Agents. **443** Courtesy Universal Pictures. **446** Henry Fuseli's *The Nightmare;* courtesy The Detroit Institute of Arts. **448** Courtesy The American Museum of Natural History. **449** Photograph courtesy Mary Evans/Freud copyrights. **450** Courtesy Wide World Photos. **454** *Top left* Photograph by Michael Cooper/Stratford Festival. *Top right* Courtesy Photofest. *Bottom* Courtesy Swarthmore College. **456** Courtesy The Kobal Collection. **457** Photograph by Burt Glinn/© 1964 Magnum Photos **459** *Left* © Sylvia Johnson/Woodfin Camp *Right* © Susan McElhinney/Woodfin Camp. **461** *Top* Mitsouko. Guerlain, Paris. *Bottom* Best Foods Baking Group. **462** Frontispiece from *The Wonderful World of American Advertising,* 1865–1900, by Leonard de Vries and Ilonka van Amstel, Chicago: Follett, 1972. **463** Photograph by James Natchwey/Magnum. **465** *Left* Photograph by Francis Laping/Black Star. *Center* Roger Sandler/Black Star. *Right* Christopher Morris/Black Star. **466** Photograph by Michael Probst/UPI, Bettmann Newsphotos. **468** Photograph by Robert C. Ragsdale/Stratford Festival. **470** British poster, 1900, John R. Freeman collection; by courtesy of the Board of Trustees of the Victoria and Albert Museum. **472** Courtesy AP/Wide World Photos. **473** Courtesy The Kobal Collection. **476** Courtesy Reuters/Bettmann Newsphotos. **477** Photograph by Suzanne Szasz. **478** Photograph by S. C. Delaney/EPA. **479** © Lee Snider/Photo Images; courtesy New York Gilbert & Sullivan Players. **483** Photograph by Michael Nichols/Magnum. **485** Photographs courtesy Dr. David Matsumoto and Dr. Paul Ekman, from the Japanese and Caucasian Facial Expressions of Emotion (JACFEE), 1989. **486** Photo by Constantine Manos/© 1968, Magnum. **487** Photograph by Suzanne Szasz. **488** Photograph by Robert C. Ragsdale/Stratford Festival. **491** Photograph by Suzanne Szasz. **495** Photograph by Hiroji Kubota/Magnum Photos. **496** *The Gifts of the Magi,* Basilica of Sant Apollinare Nuovo, Ravenna; courtesy Giorgio la Pira. **500** Luca Giordano's *The Good Samaritan,* Musée des Beaux-Arts, Rouen; courtesy Lauros-Giraudon/Art Resource. **501** UPI/Bettmann Newsphotos. **504** Grant Wood, American, 1892–1942, *American Gothic,* 1930, oil on beaver board, 76 x 63.3 cm, Art Institute of Chicago, Friends of American Art Collection, 1930.934; photograph © 1990, The Art Institute of Chicago. All Rights Reserved. **505** *Left and Center* Photographs by George K. Fuller. *Right* Photograph by John Moss/Photo Researchers. **506** *Top* Photograph from

# Name Index

# Subject Index

abnormal psychology, *see* psychopathology
absolute threshold, 156
   detection experiments and, 158–63
abstract concepts, 292
   in animals, 143–45
   concrete or formal operations and, 555
   cultural differences and, 570
   in moral reasoning, 600–601
   reference theory of meaning and, 342
abstract thought, 291–93
access to intellectual processes, 145–46
accommodation (in cognitive development),
   551, 566–67
accommodation (in vision), 177
accommodative distortions, 270
acetylcholine, 30, 31, 32–33
achievement tests, 628
achromatic colors, 186
acquisition phase, in remembering, 245
across-fiber pattern theory, 164
action potential, 22–24, 30
activation, 85, 86
active memory, 254–55
   retrieval from, 264–66
   *see also* short-term memory, working
      memory
active sentences, 355
active (REM) sleep, 8, 88, 89–91, 447, 768
actor-observer bias, 474–76
act-outcome associations, 130–32, 138–39
adaptation, 167
   of feature detectors, 209–10
   in vision, 179–81, 191
adaptive value, of behavior, 393
addiction, to drugs, 95–96, 98, 111
additive color mixture, 189–90
ADH (anti-diuretic hormone), 68
adolescence, 616–20
   competence in, related to childhood
      ability to delay gratification, 730–31
   growth in, 538

nature of transition in, 617–18
   in psychoanalytic theory, 437–38
   search for personal identity in, 619–20
adoption, maternal deprivation and,
   586–87
adoption studies:
   on bipolar disorder, 768
   on intelligence, 664–65, 666
   on personality, 707
   on schizophrenia, 761
adrenaline (epinephrine), 82–83
adrenal medulla, 82
adulthood, 620–23
   changes in intelligence during, 652–54
   Erikson's stages of, 620
   intelligence tests administered in, 641–42
   mid-life transition in, 620–21
   transition from adolescence to, 617–18
   universality of stages in, 621–23
affective disorders, *see* mood disorders
afferent nerves, 19
aftereffects, of visual movement, 209–10
afterimages, negative, 191
age, memory declines and, 653
aggression, 395–401
   in animals, 396–400
   crowd behavior and, 523, 529
   at different ages, 696
   displaced, 433
   dominance hierarchies and, 399–400
   hormones and, 396, 449, 605
   physical punishment and, 594–95
   predation and defense, 395–96
   sex differences in, 449, 604–605, 606
   territoriality and, 345–46
agnosia, 47
agoraphobia, 774, 777, 800, 811, 812
alarm signals, 170, 416$n$, 418
alcohol, 94–95, 98
Alcoholics Anonymous, 826–27
alcoholism, 814

algorithms, 309
all-or-none law, 24, 25
ally effect, 513–14
alpha males, 399–400
alpha waves, 87–88
alternative forms of mental tests, 632
alternative hypothesis, A23
altruism, 497–501
   in animals, 417, 418–19
   bystander effect and, 497–99, 522, 529
   in children, 501, 597, 598
   costs of helping and, 499–500
   empathy and, 598
   kin selection and, 418–19
   reciprocal, 419, 420, 421
   selfish benefits of, 418, 500, 597
   self-sacrifice and, 417–22
   sociobiologists' view of, 419–21
Alzheimer's disease, 57
ambiguity:
   in language, 2–3, 341, 352–53
   of reversible figures, 212
American Psychiatric Association, 612
American Sign Language (ASL), 49,
   374–75, 382
amnesia, 264, 284–87, 782
   anterograde, 250, 284, 286–87
   childhood, 280–81
   posthypnotic, 428
   retrograde, 284–86
amphetamine psychosis, 759
amphetamines, 33, 95, 96, 98
amplitude, of sound waves, 171
anal character, 717–18
analgesics, 34–35
analogical reasoning, 302, 656–57
anal stage, 435, 438, 448, 715
androgens, 406, 407, 544, 545, 607–608,
   614
anesthesia, hysterical, 427
anger, 485, 487–88

elaborative rehearsal, 260–61, 264
Electra complex, 438–39
electrical potentials, resting and action, 22–24, 30
electroconvulsive shock treatment (ECT), 804–805
electroencephalograms (EEGs), 8, 87–88
  of sociopaths, 793–94
embryos and fetuses, 406, 537–38, 539
  development of, 536, 537, 540, 544–45, 546
  differentiation of, 536, 544–45
  growth of, 537
  homosexuality and hormonal effects in, 614–15
  physical environment of, 544–45
  sensitive periods for, 546
emergency reaction, 81–86, 783–84
  central controls in, 84
  description of, 82–83
  habituation and, 103–104
  negative effects of, 84–85
emotions:
  in adolescence, 618–19
  in behavioral approach to personality, 723
  catharsis and, 428
  classical conditioning and, 110
  cognitive arousal theory of, 481–84, 486, 507–508
  complex, 487–90
  defusing of, as therapeutic goal, 820
  disorders of, in schizophrenia, 756–57
  dissonance reduction and, 464–65
  expression of, 414–15
  facial expression and, 484–86
  fundamental, 484–86, 490
  insight into, as therapeutic goal, 808–809, 815
  isolation and, 434
  James-Lange theory of, 480–82, 484, 485–86
  love, 506–10
  pity, anger, and guilt, 487–88
  prefrontal lobotomy and, 804
  regret, 488–90
  subjective experience of, 479–91
  theater and, 490–91
empathy, 501, 597–98, 731
  in humanistic psychology, 736
empiricism:
  cognitive development and, 549, 556, 560, 565–66
  perception and, 205, 207, 223, 230–31, 235
  sensory experience and, 151–54
  thinking and, 291, 292
  *see also* nativism
encoding phase of remembering, 246–59
  active memory and, 254–55
  childhood amnesia and, 280–81
  depth of processing in, 255–56, 263–64
  mnemonics in, 257–59
  organization in, 251–52, 256–57
  specificity in, 259–60
  stage theory and, 246–54

encoding strategies, in social learning theory, 726
encounters, in existential therapy, 819
endocrine system, 35–36
endorphins, 34–35, 802
environment:
  assimilation-accommodation interaction with, 551, 566–67
  after birth, 545–46
  before birth, 544–45
  diathesis-stress conception and, 752–53
  and empiricist approach to learning, 565–66
  enriched, 666
  heredity vs., as factor in intelligence, 659–71, 709
  impoverished, 665–66
  interaction between heredity and, 543–46, 661–62, 706–709
  internal, homeostasis and, 64–74
  maturation and, 546–48
  personality and, 706–709
  schizophrenia and, 761–63
  *see also* culture
epilepsy, 50
epinephrine (adrenaline), 82–83
episodic memory, 273
equipotentiality principle, 135–40
erogenous zones, 435, 715
escape learning, 122
escape reaction, *see* emergency reaction
essential hypertension, 783–85, 787
estrogen, 405, 406
estrus, 405–406, 407
ethology, 394, 422
  *see also* animal behavior
evolution:
  of courtship rituals, 404
  law of effect and, 112, 114–15
  mating systems and, 393, 407–10
  natural selection in, 392–94, 630
  and origin of displays, 404
  parent-child attachment and, 411, 412
  predispositions to behavior in, 393–94, 395
  self-sacrifice or altruism and, 417
  variability within species and, 630
excitation, 26–27
excitation transfer effects, 483–84
exercise, endorphins and, 35
existential therapy, 819–20
experimental extinction, 108
experimental groups, A4–A5
experiments, A4–A5
  variance and, A20–A21
expertise, chunking and, 297–99
expert systems, 310–12, 313–14
expressive aphasia, 48
expressive movements, 413–14
  *see also* displays
extension reflexes, 26
extensor muscles, 28
externality hypothesis, obesity and, 77–78
extinction, 107–108
  of avoidance responses, 123, 725
  partial reinforcement and, 120–21, 724–25

  in psychotherapy, 811
extroversion, 690–92, 701*n*, 704
  arousal system and, 709
  heritability of, 705–706
eye movements:
  compensation for, 207
  in perceptual selection, 226–27
  rapid, in REM sleep, 8, 88, 89–91, 447, 768
eyes:
  binocular depth cues and, 201
  color of, heredity and, 543
  *see also* retinas; vision
eyewitness testimony, 268–69

face recognition:
  difficulty in, 47
  infants and, 208, 223
facial expression, emotions and, 484–86
factor analysis, 647
  group-factor theories and, 648–49
  in taxonomy of personality traits, 692
false accepts and rejects, in aptitude tests, 635–36
false alarms, in detection experiments, 159
familiarity, attraction and, 502–503
family:
  extended, 622
  personality and differences within, 707–708
  schizophrenia and, 761, 762–63
  *see also* attachment, mother-child; child rearing; children; fathers; infants; mothers; newborns; parents
family resemblance structure, 344–45
family therapy, 827–28
fat cells, obesity and, 77
fathers:
  homosexual sons and, 613
  infants' relation to, 581–83
  in psychoanalytic theory, 436–38, 442, 443, 449–50
fat metabolism, 73–74
fear:
  anxiety vs., 128
  conditioned, 110, 123, 725
  emergency reaction and, 81–86
  panic disorder and, 777–78, 816–17
  panicky crowds and, 523, 524–28
  pheromones as signal of, 170
  of punishment, 426–27, 432, 433, 437
  of unknown and unfamiliar, 577–79
  unrealistic, behavior therapy for, 811–13, 825
  *see also* phobias
featural approach to word meaning, 343–44
feature analysis, Pandemonium model and, 218–20
feature detectors, 208–10
  adaptation of, 209–10
Fechner's law, 158
feedback systems, 63–64
feeding, 69–81, 99
  anorexia nervosa or bulimia and, 79–81
  dual-center theory of, 73–74
  external signals for, 71–72